In Afghanistan's Shadow

In Afghanistan's Shadow:
Baluch Nationalism and Soviet Temptations
Selig S. Harrison

WITHDRAWN

Carnegie Endowment for International Peace

New York   Washington, D.C.

Burgess

DS
392
B23
H37

c . 1

Credits

Photographs by David Burnett/Contact (pp. xii, 6, 13, 14, 32-bottom, 70), Abbas/Gamma (pp. 92, 114-top), Paireault/Gamma (p. 152), and the Mall Studios, London (p. 63). Photographs on p. 98 are courtesy of S. Sgt. Fred W. Karnes, USA. Other photographs were obtained or taken by the author. The maps (following p. 84) were prepared by Frank and Clare Ford of the Ford Studios, Arlington, VA.

ISBN 0-87003-029-9; 0-87003-030-2 (paper)

Library of Congress catalog card number: 81-67142

Printed in the United States of America

Contents

Foreword, by Thomas L. Hughes   vii

Acknowledgments   x

1 **After Afghanistan**   1

2 **Myths and Memories**   7
   Who Are the Baluch?
   The Search for Political Identity

3 **The Emergence of Baluch Nationalism**   21
   The Struggle Against Accession to Pakistan
   The "Broken Treaties"
   The Beginnings of Insurgency
   The War Years (1973–1977)

4 **Talking with the Triumvirate**   41
   Khair Bux Marri: Marxism and Cockfights
   Ghaus Bux Bizenjo:
       Elder Statesman or Secret Communist?
   Ataullah Mengal: "Let Them Come to Us"

5 **The Baluch Nationalist Movement in Pakistan**   71
   The Baluch People's Liberation Front
   The Baluch Students Organization
   The Pakistan National Party

6 **The Baluch Nationalist Movement in Iran**   93
   The Pahlavis and the Baluch
   Nationalism Goes Underground
   After the Shah
   Iraq and the Arab Connection

7 **Communism and Nationalism in Baluchistan** 127
Soviet Policy Toward Baluch Nationalism
Communist Strength in Baluchistan
The Afghan Communists and Baluchistan

8 **The View from Islamabad and Teheran** 149
Zia's Velvet Glove
Bhutto's Chess Game
"You Can't Trust Them"

9 **The Independence Issue: Problems and Prospects** 161
The Development Debate
Would Independence Be Viable?
The Demographic Muddle
Tribalism and Nationalism
Is Compromise Possible?

10 **Moscow, Washington and the Future of Baluchistan** 195

Notes 207

Index 221

Maps follow page 84

Foreword

In November 1977, the Carnegie Endowment selected the Afghanistan-Pakistan-Iran region as one of the danger zones on the international scene that would receive special emphasis in its Program for Journalists. Less than six months later, a Communist coup took place in Kabul, and in December 1979, Russian forces crossed the Oxus River frontier, touching off a new phase of tension in Soviet-American relations that is still continuing.

The Carnegie Journalists Program, established in 1974, attempts to anticipate "near-horizon" problems and trends that could lead to international conflict or to large-scale human suffering. By presenting independent, on-the-spot, factual reporting and analysis of such situations in their early stages, it hopes to focus attention by government and public-opinion leaders in the countries studied, as well as in the United States and the larger international community, while there is still time for ameliorative action. The findings of this program are made available in a variety of ways, ranging from magazine articles, op-ed essays, and books to radio and TV appearances, lectures, and academic seminars.

The Endowment gave the task of monitoring emergent developments in South and Southwest Asia to a widely recognized specialist, Selig S. Harrison, who has covered the area for more than three decades. Writing from Afghanistan in mid-1978, he was one of the first analysts to warn that the civil war then developing between the new Communist regime and Pakistan-based Islamic resistance groups could lead to Soviet military intervention. He sharply underlined the independent, national-communist character of the revolutionary regime in Kabul as a critical factor that could help to provoke such intervention. At the same time, looking further ahead, he emphasized that Moscow might be tempted to use its foothold in Afghanistan to fan the fires of separatism in the politically vulnerable Baluch areas of neighboring Pakistan and Iran. His 1978 *Foreign Policy* article, "After the Afghan Coup: Nightmare in Baluchistan," called attention to the explosive potential of the movement to create an independent Greater Baluchistan that would stretch for some 900 miles along the Arabian Sea up to the Strait of Hormuz.

Against the background of a deepening struggle in Afghanistan and steadily growing American involvement in Pakistan and the Persian Gulf area, Harrison presents in this book a wealth of new findings that amplify and update his earlier warnings concerning the volatility of the Baluch issue. He shows that separatist sentiment has been steadily growing in Baluchistan in recent years, reveals hitherto unpublished information concerning the character of the nationalist and Communist movements in Baluchistan, and introduces us to their leaders through extensive interviews. While it contains introductory historical chapters, the book focuses primarily on the major economic and political conflicts between the Baluch and the Pakistani and Iranian central governments and on possible ways of neutralizing separatism through constitutional adjustments. In the absence of a greater readiness for compromise on the part of Islamabad and Teheran, the book suggests, the likelihood of Soviet manipulation of Baluch nationalism will increase.

Yet Harrison offers surprising evidence indicating that Moscow is ambivalent with respect to the desirability of supporting Baluch independence. On the one hand, he contends that Baluchistan could become the focal point of a superpower confrontation if the Afghan struggle should escalate, since it is the "Baluch card" that Moscow would be most likely to play in retaliation for U.S. assistance to the Afghan resistance or for expanding U.S. military links with Pakistan. On the other, he concludes that "the Soviet approach to the Baluch issue is likely to be influenced to a significant extent by the nature of the evolving American role in Pakistan and Iran. There is still a chance to avert a superpower confrontation over Baluchistan through restraint on both sides; and by the same token, there is a growing danger that pre-emptive moves by one side or the other could set in motion an uncontrollable chain reaction of challenge and response."

This book is part of a larger continuing project in which Harrison is examining the reasons for Soviet involvement in Afghanistan, possible ways in which the situation there might develop, the impact of the Afghan crisis on surrounding countries—notably Pakistan, India, and Iran—and the policy choices confronting these countries as well as the United States, the Soviet Union, and the international community.

In its methodology, this book exemplifies the distinctive character of the Carnegie Journalists Program, which consciously seeks to combine the investigative techniques of the responsible foreign correspondent with the detachment and analytical discipline of academic research work. Thus, Harrison has relied primarily on interviews in order to open up a subject that has received almost no attention in academic, journalistic, or other writings in the West except for a handful of anthropological studies and hastily contrived journalistic accounts assembled after a few days in

Baluchistan. On a series of field trips between 1977 and 1981, he has talked with some 340 primary sources, principally Baluch leaders of all persuasions, many of them underground in Baluchistan itself and others living in exile in Europe and the Persian Gulf; political figures, officials, and scholars in Islamabad, Kabul, Teheran, and Moscow; and participants in the 1973–1977 Baluch insurgency in Pakistan, including Pakistani military officers and Baluch guerrilla leaders now hiding out in base camps in southern Afghanistan. Many of his Baluch sources have cooperated on the understanding that their anonymity would be preserved in order to avoid prosecution on treason charges. However, in most cases, Harrison has named names. He has buttressed his firsthand findings with a review of documentary material and nationalist literature in Baluchi, Urdu, Persian, and English, much of it never before obtained by foreign observers.

Harrison, one of the first Senior Associates to be appointed to the Journalists Program, brings to his work at the Endowment a rich background in scholarly journalism, with a broad stream of articles and books on Asia to his credit. His academic work has included research and teaching assignments at Harvard, Columbia, the Brookings Institution, and the Johns Hopkins School of Advanced International Studies. As a journalist, he has been a foreign correspondent in many Asian posts over a thirty-year period, has served as the *Washington Post* bureau chief in New Delhi and Tokyo, and is a former managing editor of the *New Republic*. Drawing on his background in East Asia, he conducted a pioneering study for the Endowment of the political implications of China's offshore oil development, culminating in his 1977 Endowment book *China, Oil and Asia: Conflict Ahead?* In his present work, he builds on his six years as a resident correspondent in South and Southwest Asia.

As always, Endowment sponsorship of this book implies a belief only in the importance of the subject and the credentials of the author. The views expressed are those of the author. Comments or inquiries on this and other work of the Endowment are welcome and may be addressed to the Carnegie Endowment for International Peace, 11 Dupont Circle, NW, Washington, DC, 20036, or 30 Rockefeller Plaza, New York, New York 10112.

Thomas L. Hughes
President
Carnegie Endowment for International Peace

Acknowledgments

I should like to express my appreciation to the many individuals and governments whose cooperation has made this work possible. Since more than three hundred people were interviewed, most of them on the understanding that their names would not be revealed, it is not possible to single out many of those who have been most helpful. However, I should like to record my gratitude to General Mohammed Zia Ul-Haq, President of Pakistan; Iqbal Butt, former Director-General of External Publicity in Islamabad, and his successor, Khalid Ali; Lt. Gen. Rahimuddin Khan, Governor of Pakistani Baluchistan; Lt. Gen. Arbab Jahanseb, former army commanding general in Pakistani Baluchistan; and Jafar Nadim, former Undersecretary of State in the Iranian Foreign Ministry. Others in high places, now deceased, who were particularly helpful were President Zulfiqar Ali Bhutto of Pakistan, presidents Mohammed Daud and Hafizullah Amin of Afghanistan, and Premier Amir Abbas Hoveida of Iran.

For valuable guidance in the difficult early stages of my research I would like to thank Maj. Gen. M. G. Jilani (ret.) of the Pakistan Army, Lawrence Lifschultz of the *Far Eastern Economic Review*, and K. B. Nizamani, editor of *Nedae Baluchistan*. For their help in anthropological and linguistic studies relating to the Baluch, I remain grateful to Joseph Elfenbein, Richard Frye, Stephen Pastner, Philip Salzman, and Brian Spooner. Yuri Gankovsky of the Institute of Oriental Studies in Moscow gave me a valuable elaboration of his own writings on the Baluch and enabled me to meet with other relevant Soviet specialists.

Among the many Baluch of many persuasions in Pakistan and Iran who have assisted me, a special word of appreciation is due to Ghaus Bux Bizenjo; Akbar Bukti; Aslam Gichki; Sikander Jamali; Mir Ahmed Yar Khan Baluch, the late Khan of Kalat; Mahmud Aziz Kurd; Akber Y. Mustikhan; Khair Bux Marri; Sher Mohammed Marri; Sher Baz Mazari; Ataullah Mengal; and Malik M. Towghi.

Extensive translations from eight languages, made possible by the Carnegie Endowment, have greatly enriched this work. I would like to thank the following for their translations: Iran B. Jewett (Urdu and Persian); Iftikhar Ahmad and Mujahid Iqbal (Urdu); Hamid Sultan

Baloch and Malik M. Towghi (Baluchi); Ali K. El-Amin (Arabic); Ruhul Ameen Yousufzai (Pushtu); George Liber, Jerome Ochs, and Irwin Selnick (Russian); Jeffrey Thickman (German); and Thomas Gora (French).

I am grateful to many colleagues at the Carnegie Endowment for their generous support and continuing encouragement, especially Thomas L. Hughes, President, and Larry L. Fabian, Secretary. I relied heavily on Susan C. Fisher, Manager of Publications, and her predecessor, Diane B. Bendahmane; Richard H. Moss, Staff Editor, who edited the book with care and insight; the research staff of the Endowment library; and Evelyn Morris, Anne Chong, and Margaret Byron, who transcribed and typed the manuscript at various stages of its evolution.

S.S.H.
April 1981

After Afghanistan

1

Visiting Pakistan on a troubleshooting mission for President John F. Kennedy in 1962, Henry Kissinger, then a Harvard professor, impatiently brushed aside a local journalist who asked him to comment on the insurgency then beginning to surface in the restless province of Baluchistan. "I wouldn't recognize the Baluchistan problem," Kissinger snapped, "if it hit me in the face."[1]

Until recently, Baluchistan has been all but unknown to the outside world, an obscure, exotic place of interest primarily to ethnographers and venturesome explorers. Since the Soviet occupation of neighboring Afghanistan, however, it has suddenly been discovered by Western policymakers. Warning of the historic Russian drive for warm-water ports, American officials now point to Baluchistan as one of the most likely future Soviet targets in Southwest Asia. President Jimmy Carter was deliberately vague in his pledge to defend the "Persian Gulf region," but his national security adviser, Zbigniew Brzezinski, specifically underlined the applicability of the "Carter doctrine" to Baluchistan as part of a broader U.S. commitment to Pakistan.[2] Similarly, the Reagan administration has based its policy of expanded military links with Islamabad primarily on the premise that Baluchistan's security is crucial to the security of the adjacent Persian Gulf.

A glance at the map (see Figure 1) quickly explains why strategically located Baluchistan and the five million[3] Baluch* tribesmen who live there could easily become the focal point of superpower conflict. Stretching across a vast expanse of western Pakistan and eastern Iran**—an area slightly larger than France—the Baluch homeland commands more than 900 miles of the Arabian Sea coastline, including the northern shores of the Strait of Hormuz, through which oil tankers bound for the

---

* "Baluch" is the correct form to use in describing or referring to the ethnic group. "Baluchi" refers specifically to the language.

** The overwhelming majority of Baluch live in Pakistan (3.65 million) and Iran (one million); an estimated 90,000 are native to the border areas of southern Afghanistan. Another 335,000 Baluch have migrated to the Arab sheikhdoms of the Persian Gulf. The Soviet census lists 13,000 Baluch in Turkmenistan, and some 5,000 live in East Africa.

West and Japan must pass on their way out of the Persian Gulf. Soviet control of the Baluch coast would not only give Moscow a powerful new springboard for spreading its political influence throughout the Middle East and Southwest Asia, but would also radically alter the military balance in the region. Coupled with continued Soviet access to military facilities in South Yemen, Soviet use of naval and air bases at Gwadar, Pasni, and other Baluch ports would make it difficult, if not impossible, for the United States to defend the Strait of Hormuz in a conventional war, given the limited and conditional character of projected U.S. military facilities in Oman, Somalia, and Kenya.

In the most common scenario envisaged by those who foresee further Soviet expansion, Moscow simply sends its troops and tanks across Baluchistan to the Persian Gulf, a distance of less than 350 miles, annexing the Baluch area directly to a Soviet-controlled Greater Afghanistan. But this worst-case scenario completely ignores the role of the Baluch themselves and thus grossly oversimplifies the nature of the Baluchistan issue. On the one hand, it obscures the complex political difficulties that Moscow would confront in attempting to control the Baluch through conquest. On the other, it underrates the danger that Moscow might pursue its objectives more flexibly through a combination of political and military means, perhaps using allied Baluch groups as proxies.

While not ruling out the possibility of a naked Soviet military thrust, Pakistani and Iranian leaders are more concerned that Moscow might help Baluch nationalist factions to pursue their long-standing goal of an autonomous or independent Baluchistan through guerrilla warfare. In that scenario, Moscow would give the Baluch sophisticated weaponry, technical advisers, logistical support, and funds, but would seek to avoid the risks and costs of direct aggression. Alternatively, Moscow might attempt to achieve its purposes without supporting a Baluch insurgency, using the threat of such support to pressure Pakistan or Iran, or both, into granting the use of Arabian Sea ports for military purposes.

Whether or not Moscow decides to play its "Baluch card," the Baluch nationalist movement has achieved a momentum of its own and is likely to have an increasingly significant impact on the course of events in Southwest Asia. This book seeks to fill a vacuum in knowledge about the Baluch movement and to underline its importance as a little-recognized but critical factor in a region where ethnic conflict tends to dominate political life. Baluch nationalism is among the most intractable of the seven significant separatist challenges that threaten the integrity of multiethnic Pakistan and Iran. In Pakistan, the dominant Punjabis confront serious Pushtun and Sindhi disaffection. In Iran, separatist elements in the Kurdish, Arab, Turkoman, and Azerbaijani areas have waged perennial political and military struggles against Persian* rule. As the Iran-Iraq war showed in 1980, it is not difficult to envisage situations in which regional powers, acting on their own initiative, might support Baluch separatism as part of their larger efforts to manipulate ethnic differences in pursuit of local ambitions. For example, if Baghdad is unable to bring Teheran to its knees, there will be a growing possibility of Iraqi moves to set up independent states in the non-Persian areas. Similarly, if Indo-Pakistani tensions are aggravated by superpower rivalry in Afghanistan, as chapter ten elaborates, support for the dismemberment of Pakistan is likely to increase in India.

The origins of the Baluch nationalist movement go back to the forcible incorporation of the Baluch into Iran by Reza Shah Pahlavi in 1928 and, later, into the new state of Pakistan left behind by the British Raj in 1947. The Baluch waged unsuccessful military struggles of varying magnitude to preserve their independence and have been fighting intermittently ever since to throw off Pakistani and Iranian domination. In Iran, the Shah's iron repression kept the Baluch largely under control (with the exception of a brief, Iraqi-supported insurgency) until the Khomeini revolution in 1979 led to a weakening of the central authority and an outpouring of long-suppressed nationalist feeling. In Pakistan, by contrast, Baluch insurgents have waged an on-again, off-again guerrilla struggle ever since the departure of the British, culminating in the mid-1970s in a brutal confrontation with 80,000 or more Pakistani troops in which some 55,000 Baluch were involved at various stages of the fighting. At the height of the fighting, in late 1974, U.S.-supplied Iranian combat helicopters, some manned by Iranian pilots, joined the Pakistan Air Force in raids on Baluch camps. The Baluch, lacking any substantial foreign help, were armed only with bolt-action rifles and homemade grenades.[4]

Significantly, when they started their poorly prepared insurgency in 1973, the Pakistani Baluch were fighting not for independence but rather for regional autonomy within a radically restructured, confederal Pakistani constitutional framework. By the time the shooting subsided in 1977, however, separatist feeling had greatly intensified. The wanton use of superior firepower by the Pakistani and Iranian forces, especially the indiscriminate air attacks on Baluch villages, left a legacy of bitter and

* The Farsi-speaking Persian ethnic group has traditionally dominated multiethnic Iran, which also consists of Baluch, Kurds, Arabs, Turkomans, Azerbaijanis, and tribes such as the Bakhtiaris and Lurs.

enduring hatred. Since nearly all Baluch felt the impact of Pakistani repression, the Baluch populace is now politicized to an unprecedented degree. In mid-1980, I found a pervasive mood of expectancy among the Baluch, a widespread desire to vindicate Baluch martial honor, and a readiness to renew the struggle when and if circumstances appear to be favorable.

There is still a chance to avert renewed conflict through negotiations, but the communication gap is rapidly widening between the Baluch and Pakistani and Iranian leaders. To the dominant Punjabis in Pakistan, who make up 58 percent of the population, it is unthinkable that the Baluch minority of less than 4 percent should have special claims to Baluchistan, which represents 42 percent of the land area of the country. By the same token, in Iran, where the Baluch constitute at most 2 percent of the population, the ruling Persians, who make up 52 percent, angrily reject the proposition that provincial boundaries should be demarcated in accordance with historic ethnic homelands. Both Islamabad and Teheran view the sparsely settled expanses of Baluchistan as a safety valve for surplus population, a source of badly needed raw materials, and an area of vital strategic importance over which the central government should rightfully hold undisputed sway. But for the ideologues of Pakistani and Iranian nationalism, the Baluch and other minorities cannot be permitted to stand in the way of modernization programs addressed to the overall development needs of the impoverished millions living in all parts of their respective countries.

As a report on the Baluch movement and its destabilizing potential, this book is deliberately Baluch-centered. It treats Baluch nationalism as a dynamic, self-contained phenomenon worthy of attention in its own right rather than as a subordinate aspect of the larger problems of Pakistani and Iranian nationalism. Thus, it examines Pakistani and Iranian attitudes relating specifically to the Baluch and their demands, focusing in particular on how these attitudes condition the Baluch movement and affect the prospects for compromise between the Baluch and Islamabad and Teheran. It does not give "equal time" to a consideration of Pakistani and Iranian nationalist perspectives that embrace the gamut of problems confronting Pakistan and Iran as multiethnic states. That broader examination will be part of a subsequent book.

What are the principal grievances underlying Baluch demands for autonomy, and what are the possible elements of an accommodation between the Baluch and Islamabad and Teheran? How strong is the Baluch nationalist movement in organizational terms? Does it have enough discipline and unity to wage a meaningful struggle for independence, assuming that it receives significant foreign military help? Who are its leaders? Does Moscow have a significant Communist political base in Baluchistan, or would it have to depend on alliances with non-Communist Baluch nationalists to legitimize a Soviet-sponsored independent state?

In order to assess the potential of Baluch nationalism as a flash point for intraregional tensions and superpower rivalry in Southwest Asia, it is not enough to focus on the political and economic conflicts of the recent past or even, as some have done, to search for the roots of Baluch attitudes in the stormy encounters of the Baluch with British colonial armies.[5] It is first necessary to understand how the Baluch view the larger panorama of their embattled earlier history. This report turns next, accordingly, to an exploration of the deeply ingrained historical memories that underlie Baluch nationalism, memories of a tempestuous struggle for survival stretching back more than 2,000 years. Chapter three presents a brief account of the controversial circumstances surrounding the annexation of Baluchistan to Pakistan and the early struggles of the Baluch nationalist movement there, culminating in the 1973–1977 insurgency. Chapters four and five offer a close-up look at the principal nationalist leaders and a survey of the major contemporary nationalist groups.

The special problems of the nationalist movement in Iran receive separate treatment in chapter six, setting the stage for an examination of émigré Baluch groups in the Arab states across the Persian Gulf from Iran and their links with Sunni Arab leaders seeking to destabilize the Shiite-dominated Teheran regime. Chapter seven assesses Communist strength in Baluchistan, pointing up the handicaps faced by the Baluch Communists in past years as a result of Soviet unwillingness to support Baluch independence. After an examination of Pakistani and Iranian attitudes toward Baluch demands, focusing in particular on economic issues, chapters eight and nine seek to assess the economic viability of an independent Baluchistan and weigh the possibilities for political accommodations between the Baluch and Islamabad and Teheran, taking into account the overall political prospects in the two countries. Finally, chapter ten discusses the impact of Baluch nationalism on Soviet and American policy options in Afghanistan, Pakistan, Iran, India, and the Persian Gulf.

Baluchistan lifestyle, 1981

Myths and Memories

2

If it were not for the strategic location of Baluchistan and the rich potential of oil, uranium, and other resources described in chapter nine, it would be difficult to imagine anyone fighting over this bleak, desolate, and forbidding land. Most observers compare it to the moon, but a team of U.S. Geological Survey experts on assignment in Iranian Baluchistan insisted that it was the closest thing on earth to Mars. Date groves do survive in scattered oases, and the southeastern corner of Baluch territory encompasses the rich agricultural pockets of Las Bela and Kachhi. Forests of juniper also flourish in some of the northeastern mountain ranges near the Afghan border. But for most of its 207,000 square miles, Baluchistan alternates abruptly between stark mountains and arid expanses of semidesert wasteland.

Rocky brown scrub country stretches for hundreds of miles, punctuated only by isolated formations of white or coral limestone that jut up in lurid volcanic shapes. Then suddenly, the desert gives way to precipitous peaks. Knife-backed ridges hem in tight little valleys where low stands of dwarf palm, thorny shrubs, and rough grass struggle for survival. For the uninitiated, getting from one of these valleys to the next on foot can be a precarious business: there are few passes, and many of them are not negotiable even by local donkeys accustomed to the jagged terrain. Except for mountain goats, ibex, and panthers, the Baluch have always had the barren ranges to themselves and have learned the hard way how to find safe footing and where to hide. "The lofty heights are our comrades," goes a sixteenth-century war ballad, "the pathless gorges our friends."[1]

Savage extremes of climate make mountains and plains alike almost unbearable for outsiders. In winter, the temperature often drops to –40° F. In summer, it soars to 130° F. in the shade in the more exposed areas. Rainfall is erratic, seldom exceeding five inches a year, and programs for water conservation are still insignificant, making water a scarce commodity. Few of the rivers in Baluchistan follow fixed courses. In August and September, thunderstorms and dust storms strike unpredictably and violently, often followed by torrential rains and flash floods. The lack of adequate and predictable water supplies has shaped the seminomadic lifestyle characteristic of most Baluch. Instead of relying solely on either nomadic pastoralism or on settled agriculture, most Baluch practice a mixture of the two in order to survive.

The focal points of tribal life are widely dispersed settlements of small agricultural plots, located in valleys where broad, ill-defined river-beds have been hollowed out by floods and on the northern plateaus where the rainfall is greatest. As many as ten families may have shares in a single plot. To the extent that the rains permit, the tribesmen grow such crops as wheat, millet, barley, onions, and peppers, in addition to tending their animals. But survival requires frequent migration to escape extremes of weather, replenish water supplies, and find fresh grazing lands for the flocks. The traveler through Baluchistan sees frequent evidence of this continual migration in the sporadic clusters of black goatskin tents that dot the landscape.

Goats and sheep are the mainstay of the tribal economy and are carefully herded to protect them from wolves and leopards. The favorite feast of the Baluch is *sajji*, a roast leg of lamb cooked on spits between shimmering beds of hot rocks often piled as high as five feet. The Baluch also keep donkeys, cows, and camels, but they are left to fend for themselves. The cows often stray far afield but generally stay near water; the donkeys tend to graze near the nomad camps. By contrast, camels need less water and pasturage, and some of the most bedraggled camels in the world can be seen wandering aimlessly throughout Baluchistan. There is a Baluch saying that if you see a cow, you have found water; if you see a donkey, you have found a camp; and if you see a camel, you are lost.

In many parts of Baluchistan, tribes living near date-growing oases trade their butter, milk, and grain for dates during the late summer and early autumn. The Baluch also eat a variety of wild plants, notably the heart of the hardy dwarf palm, which grows even in dry riverbeds. The leaves of the dwarf palm can be made into tents and produce a tough fiber used for rope shoes, mats, spoons, and even water pipes. Baluch women learn at an early age how to use this fiber, how to weave woolen rugs and garments, how to manipulate goatskin water bags on their backs over long distances, and how to cook in the open while the wind whistles. As in other pastoral Muslim societies, the Baluch keep their women veiled and practice arranged marriages. In the unabashedly male-centered Baluch ethos, women play a conspicuously subservient role in everyday life but are exalted in legends and folklore, which revolve around romantic triangles and martial struggles over insults to tribal honor generally involving victimized women.

The Baluch, who are Sunni Muslims of the Hanafi rite, are notably casual about religious observances. Religious leaders play a relatively marginal role in Baluch society, except in Iranian Baluchistan, where *maulavis* and *dervishes* have grown in importance in recent years. It is the tribal power structure that counts in Baluch rural society. Each of the seventeen major tribal groupings in Baluchistan is headed by a *sardar* (chieftain), and there are some 400 tribal subgroupings headed by lesser chieftains.

Out of the total Baluch population of some 5 million, nearly 1.5 million have migrated in search of work to Pakistani and Iranian cities outside Baluchistan or to the Persian Gulf. Of the remainder living in Pakistani and Iranian Baluchistan, more than 70 percent live a semi-nomadic life in rural areas. The poverty of this rural life is apparent in the fact that in Pakistani Baluchistan alone, only 3.3 million acres are cultivated out of a total acreage of some 85 million. Only 800,000 of these cultivated acres are irrigated, and most of the irrigated land is centered in the Las Bela and Kachhi areas, where non-Baluch settlers, encouraged by Islamabad, compete for the limited land available.

Some of the better-watered valleys support limited agriculture and have begun to attract light industry in recent decades. As chapter nine will elaborate, the potential for economic expansion in Baluchistan appears to be considerable, given the extent of underground water and mineral resources revealed by the limited surveys so far undertaken. But there are relatively few population centers for an area so vast in size. Pakistani Baluchistan has one town, Sibi, with a population of some 25,000, and twelve towns with populations of 7,500 or more.* Among these, the fishing ports at Gwadar, Pasni, and Ormara are often cited as possible targets of Soviet ambitions for a warm-water port on the Arabian Sea. The only city, Quetta, with a population of 122,000, sits on the border of the neighboring Pushtun tribal belt and has a more or less equal ethnic mix of Baluch, Pushtuns, and Punjabi settlers. Iranian Baluchistan has four towns with 10,000 inhabitants or more—Khash, Iranshahr, Sarawan, and Chah Bahar—as well as a multiethnic city of 75,000, Zahedan, which includes as many Sistanis and Persians as it does Baluch (see Figure 2).

As development activity has slowly increased over the years, leading to a gradual proliferation of educational facilities, there has been a steady

---

* Bhang, Dadar, Fort Sandeman, Gwadar, Kalat, Khuzdar, Mach, Mastung, Nushki, Ormara, Pasni, and Turbat. The urban-rural breakdowns in the 1961 and 1972 Pakistan censuses show an increase in the urban population of Baluchistan province from 228,468 to 399,583. The 1972 figures show 189,002 in Quetta district, 74,431 in Makran district, and 33,791 in Sibi district. ("Population [Urban/Rural by Sex, Division and District], 1961/1972," Table provided by the Information Ministry, Government of Pakistan, 16 March 1981.)

influx to urban centers. It is in these restive urban areas of Baluchistan and among Baluch migrants in Karachi and the Persian Gulf that literacy—and political consciousness—have been growing most rapidly. Most estimates suggest a literacy rate among the Baluch of 6 to 9 percent. Assuming a total Baluch population of five million, such estimates point to a literate Baluch population of 300,000 to 450,000, which is substantially higher than projections of census statistics would indicate.[2] Taking into account census projections and the available rough estimates of high school and college graduates, a credible estimate would be in the neighborhood of 250,000. This literate population provides the most volatile raw material for the organized Baluch nationalist movement. But the strength of Baluch nationalism, as we shall see, comes from the growing politicization of the countryside as a result of the 1973–1977 insurgency and the widespread acceptance of a common nationalist leadership cutting across the rural and urban areas of Pakistani Baluchistan and, more tenuously, Iranian Baluchistan as well.

Who Are the Baluch?

To the neighboring Pushtun tribes, who live in fertile riverine valleys, Baluchistan is "the dump where Allah shot the rubbish of creation."[3] But for the Baluch, their sense of identity is closely linked to the austere land where they have lived for at least a thousand years. According to the *Daptar Sha'ar* (Chronicle of Genealogies), an ancient ballad popular among all seventeen major Baluch tribes, the Baluch and the Kurds were kindred branches of a tribe that migrated eastward from Aleppo, in what is now Syria, shortly before the time of Christ in search of fresh pasturelands and water sources. One school of Baluch nationalist historians attempts to link this tribe ethnically with the Semitic Chaldean rulers of Babylon,[4] another with the early Arabs,[5] still others with Aryan tribes originally from Asia Minor.[6] In any case, there is agreement among these historians that the Kurds headed toward Iraq, Turkey, and northwest Persia, while the Baluch moved into the coastal areas along the southern shores of the Caspian Sea, later migrating into what are now Iranian Baluchistan and Pakistani Baluchistan between the sixth and fourteenth centuries.[7]

Western historians dismiss the *Daptar Sha'ar* as nothing more than myth and legend, totally unsubstantiated by verifiable evidence, and it remains for future scholars to probe into the murky origins of the Baluch. These legends are cited here not because they have serious historiographic value but because they are widely believed and are thus politically important today. For the most part, Aleppo is a unifying symbol of a common identity in the historical memories shared by all Baluch. In recent years, however, Arab attempts to attribute Arab ethnic origins to the Baluch have become a divisive factor in the nationalist movement (see chapter six).

Whatever the authenticity of the Aleppo legends, scholars in Baluchistan and in the West generally agree that the Baluch were living along the southern shores of the Caspian at the time of Christ. This consensus is based largely on linguistic evidence showing that the Baluchi language is descended from a lost language linked with the Parthian or Median civilizations, which flourished in the Caspian and adjacent areas in the pre-Christian era.[8] As one of the oldest living languages, Baluchi is a subject of endless fascination and controversy for linguists. It is classified as a member of the Iranian group of the Indo-European language family, which includes Farsi (Persian), Pushtu, Baluchi, and Kurdish. Baluchi is closely related to only one of the members of the Iranian group, Kurdish. In its modern form, it has incorporated borrowings from Persian, Sindhi, Arabic, and other languages, nonetheless retaining striking peculiarities that can be traced back to its pre-Christian origins. Until 150 years ago, the Baluch, like most nomadic societies, did not have a recorded literature. Initially, Baluch savants used the Persian and Urdu scripts to render Baluchi in written form. In recent decades, Baluch nationalist intellectuals have evolved a Baluchi script known as Nastaliq, a variant of the Arabic script.

Ethnically, the Baluch are no longer homogeneous, since the original nucleus that migrated from the Caspian has absorbed a variety of disparate groups along the way. Among these "new" Baluch were displaced tribes from Central Asia, driven southward by the Turkish and Mongol invasions from the tenth through the thirteenth centuries, and fugitive Arab factions defeated in intra-Arab warfare. Nevertheless, in cultural terms, the Baluch have been remarkably successful in preserving a distinctive identity in the face of continual pressures from strong cultures in neighboring areas. Despite the isolation of the scattered pastoral communities in Baluchistan, the Baluchi language and a relatively uniform Baluch folklore tradition and value system have provided a common denominator for the diverse Baluch tribal groupings scattered over the vast area from the Indus River in the east to the Iranian province of Kerman in the west.* To a great extent, it is the vitality of this ancient cultural heritage that explains the tenacity of the present demand for the political recognition of Baluch identity. But the strength of Baluch na-

---

* See chapter nine for a discussion of Brahui, a language spoken by certain Baluch tribes, which is increasingly converging with Baluchi.

tionalism is also rooted in proud historical memories of determined resistance against the would-be conquerors who perennially attempted, without success, to annex all or part of Baluchistan to their adjacent empires.

Reliving their past endlessly in books, magazines, and folk ballads, the Baluch accentuate the positive. They revel in the gory details of ancient battles against Persians, Turks, Arabs, Tartars, Hindus, and other adversaries, focusing on how valiantly their generals fought rather than on whether the Baluch won or lost. They point to the heroes who struggled to throw off the yoke of more powerful oppressors and minimize the role of the quislings who sold out the Baluch cause. Above all, they seek to magnify the achievements of their more successful rulers, contending that the Baluch were on the verge of consolidating political unity when the British arrived on the scene and applied their policy of divide and rule. This claim is difficult to sustain with much certainty on the basis of the available evidence. Nevertheless, the Baluch did make several significant attempts to draw together politically, and their failure to establish an enduring polity in past centuries does not prove that they would fail under the very different circumstances prevailing today. As Baluch writers argue, given the technologies of modern transportation and communication, the contemporary Baluch nationalist has new opportunities for cementing Baluch political unity that were not open to his forebears.

The Search for Political Identity

In order to validate their demands today, Baluch nationalists focus on the unification efforts made by three Baluch monarchs who ruled during the three centuries preceding the British Raj. The first nation-builder cited in Baluch historical accounts is Mir Chakar Rind,* who in the fifteenth century established a short-lived tribal confederacy reaching from the Makran coast to the present-day Marri tribal area south of Quetta. Mir Chakar ruled from his capital at Sibi from 1487 until his death in 1511, but his kingdom was destroyed by a civil war between the two leading Baluch tribal federations, the Rinds and the Lasharis. Baluch nationalist writers extol Mir Chakar for making the first serious effort to unify the Baluch politically, but reserve their highest encomiums for his brilliance as a general who personified Baluch martial virtues.

There is considerable confusion surrounding the later years of Mir

---

* *Mir* is an honorific title in the Muslim world, applied especially, but not exclusively, to descendants of the Prophet Mohammed.

"The pathless gorges, our friends"

A Baluch nomad encampment in Pakistan

Chakar's reign, especially the circumstances of his abandonment of his capital at Sibi. While some historical evidence suggests that he was defeated by the Lasharis, most Baluch nationalists are reluctant to concede that Mir Chakar was forced to leave Sibi in defeat and argue instead that he pulled up stakes in order to go on to still greater triumphs by leading a Baluch invasion of northern India. Whatever the circumstances of his departure from Sibi, it is clear that he did lead a sizable army into the Punjab, achieving "complete possession" of Multan and other areas of the south Punjab during the early sixteenth century.[9] The British historian M. Longworth Dames writes that Mir Chakar's military successes "seem to have led to something like a national migration."[10] Mir Khuda Bux Marri stresses that Mir Chakar led an army of 40,000 men into the Punjab, pointing out that Babur, founder of the Moghul Empire, conquered India with only 12,000 soldiers. With an army of 40,000, he speculates, Mir Chakar must have had some 200,000 to 300,000 followers on the march, including family members.[11]

Although never able to subdue the Lasharis, Mir Chakar is hailed in nationalist accounts as a Baluch Attila, and the exploits of his army during the Rind-Lashari war are idealized as "the Iliad of the Baluch race."[12] Similarly, his march into the Punjab, where he died, is proudly remembered, even though he failed to lay the foundations for enduring control over the areas that he conquered. The Baluch who settled in the Punjab are not closely linked to the mainstream of Baluch life today.

The principal link with their past for most Baluch is the vast body of popular ballads dating back to the days of Mir Chakar. Handed down from generation to generation and first recorded by British scholars, these ballads, sung by professional wandering minstrels, center to a considerable extent on the Rind-Lashari conflict. One of them, for example, glorifies Mir Chakar's role in the battle of Nali, where "forty thousand warriors collect on Mir's call, all descendants of one ancestor, all bedecked with coats of mail and iron armour covering their head, chest and forearms; all armed with bows and arrows, silken scarves, overcoats, red boots on their feet, silver knives, sharp daggers and golden rings on their fingers."[13]

After Mir Chakar's death in 1511, the Moghul Empire, based in Delhi, made several unsuccessful attempts to incorporate the Baluch, who were able to cooperate militarily to preserve their independence. However, the Baluch tribes were unable to restore even a modicum of political unity until the Ahmadzai tribe established the Kalat Confederacy in 1666. Based in the Kalat highlands, southwest of Mir Chakar's former capital, the new confederacy gradually encompassed an area even larger than Mir Chakar's domain. During the early eighteenth century, Abdullah Khan, the fourth Khan of Kalat,* claimed the allegiance of Baluch tribes scattered from Kandahar (now in southeastern Afghanistan) across the Makran area to Bandar Abbas (now in Iran). In the southeast, his jurisdiction included the Dera Ghazi Khan district on the edge of the Punjab. Recent indications of possible uranium deposits in Dera Ghazi Khan have led Baluch historians to emphasize that it fell within the Kalat Confederacy under Mir Abdullah and most of his successors.

Although the boundaries of Abdullah Khan's confederacy were far-flung, he was forced to pay tribute to Iranian monarchs in order to forestall their incursions in the distant western border areas of his realm. Moreover, he did little to knit the areas under his military control into a unified state. That task was left to the sixth Khan of Kalat, the dynamic Nasir Khan, who ruled for more than half a century, beginning in 1741. Nasir Khan's most notable achievement was the creation of a unified Baluch army of some 25,000 men and 1,000 camels, an impressive force by eighteenth-century Southwest Asian standards. For the first time in their history, most of the major Baluch tribes were rallied under the banner of an agreed system of military organization and recruitment.

Administratively, Nasir Khan came closer to establishing a centralized bureaucratic apparatus covering all of Baluchistan than any other Baluch ruler before or since. He had a *wazir* (prime minister), who supervised all internal administration and foreign affairs matters, and a *vakil*, whose responsibility it was to collect revenue from crown lands as well as tribute from loosely affiliated principalities or chiefdoms. There were two legislative councils, loosely described as a "Baluch parliament" by the late Khan of Kalat, consisting of a lower chamber chosen by the tribes and an upper chamber of elders serving in an advisory capacity. Members of the lower house, or their representatives, remained in Kalat at all times. The Khan built a network of roads, lined with new *caravanserais* (inns accommodating caravans), and was famed for constructing elaborate mosques.[14] There is some confusion among historians, however, as to whether he had a systematic basis for revenue collection. In political science terms, Nina Swidler writes, the Khanate of Kalat fell midway between the conventional categories of the kin-based tribe headed by an autocratic chief, with no larger political affiliation, and the centralized bureaucratic state. In her view, the khanate was never able to exact revenue from the tribes or to administer uniform tax levies on the caravan trade passing through Kalat. While the tribes did provide reliable military support, she states, the khanate relied for its financial

---

* A title of Turkish origin, *khan* is loosely applied to local chieftains or princes of varying importance.

support on irrigated crown lands in the Sarawan district commandeered at an early stage of the dynasty.[15] Challenging this view, the Khan of Kalat spoke of the collection of a traditional Islamic tax by the Kalat government dating back to the Nasir Khan period.[16] Nationalist historian Mohammed Khan Baluch states that Baluch legends attribute a treasury of four million rupees to Nasir Khan in his heyday.[17] Other sources suggest that land taxes were required from certain outlying areas that did not have a troop quota.

Nasir Khan paid tribute during the first several years of his reign to the powerful Persian emperor Nadir Shah, who had conquered the warring tribes of adjacent Afghanistan and had helped him to win the Kalat throne in the face of rival claims to the succession. Nasir Khan repudiated this tributary status following Nadir Shah's assassination in 1747 and the subsequent decline of centralized power in Iran. However, when Ahmad Shah Durrani stepped into the resulting vacuum and established the new kingdom of Afghanistan, Nasir Khan was forced to acknowledge Afghan suzerainty for eleven years, a fact cited by Afghan nationalists today to justify the idea of a Greater Afghanistan, incorporating Baluchistan. Once he had firmly established his army, Nasir Khan took on the Afghans militarily, fighting Ahmad Shah Durrani's forces to a standoff in 1758. Thereafter, Kalat enjoyed sovereign status until the arrival of the British, though it remained a military ally of Afghanistan.

At the height of his power, Nasir Khan renewed Kalat's claims of sovereignty over the Iranian Baluch areas and sent occasional expeditionary forces to his western borderlands. Nevertheless, it should be emphasized that the freewheeling Iranian Baluch tribes were for all practical purposes a law unto themselves. Separated by geography from the main body of the Baluch tribes to the east and themselves divided into several distinctive regional subgroupings, the Iranian Baluch have been on the fringes of Baluch political life throughout history and continue to be so today. Taking the self-contained character of Iranian Baluch life into account, this book treats the contemporary Baluch nationalist movements in Pakistan and Iran in separate chapters.

While they consistently rebuffed Persian and Afghan incursions, the Iranian Baluch were never able to produce a unified political or military grouping of their own, even for a brief period. Certain strong chieftains were able to establish localized confederacies, notably Dost Mohammed, who was beginning to extend his sway over southeastern Iran when Reza Shah Pahlavi subdued his forces in 1928, using air power and artillery for the first time in Iran.[18] Dost Mohammed's son, Mir Amin, former mayor of the Iranian Baluch town of Sarawan, said in a 1978 interview that his father had envisaged the creation of an independent Baluch state along the Makran coast. This state would have embraced not only the coastal areas of Baluchistan that became part of Iran, he recalled, but would also have reached into what is now Pakistani Baluchistan as far as Pasni (see Figure 2). However, at the time of Reza Shah's conquest, Dost Mohammed had in fact achieved only a shaky control over roughly one-third of the Iranian Baluch areas and had signally failed to create unifying bureaucratic or military machinery comparable to that developed by Nasir Khan.

For Baluch nationalists today, Nasir Khan's achievements remain an all-important symbol, providing some semblance of historical precedent for the concept of a unified Baluch political identity. Nationalist authors invariably cite a tribute to Nasir Khan by a British observer, Sir Henry Pottinger, who termed him "a most extraordinary combination of all the virtues attached to soldier, statesman or prince" and reported after a tour through Baluchistan that "the most distant districts were always as alert in obeying his orders as those near at hand."[19] "Forward March," the "national anthem" sung at Baluch political gatherings, invokes the name of Nasir Khan, enjoining all Baluch to

> March on, march on!
> This living slavery
> Is forbidden to the Faithful.
> Slavery is for the heathen,
> From his pen Nasir said it.
>
> March on, march on!
> With pride in your motherland,
> With devotion in body and soul,
> Come out of slavery.
> March on, march on![20]

Another patriotic song often sung in student meetings and other nationalist gatherings concludes that

> Pleasant as the homeland of another may be,
> Populous and affluent and great of name,
> Streams of honey may run there.
> But for Nasir
> The "dry wood of the homeland" is better
> than all the world.[21]

Why did the unity built by Nasir Khan collapse during the decades after his death in 1805? Was it, as most available evidence would suggest, simply because his successors succumbed to the centrifugal pulls of tribal strife?

The issue is confused in that his passing from the scene coincided with the beginnings of the "Great Game" between Britain and Russia in Afghanistan and British adoption of the "Forward Policy," designed to push the jurisdiction of the Raj to the Afghan frontier. When the British concluded that Afghanistan should become a buffer state to shield their Indian empire from Russia, Baluchistan, as a key area flanking Afghanistan, immediately acquired a new strategic significance. Determined to establish direct control over the access routes to Afghanistan, the British fought bloody battles with the Baluch for more than forty years. By 1876, they were able to subdue Kalat and obtain formal treaty rights to station troops there in return for handsome subsidies and guarantees of tribal autonomy. Playing off rival chiefs against each other during the closing decades of the century, Britain systematically proceeded to divide the Baluch area into seven parts. In the far west, the Goldsmid line gave roughly one-fourth to Persia in 1871; in the north, the Durand line assigned a small strip to Afghanistan in 1894; and in British India, the Baluch areas were divided into a centrally administered enclave (known as British Baluchistan) guarding a key mountain pass, a truncated remnant of the Kalat Confederacy, and three smaller puppet principalities.

A leading contemporary Baluch nationalist, Ghaus Bux Bizenjo, former governor of Pakistani Baluchistan, argued in a 1978 interview that Nasir Khan's successors would have consolidated an enduring polity if it had not been for the deliberate manipulation of the internal divisions in Baluch society by the British Raj. In Bizenjo's view, the Baluch failed to sustain their nationhood primarily because they happened to live in an area of vital military importance to the British. It was historical accident, he explained, that gave the Afghans the opportunity for independent statehood denied to the Baluch. Just as it served the interests of the British to foster a unified Afghanistan as a buffer state, so it was necessary, conversely, for Britain to divide the Baluch in order to make the frontiers of the Raj contiguous with Afghanistan and to assure unimpeded military dominance in the frontier region.

Nasir Khan's Kalat Confederacy might have emerged in a buffer state role instead, Bizenjo contended, if the Russians had moved south sooner than they did and if they had swallowed up Afghanistan before Britain embarked on its Forward Policy. "Remember," he said, alluding to the founding of Kalat in 1666, "we Baluch had created a state eighty years before Afghanistan was established."

Suggesting a more elemental explanation for the failure of the Baluch to achieve political unity, Brian Spooner, an anthropologist who has studied Iranian Baluchistan, stresses ecological factors. Given its forbidding topography and the fragmentation of its limited pasture lands, Spooner points out, Baluchistan lacks the large-scale nomadic settlements found in many other pastoral societies where grazing areas are more concentrated. The resulting dispersion of Baluch nomads has "made it difficult for tribal leaders to build up large confederacies," especially in the face of peculiarly severe transportation and communication problems.[22]

In ecological terms, Spooner classifies Baluchistan as "a marginal area, in the sense that at a given level of technology it can support fewer people per unit area in poorer circumstances than is the case in surrounding areas." It is generally true of such marginal areas, he concludes, that "their history is a function of the history of neighboring areas, that economic development of them is difficult except as the result of direct interest from an external power, but that unless they are important for communications, mineral deposits or other strategic considerations, such interest is not exerted. The investment required to achieve or maintain political control is not justified."[23]

Applying his analysis to the specific historical experience of Baluchistan, Spooner found only one instance in which an external power had shown much interest in the political unification of Baluchistan during the eight centuries between the Tatar invasion and the advent of the British. That was when the Persian emperor Nadir Shah gave his blessing to the young Nasir Khan, "confirming and legitimizing" a regime that lasted for the next half century. Before the Shah's intervention, the Kalat dynasty had been on the verge of collapse, Spooner maintained, and it began to fall apart once again in the early nineteenth century following Nasir Khan's death.[24]

If one accepts this interpretation of history, it logically follows that the Baluch will find it difficult, on their own, to achieve the unity necessary for a successful independence movement and for the long-term preservation of their sovereignty. By the same token, however, their prospects appear considerably brighter if one assumes even relatively limited intervention by a foreign power or powers. Surveying the Southwest Asian scene in the 1980s, it takes little imagination to envisage contingencies in which one external power or another might conclude that "the investment required to achieve and maintain political control" was fully justified by "communications, mineral deposits or other strategic considerations." Moreover, it should be remembered that the nineteenth and twentieth centuries marked a major watershed for the Baluch, who had never lost their freedom before their conquest by the modern armies of Britain, Iran, and Pakistan. The rise of Baluch nationalism now taking place in response to alien domination has posed qualitatively new questions about the nature of Baluch social and political identity for which answers are not to be found in the historical record.

The Emergence of
Baluch Nationalism

3

In both Iran and Pakistan, the contemporary Baluch nationalist movement has been steadily germinating since the subjugation of the Baluch by the Pahlavi dynasty in 1928 and by the Muslim League regime of Mohammed Ali Jinnah in 1947. As chapter six will show, however, the maturation process has been much slower in Iran, where the Pahlavis not only applied their superior military power with devastating effect, but also stifled the growth of an educated, politically conscious Baluch leadership. It is in the more favorable political climate of Pakistani Baluchistan that the nationalist movement has been able to sink its strongest roots.

In Iranian Baluchistan, Persian rulers were able to break the power of Baluch chieftains by first defeating them on the battlefield and then inducing them with carrot-and-stick techniques to act as middlemen for Teheran in dealing with their tribesmen. By contrast, British colonial administrators did not attempt to extend the administrative machinery of the Raj into the Baluch areas, with the exception of British Baluchistan, a narrow strip of territory bordering Afghanistan. So long as tribal leaders did not interfere with British military access to Afghanistan and British strategic control of frontier areas, the *sardars* enjoyed virtually complete control of their tribal affairs and were paid subsidies as well. By reinforcing the power and autonomy of the tribal chieftains, this permissive policy set the stage for subsequent conflict between the Pakistani Baluch and Islamabad.

Since the departure of the British, Pakistani leaders have attempted to reverse the policy of tribal autonomy, emulating the hard-line approach toward the *sardars* successfully applied in Iran. However, unlike the Persian rulers, who deliberately curtailed education in the Baluch areas, Pakistani leaders have fanned the fires of political awareness by providing expanded educational opportunities and other tokens of modernization. In the eyes of Pakistani nation-builders, the goal of a strong, centralized state made it imperative to break down the power of tribal chieftains as part of a larger effort to merge Baluch identity into an all-embracing Pakistani identity. But to most Baluch, tribal identity and Baluch identity are merely different layers of a single psychological whole. Islamabad's assault on the tribal social structure and its commitment to a monolithic Pakistani nationalism constitute a frontal challenge to Baluch values. The result is a simmering guerrilla struggle that has flared up with progressively increasing intensity in 1948, 1958, 1962, and finally with full force in the 1973–1977 insurgency.

The Struggle Against Accession to Pakistan

The incorporation of the Baluch into Pakistan came as a traumatic blow to nationalist leaders who had campaigned clandestinely for an independent Baluchistan during the last decades of the British Raj. The British attempted to suppress nationalist activity and resisted pressures for the introduction of education in the Baluch areas. Nevertheless, several hundred Baluch were permitted to obtain a high school and, in some cases, a college education, most of them from *sardar*-related families whose good will was valuable to the Raj. Even this limited exposure to education produced an upsurge of political consciousness under the stimulus of the October Revolution in the Soviet Union and the anti-British struggle led by Mohandas K. Gandhi and Jawaharlal Nehru.

During the twenties, recalled Mir Ahmed Yar Khan, the last ruler of Kalat, "most of the educated youth of the day" thought that Soviet objectives were progressive and would serve the Baluch cause by hastening the end of British rule and setting the stage for Baluch independence.[1] This pro-Soviet climate did not result in a significant Communist party, as chapter seven explains, but it accelerated the ferment that led to the emergence of an organized nationalist movement. One of the favorite anticolonial issues of the late twenties was the revival of British efforts to recruit Baluch soldiers into the imperial Indian army. The British had liquidated the Baluch element of the Duke of Connaught's Own Baluchis in 1910 after finding the Baluch difficult to discipline and prone to "the disconcerting habit of departing without notice."[2] When British military authorities decided to try again in 1929, Baluch nationalists, sparked by a small Communist cadre, waged a successful antirecruitment campaign. That movement culminated in an armed mutiny and the dismissal of all Baluch soldiers from what is still called the Baluch Regiment of the Pakistan Army, despite the fact that it has not included Baluch for nearly half a century.[3]

In the early 1930s, Baluch newspapers began to appear, and several underground Baluch political groups were organized, most notably Abdul Aziz Kurd's Anjuman-e-Ittehad-e-Baluchistan (Organization for the Unity of Baluchistan). In August 1933, the group's weekly newspaper, *Al-Baloch* of Karachi, published a map depicting an independent Greater

Baluchistan that embraced the Baluch areas of Iran as well as Kalat and the other Baluch principalities of Pakistan, British Baluchistan, Dera Ghazi Khan (a Baluch-claimed district in the Punjab), and the province of Sind.[4] By 1935, Kurd, Yusuf Ali Magsi, and other non-Communist nationalists had openly formed the Kalat National party, dedicated to the goal of an "independent, unified Baluchistan" following the departure of the British. As the necessary prelude to independence, the party demanded that the British restore the Baluch principalities of Kharan, Makran, and Las Bela to Kalat (see Figure 2). This party enjoyed the tacit approval of the Kalat ruler, Mir Ahmed Yar Khan, and was initially accorded a measure of freedom by the British before it was outlawed in 1939.

As the prospect of independence from Britain approached, Baluch leaders had to decide whether to seek sovereignty, as advocated by the Kalat National party, accession to Pakistan, or some intermediate status such as a confederal relationship with Pakistan. The Khan of Kalat made clear from the beginning that he sought independence and that he saw himself as heir to the tradition of Baluch nationalism personified by his ancestor Nasir Khan.

The Khan argued that the legal status of Nepal and Kalat was different from that of other princely states in the Indian subcontinent. While the other "native states" dealt with the British Indian government in New Delhi, Nepal and Kalat maintained their treaty relations directly with Whitehall. More important, the 1876 treaty which permitted Britain to occupy Baluchistan pledged that the British "would respect the sovereignty and independence of Kalat."[5]

In a memorandum submitted to the British Cabinet Mission in March 1946, the Khan asserted that the government or governments succeeding the Raj would inherit only the treaty relationships of the colonial government in New Delhi, not those of Whitehall. Once the British withdrew, the memorandum said, Kalat would retain the independence it had enjoyed prior to 1876. Similarly, the Baluch principalities that had been tributaries of Kalat, and which were later "leased" to the British under duress, would revert to Kalat. As a result, the memorandum stated, Kalat

> will become fully sovereign and independent in respect to both internal and external affairs, and will be free to conclude treaties with any other government or state.... The Khan, his government, and his people can never agree to Kalat being included in any form of Indian union. The Khan and his government will, however, always be glad to enter into an alliance with any government which succeeds the British government in India on the basis of the strictest reciprocity.[6]

The Cabinet Mission attempted to finesse the issue with a non-committal statement that left undecided the future of all of the princely states in the subcontinent. When Pakistan was formally established a year later, the issue was still unresolved, with the Khan insisting on his right to full independence and Pakistani leaders demanding unconditional accession. On August 15, 1947, one day after the creation of Pakistan, the Khan declared Kalat's independence, but offered to negotiate a special relationship with Pakistan in the spheres of defense, foreign affairs, and communications. Pakistani leaders summarily rejected this declaration, touching off a nine-month diplomatic tug of war that came to a climax in the forcible annexation of Kalat. The full story of the British role in the tangled maneuvering that resulted in Kalat's annexation has yet to be revealed by historians. But it is clear that Baluch leaders, including the Khan, were bitterly opposed to what happened.

Pakistani historians, who seek to magnify the role of the Muslim League in the annexation of Baluchistan, maintain that the Khan's stand was not representative of Baluch sentiment and point as evidence to a pro-Pakistan assembly of Baluch leaders in Quetta on June 29, 1947. These historians fail to note that the participants had been appointed by the British Raj and that the assembly's recommendations related only to the small area known as British Baluchistan.[7] Moreover, the Pakistani version of the accession debate is discredited by a study of the discussions of the Kalat Assembly on the accession issue and by interviews with a variety of Baluch leaders that confirm the authenticity of the official assembly proceedings.

The fifty-two-member lower house of the Kalat Assembly was chosen in the immediate aftermath of the Khan's declaration of independence. According to Inayatullah Baloch, a nationalist historian, the Khan staged elections in which the Kalat National party won thirty-nine seats, showing that nationalist sentiment clearly outweighed conservative tribal influence.[8] Other sources confirm that elections were held but suggest that they were hastily arranged and were not very broad-based. In any case, the assembly met for a week in early September 1947 and again in mid-December. Although most members clearly desired an alliance with Pakistan, an overwhelming consensus favored independence as a precondition for such a relationship. Speaker after speaker argued that Pakistan had shown malice toward the Baluch by perpetuating the separate status of the three "leased" Baluch principalities detached from Kalat by the British. If a unified Baluch identity had been recognized within the framework of Pakistan, several members said, it might have been possible to consider accession. But Pakistan had shown its true colors. Formalizing the dismemberment of Kalat, the Khan said, was "tantamount to the political castration of the Baluch."[9]

Assembly member Ghaus Bux Bizenjo, then twenty-nine, the principal spokesman for the independence forces, advanced many of the same arguments used by separatists today. On December 14, 1947, Bizenjo declared that

> we have a distinct culture like Afghanistan and Iran, and if the mere fact that we are Muslims requires us to amalgamate with Pakistan, then Afghanistan and Iran should also be amalgamated with Pakistan. They say we Baluch cannot defend ourselves in the atomic age. Well, are Afghanistan, Iran, and even Pakistan capable of defending themselves against the superpowers? If we cannot defend ourselves, a lot of others cannot do so either. They say we must join Pakistan for economic reasons. Yet we have minerals, we have petroleum and we have ports. The question is, what would Pakistan be without us?

Bizenjo made clear that he was prepared for close ties between a sovereign Kalat and Pakistan.

> I do not propose to create hurdles for the newly created state in matters of defense, external affairs, and communications. But we want an honorable relationship and not a humiliating one. We don't want to amalgamate with Pakistan. We cannot become such culprits in the eyes of history that we would take the Baluch into non-Baluch territory. If Pakistan wants to treat us as a sovereign people, we are ready to extend our friendship. But if Pakistan does not do so and forces us to accept this fate, flying in the face of democratic principles, every Baluch will fight for his freedom.[10]

Looking back on his 1947 speech in an interview in 1978, the sixty-year-old Bizenjo stressed that the dominant sentiment in the assembly was for a sovereign Baluch state. "We were opposed to accession, and we were not thinking of a confederation," he said, "but rather of special arrangements embodied in a treaty under which we would mutually conduct our defense, our foreign affairs, and our communications. We envisaged two sovereign countries in a treaty relationship."

The showdown between Kalat and Pakistan came on April 1, 1948, when the Pakistan Army ordered its garrison commander in Baluchistan to march on Kalat and arrest the Khan unless he signed an agreement of accession. The Khan capitulated, but his younger brother, Prince Abdul Karim, who was then governor of the newly annexed Baluch principality of Makran, gathered the arms, ammunition, and treasury funds under his control and declared a revolt against Pakistan. After leading some 700 followers across the border into Afghanistan, Abdul Karim issued a manifesto in the name of the Baluch National Liberation Committee disavowing the unconditional accession agreement signed by the Khan, proclaiming the independence of Kalat, and demanding fresh negotiations with Pakistan. K. B. Nizamani, one of the participants in this minirevolt, recalled in a 1980 interview that Abdul Karim had the tacit approval of the Khan, who saw the move as a last-ditch means of pressuring Pakistan and regaining some of his princely prerogatives. Bizenjo, Gul Khan Nasir, a prominent Baluch nationalist writer, and other leading Baluch political figures were cool to the idea of a military showdown with Pakistan, Nizamani said, fearing that it would be doomed to failure. Abdul Karim, however, embarked on his adventure confident that he would obtain Afghan support. He reasoned that since Afghanistan had objected to the inclusion of the Baluch and Pushtun areas in Pakistan and had even opposed the admission of Pakistan to the United Nations, Kabul could be persuaded to support a military initiative by the Baluch before the new Pakistani state became too well established.

According to the official Pakistani version of the episode, Abdul Karim's forces were "substantially" expanded with Afghan help and then proceeded to launch guerrilla operations against the Pakistan Army in Jhalawan district in late May. Units of General Akbar Khan's Seventh Regiment soon tracked the guerrillas down, forcing Abdul Karim to surrender in mid-June.

According to Nizamani and other Baluch nationalists, however, Abdul Karim came back without Afghan support* and had just begun to wage desultory guerrilla actions when the Khan, threatened with reprisals by Pakistani authorities, persuaded his brother to surrender with assurances of safe conduct and amnesty from the Pakistan Army. Pakistani officers reportedly signed a safe conduct agreement with Abdul Karim's representatives in the Harboi mountains and swore an oath on the Koran to uphold it. However, in this account, Pakistani forces dishonored the agreement by ambushing and arresting the Prince and 102 of his companions on their way to Kalat.

---

* Nationalist historian Inayatullah Baloch states that Afghanistan denied support to Karim because Kabul favored the inclusion of Baluchistan in an Afghan-controlled "Pushtunistan" and was opposed to an independent Baluchistan (Inayatullah Baloch, "The Emergence of Baluch Nationalism," *Pakistan Progressive*, New York, December 1980, p. 22). See my discussion of Pushtun-Baluch tension over the issue of Baluch independence in chapter seven.

The "Broken Treaties"

Abdul Karim's adventure was clearly of little immediate importance because it lacked both unified Baluch political support and Afghan military support. But what did make it significant in the long run was the widespread Baluch belief that Pakistan had betrayed the safe conduct agreement. The Baluch regard this as the first of a series of "broken treaties" which have cast an aura of distrust over relations with Islamabad. Abdul Karim and his followers were all sentenced to long prison terms and became rallying symbols for the nascent nationalist movement.

Nationalist sentiment grew rapidly among the Baluch in response to the aggressive centralizing policies pursued by Pakistani leaders. The hastily contrived Pakistani state that emerged out of the 1947 partition of the subcontinent consisted of a homogeneous, numerically dominant Bengali eastern wing and a heterogeneous western wing divided into ethnically distinct Punjabi, Sindhi, Pushtun, and Baluch regional components. Punjabi leaders, who controlled the military and bureaucratic power structure of the central government, feared that the three minority provinces in the western wing would combine with the Bengalis against them. They decided to consolidate the western wing into a single, unified province that would balance Bengali strength in a projected national governmental structure based on the concept of parity between the two wings. When central authorities began to take concrete steps designed to pave the way for this restructuring of West Pakistan, known as the One Unit plan, Baluch leaders immediately reacted by organizing open opposition in defiance of a ban on political activity. In 1955, Abdul Karim, who had completed his prison term, formed the Ustoman Gal (People's party), which opposed One Unit and demanded the formation of a unified Baluchistan province. The Khan of Kalat supported the concept of a unified Baluch state but wanted it to be under his leadership. Reviving his 1947 demand for independence and for the restoration to Kalat of other Baluch areas taken away by the British, the Khan mobilized widespread demonstrations against the One Unit idea through the tribal chieftains in his former domain.

Against a background of growing restlessness in Baluchistan, the Pakistan Army moved into Kalat on October 6, 1958—one day before martial law was declared throughout Pakistan, setting the stage for the establishment of Ayub Khan's military regime. The army arrested the Khan in his palace, commandeered his ancestral valuables, roughed up civilians who demonstrated in his favor, and detained fifty of his retainers as well as an estimated 300 Baluch political leaders in other towns. The central government charged that Abdul Karim and an uncle of the

Khan had been secretly negotiating with Afghanistan for support of a full-scale Baluch rebellion and had assembled a force of 80,000 tribesmen. However, the only evidence put forward to substantiate these charges was the fact that the Khan's Afghan wife had gone to Kabul for a holiday. The Khan's partisans maintain that these allegations were deliberately planted to provide a pretext for the nationwide imposition of martial law.[11]

The dimensions of this revolt were not as great as depicted in government accounts. Nor were the events of October 6 as bloody as depicted in the Khan's memoirs. Nevertheless, the Khan's arrest, climaxing a decade of steadily accumulating tensions, touched off a chain reaction of violence and counterviolence that has continued in Baluchistan to the present day. Aggressively patrolling the Jhalawan district, the army demanded that tribesmen turn in their weapons at local police stations. This demand outraged the Baluch, who regard the possession of guns as their birthright. The tribesmen refused to comply with this edict, provoking numerous skirmishes in which the army deployed tanks and artillery in towns and remote areas throughout the district. As tribal resistance grew and guerrilla bands began to form, the army blockaded the passes leading from Jhalawan to neighboring Sarawan (see Figure 2). The blockade led to a celebrated battle on October 10, 1958, at a remote mountain village known as Wad. Nauroz Khan, a chief of the Zehri tribe, emerged as the leader of a hastily assembled guerrilla force numbering 750 to 1,000 men.

Aroused by the bombing and confiscation of his house and property, Nauroz Khan, who was then ninety years old, led guerrilla activities against the army in Jhalawan and surrounding districts for more than a year, proclaiming that he would fight on until the Khan was returned to power and the One Unit plan was abandoned. The government responded by bombing villages suspected of harboring guerrillas and by reinforcing army units. Finally, with no end to hostilities in sight, representatives of the army and the guerrillas met in early 1960 to discuss peace terms. According to Pakistani sources, no agreement was reached. But in nationalist accounts, Nauroz Khan and his men agreed to lay down their arms in return for the withdrawal of the One Unit plan and a promise of safe conduct and amnesty. Once again, as in the case of Abdul Karim in 1948, the army representatives sanctified their safe conduct pledge with an oath on the Koran and, once again, they dishonored the pledge. In any event, Nauroz Khan was arrested, and his son and five others were hanged on treason charges in July 1960.

Popular accounts relate that the condemned cried, "Long live Baluchistan!" as they went to the gallows. One of them reputedly tied a copy of the Koran around his neck, shouting that if he were hanged, the Koran must also be hanged, since the government had broken its holy oath. Nauroz Khan's sentence was commuted to life imprisonment, and he died in Kohlu prison in 1964, a martyr to the Baluch cause. Stories of his alleged torture by the army are still a staple commodity of Baluch magazines. On a visit to the Quetta headquarters of the Baluch Students Organization in 1978, I saw a giant montage, covering an entire wall, which showed Nauroz next to scenes of his son's hanging and other atrocities.

The Beginnings of Insurgency

That a relatively small Baluch guerrilla force had been able to pin down well-equipped, numerically superior army regulars greatly disturbed military leaders and prompted them to set up new garrisons at key points in the interior of Baluchistan following the 1960 fighting. Faced with the specter of an expanding and seemingly permanent army presence, a group of politically conscious Baluch began to map plans for an organized guerrilla movement capable of defending Baluch interests. Most of the group were attracted to Marxist-Leninist ideas and wanted to emulate successful leftist guerrilla movements in other countries.

"At first we had a simple objective," Sher Mohammed Marri, the prime mover in this initiative, recalled in a 1978 interview. "We were struggling to save the Baluch nation, which was being crushed by the Pakistani government. We did not define our long-range objectives at that time on the question of independence or autonomy within Pakistan, because we were too busy concentrating on our immediate objective, namely, ousting the Pakistan Army from Baluchistan. We wanted to introduce scientific methods of guerrilla warfare into a struggle that had previously been waged in a disorganized, random manner. We wanted to give the struggle ideological firmness so that it would last from year to year. Until then, the Baluch had fought bravely on a tribal basis when they felt their dignity and honor had been insulted, but they were not organized in such a way that no one would dare to insult them in the first place."

Sher Mohammed, a towering hulk of a man with an oversized turban, a protuberant red moustache, and a long white beard, is a cousin of two leaders of the Bijarani section of the important Marri tribe and a close ally of the powerful *sardar* (chieftain) of the entire tribe, Khair Bux Marri. His father and uncle served prison terms for their anti-British activity, and Sher Mohammed himself served a total of fourteen years in prison, first for organizing a labor party during the preindependence period, despite a British ban on political activity, and later, on two different occasions, for alleged seditious activity against the interests of Pakistan. He played a pioneering role in stimulating grassroots nationalist organizing activity but has never achieved the stature of the three preeminent Baluch nationalist leaders described in the next chapter, Khair Bux Marri, Ghaus Bux Bizenjo, and Ataullah Mengal.

The late president of Pakistan, Zulfiqar Ali Bhutto, charging that Sher Mohammed had links with the Soviet Union, once dubbed him General Sherov. However, while Sher Mohammed calls himself a Marxist-Leninist, his move to create a guerrilla movement in the early 1960s was not supported by the pro-Soviet Communist party of Pakistan. Then as now, the party's line has been that communist forces should strive together to win control of all of Pakistan and that separatist movements in the minority provinces will only serve the interests of feudal and "bourgeois nationalist" elements.

For more than two years, Sher Mohammed and an initial nucleus of twenty ideologically attuned followers quietly laid their plans, seeking to get a network of base camps in place before taking on the army. As the name for their movement, they chose the Baluchi word *parari*, which is used to describe a person or group with grievances that cannot be solved by talk. For their models, Sher Mohammed and his followers looked to the experience of guerrilla struggles in China, Vietnam, Cuba, and Algeria, "but we tried to find a Baluch synthesis rather than to rely on what had happened anywhere else." By July 1963, the Pararis had established twenty-two base camps of varying sizes spread over 45,000 square miles, from the Mengal tribal areas of Jhalawan in the south, where Ali Mohammed Mengal was in command, to the Marri and Bukti areas in the north (see Figure 2). Manned by what they called a "command force" of 400 full-time volunteers, each camp could call on hundreds of loosely organized, part-time reservists.

By design, the Pararis generally attempted to avoid large-scale encounters with the army. Instead, they harassed the Pakistani forces in classic guerrilla fashion by ambushing convoys, bombing trains, sniping at sentries, and raiding military encampments. In retaliation the army staged a series of intermittent offensives marked by free-swinging reprisals and air attacks, which only served to solidify support for the guerrillas. In the first of these offensives, the army bulldozed 13,000 acres of almond trees owned by Sher Mohammed and his relatives in one of the few fertile orchard areas of the Marri region. This action provoked a major battle in December 1964, when 500 Pararis staged a raid on an army camp that resulted in heavy casualties on both sides.

Mir Hazar Ramkhani, chairman of the Revolutionary Command of the Baluch People's Liberation Front

Sher Mohammed Marri, founder of the Parari guerrilla movement (precursor of the Baluch People's Liberation Front)

*Prince Abdul Karim,
leader of the 1948
Baluch insurgency
against accession to
Pakistan*

*Akbar Bukti, former
Governor of Baluchistan
(Pakistan)*

The Pararis claim that their most spectacular success came in a series of clashes with army units in the Gharur area during December 1965. Pakistani forces allegedly suffered almost 200 casualties, a figure belittled by the Pakistani military leaders involved. Numerous witnesses confirm that the Pakistan Air Force staged air strikes during the Gharur fighting, but there is no convincing evidence to support Baluch charges that napalm was used in another battle near Bambore. In any event, stories of atrocities committed by the armed forces circulated widely in Pakistan during the late 1960s. General Tikka Khan, commander of Pakistani forces, was castigated as the Butcher of Baluchistan by anti-government leaders. The fighting in Baluchistan continued sporadically until 1969, when Yahya Khan, who succeeded Ayub Khan in that year, induced the suspicious Pararis to agree to a cease-fire by ordering the withdrawal of the One Unit plan.

Between engagements, the Pararis worked to expand the command force, which had grown to nearly 900 by 1969 and continued to increase in number slowly but steadily after the cease-fire. These full-time volunteers not only conducted military training for reservists, but also operated makeshift medical facilities, schools, and grain-marketing depots, establishing their movement as a virtual parallel government in certain areas. The authority of the guerrillas was largely unchallenged in the Marri area, where they enjoyed the active, albeit covert, support of the tribal *sardar* and received food and other necessities from the Baluch populace. Here, in particular, the Pararis hoped to establish a "liberated" zone or base area, comparable to Mao's Yenan, in the event that the Baluch embarked on a full-scale struggle for independence from Pakistan.

Despite their acceptance of the cease-fire agreement, the Pararis assumed that a renewal of hostilities with Islamabad would prove unavoidable sooner or later. Thus, they decided to keep intact as much of their organizational infrastructure as possible and to continue the training of reservists. Some of their forces in the Mengal areas fell apart once the fighting subsided in 1969, but most of the command force continued to function. When Sher Mohammed came down from the hills after the cease-fire, his young deputy in the Marri areas, Mir Hazar Ramkhani, then thirty-seven, went underground and continued to carry on clandestine organizational activities.

The War Years: 1973–1977

The Parari decision to maintain a state of combat readiness was to prove of some importance three years later, when a new and more serious phase of conflict erupted between the Baluch and Islamabad. Under Mir Hazar's leadership, the Pararis were to play a key role in the Baluch armed struggle against the Bhutto regime, which took power in 1971. The Pararis gradually evolved during the fighting into a well-established movement, now known as the Baluch People's Liberation Front.

The full story of the three-year political struggle between Islamabad and the Baluch leading up to the explosion of hostilities in 1973 does not merit detailed treatment here. On the surface, this Byzantine saga of maneuver and countermaneuver appears to constitute an instructive case study in the problems of federalism in the Pakistani context, since the conflict between Bhutto and Baluch leaders ostensibly centered around significant issues relating to the extent of autonomy to be exercised by local authorities.[12] As later chapters show, however, the specifics of the constitutional controversy between Islamabad and the Baluch were not of decisive importance in themselves. Bhutto's larger political objectives in Pakistan, pressures on Islamabad from the Shah of Iran, Iraqi-Iranian tensions, and Soviet support for Baghdad in its conflict with Teheran were also key factors that contributed to the outbreak of hostilities.

What is germane for our present purposes is that the events leading up to the 1973–1977 insurgency greatly intensified the mutual distrust between the Baluch and Islamabad which had been deepening since 1947. In Pakistani eyes, Yahya Khan had lived up to the cease-fire agreement with the Pararis by abolishing the One Unit concept in 1970, creating a consolidated Baluchistan province, and permitting the Baluch to have their first free elections along with those held in the rest of the country. Bhutto had given a further demonstration of Pakistani good faith, in this perspective, by permitting the Baluch to set up their own provincial government for the first time, based on the 1970 balloting, only to be confronted by a belligerent and uncompromising assertion of provincial prerogatives that was incompatible with the national constitution. In Baluch eyes, however, it was not out of keeping with the constitution's autonomy provisions to oust Punjabi bureaucrats from posts of authority in Baluchistan, to resist Pakistani military and paramilitary intervention in local conflicts, or to harass Punjabi farmers who had taken over the best of the limited arable farmland in the province with Islamabad's backing. Moreover, the Baluch were keenly aware that they had given an unambiguous electoral mandate to the state government headed by Ghaus Bux Bizenjo as governor and Ataullah Mengal as chief minister. The government commanded a 13–7 majority in the Baluchistan Assembly, and its opponents were almost all Pushtuns and other non-Baluch.

When Bhutto suddenly dismissed the Baluch provincial government on February 12, 1973, he did not confine himself to the charge that Bizenjo and Mengal had repeatedly exceeded their constitutional authority. He also gave his action a broader international significance by alleging that they had done so in collusion with Iraq and the Soviet Union as part of a sinister, long-term plot to dismember both Pakistan and Iran. His dismissal of the Baluch leaders was timed to coincide with the sensational disclosure that a cache of 300 Soviet submachine guns and 48,000 rounds of ammunition, allegedly consigned to Baluch leaders, had been uncovered in the Iraqi embassy in Islamabad. The arms were shown to diplomats and journalists and were undoubtedly of Soviet origin, but there was no proof that they were destined for Baluchistan, some 800 miles to the south.

Iraqi officials blamed the incident on antigovernment plotters in the Iraqi intelligence agency who were seeking to embarrass the Saddam Hussein regime.* In any event, Baghdad explained, the weapons were not destined for Pakistani Baluchistan but rather for Iranian Baluchistan, where Iraq was then openly supporting Baluch guerrilla activity in retaliation against the Shah's support of Kurdish rebels (see chapter six). Western intelligence sources have generally accepted the Iraqi explanation, contending that the arms were initially intercepted by Pakistani authorities in Karachi and were later taken north to distant Islamabad in order to maximize the impact of their exposure on the diplomats and foreign journalists, who were concentrated in the capital.

Baluch leaders contended that Bhutto deliberately contrived the "Iraqi arms conspiracy" to provide a pretext for their ouster, aided by dissidents in Baghdad. Some circumstantial evidence supports this claim, but stronger evidence suggests that the key to this still unsolved mystery may lie in the divisions within Baluch ranks in 1972 and 1973 over the tactics to be followed in dealing with Islamabad. Bizenjo, at one extreme, believed that it was possible to work within the system and avoid a costly military confrontation. Sher Mohammed, confident that a new military showdown was approaching, was anxious to get foreign arms for his

---

* The arms cache was allegedly discovered in the residence of Nasir Al-Saud, the Iraqi military attaché in Islamabad and was unveiled to diplomats and journalists there. Al-Saud disappeared from Pakistan three days before the exposure and was later executed, on July 2, 1973, together with Iraqi intelligence chief Nazim Kazzar, in connection with a coup attempt against Saddam Hussein. Antigovernment journalists in Pakistan, who linked the Baghdad coup attempt to the Iranian intelligence agency, SAVAK, said that Al-Saud had collaborated with Iranian and Pakistani intelligence agents in staging the Islamabad arms exposure.

Pararis and appears to have made arrangements for Iraqi arms deliveries on a visit to Baghdad in August 1972. The arms were to have been shared between the Pararis and Iranian Baluch groups. As many informed observers see it, one of the few top-ranking Baluch leaders who knew about this scheme, Akbar Bukti, leader of the Bukti tribe, proved to be a turncoat. By tipping off Bhutto, Bukti unseated his arch rivals, Bizenjo and Mengal—who insist they did not know about the arms—and obtained the governorship for himself. Ironically, Bhutto's dismissal of the Baluch provincial government made his prophecies of a Baluch insurgency self-fulfilling by vindicating Sher Mohammed and forcing Bizenjo, Mengal, and Khair Bux Marri to support a military struggle.

In early April 1973, less than six weeks after the ouster of the provincial government, Baluch guerrillas began to ambush army convoys. Bhutto responded dramatically by flying to Teheran, where he announced after a meeting with the Shah that Iran would provide $200 million in emergency military and financial aid. Then he challenged the Baluch by dispatching four hastily assembled divisions to reinforce the skeleton garrisons in Baluchistan and by jailing Bizenjo, Mengal, and Khair Bux Marri, who was chairman of the governing Baluch political party, the National Awami (People's) party.

To the Baluch, the dismissal of their elected government and the arrest of their leaders on what were regarded as trumped-up treason charges constituted a direct affront. The *Ryvaj,* the traditional code of honor, requires the "true" Baluch to fight, if necessary, to defend his personal and tribal honor, and the overwhelming majority of Baluch tribal leaders regarded Bhutto's action as a deliberate insult to all Baluch, requiring military redress.

Largely unnoticed by the outside world, the struggle between Islamabad and the tribesmen grew in ferocity over the next four years. More than 80,000 Pakistani troops roamed the province at the height of the war. The fighting was more widespread than it had been during the conflicts of the fifties and sixties and touched most of the Baluch population at one time or another. Every area had its legendry of Pakistani villains and Baluch heroes. One unusually dramatic example of Baluch heroism in the face of army excesses occurred in August 1973, soon after the fighting started, and immediately became as well known to Baluch as the Nathan Hale story is to Americans.

Seeking to avenge an ambush in which Pakistani forces had suffered heavy casualties, an army unit stormed into the village of Mali. The soldiers set up an improvised fortress in one corner of the village and then began to ransack huts one by one in search of concealed weapons. Men and women alike were roughly lined up in the village square. Shootouts occurred with those who resisted. Some of the older villagers were beginning to surrender when seventy-two-year-old Mir Luang Khan, elder brother of the Baluch poet and political leader Gul Khan Nasir, hobbled out of his hut on crutches to the center of the square. Shouting that he would die before permitting the troops to violate Baluch honor by intruding on the female members of his family, he picked up his outmoded muzzleloader and started to fire at the soldiers in their fortified huts. Soon most of the able-bodied men in the village had joined him in hand-to-hand fighting that lasted for four hours. Army sources concede that reinforcements had to be called in before the village could be subdued but deny Baluch eyewitness accounts claiming that fourteen Pakistani soldiers were killed before Mir Luang Khan was shot in the head while hiding with his followers in the village mosque. The Baluch bitterly acknowledge that thirty-five Mali villagers were killed by Pakistani machine gun and artillery fire, many of them women and children, and compare Mir Luang Khan to Nauroz Khan, the martyred leader of their 1958 uprising.

By July 1974, the guerrillas had been able to cut off most of the main roads linking Baluchistan with surrounding provinces and to disrupt periodically the key Sibi–Harnai rail link, thereby blocking coal shipments from Baluch areas to the Punjab. In the Marri area, as we shall see in chapter nine, attacks on drilling and survey operations effectively stymied "imperialist-sponsored" Pakistani oil exploration. Army casualties soared as the frequency and effectiveness of ambushes and raids on military encampments increased. "The hostiles were becoming quite bold as the year progressed," recalled the former army commander in Baluchistan, Lt. Gen. Arbab Jahanseb. "They thought they had reached the stage of confrontation with the armed forces in which they would actually be able to drive us out of Baluchistan. They were determined to stop oil exploration. We knew that we had to respond very forcefully or we would simply be unable to bring the situation under control." At this juncture, the Pakistan Air Force was called in. Helicopters were used not only to ferry troops but also to conduct combat operations in mountainous areas.

Initially, the Pakistanis employed the relatively clumsy Chinook helicopters that they had received from the United States under their own military aid program, fitting them with guns for combat use. But in mid-1974, Iran sent thirty U.S.-supplied Huey Cobra helicopters, many of them manned by Iranian pilots. The Huey Cobra was developed during the Vietnam war and had devastating firepower, including a six-barrel, twenty-millimeter automatic cannon with a firing rate of 750 rounds per minute. Until the Huey Cobras arrived, the only way that the

Pakistani forces could block off guerrilla escape routes after an encounter was by concentrating troops at key points on roads and trails. That tactic rarely worked, since the Baluch had much greater knowledge of the terrain. Once the Pakistanis were backed up by six or more gunships, however, special patrols could move in while the helicopters sprayed gunfire into the area ahead of them, slowly herding the guerrillas into ever-shrinking sanctuaries. Even when they sought to hide in previously secure mountain redoubts, the Baluch were often flushed out by the ubiquitous, readily maneuverable Huey Cobras.

The turning point in the war came in a brutal six-day battle at Chamalang in the Marri region (see Figure 2), which helps to explain the continuing intensity of Baluch bitterness toward Pakistan today. Every summer, the Marri nomads converge on the broad pasture lands of the Chamalang valley, one of the few rich grazing areas in all of Baluchistan. In 1974, many of the men stayed in the hills to fight with the guerrillas, but the women, children, and older men streamed down from the mountains with their flocks and set up their black tents in a sprawling, fifty-square-mile area. Chamalang, they thought, would be a haven from the incessant bombing and strafing attacks in the highlands. As the fighting gradually reached a stalemate, however, the army decided to take advantage of this concentration of Marri families as a means of luring the guerrillas down from the hills. The Pakistani officers calculated—correctly—that attacks on the tent villages would compel the guerrillas to come out into the open in defense of their families.

After a series of preliminary skirmishes in surrounding areas, the army launched Operation Chamalang on September 3, 1974, using a combined assault by ground and air forces. Interviews with Pakistani officers and Baluch participants indicate that some 15,000 Marris were massed at Chamalang. Led by the Pararis, guerrilla units formed a huge protective circle around their families and livestock. They fought for three days and nights, braving artillery fire and occasional strafing attacks by F-86 and Mirage fighter planes and Huey Cobras. Finally, when the Baluch ran out of ammunition, they did what they could to regroup and escape. Most of the important Parari units and their commanders managed to get away.

Army accounts claim that 125 guerrillas were killed and 900 captured, and independent estimates suggest that at least 50,000 sheep and 550 camels were captured at Chamalang and auctioned off by the army at bargain prices to non-Baluch in the Punjab. The Baluch minimize their own losses and claim to have killed 446 Pakistani soldiers, but it is clear that their casualties at Chamalang were damaging. They were never able to regain the military initiative in the three ensuing years of savage but increasingly uncoordinated fighting. Government statistics show that the most intensive hostilities in Baluchistan occurred between the start of the insurgency in 1973 and the end of 1975. Of 178 major recorded army encounters with the guerrillas during this period, 84 took place in the Marri area during 1974, with the rest scattered widely over other Baluch areas, especially Khuzdar and Jhalawan (see Figure 2).[13]

Faced with an unrelenting army offensive, Mir Hazar Ramkhani concluded in late 1975 that the best way to keep the Parari movement alive was to operate out of sanctuaries in southern Afghanistan. Leaving behind a skeleton force in Pakistan, he crossed the border with most of his men, their families, and their livestock. They eluded Pakistani sentries by marching stealthily at night in small groups over circuitous mountain routes. The Mohammed Daud regime permitted the Pararis to set up two large encampments and several smaller ones relatively close to the Afghan-Pakistani border (see Figure 2). Officially, they were described as refugee camps to forestall objections from Islamabad. In practice, Mir Hazar's encampments functioned as guerrilla base camps to which his lieutenants in Pakistan and the chieftains of other guerrilla bands regularly came for supplies and strategy meetings. Guerrilla units fighting in the hills periodically came to the Afghan base camps for a period of rest and medical treatment and were replaced by fresh contingents.

After they shifted their headquarters to Afghanistan, the Pararis underwent a significant transformation, as I shall elaborate in chapter five. They adopted an ambitious new program, broadened their membership base, changed their name to the Baluch People's Liberation Front, and began publishing their monthly organ, *Jabal* (Mountain).

When I visited these camps in February 1977, dozens of Baluch guerrillas returning from combat areas described bloody clashes that had just taken place and assured me that the worst of the fighting was yet to come. Later, however, touring Pakistani Baluchistan, it was clear that the degree of popular involvement in guerrilla activity was slowly ebbing. Soon after his ouster of Bhutto in July, General Zia Ul-Haq freed the imprisoned Baluch leaders, Bizenjo, Mengal, and Marri, and eventually reached an uneasy truce with them, temporarily ending the insurgency. Baluch moderates, led by Bizenjo, persuaded other Baluch leaders that it was pointless to continue fighting without adequate weapons, arguing that every effort should be made to test the good faith of the new military regime.

Interviewed in Kabul shortly after the truce started, Mir Hazar was skeptical and bitter, predicting that the agreement would collapse "within four or five years." He warned that "we will never again be caught without the proper weapons. Look what we did with those old guns! We didn't choose the time to fight this time. The fight was thrust upon us. But next time we'll choose the time and the place and we will be properly armed." Then, with a scowl, he asked, "Why doesn't anyone notice our struggle? In the beginning, the Bengalis didn't want independence, but it was forced upon them by Punjabi bullheadedness, and if Pakistan doesn't change its attitude, we'll have no alternative but to go the same way."

Zia made what he regarded as a significant concession to the Baluch in 1978 by releasing an estimated 6,000 prisoners held in controversial prisons at Kohlu and Loralai, where numerous instances of torture were alleged to have occurred. He also declared an amnesty for guerrillas who had gone to Afghanistan, an offer which was declined by the suspicious Pararis but accepted by several smaller groups. However, on substantive issues relating to autonomy for Baluchistan in a restructured Pakistani constitutional system, Zia proved to be as unresponsive to Baluch demands as previous Pakistani leaders had been.

By late 1979, after more than two years of unsuccessful negotiations between the Baluch leaders and Islamabad, Bizenjo and other moderates found it increasingly difficult to make a convincing case for continuing the dialogue with Pakistan. Zia's strict martial law regime, with its ban on political activity, forced most Baluch leaders to remain silent or to operate underground. Resuming political arrests, the police focused initially on the powerful Baluch Students Organization, staging a series of round-ups of key leaders that began in 1979 and were still continuing in early 1981. Marri and Mengal, who were increasingly circumspect in public, argued privately that Zia, a Punjabi, was prejudiced against the Baluch and that his plan to replace martial law with an electoral system based on proportional representation would virtually disenfranchise the Baluch and other ethnic minorities.

Ostensibly for medical treatment, Marri and Mengal went into voluntary political exile in Europe in November 1979 and were still there in March 1981, actively seeking foreign support for an independent Baluchistan, while leaving the door open for a resumption of negotiations with Pakistan.

Talking with the Triumvirate 4

The Baluch nationalist movement was radically transformed by five years of guerrilla warfare. Prior to the war, it was little more than a tenuous coalition of a dozen or more feuding tribal leaders patched together intermittently from crisis to crisis. It conspicuously lacked both a significant organizational base and a commonly accepted leadership transcending tribal divisions. Now, as a result of the conflict, the movement is not only becoming better organized but has also started to unite behind three loosely allied leaders who emerged as martyrs during the war years and constitute the unchallenged ruling triumvirate of Baluch politics: Khair Bux Marri, Ghaus Bux Bizenjo, and Ataullah Mengal.

Marri, Bizenjo, and Mengal share a common commitment to the objective of autonomous Baluch-majority states within the Pakistani and Iranian framework or, if this should prove impossible, ultimate independence. In temperament, style, and political philosophy, however, they are strikingly different personalities. Marri, the charismatic, idealistic, Marxist-minded *sardar* of the militant Marri tribe, favors active preparations for a renewed guerrilla struggle. He headed the now outlawed National Awami party in Baluchistan but disdained public office during the short-lived period of provincial self-rule during 1972 and 1973 and advocates a hard line against Islamabad. Bizenjo, once the youthful firebrand who sought to prevent Kalat's accession to Pakistan in 1947, is now the cautious elder statesman who hopes to win autonomy for Baluchistan through negotiations with Pakistani leaders. Bizenjo was Bhutto's choice as governor when the Baluch were given provincial self-rule. As chief minister during the Bizenjo regime, Mengal, *sardar* of the Mengal tribe, also earned a reputation as a parliamentary-minded moderate. He no longer shares Bizenjo's hopes for compromise with Islamabad but is equally chary of Marri's Marxism. It is Mengal, a skillful mediator, who holds the triumvirate together.

To a great extent, the future of Baluch nationalism will be determined by whether these three men can cooperate effectively in future crises, reconciling their differences with respect to the appropriate tactics for the nationalist cause. Until their arrest in 1973, they worked together in the National Awami party, but their organizational activities have diverged since their release from prison in 1977. Marri has covertly encouraged the underground Baluch People's Liberation Front, while Bizenjo promoted the moderate Pakistan National party until Zia banned political activity. This divergence has been reflected in factional alignments in the Baluch Students Organization and in various local nationalist groups. Nevertheless, with Mengal acting as balance wheel, the three leaders have maintained compatible personal relationships and consult each other on major decisions involving contacts with Pakistani leaders and non-Baluch political groups. All three of them are under growing pressure from younger nationalist leaders to forge a closer working unity expressed, organizationally, in some form of coordinating council of nationalist groups committed to an agreed program of action. The first signs of movement toward such unity came in February 1981, when Mengal and Marri cooperated to help create a London-based coalition of Baluch émigré groups, the World Baluch Organization. Nominally dedicated to cultural and social objectives, the new body was expected to facilitate fund-raising among Baluch living abroad in support of Baluch nationalist activity in Pakistan and Iran.

Khair Bux Marri: Marxism and Cockfights

It is not an accident that the *sardar* of the Marri tribe has been the most consistent advocate of a militant Baluch nationalism. Khair Bux II lives in the shadow of his grandfather, Khair Bux the Great, who led Marri resistance against the British in the nineteenth century, and his father, Meherullah Khan Marri, who spearheaded underground anti-British political activity in the decades immediately preceding the 1947 transfer of power. Marris are proud of the key role they have played in past Baluch struggles against foreign rule, too proud in the eyes of some other Baluch tribes who accuse them of having a "master race" complex. As the most numerous Baluch tribe, with a population of some 135,000, historically centered in a strategic, 3,300-square-mile area in the northeast corner of Baluchistan (see Figure 2), the Marris have come to think of themselves as the vanguard of the Baluch cause, especially in the wake of their pivotal role during the 1973–1977 fighting.

In spite of recurring government efforts to undermine his position, Marri has a strong hold on his tribe, which gives him a solid base for his nationalist activity. As Meherullah's eldest son, he was the unchallenged heir to tribal leadership in the patrilineal Marri society. Khair Bux is the seventh leader of the ruling Bahawalan dynasty. An American anthropologist who lived among the Marris for more than a year found a "very striking" attitude of respect for the *sardar* in Marri society "...often approaching awe. It ascribed magical and superhuman qualities to his person and encompassed attitudes which elsewhere in the Middle East are reserved for saints and other holy men."[1]

A slender, stately figure in his early fifties with a lively intellect and a deceptively gentle manner, Marri is a powerful orator and the most influential theoretician of the nationalist movement. However, he has often been indecisive, even naive, in dealing with the nitty-gritty of everyday political activity. He has cosmopolitan intellectual tastes (he reads *Time, Newsweek,* and the *Economist,* as well as Marxist periodicals) and had traveled abroad twice before going into political exile in 1979, visiting both the United States and the Soviet Union. His lifestyle, however, is distinctly Baluch. He makes a point of wearing traditional attire, even in Western countries, and is a fervent devotee of cockfighting, the closest thing to a Baluch national pastime.

Unlike many Third World nationalists who developed an ideological commitment during their college years, Marri was a late starter in politics. Former classmates who knew him as a student at Aitcheson College in Lahore remember him as a happy-go-lucky playboy typical of ruling-class families in preindependence India. Indian Ambassador to Pakistan Shankar Bajpai, who had known Marri well in college, barely recognized him at a diplomatic reception in 1977. Bajpai was astonished to find that the lighthearted youth he remembered had become an intense, introverted political crusader who bore the physical and psychological marks of five years in prison, three during the Ayub regime and two at the hands of Bhutto.

Ayub's forcible imposition of One Unit, exemplified by the arrest of *sardars* who opposed the plan and the brutal abandon of General Tikka Khan's military campaign from 1958 to 1960, transformed Marri. "They injured his self-respect," said Mukhtar Hassan, a political analyst for the newspaper *Jasarat.* "It was as simple as that, and he will never forget it." "When Ayub sent the army, Khair Bux was converted from an apolitical young man with no strong ideological leanings to an idealistic, self-educated Marxist who was hungrily searching for answers to the unexpected situation in which he found himself," said Hamida Khurro, a Sind University political scientist who met Khair Bux on a good will mission of Pakistani leaders to the Soviet Union.

Once his political consciousness had been aroused, Marri became the most vocal and unyielding hard-liner in Baluch councils. During the 1960s, his tacit support enabled the Pararis to establish a guerrilla movement with a secure network of base camps in Marri territory. In 1968, when Bizenjo and Mengal were ready to accept a compromise with Ayub, Marri balked. Two years later, openly expressing his doubts, he agreed

Khair Bux Marri, former chairman of the governing National Awami Party in Baluchistan (Pakistan)

at the eleventh hour to the more favorable settlement with Yahya that paved the way for elections in Baluchistan.

Marri won one of the Baluch seats in the Pakistan National Assembly and became chairman of the governing National Awami party during the brief period of provincial self-rule in Baluchistan. He continued to suspect Islamabad, however, and quietly helped the Pararis to maintain their guerrilla infrastructure in the hills. In 1973, when Bizenjo signed Bhutto's new constitution, Marri refused, charging that its autonomy provisions were meaningless. Marri's refusal was vindicated, in the opinion of most Baluch, when soon afterward Bhutto summarily dismissed the provincial government and arrested its principal leaders. In 1977, when the Baluch leaders were released by Zia, Marri reluctantly agreed to join with Bizenjo and Mengal in negotiations with Islamabad, but he insisted on major Pakistani concessions as the basis of any settlement. The Baluch should not support the new military regime, he argued, unless Zia agreed to withdraw the Pakistan Army completely from Baluchistan and make adequate compensation payments to the victims of military atrocities. When Zia rejected these terms, Marri was once again vindicated and became firmly established as the most steadfast guardian of Baluch interests.

Pakistani officials make no secret of their belief that Marri is the most "dangerous" of the Baluch leaders, and Marri firmly believes that the Bhutto government tried to poison him during his imprisonment. His evidence is circumstantial and inconclusive, but he continues to be so suspicious that he refused to go to a hospital when he had a hernia operation in early 1978. Instead, he went to the trouble and expense of arranging for a trusted surgeon to perform the operation in his own home in Quetta. "He was concerned that they would somehow manage to have him murdered if he went to a hospital," explained Ataullah Mengal.

Marri's Pakistani critics charge that he is simply a disgruntled feudal baron who has resisted the modernizing programs of Ayub and his successors for selfish reasons. In imposing the One Unit system, Ayub challenged the status of the forty-odd Baluch *sardars* as land-holding tribal chiefs, branding the *sardari* system as incompatible with the objective of integrating the tribal areas into a centralized Pakistani administrative system. Marri argues, however, that he was not fighting Ayub in order to preserve his privileges. As he points out, some *sardars* proved more than willing to surrender the formal trappings of their positions and cooperate with successive Islamabad regimes in return for the continuance of their privileges under a new guise.

Marri, Mengal, and other "progressive" *sardars* disdained such a bargain, charging that Islamabad did not want to modernize the Baluch areas, but only to control them. As evidence, Marri points to the fact that once Ayub found a few *sardars* who would play his game, the land reforms promised as part of the One Unit plan evaporated. In contrast, Marri and Mengal were preparing to implement land reforms of their own when Bhutto ousted the elected Baluch provincial regime in 1973. Marri even abolished many of the oppressive taxes imposed on his tribe by previous chiefs, an action that has endeared him to rank-and-file Baluch.

In addition to a reduced level of the tax revenues normally going to a *sardar* from his tribesmen, Marri receives an income from crown farms and orchards. In the early 1960s, these lands yielded an estimated 50,000 rupees ($10,000) a year. But when Marri gave moral support to the Pararis, Ayub responded by bulldozing fertile orchards and setting fire to some of his other properties. Later, during the 1973–1977 insurgency, while Marri was in prison, the Bhutto regime seized much of his other income-producing farmland, further reducing his revenues. His modest residence in Quetta, where I first interviewed him in August 1978, consists of several small adobe buildings—one of them air-conditioned—grouped around a courtyard. It is a comfortable establishment by Baluch standards but notably spartan in comparison with the opulent homes of pro-Islamabad Baluch businessmen and Punjabi officials elsewhere in the city.

Marri's opposition to the extension of central government development programs to the Marri areas is criticized even by some Baluch. "How can you take the position that there will be no roads and no schools in the Marri area, in this day and age, when you sit in Quetta in an air-conditioned room?" exploded Mahmud Aziz Kurd, a Bizenjo lieutenant. According to Munir Khan, the former chief secretary of Baluchistan, an Islamabad appointee, Marri has betrayed a sentimental desire to preserve tribal mores as well as a thinly veiled fear that development programs would undermine his leadership. In one conversation, Khan said, Marri complained that projected road-building programs would "create difficulties because when you start spending money in this way, a tribal society such as ours will get corrupted. Contractors will come in spreading money about, and people will lose their heads."

Marri himself contended that he has never opposed the modernization of the Marri area but rather what he considers the "exploitative and political character" of central government programs. As an example he cited periodic attempts by Amoco and other foreign companies to drill for oil in the Marri hills with Islamabad's encouragement, recalling with satisfaction that Marri resistance has largely blocked petroleum exploration activity and had even prevented related road-building efforts until recently. "We saw what happened in the Bukti areas, where they have 'developed' the Sui gas, 80 percent of which goes out of Baluchistan to make others rich," Marri said. "Of course we want to do these things, to modernize and to develop in ways and at a speed that we think makes sense under our conditions. We were starting to do this when we were in power. But they don't want us to carry out modernization under our own control. They want to modernize us in their own way, without listening to us." Most of the roads built in Baluchistan, he declared, were "not for our benefit but to make it easier for the military to control us and for the Punjabis to rob us. The issue is not whether to develop, but whether to develop with or without autonomy. Exploitation has now adopted the name of development."

Marri has maintained a calculated public silence since his release from prison in 1977, but he continues to carry on behind-the-scenes political activity. Although he rarely receives journalists and authors, he finally agreed after repeated requests to a "brief" interview on August 1, 1978. His manner was disarmingly modest and unpretentious, and he agonized, Hamlet-like, before responding to many of my questions. But as we talked, drank tea, and ate *sajji*, the traditional, Baluch-style roast leg of lamb, he grew more expansive. Once he started to unbend, he spoke intensely for seven uninterrupted hours in breathless, staccato outbursts only loosely held together by a logical train of thought. This proved to be the first of three extensive interviews over a period of two years.

"In earlier years our struggles had been tribal," he said, "but since 1947 they have become more and more political. It has been a natural process, like a child growing from an embryo. Our people have slowly sensed that they would destroy our identity as a nation if we did not fight back." Prince Abdul Karim's revolt was "the first expression. What did he want? He was not too clear about it, but he knew he wanted a state, something separate, and what he did, when he went to jail, had its educative effect and began the growth of a Baluch consciousness that has been advancing and maturing ever since." Later, when Abdul Karim came out of jail and formed his Ustoman Gal party, "we wanted very simple things, just for our people to be educated for jobs. We were groping for some sort of nationalism, but all we asked for were our simple human rights. Yet, every time there was a price to pay—jail, confiscation of property, being blacklisted, telephones tapped, being thrown in jail, questioned—a high price for doing what was so natural."

"When Nauroz Khan went to the hills in 1958, what did he want?"

Like Abdul Karim, "it was vague, but it was also a desire for a Baluch state. He suffered, and he believed their promise of safe conduct, and then what was the outcome? What happened to him made a great impression on educated young people, on the petty bourgeoisie, on the generation coming up. Call it an eruption, an outflow, what happened is part of history. They went to the hills and other tribes followed. I wonder what was in the mind of Nauroz Khan? He could not have explained it in terms of 'nationalism' but it was to protect his traditions, his sense of identity. There was something in his mind, some vision of freedom for the Baluch."

Repeatedly, Marri's comments revealed his preoccupation with "whether the price that was paid was worthwhile." Were the Baluch patriots who suffered and died asking for enough when they limited their demands to provincial autonomy within a new Pakistani constitutional structure? Speaking figuratively, he asked, if Nauroz Khan "lost his life for an egg, as it were, wouldn't it be worthwhile asking for a poultry farm? We Baluch live in fear that we are going to be exterminated. But for what? For seeking provincial rights? If you are going to suffer in any case, why be simple enough to ask for something small? People are asking these questions increasingly."

Reticent at first to acknowledge his attraction to the idea of an independent Greater Baluchistan, he became more and more explicit as the evening wore on, constantly returning to the theme that "whatever happens, we will suffer, we will pay the same price, we will pay through the nose, so which will we choose? Why do we continue to talk of provincial rights after all that has happened? Will we have a plastic overcoat or one made of the best material? The rain will be heavy in either case."

"It's taken for granted that the Baluch must be *with* somebody else," Marri exploded. "We are expected to accept the idea of Baluch here, Baluch there, scattered in a sort of international triangle. But what is the harm of the Baluch wanting to put themselves together? It will develop, it ought to develop. Are the Baluch really not human? Are they a lower form of human being? Look at the United Nations, look at the little member states of the U.N. like Oman or the Arab Emirates. Can you wonder why we are not satisfied to talk about provincial rights? We are told we are not viable—stretching from the Indus to Iran! Are the Maldives viable? To me there is no such thing as a small people. We are human beings, and we are small only in terms of resources. Internationalism means the equal unity of nations."

Impatiently dismissing the possibility of a satisfactory future for Baluchistan within the Pakistan framework, he declared that "unless there is a plague, we'll always remain a minority, which means we will always be exploited by the Punjabis. Even when they were outnumbered by the Bengalis, before the secession of Bangladesh, the Punjabis were not willing to give the Bengalis just representation. Now, with Bangladesh gone, the Punjabis finally have become a majority and can repress the minorities in the name of majority rule." Until recently, he reflected, "there were many who didn't think of Greater Baluchistan," but as a result of their armed encounters with Pakistan, the Baluch "have learned a little more every time. There has been a certain escalation in each stage of our struggle, and this has produced a clearer recognition that what we confront is nothing less than slow death as a people. There are scars that remain from the things that have happened in the past, the guns, the killing, the rape, and they can't erase them with a smile."

Although he is known as a leftist and has often worn a Mao badge, or in later years a Lenin badge, Marri's ideas are a bizarre mixture of assorted leftist ideology and Baluch tradition. "Sometimes he's an internationalist, sometimes he's a nationalist, and sometimes he's a Marri tribesman," said Mahmud Aziz Kurd. Marri was not wearing his customary Lenin badge on the night of our Quetta meeting, but he spoke earnestly of his interest in Lenin's writings, stressing that he did not necessarily "go all the way. I could wear badges honoring others whom I also respect, for example, the Buddha. What I see in Lenin I miss elsewhere, but it doesn't mean I feel a blind attachment to the man and his teachings. Marxism-Leninism has helped me to understand politics, though being Marxist-Leninist is not easy and I am not sure that I qualify."

Marri talks of adapting Marxist-Leninist ideas to Baluch conditions in a species of national-communism. "Anyone who believes that the problems of Baluchistan can be solved with a Western-style welfare state approach is misled. If anyone thinks the Baluch is going to get his cake —Baluchistan—through parliamentary democracy—well, I doubt it. Through law, I doubt it. If we want our rights, it can't be done in the usual Western way. Capitalist nationalism is obsolete, I am afraid. Today's poor man will not follow his landlord to fight for his freedom. You have to convince him that in a new state he will get his economic rights, and that means some adaptation of what Marx and Lenin have taught."

One of the few subjects on which I could not draw Marri out was his relationship with the Baluch People's Liberation Front guerrillas, who espouse a brand of Marxism-Leninism strikingly similar to his own. He ignored questions about the Front, saying only that he was "not a regular reader" of *Jabal* and gets a copy only "now and then." Murad Khan, a Front spokesman, explained that Marri had "not yet reached the stage of becoming part of the Front, as such, but he respects the will to resist and he respects those who have the courage to resist. He likes what we are doing because he wants his people to understand what they are fighting for. He doesn't want them to fight, as in the past, simply for honor and dignity in the old Baluch tradition." My own conclusion is that Marri has close ties with the Front, like those he had with its precursor, the Pararis, but in 1978 he had not yet left Pakistan and did not want to risk government reprisals needlessly by identifying himself with a group espousing violent action. By clear implication, he accepts the Front's view that an armed struggle will prove necessary to achieve Baluch rights.

Marri hopes that Baluchistan can be independent of great power politics and that "we will not have to hitch ourselves to some bandwagon. Ideologies are shared, they are the common property of mankind, and you don't have to owe allegiance to any one power in order to pursue a certain ideology. When you become pro-this or pro-that you lose something of yourself."

Appealing for a sympathetic American attitude toward Baluch aspirations, Marri said that U.S. support for the Zia regime and its predecessors has been "part of our problem. People think that America aids the Punjabis and that therefore our only alternative is the other camp."

As he talked, Marri returned again and again to the vulnerability of small nations caught in the struggle of big powers, observing wistfully, at one point, that "if you join a bloc, you are dominated, but I suppose that is the way of the world." Then he exploded that "people should not be puppets. We would like to be a partner, not a ward. We shouldn't deceive ourselves and go from one slavery to another. Or can we say we'll *accept* this or that slavery for our own reasons? People often say they'll try the 'new evil' rather than the 'old evil.' "

At the time of our Quetta meeting, the April 1978 Communist revolution in Kabul was four months old. Alluding to the new regime's expressions of interest in the Baluch cause, Marri mused that "before we Baluch can walk, we may be carried on the feet of others. It's a pity. Before we even begin fighting, we may lose our independence. This will be the test for us." As a result of the sanctuary given by Afghanistan to Mir Hazar's guerrillas, he said, the Baluch feel a strong sense of obligation to Kabul, and "there is a danger that the Afghans will decide for us, will think for us." If Afghanistan could remain independent of the Soviet Union, he observed, close ties with Kabul might not be too risky for the Baluch, and "we might be able to have communism without being mortgaged to another power, or at least without getting a mortgage so big that we can't pay it off."

By the time I had my second meeting with Marri on March 11, 1980, he had gone into exile in London. Soviet forces had occupied Afghanistan, and his hopes for a national-communist regime in Kabul had been swept aside. I found him in a grim mood as he surveyed the stark options confronting the Baluch. "What can we, what can the Afghans, what can any small nation do?" he asked. "You need help, but when you accept it, they feel they have their investment and they take you over. You are porous, you become saturated, you become part of something larger that you can't control." Whether it is "the Russians or the Americans, can you take help from any stronger side and retain your own image of yourself? It must be possible! If we take weapons for our struggle, it is still our own blood we are shedding, isn't it? Isn't the blood we shed for our cause worth more than their weapons? Why can't superpowers help us for what we are? Why is it smaller nations must fit in a certain mold?"

Even after the Soviet occupation, he said, "the Baluch people think, 'I don't like the Punjabis, so let the Russians come.' But those with a higher responsibility have to think, 'If the Russians come, what share do I have?'" Then he turned to me angrily, adding, "Why is it the United States always works through the established structure? If the Americans pump weapons into the Punjabis, obviously we have to stretch our hand to another superpower." In January 1981, Marri paid a flying visit to Kabul, where he conferred with Mir Hazar Ramkhani and other leaders of the Liberation Front guerrillas encamped in southern Afghanistan (see chapter five) as well as with Afghan officials. On his return to London he no longer made any secret of his links with the Front. His visit was prompted, he explained, by "some minor problems" that had arisen in relations between the guerrillas and the Karmal government. Expressing gratitude for the sanctuary given to the guerrillas by Afghanistan, he noted that the Liberation Front had never formally declared its support either for the Khalq Communist faction that took power in 1978 or for Karmal's Parchamite regime, adding that "perhaps they misunderstand our reticence." He said in response to a question that he did not meet with Soviet officials during his two-week stay in Kabul.

At times, Baluch leaders have talked of a neutral, independent Baluchistan that would refuse to grant military bases to either Moscow or Washington. Asked whether the Baluch could pursue such a middle course, seeking help for a guerrilla struggle simultaneously from both superpowers as well as from other countries, Marri declared without hesitation that "if this was ever realistic, it is not now. Either you are in one camp or the other. The question is, whose aid can we get, whose aid can we accept, without selling out completely?"

When I suggested that a settlement with Pakistan would be preferable to achieving independence under superpower tutelage, he responded after a brief pause that "if the Punjabis or the Pakistani state are prepared to talk with us in a mature way, with some kind of realism and some understanding of how our people feel, we are prepared for a settlement, as we have always been. But there is no use wasting time talking of minor matters. They must be prepared to talk in terms of a national status for us, of a relationship with us based on that status. I must confess that I cannot ever remember a Punjabi talking in such terms."

Ghaus Bux Bizenjo: Elder Statesman or Secret Communist?

"That man can't live without politics. I can do without it, but he has to have it all the time or he will perish." This is how his close colleague, Ataullah Mengal, characterizes Ghaus Bux Bizenjo, the elder statesman of Baluchistan. Unlike Khair Bux Marri, who regards parliamentary politics as a charade, Bizenjo thrives on the conventional political game. Marri often has to be coaxed into conversation, but Bizenjo holds forth readily in the stentorian tones of an orator, gravely delivering well-rounded declarations that would stand up in print without a word changed. In my view, he is one of the ablest politicians in Pakistan and could have played a major role in Islamabad but for his Baluch identity and his commitment to the Baluch cause.

A portly, fatherly-looking man with a genial personality, Bizenjo, who was sixty-three in 1981, belongs to the ruling Hamalani wing of the Bizenjo tribe but lacks the solid base of tribal power that Marri and Mengal have as *sardars*. Although his father was *sardar* of the tribe, "Ghausi," as he is widely known among the Baluch, was too young when his father died to become *sardar*, so his first cousin was chosen instead. Nevertheless, because of his princely lineage, he inherited an estimated 25,000 acres of land and received special attention from the British political agent in the Bizenjo area, who arranged for him to attend a missionary school in Quetta and Aligarh Muslim University in what is now India.

As a result of his education at Aligarh, Bizenjo received much greater exposure to the broad currents of preindependence political life in the subcontinent than his more parochially educated Baluch colleagues, with the notable exception of Oxford-educated Akbar Bukti, the urbane *sardar* of the Bukti tribe. Aligarh was the breeding ground of "nationalist Muslim" politicians who supported the Congress party of Gandhi and Nehru in its advocacy of a united, secular India and who were opposed to Mohammed Ali Jinnah's call for a separate Islamic Pakistan. It was natural for a young Baluch to feel drawn to the Congress party at Aligarh, since Baluchistan, with its homogeneous Muslim population, did

Ghaus Bux Bizenjo

not share the fear of Hindu domination that motivated Jinnah's followers in other parts of the subcontinent where Muslims were a minority. Bizenjo was more attracted by the anticolonialism of the Congress party than by the anti-Hindu doctrine of the Muslim League and joined a Congress-sponsored group active at Aligarh. At the same time, he drifted into campus Communist activities. He went back to Baluchistan armed with a battery of anti-British and leftist ideas mingled with the budding spirit of a Baluch nationalist.

According to K. B. Nizamani, who was secretary of the Sind and Baluchistan branch of the Communist party in the late 1930s, Bizenjo was a Communist in 1938 and 1939, but then broke with the party over its support of the pro-Pakistan movement. As the end of British colonial rule approached, Bizenjo and other Baluch nationalists formed the Kalat National party, discussed earlier, which was dedicated to the establishment of an independent Baluchistan. At the age of twenty-nine, Bizenjo made his memorable 1947 speech (see chapter three) opposing the accession of Kalat to Pakistan. Significantly, Bizenjo has never disowned this speech, insisting that it was not treasonous, as the Bhutto regime charged, since Kalat was not yet a part of the new state of Pakistan when he made it.

As a result of his youthful championship of independence and his respected status as the eldest top-ranking Baluch politician, Bizenjo was popularly known for many years as *Baba-i-Baluchistan* (Father of Baluchistan). More recently, his militant critics, angered by his efforts to compromise with successive Pakistani regimes, have increasingly suggested that he is selling out, dubbing him *Baba-i-Negotiations*. Talking with Bizenjo, however, I was left with little doubt that he is as dedicated as Marri and other militants to the cause of Baluch autonomy or independence. His differences with the militants are not over ultimate objectives but rather over how fast and how far to go in pursuing Baluch goals in a rapidly changing regional and global environment.

In my two conversations with Bizenjo in Quetta on July 31 and August 1, 1978, he repeatedly emphasized that the Baluch problem was part of a larger, "interlocking" set of problems confronting the artificially created, multinational states of Pakistan, Afghanistan, Iran, and India. "There will have to be changes in the way that all of these countries are constituted, or there will be no peace in our region," he declared. "They will have to change because the present situation, as a result of the colonial boundaries, is one of great confusion. No one can escape this. We have to decide what to do with these inherited artificial states lumping together diverse nationalities with no rhyme or reason. What we have in so many cases is a new type of colonialism. It is not just the Baluch.

Look at the Kurds. What will become of Iran, which is, after all, a multinational state? Look at the manner in which incompatible ethnic groups have been put together in something called Afghanistan! It was only the strategic needs of the British and the Russian czars that made it possible for Afghanistan to become an independent state in the form that it took. I don't believe in a narrow nationalism. The answer for all of us lies in regional confederations."

As the first step toward a rearrangement of regional boundaries, Bizenjo calls for the recognition of Baluchistan, Pushtunistan, Sind, and the Punjab as separate nationalities and the adoption of a new Pakistani constitution giving each national unit much wider powers than those accorded in any of the constitutions that existed before Zia's martial law regime. This stand has brought him into perennial conflict with the proponents of a unitary Pakistani constitutional structure. Provoked by an attack on his autonomy demands in a Punjabi newspaper, Bizenjo issued a much quoted statement in Lahore on August 28, 1978, ridiculing the official position that Pakistanis of all ethnic backgrounds constitute a single nationality because they share the Muslim faith. Citing the Koran, Bizenjo declared that "there is no such thing as a Muslim nation on the face of this globe. The Almighty recognized tribes, clans and nationalities, as he did a universal brotherhood of all believers."[2]

Bizenjo infuriates the Punjabis by warning that it is the advocates of a monolithic Pakistan who will be responsible if the country disintegrates. "Yesterday those who spoke of the 'ideology of Pakistan' were the ones responsible for the separation of East Pakistan," he charged in his 1978 Lahore broadside. "Today they can become guilty of breaking up what is left of Pakistan as well. We have reached a crossroad in our history where we must refrain from the practice of making unfair attacks and allegations of 'secessionist' against each other. Because to me the end result of these unfair attacks could be very fatal." To Punjabis, such statements have an implicitly threatening tone. Thus, in a *Pakistan Times* article, Bizenjo warned that "if people persist in remaining unconcerned about situations like those which developed in East Pakistan and later in Baluchistan, then every four or five years the nation will go through a period of utter confusion and chaos, frustration and despair, and as a natural consequence, martial law will come in."[3]

In this article, Bizenjo envisaged "a type of federation, not a confederation," in which the central government of Pakistan would continue to control defense, foreign affairs (including foreign trade), currency, and communications and would have the power to tax the constituent units "to the extent necessary" to fulfill these responsibilities. At the same time, he explained, the federation would be "a loose one" because "only those rights which are necessary for the common interest and for mutual survival would be *surrendered voluntarily* to the center, and in all remaining matters the federating units would retain full power in their own hands." Thus, in addition to the powers stipulated under the defunct 1973 constitution, adopted during the Bhutto regime but bypassed by Zia, each unit would also have the powers on the so-called Concurrent List that were to have been shared under the terms of that carefully negotiated charter between the central and provincial governments. The four national units would have "full control and sovereignty over their own natural resources," he said, and preference would be given to local residents in jobs, contracts, and other aspects of economic development. Asked how economic planning on a federal level would be possible under such a constitutional arrangement, Bizenjo said that "all four provinces of Pakistan depend on each other and will continue to do so. The representatives of these provinces will be able to establish joint institutions to the extent that they find it necessary to do so."

Discussing the prospects for a constitutional settlement, Bizenjo often gave me the impression that he did not really expect the Punjabis to make the necessary concessions but felt that the onus for the possible breakup of the country should be kept squarely on Islamabad. "We must do our duty before history to prevent further bloodshed if we can." Even if a settlement were reached, he cautioned, "we would have to see how such a system would work, and whether the people in the minority national units would feel secure. We would have to make some arrangements in such a constitution to prevent interference in the power and authority of the autonomous federal units. We didn't have such safeguards under the 1973 constitution, and this is why it proved to be no more than a scrap of paper when Mr. Bhutto wanted to circumvent it, using the civil service, the army, and paramilitary forces to get control over us."

When I commented that many Baluch saw no hope at all of a constitutional settlement under the Zia military regime and were thinking of another armed struggle, Bizenjo responded that "if you can't solve the problem by mutual understanding and peaceful means, naturally the militant feeling will crop up. But this is not our fault, it is because of the failure of the authorities in Pakistan to deal with the problems in a reasonable manner. I'm afraid that sentiment will grow." At the mention of the Baluch People's Liberation Front, he said, "Why have these people gone to the hills? Because of the Pakistani attitude. This movement was not created by foreigners, by the Soviet Union or China; they are just Baluch fighting for their rights."

Recalling the tense months leading up to the 1973 rupture with Bhutto, Bizenjo said, "I had been struggling to avoid a confrontation and had even gone to the extent of damaging my political image because I knew that a confrontation with Bhutto would ultimately mean the rule of the army. I was able to prevent such a confrontation for nearly one year, but Mr. Bhutto was bent on a reckless course. It was obvious to me that the ultimate result of his military adventure in Baluchistan would be his removal and the sort of military rule that we now have." Since his release from prison in 1977, Bizenjo added, "I have been trying with my colleagues to find some basis for normalization with the military leaders, but we have not been successful, and it will be damaging to me as well as to my people if we fail. I do not see any other moderating force in the picture."

In contrast to Marri, who is uneasy and ambivalent about seeking Soviet or other foreign help for an independence struggle, Bizenjo stated that "in a crisis, naturally we will seek help from somewhere, and if we get it, we will accept it. When a nationality is fighting for survival, what do you expect? If any nationality in any country faces permanent exploitation by majority nationalities, and those majority nationalities are protected and helped by the Western bloc, then in order to fight for their survival the minorities will naturally not hesitate to have help from anywhere."

Even if the Baluch did accept Soviet help to achieve their independence, Bizenjo hastened to add, "taking help and support is one thing, and the way you do things in your own country is something quite different. In most respects, we would not emulate the Russian model in our country. Of course, when other countries help, it's not a charity. They are trying to influence you politically and you incur certain obligations. But we would not forget the interests of our own people. We feel we have the capacity to stand up for our interests."

One area in which the Baluch do admire the Soviet model, Bizenjo indicated, is "their approach to the national question. We have been inspired by their idea that the existence of separate nationalities should be recognized and that each nationality should have the ultimate right of secession. However, we also recognize that the way the system works in practice is different from theory. Russia is centralized, and to them the national question is subordinate to the communist ideology. But if socialism is working there correctly, then the people of the non-Russian nationalities will be satisfied. Socialism and communism, if practiced properly, have the capacity to solve the national question."

Until recently, Bizenjo has carefully omitted references to the ultimate right of secession from his demand for a Pakistani constitution based on the recognition of four nationalities. This position was consistent with the Soviet line, which emphasizes the goal of a "united, socialist, federal" Pakistan and opposes separatism as a weapon of "bourgeois nationalists." In April 1980, however, Bizenjo explicitly included the right to secede in his response to a proposal for an antigovernment alliance between his Pakistan National party and former air marshal Asghar Khan's Tehriq Istiqlal (Movement for Integrity). A proposed joint manifesto submitted by Bizenjo for Asghar Khan's approval would have called for strictly limiting the powers of the central government to defense, foreign affairs, communications, and currency, while providing for the right of provincial units to secede if Islamabad violated their constitutional prerogatives. Before Asghar Khan could respond, he was arrested by Zia for his attacks on the martial law regime. In the meantime, Bizenjo had circulated copies of his draft, which was never published, to a small circle of Baluch leaders.

Various Baluch sources who described this highly significant change differed about its meaning. Some felt that since Bizenjo keeps in close touch with the pro-Soviet lobby in Pakistan, his shift indicates that Moscow is moving toward a newly flexible position on the issue of an independent Baluchistan. Others thought that Bizenjo simply wanted to remain in step with the militant temper of Baluch opinion and acted entirely on his own.

Bizenjo's links with pro-Soviet Communist activists have led some of his political opponents to charge that he is more of a Communist than a nationalist and that, someday, he will be Moscow's most valuable ally in Pakistan. In particular, his detractors emphasize his ties with Nawaz Butt of Karachi and Shameem Malik of Lahore, leaders of the Communist-sponsored National Progressive party. They point out that he consistently advocated a Soviet-tilted brand of neutralism as a leader of the Pakistan National party and its predecessor, the outlawed National Awami party, and opposed attempts by the Pushtun NAP leader, Abdul Wali Khan, to promote a centrist policy. These critics also point to his strong support of the "progressive" 1978 Afghan revolution and to his vocal opposition to Pakistani support of the anti-Communist Afghan rebels. Warning in early 1979 that pro-Kabul Baluch and Pushtun insurgent activity would be unleashed in the border areas if Islamabad and its Chinese and Western allies continued to support the Afghan rebels, Bizenjo urged "all concerned to take note of the delicate nature of the geopolitical situation in our region. You are playing with fire. I must make it explicitly clear that we Pakistanis, especially the Baluch and Pushtuns who live on both sides of the borders of these three neighboring countries, will resolutely oppose all attempts to push us over the precipice to disaster."

Comparatively, Bizenjo is undoubtedly more pro-Soviet in his outlook than Marri or Mengal, but it would be a mistake, in my view, to write him off as a captive of Moscow. Many student leftists and nationalist militants in Baluchistan thoroughly distrust him, branding him as a chameleonlike opportunist who would have betrayed the Baluch cause in his 1977 negotiations with Zia in return for tokens of political power and economic largesse if Marri and Mengal had not stopped him. To these leftist critics, his sympathies with Marxism-Leninism are only superficial. They charge that he has become increasingly beholden to big business interests which have backed his political activities, notably the Haroun conglomerate and Mustikhan Transcontinental, controlled by Akber Y. Mustikhan, the millionaire Baluch contractor.

Despite his long-standing criticism of the Iranian Shah as a Western puppet, Bizenjo jumped at an invitation to visit Teheran in June 1972, during his tenure as governor of Baluchistan. He had several private talks with the Shah and proudly unveiled an economic aid package for Baluchistan on his return. This visit brought sharp attacks from leftist leaders throughout Pakistan, who charged that he was plotting with Teheran and Washington to bring the Pakistani Baluch areas under Iranian hegemony. At the time of our conversations, the Shah was still in power. When I asked Bizenjo whether he could imagine circumstances in which Iran could provide help for the achievement of Baluch aspirations, his response was an enigmatic "beggars can't be choosers, after all," a smile, and a quick change of the subject.

As for his Soviet-tilted foreign policy declarations, closer examination shows that many of these were inspired directly or indirectly by American military aid policies that have bolstered Pakistani military regimes over the years and have facilitated Islamabad's repression of the Baluch. Commented Ataullah Mengal, "If strong criticism of misguided American policies that have affected us as Baluch is 'pro-Soviet,' then many of us are guilty of that." While Bizenjo might have been "more favorably disposed" toward the Russians in earlier years than some of his Baluch colleagues, Mengal said, he "cooled off considerably, like the rest of us," when Soviet representatives in Pakistan gave their blessing to the Bhutto regime at the expense of the Baluch, tacitly approving Bhutto's military offensive in Baluchistan and even belaboring Bizenjo, at one point, for opposing him. Bizenjo's disenchantment has grown, Mengal added, since the Soviet occupation of Afghanistan, though he has stopped short of open criticism of Moscow "because the Americans are also involved in the region and it is certainly not a black and white situation." If he were serious about his socialism, Mengal reflected, Bizenjo would not have objected so self-righteously when Bhutto confiscated his lands during the insurgency. "I often tease him, 'You are a socialist as long as it doesn't affect you personally.' What kind of socialist is it who prays five times a day and recites from the Koran? Ghausi is a nationalist. We are all nationalists."

Akber Y. Mustikhan, who has backed both the National Awami party and the Pakistan National party, said that Bizenjo has regained most of the lands taken by Bhutto but still owns at most a few hundred acres of cultivable farmland. Only recently has he begun to show some interest in developing his extensive mountain tracts, which have a "great potential" for orchards and dairies. "He is not interested in money," lamented Mustikhan. "He is a completely political animal, and a very pragmatic man in his sphere. He has absolutely no illusions about the Russians. He will not play their game unless you Americans, and the Pakistani author- ities, force him to do so, unless there is no other alternative. You can say that Ghausi is an opportunist, in the positive sense of the word, in the sense of what is best for the Baluch. But don't forget that he has been brought up in Western-style parliamentary politics. This is what he knows best and loves best. It is too bad that it has never been possible to play this kind of politics for very long in Pakistan."

Bizenjo himself guffaws at suggestions that he is a Communist, roar- ing, "Which of the ninety Communist factions in Pakistan would I join? They all want to be the leader, they all want Moscow to support them, and Moscow laughs at all of them. It is one thing to understand the experi- ence of socialist countries and what this means for us. It is quite another to talk of the type of Communists we have in Pakistan."

My own conclusion is that Moscow has been seriously cultivating Bizenjo as its principal potential ally in Pakistan. Communist leaders consciously flatter his ego by treating him not as a mere Baluch leader, but as the future prime minister of a "socialist, federal" regime in Is- lamabad. Bizenjo, for his part, is still ready to strike a bargain with Zia for an autonomous Baluchistan, but he no longer believes such a bargain is possible. Moscow, he calculates, is likely to become increasingly influ- ential in South Asia once it has secured its hold in Kabul. He hopes that Soviet objectives will prove to be "much more limited" in Pakistan than they were in Afghanistan and that the Baluch will be able to turn events to their advantage if they are sufficiently adroit. Thus, he suggests, the most promising way to break the grip of the Punjabi-dominated military on the country may well be to promote a "national democratic" govern- ment with Communist participation that will grant autonomy to the provinces, including the ultimate right of secession. If such a government pursued a neutralist foreign policy, he argues, the West should not ob- ject, since the only acceptable alternative in Soviet eyes may well be the dismemberment of Pakistan.

Solemnly recalling the "terrible horrors" of the 1973–1977 period, "the terrible suffering of so many innocent people," Bizenjo continually stressed the theme that it is "our duty to do what we can in the political and diplomatic arena" before countenancing another bruising military struggle for independence. In the wake of the Soviet occupation of Afghanistan, he fears that Baluchistan could become the focus of a superpower collision that could greatly damage the Baluch cause. "Now that Afghanistan can no longer play the role of a neutral buffer," he observed, "perhaps Pakistan, which is very much affiliated with the Western powers, should change its course and should play that role. If it fails to do so, there may well be a series of upheavals and conflicts leading to the breakup of Pakistan, and the superpowers will have to create a new buffer zone to preserve peace in the Persian Gulf area. We would rather become this new buffer state, with the concurrence of the superpowers, than achieve our independence through alignment with one or the other of them. The cost in blood and tears would certainly be much less for us."

Ataullah Mengal: "Let Them Come to Us"

Lean and wiry, with blazing black eyes and a carefully preened black beard, Ataullah Mengal, who was fifty-one in 1981, is a more "typical" Baluch than his two colleagues. He speaks in the straightforward and often fiery manner traditionally esteemed in Baluch culture, looking you directly in the eye. Less sophisticated in his educational background than Marri or Bizenjo, he shuns their intellectual and ideological pretensions. Like Marri, Mengal is bitter and unrelenting in his suspicion of the Punjabi-dominated Pakistani establishment. Like Bizenjo, however, he is calculating, cunning, and coldly pragmatic. He is the symbol of uncomplicated Baluch patriotism and commands broad respect in all political factions.

Next to the Marris, the Mengals are probably the most numerous Baluch tribe, with some 85,000 people spread over the Khuzdar, Kalat, and Las Bela districts (see Figure 2). Ataullah's father, Rasul Bux, was a popular *sardar* who concentrated on building the power of the ruling Shahizai clan and tending to his farmlands and orchards. Rasul Bux remained aloof from politics, but his son soon began to show an interest in liberal and nationalist ideas as a student at a small Islamic college in Karachi. Even though he was repelled by the rigidity of the Marxist thought then fashionable on the campus, he was moved by the arguments of moderate reformers who attacked the inequities of the feudal economic structure in Pakistan.

Mengal dramatically divested himself of nearly half of his inherited lands, parceling them out among his tenants. Like Marri, he earned a reputation as an incorruptible, progressive *sardar*. During the 1950s, horrified by army excesses in Baluchistan, he gradually drifted into political life. Baluchistan did not yet exist as a provincial entity under the Ayub regime, but the Baluch areas were represented in the National Assembly. Mengal ran successfully as an independent for the assembly and promptly collided with the Ayub regime by denouncing military rule and demanding autonomous provincial status for Baluchistan. Ayub then attempted to depose him as *sardar* in 1962, appointing in his stead a distant cousin, who was murdered by irate tribesmen on the day of his inauguration ceremony. Although Mengal pleads innocence, pointing out that he was far from the scene, the Ayub regime jailed him for complicity in the murder. He was released after two months, and Islamabad once again acknowledged him as *sardar* in the hope that he would prove more cooperative. But by April 1963, he was imprisoned again, this time for allegedly seditious statements, and was not released until January 1967.

Mengal emerged more politically conscious than ever from his four-year imprisonment and joined Marri and Bizenjo in organizing the Baluchistan branch of the National Awami party and in campaigning for the unification of the Baluch areas in Baluchistan province, a demand formally granted by Yahya Khan, who deposed Ayub in 1969. When the National Awami party won the 1970 elections in Baluchistan, Mengal became chief minister. When Bhutto ousted him, triggering the 1973–1977 insurgency, the Mengal tribe played a major role in the fighting. However, the Mengals proved to be less united than the Marris. Several of Mengal's five brothers sabotaged his efforts to mobilize the tribe against the government.

Mengal suffered a shattering personal tragedy during the course of the fighting when his second son, Asadullah, was shot down in broad daylight on a Karachi street by Bhutto's agents. Although Zia promised Mengal that he would find and punish the killers, Zia has never done so, claiming that the evidence has all been destroyed. Citing information supplied by former Bhutto aides, Mengal alleges that the real reason for Zia's unwillingness to deliver on his promise is that army personnel were involved, including a brigadier general.

During the three years I have known Mengal, his nationalist attitudes have progressively hardened, and he has gradually abandoned his hopes for accommodation between the Baluch and Islamabad. When I first met him, on October 14, 1977, in New York, he had just been released from prison for medical reasons by the newly installed Zia regime and had come to the United States for open-heart surgery. Marri and Bizenjo were still being held on treason charges, despite the fact that Zia had halted many of the other politically motivated judicial proceedings initiated by the Bhutto regime. Shortly before releasing Men-

Ataullah Mengal,
former Chief Minister
of Baluchistan
(Pakistan)

gal, Zia went to the prison, summoned the three leaders for a "friendly chat," and offered to improve the conditions of their confinement. "It was clear even then," Mengal said, "that the General didn't think what Bhutto had done to us was so terribly bad, after all, even though he made some comments critical of Bhutto." The meeting ended in an atmosphere of considerable tension, recalled Mengal, after Zia told his captives that "we are all Muslims, and we should not say that we are Baluch or Pushtuns." Bizenjo angrily rejoined that "we are Baluch and Pushtuns and we will never make a viable Pakistan except on that foundation."

Marri and Bizenjo were released eventually, but by freeing other political prisoners so much earlier than the Baluch, Mengal declared, Zia had "reinforced the feeling of our people that they are second-class citizens of this country. Before, we could say that it was just Bhutto, but now they can see that the Pakistani government and the Punjabis are all the same, regardless of who is in power." A delegation of student leaders came to meet him in Karachi after his release, Mengal said, and "were all talking to me about independence. They said they could see no future in Pakistan. They belittled the meaning of elections for the Baluch, even if they were ever held, since we are so few in number compared to the rest of Pakistan. They said that our vote does not count." When Mengal argued that justice could still be obtained in Pakistan through political means, Moem Khan, then president of the Baluch Students Organization, posed question after question about the circumstances of his 1973 ouster to demonstrate the futility of attempting to work with a Punjabi-dominated central government. "Then they abused the Zia regime and said that it was not just Bhutto or Zia who was to blame for what had happened, it was the Punjabi mentality. I advised them to work for a new constitution and a new type of federalism. They said nothing doing, they can't adjust to this country. They said, we will have oil, we will have uranium, so why can't we be independent?"

In 1978, when I next met Mengal in Karachi on July 19 and in Quetta on July 30, I found him increasingly disturbed by the polarization that was developing between Bizenjo's supporters, on the one hand, and hard-liners who looked to Marri as the probable leader of a new armed struggle. Mengal found himself in the middle, trying to hold the triumvirate together.

Mengal was also more doubtful of Zia than ever. The three leaders had held repeated meetings with Zia and his advisers, he said, and had been unable to get clear responses to their demands. These included "at least $10 million" in compensation for damages suffered by the Baluch during the insurgency, a comprehensive amnesty for political prisoners, and the complete withdrawal of Pakistani army and paramilitary units. Mengal was bothered most of all by the lack of any clear movement from military government back to civilian rule under a stable constitution that would protect the interests of the Baluch and other minorities. "Assuming that we could get understandings with them on immediate issues, how could they assure us that what they accepted would be honored by their successors?" he asked. "Even Zia is not a free man. He is surrounded by a tight circle of advisers and it takes a long time to implement even the smallest concession that he makes to us. That gives a handle to our hawks, who can charge with considerable credibility that he is not living up to his undertakings."

What the Baluch face, Mengal said, is a "whole gang of Punjabis" in the bureaucracy and the army, "a network that has complete control of the civil service machinery in Baluchistan and has no sympathy for the agreements we have been discussing with General Zia." This "gang" actively sabotaged the negotiations with Zia when the Baluch demanded a Baluch-controlled administrative structure for handling compensation payments. They also "put a lot of pressure on Zia" when the Baluch insisted that the Punjabi chief secretary of Baluchistan province be dismissed and replaced by a Baluch.

"They take the attitude that we have to prove our patriotism," said Mengal, "but we have had enough of this cringing. We're not going to continue going to them, paying homage to them to get their certificate of patriotism and approval. Let them come to us. If they call me a traitor a thousand times, it means I'm loyal to my people, the people of Baluchistan. I'm going to tell them that in the eyes of the Baluch, the Punjabi is enemy number one. I'll tell them, 'You satisfy the younger generation. They are deadly against you and they say to hell with Pakistan.' "

Mengal spoke grimly of the "impossible choices" confronting the older generation of Baluch leaders, who are caught between "Punjabi bullheadedness" and the demands of militant student groups pushing for an independence struggle. As a result of the intransigence shown by Pakistani leaders, he said, "I have no grounds left to plead the case for further efforts to come to an understanding with Pakistan. I tell the students that independence is not possible without a terrible price and might not be possible at all. I tell them that our location makes others feel it is necessary to control us. I ask them: 'Would you like to change masters? Will that suit you?' But still, they go on talking about independence and working secretly for independence. I tell the students, 'I won't oppose you, but I won't lead you. I'll be an ordinary follower. Let history judge who is right. You take the responsibility for the blood bath that a struggle for independence would involve. I can't take the responsibility for leading you in that direction.' "

In our 1978 conversations, Mengal talked gloomily of retiring from politics, declaring that "we will slip out of the scene, relax in our homes, and leave the whole thing to the young men. There is nothing for us to do if we are forced to choose between the betrayal of our honor and a course of reckless adventurism." By mid-1979, however, he and Marri had decided to carry on their struggle as political exiles and had left the country, ostensibly for medical treatment. Mengal's heart problems were well known, and Marri had been seeing internal medicine specialists in Pakistan, complaining of a digestive ailment. When they asked for permission to go to London, Pakistani officials could find no plausible reason for refusing. By all accounts, Islamabad concluded that the two leaders would be less of a nuisance outside the country than inside. However, the government began to have second thoughts after more than a year had passed and the leaders showed no signs of wanting to return.

In subsequent conversations with Mengal, by telephone and in London during the course of 1980, it became clear that he was reappraising his attitude toward an independence struggle. He no longer felt it would be "reckless" to pursue guerrilla activity if adequate foreign support could be arranged on acceptable terms. By remaining abroad, he felt that he could make contacts more easily than in Pakistan and could speak out more freely if, at some stage, he and Marri gave up all hope of a settlement with Islamabad and decided to establish a Baluch government-in-exile.

I also found that Mengal had radically upgraded his conditions for a political settlement with Pakistan. In 1978, he was still ready to accept a loose federation of the type advocated by Bizenjo, although he demanded built-in constitutional guarantees to safeguard provincial rights. In 1980, he insisted that the Baluch could only feel secure in a confederation based on complete parity for the four constituent units, irrespective of the size of their populations. "We can't live in a federation," Mengal said, "because the Punjabis would always dominate us. Suppose we get our rights—we would only be 9 people in an assembly of 300. They *insisted* on the principle of parity between East and West Pakistan when it was in their interests, when the western wing was outnumbered by the Bengalis. They said the Bengalis should sacrifice in order to hold the country together. Well, let them sacrifice now."

In his proposed confederation, each of the provinces would have equal representation in the armed forces and the civil service. Most of the taxing powers now wielded by the central government would be transferred to the provinces, thus assuring "equitable and adequate" revenues to the more populous provinces, while giving the minority provinces the benefits of their natural-resource endowments.

Bridling at my observation that Islamabad would be likely to reject such proposals out of hand, he exploded that "they are so arrogant, so self-centered, that they don't seem to care whether we go or stay. If they can't control us, they don't want us in Pakistan. It is true that we don't hope for much from them. But it is not our fault. It would have been acceptable to remain with them if at any stage in the last thirty years they had given us any respect."

Punjabi domination, he went on, means "tens of thousands of them coming in, civil servants and army fellows telling you what to do, people from Lahore buying up our farms, buying the best land in Quetta, more and more of them crawling all over us, annihilating us." We Baluch must choose, he concluded with a shrug, between "losing our identity at the mercy of the Punjabis or stretching our hand to others."

"If the Russians come," he said, "if it comes to that conclusion, we might at least have some kind of conditional freedom. They may send their technocrats and their soldiers, but they would not send a whole population to occupy Baluchistan as the Punjabis are doing, step by step. Russia is too far away. They might do some good things, they might educate our children. What 'freedom' do we have to lose?" Then, lamenting the fate of Afghan president Babrak Karmal, he hastily added that "we know the power would lie with someone else if the Russians came. We know there is a difference between getting freedom and changing masters. But would the Americans be better?" While Moscow would be unlikely to tolerate a neutral Baluchistan, he speculated, and would no doubt insist on having military bases, "perhaps the Americans would be satisfied if they could just keep the Russians out. They might not be as bad."

Denouncing the American role in Pakistan, Mengal urged the United States to withhold further economic and military aid to the Zia regime "until democratic values are restored, not only in the form of elections, but in fair treatment for the minority provinces. You have no reason to give assistance to such a regime, and to continue to do so would conflict with your professed dedication to human rights." He pointed to the economy as Pakistan's area of greatest vulnerability, insisting that "if the Iranians, the Arabs, and the United States would stop pumping in money, this government wouldn't last for two years. It's living on blood transfusions and glucose drips." Even with continued help, he predicted, Pakistan is in for a series of military coups which will lead to a divided, politicized army and more frequent clashes between the military and antigovernment demonstrators. Coupled with further economic deterioration, such a breakdown of authority could lead to endemic violence and strife, "a continual state of near civil war in which the Baluch, the Pushtuns, and the Sindhis will sooner or later see their opportunity to overturn the present power structure."

Much will depend, Mengal reflected, on developments in Afghanistan, since continuing border tension would enable Zia to "frighten some of the people into supporting the status quo" and would help to keep the flow of Western aid coming. Conversely, if there is some sort of diplomatic settlement, the West will "lose interest in Pakistan" and the situation will be more fluid. As Pakistan begins to collapse of its own weight, Mengal concluded, the West "might begin to see things from a different angle. After all, why should you assume that your interests can only be protected by the continuance of Pakistan in its present form? Why should the United States let the Soviet Union be the only champion of national liberation?"

The election of Ronald Reagan brought a further hardening of Mengal's position. In a London conversation in December 1980, he said angrily that "whatsoever chance of American support for our cause had existed previously has all but vanished, since the United States is more likely than ever to support reactionary regimes everywhere." By February 1981, he had decided to come out openly for Baluch independence, and to the extent that he held out hope for foreign support, it was for Soviet support.

"There was a time when we deluded ourselves with the belief that the Baluch could live in Pakistan as a respected nation," he told an interviewer for the London Baluch monthly *Nedae Baluchistan* (Voice of Baluchistan). "But now every Baluch, whether he says it or is forced to keep quiet, has reached the conclusion that there is no place in Pakistan for a self-respecting Baluch. We want to see Baluchistan as a sovereign state and the Baluch as an independent nation."

History has made clear, Mengal declared, that "the only way to gain freedom is through the muzzle of a gun." However, he saw little imminent prospect of obtaining foreign military help, especially from China, which "no longer supports socialism or people's movements and thinks only of opposing the Soviet Union," or from the United States, which "we regard as our enemy number one on the basis of past performance and which we will continue to regard as our enemy unless it proves to us, in practice, that it has changed its attitude." India, he said, "is forever trying to promote friendship with the Islamabad rulers, so why would it support the Baluch?" As for the Soviet Union, Mengal was notably milder, observing only that Moscow "has to date expressed no interest in the Baluch struggle. Perhaps they do not consider the Baluch mature enough to fight for their freedom." Referring to Afghanistan, Mengal said that "no matter how much one may disapprove of one country's interference in the affairs of another country, it would not be fair or objective to hold Soviet Russia alone responsible in the case of Afghanistan."[4]

Pakistani newspapers were not permitted to publish dispatches on Mengal's pronouncements, but news of his open advocacy of independence quickly reached Baluchistan through the underground. "Think of the irony," Mengal reflected. "When we were not in favor of independence, they claimed we were, and now that it is true, they want to keep it quiet."

Baluch People's Liberation Front guerrillas

The Baluch Nationalist Movement in Pakistan

5

The Baluch rose up swiftly and unquestioningly in 1973 to avenge what they perceived as an assault on their tribal and racial honor. Given their lack of preparation and centralized direction, however, they dissipated much of their energy fighting on a localized, ad hoc basis under free-wheeling tribal commanders. Student leaders and other urban nationalists attempted to channel this sporadic tribal resistance into organized guerrilla activity, but their efforts, too, were largely uncoordinated. Seven separate guerrilla groups operated independently in the hills under seven separate sets of leaders. Except for the Pararis, all of these groups were hastily assembled at the outbreak of the conflict and all of them were gradually disbanded following the 1977 cease-fire.

Nationalist leaders are proud that the Baluch were able to pin down Pakistani forces vastly superior in number for so long, arguing that they would have triumphed, despite their organizational deficiencies, if they had been armed with modern weaponry. Nevertheless, there is now a widespread recognition among the Baluch that their cause suffered greatly from its disorganized character. This realization has led to greatly accelerated nationalist activity designed to build upon the organizational networks established during the insurgency.

War-born political consciousness has excited unprecedented ferment in Baluch society. Newly politicized elements in the countryside are swelling the nationalist ranks. In many cases, these new elements are challenging the authority of urban-centered activists, and significant differences are developing within and between nationalist groups over issues of ideology, strategy, and tactics. Tribal animosities and personal rivalries also continue to plague the nationalist movement. Conceivably, internecine conflict will make it impossible for contending nationalist factions to cooperate effectively, but tensions have been alleviated to a great extent by the emergence, for the first time, of a broadly accepted high-level Baluch leadership, discussed in the preceding chapter.

In 1980, there were three principal vehicles of organized Baluch nationalist activity in Pakistan: the Baluch People's Liberation Front, which believes in the inevitability of a military confrontation with Pakistan and Iran; the Baluch Students Organization (BSO), which subdivides, in turn, into two rival factions; and the Pakistan National party, a moderate, nonviolent group favoring a restructured Pakistani constitutional system in which Baluchistan would have an autonomous, loosely confederated relationship with Islamabad.

The Baluch People's Liberation Front

The Baluch People's Liberation Front is an exotic amalgam of Baluch nationalism and independent Marxist-Leninist thought which explicitly rejects the primacy of either Moscow or Peking. The Liberation Front is a direct outgrowth of the Parari guerrilla movement founded by Sher Mohammed Marri in 1963 and did not adopt its present name and organizational structure until 1976. It still has close ties both to Sher Mohammed and to his tribal ally, the Marri *sardar* Khair Bux Marri, although Mir Hazar Ramkhani, who headed the Pararis during the 1973–1977 insurgency, has now been formally crowned as leader of its People's Revolutionary Command.

The Pararis were organized primarily to wage a guerrilla struggle and had only an inchoate political program. Their evolution into the more ambitious Liberation Front, which espouses political as well as military objectives and policies, began during the period of ideological reappraisal in Pakistani leftist circles that followed the 1969 cease-fire. Pointing to Parari successes on the battlefield, Sher Mohammed argued that the power structure in Pakistan could be overturned only if other minorities joined the Baluch in waging simultaneous and coordinated armed struggles to win their demands for regional autonomy. Although he was joined by like-minded allies in Bengal, Sind, the Pushtun areas, and even the Punjab, most of the entrenched leftist leadership believed that the Pakistani Left was not strong enough for a confrontation with the establishment. This group included the Communist party, which is dominated by *mahajirs* (refugees) from areas now in India and which does not have strong local roots in any of the minority provinces, including Baluchistan.

Sher Mohammed and his allies contended that nationality demands should be the cutting edge of leftist strategy in Pakistan because the economic deprivation of the masses in the three minority provinces is the result of Punjabi domination. Only by achieving autonomy within a loosely federated, socialist Pakistan, he said, or by seceding from Pakistan altogether, could these provinces escape from the economic oppression inflicted by the Punjabi-dominated political and economic hierarchy. Traditional Marxist-Leninists were deeply suspicious of this emphasis on the nationality issue, charging that leftist elements would become the tools of "bourgeois nationalist" politicians who were merely using ethnic grievances as a means of exacting economic concessions from the Punjabi elite for their own narrow class benefit.

This debate over the related issues of an armed struggle and what is known in Marxist-Leninist parlance as the "national question" echoed among Pakistani students abroad. In 1969, a group of influential non-Baluch leftist intellectuals attending various British universities rallied to Marri's standard. Baluchistan, they concluded, should be the testing ground for an armed national liberation struggle. Such an insurgency would provide a model for the rest of Pakistan and therefore should be initiated whether or not Marxist-Leninists in other parts of the country were ready to launch their own struggles. All seventeen members of the clandestine London Group are well-connected sons of prosperous businessmen and civil servants. The ringleader, Mohammed Bhabha, is the son of a Karachi import-export magnate who belongs to the Aga Khan's wealthy Ismaili sect. Two of the members of the group, Asad and Rashid Rahman, are sons of the late Justice S. A. Rahman of the Punjab High Court. Another, Najam Sethi, is a scion of the multimillionaire Sahgal family, one of the "Twenty-two Families" who were the principal targets of the Left during its successful campaign to overthrow the Ayub regime.

"We were not completely homogeneous ideologically," commented one of the members, Ghulam Mohammed, in a Kabul interview in August 1978. "But what linked us was an independent point of view in relation to the other Left tendencies then in existence. We were the kind of people who were not prepared to be linked with foreign axes. We were seeking something new, and we were all sympathetic with Baluch nationalism even though we were not Baluch." Some were admirers of the Chinese and Vietnamese models, he recalled, and wanted to create a new Marxist-Leninist party that would oversee guerrilla activity. Others were influenced by Che Guevara and by the French leftist theoretician Regis Debray, who argued that the guerrillas themselves should be the focus of political power in revolutionary movements and should not be subject to the discipline of a noncombatant political party. Ultimately, it was the Debray approach that proved most influential.

The London Group went to the hills in 1971. When word got around in the coffee shops of Karachi and Lahore, another twenty to twenty-five young leftists soon followed, including two sons of a prominent Sind politician, Mir Ali Ahmed Talpur, who was to become defense minister under Zia. For Mir Hazar Ramkhani, it was not an easy task to integrate these soft, city-bred intellectuals into his Parari ranks. Several left within a matter of months after tasting the hardships of fugitive life in the mountains. However, most of them adjusted to tribal ways, learned

Baluchi, adopted Baluch names, and eventually won the trust of their skeptical Baluch comrades by demonstrating their willingness to share the risks of combat during the war years. Mohammed Bhabha took the name Murad Khan. Asad Rahman, who called himself Chakkar Khan (a legendary leader of the Dombki tribe), played a key wartime role as one of Mir Hazar's zonal commanders. Another Punjabi, Ahmed Rashid, who adopted the name of Balach (a sixteenth-century warrior hero), led several successful Parari operations against an Amoco oil-drilling venture near Bambore, forcing a suspension of oil exploration in the Marri area for two years. The new recruits proved invaluable to Mir Hazar in organizational and propaganda activities. Their affluent sympathizers in Karachi and Lahore sent food, medical supplies, and funds to the hills. Murad Khan had contacts with George Habash's Popular Front for the Liberation of Palestine and arranged for the training of forty-odd Baluch guerrillas in Beirut in 1973.

As the insurgency began to lose steam in 1975 and 1976, it became apparent that the Pararis and the leaders of the six other organized guerrilla groups engaged in the struggle did not share the same long-term objectives. Most of the others hoped for some sort of truce with the central government and had no clear vision of the future beyond that. However, Mir Hazar and his increasingly influential brain trust from the London Group felt that the insurgency had shown what a relatively small, disciplined force could do in the face of overwhelming odds and were more committed than ever to a continuing armed struggle. This approach was also shared by many of the more militant activists in the other groups. In late 1976, Mir Hazar formally reconstituted the Pararis as the Liberation Front in order to facilitate the absorption of these militants within a broadened and restructured organizational framework. Khair Bux Marri gave his blessing to this move, and Sher Mohammed Marri was actively involved in the reorganization process. The Front subsequently attracted several hundred of the discontented followers of those guerrilla leaders, such as Khair Jan Baluch and Aslam Gichki, who accepted Zia's 1977 amnesty offer and returned to Pakistan. More recently, it has also provided a rallying point for a steady trickle of militant nationalists, especially in student groups, who want to prepare for a renewed guerrilla struggle.

On visits to the Liberation Front's base camps in southern Afghanistan between 1977 and 1980, I detected signs of tension between the strikingly divergent elements that make up the movement. Some 40 percent of its fighting forces are Ramkhanis, the Marri clan of which Mir Hazar Ramkhani is the hereditary chieftain. Marris belonging to other clans make up another 20 percent or more of the combat forces and hold most of the Liberation Front's key military command posts. A vast cultural gap exists between these largely uneducated tribesmen and the younger, detribalized nationalists from a variety of different tribes, many of them recent college graduates, who constitute the remaining 40 percent of the guerrillas. Khair Jan Baluch, one of the guerrilla leaders who broke with the Liberation Front after the 1977 truce, observed that an even more important source of tension is Marri chauvinism. "At heart, they think they are a superior race and are not really willing to share power with people from other tribes, or with the progressive Punjabis and Sindhis, like the London Group, who have joined up with them."

Since Mir Hazar will not reveal the identity of the members of his People's Revolutionary Command, it is difficult to determine the degree of non-Marri representation in the Liberation Front's top leadership. The leaders vigorously deny charges of Marri domination, citing as evidence their non-Marri zonal commanders and their explicit repudiation of tribalism as the basis for the organization of combat units. During the 1958–1960 fighting, they note, Nauroz Khan's guerrillas, primarily from the Zehri and Mengal tribes, were organized by clans. Similarly, most of the guerrilla activity from 1973 to 1977 was conducted by separate tribal groups fighting under their own tribal leadership. By contrast, as the London Group leader Balach stated, the Liberation Front combat units integrate not only different sections of the Marri tribe but also an "even balance" of members from other tribes. With the continuing influx of younger nationalists from the student movement, the Liberation Front "will become more and more a truly national movement."

While the movement's leaders make more sweeping claims, I have concluded that its presently organized combat units number at most 7,500 men. More than 2,700 (not including family members) are based in the Afghan camps, while some 1,700 are scattered in different parts of Pakistani Baluchistan and another 3,000, mostly Marris, are "active reservists" who work in Karachi and other parts of Sind. The largest single concentration that I personally have inspected—some 1,700—was encamped near Kalat-i-Gilzai, a lonely, rocky cul-de-sac deep in the Afghan hills. The camp is sixty-five miles from the nearest village and is reached only after a four-hour jeep ride from the nearest highway over a maze of bumpy mountain trails. According to Mir Hazar, the Liberation Front's organized units constitute a skeleton command structure capable of mobilizing thousands of additional troops in a future insurgency. "We could field 15,000 or 20,000 in a matter of weeks," he said, "if we had the weapons."

Despite its Marxist-Leninist rhetoric on many issues, the Liberation Front's organizational structure is not modeled after Communist parties.

When the Front was launched in 1976, Balach said, "we decided after a rather difficult debate that we would not attempt to have an elaborate organization based on democratic centralism. We made a conscious departure from the traditional way that Communist parties operate. Experience has shown the dangers of bureaucracy and egoism in Communist parties, and in a tribal society, with its hierarchical structure, we felt that the dangers of a bureaucratic approach would be peculiarly great." The organization described by Balach and other Liberation Front leaders is loosely structured and does not incorporate formal party units at the local level. Following the Debray model, the guerrilla combat units also serve as the party organization, functioning cooperatively without an internal chain of command. "If you give a man a title and a place in a structure," said Balach, "he begins to take himself too seriously, to lord it over others in a way that he would not otherwise do." Each guerrilla has a specific locale or task for which he is responsible. He reports only to a zonal commander, who reports, in turn, only to the People's Revolutionary Command.

The Liberation Front's irreverent attitude toward doctrinaire Marxism-Leninism is apparent in its acceptance of nomadism as part of its revolutionary doctrine. "We want to modernize tribal society, not to destroy it," declared Murad Khan, external affairs secretary. "We want to keep what is healthy in the tribal ethos, introducing industrialization gradually." One of the distinctly unhealthy elements in Baluch society, he added, is its denigration of women. The Liberation Front program defies traditional Baluch attitudes concerning the role of women and states that women members play a role in noncombatant educational and health programs. The Front even tried to use male paramedics to give treatment to women but has backed away from this after angry protests. On my visits to the camps, the women and children stayed in their tents, and my impression is that there are only a few women activists in the movement.

Reviewing the Liberation Front's policy pronouncements, I found a consistent emphasis on the need for an armed struggle to "liberate" Baluchistan, but a deliberate ambivalence, until recently, on the issue of whether or not liberation must come in the form of sovereign independence. In its first manifesto, the Liberation Front stressed that it was "not fighting a secessionist war for the Baluch alone, but a war of national liberation for all the nationalities of Pakistan." The manifesto pointed to Iran's growing military power and concluded that "a struggle for 'Greater Baluchistan' is not feasible in the face of the realities of the situation in this region."[1] Similarly, in the initial issue of *Jabal* in December 1976, the Front emphasized its identity with other leftist forces in Pakistan, describing Baluchistan as "a reliable base area for the liberation

Mir Hazar Ramkhani (center, seated), chairman of the Revolutionary Command of the Baluch People's Liberation Front, with followers at the Front's Kalat-i-Gilzai base camp in southern Afghanistan. The author found that the guns pictured here include British NATO-model Parker-Hale rifles captured from the Pakistan Army.

Aslam Gichki, leader of Baluch guerrilla activities 1973–1977 in the Makran Hills of Pakistan

The author joins Mir Hazar Ramkhani in a feast of sajji, *or Baluch-style roast leg of lamb, at the Baluch People's Liberation Front base camp in Kalat-i-Gilzai, southern Afghanistan*

struggles of the other oppressed nationalities, classes and democratic forces in Pakistan."[2] "We do not deny, but rather uphold, the right of nations to self-determination, including secession," *Jabal* declared in February 1977. "However, in the concrete circumstances of our country there is as yet no secessionist movement in Baluchistan. To the extent that we are able to explain the nature of the struggle and its perspective to the people of Pakistan as a whole and win their moral, political, and practical support, to that extent we shall have laid the basis for a *voluntary* union of the nationalities in Pakistan."[3]

By April 1978, Liberation Front leaders were beginning to display growing impatience with Baluch moderates and leftists in other parts of Pakistan, bemoaning their apparent readiness to accept a strengthened version of the prewar, 1973 constitution if the Zia regime could be induced to grant increased autonomy to the minority provinces. Calling once again for an armed struggle, *Jabal* declared that:

> In Baluchistan today, the armed revolution is fighting the armed counterrevolution. Here, it is no longer a question of "one unit or its breakup," or of "constitutional safeguards for the minority nationalities" or "greater power to the provinces." These are mere platitudes and totally pointless starters for resolving the problem, because the Liberation Front has raised the question to its highest point—that is, armed struggle for the national and democratic rights and the total liberation of the people of Baluchistan.[4]

This proved to be the last issue of *Jabal*. Publication was "suspended" following the 1978 Communist coup in Afghanistan and it has yet to be resumed. "We want maximum flexibility," explained Murad Khan. "The situation has been so fluid that we have felt it best to say little, while watching and waiting." In interviews with Liberation Front leaders since the suspension of *Jabal*, however, I found an increasingly explicit acknowledgment that the movement is working for independence. "We would like to see a liberation struggle in other parts of Pakistan," said Chakkar Khan, one of the founders of the London Group, interviewed in Kabul in August 1978. "But quite frankly, we do not expect this to happen very soon in Sind or the Punjab, at least not in the near future. Maybe in ten or fifteen years it may happen, but by then we'll be independent." External Affairs Secretary Murad Khan, in an interview in Paris in March 1980, said that "we are giving up our old idea of a federation of socialist republics in an all-Pakistan revolutionary structure, with Baluchistan in the vanguard." Increasingly, he explained, "new developments in the region" have pointed toward the desirability of an independent Greater Baluchistan that would unify the Baluch in Pakistan,

Afghanistan, and Iran. Militarily, the erosion of centralized authority in Iran following the Khomeini revolution has made this goal a "much more realistic one" than it was during the Shah's regime. Moreover, confronted by the Soviet military presence in Afghanistan, the Baluch in all three countries now recognize that they could well become pawns in superpower politics if they fail to unite. The Liberation Front "does not wish to take a position either for or against the Soviet presence," he said, "but we know that if the Baluch stand together, their interests will be best protected under the new circumstances."

What if Moscow should seek to promote an independent Greater Baluchistan and offer to provide military equipment? Since the Soviet occupation of Afghanistan, Front leaders have become extremely circumspect on this issue, but they had left the door wide open for Soviet assistance in earlier interviews. "We would welcome help from any side, from any government," declared Mir Hazar in August 1978, "and if any government helps those who oppress us, we will be against them." Chakkar Khan stressed that "we don't want to get involved in global blocs if we can avoid it, and we don't want to become dependent on anyone." If Iran could be neutralized, he claimed, the Baluch could defeat the Pakistan Army without much outside help, since "we would get many of the weapons we need by capturing arms in battle and through the black-market, as in the past." At the same time, he acknowledged that some source of sophisticated hardware would have to be found. It would not be possible to establish a liberated base area similar to Mao's Yenan, he reflected, "unless and until we can get more modern forms of hardware than we had the last time. We need especially something like the SAM-7, a portable anti-aircraft gun that we could use against the Pakistan Air Force."

Initially, when the Khalq wing of the Afghan Communist movement took power in 1978, the Liberation Front liked the national-communist tenor of the new Kabul regime. Murad Khan frankly expressed the hope that Afghanistan would become "a stronger and stronger ally of ours," serving as a conduit through which Soviet arms could be obtained without direct dependence on Moscow. As for the Soviet Union itself, he was more ambivalent, observing that "the shadow of the Russian bear is over us all the time, and they will either be our closest ally or our greatest foe." Two years later, when the Soviets marched into Afghanistan, Liberation Front leaders were clearly distressed. But they avoided open criticism of the Soviet presence and still appeared ready to accept Soviet aid if it were offered, albeit with greater misgivings.

Some of the Liberation Front's Soviet-leaning critics, notably former student leader Khair Jan Baluch, suggest that the Front is "basically Maoist in its ideology" and has received Chinese help. It has distributed Chinese literature in the Marri areas, Khair Jan claimed, and he had himself seen a photograph of Chairman Mao, together with boxes of Chinese Communist books, in the apartment of a Liberation Front leader in Kabul. Whatever may have been true in the past, however, I have found no evidence that the Liberation Front has a special ideological affinity with the present Chinese regime or is receiving material help from Peking.

Since setting up his camps in Afghanistan in 1975 during the Mohammed Daud regime, Mir Hazar has received a subvention of $32 monthly per person from successive Afghan governments, totaling some $875,000 per year in mid-1980. This support stems from the tradition of Baluch-Pushtun kinship dating back to Nasir Khan's tributary ties with the first Afghan kingdom in Kandahar.

Daud, who was under pressure from the late Mohammed Reza Shah Pahlavi of Iran to make peace with Pakistan, only grudgingly admitted the Baluch. He then refused to grant the guerrillas political asylum, giving them a more uncertain status as refugees. His government also declined to recognize the Liberation Front as the legitimate representative of the Baluch in the camps. Throughout his regime, he continued to give monthly subventions to the Baluch who had come in 1975. However, as a gesture to Pakistan, Daud withheld food and other assistance from 625 new recruits and their families who came to join Mir Hazar in mid-1976, forcing them to live in a makeshift camp at Shorawar, just inside the border. He hoped they would go back voluntarily. Shortly before his assassination in 1978, he was on the verge of concluding a deal with Islamabad providing for the forcible return of all Baluch "refugees" to Pakistan. By contrast, the Khalq government promptly granted the guerrillas political asylum, started giving food and other welfare aid to the Shorawar camp, and formally recognized the Liberation Front. At the annual Pushtunistan and Baluchistan National Day celebration in Kabul on August 31, 1979, Mir Hazar was invited to speak on behalf of the "Baluch liberation movement."

Even during the Daud period, Mir Hazar's followers were not treated as bona fide refugees by international relief agencies. While he has been able to feed and clothe his followers with his Afghan government subventions and from funds supplied by Liberation Front supporters in Pakistan, Mir Hazar has not been able to obtain International Red Cross medical help to combat widespread typhoid fever and tuberculosis. The Red Cross has justified its rejection of his pleas by pointing to the political and military character of the camps. Since 1975, more than 465 men, women, and children have died, including some 40 guerrillas and another 70 older men.

The guerrillas have not been treated any better or worse by Kabul since the advent of the Soviet-installed Parcham regime. However, the bitter conflict between the Khalq and Parcham factions, together with the continuing rebellion against Kabul since the 1978 Communist coup, has placed the Liberation Front in an increasingly awkward position. The feuding Afghan Communist leaders are preoccupied with their own survival and have shown little interest in the Baluch cause. The Liberation Front has attempted to keep on good terms with both factions, never knowing for sure who would come out on top. Yet at the same time, it has had to avoid overly close identification with all Kabul leaders because many of the Afghan Baluch tribes have been angered by heavy-handed Communist reform efforts, especially during the Khalq period.*

Further complicating the picture, the Liberation Front's Kalat-i-Gilzai camp is located in an area where anti-Communist rebels have been extremely active. At least one clash has occurred between the Baluch guerrillas and the Afghan resistance groups who accuse the Front of pro-Communist sympathies. By early 1981, Mir Hazar had made his peace with the resistance, but it was unclear whether the Soviet-installed Parcham regime would survive and what policy Moscow would pursue toward the Liberation Front if and when it succeeded in consolidating its control in Kabul.

The political paralysis of the Front produced by the Soviet occupation of Afghanistan, together with a simmering controversy over whether to work for independence or to cooperate with other anti-government groups in Pakistan-wide political struggles, led to the defection of several leading non-Baluch members of the London Group in March 1981, among them Asad Rahman (Chakkar Khan), a Punjabi. Mir Hazar and the Marri hard core of the Front were staunchly committed to an independent Baluchistan and were working closely with Khair Bux

---

* In the Baluch areas of isolated southwest Afghanistan, as in the Pushtun areas of the southeast, Khalq officials attempted to circumvent the established tribal leadership structure, evoking a powerful backlash. Some 10,000 of the 90,000 Afghan Baluch, notably the Nahrni, Reki, Sanjrani, and Ghur Ghesh tribes, have ancestral ties to the Baluch tribes living across the border in Iran and migrated there during the Khalq period. Some 500 Baluch from these tribes have carried on anti-Kabul resistance activity, receiving food and medical help from Afghan Baluch kinsmen now living in Zahedan and Sistan. However, this group operates independently from the Islamic fundamentalist resistance organizations based in Pakistan, which are regarded as tools of the "anti-Baluch" Zia Ul-Haq regime in Islamabad. Most Afghan Baluch have sought to keep their options open, avoiding either open identification with, or direct opposition to, the Kabul Communist regime.

Marri, who favored independence, following his exile from Pakistan (see chapter four). By contrast, some of the London Group members, echoing the current Soviet line, felt that the Baluch should join with other leftist groups in seeking to overthrow the Zia regime and build a new "anti-imperialist" Pakistan.

The Baluch Students Organization

Discussing the future of Baluchistan with President Zia in an interview (see chapter eight), I pointed to the intense nationalist feeling that I had encountered among students of all factions and the strength of student support for an armed independence struggle. Disgustedly throwing up his hands, Zia responded that "there are only a few thousand students in the whole of Baluchistan. What can *they* do?"

To be sure, the Baluch student movement, as such, does not pose a direct threat to the central government, because there is a continual turnover in its membership and government-controlled educational institutions exercise considerable leverage over individual students. In a tribally-based society like that of the Baluch, however, students play a peculiarly important political role, helping to fill the vacuum left by the absence of a significant middle class. The Liberation Front and other nationalist groups draw a steady stream of young recruits from the student movement. Moreover, the student movement is, in effect, a way station for many politically conscious young Baluch who have passed through the educational system but do not yet feel drawn to any of the existing nationalist groups. In addition to their formal membership, the two leading student organizations have almost as many active sympathizers, especially among the growing thousands of educated unemployed.

Next to the Liberation Front, the Baluch Students Organization, or BSO, and its militant dissident wing, the Baluch Students Organization–Awami (People's), or BSO-Awami, are the best organized and liveliest political forces in Baluchistan. Originally established in 1967 to combat the One Unit system, the student movement has grown steadily in strength, stimulated by the heightened political consciousness resulting from the 1973–1977 insurgency. Allowing for the turnover from year to year as students have graduated, more than 25,000 young Baluch have received their political conditioning as BSO members between 1967 and 1981.

Ironically, the expansion of student political activity has been accelerated by Pakistani government development efforts in Baluchistan. Seeking to rebut Baluch charges of neglect in the educational field,

Bhutto ordered a rapid expansion of educational facilities in the province. Twenty-seven new colleges and junior colleges were opened over a six-year period in a crash program to neutralize the insurgency by winning the "hearts and minds" of the Baluch. To keep politics off the campus, Bhutto decreed that there would be no student governments in these colleges until the end of the insurgency. Since many of these hastily launched institutions lacked adequate housing and other basic facilities, however, the net result was a restive collegiate population that flocked into the student movement not only to protest campus conditions but also to demonstrate sympathy with the insurgents.

In mid-1980, the BSO claimed a membership of 4,300 students, organized in forty-six chapters, including thirteen in Sind. It has a national council of 200 members that meets twice a year and publishes a monthly newsletter, *Girukh* (Lightning), a doctrinal monthly, *Sangat* (Truth), and a monthly literary journal, *Bam* (Morning Star). The BSO-Awami has a smaller membership, slightly less than 2,000, and a loosely knit organizational network that embraces all major campuses in Baluchistan. It has a national council of 110 members and publishes a monthly newsletter, *Pajjar* (Awakening), and a monthly literary journal, *Labzank* (Treasure of Language).

Based on the results of four meetings with thirty-two assorted student leaders in Quetta and Karachi from 1977 to 1980, I have concluded that the BSO and the BSO-Awami are strong, independent organizations and are not controlled by other groups. Nevertheless, both of them are continually subject to outside pressures, as well as a conspicuous internal tug-of-war between ideologically disparate student leaders. Some leaders are sympathetic to student and labor groups outside Baluchistan linked with the Pakistan Communist party; others lean toward the Liberation Front, and a minority prefer Bizenjo's moderate Pakistan National party.

Initially, it was the now outlawed National Awami party (NAP) that stimulated the creation of the BSO in 1967. Some of the first student leaders were NAP sympathizers. Then, in March 1978, student militants were outraged by Ghaus Bux Bizenjo's attempts to negotiate a political settlement with Zia and staged a successful revolt at the biennial BSO convention. The first leaders elected by the triumphant rebels were Razik Bukti and Habib Jalib. Bukti, then twenty-seven, generally regarded as Communist-oriented, was chosen as president. Jalib, who was five years younger and somewhat more sympathetic to the Liberation Front, was named secretary-treasurer and succeeded Bukti as president two years later. Both leaders promptly accepted invitations to the Soviet-sponsored World Conference of Students in Havana in July 1978, but the Pakistani government refused to grant them visas.

Figure 1

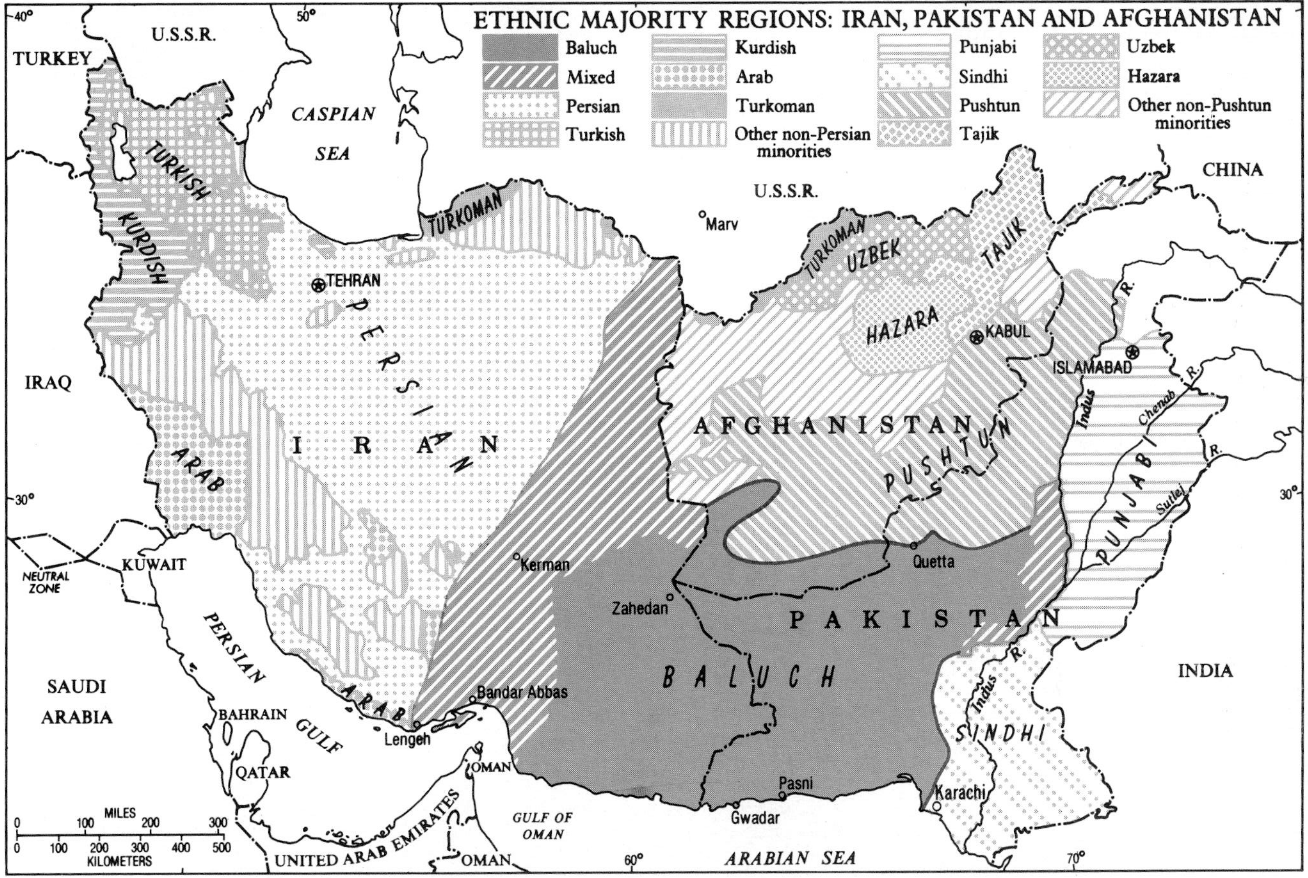

ETHNIC MAJORITY REGIONS: IRAN, PAKISTAN AND AFGHANISTAN

Baluch
Mixed
Persian
Turkish

Kurdish
Arab
Turkoman
Other non-Persian minorities

Punjabi
Sindhi
Pushtun
Tajik

Uzbek
Hazara
Other non-Pushtun minorities

U.S.S.R.

CHINA

TURKEY

TAJIK

HAZARA

KABUL

ISLAMABAD

Indus

PUNJAB

Chenab R.

Sutlej R.

Jhelum R.

CHINA

INDIA

70°

30°

TURKISH

KURDISH

TURKOMAN

CASPIAN SEA

50°

TEHRAN

I R A N

P E R S I A N

U.S.S.R.

Marv

TURKOMAN

UZBEK

A F G H A N I S T A N

P U S H T U N

Quetta

P A K I S T A N

Kabul R.

SINDHI

Indus

Karachi

IRAQ

ARAB

Kerman

Zahedan

B A L U C H

Pasni

Gwadar

ARABIAN SEA

60°

30°

NEUTRAL ZONE

KUWAIT

SAUDI ARABIA

PERSIAN GULF

BAHRAIN

QATAR

UNITED ARAB EMIRATES

Lengeh

Bandar Abbas

GULF OF OMAN

OMAN

OMAN

ARAB

0   100   200   300
MILES

0   100   200   300   400   500
KILOMETERS

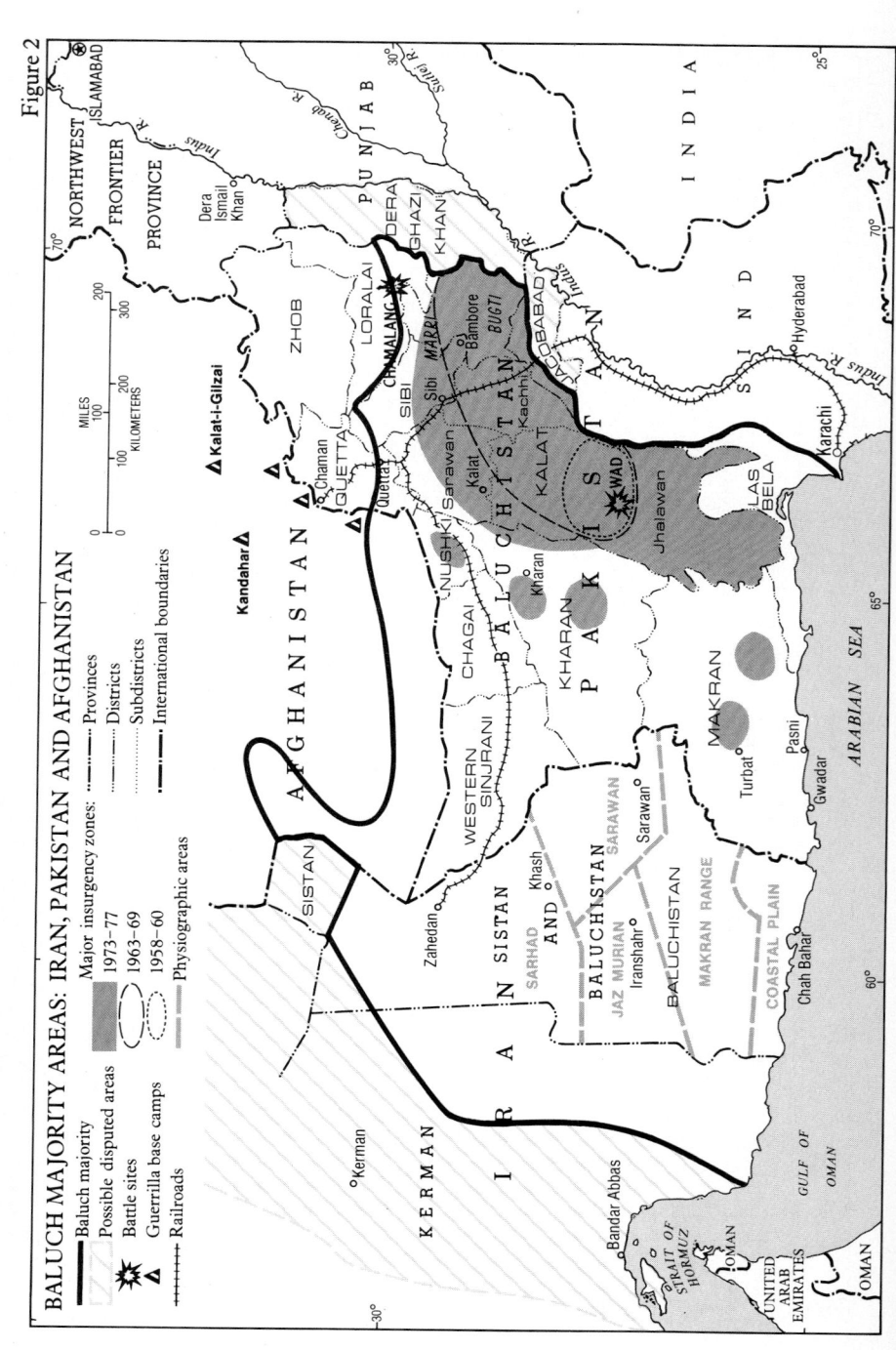

Figure 2

BALUCH MAJORITY AREAS: IRAN, PAKISTAN AND AFGHANISTAN

Baluch majority
Possible disputed areas
Battle sites
Guerrilla base camps
Railroads

Major insurgency zones:
1973–77
1963–69
1958–60

Provinces
Districts
Subdistricts
International boundaries
Physiographic areas

Figure 3

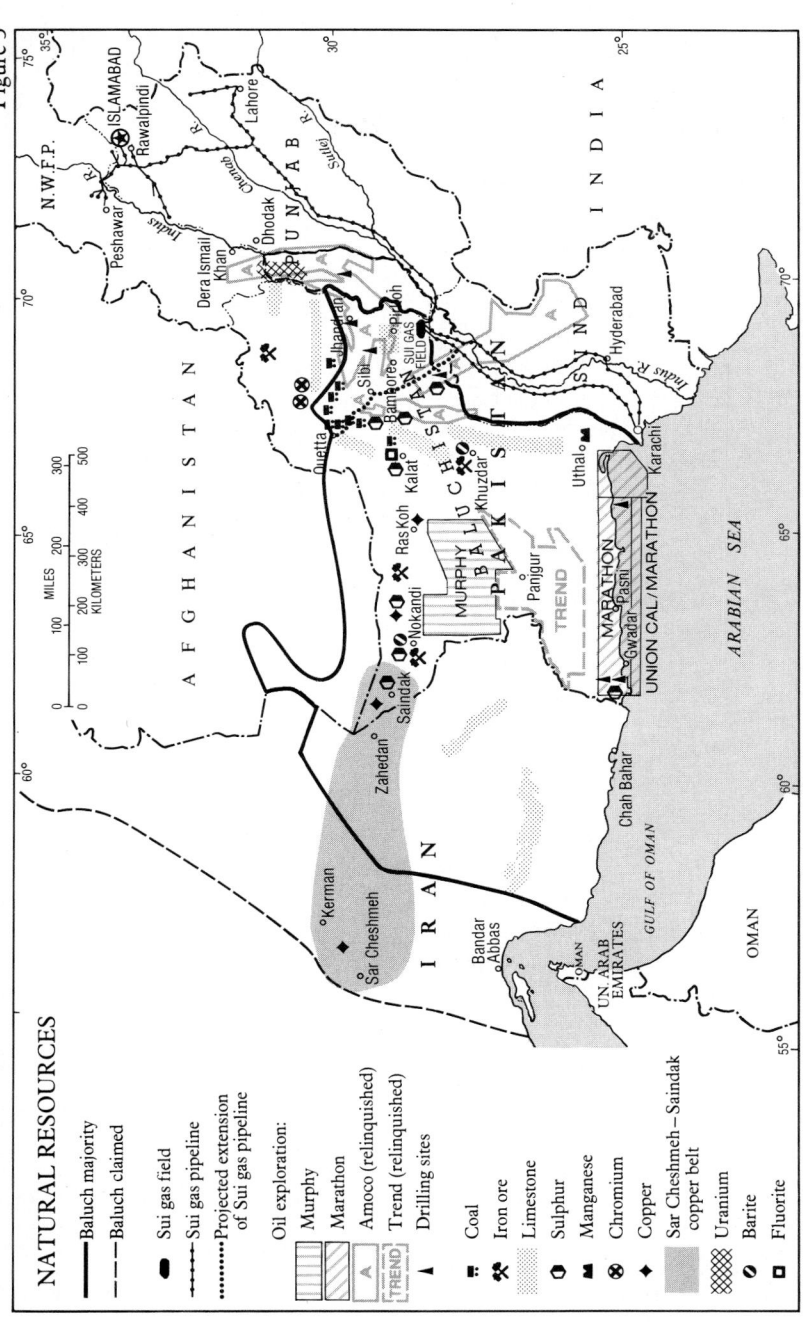

NATURAL RESOURCES

— Baluch majority
-- — Baluch claimed

● — Sui gas field
+ — Sui gas pipeline
···· — Projected extension
        of Sui gas pipeline

Oil exploration:

Murphy

Marathon

Amoco (relinquished)

TREND Trend (relinquished)

▲ — Drilling sites

▪ Coal
✾ Iron ore
◐ Limestone
◼ Sulphur
⊗ Manganese
◆ Chromium
◖ Copper
▨ Sar Cheshmeh – Saindak
    copper belt
◔ Uranium
◩ Barite
◻ Fluorite

Figure 4

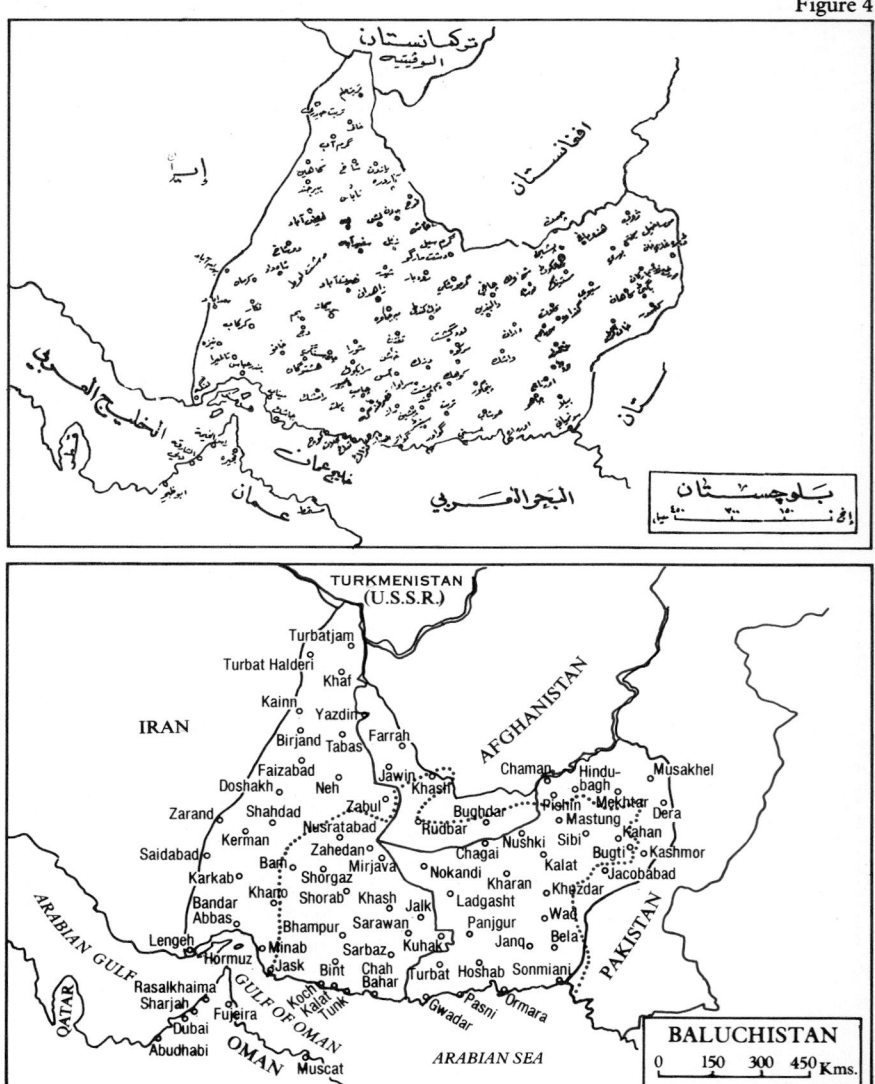

The Iraqi-supported Baluchistan Liberation Front, which conducted an insurgency against Mohammed Reza Shah Pahlavi's regime in Iran from 1968 to 1973, made far-reaching territorial claims in the above map depicting an independent "Greater Baluchistan." Many Baluch nationalist leaders today make less extensive claims (see chapter nine). In the redrawn and translated version below, solid red lines show existing national boundaries, and dotted lines indicate the extent of Baluch-majority areas as defined in Figures 1-3.

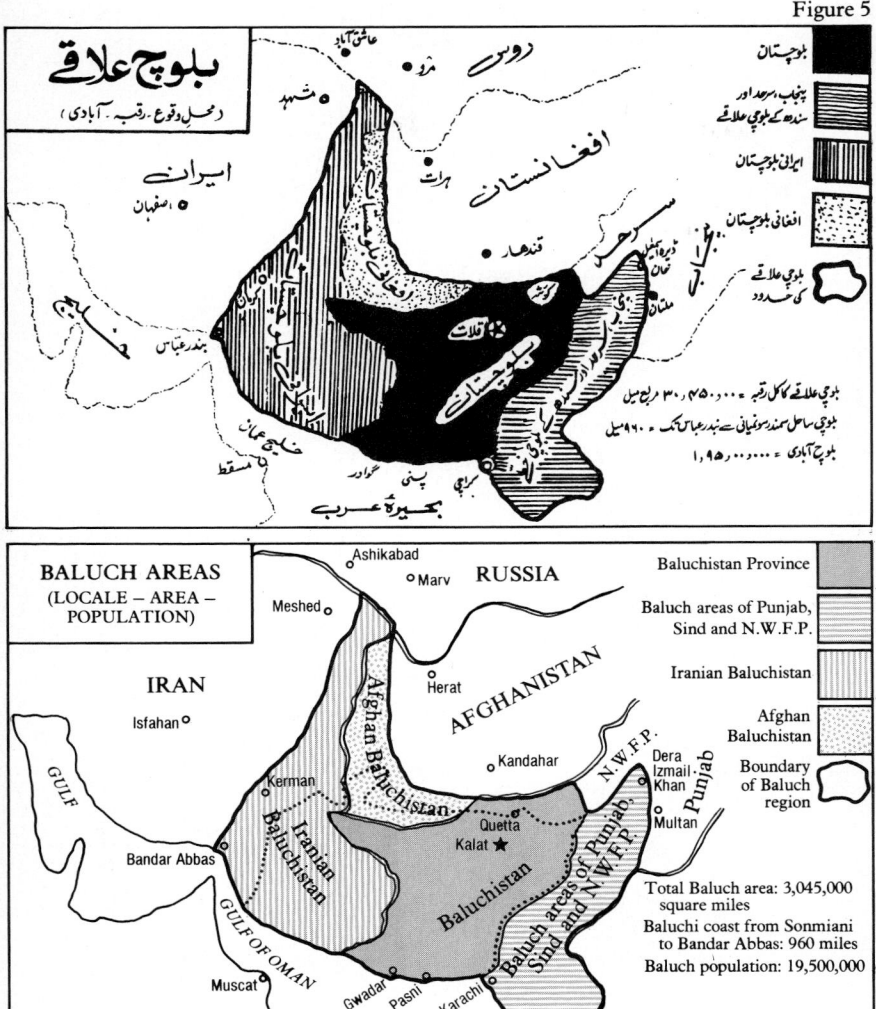

Figure 5

While not openly advocating an independent "Greater Baluchistan," the late Khan of Kalat, Mir Ahmed Yar Khan Baluch, ruler of a Baluch principality that existed for four centuries before the creation of Pakistan, depicted "Baluch Areas" on the cover of a book published in 1970 (see footnote 10, chapter 3). These areas, the Khan wrote, were encompassed by the eighteenth-century domain of Kalat and its tributaries. Two years later, when he was appointed governor of Pakistani Baluchistan, his book was banned. The redrawn and translated version (below) shows existing national boundaries in solid red lines. Dotted lines indicate the extent of Baluch-majority areas as defined in Figures 1-3.

Bukti, a "professional student" working intermittently for a law degree, has extensive connections in Karachi and Lahore leftist circles, especially with leaders of the Communist-sponsored National Progressive party. Under his leadership, the BSO spearheaded the formation of a new, countrywide student group, the Pakistan Federal Union of Students, which echoes the Progressive party line on many issues. Bukti insisted in an interview that there is "no need to be pro-Moscow or pro-Peking, and we do our work after analyzing the conditions of this country and devising programs to change the system of this country." However, he said that the Soviet Union is "very progressive, and we support progressive movements. There are two superpowers in the world, and the role of these superpowers is very different. One supports the majority while the other supports the minority and reactionary movements. People here feel that America is not the friend of the masses of the world."

Jalib, the son of a day laborer, is a political neophyte who talks more about Baluch nationalism than about ideology. When I pressed Bukti and Jalib about the BSO attitude toward the Liberation Front, Bukti was quick to say that the BSO had "no connection" with the Liberation Front, while Jalib shook his head vigorously, observing that "everyone is trying to struggle in a manner reflecting his own type of political consciousness. They are our friends, they are against the opportunist class of Baluch leaders." Similarly, while Bukti reacted negatively to mention of the Front's "armed struggle" line, Jalib was more equivocal. "We hope that we will be able to defeat the military and the bureaucracy by the strength of our united political action," he said. "But remember, it is the government that is using force. They have created the present situation, and if the Baluch people are confronted with violence indefinitely, naturally they will react in kind. The time will come when the defense will come into the offense." Jalib expressed his admiration for the Liberation Front's mentors, Khair Bux Marri and Sher Mohammed Marri, dismissing charges that they have a narrow Marri tribal outlook. "When a person has a progressive ideology," he asked, "how can anyone say he is a tribal man?" Khair Bux, he added, "has a broad outlook. He is an honest man who stands for the Baluch nation."

In contrast to the diversity of views within the BSO leadership, the BSO-Awami leans unambiguously toward the Liberation Front, an orientation which goes back to the controversy among Baluch leaders over the terms of the 1969 cease-fire. Although Sher Mohammed and the Pararis agreed to lay down their arms, they were dissatisfied with the political concessions obtained in return for the truce. Their sympathizers in the student ranks formed an "anti-*sardar* group" within the BSO to protest what they regarded as an overly soft posture on the part of Bizenjo, Ataullah Mengal, and the other tribal *sardars* who had negotiated with Islamabad. At first, the dissidents did not intend to leave the BSO, but factional lines soon hardened, and they formally seceded to form the BSO-Awami in December 1972.

Although the BSO-Awami guards its independence and is not openly linked with the Liberation Front, it makes little secret of its sympathy for the Front. An official BSO-Awami review of the group's history praised the role of Sher Mohammed and the Pararis for "reshaping the armed struggle on organized, scientific lines." The historical review saluted "those patriotic and nationalistic leaders who were not taken in by compromises" in 1969 and expressed the hope that "with their foresight, they will lead the oppressed Baluch nation until the end."[5] Similarly, condemning Bizenjo and Mengal for their "sham negotiations" with Zia in early 1978, *Pajjar,* the BSO-Awami organ, lauded Khair Bux Marri for his refusal to participate in those negotiations.[6] Sher Mohammed Marri made the major address at the annual BSO-Awami national council meeting in 1978, and I found BSO-Awami activists pouring in and out of his Quetta home on two successive visits. A former BSO-Awami president, Abdul Nabi, has served as the Liberation Front's key contact man with the student movement.

Stressing that neither student group "will let outsiders tell us what to do," Rahim Bux Baluch, a member of the BSO central committee, complained that "no existing party is really progressive in a way that the younger generation of Baluch can fully accept. We feel there is a vacuum, and we are trying to fill it ourselves with our own thinking. We don't agree with the Communists, who tell us that the Liberation Front is betraying progressivism by preparing for an armed struggle to win independence. We accept the relevance of armed struggle for the Baluch, but what the Liberation Front is doing is only part of the struggle at this stage. If we find that we cannot win our rights in Pakistan, then only will we go to the hills and fight for independence."

The student movement was an important source of guerrilla recruits during the 1973–1977 insurgency. Khair Jan Baluch, then BSO president, organized a guerrilla group of his own, and was later followed by five other erstwhile BSO veterans who drew their recruits, as he did, largely from their former colleagues in the movement. "I got more than 300 right away," he recalled, "and I could have had hundreds more if I had been able to give them guns. You see a lot of them in the coffee houses and discos now, but they're not all soft. There are plenty of young men in the movement ready to fight if we give the call and they see that it's serious."

Mahmud Aziz Kurd, a veteran Baluch politician of the older generation with moderate views, told a BBC correspondent in early 1980 that "already, quite a few of the students have gone to the hills in recent months to begin organizing themselves for an armed struggle against the present government."[7]

When I asked directly whether they favored independence, student leaders would often exchange significant glances and speak vaguely, obviously fearful that any explicit public endorsement of the independence objective would expose them to treason charges. As the hours wore on and conversation became less guarded, however, I generally found that they were fervent nationalists. Their doubts and differences concern when and how to pursue independence. Pro-Liberation Front elements favor active efforts to prepare for an insurgency now, while pro-Communist elements envisage a gradual process of political disintegration in Pakistan leading to the emergence of autonomous but closely linked leftist regimes in Baluchistan and each of the other three ethnic regions of the country.

The 1978 Communist coup in Afghanistan strengthened hopes for a leftist uprising throughout Pakistan. Baluch student leaders spoke enthusiastically to me about the "genuinely progressive" and "national" character of the Kabul government and its leaders, Nur Mohammed Taraki and Hafizullah Amin. However, when I visited Pakistan in March 1980, after the murders of Taraki and Amin in palace shootouts and the Soviet occupation of Afghanistan, many student leaders in Baluchistan were no longer confident that Pakistanis in other regions would emulate the Afghan revolutionary model. They expressed fear that the Zia regime would be able to exploit the Afghan "threat" to remain in power and that the Baluch would have to take up arms on their own against Islamabad. Most BSO and BSO-Awami leaders had gone underground after Zia's ban on political activity in October 1979, followed by periodic roundups of student activists.

Baluch student leaders were visibly less enthusiastic about the Soviet-installed Babrak Karmal regime than they had been about the Amin regime. "We don't want to be a satellite of the Soviet Union," said one of those I was able to meet clandestinely, Hamid Baluch, president of the Karachi BSO. "But we can accept their aid. The Russians will support us with modern weapons, we are sure. When the time comes, if they won't, it would mean they are not progressive, not socialist."

The Pakistan National Party

If the Zia regime were to permit elections in Pakistan, the strongest electoral force in the Baluch areas would be Ghaus Bux Bizenjo's Pakistan National party (PNP), successor to the National Awami party

(NAP), which was outlawed during the insurgency. "National" in name only, the PNP is primarily Baluch in character, but was launched as a Pakistan-wide group in order to circumvent martial law regulations banning the formation of regional parties.

Less than six months after the formation of the PNP in March 1979, Islamabad banned political activity, forcing the group to suspend overt activities. Nevertheless, according to one of Bizenjo's lieutenants, Mahmud Aziz Kurd, the party is attempting to keep its organization intact and had more than 2,200 members on its rolls in mid-1980, including 200 "very active workers." In contrast to the BSO and the Liberation Front, which draw on the more adventurous young Baluch and politically aroused tribesmen from the hinterlands, the PNP represents the detribalized Baluch middle class, not only in Quetta and smaller urban centers in Baluchistan itself, but also among Baluch migrants in Karachi and other parts of Sind. While favoring moderate, nonviolent action through parliamentary processes, PNP partisans are strong nationalists who supported the 1973–1977 insurgency and echo Bizenjo's readiness to fight once again if necessary.

As the heir to the NAP tradition, the PNP enjoys considerable prestige in Baluch eyes, because the NAP provided the only sustained organizational vehicle for the pursuit of Baluch aspirations prior to the insurgency. For two decades, the NAP, with its separate regional units in the Baluch, Pushtun, Sindhi, and Bengali areas, attempted to wrest power from the Punjabi-dominated establishment. The Bengalis alone constituted a clear majority of the Pakistani population, but the Punjabis had been able to block their assumption of power in Islamabad by playing off one Bengali political group against another and by diluting Bengali parliamentary strength through gerrymandering. The NAP strategy was to join forces in the National Assembly with the principal Bengali political party, Sheikh Mujibur Rahman's Awami League, and thereby gain control of the national government. Working closely with the Awami League, the NAP spearheaded the popular agitation that led to President Ayub Khan's overthrow in 1969, emerging as the strongest party in the Baluch and Pushtun areas in the 1970 elections.

In retrospect, it might be said that this united-front strategy was too successful, for the prospect of a dominant NAP-Awami League alliance in the National Assembly prompted Ayub's successor, Yahya Khan, to nullify the assembly's role in early 1971, heading off the possibility of a government headed by Sheikh Mujibur. This led, in turn, to the ugly chain reaction of violence that culminated in the secession of Bangladesh, a disastrous blow to the Baluch, Pushtuns, and Sindhis, who were reduced, even collectively, to minority status in what was left of Pakistan.

The NAP continued to champion the cause of Baluch autonomy, albeit shorn of Bengali support, when Bhutto took over in Islamabad following the Bangladesh debacle. Bizenjo as governor, Mengal as chief minister, and Marri as party chairman were all united behind the NAP banner during the short-lived period of Baluch self-rule during 1972 and 1973. They all proudly identified themselves as NAP leaders when Bhutto dismissed their government and arrested them in 1973. By the time they had emerged from prison, however, four years of guerrilla war had made the NAP seem obsolete, not only because its moderate, parliamentary methods had been discredited as a means of achieving Baluch rights, but also because the very idea of Baluch participation in Pakistan-wide politics was increasingly open to question.

A split had developed during the 1973–1977 insurgency between NAP's Baluch leaders, who were more embittered than ever toward Islamabad, and their Pushtun allies, who were more accommodating to the Zia regime. Even Bizenjo, anxious as he was to negotiate a Baluch settlement with Islamabad, remained staunchly committed to the concept that the minorities were separate "nationalities" and were thus entitled to autonomy. This view pitted him against Abdul Wali Khan, the Pushtun leader, who favored using terminology less objectionable to the Punjabis and moderating autonomy demands. Wali Khan hoped his approach would open the way for power-sharing in Islamabad.

The breaking point between the Baluch and Pushtun leaders came in early 1979 when they attempted to draw up a platform for a resurrected and rechristened version of the outlawed NAP, known as the National Democratic party. Wali Khan objected to Bizenjo's proposed use of the word "nationalities" to describe the provinces of Pakistan, urging instead that they be characterized as "distinctive cultural and linguistic entities." The two delegations also differed on how hard to push their autonomy demands. Equally important, Bizenjo was openly critical of the Zia regime's support for the anti-Communist rebels in Afghanistan, while Wali Khan was more equivocal. Amid angry recriminations, the Baluch abruptly walked out, called a separate convention, and formed the PNP.

Despite his past ties with the NAP, Marri refused to join the new group, declaring that there was no longer any point in participating in Pakistan-wide politics. Mengal joined the new party briefly, but withdrew soon afterward on the eve of his decision to go abroad. At the other extreme of the Baluch nationalist spectrum, Sher Baz Mazari, a leading moderate, joined Wali Khan in the National Democratic party.

The six-point manifesto adopted by the party at its founding convention stressed "constitutional and practical guarantees of equal internal autonomy to all federating units" in Pakistan, a "positive, non-aligned foreign policy" and a "national democratic revolution" designed to achieve "economic independence" and an end to "the remnants of feudalism and monopoly capitalism."[8] Zia's ban on political activity silenced the voice of the PNP almost before the ink was dry on its platform. Nevertheless, with its organization still largely intact, it could be quickly reactivated in the event of a return to parliamentary politics in Pakistan. Given Bizenjo's following, the PNP would undoubtedly win strong Baluch support even if militant Baluch groups were to boycott the elections.

Next to Bizenjo, the most important figure in the PNP is its millionaire backer Akber Y. Mustikhan, who has also given quiet help at times to Marri, Mengal, and other nationalist figures. A member of an Iranian Baluch branch of the Mengal tribe, Mustikhan's father was a self-made man who migrated to Karachi, got his start in road-building during the British Raj, and went on to become one of the biggest rubber and rice plantation owners in Burma. Mustikhan has multiplied the family fortune, partly through partnerships with the Harouns, one of Pakistan's leading business families. He now presides over his own miniconglomerate that embraces Mustikhan Transcontinental, a construction firm operating throughout the Middle East, Frigid Fish Limited, which exports shrimp, and assorted enterprises ranging from oil-marketing ventures with Gulf sheikhs to dairying, truck farming, and shipbuilding.

Until 1979, Mustikhan had kept carefully in the background, leaving open political advocacy to his son Yusuf, president of the Karachi PNP unit. Recently, however, he has started to register his political views openly in conversations with diplomats and foreign journalists and is even writing a book, to be entitled *The Baluch and Pakistan.* He is going public, he explained, because he foresees a growing danger that Islamabad's insensitivity to Baluch sentiment will open the way for Soviet-supported secessionist activity.

In an unpublished letter to General Zia on March 8, 1980, Mustikhan warned that "both of the superpowers are showing a positive interest in Baluchistan, strategically the most important and sensitive area of Pakistan, which should not be allowed to become a subject of power politics." Mustikhan set forth a detailed "Plan for National Consensus" outlining, step by step, a way for Zia to preside over a gradual transition from naked military rule to a more broad-based regime. Even though it was an extremely conservative proposal, he recalled acidly, with elections deferred until the last of four slow stages and limited initially to the federal level, Zia did not respond. Mustikhan was also instrumental in promoting an unpublished exchange of letters between Zia and Bizenjo in late 1980 in which the two leaders made an abortive attempt to define an agenda for negotiations on a restructuring of the Pakistani constitution (see chapter nine).

"We are in for trouble, lots of trouble, unless things change," he commented after a 1980 Washington visit. He had urged U.S. officials to put pressure on Zia for a more conciliatory approach to the Baluch "before it is too late," he reported, but found a tendency to discount his warnings and even to minimize the potential of the Baluch movement. Like Stalin, who asked how many divisions the pope had, some of the Americans he had encountered were "unduly influenced" by the fact that the Baluch leaders had organized guerrilla forces of less than 8,000 men in a state of combat readiness. "In the West, you think in terms of organization," Mustikhan reflected. "If you don't see a formal organization, you think we don't have a movement. But with us, the whole of Baluch society is the movement, and when the leaders give the call, and provide weapons, the people follow."

Zahedan street scene, Iranian Baluchistan

The Baluch Nationalist Movement in Iran

6

At first glance, the erosion of central authority in Iran following the overthrow of the Shah made the prospects for Baluch nationalism appear more promising in Iran than in Pakistan. The outbreak of war between Iraq and Iran strengthened that impression, leading to widespread predictions that Baghdad would seek to dismember Iran and would, therefore, support Baluch separatists in the east as well as Khuzistani Arab and Kurdish separatists in areas directly contiguous to Iraq. In reality, however, the Baluch nationalist movement in Iran was not yet sufficiently well organized in early 1981 to take advantage of Teheran's weakness or to attract large-scale Iraqi support. In marked contrast to the nationalist movement in Pakistan, it lacked a broadly accepted leadership — linking the rural Baluch tribes with politicized urban activists. Indeed, the Iranian Baluch generally looked to Pakistani Baluch leaders as their "national" leaders and waited impatiently for the call to arms while gradually building up their own organizational strength.

The relatively inchoate state of Baluch nationalism in Iran at the advent of the Khomeini revolution did not indicate that the underlying political climate in Iranian Baluchistan was less favorable for nationalist activity than in the Pakistani Baluch areas. Rather, it reflected the fact that Reza Shah and Mohammed Reza Shah Pahlavi had made a more thoroughgoing effort to contain Baluch nationalism than their British and Pakistani counterparts.

Suppressing the slightest assertion of Baluch identity, the Pahlavi dynasty used the carrot as well as the stick to control the Baluch, channeling development funds into the hands of cooperative tribal chiefs and benignly tolerating a lucrative smuggling trade. Beneath the surface, however, rebellion continually smoldered, bursting into the open from 1957 to 1959 and again from 1968 to 1973. Once the Shah left the scene, the Baluch, like the Kurdish, Arab, and Turkish minorities in Iran, soon reverted to the posture of resistance that had prevailed prior to the Reza Shah period. For the first time in fifty years, the Iranian Baluch attempted to organize open political activity. While cautiously testing the intentions and capacities of the weakened central government in Teheran, they intensified their links with the growing nationalist movement across the Pakistani border.

The Pahlavis and the Baluch

Talking with Baluch and Persians in Iran, I soon detected undercurrents of racial hostility even more powerful and deeply rooted than the tensions between the Baluch and their Punjabi overlords in Pakistan. Although the Punjabis are despised, their domination over the Baluch dates back little more than three decades. By contrast, the Baluch in Iran have been battling Persian monarchs for nearly 2,000 years. To the Baluch, the Persians are a *taarof* (effete) breed who do not deserve to rule them. To the Persians, who look with cultural and racial disdain even on the surrounding Arab states, the Baluch are virtual savages, fortunate to have the blessings of Persian conquest.

Geographically, Iranian Baluchistan is divided into five distinct areas separated by natural barriers: the Jaz Murian agricultural heartland; the wild Sarhad desert country to the north; Sarawan, punctuated by oases, to the southeast; the Makran hills; and the coastal plain (see Figure 2). Trade has been confined throughout history within each of the five regions. Even as late as 1978, travel between these different natural compartments of Iranian Baluchistan was so difficult that in order to go from Khash to Bandar Abbas, it was necessary to go circuitously by way of Zahedan to the north and Kerman to the west. It is this segmented character of the Iranian Baluch areas that has made it so difficult for would-be Baluch nationalists to establish enduring political entities comparable to Nasir Khan's Kalat Confederacy. To make matters worse for the Baluch, the Jaz Murian heartland lies on the direct access route from Kerman, the nearest Persian province, and has always been extremely vulnerable militarily to Persian conquerors. Reza Shah sent his forces over this route in 1928 when Dost Mohammed made his abortive attempt to establish an independent Baluch principality.

In his controversial study of the geopolitics of Persian Gulf oil, *The Wells of Power,* Sir Olaf Caroe observed that Baluchistan is "an empty porch to the Persian mansion, but porches, though empty, must be held by the owner of the house."[1] This was the passionate conviction of Reza Shah and later Mohammed Reza Shah Pahlavi, who displayed a relentless determination to subdue the Baluch tribes and to make Baluchistan an integrated part of a centralized Iranian state.

For most of the fifty years of Pahlavi rule, Teheran had to depend primarily on the use of overt military force to keep the Baluch areas under control, even when there was little coordinated insurgent activity. Army units permanently stationed in Iranian Baluchistan waged intermittent punitive expeditions against scattered bands of rebellious tribesmen, who often raided military camps and persistently refused to turn over hidden stocks of guns as required by law. In addition to using military power, however, Teheran enforced its authority by buying off some of the Baluch tribal chieftains and using them as middlemen. These co-opted *sardars* not only received substantial annual stipends from the Shah's regime but also handled the influx of development resources from Teheran, which provided ample opportunities for lucrative rake-offs. Describing the case of an irrigation pump in a Sarhad village where he lived for two years, Philip Salzman, a Canadian anthropologist, noted that the *sardar* kept 60 hours of pump time for himself and another 30 for his brother out of a total of 168 hours per week, selling the remaining 78 hours to his tribesmen.[2] As Salzman observed, the government had to establish its control indirectly, by co-opting as many *sardars* as it could, in those areas where the nomadic character of tribal society made it virtually impossible to set up a direct centralized administration. By contrast, in the case of the sedentary agricultural settlements in relatively fertile areas of the south, the local variant of *sardars*, known as *hakoms*, were more vulnerable, and Teheran completely displaced them, ruling through the army and the gendarmerie. This assertive central policy was in marked contrast to the pattern in Pakistan, where the British permitted the tribal chieftains to retain their power.

By the time Reza Shah's reign ended in 1941, Teheran had largely subdued the Baluch tribes, but Mohammed Reza Shah faced a new challenge in the emergence of Baluch nationalism across the border. Fearful that the Baluch in Iran would be infected by the Greater Baluchistan movement developing in Pakistan, the Shah pursued a ruthless, hard-line policy toward the Baluch designed to stifle any expressions of Baluch identity. In particular, he was determined to prevent the growth of a politicized Baluch intelligentsia. Sharply limiting education in the Baluch areas, he banned the use of the Baluchi language in the few schools attended by Baluch students and made the use of Persian mandatory. He compelled Baluch students to use history textbooks in which the Baluch were described as Persian in ethnic origin and prohibited the use of Baluchi in government offices. He also made it a criminal offense to publish, distribute, or even possess Baluchi-language books, magazines, and newspapers, a prohibition which curtailed but did not entirely choke off the flow of underground publications from Pakistan.

One of the most bitterly resented aspects of the Shah's repressive approach to the Baluch was his ban on the wearing of traditional Baluch attire in schools and other public places. James Ricciardi, a former Peace Corps volunteer who taught English in a Baluch school in Zabol, was astonished to see this rule brutally enforced on one occasion by a Persian teacher. When a Baluch seventh grader came to school wearing a typical Baluch black tunic over his bright blue Baluch pantaloons, the enraged teacher kicked him in the groin, shouting that it was for his own good to learn how to behave " in a civilized manner" and that " in this country you can't do that."

In the economic sphere, the Shah authorized just enough development spending to lubricate the machinery of control manned by the *sardar* middlemen, avoiding meaningful development programs that would stir up popular expectations. Finally, he attempted to neutralize the impact of the Baluch within the Iranian political structure with a series of gerrymandering moves. Lumping them together with another, more Persianized ethnic group, the Sistanis, he created a combined province known as Sistan and Baluchistan, which had an officially recorded population of 659,297 in 1978.[3] Nearly one-third of this total was located in Sistan, which meant that the Baluch purportedly numbered roughly 440,000, a figure bitterly ridiculed by Baluch as reflecting less than half of the actual Baluch population in the province. At the same time, the Shah attached ethnically mixed border areas, where the Baluch claim a population of 300,000, to adjacent provinces such as Kerman and Khorasan.* This policy of politically smothering and dividing the Baluch was reinforced by the systematic immigration of Persian settlers, who bought up or confiscated Baluch lands and businesses with the backing of the Persian-manned bureaucracy and 'gendarmerie. By 1978, Persian immigrants constituted almost 40 percent of the population of 75,000 in the provincial capital of Zahedan. Treated as virtual aliens in their ancestral homeland, an estimated 150,000 Iranian Baluch migrated during the Shah's reign to the Arab sheikhdoms across the Persian Gulf.

As we will see, the Shah's hard-line policies did not completely succeed in crushing separatist activity, which erupted in the 1957–1959 Dad Shah incident and in an Iraqi-assisted insurgency from 1969 to 1973. The Shah became concerned that his continuing troubles with the Baluch would be aggravated by unrest in the Pakistani Baluch areas, especially after the secession of Bangladesh. Moreover, he was obsessed with a geopolitical nightmare: that Moscow would solidify its foothold in Afghanistan and would then synchronize support for the already powerful Baluch nationalist forces in Pakistan with related attempts to intensify Baluch disaffection in Iran. The only way to be sure that his own Baluch problem would not get out of hand, the Shah concluded, was to treat

---

* Reliable data on the Baluch population in Iran does not exist. On the basis of available sources and my field inquiries, I have used an estimate of one million in this book. See chapter nine for a further discussion of this issue.

Pakistani Baluchistan as a virtual Iranian protectorate. Pressures from the Shah were largely responsible for Bhutto's decision to oust the Baluch state government in 1973 and to use air power as well as ground forces in crushing the Baluch insurgency. Bhutto told me in a 1977 interview that the Shah "had been very insistent, even threatening, and he promised us all sorts of economic and military help, much more than we actually got. He felt strongly that letting the Baluch have provincial self-government was not only dangerous in itself, for Pakistan, but would give his Baluch dangerous ideas."

Beginning in early 1973, the Shah asserted repeatedly that he regarded Pakistani Baluchistan as falling within Iran's defense perimeter. "If Pakistan disintegrates," he told *New York Times* columnist C. L. Sulzberger in April 1973, "another Vietnam situation could develop. We must see to it that Pakistan doesn't fall to pieces. This would produce a terrible mess, an Indochina situation of new and larger dimensions. I dread to think of it." And if it came anyway, Sulzberger asked, if Pakistan did fall apart? "The least we could do in our own interest," replied the Shah, "would be some kind of protective reaction in Baluchistan." What this meant, Sulzberger concluded, was that Iran would "seize it before anyone else does."[4] In a public declaration during Bhutto's visit a month later, the Shah declared that what happens in Pakistan "is vitally important to us; and should another event befall that country, we could not tolerate it. The reason for this is not only our fraternal affection for you as a Muslim nation, but because of Iranian interests, we would not be able to tolerate other changes or difficulties in Pakistan....We will not close our eyes to any secessionist movement—God forbid—in your country."[5] "What would happen if what remains of Pakistan were to disintegrate?" he asked a *Newsweek* correspondent in November 1977. "If we don't assume the security of this region, who will do it?"[6]

An interesting aspect of the Shah's preparations for a possible crisis in Baluchistan was a joint two-week Field Training Exercise held there by Iranian Special Forces units and a battalion of U.S. Army Green Berets near Chah Bahar in March 1978. The Iranian forces were accompanied by fifteen Baluch who served as guides, interpreters, and cooks. One of the Americans recalled that the Iranians "seemed very nervous" about the Baluch and would not let them take part in training sessions conducted by American specialists.

During the last decade of his regime, the Shah came under the influence of several Western-trained technocrats, especially Jamshid Amouzegar, who persuaded him that his long-term goals would be served best by a more positive approach to the Baluch, placing greater emphasis on economic inducements. In 1972, Teheran was spending

U.S. Green Berets from the 2nd Battalion of the Fifth Special Forces Group, (Fort Bragg, North Carolina) on a field training exercise in Iranian Baluchistan, April 1978

only $750,000 per year on the economic development of Sistan and Baluchistan. Yet it was the poorest of Iran's provinces, with an estimated annual per capita income of $975, less than half of the $2,200 national average for rural areas and less than one-fifth of the overall national average.

Amouzegar, who served initially as the Shah's planning commission chairman and later as prime minister and head of the governing Rastakhiz (Renascence) party, successfully pushed for greatly upgraded development allocations to the province. In 1973, the Shah created the Baluchistan Development Corporation and talked grandly of spending up to $100 million in the Baluch areas during the ensuing five years. Amouzegar also won authority to recruit "reliable" Baluch for key posts in the government bureaucracy and the Rastakhiz party in Sistan and Baluchistan. He was able to sell his liberalization policy partly because rising oil prices in the early 1970s had made more development funds available for the neglected minority provinces. But the Shah was also impressed by the argument that the prospect of ever rising oil revenues could make identification with Iran potentially more attractive to the Baluch than loyalty to the abstract ideal of a Greater Baluchistan or, for that matter, to an economically shaky Pakistan. By giving the Baluch a growing economic stake in Iran's seeming new prosperity, Amouzegar's policy was intended not only to blunt the edge of Baluch disaffection in Iran itself, but also to promote pro-Teheran sentiment among the development-starved Pakistani Baluch.

Amouzegar's choice as secretary of the Rastakhiz party in Baluchistan, Ghulam Reza Hossainborr, the first Baluch to hold this position, frankly described the Shah's liberalization policy as a step toward his broader objective of establishing a regional economic and security sphere "more or less" corresponding to the boundaries of the ancient Persian Empire. It was "inevitable" that Iran would regain most of its lost territories, Hossainborr said, "certainly" including Pakistani Baluchistan, and that the Pakistani and Iranian Baluch areas would then be united as a powerful province of an expanded Iran. "Iran today is the smallest it has ever been," Hossainborr said during an August 1978 interview in Zahedan. "We cannot forget that it used to extend over Afghanistan as well as half of Pakistan. The Indus is the natural boundary between India and Iran. Of course, the Baluch have a distinct identity and want to have relations with other Iranians on the basis of mutual respect, but we cannot say that the Baluch have feelings of a separate nationalism. Iranian culture is the ruler of the Baluch subconscious and they cannot flee from this. They have read Iranian poets and they use Persian when they have something complex or important to say."

Although Amouzegar did not envisage the decentralization of power, Hossainborr said, the premier was committed to a policy of decentralized administration linked to development programs, including expanded education, that would open up widespread new opportunities for the Baluch. Granting that the Baluch in Iran "may be dissatisfied," Hossainborr maintained that "it is not because of their nationalism but simply because they have been neglected by the central government. The government accepts the fact that they have neglected Baluchistan for many years, and it is for this reason that the government of Amouzegar has pledged to do more for Baluchistan. Maybe before they didn't do enough, but now the situation is improving and we hope that this government will pay enough attention to compensate for the past. After ten or twenty years, the degree of development here will be such that no Iranian will think it convenient to live in any country other than Iran. Even after five years, if Mr. Amouzegar rules the country, and if his policies are followed, the Baluch of Iran will certainly want to remain in Iran. They won't want to lose the economic advantages of living in Iran, and we already see that many Pakistani Baluch want to come to Iran."

As it happened, Amouzegar's tenure as prime minister ended just three months later amid the confusion preceding the Shah's downfall, and most of his plans for Baluchistan never got beyond the blueprint stage. Nevertheless, the economic impact of the oil boom unavoidably spilled over into Baluchistan during the 1970s. Already lucrative, the smuggling trade between Afghanistan, Pakistan, Iran, and the Arab sheikhdoms across the Persian Gulf became even more rewarding for the extensive network of Baluch middlemen. More important, while Teheran spent little on programs directly designed to help the Baluch, it embarked on a massive expansion of its military bases, military-related road networks, and administrative infrastructure in Baluchistan, which indirectly stimulated the local economy. Before the oil boom, wages for a construction laborer were ten tumans (US $1.50) a day, but in 1978 they had risen to fifty tumans (US $7.50). "There is definitely money floating around here," said Gurdeep Singh, the Indian consul general in Zahedan. "Look at the road-building, the new cement buildings that are being constructed, the brick factory and the ice factory here in Zahedan, the copper mine near Kerman, the military bases at Chah Bahar and Bandar Abbas, the new radio station and all that. It's bound to have some impact even on these opium-smoking people who drink too much and are too lazy to take full advantage of their new opportunities."

In addition to its economic effects, the oil boom had a significant impact on political consciousness in the Baluch areas, helping to prepare the ground for the nationalist upsurge that was to follow the Shah's overthrow. Instead of alleviating political discontent, as Amouzegar had predicted, the increased economic activity in the province stimulated new demands for development outlays geared more directly to Baluch needs. In Baluch eyes, the Shah deserved no gratitude for building roads and hospitals that were intended mainly to serve the Persian businessmen, soldiers, and civil servants coming to Baluchistan. It galled the Baluch to see millions being spent on the nearby military highway from Zahedan to Chah Bahar, while the government left a dirt road as the only link between Sarawan, with its 90,000 people, and the nearest city, Khash, more than a hundred miles away. Similarly, Baluch repeatedly pointed to the fact that the new military road from Kerman to Chah Bahar deliberately bypassed Baluch settlements that could easily have been included on the route.

Many of the younger Baluch returning from jobs in the Persian Gulf sheikhdoms during the seventies had been exposed to cosmopolitan political currents there for the first time and organized underground nationalist study groups dedicated to "Baluchistan for the Baluch." These returning migrants often brought back transistor radios, which had not been widely used in Baluch villages. As radios gradually became commonplace, more and more Baluch began listening to Baluchi broadcasts on Radio Kabul, All-India Radio, and Radio Quetta, in addition to the ninety-minute daily broadcasts in Baluchi over Radio Zahedan. Confronted with a populace that could no longer be insulated from outside political ideas, the Shah's regime hastily attempted to guide this burgeoning Baluch political awareness into safe channels by stepping up its own Baluchi-language television and radio programming and, at the same time, embarking on a crash program to expand educational facilities.

In contrast to his largely abortive economic efforts, Amouzegar's education program did lay the foundations for rapid growth in the number of schools and teachers in the Baluch areas. According to Iranian government statistics, which were dismissed as inflated by many Baluch, there were a total of 128,274 students of all ages enrolled in Sistan and Baluchistan in the 1978–1979 school year, including 91,315 in kindergartens and elementary schools, 6,815 in high schools, 19,261 in lower technical schools, 4,712 in higher technical and vocational schools, 1,075 in junior colleges, and 230 in teacher-training institutions.[7] Most of these students were concentrated in the urban centers of Zahedan, Iranshahr, Khash, Chah Bahar, Zabol, and Sarawan. The figures represented an enormous increase in enrollment over the previous year. For example, in Zahedan, official statistics showed a 59 percent increase for elementary schools and 42 percent for the teacher-training institutions. In

Khash, technical school enrollment jumped by 152 percent from 57 in 1976–77 to 144 in 1977–1978.[8]

Interviewed in Zahedan, Yusuf Khoshrou-Sefat, the Shah's provincial director of education, bemoaned the shortage of facilities resulting from such rapid expansion and showed me classes held in tents and converted private houses. However, Khoshrou-Sefat, a Persian, acknowledged that many of his new teachers—and students—were Sistanis and Persian immigrants, especially at the high school and junior college level, since "the Baluch are just beginning to come to our schools in significant numbers." Dadullah Daneshi, a young graduate in English literature from the Zahedan Teacher Training College, said that only 6 out of the 16 students in his 1978 graduating class were Baluch. The others were non-Baluch who had qualified for admission as "Baluchistanis" by fulfilling a five-year residence requirement in the province. Initially, Khoshrou-Sefat declared that "at least" 100 of the 450 students at the new University of Baluchistan were Baluch, but it turned out that he meant "Baluchistani" and that only 25 were Baluch. Sixteen high school graduates from the province were among the 62 new entrants to the university from all parts of the country in 1978, he added, and 8 of these were "actual Baluch. But we don't think in these terms. We're all Iranians. It's all the same to me."

As in the case of the economic development generated by the oil boom, the expansion of education during the 1970s failed to win Baluch support for Teheran. The expansion program was not accompanied by political reforms giving the Baluch meaningful local self-rule and was thus not administered in a way that the Baluch regarded as equitable. Most of the Baluch I met in Zahedan, Sarawan, and Khash complained bitterly that it was impossible to get justice from a school system and a bureaucracy run by Persians and their Sistani allies. "There is propaganda on the radio all the time urging us to send our children to be educated," said Ahmed Sheikhzade, a Baluch organizer for the Shah's Rastakhiz party, "but the psychological tensions encountered by Baluch children in dealing with Persian teachers keeps many of them from going." For example, he said, Persians are "very color conscious and Baluch students, whose skin is dark, are often teased as 'blacks' by their Persian teachers, which makes the students very self-conscious." Most of the teachers sent to Baluchistan, Sheikhzade explained, are serving mandatory assignments under various military and quasi-military national service programs and regard both the place and the people with undisguised contempt.

Rashid Mollazai, director of Baluchi programs for Radio Zahedan,

stressed that the ban on the use of the Baluchi language made Baluch
feel like outsiders, automatically excluded from fair treatment in school
admissions and job applications. "As education expands," he declared,
"people are becoming more sensitive about being required to learn Persian for admission to college or to get a job. They think of themselves as
something other than Persian, and so they feel shut out of the main
stream. They easily become discouraged when they encounter the ram-
pant discrimination existing in favor of Persians and Sistanis. The fact is
that the Baluch are not wanted in the university or in good jobs—and
they know they are not wanted." Even messengers had been brought to
Zahedan from Birjan, outside of the province, recalled Mohammed Sep-
ahi, a Baluch employee of a Danish construction firm near the capital.
"Persians prefer Persians," he observed, "and our only hope is that as
Baluch slowly and painfully squeeze into better jobs, they will give preference to other Baluch and build up a network of Baluch who will help
each other and give jobs to new Baluch coming out of the schools. That
is how we are beginning to count for just a little bit in the local society."

As the Shah cautiously permitted education to reach the Baluch,
Iranian Baluchistan began to look like a miniature version of Pakistani
Baluchistan, with the educated unemployed rapidly assuming politically
significant proportions. High school and junior college graduates, in
particular, had nowhere to go and were starting to think in terms of
independence even before the Shah's overthrow opened the way for an
unprecedented upsurge of political activity. "If a graduate is not getting
a job," said Shah Bakhsh, leader of the 27,000-strong Shah Bakhsh tribe,
"then he begins to feel that he should do something for the country to
create more opportunities for everyone. He begins to think there may be
greater hope if the Baluchis come together."

Nationalism Goes Underground

Until the Shah's overthrow in January 1979, the Baluch nationalist movement in Iran was a relatively insignificant force compared to the movement in Pakistan. Relentlessly pursued by the ubiquitous SAVAK
(Sazemane Attelaat Va Amneyate Keshavar, or Organization for Information and Security), its émigré leaders were forced to operate underground from a variety of shifting foreign hideouts and had little
continuing contact with their widely scattered supporters inside Iran.
Nevertheless, while it never amounted to much in organizational terms,
the pre-1979 nationalist movement proved to have great psychological
importance. The handful of Baluch activists who braved the Shah's re-

pression kept alive the spirit of resistance to Persian domination and thus directly set the stage for the resurgence of nationalist activity now taking place.

The first martyr to the Baluch cause during Mohammed Reza Pahlavi's reign was Dad Shah, a camel breeder and chieftain of a minor branch of the Mobariki tribe, who was one of the more daring opponents of Persian rule in the inaccessible southeastern corner of Iranian Baluchistan. According to Iranian authorities, he was nothing more than the leader of a "bandit gang" that operated from sanctuaries in the Ahuran mountains, terrorizing rich and poor alike. But according to the Baluch legend that later grew up around his name, Dad Shah started his exploits in the Robin Hood tradition as early as 1944, harassing Iranian police and army outposts and robbing rich Baluch feudal lords to help impoverished nomads.

On March 24, 1957, Dad Shah and a band of some twenty-four men waylaid and killed an American military aid official and his wife, Kevin and Anita Carroll, and an American contractor, Brewster Wilson, who were driving by jeep with two Iranians to the port city of Chah Bahar on the Persian Gulf. It was all a mistake, Dad Shah later explained, since his men thought they were attacking a party of Iranian officials.[9] In American eyes, however, the case had disturbing and sinister aspects that made it a front-page sensation until Dad Shah was killed in a gun battle with Iranian police ten months later. Some reports, suggesting that Carroll and Wilson wanted to size up Chah Bahar as a potential military base, saw a Communist hand in the killings.[10] When early accounts incorrectly indicated that Mrs. Carroll might still be alive, Iranian officials further fanned the fires of American press interest by explaining that she would probably be sold for a handsome profit in the slave markets of Oman or Dubai.[11] Above all, Teheran's seeming inability to ensure the safety of foreign experts raised questions in Washington concerning the stability of the Shah's regime and the advisability of continuing an aid program then costing $50 million a year. In an effort to quiet the uproar, Prime Minister Hussein Alah resigned. The Shah put a price of $10,000 on the head of each member of the Dad Shah gang, dead or alive, and the Pakistan Army and the police joined in the manhunt.

Dad Shah not only eluded his pursuers for ten months until his death but also conducted daredevil running skirmishes with them that made him a legendary figure. Although several dozen nationalist activists reportedly joined him in the hills, his forces never numbered more than forty or fifty. Yet there is general agreement that Dad Shah and his men actively attempted to engage the Shah's forces in combat by staging frequent ambushes and that they fought at least three pitched gun battles with Iranian police contingents. When they were finally cornered, Dad Shah died in battle, refusing to surrender.

"He acted the way a Baluch is supposed to act, bravely and defiantly," explained Mohammed Hussein Hossainborr, an Iranian Baluch student living in the United States. "Everyone saw himself as a potential Dad Shah." Dozens of Dad Shah ballads sprang up among the Baluch in Iran, and a *Le Monde* correspondent found in 1973 that Dad Shah was venerated as "one of the great martyrs of the Baluch movement in Iran."[12] Pakistani Baluch writers elevated him to the stature of a "national leader who raised the flag of revolt."[13] More accurately, an Iranian Baluch nationalist tract later acknowledged that Dad Shah was "a man whose aim in the beginning might not have been the independence of the whole of Baluchistan," but claimed that he had "gradually come to see his role in a larger perspective. During his last days, he gave great sacrifices for the cause of independence, for awakening the Baluch nation and fighting against imperialism."[14]

The nationalist leader who was primarily responsible for making the Dad Shah case a symbol of the Baluch cause was Jumma Khan, a dynamic young Baluch who had roots in both Pakistani and Iranian Baluchistan. He grew up in Turbat, a border town just inside Pakistani Baluchistan but oriented, socially and economically, to the neighboring Iranian Baluch tribes. After working his way through Karachi University, Jumma Khan quickly became a celebrity among both Pakistani and Iranian Baluch as a producer and announcer of Baluchi programs on Radio Karachi and as president of the leading Baluch literary group, the Baluch Academy. His political debut came when Pakistan captured Dad Shah's brother, Ahmed Shah, in late 1957. It was Jumma Khan who saw a nationalist issue in Pakistan's agreement to turn Ahmed Shah over to Iran as a gesture of Central Treaty Organization (CENTO) solidarity, despite the lack of an extradition treaty between the two countries. Denouncing the move to extradite Ahmed Shah as a violation of human rights, Jumma Khan organized a vigorous Baluch protest movement that quickly took on broader nationalist overtones. The Dad Shah case marked the first time that a Baluch leader had attempted to rally nationalist sentiment in both Pakistan and Iran around an issue of common concern under the banner of Greater Baluchistan.

Dismissed from his Radio Karachi post as a result of his nationalist activity, Jumma Khan shifted his operations in 1961 to Dubai, where he worked as a theater manager and quietly began to set up underground links in nearby Iranian Baluchistan. He was soon joined by a small group of leading Iranian Baluch political exiles, and in 1964 Jumma Khan and other exiles launched an organization known as the Baluchistan Liberation Front.* The new organization scored its biggest success when it attracted the support of one of the best-known tribal chieftains in Iranian Baluchistan, Mir Abdi Khan of the Sardarzai tribe. Permitted to leave Iran in 1965 for the ostensible purpose of making a pilgrimage to Mecca, Mir Abdi Khan never went back. Instead, for the next three years, he made Baluchi-language broadcasts beamed from Dubai to Iranian Baluchistan and regularly toured the Persian Gulf sheikhdoms, rallying Baluch émigrés and migrant workers to the Greater Baluchistan standard. Several lesser tribal notables followed his lead; one of them, Mir Mauladad, organized attacks on Iranian army units in the name of the Front. But it was Mir Abdi Khan's identification with the movement that gave it an aura of legitimacy previously lacking, not only in Iranian Baluchistan itself but also in the eyes of its sympathizers and supporters outside Iran, especially in the Arab world.

Although Mir Abdi Khan received some funds from his tribesmen in the Dashtiari and Bahu tribal areas, and Jumma Khan was also backed in a minor way by wealthy Baluch émigrés, the Front depended mainly on clandestine support from a variety of radical Arab sources. In one of its early manifestos, the Front made a bid for Arab support by endorsing the controversial thesis of some Arab and Baluch scholars that the Baluch have ethnic links to the early Arabs (see chapter two). The manifesto declared that "we consider ourselves a part of the great Arab nation, and we are wholeheartedly with our Arab brethren in their struggle against imperialism, colonialism and Zionism." The Front specifically supported Iraqi claims to the Shatt-al-Arab estuary and the Arab-populated Khuzistan area of Iran, as well as "the just rights of Palestinian Arabs over Palestine." It expressed confidence that "freedom-loving people the world over, and our Arab brothers in particular, will become more enthusiastic in helping us in our struggle for freedom."[15]

Initially, the only open Arab support that Jumma Khan received was from Iraq and from Yasser Arafat's wing of the Palestine Liberation Organization, which made him a member of its central advisory committee. Later, Syria and Egypt permitted him to open offices, and the Syrians even gave him quasi-diplomatic status during 1965 and 1966 as the representative of a provisional Baluchistan government-in-exile. Arab support was cautious and circumscribed, however, because Arab objectives differed in Iran and Pakistan. While they were happy to support the Baluch movement in Iran as a means of harassing their enemy the Shah, most Arab governments were unwilling to associate themselves with the

---

* Despite the similarity in name, this group was not related to the Baluch People's Liberation Front, discussed in chapter five.

Greater Baluchistan concept, which implied support for Baluch dissidents in Pakistan, a friendly state.[16] Pakistani pressure on Syria for the extradition of Jumma Khan eventually became so intense that he fled from Damascus in 1968 to escape arrest and ended up in Baghdad.

Unlike other Arab states, Iraq had compelling reasons to give priority to its support for the Baluch cause. Deeply embroiled in 1968 in their feud with the Shah, who was backing Kurdish rebels opposed to the Baghdad government, Iraqi leaders saw the Baluch as natural allies in their conflict with Teheran. The Iraqi Baathist regime subsidized Jumma Khan, Mir Abdi Khan, and other leaders linked with the Front for the next five years, and Baghdad became the headquarters for intensified radio broadcasting and insurgent activity in Iranian Baluchistan.

Politically, the Front attracted considerable attention during the 1968–1973 period. Shah Bakhsh, the Iranian Baluch tribal leader, recalled that "at least seventy or eighty" unemployed, educated Baluch went underground and joined Jumma Khan in the late 1960s. In military terms, however, Iraqi help to the Baluch turned out to be relatively insignificant. Most accounts indicated that Baghdad saw Baluch guerrilla activity as a mere diversion intended to tie down some of the Shah's forces in eastern Iran. Shah Bakhsh estimated that "four or five hundred" fighting men from Dad Shah's Mobariki tribe, Mir Abdi Khan's Sardarzais, and the Gamshadzais went for arms and training in Iraq, together with some of the seventy-odd educated nationalists. Baghdad was able to smuggle men and weapons into Iranian Baluchistan, he said, by sending "fishing vessels" from hidden bases along the wild Qatar coast across to Chah Bahar and other Baluch-controlled ports on the Iranian side of the Gulf of Oman. Ashraf Sarbazi, who was a Baluchi announcer on Radio Zahedan at the time, said that the largest single guerrilla force sent into Iran consisted of about a hundred men, who attacked military outposts in Mir Abdi Khan's home territory.

The Front's field commander inside Iran was a fiery Mobariki youth named Rahim Zardkoui, who continued to maintain a group of some seventy-five highly politicized tribal guerrillas after Iraqi support ended, using hideouts in the Ahuran mountains of southern Baluchistan, Dad Shah's old stronghold. With the exception of the Zardkoui group, however, the Front did not accomplish much in organizational terms during the "Baghdad period."

Seeking to account for their failure to win broader rank-and-file support, nationalist leaders generally pointed at first to the lack of education and political consciousness in the Iranian Baluch areas. But a more basic explanation, they conceded, was that the Shah had successfully pursued his policy of co-opting many of the more influential Iranian

Baluch tribal chieftains, in marked contrast to the situation in Pakistan, where Islamabad had attempted to crush the *sardari* system and the most prominent *sardars* had become leaders of the nationalist movement. Mir Abdi Khan was a lonely exception that proved the rule. From the start, the Shah was able to blunt the edge of Iraqi-supported insurgent activity by inducing cooperative *sardars* to serve as informers. "The ordinary Baluch people were sympathetic to the insurgents," said Ashraf Sarbazi, "but they were afraid to join them and were subject to a great deal of pressure from the government and some of the *sardars* if they helped them." Sarbazi was uniquely situated to gauge local support, he observed wryly, because he was broadcasting government propaganda against Iraq and was repeatedly threatened with death by irate tribesmen.

The crowning blow to Jumma Khan came in 1973 when Mir Abdi Khan succumbed to the Shah's blandishments. Uprooted from his tribal environment, the sixty-five-year-old Sardarzai chieftain had become increasingly dissolute. When the Shah's agents offered to provide him with a harem, a lifetime pension, and a handsome house in Teheran, he agreed to retire from politics—adding insult to injury, in the eyes of his erstwhile colleagues, by praising the Shah in a Radio Teheran broadcast. Iraqi help was gradually tapering off, in any case, and in March 1975, Baghdad and Teheran signed a peace agreement in which Iran promised to stop its support of the Kurds in exchange for Iraq's termination of its help to the Baluch and the Khuzistani Arabs. Fearful that some of their Iraqi "friends" might turn them over to SAVAK, disillusioned Front leaders hastily dispersed after the 1975 truce, most of them fleeing to Persian Gulf sheikhdoms. SAVAK eventually found and killed two well-known Front leaders, Abdus Samad Barakzai and Musa Khan Lashari, but Jumma Khan eluded the Shah's net and reportedly turned up in Baghdad again soon after the Shah's overthrow.

The Front's alliance with Iraq had a lasting impact on Iranian Baluch attitudes in two significant respects. First, it instilled a distrust of Iraqi intentions that is likely to affect the nature and extent of any future Baluch collaboration with Baghdad against the Khomeini regime and its successors. But more important, the alliance sharply underlined the differences between Communist and nationalist approaches to the future of Baluchistan. Iraq had close ties with the Soviet Union during the 1968–1973 period, and it was Soviet military equipment that Iraq was giving to the Baluch. Baghdad served, accordingly, as a base of operations for Iranian Communist factions opposed to the Shah, including Communist groups in the non-Persian minority areas. Iraqi leaders attempted to hold Communist and non-Communist elements together in a united anti-Teheran campaign. But this proved to be a particularly difficult task in the minority areas, since the Communists, reflecting Soviet policy, explicitly favored the retention of a "united, socialist, federal" Iran.

As early as 1952, the Moscow-oriented Tudeh party in Iran had defined a policy toward the "national question" directly emulating the Soviet model. While the Baluch and other minority nationalities were accorded the residual right of self-determination, "progressives" in all parts of Iran were enjoined to work together for the overthrow of feudalism and imperialist-controlled reaction in Teheran.[17] This policy automatically alienated most politicized Baluch, who favored ultimate independence. Nevertheless, there were a handful of Tudeh sympathizers among the Iranian Baluch, some of whom joined a Tudeh-sponsored group in Baghdad known as the National Front of the Iranian People. Led by former Iranian army general Mahmoud Panahiyan, an Azerbaijani Turk, this group championed the grievances not only of the Baluch but of the Azerbaijanis, the Kurds, and the Khuzistani Arabs. It published its own journal, *Rah-e-Ittehad* (Path of Unity), in Arabic, Kurdish, Persian, Turkish, and Baluchi, and conducted its own radio broadcasting in these languages.

With considerable difficulty, Iraqi leaders were able to persuade Panahiyan's National Front and Jumma Khan's Baluchistan Liberation Front to concentrate their fire on Teheran, avoiding attacks on each other. But the differences between the two groups were fundamental. In its political program, the Baluch branch of Panahiyan's coalition, which called itself the Democratic party of Baluchistan, advocated a "national democratic government" in Baluchistan that would be a provincial component of a "federal, socialist" Iran. Demanding a redemarcation of provincial boundaries in Iran on a linguistic basis and the right to use Baluchi as a medium of instruction in the schools, the program pointedly avoided saying whether the party's goals should be pursued peacefully or through military struggle.[18] By contrast, Jumma Khan's Front declared that "the only way of liberating Baluchistan is through the armed struggle of the masses" and rejected the idea of "compromise and political solutions. We do not believe in the so-called stage-by-stage pursuit of independence, i.e., first to struggle for linguistic, cultural, and political rights as a part of Iran, and then, afterwards, to struggle for independence. Our experience is that an oppressed people prepares itself and struggles for a cause only once. If they get something, even if it is minimal, they become contented and satisfied."[19]

Hampered by their policy on the independence issue, the Communists were even less successful in rallying the Baluch during the 1968–1973 period than Jumma Khan's Front. K. B. Nizamani, the Pakistani Baluch leftist who helped to organize the Democratic party under Iraqi auspices, recalled that the party's first and only conference, held in "a border village inside Iran" in February 1972, was "restricted to fifteen selected delegates as a result of various problems confronted by all democrats at that time." Eight years later, however, the Tudeh party had not changed its policy on the independence issue. Nuroddin Kianuri, the party's first secretary, told an interviewer in January 1980 that the party "has always supported the demands of the minority nationalities for self-government, but only within the framework of a unified Iran, giving strict priority to a political solution instead of an armed struggle."[20]

When I visited Iranian Baluchistan in August 1978, I was struck by the lack of support for the Tudeh party, despite the obvious strength of Marxist-Leninist sentiment among politically conscious youth. I was also surprised to find that anti-Teheran sentiment was not sharply focused on the personage of the Shah. While bitterly resentful of Persian domination in a generalized sense and critical of SAVAK in particular, most of the Iranian Baluch I met did not openly express the intense hatred for the Shah that I had encountered among opposition elements in the Persian heartland of Iran. This was partly explained by the prevailing atmosphere of repression. But I also sensed that I had arrived on the scene at a moment of unusual confusion and anxiety, when the possibility of a Khomeini-led revolution was just beginning to loom on the horizon. Throughout the country, religious tensions were building up between the majority Shiites and the minority Sunnis,* and the Sunni Baluch saw the Shah, with his secular emphasis, as a shield of protection against potential Shiite religious oppression.

During the course of my 1978 visits to Zahedan, Khash, and Sarawan, I was able to engage in meaningful conversations with fifteen highly articulate Baluch from varying backgrounds. Given their pervasive fears of SAVAK, however, it was extraordinarily difficult at first to win their confidence. It seemed to make little difference whether we talked in hushed tones in coffee houses and hotel rooms or in the privacy of jeeps and trucks, roaring over desert and mountain roads. I found a cautious willingness to talk in generalities about Baluch grievances relating to school admissions and job discrimination. When I asked about underground political activity or about attitudes toward independence,

* Sunnis acknowledge the first four caliphs to be the rightful successors of the Prophet Mohammed and look to the Sunnah, or traditional Koranic law, as the authoritative guide to the theory and practice of Islam. Shiites regard Ali, Mohammed's son-in-law, and his descendants as the inheritors of the Prophet's spiritual authority and have their own school of law, the Jaafari.

however, I was invariably greeted by terror-stricken silence and a degree of alarm that I had not found among Pakistani Baluch. It took three long conversations over a ten-day period before one of my informants told me of the coming "revolution." Unbeknownst to SAVAK, he said, secret visits had been paid to Baluchistan during mid-1978 by representatives of various anti-Shah groups, notably the Marxist Fedayeen-e-Khalq (Those Who Sacrifice for the People) and Paykar (Battle) factions, and the Mujahideen-e-Khalq (Crusaders for the People), which styles itself as Islamic Socialist.

Among the younger Baluch I met, the Marxist Fedayeen and Paykar appeared to have the most support, though none of these Persian-dominated leftist groups, I was told, really understood Baluch aspirations. As for the Tudeh, there was general agreement that it could not claim to be progressive, since it represented Soviet "great power chauvinism," just as the Shah's Iran had symbolized "American imperialism." The majority of these younger Baluch were clearly thinking about forming new organizations under Baluch control that would have closer links with Pakistani Baluch groups than with any political factions in Teheran and would work, in one way or another, for eventual independence. By contrast, among Baluch of the older generation, I found a more cynical appraisal of the future. Nothing would change, in their view, even if the Shah were overthrown, because one set of Persians would simply replace another in Teheran and there would always be Baluch quislings to play their game.

On the issue of independence, I found the generation gap among Iranian Baluch particularly striking. A twenty-eight-year-old personnel officer for a European firm declared that "there is an awakening now taking place among the Baluch, even among illiterate people. There is very deep anger that we do not have equal opportunity in benefiting from the economic development taking place in our own homeland. The Baluch should be treated on a par with others. Otherwise, we will go out of Iran." A young teacher who sat silently through day after day of discussion finally volunteered quietly that "every area of Iranian Baluchistan except for the Sarhad in the north would be sympathetic to a struggle for independent Baluchistan, and many would join it, if our Pakistani friends give us adequate help and leadership." He named Sarbaz, Sarawan, Chah Bahar, and Rask as areas that are still relatively immune to Teheran's control and have been most influenced by politically minded Baluch returning from the Persian Gulf. A thirty-four-year-old government employee in the communications field acknowledged that "the younger generation is very unhappy about the position of the Baluch and is thinking the situation over. The idea of independence is in their minds." But even as he said this, he added anxiously, "While we don't know about the future, for the present, I can't even think of it—I dare not—it's impossible."

Reflecting the frankly skeptical attitude of the few older tribal leaders I was able to meet, Shah Bakhsh said that while the Iranian Baluch "might have some sympathy for their brethren in Pakistan, it is unlikely that we will join them because to talk of an independent Baluchistan means that we are talking about the Russians coming here. The main objective of Russia is to get a way to Hormuz, and so the government knows that it has to keep the Baluch satisfied. They will do more for us economically, I am sure." Similarly, Mir Amin Barakzai, son of Dost Mohammed, the Baluch martyr who led the struggle against Reza Shah in 1928, said he doubted that the independence movement would succeed because it would need financial and military support that could only come from Moscow. Now that "every Baluch has a radio set," he said, "our people know that the way of life in Russia is not favorable for religion, and you must remember that our tribal people here are very conservative in their customs and their religious beliefs."

In mid-1978, the Iranian Baluch were leaderless, disorganized, and politically quiescent. They were keenly watching unfolding events in Teheran but played a relatively marginal role in the tumultuous final months of the anti-Shah struggle. Beneath the surface, however, Baluch nationalist sentiment was becoming increasingly volatile. The underground nationalist activity that had persisted during the Pahlavi years had prepared the ground, psychologically, for a relatively rapid nationalist resurgence during the post-Shah period.

After the Shah

The collapse of the Shah's regime led to an almost complete breakdown of central authority in Iranian Baluchistan, as well as in the other outlying non-Persian areas of Iran. For the first time in half a century, the Baluch suddenly found themselves free to carry on open political activity. This new freedom quickly produced a sharp struggle between the conservative Hezbe Ittehad-al-Muslimin (Islamic Unity party), organized by leading religious dignitaries, and a cluster of leftist and nationalist groups representing the young, politicized Baluch intelligentsia.

Although the Islamic Unity party embraced tribal *sardars* and other vested interests in the local power structure, its guiding spirit was the foremost Iranian Baluch *moulavi* (Muslim divine), Abdol Aziz Mollazadeh, and its strength came principally from a network of some 400 lesser *moulavis* scattered throughout Iranian Baluchistan. Mollazadeh, sixty, was the highest-ranking judge in the powerful system of religious courts that governs the application of Islamic law to the everyday lives of the Baluch. He was also one of the few public personalities well known throughout the Baluch areas as a result of his weekly Baluchi-language lectures on religion over Radio Zahedan.

The Muslim clergy in Baluchistan were largely ignored by the Shah, who relied on cooperative *sardars* as his middlemen in administering the Baluch areas. Nevertheless, at the grassroots level, the power of the *moulavis* had steadily increased during the Shah's regime. Faced with the ever-growing presence of Shiite Persian overlords, many Baluch, who belong to the orthodox Sunni sect of Islam, had turned to their Sunni faith to reinforce their sense of Baluch identity. Moreover, in the southern Baluch areas, the *moulavis* had stepped in to fill the leadership vacuum created by the Shah's destruction of the power of the *hakoms* (local chieftains) and by his failure to replace their authority with an effective centralized administration.[21]

In December 1978, the prospect of a Teheran regime dominated by Shiite clerics galvanized the Baluch Sunni *moulavis* into unprecedented political activity. Shiite influence was a clear threat to the religious freedom of the Baluch and to the *moulavis'* control over their elaborate hierarchy of Islamic courts and schools. At the same time, as Mollazadeh was quick to perceive, the *moulavis* had an opportunity to bolster their local power by assuming the intermediary role in dealing with Teheran that the *sardars* had played under the Shah. Even though Ayatollah Ruhollah Khomeini and his palace guard were Shiites, they were also fellow-clerics, Mollazadeh reasoned, and they might conceivably turn out to be more accommodating on religious issues than the Shah's Western-trained technocrats. By the time Khomeini had formally assumed power, Mollazadeh had organized the Islamic Unity party, which promptly emerged as the principal spokesman for Baluch interests during the confused early months of the new regime.

In contrast to Izza-al-din Husaini, the fire-breathing Kurdish Sunni leader who espouses a militant brand of nationalism, Mollazadeh has attempted to pursue conciliatory tactics toward Teheran. He has explicitly criticized Husaini for "excessive zeal in his actions."[22] Greeting the new regime with studied moderation, he declared that "we will give our full support to the new government, so long as there is no disrespectful behavior toward our Sunni religion and so long as our national rights are respected." By national rights, he said he meant freedom for the Baluch to practice Sunni Islam without interference, to use the hitherto-banned Baluchi language in the schools, and to make the "maximum use of local talent" in the provincial administration, including the police and military

Moulavi Abdul Aziz
Mollazadeh, leader of the
Islamic Unity Party

Karim Bakhsh Saidi, former member from
Baluchistan of the Iranian Majlis
(Parliament), who made unsuccessful overtures
to the United States for support in 1979
and 1980

Amanullah Barakzai, leader of the Baluch
Pesh Marga (Baluch Volunteer Force) in
Iranian Baluchistan

forces stationed in Sistan and Baluchistan. When he led a Baluch delegation to meet with Khomeini in March 1979, Mollazadeh did not press
for a written agreement spelling out specific concessions, as the Kurds
did, deciding instead to trust in informal guarantees given by the Ayatollah.[23] Returning from Teheran, he reported that Khomeini had promised to clear government appointments in Sistan and Baluchistan
through the Islamic Unity party and had agreed that the projected national constitution would treat Shiite and Sunni Islam on a par. He called
on the Baluch to vote for the new Islamic Republic in the April referendum. "All your national and religious wishes have been accepted," he
declared, "and will continue to be accepted in the future. There is no
cause for anxiety whatsoever."[24]

Despite Mollazadeh's conciliatory posture, the Islamic Unity party,
together with other Baluch groups, soon became embroiled in intermittent conflict with Teheran that was still continuing in mid-1981. Angered
by the initial appointment of a Persian, Tadollah Keshtkaran, as provincial governor-general, Baluch leaders persuaded Teheran in April
1979 to replace him with a Baluch mathematics professor from Baluchistan University, Danesh Naroui. Within three months, however, Naroui
quit in disgust, complaining that Teheran refused to let him exercise his
powers and had boxed him in with Khomeini-controlled Persian subordi-
nates. Naroui's successor, Habib Jaririe, a Persian, was regarded by Baluch of all shades as condescending and ethnically prejudiced against the
Baluch. More important, by late summer, the early drafts of the proposed constitution revealed that Khomeini's promised concessions to the
Baluch and other minorities had failed to materialize.

Article 13 made Shiism the state religion. Article 15 required the
study of Persian as the official language and its exclusive use as the
medium of instruction in the schools. In addition to banning the use of
Baluchi as a medium of education, Article 15 prohibited both the teaching of Baluchi as a second language and its use in textbooks, except for
those presenting Baluch literature. The only significant concession on
the language issue was permission to publish Baluchi newspapers and
magazines. Ruling out meaningful regional autonomy, Article 100 and
related provisions stated that major decisions by provincial "advisory
councils" would be subject to a central government veto. Moreover, the
members of these councils were not to be elected but were to be appointed by various Baluch religious and tribal groups.

Commenting on the draft constitution in an interview with a Teheran newspaper, Mollazadeh demanded that the provincial councils be
given stronger and more clearly defined powers. "We are not seces-
sionists," he declared. "And it is not in our interests to be independent

in all fields. Our goal is to see that the Baluch make their own decisions in the cultural and political fields, instead of being forced to accept decisions made in Teheran. At the very least, we want our provincial councils to choose our own governor general, our own governor, and our own administrators (although not our military officials). That is what the Baluch mean by autonomy."[25]

By September 1979, sentiment against Khomeini's "betrayal" had grown so intense that a split developed in the Islamic Unity party. In direct defiance of Mollazadeh's radio pleas for restraint, a rebel group led by a nationalist *moulavi* in Iranshahr, Mohammed Nazar, organized protest demonstrations throughout the province. In addition to their disenchantment over the constitution, Baluch leaders charged that Khomeini was deliberately arousing conflict between the Sunni Baluch and their Shiite neighbors, the Sistanis, giving job preference to Sistanis and even arming Sistanis with guns taken away from Baluch. Armed clashes soon became commonplace between Baluch activists and Sistanis, who were often allied with Khomeini's *pasdarans* (revolutionary guards).

When a national referendum on the constitution was held in early December, 200 Baluch set fire to the ballot boxes in Iranshahr, stormed Governor-General Jaririe's palace there, abducted Jaririe, and held him prisoner for three days until Mollazadeh intervened. Even Mollazadeh, however, called on the Baluch to boycott the referendum. As more and more *pasdarans* began patrolling the province, tensions sharpened, erupting in serious violence in Zahedan in late December in which twenty-four Baluch, Sistanis, and *pasdarans* were killed and some eighty injured. Teheran was able to quell the week-long disturbances only after it declared a state of emergency and stationed the Eighty-eighth Armored Division in the streets of Zahedan.

Alarmed by the December explosion, Khomeini attempted to appease his Baluch critics by agreeing to a constitutional amendment specifically empowering the Sunni minorities to operate their own Sunni court systems, despite the designation of Shiism as the state religion. This gesture won Mollazadeh's endorsement of Baluch participation in the presidential election in late January. Mollazadeh gradually reached an uneasy truce with Teheran, but anti-Khomeini sentiment steadily mounted among the Baluch public during 1980, leading to a growing polarization between forces supporting the Islamic Unity party and a loose coalition of embattled leftist and nationalist elements. Popular dissatisfaction was heightened by the chaotic economic conditions developing throughout Iran and the decline of the rial in relationship to Pakistani and United Arab Emirates currencies, which made smuggling less profitable than it had been during the Shah's regime.

The most significant rallying point for leftist and nationalist opinion was the Sazman-e Demokratik-e Mardom-e Baluchistan (Baluchistan People's Democratic Organization, or BPDO), which brought together Baluch adherents of the Fedayeen-e-Khalq and Paykar factions, as well as an assortment of freewheeling intellectuals. In a manifesto setting forth its objectives, the BPDO directly attacked the new constitution. It demanded the election of regional assemblies with control over law and order, education, local civil service appointments, including the selection of a provincial governor, and the exploitation of the oil, uranium, and other natural resources believed to exist in Baluchistan. At the same time, it stressed that self-rule was not a prelude to independence and pledged to "struggle against all manifestations of secessionism in the country." In the eyes of many BPDO members, this strong stand on the independence issue was a tactical ploy designed to forestall government repression. But it also reflected the influence of Fedayeen and Paykar sympathizers, who shared the Tudeh view that Baluch "progressives" should make common cause with like-minded elements in other parts of Iran.

The BPDO was linked with a short-lived monthly in Baluchi, *Makran*, named after the Arabian Sea coastal area of Baluchistan (see Figure 2). The new journal was started by one of the group's more influential covert supporters, Khalidad Arya, a sixty-year-old Baluch intellectual who has held a variety of minor Iranian government civil service posts. *Makran* was nominally dedicated to the revival of Baluchi and the promotion of Baluch literary and cultural activity. Its inaugural issue listed numerous cases in which Baluch had been punished by the Shah's regime for possessing Baluchi books and periodicals published in Pakistan. "Even those who dared to read the Holy Koran in their mother tongue," the journal alleged, "were hounded by the informers of the Pahlavi regime, arrested, and tortured." It called for the exclusive use of Baluchi as the language of government offices, schools, and radio broadcasting in Baluch-majority areas.[26]

Seeking to forestall charges of separatism, *Makran* consistently referred to the Baluch as one of the "peoples of Iran." However, its pages had unmistakable overtones of Baluch nationalism. The inaugural issue published the full text of the BPDO manifesto. It also published several poems containing thinly veiled appeals for independence and a page of "useful slogans," among them "Our unity is our power" and "Our mouths have been unlocked after fifty years." Proclaiming that *Makran* "belongs to all Baluch," including those living in Pakistan, Afghanistan, the Soviet Union, and the Persian Gulf sheikhdoms as well as Iran, Arya's inaugural editorial declared that "all of us are fully aware of the problems and difficulties faced by our oppressed people. Their grief is our grief. Let us tell the world the story of our tragedy."[27]

Ironically, Arya gave lavish praise to the new regime for permitting the minorities to publish in their mother tongues. He termed this policy "a gift by the Iranian Revolution to the peoples of Iran." As soon as his first issue reached the eyes of Teheran officials, however, *Makran* was promptly suppressed. Similarly, the authorities cracked down during 1980 on the three other publications that had been launched by Baluch intellectuals: *Mahtak* (Monthly Dispatch), a literary journal; *Graand* (Majesty), an organ of hard-core Fedayeen and Paykar opinion; and *Roshanal* (Light), the voice of militant nationalism. All three of these publications went underground and now appear irregularly. Given the lack of education in Iranian Baluchistan, the potential audience for such publications and the membership base for groups such as the BPDO is limited to some 350 Baluch college graduates and another 5,000-odd high school graduates. The BPDO claims only 200 members and "several thousand" actively involved sympathizers. Now underground, it has faced growing repression, and one of its leaders, Rahmat Hossainborr, suffered serious leg injuries during a police raid on his Iranshahr home. A loosely affiliated, more openly nationalist group, the Kanoon Siasi-Farhangi-Khalq Baluch (Baluch People's Political and Cultural Center) burst onto the scene in a fury of activity during 1979 but has also been driven underground. For six months, until evicted by the army, it used the former SAVAK office in Zahedan as its headquarters. This lively but poorly organized group, which centers around the educated unemployed, also embraces Baluch students currently attending high schools, junior colleges, and the University of Baluchistan and has loose ties with the Baluch Students Organization in Pakistan.

In addition to ideologically sensitized groups organized by urban intellectuals, there were several potentially significant guerrilla groups operating in the tribal fastnesses of Iranian Baluchistan during 1980. Like Dad Shah's followers, most of these groups were simply fighting to make it hot for their Persian rulers, in the hope of driving them out of Baluchistan. Beyond that immediate goal, their nationalist objectives were hazy, although the Baluchistan Liberation Front, led by Rahim Zardkoui until his death in a clash with *pasdarans,* represented what was left of Jumma Khan's Liberation Front and continued to espouse independence. Another group, the Baluch Pesh Marga (Baluch Volunteer Force), organized by a Sarawan aristocrat with nationalist leanings, Amanullah Barakzai, was committed more vaguely to "freedom for the Baluch people."

Barakzai, fifty-six, is a powerful personality who started out as a vocal nationalist during the 1960s but later made his peace with the Shah. A direct descendant of Dost Mohammed, who led the Baluch struggle against Reza Shah, he is one of the leading figures in the politically influential Barakzai tribe, which has traditionally been allied with the Sardarzais and Saidis in a coalition against the Mobarikis and Lasharis. The Baluch Pesh Marga and a related movement, Vahdat Baluch (United Baluch), seek to bridge this ancient rivalry and to bring urban nationalists together with tribally based guerrillas. However, Barakzai is distrusted by many intellectuals as a result of his accommodation with the Shah.

While tribal loyalties are still strong in Iranian Baluchistan, the political importance of the tribal chieftains was greatly eroded by five decades of Pahlavi rule. In southern Baluchistan, as we have seen, Teheran virtually crippled the *hakom* system, and in the north, the *sardars* who served as the Shah's agents lost much of their luster in the eyes of their tribesmen. The *hakoms* and *sardars* still continue to have loyal followers, including many who will lay down their lives for them in accordance with Baluch tradition, but the tribal chieftains are no longer the only power brokers who count in the Iranian Baluch areas. Like the *sardars* in Pakistan who allied themselves with urban nationalists in the 1950s and 1960s, the Iranian Baluch tribal chieftains are beginning to look for broader alliances in the 1980s in order to make the most of their remaining power.

Many of the tribal chieftains who aligned themselves initially with the Islamic Unity party became disillusioned as they found themselves shut off from the spoils of power by the *moulavis* and as they watched Mollazadeh, flattered by growing attention from Teheran, gradually working out a *modus vivendi* during 1980 with the Khomeini regime. Searching for a way to outflank Mollazadeh, some of these disgruntled *sardars* attempted to do business with Teheran independently, with limited success, while others supported efforts to gain Baluch autonomy or independence through military struggle. Amanullah Barakzai's movement drew some tribal support, and tribal leaders in the Chah Bahar area formed a potent partnership in 1979 with a Fedayeen-sponsored guerrilla group, the Baluch Sarmarchar (Those Ready to Offer Their Lives).

Several of the *sardars* who collaborated most closely with the Shah, notably Karim Bakhsh Saidi, a former member of the Shah's Majlis (parliament), approached the United States and other non-Communist sources on several occasions in late 1979 and early 1980, offering to organize guerrilla activities against Teheran with U.S. assistance. In the short run, they said, such activities would be helpful to former premier Shahpour Bakhtiar and others seeking to unseat Khomeini. Even if Khomeini could not be unseated, they argued, "destabilization" of his regime would be desirable in any event, especially if the United States should decide at some later stage to support an independent Baluchistan.

It would be logistically easy to smuggle arms into Baluchistan, they contended, since the United States has military links with Oman, just across the Strait of Hormuz, and many of the dock hands and other workers in Chah Bahar harbor are Baluch nationalist sympathizers. I have detailed knowledge about one of these approaches, which occurred in January 1980, from several sources who were directly involved. A group of Iranian Baluch *sardars* went to Karachi and asked a Pakistani Baluch nationalist leader for help in contacting the U.S. government. This overture was conveyed to U.S. officials by a Pakistani intermediary but, so far as I have been able to determine, was categorically rejected.

During the Iran-Iraq war, Radio Teheran and leading Iranian newspapers warned repeatedly that Washington and Baghdad were arming a group of Iranian Baluch *sardars* for a revolt to be staged in cooperation with Sultan Qabus Ibn Sa'id of Oman and his army, which consists partly of Baluch mercenaries.[28] These charges were not backed up by specific evidence and were denied by American officials. There were indications that the Iranian *sardars* were continuing to seek American help for anti-Khomeini guerrilla operations, but these approaches did not have the blessing of the principal Baluch nationalist leaders. In addition, coordination between the Iranian *sardars* and the Baluch nationalist elements in Pakistan was extremely loose in the early part of 1981.

Iraq and the Arab Connection

An explosive and imponderable factor likely to affect the Baluch movement in Iran is the possibility of renewed Arab support for the Baluch as a response to the militant Shiite regime in Teheran. As we have seen, Iraq gave support to Jumma Khan's Liberation Front as a weapon against the Shah until the 1975 truce between Baghdad and Teheran. The Yasser Arafat wing of the PLO backed the Liberation Front, and the more militant George Habash wing of the PLO trained a small group of Pakistani guerrillas in 1973.

Soon after the Shah's overthrow, Iraq once again began to express support for the Baluch and other non-Persian minorities in Iran, calling on Teheran to grant them greater autonomy. Moreover, for the first time, the Baluch movement began to attract significant interest among conservatives in the Arab world, who were outraged by Khomeini's revival of Persian expansionist claims in the Persian Gulf and by his calculated attempts to inflame Shia-Sunni tensions in the Persian Gulf sheikhdoms. Conservative Arab interest increased after the Soviet invasion of Afghanistan, which heightened Arab fears that Moscow would seek to exploit Baluch nationalism for its own purposes.

The impact of the Soviet invasion on Arab thinking was exemplified in the writings of Riyad Najib Al-Rayyes, a commentator in the influential, Saudi-backed Paris weekly *Al-Mostakbal* (The Future). Writing on Baluchistan prior to the invasion in September 1979, Al-Rayyes, a Lebanese, expressed warm sympathy for the Baluch and supported the view that they were ethnically Arab in origin. But he concluded that "their revolution is close to being defeated because nobody is ready to support it. Even Moscow does not seem enthusiastic about this revolution." While stressing that "the situation in Baluchistan concerns the Arabs, especially those of the Arabian peninsula and the Gulf," he was guarded in alluding to the possibility of Arab support for Baluch independence, observing vaguely that "the future is liable to force the Arabs to follow different policies toward Baluchistan."[29] By contrast, in February 1980, six weeks after the Soviet invasion, he argued passionately and explicitly that Arab countries should support

> an independent Baluch nation. First, because the Baluch movement is a movement of Arabs, whose Arab history goes back centuries and would fill volumes of books. Second, if the Arabs do not protect the Baluch movement, it will definitely succumb to Soviet influence. Instead of having a new Arab nation, a Communist Marxist nation will take its place, and the Arabs would have lost their chance to assert the Arab heritage of the Baluch.

The Khomeini regime, he warned, is

> threatening every political system in the Gulf, and Moscow is getting closer to the Strait of Hormuz.... The establishment of a Baluch nation would positively secure the political systems in the Gulf, and it would enhance and strengthen the Arab presence in the Gulf area by protecting it from the continuous flow of immigration from India, Korea and other places.... By helping Baluch leaders, the Gulf states will be protecting the Arabian Gulf from Persian and Asian expansion.[30]

Dismissing arguments that help for the Baluch would divide Pakistan, an Islamic country, Al-Rayyes declared that "the establishment of an Arab nation, with its Arab heritage and history, is more important than saving an already-divided Islamic country ruled by military leaders and suffering from political instability, which makes it vulnerable to every threat from outside."[31]

The most comprehensive statement of the case for Arab sponsorship of an independent Baluchistan is a 310-page book by an Iraqi, Ma'n

Shana al-Ajli Al-Hakkami, published in Bahrain in 1979, which was circulated clandestinely in several Arab countries during 1980. Titled *Baluchistan: Land of the Arabs*, it recites detailed historical evidence to establish the Arab origins of the Baluch. This version of Baluch history partially coincides with that of some Pakistani Baluch writers, since it accepts the view that the original Baluch tribes came from Aleppo, in what is now Syria. However, Al-Hakkami argues that these tribes were originally Arabs, descended from the Prophet Mohammed's uncle, Amir Hamza, who were forced to flee from Medina to Aleppo. Thus, he disputes the view expressed by other Baluch writers that the original tribes were Babylonians or linked with Aryans in Asia Minor. Moreover, he emphasizes that the majority of Baluch migrated from Aleppo to the Arabian peninsula through southern and western Iraq and then sailed from Oman across the "Arabian Gulf" to the Makran coast of southern Baluchistan. Once in Baluchistan, he maintains, they were able to keep in contact with their fellow Arabs across the Gulf, receiving periodic infusions of Arab cultural influence from the Arab invaders who continually swept through Iran and Baluchistan. Throughout history, he points out, the Baluch consistently sided with Arab armies in their struggles against Persians.[32]

While bemoaning the Baluch "loss" of the Arabic language, Al-Hakkami attempts to demonstrate that they have retained many other elements of their Arab cultural and religious identity, especially in the Makran coastal areas. He appeals to the Baluch in Pakistan and Iran for "an awakening of the Arabic spirit," contending that "the unification of Iranian and Pakistani Baluchistan should be accomplished through their common Arabic heritage." This awakening, he says, can only come if the Baluch "master the language of their ancestors and use the Arabic language in every aspect of their lives. I would like to stress to the Baluch people that the Arabic language should be the nucleus of their future bond, whether social, cultural or political." In an oblique swipe at the Baluchi language, he states that Arabic "is particularly valuable and important for the Baluch people, since the twentieth century has proven to be the least fit for any form of tribal society, with all of its social, economic and cultural complexities."

Al-Hakkami reserves special venom for Persian historians and Western orientalists who have sought to establish either the Persian ethnic origins of the Baluch, or Baluch ethnic distinctiveness, by "drawing a special historical picture. All of these writings have been intended to cover up the real ethnic background of the Baluch people, since the main fear of the enemies of the Arabs was, and still is, that when the Baluch people recognize their true ethnic background, they will form a united political front with the rest of the Arab countries."[33]

Although Al-Hakkami is an Iraqi, it is not clear whether his book was subsidized by Baghdad or by a wealthy young Baluch sheikh in Bahrain, Mohammed Bin Hassan Al-Mohammed, who claims credit for sponsoring its publication. Interviewed in Bahrain in March 1980, Sheikh Mohammed, a pudgy, affable twenty-eight-year-old businessman and a leader of the Baluch tribe known as the Hoots, presented the book to me as the "handbook and Bible, you might say" of his newly formed Islamic Arab Front for the Liberation of Baluchistan. His principal mission, the sheikh said, is to unite the 350,000 Baluch living in the Persian Gulf sheikhdoms. However, this must go hand in hand with efforts to enlist broad Arab support for the Baluch cause, he added, which makes it necessary to fly back and forth regularly between Bahrain and other Arab countries, especially Saudi Arabia, Syria, and Jordan. A licensed pilot who took his flying lessons in England and owns his own planes, Sheikh Mohammed looks like any other Bahrain sheikh, sporting a traditional Arab headdress, albeit with a mod touch in the form of a bright, red-checked scarf. Arabic is the only language he can speak or write, but he declared fervently that "all of the Baluch living here are very proud to be Baluch. We never forget our cousins across the water, and our feelings are with them in their struggles."

The Hoots, some 28,000 strong, have been centered in Bahrain and surrounding areas since 1782, the sheikh explained, having fled there to escape the depredations of the Persian shahs. Until then, Bahrain had been a Persian colony, but the arriving Hoots and other Baluch tribes joined with the locally dominant Al-Khalifa Arabs, expelled the Persians, and installed the Al-Khalifa dynasty, which still controls Bahrain today. Many Baluch intermarried with the Arabs and became part of the Bahrain power elite. The managing director of the Bank of Bahrain and Kuwait, Ismail Baluch, boasted to a reporter in London that he is worth $70 million.[34] Sheikh Mohammed's aunt is married to the present ruler of Bahrain, Isa Bin Sulman Al-Khalifa. When his father died in 1978, the sheikh, who heads the Al-Mohammed branch of the Hoots, inherited control of a thriving furniture-importing concern and extensive real estate interests. He shares leadership of his tribe with two cousins, Mir Murad Barakat of the Fujaira Oasis and Sheikh Sayeed Bin Rashid of Muscat.

In addition to the Hoots, three other Baluch tribes migrated to the Gulf from Iran centuries ago. These "old Baluch" elements have absorbed Arab culture, the sheikh said, while the "new Baluch," who have come in recent decades as migrant laborers from Pakistan and Iran, continue to speak Baluchi. Nevertheless, he insisted, the old Baluch still retain close links with affiliated branches of their own tribes that did not migrate to the Gulf sheikhdoms and with other kindred tribes living in the coastal areas of Baluchistan. Flatly declaring that "the most important leaders of the Iranian tribes are in the Gulf, especially coastal tribes like the Hoots," the sheikh declared that "all of the Baluch in this part of the world are very interconnected. We are all nationalists, we all look up to the Baluch leaders in Pakistan as our senior leaders, and nationalism is growing all the time." This affinity is especially true among the migrant workers, he added, since they are "far from home, which makes them particularly conscious of their roots. Their feelings naturally affect us old Baluch. I find the younger people coming to me. So far, no one else has organized them, and if we work for the good of all Baluch, they will support us, as their traditional leaders, rather than the Communists, who are active here, of course." Like Al-Hakkami, he argued that all Baluch should learn Arabic, but with somewhat less certitude.

Asked why Arab leaders have been hesitant to support the Baluch nationalist movement, the sheikh responded that "they are divided, because they disagree on what it would mean. Some of them agree with us that an independent Baluchistan is the best way to save the Gulf area from communism, but others are afraid that Moscow would ultimately control Baluchistan if it once became independent. Some are reluctant to have a head-on conflict with Iran and Pakistan. But it's time for them to help us. Khomeini is going to spoil the Gulf, and he is only temporary, anyway. Sooner or later Iran will go to the left. Why doesn't the United States use its influence with the Arab countries? Through your allies, you should help us to form a free Baluchistan. This is the best way to stabilize this area." Then he quickly added that an independent Baluchistan should "not be linked to either the U.S. or the Soviet Union. We want to be independent because we are working for the interest of our own people." Too often, he said, American policy has been "egocentric. You are losing support everywhere because of your attitude. For example, you are not interested in the Gulf for its own sake, but merely as a place to get oil. Why should I convince my people to be killed for America?"

Except for the sheikh's efforts and the influence of *Nedae Baluchistan*, an irregularly published London-based publication he has helped to finance (see chapter seven), there was little evidence of organized nationalist activity among the Gulf Baluch in 1980. Nor were there signs of significant Arab support for such activity. The sheikh's identification with Al-Hakkami's book led some observers to view him as a front man for Iraq, but his open appeal for American help cast doubt on this theory and suggested that his Arab encouragement, if any, has come from U.S.-oriented elements in Saudi Arabia and Jordan.

Despite their fears of Khomeini, the Arab rulers of the Persian Gulf sheikhdoms were notably ambivalent about the Baluch cause. Initially, the sheikh received qualified encouragement from the Sunni-dominated Bahrain government, which was alarmed by Khomeini's overt attempts to incite the Shia majority in Bahrain. A well-knit bloc of Sunni Baluch no doubt appeared to offer a useful counterweight to Teheran. Subsequently, however, when Khomeini adopted a more restrained approach to the Gulf, the Bahrain authorities put the sheikh under wraps.

Initially, when the Iran-Iraq war broke out in 1980, many Baluch leaders expected Iraq and its sympathizers in the Gulf to embrace the Baluch cause as a means of putting pressure on Teheran. Iraq did intensify its verbal support for greater Baluch autonomy in Iran but did not define what "autonomy" meant and gave only token financial support to Baluch nationalist groups in Iran and the Gulf. As in the case of its earlier decision to phase out support for the Baluch in 1973, Baghdad was reluctant to alienate Pakistan. Moreover, Iraqi leaders pleaded that their resources were limited and that it was all they could do to keep their own forces on the Shatt-al-Arab front well supplied.

Looking ahead, Arab support for the Baluch is likely to be closely linked with the fluctuating relations between Teheran and Arab capitals, especially those in the Gulf, just as it has been in earlier decades. Should conflict between Iraq and Iran become chronic, the possibility of Arab backing for an independent Baluchistan could grow, especially if internal economic and political conditions in Pakistan should continue to deteriorate. Significantly, in conversations with Sheikh Mohammed and Arab sources, including Iraqi diplomats, it was clear that they were preoccupied with developments in Pakistan as well as in Iran. They recognized that the growth of Baluch nationalism would make it increasingly difficult to give aid to the Iranian Baluch that would not spill over into Pakistani Baluchistan, and they were well aware that the Iranian Baluch movement was a relatively weak adjunct of the more developed nationalist movement in Pakistan. As of early 1981, Sheikh Mohammed had met on at least one occasion with Ataullah Mengal, and there were increasing Iraqi contacts with Pakistani and Iranian Baluch leaders alike as the war with Iran dragged on.

Pakistani Baluch leaders were cautiously receptive to the idea of Arab support for an independent Baluchistan during my conversations with them, but not on the terms suggested by Al-Hakkami and Sheikh Mohammed. "We are Aryans, like the Kurds!" exploded Mengal. "We are not Semites! If we give up Baluchi, as they ask, how can we call ourselves Baluch? We can be friends with the Arabs, perhaps close friends, although some of their present rulers are very reactionary. Certainly Baluchistan has much in common with the Gulf states especially. We have historical ties, and they are physically close to our tribes in Iran, very interconnected. We might want to form a special union with some of them. We could have a special relationship with them that could be very valuable to us, since they are very rich, without being threatening to us, since they are, after all, quite small. If the Arabs would allow us maneuverability, this might not be a bad idea after all. But we cannot give up our language and our identity!"

Like Mengal, Khair Bux Marri dismissed the idea of substituting Arabic for Baluchi, but he appeared ready to finesse the issue of whether the Baluch are Semites or Aryans. "If they think we are Arabs, we need not argue about our history," he mused. "What is important to us is our freedom. If we were to form a union with them, would they try to absorb us? Would they try to force some of their reactionary ideas on us? We are, after all, inspired by progressive and socialist ideals, which are essential for the development of a poor country." Marri did not rule out the idea of future links with one or more Arab states, observing that "there are a number of Arab states, and no one Arab state would necessarily be paramount if we were to join an Arab union." But he added that "most of their present leaders are reactionary, and in any case we are too weak now to talk about joining with others. We should try to buy time in which to strengthen ourselves so that we can hold our own in association with stronger partners."

Communism and Nationalism in Baluchistan

7

Given the widespread assumption that Moscow has its eye on Baluchistan, it is surprising to find that there have never been effective Soviet-oriented Communist organizations in the Baluch areas of either Pakistan or Iran. This is primarily because Soviet policy has consistently stopped short of supporting the concept of an independent Greater Baluchistan. Many Baluch regard the Soviet Union as more sympathetic to Third World aspirations than the capitalist and "imperialist" West and continue to look hopefully to Moscow as a potential supporter of their cause. But this pro-Soviet sentiment has not yet been translated into a strong Communist organizational base.

While defining the Baluch as a separate nationality and upholding their inherent right of secession, Soviet ideologues have until now advised against invoking this right, calling on their Baluch sympathizers to work with other "progressives" for overall Communist victories in Pakistan and Iran as a whole. Moreover, in addition to laboring under this doctrinal burden, Baluch Communists have been hampered by ethnic frictions with the Pakistani and Iranian Communist leadership. The faction-ridden Pakistani Communist movement has been controlled since its inception by urban, middle-class leaders who migrated from areas now in India at the time of partition and lack local roots in any of the ethnic regions now constituting Pakistan. Similarly, as we have seen, the Tudeh party in Iran is Persian-dominated and has alienated potential Baluch supporters by pushing for a loose federalism rather than for Baluch independence.

Even the Afghan Communists have been somewhat suspect in Baluch Communist eyes. For all of its expressions of sympathy with Baluch grievances, the Pushtun-dominated Afghan Communist movement has been cool to the idea of Baluch independence, promising only that the Baluch would be given autonomy within the larger framework of a Pushtunistan or a Greater Afghanistan.

Soviet Policy Toward Baluch Nationalism

The multiethnic Soviet Union employs a cynical form of ideological sleight of hand to justify strong centralized control of its diverse constituent republics while making a ceremonial bow to their separate national identities. On the one hand, communist nationality doctrine affirms the right of every nation to self-determination, including the right of secession; on the other, it stipulates that only the proletariat, whose will is embodied in the communist party, can decide whether it is in the interests of a particular nation to exercise that right on a given occasion. This doctrinal flexibility has been peculiarly suited to shifting Communist tactical priorities in the multiethnic South Asian environment.

Even before independence, the Communists in undivided India were well aware of the relevance of Soviet nationality doctrine to the Indian scene. The draft program of the nascent Indian Communist party declared in 1930 that only an "Indian Federal Soviet Republic would be capable of insuring to national minorities their right to self-determination, including that of complete separation."[1] Later, when the Hindu-Muslim conflict dominated Indian political life, Communist theoreticians turned to Soviet nationality doctrine in formulating their response to the Muslim League's demand for a separate Muslim state to be known as Pakistan. This demand was anathema to the Hindu-dominated Congress party led by Gandhi and Nehru, and its religious rationale initially made the proposal repugnant to the Communists. Seeking to maintain their popularity among Muslims, however, Indian Communist party leaders decided to support "what is just and right" in the Muslim League's demand. "The rational kernel of the Pakistan demand," wrote the party's leading theoretician on nationality, G. Adhikari, is that "wherever people of the Muslim faith living together in a territorial unit form a nationality...they certainly have the right to autonomous state existence just like other nationalities in India."[2]

In its memorandum to the British Cabinet Mission in April 1946, the Indian Communist party called on Britain to turn over power not to the provisional central government headed by Nehru, but to seventeen sovereign regional constituent assemblies, each to be empowered to decide whether or not to join the projected new Indian Union "or remain out and form a separate, sovereign state by themselves, or join another Indian Union." Four of these assemblies were to have been in Muslim-majority areas that later on became part of Pakistan—among them Baluchistan—while the other thirteen were in areas that later constituted the Indian Union.[3]

Despite the nominal allowance made for the formation of "separate, sovereign" states, the memorandum had the practical effect of supporting the Muslim League by envisaging "another Indian Union." By all indications, Moscow encouraged Communist support for the creation of Pakistan, believing that India would be "weak and disorganized, and would eventually be fragmented in the process of achieving independence."[4] In the immediate aftermath of the 1947 partition, the Indian Communist party continued to operate on the premise that India would fall apart, espousing separatist policies in Andhra and other ethnic minority regions. Fearing that the new Indian government would adopt anti-Soviet policies, the Soviet Union encouraged these separatist policies. Within less than five years, however, Moscow concluded that the Nehru government was an established fact and that India's neutralist policies would not be hostile to Soviet interests. In 1953, Moscow formally signaled its acceptance of the Indian state by decreeing that "though for India, too, the principle of self-determination means and naturally includes the right of separation, it is inexpedient for Indian nationalities to exercise the right."[5]

In the case of Pakistan, Soviet ideologues were initially less explicit, and as late as 1964, Yuri Gankovsky, a leading Soviet writer on nationality problems, asserted that "the dismemberment of India into two dominions along religious lines did not solve the national problem of Pakistan." To be sure, he conceded, "the slogan of Pakistan, albeit in an indirect, deformed way, expressed the striving for national autonomy and self-determination" of the two homogeneous Muslim regions in the subcontinent, Baluchistan and the Pushtun-dominated Northwest Frontier Province, as well as of "the Muslim parts of the Bengali, Punjabi and Sindhi peoples." But after the partition, he said, reactionary landowners, theologians, and businessmen had distorted the original intention of Mohammed Ali Jinnah and the other Muslim League founders, who had "emphasized that the areas encompassed in Pakistan would be autonomous and sovereign." Gankovsky did not directly challenge Pakistan's legitimacy or its continued right to exist, but he presented detailed historical analysis to show that it consisted of five distinct nationalities whose right to autonomy had yet to be recognized in the Pakistani state as it was then constituted.[6]

In contrast to Moscow's increasingly explicit support for Indian nationalism, Soviet policy toward Pakistan has been more ambivalent. Soviet writings have strongly advised the Baluch and other ethnic minorities against exercising their right of separation but have continued to emphasize the multinational character of Pakistan and have thus implicitly kept the separatist option open. The underlying premise of Soviet policy has been that Pakistan's chronic political instability offers fertile soil for a synchronized Communist takeover of the entire country. Rather than support uncoordinated separatist movements in the Baluch, Sindhi, and Pushtun areas without regard for the future of the Punjab, Moscow has argued, Communists should work for the conversion of the whole country into a loose multinational federation under their leadership. In effect, Moscow has treated separatism as a weapon of last resort, to be used only if and when hopes for an overall Communist victory in Pakistan must be abandoned. Similarly, as in the case of India, Moscow has attuned its evolving doctrine on the "national question" to its foreign policy priorities in Pakistan. Separatism has been consciously soft-pedaled as part of a Soviet diplomatic offensive to counter Chinese and U.S. influence in Islamabad. By implication, however, Moscow has continued to suggest that it is ready to invoke the separatist option if Islamabad should stray too far into the Sino-American orbit.

Soviet writings have treated Baluch nationalism as a nascent but growing phenomenon. The Baluch, Gankovsky wrote in his 1964 work *The Peoples of Pakistan: An Ethnic History*, "are the only one of Pakistan's major peoples who had not consolidated into a bourgeois nation by the time the colonialists left the Indo-Pakistan subcontinent." Baluchistan's economic dependence and backwardness were even greater than in other areas of British India during the colonial period, which had "a negative effect on the ethnic processes at work in the country, curbing the development of capitalist relations and arresting the rise of bourgeois-society classes and social strata." British economic neglect of Baluchistan drove many Baluch into Sind and other provinces in search of work. "This territorial dispersion did and does make the Baluch national consolidation exceedingly difficult." Nevertheless, he concluded, despite these handicaps, "the rise of the Baluchi nation is under way.... The national consolidation of the Baluchis is still on the move in our day.... The Baluchi proletariat is growing and the bourgeoisie and intelligentsia are taking shape. The birth of Baluchi national consciousness is in evidence."[7]

Parenthetically, it should be noted that when the English-language edition was published in 1971, *The Peoples of Pakistan* had been considerably toned down in keeping with a Soviet diplomatic offensive to curtail the growth of Chinese influence then taking place in Pakistan and to capitalize, if possible, on the coolness that had developed between Islamabad and Washington following the 1965 Indo-Pakistani war. The concluding chapter completely omitted the operative paragraphs in the 1964 edition that explained that the partition of the subcontinent along religious lines "did not solve the national problem in Pakistan."

Gankovsky's 1964 study marked the first extensive public scholarly Soviet treatment of the Baluch, with the exception of an economic treatise several years earlier by another author, M. G. Pikulin.[8] In 1960, Pikulin had written an article on the Baluch in Pakistan in which he concluded that the idea of a Greater Baluchistan uniting the *Pakistani*

Baluch is "a pressing issue." While expressing sympathy for Baluch self-determination, he was deliberately vague about whether it required separation from Pakistan and the creation of an independent state linking Pakistani and Iranian Baluch.[9] Similarly, Gankovsky's 1964 study, which was a historical tome focusing mainly on the preindependence period, did not offer specific policy advice to the nationalities in Pakistan. It pointedly avoided the debate then developing within Pakistani Communist ranks over the right of secession. By 1967, however, in a book devoted to postindependence "national movements," Gankovsky made clear that Moscow was opposed to separatist activity.

In his 1967 book, Gankovsky praised the "democratic movement" in Baluchistan for concentrating on the economic grievances of peasants and workers while also seeking the administrative unification of the Baluch areas into a single provincial unit which would enjoy "complete autonomy." At the same time, he directed vitriolic attacks at the "openly separatist position" of the Khan of Kalat and his uncle, Sultan Ibrahim Khan, who wanted to create an independent Baluchistan as a means of perpetuating their feudal privileges. "Imperialism and internal reaction do everything possible to sow suspicion and hatred among ethnic communities of multinational liberated states," Gankovsky concluded, "and to make their cooperative struggles for social progress impossible." He called for "incessant work" by all "progressive, patriotic forces interested in consolidating the independence and unity of their countries to prevent the spread of separatist tendencies and moods."[10]

In a 1973 book devoted entirely to the Baluch, Beknazar Ibragimov, a Gankovsky disciple, explicitly advised the Baluch against seeking independence. "The problems confronting all of the national regions of Pakistan cannot be solved on a narrowly nationalistic basis," he declared, "but require resolution on an all-Pakistan scale. This means that the national-democratic movement of the Baluchis can attain its objectives only in conjunction with all of the national and democratic forces of the country."[11] Belittling the "stubborn attitude" of those Baluch leaders who supported guerrilla activity during the 1960s, he praised the leaders of the Baluch "democratic movement who understood that the Baluch were not in a position to stand up to the military force of the government, which relied on monopolistic capital, imperialism and Maoism." He spoke contemptuously of the "weakness" of the guerrilla forces, their lack of coordination, and their shortages of supplies.[12]

Ibragimov pointed to the "major changes" that had contributed to the "integration of the Baluch into a nation" during the 1947–1970 period. Economic contacts with the more developed regions of Pakistan had disrupted the traditional economic and social structure, he said, leading to the growth of landless agricultural labor and a small but significant Baluch working class. The "Baluch national intelligentsia" had also grown progressively stronger, he added, and an "important turning point" in the Baluch struggle had come in the late 1960s, when the "national movement of the Baluchis became an indispensable part of the entire democratic movement in the country." Nevertheless, he threw up his hands at the magnitude of the social and economic problems confronting leaders of the Baluch Communist movement, pointing in particular to "inadequate organization and political literacy of the working class, the diversity of the economy, and the continuing influence of patriarchal and feudal-clerical circles." These problems would defy solution "for many decades," he said, adding that "strong nationalist traits still remain in the Baluchi movement, and this is a real danger for its successful development."[13]

In a 1977 review of nationality issues in Asia, a panel of Soviet specialists clearly ruled out Communist support for separatist movements in Pakistan, India, and Malaysia, pointing to these three cases as examples of "very unstable" multinational states marked by the absence of a "clearly-established ruling nation." By attempting to assert their dominance, the "larger and stronger nations" in these states, such as the Punjabis in Pakistan, invariably provoke a "narrowly nationalist particularism" on the part of the smaller nations. But along with the "incessant activity" of the centrifugal forces, centripetal forces are also "growing and becoming stronger," the panel concluded, reflecting the "growth of the supra-national community" in each of these countries and "the growing consciousness among the masses of the need to strengthen all-national unity."[14]

Soviet writers have been conspicuously silent on the issue of Baluch nationalism since the Soviet occupation of Afghanistan. However, Foreign Minister Andrei Gromyko made a thinly veiled threat that Moscow would seek to dismember Pakistan if Islamabad "becomes a springboard for aggression against Afghanistan." Speaking at a New Delhi banquet on February 12, 1980, Gromyko warned that "if Pakistan continues to serve as a puppet of imperialism in the future, it will jeopardize its existence and its integrity as an independent state."

Communist Strength in Baluchistan

Soviet unwillingness to support the Baluch aspiration for independence has cast a continuing pall over Communist organizing efforts in Baluchistan. "At first, in the 1930s, our prospects looked extremely promising," recalled K. B. Nizamani, who served as secretary of the Sind-Baluchistan branch of the Indian Communist party from 1935 to 1941. The party had recruited Ghaus Bux Bizenjo, then a rising young political activist, and Mohammed Hussain Unqa, one of the most popular Baluch poets of the day. As the independence of the subcontinent approached, however, Bizenjo, Unqa, and other Baluch "progressives" thought increasingly in terms of an independent Baluchistan. The Communist decision in 1941 to support the Pakistan movement "had a very bad effect, a very demoralizing effect, cutting the ground out from under us before we could really get started," Nizamani said.

In the decade preceding the 1947 partition of the subcontinent, the Indian Communist party's stand in support of the Pakistan movement reflected the marginal position of Baluch and Pushtun comrades in party councils and a corresponding dominance of party leaders from other parts of the subcontinent that has persisted since the creation of the Pakistan Communist party following partition. Both the Baluch and Pushtun regions were homogeneous Muslim areas where there was little fear of Hindu domination and little interest in the Pakistan cause. The Muslim League was not a dominant force in these areas, drawing its principal support from the Muslim-minority provinces that were destined to remain in India. Similarly, the Muslim Communist leadership was also concentrated in the Muslim-minority provinces, especially the populous Ganges Valley state of Uttar Pradesh, which happened to be the major center of political life under the British Raj.

After partition, many of the wealthier, better-educated Muslims in the Muslim-minority provinces migrated to Pakistan, where they assumed powerful positions in the bureaucratic and business worlds. As allies of the dominant Punjabis, these *mahajirs* (refugees) or "Hindustanis" became political targets of the minority Baluch, Pushtuns, and Sindhis. The Communist leaders who migrated to Pakistan were also suspect as *mahajirs* in the eyes of many of their locally rooted party comrades, but this did not prevent them from promptly asserting their claims to leadership of the new Pakistan Communist party.

Looking back on the aftermath of partition, Nizamani wrote in 1979 that

> since the areas constituting the western part of Pakistan did not have an effective Communist organization, the Pakistan Communist Party fell largely under the control of Punjabis and newly-arriving Hindustanis who had no understanding of the most acute contradictions in the country. From the very first day Pakistan was formed, the primary contradiction in the country was between the dictatorship of the ruling class and the suppression of the rights of the smaller nationalities. But since the majority of the so-called Communists were Pun-

jabis or Hindustanis, they considered this a secondary or minor contradiction.[15]

When Communist organizers came to Baluchistan, Nizamani recalled, they were looking for industrial workers and landless agricultural laborers who could be rallied on the basis of conventional Marxist-Leninist class appeals. Instead, they confronted a nomadic tribal society and generally hurried back to Karachi, concentrating their efforts on the migrant Baluch factory workers there. Nizamani cited, in particular, an organizer named Azizullah, who threw up his hands after discovering on several visits to Quetta in 1951 and 1952 that Baluch activists were primarily interested in talking about their "national" grievances. Azizullah did persuade Sher Mohammed Marri to start the short-lived Mazloom (Workers) party, but he devoted most of his attention to Pushtun students and other non-Baluch recruits.

By 1954, Nizamani was convinced that a conventional Marxist-Leninist approach could not win Baluch support without the added emotional appeal of the independence issue. He turned for help to his influential friend Prince Abdul Karim, who had staged the unsuccessful 1948 revolt against accession to Pakistan in which Nizamani had participated. Together, they attempted to organize a Baluch Marxist party dedicated to an independent Baluchistan. Abdul Karim was still serving a prison term for his revolt, but in March 1954, he was able to smuggle out a letter he had prepared for Nizamani's use in organizing the projected underground movement. The letter said that "in order to get out of a situation in which we are treated like Red Indians, and to find a place among the independent nations, we Baluch should unite in a single organization." Authorizing Nizamani to contact other Baluch on his behalf, Abdul Karim said that "the nation can achieve its independence only under the leadership of an organization formed with a Marxist outlook. We have failed in the past because of the lack of a scientific ideology."

The proposed party never got off the ground, Nizamani lamented, because he was unable to raise funds for organizational work, least of all from his former comrades within the Communist party of Pakistan, who disapproved of his emphasis on the independence issue. In the Baluch areas "there was not a semblance of a party organization from which to draw cadres, though there was a great deal of sympathy among some intellectuals," he explained. "We would have had to start from scratch." When Abdul Karim emerged from prison a year later, he had lost his appetite for underground activity and founded an open, legal party, the Ustoman Gal (People's party), which hewed to the Communist line that

Baluchistan should have autonomy, but within Pakistan. Nevertheless, Abdul Karim's flirtation with the idea of an autonomous Baluch national-communist party committed to independence makes an interesting historical footnote, since he is still a respected figure in Baluchistan, with his royal lineage as one of Nasir Khan's heirs, and could conceivably re-emerge at some future stage.

With the exception of Nizamani's abortive 1954 attempt, there has been no serious effort to alter the Pakistan Communist party's position on Baluch independence, which has consigned the party to continuing oblivion in the Baluch areas. Acknowledging that the Communists lost out during the 1960s to the Pararis, who combined nationalism with a vague Marxism-Leninism, Aijaz Ahmed, a Communist-oriented intellectual, said that "of course, many progressive elements supported the Baluch side, and almost all progressive Baluch forces participated in the fight at some time or other. That is precisely what makes the error so poignant." Since the guerrillas had survived by hiding out in remote, unpopulated areas, they were "unable to transform or politicize the masses. Ten years or more of guerrilla warfare has had little radicalizing impact on the masses." In an allusion to Khair Bux Marri and Ataullah Mengal, Ahmed declared that the "only appreciable result" of the insurgency had been to "prop up the leading *sardars* of the insurrection as the leaders of Baluchistan today. The *sardars* have retained their feudal power and have gained political legitimacy in addition."[16]

In a definitive, previously unpublished "strategy document" adopted at their second congress on May 1, 1976, Communist party leaders declared that "the question of national rights has not been solved in Pakistan." However, it warned party members

> to guard against the two erroneous lines found on this question in the country. The first line denies the existence of nationalities, thus strengthening the exploitation of the oppressed nationalities. The second line equates the struggle for national rights with the struggle for national states, leading to the breakup of the country into penny pockets which again, like the first line, serves the interests of reaction and imperialism as it divides the democratic struggle.

Referring only obliquely to the insurgency then raging, the third item in a list of seven priority political tasks called on party members to "participate in the just struggle of the people of Baluchistan," but enjoined them, at the same time, to "unite and connect the struggle in Baluchistan with the other democratic issues in the country." Imperialism and its agents "are trying to cut off the struggle of the Baluch people from the general anti-imperialist struggle in the country," it cautioned, "by propagating that the Baluch people are struggling for separation." Elsewhere, the "strategy document" stressed that the party's struggle for national rights includes "the right of self-determination, so that national barriers may be broken and class consciousness may develop." Communist party leaders made a gesture to Baluch leftists by declaring that "if the struggle develops faster in some sectors or some areas, that specific contingent of the overall democratic forces will be of great help in throwing back the enemy all along the line and bringing nearer the emancipation of the whole of Pakistan."[17]

The 1976 congress was actually the first ever held by the Communists in Pakistan; the first congress cited in the "strategy document" turns out to have been the 1948 congress of the Indian Communist party in Calcutta, which took place just after partition and was attended by delegates from Pakistan.

In contrast to the more liberal environment enjoyed by the Communist party of India, the Communist party of Pakistan has faced severe repression from the start. This harassment has aggravated built-in leadership rivalries and ideologically based factional tensions. The ranking refugee leader in the immediate aftermath of partition, Sajjad Zaheer, died in prison after his arrest for complicity in a 1952 left-wing coup attempt known as the Rawalpindi conspiracy case. Another dynamic refugee leader, Hassan Nasir, who was rapidly taking Zaheer's place, was tortured to death in prison in 1961 at the age of twenty-eight, throwing the party into a state of confusion from which it has never recovered. The nominal leader since Nasir's death, Imam Ali Nazish, is a reclusive ideologue who has failed to emerge as a commanding figure.

Attempting to play down his *mahajir* heritage, Nazish has dropped his last name, Imrohi, which reflects his origins in Imroha, a town in Uttar Pradesh state in India. Nonetheless, he personifies the refugee character of the party leadership. Leftist rivals dismiss his organization as a "*matarawa* (chickpea) communist party," likening it to the lowliest of the foodgrains used in Pakistan. In the absence of anything better, the Soviet Union has indicated its preference for Nazish's group as the closest thing to an "official" Communist party in Pakistan. Moscow clashed with Nazish openly only for a brief period in the early 1970s, when the party refused to go along completely with Soviet support of the Bhutto regime. However, Soviet representatives have also shown intermittent interest in some of the thirteen other groups vying for leadership of the Left in Pakistan and have given strong support to Bhutto's Pakistan People's party, especially since his execution.

Significantly, none of these dissident communist factions have a consequential organization in Baluchistan. The two most important of the thirteen rivals to the official organization are based in other areas: the Mazdoor-Kisan (Worker-Peasant) party, led by Afzal Bangash, which has a strong organization in the Pushtun region, and Rasul Bux Palejo's Awami Tehriq (People's League) in Sind. Bangash is an on-again, off-again Soviet partisan who has been operating out of Kabul and London since early 1980. When he attempted to unify some of the smaller leftist factions under his leadership in 1978, the leadership roster of his new leftist alliance failed to include a single Baluch. Palejo, a onetime Maoist, is basically a Sindhi nationalist, but he works closely with Baluch student and labor union factions in Sind.

It should be emphasized that despite the lack of a unified, tightly knit Communist movement in Baluchistan, the Soviet Union has enjoyed, more often than not, a favorable image among the Baluch. Soviet support of the Bhutto regime during the insurgency and the 1979 Russian invasion of Afghanistan have tarnished, but not fundamentally altered, this image. In Baluch eyes, Washington has been consistently and directly identified with the repression of the Baluch by successive Islamabad regimes through its military and economic aid, while Moscow, which has been arrayed against every Pakistani regime except Bhutto's, represents a potentially liberating alternative. In addition, the Baluch, like many Third World peoples, tend to identify the Soviet Union as a friend of the underprivileged, in contrast to the United States, with its multinational corporations, which is seen as a source of support for exploitative local capitalists. As for the Afghan invasion, Akber Y. Mustikhan, one of the leading Baluch businessmen, explained that most Baluch regard the descriptions of Soviet atrocities that appear in the Western press as "greatly exaggerated. They are reluctant to believe that the Russians, whom they don't know firsthand, could be worse than the Punjabis, whom they do know all too well. We talk to them of freedom, but they say, 'What freedom do we have to lose? We never had freedom like the Afghans.'"

Pointing to Pakistani and Western demands for free elections in Soviet-occupied Afghanistan, a London-based Baluch nationalist publication asked whether "these Punjabi politicians and foreigners would be willing to have free elections in occupied Baluchistan under the supervision of an impartial international organization."[18] British correspondent David Housego of the *Financial Times,* visiting Baluchistan in early 1980, reported that "a journalist's notebook is rapidly filled with the rhetoric of a people who feel bitter at having been cheated of self-government by successive Pakistani regimes, and who are now tempted to see in the Russians potential allies for their cause.... What would be the reaction if the Russians were to descend on the province? 'We would welcome them, of course,' says a senior tribal *sardar* with breathtaking abandon. His companion goes one further: 'We would ask them why they did not come earlier.'"[19]

As a result of this readiness to give Moscow the benefit of the doubt, there has always been a goodly scattering of active pro-Soviet "progressives" in Baluchistan linked with assorted leftist factions in Karachi and Lahore. Some of these factions are staunchly pro-Soviet, but most are freewheeling Marxist-Leninist groups with a vaguely Soviet-inclined program. In the 1960s, it should be noted, there were also a few pro-Chinese groups, but Peking's identification with Islamabad, and later the normalization of Sino-U.S. relations, have put these elements on the defensive in the Baluch areas. In one of its rare references to the Baluch issue, Peking showed little sympathy for Baluch aspirations, charging in 1980 that Moscow was "fomenting trouble among the Baluchis and other ethnic minorities in Pakistan and Iran in preparation for the dismemberment of the two countries."[20]

Many of the pro-Soviet activists in Baluchistan have played a key role in energizing left-oriented political groups, including the Ustoman Gal in the 1950s, the Baluch Ustoman Gal in the early 1960s, and more recently the National Awami party and the Baluch Students Organization. To cite an example, during his student years in the early 1970s, Khair Jan Baluch, former president of the BSO, kept in "fairly close touch" with Communist functionaries in Karachi. While the BSO "gives priority to its nationalist aims," he said, "it has played a role in the practical political field as a sort of communist party in Baluchistan, since there has been no effective Communist organization as such. We supported socialism and the role of Russia on many issues. For example, we joined them in supporting India in Bangladesh and in condemning the role of the Pakistan Army in Bangladesh." This kind of support is transitory, however, as the case of Khair Jan shows. By 1980, he had gone into business and was no longer active in leftist politics, though he still expressed vague pro-Soviet sympathies.

One of the more durable personalities in Baluch leftist circles has been K. B. Nizamani, who went into political exile in London in 1974, but who has continued to work actively to promote his own special, Soviet-oriented brand of Baluch nationalism. Using the pseudonym Karim Baluch, Nizamani, a sharp-witted, engaging political adventurer, publishes the monthly newspaper *Nedae Baluchistan* (Voice of Baluchistan), which claims some 3,500 subscribers, primarily Baluch migrant workers in the Arab sheikhdoms of the Persian Gulf. He has focused his efforts on the Gulf, Nizamani said, because the Baluch there have become "more cosmopolitan politically, more politically conscious" than many of the Baluch living under repressive regimes in Pakistan and Iran. Although his paper is banned by the Zia and Khomeini regimes, copies are smuggled into Pakistan and Iran and are then reproduced for underground use by his sympathizers. Given the absence of Communist support for Baluch nationalist aspirations, Nizamani added, *Nedae Baluchistan*, which mixes its nationalism with the "anti-imperialist" approach to global issues popular among Baluch youth, "has been filling a void in Pakistan, virtually serving as a political tendency, a political grouping or incipient party." His sympathizers are not comfortable with the "*mahajir*-dominated" Communist party of Pakistan and its occasional "opportunist" Baluch allies, such as Ghaus Bux Bizenjo. Instead, they work closely with independent Baluch leftist elements linked with the Marxist Sindhi nationalist Rasul Bux Palejo.

Nizamani's checkered political history has aroused understandable suspicions that there may be a hidden Soviet hand behind his present role. According to his own account, he studied in Moscow in 1934 and 1935 and spent nearly ten years in the Sind-Baluchistan branch of the Communist party before quitting as a result of its refusal to support Baluch independence. Still, he remained sympathetic toward the Soviet Union and worked in the information department of the Soviet embassy in Karachi until 1969. Fearing arrest after Bhutto began to crack down on Baluch activists, Nizamani went to Baghdad early in 1972, where he joined a group of émigré Baluch who were working with Iraqi encouragement to organize a Baluch uprising in Iran. The Iraqis were using the Baluch as one of their weapons against the Shah in retaliation for his support of the Kurdish rebellion. When Iraq and Iran made their peace, the Iraqis abandoned the Baluch as part of the bargain. Nizamani subsequently took refuge in London with his family and is now a British citizen.[21]

Although he expresses disillusionment with Moscow for its "opportunist, great-power attitude" and its indifference to the Baluch and other "smaller nations," Nizamani speaks more in sadness than in anger about the Russians. His newspaper, known until 1980 as *People's Front*, rarely wanders very far from the Soviet line except on issues relating directly to the Baluch. Even on the issue of independence, the paper equivocated in its early issues, hewing to the demand for a "socialist, federal" Pakistan made by the Pakistani Communists and most other Pakistani leftist groups. It was not until early 1979 that *People's Front* came out for sovereign independence. On the issue of the Afghan revolution, Nizamani has hailed with equal enthusiasm the Nur Mohammed Taraki coup of April 1978 and the advent of the Soviet-installed Babrak Karmal regime in December 1979.[22]

Nizamani's shift on the independence issue came in April 1979, just after Khomeini had taken power and Iraq had begun to reactivate its support for Kurdish, Khuzistani Arab, and Baluch rebels in Iran. This coincidence of timing has stirred speculation that his paper is financed by Baghdad. To complete the picture, however, it should be noted that in May 1979 he was invited as a government guest to Kabul, where he was received royally by both President Taraki and Prime Minister Hafizullah Amin. Nizamani himself laughed off suggestions that he receives Iraqi, Afghan, or Soviet financing, saying only that his shoestring operations are covered by contributions from wealthy Baluch in the Gulf, among them Sheikh Mohammed Bin Hassan Al-Mohammed, whose activities were discussed in chapter six.

My own impression, based on six conversations spanning the period from 1975 to 1981 as well as other inquiries, is that Nizamani is an independent Baluch nationalist who keeps his operations going by picking up help from Communist and non-Communist sources alike in a spirit of cheerfully unabashed opportunism. Ideologically speaking, however, his sympathies have remained consistently and frankly pro-Soviet, despite his continuing dissatisfaction with Moscow's attitude toward Baluchistan. He has never flirted with Maoism, Titoism, or other heresies and is not attracted to the kind of national-communist approach espoused by Khair Bux Marri or the Baluch People's Liberation Front. Should Moscow ever decide to support an independent Baluchistan, producing a polarization in the independence movement between nationalist and pro-Soviet elements, *Nedae Baluchistan* would in all likelihood be in the forefront of the pro-Soviet parade.

As one of the earliest recruits to the Baluch Communist movement in the 1930s, Nizamani presents a poignant figure four decades later, still struggling to reconcile his nationalism with his Moscow-oriented world view. Examined from one perspective, his experience illustrates the dispersion and fragmentation of the pro-Soviet forces in Baluchistan. Viewed from another, it serves as a reminder that Moscow has extensive latent Baluch support that it might well be able to convert into an effective Communist party should it embark on a separatist course in Baluchistan.

In the aftermath of the Soviet occupation of Afghanistan, unsubstantiated press reports have periodically emanated from Washington, Islamabad, and elsewhere stating that Moscow is training "thousands" of Baluch agents. I have no independent evidence to verify these reports, which have not been confirmed by American or Pakistani officials. However, Pakistani intelligence sources state that a dozen or more Baluch students have attended Lumumba University on Soviet scholarships during the past decade. An interesting variation on this theme has come from Inayatullah Baloch, a nationalist scholar at Heidelberg University's South Asian Institute. Moscow's "secret weapon" in Baluchistan, Baloch writes, is the existence of some 13,000 Soviet citizens of Baluch ancestry "who can be called upon to form part of a communist vanguard in Baluchistan if and when required."[23]

This is a provocative line of speculation, especially with respect to Iranian Baluchistan, since the Baluch tribes now living in the Merv area of Soviet Turkmenistan originally came from Iranian Baluchistan and southwestern Afghanistan. However, some of these tribes migrated to the Soviet Union nearly a century ago, and the most recent migrants came between 1918 and 1928. Eden Naby, a Harvard specialist on Soviet Central Asia, contends that their Baluch identity has been considerably diluted over the years. She specifically disputes Baloch's assertion that Moscow has encouraged the use of the Baluchi language and states that the Baluch in the Soviet Union have been forced to live together with Turkmens in collective farms where they have lost their tribal ties. "Given the small number of Baluch in the Soviet Union, their rapid assimilation into surrounding populations and the lack of Baluchi-language cultural facilities," she writes, "the Soviet Baluch role in future Baluch movements appears likely to be minimal."[24]

The Afghan Communists and Baluchistan

In contrast to the Soviet Union, which has emphasized the achievement of Baluch rights within Pakistan, Afghanistan has traditionally encouraged Baluch ambitions for some form of liberation from Islamabad. For their part, however, Baluch nationalists have always had mixed feelings concerning Afghan interest in their cause. This ambivalence is rooted in the well-founded belief that Afghan leaders, who are primarily Pushtuns, do not actually favor an independent Baluch state but rather the ultimate incorporation of Baluchistan into a Greater Afghanistan or an Afghan-controlled Pushtunistan.

As we have seen in chapter two, Afghanistan's seventeenth-century founder, Ahmad Shah Durrani, ruled over the Baluch state of Kalat as a tributary for fourteen years. Leaning on this slender historical reed, Kabul has periodically included Baluchistan in its sweeping irredentist claims to areas east of the Durand line. In its vaguely defined demand for Pushtunistan, Kabul has generally implied that the proposed state would embrace only Pushtun areas of Pakistan. But some maps have depicted

Baluchistan, in its entirety, as Southern Pushtunistan. While Afghan Communist leaders have made cosmetic gestures to the Baluch as a separate nationality, in keeping with Marxist-Leninist precepts on the "national question," their approach to the Baluch issue, in practice, has betrayed the same Pushtun bias shown by other Afghan leaders.

In their approach to the manipulation of Pushtun and Baluch separatism, the Khalq (People) and Parcham (Banner) factions of the Afghan Communist movement have followed radically different policies, reflecting the broader tactical differences that have divided the two groups. Khalq, led by Taraki and Amin, was initially committed to a "people's democracy" line, which ruled out united fronts with "bourgeois nationalist" leaders, while Parcham followed a Soviet-dictated "national democracy" line. Thus, Khalq refused to join Parcham in supporting the non-Communist Mohammed Daud regime, notwithstanding strong Soviet support for Daud, insisting that to do so would be a betrayal of Marxist-Leninist principles. Similarly, Khalq opposed the Parcham policy of collaborating with "bourgeois nationalists" in Pakistan such as National Awami party leaders Abdul Wali Khan and Ghaus Bux Bizenjo. Instead, Khalq favored efforts to build up Communist cadres under its aegis or to establish cooperative links with existing Communist factions.

Pointing to the fact that Wali Khan and most of his fellow NAP leaders in the Pakistani Pushtun areas were relatively big landholders, Khalq aligned itself with Afzal Bangash, leader of a Pushtun tenant-farmer movement linked with a Pakistani Communist faction mentioned earlier, the Mazdoor-Kisan (Worker-Peasant) party. Parcham, by contrast, worked mainly with a leftist NAP faction led by Ajmal Khattak. So far as can be determined, neither Khalq nor Parcham paid much attention to the Baluch areas until after their 1977 merger and the advent of the Khalq-dominated People's Democratic party regime in Kabul in 1978.

The significance of this Khalq-Parcham divergence is that Parcham followed a flexible line attuned to Soviet regional objectives, which called for efforts to achieve Pushtun and Baluch rights within Pakistan, while the Khalq policy foreshadowed what was to become a Greater Afghanistan approach. Strictly speaking, Wali Khan and his venerated father, Abdul Ghaffar Khan, leader of the anti-British Redshirt movement, had never indicated clearly whether their concept of Pushtunistan meant an autonomous Pushtun state within Pakistan, an Afghan-linked Pushtun state, or an independent Pushtun state. Like Afghan leaders, they had demanded only that the Pakistani Pushtuns be given the right of self-determination. As a practical matter, however, Wali Khan had made it increasingly clear that he was prepared to come to terms with

Islamabad if agreement could be reached on guarantees of regional autonomy.

In its first published program, the Khalq declared in April 1966 that the Durand line had been imposed upon Afghanistan "against the wishes of its people, and as a result, a part of the territory of the country was detached from its body." Since the Durand line serves as the de facto boundary of Afghanistan with both the Baluch and Pushtun areas of Pakistan, this declaration clearly implied that Baluchistan was part of the lost territory. However, the manifesto said only that "in accordance with their belief in the right of self-determination, the people of Afghanistan support the liberation movement of the people of Pushtunistan."[25]

Once in power, the Khalq-dominated People's Democratic party of Afghanistan (PDPA) continued to keep its Greater Afghanistan option open, treating the issue of Pushtun and Baluch aspirations with calculated ambiguity. In his first declaration of party principles, President Nur Mohammed Taraki called for "the solution of the national issue of the Pushtun and Baluch people," which gave cosmetic recognition to a separate Baluch identity but lumped Pushtun and Baluch aspirations together in a single "national issue."[26] Taraki denied the validity of the Durand line, as past Afghan regimes had done, declaring that Pushtun and Baluch grievances had to be redressed in the light of the "historical background." At the same time, he stressed that Afghanistan and Pakistan should settle their differences "through understanding and peaceful political talks," pointedly avoiding strident rhetoric in support of Pushtun and Baluch rights.[27]

The vagueness of his language left open the possibility that the new Communist regime, prodded by Moscow, might accept a solution of the dispute within the Pakistan framework. However, it soon became clear that there were significant differences on this issue between Taraki, the Khalq's elder statesman, and Hafizullah Amin, a strong Pushtun nationalist and an advocate of a Pushtun-controlled Greater Afghanistan, who controlled the party organization, including its cadres in the armed forces. Taraki had become leader of the PDPA, created by the merger of Khalq and Parcham, because he was more acceptable to Parcham. He had emerged as president after the 1978 coup, with Amin as foreign minister and Parcham leader Babrak Karmal as vice-president. But Amin gradually pushed Taraki and Karmal aside, and as his power grew, so did the stridency of his appeals to Pushtun and Baluch separatist feeling.

As soon as Amin became prime minister in March 1979, his Greater Afghanistan rhetoric began to intensify, reaching a climax in the July to September period, when the Kabul regime convened a series of meetings of Pushtun tribal notables from border areas where rebel activity was raging. His speeches were replete with imagery depicting Afghanistan as reaching from the Oxus River, which marks the northern boundary with the Soviet Union, to the Abasin (the Pushtu word for the Indus River in Pakistan). The Indus presently serves as the border between Pakistan's Punjab state and the Pushtun-majority Northwest Frontier Province, but it once marked the easternmost limits of the Afghan empire prior to the British Raj.

Addressing a meeting of Charmang and Bajaur tribal leaders on July 29, 1979, Amin declared that "all the nationalities from the Oxus to the Abasin are brothers from one homeland.... In Kabul, the roaring waves of the Abasin are mingled in revolutionary cascades with the waves of the Oxus. The waves of bravery of the Pushtuns and Baluchis of the whole region are reflected in the revolutionary emotions of the toilers here."[28] "Our revolution is revered and welcomed from the Oxus to the Abasin," he said on August 20, "from the mountains of Pamir to the beaches of Gwadar in Baluchistan."[29]

In a speech on September 20, 1979, he recited the names of several Afghan cities and made allusions, in the same breath, to Baluchistan; to Attock, the historic fort on the Indus symbolizing the high point of nineteenth-century Afghan expansion; and to Peshawar, once governed by an Afghan viceroy but now the capital of the Northwest Frontier Province. Amin hailed the

> great love of the toilers and laborers for their country, whether they are in Peshawar, Herat, Kandahar, Badakshan, Baluchistan, or Kabul.... Our sincere and honest brotherhood with the Pushtuns and Baluchis has been sanctified by history. They have been one body in the course of history and have lived together like one brother. Now the waves of their love and brotherhood extend from the Oxus to Attock, and they want to live side by side, embrace each other, and demonstrate this great love to the world at large.[30]

In two off-the-record interviews on June 6 and August 10, 1978, Amin spoke passionately about the injustice of the Durand line, which "tore us apart," assuring me that "we will do our historical duty when the time is right, when we have consolidated our revolution. The Pushtun and Baluch national movements are very dear to us." When I attempted to pin him down on the issue of an independent Baluchistan, however, he would say only that "time will decide the proper correlation between the Pushtun and Baluch nationalities." Later, Amin revealed his Greater Afghanistan sentiments more explicitly in an off-the-record interview with Feroz Ahmad, editor of the leftist *Pakistan Forum*. Dismissing Ahmad's contention that the Pushtuns in Pakistan were becoming economically integrated with the rest of the country, Amin declared that "the class struggle will solve all of these problems." Ahmad quotes Amin as saying that the Afghan leaders who acquiesced in the creation of a Pakistani state in 1947 based on the Durand line were "not patriotic. If they had been patriotic, this problem would have been solved a long time ago, and today there would have been one country."

During his visit to Kabul in early 1979 at the invitation of the Communist government, K. B. Nizamani, the pro-Soviet Baluch nationalist described earlier, received the impression that Amin envisaged autonomous status for the Baluch within a Greater Afghanistan. When the Khalq had first come to power, Nizamani observed, Baluch nationalists had seized hopefully on a number of straws in the wind suggesting that the Khalq might support Baluch independence. One such indication was the fact that the Baluch were treated on a par with the Pushtuns in Taraki's statements. Another was the inauguration of a government monthly in Baluchi, *Soub* (Victory). Baluch hopes reached a high point when the Taraki regime decided to rename the annual Pushtunistan Day celebration traditionally held in Kabul as Pushtunistan and Baluchistan Day and to give equal billing to Pushtun leaders and to Mir Hazar Ramkhani, leader of the Baluch People's Liberation Front. In conversation with Amin, however, Nizamani became skeptical about his intentions. Amin told Nizamani that he envisaged a federal constitution for Afghanistan patterned after the Soviet constitution, in which the Pushtun and Baluch areas of Afghanistan would be among the "national" units. The implication was that such a restructuring would facilitate the eventual incorporation of the adjacent Pushtun and Baluch areas of Pakistan into the "homeland."

The Baluch image of the Khalq regime was also affected by tensions that developed between Amin and the Afghan Baluch tribes. Despite the fact that it introduced the Baluchi language in the schools for the first time and promoted Baluch cultural activity in other ways, the Khalq government alienated many of the Baluch tribes by seeking to circumvent the established tribal leadership structure in carrying out its reform programs. An estimated 10,000 of the 90,000 Baluch living in Afghanistan migrated to adjacent areas of Iran during the Khalq regime. Some 500 to 700 of these Afghan Baluch carried on anti-Kabul resistance activity from bases in Iran. However, this group operated independently from the Islamic fundamentalist resistance organizations based in Pakistan, which are regarded as instruments of the "anti-Baluch" Zia Ul-Haq regime in Islamabad.

Significantly, Amin wanted Communist factions in the Pakistani Pushtun areas to become affiliates of the Khalq party. This policy contributed to a split in the Mazdoor-Kisan party between its veteran leader,

Afzal Bangash, who insisted on the continued autonomy of the party, and rebels who formed a new splinter group with links to the Khalq. Amin's plan to extend the Khalq organization into Pakistan was just getting started at the time of his death and had not yet involved the Baluch areas.

Although it is difficult to establish firmly, my own belief is that Amin's strong Pushtun nationalist commitment was one of the underlying factors that led the Soviet Union to decide on his removal. It was bad enough, in Soviet eyes, that he resisted KGB efforts to get control over the armed forces and the secret police and that he refused to heed Soviet counsels of restraint in handling the anticommunist tribal rebellion. Beyond this, what must have made his continued leadership of Afghanistan seem intolerable to Moscow was his refusal to follow Soviet dictates in dealing with Iran and Pakistan. While Moscow soft-pedaled its criticism of Khomeini after he took power, Amin continued to attack him, combining traditional Pushtun anti-Persian invective with Marxist-Leninist denunciations of the "obscurantist theocracy" in Teheran. More important, while Moscow wanted to play down the Pushtun and Baluch issues until it had a secure foothold in Kabul, Amin consciously used those issues to fortify his nationalist standing with his followers.

Viktor Lessiovsky, a special assistant to U.N. Secretary General Kurt Waldheim and long regarded as a top KGB operative, told me in early 1980 that "we were, quite seriously, afraid that he would get us involved in difficulties we did not want to get involved in. He was continually asking us to help equip them for actions across the border, in order to 'liberate' their territory, and we were continually trying to restrain him."

To some extent, Lessiovsky may have been engaging in "disinformation" as part of a Soviet effort to justify Amin's removal. Nevertheless, it is clear that Babrak Karmal promptly softened Kabul's rhetoric on the Pushtun and Baluch issues following his installation by the Russians in December 1979. In his first address to the Afghan people on January 1, 1980, Karmal made only a passing reference to "the right of the Pushtun and Baluch brethren to express their will and to decide for themselves about their own future destiny."[31] He reaffirmed past Afghan denials of the validity of the Durand line at his first press conference a week later, declaring that "there exists no border at all due to historical reasons. It is an open area."[32] Subsequently, a *Kabul Times* editorial deplored the "Machiavellian" use of the "Pushtunistan" issue by the Daud regime as a means of diverting attention from internal discontent, adding that "what lukewarm support of the Pushtun and Baluchi tribes the past Afghan governments have enjoyed was lost during the period of the sanguinary Amin and his rogue band."[33]

Asked in late February 1980, whether the Pushtuns and Baluch would be mobilized to counteract Pakistani support of the anticommunist rebels in Afghanistan, Karmal replied that "the national issue of the Pushtun and Baluchi nationalities in Pakistan is entirely their own. If the Pushtuns, Baluchis, or Sindhis are not satisfied with their regime, it is up to them to take any action. It is also quite clear that we have always nurtured warm fraternal sentiments toward Pushtuns and Baluchis, due to the common historical bonds binding us, but their problem is theirs."[34]

By mentioning the Sindhis together with the Pushtuns and Baluch, Karmal signaled that Kabul had shifted from a Greater Afghanistan line to one more in tune with Soviet policies on Pakistan. With the advent of the Parcham regime, Kabul gradually became a base of operations for Soviet-oriented leftist leaders operating in all parts of Pakistan, with the notable exception of Baluchistan. Imam Ali Nazish, secretary of the Pakistan Communist party, directed his campaign for a "socialist, federal" Pakistan from a Kabul headquarters. Nazish worked closely with Zulfiqar Ali Bhutto's oldest son, Murtaza, and several other leaders of the left wing of Bhutto's Pakistan People's party who announced plans to form a paramilitary People's Liberation Army. Karmal's old ally in the Pakistani Pushtun areas, Ajmal Khattak, was also restored to prominence after a period of eclipse during the Khalq regime. For the first time in a generation, Communist leaders in the Pushtun areas of Pakistan worked together in 1980 as part of a broader partnership with Kabul and with Communist units in other parts of Pakistan.

Given the strength of Pushtun opposition to the Soviet presence in Afghanistan, Khattak and other Pushtun Communist leaders have stressed economic appeals in 1980 much more heavily than the appeals to Pushtun solidarity with Kabul used in earlier years. This was a viable strategy in the Pushtun areas, where there are class-conscious tenant farmers in the fertile Peshawar Valley and small but significant pockets of industrial workers. By contrast, in Baluchistan the class struggle had not yet arrived. Communist leaders still confronted the same shortage of cultivable land and the same undeveloped, nomadic society that they had faced in the 1930s. Nationalism was still the horse to ride there, but the Communists were not ready to ride it.

There were some signs of a possible change brewing in mid-1980, notably Bizenjo's proposal, cited in chapter four, for an opposition platform demanding the right of secession for nationalities in Pakistan if Islamabad violated their constitutional autonomy guarantees. Did Bizenjo put this proposal forward on his own, seeking to keep in step with militant Baluch opinion, or was he reflecting a new climate in Moscow and in Pakistani Communist circles on the issue of an independent Baluchistan? The latter possibility was suggested by persistent rumors that Nazish had issued a secret party circular authorizing Communists to pursue the "piecemeal liberation" of Pakistan if the "liberation movement" developed more rapidly in some parts of the country than in others. Moreover, there have been increasing indications of Soviet efforts behind the scenes to stimulate indigenous Communist organizations in both Pakistani and Iranian Baluchistan.

In any event, Moscow would have to choose between two equally challenging alternatives if it should decide, at this late stage, to support Baluch independence. One would be a crash program to convert its extensive latent support in Baluchistan into a well-knit Communist machine. Another option, implying more limited goals, would be to support one or more of the Baluch nationalist leaders, recognizing full well that they might prove to be unusually obstreperous clients.

The View from Islamabad and Teheran 8

In attempting to assess the potential of the Baluch nationalist movement, this book has focused until now on how the Baluch feel and what Baluch leaders have done in past years to lay the foundations for future action. Let us now examine underlying Pakistani and Iranian attitudes toward the Baluch challenge before turning to a more detailed discussion of the prospects for compromise.

In the eyes of Pakistani and Iranian leaders, Baluch demands for regional autonomy constitute, at best, a thinly disguised form of blackmail designed to extort a disproportionate share of the benefits of economic progress or, at worst, a prelude to eventual secession. Not surprisingly, the dominant Punjabis in Pakistan, comprising 58 percent of the population, find it infuriating that a Baluch minority of less than 4 percent should seek to assert proprietary claims over Baluchistan, which represents 42 percent of the land area of the country. Similarly, in Iran, where the Baluch constitute at most 2 percent of the population, the ruling Persians, who make up 52 percent, ridicule the proposition that the Baluch have any special rights in Baluchistan. The idea of demarcating provincial units in accordance with historic ethnic homelands is anathema to the ideologues of Pakistani and Iranian nationalism. In both cases, a succession of authoritarian regimes, operating through highly centralized constitutional systems, have sought to minimize or obliterate regional identities in order to pursue modernization programs addressed to the overall needs and growth potential of their respective countries.

Discussing the Pakistani case, political scientist Robert G. Wirsing has pointed to the "awesome asymmetry" of a situation in which such a small minority demands recognition of special interests that conflict directly with the ambitions of such a powerfully entrenched majority. Militarily, as he observes, Baluchistan has become a strategic buffer of "incalculable importance" for the rest of Pakistan, especially in the wake of the Soviet invasion of Afghanistan.* In the context of their economic

---

* The military importance of Baluchistan was also underlined by reports in 1981 that Islamabad was preparing to use a site in the remote Chagai district for its first nuclear weapons test.

priorities, Pakistani planners are bound to view the sparsely settled expanses of Baluchistan as a safety valve for surplus population. Punjabi, Pathan, and Sindhi settlement of Baluch areas is "certain" to increase, he believes, "under the weight of one of the world's highest population growth rates." In a period of growing energy scarcity and spiraling energy costs, exploitation of Baluchistan's natural gas, coal, and mineral resources has become an increasingly crucial link in Pakistan's overall development effort. In contrast to the plight of forgotten minorities in some countries, Wirsing concludes, the problem confronted by the Baluch "is not that, having control of so little, they may be neglected by an indifferent majority. It is that, having control of so much, they are highly visible obstructions in the way of the majority's progress and are likely to be swept aside."[1]

Zia's Velvet Glove

In conversations on July 29, 1978, and March 8, 1980, General Zia Ul-Haq distinguished between Baluchistan, which he regards as important, and the "Baluch problem," which he believes has been greatly exaggerated by foreign observers. Referring to Baluchistan as "the most sensitive area of Pakistan," he warned that "if the Russians come there, it will be by naked aggression, and that is the only 'Baluch problem' we have to worry about." Given the military importance of Baluchistan, he declared, "we obviously cannot think of it as having something in particular to do with the Baluch. They have a provincial population equal to one third of the population of one city in the Punjab, Lahore. They have coal, gas, and oil that the whole country needs. We are one country, and the Baluch are part of our country. They can go anywhere to work. Why do you Americans and other foreigners make so much of this? Many countries have problems like this and they deal with them in the necessary way. People don't talk about their breaking up. Look at the Irish, Welsh, and Scotch in Britain. Look at Canada. Look at your own country. It may be a crude example, but take the case of your South Carolina. It is a depressed state, while California is a developed state. What would you think if the demand should be raised that Carolina should have the same status as California?"

On the critical autonomy issue, Zia made clear that he has little sympathy for the concept of a "multinational" Pakistan in which Baluch, Pushtuns, Sindhis, and Punjabis are entitled to local self-rule. "I simply cannot understand this type of thinking," he said earnestly, pausing to reflect on the matter. "We want to build a strong country, a unified country. Why should we talk in these small-minded terms? We should talk in terms of one Pakistan, one united, Islamic Pakistan." If circumstances should ever permit, he commented at one point in our 1978 conversation, he would "ideally" like to break up the existing provinces and replace them with fifty-three small provinces, erasing ethnic identities from the map of Pakistan altogether. President Ayub Khan's One Unit concept was a valid one, he stated, and it was "unfortunate for the country" that Yahya Khan had "surrendered to pressures," and created the existing provinces. Nevertheless, "what is done is done," he emphasized, and for the sake of national unity he would adhere to the constitution adopted in 1973, which defines a "very liberal" type of federation in which the provinces enjoy "much more power than they do in the United States or in most federations."

Zia said flatly that he would "not consider for one moment" proposals by Baluch leaders for amendments to the 1973 constitution that would rule out central intervention to dismiss an elected state regime. "We won't go beyond the 1973 constitution," Zia declared. "There was a national consensus on this constitution, more of a consensus than we have ever had before. We would be opening a Pandora's box if we were to admit the possibility of changing it by one iota." Given Pakistan's record of political instability, Zia added, it would be "suicidal" for Islamabad to relinquish its right to intervene in politically disturbed provinces. Indeed, if there is a need to alter the constitution, he went on, "it would be in the direction of strengthening it rather than weakening it." For example, he speculated, "it might be appropriate" for Pakistan to emulate the Turkish constitution, which explicitly empowers the army to take over political power when it deems such intervention necessary in the national interest.

Until taking power from Zulfiqar Ali Bhutto in July 1977, Zia reflected, "I had never met a politician, and I must confess that I am continually amazed at the way they think." He questioned the meaning of the 1970 elections held by Bhutto, in which Ghaus Bux Bizenjo, Ataullah Mengal, and Khair Bux Marri emerged as the pre-eminent leaders of the Baluch. These elections were "based on emotional grounds, on ethnic appeals, on the politics of negation," he explained, "rather than on reason and national considerations." Thus, they produced " a certain group of leaders who had a particular trend of mind" and were not representative of the Baluch as a whole. Even so, Zia maintained, Bhutto and the Baluch leaders both deserved a share of the blame for the confrontation that led to the 1973–1977 insurgency. "It was the first time they had ever had power," he said of Bizenjo, Mengal, and Marri, "and they took the bit in their teeth, even though Bhutto was holding the reins. They did childish things, saying that the police must

*President Zia Ul-Haq of Pakistan
greets a Baluch elder
on a 1980 visit to Baluchistan*

be from Baluchistan, giving out arms openly to their friends, trying to put all powers in the hands of local officials. National interests were forgotten and they had only regional interests in mind. But it should have been handled politically. You can't solve a problem like that through military means. They played into his hands, they gave him the grounds for doing what he did, and he took advantage of it. It wasn't the constitution that was at fault. If something isn't implemented properly, you shouldn't blame the system."

When he released Bizenjo, Mengal, and Marri from prison in 1977, Zia initially accorded them recognition as the legitimate spokesmen for the Baluch by holding a series of meetings with them to discuss mutually agreed machinery for the administration of amnesty and postinsurgency rehabilitation programs. As indicated in chapter four, however, these discussions broke down in 1978 when the three Baluch leaders, charging that the projected machinery would be Punjabi-controlled, insisted on the replacement of Raja Ahmad Khan, the Punjabi chief secretary who presided over the Baluchistan state government. Zia angrily refused to remove Khan. Instead, he attempted to appease the Baluch by appointing a suave, non-Punjabi military intellectual, Lt. Gen. Rahimuddin Khan, as the provincial governor in place of an unpopular, blunt Punjabi officer, Lt. Gen. Ghulam Mohammed. The new governor proved to be less abrasive than the old, but the Baluch "triumvirate" maintained that the real power in Baluchistan still rested with the Punjabi bureaucrats.

Since the rupture of the 1978 talks, Zia has gradually written off hopes for a reconciliation with Bizenjo, Mengal, and Marri and has looked for other Baluch leaders whom he considers to be "more sensible, more levelheaded, and less emotional, around whom a new consensus can emerge." As an example of such leaders, he cited Doda Khan Zarakzai, leader of the cohesive but numerically small Zarakzai tribe, who "has as much support as Mengal." Zarakzai is one of a handful of Baluch adherents of the Muslim League who have cooperated with successive Islamabad regimes. Once powerful as the party that founded Pakistan, the League was renovated by Ayub Khan as his political vehicle but became virtually inoperative during the seventies and has never had a significant following in Baluchistan except among non-Baluch.

Zia stressed that Baluchistan has a "significant" number of non-Baluch. While sidestepping the controversy over the proportion of non-Baluch in the provincial population, he said that the Pushtuns and other minorities "would continue to play an important role in the province." Zia's most effective allies in Baluchistan are among the Pushtuns, notably the powerful, landowning Jogezai family. However, the Baluchistan branch of Bhutto's former People's party is Pushtun-dominated and has been bitterly anti-Zia.

Despite Zia's refusal to hold new elections and his failure to work out a *modus vivendi* with Bizenjo, Mengal, and Marri, he sharply contrasted his own approach to the Baluch with Bhutto's "needlessly provocative" policies and said that he would be careful to avoid comparable assaults on Baluch pride. "All that these people want is sympathetic consideration," he said. "We have no grudge against them." Even Bizenjo, Mengal, and Marri, he added, had been "unnecessarily built up as having anti-Pakistan secessionist tendencies." As a result of his policy of "non-provocative" firmness, Zia contended, "what you people call the 'Baluch problem' will gradually subside." Thus, he recalled, he had shrugged it off when Akbar Bukti, leader of the Bukti tribe, had made inflammatory statements "that were secessionist in tenor and could have justified serious measures." Similarly, he had ordered army units in Baluchistan to maintain a low profile in Baluch villages, though "we will not consider, for one moment, demands that have been made for the withdrawal of the army from the interior of Baluchistan. The army has to be housed somewhere, you know. We have had cantonments in Baluchistan since the British days, and we need them there now more than ever, with the Russians breathing down our necks." When funds became available from the United States or other sources, he added, Pakistan would build new airfields at Sibi and elsewhere in the Baluch areas bordering Afghanistan.

Bhutto's Chess Game

In depicting his approach to the Baluch as a more benevolent one than his predecessor's, Zia flatly contradicted Bhutto's own version of the historical record. Shortly before his execution, Bhutto told the supreme court that Zia, as army chief of staff, had consistently blocked his efforts to wind down the 1973–1977 insurgency. Zia displayed an "almost paranoid" attitude toward the Baluch, Bhutto alleged, bitterly opposing proposals for troop withdrawals and for the release of the imprisoned Baluch leaders. "He used to argue very emotionally in meetings," recalled Bhutto, "saying that the army had given its blood against the Baluch traitors and would fight to the finish until the enemy was crushed. He repeatedly spoke of the Baluch leaders as traitors who had never wanted Pakistan in the first place." Blaming Zia for the mid-1977 breakdown of negotiations on a coalition government that provided the pretext for the army's coup, Bhutto said that the principal stumbling block in his discussions with opposition leaders was the issue of releasing the Baluch leaders and other political prisoners, on which the army was adamant. "I was willing to do this, as I had been for some time," Bhutto stated, "but the army wouldn't hear of it." Yet ironically, Bhutto observed in his submission to the supreme court, Zia promptly did an about-face on this issue after taking power "for the blatantly obvious political purpose of presenting himself as a liberator."[2]

Bhutto's allegations against Zia were broadly consistent with the tenor of statements that he made to me during conversations on December 15, 1974, and January 21, 1977. Against the background of earlier off-the-record exchanges in which we had discussed the army's political role in Pakistan, he confided in our 1974 conversation that he still faced a "delicate situation" in handling his generals but thought he would eventually be able to bring them under full control. While heatedly defending his dismissal of the Baluch state regime and his imprisonment of the Baluch leaders, Bhutto was somewhat defensive in responding to my questions about the counterinsurgency operations then in progress. He clearly implied that the army had embarked on a much bigger and more freewheeling campaign than he had sanctioned or envisioned. Similarly, in our 1977 talk, he spoke lightly of letting the generals "play their games in Baluchistan, though it's really all over, completely over."

Despite their differences, Zia and Bhutto shared broadly similar views with respect to the desirability of a unitary constitutional system for Pakistan. Bhutto would have endorsed Zia's categorical rejection of Baluch demands for a loose federalism. Since I had written a book dealing with India's problems as a multilingual state,[3] Bhutto used me as a sounding board, on several occasions, for some of his own reflections on the difficulties posed by Pakistan's ethnic diversity. One of those occasions was a conversation in Dacca on March 23, 1971, just four days before the Pakistan Army launched the brutal repression of the Bengalis that provoked the Bangladesh independence struggle. Bhutto said that he saw little chance of holding Pakistan together, blaming Sheikh Mujibur Rahman, the Bengali leader, for "a reckless attitude, typical of the unthinking emotionalism of these Bengalis that makes it impossible to talk reason to them." But he mused that a separation "might not be an undivided disaster, after all, because we are a very unwieldy country now, and the only way to keep together would be to have a type of loose constitutional arrangement that would provide a dangerous precedent for West Pakistan, where the Baluch would demand the same thing. We might be better off with a smaller but more manageable and more compact Pakistan. We would still be one of the bigger countries in the world." Clearly expecting to be the leader of such a truncated Pakistan, Bhutto said that the ethnic differences in West Pakistan were "not a small thing, but we are geographically contiguous and I can manage it. I know them and I can handle them. Baluchistan can never be Bangladesh."

When we met in December 1974, Bhutto recalled this conversation. He volunteered that he was "more convinced than ever that we have the basis for a more viable country now" and expounded at length on his plans for dealing with the rebellious Baluch. The idea of a confederation was " a ridiculous one for a country that wants to count for something in the world," he declared. "It would never work, and the smart ones know it. Bizenjo knows it very well; he's the smartest. It's a slogan. There was nothing wrong with our constitution. It wasn't Bizenjo's fault that we had to step in last year. The others pushed him." What role had the Shah played in his 1973 decision to dismiss the Baluch regime? "The Shah wanted us to take strong action, of course," Bhutto replied. "It was a convenient way to please him, but we knew what we were doing. We knew what we wanted."

In our 1977 conversation, Bhutto stressed that his approach to the Baluch differed completely from that of his predecessors, Ayub Khan and Yahya Khan, who had been correct in branding the *sardari* system a "medieval hangover," but who had erred in attempting to uproot it purely through military means. "I recognize that the *sardari* system is a symbol of their identity for many Baluch," Bhutto said. "You can't get rid of it overnight without putting something in its place, something substantial in the form of economic modernization. This is what we have been trying to do, and the *sardars* realize they are done for if we can do it, if we can get roads in, schools in, hospitals in. That is why they are opposing us. They know that if we destroy the *sardari* system, we will destroy Baluch identity, or at least begin the process of destruction." When I noted that most of the *sardars* were on his side and that Bizenjo, Mengal, and Marri professed to be in favor of land reforms, he scolded me for "talking in clichés. You know it's all a charade. We will deal with 'our' *sardars* when we don't need them any more. As for the 'progressive' Mr. Mengal and Mr. Marri, they are hypocrites. They have never really given up their power as *sardars,* and they will do so only when we force them to accept modernization."

In retrospect, one of the most significant aspects of my exchanges with Bhutto concerning the Baluch was that he did not depict the Baluch leaders as inevitably committed to secession. "Some of them have romantic notions," he said in 1977. "They don't know what they want, like Marri. But most of them are just bargaining with us, like Bizenjo and perhaps Mengal. Well, we are ready to bargain, but we're not willing to submit to blackmail." Many Pakistanis deeply resent "these blackmail tactics, these threats," he said, because "they can't forget that the Baluch leaders never wanted to be a part of Pakistan in the first place. There is a feeling of deep distrust, a feeling that if we give them an inch, they will move, bit by bit, toward secession. I don't agree; I think we have to bargain, but we won't submit to blackmail."

Bhutto's abrupt flip-flop from a soft line to a hard line in dealing with the Baluch epitomized the opportunism that marked so much of his career. In agreeing to the establishment of the first Baluch-controlled state government, headed by a popularly based Baluch leader, Bizenjo, Bhutto went far beyond what any other Pakistani leader before or since has done in seeking to work out a *modus vivendi* with the Baluch. He felt that he had a tacit understanding with Bizenjo that would preserve his own control, and he saw the Baluch as allies in his efforts to counter the power of the army. When he concluded that Bizenjo could not control the situation, Bhutto reversed course, calculating that he had more to gain politically from pursuing the repressive policies favored by the army. As it happened, however, this calculation proved to be his undoing, since his five-year embroilment in Baluchistan imposed crippling economic and political stresses on his regime that set the stage for Zia's takeover.

As a member of the Sindhi minority, Bhutto did not share what he called the "majoritarian complex" of his Punjabi allies. To him, the Baluch, like the Punjabis, were simply pawns on his personal political chessboard. By contrast, as he observed, many Punjabi and *mahajir* leaders "subconsciously equate 'Pakistan' with their own ethnic group and believe that the only way to preserve Pakistan is to dominate or absorb others. Remember, the feelings of distrust are very deep, going back to the conflicts before partition."

In the minds of Mohammed Ali Jinnah and the other Muslim League leaders in undivided India who fought for the creation of Pakistan, a new Islamic state was a sacred imperative to forestall oppression by the overwhelming Hindu majority in the subcontinent. The Muslim Leaguers saw themselves as the heirs to the noble tradition of the Moghul Empire and guardians of its cultural as well as its religious legacy. In this perspective, Baluch and Pushtun leaders who refused to support partition and gave direct or indirect help to the Hindu-dominated Congress party were nothing less than traitors to their Islamic heritage. Baluch and Pushtun leaders, citing various statements by Jinnah, have sought to prove that he would have favored a loose federation. In support of this view, they point to the original formulation of the Pakistan concept in the League's 1940 Lahore Resolution, which envisaged a loosely defined confederation (see chapter nine).[4] However, this contention is heatedly rejected by most *mahajirs* and their Punjabi allies, who identify Jinnah's "ideology of Pakistan" with a unitary state.

The contention that Baluch leaders want regional autonomy as a prelude to secession invariably emerged as a central theme in my conversations with Punjabi leaders. "It should not be surprising that we should look with some caution toward the behavior of leaders who were opposed to the original concept of Pakistan," commented Riaz Husain, a justice of the Pakistan supreme court who served as a U.N. delegate from Pakistan in 1979. "After all, as soon as he became president of Bangladesh, Sheikh Mujibur Rahman confessed that he had been working for independence since 1956. We don't understand why you Americans should raise questions about our constitution. When other countries suppress separatists, no one objects. There are other multiethnic countries in the world, you know. Look at the Philippines! Look at Nagaland! Look at Switzerland, or the USSR, or the United States itself! There is nothing defective about the constitution of Pakistan!"

Grievances voiced by the Baluch "should be objectively investigated and remedied," said Justice Husain, "and Baluchistan should, of course, be developed, since it is quite backward. But we will not be blackmailed, and we will not depart from national priorities." He laughed off Baluch complaints that it was unfair for 80 percent of the natural gas obtained from the Sui fields, in Baluchistan, to be used by industries in the Punjab and Sind. On the contrary, he declared, "it would be very unfair to the Punjab if special arrangements should be made for the use of Sui gas in Baluchistan whether or not there is commercial justification for it. If we are one country, then does it matter who uses a given product? Should we charge them a special tax for the wheat and rice that we send to them?" In any event, he added, corruption had made it difficult to promote industrialization in Baluchistan, since "if a permit for a factory is given to a Baluch, he will more often than not sell it to a Punjabi for his own private gain."

As for Baluch objections to Punjabi settlement of farm land in Baluchistan, Justice Husain countered that the Baluch "have traditionally disdained farming, and they had not farmed the land themselves, so what could they expect?" Similarly, he dismissed charges that the Baluch are underrepresented in civil service and military posts. The Baluch had been given "more than their share" of the civil service quota, he maintained, "but they didn't qualify."

"You Can't Trust Them"

Talking with Iranian leaders, I encountered attitudes toward the Baluch issue strikingly similar to those expressed in Islamabad. The late Prime Minister Amir Abbas Hoveida, interviewed in January 1977, observed that "there are not very many of them, are there? But they happen to live in a strategic part of the country. Should we let them use this accident of geography and history to provoke us into devoting precious resources to develop that wretched part of the country? Why not move them elsewhere, where development is more rational?"

Echoing the Shah's preoccupation with Soviet manipulation of Baluch nationalism, discussed in chapter six, Hoveida exclaimed that "if it were not for the Soviet Union and its friends in Iraq, we would not give such inflated importance to such a small part of our population." In a similar vein, Foreign Minister Mahmud Khalatbary, who had served as director general of the Central Treaty Organization, recalled that "in CENTO, we always assumed that the Baluch would attempt to create their own independent state some day, with Soviet support, so it was desirable to keep them as politically weak, disunited, and backward as possible."

One of those most directly concerned with the Shah's policy toward the Baluch was Manuchehr Zelli, who served as Iranian ambassador to Pakistan from 1973 to 1978 and had just returned to assume the post of undersecretary of state for political affairs when I interviewed him in Teheran. "The Baluch tribal leaders are used to having their own way," said Zelli in August 1978, "and it will take a long time to erase these attitudes left over from history and get them to become part of our countries. It's at least a twenty-five-year problem. In both countries, it will take strong, guided governments to lead the Baluch out of their difficulties." I asked him what he thought of Ghaus Bux Bizenjo's argument that a hard-line approach would only stiffen Baluch resistance to integration in Pakistan and Iran and that concessions to demands for regional autonomy would strengthen the hands of Baluch moderates. "You can't trust the Baluch leaders," he declared. "They will say anything that suits them at a particular time, but their ultimate objective is independence. They will only take advantage of weakness and concessions in order to move toward this ultimate objective."

In Pakistan and Iran alike, the specter of an independent Baluchistan tends to discourage development expenditures that are not directly related to military needs. This linkage was explicitly articulated by Mohammed Islami, the governor general of Iranian Baluchistan. Interviewed with four of his aides in Zahedan in August 1978, Islami said that the province had been "unstable in the past, and we should wait to see what happens before we make excessive financial commitments here." In any event, he said, "it would be a mistake to look on the development of Baluchistan as a particular economic challenge in and of itself. No, we should look at the province in terms of the whole nation, concentrating on how we can reform the social habits of the people while improving their welfare. We must see how we can unite this area with other, more developed areas in such a way as to advance the country as a whole. For example, it may be of no use to have educated people here, given the backwardness of the area, but we can use them in other parts of the country."

As indicated in chapter six, the Persian-dominated Khomeini regime pursued a more liberal approach toward the Baluch during early 1979 but subsequently displayed attitudes similar to those evidenced by the Shah and his aides. The only significant difference is that the new government points to the possibility of American, as well as Soviet, support for Baluch independence. "The Baluch?" said former foreign minister Ibrahim Yazdi, answering a question following a 1979 appearance in New York. "Why do you ask about the Baluch? If the superpowers would stop interfering, this would not be a problem for us."

The Independence Issue: Problems and Prospects

9

With each passing year, the angry stalemate between Baluch leaders and the Pakistani and Iranian governments continues to deepen. The Baluch nationalist struggle is steadily growing in intensity as hopes for a political settlement wane. At the same time, as the preceding analysis shows, the nationalist forces have not yet achieved a degree of unity and discipline comparable to such tightly organized guerrilla movements as the Polisario in the Sahara.[1] In the absence of large-scale foreign support, the Baluch movement appears unlikely to prevail over two determined central governments equipped with modern weaponry, and the prospects for such foreign help, or for direct foreign intervention, remained murky in early 1981.

Whether or not there is foreign involvement, the Baluch issue seems certain to trigger an ugly cycle of intermittent bloodshed and destruction unless some basis for compromise can be found between the Pakistani and Iranian governments, on the one hand, and Baluch nationalist leaders on the other. This chapter will explore the critical economic and political factors that are likely to govern the attitudes of the two sides toward possible negotiations on a political settlement: What has been accomplished, to date, in the economic development of the Baluch areas? What is the basis for Baluch charges of economic neglect and exploitation? Would an independent Baluchistan be economically viable? How secure are the political and cultural foundations of Baluch nationalism? Is compromise still possible, and if so, on what terms?

The Development Debate

By any yardstick, Baluchistan is clearly Pakistan's most impoverished province. In 1976, its per capita income was only $54 per year, compared to $80 for the Punjab, $78 for the Sind, and $60 for the Northwest Frontier.[2] Its literacy rate is only 6 to 9 percent, while the national average is 16 percent.[3] Life expectancy in rural Baluchistan was only forty-two years in 1977, as against a national average of sixty.[4]

Surveying the record of previous Pakistani regimes in overcoming this poverty, the Zia government presented a gloomy judgment. "By and large," concluded a 1980 Information Ministry review,

> it has been the general practice of the previous governments to
> hurriedly draw up a panel of development schemes sector-wise, sup-
> ported by guess estimates of costs, and to launch them without un-
> dertaking proper studies. As a result, a number of schemes used to
> drag on for years without achieving the targets. And when, at long
> last, some schemes reached a stage of fruition, these were found to
> be faulty and economically unsound or completed at tremendous
> expense to the state with enormous leakages through corrupt prac-
> tices.

When the first provincial government was formed in 1972, the review
said, "it was hoped that progressive programs would be launched to
better the lot of the people." But then came the insurgency, which the
report described as "a serious deterioration of the law and order situation." It was only after Zia stepped in to restore order in July 1977, the
study concluded, that the work of economic development could seriously
begin.[5]

At first glance, it might be assumed that Baluch nationalists would
applaud this negative appraisal of the pre-1977 Pakistani record, while
reserving judgment with respect to Zia's claim that a "new dawn" has now
broken for Baluchistan. But in reality, the nationalist perspective is an
altogether different one. In Baluch eyes, what previous regimes have
done in Baluchistan has been too much, not too little, because it has been
exploitative in character. To the extent that development efforts have
taken place at all, in this view, outside interests, backed by the Islamabad
bureaucracy, have been getting the lion's share of the profits from the
state's resources, which are rapidly being depleted without any lasting
benefit to Baluchistan itself.

As indicated earlier, natural gas has been the most significant focus
of controversy. The Sui gas fields (see Figure 3), discovered in 1953, in
the Bukti tribal area of Baluchistan, have recoverable reserves estimated
at nearly 9 trillion cubic feet and were producing more than 400 million
cubic feet a day in 1980. Originally developed by British firms, the fields
are now controlled by the central government. Sui gas provides more
than 80 percent of Pakistan's total gas production and saves an estimated
$275 million per year in foreign exchange. Yet royalties to the Ba-
luchistan state treasury from Sui gas production totaled only $1.23 mil-
lion during 1979–1980.[6] The royalty rate in 1981 was 12.5 percent of the
well-head price, as against the 45 percent rate enjoyed by the petroleum-
producing provinces of Canada, and the well-head price was $0.06 per
1,000 cubic feet, as against $1.90 in Canada.[7]

All of the gas produced from the Sui fields has been piped either northward to the Punjab and the Northwest Frontier Province or southward to the Sind. Similarly, when another gas field with reserves half as big as those at Sui was discovered at nearby Pirkoh in 1977, Pakistani officials promptly announced plans for piping it to already developed industrial centers in the Punjab and the Sind, ignoring Baluchistan altogether. As the Baluch observed, they are caught in a vicious circle in which industrialization plans have been delayed pending plans for a gas pipeline, while pipeline plans have been delayed until a commercial demand is demonstrated.

Next to natural gas, the most important mineral resource so far developed in Baluchistan is coal. Discovered during the British period, the ten principal Baluchistan mines, all of them now owned by non-Baluch operators, yielded an estimated annual value of $25 million in 1980. As in the case of gas, most of the coal produced goes to fuel industries elsewhere. Coal is scarce and expensive in Quetta, despite the city's proximity to the mines. Moreover, "we don't see any of the profits from these mines invested in Baluchistan," wrote Mir Khuda Bux Marri, the Baluch historian, who became chief justice of the Baluchistan High Court during the Zia regime.* "They take the money to the Punjab and to Karachi. Very little of it comes back to us even for the improvement of the mines, which are old and technologically obsolete." As Justice Marri noted, many of the mines still use open kerosene lamps instead of safety lamps, and there were 394 mine accidents in Baluchistan between 1973 and 1977, one of the highest rates in the world.[8]

In contrast to the coal industry, the marble-quarrying monopoly in Baluchistan is held by a Baluch entrepreneur, Nabi Bux Zehri, who has supported successive Islamabad regimes politically in exchange for government licenses and credits. There are also several lesser Baluch businessmen who have achieved their success largely through political cooperation with Islamabad, as well as one Baluch multimillionaire, Akber Y. Mustikhan, discussed in chapter five, who supports the nationalist movement. For the most part, however, the leading private entrepreneurs in Baluchistan in 1980 were non-Baluch. Nationalist leaders complain that

* Justice Marri was dismissed by General Zia Ul-Haq in March 1981 after Marri issued a stay of execution of a Baluch student leader charged with attempting to murder an Omani military officer who was recruiting Baluch as mercenaries for the Omani army. (For an account of this case, see Lawrence Lifschultz, "A Fundamental Debate," *Far Eastern Economic Review*, 13 March 1981, pp. 21–22). Marri's insistence on judicial independence touched off Zia's promulgation of a Constitutional Order that bypassed judicial authority and led to the resignation of four other state High Court judges and three justices of the Pakistani supreme court.

even Baluch businessmen show little interest in developing the province. Zehri, for example, set up his marble-carving factory in Karachi, where he lives, rather than in Baluchistan. Shortly before Bhutto dismissed their regime in 1973, Bizenjo and Mengal had announced plans to make marble a state government monopoly and to shift carving operations to several new factories in the Baluch hinterlands.

One of the principal grievances voiced by Baluch nationalists is that even in the few local mines and industries, outsiders get the best jobs. *Jabal,* the organ of the Baluch People's Liberation Front, alleged that of forty employees at the Goonga barite mine near Khuzdar in 1975, fifteen non-Baluch workers received wages three times higher than the Baluch workers there.[9] It is difficult to authenticate such charges, which are legion, or to judge the rejoinders, which generally cite the lack of appropriately trained manpower among the nomadic Baluch.

However, there is general agreement that the Baluch are grossly underrepresented in civil service jobs and thus have little or no say in the governmental decisions that shape their economic lives. According to official figures, of 830 higher civil service posts in Baluchistan, only 181 were held by Baluch in 1979, and almost all of those were minor posts. There was one Baluch among the twenty state officials holding the rank of departmental secretary, and one Baluch enjoyed the rank of director. There were no Baluch among the four local commissioners, and only one among the sixteen deputy commissioners. The inspector-general of police and his four deputies were non-Baluch, as were 70 percent of the police force.[10] Nationalist leaders contend that even these figures are misleading because many of those enumerated as Baluch are actually "Baluchistani" Pushtuns.

In any event, the Zia government, acknowledging Baluch complaints of underrepresentation in civil service posts, promised in 1980 that it would make Baluch representation in federally controlled bureaucratic posts commensurate with the 3.9 percent Baluch share of the national population. The economic review cited earlier said that "over 350" Baluch had been recruited for government jobs since the army takeover and that "the process will be continued on a recurring basis."[11] So far as can be determined, there are only a few dozen Baluch in the armed forces, mostly detribalized Baluch from Karachi. Stephen Cohen, who studied the army in 1980, said there were "very few" Sindhis or Baluch in its ranks.[12]

Pakistani officials point to a $1.97-billion Special Development Plan for Baluchistan unveiled in late 1980 as evidence that the Zia regime is more sensitive to Baluch concerns than were its predecessors. The plan envisages $765 million in road construction, much of it designed to link Baluchistan with neighboring provinces; $147 million in railroad construction; a $300-million copper-mining project at Saindak in the northwest corner of the state, near the Iranian border; a $200-million iron mine at Chagai; a $67-million, 210-mile natural gas pipeline from the Sui fields to Quetta; and a variety of smaller projects embracing education, dams, irrigation, and rural electrification. Out of the $1.97 billion total, $472 million would be required in foreign exchange, including $250 million for the Saindak project and $33 million for the Quetta gas pipeline. When Zia visited Washington in late 1980, he presented the plan to World Bank president Robert McNamara, requesting the bank's help. However, in early 1981, the fate of the Saindak project and the Quetta gas pipeline remained uncertain. Most of the other projects were still in the planning stage and did not yet figure in Islamabad's announced budgetary allocations.

The most ambitious of the projects in the Special Plan is the $300-million Saindak copper-mining venture. In the first stage of this project alone, officials said, more than 1,000 mining jobs will be created, and these will go primarily to local Baluch. Nationalist leaders point out, however, that the first stage is only the tip of the iceberg. Once the mine is built, they maintain, ancillary smelting and processing facilities could create at least 9,000 more jobs. The nationalists want assurances that these smelting and processing facilities will be set up in Baluchistan rather than in established industrial centers. Cost-conscious Islamabad planners object that local facilities would necessitate the construction of new townships and other costly infrastructural investments in order to make the desolate Saindak area suitable for industrial activity. But in the nationalist perspective, most of the profits expected to result from Saindak should rightfully flow back to Baluchistan rather than to other more developed parts of Pakistan.

According to a U.N.-assisted study, the Saindak ore deposits are likely to yield not only 412 million tons of copper, but also gold, silver, pyrite, and magnetite with an overall potential value of at least $4 billion. Steel billets can be manufactured from the magnetite and pyrite deposits, the study said, and sulfuric acid can be obtained as a by-product of the copper-smelting process. Islamabad hopes to start operations at Saindak in 1983, which could mean a production level of 22 million tons of finished blister copper per year by 1993. That level of production would bring in an estimated $92 million annually in foreign exchange, assuming a $1 per pound copper price and a $70 per ton price for sulfuric acid.[13] But in early 1981, Islamabad had not yet found adequate private foreign investment capital, and Saindak's prospects depended on a favorable response from the World Bank or assistance from private investors backed by the bank's International Finance Corporation.

Officials of the American Smelting and Refining Company (ASARCO) dismissed the U.N. study as "extremely over-optimistic." Pointing to the low grade (0.4 percent) of the Saindak deposits and the high production costs likely to result from the isolated location of the mine, ASARCO sources questioned the profitability of the Saindak venture and said that its revenues would probably not exceed $60 million per year at a $1 copper price. However, these sources said that U.S. Geological Survey aerial studies had revealed the existence of "significant" copper prospects in the vast belt to the west and north of Saindak reaching as far as the Sar Cheshmeh area of Iran, where the Shah's regime had found high-grade (2 percent) copper deposits (see Figure 3). ASARCO exploration manager R. L. Brown said that the Saindak–Sar Cheshmeh belt was "one of the five or six most promising unexplored copper areas in the world, from a strictly geological point of view, leaving politics aside." Most of this area is in Baluchistan, though Sar Cheshmeh itself is not.

The emphasis on road construction in the Special Plan is consistent with Islamabad's past approach to Baluchistan. Despite the Zia government's disparaging assessment of the economic achievements of previous regimes, there has clearly been significant progress over the past three decades in the construction of new road networks in Baluchistan. The Bhutto regime, in particular, pointed with pride to its record in road-building, blaming the lack of roads in the province on the desire of the *sardars* "to keep their feudal preserves closed to commerce and the traffic in men and ideas that would threaten their power." By 1976, said a Bhutto white paper, the army had built 562 miles of new roads, including a key link from Sibi to Maiwand, which cut down what had been a 340-mile journey to 65 miles.[14]

While grudgingly acknowledging the economic impact of Islamabad's road construction, Baluch nationalists argue that the location of many of the new roads was not determined in accordance with economic priorities. Instead, they say, the army put its roads where they were needed to penetrate to inaccessible guerrilla strongholds. In the case of the Marri area, nationalist spokesmen concede that Islamabad had an economic objective in seeking to build roads that would open up oil exploration activity. However, they contend that Islamabad's oil development program typifies the exploitative character of its economic approach to Baluchistan, since the resulting profits would go mainly to Pakistani government coffers and to foreign oil companies rather than to the Baluchistan treasury. To the leaders of the Baluch People's Liberation Front, the fact that they were able to hold up the construction of thirty-six miles of oil-related road-building for nearly five years was one of the more notable achievements of their guerrilla struggle. Conversely, to the Bhutto regime, the army's success in ultimately getting the roads finished was a momentous breakthrough that would permit the eventual resumption of the oil exploration activities abandoned during the 1973–1977 insurgency. In its 1980 economic review, the Zia government, taking credit for the army's previous road-building efforts in Baluchistan, promised to give priority to a long-pending Karachi–Quetta road, as well as to another major new highway designed to integrate Baluchistan with the Punjab.[15]

In addition to its impressive record of road construction under extremely difficult logistical conditions, Islamabad can also point to significant achievements in electrification and in the expansion of educational facilities. In 1972, the total electric power generation capacity in Quetta and a surrounding thirty-square-mile area was 17.5 million watts and in the remainder of Baluchistan only 15 million. By 1976, a 25-million-watt gas turbine had been installed in Quetta and the power-generating capacity in the rest of the province had increased to 40 million watts. Similarly, in September 1949, there were 186 primary schools, 23 secondary schools, and 60 adult education centers in the entire province, serving only 18,500 students. By 1978, there were 2,848 educational institutions of all types in Baluchistan, with 1.6 million students. These included 2,372 primary schools, 426 secondary schools, 19 junior colleges, 9 colleges, 5 technical colleges, and Baluchistan University.

Pakistan's approach to the expansion of education in Baluchistan contrasts markedly with the Shah's deliberate attempt to prevent the politicization of the Iranian Baluch by keeping educational facilities at a minimum. In most other spheres of economic development, however, Islamabad and Teheran pursued broadly similar economic policies toward Baluchistan, neglecting many critical areas, such as water development, while giving disproportionate attention to others, notably road construction, for military reasons. Ironically, under its aid program, Teheran provided funds for a cement factory and two textile mills in Pakistani Baluchistan, which surpassed what it spent on comparable industrial development ventures in the Iranian Baluch areas.

Prime Minister Amouzegar's ambitious programs for Baluchistan in Iran's fifth five-year plan, discussed in chapter six, proved to be only paper programs, as his economic spokesman, Ahmed Mesbah, frankly acknowledged in a 1977 Teheran interview. Until 1976, Mesbah said, "little had been spent in Baluchistan, I am sorry to say, but now the province is receiving attention, primarily because we have increasingly recognized its strategic importance." When I asked about projected time-tables for the steel mills, textile mills, railroad networks, and irrigation programs highlighted in the five-year plan, Mesbah replied that "we have much to do elsewhere, and these things won't get off the ground for some years." He stressed repeatedly that Baluchistan was the "poorest and least populated" part of Iran, with "very backward people, nomads and that sort of thing." Budgetary decisions concerning the future of Baluchistan were "under review," he explained, and would be incorporated in the projected sixth national five-year plan, to be unveiled in March 1978. But the sixth plan was suspended indefinitely and later scrapped amid the confusion of the Shah's last months, and as of early 1981, the Khomeini regime had not yet settled down to systematic economic planning.

Would Independence Be Viable?

In both Pakistan and Iran, Baluch nationalist demands for autonomy rest, in large part, on two closely linked economic premises. One is that the small size of their population makes it all but impossible for the Baluch to achieve economic justice within the framework of unitary constitutional systems dominated by substantially larger population groups. The other is that Baluchistan has an adequate natural resource base to support either autonomy or sovereign independence and does not require largesse from the Punjabis or the Persians in order to overcome its economic backwardness.

The first of these premises, involving as it does subjective value judgments, is inherently beyond the range of objective appraisal. Suffice it to say that Baluchistan receives much less favorable treatment in certain significant spheres (e.g., petroleum royalties) than provincial units in many other federations and that Baluch nationalists thus have little difficulty in giving credibility to their charges of injustice.

As for the second premise, the exploration of Baluchistan's resource potential has not yet been extensive enough to establish definitively the extent to which an independent state would be economically viable. Even under the most optimistic assumptions, it is clear that the development of this resource potential would require substantial foreign assistance. In nationalist eyes, however, there is already more than sufficient evidence of a resource base to make the concept of an independent state extremely attractive.

According to officials in Islamabad and Teheran, who downgrade the economic potential of an independent Baluch state, Baluchistan has been receiving development outlays in recent years much in excess of the level justified by its population and will continue to require comparable infusions of outside assistance for some time to come. Thus, in Pakistan, the National Finance Commission recommended in 1970 that Baluchistan receive a 3.9 percent share of national tax allocations on the basis of its population, as against 57.9 percent for the Punjab, 21.6 percent for the Sind, and 16.6 percent for the Northwest Frontier Province. On the basis of its population alone, noted a subsequent Bhutto government report, Baluchistan would have been entitled to receive only $8.7 million during the 1975–1976 fiscal year. Nevertheless, the report said, Islamabad adopted what was to become a well-established preferential policy toward Baluchistan, taking into account its "underdeveloped state." In 1975–1976, the report stated, Islamabad also gave Baluchistan special subventions totaling $5 million.[16] In the following year, the central government, stepping up its development programs in the province, not only gave Baluchistan $19 million in subventions over and above its population entitlement but also picked up a provincial budgetary deficit of $11.9 million.[17] By 1978–1979, the Zia regime reported, the level of special subventions had risen to $24.8 million and the annual budgetary deficit covered by Islamabad had reached $28.2 million.[18]

Confronted with these figures, Ataullah Mengal exclaimed that "first they annex us militarily! They impose unfair ground rules upon us, denying us our inheritance, our rightful control over our resources and the level of revenues from them that we rightfully deserve! Then they have the effrontery to adopt a patronizing attitude, treating us as if we are wards!"

In the kind of confederation envisaged by Mengal, Islamabad would have greatly reduced powers of taxation. Each of Pakistan's four provinces would have to raise most of its own revenues, which would vary in accordance with their respective population size and natural resources. "This would be fair to all," said Mengal. "The Punjab would have substantial revenue from the income taxes imposed on such a large population. We would obtain relatively little from income taxes, but we could live and develop by earning what we deserve from the exploitation of our natural resources, and even if this should prove to be less than fully sufficient in the early years, we would prefer this to living on the terms imposed by others." During his tenure as chief minister of Baluchistan in 1971–1972, Mengal charged, Sui gas was being sold by the Pakistani government to industries outside of Baluchistan at "one of the cheapest rates in the world." Mengal said that "if we raised the price, together with the royalty rate, we could obtain at least $35 million per year, without disrupting existing markets in the slightest."

As an example of another major source of income already in existence or on the horizon, Mengal cited projections that the Saindak copper deposits could yield $100 million yearly in foreign exchange within a decade, dismissing the doubts expressed by ASARCO officials. He also pointed to the Gadani ship repair yard, which has provided some $50 million in revenues yearly for the central government and only $15 million for the provincial government, "a most unfair arrangement, which would be reversed in a confederation." Looking ahead, however, Mengal stressed that "we could not rely on existing sources of income, and it would be necessary to move quickly into new areas of development." If a confederation should prove possible, he said, some of this new development would be undertaken in cooperation with Islamabad. He spoke of "joint institutions" in which costs, risks, and benefits would be "equitably shared, taking into account, of course, our sovereignty over the resources concerned." Alternatively, if independence should prove necessary, "we would have to obtain capital from private and public foreign sources on our own."

When I expressed skepticism with respect to the economic viability of an independent Baluchistan, Mengal replied that "the arithmetic is really very favorable, once you stop to consider it carefully. Remember that low population density can be an advantage, and don't forget that there is enormous wealth simply waiting to be exploited." For example, he said, despite Baluchistan's 750-mile coastline and an abundance of king-size shrimp in the Arabian Sea, Islamabad has done little to foster the growth of a modern fishing industry. "Enormous revenues could be obtained rather quickly, with relatively little investment" through the creation of government-owned fisheries. Above all, he declared, "the real key to our future prosperity lies in the fact that we have very substantial mineral reserves in addition to those already surveyed. If we are masters of our own destiny, we will see that proper studies are conducted. But there is already little doubt that we have iron, we have uranium, we even have oil, and none of these are being seriously exploited. Even the copper around and beyond Saindak has not been tackled seriously. They are dragging their feet. They don't want us to know the full extent of our riches."

The nationalist conviction that Baluchistan contains vast, untapped natural wealth and would thus be viable as an autonomous or independent state has deep roots in Baluch folklore. "We have a saying here," said the late Khan of Kalat, "that a Baluch child may be born without socks on his feet, but when he grows up, every step he takes is on gold." In a characteristic statement of an often-heard theme, *Jabal* declared that

> In Islamabad's calculations, Baluchistan is a vast estate for plunder, an arid desert floating on oil and minerals. A large part of their political strategy is dictated by the desire to extract this treasure for the benefit of the Pakistani bureaucratic bourgeoisie and foreign imperialist interests.... The Pakistani oligarchy needs Baluchistan's oil and minerals to overcome the severe economic crisis gripping the whole country.[19]

To some extent, it appears to be true that Baluchistan has substantial unexploited mineral resources, but the geological evidence available to date suggests that nationalist hopes may be greatly exaggerated. Even in the Saindak–Sar Cheshmeh copper belt, definitive information with respect to the extent of such resources must await a wide range of costly surveys. Moreover, even in the event of promising discoveries, the disproportionately high cost of extracting and transporting mineral deposits located in the inaccessible, undeveloped interior regions of Baluchistan could delay or discourage their exploitation.

Experts agree that Baluchistan has iron ore deposits totaling some ten million tons at Nokandi and proven reserves of at least thirteen million tons in the Chagai district. Some experts believe that the potential reserves at Chagai exceed one hundred million tons. Geologists also agree that there are large deposits of metallurgical-grade fluorite in the Kalat district and chromite at Muslimbagh, as well as the potential for expanding the existing production of limestone, magnetite, marble, sulfur, and barite. An American scholar who investigated Baluchistan's economic potential highlighted the abundant supplies of limestone throughout eastern Baluchistan. Citing as an example deposits in the northern Sarawan district, where proximity to coal and to rail transportation would facilitate establishment of a cement-manufacturing industry, he argued that the full-scale exploitation of Baluchistan's limestone deposits could give a big boost to a variety of construction activity.[20]

Scattered gold deposits have been discovered in various parts of Baluchistan, including those at Saindak, but it remains to be seen whether these are worth $5 billion or more, as some experts claim. Similarly, there is no expert consensus with respect to the uranium deposits discovered in the Dera Ghazi Khan district, which the Karachi newspaper *Dawn* has described as "extensive."[21] Dera Ghazi Khan, it should be noted, is now part of the Punjab province, and claims of a Baluch majority in the district are hotly contested.

In the case of petroleum reserves, geologists minimize the prospects in central Baluchistan, where there is a history of volcanic activity, but have long expressed keen interest in the eastern and western portions of the province. "For centuries," observed the *Financial Times* of London in a review of Pakistani oil prospects, "Baluchi tribesmen have found oil seepages coming out of the ground good enough to light their oil lamps. But the source of these seepages has eluded early oilmen—indeed, even now, its complex underground geological structures make Pakistan a notoriously difficult place to drill for oil."[22]

Surveying the prospects in Baluchistan, the Pakistan government's Oil and Gas Development Corporation reported in 1978 that four wells out of ten drilled in the province had been successful, a significantly higher ratio than the international average of one in ten.[23] Two of these were the natural gas discoveries at Sui and Pirkoh cited earlier. Another was a gas discovery at Jhandran. The fourth, at Dhodak, was located just over the border in the Punjab, but was part of a grouping of geological structures extending for a considerable distance into Baluchistan. The report pointed to a vast area enclosed by Bambore, Pirkoh, and Dhodak (see Figure 3) as "forming a golden triangle in which the future petroleum prospecting efforts of the country should be concentrated."[24]

By a strange quirk of fate, Amoco had just launched seismic survey and drilling operations at assorted sites in the mountainous part of the Marri area when the insurgency broke out in 1973. Aerial surveys had suggested the existence of "a magnificent, huge structure" in the Bambore-Jhandran-Tadri area, said J. C. Van Wagner, former director of Amoco's operations in Pakistan. By early 1976, however, the American company had pulled out of Baluchistan, despite its gas discovery at Jhandran. "There could very well be a multimillion-barrel deposit there," Van Wagner declared. "We just don't know because we did not feel that the amount of expenditure involved to find out in that difficult, mountainous terrain made sense for us in the light of our options elsewhere." In the case of the Jhandran discovery, he said, Amoco was particularly bothered by what it regarded as the low price for gas fixed by the Pakistani government.

Van Wagner denied that guerrilla attacks on its activities in Baluchistan were a "major or decisive factor" in Amoco's decision to abandon its wells at Jhandran and Tadri. This assertion was consistent with official statements in Islamabad designed to reassure other companies that the Pakistan Army could be relied upon to protect oil-drilling activities in other disturbed parts of the country. Van Wagner did not dispute a *Jabal* account of clashes between guerrilla units and the army during seismic surveys at the Tadri site in February 1975 and later during summer drilling operations.[25] However, he insisted that the only casualties were Pakistani soldiers assigned to protect the Amoco team and that only four soldiers had been killed, one in February and three in August. Van Wagner denied *Jabal*'s claims that a British engineer on the Amoco staff was killed at Jhandran and that three Americans were killed when a seismic survey patrol was ambushed near Bambore in February 1976, shortly before the cancellation of exploration activity there. "Amoco knew that to extract and transport crude oil it would need a completely stable infrastructure of roads, pipelines, electricity, housing, and water supplies," declared *Jabal*, echoing Van Wagner's explanation. That infrastructure did not exist, nor was there any prospect that it would exist in the foreseeable future in view of the Liberation Front's activities. "This is why Amoco left Baluchistan. They were unwilling to increase their investments in an area where the entire might of the Pakistan Army could not guarantee their safety."[26]

Undeterred by Amoco's withdrawal, the army finally succeeded in opening up a key sixteen-mile road link between the town of Temple Dera and the Bambore site in 1978, and the Oil and Gas Development Corporation took over the Bambore concession that same year. An agreement between Islamabad and Gulf was reached in 1978 for exploration at nearby Sibi.

Outside the Bambore-Pirkoh-Dhodak golden triangle, petroleum prospects are also regarded as favorable in parts of western Baluchistan, especially at Ras Koh in the Chagai district, where there are hopes for natural gas, and at Meshkuth, near the Pangjur oasis (see Figure 3). An American firm, Murphy Oil, holds a 10,500-square-mile concession area near the Iranian border that overlaps the Kharan and Makran districts, but Islamabad was fearful of political disturbances and asked the company to postpone exploration in January 1979. Marathon has two offshore concessions that are valid until 1984, but the company stopped exploration there in 1980 after drilling two dry holes that were only "moderately encouraging."

One of the more colorful arguments voiced by nationalists of all shades is that the Shah's Iran, in league with "imperialist interests," prevented the full-scale exploitation of Pakistani Baluchistan's petroleum resources. "The oil springs on the Pakistan side are located in the same oil belt that connects with Iran," wrote the late Khan of Kalat. "They are at a lower level. Thus, if all the oil supplies available in Pakistani Baluchistan are exploited, Iran will invariably have to face the danger of going dry. Meanwhile, the Anglo-American monopoly through world petroleum control continues undisturbed."[27] This theme was echoed by *Jabal*, which charged that "a sizable oil strike could slowly drain Iran's oil reserves, and her aid has been a form of blackmail of Pakistan, forcing her not to declare any oil find without Iran's permission."[28]

Geologists ridicule the idea of a geological linkage between the golden triangle petroleum zone in eastern Baluchistan and any petroleum deposits that may exist in distant Iranian Baluchistan. However, they agree that the Murphy concession area in the northwest corner of Pakistani Baluchistan is geologically related to adjacent border areas of Iranian Baluchistan. Similarly, a clear geological link exists between the Saindak copper site and the nearby copper deposits in Iranian Baluchistan, revealed by U.S. Geological Survey studies.

At periodic intervals, the Shah's planners invited foreign geologists and economic consultants to survey the economic potential of Baluchistan, but the findings of these surveys were closely guarded. For example, most of the report presented by the Italian firm Italconsult after an extensive survey in 1961 and 1962 was treated as confidential, with the exception of several portions relating to water development. The report of a French consulting firm in 1978 was also kept under wraps. An informed Iranian source said that the Italian study had led to the Sar Cheshmeh copper discovery and had also suggested the probability of uranium deposits of undetermined magnitude north of Chah Bahar and west of Zahedan. So far as can be determined, the Shah did little to develop copper, uranium, or other mineral resources in Baluchistan, fearing that to do so would only whet the Baluch appetite for independence.

The portions of the Italconsult report dealing with water development demonstrated in exhaustive detail how Teheran could expand the capillary water supply system in Baluchistan. In addition to the agricultural implications of such expanded water facilities, the report said, increased water supplies, together with "plentiful" existing supplies of limestone and other local raw materials, would make possible the establishment of cement factories, slaked lime factories, solid and hollow brick factories, hydraulic lime factories, and brick and tile kilns.[29]

Studies in Pakistan have also pointed to the development of water resources as the key to unlocking the economic potential of the Baluch areas. Citing a variety of favorable geological factors, M. B. Pithawalla, a Pakistani expert, concluded as early as 1952 that it was technically feasible to capture underground water resources in most parts of Baluchistan.[30] Pithawalla saw no quick fixes in one or two "magnificent barrages" or giant, multipurpose dams. Instead, he recommended a diversified program to drain rivers, develop smaller storage dams, and implement thirty-seven already projected irrigation schemes. No action was taken on his proposals, but another five-year, $25-million study of ground water resources was initiated in 1977 with foreign help. When the regime led by Bizenjo and Mengal controlled Baluchistan in 1972, ambitious plans for the installation of tubewells were outlined, only to be shelved following the outbreak of the insurgency. Bhutto later announced a program for 6,000 tubewells, including 1,185 to be built with a U.N. Development Programme grant. It was this program that became embroiled in conspicuous corruption and mismanagement, as the Zia government's economic review conceded, though many tubewells were nonetheless installed, especially on farms belonging to Baluch, Punjabis, and Pushtuns who supported the Zia regime.

Baluch nationalists and Islamabad technocrats alike emphasize the interdependence of agricultural and industrial development in Baluchistan. Thus, experts suggest, a 177-mile gas pipeline winding its way from the Sui fields through the Kohlu, Maiwand, and Kahan valleys in the Marri area and the Dera Bukti, Loti, and Singsila valleys in the Bukti area could open up an extensive network of electric power stations along the way. According to Chief Justice Mir Khuda Bux Marri, such a pipeline would facilitate the electrification of 9,000 square miles in the Marri and Bukti areas and possibly an additional million acres in the adjacent Kachhi area, setting the stage for greatly stepped-up irrigation activity as well as "all sorts of small industries." However, Marri, a moderate who has avoided identification with nationalist groups, warned against

> a repetition of the past pattern, in which development has been undertaken to provide opportunities for outside interests. The exploitation of our resources by outsiders is creating a sense of frustration which, if not checked in time, may lead to undesirable consequences. Conversely, Baluchistan will no longer be a "problem" the day that its educated and patriotic sons and daughters get their due opportunity to participate in the socio-political and economic spheres.[31]

The Demographic Muddle

Apart from the issue of Baluchistan's natural resource potential, which cannot be definitively resolved in the absence of further geological studies, nationalist leaders have inherited a variety of complex demographic and sociocultural problems that would affect the economic and political viability of an independent Baluch state.

By far the most serious of these problems is the widespread dispersion of the Baluch population. Not only is the ancestral Baluch homeland divided territorially among three countries, Pakistan, Iran, and Afghanistan; in addition, many Baluch have been compelled by the lack of development in Baluchistan itself to seek work elsewhere, most of them in other parts of Pakistan and Iran, but some in places as far away as the Persian Gulf sheikhdoms and East Africa.[32] Many of the Baluch who live in Pakistan were forced to migrate from Baluchistan to the Sind and the Punjab after losing their flocks and homes during the 1973–1977 insurgency. Most evidence indicates that there are now nearly as many Pakistani Baluch living outside the Pakistani province of Baluchistan as within it.

There is a vast discrepancy between various nationalist estimates of the Baluch population and official census figures in the countries concerned. The most far-reaching nationalist claim is an unsubstantiated figure of 30 million suggested by the Khan of Kalat in his 1975 autobiography.[33] Other nationalist writers have presented evidence to support claims of 18 million and 16 million.[34] By contrast, official estimates in Pakistan, Iran, and Afghanistan suggest a Baluch population of at most 3.2 million.

The latest Pakistani census, taken in 1972, did not contain an estimate of the Baluch population as such. It showed a population of 2.428 million in Baluchistan province, and official spokesmen estimated that the Baluch constituted some 55 percent of this figure, or 1.257 million.[35] As for Baluch migrants living outside the province, the 1961 Pakistani census, which was the last one that included linguistic data, listed 1.594 million members of Baluch tribes identified through language, including those living in the Sind and the Punjab (see Figure 2).[36]

Ridiculing these figures, Baluch leaders pointed to the logistical difficulties that have impeded thorough census-taking in mountainous Baluchistan and accused the government of undercounting for political reasons.[37] Moreover, Khair Bux Marri said, "under the prevailing political circumstances, the Baluch have been reluctant to cooperate with anything the government is doing." On the basis of local estimates by tribal leaders, Marri suggested a figure of "at least" 2.2 million Baluch living in Baluchistan province alone, and at least as many living outside of the province.

Whatever the precise extent of the Baluch population in Baluchistan itself, it should be emphasized that nearly as many Baluch live in the Sind and the Punjab. As early as 1891, the British Indian census showed 935,000 Baluch in these two provinces. In 1941, the British data indicated 725,000 in the Sind alone. Chief Justice Mir Khuda Bux Marri cited the 1941 figure in support of his contention that there are 3 million Baluch in the Sind today. Given the threefold increase in the overall population of Sind shown in the 1972 census, Marri argued, there is no reason why a comparable increase should not be assumed for the Baluch. A leading Sindhi politician of Baluch ancestry, Mir Ali Ahmed Talpur, who served as defense minister in the Zia regime, said that Marri's figure might well be low, especially if one takes into account the influx during recent years. However, he distinguished between 1.4 million Baluch who speak Baluchi, more than half of them in Karachi, and some 2 million more who are Baluch by ethnic origin but no longer speak the language. He supported his estimates by pointing to the fact that thirteen of the twenty-seven members elected to the Sind State Assembly in 1970 were Baluch.

The uranium discoveries in the Dera Ghazi Khan district of the Punjab (see Figure 3) have intensified arguments over the proportion of Baluch in the district. Nationalist sources claim that the Baluch hold a majority of 65 percent, while independent estimates suggest a lower figure, some as low as 25 percent. Nevertheless, even if one uses the 25 percent estimate, there appear to be at least 250,000 speakers of Baluchi in Dera Ghazi Khan and neighboring districts of the Punjab adjacent to Baluchistan. Thus, if one assumes a figure of 2 million Baluch in Baluchistan province, 1.4 million in Sind, and 250,000 in the Punjab, the resulting figure for the whole of Pakistan comes to 3.65 million people who identify themselves as Baluch, speak Baluchi, and function politically as part of the Baluch community.

As indicated in chapter six, the discrepancy between official census figures and nationalist claims in Iran is comparable to that in Pakistan. The 1978 official population estimate of 659,297 people in the province of Sistan and Baluchistan includes some 217,000 ethnic Sistanis and excludes many Baluch living in gerrymandered districts attached to other provinces. Shah Bakhsh, leader of the Shah Bakhsh tribe, claimed that there are more than 2 million Baluch scattered throughout Iran. This figure appears grossly exaggerated. However, responses to my inquiries in Iran among Baluch, other Iranians, and foreign observers tended to converge with respect to the location and size of Baluch migration outside Baluchistan, suggesting that the Iranian Baluch number at least one million.* If one assumes a figure of one million in Iran, 3.65 million in

* Many estimates are substantially higher. Lois Beck lists 2 million Baluch in Iran ("Revolutionary Iran and Its Tribal Peoples," *Middle East Research and Information Project Reports*, May 1980, p. 16). Richard Weekes and Stephen Pastner estimate 1.53 million (*Muslim Peoples: A World Ethnographic Survey* [Westport, CT: Greenwood Press, 1978], pp. 64, 510). One of the reasons for the wide discrepancies in these articles lies in the fact that some observers apply the term "Baluch" narrowly to nomadic Baluch tribes in Iran, excluding *shahri* (peasants) in sedentary Baluch settlements and *ghulamzai* (menial ex-slaves) who are an integral part of Baluch society and function together politically with the nomadic tribes. (See Brian Spooner, "Political and Religious Leadership in Persian Baluchistan," [Ph.D. diss., Oxford University, 1967], p. 1.)

Pakistan, 350,000 in the Persian Gulf, 90,000 in Afghanistan, and 13,000 in the Soviet Union, the figure cited in the latest Soviet census, the total Baluch population exceeds 5 million. In the absence of definitive demographic data, I have adopted this illustrative figure to suggest a rough order of magnitude of the population.

The fact that around half of the Baluch population currently lives outside Baluchistan casts a disquieting shadow over the nationalist dream. At best, the establishment of an independent state would be likely to entail large-scale population movements, with all the attendant disruption and hardship. At worst, a new Baluch state could have a serious labor shortage, at least in its early years.

In nationalist propaganda, the Baluch diaspora is attributed wholly to the economic impoverishment of the Baluch homeland. If the Baluch areas were unified and the Baluch constituted a majority, it is argued, Baluchistan would have a government dedicated to Baluch interests for the first time. Such a government, it is said, would rapidly establish industries in which the best jobs were reserved for Baluch, and the new opportunities beckoning in their homeland would draw the migrants back from the Sind, the Punjab, and the Persian Gulf. But would it be that easy? Even if there were Soviet, American, or Arab mentors ready to provide the financial backing needed for rapid industrialization, would Baluch who have become accustomed to life in large urban centers readily return to the remote interior regions of Baluchistan?

Nationalist leaders argue that most of those who have migrated in recent decades would return. One reason cited is that these later migrants have generally been separated from part or all of their families. Another is that there is little social mobility for the Baluch in many of the areas where they have migrated. Doomed to permanent status as a victimized lumpenproletariat, they huddle in Baluch ghettos like those in the Lyari and Kalakot areas of Karachi. There is undoubtedly much truth to both of these arguments. At the same time, some of the more fortunate Baluch migrant laborers have acquired new skills. It is precisely this significant minority of skilled laborers who could contribute most to an independent Baluchistan, but who would, by the same token, have the most to lose by pulling up stakes.

As for the Baluch who migrated more than two or three decades ago, notably those in the rural areas of the Sind, even nationalist leaders do not expect many of them to return to the homeland. Many of these earlier migrants came to the Sind centuries ago. Some of them, such as the Talpurs, established Baluch dynasties that once ruled the Sind. Most of these earlier migrants have melted into Sindhi life and can speak Sindhi. It should be noted, however, that they speak Baluchi at home and function as a tightly knit Baluch ethnic bloc in local politics. They are generally sympathetic to the Baluch nationalist movement, but are less actively involved in it than the more recent migrants in the industrial slums of Karachi.

The dispersion of the Baluch population could pose knotty problems in border areas where Sindhi and Baluch populations mingle. Baluch nationalists envisage the retention of mixed border areas now in Baluchistan, notably in Kachhi, Sibi, Nasirabad, and Las Bela, and the accession of Jacobabad, now in the Sind, to an independent Baluchistan or an autonomous Baluch state affiliated with a redesigned Pakistani federation (see Figure 2).* Since many of these areas are economically oriented to the Sind, however, some Sindhi nationalists would be likely to resist some of these demands. A particular bone of contention could be the Guddur Barrage in the Jacobabad district, which provides water to Sindhi and Baluch farms alike. As experience has shown in contested border areas in other parts of the world, partition plans can be extremely difficult to implement, since the populations concerned are often inextricably intermeshed.

The presence of such a large Baluch population in the Sind has led to intermittent collaboration between Sindhi and Baluch leaders. Mir Ali Ahmed Talpur told me in an August 1978 interview that "if worst should ever come to worst and Pakistan should disintegrate, the Baluch and the Sindhis would be together. They like each other and might well create a federated state of Sind and Baluchistan. But of course, we want Pakistan to survive." Two of Talpur's sons fought with the Baluch People's Liberation Front during the 1973–1977 insurgency. In Baluch eyes, many Sindhis proved to be fair-weather friends during the insurgency. Nevertheless, the idea of a Sindhi-Baluch federation has a strong latent appeal for Baluch and Sindhis alike, especially on economic grounds. With an already existing industrial base and a thriving, established port in Karachi, such a state would be much more viable economically than a separate Baluchistan. Similarly, with the natural resources of Baluchistan, it would be more viable than the independent Sind advocated by Sindhi nationalists.

In early 1981, Ataullah Mengal said that he was "in close touch" with

---

* The Jacobabad and Las Bela districts are the major focal points of controversy. The 1961 Pakistani census showed a Sindhi-speaking majority of 56.42 percent in the Jacobabad district and a Baluchi-speaking minority of 31.51 percent. In Las Bela, 66.58 percent claimed Sindhi as their mother tongue, as against 23.67 percent for Baluchi. The 1972 census did not include language data. (*Census of Pakistan*, v. 3: *West Pakistan* [Karachi: Manager of Publications, 1961], statement 7-A, pp. IV-42, IV-43.) Baluch nationalists claim that many ethnic Baluch in these districts are bilingual.

Sindhi nationalist exiles and that "we have always been very interested in consulting closely with the Sindhis to explore a possible federation." Should such efforts fail, he said, Baluchistan should retain Las Bela, Sibi, Nasirabad, and Kachhi and should acquire Jacobabad, but would not have a "rightful claim" to other areas of Sind claimed by some Baluch zealots. As for the Punjab, Mengal said that Dera Ghazi Khan "clearly" belonged within Baluchistan, recalling that Sher Baz Mazari, the principal Baluch leader there, had long advocated its accession to Baluchistan as part of any linguistic redemarcation of Pakistani provinces.

In addition to the problems posed by the dispersion of so many Baluch outside Baluchistan, the existence of a large Pushtun minority within the province could also complicate the creation of an independent or autonomous Baluch-majority state. The British deliberately split the Pushtun areas and attached some of them to Baluchistan as part of their divide-and-rule policy. Baluch nationalist leaders and a Baluchistan-based Pushtun group, the Pukhtoonkhwa (Pushtun-land) party, share the objective of a linguistic redemarcation of Pakistani provincial boundaries in which Pushtun-majority areas now in Baluchistan would be joined with the Pushtun areas of the adjacent Northwest Frontier Province, while the Baluch-majority areas of Baluchistan would be linked with adjacent Baluch areas of the Sind and the Punjab (see Figure 2). As in the case of the Sind border areas, however, there is a potential for controversy over the disposition of ethnically mixed districts in Baluchistan, notably Zhob, Loralai, Quetta, and eastern Chagai, which have Pushtun majorities but a substantial number of Baluch as well. Some Baluch nationalists claim the eastern portion of Dera Ismail Khan district in the Northwest Frontier Province, which is destined to become a fertile grain-producing area following construction of the projected Chasma Barrage on the Indus. But this demand is not supported by Mengal and other Baluch leaders.

In contrast to the rapport between Baluch and Sindhis that prompted Mir Ali Ahmed Talpur to talk of a Baluch-Sindhi union, the Baluch and Pushtuns have a troubled relationship, marked by a Baluch sense of inferiority in economic competition. The Pushtun tribal system, with its egalitarian ethos, allows more scope for individual enterprise than the hierarchical Baluch system,[38] and many Pushtuns have become prosperous moneylenders, contractors, and farmers. Some of the most productive agricultural areas of Baluchistan are in the northeastern part of the province where Pushtun tribes have increasingly encroached on what were formerly Baluch lands. In general, the Baluch who have gone to the Persian Gulf in recent years have gone—and returned—as laborers. Many enterprising Pushtuns have managed to become minor contractors and have invested their earnings in real estate, especially in Quetta, where Pushtuns now own as much land as the Baluch, if not more.

Although there is strong anti-Punjabi sentiment among the Pushtuns, the sense of alienation from Pakistan and the urge for independent statehood is not as strong among the Pushtuns as among the Baluch for a variety of reasons that I have discussed elsewhere.[39] "The Pushtuns are after a share of the cake," explained a perceptive Sindhi nationalist observer, political scientist Hamida Khurro. "They talk of independence for bargaining purposes. But the Baluch want something more—identity, self-respect, real autonomy." Pakistani leaders, recognizing that the Baluch pose a more serious separatist threat, have deliberately promoted Pushtun strength in Baluchistan as a means of offsetting Baluch power. This determination was illustrated vividly by Bhutto's selection of G. M. Barozai, a Pushtun, as chief minister of Baluchistan following the ouster of Bizenjo and Mengal in 1973.

Even Barozai did not claim that the Pushtuns constitute a majority in the province, suggesting a figure of 40 percent, or roughly one million people, with 55 percent for the Baluch, and 5 percent for Punjabis and others. Bizenjo, however, said that even 40 percent is an inflated figure. He suggested 20 to 25 percent instead, though he observed bitterly that the number of Pushtuns is steadily increasing. Even before the Soviet occupation of Afghanistan, he alleged, Islamabad had actively encouraged Pushtun immigration into Baluchistan. More recently, Bizenjo complained, Pushtun refugees from Afghanistan have been "flooding" the province, many of them wealthy landowners and traders who have immediately begun to compete for local economic and political power.

During 1980 and 1981, the continuing influx of Pushtun refugees into Baluchistan has led to acute Baluch-Pushtun tensions that have erupted in intermittent armed clashes. Against this background, the linguistic redemarcation of Pakistani provinces or the establishment of an independent Baluchistan would undoubtedly provoke serious conflict between the two groups. Pushtun spokesmen express fears that rampaging Baluch would seek to oust Pushtuns from their lands in Quetta and from other lands where Pushtuns have encroached over the years on what were once Baluch preserves. Baluch leaders stress that an autonomous or independent Baluchistan should have a clear Baluch majority and that many Pushtuns who have come in recent years would have to leave in order to make this possible. They envisage "serious discussions" with respect to certain lands recently occupied by Pushtuns. These lands were allegedly vacated by Baluch who lost their flocks during the insurgency and then migrated to the Sind in search of work with the expectation of returning. However, Ataullah Mengal said that "on the whole," Pushtun fears were exaggerated. "We will respect legitimate property rights," he said. "We will work things out in a practical and reasonable way, and we want and expect to have many of our Pushtun neighbors working with us to build Baluchistan. But certainly things cannot go on as they are. The Punjabis are trying to make us a minority in our own homeland."

Tribalism and Nationalism

Let us assume that an independent Baluch-majority state could be established through border adjustments and large-scale migrations and that it could obtain adequate financial support. Even if one makes such favorable assumptions, it does not automatically follow that such a state would prove to be politically stable. Indeed, many skeptical observers, citing the ancient tribal rivalries that divide the Baluch, predict that an independent Baluchistan would promptly collapse into hopeless factionalism. "If a Greater Baluchistan emerges," writes Pakistani author Zahurul Haq, "it will probably be destroyed in no time in a bloody shootout between the chiefs leading the various tribal groups, and nothing like a unified government will surface."[40]

A considerably more positive appraisal of Baluch nationalism is presented in this book. It emphasizes the strength of the historical memories shared by all Baluch and recounts the continuing Baluch search for political identity over the centuries, climaxed by Nasir Khan's eighteenth-century confederacy. It contrasts the obstacles to Baluch political unity in the past with the more favorable opportunities for unification provided by the technology of modern communication and transportation. It shows that the Baluch had never lost their freedom until their conquest by modern Pakistani and Iranian armies and describes the growth of the contemporary Baluch nationalist movement as a response to the unprecedented challenge posed by Punjabi and Persian domination. Above all, it underlines the vitality of the nationalist movement, pointing to the emergence of a broadly accepted leadership that transcends tribal loyalties.

Despite this positive appraisal of Baluch nationalism, it is not my intention to minimize the political problems that would confront the builders of an independent Baluch state. Chapters four and five make clear that the nationalist movement is still in a relatively early stage of development and that its tenuous unity has yet to be seriously tested. As the experience of other nationalist movements has shown, it is easier to unite against a common foe during an independence struggle than it is to consolidate that unity afterward. Moreover, given the lack of education and economic development in Baluchistan, Baluch leaders would clearly have more than their share of the characteristic social and cultural problems that accompany the transformation of fragmented traditional societies into cohesive, modern states.

For Baluch nationalists, the problem of tribalism goes beyond the division of Baluch society into seventeen distinct tribes, each continually jockeying for position in economic and political life. What makes Baluch tribalism potentially troublesome in political terms is the lack of agreement among rival tribal groups over the symbolism to be adopted by the nationalist movement. One group, claiming descent from the ancient Rinds discussed in chapter two, places Mir Chakar Rind on the highest pedestal among nationalist heroes. Another group of tribes, known as Brahuis, regards Nasir Khan as the principal symbol of Baluch nationalism. Still a third group, consisting primarily of tribes linked with the ancient Lasharis, reveres both Mir Chakar and Nasir Khan, while putting forward a few additional heroes of its own.

The smallest of these three groups, the Brahuis, number at most 500,000 of the total Baluch population in Pakistan of some 3.65 million. However, the Brahuis have historically wielded disproportionate influence in Baluch affairs because Nasir Khan and most other rulers of Kalat were Brahuis. Non-Brahui Baluch elements resent what they consider an elitist attitude on the part of the Brahui minority. While grudgingly acknowledging Nasir Khan's role in establishing a unified Baluch state, they blame the failures of the Kalat dynasty as a whole for the present position of the Baluch. Thus, extolling the memory of Mir Chakar Rind, Mohammed Khan Baluch, a Rind, bemoans the strife between the Rinds and the Lasharis that resulted in Brahui control of the Kalat highlands—an "irretrievable national misfortune." With their "narrow and bigoted spirit" and their view of the Kalat state as "a purely Brahui monopoly," he wrote, the Brahuis excluded other Baluch from political life and treated non-Brahui tribes as second-class citizens in their own domain. As an example, Mohammed Khan cited evidence that the Kalat khans gave better rations to their Brahui troops than to other Baluch troops, declaring that Brahui elitism created "a wide political gulf and a national rift between the far-flung Baluch tribes." He alleged that Nasir Khan spoke of Brahuis as "my body" and of other Baluch as his "armor."

Mohammed Khan Baluch showed an ambivalent attitude toward Nasir Khan, describing him as "the best of the line" of the Brahui rulers.[41] But his highest encomiums were reserved for Mir Chakar. By contrast, the late Khan of Kalat, reflecting his Brahui bias, mentioned "the famous Baluch hero, Mir Chakar Rind," in only one short paragraph of his book.[42] Gul Khan Nasir even ridiculed Mir Chakar as a bandit in one of his works.[43] Mir Khuda Bux Marri attempted to strike an evenhanded posture, emphasizing the need for Baluch unity and on the one hand speaking of Nasir Khan as "among the few great Baluch heroes," while on the other reserving his greatest enthusiasm for Mir Chakar as an exemplification of Baluch values.[44]

Significantly, the last Khan of Kalat played down the notion of a separate Brahui identity, charging that Islamabad was seeking to drive a wedge between Brahuis and other Baluch. He pointedly adopted the formal title of Mir Ahmed Yar Khan Baluch. In his book *Inside Baluchistan*, the Khan makes only a passing mention of the Brahuis. He presents himself as a leader of all Baluch and treats the Brahuis as merely one of the original Baluch tribes that migrated from Aleppo. The Khan's version of Baluch history is that the Brahuis separated from the rest of the Baluch tribes by going northeast to Sistan and later migrating into the Kalat highlands, while the bulk of the Baluch were migrating southward into Makran. Similarly, most leading Baluch nationalist historians, notably Mir Khuda Bux Marri[45] and Gul Khan Nasir,[46] echo the view that the Brahuis were among the early Baluch tribes who came from Iran, stressing the ethnic identity between Brahuis and other Baluch. Even a Marxist writer who stresses the weaknesses of Baluch nationalism, Aijaz Ahmed, grants that Gul Khan Nasir has demonstrated "credible ethnic links" connecting the Brahuis with the rest of the Baluch.[47]

For the most part, the Brahuis have been assimilated into the larger cultural, social, and political stream of Baluch life and think of themselves as Baluch. Warren W. Swidler, an anthropologist who lived in the Kalat area, stressed the "many similarities in culture, tradition, and political organization" between tribes that identify themselves as Brahui and other Baluch.[48] Nina Swidler also found the distinction between Brahui and other Baluch to be "problematic."[49] To the extent that a distinction should be made, it is a linguistic distinction, since Brahuis speak a language that contains Dravidian syntactical and lexical elements not found in Baluchi. However, there is a continuing controversy over whether Brahui and Baluchi should actually be treated as separate languages. Brahui enthusiasts emphasize its special characteristics, while Baluch nationalists point to the fact that Brahui and Baluchi are mutually intelligible and that Brahui has become increasingly indistinguishable from Baluchi as a result of borrowings.

Mir Khuda Bux Marri attributes the Dravidian influence in Baluchi to the impact of the Mohenjodaro civilization that flourished between 2500 B.C. and 1500 B.C. in the Indus valley and its environs, including the Kalat area. Aboriginal Dravidian speakers, he argues, left behind a "lost language," dating back to the Mohenjodaro period, that was grafted onto

Baluchi when the Brahuis arrived from the west. Marri maintains that only 25 percent of the words in the Brahui language are Dravidian in origin.[50] In terms of vocabulary, it is no doubt accurate to say, as Marri does, that Brahui is merely a variant of Baluchi. However, some authorities dispute his assertion that Dravidian elements were grafted onto a Baluchi substructure, contending that it was the other way around. Syntactically, Brahui should be classified as a Dravidian language, argues Harvard linguist Murray B. Emenau, albeit one that has been "swamped by borrowings from surrounding non-Dravidian languages."[51]

According to linguists, Brahui is gradually converging with Baluchi and will soon lose its separate identity entirely. In the meantime, there is likely to be a continuing element of tension in the cultural arena between Brahui and non-Brahui Baluch intellectuals. Baluch nationalists are attempting to develop a standardized Baluchi language as the vehicle of an ever more widely shared Baluch cultural and political life. By contrast, a small group of Brahui-language enthusiasts is seeking to promote literary activity in Brahui, which now has no written literature, and to obtain governmental recognition of Brahui as a separate language, equal in status with Baluchi and Pushtu. Alvin Moore, a Library of Congress South Asian specialist, reported in 1981 that the future of Brahui "cannot be said to be overly bright" and that "social and political trends" were hastening its demise.[52] Nevertheless, the language issue provoked a brief controversy during the Baluch-controlled National Awami party state regime in Baluchistan. It was partly to deflect Brahui pressures that Bizenjo and Mengal agreed to the designation of Urdu, the Pakistani national language, as the official language of the state government, thus providing a pretext for temporarily setting aside the choice between Baluchi, Brahui, and Pushtu.

One of the most significant indicators of the vitality of Baluch nationalism is likely to be the extent to which the Baluch are able to develop a standardized language rendered in a commonly accepted script. Although a lively literature has developed as an adjunct of the nationalist movement, Baluchi books, magazines, and newspapers reflect a widespread linguistic confusion. As one observer put it, in the absence of a standard Baluchi, "the situation is somewhat analogous to that of English before the crystallization of 'the King's English.' Each author is free to employ the grammatical apparatus, vocabulary, idioms, and pronunciation (and hence spellings) peculiar to his own region."[53]

J. H. Elfenbein, the most authoritative student of the Baluchi language, divides Baluchi into six regional dialects: the Eastern Hill, Rakshani, Sarawani, Kachhi, Lotuni, and Coastal. While there is "no doubt that all dialects are more or less mutually intelligible," Elfenbein stresses, "what differences do exist are deeply rooted" and complicate the development of a standard literary language.[54] In addition to dialectal differences, the situation is further complicated by the use of Brahui and by "classicising" and "purifying" impulses on the part of some elements of the Baluch literati. Writers well versed in Arabic, Persian, or Urdu often use literary words from those languages in an effort to underline their identification with Islamic tradition. Advocates of a "pure" Baluchi often seek to avoid loan words from other languages that are in widespread use and look instead to classical Baluchi literature for Baluchi terms that are unfamiliar to Baluch not schooled in the classical folklore. Despite these obstacles, as the authors of a standard Baluchi-language textbook observed, a "steady, gentle pressure toward standardization" is exerted by the Baluchi Academy in Quetta, by the editors of Baluchi publications, and by Baluchi broadcasts over Radio Karachi and Radio Quetta in Pakistan, Radio Zahedan in Iran, and Radio Kabul in Afghanistan.[55]

The problems of standardization are aggravated by the lack of a universally accepted alphabet for Baluchi. There is a rich and ancient Baluchi folklore that has been handed down orally from generation to generation, but the first attempts to develop a Baluchi script were not made until about 150 years ago. When M. Longworth Dames compiled his definitive anthology of Baluch literature in 1907, he used the Roman alphabet to render Baluchi words, observing that since Baluchi "has never been a literary language, it has no recognized alphabet of its own. The few Baluch who can read or write have usually received their education through the medium of Persian or Urdu and employ the Persian alphabet, as used in those languages, when they attempt to write Baluchi." By 1969, however, when a Baluchi textbook was prepared at McGill University, a distinctive Baluchi alphabet consisting of thirty-seven letters plus diacritics and special symbols, had evolved as an outgrowth of the nationalist movement. The authors of the textbook described it as a modified form of the Persianized Nastaliq style of the Arabic alphabet, which has been adapted to the sounds of Baluchi and contains a number of new letters.[56]

Nastaliq is an elaborate, calligraphic script that does not lend itself readily to use in movable type. For this reason, in part, most Baluchi books and journals must first be copied by a calligrapher and then lithographed. The Nastaliq script is not universally accepted by Baluch writers, and many Baluch nationalist works have been written in Urdu or English. Nevertheless, there are more than 125 books extant in Baluchi, including 42 issued by the Baluchi Academy in Quetta, as well as some 15 monthlies and other periodicals, many of them irregular underground publications such as those mentioned in chapters five and six. Some of these publications contain a linguistic potpourri of Baluchi and Urdu articles appearing side by side.

Baluch nationalists have long advocated the use of Roman letters for Baluchi as a natural accompaniment to the standardization of the Baluchi language and as the best way of spreading a knowledge of Baluchi. The Baluchi Academy has spearheaded this effort, and the 1971–1972 National Awami party regime pushed Romanization during its brief tenure. However, there is considerable division within the ranks of the Baluch on the desirability of using a foreign alphabet for Baluchi, and Baluchi publications continually reflect this controversy.[57] When the Baluch Students Organization–Awami literary magazine published a book on Baluchi literature in 1977, the fact that the book was published in the Nastaliq script provoked a vigorous controversy between readers advocating the Roman alphabet and the editor of the BSO journal.[58]

It should be emphasized that the number of Baluch literate in any language is not more than 300,000 to 450,000,[59] and that Baluch society is still largely nomadic. Would-be Baluch nation-builders thus confront a twofold task. They must overcome the social and cultural divisions within this politicized minority, while seeking to bridge the larger gap, at the same time, between politically sensitized urban centers and the hinterlands. As industrialization slowly displaces nomadic social patterns, class conflicts are also beginning to surface. However, class distinctions are likely to be much less of a problem for nationalist leaders in the foreseeable future than are the tribally based social and cultural conflicts.

As indicated in chapter two, the great majority of Baluch are Sunni Muslims of the Hanafi rite. However, there is a cleavage between the Sunni majority and an estimated 500,000 to 700,000 Zikri Baluch, who live in the coastal Makran area and in Karachi. The Zikris believe in the Messiah Nur Pak, whose teachings supersede those of the Prophet Mohammed himself. This heresy has led to intermittent Sunni repression of the Zikris ever since the sect originated during the fifteenth century. Nasir Khan launched a brutal and sustained crusade against the Zikris, driving most of them from the interior regions of Baluchistan to the coast.[60]

The Zikris have generally been allied with the Baluch nationalist cause in contemporary Pakistani politics, except for a significant segment in Karachi, where Bhutto's People's party mobilized substantial Zikri support. Religious riots broke out between Zikri Baluch and Sunni Baluch in various parts of Makran on several occasions in the late 1970s. Nationalist leaders blamed Pakistani agents for these incidents, but tensions between Zikris and Sunnis, like those between Brahuis and non-Brahuis, could be the cause of occasional headaches for the builders of an independent Baluch state.

In attempting to assess the potential of the independence movement, it would be a mistake to focus narrowly on the social and cultural divisions within Baluch society. It is much easier to perceive such divisions, with their many overt manifestations in everyday life, than to sense the strength of latent nationalist feelings that generally come to the surface only in time of crisis. Yet nationalist sentiment, once activated, can quickly dissolve tribal, religious, and other competing loyalties.

Experience in Baluchistan, as in other parts of the world, has shown that the dynamism of nationalist movements tends to fluctuate in accordance with the intensity of the repression inflicted by their adversaries. Thus, if Zia should continue his "velvet glove" policies toward the Baluch, nationalist leaders could well have considerable difficulty in arousing mass support for a renewed insurgency. Under such circumstances, Islamabad would have a relatively favorable climate for exploiting the internecine conflicts in Baluch ranks. Conversely, if Zia pursued a repressive course, or was goaded into one by the Baluch, nationalist prospects would brighten. Just as the 1973–1977 insurgency galvanized mass political consciousness overnight, so a renewal of hostilities would quickly polarize Baluch political life and solidify nationalist support. As this book has indicated, however, it remains to be seen whether Baluch leaders can create the unified and well-oiled organizational machinery that was so notably lacking in earlier Baluch struggles. In 1981, Mengal and Marri were openly advocating independence for the first time, and serious efforts to forge organizational unity inside and outside Baluchistan were just getting into high gear.

Is Compromise Possible?

Ever since the secession of Bengali East Pakistan in 1971, many observers have blithely compared Baluchistan to Bangladesh, predicting the inevitable emergence of an independent Baluchistan sooner or later. This comparison is valid up to a point, since the degree of psychological alienation from Islamabad now evident in Baluchistan is strikingly reminiscent of the angry climate that was developing in East Pakistan during the late 1960s.[61] On closer examination, however, it is apparent that there are important differences between the two cases.

Although the 1973–1977 insurgency aroused unprecedented political awareness in Baluchistan, Baluch nationalism has not yet acquired the cohesion and momentum that Bengali nationalism had achieved in 1971. Baluch leaders are seeking to build a nationalist movement on the uncertain social and cultural foundations of a fragmented tribal society with a minuscule middle class; low literacy levels; a relatively undeveloped literature with three competing systems of transliteration; a narrow, albeit growing, base of nationalist activists; and a relatively recent tradition of mass participation in political life. By contrast, the Awami League, which led the Bengalis to independence, operated in a relatively homogeneous society with a significant middle class, a well-established cultural and literary life, a vital, standardized language, a broad base of nationalist activists, and a heritage of mass politicization dating back to the struggle against the British Raj. Moreover, the dispersion of the Baluch population poses peculiarly complex and intractable problems for Baluch nationalists. Bengali leaders faced some demographic adjustments in dealing with their Hindu and Bihari Muslim minorities, but these problems were of a lesser magnitude than those presented by the Baluch diaspora.

In military terms, the Bangladesh independence forces were not only protected by the physical separation of East Pakistan from West Pakistan by more than 1,000 miles of Indian territory, but they also received substantial assistance from the Indian army in the critical stages of their struggle. Baluchistan is directly exposed to the adjacent provinces of Pakistan and Iran, and the Baluch had not yet found a foreign mentor in early 1981. To be sure, as earlier chapters have emphasized, it is possible that the Baluch will receive large-scale foreign support at some point in the future, which might well enable them to overcome their handicaps. But in 1981, the prospects for achieving an independent Baluchistan remained uncertain, and slender possibilities thus still existed for political settlements between the Baluch and the Pakistani and Iranian central governments.

It is not my intention to offer specific prescriptive suggestions here concerning the possible terms for such compromise arrangements. Such suggestions would be presumptuous on the part of a foreign observer because they would necessarily involve subjective value judgments. Before concluding this book, however, it is appropriate to assess the prospects for compromise by probing the stated positions of the contending parties in an effort to differentiate between what are hard and fast positions and what are mere negotiating postures. It is my hope that this effort will help to identify the broad areas where there may be some scope for accommodation when—and if—the parties should seek to resolve their differences. My implicit assumption here is that the demands for independence by Ataullah Mengal and Khair Bux Marri cited in chapter four do not completely foreclose negotiations with Islamabad and Teheran.

Reviewing the broad spectrum of Baluch attitudes recounted in these pages, it is clear that continuance of the 1973 Pakistani constitution, in its present form, would not be acceptable to any significant Baluch faction. At the very least, to win Baluch approval, the constitution would have to be amended to incorporate safeguards barring the central government from forcibly ousting an elected provincial government and unilaterally imposing central rule by executive fiat as Bhutto did in 1973.

Ghaus Bux Bizenjo's Pakistan National party made a significant compromise proposal in 1980 that attempted to define the minimum safeguards sought by the Baluch. In a memorandum to the Zia government, the PNP emphasized that the restoration of electoral processes and civilian rule by the military regime would not in itself bring political stability. In addition to demanding constitutional amendments granting "complete national autonomy," the PNP memorandum called for reinforcement of the articles providing for equal representation of the four provinces in the Senate, and a concomitant strengthening of the Senate's powers, as the key to successful federalism in Pakistan. By offsetting the control wielded by the more populous provinces in the lower chamber of the National Assembly, the memorandum said, such a reform would make central intervention acceptable under certain circumstances. It suggested that Islamabad could then be empowered to take over a province if "expressly authorized to do so for a specified and limited purpose, and for a specified and limited period of time" by a two-thirds Senate majority. Previously, Baluch leaders have ruled out central intervention in a province in the absence of a no-confidence motion in the provincial assembly.

In my view, safeguards against arbitrary central government intervention are more critical to the Baluch than the much-discussed issue of the division of powers between Islamabad and the provinces. The principal Baluch leaders have stated their position precisely with respect to the desirable division of powers in a restructured constitutional setup that would allow greater provincial autonomy. The central government would have control over only five spheres: defense, foreign affairs, foreign trade, communications, and currency. All other areas would be controlled by the provincial governments, including the areas on the "concurrent list" in the 1973 constitution, which were previously subject to the joint control of the central and provincial governments. In talking with Baluch leaders, however, I have sensed that there may be room for bargaining over the extent of provincial autonomy if meaningful guarantees against arbitrary central intervention are written into the constitution.

The Baluch are concerned not only with the substance of autonomy but also with the feeling of autonomy. This psychological factor explains why they attach so much importance to the safeguards issue. It also explains their emphasis on the need for a linguistic redemarcation of provincial boundaries that would reduce Pushtun influence in Baluchistan and give the Baluch a clear majority. Clearly, one of the key Baluch preconditions for a political settlement with Islamabad is explicit recognition of a Baluch identity in Pakistani national politics distinct from a multiethnic Baluchistani identity. But it is not clear how much room for bargaining exists concerning the form that such recognition should take.

At present, most Baluch leaders demand that the Baluch be recognized as one of four distinct "nationalities" in Pakistan, a concept which is anathema to many Pakistanis who believe in a monolithic Pakistani nationality. Some Baluch leaders, notably Ghaus Bux Bizenjo, argue that only a voluntary federal union can survive. They link the "four nationalities" concept with a companion demand that the constitution include the right of secession. Thus, as noted in chapter four, Bizenjo proposed a joint declaration with the Tehriq Istiqlal (Movement for Integrity) in 1980 calling for the right of secession in the event that the central government violated rights guaranteed to the provinces in the constitution. Conceivably, Baluch leaders would not insist on the right of secession if enough of their other major demands were met by Islamabad. However, that remains to be seen, since Bizenjo and others contend that a meaningful sense of autonomy requires acknowledgment of the residual right to secede. These Baluch leaders seek to legitimize the secession demand by citing language of the 1940 Lahore Resolution in which the Muslim League had foreshadowed its demand for Pakistan. Envisaging two Muslim states in the subcontinent following the departure of the British, the resolution called for a regrouping of "geographically contiguous . . . areas in which the Moslems are numerically in a majority, as in the northwestern and eastern zones of India . . . to constitute independent states *in which the constituent units shall be autonomous and sovereign"* (italics added).[62]

The concept of four coequal nationalities is paralleled by Ataullah Mengal's demand for complete parity for Baluch, Pushtuns, Sindhis, and Punjabis in both chambers of the National Assembly as well as in civil service and military recruitment, irrespective of population disparities. Pointedly withholding support for this position, Bizenjo's PNP has specifically limited its demand for parity in the National Assembly to the upper chamber, which suggests that Mengal's approach to the parity issue may prove to be negotiable. At the same time, all Baluch factions are united in seeking radically upgraded representation in the civil service and the armed forces. The Baluch regard the Pakistani concessions made in this sphere to date as inconsequential.

Turning to an examination of the attitudes of Pakistani leaders, it is important to distinguish between General Zia and like-minded allies, who dismiss the "Baluch problem" and thus the need for compromise, and others in the Pakistani power structure who would like to find a basis for accommodation but regard Baluch demands as extortionate. The gap between Zia and the Baluch is clearly a profound one and is likely to prove unbridgeable. But what if Zia were to be replaced by a more moderate, albeit Punjabi-dominated, regime as the result of another military coup or a successful popular agitation spearheaded by Bhutto's People's party or other opposition groups? Would it make a significant difference? How much room for compromise would exist if one assumed a liberalizing trend in Pakistani politics?

For many non-Baluch Pakistani moderates, Baluch demands for greater representation in the civil service, the armed forces, and the National Assembly would not be too difficult to swallow. Some influential Punjabi lawyers, judges, and bureaucrats have confided to me that they would welcome a Baluch prime minister as a symbol of national unity in the event of a return to civilian rule. Many of these moderates are also cautiously optimistic concerning the possibilities for working out a constitutional settlement that would provide for increased autonomy to the provinces and for safeguards against arbitrary central intervention. With regard to the terms for such a settlement, however, even moderates are greatly disturbed by the extent of Baluch demands for economic autonomy. It is in the economic sphere that a constitutional compromise is likely to be most elusive, regardless of Pakistan's future political coloration.

Economic issues are likely to be peculiarly intractable because the same moderates who respect Western democratic values—and are thus sympathetic to Baluch pleas for greater equity—also tend to be the most avid proponents of economic modernization in Pakistan. These relatively Westernized, development-minded Pakistanis want to see rising living standards in Pakistan as a whole. They are just as disturbed by poverty in the Punjab as by poverty in Baluchistan, and their liberal instincts are just as offended by the ethnocentric attitudes of some Baluch leaders on issues relating to development as by the ethnic arrogance of many Punjabis and other non-Baluch. They favor development programs and policies addressed to the greatest good for the greatest number, which leads them to emphasize the economic interdependence of the different regions of Pakistan. This approach makes them extremely unsympathetic to Baluch demands for exclusive Baluch control over the natural resources that happen to lie beneath the soil of Baluchistan.

The controversy over economic autonomy comes to a focus on two specific issues. One is the Baluch demand for much larger state government royalties on natural gas and other resources obtained in the state. The other is the Baluch desire for limitations on the role of non-Baluch entrepreneurs and central government corporations in exploiting the resources of Baluchistan and for the creation instead of state government corporations responsible for resource development. There may be substantial scope for compromise over the terms of royalty payments to Baluchistan, given the disparity cited earlier in this chapter between the 12.5 percent royalty rate received by Baluchistan and the much higher provincial share in some other countries. It might also prove possible to work out "joint arrangements" in various spheres of economic development between Baluchistan, the other provinces, and the central government, as Bizenjo has proposed. But it is unlikely that any Islamabad regime would surrender the residual authority of the central government over the exploitation of natural resources in all parts of Pakistan. Similarly, in a country subject to increasing population pressures, Baluchistan, with its vast, unpopulated expanses, is likely to attract a continuing flow of settlers from other parts of the country, especially if its water resources are developed. Just as Baluch have been free to go to other parts of Pakistan for work in the absence of employment opportunities in Baluchistan, so non-Baluch are likely to insist on the right to migrate to Baluchistan when and if the pace of economic development there should quicken.

In the interview discussed in the preceding chapter, General Zia emphasized the strategic importance of Baluchistan to Pakistan, especially in the wake of the Soviet occupation of Afghanistan. He sharply rebuffed Baluch demands for the removal of Pakistan Army units from the interior of the province. This attitude is not likely to change under any foreseeable political circumstances in Islamabad. In principle, most Baluch leaders do not challenge the right of the Pakistan Army to operate in Baluchistan, since defense is one of the five powers that would be assigned to the central government under any new constitutional division of authority. In Baluch eyes, however, there is a basic difference between military deployments that are directed toward the defense of Pakistan against a potential Soviet threat and deployments that are primarily intended for the repression of domestic political opponents. Even under a relatively favorable constitutional settlement, Baluch leaders would in all likelihood press for some type of consultative machinery that would give them a voice in the nature and location of military deployments in Baluchistan.

In a conversation with Zia in 1978, I attempted to probe his attitudes concerning the possible creation of new consultative mechanisms that would involve Baluch leaders in economic as well as military decision-making affecting their areas. He responded that Islamabad already had adequate machinery in the form of elected local councils. Then he volunteered that he did not regard Mengal, Marri, and Bizenjo as the principal leaders of the Baluch "simply because they had won some seats on emotional grounds" in the 1970 elections. One of his aides observed later that Zia could not recognize the claims of the Baluch triumvirate without inviting demands for comparable recognition from other political leaders who won local power in 1970 and have since been swept aside by the military regime.

In the case of Iran, the issues that divide the Baluch from Teheran are strikingly similar to those in Pakistan, though the two cases are different in that there have never been elections in Iranian Baluchistan comparable to the 1970 elections in Pakistani Baluchistan. As a result of the suppression of political activity, there are no leaders in the Iranian Baluch areas who can claim legitimacy comparable to that enjoyed by Mengal, Bizenjo, and Marri, and there has never been a public dialogue on the terms for a constitutional settlement comparable to the intense debate that took place both before and after the 1970 Pakistani elections. The two cases also differ in that the Baluch pose the most serious organized threat to the stability of Pakistan, while in Iran, it is the Kurds who have waged the most determined military struggle against successive Teheran regimes. If there is a Baluch independence struggle, it is likely to be led by the relatively developed Baluch nationalist movement in Pakistan rather than by the disorganized, newly emerging nationalist forces in Iran, though the Iranian Baluch would undoubtedly enter the fray.

In Pakistan and Iran alike, it is evident that the prospects for compromise settlements with the Baluch are inseparably linked with the overall course of political developments in the two countries. It is unlikely that special arrangements for autonomy would be made with the Baluch in the absence of larger processes of constitutional reform resulting from basic political upheavals in Islamabad or Teheran or both. By the same token, should compromise efforts fail, it is unlikely that the Baluch would launch an independence struggle on their own without some expectation that other disaffected minorities would eventually follow suit or, at the very least, start diversionary military actions in support of their cause. Finally, as we shall see in the next chapter, the Baluch are unlikely to embark on a new guerrilla struggle unless they are confident of substantial foreign assistance and believe that regional political trends make the odds for success favorable.

Moscow, Washington and the Future of Baluchistan 10

The Soviet occupation of Afghanistan has provoked a growing debate over Soviet intentions in Baluchistan. Many analysts argue that it is only a matter of time until Moscow annexes the Baluch areas to a Greater Afghanistan or unleashes a Soviet-supported Baluch guerrilla struggle for independence. Pointing to the traditional Russian interest in the warm-water ports, discussed in chapter one, these analysts depict the Soviet move into Afghanistan as part of an inexorable southward thrust toward the Indian Ocean, the Arabian Sea, and the Persian Gulf oil fields.[1] Some of these observers also place great emphasis on projections of a serious Soviet-bloc petroleum shortage. Since Moscow will soon be competing with the West for a major share of Persian Gulf oil, they argue, Soviet interest in military facilities along the Baluchistan coast near the Strait of Hormuz is likely to grow in direct proportion to the increasing Soviet stake in Middle East petroleum resources.[2]

Disputing this assessment, other observers have offered a variety of explanations for the Soviet move into Afghanistan that do not necessarily point to further Soviet expansionism. George Kennan and some European specialists have interpreted the Soviet occupation as a defensive response to the rise of Islamic fundamentalism in neighboring countries.[3] My own interpretation has emphasized the accidental emergence of a national-communist leader in Kabul, Hafizullah Amin, who was increasingly regarded in Soviet eyes as a potential Tito.[4]

On the issue of Soviet-bloc energy prospects, many observers argue that predictions of a Soviet-bloc shortage are exaggerated.[5] Similarly, on military issues, experts differ with respect to the strategic importance of the Baluchistan coast. Some contend that a Soviet attempt to block tanker traffic in the Strait of Hormuz could trigger a global war in which control of the strait, as such, would become a marginal factor. While Gwadar and other Baluch ports would be useful to Moscow, it is said, their development would involve disproportionately costly, multibillion-dollar outlays in order to deal with desilting and other technical problems. Proponents of this view add that Moscow is not likely to make enormous investments at Gwadar and Chah Bahar as long as it has the use of Aden. In any event, according to one military analyst, Baluchistan is too far from the oil installations at the head of the Persian Gulf to serve as a useful invasion route, and Moscow would be likely to use airborne divisions rather than infantry forces if it should ever attempt to seize the oil fields.[6]

It is not within the scope of this study to analyze the reasons for the Soviet occupation of Afghanistan or to assess the full range of specialized military and economic factors that figure in the debate over Soviet intentions in Baluchistan. Rather, by focusing on Baluch nationalism as a dynamic political phenomenon in its own right, this book has attempted to add a new dimension to analysis of the prospects in Southwest Asia and thus to help clarify the nature of the opportunities and constraints that confront Soviet and American policymakers.

Regardless of how one interprets the reasons for the Soviet move into Afghanistan, it is clear that the existence of a significant Baluch nationalist movement enlarges the options now open to the USSR in Southwest Asia and enhances the danger of further Soviet adventurism. The evidence presented here emphasizes the volatility of the Baluch issue as a target of opportunity for Moscow. At the same time, while warning of possible Soviet intervention, this study sharply underscores the ambivalence of the Soviet attitude toward Baluch nationalism.

Chapter seven shows that Moscow has explicitly opposed the Baluch nationalist goal of an independent Greater Baluchistan and has failed, accordingly, to develop strong, Soviet-oriented Communist parties in either the Pakistani or Iranian Baluch areas. Chapters three through six point to the implications of this failure, discussing the dominant role of non-Communist nationalist elements in Baluch political life. Taken as a whole, this analysis makes clear that Moscow would have to work primarily through non-Communist groups if it were to promote independence in the foreseeable future. Given the lack of a Communist organizational base in Baluchistan, would the Soviet Union be prepared to incur the costs and risks of a military adventure there, including a possible confrontation with the United States? Although far from negligible, the nationalist movement would need massive military aid, reinforced by sustained financial, technical, and logistical help, in order to conduct a successful insurgency. Moscow might well be called upon to intervene directly with its own forces if the going got rough. Yet in Soviet doctrine, non-Communist nationalists would be inherently unreliable allies both in prosecuting a Baluch insurgency and in governing an independent state.

As the interviews in chapter four reveal, the principal Baluch leaders are outspoken and freewheeling personalities who must be something of an enigma to the Russians. They do not exempt the Soviet Union from their criticisms of superpower imperialism, but they take a relatively positive view of the Soviet record with respect to the Baluch themselves and speak hopefully of the Russians as potential liberators. They condemn the United States for its military assistance to the Punjabi- and Persian-dominated governments in Islamabad and Teheran and for its "reactionary" policies in the Third World. But, they keep the door open for American and other non-Communist support, while making clear that they regard the USSR as the most likely source of military assistance.

What the Baluch leaders appear to have in mind, in the case of the Russians, is an agreement to provide military facilities or bases in exchange for unfettered internal control over an independent Baluchistan and enough economic help to make independence viable. Such an arrangement would be a high-stakes gamble for both parties. For the nationalist leaders, there would be an ever present danger that the Russians would use their military presence to build up a Communist movement, subvert the non-Communist forces, and make Baluchistan a Soviet satellite or annex it to a Soviet-controlled Afghanistan. For the Russians, the risk would be that the nationalists would turn to other sources of foreign support and would eventually oust the Soviet military presence. However, if the Russians are able to establish their control over Afghanistan, they might well feel emboldened to gamble in Baluchistan. In Soviet eyes, the risks involved in working through non-Communist leaders might be offset by the critical fact that these leaders were confirmed as the accredited spokesmen for Baluch aspirations in the 1970 Pakistani elections. A Soviet-sponsored independent Baluchistan headed collectively by Mengal, Marri, and Bizenjo would have an aura of legitimacy that might well enable Moscow to win widespread international recognition of such a new state.

In early 1981, the Soviet Union was intensifying its efforts to build up Communist networks in the Baluch areas, but Moscow continued to stop short of supporting Baluch independence. Apart from the lack of a Communist organizational base, there are other factors that explain this cautious Soviet posture. The most important of these is Moscow's overall assessment of short-term political prospects in Islamabad and Teheran. Soviet strategists appear to believe that a reasonable chance still exists to replace the Zia dictatorship in Pakistan and the Islamic fundamentalist government in Iran with more compliant regimes. Moreover, while political instability is growing in both of these multiethnic countries, Soviet planners are not persuaded that either of them has reached the breaking point and could be readily dismembered. In particular, Soviet analysts question whether Communist strength is solid enough in the other ethnic minority regions of Pakistan and Iran to ensure coordinated support for a Baluch insurgency in at least some of these regions.

Soviet sponsorship of an independent Baluchistan would not be likely to occur in isolation but rather as the first step in a larger strategy of regional Balkanization designed to set up a new constellation of Soviet satrapies in place of the existing Pakistani and Iranian states. At a minimum, Moscow would be likely to link a major move in Baluchistan with parallel action in the Sind.

In the case of Baluchistan, Soviet policymakers recognize that although Baluch nationalism is boiling, it is still at a relatively low boil. So long as it remains at a low boil, the USSR is likely to seek maximum flexibility in pursuing its broader diplomatic and political objectives in the region, especially if the prospects for increasing Soviet influence in Islamabad and Teheran appear favorable. Conversely, in a climate of growing Baluch discontent, the Soviet Union would be tempted to follow an adventurist course. The temptation would be enhanced if Moscow confronts an entrenched anti-Soviet theocracy in Teheran and if it writes off its hopes for detaching Islamabad from its military ties to Peking and Washington. Moscow can afford to bide its time in deciding whether to play the Baluch card so long as there is no movement toward political settlements between the Baluch and the central governments of Pakistan and Iran. Should Baluch leaders reach an accommodation with either Islamabad or Teheran, or both, the Baluch issue would no longer be very tempting for Moscow, since it would be difficult for the Soviet Union to organize an effective insurgency and to legitimize an independent Baluch regime in the absence of strong Baluch nationalist support.

Some observers maintain that a decisive factor deterring a Soviet adventure in Baluchistan is the likelihood that Moscow will be bogged down in Afghanistan for some time to come. Here one should think twice, though, for military realities could well compel Moscow to relieve pressure on the Afghan front by activating an insurgency in Baluchistan. Just as Soviet hopes for winning greater influence in Islamabad and Teheran deter Moscow from encouraging a Baluch insurgency, so its desire to punish Pakistan and Iran for providing sanctuaries and assistance to the Afghan resistance forces could prompt Soviet retaliatory action in the Baluch areas. In the case of Pakistan, Moscow is already using increasingly explicit threats of intervention in Baluchistan to dissuade Islamabad from serving as a conduit for Western military aid to the Afghan resistance and from upgrading its military links with Washington and Peking.

Taking into account the many factors that affect Moscow's calculations, it would be premature to assume that Soviet intervention in Baluchistan is inevitable and to base American policy on that assumption. On the contrary, American policymakers should recognize that the Soviet approach to the Baluch issue is likely to be influenced to a significant extent by the nature of the evolving American role in Pakistan and Iran. There is still a chance to avert a superpower confrontation over Baluchistan through restraint on both sides; and by the same token, there is a growing danger that pre-emptive moves by one side or the other could set in motion an uncontrollable chain reaction of challenge and response.

In shaping its policies in Southwest Asia, the United States, like the Soviet Union, must weigh a number of considerations that are beyond the scope of this book. The Baluch issue is only one of the factors conditioning American policy decisions, but it is a pivotal one because Baluchistan is so conspicuously vulnerable to Soviet political and military pressures. The impact of Baluch nationalism on Soviet and American policy options is not symmetrical. The USSR can manipulate the Baluch issue flexibly in accordance with changing circumstances. Soviet interests would be well served whether Moscow uses the threat of Baluch separatism to make Islamabad and Teheran more malleable or carves up Pakistan and Iran into smaller satrapies. For the United States, by contrast, the Baluch issue is a complicating factor, seriously inhibiting and circumscribing the choices open to American policymakers.

The issue of whether and how to aid the Afghan resistance illustrates the impact of the Baluch issue on U.S. policy options. It would be dangerously myopic for American strategists to view the Afghan struggle in isolation. Prudence dictates that they should weigh carefully the grave risks that would be incurred if Moscow were to make good on its threat to retaliate in Baluchistan. American officials should take clearly into account Islamabad's political isolation in the Baluch areas and the difficulties that would be involved in helping to defend this area in the face of pervasive local opposition. At the same time, the vulnerability of Baluchistan underlines the desirability of finding a solution to the Afghan crisis that would bring about the withdrawal of Soviet forces. The purpose of American policy in Afghanistan should not be merely to raise the costs of the Soviet presence or, as Chinese deputy premier Deng Xiao-ping has urged, to "tie them down" until the inevitable third world war.[7] Rather, the United States should explore exhaustively and persistently the possibilities for a diplomatic-*cum*-political settlement. As I have argued elsewhere,[8] the search for such a settlement need not preclude limited external military assistance that would help to keep the resistance alive and to bolster its bargaining power. But the Baluch issue makes military aid to the Afghan resistance a risky gamble and reinforces the other factors that point to the need for an Afghan policy focused on diplomacy rather than military confrontation.

The Baluch problem should also be taken into account in formulating military and economic assistance policies in Pakistan. For example, if the United States were to obtain the use of Pakistani territory for anti-Soviet intelligence monitoring in return for military aid, as it did from 1958 to 1966, there would be a significant danger of Soviet retaliation in Baluchistan and the Northwest Frontier Province. Similarly, an agreement providing for American military access to Pakistani ports and airfields would be viewed as provocative by Moscow and could lead to Soviet pressures in Pakistani border areas.

As for providing military equipment and weaponry to Islamabad, the debate over this multifaceted issue has focused largely on whether Pakistan would be likely to deploy such weaponry on the Afghan or the Indian border; on the pros and cons of using Pakistani forces as surrogates in shoring up Persian Gulf regimes; on the domestic controversy within Pakistan over ties with Washington; and on whether strengthening the armed forces would adversely affect the prospects for the democratization of Pakistani political life. Little attention has been paid to the Baluch factor. In deciding upon the scope and character of any military assistance to Pakistan, however, American officials should be clearly aware that much of such assistance would probably find its way to garrisons in Baluchistan.

Washington should not minimize the risks and costs that would be involved in helping Islamabad to suppress a renewed Baluch insurgency, even in the unlikely event that the Baluch were to embark on a military adventure without Soviet or other foreign backing. At first glance, it might appear feasible and indeed desirable under such circumstances to obtain a quick fix by providing assistance that would enable Islamabad to crush the Baluch before the Russians had a chance to intervene. On closer examination, however, this option becomes less attractive. As the account of the 1973–1977 insurgency in chapter three makes clear, there would be little or no likelihood of winning a conclusive victory over the Baluch in short order. Protracted hostilities would mean a steadily growing danger of direct or indirect Soviet involvement. Moscow could calibrate such involvement in a series of gradations short of overt participation by Soviet forces or advisers. Moreover, experience in many countries shows that popular support for guerrilla movements is generally intensified by counterinsurgency programs, which often include air attacks on civilians and other indiscriminate applications of military force. American military assistance could well add to the current polarization of political forces in Baluchistan and would thus help to create a favorable environment for Soviet intervention.

Large-scale American military inputs would accelerate the present tendency in Islamabad to view the Baluch problem in military terms. Yet as this book shows, the differences between the Baluch and Islamabad are basically political in character and are likely to be resolved only through major constitutional reforms. To the extent that external powers can have an impact on the domestic policies pursued by Islamabad, they should seek to further a liberalization of political life based on a devolution of power and resources to the provinces. In the absence of such political settlements with the Baluch and other ethnic minorities, there is a danger that any foreign weaponry supplied to Islamabad for counterinsurgency activity would be used not against Soviet-supported subversion but against dissident elements among the Baluch and other ethnic minorities who are fighting for greater autonomy within Pakistan. That is precisely what happened during the 1973–1977 Baluch insurgency against the Bhutto regime.

To some extent, the United States has shown sensitivity to the Baluch problem by seeking to earmark economic aid to Pakistan for use in the Baluch areas and other undeveloped regions of the country. However, in the absence of constitutional reforms giving Baluch nationalists a voice in economic development decisions, the political benefits of such aid for Islamabad are likely to be minimal, especially if it is addressed primarily to building a militarily focused infrastructure of roads and airfields.

While seeking to encourage political reforms, the United States should face the fact that the Baluch issue may well prove to be intractable, posing increasingly complex policy dilemmas during the years ahead. So long as hope persists for political settlements with the Baluch in Pakistan and Iran, the basic U.S. commitment to the territorial integrity of these two countries will provide a clear framework for the discussion of policy options. Some will contend, as I do, that a devolution of power offers the best hope for preserving Pakistani and Iranian unity. Others will be guided by the Punjabi-Persian argument that too much regional autonomy would only set the stage for secession. Regardless of which view prevails, the American objective will continue to be the preservation of the territorial integrity of Pakistan and Iran.

But what if Baluch leaders should abandon their hopes for constitutional settlements, set up a government-in-exile, and rekindle their insurgency with help from the Soviet Union, India, Arab countries, or some combination of foreign sources? Would the United States then invoke its 1959 security agreement with Pakistan, offering to help Islamabad and Teheran in crushing the Baluch militarily, or would Washington give its support to Baluch independence in order to pre-empt or offset Baluch reliance on Moscow?

Support for Baluch independence would conflict directly with explicit American commitments to the territorial integrity of Pakistan and Iran and is thus regarded as unimaginable by most American officials, especially in the context of the Reagan administration's effort to solidify ties with Islamabad. Significantly, however, the possibility of American support for an independent Baluchistan is treated with the utmost seriousness by many Baluch, Pakistani, and Iranian leaders. Despite its commitment to the integrity of Pakistan, these leaders point out, the Nixon administration acceded to the creation of Bangladesh, albeit at the eleventh hour.

Baluch leaders predict that Pakistan will continue to crumble internally, eventually compelling Washington to reassess its commitment to the perpetuation of the Pakistani state in its present form. Iranian leaders, for their part, fear that Washington and its Arab allies will never become reconciled to the Islamic revolution in Iran and will attempt to use the Baluch movement as leverage against Teheran. This suspicion is not surprising against the background of American support for the Kurdish revolt as a weapon against Iraq. In Iranian eyes, the Pentagon, hoping to resurrect the military bases along the Strait of Hormuz that were being developed by the Shah, might well support an independent Baluchistan as a means for obtaining these bases or at least denying them to Moscow. Islamabad, too, believes that Washington and Moscow would like to strengthen their Persian Gulf military presence by acquiring bases in Baluchistan. But Punjabi leaders have a special nightmare of their own in which India is cast as the evil genius behind the Baluch movement and Moscow or Washington or both decide to join with New Delhi in liquidating Pakistan.

Some American leaders, notably former president Richard Nixon and former secretary of state Henry Kissinger, have made no secret of their belief that the Punjabis are justified in their fears of an Indo-Soviet dismemberment strategy. Nixon and Kissinger have charged that New Delhi would have invaded what was then West Pakistan during the final stages of the Bangladesh war but for American intervention.[9] No solid evidence has been presented to substantiate this charge, which has generally been discounted, coming as it did amid a heated U.S. political controversy over the Nixon administration's pro-Pakistan "tilt." Nevertheless, the possibility of future Indian support for separatist movements in Pakistan cannot be entirely ruled out, especially in the event of a major Sino-American military build-up in Pakistan.

In Indian eyes, Islamabad wants to use the Afghan crisis as a means of bolstering its power position vis-à-vis New Delhi, just as it used the cold war for the same purpose when it entered into its earlier, ill-fated alliance with Washington in the fifties. Moreover, India sees the specter of a new

American-Pakistani alignment as part of a larger challenge embracing China. Given Peking's long-standing role as a major military supplier to Islamabad, the American decision in 1980 to extend limited military assistance to China aroused profound concern in New Delhi. Defense Secretary Harold Brown's ill-considered joint declaration with Chinese leaders that Peking and Washington share "common strategic objectives" in South Asia[10] attracted little attention in the United States. In India, however, it was viewed with alarm as the harbinger of a concerted Sino-American-Pakistani effort to block the further expansion of Indian power and influence in the South Asian region.

It should be remembered that Indian attitudes concerning the existence of Pakistan continue to be somewhat ambivalent. On the one hand, many Indian leaders stress privately that a viable Pakistan is desirable as a buffer against Soviet influence and that a Balkanization of Pakistan could turn South Asia into a battleground of contending foreign interests. Pointing to Hindu-Muslim tensions in India, these leaders say that the absorption of additional Muslims would impose a grave strain on the Indian political structure. On the other hand, the partition of 1947 left deep wounds in the Hindu psyche. For most of India's Hindu majority, it was deeply exasperating that a Muslim state should be created in part of the motherland depicted in the ancient Hindu scriptures. Partition was accepted as an unavoidable expedient, but it was assumed that the new Muslim state would be short-lived and that India could "win back the seceding children to its lap."[11] At worst, it was felt that Pakistan would eventually settle down as a deferential junior partner within an Indian sphere of influence.

Islamabad's alignment with Washington during the early cold war decades constituted an explicit challenge to New Delhi's regional aspirations and thus reinforced the underlying ambivalence in Indian attitudes concerning the acceptability of a Pakistani state. During the seventies, the reduction in Pakistani power resulting from the secession of Bangladesh, coupled with Pakistan's tentative moves toward a non-aligned foreign policy, led to a moderation of Indo-Pakistani tensions for a brief interlude. But Indian attitudes toward Islamabad have changed in the aftermath of the Soviet occupation of Afghanistan. Many Indian leaders now talk in terms of the "strategic unity" of the South Asian subcontinent and would like to have friendly ties with an economically and politically stable Pakistan. As these leaders view such a relationship, however, Pakistan would necessarily have a subordinate position and would not seek to alter substantially the existing military balance between New Delhi and Islamabad. In the wake of the Afghan crisis, New Delhi sees a danger that Pakistan will once again be able to utilize external support to achieve a disproportionately powerful diplomatic and military posture. This anxiety tends to neutralize Indian fears of a possible expansion of Soviet influence in South Asia.

One of the most significant barometers of the shifting climate of Indo-Pakistani relations in past decades has been Indian policy toward the manipulation of the non-Punjabi minorities in Pakistan. During periods of tension, India has intermittently provided support to Baluch, Sindhi, and Pushtun separatists as a means of putting pressure on Pakistan. Since 1974, as Pakistani leaders acknowledge, New Delhi has refrained from such tactics as part of its post-Bangladesh effort to stabilize relations with Islamabad. However, were the United States, China, and Pakistan to forge substantially expanded military ties, there are likely to be renewed pressures in India for efforts to destabilize Pakistan. Such sentiment has already started to grow as a result of Pakistani preparations for a nuclear explosion and would be intensified if Islamabad were to receive large-scale foreign support for its conventional forces side by side with its efforts to develop a nuclear capability.

The danger of a Balkanization of Pakistan would clearly be accentuated by a Soviet-American confrontation there and by the concomitant growth of tensions between Islamabad and New Delhi. For this reason, American strategists should tread very warily in Southwest Asia. American policies should be damage-limiting rather than risk-inviting. They should not be governed solely by immediate U.S. objectives in the Persian Gulf or Afghanistan or Pakistan, but should rest on a broader recognition of the interdependence of long-term American interests in the entire region reaching from India through Iran.

With respect to the Baluch issue, the American goal should be to forestall the necessity for a choice between the Scylla of supporting repressive counterinsurgency programs and the Charybdis of supporting Baluch independence. In the final analysis, however, it is the Punjabis, the Persians, and the Baluch who will define the choices that confront the superpowers, and these choices could well prove to be extremely unpalatable to Washington. Recognizing the limits of American power in Islamabad and Teheran, the United States should begin, even now, to consider what the nature and range of its interests and options would be in the event that Pakistan or Iran or both should prove incapable of resolving their peculiarly stubborn federal problems.

If the will for compromise on the part of the indigenous actors is strong enough, the Soviet Union is not likely to find the Baluch issue a very easy one to manipulate. If there is little hope of compromise, no amount of American leverage is likely to succeed in pushing the parties to the bargaining table. Fortunately, in both Pakistan and Iran, the avenues toward a meaningful dialogue have not yet been completely closed off. But the possibility of national disintegration is increasing in both countries, opening up new horizons of opportunity for Moscow in Southwest Asia and deepening U.S. dilemmas.

Notes

Chapter One

1. Marvin and Bernard Kalb, *Kissinger* (Boston: Little, Brown, 1974), pp. 63–64.

2. "Issues and Answers," American Broadcasting Company, 30 December 1979.

3. See chapter nine for an explanation of this estimate, which is higher than official census figures in the countries concerned but lower than Baluch nationalist estimates.

4. Estimates of casualties suffered during the 1973–1977 insurgency are based primarily on interviews with twenty-three Pakistani military officers and defense officials; thirty-five residents of Baluchistan, many of them non-Baluch, who did not participate directly in the fighting, and sixty-five Baluch combatants and members of their families, most of them interviewed in the Kalat-i-Gilzai and other guerrilla camps in southern Afghanistan, described in chapters three and five. The insurgency is discussed at length in chapter three and in my article "After the Afghan Coup: Nightmare in Baluchistan," *Foreign Policy* 32 (1978).

5. For example, see Ainslie T. Embree, "Pakistan's Imperial Legacy," in *Pakistan's Western Borderlands*, ed. Ainslie T. Embree (Durham, NC: Carolina Academic Press, 1977).

Chapter Two

1. M. Longworth Dames, *Popular Poetry of the Baloches*, vol. 1 (London: Royal Asiatic Society, 1907), p. 45. See also J. H. Elfenbein, *The Baluchi Language: A Dialectology with Text*, Royal Asiatic Society Monographs, vol. 27 (London, 1966), pp. 41–45.

2. This estimate refers to literacy in all languages among Baluch in Pakistan, Iran, and the Persian Gulf. Robert G. Wirsing found that the highest literacy rate in eight of the nine districts in Pakistani Baluchistan was 7.7 percent ("South Asia: The Baluch Frontier Tribes of Pakistan," in *Protection of Ethnic Minorities: Comparative Perspectives*, ed. Robert G. Wirsing [New York: Pergamon, forthcoming], p. 18). Alvin Moore, South Asia specialist of the Library of Congress, estimated that there were 132,000 literates in Baluchi in 1981 ("Publishing in Pushto, Baluchi and Brahui, Part 2," in *South Asia: Library Notes and Queries* [Chicago: South Asia Reference Center, University of Chicago Library, March 1980], p. 3). *The Census of Pakistan*, vol. 3 (Karachi: Manager of Publications, 1961), p. IV-94, reported 87,000 literates in Baluchistan province. The 1972 census did not contain comparable tables.

3. John C. Griffiths, *Afghanistan* (London: Pall Mall, 1967), p. 52.

4. Sardar Mohammed Khan Baluch, *History of the Baluch Race and Baluchistan*, rev. ed. (Quetta: Gosha-e-Adab, 1977), pp. 5, 16–18, 22–25.

5. Ma'n Shana al-Ajli Al-Hakkami, *Balushistan Diyal Al-Arab* [Baluchistan: Land of the Arabs] (Bahrain: 1979), an Arab work citing Baluch sources. See also Mir Ahmed Yar Khan Baluch, *Inside Baluchistan* (Karachi: Royal Book Co., 1975) for the text of the Khan of Kalat's memorandum to the 1946 British Cabinet Mission, which states (p. 262) that the ruling family of Kalat is of Arab origin, having emigrated originally from Oman to Makran and thence northward.

6. Mir Khuda Bux Bijarani Marri Baloch, *Searchlight on Baloches and Baluchistan* (Karachi: Royal Book Co., 1974), pp. 12–14. See also Mir Gul Khan Nasir, *Tarikh-e-Baluchistan* [History of Baluchistan] (Quetta: Qaumi Ghar, 1952); Malik Mohammad Saeed, *Baluchistan Maqable Tarikh* [Baluchistan in Prehistory] (Quetta: Baluchi Academy, 1971); Abdur Rahim Sabir, *Baluchistan ki Vadiyun men* [In the Valleys of Baluchistan] (Karachi: Baluchi Adabi Board, 1962); Shams Uzzuha, *Hamara Baluchistan* [Our Baluchistan] (Quetta: Bolan Book Corp., 1972); Kamil ul Qadri, *Qadim Baluchistan* [Ancient Baluchistan] (Quetta: Bolan Book Corp., 1971); Nur Ahmad Khan Faridi, *Baluch Qaum au us ki Tarikh* [History of the Baluch Nation] (Multan, Pakistan: Qasr ul Adab, 1968); and Mir Muhammad Husain 'Anqa' Baluc, *Inquilabi Baluci Tarikh* [Ancient History of the Baluch Nation] (Quetta: Gosha-e-Adab, 1974).

7. Mir Khuda Bux Bijarani Marri Baloch, *Searchlight on Baloches.*

8. J. H. Elfenbein, "Baluchi," in *Encyclopedia of Islam* (Leiden: E. J. Brill, 1960), p. 1006. See also Elfenbein, *The Baluchi Language*, esp. pp. 41–45; and Richard N. Frye, "Remarks on Baluchi History," *Central Asiatic Journal* 4, no. 1 (1961): 49. See also an unpublished study by Jozef Adamik, "The Origins and Dialect Differentiation of Balochi" (1979). Mr. Adamik is a former student in the Department of Near Eastern Languages and Civilizations, Harvard University.

9. M. Longworth Dames, *The Baloch Race: A Historical and Ethnological Sketch* (London: Royal Asiatic Society, 1904), p. 43.

10. Ibid., p. 44.

11. Mir Khuda Bux Bijarani Marri Baloch, *Searchlight on Baloches*, p. 62.

12. Sardar Mohammed Khan Baluch, *History of the Baluch Race*, p. 48.

13. Mir Khuda Bux Bijarani Marri Baloch, *Searchlight on Baloches*, p. 61. For other examples of Baluch popular ballads, see also Dames, *Popular Poetry*, pp. 43–46; Elfenbein, *The Baluchi Language*, pp. 43ff.; and M.A.R. Barker and Aqil Khan Mengal, *A Course in Baluchi*, vol. 2 (Montreal: Institute of Islamic Studies, McGill University, 1969), esp. Unit 29, pp. 263–273.

14. Mir Ahmed Yar Khan Baluch, *Inside Baluchistan*, p. 84.

15. Nina Bailey Swidler, "The Political Structure of a Tribal Federation: The Brahui of Baluchistan" (Ph.D. diss., Columbia University, 1969).

16. Mir Ahmed Yar Khan Baluch, *Inside Baluchistan*, p. 85.

17. Sardar Mohammed Khan Baluch, *History of the Baluch Race*, p. 86.

18. The definitive Persian account of Dost Mohammed's defeat was written by the general who waged Reza Shah's successful campaign to subdue Baluchistan: Gen. Amanullah Jahanbani, *Amaliyat-i Qushun dar Baluchistan* [Army Activities in Baluchistan] (Teheran: 1957). See also Sir Henry T. Holland, "A Meeting with Dost Mohammed," *Asiatic Review* 30, no. 112 (1936): 694ff. For examples of Baluch nationalist adulation of Dost Mohammed, see Mohammed Akbar Baluch, *Baluch Qaum Apni Tarikh ke Aineh men* [The Baluch Nation and Its

History] (Quetta: Bolan Book Corp., 1975), and a cover story in the defunct Baluchi monthly *Baluchi Dunya* [Baluch World] (Karachi), February 1972.

19. Sir Henry Pottinger, *Travels in Belochistan and Sinde* (London: Longman, Hurst, Rees, Orme and Brown, 1816), p. 285.

20. J. H. Elfenbein, *The Baluchi Language*, pp. 42–43.

21. Barker and Mengal, *A Course in Baluchi*, p. 400.

22. Brian Spooner, "Tribal Ideal and Political Reality in a Cultural Borderland: Ethnohistorical Problems in Baluchistan" (Paper presented at the Ethnohistory Workshop, University of Pennsylvania, 10 April 1978), p. 8.

23. Ibid., p. 15.

24. Ibid., p. 16.

Chapter Three

1. Mir Ahmed Yar Khan Baluch, *Inside Baluchistan*, (Karachi: Royal Book Company, 1975), pp. 110–114.

2. Stephen Philip Cohen, "Security Decision-Making in Pakistan" (Report prepared for the Office of External Research, U.S. Department of State, September 1980), p. 41.

3. Karim Baluch, "The Democratic Struggle in Baluchistan," *Siyasat* no. 3 (London, 1975): 3.

4. Inayatullah Baloch, "Afghanistan-Pashtunistan-Baluchistan," *Aussen Politik* no. 3 (English ed.; Hamburg, 1980): 300. See also a pioneering study of this period by the same author, "The Emergence of Baluch Nationalism: 1931–47," *Pakistan Progressive* nos. 3–4 (New York, December 1980).

5. Mir Ahmed Yar Khan Baluch, *Inside Baluchistan*, p. 294.

6. Ibid., pp. 255–296. See esp. pp. 261, 268.

7. "Baluchistan" (a Note issued by the Information Ministry of the Pakistan Government, 2 May 1980) cites studies recounting the role of the gathering on June 29, 1947. Of eight participants mentioned in the Note, three were Baluch. See also Wayne Wilcox, *Pakistan: The Consolidation of a Nation* (New York: Columbia University Press, 1963), pp. 75–76, for an account of the accession issue drawing on Pakistani and British sources.

8. Inayatullah Baloch, "The Emergence of Baluch Nationalism," p. 19.

9. *Baluch Qaum Ke Tarikh-Ke Chand Parishan Dafter Auraq* [A Few Pages from the Official Records of the History of the Baluch Nation], comp. Malik Allah Bakhsh, Protocol Minister (Quetta: Islamiyyah Press, 20 September 1957), p. 17. This publication contains the major speeches made in the September and December Assembly sessions. For further elaboration of the Khan's position on the 1947 accession issue, see also *Mukhtasir Tarikh-Qaum-e-Baluch Wa Khawaneen-e-Baluch* [Short History of the Baluch Nation and the Baluch Khans], written under the orders and instructions of Mir Ahmed Yar Khan Baluch, Khan-I-Azam of Kalat (Quetta: Islamiyyah Press, 1970); and Mir Ahmed Yar Khan Baluch, *Baluch Qaum Ke Nam Khan-e-Baluch Ka Paigham* [Message from the Khan of the Baluch to the Baluch Nation] (Karachi: Litho Art Press, 1972).

10. Ibid., p. 43.

11. Mir Ahmed Yar Khan Baluch, *Inside Baluchistan*, pp. 180–190. See also Wilcox, *Pakistan*, p. 206; Herbert Feldman, *Revolution in Pakistan* (London: Ox-

ford University Press, 1967), pp. 42–43; Karim Baluch, "Democratic Struggle in Baluchistan," p. 5; and Sylvia A. Matheson, *The Tigers of Baluchistan* (London: Oxford University Press, 1967). Mrs. Matheson said in an interview in Teheran in 1978 that the blocking-out of certain portions of page 186 of her book included a description of the bombing of the Khan's palace by the Pakistan Air Force and a skeptical reference to the charge of a conspiracy with Afghanistan.

12. For a perceptive study of center-state tensions during the short-lived Baluch National Awami party regime in Baluchistan, see Philip Jones, "Center-Province Relations in Pakistan: The Case of Bhutto and the Regionalists" (Paper delivered at the 32nd Annual Convention of the Association for Asian Studies, Washington, DC, 23 March 1980). See also Robert G. Wirsing, ed., *Protection of Ethnic Minorities: Comparative Perspectives* (New York: Pergamon, forthcoming). The Pakistan government's view of the events leading up to the 1973 insurgency can be found in *White Paper on Baluchistan* (Rawalpindi: Government of Pakistan, 19 October 1974) and in the concluding address in the Pakistan Supreme Court by Yahya Bakhtiar in *Government's Reference on NAP's Dissolution* (Rawalpindi, 8–17 September 1975).

13. "List of Incidents Showing Firing Cases in Baluchistan from February 22, 1973 to December 31, 1975," Annexure G-5, pp. 108–113, and "Details of Firing and Other Acts of Sabotage/Terrorism in Baluchistan during 1974–75," Annexure G-3, pp. 99–103, in *State (Through Secretary, Minister of Interior)* v. *Abdul Wali Khan and Others*, a Complaint filed by the Government of Pakistan, Islamabad, before the Special Court, Hyderabad, 15 April 1976 (Notification F 44 (1)/76-A of 20 February 1976). See also the Supplementary Complaint filed before the Special Court. For a Pakistan Army officer's view of the insurgency, see Brigadier Muhammad Usman Hasan, *Baluchistan: Mazi, Hal Aur Mustaqbil* [Baluchistan: Past, Present and Future] (Karachi: Indus Publications, 1976), pp. 113–116. Among the few accounts of the insurgency published by the Western press were "Pakistan's Civil War," *Manchester Guardian*, 24 January 1975; and Alexander Dastarac and Robert Dersen, "Baluchistan: The Forgotten War," *Le Monde Diplomatique*, August 1976.

Chapter Four

1. Robert N. Pehrson, *The Social Organization of the Marri Baluch*, Viking Fund Publications in Anthropology, no. 43 (New York: Wenner Gren Foundation for Anthropological Research, 1966), p. 20.

2. "Bizenjo's Statement," *Imroze* (Lahore), 29 August 1978, p. 1. See also "Bijenjo and Nationalities," *Pakistan Times* (Lahore), 28 August 1978, p. 1; Salamat Ali, "Shaking the Foundations," *Far Eastern Economic Review*, 15 September 1978, pp. 24–25; and Mir Ghaus Bux Bizenjo, "The Basics of Our Politics," *Viewpoint* (Lahore), 28 August 1978, pp. 7–8.

3. Mir Ghaus Bux Bizenjo, "The Problems of Pakistan," *Pakistan Times*, 8 February 1978. See also a Punjabi rejoinder in a letter from Lt. Col. Rafi Nasim, *Pakistan Times*, 16 February 1978.

4. "Hum Apne Wattan Baluchistan Ko Azad Dekhna Chahte Hain" [We Want to See Our Country Baluchistan Free], *Nedae Baluchistan* [Voice of Baluchistan] 1, no. 4 (London), February 1981, pp. 2–4. See also a letter from Mengal in the January 1981 issue of *Nedae Baluchistan*.

Chapter Five

1. *Strategy for Liberation: The War in Baluchistan* (Paris: Baluchistan People's Liberation Front, 1976), p. 8.

2. *Jabal* (Bulletin of the Baluchistan People's Liberation Front), December 1976, p. 1. The London Group, which edited *Jabal*, used the name *Baluchistan People's Liberation Front*, reflecting their desire to play down the group's ethnic identity and emphasize its character as a Marxist-Leninist organization championing a cause related to leftist objectives throughout Pakistan. However, Sher Mohammed Marri and Mir Hazar said this was an "error" and that the proper nomenclature is the Baluch People's Liberation Front. This dispute exemplified the tensions between the London Group and other Front leaders that led to the defection of some London Group adherents in 1981.

3. *Jabal*, February 1977, p. 10A.

4. *Jabal*, February 1978, p. 2.

5. "Talib Ilm Tanzeem Aur Harawal Party May Farq Karna Lazimee Hay" [It Is a Must to Differentiate between Student Organization and the Vanguard Party], Excerpts from a report of the BSO-Awami National Council, 4th sess., in *Pakistan Forum* (Karachi), September 1978, p. 10.

6. "Mazakarat Aur Aam Maafi Ka Nushk" [Negotiation and the General Amnesty], *Pajjar*, January-February 1978, p. 2. See also the references to Sher Mohammed Marri in Nargis Latif, "BSO (Awami) on Student Politics," *Viewpoint* (Lahore), 10 January 1979, p. 13. For a useful summary of BSO activities and policies, see the special issue of *Baluchi Dunya* [Baluch World], October 1972, on the BSO, esp. the lead article, "Baluch Talaba Ka Ittehod Zindabod" [Long Live the Unity of Baluch Students], pp. 5–8.

7. See the transcript of "Panorama," (BBC Transmission 1925(2), 31 January 1980), p. 10, in which Kurd is interviewed by correspondent Tom Mangold.

8. "What PNP Stands For," *Viewpoint* (Lahore), 19 August 1979, p. 7. See also "A National Party Is Born," *Viewpoint*, 10 June 1979, p. 10.

Chapter Six

1. Sir Olaf Caroe, *Wells of Power: The Oil Fields of Southwestern Asia*, History and Politics of Oil Series (1951; reprint ed., Westport, CT: Hyperion Press, 1976).

2. Philip C. Salzman, "Adaptation and Change among the Yarahmadzai Baluch" (Ph.D. diss., University of Chicago, 1972), pp. 266–268. For an excellent overview of tribal society in Iranian Baluchistan, see Brian Spooner, "Political and Religious Leadership in Persian Baluchistan," (Ph.D. diss., Oxford University, 1967) and "Politics, Kinship and Ecology in Southeast Persia," *Ethnology* 8, no. 2 (1969). See also Philip C. Salzman, "The Proto-State in Iranian Baluchistan," in *Origins of the State: The Anthropology of Political Evolution*, ed. R. Cohen and E. Service (Philadelphia: ISHI, 1978); "Adaptation and Political Organization in Iranian Baluchistan," *Ethnology* 10, no. 4 (1971); and "Continuity and Change in Baluchi Tribal Leadership," *International Journal of Middle East Studies* 4, no. 4 (1973).

3. *Sistan va Baluchistan: Mutala'at Bar Nameh Tavaso'i Iqtisadi va Ijtimai'l* [Sistan and Baluchistan: Studies in Economic and Social Development] (Zahedan:

Planning Office, Sistan and Baluchistan, 1976), Table 3-A. For earlier official census figures relating to the Baluch, see *Census Report* (Teheran: Iranian Statistical Center, 1968) and Zabibullah Nasih, *Introduction to the Culture and Civilization of Iran*, vol. 8 (Teheran: Kitab Khanae Ibnsina, 1965), which cites a figure of 271,584 Baluch in Iran in 1930.

4. C. L. Sulzberger, "Belief in Crude Reality," *New York Times*, 22 April 1973.

5. *Middle East Monitor*, 1 June 1973. See also "Pakistani Leader Ends Stay in Iran," *New York Times*, 15 May 1973.

6. "The Shah on War and Peace," *Newsweek*, 14 November 1977. p. 70.

7. *Natije Amaar Giri Edareh Kohl Amouzesh Va Parvaresh Ostan, Sistan Va Baluchistan Dar Sall Tahsili 2536–2537* [The Results of the Statistics Done by the Department of Education, Provinces of Sistan and Baluchistan, in the Educational Year 1977–1978] (Zahedan: Department of Education, Provinces of Sistan and Baluchistan, 1978), Table 19.

8. Ibid., Tables 1, 7, 3, 12.

9. "U. S. Aides Slain in Ambush in Iran," *New York Times*, 26 March 1957.

10. "Pakistanis Press Iran Killer Hunt," *New York Times*, 11 April 1957. See also "U. S. Halts Aid in Southeast Iran," *New York Times*, 2 April 1957.

11. "Iranian Troops Seek Seized U. S. Woman," *New York Times*, 29 March 1957.

12. Jean Viennot, "Baluchistan: A New Bangladesh?" *Le Monde Diplomatique*, November 1973.

13. For example, see repeated references to Dad Shah in Mohammed Akbar Baluch, *Baluch Qaum Apni Tarikh ke Aineh Men* [The Baluch Nation and Its History] (Quetta: Bolan Book Corp., 1975).

14. *Baluchistan: Introduction and Liberation Struggle* (Baluchistan Liberation Front, n.d.), p. 12. This pamphlet, issued clandestinely and bearing no name of a publisher or printer, was obtained in Teheran in December 1972 by Philip Salzman, professor of Anthropology at McGill University, Montreal. The author is grateful to Professor Salzman for making it available.

15. Ibid., p. 18.

16. For a description of Baluch links with the Arabs in the mid-sixties, see "Arab Support for Baluchistan," *Foreign Report* (London, Economist Newspaper Limited), 14 February 1973, p. 5.

17. Sepehr Zabih, *The Communist Movement in Iran* (Berkeley: University of California Press, 1966), pp. 180–183.

18. "Political Program of the Democratic Party of Baluchistan," in Mahmoud Panahiyan, *Farhang Gughraphia-e-Milli Baluchistan Iran* [Culture and Geography of the Baluch Nation in Iran] (Baghdad: 1971), pp. 8, 11, 15–19. This program was ratified at the first and only conference of the Democratic party of Baluchistan (Iranian), 20–23 February 1972, according to K. B. Nizamani.

19. *Baluchistan: Introduction and Liberation Struggle*, p. 17.

20. Kianuri's interview in *Nepszabadsag* (Budapest) was reported in *Foreign Broadcast Information Service Daily Report (Iran)*, 22 January 1980, pp. 12–13.

21. Brian Spooner, "Religion and Society Today: An Anthropological Perspective," in *Iran Faces the Seventies*, ed. E. Yar-Shater (New York: Praeger, 1971). See also Spooner, "Political and Religous Leadership in Persian Baluchistan," p. 446–448; and Philip C. Salzman, "Islam and Authority in Tribal Iran: A Comparative Comment," *Muslim World* (Hartford Seminary Foundation) 1975, no. 3, pp. 186–192.

22. Interview in *Ayandegan* (Teheran), 22 July 1979, trans. in *Review of Iranian Political Economy and History* 4, no. 1 (1980): 75.

23. See "Baluchi Movement Congratulates Revolution," *Foreign Broadcast Information Service Daily Report (Iran)*, 12 February 1979, p. R-32; and "Khomeini Sends Envoy to Sistan-Baluchistan," *FBIS Daily Report (Iran)*, 2 April 1979, p. R-13.

24. "Sunni Leader in Baluchistan," *FBIS Daily Report (Iran)* 28 March 1979, p. R-6.

25. *Review of Iranian Political Economy and History* 4, no. 1 (1980): 75–77.

26. *Makran* 1, no. 1 (Teheran, 1979): 2.

27. Ibid., p. 1.

28. "America Mesr Iraq Arabistan va Ordon Barai Ejade Eghteshash va Tajzeye Iran de Tavafuq Rasedand" [America, Egypt, Iraq, Arabistan, and Saudi Arabia Have Reached Agreement for Creating Disturbances and Dividing Up Iran), *Kayhan* (Teheran), 29 January 1981. See also Radio Teheran commentary in Arabic, reported in *FBIS Daily Report (Iran)* 2 February 1981, p. I-16.

29. Najib Al-Rayyes, "Balushistan: Thawrah Tabhath An Sha'ir" [Baluchistan: A Revolution in Search of a Poet], *Al-Mostakbal* [The Future] (Paris), 29 September 1979, p. 15.

30. "Tahridan Ala Urubat Balushistan" [Calling for the Arabization of Baluchistan], *Al-Mostakbal*, 2 February 1980, p. 10.

31. Ibid., p. 12.

32. Ma'n Shana al-Ajli Al-Hakkami, *Balushistan Diyal Al-Arab* [Baluchistan: Land of the Arabs] (Bahrain: 1979), p. 7.

33. Ibid., p. 35.

34. Sally Quinn, "The Arabs in London: The Merchant," *Washington Post*, 18 July 1977.

Chapter Seven

1. "Draft Program of Action of the Communist Party of India," *International Press Correspondence*, 18 December 1930, cited in "The Communist Party of India," U. S. Office of Strategic Services, Research and Analysis Branch, Report no. 2681 (August 1945).

2. G. Adhikari, *Pakistan and Indian National Unity*, (Bombay: People's Publishing House, 1944), p. 8. See a discussion of the Congress-Communist debate over this issue in Selig S. Harrison, *India: The Most Dangerous Decades* (Princeton: Princeton University Press, 1960), pp. 150–156.

3. Memorandum of the Communist party of India to the British Cabinet Mission, mimeographed, (15 April 1946). See related sources cited in Harrison, *India*, p. 154.

4. Gene D. Overstreet and Marshall Windmiller, *Communism in India* (Berkeley: University of California Press, 1958), p. 81.

5. "Questions and Answers: Nationalities and the Right of Secession," *Crossroads* (New Delhi), 6 September 1953, p. 10.

6. Yuri V. Gankovsky, *Narody Pakistane: Etnicheskaia Istoriia* [The Peoples of Pakistan: An Ethnic History] (Moscow: Nauka Publishing House, 1964), p. 225. An English edition was brought out by the same publisher in 1971.)

7. Ibid., p. 208.

8. M. G. Pikulin, *Beludzhei: Istoriia i Ekonimiia* [The Baluch: History and Economy] (Moscow: Nauka Publishing House, 1959).

9. M. G. Pikulin, "K Voprosy o Natsional'noi Konsolidatsii Beludzhei Pakistanskogo Beludzhanistana" [On the Question of the National Consolidation of the Baluch of Pakistan], *Izvestiia Akademii Nauk UzSSR* [News of the Academy of Sciences of the Uzbek SSR], 1960, no. 4, p. 20.

10. Yuri V. Gankovsky, *Natsional'nyi Vopros i Natsional'nye Dvizheniia v Pakistane* [The National Question and National Movements in Pakistan] (1967; reprint ed., Moscow: Nauka Publishing House, 1977), pp. 206, 250.

11. Beknazar Ibragimov, *Beludzhei Pakistane* [The Baluch of Pakistan] (Moscow: Nauka Publishing House, 1973), p. 4.

12. Ibid., p. 94.

13. Ibid., p. 210.

14. M. S. Lazarev, "K Natsional'noi Situatsii na Sovremennom Vostoke" [On the National Situation in the Contemporary Orient] in *Natsional'nye Problemy Sovremennogo Vostoka* [National Problems in the Contemporary Orient] (Moscow: Institute of Oriental Studies, 1977), p. 50.

15. "Pakistan's So-Called Left," *People's Front* (London), February 1979, p. 3.

16. Aijaz Ahmed, "The National Question in Baluchistan," in *Focus on Baluchistan and the Pushtun Question,* ed. Feroz Ahmad (Lahore: People's Publishing House, 1975), pp. 30–31. The article first appeared in *Pakistan Forum* (June 1973).

17. "Strategy Document: Struggle for Independent National Democracy in Pakistan," mimeographed (1 May 1976), pp. 44–45.

18. " 'Free' Elections in Afghanistan," *People's Front,* April 1980, p. 1.

19. David Housego, "Baluchis Bitter At Army Occupation," *Financial Times* (London), 5 February 1980.

20. Han Xu, "Peaceful Coexistence in the Asia-Pacific Region," in *Day after Tomorrow in the Pacific Region, 1981* (New York: Worldview Magazine and the Asia Society, 1981), p. 27.

21. Interview with the author.

22. *People's Front* first advocated independence in April 1979 (see "Our Aim: National Freedom," 19 April 1979, p. 1).

23. Inayatullah Baloch, "Afghanistan-Pashtunistan-Baluchistan," *Aussen Politik* 3 (English ed.; Hamburg, 1980): 291–292.

24. Eden Naby, "The Iranian Frontier Nationalities: The Kurds, the Assyrians, the Baluchis, and the Turkmens," in *Soviet Asian Ethnic Frontiers,* ed. William O. McCagg, Jr., and Brian D. Silver (New York: Pergamon, 1979), p. 105.

25. "For the Oppressed Peoples of Afghanistan," Program of the People's Democratic party of Afghanistan, *Khalq* (Kabul), 11 April 1966.

26. *Basic Lines of Revolutionary Duties of the Government of the Democratic Republic of Afghanistan,* Broadcast by Prime Minister Nur Mohammed Taraki (Kabul: Democratic Republic of Afghanistan, 9 May 1978), p. 33.

27. Ibid., p. 34.

28. "H. Amin's Address to Charmang and Bajaur People," *Kabul Times,* 5 August 1979.

29. "H. Amin: This Is a Revolution Which Handed Power From One Strata to the Other," *Kabul Times,* 21 August 1979.

30. "Spongers, Oppressors Have No Power Now in Afghanistan," *Kabul Times,* 20 September 1979.

31. "Babrak Karmal Greets Afghan Nation," *Kabul New Times*, 1 January 1980.
32. "An Honest Leader: Press Conference," *Kabul New Times*, 8 January 1980.
33. "Unbreakable Links with Our Brothers," *Kabul New Times*, 17 January 1980.
34. "U. S. Arming Pakistan," *Kabul New Times*, 20 February 1980.

Chapter Eight

1. Robert G. Wirsing, "South Asia: The Baluch Frontier Tribes of Pakistan," in *Protection of Ethnic Minorities: Comparative Perspectives*, ed. Robert G. Wirsing (New York: Pergamon, forthcoming), p. 25.
2. In the Supreme Court of Pakistan (Rawalpindi), *Constitutional Petition No. One-R of 1977*, Begum Nusrat Bhutto v. Chief of Army Staff, etc., p., 18. See also pp. 33, 47, 104. See also In the Supreme Court of Pakistan, *Criminal Appeal No. 11 of 1978*, The State v. Zulfiqar Ali Bhutto, pp. 23–28.
3. Selig S. Harrison, *India: The Most Dangerous Decades* (Princeton: Princeton University Press, 1960).

Chapter Nine

1. Alex Beam, "Polisario War in the Sahara," *Nation*, 21 January 1978, p. 43. See also "Shifting Sands," *Time*, 3 September 1979, p. 31.
2. Shahid Javed Burki, *Pakistan under Bhutto* (New York: St. Martin's, 1980), Table 5.1, p. 94.
3. See chapter two, note 2.
4. Robert G. Wirsing, "South Asia: The Baluch Frontier Tribes of Pakistan," in *Protection of Ethnic Minorities: Comparative Perspectives*, ed. Robert G. Wirsing (New York: Pergamon, forthcoming), p. 18.
5. "Baluchistan," mimeographed (A Note issued by the Information Ministry of the Pakistan Government, 2 May 1980), pp. 3–4. See also *The New Face of Baluchistan* (Islamabad: Pakistan Publications, May 1980).
6. Letter to Harrison from Khalid Ali, Press Counselor, Embassy of Pakistan (Washington, DC), 2 February 1981, citing Article 160 of the Pakistani constitution.
7. Letter to Harrison from Khalid Ali, 19 December 1980, citing a notification in the *Gazette of Pakistan*, 9 June 1975. See also Lukin Robinson, "Equalization and the Price of Oil," *Canadian Forum* (Ottawa), October 1980.
8. Mir Khuda Bux Bijarani Marri Baloch, *Searchlights on Baloches and Balochistan* (Karachi: Royal Book Co., 1974), pp. 269–271.
9. "Production of Barytes in Baluchistan," *Jabal*, November 1977, p. 3.
10. "Baluchistan ki Mulazemataun se Baluchaun ki Mahrumi" [The Baluch Are Deprived of Jobs in Baluchistan], *Nedae Baluchistan* 1, no. 1 (London, 1980): 1. See also "Baluchistan: Turbulent Fragment," *Time*, 15 January 1979, p. 33.
11. "Baluchistan," (Information Ministry), p. 11.
12. Stephen Philip Cohen, "Security Decision-Making in Pakistan," (Report

prepared for the Office of External Research, U.S. Department of State, September 1980), p. 37.

13. "A Note on the Resource Development Corporation's Saindak Porphyry Copper Deposits, Chagai District, Baluchistan" (U.S. Embassy, Rawalpindi, 1978). See also "Riches on a Troubled Border," *Far Eastern Economic Review*, 21 March 1980, p. 86.

14. *White Paper on Baluchistan*, (Rawalpindi: Government of Pakistan, 19 October 1974), p. 31.

15. "Baluchistan" (Information Ministry), p. 10.

16. *Achievements of the People's Government, 1972–76: Baluchistan* (Islamabad: Ministry of Information and Broadcasting, 1976), pp. 6–7.

17. *White Paper on Baluchistan*, p. 33. See also "Pledges Made in 1970 Fulfilled," *Pakistan Times* (Karachi), 25 January 1977.

18. "Baluchistan" (Information Ministry), p. 5.

19. "Imperialism, Oil and the Baluchistan Revolution," *Jabal*, July 1977, p. 6.

20. Charles C. Yahr, "The Economic Development Potential of the Baluchistan States of Pakistan" (Ph.D. diss., University of Illinois, 1956), pp. 201–202.

21. "Mineral Development," *Dawn* (Karachi), 9 January 1978, p. 6. See also "Search for Mineral Wealth On," *Pakistan Affairs* (Pakistan Embassy, Washington, DC), 10 April 1978, p. 3.

22. "Abundant Promise in New Oil and Gas Finds," *Financial Times* (London), 11 August 1978, Pakistan Supplement, pp. 13–14.

23. "Oil Prospecting Soon," *Pakistan Times*, 3 November 1977.

24. "Golden Triangle Seen," *Dawn*, 22 December 1976.

25. Letter to Harrison from J. C. Van Wagner, Resident Manager, Amoco Far East Exploration Company (Singapore), 26 July 1978. Mr. Van Wagner served as Amoco's resident manager in Pakistan from 1973 to 1977.

26. "Imperialism, Oil and the Baluchistan Revolution," p. 7.

27. Mir Ahmed Yar Khan Baluch, *Inside Baluchistan* (Karachi: Royal Book Co. 1975), p. 42.

28. "Imperialism, Oil and the Baluchistan Revolution," p. 5.

29. Societa Generale per Progettazioni, Consulenze e Partecipazioni (Italconsult), "Economic and Social Development Plan for the Southeastern Region" (Project 37, Buildings Materials Research, Rome, May 1962), esp. pp. 3, 6, 9, 17, 28, 219.

30. M. B. Pithawalla, *The Problem of Baluchistan: Development and Conservation of Water Resources, Soils and Natural Vegetation* (Karachi: Ministry of Economic Affairs, 1952), esp. pp. 17, 48, 55, 90.

31. Mir Khuda Bux Bijarani Marri Baloch, *Searchlight on Baloches*, p. 303.

32. The Baluch settlers in East Asia are discussed in Walter T. Brown, "A Pre-Colonial History of Bagamoyo (Tanzania)" (Ph.D. diss., Boston University, 1971), pp. 256–266.

33. Mir Ahmed Yar Khan Baluch, *Inside Baluchistan*, p. 207.

34. Sardar Mohammed Khan Baluch, *History of the Baluch Race and Baluchistan*, rev. ed. (Quetta: Gosha-e-Adab, 1977), Prologue; and Mir Khuda Bux Bijarani Marri Baloch, *Searchlight on Baloches*, pp. 15–24.

35. Interview with Chief Minister G. M. Barozai of Baluchistan province, 3 February 1977. Data relating to the 1972 census was provided by the Information Ministry, Government of Pakistan.

36. *Census of Pakistan,* vol. 3, *West Pakistan, Tables and Report, Population, 1.* (Karachi: Ministry of Home and Kashmir Affairs), Statement 7-B.

37. For example, Mir Khuda Bux Bijarani Marri Baloch, *Searchlight on Baloches,* p. 16.

38. Frederik Barth, "Ethnic Processes on the Pathan-Baluch Boundary," in *Indo-Iranica,* ed. G. Renard (Wiesbaden: Harrassowitz, 1964).

39. Selig S. Harrison, "After the Afghan Coup: Nightmare in Baluchistan," *Foreign Policy* 32 (1978): 153.

40. Letter to Harrison, 20 January 1981.

41. Sardar Mohammed Khan Baluch, *History of the Båluch Race,* pp. 124–127.

42. Mir Ahmed Yar Khan Baluch, *Inside Baluchistan,* pp. 66, 71.

43. Gul Khan Nasir, *Tarikh-e-Baluchistan* [History of Baluchistan] (Quetta: Quami Ghar, 1952), p. 112.

44. Mir Khuda Bux Bijarani Marri Baloch, *Searchlight on Baloches,* p. 239.

45. Ibid., p. 110.

46. Mir Gul Khan Nasir, *Tarikh-e-Baluchistan* [History of Baluchistan] (Quetta: Qaumi Ghar, 1952), p. 11.

47. Feroz Ahmad, *Focus on Baluchistan and Pushtoon Question* (Lahore: People's Publishing House, 1975), p. 16.

48. Warren W. Swidler, "Technology and Social Structure in Baluchistan, West Pakistan" (Ph.D. diss., Columbia University, 1968), p. 29.

49. Nina Bailey Swidler, "Brahui Political Organization and the National State," in *Pakistan's Western Borderlands,* ed. Ainslie T. Embree (Durham, NC: Carolina Academy Press, 1977), p. 112. See also Nina Bailey Swidler, "The Political Structure of a Tribal Federation: The Brahui of Baluchistan" (Ph.D. diss., Columbia University, 1969), p. 29.

50. Mir Khuda Bux Bijarani Marri Baloch, *Searchlight on Baloches,* pp. 110, 226.

51. Murray B. Emeneau, *Brahui and Dravidian Comparative Grammar* (Berkeley and Los Angeles: University of California Press, 1962), and "Linguistic Desiderata in Baluchistan," in *Indo-Iranica,* ed. G. Renard (Wiesbaden: Harrassowitz, 1964), pp. 73–77.

52. Alvin Moore, Jr., "Publishing in Pushto, Baluchi, Brahui, and Other Minor Languages of Pakistan, Part 3," *South Asia: Library Notes and Queries* (Chicago: South Asia Reference Center, University of Chicago Library, June 1980), p. 3.

53. M.A.R. Barker and Aqil Khan Mengal, *A Course in Baluchi,* vol. 2 (Montreal: Institute of Islamic Studies, McGill University, 1969), p. 7.

54. J. H. Elfenbein, *The Baluchi Language: A Dialectology with Text,* Royal Asiatic Society Monographs, vol. 27, (London, 1966), pp. 3, 10.

55. Barker and Mengal, *A Course in Baluchi,* p. 8. However, Baluchi publications continually carry complaints that Radio Karachi, Radio Quetta, and Radio Teheran do not use Baluchi often enough. For example, see "Baluchi Zaben Se Imtiazi Suluk Kun?" [Why Is There Discrimination against the Baluchi Language?], *Baluchi Dunya* [Baluch World] (Karachi), December 1971, p. 33–34.

56. M. Longworth Dames, *Popular Poetry of the Baloches,* vol. 2 (London: Royal Asiatic Society, 1907), p. 201. Barker and Mengal in *A Course in Baluchi,* p. 1, describe the Baluchi alphabet. The author is indebted to Richard N. Frye for a clarification of the relationship between Baluchi and the Arabic alphabet.

57. For example, see "A Plea for the Use of the Roman Script," *Baluchi Dunya,* November 1971, p. 14; and A. S. Sorbazi, "Baluch Ka Rasm Ul Khat Kia Ho" [What Script Should Be Used for Baluchi?], *Baluchi Dunya,* January 1973. See also *Jabal,* May-June 1978, p. 3.

58. See letters from advocates of the Roman script in *Labzank* [Treasure of Language], June 1977, pp. 78–79.

59. See chapter two, note 2.

60. Stephen Pastner, "A Nudge from the Hand of God," *Natural History,* March 1978, pp. 32–34. See also Pastner, "Power and Pirs among the Pakistani Baluch," *Journal of Asian and African Studies* 13, nos. 3–4 (1978): 231–243; and Stephen and Carroll McC. Pastner, "Secular and Sacred Leadership among the Pakistani Baluch" (Paper prepared for a U.S. Department of State Conference on Baluchistan, 10 March 1980). For an account of alleged Pakistani government efforts to exploit differences between Zikris and other Baluch, see "Baluchistan Main Fir Qa Warana Fasadat Karane Key Sazish" [Conspiracy to Instigate Sectarian Riots in Baluchistan], *Pajjar,* May-June 1978, p. 3.

61. For an analysis of this climate two years before the secession of Bangladesh, see Selig S. Harrison, "East Pakistanis Resent Army Takeover," a two-part series from Dacca, *Washington Post,* 30 March and 1 April 1969.

62. Cited in Zulfiqar Ali Bhutto, "Pakistan Builds Anew," *Foreign Affairs* 51, no. 3 (1973): 545. See also Mohammed Iqbal's 1930 proposal for a "loose federation of all India" in Sir Reginald Coupland, *India: A Restatement* (London: Oxford University Press, 1945), p. 189.

Chapter Ten

1. For example, see Richard Pipes, "Soviet Global Strategy," *Commentary,* April 1980, pp. 31–39; and Sol W. Sanders, "Moscow's Next Target in Its March Southward," *Business Week,* 21 January 1980, p. 51.

2. Herbert E. Meyer in "Why We Should Worry about the Soviet Energy Crunch," *Fortune,* 25 February 1980, pp. 82–88, presents the view that the Soviet bloc will have a growing energy shortage.

3. See Kennan's testimony on 27 February 1980 in *U.S. Security Interests and Policies in Southwest Asia,* Hearings before the Committee on Foreign Relations, U.S. Senate, 96th Cong., 2nd sess., pp. 87–120.

4. Selig S. Harrison, "Dateline Afghanistan: Exit Through Finland?" *Foreign Policy* 41 (1980-81): 163–187.

5. Marshall Goldman in "Is There a Russian Energy Crisis?" *Atlantic,* September 1980, pp. 55–64, disputes projections of a Soviet-bloc energy shortage.

6. Edward N. Luttwak in "After Afghanistan, What?" *Commentary,* April 1980, pp. 43–44, argues that its low population density makes Baluchistan more advantageous as a Soviet invasion route than a route farther west originating from bases in the Caucasus. But he concludes that an airborne attack on the oil fields would be more likely than a land invasion. See also Vernon V. Aspaturian, "Moscow's Afghan Gamble," *New Leader,* 28 January 1980, pp. 7–13; and David Lynn Price, "Moscow and the Persian Gulf," *Problems of Communism,* March-April 1979.

7. "Deng: A Third World War Is Inevitable," *Washington Post,* 1 September 1980.

8. Harrison, "Dateline Afghanistan," pp. 180-181.

9. For a perceptive account of the Nixon-Kissinger policy toward India and Pakistan, see William J. Barnds, "India, Pakistan and American Realpolitik," *Christianity and Crisis,* 12 June 1972. See also Joseph Alsop, "U.S. Role in South Asia," *Washington Post,* 14 January 1972.

10. Transcript of a Press Conference by U.S. Secretary of Defense Harold Brown (Beijing: 9 January 1980), p. 1.

11. *Congress Bulletin* (New Delhi), All-India Congress Committee, 10 July 1947.

Index

Afghanistan: and Baluch guerrillas, 39, 50, 51, 81; as buffer state to British Indian empire, 19; Communist movement in, 80, 81, 82, 142–148; Durand line, 19, 143, 144, 146; Greater, 143; and Kalat revolt, 26; and Liberation Front, 80–83; Parcham regime, 82; Soviet occupation, 1, 51, 59, 121, 137, 195, 196, 203; U.S. and, 199. *See also* Baluch, Afghan; Soviet Union

Agriculture, Baluchistan, 8, 9
Ahmad, Feroz, 144–45
Ahmadzai tribe, 15
Ahmed, Aijaz, 135
Ahmed Shah, 105
Al-Hakkami, Ma'n Shana al-Ajli, 121–23, 124
Al-Khalifa dynasty, 123
Al-Mohammed, Sheikh Mohammed Bin Hassan, 123, 124, 125, 140
Al-Rayyes, Riyad Najib, 121
American Smelting and Refining Company (ASARCO), 166, 170
Amin, Hafizullah, 87, 140, 195; on Greater Afghanistan, 143–45; Soviet removal of, 146
Amoco, petroleum operations in Baluchistan, 172–73
Amouzegar, Jamshid, and economic development of Iranian Baluchistan, 99–100, 167
Anjuman-e-Ittehad-e-Baluchistan. *See* Organization for the Unity of Baluchistan
Arabian Sea, 1, 2, 195
Arabs: and independent Baluchistan, 106–07, 121–22, 125
Arafat, Yasser, 106, 120
Arya, Khalidad, 117

ASARCO. *See* American Smelting and Refining Company
Awami League, 88
Awami Tehriq. *See* People's League
Ayub Khan, 27; imposition of One Unit plan, 43, 45; and Khair Bux Marri, 45, 46; and Muslim League, 153

Bahrain sheikhdom, 123, 125
Bajpai, Shankar, 43
Bakhsh, Shah, 107, 112, 177
Bakhtiar, Shahpour, 199
Baloch, Inayatullah, 24, 26n, 141
Baluch, Hamid, 87
Baluch, Khair Jan, 74, 75, 81; Communist associations, 138; guerrilla activity, 86
Baluch, Mohammed Khan, 17, 183
Baluch, Rahim Bux, 86
Baluch: cultural heritage, 11–12; early efforts at political unification, 12, 15–19; origins, 10–11
Baluch, Afghan, 82; number of, 178; Pushtuns versus, 89, 142–47, 158, 180–82
Baluch, Iranian: different views on independence, 111–12; employment discrimination against, 103; expanded educational facilities, 101–03; gerrymandering to reduce political force of, 96; migration of, 96; military control over, 94–95; number of, 177; oil boom effect on, 100–01; tribal differences in reaction to Shah, 110; and U.S., 119–20
Baluch, Pakistani: employment discrimination against, 164; fight for regional autonomy, 3; number of, 177–78; politicization, 4; Pushtuns

versus, 89. *See also* Guerrilla movement, in Pakistan

Baluchi. *See* Language

Baluchistan: agriculture, 8, 9; Al-Hakkami on history of, 122; climate, 7; ecological factors influencing political unity, 19–20; economy, 8; physical features, 1, 7; as potential Soviet target, 1–2; tribal power structure, 9. *See also* Independence of Greater Baluchistan

Baluchistan, British, 19, 21, 24

Baluchistan, Iranian: breakdown of central authority, 112; cities and towns, 9; defeat of Baluch chiefs, 21; economic development, 97, 99–100, 159–60, 167–68; education, 101–03, 167; five regions of, 94. *See also* Baluch, Iranian; Nationalist movement (Baluch), in Iran

Baluchistan, Pakistani: Baluch provincial government, 34, 35; cities and towns, 9; coal, 163; copper deposits, 165–66, 170, 174; development program for, 159–60, 161–63, 169; education, 22, 84, 167; guerrilla warfare, 3, 22, 28, 29, 30; importance to rest of Pakistan, 149–50; as Iranian protectorate, 97; marble-quarrying, 163–64; natural gas, 158; poverty of, 161–62; road-building, 166–67; share of national tax allocation, 169; Special Development Plan, 164–66; unexploited mineral resources, 171–72; water resources, 174–75. *See also* Baluch, Pakistani; Nationalist movement (Baluch), in Pakistan

Baluchistan Development Corporation, 99

Baluchistan Liberation Front (Iran), 105, 118; Iraqi support for, 106–07, 108; Tudeh party versus, 109

Baluchistan People's Democratic Organization (BPDO) (Sazman-e-Demokratik-e Mardom-e Baluchistan): formation, 117; publications, 117–18

Baluch Marxist party, 134

Baluch People's Liberation Front (Pakistan), 34, 39, 71, 118; Bizenjo and,

56; BSO and, 85; divergent elements in, 74–75; ideology, 72, 76, 81; Khair Bux Marri and, 42, 49; Marxist-Leninist doctrine, 76; number of members, 75; organizational structure, 75–76; reaction to Soviet occupation of Afghanistan, 80; recruits from student movement, 83; on sovereign independence versus national liberation, 76, 79. *See also* People's Revolutionary Command

Baluch People's Political and Cultural Center (Kanoon Siasi-Farhangi-Khalq Baluch), 118

Baluch Pesh Marga. *See* Baluch Volunteer Force

Baluch Students Organization (BSO), 40, 71, 118, 138; guerrilla activity, 86–87; membership, 83, 84; and Pakistan Federal Union of Students, 85; political leanings, 84–86; publications, 84, 187; and Soviet Union, 87

Baluch Students Organization–Awami, 83; membership, 84; political leanings, 84–85; publications, 84

Baluch Volunteer Force (Baluch Pesh Marga), 118

Bangash, Afzal, 146

Bangladesh, 155, 188, 189, 202

Barakzai, Amanullah, 118–19

Barakzai, Mir Amin, 112

Barozai, G. M., 181

Bengalis: nationalism, 188; Punjabis versus, 88

Bhabba, Mohammed. *See* Khan, Murad

Bhutto, Zulfiqar Ali, 30; and Baluch provincial government, 34, 35, 46, 97; expansion of education by, 84; on potential Baluch secession, 156–57; on *sardari* system, 156; on unitary constitutional government, 155–56; water resources development program, 175; on Zia and Baluch, 154–55

Bizenjo, Ghaus Bux, 19; and Baluch independence, 25, 54; in Baluch provincial government, 34; in Baluch triumvirate, 41, 89; Bhutto accusations against, 35, 157; and Communist party, 133; on federation of Pakistani states, 55–56, 57–58, 191; imprisonment, 36; and Iranian Shah, 59; on Kalat-Pakistan relations, 25; opposition to alignment with superpowers, 61; plans for state marble monopoly, 164; profile of, 52, 54; on regional confederations, 54–55, 147; and Soviet Union, 57–59, 60; and Zia, 39–40, 84, 151, 153–54

BPDO. *See* Baluchistan People's Democratic Organization

Brahui tribe, 183–84; language, 185

British Raj: efforts to expand, 19; incorporation of Baluch into Pakistan by, 3; suppression of nationalism under, 22

BSO. *See* Baluch Students Organization

BSO-Awami. *See* Baluch Students Organization–Awami

Bukti, Akbar, 36, 52, 154

Bukti, Razik, 84, 85

Bukti tribal area, 162, 175

Butt, Nawaz, 58

Caroe, Sir Olaf, 94

Carter doctrine, applied to Baluchistan, 1

Central Treaty Organization (CENTO), 105, 159

Chah Bahar, 119, 120; Baluch-controlled, 107; 111

Chamalang, battle of, 38

Chronicle of Genealogies. *See Daptar Sha'ar*

Coal, in Pakistani Baluchistan, 163

Communists: Afghan, 127; and Baluch independence, 22, 127, 134–41; Iranian, 111; Pakistani, 54, 72, 133, 136, 147–48; Soviet Union and Baluch, 127–32, 136–40. *See also* Marxism-Leninism

Copper deposits, in Pakistani Baluchistan, 165–66, 170, 174

Dad Shah, 96, 104–05

Dames, M. Longworth, 15, 186

Daptar Sha'ar (Chronicles of Genealogie), 10

Daud, Mohammed, 39, 81

Debray, Regis, 73, 76

Dera Ghazi Khan district, 16, 177, 180

Dost Mohammed, 17

Durand line, 19, 143, 144, 146

Durrani, Ahmed Shah, establishment of Afghanistan, 17, 141

Education, Baluch, 9; in Iran, 101–03, 167; in Pakistan, 22, 84, 167

Elfenbein, J. H., 185

Emenau, Murray B., 185

Employment, Baluch: discrimination in, 103, 164; migration to find, 176

Federalists, 55–58, 191

Forward Policy, 19

Gamshadzai tribe, 107

Gankovsky, Yuri, 129–31

Gold deposits, in Pakistani Baluchistan, 171

Great Britain; battles with Baluch, 19; recruitment of Baluch soldiers, 22; role in Pakistani annexation of Kalat, 24; treaty for Kalat independence, 23. *See also* British Raj

Gromyko, Andrei, 132

Guerrilla movement, 3, 22, 28, 29, 30; Afghanistan and, 39, 50, 51, 81; during Bhutto regime, 36–39; BSO and, 86–87; cease-fire, *1969*, 33, 72; Marri support for, 41, 43; People's Revolutionary Command and, 76; popular involvement in, 39; tribal combat units in, 75

Hakoms, 95, 113, 119

Haq, Zahurul, 182

Haroun family, 59, 90

Hassan, Mukhtar, 43

Hezbe Ittehad-al-Muslimin. *See* Islamic Unity party

Hoots, 123, 124

Hossainborr, Ghulam Reza, 99–100

Hossainborr, Mohammed Hussein, 105

Housego, David, 137

Hoveida, Amir Abbas, 158–59

Husain, Riaz, 158

Husaini, Izza-al-din, 113

Ibragimov, Beknazar, 131–32
Independence of Greater Baluchistan:
Bizenjo and, 25, 54; Iranian Baluch
differences on, 111–12; Liberation
Front policy on, 76, 79–80; Khair
Bux Marri and, 48–49, 82–83, 188,
189; Mengal and, 65–66, 188, 189;
outside help for, 80–81, 161, 189;
potential for achieving, 20, 188–89,
194; and potential natural resources
development, 168–75; Soviet Union
and, 127–32, 136–41, 195–98; U.S.
and, 199–202. *See also* Nationalist
movement
India: and Pakistan, 3, 130, 204; and
U.S.-Pakistani alignment, 202–03;
and Soviet Union, 128–29
Indian Communist party, 128, 133,
136
Iran: Khomeini revolution in, 3, 80,
113, 202; Mollazadeh and, 112–16,
119; U.S. and, 119–20, 202; war
with Iraq, 3, 120, 125. *See also* Baluchistan, Iranian; Baluch, Iranian;
Nationalist movement (Baluch), in
Iran; Pahlavi, Mohammed Reza
Shah
Iraq: and Pakistani Baluch, 35; and Soviet Union, 108; support for Iranian
nationalists, 106–07, 108; war with
Iran, 3, 120, 125
Islamic Unity party (Hezbe Ittehad-al-
Muslimin), 112–13, 115; split within,
116

Jabal, 39, 49, 76, 164, 170, 173–74;
suspension of publication, 79
Jahanseb, Arbab, 37
Jalib, Habib, 84, 85
Jaririe, Habib, 115
Jinnah, Mohammed Ali, 129, 157

Kalat, 17; detachment of three Baluch
principalities from, 24; independence, 23, 24, 26; founding, 19; Pakistani takeover of, 27–28. *See also*
Baluchistan, Pakistani
Kalat Confederacy, 15; Nasir Khan
and, 16, 19
Kalat-i-Gilzai guerrilla camp, 75

Kalat National party, 23, 54
Kanoon Siasi-Farhangi-Khalq Baluch.
See Baluch People's Political and
Cultural Center
Karim, Abdul, 25; and Baluch Marxist
party, 134; formation of People's
party, 27, 47, 134–35; revolt against
Pakistan, 26
Karmal, Babrak, 67, 146
Kennan, George, 195
Keshtkaran, Tadollah, 115
Khalq faction, Afghanistan, 80, 81, 82;
extension into Pakistan, 146; and
Greater Afghanistan, 143; Parcham
faction versus, 142
Khan, Abdul Wali, 58, 89, 142–43
Khan, Asghar, 58
Khan, Chakkar (pseudonym of Asad
Rahman), 73, 74, 82; on an indepen-
dent Greater Baluchistan, 79; on
outside help for independence, 80
Khan, Jumma, 105–08
Khan, Mir Abdi, 106–07
Khan, Mir Abdullah, 16
Khan, Mir Ahmed Yar, 22, 23; arrest
of, 27–28; declaration of Kalat inde-
pendence, 24; opposition to One
Unit plan, 27
Khan, Mir Luang, 37
Khan, Moem, 64
Khan, Munir, 46
Khan, Murad (pseudonym of Mo-
hammed Bhabba), 49, 73, 74, 76; on
an independent Greater Baluchi-
stan, 79
Khan, Raja Ahmad, 153
Khan, Tikka, 33, 43
Khanate of Kalat, 16–17
Khattak, Ajmal, 147
Khomeini, Ayatollah Ruhollah, 113;
and Baluch, 115, 116, 160; efforts to
unseat, 119; expansionism in Per-
sian Gulf, 120, 121; revolution, 3,
80, 113
Khoshrou-Sefat, Yusuf, 102
Khurro, Hamida, 43, 181
Kianuri, Nuroddin, 110
Kissinger, Henry, 1, 202
Kurd, Abdul Aziz, 22
Kurd, Mahmud Aziz, 46; on PNP, 88;
on student movement, 86–88

Lahore Resolution, 157, 191
Language, Baluchi, 11, 113, 141; Arabic in place of, 122, 126; convergence with Brahui language, 185; dialects of, 185–86; Dravidian influence on, 184–85; problems in standardizing, 186–87
Lashari tribe, 12; war with Rinds, 12, 15, 183
Lessiovsky, Viktor, 146
Liberation Front. *See* Baluch People's Liberation Front
Literacy, 10, 187
London Group, 73, 82–83

Mahajirs 72, 136, 157
Makran, 117, 118
Mali, battle of, 36–37
Malik, Shameem, 58
Marble-quarrying, in Pakistani Baluchistan, 163–64
Marri, Khair Bux, 29, 36, 39, 74, 85; and Baluch independence, 48–49, 82–83, 188, 189; on Baluch population, 176–77; in Baluch triumvirate, 41–42, 89; on coal profits in Baluchistan, 163; on electric power development, 175; and guerrilla movement, 41, 43; and Marxist-Leninist ideology, 49; and modernization of Marri area, 45–47; One Unit plan effect on, 43; and PNP, 89; profile of, 43; reaction to Soviet occupation of Afghanistan, 51; relations with Pakistani officials, 45; role in Marri tribe, 42; on U.S. aid to Pakistan, 50; voluntary exile of, 40, 50; and Zia, 151, 153, 154
Marri, Khuda Bux, 15, 163, 176, 184–85
Marri, Sher Mohammed, 33, 74, 85; and BSO–Awami, 86; emphasis on nationality issue, 72; and guerrilla warfare, 29, 35–36; role in nationalist movement, 30
Marri tribe, 29; guerrilla fighting by, 36–39; in Liberation Front, 74–75; role of *sardars* in, 42–43
Martial law, under Zia, 40
Marxism-Leninism: Baluch Marxist party and, 134; Liberation Front

and, 76; Pararis and, 135; Tudeh party and, 110
Mazari, Sher Baz, 180
Mazdoor-Kisan party. *See* Worker-Peasant party
Mengal, Ali Mohammed, 30
Mengal, Ataullah, 30, 34, 36, 39, 179–80, 181; and Ayub regime, 62; and Baluch independence, 65–66, 188, 189; in Baluch triumvirate, 41–42, 64, 89; on Baluch share of national tax allocation, 169; in Baluch provincial government, 34, 62; Bhutto accusations against, 35; on Bizenjo's pro-Soviet policy, 59–60; plans for state marble monopoly, 164; and PNP, 89; profile of, 61–62; proposed confederation of provinces, 66–67, 191; on relations with Arabs, 125–26; on Soviet and U.S. influence in Pakistan, 67–68; voluntary exile, 40, 66; and Zia, 62, 64–65, 151, 153, 154
Mengal, Rasul Bux, 61
Mengal Tribe, 61, 62
Mesbah, Ahmed, 167–68
Mir Chakar Rind, *See* Rind, Mir Chakar
Mir Hazar Ramkhani, *See* Ramkhani, Mir Hazar
Mohammed, Ghulam, 73, 153
Mohenjodaro civilization, 184
Mollazadeh, Abdol Aziz: and Islamic Unity party, 112–13; and Khomeini, 115; request for Baluch autonomy, 115–16; tribal chieftains and, 119
Mollazai, Rashid, 102
Moore, Alvin, 185
Moulavis, 112–13
Movement for Integrity (Tehriq Istiqlal), 58
Muslim League, 24, 128, 129, 133, 153, 191
Mustikhan, Akber Y., 59, 60, 163; plan for national consensus for Zia, 90–91; and PNP, 90, on Soviet invasion of Afghanistan, 137
Mustikhan Transcontinental, 59

Nabi, Abdul, 86
Nadir Shah, 17, 20

NAP, *See* National Awami party
Naroui, Danesh, 115
Nasir, Gul Khan, 183, 184
Nasir, Hassan, 136
Nasir Khan, 20; and Afghanistan, 17; tribute to Nadir Shah, 17; tributes to, 18; unification of Baluch tribes, 16, 183
National Awami party (NAP), 36, 41, 45, 58, 138; and BSO formation, 84; leaders of, 89; outlawing of, 88, 89; Pakistan National party as successor to, 87
Nationalist movement: Communists and, 22, 127, 134–41; from politicization of countryside, 10; impact on events in Southwest Asia, 2; lack of cohesion and momentum in, 188–89; origins, 3, 11–12; ruling triumvirate and, 41–42; tribal rivalries affecting, 182–83, 188; versus Iranian and Pakistani nationalism, 4
Nationalist movement, in Iran, 21; Dad Shah and, 104–05; following Shah's overthrow, 100–01; Jumma Khan and, 105–07; Mir Abdi Khan and, 106–07; suppression of, 3, 17, 21, 93, 95–96, 103–04
Nationalist movement, in Pakistan, 21, 22; lack of cooperation in, 71; non-Baluch leftist support for, 73. *See also* Baluch People's Liberation Front
Natural gas, in Pakistani Baluchistan, 158, 162–63
Natural resources, 158, 162–63, 168–74; royalty payments for development of, 169, 193
Nauroz Khan, 28–29, 47–48
Nazish, Iman Ali, 136, 147, 148
Nedae Baluchistan. See Voice of Baluchistan
Newspapers, Baluch, 22–23, 115
Nixon administration, Pakistan policy, 202
Nizamani, K. B., 26, 54, 109–10, 145; and Baluch Marxist party, 134; and Indian Communist party, 132–133; on Pakistan Communist party, 133; publication of *People's Front*, 139; publication of *Voice of Baluchistan*,

138, 139; and Soviet Union, 139, 140

One Unit plan, 27, 151; BSO-Awami to combat, 83; withdrawal of, 28, 33, 34
Organization for the Liberation of Baluchistan (Anjuman-e-Ittehad-e-Baluchistan), 22

Pahlavi, Mohammed Reza Shah, 81, 168; Baluch tribal differences in reaction to, 110; and economic development of Baluch, 97, 99–100; and Pakistani Baluchistan, 96–97; *sardari* cooperation with, 108; suppression of Baluch nationalism, 93, 95–96
Pahlavi, Reza Shah, suppression of Baluch nationalism, 3, 17, 93
Pakistan: efforts to reduce tribal autonomy in, 21; importance of Baluchistan to, 150, 192–93; incorporation of Kalat into, 22, 24, 27–28; Kalat revolt against, 26; One Unit plan for restructuring, 27, 28, 33, 34, 83, 151; Soviet Union and, 128, 129, 130, 193, 197; U.S. and, 67–68, 200–03
Pakistan Communist party, 72, 133, 136; and Baluch independence, 135
Pakistan Federal Union of Students, 85
Pakistan National party (PNP), 72; Bizenjo and, 42, 58, 87, 190; constitutional safeguards for Baluch, 190; formation, 88, 89; six-point manifesto, 89–90
Pakistan People's party, 136
Palestine Liberation Organization, 106, 120
Pararis: evolution into Baluch People's Liberation Front, 34, 39, 72; guerrilla warfare, 30, 33, 43, 45; integration of non-Baluch with, 73–74; and Marxism-Leninism, 135; shift of headquarters to Afghanistan, 39. *See also* Baluch People's Liberation Front
Parcham faction, 142
Pasdarans (revolutionary guards), 116
PDPA. *See* People's Democratic party of Afghanistan

People's Democratic party of Afghanistan (PDPA), 142, 143
People's Front, 139
People's League, Pakistan, 137
People's party (Ustoman Gal), 27, 134, 138
People's Revolutionary Command, 72, 75, 76
Persian Gulf area, 1, 5, 195, 196, 204
Persians, 9; and Baluch claims, 4, 94, 149
Petroleum, in Pakistani Baluchistan: guerrilla warfare effect on, 37, 172–73; reserves, 171–72, 173–74
Pikulin, M.G., 130-21
Pithawalla, M. B., 174
PNP. *See* Pakistan National party
Population, Baluch, 9; dispersion of, 175–76, 179; estimates of, 176–78; migration of, 177–78
Pottinger, Sir Henry, 18
Pukhtoonkhwa party. *See* Pushtunland party
Punjabis, 9, 34, 40; and Baluch claims to Baluchistan, 4, 149; Bengalis versus, 88; Bizenjo and, 55; dominance of, 72; Khair Bux Marri on, 49, 51–52; Mengal on, 67
Punjab province: Baluch population, 176–77; uranium discoveries in, 177
Pushtun-land party (Pukhtoonkhwa party), 180
Pushtunistan, 141, 146
Pushtuns, 9, 88, 129; Baluch versus, 89, 142–47, 158, 180–82; separate state for, 141–42; and Zia, 153

Rahman, Asad. *See* Khan, Chakkar
Rahman, Sheikh Mujibur, 88, 155, 158
Ramkhani, Mir Hazar, 33, 51, 80, 82; in fight against Bhutto regime, 34, 39; integration of non-Baluch with Pararis, 73–74; and international relief for guerrillas, 81–82; and People's Revolutionary Command, 75
Rastakhiz party, Iran, 99
Religion, Baluch, 8–9
Ricciardi, James, 95
Rind, Mir Chakar, 12, 15, 183–84

Rind tribe, war with Lasharis, 12, 15, 183
Road Construction in Pakistani Baluchistan, 166–67
Royalty rate, for natural resources development, 169, 193
Ryvaj (code of honor), 36

Saindak copper mines, 165–66, 169
Sarbazi, Ashraf, 107, 108
Sardars: in Iran, 21, 95, 108, 112, 113, 119–20; in Pakistan, 21, 42–43, 45, 156; political power, 135
Sardarzai tribe, 106, 107
SAVAK, 103, 108, 110–11
Sazman-e Demokratik-e Mardom-e Baluchistan. *See* Baluchistan People's Democratic Organization
Sethi, Najam, 73
Sheikhzade, Ahmed, 102
Sher Mohammed Marri. *See* Marri, Sher Mohammed
Shiite sect, 113, 115, 116, 120
Shorawar guerrilla camp, 81
Sibi–Harnai railroad, 37
Sindhis, 88, 129, 137, 157; proposed federation with Baluch, 179–80
Sind province, Baluch population, 176–79
Sistani tribe, 9, 116
Sistan and Baluchistan province, Baluch population, 177
Soviet Union: Afghanistan occupation, 1, 51, 59, 120, 121, 195, 196, 203; and Baluch independence, 2, 127–32, 136–41, 195, 196–98; and Baluch leaders, 196–97; Baluch population of, 178; and India, 128–29; and Iraq, 108; and Pakistan, 128, 129, 130, 193, 197; potential targets in Southwest Asia, 1–2
Special Development Plan, 164–66
Spooner, Brian, 19–20
Strait of Hormuz, 1, 2, 195
Student movement. *See* Baluch Students Organization; Baluch Students Organization–Awami
Sunni Muslims, 8, 113, 115; conflict with Sistanis, 116; repression of Zikris, 187–88

Swidler, Nina, 16, 184
Swidler, Warren W., 184

Talpur, Mir Ali Ahmed, 73, 177, 179, 180
Taraki, Nur Mohammed, 87, 139, 140; on Durand line, 143
Tehriq Istiqlal. *See* Movement for Integrity
Tribes, Baluch, 9; absorption of Arab culture, 123–124; loyalties among Iranian, 119; and Nationalist movement, 182–83
Tudeh party, Iran, 109–10

United States: and Baluch independence, 199–202, 204; and Iranian Baluch, 119–20; and Iranian revolution, 202; options on Baluch policy, 204–05; and Pakistan, 67–68, 200–03; policy in Afghanistan, 199
Unqa, Mohammed Hussain, 133
Uranium deposits, 16, 177
Urban areas, 9–10
Urdu language, 185, 186
Ustoman Gal. *See* People's party

Van Wagner, J. C., 172–73
Voice of Baluchistan (Nedae Baluchistan), 68, 138, 139, 140

Water resources development, in Pakistani Baluchistan, 174–75
Wirsing, Robert G., 149–50
Women, Liberation Front and, 76
Worker-Peasant party, Pakistan, 137, 142, 145
World Baluch Organization, 42

Yahya Khan, 88; Khair Bux Marri and, 45; withdrawal of One Unit plan, 33, 34, 151

Zaheer, Sajjad, 136
Zarakzai tribe, 153
Zardkoui, Rahim, 107
Zehri, Nabi Bux, 163, 164
Zelli, Manuchehr, 159
Zia Ul-Haq, Mohammed, 39, 192; Baluchistan development program under, 161–67; and Baluch leaders, 62, 64–65, 151, 153–54, 193–94; ban on Baluch political activity, 87, 88, 90; on Bhutto relations with Baluch leaders, 151; concessions to Baluch, 40; on importance of Baluchistan to Pakistan, 150, 193; martial law regime, 40; PNP pressure on, 90–91; on provincial self-rule, 150–151; and student movement, 83, 87
Zikris, repression by Sunnis, 187–88

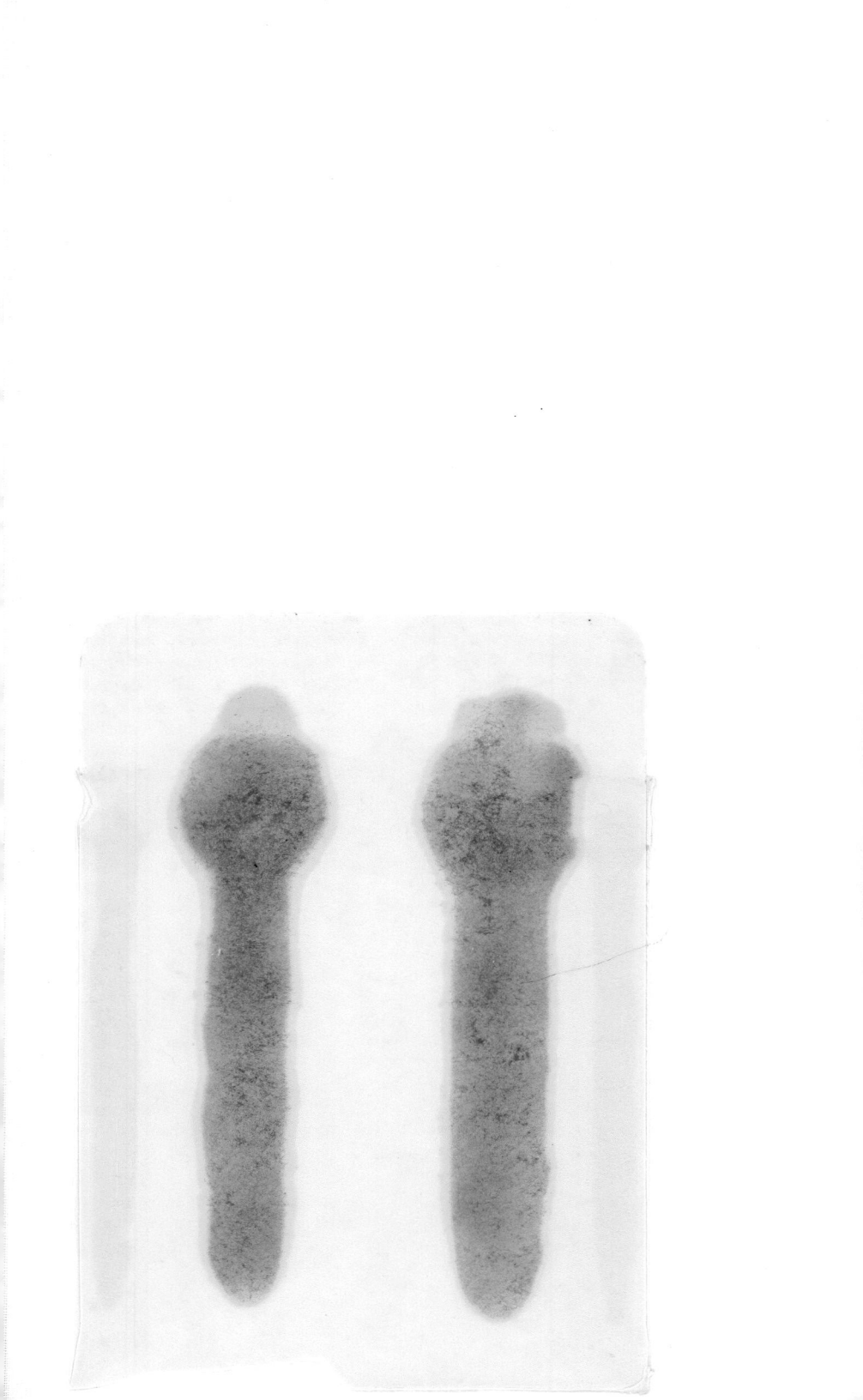

In Afghanistan's shadow lies Baluchistan, a little known but strategically located area stretching across eastern Iran, western Pakistan, and a strip of southern Afghanistan. For more than 1,000 years, Baluch tribesmen have regarded this vast expanse of desert and mountains as their rightful homeland, resisting its annexation into surrounding empires. In recent decades they have fought four guerrilla wars to win either autonomy within Pakistan and Iran or, failing that, an independent Greater Baluchistan that would unite the five million Baluch under one flag. Against a background of deepening conflict in Afghanistan and growing American involvement in Pakistan, the Baluch nationalist movement has acquired new importance as a potential focal point of regional or superpower conflict. Baluchistan commands more than 900 miles of the Arabian Sea coastline, including the northern shores of the Strait of Hormuz, through which oil tankers bound for the West and Japan must pass on their way out of the Persian Gulf. Soviet sponsorship of an independent Baluchistan or the annexation of Baluchistan to a Greater Afghanistan would radically alter the military balance in the Persian Gulf area and would give Moscow a powerful new springboard for spreading its political influence throughout the Middle East and Southwest Asia.

This book presents the first in-depth assessment of the Baluch nationalist movement and its growing significance in a region troubled by ethnic conflict. Author Selig S. Harrison talked with some 340 primary sources: Baluch leaders of all persuasions (many of them underground in Baluchistan or living in exile), political figures, Pakistani and Iranian officials, scholars, and participants in the 1973–1977 Baluch insurgency in Pakistan, including Pakistani military officers and Baluch guerrillas now hiding out in base camps in southern Afghanistan. Probing the attitudes of Baluch, Pakistani, and Iranian leaders, Harrison concludes that there is still a slender possibility for political settlements between the Baluch and Islamabad and Teheran. In the absence of such settlements, he warns, Moscow may be increasingly tempted to manipulate Baluch nationalism. Significantly, however, he shows that the Soviet Union has been ambivalent about supporting an independent Baluchistan, has failed to build up to a strong Communist movement in the Baluch areas, and would have to work primarily through non-Communist Baluch nationalist leaders if it decided to play its "Baluch card."

Five maps in two colors, many hitherto unpublished photographs of Baluch leaders, and an unusual range of documentary sources make In Afghanistan's Shadow an invaluable reference as well as a work of contemporary importance for all those interested in Soviet-American relations, South and Southwest Asian affairs, the geopolitics of the Persian Gulf region, and the problems of multiethnic states in the Third World.

Cover Photograph by David Burnett/Contact
Book design by Sheila Freeman/Graphic Design
I.S.B.N. 0–87003–030–2 (paper)

$6.00

Table B.3 (Continued)

z	.00	.01	.02	.03	.04	.05	.06	.07	.08	.09
1.5	.4332	.4345	.4357	.4370	.4382	.4394	.4406	.4418	.4429	.4441
1.6	.4452	.4463	.4474	.4484	.4495	.4505	.4515	.4525	.4535	.4545
1.7	.4554	.4564	.4573	.4582	.4591	.4599	.4608	.4616	.4625	.4633
1.8	.4641	.4649	.4656	.4664	.4671	.4678	.4686	.4693	.4699	.4706
1.9	.4713	.4719	.4726	.4732	.4738	.4744	.4750	.4756	.4761	.4767
2.0	.4772	.4778	.4783	.4788	.4793	.4798	.4803	.4808	.4812	.4817
2.1	.4821	.4826	.4830	.4834	.4838	.4842	.4846	.4850	.4854	.4857
2.2	.4861	.4864	.4868	.4871	.4875	.4878	.4881	.4884	.4887	.4890
2.3	.4893	.4896	.4898	.4901	.4904	.4906	.4909	.4911	.4913	.4916
2.4	.4918	.4920	.4922	.4925	.4927	.4929	.4931	.4932	.4934	.4936
2.5	.4938	.4940	.4941	.4943	.4945	.4946	.4948	.4949	.4951	.4952
2.6	.4953	.4955	.4956	.4957	.4959	.4960	.4961	.4962	.4963	.4964
2.7	.4965	.4966	.4967	.4968	.4969	.4970	.4971	.4972	.4973	.4974
2.8	.4974	.4975	.4976	.4977	.4977	.4978	.4979	.4979	.4980	.4981
2.9	.4981	.4982	.4982	.4983	.4984	.4984	.4985	.4985	.4986	.4986
3.0	.4987	.4987	.4987	.4988	.4988	.4989	.4989	.4989	.4990	.4990
3.1	.4990	.4991	.4991	.4991	.4992	.4992	.4992	.4992	.4993	.4993
3.2	.4993	.4993	.4994	.4994	.4994	.4994	.4994	.4995	.4995	.4995
3.3	.4995	.4995	.4995	.4996	.4996	.4996	.4996	.4996	.4996	.4997
3.4	.4997	.4997	.4997	.4997	.4997	.4997	.4997	.4997	.4997	.4998
3.5	.4998	.4998	.4998	.4998	.4998	.4998	.4998	.4998	.4998	.4998
3.6	.4998	.4998	.4999	.4999	.4999	.4999	.4999	.4999	.4999	.4999
3.7	.4999	.4999	.4999	.4999	.4999	.4999	.4999	.4999	.4999	.4999
3.8	.4999	.4999	.4999	.4999	.4999	.4999	.4999	.4999	.4999	.4999
3.9	.49995	.49995	.49996	.49996	.49996	.49996	.49996	.49996	.49997	.49997
4.0	.49997									
4.5	.499997									
5.0	.4999997									

Adapted from *Standard Mathematical Tables,* 25th ed., Boca Raton: Chemical Rubber Company Press, 1978, p. 524. Reprinted with permission.

GENERAL STATISTICS

GENERAL STATISTICS

THIRD EDITION

WARREN CHASE
FRED BOWN
Framingham State College

JOHN WILEY & SONS, INC.

New York • Chichester • Brisbane • Toronto • Singapore

ACQUISITIONS EDITOR	Brad Wiley II
MARKETING MANAGER	Jay Kirsch
PRODUCTION MANAGER	Lucille Buonocore
SENIOR PRODUCTION EDITOR	Tracey Kuehn
PRODUCTION COORDINATOR	Susan L. Reiland
DESIGNER	Ann Marie Renzi
MANUFACTURING MANAGER	Dorothy Sinclair
ILLUSTRATION	Jaime Perea
COVER DESIGN	Kenny Beck
COVER PHOTO	Charles Krebs/Tony Stone Images

This book was set in Palatino by Publication Services
and printed and bound by R. R. Donnelley/Willard. The cover was printed by Lehigh Press.

Recognizing the importance of preserving what has been written, it is a
policy of John Wiley and Sons, Inc., to have books of enduring value published
in the United States printed on acid-free paper, and we exert our best
efforts to that end.

The paper in this book was manufactured by a mill whose forest management programs include
sustained yield harvesting of its timberlands. Sustained yield harvesting principles ensure that
the number of trees cut each year does not exceed the amount of new growth.

Library of Congress Cataloging-in-Publication Data:
Chase, Warren.
    General statistics / Warren Chase, Fred Bown. – 3rd ed.
        p.   cm.
    Includes bibliographical references and index.
    ISBN 0-471-05584-0 (cloth : alk. paper)
    1. Statistics.   I. Bown, Fred.   II. Title.
QA276.12.C456   1996
519.5–dc20   96-11200
                                                      CIP

ISBN 0-471-05584-0

Printed in the United States of America

10 9 8 7 6 5 4 3 2

The purpose of this book is to present a first course in statistics appropriate for students in a wide variety of disciplines, the only prerequisite being a knowledge of high school algebra. We feel that the objective of such a course should be to acquaint the student with the basic ideas of descriptive and inferential statistics. Great care has been taken in writing this book to make the subject matter understandable. All technical terms are defined in easy-to-grasp language; definitions, important formulas, and summaries of statistical tests are set off in boxes for quick reference. Concepts are introduced and reinforced with examples and exercises from a wide range of fields, from sports to medicine. All chapters begin with an introduction and end with a summary of the important ideas of the chapter. As in the second edition of the book, most exercises on hypothesis testing do not specify whether the traditional approach (finding the critical region), or the P-value approach should be used. We give answers in terms of both approaches. The instructor can then decide which to use.

New Features of the Third Edition

The third edition involves more use of **exploratory data analysis** (EDA). There is a growing consensus that all too often statistical formulas and techniques are blindly applied without looking carefully at the data to see whether these methods are appropriate. Techniques of exploratory data analysis, such as **stem-and-leaf plots** and **boxplots,** are used throughout the book to investigate these issues. For example, when investigating a population mean using a small sample, a t test would be inadvisable if the sample is strongly skewed or contains extreme outliers. A stem-and-leaf plot will detect these conditions.

Structural changes:

- Chapter 1 includes expanded coverage of sampling and design of experiments.
- Descriptive aspects of regression and correlation are treated earlier (Chapter 4) than in the second edition. Inference concerning regression and correlation is dealt with in Chapter 10, and has been expanded to include inference concerning slope of the regression line.
- The chapter on probability (Chapter 5) has been extensively reworked. All but the first four sections are optional. Traditionally, probability has been the topic that students find most difficult in a first course in statistics. We have tried to segregate the stumbling points into optional sections. For example, students do not seem to have trouble with the Addition Rule when the events are mutually exclusive, or the Multiplication Rule when the events are independent. But when the events are not mutually exclusive, or are dependent and conditional probability is involved, students encounter difficulty. We have placed these cases in Section 5, which is optional.

- The chi-square test for variance and the F test for comparing two variances have been placed in the Appendix. In practice, statisticians rarely use these tests due to their extreme sensitivity to departures from normality of the underlying populations.

- We have attempted to streamline various parts of the book. For example, all the introductory material on inference (both large- and small-sample inference for a mean μ and inference for a proportion p) are now in one chapter (Chapter 8).

- The exercise sets have been expanded and include more data sets.

Pedagogical changes:

- We have included an appendix containing data on 1000 randomly selected subjects from the Framingham Heart Study. These data are also available on a floppy disk. At the end of most chapters we have included optional sections entitled "Working with Data." These sections enable the student to apply the procedures developed in the chapter on data from the Framingham Heart Study.

- As in the second edition, most chapters have optional self-contained Minitab sections. In addition, we have included examples and exercises throughout the text that illustrate the interpretation of computer output from a variety of statistical packages. Also a number of exercises involve the use of output from Resampling Stats.

- A number of case studies have been added. We have chosen to integrate these within the exposition and exercises, rather than putting them in stand-alone boxes that can be ignored. Thus the Hazelwood race discrimination case is the principal vehicle for explaining hypothesis testing concerning a population proportion, rather than merely an appendage to the textual material. The Game Show Paradox of *Parade Magazine*'s Marilyn Vos Savant is used to illustrate most of the probability techniques involving compound events.

Chapters 1–8 would be suitable for the core of a three-semester-hour introductory course, and Chapters 1–10 would form the core of a 4-semester-hour course. In each case, additional material could be covered. After Chapter 8, the remaining chapters can be covered in any order. (See prerequisite chart in Figure 1.)

Supplements

- An *Instructor's Manual*, which includes complete solutions to all exercises, chapters on the Poisson distribution, the hypergeometric distribution, and multiple regression, and a list of answers to the even exercises. Any portion may be reproduced for class use.

- A *Student's Solutions Manual* with complete solutions to all odd-numbered exercises.

- A *Study Guide*, which includes a review of algebra and notation.

- A *Test Bank* with true–false, fill-in-the-blank, multiple choice, and computational exercises. This is available in hard copy and on a floppy disk that may be edited to include the instructor's test items.

- A Data Disk in ASCII file format is available from the publisher for each adopter of this text. The floppy disk contains data on 1000 randomly selected subjects from the Framingham Heart Study (which also appears in the Appendix).

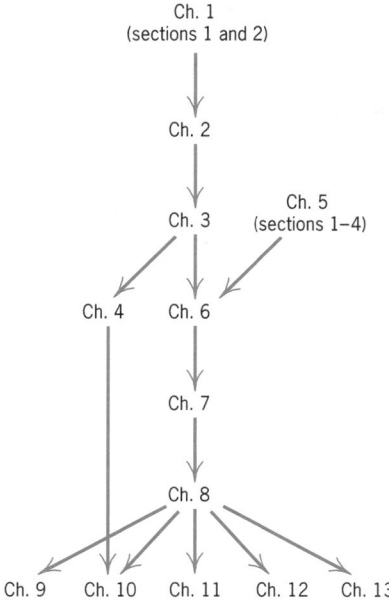

Figure 1
Prerequisite Chart. Chapter at Tail of Arrow Is a Prerequisite for Chapter at Point of Arrow.

Acknowledgments

We wish to thank Dr. William Castelli of the Framingham Heart Study for providing us with data and reprints of papers from the heart study. We also wish to thank Robert Garrison, Michael Hartman, and Paul Sorlie of the National Institutes of Health for their role in compiling the heart study data and for providing us with computer tapes containing the data.

We want to thank the following reviewers of the third edition for their many valuable suggestions:

Susan Barton
Brigham Young University-Hawaii

Beverly R. Broomell
Suffolk Community College

James Curl
Modesto Junior College

Stanley Fraser
State University of New York at Canton

R. K. Goodrich
University of Colorado-Boulder

Lawrence J. Kratz
Idaho State University

Susan Mills
Riverside Community College

Mike Scroggins
Lewis and Clark Community College

Thomas Short
Villanova University

Special thanks are in order for Mack Hill of Worcester State College, who worked through all the examples and exercises and checked the manuscript of the third edition for accuracy. We also want to express our gratitude to our editor, Brad Wiley; his hard work, enthusiasm, and encouragement contributed in large part to making the third edition a reality.

W.C.
F.B.

CONTENTS

CHAPTER 1

INTRODUCTION 1

1.1 THE NATURE OF STATISTICS 1
1.2 SAMPLING 5
1.3 TOPICS IN THE DESIGN OF EXPERIMENTS 12
1.4 SUMMARY 17

PART ONE

DESCRIPTIVE STATISTICS 19

CHAPTER 2

ORGANIZATION OF DATA 21

2.1 INTRODUCTION 21
2.2 SUMMARIZING DATA 22
2.3 GRAPHIC REPRESENTATIONS 31
2.4 THE SHAPE OF A DISTRIBUTION 39
2.5 STEM-AND-LEAF PLOTS 41
2.6 MISLEADING GRAPHS (OPTIONAL) 46
2.7 USING MINITAB (OPTIONAL) 50
2.8 WORKING WITH DATA (OPTIONAL) 61
2.9 SUMMARY 63
    REVIEW EXERCISES 64

CHAPTER 3

MEASURES OF CENTRAL TENDENCY, DISPERSION,
AND POSITION 75

3.1 INTRODUCTION 75
3.2 MEASURES OF CENTRAL TENDENCY 76
3.3 MEASURES OF DISPERSION 85
3.4 PERCENTILES, QUARTILES, AND THE INTERQUARTILE
    RANGE 95
3.5 BOXPLOTS 102
3.6 USING MINITAB (OPTIONAL) 109
3.7 WORKING WITH DATA (OPTIONAL) 118
3.8 SUMMARY 119
    REVIEW EXERCISES 119

CHAPTER 4

REGRESSION AND CORRELATION   131

4.1   INTRODUCTION   131
4.2   THE LEAST SQUARES REGRESSION LINE   132
4.3   THE LINEAR CORRELATION COEFFICIENT   152
4.4   SOME WORDS OF CAUTION CONCERNING CORRELATION
       AND REGRESSION   169
4.5   USING MINITAB (OPTIONAL)   170
4.6   WORKING WITH DATA (OPTIONAL)   173
4.7   SUMMARY   173
       REVIEW EXERCISES   174

PART TWO

PROBABILITY   183

CHAPTER 5

PROBABILITY   185

5.1   INTRODUCTION   185
5.2   SAMPLE SPACES AND EVENTS   186
5.3   THE PROBABILITY OF AN EVENT   191
5.4   COMPOUND EVENTS   197
5.5   MORE ON COMPOUND EVENTS (OPTIONAL)   205
5.6   COMBINATORICS (OPTIONAL)   213
5.7   SUMMARY   218
       REVIEW EXERCISES   220

CHAPTER 6

PROBABILITY DISTRIBUTIONS FOR DISCRETE RANDOM
VARIABLES   227

6.1   INTRODUCTION   227
6.2   RANDOM VARIABLES   227
6.3   DISCRETE PROBABILITY DISTRIBUTIONS   231
6.4   MEAN AND VARIANCE   237
6.5   THE BINOMIAL PROBABILITY DISTRIBUTION   245
6.6   USING MINITAB (OPTIONAL)   255
6.7   SUMMARY   259
       REVIEW EXERCISES   260

CHAPTER 7

PROBABILITY DISTRIBUTIONS FOR CONTINUOUS RANDOM
VARIABLES; THE NORMAL DISTRIBUTION   267

7.1   INTRODUCTION   267
7.2   CONTINUOUS PROBABILITY DISTRIBUTIONS   268
7.3   THE NORMAL DISTRIBUTION   273
7.4   THE STANDARD NORMAL DISTRIBUTION   274
7.5   MORE ON NORMAL PROBABILITY   282

7.6 NORMAL APPROXIMATION TO THE BINOMIAL
DISTRIBUTION 294
7.7 THE CENTRAL LIMIT THEOREM 300
7.8 USING MINITAB (OPTIONAL) 310
7.9 SUMMARY 317
REVIEW EXERCISES 317

PART THREE

STATISTICAL INFERENCE 323

CHAPTER 8
STATISTICAL INFERENCE CONCERNING MEANS
AND PROPORTIONS 325

8.1 INTRODUCTION 325
8.2 ESTIMATING A POPULATION MEAN (Large-Sample Case) 326
8.3 HYPOTHESIS TESTING CONCERNING A POPULATION MEAN
(Large-Sample Case) 338
8.4 *P*-VALUES 353
8.5 INFERENCE CONCERNING A POPULATION MEAN
(Small-Sample Case) 358
8.6 INFERENCE CONCERNING A POPULATION PROPORTION 378
8.7 USING MINITAB (OPTIONAL) 391
8.8 WORKING WITH DATA (OPTIONAL) 394
8.9 SUMMARY 395
REVIEW EXERCISES 396

CHAPTER 9
INFERENCE CONCERNING TWO POPULATION PARAMETERS 405

9.1 INTRODUCTION 405
9.2 INFERENCE CONCERNING TWO POPULATION MEANS:
DEPENDENT SAMPLES 406
9.3 INFERENCE CONCERNING TWO POPULATION MEANS BASED
ON INDEPENDENT SAMPLES: Large-Sample Case 415
9.4 INFERENCE CONCERNING TWO POPULATION MEANS BASED
ON INDEPENDENT SAMPLES: Small-Sample Case 421
9.5 INFERENCE CONCERNING TWO POPULATION
PROPORTIONS 432
9.6 USING MINITAB (OPTIONAL) 440
9.7 WORKING WITH DATA (OPTIONAL) 443
9.8 SUMMARY 443
REVIEW EXERCISES 445

CHAPTER 10
INFERENCE CONCERNING REGRESSION AND CORRELATION 453

10.1 INTRODUCTION 453
10.2 INFERENCE CONCERNING SLOPE 453

10.3 INFERENCE CONCERNING CORRELATION 467
10.4 PREDICTION INTERVALS AND CONFIDENCE INTERVALS
      (OPTIONAL) 473
10.5 USING MINITAB (OPTIONAL) 479
10.6 WORKING WITH DATA (OPTIONAL) 483
10.7 SUMMARY 483
      REVIEW EXERCISES 484

CHAPTER 11
ANALYSIS OF VARIANCE 491

11.1 INTRODUCTION 491
11.2 THE IDEA BEHIND ANALYSIS OF VARIANCE; THE CASE OF
      EQUAL SAMPLE SIZES 492
11.3 ANALYSIS OF VARIANCE WHEN SAMPLE SIZES ARE NOT
      NECESSARILY EQUAL; CONVENTIONAL TERMINOLOGY 505
11.4 ALTERNATE FORMULAS (OPTIONAL) 518
11.5 USING MINITAB (OPTIONAL) 521
11.6 WORKING WITH DATA (OPTIONAL) 522
11.7 SUMMARY 523
      REVIEW EXERCISES 524

CHAPTER 12
ANALYSIS OF CATEGORICAL DATA 531

12.1 INTRODUCTION 531
12.2 THE CHI-SQUARE TEST FOR GOODNESS-OF-FIT 532
12.3 TESTS OF INDEPENDENCE; CONTINGENCY TABLES 541
12.4 TESTS OF HOMOGENEITY 551
12.5 USING MINITAB (OPTIONAL) 554
12.6 WORKING WITH DATA (OPTIONAL) 556
12.7 SUMMARY 556
      REVIEW EXERCISES 557

CHAPTER 13
NONPARAMETRIC STATISTICS 561

13.1 INTRODUCTION 561
13.2 THE SIGN TEST 562
13.3 THE WILCOXON SIGNED-RANK TEST 569
13.4 THE MANN–WHITNEY U TEST 581
13.5 THE RUNS TEST 589
13.6 A DISCUSSION OF PARAMETRIC VERSUS NONPARAMETRIC
      TESTS 594
13.7 USING MINITAB (OPTIONAL) 595
13.8 WORKING WITH DATA (OPTIONAL) 598
13.9 SUMMARY 598
      REVIEW EXERCISES 599

APPENDIX A
USE OF THE RANDOM NUMBER TABLE A-1

APPENDIX B
TABLES A-3

APPENDIX C
INFERENCE CONCERNING VARIANCES A-39

APPENDIX D
BIBLIOGRAPHY A-65

ANSWERS ANS-1

INDEX I-1

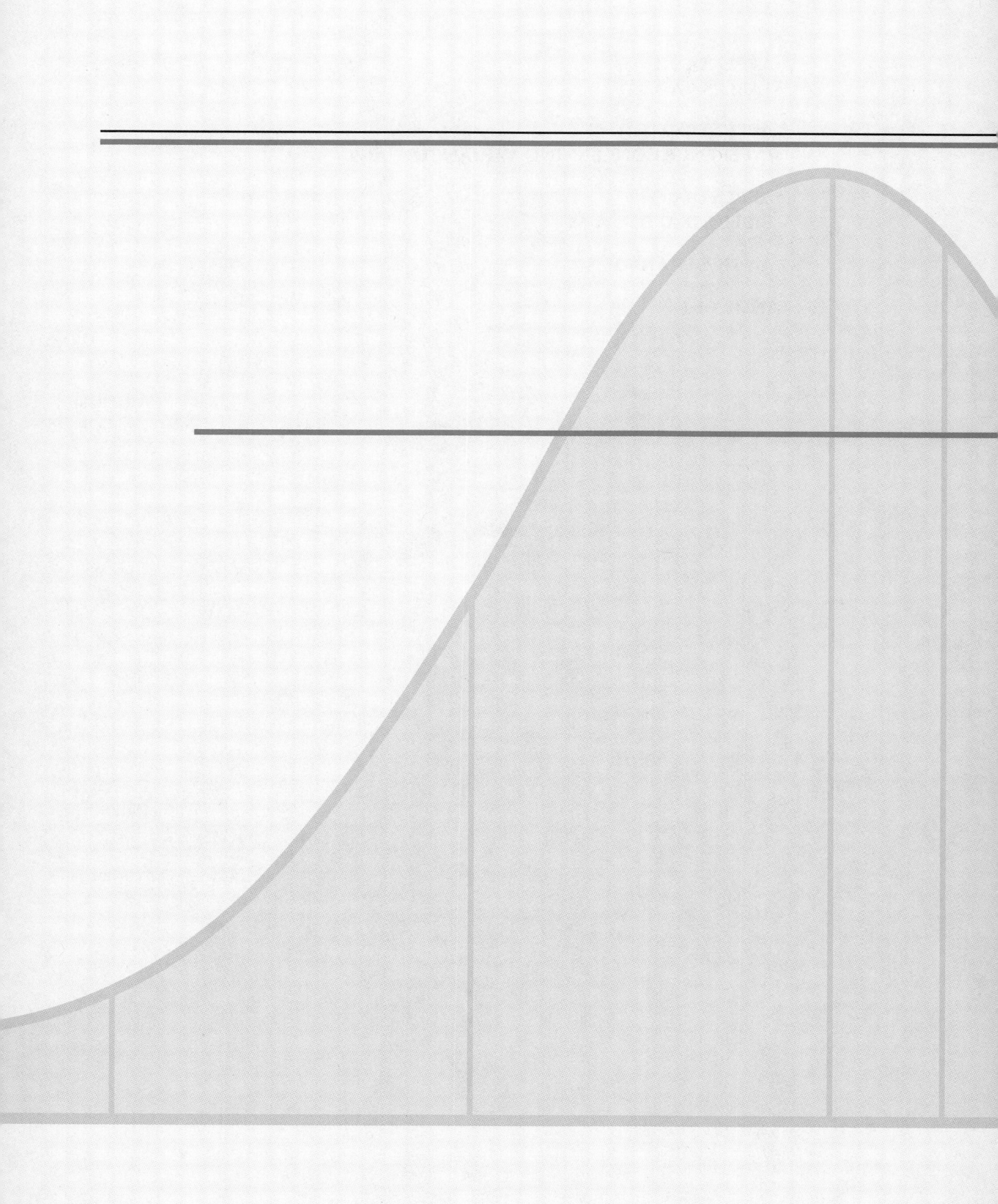

CHAPTER 1

INTRODUCTION

1.1 THE NATURE OF STATISTICS

1.2 SAMPLING

1.3 TOPICS IN THE DESIGN OF EXPERIMENTS

1.4 SUMMARY

    NOTES

1.1

THE NATURE OF STATISTICS

To get an idea of what statistics is all about, we consider a few concrete illustrations of the kinds of problems that involve statistics.

- A pollster interested in the outcome of an upcoming election interviews a certain number of voters and, based on the results obtained, makes a prediction as to who will probably win the election.

- The Environmental Protection Agency conducts tests on a certain number of cars of the same make and model to estimate the average gas mileage for all cars of that make and model.

- Each year the Federal Bureau of Investigation publishes the *Uniform Crime Reports*. Among other things, this document reports the violent crime rate (number per 100,000 people) for each of the Metropolitan Statistical Areas in the United States.

- To get an idea of the economic status of a town, an economist obtains the salaries of all wage earners in the town and then computes the average.

1

- To estimate the average age of all adult Americans, a sociologist selects 1000 adults, computes their average age, and then uses this figure as an estimate.

All of these illustrations make use of the raw material of statistics, namely, **data** (or **data values**), also called **observations.** We use these terms in a very broad sense. That is, a data value is simply a piece of information that might be numerical, such as the annual snowfall in Boston, or a person's weight or age. Or the information might be nonnumerical, such as the color of a car, a person's ethnic status, or whom you favor in the next presidential election. We give the following definition of **statistics:**

Definition *Statistics* is the science of collecting, simplifying, and describing data, as well as making inferences (drawing conclusions) based on the analysis of data.

As the definition suggests, there are two branches of statistics. The branch that deals with collecting, simplifying, and giving properties of data is called **descriptive statistics.** An important objective of descriptive statistics is to organize, summarize, or describe the data to make it more comprehensible. For example, suppose that we obtained a list of the salaries of all the wage earners in Boston. This list would be so long that it would be incomprehensible. But if we were to find the average of all these salaries, then we would understand something about the economic status of the residents of Boston.

The other branch of statistics, which involves drawing conclusions based on the analysis of data, is called **inferential statistics.** The pollster who predicts the outcome of an election based on a knowledge of only *some* of the votes, and the sociologist who estimates the average age of *all* adult Americans based on a knowledge of the average of the ages of *some* of these adults, are both using inferential statistics. Apparently, it was impractical for these researchers to obtain all the data they were interested in (i.e., all the votes or all the ages); therefore, in both cases a judgment was made about the larger body of data that was being studied by means of information obtained from only some of these data values. This leads to the following definition:

Definition The entire collection of all the elements we are interested in is called a *population.* (These elements might be people, automobiles, data values, etc.) A collection of some of the elements obtained from the population is called a *sample* from the population.

In an investigation such as a voter preference study, we may think of the population as consisting of all the voters or all the votes they will cast. The votes are the **data values** of interest, and it is these values that we are really investigating. In general, we are ultimately interested in data values in statistics. For this reason, in this book, we will often think of populations as consisting of data values.

Now that we have introduced the terms *population* and *sample,* we can give a more precise definition of inferential statistics.

> Definition   *Inferential statistics* is concerned with making judgments (or inferences) about a population based on the properties of some sample obtained from the population.

We said that trying to estimate the average age of all adult Americans by using the average of the ages of some of these adults is a typical problem in inferential statistics. The average age for the population of all adult Americans is an example of what is called a **parameter.** The average of the ages for a sample of adult Americans is an example of a **statistic.**

> Definition   A numerical property of a population is called a *parameter.* A numerical property of a sample is called a *statistic.* (By numerical property we mean a property that can be expressed as a number.)

Consider the population of all voters in the 1936 presidential election. The percentage of the voters that were for Roosevelt is a parameter. Viewing the voters in Peoria, Illinois, as a sample from this population, we see that the percentage in this sample that were for Roosevelt is a statistic.

Many problems in inferential statistics involve estimating the value of, or making some decision concerning, a parameter based on the value of a statistic.

The methods used in making inferences in statistics are probabilistic. For example, suppose that a pollster interviews 100 voters selected by chance and finds that 96 of them favor candidate A in an upcoming election. Then the pollster would say that the evidence points to candidate A winning the election, because it would be highly unlikely or improbable that so many voters (in the sample of 100 voters) would be in favor of candidate A if candidate A were not going to win the election. **Probability, which deals with the laws of chance, plays an important role in statistics.** Therefore, we will study this topic in some detail in this book.

EXERCISES

In Exercises 1.1 and 1.2, discuss similarities and differences between the following terms.

1.1   Population and sample
1.2   Parameter and statistic

In Exercises 1.3–1.5, which are true?

1.3   Often, the value of a parameter is unknown.
1.4   The value of a parameter always remains unchanged from sample to sample.
1.5   The value of a statistic always remains unchanged from sample to sample.

In Exercises 1.6–1.10, determine whether the results given are examples of descriptive or inferential statistics.

1.6   In the 1992 presidential election, voters in Massachusetts cast 1,315,016 votes for Bill Clinton, 803,974 for George Bush, and 630,440 for H. Ross Perot (*Source: World Almanac,* 1993, p. 73).

1.7   As of January 1, 1992, the Nielsen Company estimated various percentages for United States homes (*Source: World Almanac,* 1993, p. 305). Percentage with

Color TV sets	98%	Black and white only	2%
Two or more sets	65%	One set	35%

1.8   The mid-1993 population of the United States was estimated to be 258.3 million, and the 1990 median age was estimated to be 32.9 years (*Source: The 1994 Information Please Almanac,* 1994, p. 3). *Note:*   Estimating a median age of 32.9 years is saying that 50% of the population is estimated to be younger than 32.9 years of age.

1.9   In the 1992 presidential election, Bill Clinton, George Bush, and H. Ross Perot received 370, 168, and 0 electoral votes, respectively (*Source: World Almanac,* 1993, p. 73).

1.10   The population of Worcester, Massachusetts, in 1990 was 169,759, an increase of 4.92% from the 1980 population of 161,799 (*Source: World Almanac,* 1993, p. 412).

1.11   The Bureau of the Census estimates that 5% of the black population was missed in the 1980 population census (*Source: Hansen, M. H., and B. A. Bailar, "How to Count Better," in *Statistics: A Guide to the Unknown,* 3rd ed., p. 209). Is 5% the value of a parameter or a statistic?

1.12   A researcher is looking into aspects of life at a large eastern university. The researcher wishes to estimate the proportion of students at the university who are commuters. The researcher does not know that 4/10 of the students are commuters. Is 4/10 the value of a parameter or a statistic?

1.13   A linguist was interested in the population of words in James Joyce's *Ulysses.* The word *the* occurs 14,887 times (*Source: Simon, H. A., "The Sizes of Things," in *Statistics: A Guide to the Unknown,* 3rd ed., p. 143). Is 14,887 the value of a parameter or a statistic?

1.14   A sample of 50 federal employees in a large midwestern city showed an average age of 38.2 years. Is 38.2 the value of a parameter or a statistic?

1.15   Consider the problem of estimating the average grade point average (GPA) of the 750 seniors at a college. (The average, which is unknown, is the sum of 750 GPAs divided by 750.)

(a)   What is the population? How many data values are in the population?

(b)   What is the parameter of interest?

(c)   Suppose that a sample of 10 seniors is selected, and their GPAs are 2.72, 2.81, 2.65, 2.69, 3.17, 2.74, 2.57, 2.17, 3.48, 3.10. Calculate a statistic that you would use to estimate the parameter.

(d)   Suppose that another sample of 10 seniors was selected. Would it be likely that the value of the statistic is the same as in part (c)? Why or why not? Would the value of the parameter remain the same?

1.16   Unaware that 35% of the 10,000 voters in his district still support him, a politician decides to estimate his political strength. A sample of 200 voters shows that 40% support him.

(a)   What is the population?

(b)   What is the value of the parameter of interest?

(c)   What is the value of the statistic of interest?

(d) Compare your answers in (b) and (c). Is it surprising they are different? If the politician were to sample another 200 voters, which of the two numbers would most likely change? Explain.

1.17 A sociologist was interested in estimating some aspects of family life in a town. Information about the entire town (unknown to the sociologist) and the results of a sample obtained by the sociologist follow.

Number of Children per Family	Number of Families in Town	Number of Families in Sample
0	120	6
1	180	10
2	270	12
3	300	8
4	80	6
5	50	8

(a) Identify the elements of the population and give the population size.

(b) Identify the elements of the sample and give the sample size.

(c) Suppose that the sociologist were interested in the *number* of families with more than two children.
  (i) Calculate a statistic to estimate the parameter of interest. (*Hint:* Assume that the sociologist knows that the population is 20 times the size of the sample.)
  (ii) What is the value of the parameter?

(d) Suppose that the sociologist were interested in the *proportion* of families with less than four children.
  (i) What is the value of the statistic?
  (ii) What is the value of the parameter?

1.18 In the Massachusetts State Lottery Megabucks game, six numbers are selected from the set of 42 numbers $\{1, 2, 3, 4, \ldots, 39, 40, 41, 42\}$. A player thought that too high a percentage of single-digit numbers was being selected. He obtained a partial list of past drawings and observed that 26.4% of the numbers were single digit.

(a) If the numbers were generated randomly, what would the value of the parameter of interest be?

(b) What is the value of the statistic?

1.2

SAMPLING

We said that in inferential statistics we use samples to make judgments about populations. We want the samples we obtain to be **representative** of the population, that is, to resemble the population. There are many ways of obtaining samples; we mention only a few here.

Random Samples

Random sampling is one of the most important types of sampling in statistics.

> **Definition**   A *random sample* is a sample obtained from the population in such a manner that all samples of the same size have equal likelihood of being selected. Any method of obtaining random samples is called *random sampling*.

For example, one method of random sampling is the **lottery method.** With this method, elements in the population are identified by a name or number written on a tag. The tags are placed in a container and are then well mixed. A tag is drawn by chance from the container, and this process is repeated until the desired number of tags is obtained.

When the elements in the population are identified by numbers (such as employee identification numbers for employees of a large corporation), we may use the **random number method** to obtain random samples. Random numbers are found in Appendix Table B.1. Instructions on how to use the table are found in Appendix A. Suppose there are 9000 employees with ID numbers 0001, 0002, 0003, and so on, up to 9000. We can use the random number table to obtain a random sample of, say, five employees, by choosing a sequence of five ID numbers that occurred in a purely random manner. When the sampling is done in such a way that there are no repetitions in the sample (for example, by ignoring ID numbers that repeat), we call the resulting sample a **simple random sample** (SRS).

Stratified Samples

Another type of sample frequently encountered is a **stratified sample.**

> **Definition**   If the population is divided into subpopulations, called *strata*, and we take a random sample from each stratum, the resulting sample is a *stratified sample.*

For example, the students at a college could be divided into strata according to class: freshmen, sophomores, juniors, seniors. To obtain a stratified sample, we could take a random sample from each class. In stratified sampling, the size of the sample from each stratum is often proportional to the size of the stratum in the population. For example, suppose 40% of the student body are freshmen, 25% sophomores, 20% juniors, and 15% seniors. To obtain a stratified sample of size 100, we could sample 40 freshmen, 25 sophomores, 20 juniors, and 15 seniors. The result would be a **proportional stratified sample.**

Stratified samples are often easier to obtain than true random samples. For example, if we wanted a sample of Massachusetts voters, it would be inconvenient to compile a list or computer file of all voters from which to select a random sample. However, we could sample voters from each voting precinct, thereby obtaining a stratified sample.

Cluster Samples

Even though a population can be divided into strata, it may not be convenient to sample from each stratum. For example, instead of sampling from each voting precinct in the state, we could randomly select some of the precincts and sample from each of these. Thus if we wanted a sample of 1000 voters, we might select 20 precincts and randomly sample 50 voters from each precinct. This kind of sample is called a **cluster sample.**

Definition A *cluster sample* is obtained by selecting some of the strata and then sampling from each of these.

In stratified sampling, the strata are frequently quite different from one another but are homogeneous internally. In cluster sampling, however, the strata are often defined in such a way that the clusters are as internally diverse as possible, yet easy to access by the interviewer. This could be accomplished by defining the clusters as compact geographical regions, saving the interviewer's travel time.

In practice, most large surveys, such as the Current Population Survey (CPS) of the Census Bureau, use **multistage cluster sampling.** To obtain a multistage cluster sample of U.S. households, we could start with a list of all U.S. counties. These are called **primary sampling units** (PSUs). The procedure is as follows:

- Take a sample of PSUs.
- Take a sample of towns in each PSU.
- Take a sample of streets in each town.
- Take a sample of households on each street.

At each stage, simple random sampling could be used.

The multistage cluster sample used for the Current Population Survey differs from this scheme in a number of respects. For example, the PSUs are placed in strata based on various criteria, such as size. A stratified sample of the PSUs is then obtained. Also, instead of streets, the CPS uses enumeration districts (EDs) selected from a list by a procedure called **systematic sampling,** to be discussed next.

Systematic Samples

If we have a list of the elements in the population, an easy way to obtain a sample is by **systematic sampling.** For example, from a list of all employees of a corporation, we could choose by chance some starting point on the list and then select perhaps every fifth name on the list. The starting point could be chosen by selecting an ID number from the random number table.

Definition From a list of members of a population, choose a starting point by chance and then select every nth element on the list (for some appropriate value of n). The result is a *systematic sample.*

For example, suppose you have a list of 100 ID numbers, and you want a sample of size 12. Notice that $100/12 \doteq 8.33$ (where $\doteq$ means "is approximately equal to").

Round *up* to get 9. Randomly select a starting point. Then select every 9th ID number until you have 12 numbers. You could use the random number table to select a starting ID number. If the starting point was 004, the next number would be 013.

The samples discussed thus far involve a chance process and fall under the general heading of **probability samples.** However, occasionally we encounter samples that are not probability samples. An example of this is a **sample of convenience.**

Samples of Convenience

A statistics instructor who was teaching two sections of statistics wanted to compare two books, so one book was used in one section and the other book was used in the other section. The two statistics sections are examples of **samples of convenience.**

Definition A *sample of convenience* is a sample that already exists and is available for study; the elements in the sample are not chosen by a chance process. By contrast, a *probability sample* is obtained by a chance process; each element in the population has a certain probability of being selected.

A sample of convenience can be useful provided we can be fairly confident that the sample is not biased for some reason. For example, we should not choose a statistics section as representative of statistics students if it is a section consisting of honors students.

In Part III of this book (Statistical Inference), we use samples to study populations. The methods we use are valid for random samples. However, many statisticians would use these techniques on samples of convenience as well.

Some Problems with Sampling

Sometimes common sense is the most important element of a sampling strategy. In the 1936 presidential campaign between Franklin Roosevelt and Republican opponent Alf Landon, the publishers of *Literary Digest* magazine conducted a survey of some 2.4 million people—an enormous sample by today's standards. On the basis of the survey, the magazine predicted a landslide win for Alf Landon, but the opposite occurred. The flaw in the sampling scheme was that the participants in the survey included many whose names were taken from telephone directories, lists of clubs, and other organizations where the affluent (many of whom were Republican) would be overrepresented. (In 1936 only the relatively well-to-do possessed telephones.) In other words, the sample was biased.

The A. C. Nielsen Company conducts surveys to determine the percentage (share) of TV viewers watching various shows. In the 1960s, some 1600 families were used in a sample selected as representative of television-viewing families in America. A device called an audometer was attached to their TV sets to record the shows being viewed. The audometer was connected by telephone lines to Nielsen computers. A Texas viewer who happened to be in the sample had a strong aversion to then president of the United States Lyndon Johnson. One night he became enraged at something Johnson said on the news, and fired his shotgun into the

TV, destroying the TV and the audometer. He bought a new TV the next day and called the Nielsen Company to have them install a new audometer. A few weeks later the same thing happened. After this occurred a number of times, the Nielsen Company became tired of installing new audometers, and officials decided to remove this individual from their sample. However, they were overruled by Mr. Nielsen, the president of the company. His reasoning was that for the sample to be representative, the lunatic fringe must also be included.

Nonresponse Bias

The ideas just presented are related to the problem of **nonresponse bias** in a sample. Nonresponse bias occurs when a segment of the population is inadequately reflected in the sample. Nonresponse can range from people in a survey not answering some of the questions or refusing to participate at all, to whole categories of people being left out of the sample. People who refuse to participate are different from people who do participate, at least in their unwillingness to participate, and they may be different in other respects as well. In this case, the sample will not be representative of the population, and bias has been introduced. Sometimes entire categories of people are left out of surveys: Telephone surveys will miss those too poor to have a telephone. Interviewers who visit homes to interview subjects will miss the homeless.

Some of the surveys conducted by the media suffer from severe nonresponse bias. TV shows that ask viewers to call 900 numbers to vote on some controversial issue, such as gun control, will attract viewers with strong feelings on the subject. The sample would have an unusually large concentration of members of the National Rifle Association and Handgun Control Inc. People who do not have strong feelings on the subject will tend not to call with such frequency. This nonresponse results in a biased sample. In a similar vein, magazines sometimes include a tear-out questionnaire, and invite their readers to participate in a survey. Such surveys usually have nonresponse bias as well. These kinds of media surveys that use self-selected samples are usually worthless.

Every effort should be made to cut down on nonresponse. In the case of the U.S. Census, response is required by law. With private surveys, nonresponse is a greater problem. Telephone surveys use callbacks to people who were not home when first called. Some surveys use incentives to elicit response: "Complete this survey and you may choose any one of the following products free." However, nonresponse sometimes cannot be avoided. Sometimes researchers assume a nonrespondent resembles some subset of the respondents with similar characteristics. If the nonrespondent failed to answer the question on salary, the average salary of these similar respondents could be used. For a discussion of methods for dealing with missing data, see Madow, Nisselson, and Olkin (1983) and Deming (1968).

Response Bias

In surveys, respondents may lie or have a failure of memory. Or the questionnaire or interview process may be flawed. These situations lead to **response bias.** Response bias can occur when questions are phrased to elicit a certain response, for example, "In view of the fact that last year's increase in the school budget did not produce any increase in students' scores, do you favor or oppose an increase in next year's school budget?" Of course, the designer of the survey controls the wording of the question. But it is more difficult to control for lying. Respondents might be afraid or embarrassed to answer some questions truthfully, for example, "Have you ever cheated on your income tax?"

Here is a way to get around this problem: Suppose you have 1000 respondents in your survey. Tell each respondent to flip a coin. If it comes up heads, then they are told to answer Yes to the above question (even if they have never cheated on their income tax). If it comes up tails, they are to answer the question truthfully. This way the interviewer has no idea who has really cheated. Now suppose 600 respondents answer Yes and 400 answer No. You can expect 500 heads, and hence 500 Yes answers due only to the heads. The 500 who got tails presumably answered truthfully, and these account for the remaining 100 Yes answers. So, assuming we have a good sample, we would estimate that 20% of people have cheated on their income tax.

EXERCISES

1.19   List all simple random samples of size 3 from the population {a, b, c, d}.

1.20   For the population {0, 1, 2, 3, 5, 7},

  (a)   Give an example of a proportional stratified sample of size 3 where the strata are {0, 1, 2, 3}, {5, 7}.

  (b)   Give a cluster sample of size 2 where the clusters are {0, 1}, {2, 3}, {5, 7}.

  (c)   Give a systematic sample of size 3 where the elements are listed in order: 0, 1, 2, 3, 5, 7.

1.21   A business has 100 employees, and each employee is identified with a two-digit ID number. A complete list of the identification numbers is 00, 01, 02, 03, . . . , 99. Assume there are four departments, A, B, C, and D, within the business consisting of the following employees:

$$
\begin{array}{ll}
\text{A:} \quad 00, 01, \ldots, 09 & \text{B:} \quad 10, 11, \ldots, 29 \\
\text{C:} \quad 30, 31, \ldots, 59 & \text{D:} \quad 60, 61, \ldots, 99
\end{array}
$$

  (a)   Give a systematic sample of 10 ID numbers.

  (b)   Give a sample of 10 ID numbers using Appendix Table B.1. Start with the first column of numbers 10, 37, 08, ... List the elements sampled for each of the following cases:
      (i)   Simple random sample
      (ii)   Proportional stratified sample
      (iii) Cluster sample, assuming department D is randomly selected

1.22   There are 10 males and 15 females in a statistics class of 25 students. Five are to be sampled. Explain how you would use Appendix Table B.1 to obtain the following samples:

  (a)   A simple random sample

  (b)   A proportional stratified sample where the strata are males and females

  (c)   A cluster sample where one of the strata is randomly selected

  (d)   A systematic sample where a starting point is determined and then every fifth element in a list is selected

1.23   A local automobile company that employs 600 males and 400 females operates three shifts (I, II, III). Company officials hired a statistician to conduct a survey to obtain information on employees' attitudes toward the company. The statistician is going to survey 40 employees. The numbers of males and females working various shifts are as follows:

	Shift I	Shift II	Shift III	Totals
Male	300	200	100	600
Female	200	100	100	400
Totals	500	300	200	1000

To conduct a sample, the statistician uses the following coding:

Male and shift I: {000, 001, 002, ..., 299}
Male and shift II: {300, 301, 302, ..., 499}
Male and shift III: {500, 501, 502, ..., 599}
Female and shift I: {600, 601, 602, ..., 799}
Female and shift II: {800, 801, 802, ..., 899}
Female and shift III: {900, 901, 902, ..., 999}

The statistician is considering many different sampling schemes to obtain a sample of 40 employees.

(a) To select a simple random sample, use Appendix Table B.1 and start with the first row of numbers 100, 973, 253, 376, ... Use the table below to fill in the number sampled in each category.

	Shift I	Shift II	Shift III	Totals
Male				
Female				
Totals				

(b) Consider the six strata: Male and shift I, Male and shift II, Male and shift III, Female and shift I, Female and shift II, Female and shift III. The statistician decides to obtain a proportional stratified sample and starts with the sixth row of numbers, 660, 657, 471, 734, ..., in Appendix Table B.1. Use the table below and fill in the number required in each stratum. List the elements obtained for the stratum Male and shift I.

	Shift I	Shift II	Shift III	Totals
Male				
Female				
Totals				

(c) Obtain a systematic sample using 321 as the starting point and then select every 25th element. Assume the list is 000, 001, 002, ..., 998, 999. How many females are included in this sample? How many people from shift I are included? Note that Appendix Table B.1 is not needed.

(d) Suppose a cluster sample is obtained by selecting shifts II and III from the three shift strata. If the sampling is proportional, how many employees should be chosen from each stratum?

1.24 Suppose that a computer outlet firm has ten stores, and each store has four departments. Describe a multistage sampling scheme to select a sample of employees. Assume that a department is selected from each of four stores.

1.3

TOPICS IN THE DESIGN OF EXPERIMENTS

Many colleges now offer short courses or seminars to improve study skills. To assess the effectiveness of such experiences, we might obtain a sample of students who took the course and compare them with a sample of students who did not take the course. It would seem natural to compare the grade point averages for the two groups. The skills course is referred to as the **treatment,** and the students who took the course as the **treatment group.** The other students are the **control group.**

Definition

- The *treatment* is the property being studied.
- The *treatment group* is the group possessing the property.
- The *control group* is the group not possessing the property.

There is a possible problem with the study just discussed. The students who took the study skills course may have been more highly motivated than the other students, and this alone might cause them to study harder and therefore do better. We might conclude that the skills course was effective, when in fact it was the higher motivation that accounted for the students' better performance. Motivation is an example of a **confounding factor.**

To overcome this, we might have designed the study differently. We could obtain a group of students and ask half to take the course. This way motivation would not determine who took the course. When the researcher has control over which subjects obtain the treatment, it is a **controlled experiment.** When the researcher does not have this control, it is an **observational study.** Note that in both of the experiments described, there is a control group. *Having a control group does not necessarily mean that we have a controlled experiment.*

In the controlled experiment just described, there can still be a problem. The researcher involved may be partial to the skills course and thus may assign the better students to take the course (perhaps even subconsciously). To overcome this, the students could be randomly assigned to the treatment and control groups, perhaps by the toss of a coin. This is called a **randomized controlled experiment.**

Definition When the researcher can control which subjects are assigned to the treatment, it is a *controlled experiment.* Otherwise, it is an *observational study.* When the subjects are assigned by chance to the treatment and control groups, it is a *randomized controlled experiment.* The purpose of a controlled experiment is to eliminate *confounding factors,* which are properties other than the treatment that can influence a study.

Even with randomized controlled experiments there can be problems. The students who are randomly assigned to take the skills course might feel compelled to do better, and thus study harder, thereby confounding the results. It is difficult to know how to overcome this in the study described, but in some situations, we can get around this difficulty. For example, if we wanted to study the effectiveness of vitamin C in combating colds, we might randomly assign some subjects to take regular doses of vitamin C (the treatment) and other subjects to take a placebo (the control). Further, we would not allow the subjects to know whether their pills were vitamin C or placebos. This way, the subjects who took vitamin C would not know whether they were "expected" to have fewer colds. At the end of a year's time, the subjects would be interviewed to determine how many colds each got. We should be sure that the interviewers do not know which subjects received the vitamin C and which received the placebos. This would be called a **double-blind randomized controlled experiment.** Whenever possible, this is the type of experimental design we should use.

> **Definition** In a *double-blind randomized controlled experiment,* neither the subjects nor those who evaluate the effects know which subjects are assigned to the treatment group and which are in the control group.

Although controlled experiments are in general preferable to observational studies, we should keep in mind that a controlled experiment is not always possible or even ethical. If we were studying the effects of heavy drinking on health, it would hardly be ethical to tell some of the subjects to become heavy drinkers in the interest of science.

Cross-Sectional Studies and Longitudinal Studies

In a **cross-sectional study,** different subjects are compared to one another at the same point in time. In a **longitudinal study,** the same subjects are compared to themselves at different points in time. For example, to study the effects of smoking on blood pressure using a cross-sectional study, we might obtain a sample of people and compare the smokers with the nonsmokers. In a longitudinal study, we could look at a group of smokers who gave up smoking and compare their blood pressures before and after giving up smoking.

Politicians and journalists sometimes confuse cross-sectional studies done at different points in time with a longitudinal study, particularly when analyzing income data. Income data are often analyzed by grouping people into **fifths** or **quintiles.** Then the average income of the lowest fifth of workers is computed, the average of the next lowest fifth is computed, and so forth.

Table 1.1 (page 14) contains the average family income of each quintile in 1977 and 1986. Such figures are often the cause of great hand wringing. We hear about the poor getting poorer and the rich getting richer. But notice the phrases: *the* poor and *the* rich. The people who were in the lowest quintiles in 1977 and 1986 are generally not the same people. The same applies to the other quintiles. Since Table 1.1 does not compare the same people in 1977 and 1986, **it is not a longitudinal study of people.**

To do a longitudinal study, we should look at the average income of each quintile in 1977 and then look at the incomes of the same people in 1986. For

Table 1.1
Two Cross-Sectional Studies: Average Family Income by Quintile (in 1991 dollars)

Quintile	1977	1986	Percent Change
Lowest	$10,282	$ 9,990	−2.8
Second	22,865	23,501	2.8
Third	34,483	36,471	5.8
Fourth	47,588	52,115	9.5
Top	81,584	94,926	16.4

Source: Money Income of Households, Families, and Persons in the United States: 1991, U.S. Bureau of the Census, B-13.

example, we should compare the average income of the people in the lowest quintile in 1977 with the average income of those *same people* in 1986, regardless of what quintile those people happen to belong to in 1986. Isabel V. Sawhill and Mark Condon did such a longitudinal study (see Sawhill and Condon, p. 3). The University of Michigan's Panel Study on Income Dynamics (PSID) has followed a representative group of households over a period of years. Using these data, Sawhill and Condon compared the average income of each quintile in 1977 with the average income of those same people in 1986. The results are in Table 1.2. This table presents a very different picture from Table 1.1. The figures in the first column in Table 1.1 are not the same as those in the first column of Table 1.2. This is because Sawhill and Condon limited their sample to adults age 25–54. This eliminated younger people (such as college students), whose incomes are likely to grow dramatically, and older people, who retire and show a dramatic drop in income.

Table 1.2
A Longitudinal Study: Average Family Income of 1977 Quintile Members in 1977 and 1986 (in 1991 dollars)[a]

	Average Family Income of		
Quintile	1977 Quintile Members in 1977	1977 Quintile Members in 1986	Percent Change
Bottom	$15,853	$27,998	77
Second	31,340	43,041	37
Third	43,297	51,796	20
Fourth	57,486	63,314	10
Top	92,531	97,140	5

[a]Sample limited to adults age 25 to 54

Source: Sawhill, Isabel V., and Mark Condon, "Is U.S. Income Inequality Really Growing?" *Policy Bites,* No. 13, June 1992, p. 3, The Urban Institute.

Although Table 1.1 does not show that the rich are getting richer and the poor are getting poorer, it does show a growing income disparity, a troubling trend in itself.

Simpson's Paradox or the Danger of Aggregating Data

Beginning in 1987, the Department of Transportation required U.S. airlines to report each month the percentage of their flights that are on time in the 30 busiest airports in the United States. Reporting an overall percentage of on-time flights can favor airlines that frequently serve fair-weather cities and disadvantage airlines that serve cities with rain or fog.

Alaska Airlines serves only 5 of the 30 busiest airports. America West Airlines has a higher overall percentage of on-time flights for the five cities than Alaska Airlines. But a careful look at the data reveals something interesting. Table 1.3 is the record for June 1991. Although America West had a higher overall percentage of on-time flights, Alaska Airlines had a better on-time record in each of the five cities!

Table 1.3

Destination	Alaska Airlines			America West Airlines		
	Number of Arrivals	Arrivals on Time	% On Time	Number of Arrivals	Arrivals on Time	% On Time
Los Angeles	559	497	88.9%	811	694	85.6%
Phoenix	233	221	94.8	5255	4840	92.1
San Diego	232	212	91.4	448	383	85.5
San Francisco	605	503	83.1	449	320	71.3
Seattle	2146	1841	85.8	262	201	76.7
Five-airport totals	3775	3274	**86.7%**	7225	6438	**89.1%**

Source: Barnett, Arnold, "How Numbers Can Trick You," *Technology Review,* Oct. 1994, p. 42. Reprinted with permission from *Technology Review,* copyright 1994.

The reason for this paradox (called **Simpson's Paradox**) can be appreciated by closely examining Table 1.3. Most of America West flights went to Phoenix, a fair-weather airport; America West had an excellent on-time record for this city (although Alaska Airlines did better). On the other hand, most of Alaska Airlines' flights went into Seattle, which has rather inclement weather.

This example shows the danger that can arise if one looks only at summary data. A similar effect occurred in 1973 at the University of California at Berkeley Graduate School.[*] The overall percentage of female applicants rejected was much higher than the percentage of males rejected. But when each academic department was examined, it was found that the rejection rate was about the same for females as for males, or, in a few cases, the rejection rate was somewhat higher for males. The explanation lies in the fact that females tend to apply to programs that have a large number of applicants, and therefore a higher rejection rate (psychology, sociology). Males tend to apply to programs that have fewer applicants, and therefore a lower rejection rate (engineering, the sciences).

EXERCISES

1.25 A government agency initiated a program in substance abuse therapy for alcoholics eligible for supplemental security income (SSI). Participation in the program was voluntary. When the participants were compared with another group of alcoholics

---

[*]See Bickel, P., E. A. Hammel, and J. W. O'Connell, "Sex Bias in Graduate Admissions: Data from Berkeley." *Science,* Vol. 187, Feb. 7, 1975, pp. 398–404.

receiving SSI who did not participate, it was found that a higher proportion of the participants were off SSI and working within 2 years.

(a) What is the treatment?

(b) Identify the treatment group and the control group.

(c) Is this a controlled experiment?

(d) What factor could confound the result?

(e) If your answer to part (c) was No, how could a controlled experiment be done?

1.26 Keypunchers find that keypunching over a period of time can be stressful and painful. For example, one source of discomfort is that the wrist and forearm become quite painful. A computer company designed a new keyboard and believed that it would relieve the discomfort. To test whether this was so, 20 employees were selected and 10 were randomly chosen to use the new keyboard. The other 10 were assigned to the keyboard in current use. The 20 participants spent a specified amount of time keypunching. Then each was asked their level of discomfort on a scale of 0–6, with 0 being pain-free and 6 the most severe pain. The company wanted to compare the levels of discomfort for the two groups.

(a) What is the treatment?

(b) Identify the treatment group and the control group.

(c) Is this a controlled experiment?

1.27 The following data were reported concerning drinking habits of college students:

Class	Average Number of Drinks per Week
Freshmen	6.1
Sophomores	6.0
Juniors	5.7
Seniors	5.4

Source: U.S. News and World Report, June 20, 1994, p. 21.

(a) On seeing these numbers, one of our students concluded that "students tend to drink less as they get older." Do you agree with this? If not, what other factor could account for the fact that lower alcoholic consumption is associated with higher class standing?

(b) In order to study college students' drinking habits as they progress through four years of college, how might you design a study?

1.28 Forty-eight of 127 Central High School graduates had an overall scholastic average of more than 85. A school administrator was interested in comparing satisfaction with life for this group as compared to the rest of the graduates 1 year after graduation. The 127 graduates were asked a year after graduation whether they were satisfied with their lives. Is this a controlled experiment or an observational study? Would this study be classified as cross-sectional or longitudinal?

1.29 Refer to Exercise 1.28. Suppose that the administrator wanted to compare satisfaction with life at graduation with satisfaction 5 years later for those with an overall average of more than 85. Would this study be classified as cross-sectional or longitudinal?

1.30 A sociologist was interested in whether people's attitudes about raising taxes to support building a new school were related to whether they had children in school. One hundred voters with children in the ninth grade were asked whether they supported the idea of higher taxes for the purpose of building a new high school. Five years later they were again asked the same question. Would this study be classified as cross-sectional or longitudinal?

1.31 Fifty voters with children in a public school and 50 with no children in school were sampled and asked whether they would support an increase in taxes to help pay for a new school. The town finance manager wanted to compare results between voters with children in school and others. Would this study be classified as cross-sectional or longitudinal?

1.32 At the beginning of the work stoppage in 1994, management of a baseball franchise sampled 100 current and 100 former season ticket holders. Management was trying to determine whether attitudes were different in the two groups regarding blame for the stoppage. Would this study be classified as cross-sectional or longitudinal?

1.33 At the beginning of the work stoppage in 1994, management of a baseball franchise sampled 100 season ticket holders. They were interviewed at the beginning and end of the strike. The management wanted to obtain information on whether the fans believed management was more at fault for the stoppage than the players and whether their attitudes had changed by the end of the strike. Would this study be classified as cross-sectional or longitudinal?

1.34 Between 1976 and 1979, the nominal tax rate as a percent of personal income was decreased in each tax bracket by Congress. But the overall percentage of income paid in taxes increased for the country as a whole (*Source:* Wagner, C. H., "Simpson's Paradox in Real Life," *American Statistician*, 36, 1982, pp. 46–48). To see how this can happen, consider the following hypothetical data:

1976:	Tax Brackets	20%	40%	50%
	Percentage of Taxpayers	70%	20%	10%

1979:	Tax Brackets	18%	38%	48%
	Percentage of Taxpayers	10%	30%	60%

The overall rates for 1976 and 1979 were 27% and 42%, respectively. What explains the increase in spite of the decrease in each bracket?

1.35 The following table gives information on job applicants at a hypothetical company with four job categories. Complete the table in such a way that

(a) in each job category the percentage of males accepted is the same as the percentage of females accepted.

(b) the overall percentage of females accepted is lower than the overall percentage of males accepted.

(There is more than one correct answer.)

Job Applicants	A		B		C		D		Total	
	M	F	M	F	M	F	M	F	M	F
Accepted	50		40		60		50			
Rejected	100		60		300		400			
% accepted										

1.4

SUMMARY

Statistics is the science of collecting, simplifying, and describing data, as well as making inferences based on the analysis of data.

The collection of all the elements (often data values) we are interested in is called a **population.** A collection of some of the elements obtained from the population is called a **sample** from the population.

Descriptive statistics involves collecting, simplifying, and giving the properties of data. **Inferential statistics** is concerned with making judgments about a population based on properties of some sample obtained from the population.

A number representing a numerical property of a population is called a **parameter.** A number representing a numerical property of a sample is called a **statistic.**

A **random sample** is a sample obtained from the population in such a manner that all samples of the same size have equal likelihood of being selected. A **stratified sample** is obtained by dividing the population into strata or subpopulations and sampling from each stratum. A **cluster sample** is obtained by selecting some of the strata and sampling from these. A **systematic sample** can be chosen from a list of the members of the population by selecting a starting point on the list by chance, and then choosing every nth element on the list for some appropriate n. A **sample of convenience** is a sample that already exists and is available for study; the elements of the sample are not selected by any chance process. **Nonresponse bias** occurs when a segment of the population is inadequately reflected in a sample. **Response bias** occurs if respondents lie or fail to remember, or if the questionnaire or interview is in some way flawed.

A **treatment** is a property being studied (such as smoking cigarettes). The **treatment group** is the group possessing the property. The **control group** does not possess the property. When the researcher can control which subjects can be assigned to the treatment, the study is called a **controlled experiment;** otherwise, it is an **observational study.** When the subjects are randomly assigned to the treatment group, we have a **randomized controlled experiment.** A **confounding factor** is a property other than the treatment that can influence a study. In a **double-blind** study, neither the subjects nor those evaluating the results know which subjects are in the control group and which are in the treatment group. In a **cross-sectional study,** different subjects are compared at the same point in time. In a **longitudinal study,** the same subjects are compared to themselves at different points in time.

Notes

Barnett, Arnold, "How Numbers Can Trick You," *Technology Review,* Oct. 1994.

Bickel, P. E., A. Hammel, and J. W. O'Connell, "Sex Bias in Graduate Admissions: Data from Berkeley," *Science,* Vol. 187, Feb. 7, 1975.

Deming, W. E., *Sample Surveys I: The Field* (1968), Updated in 1978 in *International Encyclopedia of Statistics,* eds. W. H. Kruskal and J. M. Tanur. New York: Macmillan.

The 1994 Information Please Almanac. Boston: Houghton Mifflin Company, 1994.

Madow, W. G., H. Nisselson, and I. Olkin, *Incomplete Data in Sample Surveys* (3 vols.). New York: Academic Press, 1983.

Money Income of Households, Families, and Persons in the United States: 1991. Washington: U.S. Bureau of the Census, 1992.

Sawhill, I., and M. Condon, "Is U.S. Income Inequality Really Growing?" *Policy Bites,* No. 13. Washington D.C.: Urban Institute, 1992.

Tanur, J. M., et al., eds., *Statistics: A Guide to the Unknown,* 3rd ed. Pacific Grove, Calif.: Wadsworth and Brooks/Cole, 1989.

U.S. News & World Report, June 20, 1994.

Wagner, C. H., "Simpson's Paradox in Real Life," *American Statistician,* Vol. 36, 1982.

The World Almanac and Book of Facts. New York: Newspaper Enterprise Association, 1993.

PART ONE

DESCRIPTIVE STATISTICS

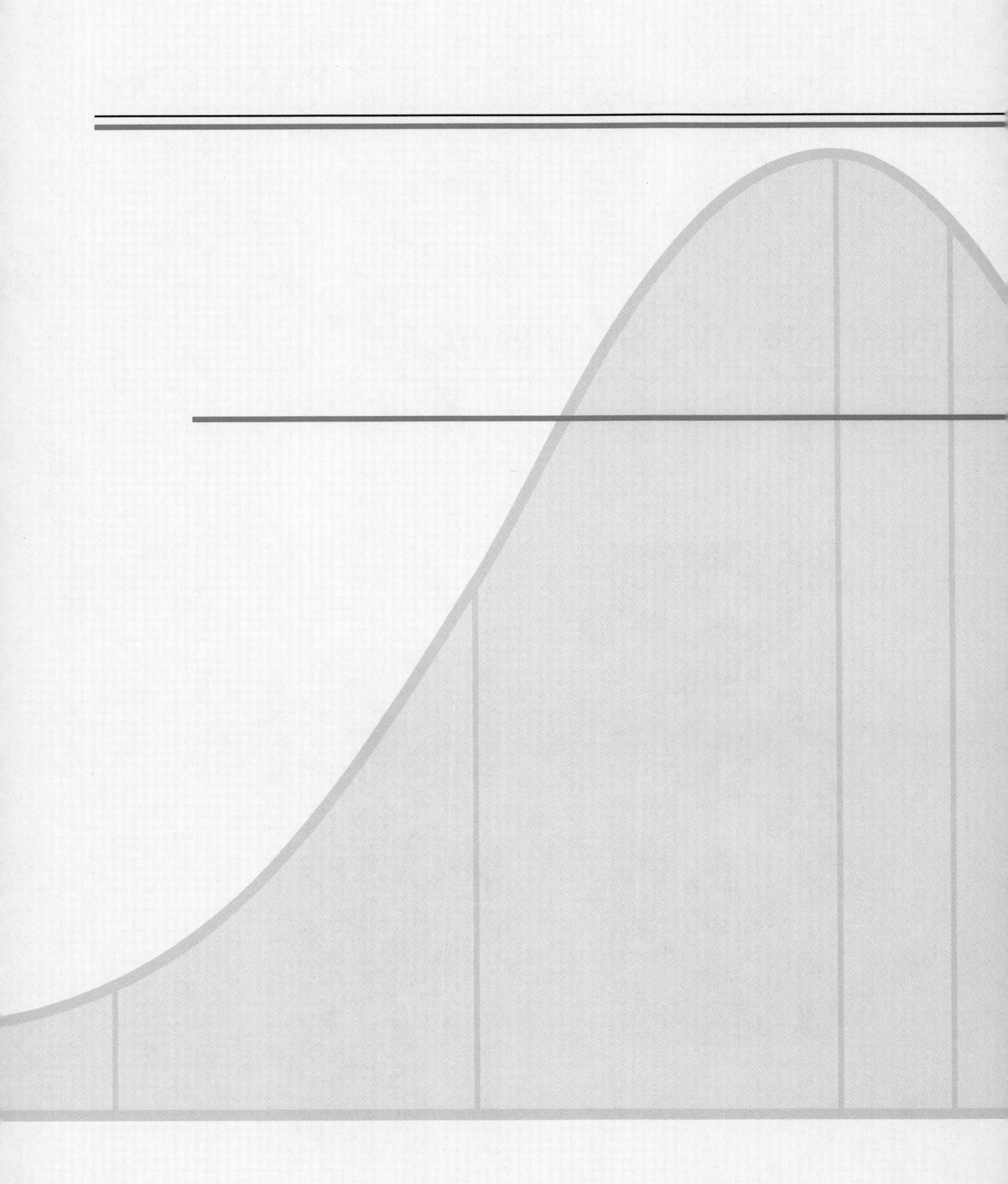

CHAPTER 2

ORGANIZATION OF DATA

2.1 **INTRODUCTION**

2.2 **SUMMARIZING DATA**

2.3 **GRAPHIC REPRESENTATIONS**

2.4 **THE SHAPE OF A DISTRIBUTION**

2.5 **STEM-AND-LEAF PLOTS**

2.6 **MISLEADING GRAPHS (OPTIONAL)**

2.7 **USING MINITAB (OPTIONAL)**

2.8 **WORKING WITH DATA (OPTIONAL)**

2.9 **SUMMARY**

REVIEW EXERCISES

NOTES

2.1

INTRODUCTION

In Chapter 1, we said that descriptive statistics involves organizing and describing data in such a way as to make it more comprehensible. In this chapter, we concentrate on how to organize or summarize the data. This involves presenting the data in a form that is easy to comprehend. It also involves representing the data graphically. In the next chapter, we will continue our study of descriptive statistics by discussing how to describe data by means of certain numerical characteristics (such as the average of the data values).

Occasionally, the data values we study constitute all the data values we are interested in; that is, they may constitute all the data values from a population.

But more often, we can obtain only a sample from the population, in which case we hope that the sample is *representative* of the population, that is, resembles the population. If this is the case, the essential information we obtain from the sample would also be true of the population as a whole.

Notation

If we have a collection of data values, generally we will represent an arbitrary or unspecified data value from this collection by a lowercase letter from near the end of the alphabet, such as x, y, or z.

2.2

SUMMARIZING DATA

Frequency Distributions

Rather than write out all the data values in a collection of data, including repetitions, it is sometimes more convenient simply to list the distinct values in the collection together with the number of times each value occurs.

Definition Given a collection of data values, the specification of all the distinct values in the collection together with the number of times each of these values occurs in the collection is called a *frequency distribution*. The number of times a value occurs is called its *frequency*. The frequency of a data value x is denoted by f_x (or just f).

EXAMPLE 2.1

Construct a frequency distribution for the following data, which represent the number of breakdowns for each truck in a fleet of 20 delivery trucks in 1 year:

6   11   5   1   6   6   7   5   7   6   1   7   5   3   6   3   5   6   7   6

Solution
The distinct values are 1, 3, 5, 6, 7, 11, which occur 2, 2, 4, 7, 4, 1 times, respectively. It is customary to organize this information in a table. The first column of the table contains the distinct values. In the second column next to each distinct value, we record its frequency. So the frequency distribution is represented as follows:

x	f
1	2
3	2
5	4
6	7
7	4
11	1

EXAMPLE 2.2

Frequency distributions may also be used to summarize nonnumerical data. The Federal Bureau of Investigation gathered information on all murders committed in 1992. The data value associated with each murder was the type of weapon used. Table 2.1 gives the number of murders (f) for each weapon type (x). For convenience, we have added a column giving the percentage for each weapon type.

Table 2.1
Murders by Type of Weapon

Type of Weapon (x)	Frequency (f)	Percentage (approximate)
Handgun	12,489	55.4
Rifle	698	3.1
Shotgun	1,104	4.9
Knife	3,265	14.5
Personal weapon (hands, fists, etc.)	1,121	5.0
Other weapon[a] (club, poison, etc.)	3,863	17.1
Total	22,540	100.0

[a]Includes weapons not specified.

Source: Data based on *Crime in the United States—Uniform Crime Reports,* Washington, D.C.: Federal Bureau of Investigation, 1993, p. 18.

Grouped Frequency Distributions

The frequency distributions just discussed can be helpful in simplifying data if the number of distinct data values is not too large. But if the number of distinct data values is large, which is often the case with numerical data, the frequency distribution will not be of much value in simplifying the data.

Given a large collection of numerical data values, we can simplify these data and make them more comprehensible as follows: Divide an interval containing these data into a small number of line segments (or subintervals), usually of equal width. These segments are called **classes.** We then tell how many data values fall into each class. The result is called a **grouped frequency distribution.**

For example, a department store described the ages of its 100 employees with the following grouped frequency distribution:

	Age	Number of Employees	
	20–29	30	
	30–39	35	
Classes	40–49	20	Class frequencies
	50–59	10	
	60–69	5	

The values 20, 30, 40, 50, and 60 are called **lower class limits.** The values 29, 39, 49, 59, and 69 are called **upper class limits.** The distance from one lower class limit to the next lower class limit is called the **class width.** For the grouped frequency distribution of employees, the class width is 10. (*Note:*   This is the distance from lower class limit to lower class limit, not from lower class limit to upper class limit.)

We illustrate the procedure for constructing a grouped frequency distribution for the data in Table 2.2, which represent the scores of 40 high school students on a scientific achievement test.

Table 2.2
**Scores on a Scientific
Achievement Test**

46	58	65	70	76
49	59	66	71	78
50	59	66	71	79
53	60	66	72	80
54	62	66	73	82
55	63	68	73	83
55	64	68	73	84
57	65	69	74	88

Notice that the data in Table 2.2 are ranked, that is, arranged in order of increasing magnitude. When the data values are ranked, it is easier to count the number of values in each class. However, it is not essential to rank the data to construct a grouped frequency distribution. But if we are working with unranked data, we must be very careful when counting the number of data values in each class.

Procedure for Constructing a Grouped Frequency Distribution

1.   Decide on the starting point, that is, the lower class limit of the first class. The lowest data value in Table 2.2 is 46. The lower class limit should be 46 or a number somewhat less than this. The number 45 seems convenient, so we will use this.

2.   Choose the number of classes and the class width W. Each class will have the same width. The distance from our starting point (45) to the highest data value (88) is 43 units. We can cover the distance 43 with 9 classes having width 5. Notice that we chose the number of classes and the class width so that their product (45) is somewhat larger than the distance we wish to cover (43).

3.   Describe the classes by giving the class limits. The lower and upper class limits for a class will be the smallest and largest numbers, respectively, that could be data values for the class. We have said that the lower class limit for the first class will be 45. The lower class limit for the second class is obtained by adding the class width ($W = 5$) to this, giving 50. The upper class limit for the first class is the largest possible value that could conceivably be a data value in that class. Since we are dealing with integers, that value would be 49. Proceeding in this manner, we obtain the following classes:

45–49

50–54

55–59

60–64

65–69

70–74

75–79

80–84

85–89

4. List each class with its class limits to complete the grouped frequency distribution. To the right of each class, we record the **frequency of the class, f.** This is the number of data values in the class. In Table 2.3, we display the grouped frequency distribution for the data in Table 2.2. (Keeping tallies is optional but is especially recommended when the data are unranked.)

Table 2.3
Grouped Frequency Distribution for the Data in Table 2.2

Class	Limits	Tally	Class Frequency (f)
1	45–49	II	2
2	50–54	III	3
3	55–59	⊞ I	6
4	60–64	IIII	4
5	65–69	⊞ IIII	9
6	70–74	⊞ III	8
7	75–79	III	3
8	80–84	IIII	4
9	85–89	I	1

In some situations, we may have a predetermined value in mind for the number of classes (or class width). For example, suppose we had decided beforehand that we wanted nine classes for the data in Table 2.2. To find an appropriate class width, divide the distance we wish to cover (43) by the number of classes: $\frac{43}{9} = 4.78$. We then choose a convenient number somewhat larger than this to be sure we cover the entire distance with our classes. Since the data values are whole numbers, we would choose 5 as the class width.

Suppose H is the highest data value in a data set, and we wish to have k classes with L as the lower class limit of the first class. The *class width W* should be a convenient number somewhat larger than

$$\frac{H - L}{k}$$

The *lower class limits* are $L, L + W, L + 2W, \ldots$. (There will be k of these.) The *upper class limits* are the largest conceivable data values for each class.

Sometimes it is of interest to have a **grouped relative frequency distribution.** This is similar to a grouped frequency distribution except that instead of the frequency f of each class, we list the relative frequency f/n of each class (where n = the total number of data values). For example, in Table 2.3, which describes the scores of 40 high school students on a scientific achievement test, the relative frequency of the fifth class with limits 65–69 is

$$\frac{f}{n} = \frac{9}{40} = .225$$

The relative frequency can be important if we wish to generalize the properties of our sample. For instance, since the fraction of students in our sample receiving scores between 65 and 69 was $\frac{9}{40} = .225$, we would expect a similar property to hold for the population of scores of all high school students on this test, provided that our sample was representative of the population. In other words, we would expect about 22.5% of all high school students to have scores between 65 and 69. The relative frequencies are in Table 2.4. Some additional types of grouped distributions are discussed in Exercises 2.25 and 2.26.

Table 2.4

Class	Class Limits	f	Relative f
1	45–49	2	.050
2	50–54	3	.075
3	55–59	6	.150
4	60–64	4	.100
5	65–69	9	.225
6	70–74	8	.200
7	75–79	3	.075
8	80–84	4	.100
9	85–89	1	.025

Sometimes it is useful to describe the classes in terms of **class boundaries.** For example, for the grouped distribution discussed previously, the upper class boundary for the first class is halfway between the upper class limit of the first class (49) and the lower class limit of the second class (50). So the upper class boundary of the first class is 49.5. This is also the lower class boundary of the second class. The distance between the upper and lower class boundaries of a class is equal to the class width 5. Therefore, the lower class boundary of the first class is 44.5. The classes described in terms of the class boundaries are

44.5–49.5

49.5–54.5

54.5–59.5

59.5–64.5

64.5–69.5

69.5–74.5

74.5–79.5

79.5–84.5

84.5–89.5

Note that since these class boundaries involve the decimal .5, none of the data values in Table 2.2 will fall exactly on a class boundary.

Another useful device is the **class mark** of a class. This is the number halfway between the lower and upper class limits of a class. For example, the class mark of the first class in Table 2.4 is the number halfway between 45 and 49, namely, 47. The class marks of the remaining classes are 52, 57, 62, 67, 72, 77, 82, and 87. (Notice that these class marks are whole numbers. When the class width is an odd number, the class marks will be whole numbers, which is convenient but not necessary.) Class marks can be useful when performing computations involving the data. For example, we can simplify computations by approximating each data value in a class by the class mark. Also, this may be necessary if the original data are unavailable.

Sometimes the original data will involve decimals. For example, suppose we had data with one decimal place of accuracy, and the data values ranged from a low of 3.5 to a high of 15.1. Further, suppose we want to have five classes with 3.5 as the lower class limit of the first class. To determine the class width, we first calculate

$$\frac{15.1 - 3.5}{5} = \frac{11.6}{5} = 2.32$$

Now we choose a convenient value somewhat larger than 2.32 for the class width. Since our data are assumed to have one decimal place, we will choose a class width of $W = 2.4$. The class limits and class boundaries are then described as follows:

Class Limits	Class Boundaries
3.5–5.8	3.45–5.85
5.9–8.2	5.85–8.25
8.3–10.6	8.25–10.65
10.7–13.0	10.65–13.05
13.1–15.4	13.05–15.45

We should keep in mind that the number of classes should not be too large; otherwise not much simplification of the data will result. On the other hand, if the number of classes is too small, too much simplification may result and we would lose too much information. It seems reasonable to have between 5 and 15 classes.

Finally, we should point out that there is a trade-off in the use of any grouped distribution. We gain simplicity but lose certain information. For example, a grouped frequency distribution tells us how many data values are in each class but not what the data values are.

EXERCISES

2.1 **(a)** A new business recorded the number of incoming telephone calls over the first 25 days of business. The numbers of calls received were 4, 4, 1, 10, 12, 6, 4, 6, 9, 12, 12, 1, 1, 1, 12, 10, 4, 6, 4, 8, 8, 9, 8, 4, 1. Construct the frequency distribution.

(b) In part (a), note how the frequency distribution simplified the data. Now give an example of 25 data values such that a frequency distribution does not simplify the data very much.

2.2 Over a 15-day period, the number of employee absences from work recorded by the owner of a landscaping business was

3 2 0 0 1 1 2 1 0 0 4 0 1 3 1

(a) Construct the frequency distribution.

(b) What percentage of days were three or more employees not at work?

2.3 A podiatrist recorded the recovery time, measured in days, for 36 patients. He was trying out a new procedure and hoped the recovery time would be less than the usual 6 days. The recorded times were

```
8   7   6   9   4   5   3   7   8   10   7   7   6   4   10   3   6   8
2   5   4   5   3   8   7   4   6   3    7   12  4   3   6    6   9   4
```

(a) Construct the frequency distribution.

(b) What percentage of recovery days were fewer than 6?

2.4 The following data are the ages at inauguration of United States presidents (*Source: The 1994 Information Please Almanac*, 1994, p. 634).

```
42   43   46   46   47   48   49   49   50   50   51   51   51   51
52   52   54   54   54   54   55   55   55   55   56   56   56   57
57   57   57   58   60   61   61   61   62   64   64   65   68   69
```

(a) Construct the frequency distribution.

(b) Using 40 as the starting point, construct a grouped frequency distribution with six classes.

(c) To describe the distribution of data values to a friend, would you use the frequency distribution in part (a) or the grouped frequency distribution in part (b)? Give reasons for your choice.

2.5 The accompanying data are the numbers of home runs hit by American League home run leaders in the years 1954–1993 (*Source: The 1994 Information Please Almanac*, 1994, p. 989).

```
32   37   52   42   42   42   40   61   48   45   49   32   49   44
44   49   44   33   37   32   32   36   32   39   46   45   41   22
39   39   43   40   40   49   42   36   51   44   43   46
```

(a) Construct the frequency distribution.

(b) Using 22 as the starting point, construct a grouped frequency distribution with eight classes.

(c) To describe the distribution of data values to a friend, would you use the frequency distribution in part (a) or the grouped frequency distribution in part (b)? Give reasons for your choice.

2.6 The following data are the numbers of home runs hit by National League home run leaders in the years 1954–1993 (*Source: The 1994 Information Please Almanac*, 1994, p. 990).

```
49   51   43   44   47   46   41   46   49   44   47   52   44   39
36   45   45   48   40   44   36   38   38   52   40   48   48   31
37   40   36   37   37   49   39   47   40   38   35   46
```

Using 31 as the starting point with a class width of 3, construct a grouped frequency distribution.

2.7 Refer to the data in Exercise 2.3.

(a) Using 1 as the starting value, and a class width of 2, construct a grouped frequency distribution.

(b) What is the class mark for the third class?

(c) What is the upper class boundary of the second class?

(d) What is the relative frequency of the fourth class?

2.8 The following data are the numbers of English-language Sunday newspapers (per state) in the United States as of February 1, 1993 (*Source: The 1994 Information Please Almanac*, 1994, p. 315).

2	2	3	3	4	4	4	4	5	5	6	7	7
7	7	10	10	10	11	11	11	12	13	14	14	14
14	15	16	16	16	17	17	17	18	20	20	21	
21	22	27	28	32	35	36	37	42	44	71	87	

  (a) Using 1 as the starting value, construct a grouped frequency distribution with 6 classes.

  (b) What is the class width?

  (c) What is the class mark for the fifth class?

  (d) What is the lower class boundary of the first class?

  (e) What is the relative frequency of the third class?

2.9 A state policeman issued 200 speeding tickets over a 1-year period. The speeds ranged from 61 to 84 miles per hour. Suppose you were to construct a grouped frequency distribution with 8 classes. Give upper and lower class limits, upper and lower class boundaries, and the class mark for each class. Use 61 as the starting point.

2.10 The 1991 birth rates (per 1000 population) for 29 selected countries range from 9.8 to 21.4 (*Source: The 1994 Information Please Almanac*, 1994, p. 135). Suppose you were to construct a grouped frequency distribution with a starting point of 9.4 and class width of 2.1. Give upper and lower class limits, upper and lower class boundaries, and the class mark for each class. (*Note: Since the data values are in decimal form, it is reasonable to have a class width with the same number of decimal places.)

2.11 The following data represent weights (in pounds) of meat obtained from 30 beef cattle:

204.0	205.1	214.9	222.6	222.8	198.4	222.2	230.9	220.0	222.4
215.9	207.6	208.2	228.0	208.4	219.5	194.2	192.9	196.4	202.1
212.9	203.8	208.9	206.3	210.6	195.9	235.9	228.5	216.9	189.8

  (a) Complete the following table.

Class	Class Boundaries	Frequency
1	189.75–196.75	

  (b) What is the class mark for the third class?

  (c) What is the class width?

2.12 The following data give the 1991 death rates (per 1000 population) for selected countries (*Source: The 1994 Information Please Almanac*, 1994, p. 135).

Singapore	5.0	Australia	6.9	United States	8.6
Israel	6.3	Canada	7.3	Spain	8.7
Cuba	6.6	Malta	7.8	Ireland	8.9
Mauritius	6.6	New Zealand	7.8	Switzerland	9.0
Japan	6.7	The Netherlands	8.6	France	9.2

(*continued*)

Italy	9.7	Austria	10.6	Germany	11.1
Luxembourg	9.7	Poland	10.6	United Kingdom	11.2
Portugal	9.7	Belgium	10.7	Denmark	11.6
Finland	9.8	Romania	10.9	Hungary	14.0
Norway	10.5	Sweden	11.0		

(a)   Complete the following table:

Class	Class Limits	Frequency	Class Mark
3	8.6–10.4		

(b)   What is the class width?

(c)   What is the relative frequency of the third class?

2.13   The owner of a small business wants to analyze profits over the past 30 years. Profits (in thousands of dollars) were obtained for the 30-year period. The ranked data values are

15	17	18	19	20	20	20	21	23	23	24	24	24	24	24
25	25	25	25	25	26	26	27	27	28	29	30	30	31	32

(a)   Complete the following grouped frequency distribution.

Class	Class Limits	Frequency
2	18–20	

(b)   What is the class width?

(c)   What is the lower class boundary of the first class?

(d)   What is the relative frequency of the second class?

2.14   The following data represent cholesterol readings (mg/dl) for randomly selected women from the Framingham Heart Study:

287	242	200	260	298	278	195	265	230	300	215	224
228	291	236	244	234	278	302	244	281	217	221	156
198	267	198	204	280	182	185	204	256	234	172	

(a)   Complete the following grouped frequency distribution.

Class	Class Boundaries	Frequency
2	171.5–190.5	

(b)   What is the class mark for the fourth class?

(c)   What is the class width?

(d)   What is the relative frequency of the third class?

2.3

GRAPHIC REPRESENTATIONS

Graphic representations are, in a sense, pictures of data and as such sometimes make the data easier to comprehend.

One way to graphically represent a frequency distribution is by means of a **dot diagram.** We construct a dot diagram as follows: We use a horizontal axis to represent the data values. Above each distinct data value on the horizontal axis we place dots, the number of dots being equal to the frequency of the data value.

EXAMPLE 2.3

Construct a dot diagram for the data in Example 2.1.

Solution

Recall that the frequency distribution is

x	f
1	2
3	2
5	4
6	7
7	4
11	1

The dot diagram is shown in Figure 2.1.

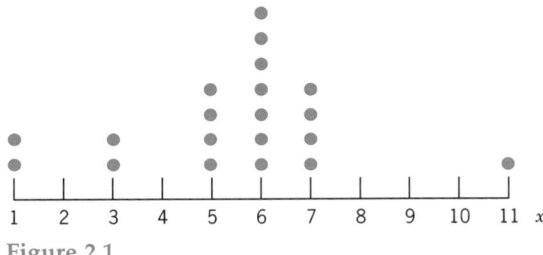

Figure 2.1
A Dot Diagram

A **bar graph** or a **pie chart** can be used to depict a frequency distribution, especially when the data values are nonnumerical. These are illustrated in the following example.

EXAMPLE 2.4

In this example, we construct a bar graph and pie chart for the frequency distribution of Example 2.2 (murders by type of weapon for 1992). We construct a bar graph as follows: Along the horizontal axis we indicate the types of weapon. (These are the distinct data values.) The vertical axis measures the frequency with which each type of weapon was used. Above each type of weapon, we construct a bar having a height equal to the frequency for that type of weapon. See Figure 2.2(a). Notice that the bars are separated (*noncontiguous* is the term often used). This is always the case when we are dealing with nonnumerical categories such as the type of weapon.

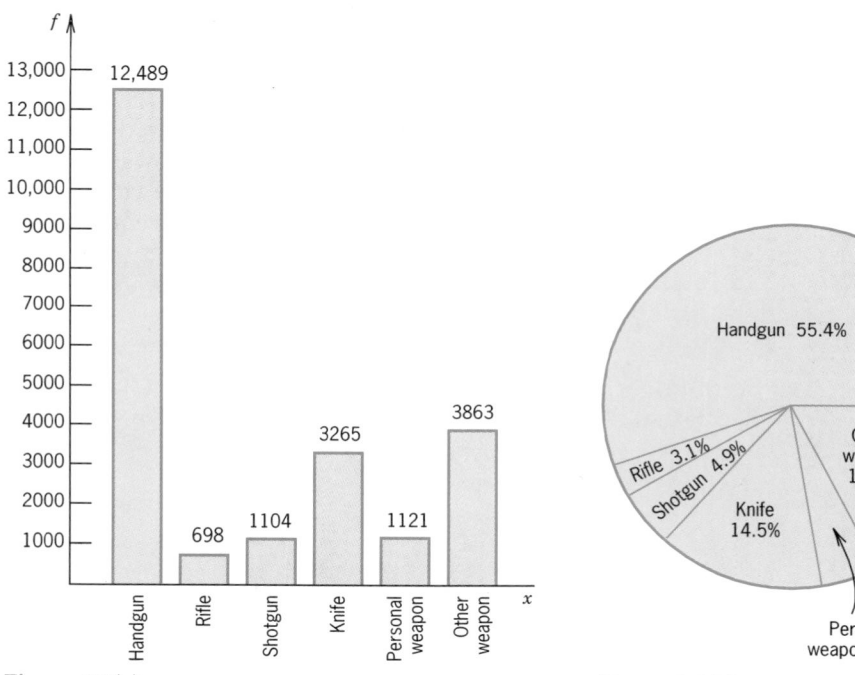

Figure 2.2(a)
A Bar Graph (Murders by Type of Weapon)

Figure 2.2(b)
A Pie Chart (Percentage of Murders by Type of Weapon)

A pie chart is often used to represent the frequency of each data value as a percentage of the total number of data values. We construct a circle, then divide the circle into sectors, one for each distinct data value (type of weapon). The size of a given sector is proportional to the percentage of murders committed with that type of weapon. See Figure 2.2(b) and refer to Example 2.2.

Notice how the sectors of the circle were constructed. For example, handguns accounted for 55.4% of all 1992 murders; therefore the degree measure of the sector is

$$(.554) \times (360°) = 199.4°$$

A graphic representation of a grouped frequency distribution that is often used is a type of bar graph called a **frequency histogram.** Here again the horizontal or x-axis represents the data and the vertical or f-axis represents the frequency. Along the x-axis, we display the classes by labeling the class boundaries. Above each class we draw a bar having a width equal to the class width and a height equal to the class frequency. Each axis should be labeled. This idea is illustrated in the following example.

EXAMPLE 2.5

Construct a frequency histogram for the grouped frequency distribution of Table 2.3, which summarized 40 test scores on a scientific achievement test.

Solution
Recall that the class boundaries are 44.5, 49.5, 54.5, and so on. The histogram is displayed in Figure 2.3.

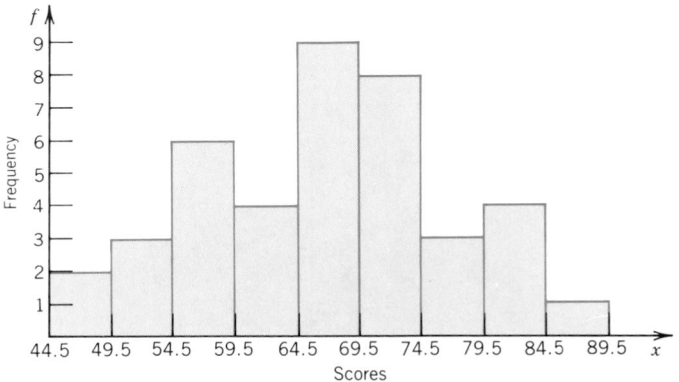

Figure 2.3
Frequency Histogram for the Data in Table 2.3

Remark If, in a histogram, we make the heights of the bars equal to the relative frequencies of the classes rather than the frequencies, we have a **relative frequency histogram.**

Another way of graphically displaying a grouped frequency distribution is by means of a **frequency polygon.** (The frequency polygon is especially useful in conveying the shape of the distribution.) The following example illustrates how a frequency polygon is constructed for the test score data.

EXAMPLE 2.6

We will construct a frequency polygon using the grouped frequency distribution in Table 2.3. This grouped frequency distribution is summarized in Table 2.5 (page 34) along with the class marks. First draw a horizontal x-axis and a vertical frequency axis. Label the class marks on the x-axis; above each class mark, place a dot at a height equal to the frequency of the class. Then connect the dots by line segments (see Figure 2.4). The first and last dots are connected to two points on the x-axis;

one of the points is one class width to the left of the first class mark, the other is one class width to the right of the last class mark. These two points are usually not labeled. The class width in this case is 5; therefore we connect the first and last dots to the points 42 and 92, respectively.

Table 2.5

Class	Class Limits	Frequency (f)	Class Mark
1	45–49	2	47
2	50–54	3	52
3	55–59	6	57
4	60–64	4	62
5	65–69	9	67
6	70–74	8	72
7	75–79	3	77
8	80–84	4	82
9	85–89	1	87

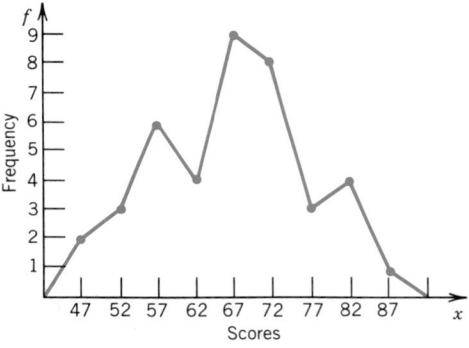

Figure 2.4
Frequency Polygon for Table 2.5

A **relative frequency polygon** is constructed in a manner similar to a frequency polygon with the exception that the dots are placed at a height equal to the relative frequency of the class, f/n, rather than the frequency of the class.

Other Graphs

Figures 2.5(a) and (b) are **pictograms.** In Figure 2.5(a), the wine glasses measure mortality rate (deaths per 1000 people in 10 years). Note that people who drink in moderation have a lower mortality rate than those who do not drink at all or those who drink in excess. Figure 2.6 is a **segmented bar graph** showing a trend in percentage of children living with a single parent. Figure 2.7 is a **line graph** or a **time series** showing number of employees of the Department of Defense over time. Note the upward surge of employment during the Korean and Vietnam wars.

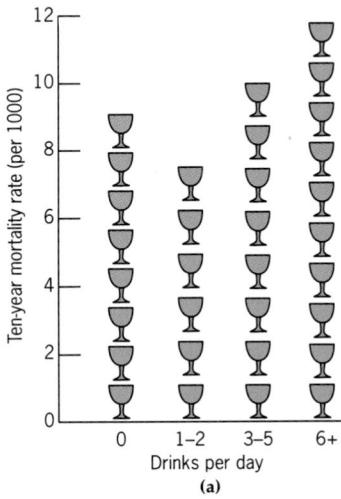

Figure 2.5(a)
Total Mortality Rate Compared to Alcohol Consumption [*Source: Food and Wine,* Sept. 1992, p. 27. Used with permission of *Food and Wine* magazine, Sept. 1992 ©1992. American Express Publishing Corp. All rights reserved.]

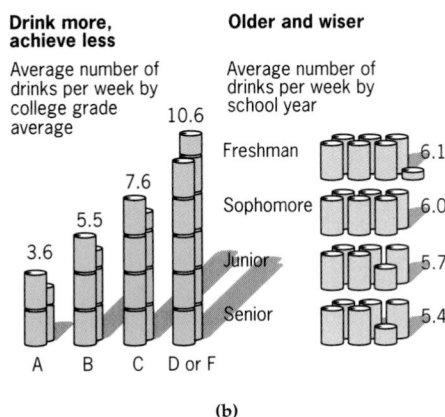

Figure 2.5(b)
Number of Drinks Per Week Compared to Grade and Class [Copyright, June 20, 1994, *U.S. News and World Report,* p. 21]

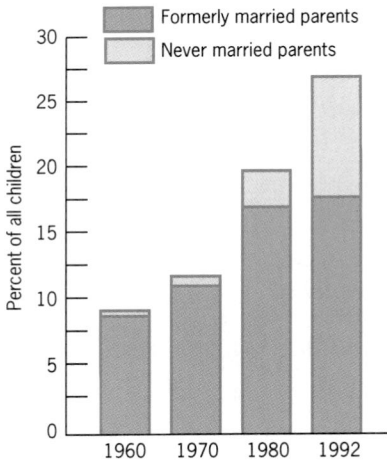

Figure 2.6
The Percentage of Children Living with a Single Parent Has Tripled in 30 Years. Since 1980, the increase has come almost entirely among children living with a parent who has never married. [*Source: Budget of the United States Government, Fiscal Year 1995,* Office of Management and Budget, p. 109]

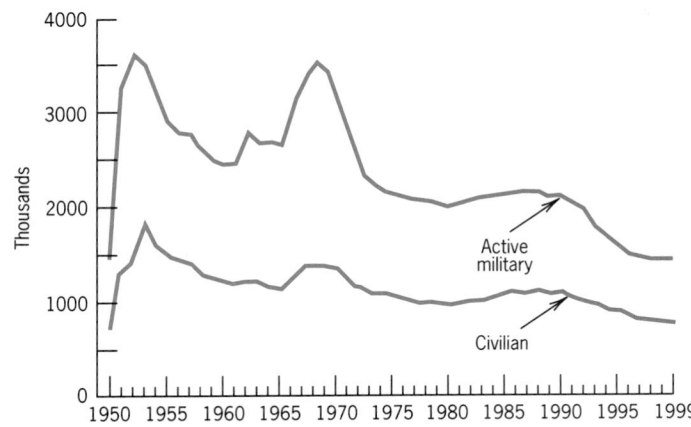

Figure 2.7
Historical Defense Personnel Levels [*Source: Budget of the United States Government, Fiscal Year 1995,* Office of Management and Budget, p. 227]

EXERCISES

2.15 For each of the following frequency distributions, construct a dot diagram:

(a)	x	f	(b)	x	f
	0	3		1	2
	1	6		2	2
	2	5		3	2
	3	2		4	2
	4	2		5	2
				6	2

2.16 In the Massachusetts State Lottery Numbers game, four numbers are selected randomly with replacement from the set of 10 numbers $\{0, 1, 2, 3, 4, 5, 6, 7, 8, 9\}$.

(a) Over a long period of time, what percentage of times would you expect each digit to appear?

(b) The dot diagram shown here represents five drawings (five games, 20 digits in all) during the period June 2–6, 1994. Construct a frequency distribution for the data set (*Source: The Boston Globe*, p. 22, June 7, 1994).

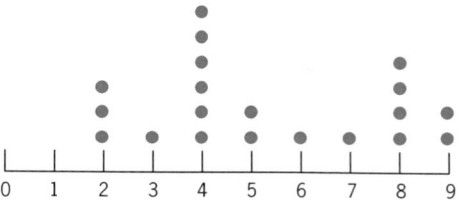

For each of Exercises 2.17–2.20, construct (a) a frequency histogram and (b) a frequency polygon. (c) Find the class width for each grouped frequency distribution.

2.17 The following grouped frequency distribution represents the time (in minutes) for students in an economics class to complete a quiz.

Class	Class Limits	Frequency
1	10–14	1
2	15–19	5
3	20–24	10
4	25–29	12
5	30–34	4

2.18 The following grouped frequency distribution represents the distance (in feet) from the pin of the shots of 32 golfers in a hole-in-one contest.

Class	Class Limits	Frequency
1	10–14	4
2	15–19	12
3	20–24	10
4	25–29	5
5	30–34	1

2.19   The following grouped frequency distribution represents the age (in years) of 59 patients of a psychiatric counseling center.

Class	Class Limits	Frequency
1	21–27	3
2	28–34	7
3	35–41	12
4	42–48	15
5	49–55	12
6	56–62	7
7	63–69	3

2.20   The grouped frequency distribution shown here represents the weight (in pounds) of 30 elementary school children selected to participate in a physical fitness study.

Class	Class Limits	Frequency
1	46–48	6
2	49–51	6
3	52–54	6
4	55–57	6
5	58–60	6

2.21   Using Exercise 2.11, construct
   (a)   A frequency histogram.
   (b)   A frequency polygon.

2.22   Using Exercise 2.14, construct
   (a)   A frequency histogram.
   (b)   A frequency polygon.

2.23   The following is a grouped frequency distribution for the number of home runs hit by American League home run leaders for the years 1954–1993. See Exercise 2.5.

Class limits	22–26	27–31	32–36	37–41	42–46	47–51	52–56	57–61
Number of home runs	1	0	8	9	14	6	1	1

Construct
   (a)   A relative frequency histogram.
   (b)   A relative frequency polygon.

2.24   This grouped frequency distribution represents the number of home runs hit by National League home run leaders for the period 1954–1993. See Exercise 2.6.

Class limits	27–31	32–36	37–41	42–46	47–51	52–56
Number of home runs	1	4	13	10	10	2

Construct

(a)   A relative frequency histogram.

(b)   A relative frequency polygon.

2.25   This exercise illustrates what is called a *grouped cumulative frequency distribution*. The class boundaries are labeled on the horizontal axis. Above the upper class boundary of each class, a dot is placed. The height of the dot is equal to the number of data values in the data set that are less than the upper class boundary of that class. Notice that there are 7 classes.

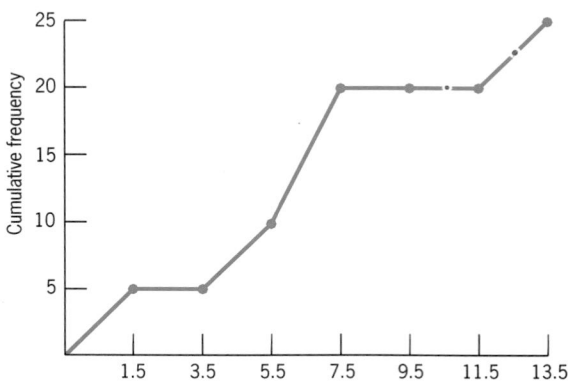

(a)   How many data values are there?

(b)   What are the class limits for the second class?

(c)   Which class contains the most data values?

(d)   What is the frequency for the third class?

(e)   What is the frequency for the fifth class?

2.26   This exercise illustrates what is called a *grouped cumulative relative frequency distribution*. This is similar to the grouped cumulative frequency distribution discussed in Exercise 2.25, except that we plot the *proportion* of data values in the data set that are less than the upper class boundary for each class. The following cumulative relative frequency polygon is for the age at inauguration of United States presidents, discussed in Exercise 2.4.

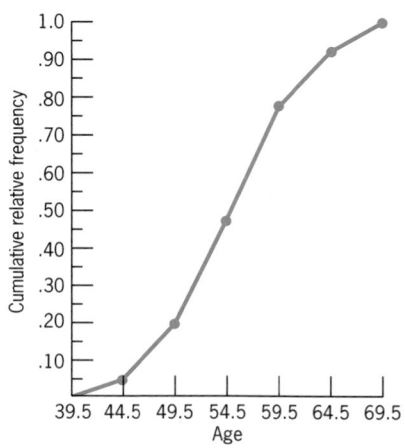

(a) Use the graph to estimate the age that separates the bottom 75% from the top 25% of ages. (This is called the 75th percentile. Percentiles are discussed more fully in the next chapter.)

(b) Use the graph to estimate the percentage of presidents younger than 50 at inauguration. (This is called the percentile rank of 50.)

2.27 The following data give the unemployment rates in the civilian labor force for the years 1980–1992 (*Source: The 1994 Information Please Almanac*, 1994, p. 61).

Year	1980	1981	1982	1983	1984	1985	1986
Rate	7.1	7.6	9.7	9.6	7.5	7.2	7.0

Year	1987	1988	1989	1990	1991	1992
Rate	6.2	5.4	5.3	5.5	6.7	7.4

Construct a line graph.

2.28 Construct a line graph for the accompanying data on median family income in thousands of dollars (in current dollars) for the years 1980–1992 (*Source: The 1994 Information Please Almanac*, 1994, p. 48).

Year	1980	1981	1982	1983	1984	1985	1986
Median Family Income	21.0	22.4	23.4	24.6	25.9	27.1	28.2

Year	1987	1988	1989	1990	1991	1992
Median Family Income	29.7	31.0	32.4	34.0	34.8	35.8

2.29 The following data are the numbers of hazardous waste sites in the eastern north-central United States (*Source: World Almanac and Book of Facts*, 1993, p. 675).

Ohio	33	Michigan	77
Indiana	32	Wisconsin	39
Illinois	36		

(a) Construct a bar graph.

(b) Construct a pie chart.

2.30 The following is the world distribution of nuclear reactors in operation (*Source: World Almanac and Book of Facts*, 1993, p. 175).

United States	111	United Kingdom	37
France	56	Germany	21
former U.S.S.R.	45	Canada	20
Japan	42	Other countries	88

(a) Construct a bar graph.

(b) Construct a pie chart.

2.4

THE SHAPE OF A DISTRIBUTION

The shapes of frequency polygons (or frequency histograms) often resemble certain commonly observed types, which we display in Figure 2.8 (page 40).

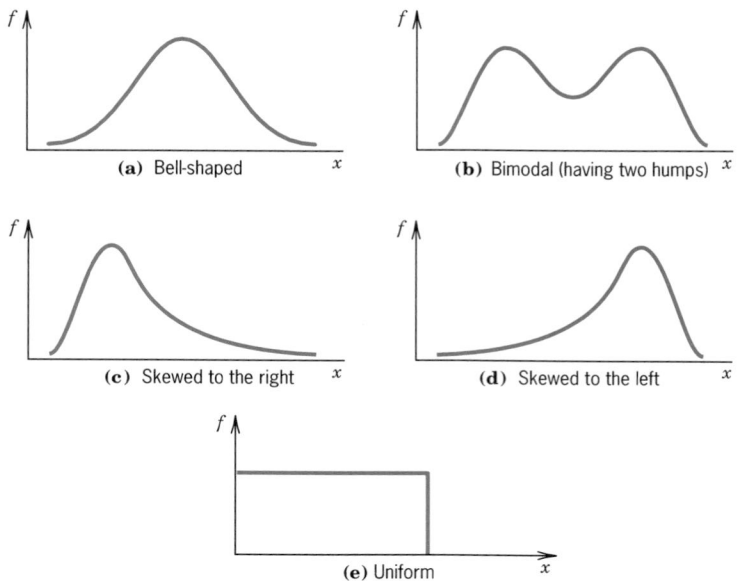

Figure 2.8
Common Distribution Shapes

In Figure 2.8(a) and (b), the distributions are **symmetric** because if we draw a vertical line through the center of the graph, we see that the portion of the graph on one side of the line is a mirror image of the portion of the graph on the other side. It may be useful to know whether a distribution is symmetric, as we will see in Chapter 7.

The distributions in Figure 2.8(a) and (b) are often encountered when the data or x values represent test scores and f, of course, represents frequency. Perhaps Figure 2.8(a) is the most commonly encountered shape in this context. However, many college professors claim that Figure 2.8(b) is more often being encountered. This situation can occur in a class where there is one group of well-prepared students, another group of students with weak backgrounds, and not many in between.

Figure 2.8(c) is encountered with variables such as personal income and length of life of automobiles or other machines. Figure 2.8(d) is encountered when x represents heights of people, including children and adults. (The children's heights account for the skewing to the left.) Figure 2.8(e) might represent the number of phone calls f received by a switchboard at a department store at various times x of the business day. (The idea conveyed is that the calls come in at approximately the same rate all day.)

Frequency polygons for data tend to assume certain shapes, not by accident, but because of the nature of the population from which the data were obtained. For example, in Chapter 7 we will study a class of populations called **normal populations.** A large collection of data from a normal population will usually give rise to a frequency polygon that resembles approximately Figure 2.8(a). It may be important to know whether a population is normal, as we will see later. By examining the frequency polygon for a collection of data, we may be able to tell whether a population is approximately normal.

EXERCISE

2.31   Characterize the distribution shapes in each of Exercises 2.17–2.20 by selecting the name of the distribution that most closely approximates the data.

2.5

STEM-AND-LEAF PLOTS

Stem-and-leaf plots are a way of organizing data in such a way that the data values themselves are used to construct the bars of a figure that resembles a histogram. Thus the stem-and-leaf plot portrays the shape of a distribution and gives the individual data values as well. A stem-and-leaf plot is also useful for spotting **outliers,** which are individual data values that are atypical because they stand considerably apart from the general pattern of the data. Outliers should be investigated to make sure that they are not mistakes, such as typographical errors. Of course, outliers resulting from such errors should be corrected or eliminated.

To see how a stem-and-leaf plot works, consider the following data, which represent annual salaries (in thousands of dollars) for 20 employees of a small business:

27	32	47	54	36	44	56	49	53	51
35	29	62	19	65	37	48	33	41	45

The data range from 27 to 65. We could group the data into categories according to the tens digit. For example, the data values between 40 and 49 inclusive have 4 as a tens digit, and so on. To construct a stem-and-leaf plot, list the tens digits: 2, 3, 4, 5, 6 in a vertical column. These are called **stems.** Just to the right of this, draw a vertical line. Record the last digit (units digit) of each data value to the right of the appropriate stem. These are called **leaves.** For example, there are two data values with the first digit 6: 62 and 65. Therefore, next to 6 we would write a 2 and a 5:

$$6 \mid 2 \ 5$$

The entire stem-and-leaf plot is shown in Figure 2.9(a). Notice that the stems are equivalent to classes. For example, the data values with stem 3 fall in the class 30–39. The number of leaves is the frequency of the class. The display of the leaves resembles the bars of a histogram.

```
1 | 9                          1 | 9
2 | 7  9                       2 | 7  9
3 | 2  6  5  7  3              3 | 2  3  5  6  7
4 | 7  4  9  8  1  5           4 | 1  4  5  7  8  9
5 | 4  6  3  1                 5 | 1  3  4  6
6 | 2  5                       6 | 2  5
```

Figure 2.9(a)
Stem-and-Leaf Plot
for the Salaries
(3|2 = $32,000)

Figure 2.9(b)
Ordered Stem-and-Leaf
Plot for the Salaries

If we rotated Figure 2.9(a) counterclockwise by 90°, it would resemble a histogram. This distribution of data looks bell-shaped.

If we arrange the leaves on each stem in increasing order of magnitude, we have an **ordered stem-and-leaf plot,** as shown in Figure 2.9(b). What this accomplishes is a ranked list of all the data values in increasing order. This can be helpful in finding quantities such as medians and percentiles (to be discussed in Chapter 3).

EXAMPLE 2.7

Construct a stem-and-leaf plot for the data in Table 2.6, which represent student dropout rates in the public schools in Boston-area towns within Route 128.

Solution

Notice that the data range from 0.0 to 13.3. We could use the units and tens digits for the stems and the tenths digits for the leaves. For example, the value 3.7 would be represented as 3 | 7. The value 13.3 would be represented as 13 | 3. From the stem-and-leaf plot in Figure 2.10, we can see that the data are skewed positively (i.e., to the right). Also there are two outliers: Boston (10.7%) and Chelsea (13.3%).

Table 2.6

Dropout Rate (%)

Arlington	0.1	Medford	3.0
Belmont	1.1	Melrose	0.7
Beverly	2.8	Milton	0.5
Boston	10.7	Needham	0.0
Braintree	1.6	Newton	0.6
Brookline	0.3	Peabody	3.7
Cambridge	2.4	Quincy	5.2
Chelsea	13.3	Revere	6.5
Cohasset	0.3	Salem	6.1
Dedham	1.7	Saugus	0.0
Everett	3.3	Somerville	5.4
Gloucester	4.1	Stoneham	1.1
Hingham	0.2	Swampscott	0.5
Hull	2.8	Wakefield	2.4
Lexington	0.1	Waltham	3.3
Lynn	7.8	Watertown	1.6
Lynnfield	0.9	Weymouth	2.4
Malden	6.6	Winchester	0.7
Marblehead	0.3	Woburn	1.6

Source: *The Boston Globe,* June 6, 1993.

```
 0 | 1  3  3  2  1  9  3  7  5  0  6  0  5  7
 1 | 1  6  7  1  6  6
 2 | 8  4  8  4  4
 3 | 3  0  7  3
 4 | 1
 5 | 2  4
 6 | 6  5  1
 7 | 8
 8 |
 9 |
10 | 7
11 |
12 |
13 | 3                        5 | 2 = 5.2%
```

Figure 2.10
Stem-and-Leaf Plot for the Dropout Rates in Table 2.6

Choosing the Stems and Leaves

The following conventions are usually followed for stem-and-leaf plots:

- Each leaf consists of a single digit.
- A stem can have any number of digits.

Suppose the data ranged from 96 to 1137. If we used the last digit for the leaves, then the stems would be

$$9, 10, 11, \ldots, 112, 113$$

That is 105 stems! Such a stem-and-leaf plot would not tell us much about shape. There might be fewer than two leaves per stem. In this case, it is customary to **cut the data.** This involves replacing a certain number of digits on the right by zeros. Suppose we replaced the last digit by 0. Then our data would range from 90 to 1130 or (to write it more conveniently) from 090 to 1130. The tens digits could be used as the leaves. The stems would be:

$$0, 1, 2, \ldots, 11$$

So, 090 would be represented as 0 | 9, and 1130 would be 11 | 3.

Similar remarks would apply if the data ranged from 9.6 to 11.37. If we cut the data by one digit, the data would range from 09.0 to 11.30. The stems would be the same as just described. So, 09.0 would be represented as 0 | 9 and 11.30 would be 11 | 3.

You may be wondering: If a stem-and-leaf plot displays a data value as 12 | 3, how is this to be interpreted? Is it 123 or 12.3 or 1.23? The answer is that it is up to the maker of the stem-and-leaf plot to explain the plot. For example, you could include a note saying 12 | 3 represents 12.3.

Suppose your data include both positive and negative numbers. Positive and negative numbers should be on separate stems. For example, suppose your data include −12, −1, 2, 14. If we use the tens digits as the stems and the units digits as the leaves, these numbers would be represented as:

$$
\begin{array}{r|l}
-1 & 2 \\
-0 & 1 \\
0 & 2 \\
1 & 4 \\
\end{array}
$$

Splitting the Stems

Sometimes there will be only a few stems with the leaves "loading up" on these stems. Shape is not very well displayed in such a situation. Figure 2.11(a) is such a stem-and-leaf plot for 30 systolic blood pressure readings from the Framingham Heart Study. (Note that 13 | 2 represents 132 mm.) We could split each stem into two parts with leaves 0–4 on one part, and leaves 5–9 on the other. This is displayed in Figure 2.11(b), which portrays shape better. As a rule of thumb, you should consider splitting the stems if there are fewer than, say, five stems.

```
11 | 1  2  6  6  7
12 | 0  1  3  4  5  6  8  8  8  9  9
13 | 2  2  3  4  4  5  7  9  9
14 | 1  2  3  5  7                      13 | 2 = 132 mm
```

Figure 2.11(a)
Stem-and-Leaf Plot for 30 Systolic Blood Pressure Readings

```
11 | 1  2
11 | 6  6  7
12 | 0  1  3  4
12 | 5  6  8  8  8  9  9
13 | 2  2  3  4  4
13 | 5  7  9  9
14 | 1  2  3
14 | 5  7
```

Figure 2.11(b)
Stem-and-Leaf Plot Obtained by Splitting the Stems in Figure 2.11(a)

Side-by-Side Stem-and-Leaf Plots

Occasionally side-by-side stem-and-leaf plots are helpful when comparing two data sets, as the following example shows.

EXAMPLE 2.8

The following data are the winning American League batting averages in the 1920s and 1980s:

| 1920s: | .407 | .394 | .420 | .403 | .378 | .393 | .378 | .398 | .379 | .369 |
| 1980s: | .390 | .336 | .332 | .361 | .343 | .368 | .357 | .363 | .366 | .339 |

Source: World Almanac and Book of Facts, 1993, p. 922.

We will use the first two digits as the stem, and the third as the leaf. Place the stems in the center of the page. The leaves for the 1920s will be on the left of this; the 1980s will be on the right. See Figure 2.12.

```
        1920s              1980s

              | 33 | 6  2  9
              | 34 | 3
              | 35 | 7
         9    | 36 | 1  8  3  6
    9  8  8   | 37 |
              | 38 |
    8  3  4   | 39 | 0
       3  7   | 40 |
              | 41 |
         0    | 42 |          36 | 8 = .368
```

Figure 2.12
Leading American League Batting
Averages: 1920s versus 1980s

The 1920s show a pattern of higher leading averages. Some of this can be accounted for by the players themselves. On the other hand, Wade Boggs was no slouch in the 1980s, and Babe Ruth won the batting title only once—in 1924. Another factor that might explain some of the difference is the elaborate system of relief pitchers currently in use that was not in place in the 1920s. Such a system has been hard on hitters.

EXERCISES

2.32   The ordered data shown here (from Exercise 2.8) represent the numbers of English-language Sunday newspapers in the 50 states. Construct a stem-and-leaf plot using 0, 1, 2, . . . , 8 as stems. Describe the shape of the distribution.

2	2	3	3	4	4	4	4	5	5	6	7	7
7	7	10	10	10	11	11	11	12	13	14	14	14
14	15	16	16	16	17	17	17	18	20	20	21	
21	22	27	28	32	35	36	37	42	44	71	87	

2.33   The following data are test scores for an introductory economics class given in the evening. A perfect score is 80. The instructor was interested in the distribution of scores and potential outliers. (Data provided by Walter Block, Holy Cross College.)

60	42	61	70	59	65	68	67
78	68	67	74	61	74	61	71

(a) Use 4, 5, 6, and 7 as stems and construct a stem-and-leaf plot.

(b) Split the stems 4, 5, 6, and 7 into two parts with leaves 0–4 on one part and 5–9 on the other. Construct a stem-and-leaf plot. Characterize the shape of the distribution of scores. What seems to be a typical score? Which scores, if any, appear to be outliers?

(c) Which stem-and-leaf plot gives a better description of the distribution of scores?

2.34 The accompanying data are test scores for an introductory economics class given in the afternoon. A perfect score is 80. Among other things, the instructor was interested in the distribution of scores and potential outliers. (Data provided by Walter Block, Holy Cross College.)

59	63	63	63	64	60	71	55	70
54	65	66	69	69	60	52	61	

Split the stems 4, 5, 6, and 7 into two parts with leaves 0–4 on one part and 5–9 on the other. Construct a stem-and-leaf plot. Characterize the shape of the distribution of scores. What seems to be a typical score? What scores, if any, appear to be outliers?

2.35 The following data are the averages (points per game) of the leading scorers in the National Basketball Association for 1992–1993.

32.6	29.9	27.0	26.1	25.6	24.2	23.5	23.4	23.4	22.8
22.3	22.1	21.5	21.2	21.0	20.8	20.7	20.3	20.2	19.9

(a) Construct a stem-and-leaf plot. Split the stems 1, 2, and 3 into five parts with leaves 0–1, 2–3, 4–5, 6–7, and 8–9. Cut the data by dropping the decimal. (*Note:* To get enough lines in the stem-and-leaf plot, we have split the stems into five parts.)

(b) What average appears to be an outlier?

(c) What average is represented with stem 2 and leaf 6?

2.36 An economics instructor wished to compare test scores for his evening and afternoon classes. Use the results of Exercises 2.33(b) and 2.34(a) to construct a side-by-side stem-and-leaf plot. Split the stems 4, 5, 6, and 7 into two parts with leaves 0–4 on one part and 5–9 on the other. Comment on your comparisons.

2.37 On January 28, 1986, the space shuttle *Challenger* exploded because of O-ring failure.* (O-rings are supposed to prevent the leak of combustible gases, and damage can lead to an explosion.) The accompanying data on the 23 previous shuttle flights give the temperatures at time of launch for those flights for which there was O-ring damage versus those flights with no O-ring damage. The temperature is that of the joints between sections of the solid rocket boosters prior to ignition.

Launch Temperatures (°F)

Flights with O-ring Damage	53	57	58	63	70	70	75								
Flights with No O-ring Damage	66	67	67	67	68	69	70	70	72	73	75	76	76	78	79	81

Source: Report of the Presidential Commission on the Space Shuttle Challenger Accident, Washington, D.C., 1986, pp. 129–131.

_____

*Christa Corrigan McAuliffe, who was killed in the *Challenger* disaster, was a 1970 graduate of Framingham State College.

Make a side-by-side stem-and-leaf plot for the two data sets. Split the stems 5, 6, 7, and 8 into two parts with leaves 0–4 on one part and 5–9 on the other. Note that the launch temperatures tend to be lower for the flights with O-ring damage. It is believed that low temperature can cause O-ring damage. The temperature at the time of the *Challenger* launch was 31° F.

2.38 The following data (discussed in Exercise 2.14) give the cholesterol readings of randomly selected women from the Framingham Heart Study. Use stems 15, 16, 17,..., 30 and construct a stem-and-leaf plot.

287	242	200	260	298	278	195	265	230	300	215	224
228	291	236	244	234	278	302	244	281	217	221	156
198	267	198	204	280	182	185	204	256	234	172	

2.39 The data (see Exercise 2.11) represent the weights (in pounds) of meat obtained from 30 beef cattle.

204.0	205.1	214.9	222.6	222.8	198.4	222.2	230.9	220.0	222.4
215.9	207.6	208.2	228.0	208.4	219.5	194.2	192.9	196.4	202.1
212.9	203.8	208.9	206.3	210.6	195.9	235.9	228.5	216.9	189.8

(a) Construct an ordered stem-and-leaf plot. Cut the data by dropping the decimals. Split the stems 18, 19, 20, 21, 22, and 23 into two parts with leaves 0–4 on one part and 5–9 on the other.

(b) Describe the shape of the distribution.

(c) Which scores, if any, appear to be outliers?

2.40 The following ordered data (discussed in Exercise 2.12) represent death rates (per 1000 population) for selected countries. Construct a stem-and-leaf plot using 5, 6, 7,..., 14 as stems.

5.0	6.3	6.6	6.6	6.7	6.9	7.3	7.8	7.8	8.6
8.6	8.7	8.9	9.0	9.2	9.7	9.7	9.7	9.8	10.5
10.6	10.6	10.7	10.9	11.0	11.1	11.2	11.6	14.0	

2.41 The following data represent the percent changes in population between the 1980 census and the 1990 census for the 50 largest cities in the United States (*Source: The 1994 Information Please Almanac*, 1994, p. 792).

3.5	17.4	−7.4	2.2	−6.1	26.8	−14.7	11.3	24.5	19.1
24.3	4.3	−6.4	6.6	17.9	12.0	−1.3	−5.5	−4.9	2.0
4.5	21.2	6.9	−11.9	−10.9	−5.1	34.6	16.2	10.1	18.8
−2.9	18.8	22.6	−12.4	25.5	−7.3	49.9	15.6	9.7	−12.8
34.0	−0.7	1.8	0.1	−5.5	3.4	62.9	7.0	−6.1	−8.3

(a) Construct a stem-and-leaf plot. Cut the data by dropping the decimals. Split the stems −1, −0, 0, 1, 2, 3, 4, 5, and 6 into two parts with leaves 0–4 on one part and 5–9 on the other.

(b) Describe the shape of the distribution.

(c) Which scores, if any, appear to be outliers?

2.6

MISLEADING GRAPHS (OPTIONAL)

There are many abuses of statistics. We cite some of the more common abuses of graphical methods in the following examples.

EXAMPLE 2.9

The treasurer of a company was instructed to prepare a report to the board of directors describing the company's profits as a percentage of sales for a 5-year period. The data are

Year	Profit (percent of sales)
1991	6.1
1992	6.7
1993	7.3
1994	7.5
1995	8.0

Such data are often described by a type of bar graph shown in Figure 2.13 (in an acceptable form).

Figure 2.13 shows a modest growth in profits over the years. However, the treasurer was overanxious to impress the board and instead constructed a **truncated bar graph,** shown in Figure 2.14. Notice how this graph exaggerates the growth in profits. The word *truncated* refers to the fact that the graph is cut off at the bottom and starts at 5.5. This sort of thing is generally frowned upon.

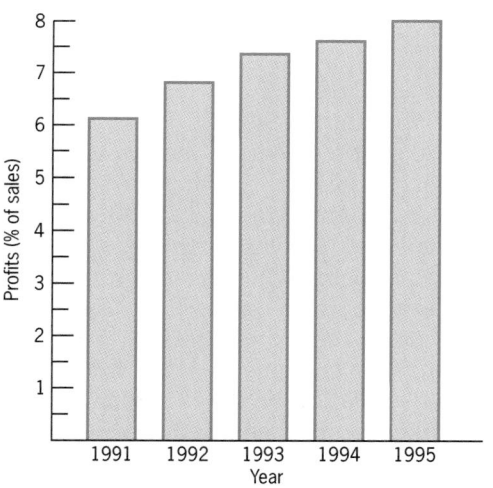

Figure 2.13
Bar Graph

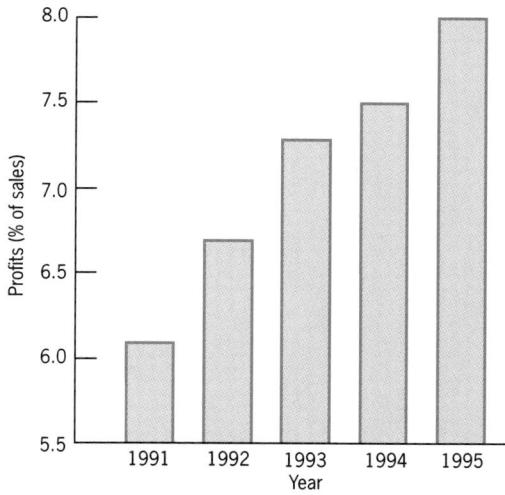

Figure 2.14
Truncated Bar Graph

EXAMPLE 2.10

A railroad company prepared some advertising material in which it portrayed a doubling of its yearly freight (measured in carload lots) between 1990 and 1995. In 1990, it shipped 4000 carload lots; in 1995, it shipped 8000 carload lots. This growth was represented graphically in Figure 2.15 (page 48) by means of two freight cars, one for 1990 and the other for 1995.

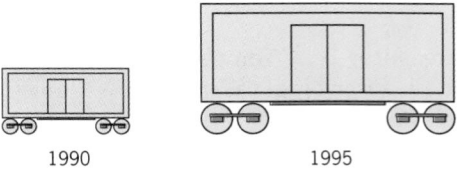

1990   1995

Figure 2.15
Misleading Pictogram

The freight car for 1995 in Figure 2.15 is twice as high as the one for 1990, which the railroad management believes is justified because its freight doubled. But it is also twice as long. Therefore, its area is four times the area of the freight car for 1990, which might suggest a quadrupling of business to the unwary reader. Figure 2.16 shows a more reasonable way to represent the growth. This is called a **pictogram.**

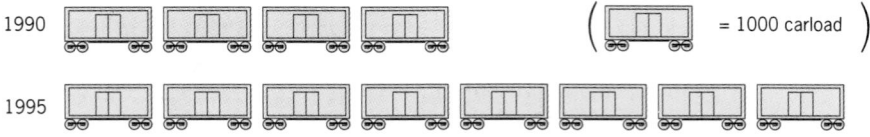

Figure 2.16
Pictogram Showing Growth in Freight from 1990 to 1995

EXAMPLE 2.11   Albert Shanker Was Right—Sort of

On February 4, 1988, Albert Shanker, president of the American Federation of Teachers, placed an ad in the *New York Times* sharply critical of a graph distributed by the Department of Education. The graph was supposed to show that as educational expenditures rose, scores on the combined Scholastic Aptitude Test (SAT) declined. [See Figure 2.17(a).] There are two problems with this graph. First, the bar graph for SAT scores is truncated, thus exaggerating the decline. Combined SAT scores start at 400, not 800. Second, the growth in expenditures is exaggerated because they are not adjusted for inflation. (For example, a 1980 dollar is equivalent to $1.50 in 1990 dollars because of 50% inflation between 1980 and 1990.) These two problems are corrected in Mr. Shanker's graph, which shows a full range bar chart and expenditures in constant (1986) dollars.* [See Figure 2.17(b).]

Mr. Shanker's graph is correct insofar as it goes. But some would say we should be measuring academic performance against per pupil expenditures, rather than total expenditures. Figure 2.17(c) shows per pupil expenditures in constant dollars adjusted for inflation. These are seen to be sharply increasing. So SAT scores are declining slightly, probably because a broader range of students is taking the tests in recent years. And per pupil expenditures are rising, perhaps in part because of the increasing costs of special education and bilingual education.

---

*The source for the graphs was Dr. Joan Baratz-Snowden and ETS.

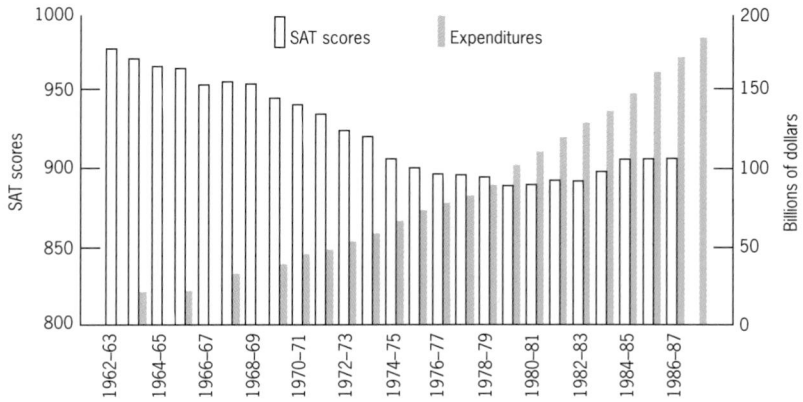

Figure 2.17(a)

Misleading Graph of SAT Scores (Truncated) and School Expenditures (Not Adjusted for Inflation) (*Source:* *New York Times*, Sept. 4, 1988)

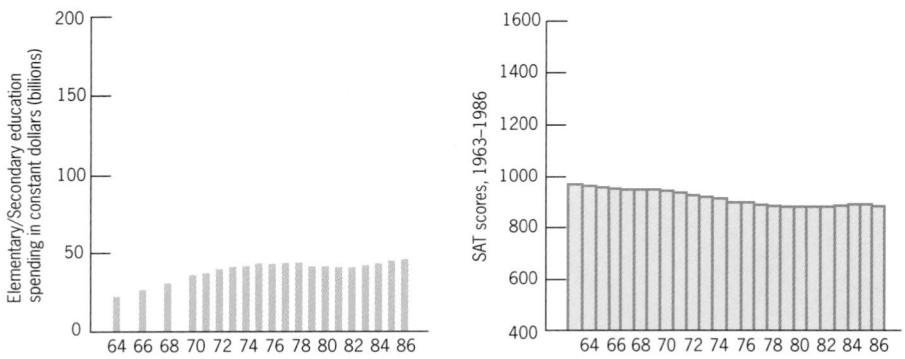

Figure 2.17(b)

Expenditures Adjusted for Inflation and Nontruncated SAT Scores
(*Source:* Albert Shanker, "Where We Stand," *New York Times*, Sept. 4, 1988)

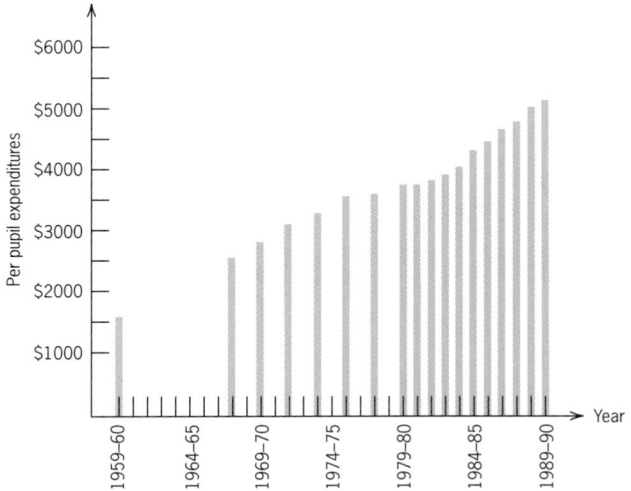

Figure 2.17(c)

Per Pupil Expenditures in Public Elementary and Secondary Schools in Constant 1990–1991 Dollars (*Sources:* *Digest of Education Statistics, 1993,* National Center for Education Statistics, Office of Educational Research and Improvement, NCES 93-292, p. 163; *Statistical Abstract of the United States,* U.S. Bureau of the Census, 100th ed., 1979, p. 149)

2.7

USING MINITAB (OPTIONAL)

Minitab for Windows

Most chapters in this textbook have an optional section that shows the reader how to use the Minitab computer package to solve statistical problems. We will be using Minitab's Release 10 for Windows. We assume the reader knows the basics of using Windows. The Minitab window shows two windows on your screen: the **Session window** and the **Data window** (see Figure 2.18).

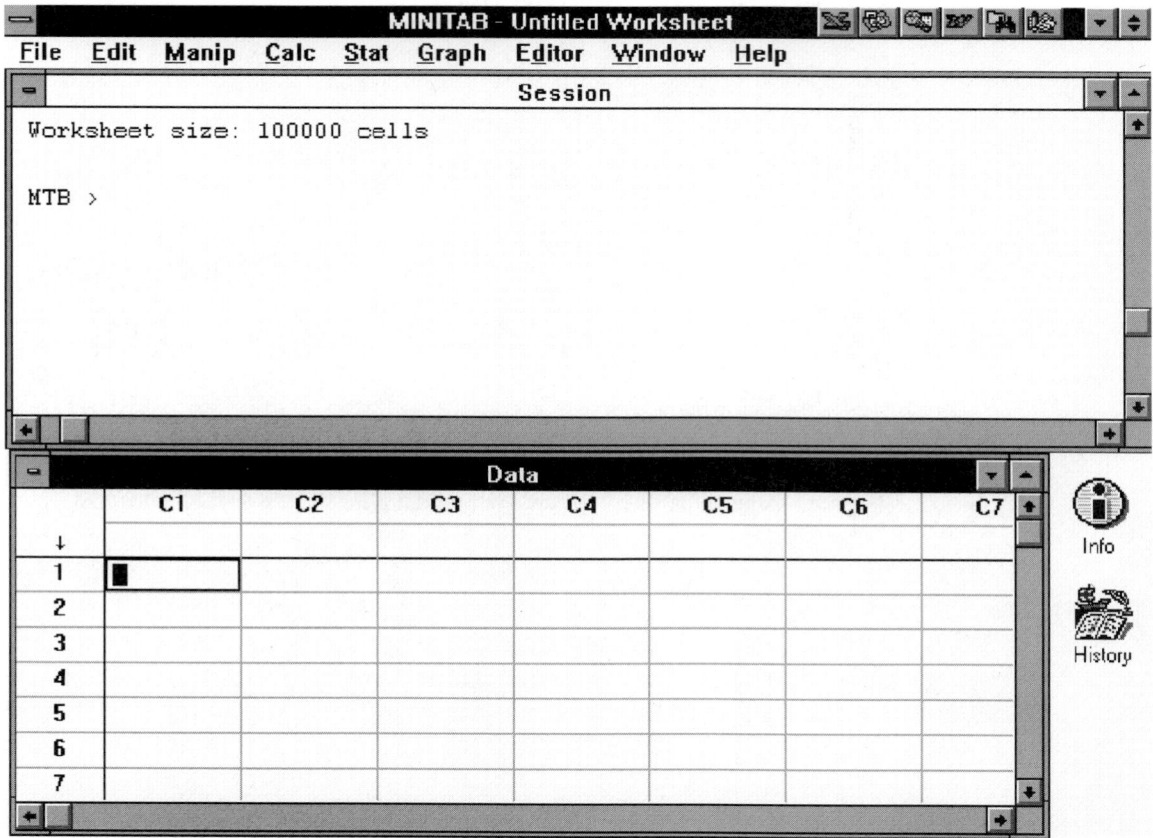

Figure 2.18

Two other windows are shown as icons: the **History window** and the **Info window.** To view these windows, click on them. The History window keeps a record of your commands. The Info window keeps track of what columns of data and stored constants you have created.

If you are not using the Windows version of Minitab, then you will essentially be typing commands and data in what amounts to the Session window, so just concentrate on our discussion of this.

Entering Data

The Minitab **worksheet** consists of a collection of columns internal to the computer. These columns will contain your data and the results of your computations. The columns are labeled C1 and C2 for columns 1 and 2, and so forth. Data and commands can be entered at a computer terminal keyboard. The easiest way to enter data is in the Data window. Just click the first row of the column where you want your data and start typing. There is a small arrow in the upper left of the Data window. Normally it is pointing down ($\downarrow$). This means that when you press ENTER, the cursor will drop down to the next line. If you want to enter data horizontally across columns, click on the arrow. It will then point horizontally ($\rightarrow$). Now when you press ENTER, the cursor will move horizontally to the next column.

You may also enter data from the Session window using the SET command. Click on the Session window. If you type

SET THE FOLLOWING DATA IN C1
1 4 3 6
END

the four data values will be placed in column 1 in computer memory. These data values will also be displayed in column 1 of your Data window. With the SET command, you may type data on more than one line if you wish. (You may also type data in a column.) Make sure your data values are separated by spaces or commas. Do not use commas in numbers. Do not write 1,500: Minitab will interpret this as two numbers. Instead, type 1500. After you have typed your data, you should type END to instruct Minitab that you are finished entering the data.

When typing Minitab commands, you need type only the first four letters of the command name (or three letters with a command like SET). You must also specify columns where data are located and occasionally constants or expressions that may be needed. Additional text after the command name is optional. (However, additional text is *not* allowed in high-resolution graphics commands, such as HISTOGRAM.) Thus, you may type

SET C1

This would achieve the same result as

SET THE FOLLOWING DATA IN C1

Be careful, however, not to include any unnecessary numbers in the additional text. Do not type, for example,

SET THE FOLLOWING 30 DATA VALUES IN C1

(Certain other symbols should be avoided in additional text because they have special meaning in Minitab. These are the symbols $+ ; - * \&.$)

When Minitab is expecting a command, it prompts you with the symbol

MTB >

You then type the command. When data are expected, Minitab types

DATA >

after which you enter your data. If you have a large collection of data, and you come to the end of a line, press ENTER. Minitab will respond with the DATA > prompt. Continue typing your data. When you are finished, press ENTER, type END, and press ENTER again. In any Minitab program, when you press ENTER, Minitab will respond with the appropriate prompt, or it will print the desired output. When reading Minitab printouts in this text, keep in mind that those lines preceded by prompts (such as MTB > or DATA >) are typed by the user. All other lines are output from the computer.

Alpha Data

An **alpha data value** is a group of letters or other characters. Often it is a word or phrase. Again, the easiest way to enter alpha data is to type them in the Data window. In the Sessions window, you can use the SET command, but you also need a **subcommand** called FORMAT. When you want to use a subcommand, you type a semicolon (;) at the end of the main command, then press ENTER. Minitab then expects a subcommand and prompts you with the symbol

SUBC >

Sometimes subcommands are indented to help distinguish them from main commands, but this is optional.
   To see how the FORMAT subcommand works, recall the data in Example 2.2, number of murders by weapon type. The weapon types are alpha data. Using one-word abbreviations for weapon type, we see that the maximum number of characters is 8 for *personal* (hands, feet, etc.). The following program puts weapon types in column 1.

```
MTB > SET C1;
SUBC>    FORMAT(A8).
DATA> HANDGUN
DATA> RIFLE
DATA> SHOTGUN
DATA> KNIFE
DATA> PERSONAL
DATA> OTHER
DATA> END
```

Notice that the FORMAT subcommand is followed by a period. Also alpha data must be typed in columns. Column 1 in the Data window is shown here.

Untitled Worksheet		
	C1-A	**C2**
↓		
1	HANDGUN	
2	RIFLE	
3	SHOTGUN	
4	KNIFE	
5	PERSONAL	
6	OTHER	
7		
8		
9		

The "A" indicates alpha data

Bar Graphs

In Example 2.4, we constructed a bar graph for the homicide data in Example 2.2 (murders by weapon type). Assume the weapon types are in column 1 and the frequencies are in column 2. The following program in the Session window produces a bar graph:

$$\text{MTB} > \text{CHART C2*C1}$$

Output

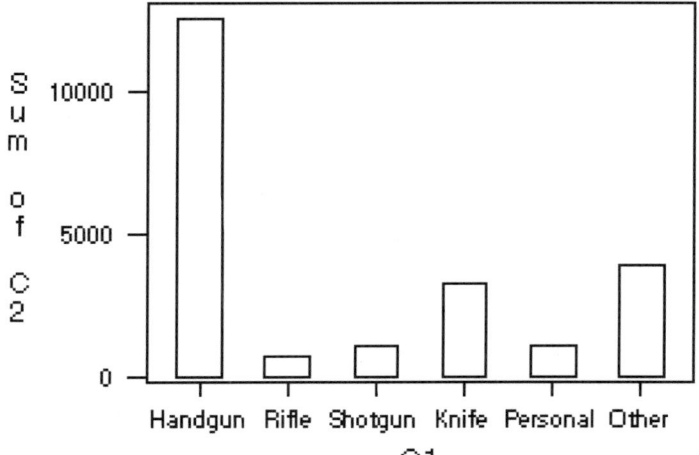

The Menu Bar and Dialog Box

This graph could be obtained with your mouse by clicking on the appropriate choices on the Menu bar and dialog box. Across the top of the screen is the Menu bar. Click on **Graph** and a menu will pop down. Click on **Chart.** A dialog box will appear. Type *C2* under **Y** and *C1* under **X**. Click **OK.** The bar graph shown on page 53 will appear. A shorthand way of explaining the use of a dialog box to produce the graph is:

Graph ▶ Chart

Type *C2* under **Y** and *C1* under **X**. Click **OK.**

In this book, we will give Session commands along with the corresponding dialog box choices.

Pie Charts

In Example 2.4, we also gave a pie chart for the homicide data. Assuming the weapon types are in column 1 and the frequencies are in column 2, a pie chart is produced as follows:

Session Commands	**Dialog Box**
MTB > %PIE C1; SUBC> COUNTS C2.	**Graph ▶ Pie Chart** Type *C1* in **Categories** Type *C2* in **Frequencies in** Click **OK**

Output

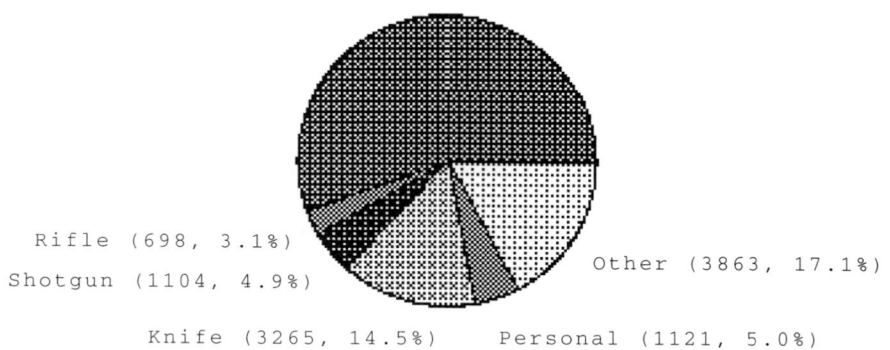

Pie Chart of C1

Handgun (12489, 55.4%)

Rifle (698, 3.1%)

Shotgun (1104, 4.9%)

Other (3863, 17.1%)

Knife (3265, 14.5%)

Personal (1121, 5.0%)

Histograms

Table 2.2 consisted of 40 scores on a science achievement test. Assume the data are in column 3. A histogram for these data can be obtained as follows:

Session Command	**Dialog Box**
MTB >HISTOGRAM C3	**Graph ▶ Histogram**
	Type C3 under **X**
	Click **OK**

Output

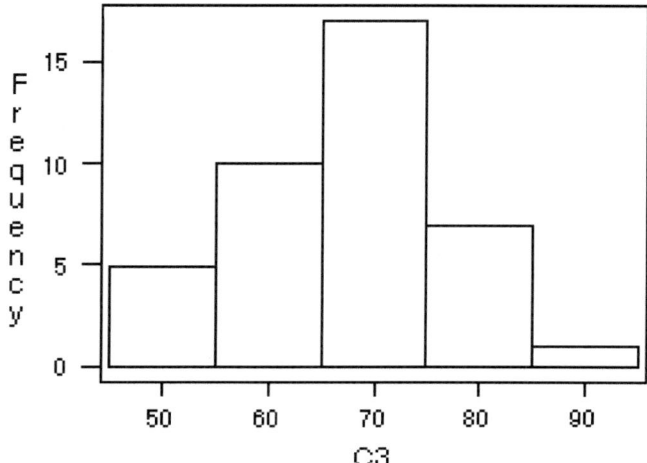

For each interval (class), the midpoint is given along with a bar with height equal to the class frequency. In this histogram, the distance between the midpoints is 10, so this is the class width. The intervals are defined in terms of the midpoints. Since the midpoint of the first interval is 50, this interval contains all data values greater than or equal to 45 and less than 55. If the value 55 had occurred in the data, it would be counted in the next interval.

In this histogram, the computer selected a convenient class width and the midpoints, since it was not told to do otherwise. If we want to select the midpoints, we could do so by means of a subcommand.

Suppose you want the midpoints to be 50, 55, 60, 65, 70, 75, 80, 85, and 90. In the Sessions window, you would type

HISTOGRAM C3;
MIDPOINTS 50 55 60 65 70 75 80 85 90.

There is an easier way to specify these midpoints, namely, by using **patterned data.** Minitab shorthand for the integers from 0 to 100 is 0:100. The numbers 50, 55, ..., 90 can be represented as 50:90/5. (This indicates that the numbers from 50 to 90 in increments of 5 are selected.) The program to accomplish this follows:

Session Commands	**Dialog Box**
MTB >HISTOGRAM C3,	**Graph ▶ Histogram**
SUBC> MIDPOINTS 50:90/5.	Type C3 under **X**
	Click **Options**
	Click **Midpoint/Cutpoint Positions**
	Type *50:90/5* in box.
	Click **OK** twice.

You may wish to use these midpoints more than once. If so, you could place them in column 4 by typing

SET C4

50:90/5

END

Then any time you want to specify these midpoints in a Session command or Dialog box, just type C4. For example, type MIDPOINTS C4.

Cutpoints are the endpoints at the base of each bar of the histogram. If you wish Minitab to display cutpoints on the horizontal axis instead of midpoints, use the CUTPOINT subcommand. If you do not specify any cutpoints, Minitab will choose its own. But you may specify cutpoints the same way you specify midpoints. Figure 2.3 (in Section 2.3) is a histogram for the test scores using the class boundaries 44.5, 49.5, ..., 89.5. The following program reproduces this histogram:

Session Commands	**Dialog Box**
MTB >HISTOGRAM C3; SUBC> CUTPOINTS 44.5:89.5/5.	**Graph ▶ Histogram** Type C3 under **X** Click **Options**. Click **Cutpoint** Click **Midpoint/Cutpoint Positions** Type *44.5:89.5/5* in box. Click **OK** twice.

Output

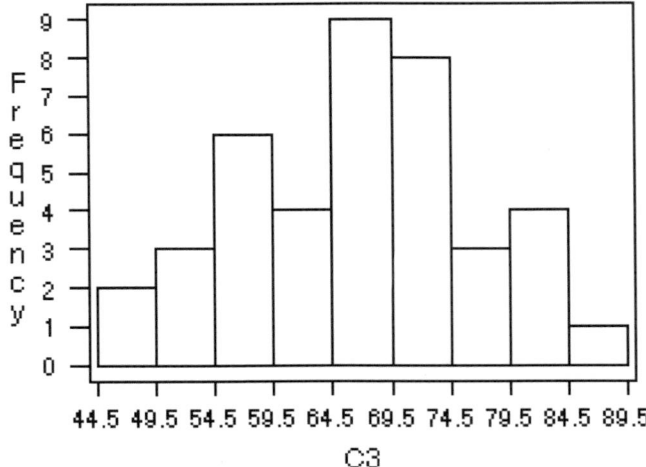

Cutpoints are not always class boundaries. If your data are whole numbers, and you choose whole numbers for the cutpoints, the cutpoints will be lower class limits.

Frequency Polygons

A subcommand of HISTOGRAM called CONNECT can be used to produce a frequency polygon. When more than one subcommand is used, each is followed by a semicolon except the last, which is followed by a period. The following will produce a frequency polygon for the 40 scores in column 3. Recall that the class marks are 47, 52, ..., 87.

Session Commands	Dialog Box
MTB >HISTOGRAM C3;	**Graph ▶ Histogram**
SUBC> MIDPOINTS 47:87/5;	Type *C3* under **X**
SUBC> CONNECT.	Click **Display.** Menu drops down
	Click **Connect.** Click **Options.**
	Click **Midpoint/Cutpoint Positions.**
	Type *47:87/5* in box.
	Click **OK** twice.

Output

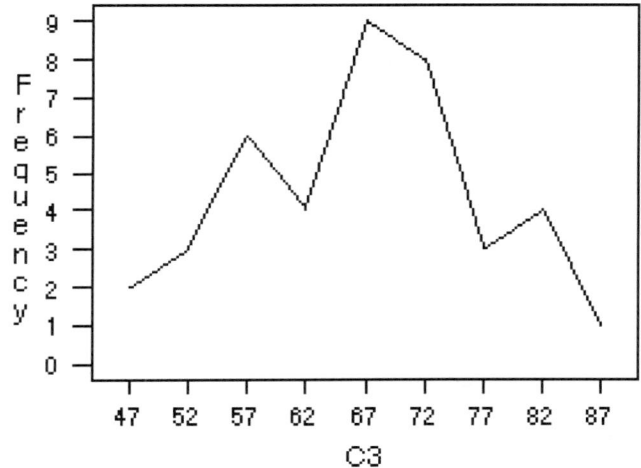

You can produce more than one histogram in the same program. Follow these steps to produce a histogram for the data in, say, columns 5, 6, and 7:

Session Command	Dialog Box
MTB >HISTOGRAM C5 C6 C7	**Graph ▶ Histogram**
	For graphs 1, 2, 3, under **X**
	Type *C5*
	C6
	C7

Remark Before deciding on your midpoints (or cutpoints), you must know the range of the data (i.e., the maximum and minimum values). If the data are ranked, it is easy to see what these are. But if the data are unranked, the following Session command will quickly give you the maximum and minimum values:

MAXIMUM C3
MINIMUM C3

Dotplots

A histogram groups the data into relatively few intervals. A **dotplot** is a variation on the histogram that does as little grouping as possible. Thus the data are grouped into many intervals of small width. A dot is given for each data value. Hence a dotplot resembles a dot diagram and is useful for small data sets, whereas a histogram is useful for large data sets. A dotplot for the 40 test scores follows.

Session Command	**Dialog Box**
MTB >DOTPLOT C3	**Graph** ▶ **Histogram** ▶ **Character Graphs** ▶ **Dotplots** Type C3 in Variables Box.

Output

Character Dotplot

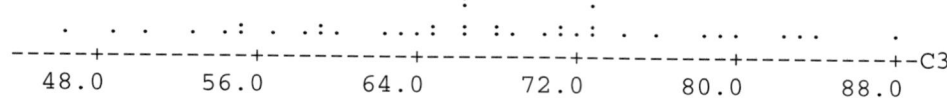

```
                                   :            .
          .   .   .   . .:  . .:.  ...: : :. .:.:  . .   ...   ...      .
      ----+---------+---------+---------+---------+---------+---------+-C3
          48.0      56.0      64.0      72.0      80.0      88.0
```

Stem-and-Leaf Plots

Use the following commands to generate a stem-and-leaf plot for the same 40 data values in column 3.

Session Command	**Dialog Box**
MTB >STEM-AND-LEAF C3	**Graph** ▶ **Character Graph** ▶ **Stem-and-Leaf** Type C3 under **Variables** Click **OK**

Output

Character Stem-and-Leaf Display

```
Stem-and-leaf of C3        N   = 40
Leaf Unit = 1.0

       2      4 69
       5      5 034
      11      5 557899
      15      6 0234
      (9)     6 556666889
      16      7 01123334
       8      7 689
       5      8 0234
       1      8 8
```

Notice that Minitab tells you the leaf digit unit is 1; this means it is the ones digit. For example, 6 5 represents the number 65. If the leaf unit were 10, then 6 5 would mean 650. With a leaf unit of .01, we would read 6 5 as .65. The first column gives the number of data values on that line plus the number of values in the lines toward the outer tail of the distribution (that is, the outer tail nearest the line). For example, the 15 on the fourth line means there are 15 data values in the nearest tail: lines 1 through 4. The exception to this rule is the line containing the median (a kind of central value, to be discussed in Chapter 3). Next to the line containing the median, the number of data values on *that* line is given in parentheses. The median for these data is 66, which is on the fifth line.

Sometimes the leaves for each stem are stretched over more than one line. The number of lines is usually 1, 2, or 5. In the previous printout, there are two lines per stem. Thus we see the values 60 and 65 as

$$6 \quad 0$$
$$6 \quad 5$$

instead of

$$6 \quad 05$$

The values 60–64 go on the fourth line and 65–69 on the fifth line. Note the distance between the lowest possible value on the first line (40) and the lowest possible value on the second line (50) is 5. This is called the **increment.** We can control the increment with a subcommand. If we wanted all the values with the same tens digits on the same line, then the distance (increment) between lines would be 10. We would then type the following:

Session Commands	**Dialog Box**
MTB >STEM-AND-LEAF C3;	**Graph ▶ Character Graph ▶ Stem-and-Leaf**
SUBC > INCREMENT = 10.	Type *C3* under **Variables**
	Type *10* for **Increment**
	Click **OK**

The increment must always be 1, 2, or 5 perhaps with leading or trailing zeros, such as 10, .1, .01, 2, .2, .02, 200, etc.

Stored Constants

Although data sets are stored in columns, single numbers may also be stored, and as such are referred to as **stored constants.** Locations of stored constants are labeled K1, K2, etc. For the data discussed previously, the maximum value was 88. We could have stored this for future reference with the following variation of the MAXIMUM command given previously:

MAXIMUM C3, STORE IN K1

The value of 88 would be stored in K1. Later if we wanted to see the maximum value, we could type

PRINT K1

Minitab would print the value of K1. The PRINT command can be used to print columns and constants. For example,

PRINT C1, C3-C5, K1

would print columns C1, C3, C4, C5, and constant K1.

Annotating a Program

If you wish to type any explanatory comment on your output, you can use the symbol # followed by your comment. Minitab ignores everything on the line following #. For example,

HISTOGRAM C3 # 40 TEST SCORES

Naming Columns

We may use the NAME command to name columns. Minitab will then use the names when printing information about these columns. Enclose the name in single quotes. For example,

NAME FOR C3 IS 'SCORES'

We can abbreviate this command as

NAME C3 'SCORES'

If you wish, you may use this name in subsequent commands. For example,

HISTOGRAM 'SCORES'

We can name more than one column at a time:

NAME FOR C4 IS 'PRICE', FOR C5 IS 'QUANTITY'

A name may be up to 8 characters long, but it may not begin or end with a blank, or contain the symbol # or a single quote. You may use the NAME command to change a column name. To erase a column name, but not the column contents, give it a blank name:

NAME FOR C3 IS ' '

When you are through using Minitab, type STOP (and press ENTER).

MTB >STOP

PRACTICE QUIZ (Answers follow the Review Exercises.)

Find the errors (if any) in the following Session commands.

1. SET THE FOLLOWING DATA IN C1: 1 4 5
   END
2. SET THE FOLLOWING DATA IN C1
   913 847 312 2,104
   END
3. SET THE FOLLOWING DATA IN COLUMN 1
   5 3 7
   END
4. MAXIMUM FOR C1
   MINIUM FOR C1
5. SETTHE FOLLOWING DATA IN C1
   1 2 3 4
   END
6. PLEASE SET THE FOLLOWING DATA IN C1
   1 2 3 4
   END
7. SET IN C1
   2 7   32
      12
   END
8. SET THE DATA FOR BRAND 1 in C1
   11 8 2 3 9
   END
9. MAXIMUM FOR C1, MINIMUM FOR C1
10. STEM-AND-LEAF FOR C5;
    INCREMENT = 13.

EXERCISES

Suggested exercises to use with Minitab are 2.48, 2.54(b), 2.55(b), and 2.57. Some of these exercises ask you to construct a frequency histogram based on grouped frequency distributions found in previous exercises. The histogram command in Minitab does not require that you first construct a grouped frequency distribution; it does everything at once. Use the previous exercises only to determine necessary information about the grouped distribution, such as the starting point for the first class.

2.8

WORKING WITH DATA (OPTIONAL)

In most of the chapters of this book, we include a section that enables the reader to work with data from the Framingham Heart Study. This study followed a cohort of 5209 men and women for over 25 years. Biennial cardiovascular examinations included a cardiovascular history and physical examination, blood lipid and glucose examinations, as well as other medical exams. The study has been important in identifying risk factors associated with cardiovascular disease.

With the kind assistance of Dr. William Castelli, Director of the Framingham Heart Study, as well as Robert Garrison, Michael Hartman, and Paul Sorley of the National Institutes of Health, we obtained a large body of data pertaining to the entire Framingham cohort.

Appendix Table B.11 contains data for a random sample of 1000 subjects from the Framingham Heart Study. The following is a description of the variables we have selected from the study:

Column	Description of Variable
1	ID number 0001 to 1000
2	Sex 1 Man 2 Woman
3	Age 30–64 years
4	Systolic blood pressure 082–300 mm
5	Diastolic blood pressure 020–148 mm
6	Serum cholesterol 115–568 mg/100 ml (9999: Unknown)
7	First evidence of coronary heart disease (CHD) 0 No evidence of CHD 1 Pre-existing CHD at Exam 1 2–10 Exam at which CHD first diagnosed
8	Number of cigarettes smoked per day (9999: Unknown)

This data set (without the ID column) is also available from the publisher on a floppy disk.

A random sample of subjects can be obtained from Appendix Table B.11 by choosing the desired number of ID numbers from the random number table (Appendix Table B.1). Alternatively, you could start at any point in the Heart Study table and sequentially select the desired number of subjects.

PROBLEM SET

To do the following problems, it would be helpful (though not absolutely necessary) to use a statistical software package such as Minitab. Using the Heart Study data in Appendix Table B.11, randomly select 35 males and 35 females. Consider the variables sex, age, systolic blood pressure, diastolic blood pressure, serum cholesterol level, and number of cigarettes smoked per day. (Ignore any subject with the missing data code of 9999.) These data will be used in the problems below unless otherwise specified. Save your data for use in later chapters.

1. Construct a grouped frequency distribution of systolic blood pressure for the following:
   (a) Males and females combined
   (b) Males
   (c) Females
2. Construct frequency histograms for parts (a), (b), and (c) of Problem 1. In each case, describe the shape of the distribution.
3. Construct a grouped frequency distribution of serum cholesterol level for the following:
   (a) Males and females combined
   (b) Males
   (c) Females
4. Construct frequency polygons for parts (a), (b), and (c) of Problem 3. In each case, describe the shape of the distribution.
5. Construct (ungrouped) frequency distributions of the number of cigarettes smoked for the following:
   (a) Males and females combined
   (b) Males
   (c) Females
6. Construct dot diagrams for parts (a), (b), and (c) of Problem 5.
7. Construct a stem-and-leaf plot of diastolic blood pressures for the following:
   (a) Males and females combined
   (b) Males
   (c) Females
   (d) Which samples, if any, appear to have come from normal populations? (*Hint:* Samples from normal populations tend to have graphs that are roughly mound-shaped, are not strongly skewed, and do not contain extreme outliers.)
8. Biological measurements from homogeneous populations often constitute approximately normal populations. Randomly select 25 males age 30–39 from Appendix Table B.11. Make a stem-and-leaf plot of their diastolic blood pressures. Does it appear that the sample may have come from an approximately normal population? (Your answer should be Yes if the stem-and-leaf plot is roughly mound-shaped, is not strongly skewed, and contains no extreme outliers.)

2.9

SUMMARY

Various ways of summarizing and simplifying data were presented in this chapter. A **frequency distribution** gives us the distinct data values in a collection of data together with the number of times each occurs. A **grouped frequency distribution** is obtained by giving classes or intervals together with the number of data values in each class. The **grouped relative frequency distribution** gives the frequency for each class divided by the total number of data values for the data set.

Describing data graphically can also be useful. **Dot diagrams, bar graphs,** and **pie charts** are used to represent frequency distributions. A grouped frequency distribution can be represented by means of a **frequency histogram** or a **frequency polygon.**

Stem-and-leaf plots are also useful for displaying data.

REVIEW EXERCISES

2.42 The following data are the numbers of deaths by horsekicks in the Prussian Army from 1875 to 1894 for 14 corps (*Source:* Andrews, D. F., and A. M. Herzberg, "The Number of Deaths by Horsekicks in the Prussian Army," in *Data,* p. 18. New York: Springer-Verlag):

$$
\begin{array}{cccccccccc}
3 & 4 & 5 & 5 & 6 & 6 & 7 & 8 & 9 & 9 \\
10 & 11 & 11 & 11 & 12 & 14 & 15 & 15 & 17 & 18
\end{array}
$$

(a) Construct the frequency distribution.

(b) Construct a dot diagram.

2.43 The accompanying data are magnitudes on the Richter scale of 20 earthquakes selected from 1000 seismic events occurring near the Fiji Islands between 1964 and 1974 (*Source:* Extracted from the World Wide Seismic Network Tape by Professor John Woodhouse of Harvard University. Data from Donoho, A., D. Donoho, and M. Gasko, *MacSpin Graphical Data Analysis Software,* p. 115). The data are

$$
\begin{array}{cccccccccc}
4.7 & 4.3 & 4.5 & 4.8 & 5.1 & 5.5 & 4.7 & 4.4 & 4.7 & 4.6 \\
4.5 & 5.7 & 4.9 & 4.5 & 4.3 & 4.1 & 4.3 & 4.6 & 5.1 & 4.7
\end{array}
$$

(a) Construct the frequency distribution.

(b) Give the percentage of earthquakes with magnitude less than 5.0.

(c) Construct a dot diagram.

In Exercises 2.44–2.46, use the following data. An interviewer was interested in the television-viewing habits of people 18 years or older in a large city. She selected 20 homes and obtained the information in Table 2.7 from one adult in each home.

Table 2.7

Age	Gender	Number of Hours Watching TV per Week	Number of Children
71	F	16	3
30	M	23	2
63	F	19	4
66	F	31	5
47	M	28	1
29	F	4	2
26	F	11	2
47	F	21	3
31	F	17	4
82	M	13	2
74	F	29	5
53	F	7	3
32	F	3	3
40	M	18	0
30	F	21	1
19	F	28	0
68	F	12	2
55	F	3	3
24	F	24	2
38	F	27	3

2.44 Construct a frequency distribution for the number of children.

2.45 Would it be worthwhile to construct a frequency distribution for "Age"? For "Number of hours watching TV per week"? Give your reasons.

2.46 What proportion of those sampled are female? What might account for such a large proportion of females?

In Exercises 2.47–2.50, use the information in Table 2.7 but assume that the interviewer categorized the number of hours of watching TV as follows: seldom (0–6 hours inclusive), occasional (7–13 hours inclusive), frequent (14–20 hours inclusive), very frequent (21–27 hours inclusive), and excessive (28 or more hours). (For consistency, you may regard this last category as 28–34 hours.)

2.47 Construct a grouped frequency distribution for "Number of hours" with classes based on the categories defined previously.

2.48 Using Exercise 2.47, construct the following:
   (a) A frequency histogram
   (b) A frequency polygon

2.49 Construct a grouped frequency distribution for "Age". Use a starting point of 10 and a class width of 10.

2.50 Using Exercise 2.49, construct the following:
   (a) A frequency histogram
   (b) A frequency polygon

2.51 The finance committee of a town was interested in the economic makeup of families in that town. A sample of 200 families was taken to determine their incomes. Assume, for example, that 34 is taken to be $34,000 and that income was recorded to the nearest thousand.
   (a) Complete Table 2.8.

Table 2.8

Class	Class Boundaries	Frequency	Relative Frequency
1			.05
2		30	
3		12	
4	32.5–35.5	47	
5			.25
6		28	
7		5	
8			
Total		200	

   (b) Construct a frequency histogram.
   (c) Construct a frequency polygon.
   (d) If you believed that the sample was representative of the economic status of families in this town, what would you estimate the proportion of families to be that
   (i) Earn more than $35,500?
   (ii) Earn between $32,500 and $35,500?

2.52 The frequency distribution for magnitudes of 1000 earthquakes, discussed in Exercise 2.43, is as follows:

x	4.0	4.1	4.2	4.3	4.4	4.5	4.6	4.7	4.8	4.9	5.0	5.1	5.2
f	46	55	90	85	101	107	101	98	65	54	47	43	29

x	5.3	5.4	5.5	5.6	5.7	5.8	5.9	6.0	6.1	6.2	6.3	6.4
f	21	20	14	9	8	0	2	3	1	0	0	1

(a) Use 4.0 as a starting point and construct a grouped frequency distribution with five classes.

(b) What is the class width?

(c) Find the percentage of magnitudes 5.0 or larger.

(d) Construct a frequency histogram.

(e) Characterize the distribution shape by selecting the name of the distribution that most closely approximates the data.

2.53 Select 60 digits from the random number table (Appendix Table B.1) as follows: Start at the beginning of some column in the table. Record the first 60 digits by moving down this column to the next column, and so on.

(a) Construct a dot diagram.

(b) If the entire random number table generates numbers in a chance manner, approximately what proportion of times should each integer occur? Do your data reflect this? What should be the approximate shape of the distribution?

2.54 A psychologist observed reaction times to a stimulus and recorded the following 50 reaction times, in seconds:

2.7	3.1	4.0	3.3	3.6	2.1	1.3	1.8	3.7	3.7
3.7	3.4	6.4	3.4	3.3	2.9	1.6	3.3	4.5	3.1
3.5	2.6	3.0	3.3	1.6	.9	1.5	2.7	2.7	2.6
2.3	1.3	1.7	2.2	3.2	2.8	3.1	3.4	2.6	1.7
2.5	3.8	2.0	3.8	1.4	2.8	2.4	4.5	3.2	2.3

(a) Using eight classes, construct a table with columns for class limits, class boundaries, class marks, frequencies, and relative frequencies. What is the class width? (Use the minimum data value as a starting point, i.e., lower class limit of first class.)

(b) Construct a frequency histogram.

(c) Construct a frequency distribution. Compare with the grouped frequency distribution. Was it worthwhile to group the data? Give your reasons.

2.55 The following data are observations of time in days from remission induction to relapse for 51 patients with acute nonlymphoblastic leukemia (*Source:* Matthews, D. T., and V. T. Farewell, "On Testing for a Constant Hazard Against a Change-point Alternative." *Biometrics*, Vol. 38; pp. 463–468, 1982.)

24	46	57	57	64	65	82	89	90	90	111	117	128
143	148	152	166	171	186	191	197	209	223	230	247	249
254	258	264	269	270	273	284	294	304	304	332	341	393
395	487	510	516	518	518	534	608	642	697	955	1160	

(a) Construct a grouped frequency distribution with 6 classes. Use 24 as a starting point.

(b) Construct a frequency polygon.

(c) Characterize the distribution shape by selecting the name of the distribution that most closely approximates the data.

(d) What is the percentage of observations for which the time to relapse lasted more than 403 days?

2.56 Consider the following grouped frequency distribution:

Class	Class Limits	Frequency
1	60–61	13
2	62–63	27
3	64–65	45
4	66–67	43
5	68–69	32
6	70–71	38
7	72–73	21
8	74–75	14
9	76–77	2

(a) Find the class width.

(b) Give the class boundaries for the third class.

(c) Find the class mark of the fifth class.

(d) Construct a frequency histogram.

(e) Construct a frequency polygon.

2.57 The following data, used in Exercise 2.13, are profits over the past 30 years for a small business (in thousands of dollars).

| 15 | 17 | 18 | 19 | 20 | 20 | 20 | 21 | 23 | 23 | 24 | 24 | 24 | 24 | 24 |
| 25 | 25 | 25 | 25 | 25 | 26 | 26 | 27 | 27 | 28 | 29 | 30 | 30 | 31 | 32 |

(a) Construct a stem-and-leaf plot. Split the stems 1, 2, and 3 into five parts with leaves 0–1, 2–3, 4–5, 6–7, and 8–9. (*Note:* To get enough lines in the stem-and-leaf plot, we have split the stems into five parts.)

(b) Characterize the distribution shape by selecting the name of the distribution that most closely approximates the data.

2.58 The following data are test scores for an introductory economics class given in the morning. A perfect score is 80. The distribution of scores and potential outliers were of interest to the instructor. (Data provided by Walter Block, Holy Cross College.)

| 55 | 50 | 70 | 65 | 68 | 73 | 57 | 66 | 66 |
| 68 | 46 | 63 | 69 | 68 | 70 | 61 | 61 | |

(a)   Use 4, 5, 6, and 7 as stems and construct a stem-and-leaf plot.

(b)   Split the stems 4, 5, 6, and 7 into two parts with leaves 0–4 on one part and 5–9 on the other. Construct a stem-and-leaf plot. Characterize the shape of the distribution of scores. What seems to be a typical score? Which scores, if any, appear to be outliers?

(c)   Which stem-and-leaf plot gives a better description of the distribution of scores?

2.59   The following data are the per capita property tax collections by state (in 1991 dollars) (*Source: The 1994 Information Please Almanac, 1994, p. 80*).

171	1213	662	242	639	690	1138	311	687	506
430	427	785	571	686	691	277	275	796	617
830	894	718	344	377	523	744	456	1341	1257
222	1101	382	505	541	250	877	562	880	423
580	329	679	416	925	638	625	273	797	912

(a)   Construct a stem-and-leaf plot. Use stems 1, 2, 3, ..., 13, and cut the data by dropping the units digit.

(b)   Characterize the distribution shape by selecting the name of the distribution that most closely approximates the data.

(c)   Construct a frequency polygon.

2.60   The following data are the percentages of mothers with children under 18 years of age participating in the labor force (*Source: The 1994 Information Please Almanac, 1994, p. 56*).

Year	1983	1984	1985	1986	1987	1988
%	58.9	60.5	62.1	62.8	64.7	65.0

Construct a line graph.

2.61   The following data are the percentages of mothers participating in the labor force who have children under 6 years of age (*Source: The 1994 Information Please Almanac, 1994, p. 56*).

Year	1983	1984	1985	1986	1987	1988
%	50.5	52.1	53.5	54.4	56.7	56.1

Construct a line graph.

2.62   The following data give the marriage rates (per 1000 population) (*Source: The 1994 Information Please Almanac, 1994, p. 839*).

Year	1978	1979	1980	1981	1982	1983	1984	1985
%	10.5	10.6	10.6	10.6	10.8	10.5	10.5	10.2

Year	1986	1987	1988	1989	1990	1991	1992
%	10.0	9.9	9.7	9.7	9.8	9.4	9.2

Construct a line graph.

2.63 There were 6000 full-time state jobs created between fiscal 1984 and fiscal 1989 in the commonwealth of Massachusetts (*Source: The Boston Globe*, Feb. 22, 1989, p. 14). The numbers of jobs (rounded off) within governmental departments were

Human Services	3000
Higher Education	1200
Public Safety	500
Administration and Finance	900
Environmental	400

(a) Construct a bar graph.

(b) Construct a pie chart.

2.64 The following data are the numbers of persons (in thousands by educational level) of voting age in the 1992 presidential election (*Source: The 1994 Information Please Almanac*, 1994, p. 37).

Education	8 years or less	9–11 years	12 years	16 or more
Number	15,391	20,970	65,281	37,351

(a) Construct a bar graph.

(b) Construct a pie chart.

2.65 The accompanying data are the numbers of persons (in thousands by educational level) reporting they voted in the 1992 presidential election (*Source: The 1994 Information Please Almanac*, 1994, p. 37).

Education	8 years or less	9–11 years	12 years	16 or more
Number	5406	8638	37,517	30,236

(a) Construct a bar graph.

(b) Construct a pie chart.

2.66 The graphs at the top of page 70 are called a *cumulative frequency polygon* and a *cumulative relative frequency polygon*. Cumulative frequency and cumulative relative frequency of a class are the total number and the proportion, respectively, of data values less than the upper class boundary of the class. These are plotted above the upper class boundaries. The data represent heights (to the nearest inch) of tenors in the New York Choral Society in 1979 (*Source:* Chambers, J., W. Cleveland, B. Kleiner, and P. Tukey, *Graphical Methods for Data Analysis*. Boston: Duxbury Press, 1983, p. 350).

(a) How many classes are there?

(b) Find the class width.

(c) How many data values are there?

(d) What are the class limits for the second class?

(e) Find the frequency of the second class.

(f) Use the cumulative relative frequency polygon to estimate the data value that separates the lower 50% of the data from the upper 50% of the data. (This is called the 50th percentile.)

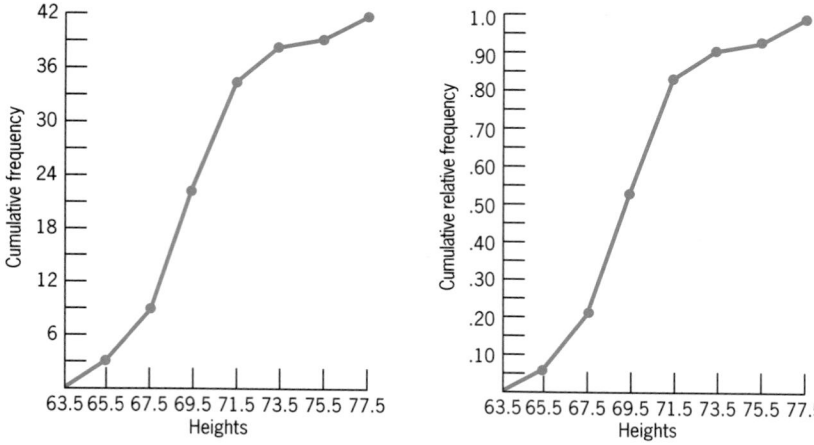

(g) Use the cumulative relative frequency polygon to estimate the percentage of heights less than 71.5.

For Exercises 2.67–2.71, use the data in Table 2.9. A Florida city hospital and a Massachusetts city hospital maintained records in a certain year indicating the age at admittance for those patients who spent at least 3 days at the hospital. The data are given in Table 2.9. These incidence rates were based upon the previous year's population census of the respective cities. (By incidence rate, we mean the number of admittances per 100,000 of the city population with ages in this category.)

Table 2.9

Age at Admittance	Number at Florida Hospital	Number at Massachusetts Hospital	Incidence Rate (per 100,000)	
			Florida	Massachusetts
0–9	27	41	.3	.4
10–19	19	32	.7	.6
20–29	31	60	1.6	1.9
30–39	47	72	6.2	5.8
40–49	42	70	11.4	12.1
50–59	68	40	13.6	13.8
60–69	87	37	17.2	17.8
70–79	145	33	28.3	26.4
80–89	34	15	44.2	49.4
Total	500	400		

2.67 Use the columns for number of admittances.
(a) Construct a frequency polygon for the Florida hospital.
(b) Construct a frequency polygon for the Massachusetts hospital.
(c) Comment on differences between the polygons.

2.68   Consider the incidence rate per 100,000.

(a)   Construct an incidence polygon* for the Florida hospital.

(b)   Construct an incidence polygon* for the Massachusetts hospital.

(c)   Comment on any similarities and differences between the polygons.

2.69   This exercise illustrates a cumulative frequency polygon. The *cumulative frequency* of a class is the total number of data values in the data set that are less than the upper class boundary of the class. The cumulative frequency polygon is constructed by plotting above each upper class boundary the cumulative frequency of the class. Consider the number of admittances.

(a)   Construct a cumulative frequency polygon for the Florida hospital.

(b)   Construct a cumulative frequency polygon for the Massachusetts hospital.

2.70   Compare the frequency polygon and the cumulative frequency polygon for the Massachusetts hospital. [See Exercises 2.67(b) and 2.69(b).] Do you see any connection between the two? Could you have drawn the cumulative frequency polygon (roughly) from the frequency polygon if no numbers had been displayed?

2.71   Refer to Exercise 2.69. Construct a column of cumulative frequencies for the Florida hospital regarding the number of admittances. Using this column, find the following:

(a)   The number admitted who were 40 years or older

(b)   The number admitted who were 69 years or younger

(c)   The number admitted who were more than 29 but less than 80 years of age

2.72   (a)   Use the data for "Age" in Table 2.7 to construct a stem-and-leaf plot. For stems, use the tens digit. Thus 63 is represented as 6 | 3.

(b)   Construct a frequency histogram with classes 10–19, 20–29, etc.

(c)   Rotate your stem-and-leaf plot 90° counterclockwise and compare its appearance with the frequency histogram in part (b). Could the stem-and-leaf plot be used as a frequency histogram?

2.73   This problem deals with frequency histograms for grouped frequency distributions in which not all classes are of equal width. It illustrates that the area of each rectangle should be proportional to the frequency for that class. Consider the following data indicating profits in millions of dollars for a large corporation over the indicated time period.

Time Period	Profit
1980–1981	4
1982–1985	6
1986–1991	6
1992–1993	1
1994	2
1995	3

(a)   Construct a frequency histogram for the data in the usual manner. Does the histogram accurately reflect the fact that 1995 was the best year for profits for the company? Why?

---

*By "incidence polygon," we mean a graph similar to a frequency polygon, except that frequencies are replaced by incidence rates. The height of a dot is the incidence rate rather than frequency.

(b) To adjust for the different lengths of times recorded, consider the amount of profit per year's time over a specified interval. For example, the 2-year period of 1980–1981 indicates a profit of $4 \div 2 = \$2$ million per year. Construct a frequency histogram using the amount of profit per year's time as the height of the bars. Is this histogram quite different from that of part (a)? Which gives more accurate information?

ANSWERS TO PRACTICE QUIZ

1. The data must be on a separate line (or lines) from the command line.

2. This program probably does not accomplish what the user intended. The 2,104 will be interpreted by Minitab as two numbers: 2 and 104. Type 2104 instead.

3. Do not type COLUMN 1. Type C1.

4. This program is all right. The user will not get high marks for the spelling of minimum, but Minitab is friendly and does not care about this as long as the first four characters of the command can be found in its dictionary of commands.

5. Minitab is friendly, but not this friendly. It looks at the first four characters of the first word of a command (including blanks). There is no SETT command in its dictionary.

6. The user who wrote this program forgot that Minitab expects the command to be the first word. If you insist on being this polite, put the PLEASE somewhere after the first word.

7. Nothing is wrong.

8. The 1 in BRAND 1 is an unnecessary constant, but Minitab is expecting a column. Minitab can ignore letters but not numbers in explanatory text. The following error message will be returned:

ERROR ARGUMENT IS A CONSTANT OR MATRIX BUT A COLUMN WAS EXPECTED

You can avoid this difficulty by typing BRAND ONE.

9. You should put only one command to a line.

10. The value for INCREMENT must be 1, 2, or 5 times a power of 10.

Notes

Andrews, D. F., and A. M. Herzberg. "The Number of Deaths by Horsekicks in the Prussian Army." *Data*. New York: Springer-Verlag, 1985.

Budget of the United States Government, Fiscal Year 1995. Washington, D.C.: Office of Management and Budget, 1994.

Chambers, J., W. Cleveland, B. Kleiner, and P. Tukey. *Graphical Methods for Data Analysis*. Boston: Duxbury Press, 1983.

Crime in the United States—Uniform Crime Reports. Washington, D.C.: Federal Bureau of Investigation, 1993.

Food and Wine, September 1992.

The 1994 Information Please Almanac. Boston: Houghton Mifflin Company, 1994.

Matthews, D. E., and V. T. Farewell. "On Testing for a Constant Hazard Against a Change-Point Alternative." *Biometrics*, Vol. 38, 1982, pp. 463–468.

The Boston Globe. Boston: Globe Newspaper Company, June 6, 1993; June 7, 1994.

The World Almanac and Book of Facts. New York: Newspaper Enterprise Association, 1993.

Woodhouse, J., "World Wide Seismic Network Tape." Data in Donoho, A. W., D. L. Donoho, and M. Gasko, *MacSpin User Manual.* Austin, Texas: D^2 Software Inc.

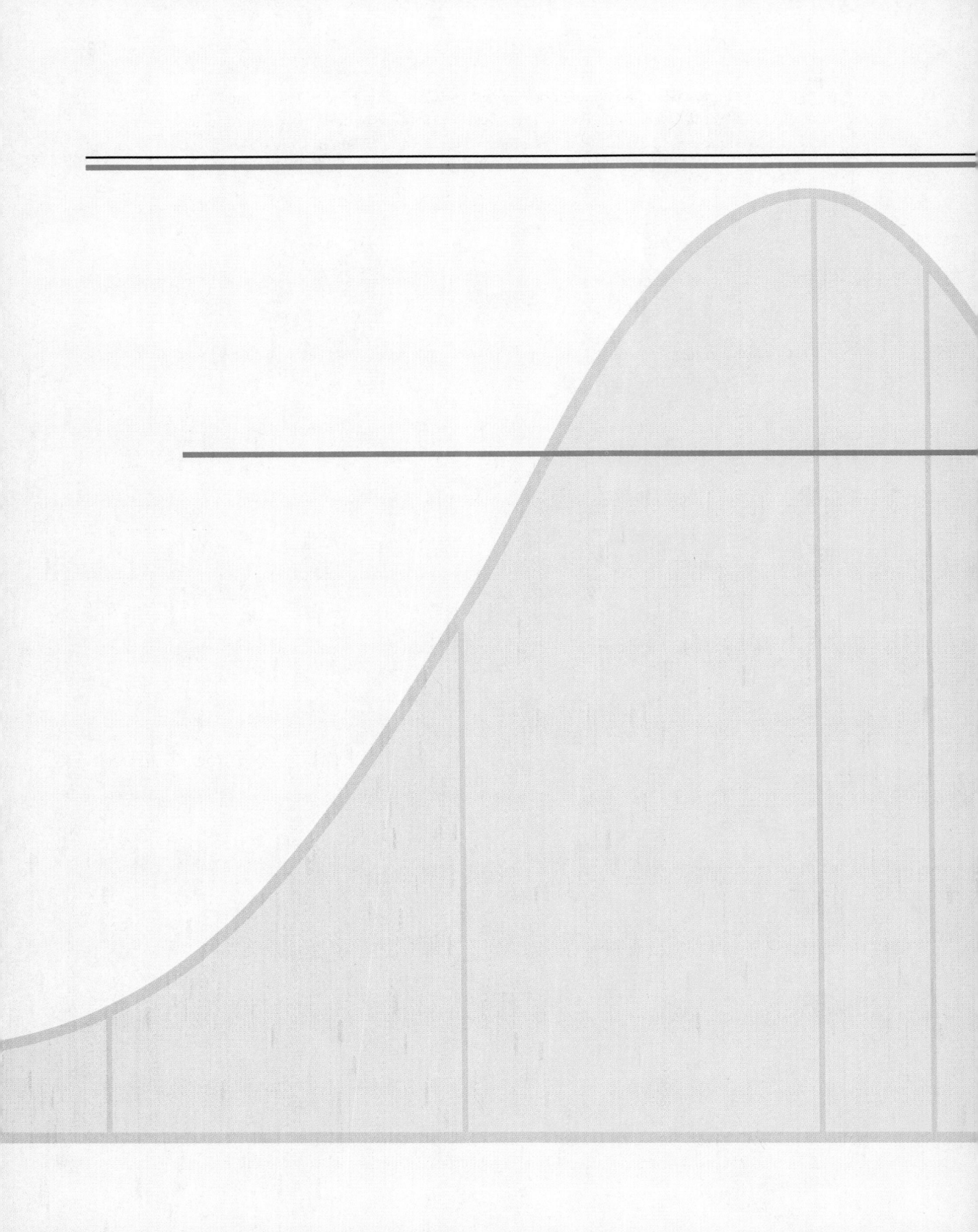

CHAPTER 3

MEASURES OF CENTRAL TENDENCY, DISPERSION, AND POSITION

3.1 INTRODUCTION

3.2 MEASURES OF CENTRAL TENDENCY

3.3 MEASURES OF DISPERSION

3.4 PERCENTILES, QUARTILES, AND THE INTERQUARTILE RANGE

3.5 BOXPLOTS

3.6 USING MINITAB (OPTIONAL)

3.7 WORKING WITH DATA (OPTIONAL)

3.8 SUMMARY

REVIEW EXERCISES

NOTES

3.1

INTRODUCTION

In this chapter, we continue our study of certain topics in descriptive statistics. We investigate ways of describing numerical data by giving certain properties of the data. Specifically, we discuss the concept of a **measure of central tendency.** A measure of central tendency for a collection of data values is a number that is meant to convey the idea of a center or a typical value for the data set. We study two measures of central tendency: the **mean** and the **median.** However, the one we will use most often in later chapters is the mean.

We also study **measures of dispersion,** which reflect the amount of spread or variability in a collection of data. Measures of dispersion include the **variance,** the

standard deviation, and the **interquartile range.** We also discuss **percentiles** and **quartiles.** These describe how a data value relates to the other data in a collection of data values. For example, if your score on a test was at the 99th percentile, this would be a **measure of position** because it means that 99% of the scores were lower than yours.

In this and subsequent chapters, we need a rule for rounding off decimal answers. In statistics, it is common to retain one or two more decimal places than were present in the original data. In this book, we favor retaining two more decimal places than were present in the original data. Only the final answer should be rounded; do not round off during intermediate steps. When we round off a number, our answer will be approximate; this is indicated by using the symbol $\doteq$, which means "is approximately equal to."

3.2

MEASURES OF CENTRAL TENDENCY

The Mean

Definition Given a collection of n data values, the *mean* of these data is simply the average of these data values. Therefore, the mean is the sum of the data values divided by n:

$$\text{mean} = \frac{\text{sum of the data values}}{n}$$

The collection of data we are working with may constitute a population or a sample from a population. We use the Greek letter μ to represent a population mean and the symbol $\bar{x}$ to represent a sample mean (if x represents an arbitrary data value from the sample). In many cases, we do not know enough about the population to find the value of μ exactly. In such cases, we can often estimate μ by the sample mean $\bar{x}$ for some appropriate sample from the population.

Many of the formulas involving the mean are equally valid whether we are talking about the mean μ of a population or the mean $\bar{x}$ of a sample. When this is the case, we represent the mean simply by writing the word *mean*.

EXAMPLE 3.1
The following sample data are the temperature readings (°F) at time of launch for the seven space shuttle flights that experienced O-ring damage prior to the space shuttle *Challenger*.* (The *Challenger* exploded due to O-ring failure on Jan. 28, 1986.)

$$53 \quad 57 \quad 58 \quad 63 \quad 70 \quad 70 \quad 75$$

Find the mean of these launch temperatures.

---

*For more details, see Exercise 2.37.

Solution
The number of data values is $n = 7$. Thus

$$\bar{x} = \frac{53 + 57 + 58 + 63 + 70 + 70 + 75}{7} = \frac{446}{7} \doteq 63.71°$$

(*Note:* You will be asked to compare this result with the mean launch temperature for those flights with *no* O-ring damage in Exercise 3.5.)

Remark A graphic interpretation of the mean is that it is the balancing point for the frequency distribution. That is, if equal weights are placed along the number axis, one for each data value, the number axis will balance when a fulcrum is placed at the mean. Figure 3.1(a) illustrates this idea for the data in Example 3.1.

The same is true for a histogram for a grouped frequency distribution: The histogram will balance at the mean. Figure 3.1(b) shows the histogram that was constructed in Example 2.5 for the data in Table 2.2. The mean for the data is 66.75, the balancing point for the histogram.

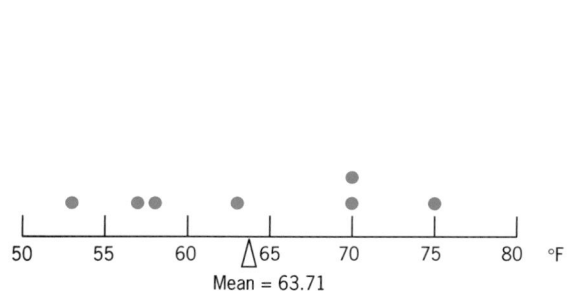

Mean = 63.71

Figure 3.1(a)
A Frequency Distribution Balances at the Mean. (Launch Temperatures for Flights with O-ring Damage)

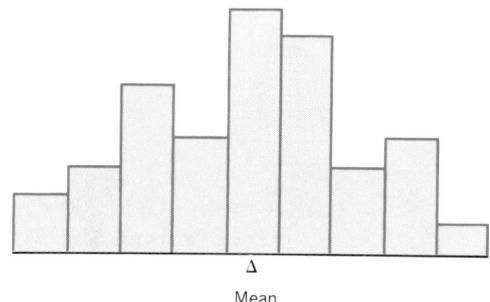

Mean

Figure 3.1(b)
A Histogram Balances at the Mean (66.75).

Summation Convention

We said that we can use a symbol such as x to represent any data value from some collection of data. We use the symbol $\sum x$ to represent the sum of these values. The Greek letter sigma, $\sum$, is used to represent summation of the values of whatever symbol follows. So $\sum x$ means sum the values of x.

For instance, consider the data values 5, 10, 6, 9, 4, 3, and 5. If we use the symbol x to represent any of these values, then

$$\sum x = 5 + 10 + 6 + 9 + 4 + 3 + 5 = 42$$

Suppose that we wish to sum the squares of these data values. We use the symbol $\sum x^2$ for this. Thus,

$$\sum x^2 = 5^2 + 10^2 + 6^2 + 9^2 + 4^2 + 3^2 + 5^2 = 292$$

Notice that $(\sum x)^2 = 42^2 = 1764$. So $(\sum x)^2$ is not the same as $\sum x^2$.

Using our summation convention, we can write the formula for the mean of a collection of n data values as

$$\text{mean} = \frac{\sum x}{n}$$

For the data values 5, 10, 6, 9, 4, 3, and 5, we have $n = 7$. Therefore

$$\text{mean} = \frac{\sum x}{n} = \frac{42}{7} = 6$$

With some data sets, there can be a problem with the mean if you try to use it as a typical value for the data set. For example, consider the following 11 salaries (in thousands of dollars):

$$46 \quad 44 \quad 43 \quad 38 \quad 45 \quad 42 \quad 45 \quad 44 \quad 46 \quad 44 \quad 135$$

The mean is

$$\bar{x} = \frac{\sum x}{n} = \frac{46 + 44 + 43 + 38 + 45 + 42 + 45 + 44 + 46 + 44 + 135}{11}$$

$$= \frac{572}{11} = 52$$

A mean of $52,000 hardly seems typical. After all, 10 of the 11 salaries are a good deal less than $52,000. The problem is caused by one salary—$135,000—that is considerably larger than the rest of the data. In other words, it is an **outlier.** The mean is quite sensitive to outliers. The presence of outliers can inflate (or deflate) the numerator in the formula for $\bar{x}$, resulting in an atypically large (or small) value for $\bar{x}$. The same thing happens if the data set is skewed. In general, the mean is sensitive to **extreme observations.** Extreme observations are data values that are substantially greater than or less than most of the other data values in a data set. Extreme observations might be outliers. But they need not be outliers; data values toward the long end of a skewed distribution are also extreme observations. Extreme observations can distort the mean so that it is not typical of the data set. Because of this sensitivity to extreme observations, we say the mean is not a **resistant measure.** It does not resist the effect of extreme observations. A measure of central tendency that *is* resistant is the median.

The Median

Definition   The *median* for a collection of data values is the number that is exactly in the middle position of the list when the data are ranked (i.e., arranged in increasing order). If we use the symbol x to represent an arbitrary data value in the collection, then the median is represented by the symbol $\tilde{x}$ (read "x tilde").

Assume that we have an odd number of data values. For example, consider the ranked list of five data values 5, 6, 9, 11, and 15. Clearly, the middle number is the third data value; that is, the location of the median is 3. The median itself is 9.

Now suppose that we have an even number of data values. For example, consider the ranked list of four data values 1, 4, 7, and 9. There is no middle data value. We will agree that the median in a case like this is the number that is halfway between the two data values closest to the middle. So the median here is the number that is halfway between the second and third data values in the ranked list. This is also the average of the second and third data values; that is, the median is

$$\frac{4+7}{2} = 5.5$$

In a case like this, we say that the location of the median is 2.5, since the median is the number halfway between the second and third data values (in the ranked list).

To find the location of the median in a ranked list of n data values, we can use the formula

$$\text{location of } \tilde{x}: \quad \frac{n+1}{2}$$

Notice that this formula works for both of the data sets we discussed. For the first set, $n = 5$; so the location of the median is $\frac{6}{2} = 3$. For the second set, $n = 4$; so the location is $\frac{5}{2} = 2.5$. When the location involves .5, as in 2.5, the median is halfway between the two data values nearest to the location. (When these two have the same value, this value is the median.) *Note:* Do not confuse the *location* of $\tilde{x}$ with the *value* of $\tilde{x}$.

EXAMPLE 3.2

Find the median for the following salaries (in thousands) that were just discussed:

46   44   43   38   45   42   45   44   46   44   135

Solution

First, rank the data:

38   42   43   44   44   44   45   45   46   46   135

The number of data values is $n = 11$. Thus

$$\text{location of } \tilde{x}: \quad \frac{n+1}{2} = \frac{11+1}{2} = 6$$

So $\tilde{x}$ is the sixth data value in the ranked list. Therefore,

$$\tilde{x} = 44$$

Compare this with the mean of 52 (thousand) for these data; 44 (thousand) seems much more typical of the data set.

EXAMPLE 3.3

Table 3.1 gives per-pupil expenditures (in hundreds of dollars) for 1992 in the 10 western suburbs of Boston within Route 128.

Table 3.1

Town	Per-Pupil Spending (in hundreds of dollars)
Arlington	59
Belmont	56
Brookline	67
Cambridge	86
Dedham	58
Lexington	65
Newton	63
Somerville	59
Waltham	61
Watertown	64

Source: *The Boston Globe,* June 6, 1993.

```
5 |
5 | 6  8  9  9
6 | 1  3  4
6 | 5  7
7 |
7 |
8 |
8 | 6
```

Figure 3.2
Ordered Stem-and-Leaf Plot
for Per-Pupil Expenditures

(a)   Construct a stem-and-leaf plot. This should support your suspicion that the Cambridge expenditure is an outlier.

(b)   Find the median.

Solution

(a)   The first digit will be the stem and the second digit will be the leaf. Since there are only four stems, we will split each stem, putting leaves 0 to 4 on one stem and 5 to 9 on the other. The stem-and-leaf plot is in Figure 3.2. Notice that it is ordered; that is, the leaves are arranged in increasing order. This results in a ranking of the whole data set, making it easy to find the median from the stem-and-leaf plot.

(b)   The stem-and-leaf plot in Figure 3.2 suggests that the Cambridge expenditure of $8600 is an outlier. The per-pupil expenditures in the other towns are between $5600 and $6700. The number of data values is $n = 10$. So

$$\text{location of } \tilde{x}: \quad \frac{n + 1}{2} = \frac{10 + 1}{2} = 5.5$$

Thus the median is halfway between the fifth and sixth data values. Reading down from the top of the stem-and-leaf plot, the fifth value is 61 and the sixth is 63. So

$$\tilde{x} = 62$$

In the previous examples, the median was not influenced by the size of the extreme observations. In Example 3.2, the median would have been the same if 135 were replaced by 135,000 or 135,000,000. The median is a **resistant measure of central tendency.**

> **Definition** A measure that is not influenced by extreme observations is called a *resistant measure*.

If a data set contains outliers, or if it is skewed, the median will usually be a better measure of central tendency than the mean. That is, the median will be more typical or representative of the data. A graph, such as a stem-and-leaf plot, can be used to determine whether outliers or skewness indicate that the median should be used instead of the mean.

However, such generalizations are risky. You should not *automatically* compute the median just because an outlier is present. Investigate the data. Perhaps the outlier is a mistake. For example, in recording the weights of laboratory rats, someone types 112 pounds instead of 1.12 pounds. In this case, try to correct the value. If an outlier cannot be corrected but you are reasonably sure it is wrong, delete it. Also, sometimes the mean is a better measure even if the data are skewed or outliers are present. A company that keeps a daily record of sales is more interested in the mean than the median. If we know that a company's mean sales is $1000 per day, then in 30 days the company's total sales are $30,000. From the mean, we can compute the total. We cannot do so with the median.

You should not abandon the mean unnecessarily. The mean has certain advantages over the median. There is a formula for the mean. There is no formula for the median, only for the location of the median. Also, the mean uses all the information contained in the data, which is usually desirable. The median depends only on the value in the middle position in a ranked list of the data. The other data values affect the median only insofar as they are used to determine which value is in the middle position.

Figure 3.3 shows the relationship between the mean and the median for three distributions (as described by smoothed-out frequency polygons). Note how

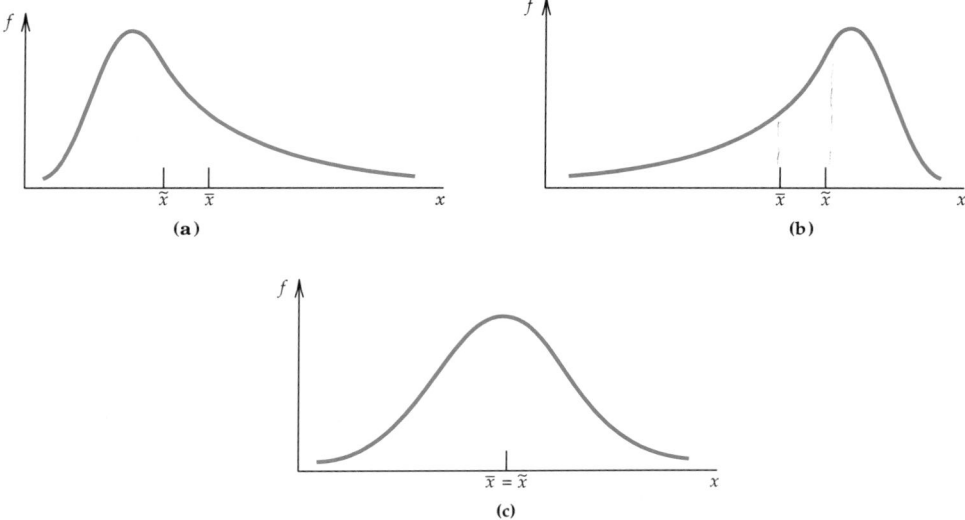

Figure 3.3
Relationships Between the Mean and the Median: (a) Skewed to the Right; (b) Skewed to the Left; (c) Symmetric

the mean is pulled away from the median toward the long tail of the skewed distributions. Outliers have a similar effect.

A much less commonly used measure of central tendency is the mode, which is discussed in Exercise 3.18.

EXERCISES

In Exercises 3.1–3.4, find (a) the mean, (b) the location of the median, and (c) the median.

3.1 The following list gives the numbers of copies of a book sold by a bookstore over a 6-day period:

$$7 \quad 12 \quad 6 \quad 12 \quad 2 \quad 9$$

3.2 The diastolic blood pressure readings of 12 randomly selected males aged 45–49 from the Framingham Heart Study were

$$94 \quad 84 \quad 74 \quad 90 \quad 98 \quad 92 \quad 74 \quad 90 \quad 80 \quad 98 \quad 78 \quad 80$$

3.3 The numbers of traffic tickets issued by a police department over a 7-day period were

$$19 \quad 17 \quad 14 \quad 21 \quad 19 \quad 16 \quad 20$$

3.4 The weights (in pounds) of nine newborn babies at a local hospital were recorded as

$$7.4 \quad 7.6 \quad 9.4 \quad 7.6 \quad 6.4 \quad 7.6 \quad 8.3 \quad 8.5 \quad 7.1$$

3.5 In Exercise 2.37, we discussed O-ring damage and temperature at time of launch of the 23 space shuttle flights that preceded the ill-fated *Challenger* which exploded due to O-ring failure. The data are reproduced below.

Launch Temperatures (°F)

Flights with O-ring Damage	53	57	58	63	70	70	75									
Flights with No O-ring Damage	66	67	67	67	68	69	70	70	72	73	75	76	76	78	79	81

(a) The mean launch temperature for the flights with O-ring damage was found in Example 3.1 to be 63.71°. Now compute the mean launch temperature for the flights without O-ring damage and compare the two means.

(b) Find the median launch temperatures for each data set and compare them.

Note that it does not much matter which measure of central tendency is used. In either case, the typical launch temperature for flights with O-ring damage was substantially less than for flights without O-ring damage. In Exercise 4.15 you will show that the chance of O-ring damage at 53° (the lowest launch temperature prior to the *Challenger*) is about 92%. As noted in Chapter 2, the temperature at the launch of the *Challenger* was 31°.

3.6 The following data are test scores for an introductory economics class given in the evening. The data are

$$60 \quad 42 \quad 61 \quad 70 \quad 59 \quad 65 \quad 68 \quad 67$$
$$78 \quad 68 \quad 67 \quad 74 \quad 61 \quad 74 \quad 61 \quad 71$$

(a) Split the stems 4, 5, 6, and 7 into two parts with leaves 0–4 on one part and 5–9 on the other. Construct an ordered stem-and-leaf plot. (*Note:* You may have done this in Exercise 2.33.) Confirm that 42 is an outlier. (Data provided by Walter Block, Holy Cross College.)

(b) **(i)** Find the mean.
   (ii) Find the median.

Which do you prefer as a measure of central tendency?

3.7 The following data are the test scores in Exercise 3.6 with the outlier 42 removed.

$$60 \quad 61 \quad 70 \quad 59 \quad 65 \quad 68 \quad 67 \quad 78$$
$$68 \quad 67 \quad 74 \quad 61 \quad 74 \quad 61 \quad 71$$

(a) Construct an ordered stem-and-leaf plot. Split the stems 5, 6, and 7 into two parts with leaves 0–4 on one part and 5–9 on the other.

(b) **(i)** Find the mean.
   (ii) Find the median.

Which do you prefer as a measure of central tendency?

3.8 The following data are profits over the past 30 years in a small business (in thousands of dollars).

$$15 \quad 17 \quad 18 \quad 19 \quad 20 \quad 20 \quad 20 \quad 21 \quad 23 \quad 23 \quad 24 \quad 24 \quad 24 \quad 24 \quad 24$$
$$25 \quad 25 \quad 25 \quad 25 \quad 25 \quad 26 \quad 26 \quad 27 \quad 27 \quad 28 \quad 29 \quad 30 \quad 30 \quad 31 \quad 32$$

(a) Construct a stem-and-leaf plot. Split the stems 1, 2, and 3 into five parts with leaves 0–1, 2–3, 4–5, 6–7, and 8–9. (*Note:* You may have done this in Exercise 2.57.)

(b) **(i)** Find the mean.
   (ii) Find the median.

Which do you prefer as a measure of central tendency?

3.9 The accompanying data values are the numbers of cars passing through an intersection between noon and 12:10 P.M. over a 10-day period.

$$21 \quad 17 \quad 20 \quad 34 \quad 18 \quad 15 \quad 22 \quad 38 \quad 21 \quad 19$$

(a) Construct an ordered stem-and-leaf plot. Split the stems 1, 2, and 3 into two parts with leaves 0–4 on one part and 5–9 on the other.

(b) **(i)** Find the mean.
   (ii) Find the median.

Which do you prefer as a measure of central tendency?

3.10 In Table 2.7, we considered the number of hours per week 20 adults watch television. The data are

$$16 \quad 23 \quad 19 \quad 31 \quad 28 \quad 4 \quad 11 \quad 21 \quad 17 \quad 13$$
$$29 \quad 7 \quad 3 \quad 18 \quad 21 \quad 28 \quad 12 \quad 3 \quad 24 \quad 27$$

(a) Find the mean.

(b) Find the median.

(c) Which do you prefer as a measure of central tendency?

3.11 The following data are observations of time in days from remission induction to relapse for 51 patients with acute nonlymphoblastic leukemia (see Exercise 2.55):

24	46	57	57	64	65	82	89	90	90	111
117	128	143	148	152	166	171	186	191	197	
209	223	230	247	249	254	258	264	269	270	
273	284	294	304	304	332	341	393	395	487	
510	516	518	518	534	608	642	697	955	1160	

(a)   Find the mean. (*Note:* The sum of the data values is 14,912.)

(b)   Find the median.

(c)   Which do you prefer as a measure of central tendency?

3.12   A statistics student claimed that the median of the data values 9, 8, 12, 4, and 6 must be 12. The student reasoned that the location of the median is 3 and the third value in the list is 12. Is there anything wrong with the student's reasoning?

3.13   The median family income in current dollars in the United States for 1992 was reported to be $35,776. Interpret this statement (*Source:* *The 1994 Information Please Almanac,* 1994, p. 48).

3.14   The following data are the percentages of annual salary typically awarded employees who are fired or laid off. Figures are the percentages of total annual salary plus bonuses, if any, typically paid to anyone whose employment is involuntarily terminated for reasons other than misconduct (*Source:* *U.S. News & World Report,* Dec. 19, 1988, p. 70).

Country	Manufacturing Workers	Chief Executives
Japan	102	261
The Netherlands	25	228
Germany	100	200
Spain	183	185
Britain	22	156
Italy	46	154
Korea	125	125
Canada	23	115
Mexico	110	146
France	54	83
United States	29	79
Sweden	42	42
Brazil	19	27
Argentina	24	131
Hong Kong	18	77

(a)   Find the median percentage for manufacturing workers. Would your answer change if the five largest percentages were increased by 25 percentage points?

(b)   Find the median percentage for chief executives. Would your answer change if the five smallest percentages were decreased by 25 percentage points?

3.15   For data values 2, 5, 2, 6, 0, calculate each of the following:

(a) $\sum x$ (b) $\sum(x - \bar{x})$ (c) $\sum(x - \bar{x})^2$

(d) $\sum x^2$ (e) $(\sum x)^2$

(f) $\sum 7x$ [Compare your answer with $7\sum x$.]

Note: The answers for parts (d) and (e) are not the same.

3.16   Answer each of the following either True or False.

(a)   For a symmetric distribution, the mean and the median have the same value.

(b)   For a distribution that is skewed to the left, the value of the median is smaller than the value of the mean.

(c)   The value of the mean for a finite collection of data values is necessarily one of the data values.

(d)   The value of the median for a finite collection of data values is necessarily one of the data values.

3.17   The dot diagram represents the distribution of 25 data values.

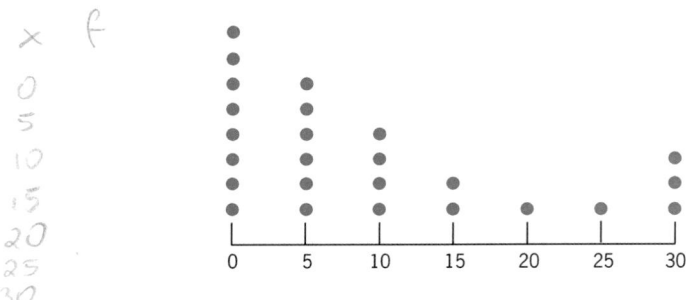

(a)   Without calculating, which is larger, the mean or median value?

(b)   Which measure would better summarize the data in terms of a typical value?

(c)   Calculate the mean and median.

3.18   Another measure of central tendency is the *mode*. The mode for a collection of data values is the data value that occurs most frequently (if there is one). Find the mode (if it exists) for each of the following data sets:

(a)   3 2 4 5 1 2 3 3 4 2 5 3 3 0 1 0 2 3 2 3

(b)   4 2 0 1 0 0 3 5 5 0

(c)   2 4 6 8 8 0 6 5 3 1

3.3

MEASURES OF DISPERSION

In Section 3.2, we studied the notion of a measure of central tendency, but measures of central tendency may not be completely adequate in describing certain properties of data. For example, consider the following two collections of data: 99, 100, 100, 101; and 50, 100, 100, 150. Both have the same mean and median (namely, 100), and yet the second set of data values possesses much more spread or variability than the first. Apparently, a measure of central tendency is incapable of detecting differences in the spread or variability in a collection of data values.

Yet it may be of great importance to know how much variability there is. For instance, a manufacturer of steel girders advertises the strength of the girders as being 10,000 pounds per square inch on the average. Consider the collection of data values, which consists of the actual strengths of the various girders to be used in the construction of a bridge. This manufacturer would want the variability of these data values from the mean of 10,000 pounds to be at a minimum.

In contrast, if an educator develops an examination to be used by a college to screen applicants for admission, it would be desirable for the scores on this exam to have as much variability as possible so that the college could more easily distinguish between applicants.

For these reasons, statisticians have developed ways of measuring variability—measures of dispersion. The measure of dispersion that is perhaps the simplest and easiest to calculate is the **range.**

Definition The *range R* for a collection of data values is the difference between the highest (H) and lowest (L) data values.

$$R = H - L$$

EXAMPLE 3.4
The following is a list of the number of books the 10 students in a history class read while doing research for a term paper: 6, 11, 5, 1, 6, 6, 7, 5, 7, 6. Find the range of the data.

Solution
For these data, $L = 1$ and $H = 11$. Thus

$$R = H - L$$
$$= 11 - 1 = 10$$

The range is a rather rough measure of dispersion: It depends only on the highest and lowest data values and ignores the ones in between. Hence it may not give us all the information we need about the variability of all the data values. To get a better understanding of this, we construct a dot diagram for the data in Example 3.4 [Figure 3.4(a)]. Now compare this with a dot diagram for the following data: 10, 3, 9, 2, 2, 11, 2, 1, 9, 11 [Figure 3.4(b)]. These data represent the number of books read by 10 students in a sociology class preparing for a term paper.

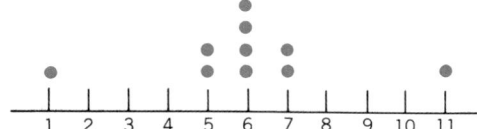
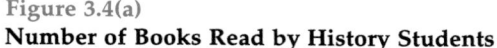
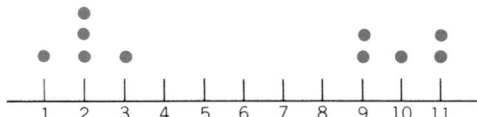

Figure 3.4(a)
Number of Books Read by History Students

Figure 3.4(b)
Number of Books Read by Sociology Students

Both sets of data have the same range (10) and the same mean (6), but somehow there appears to be less variability among the data in Figure 3.4(a). This is because more of the data values appear to cluster near the middle (in fact, the mean 6), whereas there are fewer near the extreme values of 1 and 11. Apparently, the range is incapable of detecting these differences in the two sets of data. We would like to have a measure of dispersion that is more sensitive to such differences. More precisely, we would like to have a measure of dispersion that would somehow indicate that there is less variability for the data of Figure 3.4(a) than the data of Figure 3.4(b). We discuss such a measure next.

We will find it convenient to measure variability in a collection by examining the degree to which the data values cluster about (or deviate from) their mean. For simplicity, we consider the following data: 1, 5, and 6. The mean of these data values is 4. To study variability from the mean, perhaps we should find the difference between each data value and the mean, and then average these differences. These differences, called **deviations,** are

$$1 - 4 = -3$$
$$5 - 4 = 1$$
$$6 - 4 = 2$$

The average of these deviations is

$$\frac{-3 + 1 + 2}{3} = 0$$

It turns out that no matter what data values we use, the average of the differences between the data values and their mean is always 0. Therefore, such an average will not be a satisfactory measure of dispersion. The average of these deviations is 0 because their sum is 0—the negative values cancel the positive values. We can get around this difficulty by squaring the deviations. This eliminates the negative signs.* The squares of the deviations are

$$(1 - 4)^2 = (-3)^2 = 9$$
$$(5 - 4)^2 = 1^2 = 1$$
$$(6 - 4)^2 = 2^2 = 4$$

The average of these is

$$\frac{9 + 1 + 4}{3} = \frac{14}{3} \doteq 4.67$$

Note that to calculate this, we added each value of $(x - \text{mean})^2$ and divided by the number of data values. Using the summation convention, we can write this average symbolically as

$$\frac{\sum (x - \text{mean})^2}{n}$$

(where n is the number of data values).

Although averaging squares of numbers may not be a familiar part of our experience, this average does lead to a valid measure of dispersion in the following sense: If we have two collections of data, the one for which this average is larger is the one whose values tend to deviate more from their mean.

The reader might get the feeling that the above average would be a satisfactory measure of dispersion for either a population or a sample. However, most statisticians prefer to use it only for a population. (They prefer to use a slightly different expression for samples, which we will discuss shortly.) When the collection of data values we are dealing with is a population and not a sample, we often use N to represent the number of data values rather than n. We are now in a position to define the term **population variance.**

---

*If we used the absolute value of each deviation, this would also eliminate the negative signs. But it turns out that for technical reasons, it is mathematically more convenient to use the squares of the deviations.

> **Definition**   Given a population of N data values, we define the *population variance*, represented by the symbol σ^2 (where σ is the Greek lowercase sigma), as
>
> $$\sigma^2 = \frac{\sum (x - \mu)^2}{N}$$
>
> where μ is the population mean $\sum x / N$.

EXAMPLE 3.5

In Example 3.4, we discussed the number of books read by each student preparing for a term paper in a history class of 10 students: 6, 11, 5, 1, 6, 6, 7, 5, 7, 6. Viewing this collection of data values as a population, find the population variance, σ^2.

Solution

First, find the population mean, μ. Now $N = 10$ so

$$\mu = \frac{\sum x}{N}$$

$$= \frac{6 + 11 + 5 + 1 + 6 + 6 + 7 + 5 + 7 + 6}{10} = \frac{60}{10} = 6$$

Some find it convenient to use a table such as Table 3.2 to calculate variance.

Table 3.2

x	$x - \mu$	$(x - \mu)^2$
6	0	0
11	5	25
5	−1	1
1	−5	25
6	0	0
6	0	0
7	1	1
5	−1	1
7	1	1
6	0	0
		Sum = $\overline{54}$
		↑
		$\sum (x - \mu)^2$

Hence

$$\sigma^2 = \frac{\sum (x - \mu)^2}{N}$$

$$= \frac{54}{10} = 5.4$$

If you were to calculate the population variance for the number of books read by the sociology class in Figure 3.4(b), you would find it to be 16.6. Comparing this with the variance of 5.4 for the history class confirms our feeling that the sociology class shows more variability.

Many results in statistics involve the square root of the variance. We call the square root of the population variance the **population standard deviation.** Some statisticians like to think of standard deviation as a sort of typical distance from the mean for the data values. The units of standard deviation will be the same as the units of the data set.

Definition   Given a population of N data values, we define the *population standard deviation* as the square root of the population variance, $\sqrt{\sigma^2} = \sigma$. Therefore,

$$\sigma = \sqrt{\frac{\sum(x - \mu)^2}{N}}$$

For example, for the population of Example 3.5, the population standard deviation is $\sigma = \sqrt{5.4} \doteq 2.32$.

Variance and Standard Deviation for a Sample

In practice, the populations we study are usually enormous, and we rarely know enough about them to find σ^2 exactly. What we usually do is obtain a sample from the population and then try to estimate σ^2 using information from the sample. Suppose that there are n data values in a sample obtained from our population of interest. Our first impulse might be to try to estimate σ^2 as follows: Assuming that we do not know μ, we can estimate μ by $\bar{x}$, and then estimate σ^2 by

$$\frac{\sum(x - \bar{x})^2}{n}$$

This does provide an estimate for σ^2 and, in fact, is used as such by some statisticians. However, it can be shown (using more advanced techniques than we have at our disposal) that this expression tends to underestimate σ^2, on the average. Replacing the n in the denominator of this expression by $n - 1$ gives us a slightly larger ratio. The resulting expression provides an estimate for σ^2 that many statisticians think is more desirable. With this in mind, we give the following definitions.

Definitions   Assume that we have a sample of n data values from some population. We define the *sample variance*, s^2, by the equation

$$s^2 = \frac{\sum(x - \bar{x})^2}{n - 1}$$

The square root of the sample variance is the *sample standard deviation, s:*

$$s = \sqrt{\frac{\sum(x - \bar{x})^2}{n - 1}}$$

In the future, when it is impossible or impractical to calculate the exact value of σ^2 for a population, we can think of s^2 for some appropriate sample from the population as an estimate for σ^2. Of course, s^2 may also be viewed as a measure of variability of the data values in the sample from their mean $\bar{x}$.

EXAMPLE 3.6

Find the sample variance and sample standard deviation for the following data, which represent the numbers of fire alarms answered by Boston Engine Company 10 over a 5-day period: 4, 3, 7, 4, 2.

Solution

The sample mean is

$$\bar{x} = \frac{4 + 3 + 7 + 4 + 2}{5} = \frac{20}{5} = 4$$

Table 3.3 is helpful in calculating the variance.

Table 3.3

x	$x - \bar{x}$	$(x - \bar{x})^2$
4	0	0
3	−1	1
7	3	9
4	0	0
2	−2	4
	Sum =	14

$$\uparrow$$
$$\sum (x - \bar{x})^2$$

$$s^2 = \frac{\sum (x - \bar{x})^2}{n - 1} = \frac{14}{4} = 3.5$$

$$s = \sqrt{3.5} \doteq 1.87$$

Alternative Formulas for Finding Variance

There is a way of computing variance that is often more convenient, because it does not require finding the mean first. Even if the mean is known, this method can result in less error due to round off when the original data are whole numbers and the mean involves a decimal. This method consists of using the following formulas to find σ^2 and s^2; these formulas are equivalent to the original formulas given for σ^2 and s^2. That is, they will give the same result.

Alternative Formulas for Computing Variance
For a population of N data values

$$\sigma^2 = \frac{N(\sum x^2) - (\sum x)^2}{N^2}$$

For a sample of n data values

$$s^2 = \frac{n(\sum x^2) - (\sum x)^2}{n(n-1)}$$

You will usually find that **these formulas are more convenient than the original formulas unless the mean is a known whole number.** For example, consider the sample data 1, 3, and 4. The sample mean is

$$\bar{x} = \frac{\sum x}{n} = \frac{1 + 3 + 4}{3} = \frac{8}{3} \doteq 2.67$$

To find s^2 using the original formula would be slightly unpleasant. But refer to Table 3.4 and observe how the alternative formula avoids working with such decimals:

Table 3.4

x	x^2
1	1
3	9
4	16
Sums: 8	26
↑	↑
$\sum x$	$\sum x^2$

$$s^2 = \frac{n(\sum x^2) - (\sum x)^2}{n(n-1)} = \frac{3(26) - 8^2}{(3)(2)}$$

$$= \frac{78 - 64}{6} = \frac{14}{6} \doteq 2.33$$

EXAMPLE 3.7

The actual voltages of 6-volt batteries will vary somewhat, but a battery manufacturer wanted to keep this variability to a minimum. A quality control procedure was put in place whereby, periodically, a sample of six batteries were measured for voltage. If the standard deviation exceeds .3 volt, the production process is checked. The following voltage readings were obtained:

$$6.1 \quad 5.7 \quad 5.8 \quad 6.0 \quad 5.8 \quad 6.3$$

Using the alternative formula, find the sample variance and the sample standard deviation.

Solution

See Table 3.5.

Table 3.5

x	x^2
6.1	37.21
5.7	32.49
5.8	33.64
6.0	36.00
5.8	33.64
6.3	39.69
Sums: 35.7	212.67

Therefore, $\sum x = 35.7$ and $\sum x^2 = 212.67$. Thus

$$s^2 = \frac{n(\sum x^2) - (\sum x)^2}{n(n-1)} = \frac{6(212.67) - (35.7)^2}{(6)(5)}$$

$$= \frac{1276.02 - 1274.49}{30} = \frac{1.53}{30} = .051$$

$$s = \sqrt{.051} \doteq .226$$

Since $s < .3$, the process was judged to be in control.

Measures of Dispersion and Resistance

None of the measures of dispersion discussed so far is resistant. They are strongly influenced by extreme observations. The most commonly used measure of spread, the standard deviation, is even more sensitive to extreme observations than the mean. For example, if x is much larger than most of the other data values, then $x - \bar{x}$ will be similarly inflated relative to other values of $x - \bar{x}$. Squaring $x - \bar{x}$ will compound the problem.

If you do not use $\bar{x}$ as a measure of central tendency for a data set, you probably should not use the standard deviation (or variance) as a measure of variability. In the next section, we discuss a resistant measure of variability, the **interquartile range.** The interquartile range is sometimes used to describe variability when the median is used as a measure of central tendency.

EXERCISES

In Exercises 3.19–3.23, find the (a) range, (b) sample variance, and (c) sample standard deviation.

3.19   A public library employee in a small town reported the numbers of books signed out each day over a 10-day period as

$$18 \quad 14 \quad 12 \quad 16 \quad 23 \quad 14 \quad 17 \quad 16 \quad 20 \quad 10$$

3.20   A grocery store owner recorded the numbers of cases of a soft drink sold each month over a 6-month period. The numbers recorded were

$$24 \quad 16 \quad 27 \quad 34 \quad 36 \quad 25$$

3.21 The following data represent systolic blood pressures of randomly selected females aged 30–34 from the Framingham Heart Study:

138   124   116   128   140   136

3.22 A high school guidance counselor sampled 10 college-bound seniors and recorded their mathematics SAT scores. They were

623   504   519   473   629   705   513   510   630   594

3.23 The numbers of absentees at a large plant over a 10-day period were

30   17   18   18   29   22   14   10   8   23

3.24 Which of the following measures of dispersion use all data values in its calculation? Assume that there are more than two distinct data values.

(a)   The range   (b)   The standard deviation

3.25 For the data set 5, 5, 5, 5, 5, 5, compute the sample standard deviation. Does your answer reflect the fact that there is no spread in the data?

3.26 Consider these two data sets:

(i)   1 2 3 7 8 12 13 14   (ii)   1 7 7 7 8   8   8 14

(a)   Construct a dot diagram for each set. Locate the mean of each data set.

(b)   Which of the two sets appears to have less spread about the mean?

(c)   Compute the sample standard deviations for both sets. Do these values agree with your conclusion in part (b)?

3.27 Suppose that you are undecided between two cans of tennis balls (three balls per can) to use in a match. Upon testing, you find that both cans of balls bounce the same height on the average. How do you choose which can of balls to use? (*Hint:* Is the average bounce your only consideration?)

3.28 A trucking firm wished to compare the shipping time (in hours) for two routes (A and B). The firm believed that the average shipping time for the two routes would be about the same, but they hoped to increase reliability by choosing the route with smaller variability. The 15 shipping times for each route were as follows:

A   51 50 55 50 49 52 53 52 51 52 52 54 50 51 48
B   45 52 59 54 51 53 55 55 51 55 50 50 52 52 44

(a)   Construct a side-by-side stem-and-leaf plot. Split stem 4 into three parts with leaves 4–5, 6–7, 8–9 and split stem 5 into five parts with leaves 0–1, 2–3, 4–5, 6–7, and 8–9. Which of the two routes appears to have the smaller variability?

(b)   Find the sample standard deviation for both routes.

3.29 The following data give average temperatures per month over a 12-month period for Bismarck, North Dakota, and San Diego, California:

Bismarck   8   14   25   43   54   64   71   69   58   47   29   16
San Diego   56   60   58   62   63   68   69   71   69   67   61   58

(a)   Which of the two cities do you suspect is warmer on average? Which has more temperature variability?

(b)   Construct a side-by-side stem-and-leaf plot. Use stems 0–7. Does the plot confirm your suspicions in part (a)?

(c) Use the following information to compute the mean and standard deviation for both cities. Do the calculations confirm your suspicions in part (a)?

Bismarck	$\sum x = 498$	$\sum x^2 = 26{,}218$
San Diego	$\sum x = 762$	$\sum x^2 = 48{,}674$

3.30 The ordered side-by-side stem-and-leaf plot shown here represents verbal and math SAT scores, respectively, of 25 randomly selected students from a northeastern university. Notice, for example, that stem 6 and leaf 2 can be any score between 620 and 629 inclusive.

Verbal		Math
9	4	
	5	0
23	5	
5	5	5
6677	5	77
88899	5	8
001	6	01111
23	6	223
45	6	55
6666	6	67
	6	
1	7	0011
	7	223
	7	4

(a) Which set of scores appears to have a larger mean? Which set is more variable?

(b) Use the following information to compute the mean and standard deviation for both data sets. Do the calculations confirm your suspicions in part (a)?

Verbal SAT	$\sum x = 15{,}083$	$\sum x^2 = 9{,}166{,}759$
Math SAT	$\sum x = 16{,}158$	$\sum x^2 = 10{,}539{,}379$

3.31 Find the *population* variance σ^2 for the following data sets.

(a) 14 14 14 14 0 0 0 0

(b) 1 2 3 4 5 6 7   **(c)** 5 4 4 6 0 1

3.32 For a fairly large sample from a normal population, we expect approximately 68% of the observations to be between $\bar{x} - s$ and $\bar{x} + s$, 95% between $\bar{x} - 2s$ and $\bar{x} + 2s$, and 99.7% between $\bar{x} - 3s$ and $\bar{x} + 3s$. This is known as the Empirical Rule. The mean and standard deviation of a sample of 50 data values are 73.38 and 4.54, respectively. The data and frequency histogram follow. Find the percentage of data values within 1, 2, and 3 standard deviations of the mean. Compare with the Empirical Rule.

$73.38 \pm 3(4.54)$

$(59.76, 87)$

$\approx 100\%$

63	65	66	66	67
67	70	70	70	70
70	71	71	71	71
71	71	72	72	72
72	72	72	72	72
72	73	73	74	74
75	75	75	75	75
76	76	77	77	77
78	78	78	78	79
80	80	81	83	84

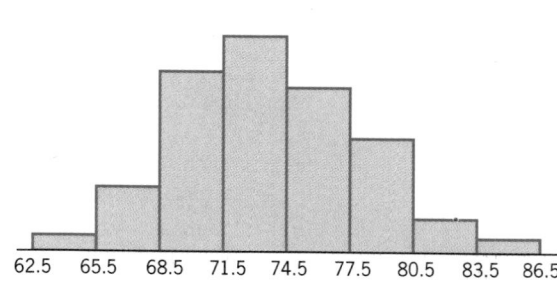

3.4

PERCENTILES, QUARTILES, AND THE INTERQUARTILE RANGE

Suppose you are told that you received a raw score of 733 on a standard test. This does not give you much of an idea of how well you did. But if you are told that relative to the other scores on the test, your score was the 99th percentile, then this means that 99% of the people taking the test had scores that were between the lowest score and your score, whereas 1% of the people had scores between your score and the highest score. This gives you a better idea of how well you did. In general, the **mth percentile** is the number that separates the bottom m% of the data from the top $(100 - m)$% of the data. It is denoted by the symbol P_m. (We have already discussed a percentile in Section 3.2—the median is the 50th percentile.)

To find percentiles, we first rank the data; that is, we list the data values in ascending order. For example, Table 3.6 contains the ranked scores of 40 high school seniors on a scientific achievement test. (These were discussed in Chapter 2.)

Table 3.6
Scores on a Scientific Achievement Test

46	58	65	70	76
49	59	66	71	78
50	59	66	71	79
53	60	66	72	80
54	62	66	73	82
55	63	68	73	83
55	64	68	73	84
57	65	69	74	88

Suppose that we want to find the 80th percentile, P_{80}. We first find the location of P_{80} in the ranked list. Since about 80% of the data values will be less than P_{80}, the location of P_{80} should be about 80% of the way down the ranked list of data. There are $n = 40$ data values and 80% of 40 is $(.80)(40) = 32$. Notice that 32 is a whole number. In this case, we will agree that the location of P_{80} is 32.5. This means that P_{80} is halfway between the 32nd and 33rd data values. In other words, it is the average of the 32nd and 33rd data values (74 and 76). So $P_{80} = 75$.

Now suppose that we want to find the 83rd percentile, P_{83}. Eighty-three percent of 40 is $(.83)(40) = 33.2$. When we get a decimal, we agree that the location is the next higher whole number. So the location of P_{83} is 34. From Table 3.6, we see that the 34th data value is 78. So $P_{83} = 78$.

Procedure for Finding Percentiles To find the mth percentile, P_m, we first find its location in the ranked list of n data values. Evaluate $(m/100)n$.

(a) If $(m/100)n$ is a whole number, then

$$\text{location of } P_m \text{ is } \left(\frac{m}{100}\right)n + .5$$

So P_m is halfway between the data value in position $(m/100)n$ and the data value in the next position; that is, it is the average of these two data values.

(b) If $(m/100)n$ is not a whole number, then

location of P_m is next higher whole number

The percentile P_m is the data value in this location.

EXAMPLE 3.8

For the data in Table 3.6, find the following:

(a) P_{10}

(b) P_{66}

Solution

(a) In this case, $m = 10$. Now

$$\left(\frac{m}{100}\right)n = \left(\frac{10}{100}\right)(40) = (.10)(40) = 4$$

Thus

location of P_{10}: $4 + .5 = 4.5$

This means that P_{10} is the average of the fourth and fifth data values. Therefore, from Table 3.6, $P_{10} = 53.5$.

(b) In this case, $m = 66$ and

$$\left(\frac{m}{100}\right)n = \left(\frac{66}{100}\right)(40) = (.66)(40) = 26.4$$

Thus

location of P_{66} is 27

Since the 27th data value in Table 3.6 is 71, $P_{66} = 71$. *Note:* Do not confuse the location of a percentile with the value of the percentile itself.

Closely related to the idea of percentile is the **percentile rank** of a data value. We previously discussed a standard test for which the score 733 was the 99th percentile. We then say that 99 is the percentile rank of the score 733.

Definition   If a data value x is the mth percentile, that is, if $x = P_m$, then we say that m is the *percentile rank* of x.

We can find the approximate percentile rank of a data value as follows: Look at the data value 62 in Table 3.6. There are 12 out of 40 data values that precede 62 in the ranked list. Since

$$\frac{12}{40} = .30$$

then 30% of the scores are less than 62. So the percentile rank of 62 is 30.

Formula for Percentile Rank of a Data Value x The percentile rank m is (approximately)

$$m = \left(\frac{\text{number of data values less than } x}{\text{total number of data values}} \right) \cdot 100$$

EXAMPLE 3.9
Find the percentile rank of the data value 58 in Table 3.6.

Solution
There are eight data values less than 58 in the list of 40 data values. So the percentile rank is

$$m = \left(\frac{8}{40} \right) \cdot 100 = 20$$

We often see the term **quartile** in statistics. Quartiles are defined as follows.

Definitions The *first quartile* Q_1, the *second quartile* Q_2, and the *third quartile* Q_3 are defined as

$$Q_1 = P_{25} \qquad Q_2 = P_{50} \qquad Q_3 = P_{75}$$

The quartiles divide the data into quarters. Also note that the second quartile is the 50th percentile, which is also the median.

EXAMPLE 3.10
Find the quartiles for the data in Table 3.6.

Solution
According to our definitions, we must find the percentiles P_{25}, P_{50}, and P_{75}.

(a) Find P_{25}. Now $(.25)(40) = 10$. Thus

$$\text{location of } P_{25} \text{ is } 10.5$$

This means that P_{25} is the average of the 10th and 11th data values. Thus

$$Q_1 = P_{25} = 59$$

(b) Find P_{50}. Now $(.50)(40) = 20$. Thus

$$\text{location of } P_{50} \text{ is } 20.5$$

This means that P_{50} is the average of the 20th and 21st data values. Thus

$$Q_2 = P_{50} = 66$$

(c) Find P_{75}. Now $(.75)(40) = 30$. Thus

$$\text{location of } P_{75} \text{ is } 30.5$$

This means that P_{75} is the average of the 30th and 31st data values so that

$$Q_3 = P_{75} = 73$$

JMP Printout

JMP is a statistical software package produced by SAS Institute, Inc. The following is a JMP printout of quartiles and percentiles (sometimes called "quantiles") for the data in Table 3.6. Columns of various percentile ranks and the corresponding percentiles are given. Statistical packages use a method of calculating percentiles that is slightly different from the one we gave. Notice that the 10th percentile in the printout is 53.1, whereas in Example 3.8, we calculated it to be 53.5.

Quantiles		
maximum	100.0%	88.000
	99.5%	88.000
	97.5%	87.900
	90.0%	81.800
quartile	75.0%	73.000
median	50.0%	66.000
quartile	25.0%	59.000
	10.0%	53.100
	2.5%	46.075
	0.5%	46.000
minimum	0.0%	46.000

A Resistant Measure of Dispersion

The more spread there is in a data set, the farther apart are the quartiles Q_1 and Q_3. This leads to the definition of another measure of dispersion.

Definition The *interquartile range*, or *IQR*, is the difference between Q_3 and Q_1.

$$IQR = Q_3 - Q_1$$

EXAMPLE 3.11
Find the interquartile range for the data in Table 3.6.

Solution

In Example 3.10, we saw that $Q_1 = 59$ and $Q_3 = 73$ for the data in Table 3.6. Therefore

$$\text{IQR} = Q_3 - Q_1 = 73 - 59 = 14$$

This tells us that the middle 50% of the data is spread over a range of 14 points.

If we changed the largest data value in Table 3.6 from 88 to 88,000, the quartiles would not change. So the interquartile range would not change. **The interquartile range is not influenced by extreme observations; it is a resistant measure of dispersion.**

Many statisticians think that if the median is used (instead of the mean) as a measure of central tendency because of the presence of extreme observations, then the interquartile range should be used (instead of the standard deviation) to describe variability.

EXERCISES

3.33 The following ranked data represent the miles driven each day by a salesman over a 30-day period:

33	37	43	44	44	55	58	65	65	66	71	74	75	75	78
81	81	81	82	84	86	86	87	89	89	92	92	93	93	95

In parts (a)–(f), find the following:

(a) P_{33} **(b)** P_{87} **(c)** Q_1 **(d)** Q_3

(e) The interquartile range

(f) The percentile rank of 74

(g) The nine deciles are defined as follows: The first decile D_1 is the 10th percentile P_{10}; the second decile D_2 is the 20th percentile P_{20}; ...; and the 9th decile D_9 is the 90th percentile P_{90}. Find D_3.

3.34 Consider the following ranked data:

.02	.09	.14	.25	.37	.55	.55	.56	.60
.77	.86	.93	1.15	1.34	1.41	1.75	2.01	
2.16	2.23	3.69	3.90	4.50	4.88	7.79	9.56	

Find the following:

(a) P_{20} **(b)** P_{95} **(c)** Q_2

(d) The percentile rank of 3.69

3.35 Consider the following 50 data values that represent the nearest hour of births in a city hospital in a 6-day period. Note that 0 represents a birth between 11:31 P.M. and 12:30 A.M., inclusive, whereas 23 represents a birth between 10:31 P.M. and 11:30 P.M. inclusive.

19	13	6	1	5	17	19	22	16	14	5	17	11	18	2	7	11
19	21	19	15	22	12	20	23	9	17	12	19	9	5	21	11	6
6	17	5	6	16	7	22	21	5	8	22	12	6	9	6	9	

Find the following:

(a) P_{20} (b) P_{80} (c) Q_1

(d)   The percentile rank of 8

3.36   The following data (discussed in Exercise 2.55) give time (in days) from remission to relapse for 51 patients with acute nonlymphoblastic leukemia.

24	46	57	57	64	65	82	89	90	90	111
117	128	143	148	152	166	171	186	191	197	
209	223	230	247	249	254	258	264	269	270	
273	284	294	304	304	332	341	393	395	487	
510	516	518	518	534	608	642	697	955	1,160	

Find the following:

(a)   The first and third quartiles $Q = 128$ $Q_3 = 393$

(b)   The interquartile range 215

(c)   The median 249

(d)   The 95th percentile

(e)   The percentile rank of 111

3.37   The following frequency distribution represents the magnitude on the Richter scale of 1000 seismic events occurring near the Fiji Islands during 1964–1974. (*Source: Extracted from the World Wide Seismic Network Tape by Professor John Woodhouse of Harvard University. Data from Donoho, A., D. Donoho, and M. Gasko, MacSpin Graphical Data Analysis Software, 1985, p. 115*)

x	4.0	4.1	4.2	4.3	4.4	4.5	4.6	4.7	4.8
f	46	55	90	85	101	107	101	98	65

x	4.9	5.0	5.1	5.2	5.3	5.4	5.5	5.6
f	54	47	43	29	21	20	14	9

x	5.7	5.8	5.9	6.0	6.1	6.2	6.3	6.4
f	8	0	2	3	1	0	0	1

Find the following:

(a)   The quartiles

(b)   The interquartile range

(c)   The 90th percentile

(d)   The percentile rank of 5.7

3.38   The data shown here, from Exercise 2.4, represent the age at inauguration for United States presidents.

42	43	46	46	47	48	49	49	50	50	51	51	51	51
52	52	54	54	54	54	55	55	55	55	56	56	56	57
57	57	57	58	60	61	61	61	62	64	64	65	68	69

Find the following:

(a)   The quartiles

(b)   The interquartile range

(c)   The 80th percentile

(d)   The percentile rank of 60

3.39   In each of the following parts, do you prefer the mean and standard deviation, or the median and interquartile range, as measures of central tendency and variability?

(a)   0   1   1   4   5   7   8   10   12   15   16   45

(b)   14   17   18   19   20   20   20   21   21   23   25   26

(c)   7   31   33   33   35   36   38   41   41   42   44   47

3.40   In Exercise 2.8, we discussed the number of English-language Sunday newspapers (per state) in the United States as of February 1, 1993. The data are

2	2	3	3	4	4	4	4	5	5	6	7	7
7	7	10	10	10	11	11	11	12	13	14	14	14
14	15	16	16	16	17	17	17	18	20	20	21	
21	22	27	28	32	35	36	37	42	44	71	87	

Verify the following output from Data Desk.* In computing the mth percentile, P_m, Data Desk calculates the location of P_m as $(m/100)(n + 1)$, with n being the number of data values. If the result is an integer, the corresponding data value is used. If the result is not an integer, P_m is found by interpolation. For example, the location of P_{95} is $(95/100)(50 + 1) = 48.45$. So P_{95} is the 48th value in the ranked list plus .45 times the distance between the 48th and 49th values. That is, $P_{95} = 44 + (.45)(71 - 44) = 56.15$.

Summary statistics

Median 14   Numeric 50   (*This means that there are 50 data values.*)

Interquartile 14   Range 85

25th%ile 7   75th%ile 21   90th%ile 36.900000

3.41   In Exercise 2.5, we discussed the number of home runs hit by American League home run leaders in the years 1954–1993. The ordered data are

22	32	32	32	32	32	33	36	36	37	37	39	39	39
40	40	40	41	42	42	42	42	43	43	44	44	44	44
45	45	46	46	48	49	49	49	49	51	52	61		

A JMP printout follows. In computing the mth percentile, P_m, JMP calculates the location of P_m as $(m/100)(n + 1)$, with n being the number of data values. If the result is an integer, the corresponding data value is used. If the result is not an integer, P_m is found by interpolation. For example, the location of P_{80} is $(80/100)(40 + 1) = 32.8$. So P_{80} is the 32nd value in the ranked list plus .8 times the distance between the 32nd and 33rd values. That is, $P_{80} = 46 + (.8)(48 - 46) = 47.6$.

(a)   Verify the printout for the 25th and 75th percentiles.

(b)   Give the interquartile range.

(c)   Without looking at a graph of the data, do you think the data are strongly skewed? (*Hint:*   Compare the mean and the median.)

---

*Data Desk is statistical software from Data Description, Inc.

Quantiles		
maximum	100.0%	61.000
	99.5%	61.000
	97.5%	60.775
	90.0%	49.000
quartile	75.0%	45.750
median	50.0%	42.000
quartile	25.0%	37.000
	10.0%	32.000
	2.5%	22.250
	0.5%	22.000
minimum	0.0%	22.000

Moments	
Mean	41.47500
Std Dev	7.11440
Std Err Mean	1.12489
upper 95% Mean	43.75029
lower 95% Mean	39.19971
N	40.00000
Sum Wgts	40.00000

Note: Under *Moments* we see, besides the mean and standard deviation, the standard error of the mean $s/\sqrt{n}$. Also given are *upper* and *lower 95% Means*. These are endpoints of an interval that we are 95% sure will contain the *population* mean (such intervals are discussed in Chapter 8). Each data value has the same weight (1). So the sum of the weights is 40.

3.5

BOXPLOTS

A **boxplot** (sometimes called a box-and-whisker plot) can be used to display graphic and numerical features of collections of data. We illustrate this idea using the exam score data in Table 3.6 (Section 3.4).

- First, we compute five numbers: the lowest data value (L), the highest value (H), and the three quartiles, Q_1, Q_2, and Q_3. We see from the ranked data in Table 3.6 that

$$L = 46 \qquad H = 88$$

Furthermore, we have already computed the three quartiles in Example 3.10:

$$Q_1 = 59 \qquad Q_2 = 66 \qquad Q_3 = 73$$

- Next, we draw a horizontal axis with the five numbers marked on the axis. Above the axis, we construct a **box** with the two vertical sides above Q_1 and Q_3 on the axis (see Figure 3.5). These sides are called the **hinges.** Also we construct a vertical line in the box above Q_2.

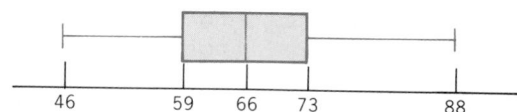

Figure 3.5
Boxplot for the Achievement Test Scores in Table 3.6

- Finally, we draw vertical lines above L and H, and connect these to the hinges using horizontal lines. These horizontal lines are called **whiskers.** Note that each portion of the box and each whisker contains about one-fourth of the data.

An examination of Figure 3.5 suggests that the data between Q_1 and Q_3 are quite symmetrically distributed since Q_2 (the median) is exactly halfway between Q_1 and Q_3. The right whisker is only slightly longer than the left whisker, indicating only a very slight skewing to the right. Overall, however, the data appear to be rather symmetrically distributed.

EXAMPLE 3.12

The following data represent the lengths of long-distance phone calls (in minutes) made by a business office in 1 day:

$$3 \quad 7 \quad 2 \quad 14 \quad 4 \quad 29 \quad 3 \quad 9 \quad 1 \quad 20 \quad 10 \quad 7 \quad 2 \quad 42 \quad 3 \quad 5$$

Construct a boxplot for the data. What does the boxplot tell us about the way the data are distributed?

Solution

Since the data are unranked, we must first rank them:

$$1 \quad 2 \quad 2 \quad 3 \quad 3 \quad 3 \quad 4 \quad 5 \quad 7 \quad 7 \quad 9 \quad 10 \quad 14 \quad 20 \quad 29 \quad 42$$

Now, $L = 1$ and $H = 42$. Find Q_1 (which is the 25th percentile, P_{25}). There are $n = 16$ data values and $(.25)(16) = 4$, so

$$\text{location of } Q_1 \text{ is } 4.5$$

Thus Q_1 is the average of the fourth and fifth data values in the ranked list. Therefore,

$$Q_1 = 3$$

Find Q_2 (the 50th percentile). Now $(.50)(16) = 8$. So

$$\text{location of } Q_2 \text{ is } 8.5$$

Hence Q_2 is the average of the eighth and ninth data values:

$$Q_2 = 6$$

Find Q_3 (the 75th percentile). Now $(.75)(16) = 12$. So

$$\text{location of } Q_3 \text{ is } 12.5$$

and

$$Q_3 = 12$$

The boxplot is given in Figure 3.6. The right portion of the box is longer than the left

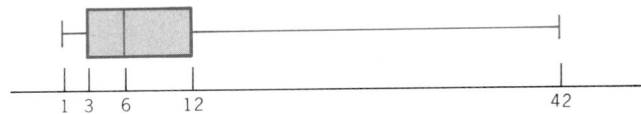

Figure 3.6
Boxplot for the Telephone Data

portion, and the right whisker is considerably longer than the left. This indicates that the data are skewed to the right.

Modified Boxplot

Sometimes it is helpful to plot suspected outliers. The **modified boxplot** can be used to do this. Instead of drawing the whiskers from hinges Q_1 and Q_3 to the lowest and highest data values, draw the upper whisker from Q_3 to the largest data value between

$$Q_3 \quad \text{and} \quad Q_3 + 1.5 \times \text{IQR}$$

(where $\text{IQR} = Q_3 - Q_1$). Draw the lower whisker from Q_1 to the smallest data value between

$$Q_1 - 1.5 \times \text{IQR} \quad \text{and} \quad Q_1$$

Plot with a dot any data value that is less than $(Q_1 - 1.5 \times \text{IQR})$ or greater than $(Q_3 + 1.5 \times \text{IQR})$. These are suspected outliers. Note that when there are no outliers, boxplots and modified boxplots are the same.

EXAMPLE 3.13
Construct a modified boxplot for the data in Example 3.12.

Solution
We saw in Example 3.12 that $Q_1 = 3$, $Q_2 = 6$, and $Q_3 = 12$. So

$$\text{IQR} = Q_3 - Q_1 = 12 - 3 = 9$$
$$1.5 \times \text{IQR} = 13.5$$
$$Q_1 - 1.5 \times \text{IQR} = 3 - 13.5 = -10.5$$
$$Q_3 + 1.5 \times \text{IQR} = 12 + 13.5 = 25.5$$

The smallest data value between 3 and -10.5 is 1. The largest data value between 12 and 25.5 is 20. No data values are less than -10.5, but two are greater than 25.5: 29 and 42. These are suspected outliers. The modified boxplot is in Figure 3.7.

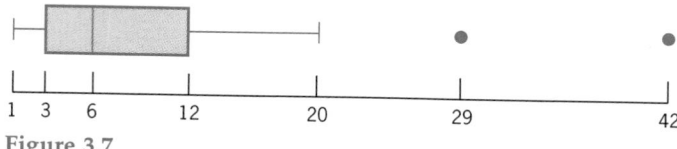

Figure 3.7
Modified Boxplot for the Data in Example 3.12

Data Desk Printout for Example 3.13

The following Data Desk printout is a modified boxplot for the data discussed in Example 3.13. Statistical software packages often use vertical boxplots. Data Desk differentiates outliers as follows: A circle represents an outlier, for example, 29 in the Data Desk printout. An asterisk corresponds to an extreme outlier, for example, 42 in the printout. An extreme outlier is one that is less than $Q_1 - 3 \times \text{IQR}$ or more than $Q_3 + 3 \times \text{IQR}$.

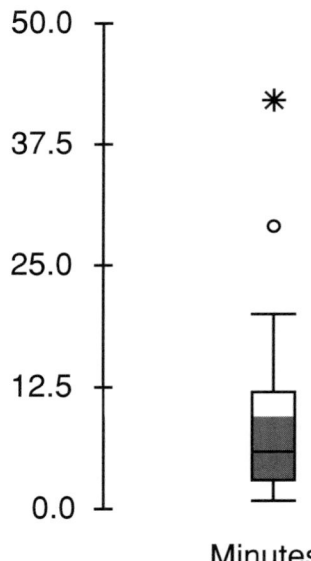

Minutes

A stem-and-leaf plot gives a better picture of shape for a data set than a boxplot. But boxplots are more useful when comparing two or more data sets. To do this you can arrange the boxplots one above the other or vertically side by side.

EXAMPLE 3.14

In Example 2.8, we discussed the leading batting averages in the 1920s and 1980s. Compare the two data sets using modified boxplots.

Solution

First, rank the data:

1920s: .369   .378   .378   .379   .393   .394   .398   .403   .407   .420

location of Q_1 is 3 $Q_1 = .378$
location of Q_2 is 5.5 $Q_2 = .3935$
location of Q_3 is 8 $Q_3 = .403$
$IQR = Q_3 - Q_1 = .025$
$Q_1 - 1.5 \times IQR = .3405$
$Q_3 + 1.5 \times IQR = .4405$
Smallest data value between .3405 and .378:   .369
Largest data value between .403 and .4405:   .420

1980s: .332   .336   .339   .343   .357   .361   .363   .366   .368   .390

$Q_1 = .339$
$Q_2 = .359$
$Q_3 = .366$

$$\text{IQR} = Q_3 - Q_1 = .027$$
$$Q_1 - 1.5 \times \text{IQR} = .2985$$
$$Q_3 + 1.5 \times \text{IQR} = .4065$$

Smallest data value between .2985 and .339: .332

Largest data value between .366 and .4065: .390

The boxplots are in Figure 3.8. For purposes of comparison, we have provided a common number axis. The boxplots show the overall pattern of higher leading averages in the 1920s. No outliers are indicated by the boxplots.

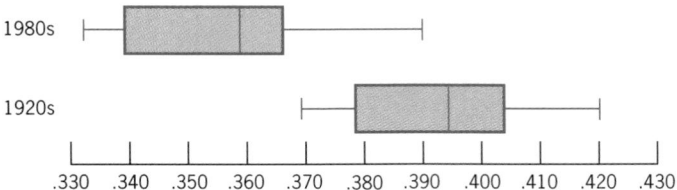

Figure 3.8
Boxplots of Leading American League Batting Averages of 1920s and 1980s

---

EXERCISES

3.42   The following ranked data (see Exercise 3.33) represent the miles driven each day by a salesman over a 30-day period:

33	37	43	44	44	55	58	65	65	66	71	74	75	75	78
81	81	81	82	84	86	86	87	89	89	92	92	93	93	95

Construct a boxplot for the data. Characterize the distribution shape by selecting the name of the distribution that most closely approximates the data.

3.43   The following ranked data give the 1991 death rates (per 1000 population) for 29 selected countries (see Exercise 2.12):

Singapore	5.0	United States	8.6	Austria	10.6
Israel	6.3	Spain	8.7	Poland	10.6
Cuba	6.6	Ireland	8.9	Belgium	10.7
Mauritius	6.6	Switzerland	9.0	Romania	10.9
Japan	6.7	France	9.2	Sweden	11.0
Australia	6.9	Italy	9.7	Germany	11.1
Canada	7.3	Luxembourg	9.7	United Kingdom	11.2
Malta	7.8	Portugal	9.7	Denmark	11.6
New Zealand	7.8	Finland	9.8	Hungary	14.0
The Netherlands	8.6	Norway	10.5		

Construct a boxplot for the data. Characterize the distribution shape by selecting the name of the distribution that most closely approximates the data.

3.44   The following ranked data from Exercise 2.8 represent the numbers of English-language Sunday newspapers in the 50 states:

2	2	3	3	4	4	4	4	5	5	6	7	7
7	7	10	10	10	11	11	11	12	13	14	14	14
14	15	16	16	16	17	17	17	18	20	20	21	
21	22	27	28	32	35	36	37	42	44	71	87	

Construct a boxplot for the data. Characterize the distribution shape by selecting the name of the distribution that most closely approximates the data.

3.45 The following ranked data are observations of time in days from remission induction to relapse for 51 patients with acute nonlymphoblastic leukemia. (See Exercise 2.55.)

24	46	57	57	64	65	82	89	90	90	111
117	128	143	148	152	166	171	186	191	197	
209	223	230	247	249	254	258	264	269	270	
273	284	294	304	304	332	341	393	395	487	
510	516	518	518	534	608	642	697	955	1160	

(a) Construct a boxplot for the data.

(b) Construct a modified boxplot for the data. Which observations are suspected outliers?

(c) Characterize the distribution shape by selecting the name of the distribution that most closely approximates the data.

3.46 The following ranked data (from Exercise 2.4) are the ages at inauguration of United States presidents:

42	43	46	46	47	48	49	49	50	50	51	51	51	51
52	52	54	54	54	54	55	55	55	55	56	56	56	57
57	57	57	58	60	61	61	61	62	64	64	65	68	69

(a) Construct a boxplot for the data.

(b) Construct a modified boxplot for the data. What observations are suspected outliers?

3.47 The following data represent the 1990 populations (in 100,000s) for the 50 largest cities in the United States (*Source: The 1994 Information Please Almanac,* 1994, p. 792). The data are rounded off.

73	35	28	16	16	11	10	10	9.8	9.4
7.8	7.4	7.4	7.2	6.7	6.3	6.3	6.1	6.1	5.7
5.2	5.2	5.1	5.1	5.0	4.7	4.7	4.5	4.4	4.4
4.4	4.3	4.1	4.0	4.0	3.9	3.9	3.8	3.7	3.7
3.7	3.7	3.7	3.7	3.6	3.6	3.5	3.4	3.3	3.3

Construct a modified boxplot for the data. Which observations are suspected outliers?

3.48 In Exercise 3.29, we looked at average temperatures per month over a 12-month period for Bismarck, North Dakota, and San Diego, California. We now compare the distributions with boxplots, one on top of the other.

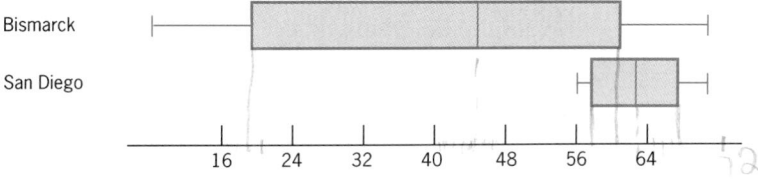

Use the boxplots to answer the following:

(a)   How do the median temperatures per month compare?

(b)   Which of the two cities appears to have smaller month-to-month variability in temperature?

(c)   Estimate the 25th percentiles for the two cities.

(d)   Estimate the 75th percentiles for the two cities.

3.49   In 1969, an executive order was issued by President Richard M. Nixon requiring that a random method be used to draft men into military service. The 1970 draft lottery was held on December 1, 1969, to determine the order in which men would be called. The lottery system was based on a person's birthday. The data values are from 1 through 366, with 1 corresponding to September 14 (the first one drawn), 2 corresponding to April 24 (the second birthdate drawn), and so forth.

(a)   Compare the January–June and July–December boxplots shown here. Comment on whether people born in the July–December range were more likely to be called sooner into service than people in the January–June range.

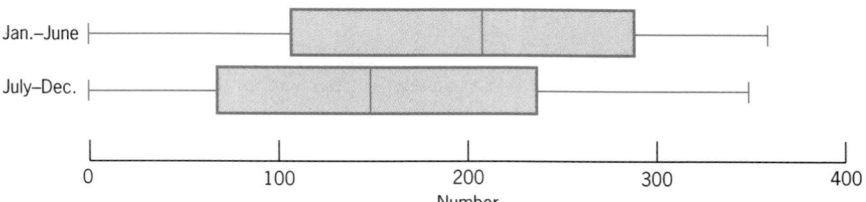

(b)   Following the drawing, many scientists complained that the method used was not random. A new system was drawn up by Selective Service officials for the 1971 draft. The following boxplot describes the 1971 selection process. Does the new system appear to be a more random process than that in part (a)?

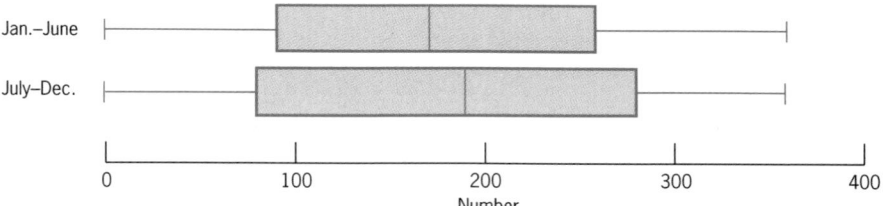

(For an excellent discussion, see *Randomization for the Selective Service Draft Lotteries* by Stephen E. Fienberg in *Statistics by Example, Finding Models,* Addison-Wesley Publishing Company, pp. 1–13.)

3.50   The two modified boxplots shown here represent heights (in inches) of 123 female and 107 male singers in the New York Choral Society in 1979. (Data from Chambers, J., W. Cleveland, B. Kleiner, and P. Tukey, *Graphical Methods for Data Analysis,* Boston: Duxbury Press, 1983, p. 350.)

(a)   What is the height of the suspected outlier? What percentage of male singers in the New York Choral Society in 1979 were no taller than the tallest woman?

(b)   What percentage of males were taller than all females, excluding the tallest woman?

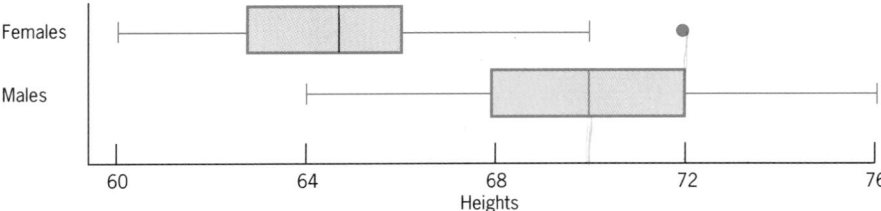

3.51 The four modified boxplots shown here represent heights (in inches) of 66 soprano, 57 alto, 42 tenor, and 65 bass singers in the New York Choral Society in 1979. (See Exercise 3.50.)

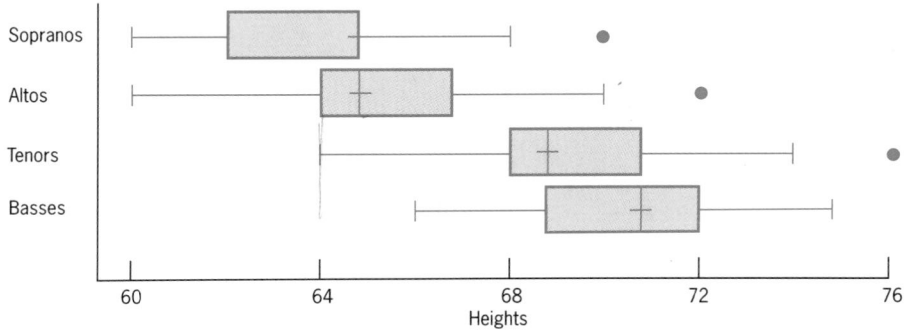

(a) How do the median heights of singers compare across the four categories? Does there appear to be a trend between median heights and the four groups?

(b) Approximately what percentage of altos are shorter than all tenors?

(c) Would the suspected soprano outlier be a suspected tenor outlier?

3.6

USING MINITAB (OPTIONAL)

READ and LET Commands

As indicated in Section 2.7, the easiest way to enter a data set is to type it directly into the Data window; but it may also be entered from the Session window. When you have more than one collection of data, you can use the SET command repeatedly to enter the data. However, when each collection of data has the same number of data values, it is sometimes more convenient to use the READ command. With this command, each collection of data is entered in a column.

The following printout deals with the increase in income for a chain of 10 fast-food restaurants after an advertising campaign. In the Session window, we enter the average daily income for each restaurant for the month preceding and for the month following the advertising campaign into columns 1 and 2. The difference (after minus before) for each restaurant is computed and stored in column 3 by the command

$$\text{LET C3} = \text{C2} - \text{C1}$$

This gives the increase for each restaurant. Finally, we print the increases for the 10 restaurants.

```
MTB > READ THE FOLLOWING DATA INTO C1, C2
DATA> 3815 5820
DATA> 3652 5571
DATA> 4080 6523
DATA> 4958 7042
DATA> 5637 6784
DATA> 3562 4011
DATA> 4579 6018
DATA> 6594 8350
DATA> 5716 6824
DATA> 4203 6110
DATA> END
      10 ROWS READ
MTB > LET C3 = C2 - C1
MTB > PRINT C3

C3
   2005    1919    2443    2084    1147    449    1439    1756    1108    1907
```

Note: A list of consecutive columns may be abbreviated with a dash. For example, we could type

READ INTO C1–C3

instead of

READ INTO C1, C2, C3

If a collection of data is already in a column, and you SET or READ a new collection of data into the same column, the old data are automatically erased.

Dialog Box

Once the previous data were in columns 1 and 2, column 3 could have been computed using a dialog box. Click **Calc** on the menu bar. Then click **Mathematical Expressions** on the pull-down menu. A dialog box will appear. In the **Variable** box, type *C3*. In the **Expression** box, type *C2 − C1*. Then click **OK**. Column 3 will appear in the Data window.

Arithmetic

We saw how the LET command or the dialog box can be used to compute a column of differences. Minitab performs arithmetic operations on columns term by term. The operations of addition, subtraction, multiplication, and division are denoted +, −, *, and /, respectively. Exponentiation (raising to a power) is denoted by **. For example, suppose we have the columns

C1	C2
9	3
4	2
8	2

Then

$$C1 + C2 = \begin{array}{c} 12 \\ 6 \\ 10 \end{array} \qquad C1 - C2 = \begin{array}{c} 6 \\ 2 \\ 6 \end{array} \qquad C1 + 5 = \begin{array}{c} 14 \\ 9 \\ 13 \end{array}$$

$$C1 * C2 = \begin{array}{c} 27 \\ 8 \\ 16 \end{array} \qquad C1/C2 = \begin{array}{c} 3 \\ 2 \\ 4 \end{array}$$

The square of column 1 is

$$C1 ** 2 = \begin{array}{c} 81 \\ 16 \\ 64 \end{array}$$

Using the LET command, we can form new columns by means of expressions involving various combinations of these operations. For example, suppose we type

$$\text{LET } C4 = (C1 - C2) ** 2/C2$$

Minitab would first compute the difference $C1 - C2$, square this, and then divide by C2, giving

C4
12
2
18

Minitab evaluates expressions as follows: Expressions are repeatedly scanned from left to right. Expressions within parentheses are evaluated first, then exponentiation

$**$ is performed, followed by multiplication and division, and lastly addition and subtraction. Note the differences in the following:

C5
24
12
20

$$\text{LET C5} = 2*(C1 + C2) \rightarrow$$

C6
21
10
18

$$\text{LET C6} = 2*C1 + C2 \rightarrow$$

The LET command is used in the Session window. But the same expressions may be computed using the dialog box. For example, column 6 mentioned above is created as follows:

Calc ▶ Mathematical Expressions
Type *C6* in **Variable** box
Type *2*C1 + C2* in **Expression** box
Click **OK**

Describing Data

The scores of 30 males on a test of aggressiveness are entered into column 1 from the Session window as follows:

```
MTB > SET THE FOLLOWING DATA IN C1
DATA> 136 133 122 105 141 118 148 113 128 125 120 146
DATA> 137 135 98 126 108 93 140 110 134 131 102 115
DATA> 106 110 118 147 136 146
DATA> END
```

For the remainder of this section, we assume these data are in column 1. We can produce a variety of statistics for column 1, such as the mean, median, standard deviation, either from the Session window or with a dialog box. For example, the mean is obtained as follows:

Session Command	**Dialog Box**
MTB>MEAN C1	**Calc ▶ Column Statistics**
	Click **Mean** from a list of options
	Type *C1* in Input Variable(s)
	Click **OK**

Output

Column Mean

Mean of C1   =   124.23

We can produce a number of other statistics (such as the median or standard deviation) by typing the desired statistic (MEDIAN C1) in the Session window or by clicking on that statistic in the dialog box.

To store the mean in K1, we would do the following:

Session Command	Dialog Box
MTB>MEAN C1, STORE K1	Calc ▶ Column Statistics
	Click **Mean**
	Type *C1* in Input Variable Box
	Click on **Store Results**
	Type *K1* in box
	Click **OK**

There is an alternative way of doing this in the Session window using the LET command. Type

LET K1 = MEAN (C1)

When another command is used in a LET command, we must use parentheses around the column. The same applies to the creation of mathematical expressions in a dialog box:

Calc ▶ **Mathematical Expressions**
Type *K1* in the **Variable** box
Type *MEAN (C1)* in the **Expression Box**

The DESCRIBE command gives the number of data values, the mean, median, standard deviation, and other information.

Session Command	Dialog Box
MTB>DESCRIBE C1	Stat ▶ **Basic Statistics** ▶ **Descriptive Statistics**
	Under **Variable,** type *C1* in box
	Click **OK**

Output

Descriptive Statistics

Variable	N	Mean	Median	TrMean	StDev	SEMean
C1	30	124.23	125.50	124.65	15.75	2.88

Variable	Min	Max	Q1	Q3
C1	93.00	148.00	110.00	136.25

The TrMean in this printout is the **trimmed mean.** This can be useful when there are atypical extreme data values, because it is obtained by discarding the top 5% and bottom 5% of the data values and computing the mean of the remaining 90%. The SEMean is the **standard error of the mean.** This is the standard deviation divided by the square root of the sample size. (We will see how this is used in Chapter 7.) Note that the first quartile Q_1 and the third quartile Q_3 are also given. (The median is the second quartile and also the 50th percentile.)

Percentiles

Suppose we want to find some percentiles (other than those given by DESCRIBE). We first rank the data and store them in, say, column 2. This is accomplished in the Session window as follows:

```
MTB > SORT C1 PUT INTO C2
```

Suppose we want the 35th percentile of the 30 data values in column 2. Since $(.35)(30) = 10.5$, the location of P_{35} is 11. The 11th data value in column 2 is denoted by C2(11). The printout of this is obtained as follows:

```
MTB > LET K1 = C2(11)
MTB > PRINT K1
```

Data Display

```
K1    118.000
```

Suppose we want the 60th percentile. Since $(.60)(30) = 18$, the location of P_{60} is 18.5. So P_{60} is the average of the 18th and 19th data values in column 2:

```
MTB > LET K2 = (C2(18) + C2(19)) / 2
MTB > PRINT K2
```

Data Display

```
K2    132.000
```

You can get the same results using dialog boxes. To get the 35th percentile:

Manip ▶ Sort
Type *C1* under **Sort column(s) in:**
Type *C2* under **Store sorted column(s) in:**
Type *C1* in **Sort column(s) by:**
Click **OK**

Calc ▶ Mathematical Expressions
Type *K1* in **Variable** box
Type *C2(11)* in **Expression** box
Click **OK**

File ▶ **Display Data**
Type *K1* in **Display** box
Click **OK**

To get the 60th percentile:

Calc ▶ **Mathematical Expressions**
Type *K2* in **Variable** box
Type *(C2(18) + C2(19)) / 2* in **Expression** box
File ▶ **Display**
Type *K2* in **Display** box

COUNT and COPY Commands

The COUNT command gives us the number of data values in a column. If we type

COUNT C1

the computer will print the number of data values in column 1. If we wish to store the number of data values (as a stored constant), we can type

Let K1 = COUNT(C1)

The COUNT command can be used along with the COPY command to find the percentile rank of a data value. Suppose we want to find the percentile rank of the data value 115 in column 1. This would be the percentage of data values that are less than 115. The next lower possible value is 114 (since we are dealing with whole numbers), and 0 is the smallest possible value for these data. The following COPY command, along with the USE subcommand, will take the values in column 1 between 0 and 114 (inclusive) and place them in column 2. (Any values previously in column 2 will automatically be erased.)

COPY C1 INTO C2;
USE ROWS WHERE C1 = 0:114.

Note that 0:114 means 0 to 114 inclusive. If we had said 0,114 or 0 to 114, only the values 0 and 114 would be selected.*

The percentage of data values less than 115 is then obtained by multiplying 100 by the number of data values in C2 and then dividing by the number of data values in C1.

100 * COUNT(C2)/COUNT(C1)

The printout at the top of page 116 shows that the percentile rank is 30:

---

*With the USE subcommand, we can also specify *rows* to be used by giving row numbers:

USE ROWS 3 5 7:9.

will select rows 3, 5, 7, 8, 9. That is, the 3rd, 5th, 7th, 8th, and 9th values in column 1 would be selected.

```
MTB > COPY C1 INTO C2;
SUBC>   USE ROWS WHERE C1 = 0:114.
MTB > LET K1 = 100 * COUNT(C2) / COUNT(C1)
MTB > PRINT K1
```

Data Display

```
K1     30.0000
```

Obtain the 30th percentile using dialog boxes as follows:

Manip ▶ Copy Columns
Type *C1* under **Copy from columns:**
Type *C2* under **To columns:**
Click **Use Rows**
Click **Use rows with columns,** and type *C1* in box
Type *0:114* in box (after **equal to**)
Click **OK** twice

Calc ▶ Mathematical Expressions
Type *K1* in **Variable** box
Type *100*count(C2) / count(C1)* in **Expression** box
File ▶ Display Data
Type *K1* in **Display** box
Click **OK**

Boxplots

Minitab produces a modified boxplot (discussed in Section 3.5). Suspected outliers are identified with an asterisk (*). We produce a boxplot for the data in column 1 as follows:

Session Command	**Dialog Box**
MTB>BOXPLOT C1	**Graph ▶ Boxplot**
	Type *C1* under **Y**
	Click **OK**

Output

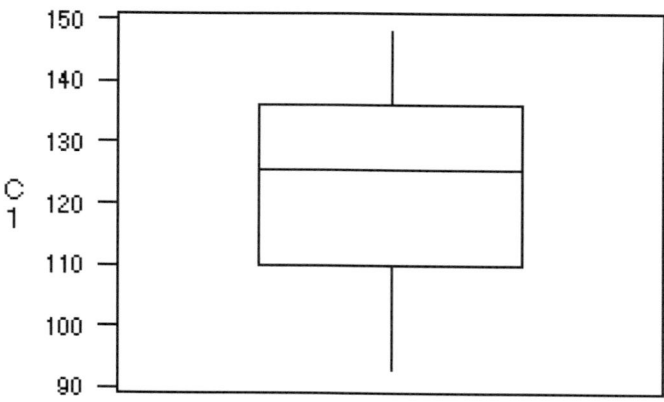

PRACTICE QUIZ (Answers follow the Review Exercises.)

1. Show how one READ command can be used to accomplish what the following SET commands do.

$$\begin{aligned}
&\text{SET C1}\\
&10\ \ 11\ \ 15\ \ 3\\
&\text{END}\\
&\text{SET C2}\\
&4\ \ 8\ \ 1\ \ 5\\
&\text{END}
\end{aligned}$$

2. Describe the status of the Minitab worksheet after running the following program:

$$\begin{aligned}
&\text{READ INTO C1 C2}\\
&2\ \ 4\\
&1\ \ 2\\
&3\ \ 3\\
&\text{END}\\
&\text{LET C3} = 4 * (\text{C1} + \text{C2})\\
&\text{LET C4} = 4 * \text{C1} + \text{C2}\\
&\text{LET C5} = 12/\text{C1} + \text{C2}\\
&\text{LET C6} = 12/(\text{C1} + \text{C2})\\
&\text{LET C7} = \text{C1} ** 2 + \text{C2}
\end{aligned}$$

3. The COPY command can be used to copy rows from more than one column. What will columns 3 and 4 look like after the following program?

$$\begin{aligned}
&\text{READ INTO C1 C2}\\
&1\ \ 5\\
&4\ \ 7\\
&2\ \ 8\\
&3\ \ 6\\
&\text{END}\\
&\text{COPY C1 C2 INTO C3 C4;}\\
&\ \ \text{USE ROWS WHERE C1} = 2\ \ 4.
\end{aligned}$$

In Questions 4–10, determine what is wrong, if anything.

4. READ INTO C1, C2
    4 6
    8 1
    3 9
    7
    END

5. SET C1
    11 14 21 18 9
    END
    MEAN FOR C1
    MEDIUM FOR C1

6. SET C1, C2
    4 8
    7 2
    3 9
    END
7. READ C1, C2
    3 8
    7 4
    1 9
    END
    LET K1 = C1 + C2
8. DESCRIBE THE 3 DATA VALUES IN C1
9. LET K1 = MEAN C1
10. PRINT K1/K2

EXERCISES

Suggested exercises for use with Minitab are 3.44, 3.54, 3.55, 3.63(b)–(f), and 3.67.

3.7

WORKING WITH DATA (OPTIONAL)

Refer to the Framingham Heart Study data sets you obtained in Section 2.8.

1. Find the mean and median systolic blood pressure for
    (a)   Males   **(b)**   Females
    (c)   In each case, indicate whether one measure of central tendency is preferable to the other. (*Hint:*   It may help to refer to the results of Problem 2 of Section 2.8.)
2. Find the mean and median serum cholesterol level for
    (a)   Males   **(b)**   Females
    (c)   In each case, indicate whether one measure of central tendency is preferable to the other.
3. Find the mean and median for the number of cigarettes smoked per day for
    (a)   Males   **(b)**   Females
    (c)   In each case, which is a better measure of central tendency?
    Note: The dot diagrams constructed in Problem 6 (of Section 2.8) may be of help in answering part (c).
4. Find the systolic blood pressure standard deviation for
    (a)   Males   **(b)**   Females
5. Find the serum cholesterol level standard deviation for
    (a)   Males   **(b)**   Females
6. Find the standard deviation for number of cigarettes smoked per day for
    (a)   Males   **(b)**   Females
7. For systolic blood pressure, find the quartiles and the interquartile range for
    (a)   Males   **(b)**   Females
    (c)   In each case, indicate whether the interquartile range is preferable to the standard deviation as a measure of dispersion. (*Hint:*   Your answer to Problem 1 should influence your answer here.)

_____ **3.8**

SUMMARY

In this chapter, we studied the notion of a **measure of central tendency,** which is a number that is a typical or representative value for a collection of data. We investigated two measures of central tendency: the **mean** (the average value) and the **median** (the middle value in a ranked list).

In this text, the measure we will use the most is the mean. The mean of a population is denoted by the Greek letter μ, whereas we use the symbol $\bar{x}$ to represent the mean of a sample (when x is used to represent an arbitrary data value). In practice, we rarely have enough information about a population to calculate μ. In this case, we might estimate the value of μ by $\bar{x}$.

The **mth percentile,** P_m, separates the bottom $m\%$ of the data from the top $(100 - m)\%$. The **quartiles,** Q_1, Q_2, and Q_3, divide the data into quarters.

A **measure of dispersion** is a number that conveys an idea of how much spread or variability there is in a collection of data values. In this chapter, we studied the following measures of dispersion:

1. The **range** R is the difference between the highest (H) and the lowest (L) data values:

$$R = H - L$$

2. The **population variance** σ^2 for a population of N data values is the average of the squares of the deviations of the data values from the population mean μ:

$$\sigma^2 = \frac{\sum(x - \mu)^2}{N} = \frac{N(\sum x^2) - (\sum x)^2}{N^2}$$

3. The **population standard deviation** σ is the square root of the population variance.

4. The **sample variance** s^2 for a sample of n data values is a "modified average" of the squares of the deviations of the data values from their (sample) mean $\bar{x}$:

$$s^2 = \frac{\sum(x - \bar{x})^2}{n - 1} = \frac{n(\sum x^2) - (\sum x)^2}{n(n - 1)}$$

5. The **sample standard deviation** s is the square root of the sample variance.

6. The **interquartile range** is the difference between the third and first quartiles, $\text{IQR} = Q_3 - Q_1$

When a data set contains extreme observations, the median and interquartile range are often used instead of the mean and standard deviation.

Boxplots can be useful in portraying how data are distributed.

REVIEW EXERCISES

3.52   Consider the following data:

$$27 \quad 25 \quad 28 \quad 24 \quad 26 \quad 26 \quad 27 \quad 25 \quad 29 \quad 26$$

Find each of the following:

(a)   Mean   (b)   Median   (c)   Range

(d)   Sample variance

(e)   Sample standard deviation   (f) P_{85}

(g)   Percentile rank of 29

3.53   Consider the following ranked data:

$$3 \quad 5 \quad 6 \quad 6 \quad 7 \quad 8 \quad 9 \quad 11 \quad 11 \quad 12 \quad 14 \quad 16$$

Find each of the following:

(a)   Mean   (b)   Median   (c)   Range

(d)   Sample variance

(e)   Sample standard deviation

(f)   The quartiles Q_1 and Q_3

(g)   Interquartile range

(h)   Percentile rank of 8

(i)   Would you use $\bar{x}$ and s, or the median and interquartile range, to describe the data?

3.54   The following data are heights (in inches) of 65 bass singers in the New York Choral Society in 1979. (See Exercise 3.51.)

66	66	66	67	67	68	68	68	68	68	68	68	68
69	69	69	69	70	70	70	70	70	70	70	70	70
70	70	70	71	71	71	71	71	71	71	72	72	72
72	72	72	72	72	72	72	72	72	72	73	73	73
74	74	74	74	74	75	75	75	75	75	75	75	75

Find each of the following. (*Note:* $\sum x = 4614$ and $\sum x^2 = 327{,}928$)

(a)   Mean   (b)   Median   (c)   Sample variance

(d)   Sample standard deviation

(e)   The quartiles Q_1 and Q_3

(f)   The interquartile range

(g)   The 90th percentile

3.55   The following distribution gives the life spans (in days) for 144 hamsters (*Source:* Lyman et al., 1981):

x	116	264	314	331	364	397	430	446	496	512	545
f	1	2	1	1	2	1	1	2	2	1	3

x	562	579	612	645	678	694	711	727	744	760	777
f	2	3	1	1	4	1	4	4	2	10	1

x	793	810	826	843	860	876	884	893	909	942	959
f	1	5	6	3	4	3	1	3	3	1	1

x	975	992	1008	1025	1041	1058	1074	1091	1107	1124	1132
f	4	1	3	1	2	2	4	1	6	4	1

x	1140	1157	1174	1190	1207	1223	1256	1273	1289	1306	1355
f	3	1	3	1	3	2	3	3	5	1	1

x	1372	1388	1421	1438	1504	1587	1620
f	1	1	1	1	1	2	1

Find the following:

(a)   The quartiles Q_1 and Q_3

(b)   The interquartile range

(c)   The 10th and 90th percentiles

(d)   The percentile rank of each of the following:
    (i)   884   **(ii)**   1091

3.56   In Exercise 2.6, we discussed the numbers of home runs hit by National League home run leaders in the years 1954–1993. The ordered data are

```
31   35   36   36   36   37   37   37   38   38   38   39   39   40
40   40   40   41   43   44   44   44   44   45   45   46   46   46
47   47   47   48   48   48   49   49   49   51   52   52
```

A Minitab printout is given. For the home run data, the Minitab command DESCRIBE 'HOMERUNS' gave

Descriptive Statistics

```
Variable          N      Mean    Median    TrMean     StDev    SEMean
HomeRuns         40    42.800    44.000    42.833     5.321     0.841

Variable        Min       Max        Q1        Q3
HomeRuns     31.000    52.000    38.000    47.000
```

(a)   Verify the output given for Mean, Median, Min, and Max.

(b)   Give the interquartile range.

(c)   Without using a graph, determine whether the data are strongly skewed.

3.57   The following 27 scores are the winning teams' scores for selected New England college basketball games on February 11, 1995. The scores are

```
54   55   59   69   70   71   75   76   77   81   81   82   85   86
86   86   86   87   88   89   90   99   103   105   106   108   108
```

A Maple V printout is given at the top of page 122. Maple V computes the mth percentile, P_m, as follows: The location of P_m is $(m/100)(n)$ with n being the number of data values. If the result is an integer, the corresponding data value is used. If the result is not an integer, P_m is found by interpolation. For example, the location of P_{10} is $(10/100)(27) = 2.7$. So P_{10} is $\frac{7}{10}$ of the way between the second and third values. That is, $P_{10} = 55 + (7/10)(59 - 55) = 289/5$. Verify the printout for the quartiles and the 30th and 80th percentiles.

quartiles; $\left[74, \dfrac{171}{2}, \dfrac{357}{4}\right]$ percentile[30]; $\dfrac{761}{10}$ percentile[80]; $\dfrac{477}{5}$

3.58 Consider the following data:

$$19 \quad 20 \quad 23 \quad 27 \quad 1 \quad 22$$

(a) Find the mean.

(b) Find the median.

(c) Which do you prefer as a measure of central tendency?

3.59 Consider the following data:

$$12 \quad 14 \quad 12 \quad 16 \quad 17 \quad 19 \quad 12 \quad 13 \quad 20 \quad 175$$

(a) Find the mean.

(b) Find the median.

(c) Which do you prefer as a measure of central tendency?

(d) Without computing, would you use s or the interquartile range to describe the variability of this data set? Explain.

3.60 The following data are the 1993 estimated populations (in millions) of the world's 20 most populous countries (*Source:* *The 1994 Information Please Almanac,* 1994, p. 133).

Country	Population	Country	Population
China	1178.5	Mexico	90.0
India	897.4	Germany	81.1
United States	258.3	Vietnam	71.8
Indonesia	187.6	Philippines	64.6
Brazil	152.0	Iran	62.8
Russia	149.0	Turkey	60.7
Japan	124.8	Egypt	58.3
Pakistan	122.4	United Kingdom	58.0
Bangladesh	113.9	Italy	57.8
Nigeria	95.1	France	57.7

The following is a modified boxplot:

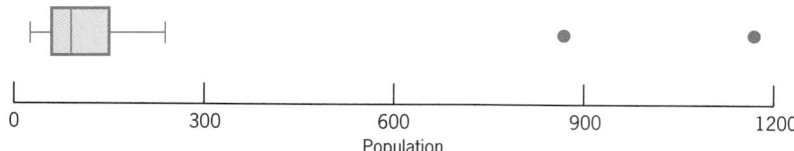

(a) Characterize the distribution of data values as skewed to the left, symmetric, or skewed to the right. Which measure, the mean or median, do you prefer as a measure of central tendency? Which is most likely larger?

(b) Find the mean. (*Note:* The sum of the 20 data values is 3941.8.)

(c) Exclude China and India, and find the mean for the remaining 18 countries. Compare your answer with that obtained in part (b). Did deleting China and India make a big difference in the mean population?

(d) Find the median.

(e) Exclude China and India, and find the median for the remaining 18 countries. Compare your answer with that obtained in part (d). Did deleting China and India make a big difference in the median population?

3.61 The following list gives the production of crude petroleum, in thousands of barrels, for countries in the western hemisphere in 1987 (*Source: The 1989 Information Please Almanac*, 1989, p. 377).

Country	Production	Country	Production
United States	3,041,910	Ecuador	98,915
Mexico	914,690	Peru	63,875
Venezuela	547,500	Trinidad and Tobago	60,225
Canada	538,375	Chile	10,950
Brazil	208,415	Bolivia	6,570
Argentina	141,255	Guatemala	1,460
Colombia	132,130		

(a) Characterize the distribution of data values as skewed to the left, symmetric, or skewed to the right. Which measure, the mean or median, do you prefer as a measure of central tendency? Which is most likely larger?

(b) Find the mean production per country. (*Note:* The sum of the 13 data values is 5,766,270.)

(c) Exclude the United States, and find the mean production per country of the remaining 12 countries. Compare your answer with that obtained in part (b). Did deleting the United States make a big difference in the mean production?

(d) Find the median production per country.

(e) Exclude the United States, and find the median production per country of the remaining 12 countries. Compare your answer with that obtained in part (d). Did deleting the United States make a big difference in the median production?

3.62 A businessman was trying to decide whether to accept a new position in Albany, New York, or Reno, Nevada. Being an avid golfer, he wanted to compare temperatures in the two cities. The following data represent the average monthly temperatures in degrees Fahrenheit for Albany and Reno based on a standard 30-year period (*Source: Statistical Abstract of the United States*, 1984, p. 217).

Albany

January	21.1	July	71.4
February	23.4	August	69.2
March	33.6	September	61.2
April	46.6	October	50.5
May	57.5	November	39.7
June	66.7	December	26.5

Reno

January	32.2	July	69.5
February	37.4	August	66.9
March	40.6	September	60.2
April	46.4	October	50.3
May	54.6	November	39.7
June	62.4	December	32.5

Consider the following boxplots:

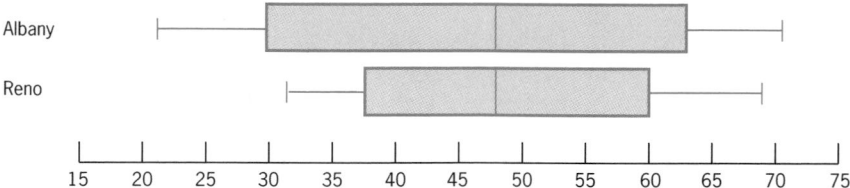

(a) **(i)** Without computing, estimate the median temperature and the interquartile range for each city from the boxplots.

 (ii) Based on consideration of median temperatures along with interquartile ranges, which city would the businessman prefer?

(b) If you had made your decision in part (a)(ii) using the mean and the standard deviation, do you think your decision would be the same? Explain.

3.63 A midwestern company that uses railways to transport its goods wants to open a factory in another city. A major consideration is the railroad distance between that city and other cities. One of the cities being considered is Boston. The following data represent railroad distances (in hundreds of miles) between Boston and various cities (*Source: Hammond Almanac*, 1983, p. 222).

City	Miles to Boston (× 100)	City	Miles to Boston (× 100)
New York City	2.3	St. Paul	14.1
Philadelphia	3.2	Mobile	14.4
Baltimore	4.2	Kansas City	15.7
Washington, D.C.	4.5	New Orleans	15.7
Buffalo	4.9	Miami	15.8
Pittsburgh	6.7	Oklahoma City	17.4
Cleveland	6.8	Dallas	18.6
Detroit	7.5	Houston	19.3
Cincinnati	9.4	Denver	20.4
Indianapolis	9.6	Albuquerque	23.6
Chicago	10.2	El Paso	24.1
Atlanta	10.9	Salt Lake City	25.3
St. Louis	12.0	Seattle	31.6
Jacksonville	12.1	Portland	32.2
Birmingham	12.2	Los Angeles	32.4
Des Moines	13.8	San Francisco	32.8
Memphis	13.8		

Consider the following boxplot:

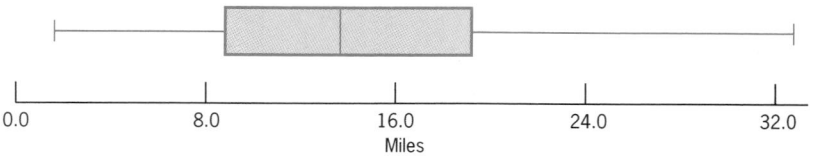

(a) Characterize the distribution of data values as skewed to the left, symmetric, or skewed to the right. Do you expect the mean or median to be larger?

Find the following:

(b) The mean and the median

(c) The quartiles Q_1 and Q_3

(d) The interquartile range

(e) P_{10}

(f) The city for which the corresponding data value has approximate percentile rank 12

3.64 Chicago is known as "The Windy City." The following display gives average wind speeds per month for Boston and Chicago based on records kept for a period of 20 years.

Month	Boston	Chicago
January	14.2	11.5
February	14.1	11.6
March	13.9	11.9
April	13.3	12.1
May	12.2	10.6
June	11.4	9.1
July	10.9	8.1
August	10.7	8.1
September	11.3	8.7
October	12.0	9.8
November	12.9	10.9
December	13.7	10.9

Consider the following boxplot:

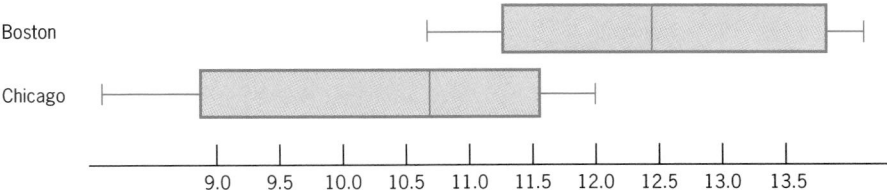

(a) Using the boxplot, which data set has a smaller median? A smaller mean?

(b) Find the median of the monthly wind speeds for each city.

(c) Find the mean of the monthly wind speeds for each city.

3.65 The accompanying data give the cholesterol readings of 35 randomly selected women from the Framingham Heart Study:

287	242	200	260	298	278	195	265	230	300	215	224
228	291	236	244	234	278	302	244	281	217	221	156
198	267	198	204	280	182	185	204	256	234	172	

Construct a modified boxplot. Are there any suspected outliers?

3.66 A trucking firm wished to compare the shipping time (in hours) for two routes (A and B). The firm believed that the average shipping time for the two routes would be about the same, but they hoped to increase reliability by choosing the route with smaller variability. (See Exercise 3.28.) The 15 shipping times for each route were as follows:

A	51	50	55	50	49	52	53	52	51	52	52	54	50	51	48
B	45	52	59	54	51	53	55	55	51	55	50	50	52	52	44

(a)   Construct boxplots for both routes, and place one on top of the other for comparison purposes.

(b)   Use the boxplots to determine which of the two routes appears to have smaller variability in delivery time.

3.67   The following data are the per capita property tax collections by state (in 1991 dollars). (See Exercise 2.59.)

171	1213	662	242	639	690	1138	311	687	506
430	427	785	571	686	691	277	275	796	617
830	894	718	344	377	523	744	456	1341	1257
222	1101	382	505	541	250	877	562	880	423
580	329	679	416	925	638	625	273	797	912

(a)   Construct a boxplot.

(b)   Characterize the shape of the distribution of the data.

(c)   Without computing, do you believe the mean or median is larger?

3.68   The eight modified boxplots shown here represent heights (in inches) of 36 soprano 1, 30 soprano 2, 35 alto 1, 22 alto 2, 21 tenor 1, 21 tenor 2, 39 bass 1, and 26 bass 2 singers in the New York Choral Society in 1979 (see Exercise 3.50). This is a parallel display of the boxplots for the eight voice parts.

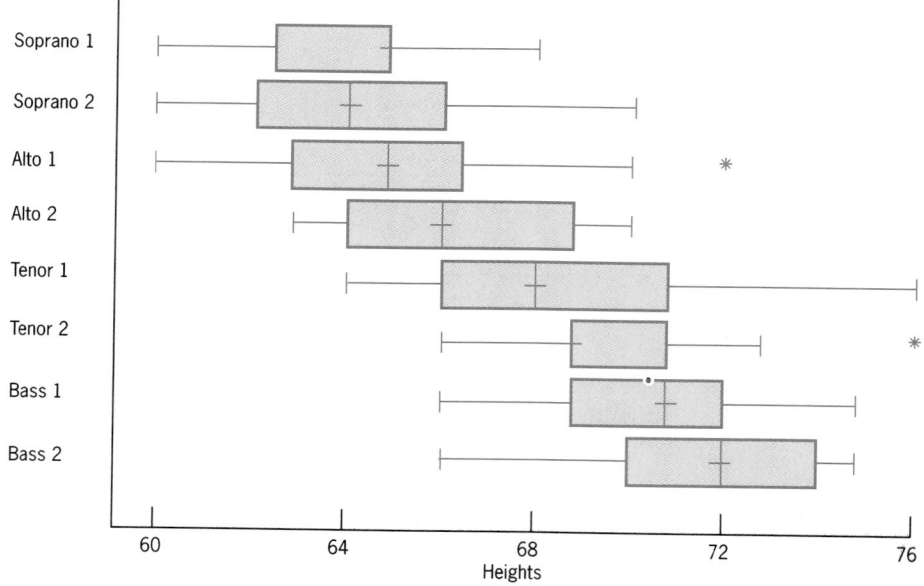

(a)   Compare the median heights of singers across the categories of voice. Ignoring soprano 1, does there appear to be a trend between median heights and categories?

(b) Approximately what percentage of bass 2 singers are taller than all alto 2 singers?

(c) Would the height of a suspected alto 1 outlier also be a suspected tenor 2 outlier?

In Exercises 3.69 and 3.70, use the following. For a fairly large sample from a normal population, we expect approximately 68% of the observations to be between $\bar{x} - s$ and $\bar{x} + s$, 95% between $\bar{x} - 2s$ and $\bar{x} + 2s$, and 99.7% between $\bar{x} - 3s$ and $\bar{x} + 3s$. This is known as the Empirical Rule.

3.69 The data given here, discussed in Exercise 2.5, are the numbers of home runs hit by American League home run leaders in the years 1954–1993:

32	37	52	42	42	42	40	61	48	45	49	32	49	44
44	49	44	33	37	32	32	36	32	39	46	45	41	22
39	39	43	40	40	49	42	36	51	44	43	46		

The mean and sample standard deviation of the data are 41.47 and 7.11, respectively. Find the percentage of data values within 1, 2, and 3 standard deviations of the mean. Compare with the Empirical Rule.

3.70 The following data, discussed in Exercise 2.6, are the numbers of home runs hit by National League home run leaders in the years 1954–1993:

49	51	43	44	47	46	41	46	49	44	47	52	44	39
36	45	45	48	40	44	36	38	38	52	40	48	48	31
37	40	36	37	37	49	39	47	40	38	35	46		

The mean and sample standard deviation of the data are 42.80 and 5.32, respectively. Find the percentage of data values within 1, 2, and 3 standard deviations of the mean. Compare with the Empirical Rule.

In Exercises 3.71 and 3.72, use Chebyshev's Theorem, which states that given a collection of data values, then for any number $k > 1$, the proportion of these data values that fall within k standard deviations of the mean is at least $1 - 1/k^2$.

3.71 Suppose that a collection of data values has mean 150 and standard deviation 15. At least what proportion of data values lie between

(a) 120 and 180?   **(b)** 132 and 168?   **(c)** 90 and 210?

3.72 Assume that a collection of 1000 data values has mean 400 and standard deviation 25.

(a) At least how many data values lie between 325 and 475?

(b) At least how many data values lie between 300 and 500?

(c) At *most* how many scores are smaller than 350 or larger than 450?

3.73 This exercise demonstrates that the mean can be viewed in terms of proportions. Consider the data values 2, 3, 3, 3, 3, 3, 3, 5, 5, 10, which have a mean of 4.

(a) Write an expression that gives the value of $\bar{x}$ in terms of the distinct data values and their proportions (i.e., relative frequencies).

(b) What would be the mean of a collection of data values consisting of 1000 2's, 6000 3's, 2000 5's, and 1000 10's?

3.74 In Section 3.2, we mentioned that the mean is the balancing point for a set of data. This is reflected by the fact that $\sum(x - \bar{x}) = 0$.

(a) Consider the data values 0, 2, 5, 8, 9, 12. Verify that $\sum(x - \bar{x}) = 0$.

(b) Given these six data values, suppose that we supplement the data with a 4 (giving the data 0, 2, 5, 8, 9, 12, 4). If we were to supplement another value, what must it be so that the mean is 6 again? (*Hint:*   We do not want to disturb the balancing point.)

3.75   Over a five-game period, a basketball player scored 9, 12, 8, 5, and 6 points. Therefore the mean number of points scored per game was $\bar{x} = 8$.

  (a)   Suppose the player had scored four more points in each game. What would be the mean number of points per game? Compare your answer with $\bar{x} = 8$.

  (b)   Suppose the player had scored c additional points per game, where c is a constant value. What would be the mean number of points scored per game? Express your answer in terms of $\bar{x}$ and c.

  (c)   Suppose the player had doubled the number of points scored in each game. What would be the mean number of points scored per game? Compare your answer with $\bar{x} = 8$.

  (d)   Suppose the player had scored k times as many points in each game, where k is a constant value. What would be the mean number of points scored per game? Express your answer in terms of $\bar{x}$ and k.

  (e)   Now consider the data values 0, 2, 5, 8, 9, 12. A new collection of data values is obtained in the following way. Each of these six data values is multiplied by 4, and the resulting product is increased by 7. Use the results of parts (b) and (d) to find the mean of the new collection of data values. Note that $\bar{x} = 6$ for the original set of data (that is, 0, 2, 5, 8, 9, 12).

3.76   Each week a newspaper carrier notes the number of new subscribers. Over a 6-week period, the carrier recorded 0, 2, 5, 8, 9, and 12 new subscribers. The sample variance is $s^2 = 20.4$.

  (a)   Suppose 3 were added to each of the above data values. What would the new sample variance be? Compare your answer with $s^2 = 20.4$.

  (b)   Suppose the carrier added a constant c to each data value. What would the new sample variance be?

  (c)   Suppose the number of subscribers per week doubled. What would the new sample variance be? Compare your answer with $s^2 = 20.4$.

  (d)   Suppose the carrier obtained k times as many new subscribers per week, where k is a constant value. What would the new sample variance be? Express your answer in terms of s^2 and k.

  (e)   Consider the data values 1, 1, 4, 4, 5, which have sample variance 3.50. A new collection of data values is obtained in the following way. Each of the above data values is multiplied by 3, and the resulting product is increased by 6. Use the results of parts (b) and (d) to find the sample variance of the new collection of data values.

ANSWERS TO PRACTICE QUIZ

1.   READ IN C1, C2
     10 4
     11 8
     15 1
     3 5

2.

C3	C4	C5	C6	C7
24	12	10	2	8
12	6	14	4	3
24	15	7	2	12

3.

C3	C4
4	7
2	8

4. Columns are not of equal length, which is a requirement for use of the READ command.

5. Nothing is wrong. Median is misspelled, but Minitab looks only at the first four letters.

6. SET command can be used to enter only one collection of data at a time. Use the READ command instead.

7. K1 is a constant, but C1 + C2 will be a column (the column of sums). Type

LET C3 = C1 + C2

8. Here 3 is an unnecessary constant. Type

DESCRIBE C1

9. Since MEAN is used in the LET command, we must have parentheses around C1. Type

LET K1 = MEAN (C1)

10. PRINT is used only to print stored constants or columns. Type

LET K3 = K1/K2

PRINT K3

Notes

The Hammond Almanac. Maplewood, NJ: Hammond Almanac, Inc., 1983.

Information Please Almanac. Boston: Houghton Mifflin Company, 1989, 1994.

Lyman, C. P., R. C. O'Brien, G. C. Greene, and E. D. Papafrangos. "Hibernation and Longevity in the Turkish Hamster *Mesocricetus brandti.*" *Science,* Vol. 212, 1981, pp. 668–670.

Statistical Abstract of the United States. Washington, D.C.: U.S. Bureau of the Census, 1984.

U.S. News & World Report. Washington, D.C.: U.S. News & World Report, Inc., Dec. 19, 1988.

Woodhouse, J. "Worldwide Seismic Network Tape." Data in Donoho, A. W., D. L. Donoho, and M. Gasko, *MacSpin User Manual.* Austin, Texas: D^2 Software Inc., 1985.

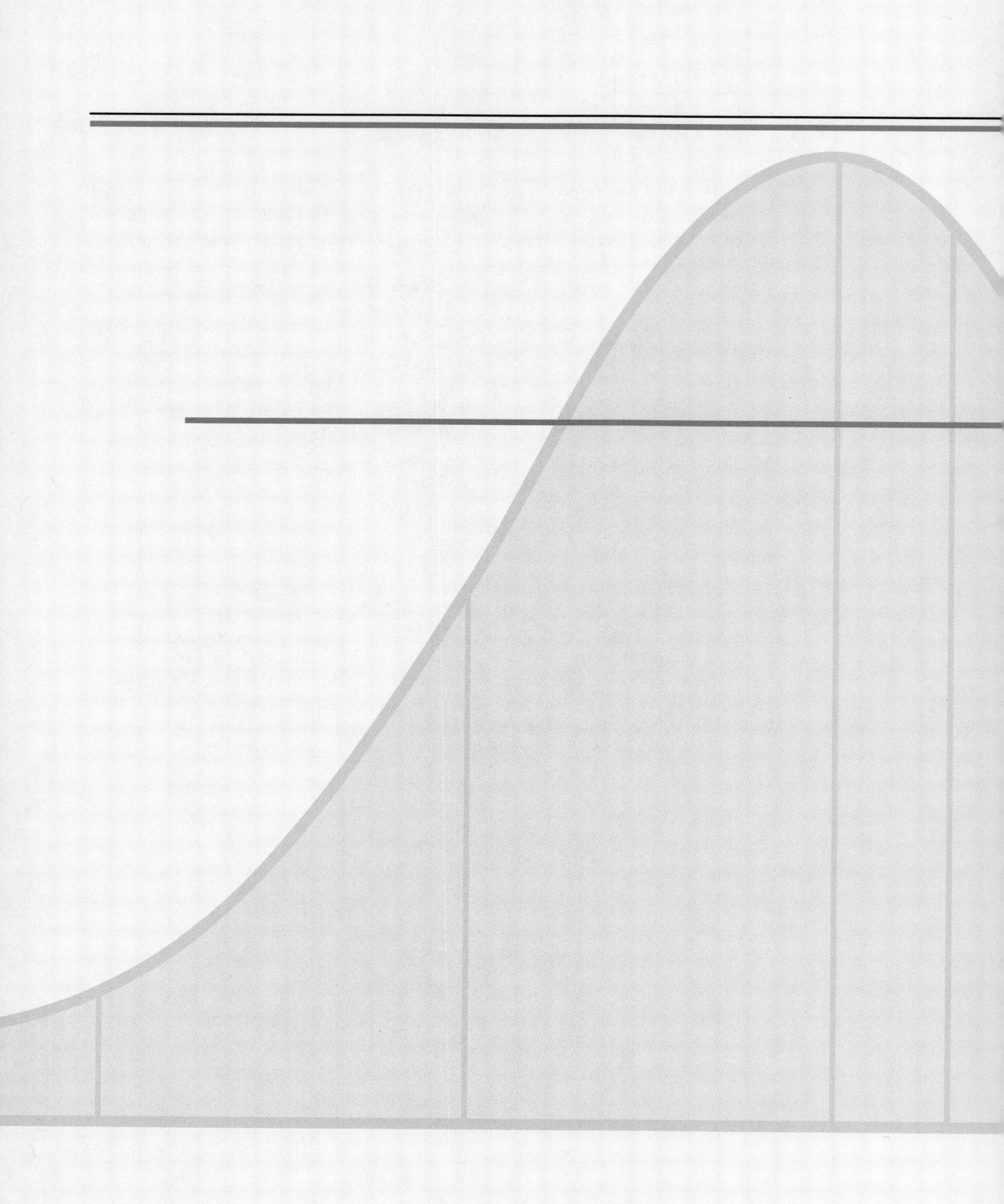

CHAPTER 4

REGRESSION AND CORRELATION

4.1 INTRODUCTION

4.2 THE LEAST SQUARES REGRESSION LINE

4.3 THE LINEAR CORRELATION COEFFICIENT

4.4 SOME WORDS OF CAUTION CONCERNING CORRELATION AND REGRESSION

4.5 USING MINITAB (OPTIONAL)

4.6 WORKING WITH DATA (OPTIONAL)

4.7 SUMMARY

REVIEW EXERCISES

NOTES

4.1

INTRODUCTION

Statistics is often used to investigate the relationship between two variables of interest. The following are examples of some of the kinds of issues that are often studied:

- Is there a relationship between years of schooling and level of income?
- What is the relationship between the inflation rate and the prime lending rate (the interest rate that banks charge their best customers)?
- Is there a relationship between high school grade point average and college grade point average? If so, what is the relationship?
- What is the relationship between a person's age and remaining years of life?

131

In these examples, there are two basic kinds of questions of interest concerning a pair of variables:

1. Is there a relationship between the two variables?
2. What is the relationship (if any) between the two variables? This is the question asked in the last item in the list of examples. Actuarial scientists would be interested in the (approximate) relationship between age and the remaining years of life. To answer this, we might look for a formula that would enable us to predict the approximate expected remaining years of life for a person of any given age. Such information would be of use to determine the amount of money needed to provide a retirement annuity of a fixed amount for a person of a certain age.

In this chapter, we study these two questions. We study **correlation analysis,** which is concerned with the question of whether there is a relationship between variables. We also discuss **regression analysis,** where our objective is to find a relationship (or approximate relationship) between the variables. This relationship takes the form of an equation relating the two variables. Then for a given value of one variable, we can solve for the approximate value of the other variable.

4.2

THE LEAST SQUARES REGRESSION LINE

In many cases, there is a linear or straight-line relationship between two variables of interest. For example, suppose a TV repair technician charges $15 for driving to your house, plus $20 for each hour of work on your TV. If we let $y =$ the total charge (excluding parts) and $x =$ the number of hours of work, the relationship between x and y is

$$y = 15 + 20x$$

Then if $x = 2$ hours of work is done, the cost is

$$y = 15 + (20)(2) = \$55$$

Notice that if the problem is fixed immediately, then $x = 0$. But you still pay the amount $y = 15 + (20)(0) = \$15$. A few of the values of x and y are given in Table 4.1.

Table 4.1

Hours Worked (x)	Cost for Labor and Service Charge (y)
0	15
1	35
2	55
3	75

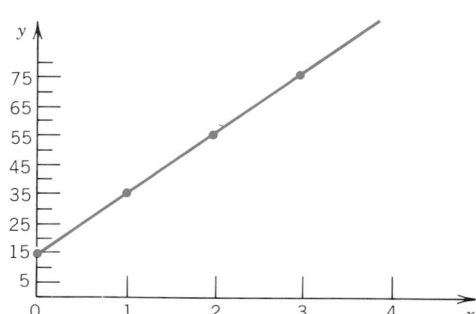

Figure 4.1

The graph of the equation $y = 15 + 20x$ is the collection of all points in the xy-plane that satisfy the equation, such as the points $(0, 15)$, $(1, 35)$, $(2, 55)$, etc. Figure 4.1 is a graph of the equation showing the points in Table 4.1.

The graph in Figure 4.1 is, of course, a straight line. This is why we say that the relationship between x and y is **linear.** There are two terms that should be mentioned in connection with straight lines. Observe that an increase of 1 hour in the technician's labor corresponds to an increase of $20 in the fee. This value is called the **slope** of the line. Note that the slope is the coefficient of the x term in the equation of the line. This is true for any line. When the slope is a positive number, an increase in x is accompanied by an increase in y. In this case, we say there is a *positive linear relationship* between x and y. If the slope were negative, it would mean that an increase in x was accompanied by a decrease in y. In this case, we say there is a *negative linear relationship* between x and y. When the slope is 0, the line is horizontal. When the technician fixes the problem immediately, then $x = 0$ and $y = \$15$. This value is called the **y-intercept,** because it is the value on the y-axis where the line crosses the y-axis. The y-intercept is the constant term in the equation.

In general, the equation of a (nonvertical) straight line may be written in the form

$$y = b_0 + b_1 x$$

where b_0 and b_1 are constants. Conversely, any equation in this form has as its graph a straight line. The constant b_0 is the y-intercept and b_1 is the slope.

If such a straight-line (or linear) relationship exists between two variables, and if we can find the values of b_0 and b_1, then it is a simple matter to find the y value when we know the corresponding x value. We simply "plug" the x value into the equation. We sometimes call x the **independent variable** and y the **dependent variable.**

In the example discussed previously, all the possible points, that is, pairs (x, y), lie exactly on the line. We say that there is a *perfect linear relationship* between the x and y values. However, in many situations, the points are not exactly on a line but rather tend to cluster around a line. In this case, the line and its equation may still be of use because we might use the line to predict the approximate y value associated with a given x value.

To understand this, consider the following example: An electronics firm was planning to expand its product line and wanted to get an idea of the salary picture for the technicians it would hire in this field. A company official obtained the following information on annual salary in thousands of dollars (y) and years of experience (x) for 12 technicians employed at various firms involved in this field (see Table 4.2 on page 134). In Figure 4.2(a), we have plotted the (x, y) values; this is called a **scatter diagram.**

Notice how the points in the scatter diagram tend to cluster about the straight line in Figure 4.2(b). Using this line, the company could estimate the approximate salary it could expect to pay a technician with, say, 15 years of experience. Locate the value 15 on the x-axis; then read up to the line and across to the value on the y-axis as shown. This value appears to be about 30. This means that the company can expect to pay a salary of about $30,000 per year to a technician with 15 years of experience in the field. (We also think of $30,000 as an estimate of the mean salary of all technicians with 15 years experience in the field.) Instead of reading a y value from a graph, it would be more convenient to use the equation of the line and substitute the value $x = 15$ into the equation to obtain y. *When the points*

Table 4.2
Salary Data for 12 Technicians

Years of Experience (x)	Salary in Thousands of Dollars (y)
12	29
16	31
6	23
23	34
27	38
8	24
5	22
19	34
23	36
13	27
16	33
8	27

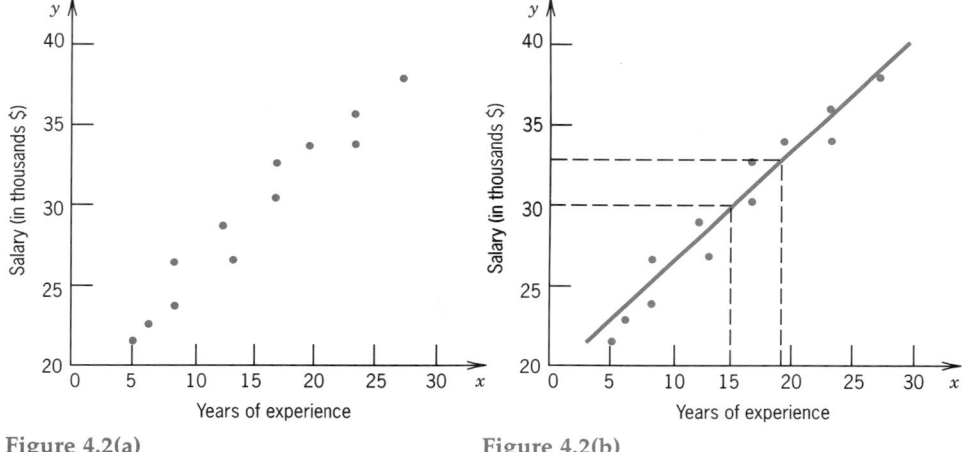

Figure 4.2(a)
Scatter Diagram for Salary Data

Figure 4.2(b)
Salary Data Cluster about a Line

in the scatter diagram cluster about a straight line as in Figure 4.2(b), it would be worthwhile to find the equation of the line. However, note that the line in Figure 4.2(b) is *nonhorizontal.* If the line were horizontal (with slope 0), it would indicate there is no relationship between experience and salary. In that case the line would not be useful for estimating salary.

> When the points in a scatter diagram cluster about a line with nonzero slope, the relationship between the x and y values is (approximately) linear.

The question is, How does one find the line in Figure 4.2(b), and what is its equation? The line drawn there was not drawn by eye. There is a way of finding the equation of the line that "best fits" the data. Before showing how this is done, we should discuss what we mean when we say that a particular line best fits the data. When we use a straight line to predict or estimate a y value corresponding to a particular x value, we denote the estimate by $\hat{y}$. So we will denote the y values on the line by $\hat{y}$. The difference between the observed value y and the estimate $\hat{y}$ is called the **error** of the estimate. It is also called a **residual** and is denoted by e (Figure 4.3):

$$e = y - \hat{y}$$

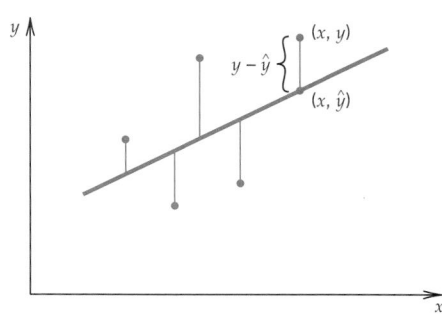

Figure 4.3
Residuals

For a concrete example, consider the salary data in Table 4.2. One of the technicians in the study has an annual salary of $y = 34$ (thousand dollars) with $x = 19$ years experience. If we examine Figure 4.2(b), we see that for a technician with 19 years experience, the estimated salary (from the line) appears to be about $\hat{y} = 33$. Therefore, in this case, the error or residual is

$$e = y - \hat{y} = 34 - 33 = 1 \quad \text{(thousand dollars)}$$

For a scatter diagram, we would want to choose the line that somehow minimizes the errors taken as a whole. But just what is to be minimized? If we considered the sum of the errors, we may get a small value just because the negative errors cancel the positive errors. If we square the errors, we eliminate the problem of negative values. Thus the sum of the squares of the error terms will be a measure of how close the line fits the points: the smaller this sum, the better the fit. We will agree that the line that best fits the data is the one for which the sum of the squares of the error terms is smallest. This is called the **least squares criterion.**

Least Squares Criterion   We define the sum of squares for error, SSE, to be the sum of the squares of the error terms

$$\text{SSE} = \sum e^2 = \sum (y - \hat{y})^2$$

We agree that the line that best fits the data is the line for which the sum of squares for error, SSE, is minimum. This line is called the *line of best fit* or the *regression line.*

There are many lines that can be drawn through the points in a scatter diagram. How do we find the line of best fit? Using techniques beyond the scope of this book, it can be shown that the line of best fit is obtained as follows:

Suppose that we have a scatter diagram with n points. The *line of best fit*, also called the *regression line*, has the equation

$$\hat{y} = b_0 + b_1 x$$

where

$$b_1 = \frac{n(\sum xy) - (\sum x)(\sum y)}{n(\sum x^2) - (\sum x)^2}$$

and

$$b_0 = \bar{y} - b_1 \bar{x}$$

The meaning of the terms in these formulas is explained in the following example.

EXAMPLE 4.1

For the data in the accompanying table, plot the scatter diagram. Find the line of best fit, and sketch the graph of the line.

x	y
1	2
2	4
3	4
4	6

Solution

The scatter diagram is given in Figure 4.4(a). It suggests clustering about a line. We now find the line of best fit. To find the slope b_1 and the y-intercept b_0, it will be helpful to set up Table 4.3.

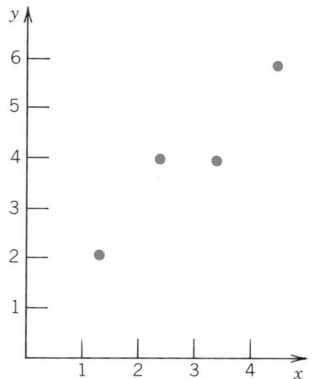

Figure 4.4(a)
Scatter Diagram

Table 4.3

x	y	xy	x^2
1	2	2	1
2	4	8	4
3	4	12	9
4	6	24	16
10	16	46	30
$\uparrow$	$\uparrow$	$\uparrow$	$\uparrow$	
$\sum x$	$\sum y$	$\sum xy$	$\sum x^2$	$n = 4$

From Table 4.3, we see that $\sum x = 10$, $\sum y = 16$, $\sum xy = 46$, and $\sum x^2 = 30$. Using these sums, we can find the line of best fit with the equation $\hat{y} = b_0 + b_1 x$, where

$$b_1 = \frac{n(\sum xy) - (\sum x)(\sum y)}{n(\sum x^2) - (\sum x)^2} = \frac{(4)(46) - (10)(16)}{4(30) - (10)^2}$$

$$= \frac{184 - 160}{120 - 100} = \frac{24}{20} = 1.2$$

$$b_0 = \bar{y} - b_1 \bar{x} = \frac{16}{4} - (1.2)\left(\frac{10}{4}\right) = 1$$

Hence the line of best fit (regression line) has the equation

$$\hat{y} = 1 + 1.2x$$

To graph the line, we need to find just two points that satisfy the equation. Then we draw the line through these two points. (Two points determine a line.) When $x = 0$, $\hat{y} = 1$ (the y-intercept). When $x = 1$, $\hat{y} = 2.2$. So $(0, 1)$ and $(1, 2.2)$ are points on the line. The line is sketched in Figure 4.4(b).

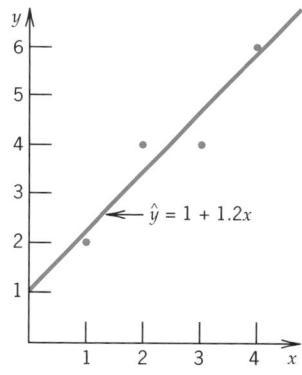

Figure 4.4(b)
Line of Best Fit

The line of best fit in Figure 4.4(b) is the line with the smallest possible sum of squares for error calculated for the points in Figure 4.4(a). We will now calculate the SSE for the line of best fit, and compare it with the SSE for some other line through the scatter diagram. We will compare the following two lines (which are shown in Figure 4.5 on page 138):

Line 1: $\hat{y} = 1 + 1.2x \leftarrow$ line of best fit

Line 2: $\hat{y} = 4 \leftarrow$ horizontal line through the value 4 on the y-axis

The SSE for line 1 should be smaller than the SSE for line 2.

The calculations are shown in Table 4.4. Note that in these calculations, the value of $\hat{y}$ corresponding to a particular x is obtained from the equation of the line. For example, for line 1, the value of $\hat{y}$ corresponding to $x = 1$ is obtained by substituting $x = 1$ into the equation of the line, so $\hat{y} = 1 + (1.2)(1) = 2.2$. Line 2 is a horizontal line; therefore each value of $\hat{y}$ is the same: $\hat{y} = 4$. This situation is displayed graphically in Figure 4.5.

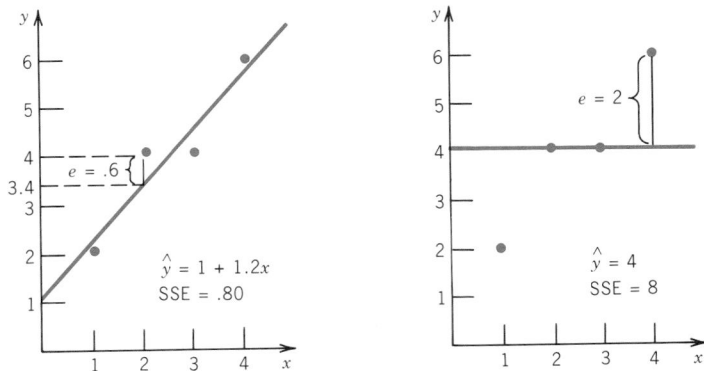

Figure 4.5
The Line of Best Fit Has the Smallest Possible Value for SSE.

Table 4.4

| Line 1: $\hat{y} = 1 + 1.2x$ | | | | | Line 2: $\hat{y} = 4$ | | | | |
x	y	$\hat{y}$	$e = y - \hat{y}$	e^2	x	y	$\hat{y}$	$e = y - \hat{y}$	e^2
1	2	2.2	$-.2$	.04	1	2	4	-2	4
2	4	3.4	.6	.36	2	4	4	0	0
3	4	4.6	$-.6$	.36	3	4	4	0	0
4	6	5.8	.2	.04	4	6	4	2	4
			SSE $= \sum e^2 =$ .80					SSE $=$ 8	

As expected, line 2 has a larger SSE than the line of best fit. This will always be the case, no matter what line is used in place of line 2.

We will now find the line of best fit for the salary data discussed at the beginning of this section. (See Table 4.2.)

EXAMPLE 4.2
Find the line of best fit for the salary data in Table 4.2.

Solution
We have already seen that the points in the scatter diagram tend to cluster about a line [see Figures 4.2(a) and (b)]. The calculations for the line of best fit are shown in Table 4.5.

$$b_1 = \frac{n(\sum xy) - (\sum x)(\sum y)}{n(\sum x^2) - (\sum x)^2}$$

$$= \frac{(12)(5661) - (176)(358)}{(12)(3162) - (176)^2} = \frac{4924}{6968}$$

$$= .706659 \doteq .71$$

$$b_0 = \bar{y} - b_1 \bar{x} = \frac{358}{12} - (.706659)\left(\frac{176}{12}\right) \doteq 19.47$$

Table 4.5

x	y	xy	x^2
12	29	348	144
16	31	496	256
6	23	138	36
23	34	782	529
27	38	1026	729
8	24	192	64
5	22	110	25
19	34	646	361
23	36	828	529
13	27	351	169
16	33	528	256
8	27	216	64
Sums: 176	358	5661	3162 $n = 12$

(Note that we substituted the value .706659 for b_1 in the formula for b_0 rather than the rounded value of .71. This is in keeping with the practice of rounding as little as possible during intermediate steps and rounding only the final answer.) The equation of the line of best fit is

$$\hat{y} = 19.47 + .71x$$

Using this equation, we could construct a salary schedule for technicians. The equation suggests a base salary of 19.47 thousand dollars (or $19,470) plus .71 thousand dollars ($710) for each year of experience in the field. For a technician with $x = 15$ years, the company could expect to pay an annual salary (in thousands) of

$$\hat{y} = 19.47 + (.71)(15) = 30.12$$

or $30,120.

EXAMPLE 4.3

An economist was interested in the production costs for companies supplying chemicals for use in fertilizers. The data in Table 4.6 represent the numbers of tons produced during a year in thousands (x) along with the production costs per ton (y) for seven companies. (Note that $x = 2.4$ means 2400 tons.)

Table 4.6

Number of Tons (in Thousands) x	Cost per Ton (in Dollars) y
3.0	40
4.0	40
2.4	50
5.0	35
2.6	55
4.0	35
5.5	30

(a) Plot the points and find the line of best fit for the data. Sketch its graph on the scatter diagram.

(b) What cost per ton would you predict for a company producing 3500 tons?

Solution

(a) The points of the scatter diagram are displayed in Figure 4.6 and suggest a clustering about a line.

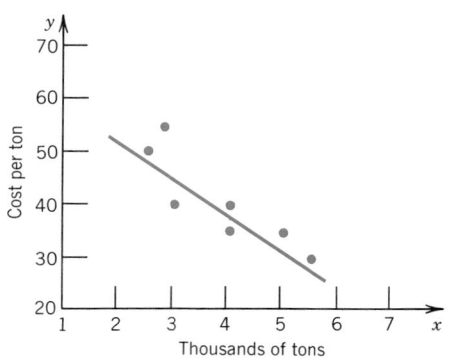

Table 4.7

	x	y	xy	x²
	3.0	40	120	9.00
	4.0	40	160	16.00
	2.4	50	120	5.76
	5.0	35	175	25.00
	2.6	55	143	6.76
	4.0	35	140	16.00
	5.5	30	165	30.25
Sums:	26.5	285	1023	108.77	n = 7

Figure 4.6
Production Costs

$$b_1 = \frac{n\left(\sum xy\right) - \left(\sum x\right)\left(\sum y\right)}{n\left(\sum x^2\right) - \left(\sum x\right)^2}$$

$$= \frac{(7)(1023) - (26.5)(285)}{(7)(108.77) - (26.5)^2} = \frac{7161 - 7552.5}{761.39 - 702.25} = \frac{-391.5}{59.14} = -6.619885 \doteq -6.62$$

$$b_0 = \bar{y} - b_1\bar{x} = \frac{285}{7} - (-6.619885)\left(\frac{26.5}{7}\right) \doteq 65.78$$

The equation of the line of best fit is

$$\hat{y} = 65.78 - 6.62x$$

This line is also displayed in Figure 4.6. The negative slope indicates that an increase in the number of tons is accompanied by a decrease in the cost per ton. (Of course, we would not expect this equation to apply to firms with a production capacity outside the range studied by the economist, which happened to be companies in the range of 2000 to 6000 tons.)

(b) For a company producing 3500 tons, x = 3.5. The predicted cost per ton is obtained by substituting 3.5 for x:

$$\hat{y} = 65.78 - 6.62(3.5) = \$42.61$$

JMP Printout for Example 4.3

The following is a portion of a JMP printout corresponding to Example 4.3. Below the scatter diagram is information on the line of regression. Under Estimate, we see the value of b_0 next to Intercept and the value of b_1 next to x. Also given are estimates of the standard deviations for b_0 and b_1, listed under Std Error. With repeated sampling, the values of b_0 and b_1 would change from sample to sample. Hence they are variables; so it makes sense to talk about their standard deviations. The last two columns will be discussed in Chapter 10. The output from most statistical programs resembles the JMP output given here. The second column, which contains b_0 and b_1, is usually labeled *Estimate* or *Coefficient*.

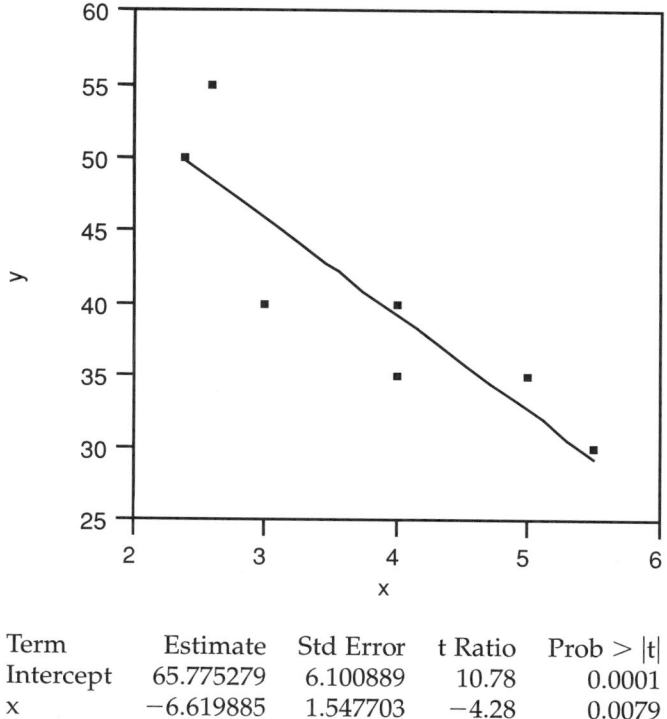

Term	Estimate	Std Error	t Ratio	Prob > |t|
Intercept	65.775279	6.100889	10.78	0.0001
x	−6.619885	1.547703	−4.28	0.0079

Appropriateness of Linear Regression

The previous examples should suggest that it is prudent to take some measure, such as looking at a scatterplot, to investigate linearity before finding the regression line. Do not just blindly compute the regression line. After all, the regression line is useful only when the points in the scatter diagram cluster about a straight line. There are many situations, however, when this is not the case, as shown in Figure 4.7 (page 142).

In Figure 4.7(a), the points appear to cluster about a curve. There appears to be some relationship between the x and y values, although not a linear relationship. In Figure 4.7(b), the points do not appear to cluster about a curve or a straight line, indicating no relationship of any kind.

Our method of finding the line of best fit will work even for the data in Figure 4.7. However, the line so obtained may be of little value in predicting a y value for a given x value (see Figure 4.8).

Until now we have relied upon a scatter diagram to determine whether the points are clustered about a straight line. In the next section, we introduce the **linear correlation coefficient.** This is a number calculated from the data; it measures the degree of linear relationship between the x and y values.

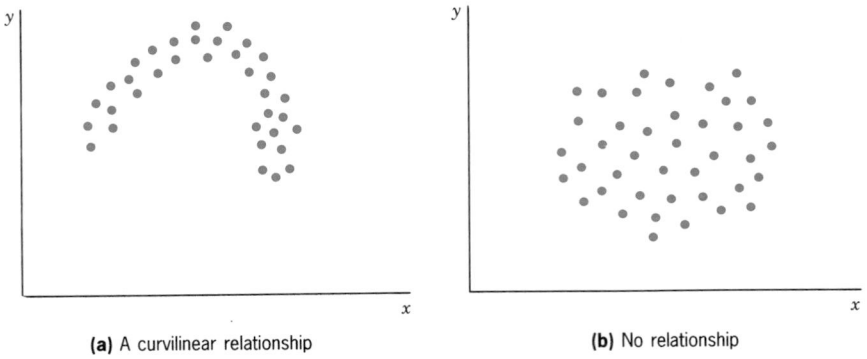

(a) A curvilinear relationship   **(b)** No relationship

Figure 4.7

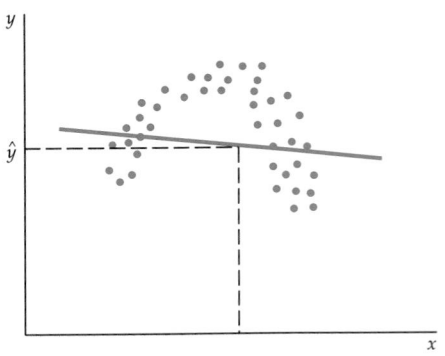

Figure 4.8

Unusual Observations

Although there may be an overall linear pattern for the points in a scatter diagram, there may occasionally be a few points that deviate in some sense from the other points. These are called **unusual observations.** A point may be unusual for the following reasons:

1.   It is far from the regression line in the y direction, or
2.   Its x value is a considerable distance from the x values of the other points. In other words, the x value is an outlier relative to the other x values.

The Minitab statistical package prints a list of any unusual observations and indicates which of these two conditions makes them unusual.

Unusual observations should be investigated to see whether they have a large influence on the regression line. If they do, they are called **influential observations.** Influential observations are often dropped from the data set.

Table 4.8 contains average teacher salaries and pupil-to-staff ratios for the 10 western suburbs of Boston within Route 128 in 1992.

In Figure 4.9, we see the scatter diagram and the regression lines with and without Newton. Newton is clearly an influential observation. With Newton included, there seems to be a positive linear relationship, suggesting an association between high teacher salaries and larger class sizes. But without Newton, there does not appear to be much of a relationship. Notice how Newton pulls the regression line

Table 4.8

Town	Average Teacher Salaries in $ Thousands (x)	Pupil-to-Staff Ratio (y)
Arlington	40	13.4
Belmont	44	14.4
Brookline	35	11.7
Cambridge	42	11.7
Dedham	37	13.0
Lexington	48	13.9
Newton	56	17.8
Somerville	40	14.3
Waltham	38	13.9
Watertown	41	13.1

Source: *The Boston Globe*, June 6, 1993.

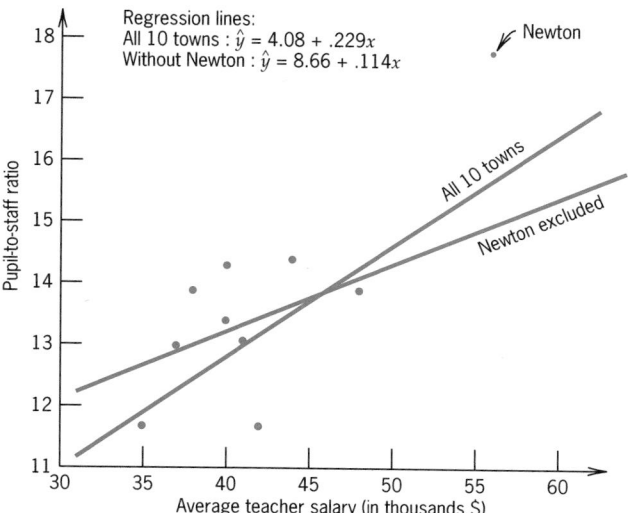

Figure 4.9
Scatter Diagram and Regression Lines for Pupil-to-Staff Ratio Versus Average Teacher Salary, With and Without Newton

toward itself. This often happens with points that are far from the other points in the *x* direction. Such points are said to have **high leverage.**

> **Definition**   A point in a scatter diagram is an *influential observation* if removing it would substantially alter the regression line.

Influential observations are akin to extreme observations, discussed in Chapter 3. A point may be atypical enough to substantially influence the regression line. In other words, **the regression and correlation techniques of this chapter are not resistant.**

Not all unusual observations are extreme enough to be influential. The data in Table 4.9 (page 144) give fat consumption in kilograms per person per year (*x*) and the death rate from atherosclerosis per 100,000 people per year (*y*) in Norway from 1938 to 1947. Norway was an occupied country during World War II, and it was difficult to obtain foods rich in fat. Along with the decline in consumption of fat there was a corresponding decline in the death rate from atherosclerosis.*

Figure 4.10 gives the scatter diagram and regression line for the data in Table 4.9. There is one point (corresponding to 1940) that seems quite far from the regression line. Indeed, Minitab would identify this as an unusual observation. The equation for the regression line is

$$\hat{y} = 13.5 + 1.06x$$

---

*Although atherosclerosis is a disease that takes years to develop, the decrease in mortality was immediate with the change in dietary habits. It has been suggested that this could be explained by the possibility that once fat in the arteries accumulates to a certain level, a triggering event (such as a blood clot) is associated with mortality. It is possible that the low-fat diet reduced the tendency of the blood to clot.

Table 4.9
Norway Data

Year	Fat Consumption (x)	Death Rate (y)
1938	14.4	29.1
1939	16.0	29.7
1940	11.6	29.2
1941	11.0	26.0
1942	10.0	24.0
1943	9.6	23.1
1944	9.2	23.0
1945	10.4	23.1
1946	11.4	25.2
1947	12.5	26.1

Source: The data are estimated from a graph in Williams, C. L., "Nutrition and Coronary Heart Disease" in *Bank of Epidemiology Exercises*, Exercise 13, 1st ed. New York: Dept. of Community and Preventive Medicine, New York Medical College, 1978.

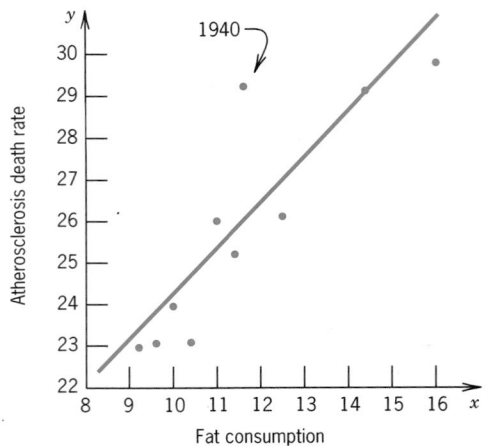

Figure 4.10
Line of Best Fit for Data in Table 4.9

If 1940 is deleted, the remaining points have the following regression line:

$$\hat{y} = 13.1 + 1.07x$$

There is hardly any difference between the two lines, so 1940 is not influential and probably should not be deleted.

EXERCISES

4.1 Find the y-intercept (b_0) and the slope (b_1) of each of the lines given by the following equations. Then graph the line.

(a) $y = 4 + 7x$

(b) $y - 3 = 5(x + 2)$

(c) $y = 8$

(d) $4x + 2y - 9 = 0$

(e) $3y = 9x + 12$

In Exercises 4.2–4.6, (a) plot the scatter diagram, (b) find the line of best fit for estimating y from x, and (c) sketch the line of best fit on the same paper as the scatter diagram.

4.2

x	y
2	9
2	7
4	5
4	5
6	3
6	1

4.3

x	y
0	2
0	4
0	6
1	6
2	7
2	8
2	9

4.4

x	y
1	2
2	6
4	14
5	18

4.5

x	y
1	2
2	2
3	1
4	0
5	0

4.6

x	y
0	5
0	4
1	3
2	2
2	1

4.7 For the following data, $\hat{y} = 4 + 2x$ represents the line of best fit:

x	y
0	2
0	4
0	6
1	6
2	7
2	8
2	9

(a) Compute the value of SSE for the line of best fit.

(b) Without computing, would SSE for the line $\hat{y} = 6$ be smaller or larger than the value computed in part (a)?

(c) Now compute SSE for the line $\hat{y} = 6$.

4.8 For the following data, one of the equations $\hat{y} = -1.2 + 1.2x$ or $\hat{y} = x$ represents the line of best fit:

x	y
2	2
4	2
6	6
8	10
10	10

Using the value of SSE for each line, determine which line is the line of best fit.

4.9 The owner of a liquor store wanted to investigate the relationship between the intensity of advertising (x) and the number of cases (y) of Samuel Adams Boston Ale sold per day. The intensity of advertising was indexed from 1 for no advertising to 5 for the most intensive advertising. The data are given in the following table.

Intensity of Advertising (x)	Number of Cases Sold (y)
1	4
2	7
3	8
4	14
5	15

(a) Draw a scatter diagram. Does the number of cases sold appear to increase as intensity of advertising increases?

(b) Find the line of best fit for estimating the number of cases sold given the intensity of advertising. Sketch the line on the same paper as the scatter diagram.

(c) Estimate the number of cases sold for an intensity of advertising 3.5.

4.10 A town assessor was trying to determine a relationship between the size of a parcel of land (x) and the selling price (y). The assessor used the data in the following table.

Size in Acres (x)	Selling Price in Thousands of Dollars (y)
.5	25
1.0	40
1.5	55
2.0	65
2.5	75
3.0	80

(a) Draw a scatter diagram. Does the selling price appear to increase as acreage increases?

(b) Find the line of best fit for estimating the selling price given the acreage. Sketch the line on the same paper as the scatter diagram.

(c) Estimate the selling price for a 1.7-acre piece of land.

4.11 A state official was investigating the relationship between salary (x) and the number of absences (y) for state employees. The variable y in the following table represents the average number of absences per year for employees at that salary.

Salary in $ Thousands (x)	Number of Absences (y)
20.0	2.3
22.5	2.0
25.0	2.0
27.5	1.8
30.0	2.2
32.5	1.5
35.0	1.2
37.5	1.3
40.0	.6

(a) Find and sketch the line of best fit for estimating the number of absences given the salary.

(b) Estimate the average number of absences for employees earning $29,000.

4.12 The data in the following table represent trends in cigarette consumption (x) and lung cancer mortality (y) for Canadian males. The data have been rounded off for convenience. Find the line of best fit for predicting the mortality rate from the cigarette consumption.

Cigarette Consumption per Capita in Hundreds (x)	Mortality Rate per 100,000 (y)
11.8	10.4
12.5	16.5
15.7	22.9
19.2	26.6
21.9	33.8
23.3	42.8

Source: Phillips, A. J., "Smoking Control Programs for Canadian Adults," *Proceedings of the Third World Conference, Smoking and Health,* Vol. II, p. 273.

4.13 An owner of a health spa wished to study the relationship between the temperature (x) in degrees Fahrenheit at 11 A.M. and the number (y) of customers using the facilities at that time for randomly selected days during the summer. The data follow.

Temperature (x)	Number of Customers (y)
65	27
67	25
75	20
81	22
85	16
87	10

(a) Draw a scatter diagram. Do the sample data appear to indicate a linear relationship between temperature and number of customers?

(b) Find the line of best fit for estimating the number of customers using the facilities given the temperature.

(c) Estimate the number of customers using the facilities when the temperature is 70°F.

4.14 A farmer was interested in the relationship between the amount of fertilizer (x) and the number of bushels (y) of soybeans produced. The farmer conducted an experiment and obtained the following data:

Hundreds of Pounds per Acre (x)	Bushels per Acre (y)
1.0	25
2.5	32
3.0	35
3.0	32
3.4	35
4.0	39
4.0	41
4.5	40

(a) Draw a scatter diagram. Do the sample data appear to indicate a linear relationship between amount of fertilizer and bushels per acre?

(b) Find the line of best fit for estimating the bushels per acre given hundreds of pounds of fertilizer.

(c) Estimate the number of bushels given 3.5 hundreds of pounds of fertilizer.

4.15 On January 28, 1986, the space shuttle *Challenger* exploded because of O-ring failure shortly after it was launched. (O-rings are supposed to prevent the release of combustible gases.) The accompanying data are a history of O-ring damage and temperature at time of launch for 23 previous shuttle flights. The variable x is temperature (°F), and y represents O-ring damage, where $0 =$ no damage and $1 =$ O-ring damage.

x	53	57	58	63	66	67	67	67	68	69	70	70
y	1	1	1	1	0	0	0	0	0	0	0	0
x	70	70	72	73	75	75	76	76	78	79	81	
y	1	1	0	0	0	1	0	0	0	0	0	

Source: *Report of the Presidential Commission on the Space Shuttle Challenger Accident*, Washington, D.C., 1986, pp. 129–131.

The summary statistics are

$$\sum xy = 446 \quad \sum x = 1600 \quad \sum y = 7 \quad \sum x^2 = 112{,}400$$

(a) Make a scatter diagram of O-ring damage versus temperature. Since y can be only 0 or 1, you will not see a clustering about a line. Yet there does appear to be a relationship between temperature and O-ring damage: The lower the temperature, the greater the tendency toward O-ring damage.

(b) Find the line of regression.

(c) We said that $\hat{y}$ from a regression line can be thought of as an estimate of the *average* of all possible y values for a fixed x value. Since our y values here are 0's and 1's, there is another interpretation. Suppose for some particular temperature, there were nine 1's and one 0. Nine flights with O-ring damage in 10 flights suggests a 90% chance of O-ring damage for that temperature. Expressed as a decimal, this is .9, and is referred to as a *probability*. But notice that .9 is also the *average* of the nine 1's and one 0. So the $\hat{y}$ we compute from the regression line not only estimates an average, but in this situation it is also an estimate of a probability. That is, $\hat{y} \doteq$ *probability of O-ring damage for a given temperature.* Using the regression line from part (b), estimate the probability of O-ring damage for a launch temperature of 53°.

Comment: The lowest temperature at launch for any previous shuttle flight was 53°. The temperature at the time of the *Challenger* launch was 31°! This temperature is too far out of the range of all other launch temperatures to use the regression line of part (b) to estimate the probability of O-ring damage. But the analysis you performed here clearly suggests that O-ring damage at 31° should not be surprising.

4.16 The data in the following table represent the inflation rate (x) and prime lending rate (y) over a 7-year period. Plot a scatter diagram. Find the line of best fit for predicting the prime lending rate from the inflation rate.

Inflation Rate (x)	Prime Lending Rate (y)
3.3	5.2
6.2	8.0
11.0	10.8
9.1	7.9
5.8	6.8
6.5	6.9
7.6	9.0

Source: Statistical Abstract of the United States, 100th ed. Washington, D.C.: U.S. Bureau of the Census, pp. 419 and 541.

4.17   Education and crime ratings for selected U.S. cities are given in the following table. Education is a composite rating including pupil/teacher ratio, academic options in higher education, etc. The higher the rating, the better. Crime is the crime rate per 100 people.

City	Education (x)	Crime (y)
Boston	35	12
Chicago	35	10
Detroit	31	16
Los Angeles	32	20
New York	30	25
Washington, D.C.	36	13

Source: Boyer, R., and D. Savageau. Places Rated Almanac (Rand McNally), as reported in *MacSpin Release 1.1,* 1986.

(a)   Draw a scatter diagram. Does there appear to be a strong linear relationship between education and crime rate?

(b)   Find and sketch the line of best fit for predicting crime rate from an education rating.

(c)   Estimate the crime rate for an education rating of 34.

4.18   The following data give average salaries and fringe benefits (in thousands of dollars) for full professors in private (y) and public (x) institutions of higher learning for the years 1984–1991 (*Source: The 1994 Information Please Almanac,* 1994, p. 865):

Year	1984	1985	1986	1987	1988	1989	1990	1991
Public (x)	37.1	39.6	42.3	45.3	47.2	50.1	53.2	55.8
Private (y)	41.5	44.1	47.0	50.3	52.2	55.9	59.6	61.6

Consider the following summary information:

$$\sum xy = 19{,}425.13 \quad \sum x = 370.6 \quad \sum y = 412.2 \quad \sum x^2 = 17{,}467.68$$

(a)   Draw a scatter diagram. Does there appear to be a strong linear relationship between x and y?

(b)   Find the line of best fit for y in terms of x.

(c)   By examining the line of best fit, determine the approximate average increase per year at private institutions for each $1000 increase at public institutions.

4.19   The following scatter diagram represents measurements on 38 1978–1979 model automobiles. Gas mileage (MPG) in miles per gallon (y) was measured by Consumers' Union on a test track. The variable Weight (x) was reported by the automobile manufacturer. (*Source:*   Henderson, H. and P. F. Velleman. "Building Regression Models Interactively." *Biometrics,* Vol. 37, p. 400, 1981.)

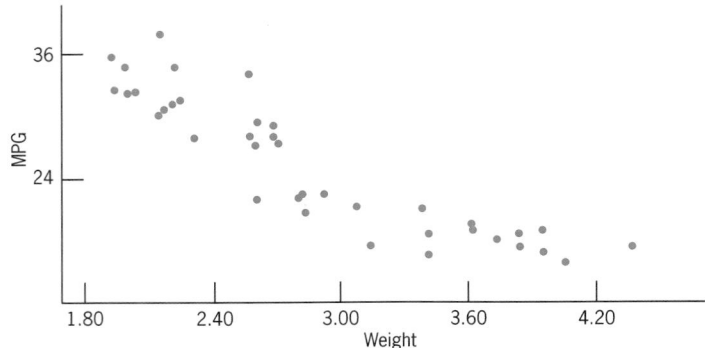

The summary information, rounded off, is

$$\sum xy = 2539 \quad \sum x = 109 \quad \sum y = 941 \quad \sum x^2 = 330$$

(a)   Does there appear to be a reasonably strong linear relationship between x and y?

(b)   Find the line of best fit for estimating miles per gallon given the weight.

(c)   What is the estimated average change in miles per gallon per increase of 1 unit in weight?

(d)   Estimate the average miles per gallon for a car with weight 2.5.

4.20   A sample of 31 black cherry trees was obtained in Allegheny National Forest, Pennsylvania (*Source:*   Ryan, B. F., B. L. Joiner, and T. A. Ryan, Jr., *Minitab Handbook,* 2nd ed. Boston: PWS-Kent, 1985, pp. 328–329). Among the variables measured were the volume (y) and diameter (x). The diameter was measured in inches at 4.5 feet above ground level, and the volume was measured in cubic feet. The diameter is easy to measure; the volume, difficult. The goal was to obtain an equation in which volume could be estimated from a tree's diameter. The data are as follows:

x	8.3	8.6	8.8	10.5	10.7	10.8	11.0	11.0	11.1	11.2	11.3
y	10.3	10.3	10.2	16.4	18.8	19.7	15.6	18.2	22.6	19.9	24.2

x	11.4	11.4	11.7	12.0	12.9	12.9	13.3	13.7	13.8	14.0	14.2
y	21.0	21.4	21.3	19.1	22.2	33.8	27.4	25.7	24.9	34.5	31.7

x	14.5	16.0	16.3	17.3	17.5	17.9	18.0	18.0	20.6
y	36.3	38.3	42.6	55.4	55.7	58.3	51.5	51.0	77.0

Consider the following rounded summary information and the scatter diagram:

$$\sum xy = 13{,}888 \quad \sum x = 411 \quad \sum y = 935 \quad \sum x^2 = 5737$$

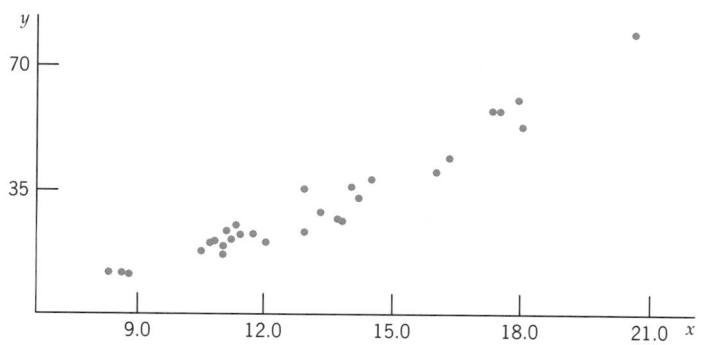

(a)   Does there appear to be a strong linear relationship between x and y?

(b)   Find the line of best fit for estimating the volume given the diameter.

(c)   Estimate the volume of a black cherry tree in Allegheny National Forest that has a diameter of 15 inches.

(d)   Minitab identifies the observation $x = 20.6$, $y = 77.0$ as unusual. Delete this observation and repeat parts (a), (b), and (c). Compare the difference in estimating the volume given a diameter of 15 inches with and without the unusual observation. Use the following rounded summary information (with the unusual observation deleted):

$$\sum xy = 12{,}302 \quad \sum x = 390 \quad \sum y = 858 \quad \sum x^2 = 5312$$

(e)   Are the lines different enough so that the unusual observation should be deleted and the second line used?

4.21   In this exercise, we are interested in the relationship between the per capita tax collection by the 50 states for the years 1980 (x) and 1991 (y) in 1991 dollars (*Source: The 1994 Information Please Almanac,* 1994, p. 80). The scatter diagram shows that there is one observation with an x value far removed from the others.

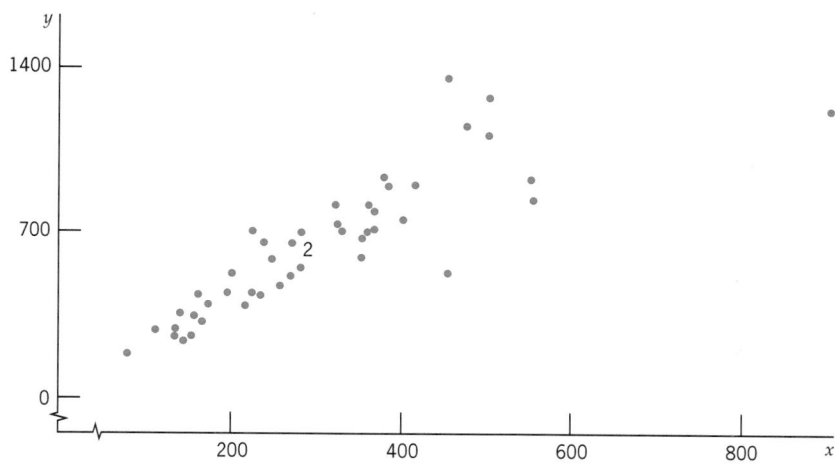

(a) Find the line of best fit for y in terms of x. Use the following information:

$$\sum xy = 11{,}235{,}240 \quad \sum x = 15{,}149 \quad \sum y = 31{,}215 \quad \sum x^2 = 5{,}677{,}175$$

(b) When we delete the unusual observation, the remaining 49 observations give the following:

$$\sum xy = 10{,}143{,}540 \quad \sum x = 14{,}249 \quad \sum y = 30{,}002 \quad \sum x^2 = 4{,}867{,}176$$

Find the line of best fit.

(c) Are the lines different enough so that the unusual observation should be deleted and the second line used?

4.22 The salary data with experience in years (x) and salary in thousands of dollars (y) were discussed in Example 4.2. Use the JMP printout to answer the following questions.

Parameter Estimates

Term	Estimate	Std Error	t Ratio	Prob>ltl
Intercept	19.469001	0.94552	20.59	0.0000
x	0.706659	0.05825	12.13	0.0000

(a) Give the equation for the line of best fit. Find the estimated salary for a person with 15 years of experience.

(b) What is the estimated increase in salary per year?

4.23 The following Data Desk output represents measurements, discussed in Exercise 4.19, on 38 1978–1979 model automobiles. Gas mileage (MPG) in miles per gallon (y) was measured by Consumers' Union on a test track. The variable Weight (x) was reported by the automobile manufacturer. Use the printout to answer the following questions. (*Note:* Due to roundoff error, your answers may differ from the computer output.)

(a) Give the equation for the line of best fit.

(b) Find the estimated gas mileage for a weight of 3.

Variable	Coefficient	s.e. of Coeff	t-ratio	prob
Constant	48.7075	1.954	25.0	≤ 0.0002
Weight	-8.36459	0.6631	-12.6	≤ 0.0002

4.3

THE LINEAR CORRELATION COEFFICIENT

We said that we can always find the regression line (or line of best fit) for a scatter diagram. However, such a line will be of use only if the x and y values show some degree of **linear relationship.** By this we mean that the points in the scatter diagram tend to cluster about a nonhorizontal line. The closer the points are to the line, the stronger the degree of linear relationship (also called *linear correlation*).

In this section, we show how to calculate a number from the data, called the **linear correlation coefficient,** r. *This number measures the degree of linear relationship* *between the x and y values.* Using the value of r, we can determine whether it is worthwhile to find the regression line. In addition, there are situations when we are not particularly interested in a regression line or in predicting y values, but instead we may simply wish to know whether some degree of linear relationship exists between the x and y values. The linear correlation coefficient can be used to study this question.

Definition The (linear) *correlation coefficient* r for a collection of n pairs of data values is

$$r = \frac{\sum (x - \bar{x})(y - \bar{y})}{(n-1)s_x s_y}$$

where s_x and s_y are the standard deviations of the x values and y values, respectively. Instead of using this formula to find r, we will use an alternative formula that gives the same result. Although the alternate formula looks more complicated, it actually simplifies our computations:

$$r = \frac{n\left(\sum xy\right) - \left(\sum x\right)\left(\sum y\right)}{\sqrt{n\left(\sum x^2\right) - \left(\sum x\right)^2} \cdot \sqrt{n\left(\sum y^2\right) - \left(\sum y\right)^2}}$$

Before giving the properties of r, we illustrate how to use the formula on the data of Example 4.1 (see Figure 4.11 and Table 4.10).

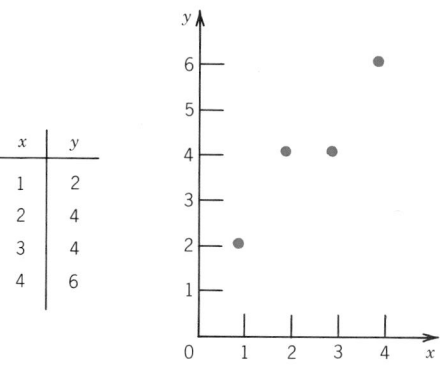

x	y
1	2
2	4
3	4
4	6

Table 4.10

	x	y	xy	x^2	y^2
	1	2	2	1	4
	2	4	8	4	16
	3	4	12	9	16
	4	6	24	16	36
Sums:	10	16	46	30	72	$n = 4$

Figure 4.11
Scatter Diagram

$$r = \frac{n\left(\sum xy\right) - \left(\sum x\right)\left(\sum y\right)}{\sqrt{n\left(\sum x^2\right) - \left(\sum x\right)^2} \cdot \sqrt{n\left(\sum y^2\right) - \left(\sum y\right)^2}}$$

$$= \frac{(4)(46) - (10)(16)}{\sqrt{(4)(30) - (10)^2} \cdot \sqrt{(4)(72) - (16)^2}} = \frac{24}{\sqrt{20} \cdot \sqrt{32}}$$

$$= .9486833 \doteq .95$$

Properties of r

1. The value of r is always between -1 and 1; that is, $-1 \leq r \leq 1$.

2. $r = 1$, provided that all of the points in the scatter diagram lie exactly on a line with a positive slope. (As would be expected, this is the regression line.) Also, $r = -1$, provided that all of the points lie exactly on a line with a negative slope. See Figure 4.12.

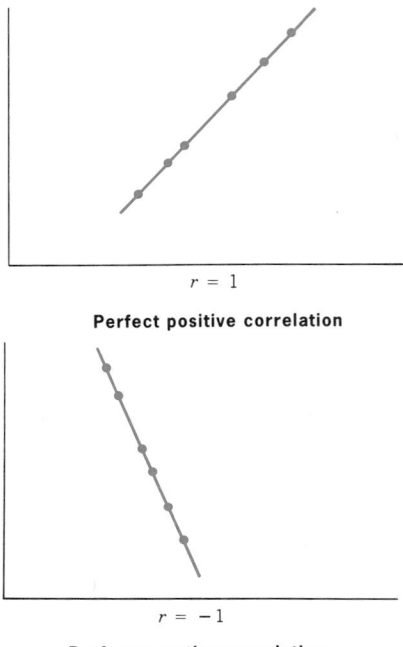

$r = 1$

Perfect positive correlation

$r = -1$

Perfect negative correlation

Figure 4.12

3. Suppose $r \neq 0$. Then the points in the scatter diagram are grouped around a nonhorizontal line (the regression line). If r is positive, the line has positive slope (i.e., sloping upward to the right). If r is negative, the line has negative slope. The closer r is to 1 or -1, the closer the points tend to cluster about the line. Therefore, a value of r close to 1 or -1 indicates a strong degree of linear relationship. The closer r is to 0, the more dispersed the points will be from the line. Figure 4.13 shows linear relationships for various values of r.

4. If $r = 0$, there is no linear relationship between the x and y values for the data. When $r = 0$, it can be shown that the line of best fit (the regression line) is a horizontal line through the points (Figure 4.14). If r is near 0, there will be only a very weak linear relationship.

We should stress that when $r = 0$, we can say that there is no degree of *linear* relationship between the x and y values of the data. This does not mean that there can be no other kind of relationship for the data. The points in Figure 4.15 suggest a strong relationship between the x and y values, although not a linear relationship. In fact, this is a quadratic relationship. This is the type of scatter diagram that occurs if x represents a person's age and y is the maximum weight the person can lift.

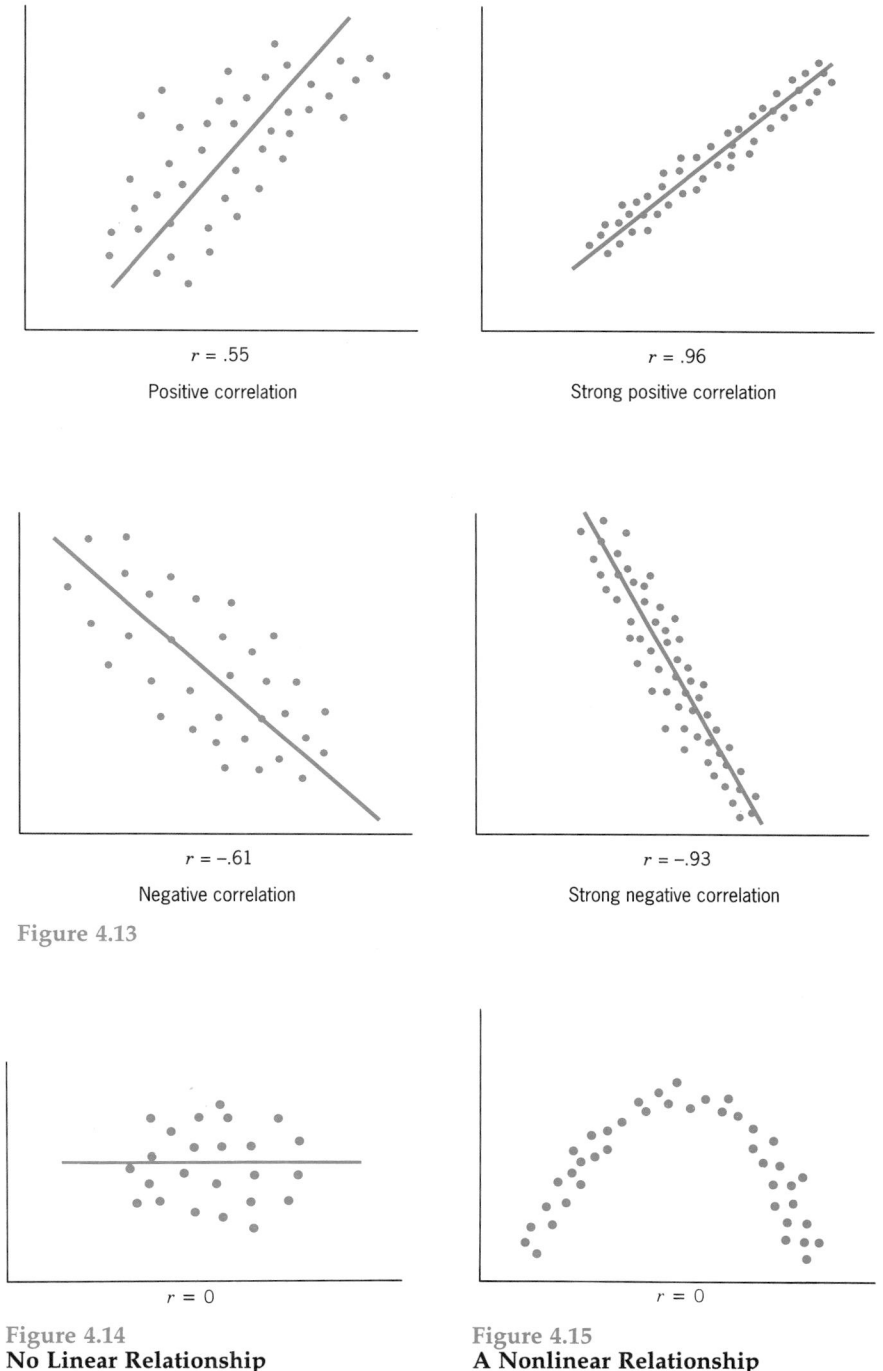

$r = .55$

Positive correlation

$r = .96$

Strong positive correlation

$r = -.61$

Negative correlation

$r = -.93$

Strong negative correlation

Figure 4.13

$r = 0$

Figure 4.14
No Linear Relationship

$r = 0$

Figure 4.15
A Nonlinear Relationship

When $r \neq 0$, the points are scattered about a nonhorizontal line, and there will be at least some degree of linear relationship between the x and y values for the data. But as we said, if r is close to 0, there will be only a very small degree of linear relationship, and the regression line will not be very helpful in predicting y values. In this case, it may be advisable to look for some suitable nonlinear relationship. A scatter diagram might suggest such a relationship. We will not discuss nonlinear relationships in this text. Another possibility is that there are other independent variables that are important. **Multiple regression** is concerned with relationships involving more than one independent variable. We will restrict our attention to **simple regression,** which involves one independent variable.

If, on the other hand, the value of r is reasonably close to 1 or -1, a worthwhile linear relationship will exist. It would then make sense to find the regression line if we wanted to predict y values. We will examine what we mean by "close to ± 1" more carefully later in this section. For now, we rely on intuition.

EXAMPLE 4.4

Find the linear correlation coefficient for the salary data in Table 4.2. Interpret the result.

Solution

Most of the calculations were done in Example 4.2. The only additional information we need is $\sum y^2$; therefore, we add a column of y^2 values in Table 4.11.

Table 4.11

	x	y	xy	x^2	y^2	
	12	29	348	144	841	
	16	31	496	256	961	
	6	23	138	36	529	
	23	34	782	529	1,156	
	27	38	1,026	729	1,444	
	8	24	192	64	576	
	5	22	110	25	484	
	19	34	646	361	1,156	
	23	36	828	529	1,296	
	13	27	351	169	729	
	16	33	528	256	1,089	
	8	27	216	64	729	
Sums:	176	358	5,661	3,162	10,990	$n = 12$

$$r = \frac{n\left(\sum xy\right) - \left(\sum x\right)\left(\sum y\right)}{\sqrt{n\left(\sum x^2\right) - \left(\sum x\right)^2} \cdot \sqrt{n\left(\sum y^2\right) - \left(\sum y\right)^2}}$$

$$= \frac{(12)(5661) - (176)(358)}{\sqrt{(12)(3162) - (176)^2} \cdot \sqrt{(12)(10,990) - (358)^2}}$$

$$= \frac{4924}{\sqrt{6968} \cdot \sqrt{3716}} = .9676674 \doteq .97$$

This value is close to $+1$, indicating a strong degree of positive linear relationship for the data. This is consistent with Figure 4.2(b), which shows the points in the scatter diagram clustered closely about the line.

Note: You may have noticed that the numerator in the formula for r is the same as the numerator in the formula for b_1, and the expression under the first square root in the denominator of r is the denominator of b_1. Thus, if you have already found b_1, these calculations can simplify the process for finding r even further. We have not made use of this fact in this section, because we have chosen to keep the calculations self-contained. But it is something to keep in mind.

EXAMPLE 4.5

Find the linear correlation coefficient for the production cost data in Example 4.3.

Solution

We reproduce the calculations from Example 4.3 along with a column of y^2 values in Table 4.12.

Table 4.12

x	y	xy	x^2	y^2	
3.0	40	120	9.00	1,600	
4.0	40	160	16.00	1,600	
2.4	50	120	5.76	2,500	
5.0	35	175	25.00	1,225	
2.6	55	143	6.76	3,025	
4.0	35	140	16.00	1,225	
5.5	30	165	30.25	900	
Sums: 26.5	285	1,023	108.77	12,075	$n = 7$

$$
r = \frac{n\left(\sum xy\right) - \left(\sum x\right)\left(\sum y\right)}{\sqrt{n\left(\sum x^2\right) - \left(\sum x\right)^2} \cdot \sqrt{n\left(\sum y^2\right) - \left(\sum y\right)^2}}
$$

$$
= \frac{(7)(1023) - (26.5)(285)}{\sqrt{(7)(108.77) - (26.5)^2} \cdot \sqrt{(7)(12{,}075) - (285)^2}}
$$

$$
= \frac{-391.5}{\sqrt{59.14} \cdot \sqrt{3300}} = -.8862049 \doteq -.89
$$

This is consistent with Figure 4.6 and indicates a negative linear relationship for the data.

The Coefficient of Determination

Before finding the regression line, we want to be sure that there is a reasonable degree of linear relationship between x and y. The correlation coefficient r is a measure of this relationship. A value of $r = .99$ would seem to indicate that a useful linear relationship exists. But what if $r = .70$? Is this value close enough to 1 to indicate a reasonable degree of linear relationship? It is difficult to answer this question because, although r measures the degree of linear relationship, it does not do so in familiar terms. In other words, what does $r = .70$ mean? How do we interpret it?

We will discuss two approaches to this problem. One approach is to establish cutoff values for r so that if a value of r is within a certain distance of ± 1, we can conclude that there is a significant degree of linear relationship between the x and y values. This approach is discussed in Chapter 10. The other approach is to look at the square of the correlation coefficient, r^2. It turns out that this quantity, called the **coefficient of determination,** enables us to interpret the degree of linear relationship in more familiar terms, so that we can make a judgment about whether a useful relationship exists between the x and y values.

Suppose that we consider the variables Age (x) and Height (y) for males 18 years and older. We would expect little relationship between age and height for this group. After all, we would not expect a difference in height of 1 foot between two men to be "explained" by the fact that one of the men is 30 years old and the other is 40. However, if we considered age and height for males age 1 to 16, then we would expect some relation between these variables for this group. If we were told that one such male was 1 foot tall and the other 6 feet tall, it would be a pretty safe bet that the 6-foot male was older. In other words, we believe that a good portion of the variation in heights for this group can be accounted for, or explained by, the relationship between height and age.

It turns out that for a collection of pairs of (x, y) values, the coefficient of determination r^2 gives the proportion of the variation in y values that is accounted for, or explained by, the linear relationship with the x values. So if $r = .9$, then $r^2 = .81$. Thus 81% of the variability in y is explained by x.

Let's clarify this idea using the data in Example 4.1. We reproduce these data along with the regression line in Figure 4.16.

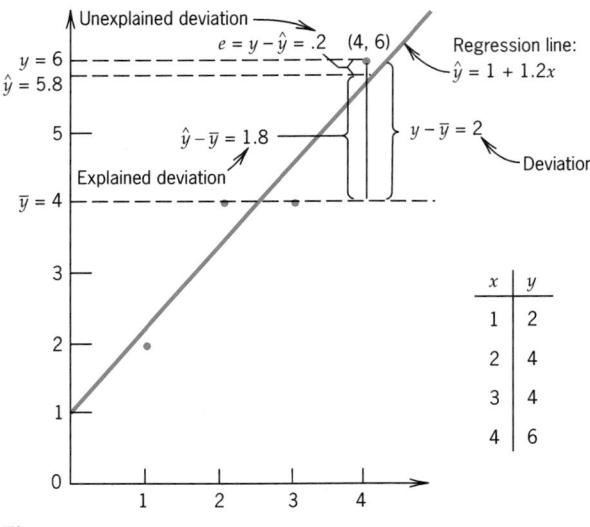

Figure 4.16

The deviation of a y value from the mean $\bar{y}$ is $y - \bar{y}$. This is also called the **total deviation.** Look at the point $(4, 6)$ in Figure 4.16. Now $\bar{y} = 4$, so the total deviation of 6 from the mean is

$$y - \bar{y} = 6 - 4 = 2$$

If we did not know the y value when $x = 4$, we would estimate it from the regression line. This estimate is

$$\hat{y} = 1 + 1.2x = 1 + (1.2)(4) = 5.8$$

If we wanted to estimate $y - \bar{y}$, we could use $\hat{y} - \bar{y}$:

$$\hat{y} - \bar{y} = 5.8 - 4 = 1.8$$

In a sense, we have "explained" 1.8 out of 2 units of the total deviation by using the regression line. See Figure 4.16. We call $\hat{y} - \bar{y}$ the **explained deviation.** That still leaves .2 unit of deviation unexplained:

$$y - \hat{y} = 6 - 5.8 = .2$$

We call $y - \hat{y}$ the **unexplained deviation** or the **error** or **residual.** In Figure 4.16, we see the relationship between the deviations for the point $(4, 6)$:

$$2 = 1.8 + .2$$

In general

$$y - \bar{y} = (\hat{y} - \bar{y}) + (y - \hat{y})$$

or

Total deviation = Explained deviation + Unexplained deviation

Instead of looking at individual y values, we must look at the variation of *all* the y values taken together. Variation is often measured by a sum of squares of deviations. It can be shown (we omit the proof) that

$$\sum(y - \bar{y})^2 = \sum(\hat{y} - \bar{y})^2 + \sum(y - \hat{y})^2$$

This equation is often stated as

Total variation = Explained variation + Unexplained variation

or

$$\begin{pmatrix} \text{Total sum} \\ \text{of squares} \end{pmatrix} = \begin{pmatrix} \text{Sum of squares} \\ \text{for regression} \end{pmatrix} + \begin{pmatrix} \text{Sum of squares} \\ \text{for error} \end{pmatrix}$$

or, in abbreviated form,

$$\text{TSS} = \text{SSR} + \text{SSE}$$

In Table 4.13, we calculate TSS, SSR, and SSE for the data in Figure 4.16.

Table 4.13

x	y	$\hat{y} = 1 + 1.2x$	$(y - \bar{y})^2$	$(\hat{y} - \bar{y})^2$	$(y - \hat{y})^2$
1	2	2.2	$(2 - 4)^2 = 4$	$(2.2 - 4)^2 = 3.24$	$(2 - 2.2)^2 = .04$
2	4	3.4	$(4 - 4)^2 = 0$	$(3.4 - 4)^2 = .36$	$(4 - 3.4)^2 = .36$
3	4	4.6	$(4 - 4)^2 = 0$	$(4.6 - 4)^2 = .36$	$(4 - 4.6)^2 = .36$
4	6	5.8	$(6 - 4)^2 = 4$	$(5.8 - 4)^2 = 3.24$	$(6 - 5.8)^2 = .04$
Sums:			TSS = 8	SSR = 7.20	SSE = .80

Notice that for the sum of squares

$$8 = 7.20 + .80$$

or

$$TSS = SSR + SSE$$

The total variation (TSS) is a measure of the variability in the y values. The explained variation (SSR) is the portion of that variability explained or accounted for by the regression line.

The *proportion* of total variation explained by the regression line is

$$\frac{\text{Explained variation}}{\text{Total variation}} = \frac{SSR}{TSS}$$

The closer the points are to the line, the greater the proportion of explained variation. For the data in Table 4.13, this is

$$\frac{7.20}{8} = .90$$

So 90% of the variation in y values is explained by the regression line. Recall that, at the beginning of this section, we showed that for these data, $r = .9486833$. Observe that

$$r^2 = (.9486833)^2 = .90$$

This result holds in general.

$$r^2 = \frac{\text{Explained variation}}{\text{Total variation}} = \frac{SSR}{TSS}$$

So the coefficient of determination, r^2, gives the proportion of variation in y values explained by the linear relationship with x (the regression line). Since we are really using the x's to calculate the $\hat{y}$'s, sometimes we say r^2 gives the proportion of variation in y values explained by x.

The square of the linear correlation coefficient is the **coefficient of determination r^2:**

> $r^2 =$ proportion of variation in y values that is explained
> by (the linear relationship with) x

The greater the proportion of explained variation, the closer are the y values and $\hat{y}$ values, hence the stronger the linear relationship. The simplest way to calculate the proportion of explained variation is to compute r and square it.

The coefficient of determination is an intuitively appealing measure of linear relationship because it measures the strength of the relationship in rather familiar terms.

EXAMPLE 4.6

Calculate and interpret the coefficient of determination for the salary data in Example 4.4.

Solution

We have seen that for these data, $r \doteq .97$. Therefore,

$$\text{Coefficient of determination} = r^2 \doteq .94$$

This means that about 94% of the variation in the salaries is explained by years of experience (i.e., by the linear relationship). About 6% of the variability is unexplained. Perhaps this portion of the variation is due to chance or other variables not considered.

EXAMPLE 4.7

Table 4.14 gives the size of the youth population, that is, the number of 14- to 24-year-olds per 1000 of the population (x) versus the homicide rate measured in number of homicides per 100,000 of the population (y) in the six New England states in 1 year.

Table 4.14

State	Number of 14- to 24-Year-Olds per 1000 (x)	Number of Homicides per 100,000 (y)
Maine	206	2.7
New Hampshire	204	1.4
Vermont	211	3.3
Massachusetts	211	3.7
Rhode Island	204	4.0
Connecticut	203	4.2

Source: Statistical Abstract of the United States, 100th ed. Washington, D.C.: U.S. Bureau of the Census, p. 178.

Find the linear correlation coefficient and the coefficient of determination. Interpret the results.

Solution

Table 4.15

	x	y	xy	x^2	y^2	
	206	2.7	556.2	42,436	7.29	
	204	1.4	285.6	41,616	1.96	
	211	3.3	696.3	44,521	10.89	
	211	3.7	780.7	44,521	13.69	
	204	4.0	816.0	41,616	16.00	
	203	4.2	852.6	41,209	17.64	
Sums:	1,239	19.3	3,987.4	255,919	67.47	$n = 6$

$$r = \frac{n\left(\sum xy\right) - \left(\sum x\right)\left(\sum y\right)}{\sqrt{n\left(\sum x^2\right) - \left(\sum x\right)^2} \cdot \sqrt{n\left(\sum y^2\right) - \left(\sum y\right)^2}}$$

$$= \frac{(6)(3987.4) - (1239)(19.3)}{\sqrt{(6)(255,919) - (1239)^2} \cdot \sqrt{(6)(67.47) - (19.3)^2}}$$

$$= \frac{11.7}{\sqrt{393} \cdot \sqrt{32.33}} = .1037975 \doteq .10$$

This value is quite small, indicating almost no linear relationship for the data. The coefficient of determination is

$$r^2 = (.1037975)^2 = .0107739 \doteq .01$$

This confirms the fact that there is virtually no degree of linear relationship between the x and y values. It says that only about 1% of the variation in the homicide rate can be explained by (the linear relationship with) the number of 14- to 24-year-olds per 1000. The scatter diagram in Figure 4.17 does not suggest any other kind of plausible relationship.

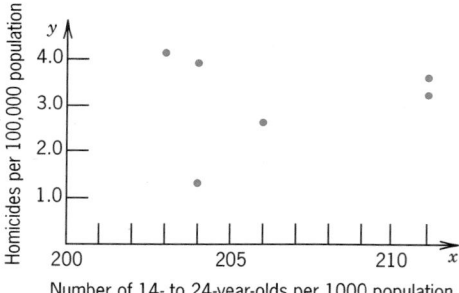

Figure 4.17

Minitab Output for Example 4.7

The following printout contains the regression equation (which we did not find in Example 4.7) and information about the regression coefficients. Some of this information was explained in the JMP printout following Example 4.3. The coefficient of determination is given as R-sq, and agrees with the value computed in Example 4.7 except for a slight difference due to round-off. R-sq(adj) is r^2 adjusted, which is an estimate of the coefficient of determination for a hypothetical population from which the data were obtained. Under SS we see the sums of squares:

$$\text{SSR} = 0.058 \quad \text{SSE} = 5.330 \quad \text{TSS} = 5.388$$

Other information in the printout relates to statistical inference, and will be discussed in Chapter 10.

Regression Analysis

```
The regression equation is
y = - 2.9 + 0.030 x

Predictor         Coef        Stdev      t-ratio          p
Constant         -2.93        29.46        -0.10      0.926
x                0.0298      0.1426         0.21      0.845

s = 1.154       R-sq = 1.1%        R-sq(adj) = 0.0%

Analysis of Variance

SOURCE          DF            SS           MS         F          p
Regression       1         0.058        0.058      0.04      0.845
Error            4         5.330        1.333
Total            5         5.388
```

EXERCISES

In Exercises 4.24–4.28, (a) find the linear correlation coefficient, and (b) find the coefficient of determination and give its interpretation. (The data were used in Exercises 4.2–4.6.)

4.24

x	y
2	9
2	7
4	5
4	5
6	3
6	1

4.25

x	y
0	2
0	4
0	6
1	6
2	7
2	8
2	9

4.26

x	y
1	2
2	6
4	14
5	18

4.27

x	y
1	2
2	2
3	1
4	0
5	0

4.28

x	y
0	5
0	4
1	3
2	2
2	1

4.29   In Exercise 4.17, we considered education and crime ratings for six U.S. cities. Find the proportion of variation in crime rating explained by education. The data are given in the table.

City	Education (x)	Crime (y)
Boston	35	12
Chicago	35	10
Detroit	31	16
Los Angeles	32	20
New York	30	25
Washington, D.C.	36	13

4.30   As a result of an overpopulation of deer in the Crane Reservation, in the coastal community of Ipswich, Massachusetts, there was a local epidemic of Lyme disease. Lyme disease is transmitted by a tick (*Ixodes dammini*) that winters and mates on deer. In the accompanying table the zone is based on the distance from the reservation, with 1 being closest. The table also gives the percentage of residents in each zone who have been infected with Lyme disease.

Lyme Disease Data

Zone (x)	Percentage of Residents Infected (y)
1	66
2	42
3	32
4	13
5	21

Source: Lastavica, C., et al., "Rapid Emergence of a Focal Epidemic of Lyme Disease in Coastal Massachusetts." *New England Journal of Medicine,* Vol. 320, 1989, pp. 133–137.

Find the correlation coefficient. Find the coefficient of determination and interpret the value.

4.31   A study was published in 1965 concerning malignancy rates in counties along the Columbia River, downstream from the Hanford Washington Atomic Storage Preserve.* Since World War II, plutonium for nuclear weapons had been produced at Hanford. Some nuclear waste leaked into the Columbia River. An index of exposure to contaminants and the cancer incidence for nine Oregon counties downstream from Hanford on the Columbia River are given in the table. *Index of exposure* is a measure of exposure to the river and closeness to Hanford; the higher the index, the more exposure to contaminants. *Cancer incidence* is defined as the number of deaths due to cancer per 100,000 people.

Exposure to Contaminants from the Hanford Nuclear Facility and Cancer Incidence

County	Index of Exposure (x)	Cancer Incidence (y)
Umatilla	2.49	147.1
Morrow	2.57	130.1
Gilliam	3.41	129.9
Sherman	1.25	113.5
Wasco	1.62	137.5
Hood River	3.83	162.3
Portland	11.64	207.5
Columbia	6.41	177.9
Clatsop	8.34	210.3

*Fedeley, R. C., "Oregon Malignancy Pattern Physiographically Related to Hanford Washington Radioisotope Storage." *Journal of Environmental Health,* Vol. 27, No. 6, 1965, pp. 883–897.

Summary statistics are

$$\sum x = 41.56 \qquad \sum y = 1416.1 \qquad \sum xy = 7439.37$$
$$\sum x^2 = 289.4222 \qquad \sum y^2 = 232,498.97$$

(a) Find the linear correlation coefficient.

(b) Give the coefficient of determination and its interpretation.

4.32 In Exercise 4.14, we considered the relationship between the amount of fertilizer (x) and the number of bushels (y) of soybeans produced. The data follow.

Hundred of Pounds per Acre (x)	Bushels per Acre (y)
1.0	25
2.5	32
3.0	35
3.0	32
3.4	35
4.0	39
4.0	41
4.5	40

(a) Draw a scatter diagram (you may have done this in Exercise 4.14). Do the data appear to be positively or negatively correlated?

(b) Find the correlation coefficient.

(c) Find the coefficient of determination and interpret the value.

4.33 In Exercise 4.21, we considered the relationship between x and y, the per capita tax collection by the states for the years 1980 and 1991, respectively (in 1991 dollars).

(a) Find the coefficient of determination and interpret the value for the 50 states. Use the following information:

$$\sum x = 15,149 \qquad \sum x^2 = 5,677,175 \qquad \sum y = 31,215$$
$$\sum y^2 = 23,432,726 \qquad \sum xy = 11,235,240$$

(b) One of the 50 observations had a large x value compared with the x values of the other 49. Deleting the observation with the large x value, find the coefficient of determination and give its interpretation for the remaining 49 states. The summary information follows:

$$\sum x = 14,249 \qquad \sum x^2 = 4,867,176 \qquad \sum y = 30,002$$
$$\sum y^2 = 21,961,358 \qquad \sum xy = 10,143,540$$

(c) Is there a substantial difference in the values of r^2 in parts (a) and (b)?

4.34 The scatter diagram at the top of page 166 plots the variable PRO, the percentage of people who approve of the way President Carter was doing his job (y), versus the variable UNEMP, the unemployment rate in percent (x) (*Source:* Compiled by Paul Robertson from issues of *Public Opinion Quarterly and Business Conditions Digest,* as reported in *MacSpin Release* 1.1). The data are for the period February 1977 through September 1980.

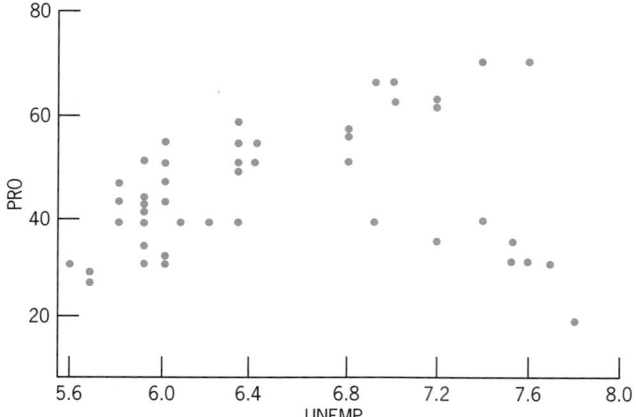

(a) Do the data indicate a positive or negative relationship between the variables? Is this what you would expect?

(b) Interpret the coefficient of determination $r^2 \doteq .08$.

(c) What is the value of the linear correlation coefficient r?

4.35 The following scatter diagram plots the variable PRO, the percentage of people who approve of the way President Reagan was doing his job (y), versus the variable UNEMP, the unemployment rate in percent (x) (*Source:* Compiled by Paul Robertson from issues of *Public Opinion Quarterly* and *Business Conditions Digest*, as reported in *MacSpin Release* 1.1). The data are for the period January 1981 through October 1985.

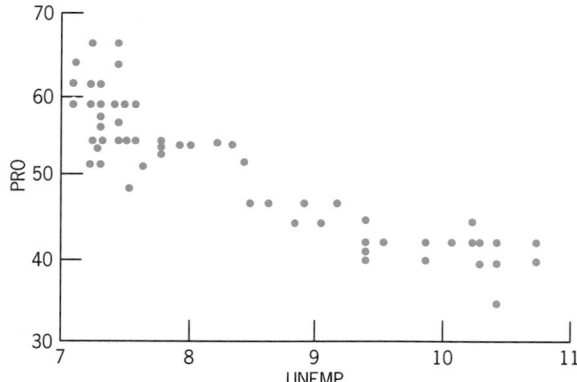

(a) Do the data indicate a positive or negative relationship between the variables? Is this what you would expect?

(b) Interpret the coefficient of determination $r^2 \doteq .814$.

(c) What is the value of the linear correlation coefficient r?

4.36   In Exercise 4.3, we considered the following data:

x	y
0	2
0	4
0	6
1	6
2	7
2	8
2	9

(a)   Complete the following table. Then find (i) TSS $= \sum(y - \bar{y})^2$ and (ii) SSR $= \sum(\hat{y} - \bar{y})^2$. Use TSS and SSR to find the coefficient of determination r^2. (*Note:* $\hat{y} = 4 + 2x$)

x	y	$\hat{y}$	$\bar{y}$	$(y - \bar{y})^2$	$(\hat{y} - \bar{y})^2$

(b)   Now use the formula given in the text to find r for the same data. Then compute r^2 and compare with your answer in part (a).

4.37   In Exercise 4.11, we considered the relationship between salary (x) and the number of absences (y) for state employees. The data are given in the table.

Salary in $ Thousands (x)	Number of Absences (y)
20.0	2.3
22.5	2.0
25.0	2.0
27.5	1.8
30.0	2.2
32.5	1.5
35.0	1.2
37.5	1.3
40.0	.6

(a)   Draw a scatter diagram. Do the data appear to be positively or negatively correlated?

(b)   Find the correlation coefficient.

(c)   Find the coefficient of determination and interpret the value.

4.38   In Exercise 4.9, we looked at the variables Intensity of advertising and Number of cases sold. The data are reproduced here.

Intensity of Advertising (x)	Number of Cases Sold (y)
1	4
2	7
3	8
4	14
5	15

(a)   Complete the following table. Then find (i) TSS $= \sum(y - \bar{y})^2$ and (ii) SSR $= \sum(\hat{y} - \bar{y})^2$. Use TSS and SSR to find the coefficient of determination r^2. (*Note:* $\hat{y} = .9 + 2.9x$)

x	y	$\hat{y}$	$\bar{y}$	$(y - \bar{y})^2$	$(\hat{y} - \bar{y})^2$

(b)   Now use the formula given in the text to find r for the same data. Then compute r^2 and compare with your answer in part (a).

4.39   In parts (a)–(d), find the missing entries.

	SSR	SSE	TSS	r^2
(a)	40	60		
(b)	100		300	
(c)	80			.4
(d)		27		.7

4.40   In parts (a)–(d), find the missing entries.

	SSR	SSE	TSS	r^2
(a)		20	50	
(b)			40	.2
(c)	25			1.0
(d)	30	0		

4.41   This exercise illustrates the relationship between the linear correlation coefficient r and the line of best fit. Consider the data given in the table.

x	y
1	2
1	4
3	3
4	2
6	9

(a)   Find the sample standard deviations s_x and s_y.

(b)   Find the linear correlation coefficient r.

(c)   Find the line of best fit.

(d)   Using your results in parts (a), (b), and (c),

    (i)   Verify that $r(s_y/s_x) = b_1$.

    (ii)   Verify that $\bar{y} - r(s_y/s_x)\bar{x} = b_0$.

(e)   Using part (d), verify that the equation of the line of best fit for these data may be written as

$$\hat{y} = \bar{y} + r\left(\frac{s_y}{s_x}\right)(x - \bar{x})$$

(*Note:*   It can be shown that the line of best fit can always be written in this form.)

4.42   This exercise uses the results of Exercise 4.41. A company gave a course for its typists to improve typing speed. A pretest (x) and posttest (y) were given to each typist. The results were

$$\bar{x} = 60 \text{ words per minute} \qquad \bar{y} = 61 \text{ words per minute}$$
$$s_x = 5 \text{ words per minute} \qquad s_y = 5 \text{ words per minute}$$
$$r = .6$$

(a)   Refer to Exercise 4.41, and write the equation of the regression line.

(b)   What is the expected (average) posttest score for a typist who typed 80 words per minute on the pretest?

(c)   What is the expected posttest score for a typist who typed 40 words per minute on the pretest?

Observe that the results of parts (b) and (c) suggest that those who did well on the pretest did not do as well on the posttest, and those who did not do well on the pretest showed an improvement on the posttest. This is called the *regression effect,* and it is due to the structure of the regression equation rather than to any effect from the typing course. Specifically, this result is due to the fact that r in the regression equation is less than 1. If you replace .6 by the value 1 and repeat parts (b) and (c), you will get very different results.

4.4

SOME WORDS OF CAUTION CONCERNING CORRELATION AND REGRESSION

A number of misuses of the ideas we have discussed in this chapter can occur. We mention two of them here.

1.   *Equating correlation with causality*   Suppose that we were to record for each month the number of snakebites (y) and the amount of ice cream consumed in the United States (x). It is a fact that a strong positive correlation exists between these two variables. Does it mean that eating ice cream causes snakebite? Hardly so. Instead, there is a third factor that explains the relationship. As the weather gets warmer, snakes come out of hibernation and become more active. At the same time, our appetite for cool refreshments increases. Therefore, we cannot assert that correlation equals causality. This does not mean that correlation

analysis may never be used in drawing conclusions about causal relationships, but some common sense should be used. For example, a correlation study contributed heavily to the Surgeon General's report linking cigarette smoking with lung cancer.* Furthermore, other studies have shown an association between smoking and lung cancer. Also, there does not appear to be a plausible third factor that might explain changes in both smoking and rate of lung cancer. Clinical evidence as well shows the deleterious effects of smoking on the lungs, so a conclusion asserting a causal link would not be unreasonable.

2. *Unwarranted extrapolation*   In Example 4.3, we found the regression line relating production cost per ton (y) to the number of tons of a chemical produced (x). The data used were obtained from companies that produced 2000–6000 tons per year. It might be reasonable to use this line to predict the cost per ton for a company in this range. But to use this line to predict the cost per ton for a company producing, say, 1 million tons per year would be questionable.

4.5

USING MINITAB (OPTIONAL)

The following Minitab printout deals with the data in Table 4.2, where x represents years of experience and y represents annual salary (in thousands of dollars) for 12 technicians. In the Session window, we read the years (x) into column C1 and salaries (y) into C2. The PLOT command produces the scatter diagram that we saw in Figure 4.2(a):

PLOT C2 * C1

The REGRESS command produces the regression equation given in Example 4.2. Since the x values in C1 are used to predict y values in C2, we typed

REGRESS C2 ON 1 PREDICTOR IN C1

Remember that Minitab requires only the bare essentials, and any other text is optional. We could have typed

REGR C2 1 C1

We also produce the correlation coefficient by using the command

CORRELATION BETWEEN DATA IN C1 C2

```
MTB > READ THE FOLLOWING DATA INTO C1 C2
DATA> 12 29
DATA> 16 31
DATA> 6 23
DATA> 23 34
DATA> 27 38
DATA> 8 24
```

---

*See Doll, R., "Etiology of Lung Cancer." *Advances in Cancer Research*, Vol. 3, 1955, pp. 1–50; Report of the U.S. Surgeon General, *Smoking and Health*, 1964.

```
DATA> 5 22
DATA> 19 34
DATA> 23 36
DATA> 13 27
DATA> 16 33
DATA> 8 27
DATA> end
12 ROWS READ
MTB > PLOT C2 * C1
```

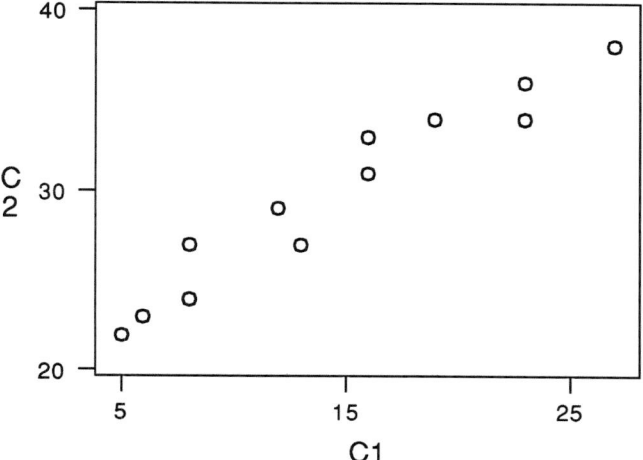

```
MTB > REGRESS C2 ON 1 PREDICTOR IN C1
```

Regression Analysis

```
The regression equation is
C2 = 19.5 + 0.707 C1
```

Predictor	Coef	Stdev	t-ratio	p
Constant	19.4690	0.9455	20.59	0.000
C1	0.70666	0.05825	12.13	0.000

```
s = 1.404      R-sq = 93.6%      R-sq(adj) = 93.0%
```

Analysis of Variance

SOURCE	DF	SS	MS	F	p
Regression	1	289.97	289.97	147.18	0.000
Error	10	19.70	1.97		
Total	11	309.67			

```
MTB > CORRELATION BETWEEN DATA IN C1 C2
```

Correlations (Pearson)

```
Correlation of C1 and C2 = 0.968
```

Dialog Box

We can obtain the above results using a dialog box. To obtain the plot, click

> **Graph ▶ Plot**
> Type *C2* under **Y** and *C1* under **X**
> Click **OK**

To obtain the regression output, click

> **Stat ▶ Regression ▶ Regression**
> Type *C2* in **Response** box and *C1* in **Predictors** box
> Click **OK**

To obtain the correlation, click

> **Stat ▶ Basic Statistics ▶ Correlation**
> Type *C1 C2* in **Variables** box
> Click **OK**

Interpreting Output

In addition to the regression equation, the Minitab output includes other information, such as b_0 and b_1 displayed under Coef. Notice that $b_0 = 19.4690$ and $b_1 = .70666$, which agree with the values we found in Example 4.2. Under Stdev, we see that the standard deviations of b_0 and b_1 are estimated as .9455 and .05825, respectively. You might ask, How can a constant have a standard deviation? Often our data are viewed as a sample from a population. Repeated samplings could produce different values for b_0 and b_1, and Minitab estimates the standard deviations of these values. We sometimes view the regression line as an estimate of the population regression line

$$y = \beta_0 + \beta_1 x$$

where β_0 is estimated by b_0 and β_1 is estimated by b_1. The standard deviation gives an idea of how much an estimator can vary from what is being estimated. The larger the standard deviation, the less likely it is that we will have a close estimate.

The t ratios and P-values will be discussed when we study inference in correlation and regression in Chapter 10. In the printout, $s = 1.404$. This is an estimate of the population standard deviation σ of the y values from the population regression line.

The coefficient of determination is given as R-sq and (except for a difference in roundoff) agrees with the value we found in Example 4.7. The printout also gives R-sq(adj), which is adjusted for degrees of freedom. (For a more complete discussion of this, consult a Minitab reference manual.) It suffices to say that r^2 adjusted for degrees of freedom is a certain type of estimate for the *population* coefficient of determination—an *unbiased estimator*.

Under Analysis of Variance, we see the breakdown of the total sum of squares (TSS) into sum of squares for regression (SSR) and sum of squares for residual or error (SSE). Observe that the proportion of variation explained by regression is

$$\frac{\text{SSR}}{\text{TSS}} = \frac{289.97}{309.67} \doteq .936 \text{ or } 93.6\%$$

This value is r^2. Under Analysis of Variance, we also see MS, F, and P. These will be discussed in Chapter 10.

Notice that the CORRELATION command produces the value of r (.968), which agrees with the value we found in Example 4.4.

EXERCISES

Suggested exercises for use with Minitab are 4.16, 4.18, 4.44, and 4.45.

4.6

WORKING WITH DATA (OPTIONAL)

Obtain a random sample of 20 females from the Framingham Heart Study data in Appendix Table B.11. Record age, systolic blood pressure, and serum cholesterol levels. Omit any subjects with missing data code (9999). Save your data for use in Chapter 10.

1. **(a)** Make a scatter diagram of systolic blood pressure (y) versus age (x).
   (b) Find the regression line relating systolic blood pressure to age.
   (c) Find the correlation coefficient.
   (d) Give the coefficient of determination and its interpretation.
2. Are there any unusual observations in Problem 1? If so, delete each, and recompute the regression line to see which observations are influential.
3. **(a)** Make a scatter diagram of serum cholesterol (y) versus age (x).
   (b) Find the regression line relating serum cholesterol to age.
   (c) Estimate the cholesterol level of a woman 45 years old.
   (d) Find the correlation coefficient.
   (e) Find the coefficient of determination and interpret the value.
4. Are there any unusual observations in Problem 3? If so, delete each, and recompute the regression line to see which observations are influential.
5. Results will vary from sample to sample, but often it is found that there is not a strong correlation between blood pressure and age (or cholesterol and age) for men; nevertheless, there is a stronger correlation for women. Can you think of any reason why this might be so? (*Hint:* Ask some friends majoring in biology.)

4.7

SUMMARY

We use correlation analysis to study the question of whether there is a relationship between two variables x and y. In regression analysis, we attempt to find the particular relationship. Such a relationship can be used to predict the approximate value for an unknown y associated with a known x value. In this chapter, we restricted our attention to *linear* correlation and regression. In the linear case, we investigate the possibility of a linear or straight-line relationship between the x and y values.

The **line of regression** (or line of best fit) for a collection of (x, y) values has the equation

$$\hat{y} = b_0 + b_1 x$$

where

$$b_1 = \frac{n\left(\sum xy\right) - \left(\sum x\right)\left(\sum y\right)}{n\left(\sum x^2\right) - \left(\sum x\right)^2}$$

$$b_0 = \bar{y} - b_1\bar{x}$$

To study the question of whether there is a linear relationship between x and y values, we use the **linear correlation coefficient, r:**

$$r = \frac{n\left(\sum xy\right) - \left(\sum x\right)\left(\sum y\right)}{\sqrt{n\left(\sum x^2\right) - \left(\sum x\right)^2} \cdot \sqrt{n\left(\sum y^2\right) - \left(\sum y\right)^2}}$$

Values of r near ± 1 indicate a strong linear relationship. Values of r near 0 indicate little or no degree of linear relationship.

The **coefficient of determination** is r^2:

r^2 = the proportion of the variation in y values that is explained by the linear relationship (line of best fit)

REVIEW EXERCISES

4.43 Consider the data given in the table.

x	y
3	7
3	5
5	3
6	3
8	2

(a) Find the line of best fit.

(b) Find SSE $= \sum(y - \hat{y})^2$, with $\hat{y}$ corresponding to the line of best fit.

(c) Find SSE $= \sum(y - \hat{y})^2$, using the line with the equation $\hat{y} = \bar{y} = 4$.

(d) Compare the SSE in parts (b) and (c). Comment on the fact that SSE in part (b) is less than SSE in part (c).

4.44 The data in the following table represent average cholesterol intake (x) and male population death rate (y) from arteriosclerotic and degenerative heart disease. The males were aged 55–59 and were chosen from selected countries. (*Source:* Data estimated from a graph in Williams, 1978, p. 6.)

Country	Cholesterol Intake in Tens of mg/day (x)	Death Rate per 10,000 (y)
United States	59	72
Finland	31	65
Holland	30	30
Italy	19	21
Greece	15	9
Yugoslavia	12	9
Japan	8	12

(a) Draw a scatter diagram. Does there appear to be a positive or negative linear relationship between average cholesterol intake and male population death rate?

(b) Find the linear correlation coefficient. Find and interpret the coefficient of determination.

(c) Find the line of best fit.

(d) Estimate the death rate for a cholesterol intake of 40.

4.45 The owner of a one-bedroom apartment was undecided what to charge per month. The apartment was located 1.5 miles from a rapid transit station. The owner obtained the following information pertaining to one-bedroom apartments in the city. The variable x represents the distance from a rapid transit station, and y is the rent.

Distance in Miles (x)	Rent in Hundreds of Dollars (y)
.3	8.5
.5	8.0
.7	8.2
1.1	7.1
1.2	7.6
2.3	6.8
2.9	7.0
3.0	6.8

(a) Draw a scatter diagram. Does there appear to be a positive or negative linear relationship between x and y?

(b) Find the linear correlation coefficient. Find and interpret the coefficient of determination.

(c) Find the line of best fit for estimating rent given the distance from a rapid transit station.

(d) What should the owner charge for rent?

4.46 A business school dean was interested in the relationship between quantitative GMAT scores (QUANT) and first-year grade point average (GPA) at the school. Use the following data to find the proportion of variation in GPA explained by QUANT.

QUANT	GPA
38	3.2
40	3.7
25	3.3
32	3.1
33	2.9
36	3.7

4.47 The following data, taken from 10 towns in Massachusetts, are the percentages of residents who are college graduates (x) and the median household incomes (in $ thousands) for all households (y) (*Source:* Egan, Margery. *"Public Schools: You Get What You Pay For." Boston Magazine,* October 15, 1985, Boston):

x	61.7	50.9	47.0	57.1	56.4	42.8	42.1	33.2	52.8	29.1
y	47.6	34.1	31.5	41.3	34.5	29.1	23.1	20.4	34.0	28.8

Consider the following summary information:

$\sum x = 473.1$ $\sum y = 324.4$ $\sum xy = 15{,}985.69$ $\sum x^2 = 23{,}389.21$ $\sum y^2 = 11{,}098.78$

(a) Draw a scatter diagram. Comment on whether there appears to be a linear relationship between y and x.

(b) Find the linear correlation coefficient. Find and interpret the coefficient of determination.

(c) Find the line of best fit for estimating median household income from the percentage of residents who are college graduates.

(d) Estimate the median household income if the percentage of college graduates is 40.

4.48 In 1969, an executive order was issued by President Richard M. Nixon requiring that a random method be used to draft men into military service (see Exercise 3.49). The 1970 draft lottery was held on December 1, 1969, to determine the order in which men would be called. The lottery system was based on a person's birthday. The data values are from 1 through 366 (which includes February 29), with 1 corresponding to September 14 (the first birthday drawn), 2 corresponding to April 24 (the second birthday drawn), etc. In effect, the purpose was to randomly assign a rank to each day of the year. The following data are the means of the ranks for the days of each month.

Month	Jan.	Feb.	March	Apr.	May	June	July	Aug.	Sept.	Oct.	Nov.	Dec.
(x)	1	2	3	4	5	6	7	8	9	10	11	12
Mean (y)	201.2	203.0	225.8	203.7	208.0	195.7	181.5	173.5	157.3	182.5	148.7	121.5

Consider the following summary information:

$$\sum x = 78 \quad \sum y = 2202.4 \quad \sum xy = 13{,}306.5 \quad \sum x^2 = 650 \quad \sum y^2 = 413{,}700.24$$

(a) Draw a scatter diagram. Comment on whether people born in the latter part of the year were more likely to be called sooner into service than people born in the early part of the year. Based on this, do you think the process was random?

(b) Find the linear correlation coefficient. Find and interpret the coefficient of determination.

4.49 Following the draft lottery of 1970 (see Exercise 4.48), there were many complaints that the method used was not random. A new system was drawn up by Selective Service officials for the 1971 draft. The following data give the means of the ranks for each day of the month.

Month	Jan.	Feb.	March	Apr.	May	June	July	Aug.	Sept.	Oct.	Nov.	Dec.
(x)	1	2	3	4	5	6	7	8	9	10	11	12
Mean (y)	151.8	198.9	179.8	182.2	181.9	194.6	183.6	194.4	209.9	173.0	163.1	183.5

Consider the following summary information:

$$\sum x = 78 \quad \sum y = 2196.7 \quad \sum xy = 14{,}350.5 \quad \sum x^2 = 650 \quad \sum y^2 = 404{,}847.29$$

(a) Draw a scatter diagram. Does it suggest that the process is random?

(b) Find the linear correlation coefficient. Find and interpret the coefficient of determination.

(c) Compare with Exercise 4.48, and comment on whether the 1971 draft lottery seems to have been more random than the 1970 draft lottery. (The coefficient of determination for the 1970 draft lottery is approximately .751.)

4.50 The following scatter diagram represents measurements (see Exercise 4.19) on 38 1978–1979 model automobiles. Weight (y) and horsepower (x) were reported by the automobile manufacturer.

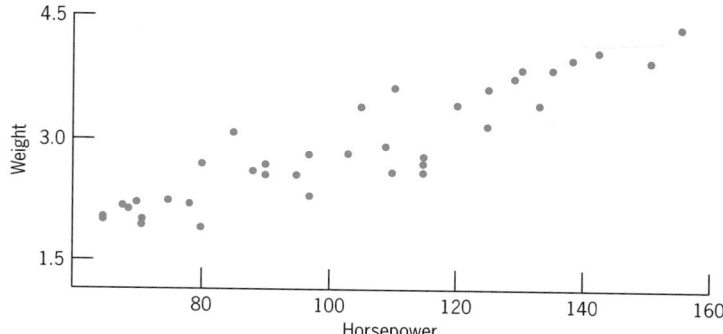

The summary information follows:

$$\sum x = 3866 \quad \sum y = 108.79 \quad \sum xy = 11{,}702.343 \quad \sum x^2 = 419{,}190 \quad \sum y^2 = 329.941952$$

(a)   From the scatter diagram, does there appear to be a linear relationship between weight and horsepower?

(b)   Find the linear correlation coefficient. Find and interpret the coefficient of determination.

(c)   Find the line of best fit for estimating weight given the horsepower.

(d)   Estimate the weight for a car with horsepower 100.

4.51   The following scatter diagram represents measurements (see Exercise 4.19) on 38 1978–1979 model automobiles. Gas mileage (MPG) in miles per gallon (y) was measured by Consumers' Union on a test track. The variable cylinders (x) was reported by the automobile manufacturer.

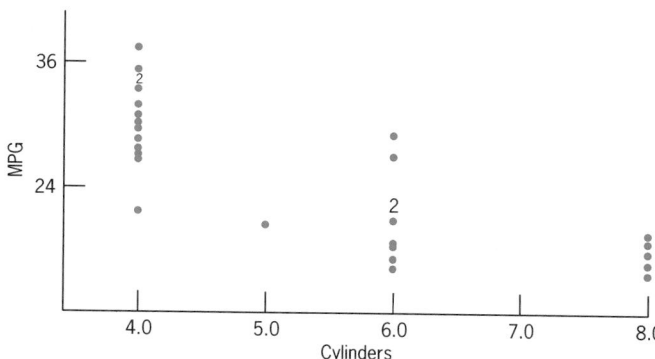

The summary information follows:

$$\sum x = 205 \quad \sum y = 940.9 \quad \sum xy = 4763.1 \quad \sum x^2 = 1201 \quad \sum y^2 = 24{,}883.27$$

(a)   From the scatter diagram, does there appear to be a linear relationship between miles per gallon and number of cylinders?

(b)   Find the linear correlation coefficient. Find and interpret the coefficient of determination.

(c)   Find the line of best fit for estimating miles per gallon given the number of cylinders.

4.52 The following data represent age (x) and time in minutes (y) to finish the 1986 Boston Marathon for 20 randomly selected male runners under 40 years of age (*Source: The Boston Marathon Racer's Recordbook 1986 Official Computer Results*, Honeywell Information Systems, 1986).

Age (x)	34	23	30	37	29	33	39	29	31	20
Time (y)	147.68	152.68	156.15	158.25	159.72	163.57	166.13	161.27	164.88	167.07

Age (x)	28	32	39	26	18	30	38	28	29	28
Time (y)	168.85	170.97	172.00	173.08	174.85	176.77	178.30	179.87	193.45	195.45

Consider the following summary information:

$$\sum x = 601 \quad \sum y = 3380.99 \quad \sum xy = 101{,}462.51 \quad \sum x^2 = 18{,}689 \quad \sum y^2 = 574{,}386.6793$$

(a) Draw a scatter diagram. Comment on whether there appears to be a linear relationship between y and x.

(b) Find the linear correlation coefficient. Find and interpret the coefficient of determination.

4.53 The following data represent age (x) and time in minutes (y) to finish the 1986 Boston Marathon for 20 randomly selected male runners 40 or more years of age (see Exercise 4.52):

Age (x)	47	49	40	49	43	42	46	53	46	43
Time (y)	168.03	169.92	174.03	175.72	186.42	189.45	191.22	193.48	192.02	194.65

Age (x)	41	41	53	40	45	52	40	59	50	43
Time (y)	196.25	197.10	198.80	199.85	201.25	204.12	206.37	109.98	212.87	214.48

Consider the following summary information:

$$\sum x = 922 \quad \sum y = 3776.01 \quad \sum xy = 172{,}959.36 \quad \sum x^2 = 43{,}044 \quad \sum y^2 = 722{,}664.4237$$

(a) Draw a scatter diagram. Comment on whether there appears to be a linear relationship between y and x.

(b) Find the linear correlation coefficient and the coefficient of determination.

(c) Notice in the scatter diagram that one observation (59, 109.98) is separated from the bulk of the data. Removing this observation gives the following summary information:

$$\sum x = 863 \quad \sum y = 3666.03 \quad \sum xy = 166{,}470.54 \quad \sum x^2 = 39{,}563 \quad \sum y^2 = 710{,}568.8233$$

With the observation removed, find the linear correlation coefficient and the coefficient of determination. Compare your results with those in part (b). Comment on the influence of the extreme observation on the linear correlation coefficient and the coefficient of determination.

4.54 Let x and y be the content (mg/cigarette) of nicotine (N) and carbon monoxide (CO), respectively, from 203 brands of cigarettes (*Source:* Data compiled by David Donoho and Liat Kulwarski from *San Francisco Examiner*, April 4, 1983, as reported in *MacSpin Release* 1.1). Consider the following summary information:

$$\sum x = 169.1 \quad \sum y = 2240.4 \quad \sum xy = 2243.7 \quad \sum x^2 = 173.6 \quad \sum y^2 = 30{,}390$$

(a)   Find the coefficient of determination and interpret the value.

(b)   Find the line of best fit for predicting CO content from N content.

(c)   Estimate the CO content for $x = 1$ mg/cigarette.

4.55   The following data are the numbers of home runs (y) and the numbers of hits (x) for 14 American League baseball teams in the 1993 season (*Source: The 1994 Information Please Almanac,* 1994, p. 998).

x:	1568	1556	1546	1547	1472	1470	1454
y:	178	159	178	141	181	157	162

x:	1480	1451	1455	1429	1399	1426	1408
y:	121	114	125	161	114	125	158

Consider the following Mathematica printout:

	Estimate	SE	TStat	PValue
1	-151.07	161.608	-0.934792	0.368326
x	0.202748	0.109432	1.85274	0.0886627

RSquared -> 0.222427

(a)   Give the coefficient of determination and its interpretation.

(b)   Give the equation for the line of best fit. Find the estimated number of home runs for 1500 hits.

(c)   On average, about how many hits are needed to increase the average number of home runs by 1? [*Hint:*   How much does one more hit increase home runs?]

4.56   The following data are the numbers of home runs (y) and the numbers of hits (x) for 14 National League baseball teams in the 1993 season (*Source: The 1994 Information Please Almanac,* 1994, p. 998).

x:	1534	1555	1507	1508	1521	1482	1459
y:	168	156	142	118	161	110	138

x:	1457	1444	1458	1410	1386	1350	1356
y:	137	169	130	122	153	158	94

Consider the following Mathematica printout:

	Estimate	SE	TStat	PValue
1	-9.39694	142.216	-0.0660753	0.948406
x	0.102196	0.0973812	1.04944	0.314651

RSquared -> 0.0840625

(a)   Give the coefficient of determination and its interpretation.

(b)   What is the value of the linear correlation coefficient r?

4.57 Consider the following data:

x	y
2	0
5	0
5	3
6	4
6	4
6	7

(a) Find the line of best fit.

(b) Complete the following table:

y	$\hat{y}$	$\bar{y}$	$(y - \bar{y})^2$	$(\hat{y} - \bar{y})^2$

(c) Find TSS and SSR.

(d) Use TSS and SSR to find the coefficient of determination and interpret the value.

4.58 Construct a set of four data points (x, y) so that

(a) $r = 1$ (b) $r = -1$ (c) $r = 0$

4.59 In parts (a)–(h), find the missing entries.

	SSR	SSE	TSS	r^2
(a)	50	50		
(b)	100		400	
(c)		40	50	
(d)	90			.6
(e)		28		.3
(f)			40	.8
(g)	50			1.0
(h)		0	75	

Notes

The Boston Globe, June 6, 1993.

The Boston Marathon Racer's Handbook 1986 Official Computer Results. Honeywell Information Systems, 1986.

Boyer, R., and D. Savageau, *Places Rated Almanac.* Data in Donoho, A., D. Donoho, M. Gasko, A. Ledbetter, and C. Olson, *MacSpin Release* 1.1. Austin, Texas: D² Software Inc.

Egan, M., "Public Schools: You Get What You Pay For." *Boston Magazine,* October 15, 1985, Boston.

Fedeley, R. C., "Oregon Malignancy Pattern Physiographically Related to Hanford Washington Radioisotope Storage." *Journal of Environmental Health,* Vol. 27, No. 6, 1965, p. 888.

Fortune magazine; Data compiled by Donoho, D. and L. Kulwarski, in Donoho, A., D. Donoho, M. Gasko, A. Ledbetter, and C. Olson, *MacSpin Release* 1.1. Austin, Texas: D² Software Inc.

Henderson, H., and P. F. Velleman, "Building Regression Models Interactively." *Biometrics,* Vol. 37, p. 400, 1981.

Information Please Almanac. Boston: Houghton Mifflin, 1994.

Lastavica, C., M. Wilson, V. Berardi, A. Spielman, and R. Deblinger, "Rapid Emergence of a Focal Epidemic of Lyme Disease in Coastal Massachusetts." *New England Journal of Medicine,* Vol. 320, 1989.

Phillips, A. J., "Smoking Control Programs for Canadian Adults." Proceedings of the Third World Conference, *Smoking and Health,* Vol. II. Department of Health, Education and Welfare, Publication Number (NIH) 77-1413.

Public Opinion Quarterly and Business Conditions Digest; Data compiled by P. Robertson, in Donoho, A., D. Donoho, M. Gasko, A. Ledbetter, and C. Olson, *MacSpin Release* 1.1. Austin, Texas: D² Software Inc.

Report of the Presidential Commission on the Space Shuttle Challenger Accident. Washington, D.C., 1986, pp. 129–131.

Ryan, B. F., B. L. Joiner, and T. A. Ryan, Jr., *Minitab Handbook,* 2nd ed. Boston: PWS-Kent, 1985.

San Francisco Examiner; Data compiled by Donoho, D. and L. Kulwarski, in Donoho, A., D. Donoho, M. Gasko, A. Ledbetter, and C. Olson, *MacSpin Release* 1.1. Austin, Texas: D² Software Inc.

Statistical Abstract of the United States, 100th ed. Washington, D.C.: U.S. Bureau of the Census, 1979.

Williams, C. L., "Nutrition and Coronary Heart Disease." *Bank of Epidemiology Exercises,* Exercise 13, edition 1. Dept. of Community and Preventive Medicine, New York Medical College, 1978. Data obtained from G. Biorck.

PART TWO

PROBABILITY

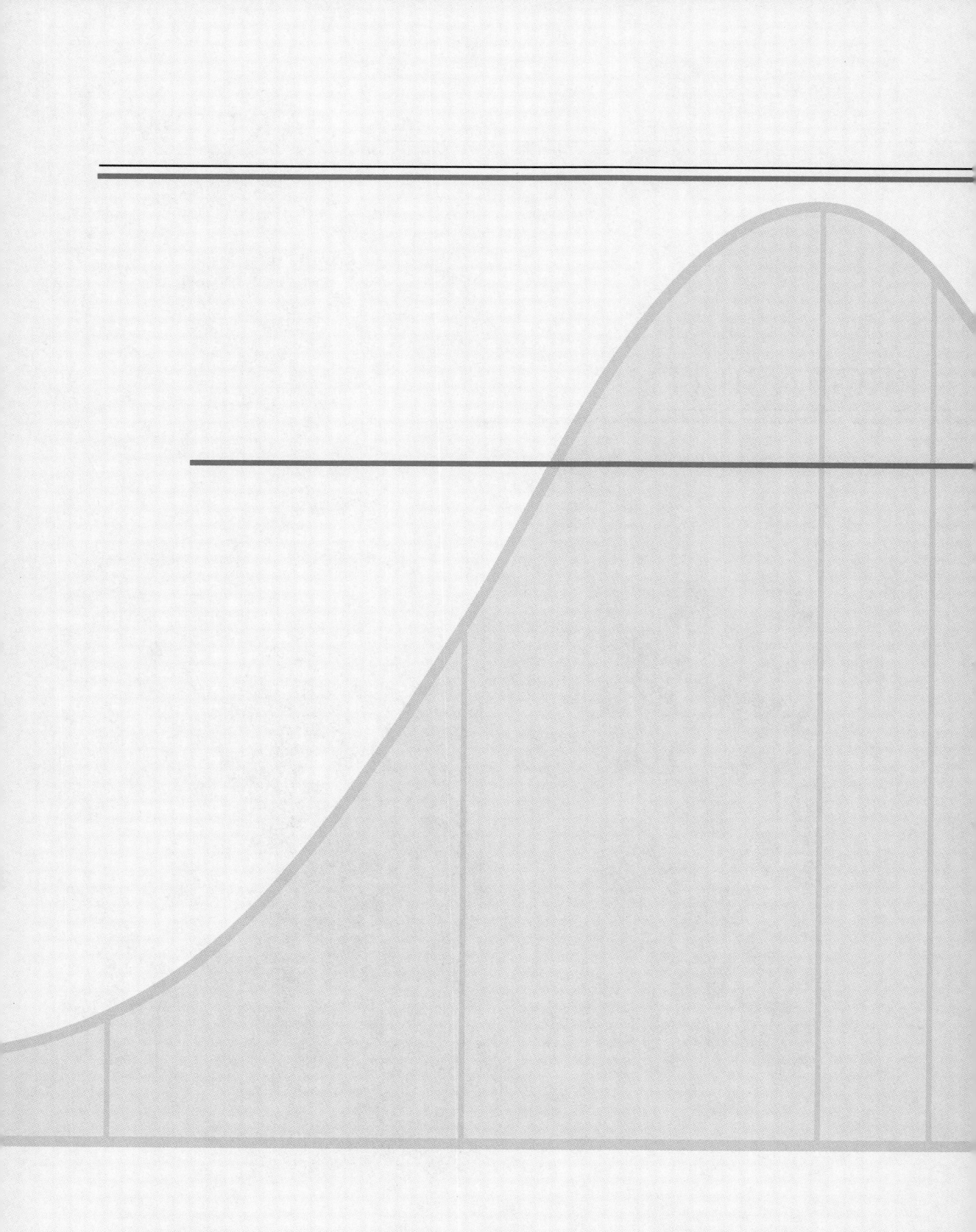

CHAPTER 5

PROBABILITY

5.1 INTRODUCTION

5.2 SAMPLE SPACES AND EVENTS

5.3 THE PROBABILITY OF AN EVENT

5.4 COMPOUND EVENTS

5.5 MORE ON COMPOUND EVENTS (OPTIONAL)

5.6 COMBINATORICS (OPTIONAL)

5.7 SUMMARY

REVIEW EXERCISES

NOTES

5.1

INTRODUCTION

In Chapter 1, we pointed out that probability, which deals with the laws of chance, plays an important role in statistical inference. We discussed a hypothetical situation in which a pollster interviews 100 voters selected by chance and finds that 96 of them plan to vote for a certain political candidate, candidate A, in an upcoming election. Based on this information, the pollster would predict that candidate A would win the election. The reason for this is that it seems highly unlikely or improbable that so many voters in the sample would be for candidate A if candidate A were not going to win the election.

On the basis of the sample of 100 voters, the pollster made a decision about the population of all voters. The decision that candidate A would win the election was equivalent to saying that the percentage of all voters in the population that are (or will be) in favor of candidate A is greater than 50%. (We are assuming a two-candidate race.)

This was not a difficult decision to make given the results of the survey. It seems intuitively clear that the chances or probability of so many voters being in favor of candidate A would be very small if candidate A were not going to win. But what if only 66 of the 100 voters were for candidate A? Can it also be said that this many votes would be very unlikely unless candidate A were going to win? The answer to this is not so obvious.*

In later chapters dealing with statistical inference, we will need to be able to deal with questions such as this. Therefore, we will develop the fundamentals of probability theory in this chapter. We will talk about what is meant by the probability or likelihood associated with various occurrences or events and also show how to calculate the probability of certain types of events.

5.2

SAMPLE SPACES AND EVENTS

The first technical term we discuss is **experiment.** We will see that most of the other terms in probability follow quite naturally from this term.

> **Definition**   Any activity that yields a result or an outcome is called an *experiment.*

Normally, there are a variety of possible outcomes of an experiment and the one that occurs when the experiment is performed is a matter of chance.

EXAMPLE 5.1
Consider the experiment of tossing a coin. There are two possible outcomes: heads (*H*) or tails (*T*).

EXAMPLE 5.2
Consider the experiment of interviewing a voter to determine whether he or she favors nuclear power. Here the possible outcomes might be yes, no, or undecided.

EXAMPLE 5.3
Consider the experiment of randomly selecting an adult American. This means selecting an adult in such a way that each adult has an equal likelihood of being selected.† The adult selected is the outcome of this experiment. Since any adult

---

*Actually, it can be shown that if candidate A were not going to win the election, the odds against candidate A getting more than 65 votes out of the 100 are about 1000 to 1 (if the voters are selected by a truly random process, which is not always so easy).
†In practice, this may be very difficult to do, but we need not worry about this for now.

could be selected, the collection of all adult Americans constitutes the possible outcomes.

We will be interested in the collection of all possible outcomes of an experiment. An important thing to keep in mind about this collection is that not only will it include all possibilities, but no two outcomes in this collection can occur at the same time. For instance, in Example 5.1, when we toss a coin, we must get either H or T, but we cannot get both of these at the same time.

> **Definition** The collection (or set) of all possible distinct outcomes that can occur when an experiment is performed is called the *sample space* for the experiment. This collection of outcomes must have the property that when the experiment is performed, one and only one of these outcomes must occur.

We often use a symbol such as S to represent a sample space, and we sometimes describe this set by specifying the outcomes inside braces. So, for Example 5.1, we could describe S as

$$S = \{H, T\}$$

(The outcomes may be listed in any order inside the braces.)

The sample spaces associated with the experiments discussed so far are finite, but sample spaces associated with some experiments are infinite, as the following example shows.

EXAMPLE 5.4

Consider the following experiment: A coin is flipped until a tail occurs. We could get a tail on the first flip, represented symbolically by T; or we could get a head on the first flip and a tail on the second flip, represented by HT; or we could get two heads followed by a tail represented by HHT; and so on. Notice that the number of possible outcomes is infinite. We could represent the sample space as

$$S = \{T, HT, HHT, HHHT, \ldots\}$$

EXAMPLE 5.5

Microscopic particles known as "genes" are present in the cells of all living organisms and determine the inherited characteristics of each organism. Most genes occur in pairs called "genotypes"; one of the pair comes from the mother, the other from the father. If the mother contributes gene A and the father gene B, we represent the genotype as AB. In humans, a single gene pair determines whether the body will have normal pigmentation (coloring) or complete lack of pigmentation (albinism). We will use the symbol C to represent the gene that calls for normal pigmentation and the symbol c will represent the gene for albinism. A person might have each of these in a gene pair. We could represent this pair by the symbol Cc. A human with this genotype will have normal pigmentation because the gene C is "dominant," whereas the gene c is "recessive."

The particular combination of genes (genotype) that occurs is a matter of chance. Observing the pigmentation genotype of an offspring is an experiment. Let us find the sample space of the experiment when both parents have the genotype Cc. The following diagram gives the possible genotypes that can occur.

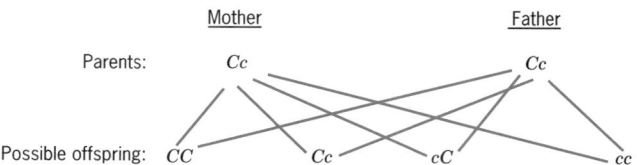

The sample space for the experiment is

$$S = \{CC, Cc, cC, cc\}$$

Since C is a dominant gene, each of these genotypes will result in a child with normal pigmentation, except cc, which will result in albinism. Also note that both parents have normal pigmentation.

EXAMPLE 5.6

Sickle-cell anemia is a disorder of the blood characterized by red blood cells that are crescent shaped. People with sickle-cell anemia can exhibit severe anemia, headaches, nausea, and other symptoms. Until recently, few lived beyond age 40. Sickle-cell anemia is found predominantly in blacks. This disease is inherited and is determined by a single gene pair that affects the hemoglobin in the blood. We will call

$$H = \text{normal hemoglobin gene}$$
$$h = \text{altered hemoglobin gene for sickle-cell anemia}$$

Each person has a pair of hemoglobin genes (a genotype), one gene inherited from the mother and one from the father. A person with genotype HH will have normal blood cells. Someone with genotype hh will have sickle-cell anemia. A person with mixed genotype Hh is called a "carrier" of the sickle-cell trait. The gene h is not completely recessive. That is, someone with genotype Hh will not actually have sickle-cell anemia but will exhibit episodes of the sickle-cell trait that can be brought on by stress. As in Example 5.5, observing the hemoglobin genotype of an offspring is an experiment in which the possible hemoglobin genotypes are the outcomes. If a normal mother and a father who is a carrier produce an offspring, find the sample space and use this to show that this couple cannot produce a child with sickle-cell anemia.

Solution

We use the same procedure that we used in Example 5.5.

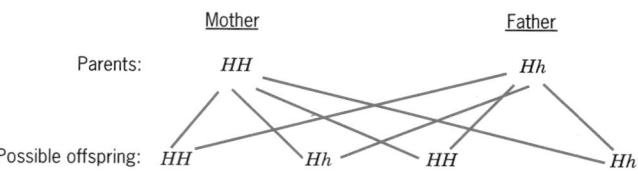

The sample space consists of the possible distinct outcomes. Since there are only two different outcomes listed,

$$S = \{HH, Hh\}$$

It is clear that these parents cannot produce a child with sickle-cell anemia (but they could produce a carrier).

Events

A student, who has not studied, randomly guesses at the answers on a two-question true–false quiz (perhaps by the toss of a coin). This can be viewed as an experiment. The outcome of guessing correctly on the first question and wrongly on the second question can be represented as CW. The sample space is

$$S = \{CW, WC, WW, CC\}$$

Getting exactly one question correct is an example of what is called an **event.** One correct can occur in two ways, namely, if either of the outcomes CW or WC occurs. It is important to stress that for the event "one correct" to occur, just one of these outcomes need occur. (Indeed when an experiment is performed, only one outcome *can* occur at one time.) Since we can describe "one correct" by listing the outcomes that constitute getting one correct, we will simply view "one correct" as the collection of outcomes

$$\{CW, WC\}$$

Notice that this is a subset of the sample space. This leads to the following definition:

> **Definition** An *event* is a collection (or set) of some of the possible outcomes from the sample space. In other words, an event is a subset of the sample space. We say that the event *occurs* if, when we perform the experiment, one of its constituent outcomes occurs.

The outcomes that define an event are usually listed inside braces. We often use capital letters, especially from the beginning of the alphabet, to represent events. If A is some finite event, we will use the symbol $n(A)$ to represent the number of distinct outcomes in A.

Notice that an event can consist of a single outcome. Therefore, each possible outcome in the sample space is an event, sometimes called a **simple event.** Also, an event could consist of all the possible outcomes in the sample space; that is, S is an event. This event must occur each time the experiment is performed.

EXAMPLE 5.7

A randomly selected citizen is interviewed and the following information is recorded: gender and ethnic status. The symbols for ethnic status will be A = Asian, B = Black, H = Hispanic, I = American Indian, W = White, and O = Other. If the person interviewed was a female Hispanic, we could represent this outcome as FH. Complete the description of the sample space S. Let E be the event that the person interviewed was female and nonwhite. Describe E as a subset of the sample space.

Solution

The sample space is

$$S = \{FA, MA, FB, MB, FH, MH, FI, MI, FW, MW, FO, MO\}$$

The event of interest is

$$E = \{FA, FB, FH, FI, FO\}$$

EXAMPLE 5.8

Consider the experiment and sample space of Example 5.5. Let E be the event that occurs if the offspring has normal pigmentation. Describe this as a subset of the sample space.

Solution

Remember that the gene for normal pigmentation C is dominant, so any one of the following genotypes will result in normal pigmentation: CC, Cc, and cC. Therefore,

$$E = \{CC, Cc, cC\}$$

EXERCISES

5.1 People's blood types are classified as O, A, B, and AB.

    (a) Suppose that one person is to be selected and the blood type observed. List the elements of the sample space.

    (b) Suppose that a husband and wife are selected and both of their blood types are observed. List the elements of the sample space.

5.2 A coin is tossed three times, and H or T (H = head, T = tail) is recorded each time. List the elements of the sample space S, and list the elements of the event consisting of

    (a) All heads

    (b) A head on the second toss

    (c) Exactly two tails

5.3 Suppose that a lottery number is determined by selecting four digits in succession and recording each digit when selected. Repeated digits are allowed. List the elements of the event where

    (a) The digits 426 are the first three digits in this order.

    (b) The four digits consist of 4, 2, and 6 in the first three positions (not necessarily in that order) and 8 in the fourth position.

5.4 A randomly selected citizen is interviewed and the following information is recorded: employment status and level of education. The symbols for employment status are Y = employed and N = unemployed, and the symbols for level of education are 1 = did not complete high school, 2 = completed high school but did not complete college, and 3 = completed college. List the elements of the sample space, and list the elements of the following events:

    (a) Did not complete high school   **(b)** Is unemployed

5.5 In genetics, there are two genes that determine gender: X and Y. Each individual has a pair of these (a sex genotype). A female has the pair XX; a male, the pair XY.

In producing an offspring, each parent contributes one gene. Some inherited characteristics are carried by, or linked to, the X gene. They are called "sex-linked inherited characteristics." For example, colorblindness is one such characteristic. When this gene carries the colorblind trait, we use the lowercase x. A female with the pair xx will be colorblind. A female with sex genotype xX will not be colorblind but will be a carrier of the colorblindness gene. A male with sex genotype xY will be colorblind. For a carrier mother and a normal father, find the sample space of sex genotypes for the experiment of observing the sex genotype of an offspring.

5.6 Repeat Exercise 5.5 with a normal mother and a colorblind father. Use the sample space to show that a child of this couple cannot inherit colorblindness.

5.7 A hospital administrator records a 0 if a patient has no medical insurance and a 1 if the patient does have medical insurance. The administrator also records an A, B, C, D, or E representing good, fair, poor, serious, or critical condition, respectively. List the elements of the sample space S, and list the elements of the event consisting of a selected patient

(a) With no medical insurance and in serious or critical condition

(b) With medical insurance and not in critical condition

(c) In good or fair condition

(d) With medical insurance

5.8 Two cards are selected in succession from an ordinary deck of cards. The suit of the first card is recorded, and then the suit of the second card is recorded. For the suits, let C = clubs, D = diamonds, H = hearts, and S = spades. List the elements of the events consisting of

(a) Both spades   (b) Either both spades or both clubs

(c) At least one heart   (d) A diamond as the second card

5.9 A study is to be made in a large university to try to determine a relationship, if any, between the gender of a faculty member and his or her salary. Faculty are to be interviewed and classified according to gender and salary category. Suppose that M = male, F = female, 1 = less than \$30,000, 2 = less than \$35,000 but greater than or equal to \$30,000, 3 = less than \$40,000 but greater than or equal to \$35,000, 4 = less than \$45,000 but greater than or equal to \$40,000, 5 = less than \$50,000 but greater than or equal to \$45,000, and 6 = greater than or equal to \$50,000. List the elements of the event consisting of a selected faculty member

(a) With a salary less than \$40,000

(b) Who is female or has a salary greater than or equal to \$40,000

(c) Who is male with a salary greater than or equal to \$50,000

(d) Who is male with a salary less than \$40,000 and greater than or equal to \$35,000

5.3

THE PROBABILITY OF AN EVENT

In this section, we are interested in the chance that a particular event will occur when an experiment is performed.

In the last section, we talked about the sample space for the student who guesses on a two-question true–false quiz:

$$S = \{CW, WC, WW, CC\}$$

Let A be the event that consists of getting exactly one correct. As a subset

$$A = \{CW, WC\}$$

Each time you randomly guess at a true–false question there is a 50–50 chance of getting it correct. So it seems intuitively clear that each outcome in the sample space has equal likelihood of occurring. If the experiment were repeated many times, say, by 1000 students all guessing, we would expect each outcome to occur about 250 times. So we expect event A to occur about 500 times. The number of occurrences of A divided by the number of times the experiment is performed is called the **proportion of occurrences of A** or the **proportion of times A occurred.** In this case, the expected proportion of occurrences of A is

$$\frac{500}{1000} = \frac{1}{2}$$

This expected proportion is also called the **probability of A.** Symbolically, we write

$$P(A) = \frac{1}{2}$$

Note: The symbol $P(A)$ is read "P of A" or the "probability of A."

Let us generalize the foregoing ideas. First, we will agree that if A is some event, then the number of times A occurs divided by the total number of times the experiment is performed is called the **proportion of occurrences of A** or the **relative frequency of A.** From the preceding discussion, we see that the **probability of A** is the proportion of occurrences of A we expect in the long run, that is, if the experiment is performed over and over many times.

Definition   Suppose that A is some event. The *probability of A*, denoted by $P(A)$, is the expected proportion of occurrences of A if the experiment were to be repeated many times.

If we perform the experiment many times, $P(A)$ is the proportion or fraction of the times we expect to see A occur. Therefore, $P(A)$ is a proportion that will be at least 0 and at most 1. So $0 \le P(A) \le 1$. Also recall that the sample space S is itself an event that must occur each time the experiment is performed. Hence, $P(S) = 1$.

Notice that for the event A (getting exactly one correct)

$$P(A) = \frac{1}{2} = \frac{2}{4} = \frac{\text{number of outcomes in } A}{\text{number of outcomes in } S}$$

This formula generalizes to any event from a finite sample space in which each outcome is equally likely.

Rule 5.1   Suppose that A is an event in a finite sample space S and each outcome in S is equally likely. Let $n(A)$ represent the number of distinct outcomes in A and $n(S)$ represent the total number of distinct outcomes in S. Then

$$P(A) = \frac{n(A)}{n(S)} = \frac{\text{number of ways } A \text{ can occur}}{\text{total number of possible outcomes}}$$

EXAMPLE 5.9

Consider the experiment of rolling two ordinary dice. Find the probability that a sum of 7 will occur.

Solution

To understand this situation, it will help if we imagine one die as painted red and the other as painted green. We could get a 4 on the red die and 3 on the green die. This outcome could be represented as $(4, 3)$. Note that $(3, 4)$ is a different outcome.* The sample space S will have 36 possible outcomes:

$$S = \{(1, 1), (1, 2), (1, 3), (1, 4), (1, 5), (1, 6),$$
$$(2, 1), (2, 2), (2, 3), (2, 4), (2, 5), (2, 6),$$
$$(3, 1), (3, 2), (3, 3), (3, 4), (3, 5), (3, 6),$$
$$(4, 1), (4, 2), (4, 3), (4, 4), (4, 5), (4, 6),$$
$$(5, 1), (5, 2), (5, 3), (5, 4), (5, 5), (5, 6),$$
$$(6, 1), (6, 2), (6, 3), (6, 4), (6, 5), (6, 6)\}$$

Each outcome is equally likely. Now let A be the event consisting of a sum of 7. Describing A as a set, we see that

$$A = \{(6, 1), (5, 2), (4, 3), (3, 4), (2, 5), (1, 6)\}$$

that is, A will occur if any one of these outcomes occurs. Applying Rule 5.1, we see that

$$P(A) = \frac{n(A)}{n(S)} = \frac{6}{36} = \frac{1}{6}$$

EXAMPLE 5.10

For the sample space of Example 5.5, assign probabilities to each outcome. Also, find the probability that an offspring will have normal pigmentation.

Solution

Each of the four possible pairings of genes from the parents is equally likely. So the probability associated with each pairing is $\frac{1}{4}$. Let E be the event that an offspring has normal pigmentation. We pointed out in Example 5.8 that since C is a dominant gene, CC, Cc, and cC will all result in normal pigmentation. Therefore, as a set

$$E = \{CC, Cc, cC\}$$

Since each outcome in the sample space is equally likely, we can use Rule 5.1 to obtain

$$P(E) = \frac{n(E)}{n(S)} = \frac{3}{4}$$

---

*In mathematics, parentheses ( ) are often used to enclose elements when order is important. When order is not important, braces { } are usually used.

Fundamental Principle of Counting

Because of Rule 5.1, it is important to be able to find the number of outcomes in a set. Yet writing out all the outcomes in a set may be tedious. The **Fundamental Principle of Counting** can in many cases make this unnecessary.

Suppose a fast-food restaurant sells ice cream cones in two sizes (regular and large) and three flavors (vanilla, chocolate, and strawberry). The task of ordering an ice cream cone can be broken down into two tasks:

Task 1 = specify the size

Task 2 = specify the flavor

We illustrate the process with a **tree diagram** (Figure 5.1).

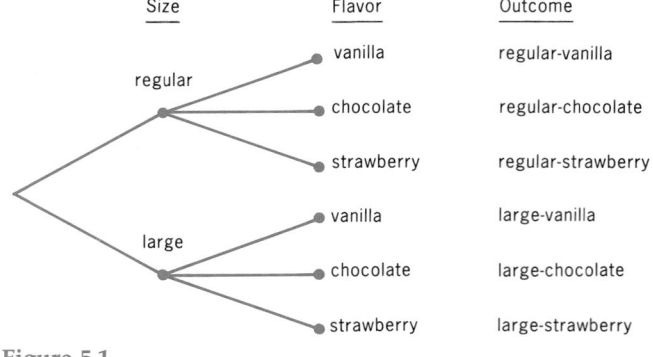

Figure 5.1

Notice that six possible ice cream cones could be ordered. Task 1 can be done 2 ways, Task 2 can be done 3 ways, and $2 \times 3 = 6$.

Task: Order ice cream cone = specify size and specify flavor

Number of ways: $6 = 2 \times 3$

Rule 5.2 Fundamental Principle of Counting   If Task 1 can be done in n_1 ways and Task 2 can be done in n_2 ways, then Task 1 *and* Task 2 performed together can be done in $n_1 \cdot n_2$ ways.

This can be extended to three or more tasks. For example, if Task 1 can be done in n_1 ways, Task 2 can be done in n_2 ways, and Task 3 can be done in n_3 ways, then Task 1 *and* Task 2 *and* Task 3 performed together can be done in $n_1 \cdot n_2 \cdot n_3$ ways.

EXAMPLE 5.11

In a family with four children, find the probability that the oldest three are boys. Assume that for each birth the probability of a boy is $\frac{1}{2}$.

Solution

If the oldest three are boys and the youngest is a girl, we represent this outcome as *BBBG*. The event in question is

$$A = \text{oldest 3 are boys} = \{BBBG, BBBB\}$$

Writing out the sample space amounts to performing four tasks: Specify the gender of each child. Each task can be performed two ways (*B* or *G*). Hence the overall task can be performed

$$2 \cdot 2 \cdot 2 \cdot 2 = 16$$

ways. Therefore the sample space has 16 outcomes. Since for each birth the probability of a boy or girl is the same, each outcome in the sample space is equally likely. So by Rule 5.1

$$P(A) = \frac{n(A)}{n(S)} = \frac{2}{16} = \frac{1}{8}$$

EXERCISES

5.10   A statistics class contains 14 males and 20 females. A student is to be selected by chance and the gender of the student recorded.

    (a)   Give a sample space *S* for the experiment.

    (b)   What is the probability that the selected student is female?

5.11   In Example 5.9, we considered the experiment of tossing two fair dice. Find the probability of each of the following events:

    (a)   The sum of the two dice is less than 5.

    (b)   We get one or two 6's.

    (c)   Neither is a 6.

    (d)   The sum is either 7 or 11.

5.12   A health clinic in the city of Worcester employs 50 people. Four live in the town of Shrewsbury, 10 in Auburn, 12 in Grafton, and the rest live in Worcester. One employee is needed to participate in a clinic project. If one employee is randomly selected, find the probability that

    (a)   The person lives in Shrewsbury.

    (b)   The person lives in Worcester.

5.13   A digit is to be selected by chance.

    (a)   Give a sample space *S*.

    In parts (b) and (c), list the elements of the event. Then find the probability that the event will occur.

    (b)   The event consisting of an odd digit

    (c)   The event consisting of a number larger than 6

5.14   An experiment consists of selecting by chance four digits and recording each in succession as *E* (even) or *O* (odd).

    (a)   List the elements of a sample space *S*.

    In parts (b)–(d), find the probability of each event.

    (b)   The event consisting of all evens

    (c)   The event consisting of one or more evens

    (d)   The event consisting of two or more evens occurring in succession

5.15   Assume a 50–50 chance that a newborn child will be a boy. In a family of four children, find the probability that

    (a)   There are exactly two boys.

    (b)   The oldest two children are boys.

(c)   All the children are girls.

(d)   Not all the children are girls.

5.16   Megabucks, a lottery game conducted by the Massachusetts State Lottery Commission, consists of selecting 6 numbers from the 42 numbers, $\{1, 2, 3, 4, \ldots, 41, 42\}$. (No repetitions are allowed and order does not matter.) The commission selects by chance the six winning numbers. You pay \$1 to play. You get a free ticket if three of your numbers match three of the winning numbers, \$75 for matching four numbers, \$1500 for matching five numbers, and a large prize if you match all six numbers. The sample space S consists of all possible six-number combinations that can be selected. It can be shown that $n(S) = 5{,}245{,}786$. The number of elements in S that match 0, 1, 2, 3, 4, 5, or 6 winning numbers is as follows:

Number of Matches	Number of Possibilities
0	1,947,792
1	2,261,952
2	883,575
3	142,800
4	9,450
5	216
6	1

Find the probability of the following:

(a)   Not winning anything

(b)   Getting one or more matches

(c)   Winning a free ticket

(d)   Winning either \$75 or \$1500

(e)   Winning Megabucks

5.17   The following data represent the numbers of earned degrees conferred in the United States and Puerto Rico for the years 1960, 1970, and 1980 (*Source: Statistical Abstract of the United States*, 1984, p. 168). The data values are in thousands.

Year	Bachelor's	Master's
1960	395	75
1970	833	209
1980	999	298

A degree recipient is selected by chance (assume one degree per recipient). Find the probability that the recipient

(a)   Received a Master's degree

(b)   Received a degree in 1970

5.18   Assume that there are four roads between towns A and B, five roads between towns B and C, and eight roads between towns C and D.

(a)   How many different routes are possible in traveling from A to B to C?

(b)   How many different routes are possible in traveling from A to B to C to D?

5.19   A license plate consists of three letters followed by three digits. How many license plates can be issued? (*Note:* Repetitions are allowed.)

5.20   Some computers use the binary coded decimal (BCD) system to represent characters such as A, B, 3, 4, etc. This is a system that uses a sequence of six bits to represent a character, where each bit is a 0 or 1. How many characters can be represented?

5.21 Assume that a telephone number consists of ten digits, and the first and fourth digits cannot be 0.

    (a) How many telephone numbers are possible?

    (b) How many telephone numbers are possible within the 617 area code?

    (c) How many telephone numbers are possible within the 617–661 telephone exchange?

5.22 Suppose four digits are to be randomly selected (repetitions allowed). [*Note:* The set of digits is $\{0, 1, 2, 3, 4, 5, 6, 7, 8, 9\}$.] Find the probability that

    (a) 5562 is selected.

    (b) 0000 is selected.

    (c) All four digits are the same.

    (d) 2 is the first digit selected.

5.23 Three dice are to be tossed followed by two dimes. Find the probability of getting

    (a) Three 6's and two heads

    (b) Three 6's   **(c)** Two heads

5.4

COMPOUND EVENTS

We will use the term **compound event** to mean an event that is expressed in terms of, or as a combination of, other events. It is often convenient to view an event as a compound event because there are rules for finding the probabilities of such events.

Suppose A, B are events from some sample space. In this and the next section, we will be interested in properties of the following three events:

$$A \ or \ B \qquad A \ and \ B \qquad complement \ of \ A$$

We begin by giving concrete examples of these events followed by a formal definition of each.

EXAMPLE 5.12

Suppose that we consider the experiment of randomly selecting a voter from a particular town. Let the event A correspond to selecting a voter who favors universal health care. Let the event B correspond to selecting a voter who is a member of a union. Now ($A \ or \ B$) is the event that occurs if the person selected either favors universal health care *or* is a member of a union *or* both. The event ($A \ and \ B$) occurs if the voter selected favors universal health care *and* at the same time is a union member. The (*complement of A*) is the event that occurs if the voter selected does not favor universal health care.

Definitions   Let A, B be events from a sample space S.

1. **$A \ or \ B$** is the event that will occur if either A occurs or B occurs or both occur. As a set, the event ($A \ or \ B$) consists of those outcomes in A together with those outcomes in B. (This set is sometimes called the union of A with B, denoted by $A \cup B$.)

2. *A and B* is the event that will occur if both *A* occurs and *B* occurs at the same time. As a set, the event (*A and B*) consists of those outcomes which are both in *A* and at the same time in *B*, in other words, those outcomes common to both events. (This set is sometimes called the intersection of *A and B*, denoted by $A \cap B$.)

3. The *complement of A*, denoted by $\overline{A}$, is the event that consists of those outcomes in *S* that are not in *A*. (Therefore, $\overline{A}$ will occur whenever *A* does not. In this sense, $\overline{A}$ is the opposite of *A*.)

Figure 5.2 is a graphic representation of the events just described. These are called **Venn diagrams.**

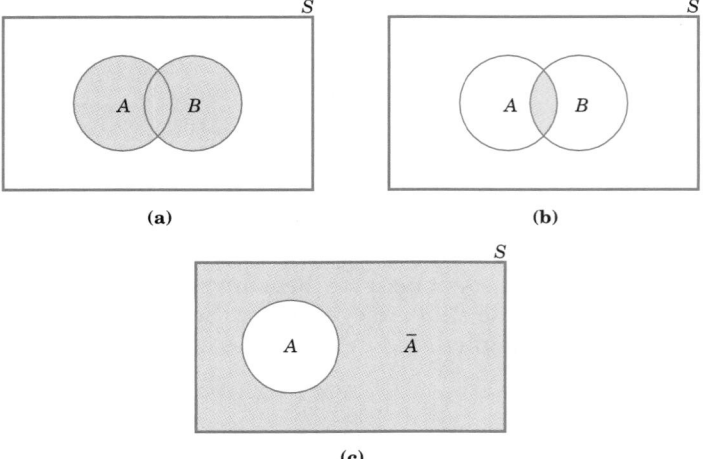

(a)   (b)

(c)

Figure 5.2
Compound Events: (a) *A or B* (shaded); (b) *A and B* (shaded);
(c) $\overline{A}$ (shaded)

Mutually Exclusive Events

At a meeting of a college student government council, 50 students are present: 20 freshmen, 15 sophomores, 10 juniors, and 5 seniors. One student is to be randomly selected to deliver a petition to the school administration. Call *A* the event that occurs if the student is a freshman and *B* the event that the student is a sophomore. Now the sample space consists of all 50 students. Event *A* is the set of 20 freshmen, and event *B* is the set of 15 sophomores. All outcomes (students) are equally likely, so by Rule 5.1

$$P(A) = \frac{n(A)}{n(S)} = \frac{20}{50} \quad \text{and} \quad P(B) = \frac{n(B)}{n(S)} = \frac{15}{50}$$

What about the probability of selecting a freshman or a sophomore? Notice that there are $20 + 15 = 35$ who are freshmen or sophomores. So the probability of selecting a freshman or sophomore is

$$P(A \text{ or } B) = \frac{35}{50} = \frac{20 + 15}{50} = \frac{20}{50} + \frac{15}{50} = P(A) + P(B)$$

This property generalizes, but only when the events A, B cannot both occur at the same time. Such events are called **mutually exclusive.**

Definition Events A, B are said to be *mutually exclusive* if they cannot both occur together when the experiment is performed (i.e., they have no outcomes in common).

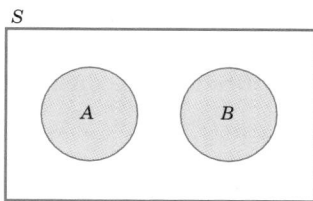

Figure 5.3
Mutually Exclusive Events

Rule 5.3 Addition Rule for Mutually Exclusive Events If A, B are mutually exclusive events, then

$$P(A \text{ or } B) = P(A) + P(B)$$

This generalizes to three or more mutually exclusive events (no two of them have any outcomes in common). For mutually exclusive events A, B, C,

$$P(A \text{ or } B \text{ or } C) = P(A) + P(B) + P(C)$$

EXAMPLE 5.13

If a pair of dice is rolled, find the probability of getting a sum of 7 or a match.

Solution

Refer to Example 5.9 for the sample space. Let

$$A = \text{sum of } 7 = \{(6,1),(5,2),(4,3),(3,4),(2,5),(1,6)\}$$

and

$$B = \text{a match} = \{(1,1),(2,2),(3,3),(4,4),(5,5),(6,6)\}$$

Events A, B have no outcomes in common, so they are mutually exclusive. All outcomes in the sample space are equally likely, so by Rule 5.1,

$$P(A) = \frac{n(A)}{n(S)} = \frac{6}{36} = \frac{1}{6} \qquad P(B) = \frac{n(B)}{n(S)} = \frac{6}{36} = \frac{1}{6}$$

By Rule 5.3,

$$P(A \text{ or } B) = P(A) + P(B) = \frac{1}{6} + \frac{1}{6} = \frac{1}{3}$$

A more general Addition Rule that applies even when the events are not mutually exclusive will be discussed in the next section.

Suppose event A consists of outcomes o_1, o_2, o_3. That is,

$$A = \{o_1, o_2, o_3\}$$

Now the outcomes are themselves events (which are mutually exclusive), and A can be described as

$$A = o_1 \text{ or } o_2 \text{ or } o_3$$

Hence, by the Addition Rule

$$P(A) = P(o_1) + P(o_2) + P(o_3)$$

We can state this more generally as follows: **The probability of an event is the sum of the probabilities of its constituent outcomes.**

Independent Events

Recall the discussion in the previous section of the student randomly guessing on a two-question true–false quiz. The sample space was

$$S = \{CW, WC, WW, CC\}$$

We said each outcome is equally likely, so each can be expected to occur about $\frac{1}{4}$ of the time. That is, each outcome has probability $\frac{1}{4}$. Define events A, B as

$$A = \text{correct on first question} = \{CW, CC\}$$
$$B = \text{wrong on second question} = \{CW, WW\}$$

The probability of guessing correctly on the first question is $\frac{1}{2}$, and the probability of guessing wrongly on the second is $\frac{1}{2}$. So

$$P(A) = \frac{1}{2} \qquad P(B) = \frac{1}{2}$$

Notice that

$$A \text{ and } B = \{CW\}$$

and

$$P(A \text{ and } B) = P(CW) = \frac{1}{4} = \frac{1}{2} \cdot \frac{1}{2}$$
$$= P(A) \cdot P(B)$$

What you guess on one question is independent of your guess on the other question. The events A, B are said to be **independent.** The preceding result is valid whenever the events are independent.

Definition   Events A, B are *independent* if the occurrence of one has no effect on the probability of the occurrence of the other.

Rule 5.4 Multiplication Rule for Independent Events   Suppose A, B are independent events; then

$$P(A \text{ and } B) = P(A) \cdot P(B)$$

This generalizes to more than two independent events. For example, if A, B, C are independent,

$$P(A \text{ and } B \text{ and } C) = P(A) \cdot P(B) \cdot P(C)$$

EXAMPLE 5.14   Found Guilty by the Multiplication Rule!
In 1964 in Los Angeles, a couple snatched a woman's purse and fled. Later a couple apprehended by the police had all the characteristics described by witnesses. Think of the experiment as randomly selecting a couple in the Los Angeles area. The characteristics can be thought of as events. The following are the characteristics (events) described by the prosecutor in court, along with their supposed probabilities:*

Event	Probability
E_1 = drove yellow car	1/10
E_2 = man had moustache	1/4
E_3 = woman had ponytail	1/10
E_4 = woman had blonde hair	1/3
E_5 = black man with beard	1/10
E_6 = interracial couple in car	1/1000

The prosecutor claimed these events were independent. Assuming this is true, find the probability that a randomly selected couple has all of these characteristics.

Solution
Using the Multiplication Rule,

$$P(E_1 \text{ and } E_2 \text{ and } E_3 \text{ and } E_4 \text{ and } E_5 \text{ and } E_6)$$
$$= P(E_1) \cdot P(E_2) \cdot P(E_3) \cdot P(E_4) \cdot P(E_5) \cdot P(E_6)$$
$$= \frac{1}{10} \cdot \frac{1}{4} \cdot \frac{1}{10} \cdot \frac{1}{3} \cdot \frac{1}{10} \cdot \frac{1}{1000}$$
$$= \frac{1}{12,000,000}$$

The prosecutor argued that since this probability was so small, this must be the guilty couple. The jury agreed and convicted the couple, even though there was no other evidence!

The case was appealed to the California Supreme Court. There the defense used a probability argument to show that, given there is at least one couple in the Los Angeles area having all six characteristics, then there is an 8% chance that there is more than one couple having all the characteristics. This was a large enough probability to raise a reasonable doubt, and the conviction was overturned.

In the next section, we discuss a more general Multiplication Rule, one that applies even when the events are not independent.

Source: Fairley, W. B., and F. Mosteller, "A Conversation about Collins," in *Statistics and Public Policy,* Fairley, W. B., and F. Mosteller, eds. Reading, Mass.: Addison-Wesley, 1977.

Probability for Complementary Events

For any event A, its complement $\overline{A}$ is its opposite. Hence whenever A occurs, $\overline{A}$ does not occur, and when A does not occur, $\overline{A}$ does occur. It follows that if A has probability, say, $\frac{1}{3}$, then A will occur $\frac{1}{3}$ of the time and $\overline{A}$ will occur $\frac{2}{3}$ of the time. Hence the probabilities of A and $\overline{A}$ will add up to 1:

$$P(A) + P(\overline{A}) = 1$$

This result holds in general. As a consequence, if we know the probability of A, we can find the probability of $\overline{A}$ from the following formula.

Rule 5.5   For any event A, the probability of its complement is

$$P(\overline{A}) = 1 - P(A)$$

EXAMPLE 5.15

A six-person jury for a civil trial was selected by chance. The defense attorney, whose client was female, was surprised that the jury did not have at least one female. Assuming the population is half female, find the probability that such a jury will have at least one female.

Solution
"At least one" is the opposite of "none." So if we let

$$A = \text{no females}$$

then

$$\overline{A} = \text{at least one female}$$

We can think of the jury as being composed of six males selected sequentially:

$$A = \text{all males} = MMMMMM$$

We assume the population is large and one-half male; hence the probability of any selection being a male is $\frac{1}{2}$. We assume the probability of a male on one selection is independent of any other selection. The event $MMMMMM$ is the compound event: (first juror is male) *and* (second juror is male) *and* ... *and* (sixth juror is male). Using the Multiplication Rule for independent events, we get

$$P(A) = P(MMMMMM) = P(M) \cdot P(M) \cdot P(M) \cdot P(M) \cdot P(M) \cdot P(M)$$
$$= \left(\tfrac{1}{2}\right)^6 = \tfrac{1}{64}$$

Using Rule 5.5,

$$P(\overline{A}) = 1 - P(A) = 1 - \tfrac{1}{64} = \tfrac{63}{64} \doteq .98$$

So the chance of at least one female on the jury is about 98%.

The Game Show Paradox

The following application uses all the ideas in this section. *Parade* columnist Marilyn Vos Savant described the following game show to her readers: Behind one of three closed doors there is a prize—a car. The contestant is asked to select one of the doors. There is a $\frac{1}{3}$ probability the contestant selects the right door. The host of the show then deliberately opens one of the other doors not containing the car. The contestant is then given the opportunity to switch to the other unopened door. The question is, Should the contestant switch? Marilyn Vos Savant said yes. This started a firestorm of protest in the form of indignant letters, some from college professors. But Ms. Vos Savant was quite right.

We said there is a $\frac{1}{3}$ probability the car is behind the door initially selected. So if the contestant does not use the switching strategy, there is a $\frac{1}{3}$ probability of winning the car. But suppose the contestant decides to switch. If the contestant initially selects door 1, represent this event by S_1. If the car is behind door 2, represent this by C_2. When the contestant initially selects door 1 and the car is behind door 2, the host will open door 3. The contestant would then switch to door 2 and win the car. We can represent this event symbolically as S_1 *and* C_2.

If you think about it, you will see that the only time the contestant who uses the switching strategy will lose is when the door initially selected is the one containing the car. For example, suppose the contestant initially selects door 1 and the car is behind door 1. This is the event S_1 *and* C_1. The host might then open door 2, and the contestant then switches to door 3 and loses. Let's call

$$L_1 = S_1 \text{ } and \text{ } C_1$$
$$L_2 = S_2 \text{ } and \text{ } C_2$$
$$L_3 = S_3 \text{ } and \text{ } C_3$$

We will find the probability that the contestant will lose when using the switching strategy. Then subtract this from 1 to find the probability of winning. Let L represent the event of losing. You can lose if L_1 *or* L_2 *or* L_3 occurs. That is,

$$L = L_1 \text{ } or \text{ } L_2 \text{ } or \text{ } L_3$$

Events L_1, L_2, L_3 are mutually exclusive. So, by the Addition Rule

$$P(L) = P(L_1) + P(L_2) + P(L_3)$$

Now $L_1 = S_1$ *and* C_1. Further S_1, C_1 are independent. (The door first selected is independent of where the show's producer put the car.) Further, the probability the contestant selects door 1 is $\frac{1}{3}$, and the probability the car is behind door 1 is $\frac{1}{3}$. So, by the Multiplication Rule

$$P(L_1) = P(S_1 \text{ } and \text{ } C_1) = P(S_1) \cdot P(C_1) = \frac{1}{3} \cdot \frac{1}{3} = \frac{1}{9}$$

Similarly, $P(L_2) = \frac{1}{9}$ and $P(L_3) = \frac{1}{9}$. So

$$P(L) = P(L_1) + P(L_2) + P(L_3) = \frac{1}{9} + \frac{1}{9} + \frac{1}{9} = \frac{1}{3}$$

The event of winning is the complement of losing ($\overline{L}$). Hence, the probability of winning by using the switching strategy is

$$P(\overline{L}) = 1 - P(L) = 1 - \frac{1}{3} = \frac{2}{3}$$

EXERCISES

5.24 In Example 5.9, we considered the tossing of two fair dice. Consider the following events: A = sum is 7 or more, B = sum is even, C = sum is 7, and D = sum is less than 11.

(a)   Verify that the only pair of mutually exclusive events is *B, C*.

(b)   Use the Addition Rule to find *P(B or C)*.

(c)   Let *E* = sum is less than 4, and *F* = {(3, 3)}. Find *P(A or E or F)*. (*Hint:*   *A, E,* and *F* are mutually exclusive.)

5.25   A card is to be randomly selected from an ordinary deck of 52 cards. Consider the following events: *A* = ace, *B* = face card, and *C* = club.

(a)   Verify that the only pair of mutually exclusive events is *A, B*.

(b)   Use the Addition Rule to find *P(A or B)*.

5.26   Refer to Exercise 5.5, where the mother was a carrier for colorblindness and the father was normal. Assume that when a parent contributes a gene from a gene pair, either gene is equally likely to be contributed. Let event *A* = carries gene for colorblindness and event *B* = is colorblind.

(a)   Assign probabilities to each outcome.

(b)   Are the events *A, B* mutually exclusive?

(c)   Find the probability that an offspring will either carry the colorblindness gene or be colorblind.

5.27   The following data are characteristics of the voting-age population regarding the 1992 presidential election in the United States. Number of persons is measured in thousands (*Source:*   *The 1994 Information Please Almanac*, 1994, p. 37).

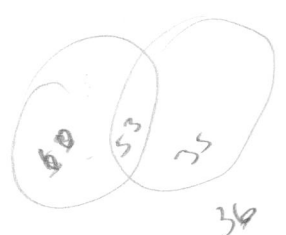

	A Voted	*Ā* Did Not Vote
B Males	53,312	35,245
B̄ Females	60,554	36,573

For a randomly selected person from the population, let *A* be the event that the person selected voted, and *B* be the event that the person selected is a male. Find each of the following:

(a)   *P(B)*

(b)   *P(Ā)*

(c)   *P(Ā and B̄)*

5.28   There are 2000 voters in a town. Consider the experiment of randomly selecting a voter to be interviewed. (The voters in the town are the possible outcomes of the experiment.) The event *A* consists of being in favor of more stringent building codes; the event *B* consists of having lived in the town less than 10 years. The following table gives the numbers of voters in various categories.

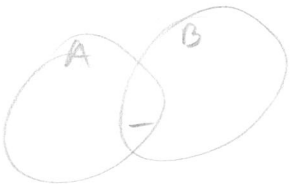

	A Favor More Stringent Codes	*Ā* Do Not Favor More Stringent Codes
B Less Than 10 Years	100	700
B̄ At Least 10 Years	1000	200

Find each of the following:

(a) $P(A)$

(b) $P(\overline{B})$

(c) $P(A \text{ and } B)$

5.29 Two cards are to be selected from an ordinary deck of 52 cards. Assume the first card is replaced before the second card is selected. Consider the following events: A = the first card is an ace; B = the second card is an ace; C = the second card is a king.

(a) Find each of the following:

  (i) $P(A \text{ and } B)$

  (ii) $P(B \text{ or } C)$

(b) Now suppose a third card is selected after replacing the first and second cards. Let D = third card is not an ace. Find $P(A \text{ and } B \text{ and } D)$.

5.30 A sporting goods store has a large batch of cans of tennis balls on hand. Ten percent of the cans are unacceptable (that is, contain at least one defective ball).

(a) A customer decides to purchase one can. What is the probability that the customer will be satisfied?

(b) A customer is to purchase two cans. Find the probability that

  (i) Both cans will be satisfactory.

  (ii) Exactly one can will be satisfactory.

  (iii) At least one can will be satisfactory.

5.31 Suppose that the probability that a child produced by a couple will have a particular disease is $\frac{1}{10}$. If they plan to have four children, what is the probability that at least one child will have the disease?

5.32 A large shipment of items contains 2% defective items. Five items are to be selected. What is the probability of getting at least one defective item?

5.33 In an effort to present sufficient evidence to bring O. J. Simpson to trial, a prosecution expert testified that "several factors in Simpson's blood closely matched a bloodstain found at the murder scene and concluded that fewer than one in 200 individuals would have the same pattern" (*Source: The Boston Globe,* July 9, 1994, p. 5). The evidence presented was as follows:

Test	Sample at Crime Scene	O. J. Simpson	Probability of a Match
Blood Group	A	A	.337
Esterase D	1	1	.796
PGM	2^+2^-	2^+2^-	.016

Let events L = blood type A, M = esterase D is 1, and N = PGM is 2^+2^-. Assuming independent events, find $P(L \text{ and } M \text{ and } N)$. Does your answer support the expert's contention that "fewer than one in 200 individuals would have the same pattern"? (*Note:* An attorney for the defense questioned the assumptions of independent events and whether the probabilities used applied to the general population. The probabilities used by the prosecution were obtained from police files.)

5.5

MORE ON COMPOUND EVENTS (OPTIONAL)

In this section, we develop an Addition Rule that does not require that the events are mutually exclusive, and a Multiplication Rule that does not require independence of events.

Addition Rule—General Form

In Example 5.12, we talked about the experiment of randomly selecting a voter from a town. The possible outcomes are the voters in the town. Therefore the sample space is

$$S = \{\text{all voters in town}\}$$

The event A corresponds to selecting a voter favoring universal health care. As a set of outcomes

$$A = \{\text{all voters in town favoring universal health care}\}$$

The event B consists in selecting a union member. As a set,

$$B = \{\text{all voters in town belonging to a union}\}$$

Now suppose that there are 1000 voters in the town. Then $n(S) = 1000$. Also, suppose $n(A) = 500$ and $n(B) = 400$. Further breakdown of the voters is given in Table 5.1.

Table 5.1
Voter Preference on Universal Health Care (UHC) Versus Union Membership in a Town With 1000 Registered Voters

	A (Favor UHC)	$\overline{A}$ (Oppose UHC)	Row Totals
B (Union)	100	300	400 ← $n(B)$
$\overline{B}$ (Nonunion)	400	200	600 ← $n(\overline{B})$
Column Totals	500	500	1000 (Grand total)
	↑ $n(A)$	↑ $n(\overline{A})$	↑ $n(S)$

This table is not difficult to interpret. For example, the number in the intersection of column A and row B is 100, meaning 100 voters favor universal health care and are also members of a union. Thus, $n(A \text{ and } B) = 100$. Now each outcome (voter) is equally likely. Therefore let's use Rule 5.1 to evaluate some probabilities:

$$P(A) = \frac{n(A)}{n(S)} = \frac{500}{1000} = .5 \qquad P(\overline{A}) = \frac{n(\overline{A})}{n(S)} = \frac{500}{1000} = .5$$

$$P(B) = \frac{n(B)}{n(S)} = \frac{400}{1000} = .4 \qquad P(\overline{B}) = \frac{n(\overline{B})}{n(S)} = \frac{600}{1000} = .6$$

$$P(A \text{ and } B) = \frac{n(A \text{ and } B)}{n(S)} = \frac{100}{1000} = .1$$

$$P(A \text{ or } B) = \frac{n(A \text{ or } B)}{n(S)} = \frac{?}{1000}$$

We can find $n(A \text{ or } B)$, the number of voters who favor universal health care or are members of a union, from the table. We want the number of *distinct* voters in $(A \text{ or } B)$; that is, we do not want to count anyone twice. Now there are 500 voters in A and 400 in B. But 100 voters are in both A and B [$n(A \text{ and } B) = 100$]. If we tried to count the number of voters, $n(A \text{ or } B)$, by adding $500 + 400$, we would be counting 100 of them twice. What we should do is subtract 100 from this sum:

$$n(A \text{ or } B) = n(A) + n(B) - n(A \text{ and } B)$$
$$= 500 + 400 - 100 = 800$$

Therefore,

$$P(A \text{ or } B) = \frac{n(A \text{ or } B)}{n(S)} = \frac{800}{1000} = .8$$

Note that

$$P(A \text{ or } B) = \frac{n(A \text{ or } B)}{n(S)} = \frac{n(A) + n(B) - n(A \text{ and } B)}{n(S)}$$
$$= \frac{n(A)}{n(S)} + \frac{n(B)}{n(S)} - \frac{n(A \text{ and } B)}{n(S)}$$
$$= P(A) + P(B) - P(A \text{ and } B) = .5 + .4 - .1 = .8$$

Thus

$$P(A \text{ or } B) = P(A) + P(B) - P(A \text{ and } B)$$

This is a more general **Addition Rule.** The technique we have used could be used to show that the Addition Rule is valid for any events A, B in a finite sample space in which each outcome is equally likely. (Remember, we have used Rule 5.1.) However, the Addition Rule can be shown to be valid in general—even in sample spaces where not all outcomes are equally likely. This is an important result because it enables us to find the probability on the left if we know the three probabilities on the right. In fact, if we know any three of the probabilities in the equation, we can solve for the fourth.

Rule 5.6 Addition Rule   If A, B are events from some sample space, then

$$P(A \text{ or } B) = P(A) + P(B) - P(A \text{ and } B)$$

EXAMPLE 5.16
A die is rolled. Find the probability that the number on the top face is even or greater than 4 using the Addition Rule.

Solution
There are six possible outcomes: 1, 2, 3, 4, 5, and 6. As sets,

$$\text{even} = \{2, 4, 6\} \qquad \text{greater than } 4 = \{5, 6\}$$

so that

$$P(\text{even}) = \tfrac{3}{6} = \tfrac{1}{2} \qquad P(\text{greater than } 4) = \tfrac{2}{6} = \tfrac{1}{3}$$

Therefore,

$$P(\text{even } or \text{ greater than } 4)$$
$$= P(\text{even}) + P(\text{greater than } 4) - P(\text{even } and \text{ greater than } 4)$$
$$= \tfrac{1}{2} + \tfrac{1}{3} - P(6)$$
$$= \tfrac{1}{2} + \tfrac{1}{3} - \tfrac{1}{6} = \tfrac{2}{3}$$

When A, B are mutually exclusive, they have no outcomes in common. Hence, $P(A \text{ and } B) = 0$. Thus Rule 5.6 reduces to $P(A \text{ or } B) = P(A) + P(B)$, which is Rule 5.3.

Multiplication Rule—General Form

Now we return to our discussion of the data in Table 5.1. The experiment is randomly selecting a voter from the town of 1000 voters. First, consider the probability of event B occurring, given that A has definitely occurred. In other words, we want the probability that the voter selected is a union member if we know this voter favors universal health care. This probability is called the *conditional probability of B given that A has occurred*, denoted by $P(B \mid A)$. Now 500 voters favor universal health care [$n(A) = 500$] and 100 of those are also union members [$n(A \text{ and } B) = 100$]. Thus the probability that the person selected is a union member given that this person favors universal health care is $\frac{100}{500} = .2$. Therefore,

$$P(B \mid A) = \frac{n(A \text{ and } B)}{n(A)} = \frac{100}{500} = .2$$

By performing a simple algebraic operation on this equation, we can discover a useful relationship. We can divide both the numerator and denominator of the fraction in the equation by the same number, $n(S) = 1000$, without affecting the equality. Dividing by $n(S)$ and using Rule 5.1, we obtain

$$P(B \mid A) = \frac{n(A \text{ and } B)/n(S)}{n(A)/n(S)} \leftarrow \left(\frac{100/1000}{500/1000} = \frac{.1}{.5} = .2 \right)$$

So we see that

$$P(B \mid A) = \frac{P(A \text{ and } B)}{P(A)}$$

This relationship is usually written in the following form:

$$P(A \text{ and } B) = P(A) \cdot P(B \mid A)$$

This is a more general **Multiplication Rule.** Although this discussion involved events in a finite sample space where each outcome is equally likely, this result is valid for events in any sample space.

Rule 5.7 Multiplication Rule   If A, B are events in some sample space, then

$$P(A \text{ and } B) = P(A) \cdot P(B \mid A)$$

where $P(B \mid A)$ is the (conditional) probability that B will occur, given that A has occurred.

The Multiplication Rule can be extended to more than two events. For example,

$$P(A \text{ and } B \text{ and } C) = P(A) \cdot P(B \mid A) \cdot P(C \mid A \text{ and } B)$$

EXAMPLE 5.17

Two cards are dealt from a deck. Find the probability that the first is an ace and the second is a king.

Solution

Let A be the event consisting of an ace on the first card and B the event of a king on the second card. We want to find $P(A \text{ and } B)$. By Rule 5.7,

$$P(A \text{ and } B) = P(A) \cdot P(B \mid A)$$

Four cards in the deck of 52 are aces. Thus

$$P(A) = \tfrac{4}{52}$$

Now suppose the first card was an ace. Then there are 51 cards left, and 4 of them are kings. Hence, the probability of a king on the second card, given the first was an ace, is

$$P(B \mid A) = \tfrac{4}{51}$$

Therefore,

$$P(A \text{ and } B) = P(A) \cdot P(B \mid A) = \tfrac{4}{52} \cdot \tfrac{4}{51} = \tfrac{16}{2652} \doteq .006$$

EXAMPLE 5.18

At a large bank, 6% of the employees are computer programmers, 50% of the employees are female, and 2% of the employees are female computer programmers. If an employee is selected by chance, what is the probability that

(a) The employee is a computer programmer, given that the employee is female.

(b) The employee is female, given that the employee is a computer programmer.

Solution

Let $F =$ employee is female, and $C =$ employee is a computer programmer. We are given

$$P(F) = .5 \qquad P(C) = .06$$
$$P(F \text{ and } C) = .02$$

(a) We want $P(C \mid F)$. Now from the Multiplication Rule

$$P(F \text{ and } C) = P(F) \cdot P(C \mid F)$$

Therefore

$$P(C \mid F) = \frac{P(F \text{ and } C)}{P(F)} = \frac{.02}{.50} = \frac{2}{50} = \frac{1}{25} = .04$$

(b) This asks for $P(F \mid C)$. We can also write (by the Multiplication Rule)

$$P(C \text{ and } F) = P(C) \cdot P(F \mid C)$$

Therefore

$$P(F \mid C) = \frac{P(C \text{ and } F)}{P(C)} = \frac{.02}{.06} = \frac{1}{3}$$

When events A, B are independent, the probability of B occurring is not affected by whether A has occurred. In other words, $P(B \mid A) = P(B)$. In this case, Rule 5.7 reduces to

$$P(A \text{ and } B) = P(A) \cdot P(B)$$

which is Rule 5.4. The next example brings out the difference between independent and dependent events.

EXAMPLE 5.19

A box contains seven red poker chips and three white ones. Two chips are randomly selected from the box. Find the probability that we get a red chip on the first draw and a white one on the second draw if

(a)   The chips are selected without replacement (i.e., the first is not returned to the box before the second is selected).

(b)   The chips are selected with replacement (i.e., the first chip is returned before selecting the second).

Solution

Let $R1 =$ red on first draw, $W2 =$ white on second draw.

(a) $P(R1 \text{ and } W2) = P(R1) \cdot P(W2 \mid R1)$

Now

$$P(R1) = \tfrac{7}{10}$$

If we draw a red on the first selection and if we do not replace the chip, there are 9 left, of which 3 are white. Hence

$$P(W2 \mid R1) = \tfrac{3}{9} = \tfrac{1}{3}$$

and so

$$P(R1 \text{ and } W2) = \tfrac{7}{10} \cdot \tfrac{1}{3} = \tfrac{7}{30}$$

(b)   To find the probability when the chips are selected with replacement, we can use the same formula as in part (a). The only difference occurs with the term $P(W2 \mid R1)$. Since the first chip is replaced, the probability of a white on the second draw is unaffected by whether we get a red on the first. In other words, $R1$, $W2$ are independent. So

$$P(W2 \mid R1) = P(W2) = \tfrac{3}{10}$$

Therefore

$$P(R1 \text{ and } W2) = P(R1) \cdot P(W2)$$
$$= \tfrac{7}{10} \cdot \tfrac{3}{10} = \tfrac{21}{100}$$

Sometimes a *tree diagram* is helpful in analyzing probabilities of the type found in Example 5.19. Conditional probabilities may be written on the branches of the tree. Multiplying the probabilities along the branches leading to an outcome at the end of a tree gives the probability of the outcome. Figure 5.4 is a representation of selecting two poker chips without replacement, as in Example 5.19(a).

	Chip 1	Chip 2	Outcome	Probability
	$P(R2 \mid R1) = \frac{6}{9}$	R	R1 and R2	$\frac{7}{10} \cdot \frac{6}{9} = \frac{42}{90}$
$P(R1) = \frac{7}{10}$ R				
	$\frac{3}{9}$	W	R1 and W2	$\frac{7}{10} \cdot \frac{3}{9} = \frac{21}{90}$
	$\frac{7}{9}$	R	W1 and R2	$\frac{3}{10} \cdot \frac{7}{9} = \frac{21}{90}$
$\frac{3}{10}$ W				
	$\frac{2}{9}$	W	W1 and W2	$\frac{3}{10} \cdot \frac{2}{9} = \frac{6}{90}$

Figure 5.4
Selecting Two Poker Chips Without Replacement. See Example 5.19(a).

EXERCISES

5.34   In Example 5.9, we tossed two fair dice. Consider the following events: A = sum is 7 or more, B = sum is even, C = sum is 7, and D = sum is less than 11. Find

   (a) $P(A$ or $B)$ **(b)** $P(A$ or $C)$ **(c)** $P(A$ or $D)$

5.35   In a small college, 1500 of the 4000 students are male. Also, 1200 of the 3600 students under the age of 25 are male. What proportion of the student body is either male or under the age of 25?

5.36   There are 2000 voters in a town. Consider the experiment of randomly selecting a voter to be interviewed. (The voters in the town are the possible outcomes of the experiment.) The event A consists of being in favor of more stringent building codes; the event B consists of having lived in the town less than 10 years. The following table gives the numbers of voters in various categories.

	A Favor More Stringent Codes	$\overline{A}$ Do Not Favor More Stringent Codes
B Less Than 10 Years	100	700
$\overline{B}$ At Least 10 Years	1000	200

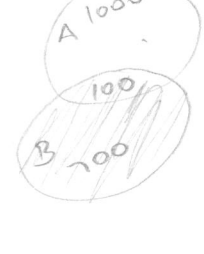

   (a)   Find $P(A$ or $B)$.   **(b)**   Find $P(A$ or $\overline{B})$.

5.37   Two cards are to be selected from an ordinary deck of 52 cards. Assume that the first card is not replaced before the second one is drawn. Consider the following events: A = the first card is an ace, B = the second card is an ace.

(a)   Find P(*A and B*).

(b)   Find P(*B*). [*Hint:*   Let $\bar{A}$ = the first card is not an ace. Now *B* = (*A and B*) or ($\bar{A}$ *and B*).] Are the events *A* and *B* independent?

(c)   Find P(*A or B*).

5.38   In Example 5.9, we considered the experiment of tossing two fair dice. Consider the following events: *A* = the sum is even, *B* = a match (both numbers are the same), *C* = the sum is larger than five, and *D* = the sum is odd.

(a)   Use the Multiplication Rule to find each of the following:

   (i) $P(A \mid C)$ (ii) $P(C \mid A)$ (iii) $P(B \mid C)$

(b)   Find the following:

   (i) $P(A \mid B)$ (ii) $P(D \mid B)$

(c)   Which pairs of events are independent?

5.39   Refer to the parents of Exercise 5.5, where the mother is a carrier for colorblindness and the father is normal.

(a)   Find the probability that a child will be colorblind if it is male.

(b)   Find the probability that a child will be colorblind if it is female.

5.40   A committee of seven consists of two males and five females. Two members are to be chosen randomly to look into a specific problem. What is the probability that both males will be chosen? (*Hint:*   Imagine the selection as a two-stage process—select one member then another, without replacement.)

5.41   A business employs 600 men and 400 women. Five percent of the men and 10% of the women have been working there for more than 20 years. If an employee is selected by chance, what is the probability that the employee is male, given that the length of employment is more than 20 years?

5.42   In a town, 70% of the men are employed. The probability that a man will commit a crime is .10, and the probability that a man is employed, given he will commit a crime, is .05. A man is selected by chance and is employed. What is the probability that he will commit a crime?

5.43   A change was proposed in the mathematics curriculum at a college. The mathematics majors were asked whether they approved of the proposed change. The results of the survey follow.

	Approved	No Opinion	Did Not Approve	
Male	21	6	12	-39
Female	14	10	7	31
	35	16	19	

Suppose that a mathematics major is selected by chance. Find the probability that

(a)   The student is female, given no opinion.

(b)   The student approves of the proposed change, given the student is male.

(c)   The student is male, given the student does not approve of the proposed change.

(d)   The student is male and approves of the proposed change. (Use the Multiplication Rule.)

5.44   In Exercise 5.27, we discussed the events *A* (person randomly selected voted in the 1992 presidential election) and *B* (person was a male). The following table gives the number of people in various categories. Number of persons is measured in thousands.

	A Voted	$\overline{A}$ Did Not Vote
B Males	53,312	35,245
$\overline{B}$ Females	60,554	36,573

Find

(a) $P(A \text{ or } B)$ **(b)** $P(\overline{A} \text{ or } B)$ **(c)** $P(B \mid A)$ **(d)** $P(\overline{A} \mid \overline{B})$

5.45 A city has 1000 married couples with both husband and wife working. Each person was asked whether their salary exceeded $30,000. The following information was obtained.

		Husband	
		Less Than $30,000	More Than $30,000
Wife	Less Than $30,000	430	410
	More Than $30,000	60	100

If one of the couples is selected by chance,

(a) Find the probability that a husband earns less than $30,000, given that the wife earns less than $30,000.

(b) Find the probability that a wife earns more than $30,000, given that the husband earns more than $30,000.

(c) Are the salaries of husband and wife statistically independent?

5.46 Suppose that 2% of the people in a town have a particular disease. A test designed to detect the disease has the following properties: If a person has the disease, the test will detect it with probability .99. If the person does not have the disease, the test will indicate the disease is present with probability .005. If the test indicates a person has the disease, what is the probability that the person actually has the disease? Assume that the probability that the test indicates the disease is .0247.

5.47 A study is being conducted on families with two children. Consider the following events: A = the older child is a boy, and B = the younger child is a boy. A family with two children is selected by chance. Find each of the following probabilities (assume a probability of $\frac{1}{2}$ that a particular child is a boy).

(a) $P[(A \text{ and } B) \mid A]$ **(b)** $P[(A \text{ and } B) \mid (A \text{ or } B)]$

5.48 A subcommittee of two is to be selected by chance from a committee consisting of eight men and two women. What is the probability that at least one of the two women will be selected?

5.6

COMBINATORICS (OPTIONAL)

Combinatorics is the study of counting techniques. In probability, it is sometimes important to count the number of elements in a set (see Rule 5.1).

A lottery game consists of selecting a sequence of three digits by filling in three boxes on a lottery ticket. No repetitions are allowed. We can look at this as performing three tasks, as follows:

$$\text{Task 1} = \text{select the first digit}$$

$$\text{Task 2} = \text{select the second digit}$$

$$\text{Task 3} = \text{select the third digit}$$

The digits are selected from the set $\{0, 1, 2, 3, 4, 5, 6, 7, 8, 9\}$. There are 10 digits to choose from for Task 1, so Task 1 can be performed 10 ways. Since no repetitions are allowed, there are only nine digits available for Task 2, and thus Task 2 can be done nine ways. And for Task 3, there are only eight possibilities. So the three digits can be selected

$$10 \cdot 9 \cdot 8 = 720 \text{ ways}$$

This process can be viewed as follows: Imagine the 10 digits 0, 1, 2, 3, 4, 5, 6, 7, 8, 9 written on 10 tags. We then choose three tags and arrange them in the desired order, such as

5	2	8

(Note that there will not be any repetitions.) Such an arrangement is called a **permutation,** or more precisely, a **permutation of 10 objects taken 3 at a time.**

To be able to conveniently count the number of possible permutations, it is helpful to introduce the concept of **factorials.** If n is a positive whole number, n **factorial,** denoted by $n!$, is defined as the product

$$n! = 1 \cdot 2 \cdot 3 \cdot \cdots \cdot n$$

Thus

$$4! = 1 \cdot 2 \cdot 3 \cdot 4 = 24$$
$$3! = 1 \cdot 2 \cdot 3 = 6$$
$$2! = 1 \cdot 2 = 2$$
$$1! = 1$$

By definition $0! = 1$.

Factorials can get large very quickly. For example,

$$7! = 5{,}040$$

$$10! = 3{,}628{,}800$$

Many calculators have factorial keys, and there are also mathematical tables of factorials.

We have seen that there are 720 permutations of the 10 digits taken 3 at a time. Notice that

$$720 = \frac{3{,}628{,}800}{5{,}040} = \frac{10!}{7!} = \frac{10!}{(10-3)!}$$

So the number of permutations of 10 objects taken 3 at a time is

$$\frac{10!}{(10-3)!} = 720$$

We generalize these ideas as follows.

Permutations   An ordered arrangement of r objects selected from a set of n objects is a *permutation of n objects taken r at a time.* The total number of such permutations, denoted by $_nP_r$, is

$$_nP_r = \frac{n!}{(n-r)!}$$

It may seem that the use of factorials is a more complicated way to compute the number of permutations. But remember, there are tables of factorials, and factorials can be computed with calculators. So factorials can shorten our work.

EXAMPLE 5.20

A TV news department decided to interview four celebrities for the evening news. If the news department employs six reporters, how many different ways are there to assign the interviewers? (Assume that no reporter will interview more than one celebrity.)

Solution

The assignment of reporters to celebrities 1, 2, 3, and 4 can be thought of as an arrangement or permutation of the reporters. So we want the number of permutations of six reporters taken four at a time.

$$_6P_4 = \frac{6!}{(6-4)!} = \frac{6!}{2!} = \frac{720}{2} = 360$$

Suppose three friends wish to play each other at chess. How many different matches are possible? Suppose we call the players A, B, and C. We are asking how many ways there are of selecting two players. But notice that order does not matter here. A list of elements in which order does not matter is simply a set. The sets consisting of two elements are

$$\{A, B\} \qquad \{A, C\} \qquad \{B, C\}$$

Such sets are also called **combinations,** or more precisely, **combinations of 3 things taken 2 at a time.** Note there are three of them. Observe that

$$\frac{3!}{2!(3-2)!} = \frac{6}{(2)(1)} = 3$$

This generalizes to a computational formula for combinations.

> **Combinations** A collection of r objects selected from a set of n objects is called a *combination of n objects taken r at a time*. The total number of such combinations, denoted by $_nC_r$, is
>
> $$_nC_r = \frac{n!}{r!(n-r)!}$$
>
> This is also denoted by $\binom{n}{r}$.

Note: **When order matters, use the permutation formula; when order does not matter, use the combination formula.**

EXAMPLE 5.21

To complete the requirements for a major, a student must select three courses from a list of seven. How many different three-course combinations are there?

Solution

We want the number of combinations of seven courses taken three at a time.

$$_7C_3 = \frac{7!}{3!(7-3)!} = \frac{7!}{3!4!} = \frac{\cancel{1} \cdot \cancel{2} \cdot \cancel{3} \cdot \cancel{4} \cdot 5 \cdot 6 \cdot 7}{(1 \cdot 2 \cdot 3)(\cancel{1} \cdot \cancel{2} \cdot \cancel{3} \cdot \cancel{4})}$$

$$= \frac{5 \cdot 6 \cdot 7}{1 \cdot 2 \cdot 3} = \frac{5 \cdot \cancel{6} \cdot 7}{\cancel{6}} = 35$$

EXAMPLE 5.22

The Massachusetts Megabucks lottery consists of selecting six numbers from the numbers: $1, 2, \ldots, 42$. Order does not matter.

(a) If you play the game once, what is the probability that your six numbers are the same as the winning six numbers?

(b) How many six-number combinations match exactly four of the six winning numbers?

(c) What is the probability that you will match exactly four of the six winning numbers?

Solution

(a) First, we must calculate the number of possible six-number combinations. We want the number of combinations of 42 things taken 6 at a time:

$$_{42}C_6 = \frac{42!}{6!(42-6)!} = \frac{42!}{6!36!}$$

$$= \frac{\cancel{1} \cdot \cancel{2} \cdot \cancel{3} \cdot \cancel{4} \cdot \cdots \cdot \cancel{35} \cdot \cancel{36} \cdot 37 \cdot 38 \cdot 39 \cdot 40 \cdot 41 \cdot 42}{6!\cancel{1} \cdot \cancel{2} \cdot \cancel{3} \cdot \cancel{4} \cdot \cdots \cdot \cancel{35} \cdot \cancel{36}}$$

$$= \frac{37 \cdot \overset{19}{\cancel{38}} \cdot \overset{13}{\cancel{39}} \cdot \overset{10}{\cancel{40}} \cdot 41 \cdot \overset{7}{\cancel{42}}}{1 \cdot \cancel{2} \cdot \cancel{3} \cdot \cancel{4} \cdot 5 \cdot \cancel{6}} = 5{,}245{,}786 \text{ combinations}$$

Each combination is equally likely. Therefore, the probability of selecting all six winning numbers is

$$\frac{1}{5{,}245{,}786} \doteq .00000019$$

This minuscule probability shows that your chance of winning at Megabucks is about the same, whether you buy a ticket or not. So your chance of winning is about 1 in 5.2 million.

(b) To count the number of possibilities that match the winning combination in exactly four numbers, we can imagine counting the ways we can perform two tasks sequentially:

> Task 1 = specify which four of the six numbers in the winning
> combination are to be matched
>
> Task 2 = specify the remaining two numbers

Task 1 consists of selecting a subset of four elements from the winning set of six elements. We have seen that the number of ways of doing this is

$$_6C_4 = \frac{6!}{4!(6-4)!} = \frac{6!}{4!2!} = \frac{\cancel{1} \cdot \cancel{2} \cdot \cancel{3} \cdot \cancel{4} \cdot 5 \cdot \overset{3}{\cancel{6}}}{(\cancel{1} \cdot \cancel{2} \cdot \cancel{3} \cdot \cancel{4})(1 \cdot \cancel{2})} = 15$$

To specify the remaining two numbers, we must be sure not to use any of the remaining two numbers of the winning combination (otherwise we would have more than four matching numbers). Thus we have to choose the remaining two numbers from the 36 nonwinning numbers. Therefore Task 2 can be done $_{36}C_2$ ways:

$$_{36}C_2 = \frac{36!}{2!(36-2)!} = \frac{36!}{2!34!} = \frac{1 \cdot 2 \cdot 3 \cdot \,\cdots\, \cdot 34 \cdot 35 \cdot 36}{(1 \cdot 2)(1 \cdot 2 \cdot 3 \cdot \,\cdots\, \cdot 34)}$$

$$= \frac{35 \cdot 36}{1 \cdot 2} = (35)(18) = 630$$

Using the Fundamental Principle of Counting, Task 1 and Task 2 taken together can be done

$$(15) \cdot (630) = 9450$$

ways. This is the number of combinations that match exactly four of the six winning numbers.

(c) The probability of matching exactly four of the six winning numbers is

$$P(\text{matching 4}) = \frac{\text{number of combinations that match four winning numbers}}{\text{total number of possible combinations}}$$

$$= \frac{9450}{5{,}245{,}786} \doteq .0018$$

When you match four numbers, you win \$75.

EXERCISES

5.49   Evaluate each of the following:

   (a) 6!   **(b)** $_{12}P_3$ **(c)** $_5P_5$ **(d)** $_{12}C_3$ **(e)** $_{12}C_9$ **(f)** $_5C_5$

5.50   Consider the set $S = \{a, b, c, d\}$.

   (a)   Find $_4C_2$ and list the combinations.

   (b)   Find $_4P_2$ and list the permutations.

5.51   Ten people are in a line to purchase tickets. In how many different ways can the 10 people be lined up?

5.52   A newspaper editor is going to assign two reporters to cover a political convention. The assignment will be made from a pool of six women and four men. How many groups of two reporters can be assigned if

   (a)   Both are to be women?

   (b)   Both are to be men?

   (c)   There is to be one woman and one man?

5.53   A group of six women and four men have volunteered to participate in an experiment. Three of them will be randomly selected to participate in one phase of the experiment.

   (a)   Find the probability that all are men.

   (b)   Find the probability that exactly two are women.

5.54   Suppose four digits are to be randomly selected (repetitions allowed). [*Note:*   The set of digits is $\{0, 1, 2, 3, 4, 5, 6, 7, 8, 9\}$.] Find the probability that 1, 2, and 3 are the first three digits selected, not necessarily in the order 123.

5.55   The letters A, B, C, D, E, and F are to be randomly arranged in a row. Find the probability that

   (a)   The arrangement is ABCDEF.

   (b)   The first three letters, in order, are ABC.

   (c)   The letters A and B appear next to each other in either order.

5.56   Megabucks, a lottery game conducted by the Massachusetts State Lottery Commission, consists of selecting six numbers from the 42 numbers $\{1, 2, 3, 4, \ldots, 41, 42\}$. (No repetitions are allowed, and order does not matter.) The commission selects by chance the six winning numbers. You pay \$1 to play. You get a free ticket if three of your numbers match three of the winning numbers, \$75 for matching four numbers, \$1500 for matching five numbers, and a large prize if you match all six numbers. The sample space S consists of all possible six-number combinations that can be selected. Without using Exercise 5.16, find the probability of

   (a)   Winning a free ticket   **(b)**   Winning \$1500

5.57   In a 13-card bridge hand, find each of the following:

   (a)   The probability of getting 4 aces

   (b)   The probability of getting 7 diamonds and 6 hearts

_____ **5.7**

SUMMARY

In this chapter, we discussed the notion of an **experiment,** which is any activity yielding an outcome. The collection of all distinct possible outcomes is the **sample space** of the experiment. An **event** is a subset of the sample space. A major objective of the chapter is to be able to find the chances or the probability that an event will occur. We developed some techniques in the form of rules for finding such probabilities.

Rule 5.1

If A is an event in a finite sample space in which each outcome is equally likely, then

$$P(A) = \frac{n(A)}{n(S)}$$

where $n(A)$ = the number of distinct outcomes in A (i.e., the number of different ways A can occur) and $n(S)$ is the total number of possible distinct outcomes in S.

Rule 5.2 (Fundamental Principle of Counting)

If Task 1 can be done in n_1 ways and Task 2 can be done in n_2 ways, then Task 1 *and* Task 2 performed together can be done in $n_1 \cdot n_2$ ways.

Rule 5.3 (Addition Rule for Mutually Exclusive Events)

If A, B are *mutually exclusive* (cannot occur at the same time), then

$$P(A \text{ or } B) = P(A) + P(B)$$

Rule 5.4 (Multiplication Rule for Independent Events)

When events A, B are *independent*, that is, the occurrence of A has no effect on the probability of B occurring, then

$$P(A \text{ and } B) = P(A) \cdot P(B)$$

Rule 5.5

For an event A, its *complement* $\overline{A}$ is the event that occurs provided that A does not occur ($\overline{A}$ is the opposite of A).

$$P(\overline{A}) = 1 - P(A)$$

Rule 5.6 (Addition Rule—General Form)

For events A, B

$$P(A \text{ or } B) = P(A) + P(B) - P(A \text{ and } B)$$

Rule 5.7 (Multiplication Rule—General Form)

For events A, B

$$P(A \text{ and } B) = P(A) \cdot P(B \mid A)$$

where $P(B \mid A)$ = probability of B occurring if A has occurred.

A **permutation** is an arrangement of objects in a particular order. The number of possible permutations of n objects taken r at a time is denoted by $_nP_r$:

$$_nP_r = \frac{n!}{(n-r)!}$$

A **combination** is a set of objects (order does not matter). The number of possible combinations of n objects taken r at a time is denoted by $_nC_r$:

$$_nC_r = \frac{n!}{r!(n-r)!}$$

REVIEW EXERCISES

5.58   A lottery ticket has a color, R = red, B = blue, or G = green, followed by a 1, 2, 3, or 4. One ticket is to be selected and the combination of color and number observed. List the elements in the sample space. Use the set notation $S = \{\ \}$.

5.59   A study of 1000 couples is designed to determine the relationship, if any, between educational backgrounds of husbands and wives. It has been decided to categorize the educational levels in terms of the highest degree attained. The labels are 1 = Doctorate, 2 = Master's degree, 3 = Bachelor's degree, and 4 = other. Both husband and wife are asked their educational status. List the elements in the sample space. Use the set notation $S = \{\ \}$.

5.60   Refer to Example 5.5. The sample space S was given as $S = \{CC, Cc, cC, cc\}$. List the elements of the following events: (a) albinism, and (b) offspring is a carrier of albinism (but has normal pigmentation).

5.61   A man buys 10 chances for a large raffle. Two tickets are to be drawn in the raffle. (Thus the man could possibly win two prizes.) For each ticket drawn, it is noted whether the man wins or loses.

   (a)   Give a sample space.

   (b)   List the elements of the following events:

   (i)   The man wins two prizes.

   (ii)   The man wins exactly one prize.

5.62   A large city hospital is doing a study on the safety of certain anesthetics and is collecting data on the type used, the physical status of the patient at the time of surgery, and whether the patient survived the surgery. For the type of anesthetic used, let 1 = cyclopropane, 2 = ether, 3 = halothane, 4 = pentothal, and 5 = other. Also, let a = good physical status, b = poor physical status, x = survived surgery, and y = did not survive surgery. List the elements of the following events:

   (a)   Survived surgery

   (b)   Received either cyclopropane or halothane, and was in good physical shape

   (c)   Was in poor physical shape and survived surgery

5.63   An urn contains 365 chips representing the days of the year. One chip is to be selected by chance. Find the probability that

   (a)   Your birth date is selected.

   (b)   A day in the month of July is selected.

   (c)   The first day of any month is selected.

   (d)   A day in a month beginning with a J is selected.

5.64   The voting list in a small town contains the names of 417 Democrats, 335 Republicans, and 248 Independents. One name is to be selected by chance. Find the probability that the name selected is

   (a)   A Democrat

   (b)   A Democrat or an Independent

   (c)   Not an Independent

5.65   The Mass Millions lottery game involves selecting six numbers (no repetitions and order does not matter) from a collection of 46 numbers, $\{1, 2, 3, 4, \ldots, 44, 45, 46\}$. Let the sample space S consist of all possible six-number combinations that can be selected. It can be shown that $n(S) = 9{,}366{,}819$. Suppose you select six numbers. The number of elements in S that match 0, 1, 2, 3, 4, 5, or 6 numbers of the winning combination are

Number of Matches	Number of Possibilities
0	3,838,380
1	3,948,048
2	1,370,850
3	197,600
4	11,700
5	240
6	1

(a) Find the probability of matching three numbers (and thereby winning a free ticket). Compare with Exercise 5.16, part (c).

(b) Find the probability of matching zero or one number.

(c) On average, approximately how many times per 10,000 would you expect to match either four, five, or six numbers?

5.66 A person purchases a package of 10 ballpoint pens that, unknown to the purchaser, contains three defective pens. Of the first two pens to be used by the purchaser, find the probability that

(a) Both are defective.

(b) At least one is defective.

(c) Exactly one is defective.

5.67 Refer to the parents of Exercise 5.5 (i.e., for a carrier mother and a normal father). Assume that these parents have two children (not twins).

(a) Find the probability that the older is colorblind and the other is not.

(b) Find the probability that exactly one is colorblind.

(c) Find the probability that both are colorblind.

(d) Find the probability that at least one is colorblind.

5.68 It is claimed that 70% of the residents in a large town approve of the current zoning law. Four residents are to be randomly selected. Find the probability that

(a) None of the four approves.

(b) Exactly two approve.

(c) At least one approves.

5.69 A family owns two cars. The probabilities that cars S and T will fail to start on a cold morning are $\frac{2}{10}$ and $\frac{3}{10}$, respectively. Assuming that the failure of one car to start is independent of the starting of the second car, find the probability that on a cold morning

(a) Both cars will fail to start.

(b) At least one of the cars will fail to start.

(c) Exactly one of the cars fails to start.

5.70 Teams S and T are in the World Series, and the first team to win four games is the series winner. Assume that the probability that team S wins any particular game is $\frac{3}{5}$. Find the probability that

(a) S wins the series in four games.   (b) The series lasts exactly five games.

5.71 Two people, S and T, agree to meet at a restaurant. Each person will arrive, independently of the other, at 1:00, 1:30, or 2:00 P.M. Assume that each person has probability $\frac{1}{3}$ of arriving at any of the three times. Find the probability that

(a) They both arrive at 1:30.

(b) They both arrive at the same time.

(c) S arrives 30 minutes before T.

5.72 A state lottery selects a four-digit number as follows: Four digits are selected one at a time (at random) from {0, 1, 2, 3, 4, 5, 6, 7, 8, 9}. Assume sampling with replacement so that repetitions are allowed. (*Note:* 0939 is a possible outcome.) Suppose that you purchase a lottery ticket. Find the probability that your number is selected.

5.73 Suppose the chances that a particular husband and wife live for 25 more years are $\frac{7}{10}$ and $\frac{9}{10}$, respectively. Assume that survival of one is independent of the other. Find the probability that

(a) The husband does not live for 25 more years.

(b) Both husband and wife live for 25 more years.

(c) At least one of the two lives for 25 more years.

5.74 At one time, it was thought that an enlarged thymus in infants increased the risk of sudden infant death syndrome. Subsequently, this was found to be incorrect, but at the time many such infants were treated with radiation to shrink the thymus. Over the next 40 years, about 25% of those treated developed thyroid tumors and about 6% of those treated developed cancerous thyroid tumors. (There is some debate about the latter figure, but let us assume that it is correct.) Suppose that during a medical checkup one of those treated is found to have a thyroid tumor. What is the probability that it is cancerous?

5.75 One thousand young adults (18–25 years old) from a large city were asked whether they had used certain drugs at least once during the month prior to the study. The results were as follows:

Type of Drug	Number
Only marijuana	400
Only cocaine	190
Only heroin	35
Marijuana and cocaine	75
Marijuana and heroin	15
Cocaine and heroin	10
All three drugs	5
No drugs	270

Find the proportion of the young adults who used

(a) Marijuana

(b) Either cocaine or heroin

(c) Either marijuana or cocaine

5.76 At a liberal arts college, 90% of the freshmen are enrolled in English I, 80% are enrolled in Mathematics I, and 75% are enrolled in both courses. A freshman is to be randomly selected. Find the probability that the student is

(a) Not enrolled in English I   .10

(b) Enrolled in either English I or Mathematics I   .95

(c) Enrolled in English I, given that the student is enrolled in Mathematics I

5.77 A survey was taken of 150 residents of a small resort town to determine attitudes of the residents toward a proposed hotel development. The occupations of the residents were determined along with whether they approved of the hotel being built. The results follow.

	Building and Trade	Businessmen	Other
Approve	40	40	5
Disapprove	10	20	35

In parts (a)–(e), find the proportion of the 150 residents who

(a)   Are businessmen

(b)   Approve of the hotel being built

(c)   Approve of the hotel being built, given that they are in building and trade

(d)   Are businessmen, given that they approve of the hotel being built

(e)   Are businessmen or approve of the hotel being built

(f)   Are the events "Businessmen" and "Approve" independent? Explain. Are they mutually exclusive? Explain.

5.78   The following data represent characteristics of the voting-age population in the November 1988 election in the United States. Number of persons is measured in thousands.

	A Registered	$\overline{A}$ Not Registered
B Males	55,114	29,417
$\overline{B}$ Females	63,439	30,129

In parts (a), (b), and (c), evaluate the following probabilities and describe the proportions they represent:

(a) $P[(\overline{B} \text{ and } A) \text{ or } (\overline{B} \text{ and } \overline{A})]$ **(b)** $P(A \mid B)$ **(c)** $P(\overline{B} \mid \overline{A})$

5.79   Evaluate each of the following:

(a) $12!$ **(b)** $_{20}P_3$ **(c)** $_{20}C_3$ **(d)** $100!/98!$

5.80   A man has four pairs of trousers, six shirts, and three sweaters. How many different outfits can he choose to wear?

5.81   Consider the set $S = \{A, B, C, D, E\}$.

(a)   Find $_5C_2$ and list the combinations.

(b)   Find $_5P_2$ and list the permutations.

5.82   A hand in cribbage consists of six cards dealt from an ordinary deck of 52 cards. How many possible cribbage hands are there?

5.83   A basketball team has 12 players, only five of whom can be on the court at once. How many different sets of five players are there?

5.84   The letters A, B, C, D, E, F, and G are to be randomly arranged in a row. Find the probability that

(a)   The arrangement is ABCDEFG.

(b)   The first 3 letters, in order, are ABC.

(c)   The letters ABC appear together in that order.

(d)   The letters A, B, and C appear together in any order.

5.85   A hand in five-card draw poker consists of five cards dealt from an ordinary deck of 52 cards. Find the probability of being dealt

(a)   4 aces   **(b)**   5 hearts   **(c)**   3 aces and 2 kings

5.86   A hand in bridge consists of 13 cards dealt from an ordinary deck of 52 cards. The probability of being dealt seven or more spades is

$$[(_{13}C_7)(_{39}C_6) + (_{13}C_8)(_{39}C_5) + (_{13}C_9)(_{39}C_4) + (_{13}C_{10})(_{39}C_3)$$
$$+ (_{13}C_{11})(_{39}C_2) + (_{13}C_{12})(_{39}C_1) + (_{13}C_{13})(_{39}C_0)]/(_{52}C_{13})$$

Notice that this is a tedious calculation using a calculator. With some calculators, the calculation is not possible. Resampling Stats is a program that allows for approximate answers by simulation. We use Resampling Stats to select 1000 bridge hands and keep track of the number of spades each time. The following is a histogram of the number of spades for the 1000 bridge hands. From this, estimate the probability of seven or more spades. (For this simulation, the largest number of spades observed was 7.)

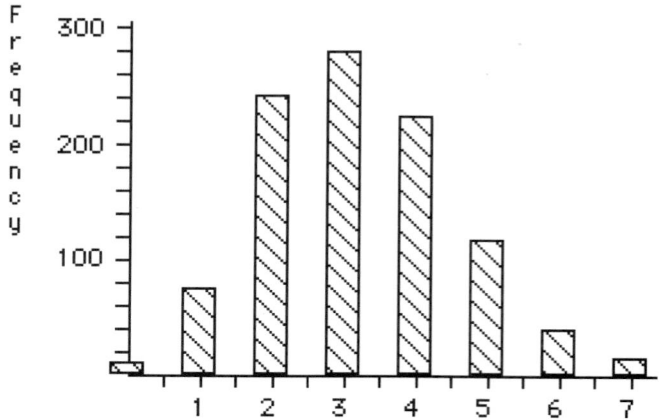

5.87   Resampling Stats is a program that allows for approximate answers by simulation. Consider the following "birthday problem" probability question. In a class of 35 students, what is the probability that two or more students have the same birthday? Resampling Stats simulated the birthday problem 1000 times. In each set of the 1000 outcomes, Resampling Stats sampled 35 numbers with replacement from the set of numbers $1, 2, 3, \ldots, 365$, which represent 365 days in a year. (Leap year was omitted.) For example, if the ordered result of one such simulation were

1	2	5	5	6	6	7	9	11	13	13	13	13
14	18	19	22	22	23	25	28	30	34	35	35	39
39	39	41	42	42	45	47	49	49				

then there were eight sets of "people" with the same birthday; those birthdays were days 5, 6, 13, 22, 35, 39, 42, 49.

The results of the Resampling Stats simulation are shown here. Displayed are the number of times there were 0, 1, 2, 3, 4, 5, and 6 or more sets of people with the same birthday. What is the estimated probability that two or more people in a class of 35 will have the same birthday? (*Hint:*   Two or more people will have the same birthday if one or more sets of people have the same birthday.)

Bin Center	Freq	Pct	Cum Pct
0	175	17.5	17.5
1	358	35.8	53.3
2	297	29.7	83.0
3	129	12.9	95.9
4	31	3.1	99.0
5	9	0.9	99.9
6	1	0.1	100.0

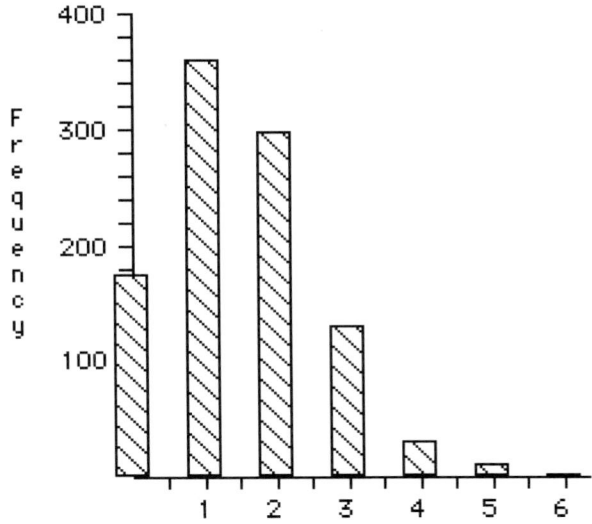

Notes

The Boston Globe, Boston, 1994.

Fairley, W. B., and F. Mosteller, "A Conversation about Collins," in *Statistics and Public Policy,* Fairley, W. B., and F. Mosteller, eds. Reading, Massachusetts: Addison-Wesley, 1977.

The 1994 Information Please Almanac. Boston: Houghton Mifflin, 1994.

Statistical Abstract of the United States. Washington, D.C.: U.S. Bureau of the Census, 1984.

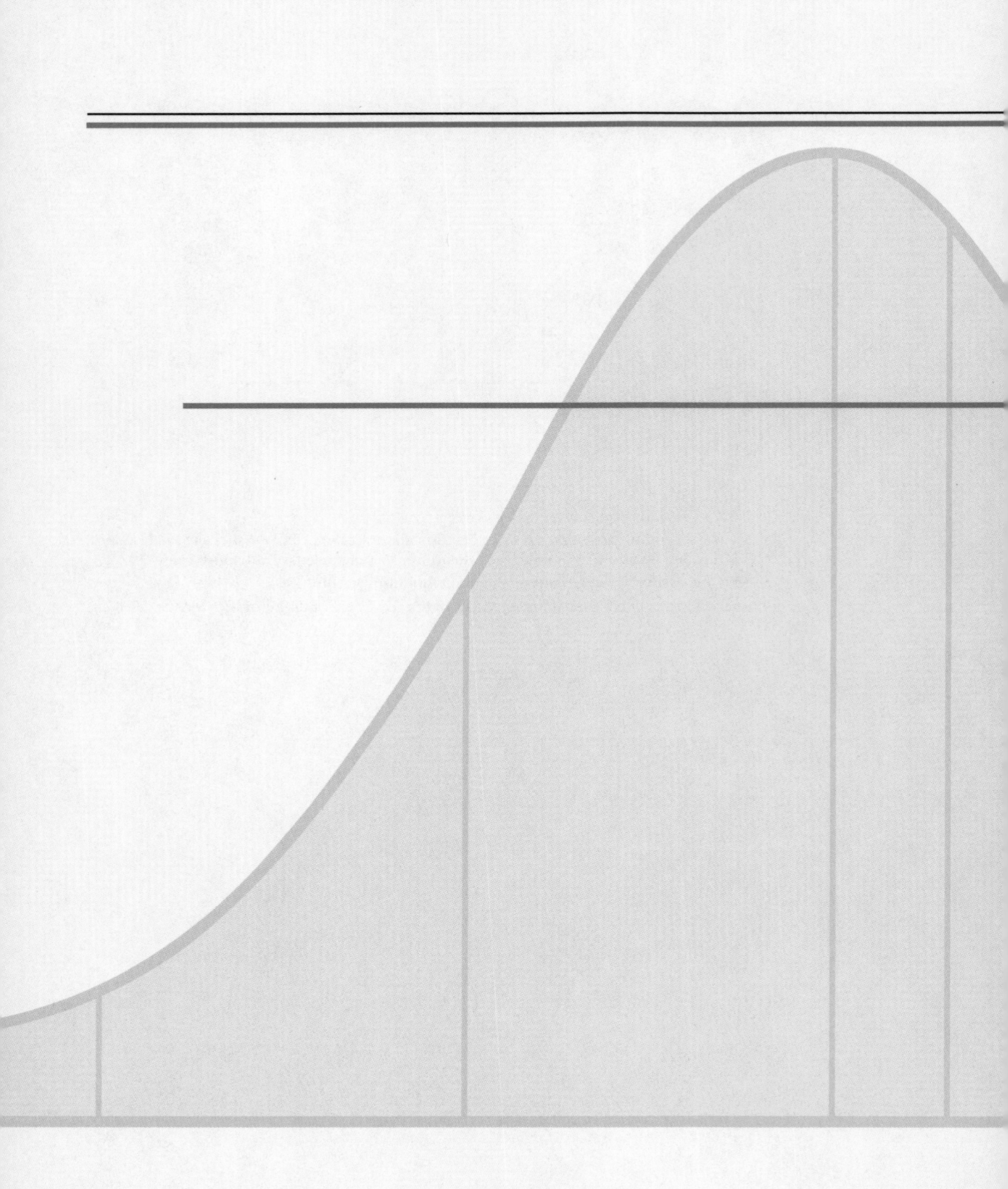

CHAPTER 6

PROBABILITY DISTRIBUTIONS FOR DISCRETE RANDOM VARIABLES

6.1 INTRODUCTION

6.2 RANDOM VARIABLES

6.3 DISCRETE PROBABILITY DISTRIBUTIONS

6.4 MEAN AND VARIANCE

6.5 THE BINOMIAL PROBABILITY DISTRIBUTION

6.6 USING MINITAB (OPTIONAL)

6.7 SUMMARY

REVIEW EXERCISES

6.1

INTRODUCTION

In Chapters 2 and 3, we were concerned with the analysis of numerical data. In Chapter 5, we studied the concepts of experiment, outcome, sample space, and probability. In this chapter, we bring these ideas together by introducing **random variables,** which describe numerical properties of the elements of a sample space.

In this text, we will ultimately be interested in the study of populations. We will see that **probability distributions,** which are studied in this chapter and Chapter 7, can be used to summarize the essential features of a population of data values.

6.2

RANDOM VARIABLES

In any scientific inquiry, it is helpful to translate that which is being studied into numbers. For instance, if we are interested in the fuel efficiency of various kinds of automobiles, we would look at the mileage rating (number of miles per gallon of fuel) for each kind of car. The process of assigning numbers to the objects being studied seems to be a natural one.

Given a sample space, we often study some numerical property of the various outcomes in the sample space. For example, consider the collection of adult Americans. (This is the sample space associated with the experiment of selecting an adult American at random.) One possible numerical property of interest might be the age of each person. Once we have specified the numerical property of interest, we have in essence given a rule for assigning a certain number to each element of the sample space. (Next to the name of each adult American, we assign the number that represents that person's age.) A rule for assigning such numbers is called a **random variable.**

> **Definition** A rule that enables us to assign a number to each outcome of a sample space is called a *random variable* on the sample space. The actual number associated with a particular outcome is called the value (or data value) of the random variable associated with this outcome. When the experiment is performed, the value associated with the outcome is said to have *occurred* or been observed.

EXAMPLE 6.1

In the 1992 presidential election, a pollster was assigned to interview the oldest male and female in various households. Each was asked whether he or she voted for George Bush. If the male said "Yes" and the female said "No," the pollster recorded *YN*. The interview of one household can be viewed as an experiment with sample space

$$S = \{YN, NY, YY, NN\}$$

Consider the random variable "number of yes responses" from the two voters. The possible values are 0, 1, and 2, as shown in the following table:

Outcome	YN	NY	YY	NN
Number of Yes Responses	1	1	2	0

EXAMPLE 6.2

Consider the collection (sample space) of all working people in the United States. We could consider a number of random variables, such as weight, height, age, salary, and so on.

We often use a symbol such as x, y, or z to represent an arbitrary or unspecified value of a random variable. Thus in Example 6.1, we could have used x to represent any one of the values 0, 1, or 2. We could also use the symbol more abstractly to represent the random variable itself. Thus we could say: Consider the random variable x, where $x =$ the number of yes responses.

Suppose we let $x =$ the water temperature at some randomly selected point in Lake Erie next September 1. Then x could potentially be any value between freezing (32°F) and boiling (212°F). (A spot containing industrial waste might account for the possibility of extremely high temperatures.)

$$32°F < x < 212°F$$

This inequality says that x must be greater than 32°F and less than 212°F. The numbers that satisfy this inequality constitute what is called an **interval** or **line segment.** The random variable "Water temperature" is a **continuous** random variable; it can potentially assume any value on an interval [Figure 6.1(a)].

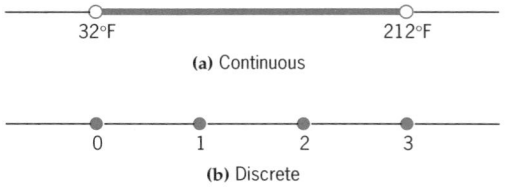

(a) Continuous

(b) Discrete

Figure 6.1

On the other hand, suppose that we select three light bulbs from a production line. Let y be the random variable that counts the number of defectives. So y can potentially assume any one of the values 0, 1, 2, or 3. We call y a **discrete** random variable; the values it can potentially assume constitute separated or isolated points on the real number axis. For example, we could get 1 or 2 defectives but not 1.5 defectives. See Figure 6.1(b).

> **Definitions** A random variable is *continuous* if it potentially can take on any value on some line segment or interval (that is, there are no "breaks" between possible values). A random variable is *discrete* if the values it can potentially assume constitute a sequence of isolated or separated points on the real number axis.

Continuous random variables usually measure the amount of something, whereas discrete random variables usually count something.

Here are some additional examples of continuous random variables: a person's height, the length of time to run a marathon, the mass in kilograms of a celestial object (planet, star, meteor, piece of space dust, etc.). In this last example, we could consider the mass to be theoretically any value greater than 0, showing that sometimes the interval of possible values of a random variable is considered to be infinite in length.

Additional examples of discrete random variables are the number of children in a family, the number of times a person catches a cold in a given year, and the number of tosses of a coin before a tail appears. This last example shows that sometimes the sequence of potential values of a discrete random variable can be infinite because the sequence in this example would be 1, 2, 3, ...

We will ultimately be interested in probabilities associated with various values of a random variable. A formula or table that enables us to find such probabilities is called a **probability distribution** for the random variable. We investigate probability distributions for discrete random variables in this chapter. In Chapter 7, we will study probability distributions for continuous random variables.

EXERCISES

6.1   Classify the following random variables as discrete or continuous:
  (a)   The number of automobile fatalities over a 72-hour period
  (b)   The length of time to run a 100-yard dash
  (c)   The diameter of pebbles from a stream
  (d)   The number of incoming phone calls to a switchboard at a city hospital
  (e)   The barometric pressure at noon at a specific location
  (f)   The number of bills paid on time per month to a plumber

6.2   One word is randomly selected from the following sentence: The grass needs cutting and should be cut by tomorrow afternoon. Let x be the number of letters in the selected word.
  (a)   What values can x assume?
  (b)   Is x a discrete or continuous random variable?

6.3   A green, a red, and a blue die are tossed. In each of the following, find the values that x can assume:
  (a)   Let x = the sum of the three dice.
  (b)   Let x = the minimum number of dots showing on any die.
  (c)   Let x = two times the number of dots on the green die.

6.4   One hundred voters in a suburban town are to be selected and asked whether they approve of a civic arena being built. Let x = the number of voters in the sample who approve.
  (a)   What values can x assume?
  (b)   Is x a discrete or continuous random variable?

6.5   A manufacturer of light bulbs is interested in various properties about the length of life of his product. Let x = length of life of a light bulb (measured in hours).
  (a)   What values can x assume?
  (b)   Is x a discrete or continuous random variable?

6.6   An engineer is testing samples of steel cables to be used in the construction of a suspension bridge.
  (a)   Describe one random variable of possible interest.
  (b)   Is the random variable discrete or continuous?

6.7   A health official wanted to investigate the relationship between females with no children and the incidence of breast cancer. Five hundred women, 40–45 years of age, with no children and no prior breast cancer, are selected. Let x = the number of women who develop breast cancer during the following 5 years.
  (a)   What values can x assume?
  (b)   Is x a discrete or continuous random variable?

6.8   A known health effect associated with exposure to elevated levels of radon is an increased risk of developing lung cancer. The alpha track detector is a device for measuring the amount of radon in the air. The amount is measured in picocuries of radon per liter of air (pCi/l). The Environmental Protection Agency (EPA) action level for radon in air is 4.0 pCi/l. An alpha track detector is placed in the cellars of 50 randomly selected homes. Classify the random variable in parts (a) and (b) as continuous or discrete, and state the values it can assume.

(a)   Let x = the mean pCi/l level of the 50 measurements.

(b)   Let x = the number of homes that exceed the EPA action level for radon in air.

———— 6.3

DISCRETE PROBABILITY DISTRIBUTIONS

In a study of families with one child, a researcher coded families as follows:

$$x = \begin{cases} 0, & \text{if child is a boy} \\ 1, & \text{if child is a girl} \end{cases}$$

Imagine the experiment of randomly selecting a family with one child and recording whether the child is a boy (B) or a girl (G). The sample space is

$$S = \{B, G\}$$

and x is a random variable on this sample space. We can view x as the number of girls in a randomly selected family with one child (0 or 1). We assume that a boy and a girl are equally likely. Hence, the probability that $x = 0$ (a boy) is $\frac{1}{2}$ and the probability that $x = 1$ (a girl) is $\frac{1}{2}$. We sometimes write

$$P(0) = \tfrac{1}{2} \qquad P(1) = \tfrac{1}{2}$$

The specification of the probabilities associated with the distinct values of this random variable is called its **probability distribution.** We generalize this idea with the following definition.

> **Definition**   The specification of the probabilities associated with the various distinct values of a discrete random variable is called a *discrete probability distribution.* The probability associated with the value x is denoted by the symbol $P(x)$.

If many one-child families were selected, and the number of girls (0 or 1) were recorded for each family, a population of data values would be generated. The probability distribution for x (the number of girls) provides a theoretical description of what this population should look like: Since the probability of observing a 0 is $\frac{1}{2}$ and the probability of observing a 1 is $\frac{1}{2}$, the 0's and 1's should occur in equal proportions (in the long run).

It is often convenient to think of a conceptual population of data values associated with a random variable x. This is the collection of values x that would result if the experiment were performed many times. Sometimes we imagine the experiment as being performed repeatedly for an unlimited number of times. In this case, the population is viewed as infinite, because there is no reason to impose a specific limit on the number of times the experiment is performed.

EXAMPLE 6.3

In Chapter 5, we discussed the experiment where a student randomly guesses at the two questions on a true–false quiz. Let x = the number of correct guesses. Find the probability distribution for x.

Solution

Recall that correct on the first question and wrong on the second is CW. The sample space associated with the experiment of taking the quiz by guessing is

$$S = \{CW, WC, WW, CC\}$$

Each outcome in S is equally likely. Therefore, each has the probability $\frac{1}{4}$. The values of the random variable x are given by the following table:

Outcome	x
CW	1
WC	1
WW	0
CC	2

The value 0 will occur if WW occurs. Thus

$$P(0) = P(WW) = \tfrac{1}{4}$$

The value 1 will occur if either CW or WC occurs—that is, if the event $\{CW, WC\}$ occurs:

$$P(1) = P(\{CW, WC\}) = \tfrac{1}{4} + \tfrac{1}{4} = \tfrac{1}{2}$$

The value 2 will occur if CC occurs. Therefore

$$P(2) = P(CC) = \tfrac{1}{4}$$

The probability distribution is summarized in the following table:

x	$P(x)$
0	$\frac{1}{4}$
1	$\frac{1}{2}$
2	$\frac{1}{4}$

where x is the number of correct guesses.

EXAMPLE 6.4

A college statistics class has 20 students. The ages of these students are as follows: One student is 16 years old, four are 18, nine are 19, three are 20, two are 21, and one is 30. Let $x =$ the age of any student (randomly selected). Find the probability distribution for x.

Solution

Since each student has an equal likelihood of being selected, the probability of selecting a particular student is $\frac{1}{20}$. The probability of selecting a student that is 19 years old is $P(19) = \frac{9}{20}$, since there are nine students of that age. The probability distribution is summarized in the following table:

x	$P(x)$
16	$\frac{1}{20}$
18	$\frac{4}{20}$
19	$\frac{9}{20}$
20	$\frac{3}{20}$
21	$\frac{2}{20}$
30	$\frac{1}{20}$

In reading the preceding examples, you may have noted the following properties, which generalize to all discrete probability distributions.

1. Since $P(x)$ is a probability, it will always be a number between 0 and 1 inclusive:

$$0 \le P(x) \le 1$$

2. The sum of the values of $P(x)$ for each distinct value of x is 1:

$$\sum P(x) = 1$$

Another point worth noting is this: Suppose in Example 6.3 that we were interested in the probability that the number of correct guesses on the two-question quiz is either 0 or 1. We write this probability as $P(x = 0 \text{ or } x = 1)$. Now x will be 0 for two wrong guesses, WW, and x will be 1 with the guesses CW or WC. So $x = 0$ or $x = 1$ corresponds to the event $\{WW, CW, WC\}$. Notice that

$$P(x = 0 \text{ or } x = 1) = P(\{WW, CW, WC\}) = \tfrac{3}{4} = \tfrac{1}{4} + \tfrac{1}{2}$$
$$= P(0) + P(1)$$

This result generalizes to any discrete distribution:

$$P(x = a \text{ or } x = b) = P(a) + P(b)$$

Every discrete probability distribution must satisfy properties 1 and 2 in the preceding box. Conversely, if we are given values for x and $P(x)$ such that properties 1 and 2 are satisfied, then these values define a discrete probability distribution for some random variable x. The following example illustrates this point.

EXAMPLE 6.5

Consider the expression $P(x)$ defined by the equation

$$P(x) = \frac{x}{6} \quad \text{for } x = 1, 2, 3$$

(a)   Show that $P(x)$ defines a probability distribution:

(b)   Give an example of an experiment, a sample space, and a random variable on the sample space for which $P(x)$ is the probability distribution.

Solution

(a)   To show that $P(x)$ is a probability distribution, we need only show that the two basic properties of a distribution are satisfied.

(1)   Clearly, $0 \le \frac{x}{6} \le 1$ for $x = 1, 2, 3$.

(2) $\sum P(x) = P(1) + P(2) + P(3)$
$$= \frac{1}{6} + \frac{2}{6} + \frac{3}{6} = 1$$

Therefore, $P(x)$ is a probability distribution.

(b)   Construct an experiment and sample space as follows: Place six balls in a box. Label one ball with the number 1, label two balls with the number 2, and three balls with the number 3. Let the experiment be to select a ball at random. The sample space consists of the six balls. For the random variable, we would let x be the number on the ball selected. It should be clear that $P(x) = x/6$ gives the probability associated with each value of x.

Graphic Representations

We can represent a probability distribution graphically by constructing a type of bar graph called a **probability histogram.** This is constructed by displaying the possible distinct values of the random variable along a horizontal axis. Above each value x of the random variable, we draw a vertical bar having height equal to the probability $P(x)$. We will restrict our attention to those cases where the possible values of x are whole numbers. In such cases, we make the width of each bar 1.

EXAMPLE 6.6
Construct a probability histogram for the distribution of Example 6.3.

Solution
The probability distribution is given by

x	$P(x)$
0	$\frac{1}{4}$
1	$\frac{1}{2}$
2	$\frac{1}{4}$

The probability histogram is shown in Figure 6.2.

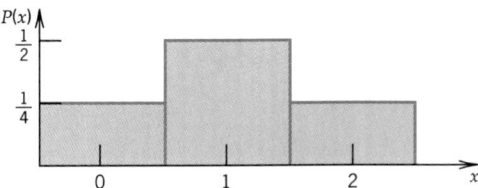

Figure 6.2
A Probability Histogram

Remark   In Example 6.6, notice that the probability associated with a value x is not only the height of the bar above x, but it is also equal to the area of the bar above x, since the width of each bar is 1. That is,

$$P(x) = \text{area of the bar above } x$$

This will be the case for all discrete distributions we consider. This seemingly insignificant observation will be of great importance in future applications.

EXERCISES

6.9   An electronics firm employs 15 people whose yearly salaries (in thousands of dollars) are

25.0	25.7	25.7	26.6	27.2	27.3	27.3	27.3
27.3	27.8	27.8	28.4	28.4	29.0	29.0	

Let x be the yearly salary for any employee. Find the probability distribution for x.

6.10   Ten thousand Instant Money lottery tickets were sold. One ticket has a face value of $1000, five tickets have face values of $500 each, 20 tickets are worth $100 each, 500 are worth $1 each, and the rest are losers. Let x = the value of a ticket that you buy. Find the probability distribution for x.

6.11   The following table gives information on the range of holdings for 50 major U.S. college and university libraries in 1991–1992 (*Source: The 1994 Information Please Almanac, 1994*, p. 864). The value of x gives a code for each range, with 1 representing the lowest range, and 9 representing the highest range. Find the probability distribution of x.

Number of Libraries	Range of Holdings	x
20	2–3 million	1
12	3–4 million	2
4	4–5 million	3
5	5–6 million	4
5	6–7 million	5
1	7–8 million	6
1	8–9 million	7
1	9–10 million	8
1	10 million or more	9

Note: 2–3 million means at least 2 million and less than 3 million.

6.12   A box has five tickets numbered 1, 2, 3, 4, and 5. Two are to be randomly selected without replacement. Let x be the number of occurrences of either 4 or 5. For example, if 2 and 5 are selected, then $x = 1$. If both 4 and 5 are selected, then $x = 2$. Find the probability distribution for x.

6.13   The following data are characteristics of the voting-age population regarding the 1992 presidential election in the United States. Number of persons is measured in thousands.

	Number Voted	Number Did Not Vote
Males	53,312	35,245
Females	60,554	36,573

Find the probability distribution of x in parts (a) and (b):

(a) A name is to be randomly selected from those who voted. Let $x = 0$ if a male is selected. Otherwise, let $x = 1$.

(b) A name is to be randomly selected from the female voting-age population. Let $x = 0$ if the selected female voted. Otherwise, let $x = 1$.

6.14 For adults without known heart disease, a desirable total cholesterol level is less than 200. Between 200 and 239 is categorized as borderline, and above 239 is too high. The following data are from a sample of 825 participants in the Framingham Heart Study with no prior heart disease:

Category	Frequency
Desirable	234
Borderline	297
Too high	294

Let x equal 1, 2, or 3 for desirable, borderline, or too high, respectively. Find the probability distribution for x.

6.15 In a population of 3000 people, 1470 were classified as blood type O, 1140 as type A, 300 as type B, and the remaining as type AB. Let $x = 0$, 1, 2, or 3 if a person's blood type is O, A, B, or AB, respectively. Find the probability distribution for x.

In Exercises 6.16–6.19, determine whether each is a probability distribution. Give reasons for your answer.

6.16

x	$P(x)$
2	$\frac{1}{2}$
4	$\frac{1}{4}$
6	$\frac{1}{2}$

6.17

x	$P(x)$
3	$\frac{2}{5}$
9	$\frac{2}{5}$
11	$\frac{2}{5}$
13	$-\frac{1}{5}$

6.18

x	$P(x)$
-3	$\frac{1}{3}$
-1	$\frac{1}{3}$
5	$\frac{1}{3}$

6.19

x	$P(x)$
0	$\frac{2}{3}$
1	$\frac{1}{6}$
2	$\frac{1}{6}$

6.20 The probability distribution for the number of electronic instruments produced per hour by an assembly line is as follows:

x	$P(x)$
1	$\frac{1}{36}$
2	$\frac{3}{36}$
3	$\frac{5}{36}$
4	$\frac{7}{36}$
5	$\frac{9}{36}$
6	$\frac{11}{36}$

Construct a probability histogram.

6.21 A business executive was sensitive to the possibility of being accused of religious discrimination in his hiring practices. He found that of 600 employees, 204 were Catholic, 228 were Protestant, 72 were Jewish, with the rest classified as Other. Let $x = 0, 1, 2,$ or 3 if a person's religion is Catholic, Protestant, Jewish, or Other, respectively. Find the probability distribution and construct the probability histogram.

6.4

MEAN AND VARIANCE

In Example 6.3, we discussed an experiment that consisted of a student randomly guessing at the answers to a two-question true–false quiz. The random variable was $x =$ number of correct guesses (0, 1, or 2). The probability distribution was given by

x	$P(x)$
0	$\frac{1}{4}$
1	$\frac{1}{2}$
2	$\frac{1}{4}$

The population for this random variable would be the string of values of x that would occur if this experiment were performed over and over by many students. The probability distribution provides a theoretical description of this population, and we ought to be able to use it to predict the mean and variance of all these values.

We will try to simulate this population by considering what the data values should theoretically look like if the experiment is performed by a large number of students, say $N = 40,000$ students, and the number x of correct guesses is recorded for each student. Examining the probability distribution $P(x)$, we see that in an ideal situation we should expect 0 to occur about $\frac{1}{4}$ of the time. Thus we expect about 10,000 zeros. Similarly, we expect about 20,000 ones and 10,000 twos.

$x =$ Number Correct	Frequency
0	10,000
1	20,000
2	10,000

Therefore, we expect the mean of all these values to be

$$\mu = \frac{\text{sum of all } x \text{ values}}{N}$$

$$= \frac{(0)(10{,}000) + (1)(20{,}000) + (2)(10{,}000)}{40{,}000}$$

$$= (0) \cdot \left(\frac{10{,}000}{40{,}000}\right) + (1) \cdot \left(\frac{20{,}000}{40{,}000}\right) + (2) \cdot \left(\frac{10{,}000}{40{,}000}\right)$$

$$= (0) \cdot \left(\tfrac{1}{4}\right) + (1) \cdot \left(\tfrac{1}{2}\right) + (2) \cdot \left(\tfrac{1}{4}\right) = 1$$

Notice that

$$(0) \cdot (\tfrac{1}{4}) = (0) \cdot P(0) \qquad (1) \cdot (\tfrac{1}{2}) = (1) \cdot P(1) \qquad (2) \cdot (\tfrac{1}{4}) = (2) \cdot P(2)$$

So we can write

$$\mu = 0 \cdot P(0) + 1 \cdot P(1) + 2 \cdot P(2) = 1$$

This is the sum of the values of $x \cdot P(x)$ for each distinct value of x. We write this as

$$\mu = \sum x \cdot P(x)$$

(which works out to be 1 for the random variable under discussion).

The equation for the mean does not involve the population size N anywhere. In fact, no matter how large the value of N, we would be led by the preceding reasoning to the same formula for predicting the mean. Therefore, we will agree that the mean will be given by this formula.

We generalize this idea in the following definition.

Definition   Given a discrete random variable x with probability distribution $P(x)$, the *mean* of the random variable x is defined as

$$\mu = \sum x \cdot P(x)$$

Note: μ is also referred to as the mean of the probability distribution $P(x)$.

We could go through a discussion very similar to the one just given to discover a suitable formula for population variance in terms of $P(x)$. However, this would be unnecessarily repetitious. Perhaps the simplest thing to do is to observe that whereas the population mean is an average of x values, the population variance is an average of values of $(x - \mu)^2$. Then the same discussion that led to a formula for the mean, μ, would lead to a similar formula for σ^2. The only difference is that instead of summing the values of $x \cdot P(x)$, we would sum values of $(x - \mu)^2 \cdot P(x)$. This leads to the following definitions.

Definitions   Given a discrete random variable x with probability distribution $P(x)$, the *variance* of the random variable x is defined as

$$\sigma^2 = \sum (x - \mu)^2 \cdot P(x)$$

The *standard deviation* σ is the square root of the variance. We also use the phrase variance or standard deviation of the distribution $P(x)$.

We often do not know enough about the population to find $P(x)$. In this case, we might obtain a sample from the population and use the sample mean $\bar{x}$ to estimate μ, and s^2 to estimate σ^2.

EXAMPLE 6.7

Consider the experiment of randomly selecting a family with one child. Let $x =$ the number of girls (0 or 1). For this random variable, calculate the mean, variance, and standard deviation.

Solution

Assuming a girl and boy are equally likely, the probability distribution is given by

x	$P(x)$
0	$\frac{1}{2}$
1	$\frac{1}{2}$

Now

$$\mu = \sum x \cdot P(x) = 0 \cdot P(0) + 1 \cdot P(1)$$
$$= (0) \cdot (\tfrac{1}{2}) + (1) \cdot (\tfrac{1}{2}) = \tfrac{1}{2}$$

By definition, the variance is

$$\sigma^2 = \sum (x - \mu)^2 \cdot P(x)$$
$$= (0 - \tfrac{1}{2})^2 \cdot P(0) + (1 - \tfrac{1}{2})^2 \cdot P(1)$$
$$= (\tfrac{1}{4}) \cdot (\tfrac{1}{2}) + (\tfrac{1}{4}) \cdot (\tfrac{1}{2}) = \tfrac{1}{4}$$
$$\sigma = \sqrt{\tfrac{1}{4}} = \tfrac{1}{2}$$

There is an **alternative formula for σ^2** that is a little simpler computationally, but which gives the same result. The formula is

$$\boxed{\sigma^2 = [\sum x^2 \cdot P(x)] - \mu^2}$$

This formula tells us to square each distinct value of x, multiply this by $P(x)$, and then add all these products. We then subtract μ^2 from this sum. *In future work, we recommend using the alternative formula unless μ is a whole number.*

EXAMPLE 6.8

For the random variable of Example 6.7 (number of girls in a one-child family), calculate the variance and standard deviation using the alternative formula.

Solution

We saw in Example 6.7 that $\mu = \tfrac{1}{2}$. Hence

$$\sigma^2 = [\sum x^2 \cdot P(x)] - \mu^2 = 0^2 \cdot P(0) + 1^2 \cdot P(1) - (\tfrac{1}{2})^2$$
$$= (0) \cdot (\tfrac{1}{2}) + (1) \cdot (\tfrac{1}{2}) - (\tfrac{1}{4}) = \tfrac{1}{4}$$
$$\sigma = \sqrt{\tfrac{1}{4}} = \tfrac{1}{2}$$

Sometimes it is helpful to organize our computations in the form of a table. This is especially recommended if there are more than, say, four or five values for x. We illustrate how such a table is used in the following example.

EXAMPLE 6.9

Consider the following probability distribution:

x	$P(x)$
1	$\frac{4}{10}$
2	$\frac{4}{10}$
3	$\frac{1}{10}$
4	$\frac{1}{10}$

We will use Table 6.1 to find the mean, variance, and standard deviation.

Table 6.1

x	$P(x)$	$x \cdot P(x)$	$x^2 \cdot P(x) = x[x \cdot P(x)]$
1	$\frac{4}{10}$	$\frac{4}{10}$	$\frac{4}{10}$
2	$\frac{4}{10}$	$\frac{8}{10}$	$\frac{16}{10}$
3	$\frac{1}{10}$	$\frac{3}{10}$	$\frac{9}{10}$
4	$\frac{1}{10}$	$\frac{4}{10}$	$\frac{16}{10}$
Totals		$\frac{19}{10}$	$\frac{45}{10}$
		$\sum x \cdot P(x)$	$\sum x^2 \cdot P(x)$

$$\mu = \sum x \cdot P(x) = \tfrac{19}{10} = 1.9$$
$$\sigma^2 = [\sum x^2 \cdot P(x)] - \mu^2 = \tfrac{45}{10} - (1.9)^2 = 4.5 - 3.61 = .89$$
$$\sigma = \sqrt{.89} \doteq .94$$

Remark Note that the mean of the distribution in Example 6.9 is 1.9. This is different from the mean of the individual x values (1, 2, 3, 4), which is 2.5. Occasionally, the mean of the distribution is the same as the mean of the individual x values. One example is when the distribution is symmetric. (See the distribution discussed at the beginning of this section.)

Expected Value

Expected value is just another name for the mean of a random variable. Using this name for the mean is often helpful, because many problems are stated in terms of expectation when the mean is involved. For example, an insurance company might be interested in its expected earnings per customer. This is really just the average.

> **Definition** For a random variable x, we define the *expected value* of the random variable, denoted by $E(x)$, to be the mean of the random variable. Therefore, for a discrete random variable,
>
> $$E(x) = \mu = \sum x \cdot P(x)$$

EXAMPLE 6.10

An insurance company sells a life insurance policy with a face value of $1000 and a yearly premium of $20. If .2% of the policyholders can be expected to die in the course of a year, what would be the company's expected earnings per policyholder in any year?

Solution

Let x = the amount of money earned by the company from an arbitrary (randomly selected) policyholder in a year. If the policyholder survives the year, then x = $20. If the policyholder dies, the company must pay out $1000. This minus the $20 premium means that the company loses $980. In other words, on this policyholder, the company earns −$980 (i.e., $x = -\$980$). The probability that the policyholder dies (i.e., $x = -980$) is .002. So the probability that the policyholder lives (i.e., $x = 20$) is .998. Therefore, the probability distribution is

x	$P(x)$
20	.998
−980	.002

The expected earnings per policyholder are

$$
\begin{aligned}
E(x) &= \sum x \cdot P(x) \\
&= (20)(.998) + (-980)(.002) \\
&= 19.96 - 1.96 = 18
\end{aligned}
$$

The company can expect to earn $18 per policyholder (on the average).

EXAMPLE 6.11 (The Numbers Game*)

This game consists of selecting a three-digit number. If you guess the right number, you are paid $700 for each dollar you bet. Each day there is a new winning number. If a person bets $1 each day for 1 year, how much money can he expect to win (or lose)?

Solution

Let x = the amount won on a given day. If the correct number is guessed, then he wins $700 − $1 = $699. (Do not forget that it costs $1 to bet.) Otherwise, he loses, so his winnings in this case would be −$1. There are 1000 possible three-digit

---

*For a discussion of this and other casino games, see Koshy, T., *Finite Mathematics and Calculus with Applications*, Santa Monica, Calif.: Goodyear, 1979, Section 4.2.

numbers: 000 to 999. The probability of winning (selecting the correct three digits) is $\frac{1}{1000} = .001$. The probability of losing is $\frac{999}{1000} = .999$. The probability distribution is

x	$P(x)$
-1	.999
699	.001

Now we find the *expected daily winnings, E(x)*:

$$E(x) = \sum x \cdot P(x) = (-1)(.999) + (699)(.001)$$
$$= -.999 + .699 = -\$.30$$

Thus he can expect to lose 30 cents per day (on the average). For the year, he can expect to lose $(.30)(365) = \$109.50$.

EXAMPLE 6.12[*]

A clinic tests blood for a disease that occurs in 1% of the population. The blood samples arrive in batches of 50. The clinic director wondered whether a portion of the blood from each vial should be taken and one test performed on the pooled samples. Then if the test were negative, all samples would be negative. If the test were positive, then each sample would be tested to see which were positive. Under this procedure, what is the expected number of tests that will be performed?

Solution

Let x = number of tests. If all 50 people are free of the disease, only one test will be performed ($x = 1$). If the pooled samples test positive, another 50 tests will be done, so $x = 51$. So

$$x = \begin{cases} 1, & \text{if all 50 people are negative} \\ 51, & \text{if at least one person is positive} \end{cases}$$

Since 1% of the population has the disease, 99% do not. So the probability that one person will be negative (does not have the disease) is .99. The probability that all 50 people are negative is the probability that

(first is negative) *and* (second is negative) *and* ... *and* (50th is negative)

Using the Multiplication Rule for Independent Events, the probability of this is $(.99)^{50}$. At least one person being positive is the opposite (or complement) of all being negative. Hence the probability that at least one person is positive is $1 - (.99)^{50}$. The probability distribution for x is

x	$P(x)$
1	$(.99)^{50}$
51	$1 - (.99)^{50}$

---

[*]Adaptation of a problem from *Innumeracy—Mathematical Illiteracy and Its Consequences*, New York: Vintage Books, 1990, p. 47 ©1988 by John Allen Paulos. Reprinted by permission of Hill & Wang, a division of Farrar, Strauss & Giroux, Inc. The same problem is discussed for various sample sizes by Richard J. Larsen and Morris L. Marx in *Introduction to Mathematical Statistics and Its Applications*, Englewood Cliffs, N.J.: Prentice-Hall, 1986, p. 158.

The expected number of tests is

$$E(x) = \sum x \cdot P(x) = (1)(.99)^{50} + (51)[1 - (.99)^{50}]$$
$$= .605006 + 20.144691 = 20.749697$$

So by pooling the samples, we expect only about 21 tests to be performed on average as opposed to 50 tests if each sample were to be tested.

EXERCISES

For the probability distributions in Exercises 6.22–6.25, find (a) the mean, (b) the variance, and (c) the standard deviation. Also, (d) describe each of the distributions as skewed to the left, skewed to the right, or symmetric. (To organize your computations, it may help to use a table like Table 6.1.)

6.22

x	$P(x)$
0	$\frac{1}{10}$
1	$\frac{2}{10}$
2	$\frac{3}{10}$
3	$\frac{4}{10}$

6.23

x	$P(x)$
0	$\frac{4}{10}$
1	$\frac{3}{10}$
2	$\frac{2}{10}$
3	$\frac{1}{10}$

6.24

x	$P(x)$
0	$\frac{1}{8}$
1	$\frac{3}{8}$
2	$\frac{3}{8}$
3	$\frac{1}{8}$

6.25

x	$P(x)$
2	$\frac{1}{4}$
3	$\frac{1}{4}$
4	$\frac{1}{4}$
5	$\frac{1}{4}$

6.26   A dentist has determined that the number of patients x treated in an hour is described by the probability distribution given here. Find (a) the mean, (b) the variance, and (c) the standard deviation.

x	$P(x)$
1	$\frac{2}{15}$
2	$\frac{10}{15}$
3	$\frac{2}{15}$
4	$\frac{1}{15}$

6.27   The manager of a baseball team has determined that the number of walks x issued in a game by one of the pitchers is described by the probability distribution given here. Find (a) the mean, (b) the variance, and (c) the standard deviation.

x	$P(x)$
0	$\frac{1}{20}$
1	$\frac{2}{20}$
2	$\frac{3}{20}$
3	$\frac{11}{20}$
4	$\frac{3}{20}$

6.28 Appendix Table A describes how to select random numbers from Appendix Table B.1, a table of random numbers. Let x = a randomly selected single digit.

(a) Assume that the probability distribution of x is as follows:

$$P(x) = \frac{1}{10} \quad \text{for } x = 0, 1, 2, 3, 4, 5, 6, 7, 8, 9$$

(i) Find the mean of x.   (ii) Find the standard deviation of x.

(b) Randomly select 25 digits from Appendix Table B.1. Calculate the sample mean and the sample standard deviation. Compare these sample results with the population mean and standard deviation in part (a).

6.29 An altered die has one dot on one face, two dots on three faces, and three dots on two faces. The die is to be tossed once. Let x be the number of dots on the upturned face. Find the mean and variance of x.

6.30 A card is to be selected from an ordinary deck of 52 cards. Suppose that a casino will pay $10 if you select an ace. If you fail to select an ace, you are required to pay the casino $1.

(a) If you play this game once, how much money does the casino expect to win?

(b) If you play the game 26 times, how much money does the casino expect to win?

6.31 In the game of craps, a player rolls two dice. If the first roll results in a sum of 7 or 11, the player wins. If the first roll results in a 2, 3, or 12, the player loses. If the sum on the first roll is 4, 5, 6, 8, 9, or 10, the player keeps rolling until he throws a 7 or the original value. If the outcome is a 7, the player loses. If it is the original value, the player wins. The probability that a player will win is .493. Suppose that a player pays $5 to a casino if he loses and is paid $4 for a win. What is the expected loss for the player if he plays (a) one game? (b) ten games?

6.32 A bus company is interested in two potential contracts, one for an express and the other for local stops. The probabilities that the bids will be accepted are .70 and .50 with costs of $500 and $750, respectively. The estimated total incomes are $6000 and $10,000, respectively. If the company were allowed only one bid, which bid should they enter?

6.33 A high school class decides to raise some money by conducting a raffle. The students plan to sell 2000 tickets at $1 apiece. They will give one prize of $100, two prizes of $50, and three prizes of $25. If you plan to purchase one ticket, what are your expected net winnings? (*Hint:* The probability of getting the $100 ticket is $\frac{1}{2000}$, of getting a $50 ticket is $\frac{2}{2000}$, and of getting a $25 ticket is $\frac{3}{2000}$.)

6.34 In Exercises 5.16 and 5.56, we considered Megabucks, a lottery game conducted by the Massachusetts State Lottery Commission. Megabucks consists of selecting six numbers from the 42 numbers $\{1, 2, 3, 4, \ldots, 41, 42\}$ (no repetitions and order does not matter). The commission selects by chance the six winning numbers. You pay $1 to play. You get a free ticket if three of your numbers match three of the winning numbers, $75 for matching four numbers, $1500 for matching five numbers. Assume you get $1,000,000 if you match all six numbers. The sample space S consists of all possible six-number combinations that can be selected. It can be shown that $n(S) = 5,245,786$. The number of elements in S that match 0, 1, 2, 3, 4, 5, or 6 winning numbers is given here. What is your expected loss?

Number of Matches	Number of Possibilities
0	1,947,792
1	2,261,952
2	883,575
3	142,800
4	9,450
5	216
6	1

6.5

THE BINOMIAL PROBABILITY DISTRIBUTION

Consider the experiment of rolling a single die and recording whether the number (of dots) on the top face is odd (O) or even (E). This experiment has two possible outcomes: O or E. We can construct a new experiment by performing this basic experiment over and over a certain number of times. (In a situation like this, the basic experiment is called a *trial*.) For example, suppose that we perform this basic experiment three times. If we observed an even number, then an odd, and then an even, we would represent this outcome by EOE. The sample space for the new experiment is

$$\{OOO, EOO, OEO, OOE, OEE, EOE, EEO, EEE\}$$

This experiment consisted of repeating a trial a certain number of times; each trial had two possible outcomes. Such an experiment is called a **binomial experiment.**

There are many practical situations that are in essence binomial experiments. For example, we may interview 10,000 voters to see how many favor candidate A. Here the trial is to interview a voter. This trial has two possible outcomes: Voter favors candidate A or does not favor candidate A. The trial is repeated 10,000 times. As another example, a manufacturer of transistors may select 1000 transistors, then repeatedly perform the trial of checking each transistor to see whether it is defective.

We summarize these ideas in the following definition.

Definition A *binomial experiment* is an experiment that has the following properties:

1. It consists of performing some basic experiment a fixed number of times, n. Each time the basic experiment is performed, we call this a *trial*.

2. Each trial is identical and has two possible outcomes. We arbitrarily call one outcome success (S) and the other failure (F). We call the probability of success $P(S) = p$ and the probability of failure $P(F) = q$. Note that $p + q = 1$. (So $q = 1 - p$.) The values of p and q do not change from one trial to another.

3. The trials are independent of one another, that is, the outcome of one trial has no bearing on the outcome of any other trial.

The random variable of interest, the *binomial random variable x*, is the number of successes in n trials. Note that x can assume the values $0, 1, 2, \ldots, n$. The probability distribution of x is called a *binomial probability distribution*.

EXAMPLE 6.13

Consider the binomial experiment of rolling a die three times. Each time we record whether the number of dots showing is odd (O) or even (E). Let $x =$ the total number of evens recorded. Find the binomial probability distribution $P(x)$.

Solution

The trial is to roll the die and record O or E. We will call E a success. So $S = E$ and failure $F = O$. Since half the numbers on a die are even and half are odd, $p = P(S) = \frac{1}{2}$ and $q = P(F) = \frac{1}{2}$. We have seen that the sample space is

$$\{OOO, EOO, OEO, OOE, OEE, EOE, EEO, EEE\}$$

Each outcome is equally likely and therefore has the probability $\frac{1}{8}$. The binomial random variable is $x =$ the number of successes $=$ the number of evens. We must have $x = 0, 1, 2,$ or 3.

Now $x = 0$ corresponds to OOO, so $P(0) = P(OOO) = \frac{1}{8}$. The value $x = 1$ corresponds to the event $\{EOO, OEO, OOE\}$. So

$$P(1) = P(\{EOO, OEO, OOE\}) = \frac{3}{8}$$

The value $x = 2$ corresponds to the event $\{OEE, EOE, EEO\}$. Therefore,

$$P(2) = P(\{OEE, EOE, EEO\}) = \frac{3}{8}$$

Finally, the value $x = 3$ corresponds to EEE, so that $P(3) = P(EEE) = \frac{1}{8}$. The binomial probability distribution for this situation is summarized as follows:

x	$P(x)$
0	$\frac{1}{8}$
1	$\frac{3}{8}$
2	$\frac{3}{8}$
3	$\frac{1}{8}$

Given a binomial experiment consisting of n trials where the probability of success on an individual trial is p and the probability of failure is q (where $q = 1 - p$), it can be shown that the probability of exactly x successes in n trials is given by the following formula*:

$$P(x) = \frac{n!}{x!(n-x)!} \cdot p^x \cdot q^{n-x} \quad \text{for } x = 0, 1, 2, \ldots, n$$

---

*If you have read Sections 5.4 and 5.6, it is not difficult to see why this formula works. First, consider the event consisting of success on the first x trials and failure on the next $n - x$ trials:

$$\underbrace{SS \cdots S}_{x} \underbrace{FF \cdots F}_{n-x} \quad \leftarrow n \text{ trials}$$

The trials are independent. Hence the Multiplication Rule for independent events tells us the probability of this is

$$\underbrace{p \cdot p \cdot \cdots \cdot p}_{x} \cdot \underbrace{q \cdot q \cdot \cdots \cdot q}_{n-x} = p^x \cdot q^{n-x}$$

Now there are a number of different arrangements that can result in x successes and $n - x$ failures, all having the same probability, $p^x q^{n-x}$. To count how many ways this can happen, just calculate how many ways we can specify which x trials out of the n trials are the successes. In Section 5.6, we saw that this number is

$$_nC_x = \frac{n!}{x!(n-x)!}$$

So there are this many ways of getting x successes and $n - x$ failures, all having probability $p^x q^{n-x}$. Hence, the probability of x successes in n trials is

$$P(x) = \frac{n!}{x!(n-x)!} \cdot p^x \cdot q^{n-x}$$

The symbol $n!$ (read "n factorial") is defined for any positive integer to be

$$n! = 1 \cdot 2 \cdot 3 \cdot \ \cdots \ \cdot n$$

Therefore

$$3! = 1 \cdot 2 \cdot 3 = 6$$

$$5! = 1 \cdot 2 \cdot 3 \cdot 4 \cdot 5 = 120$$

$$1! = 1$$

We will agree that $0! = 1$.

The values of $P(x)$ constitute the **binomial probability distribution.** The word *binomial* is used because the values of $P(x)$ for the various values of x are precisely the terms in the binomial expansion of $(p + q)^n$. For example, when $n = 2$, the values of $P(x)$ for $x = 0, 1$, and 2 are the three terms on the right-hand side of the following equation:

$$(p + q)^2 = p^2 + 2pq + q^2$$

In Figure 6.3, we display probability histograms for two binomial probability distributions.

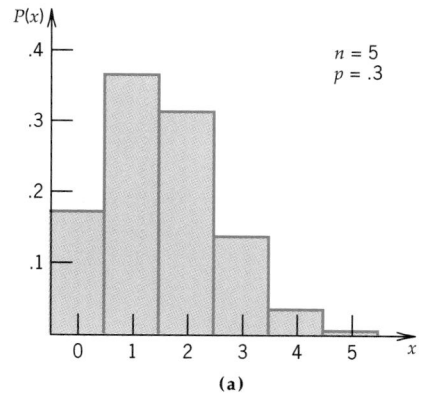

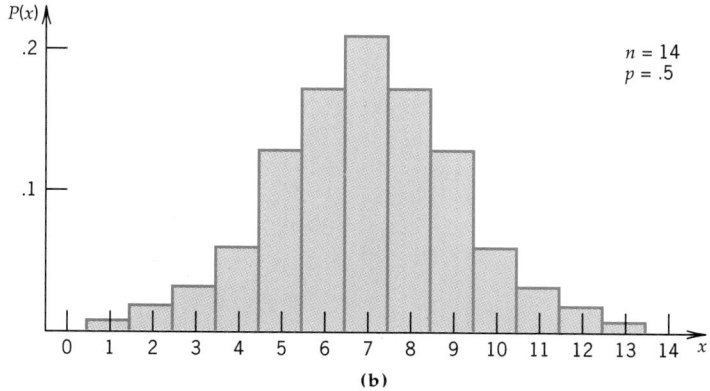

Figure 6.3
Binomial Probability Distributions

EXAMPLE 6.14

Verify that the formula for $P(x)$ in the preceding box does give the probability distribution for the binomial variable of Example 6.13.

Solution

For this experiment, $n = 3$. Also, success = record even (E) and failure = record odd (O). Thus $p = P(E) = \frac{1}{2}$ and $q = P(O) = 1 - p = \frac{1}{2}$. Finally, x = number of evens recorded in three rolls of the die. Therefore,

$$P(x) = \frac{3!}{x!(3-x)!} \cdot (\tfrac{1}{2})^x \cdot (\tfrac{1}{2})^{3-x}$$

Observe that

$$(\tfrac{1}{2})^x \cdot (\tfrac{1}{2})^{3-x} = (\tfrac{1}{2})^{x+3-x} = (\tfrac{1}{2})^3 = \tfrac{1}{8}$$

and so

$$P(x) = \frac{3!}{x!(3-x)!} \cdot \tfrac{1}{8}$$

Now

$$P(0) = \frac{3!}{0!(3-0)!} \cdot \tfrac{1}{8} = \frac{6}{(1) \cdot (6)} \cdot \tfrac{1}{8} = \tfrac{1}{8}$$

$$P(1) = \frac{3!}{1!(3-1)!} \cdot \tfrac{1}{8} = \frac{6}{(1) \cdot (2)} \cdot \tfrac{1}{8} = \tfrac{3}{8}$$

$$P(2) = \frac{3!}{2!(3-2)!} \cdot \tfrac{1}{8} = \frac{6}{(2) \cdot (1)} \cdot \tfrac{1}{8} = \tfrac{3}{8}$$

$$P(3) = \frac{3!}{3!(3-3)!} \cdot \tfrac{1}{8} = \frac{6}{(6) \cdot (1)} \cdot \tfrac{1}{8} = \tfrac{1}{8}$$

These results agree with the results of Example 6.13.

EXAMPLE 6.15

Assume that when a certain hunter shoots at a pheasant, the probability of hitting it is .6. Find the probability that the hunter

(a)   Will hit exactly four of the next five pheasants at which he shoots.

(b)   Will hit at least four of the next five.

(c)   Will hit at least one of the next five.

Solution

(a)

$$\text{trial} = \text{shoots at a pheasant}$$
$$\text{success} = \text{hits the pheasant}$$
$$\text{failure} = \text{does not hit the pheasant}$$
$$P(S) = p = .6$$
$$P(F) = q = 1 - p = .4$$

The trial is repeated five times, so $n = 5$. The binomial distribution giving the probability of exactly x successes in five trials is

$$P(x) = \frac{5!}{x!(5-x)!} \cdot (.6)^x \cdot (.4)^{5-x}$$

The probability of hitting exactly four of the next five pheasants is

$$P(4) = \frac{5!}{4!(5-4)!} \cdot (.6)^4 \cdot (.4)^{5-4}$$

$$= \frac{1 \cdot 2 \cdot 3 \cdot 4 \cdot 5}{(1 \cdot 2 \cdot 3 \cdot 4) \cdot (1)} \cdot (.6)^4 \cdot (.4) = (5) \cdot (.6)^4 \cdot (.4)$$

$$= .25920$$

(b) Now the probability that he hits at least four of the next five pheasants is $P(x = 4 \ or \ x = 5)$. But we know that

$$P(x = 4 \ or \ x = 5) = P(4) + P(5)$$
$$= .25920 + P(5)$$

and

$$P(5) = \frac{5!}{5!(5-5)!} \cdot (.6)^5 \cdot (.4)^{5-5}$$

$$= \frac{5!}{5!0!} \cdot (.6)^5 \cdot (.4)^0$$

Keeping in mind that $0! = 1$ and $(.4)^0 = 1$, we get

$$P(5) = (.6)^5 = .07776$$

Thus

$$P(x = 4 \ or \ x = 5) = P(4) + P(5)$$
$$= .25920 + .07776 = .33696$$

(c) Now we find the probability that he hits at least one out of the next five pheasants. Call A the event consisting of *no* hits in the next five shots. Then the complement of this event, $\overline{A}$, consists of hitting at least one. Since $P(A) + P(\overline{A}) = 1$, we have

$$P(\text{hitting at least 1}) = P(\overline{A}) = 1 - P(A) = 1 - P(0)$$

Now we need only evaluate $P(0)$ and subtract from 1:

$$P(0) = \frac{5!}{0!(5-0)!} \cdot (.6)^0 \cdot (.4)^{5-0}$$

$$= \frac{5!}{5!} \cdot (1) \cdot (.4)^5 = (.4)^5$$

$$= .01024$$

Therefore,

$$P(\text{hitting at least one}) = 1 - P(0)$$
$$= 1 - .01024$$
$$= .98976$$

The formula for calculating binomial probabilities $P(x)$ can be rather unpleasant to use for all but very small values of n. Appendix Table B.2 gives values of $P(x)$ for various values of n and x up to $n = 25$. [In Chapter 7, we develop a method of finding $P(x)$ for values of $n > 25$.]

Let's use Appendix Table B.2 to find $P(x)$ when $n = 5$, $p = .60$, and $x = 4$. In Example 6.15, we found this value to be .259 rounded to three decimal places. In the far left column, locate the desired value of n, in this case $n = 5$. To the right and below this, locate the row containing the desired value of x, here $x = 4$. At the top of the table, locate the column containing the desired value of p, here $p = .60$. Now where the row containing $x = 4$ and the column containing $p = .60$ intersect, we find the value of $P(4)$, namely, .259. (See Table 6.2, which shows a portion of Appendix Table B.2.)

Table 6.2

n	x	.01	.05	.10	.20	.30	.40	.50	.60	.70	.80	.90	.95	.99
5	0								.010					
	1								.077					
	2								.230					
	3								.346					
	4								.259					
	5								.078					

Notice that some of the probabilities in Appendix Table B.2 are represented as 0+. This means that the probability is so small as to be negligible and hence may be assigned the value 0 in calculations.

EXAMPLE 6.16
Thirty percent of the voters in a large voting district are veterans. If 10 voters are randomly selected, find the probability that less than five will be veterans.

Solution
This is a binomial experiment.

trial = select voter

success = voter is a veteran

$P(S) = p =$ proportion of voters in district who are veterans

$= .30$

$n = 10$ (repeat the trial 10 times)

$x =$ number of veterans

We want to find $P(x < 5)$. Using Appendix Table B.2, we get

$$P(x < 5) = P(0) + P(1) + P(2) + P(3) + P(4)$$
$$= .028 + .121 + .233 + .267 + .200$$
$$= .849$$

Note: Since the voting district is large, we can safely assume that the value of p remains essentially the same from one trial to the next.

EXAMPLE 6.17
A company that manufactures color television sets claims that only 5% of its sets will need to be adjusted by a technician before being sold. If an appliance dealer

sells 20 of these sets, how likely is it that more than three of them will need to be adjusted?

Solution

$$\text{trial} = \text{check one of the sets}$$

$$\text{success} = \text{it needs adjustment}$$

$$P(S) = p = .05$$

$$n = 20 \text{ (repeat the trial 20 times)}$$

$$x = \text{number out of 20 that need adjustment}$$

We want to find $P(x > 3)$. Using Appendix Table B.2, add the values of $P(x)$ for x from 4 to 20:

$$P(x > 3) = P(4) + P(5) + \cdots + P(19) + P(20)$$
$$= .013 + .002 + \text{(negligible terms)}$$
$$= .015$$

We conclude that if the manufacturer is right, it is very unlikely that more than three sets will need to be adjusted.

Example 6.17 provides some insight into how the binomial distribution might be used in statistical inference. For example, the manager of an appliance store chain received a large shipment of these TV sets, and she wished to test the manufacturer's claim that only 5% (or perhaps less) will need adjustment. She might randomly select 20 sets from the shipment and determine how many of these sets need adjustment. We can view the population as consisting of the entire shipment of TV sets from the manufacturer. The 20 sets then constitute a sample from the population. Based on the number of TV sets out of the 20 that are in need of adjustment, she will decide whether there is strong evidence to suggest that more than 5% of the sets in the population will be in need of adjustment. She would want the evidence to be strong because if she concludes that more than 5% of the population need adjusting, she will return the entire shipment—a drastic step. What criterion might she use? That is, if $x = $ the number of TV sets out of the 20 needing adjustment, how large should x be for the manager to conclude that the shipment should be returned?

Since the manufacturer claims 5% (or less) will need adjusting, it would not be alarming if we found 5% of the 20, or one TV set, needing adjusting. Perhaps two sets would not even be alarming. (After all, we can expect some fluctuation from one batch of 20 sets to the next.) But the larger the value of x, the more we are inclined to believe that more than 5% of the population will need adjusting. If the value of x is large enough (relative to 1), the manager would reject the manufacturer's claim (and the shipment as well). By "large enough" we mean so large that it would be highly unlikely that we would observe such a large value of x if the manufacturer's claim were true. Note that we have already seen a range of such unlikely values in Example 6.17. We said that it would be very unlikely (only a 1.5% chance) that we would get a value of x greater than 3 if in fact the manufacturer were correct. Therefore, the manager could use this as her criterion: If more than three of the TV sets do need adjusting, the evidence would strongly suggest that the manufacturer's claim should be rejected.

We will see in later chapters that a binomial experiment is a very important concept in a variety of statistical inference problems ranging from industrial quality control to voter preference studies. The reason for this is that *the proportion of elements in a population possessing a certain characteristic of interest may be viewed as the probability of success in a binomial experiment.* In Example 6.16, we discussed the proportion of voters in a district who were veterans. This proportion was .30. A trial consisted of selecting a voter by chance. A success occurs if the voter selected is a veteran. The binomial experiment consisted of performing the trial 10 times. Since 30% of the voters are veterans, the probability that a voter selected on a single trial will be a veteran is .30. This is the probability of success, so that $P(S) = p = .30$. Sometimes such proportions are unknown, and we can use a binomial variable to study these proportions. We investigate these proportions, known as **population proportions,** in Chapter 9.

Mean and Variance of a Binomial Random Variable

Suppose that we consider the binomial experiment of tossing a fair coin $n = 100$ times. Let success = heads. Clearly, $p = .5$. Let $x =$ the number of heads. When the coin is tossed 100 times, how many heads would you expect to get, that is, what is your best guess? We would guess that half (or 50) would be heads. In other words, the expected value of x is 50. This can be obtained from the formula

$$E(x) = n \cdot p = 100 \cdot \left(\tfrac{1}{2}\right) = 50$$

This formula, in fact, works in general. That is, it can be proved rigorously, using the formula for μ given previously in this chapter, that **for a binomial experiment** consisting of n trials with the probability of success p, the mean or expected value of x is

$$\mu = E(x) = n \cdot p$$

It can also be proved, using the formula for variance given previously in the chapter, that for a binomial variable

$$\sigma^2 = n \cdot p \cdot q$$

Thus, for the number of heads when a coin is tossed 100 times

$$\sigma^2 = n \cdot p \cdot q = (100)\left(\tfrac{1}{2}\right)\left(\tfrac{1}{2}\right) = 25$$
$$\sigma = \sqrt{25} = 5$$

EXERCISES

6.35   Which of the following are binomial experiments? For those that are not, indicate which part of the definition of a binomial experiment does not apply.

   (a)   Tossing a fair coin 1000 times and counting the number of times a head appears

   (b)   Tossing a fair coin and counting the number of tosses before a head appears

(c)   Checking five students for drug use from a class of 30 students in which 10% use drugs

(d)   A state agency randomly selects 20 liquor stores, with replacement, and counts the number of stores involved in price fixing

(e)   A shipment of 40 appliances contains two defectives. A dealer tests 15 of the appliances and counts the number that fail to meet specifications.

6.36   Consider a binomial experiment with $n = 4$, $p = .6$, and $x =$ the number of successes. Use the formula for $P(x)$ to find the probability that

    (a) $x = 0$ **(b)** $x = 1$ **(c)** $x = 2$

6.37   Consider a binomial experiment with $n = 5$, $p = .7$, and $x =$ the number of successes. Use the formula for $P(x)$ to find the probability that

    (a) $x = 3$ **(b)** $x = 4$ **(c)** $x = 5$

6.38   Consider a binomial experiment with $n = 11$, $p = .4$, and $x =$ the number of successes. Use Appendix Table B.2 to find the probability that

    (a) x is less than 2.

    (b) x is greater than 5 and less than 8.

    (c) x is greater than or equal to 5 and less than or equal to 8.

    (d) x equals 6.

    (e) x is greater than 0.

6.39   Consider a binomial experiment with $n = 9$, $p = .7$, and $x =$ the number of successes. Use Appendix Table B.2 to find the probability that

    (a) x is less than 3.

    (b) x equals 3.

    (c) x is greater than 3 and less than 5.

    (d) x is greater than or equal to 3 and less than or equal to 5.

    (e) x is less than 9.

6.40   Sixty percent of the voters in a large town are opposed to a proposed development. If 20 voters are selected at random, find the probability that

    (a)   10 are opposed to the proposed development.

    (b)   More than 13 are opposed to the proposed development.

    (c)   Less than 10 are opposed to the proposed development.

6.41   Forty percent of the student body at a large university are in favor of a ban on drinking in the dormitories. Suppose 15 students are to be randomly selected. Find the probability that

    (a)   Seven favor the ban.

    (b)   Fewer than four favor the ban.

    (c)   More than two favor the ban.

6.42   It has been reported that 30% of the population of women who had given birth in the last year and had less than a high school education were in the labor force (*Source: The 1994 Information Please Almanac*, 1994, p. 843). In a random sample of 25 from this population, find the probability that

    (a)   Ten are in the labor force.

    (b)   The sample will contain 4, 5, 6, or 7 women in the labor force.

6.43   Sixty percent of the Framingham Heart Study participants have a total serum cholesterol level below 238. An HMO statistician is interested in interviewing 15 people. If 15 people are randomly selected, find the probability that

    (a)   Eight people will have a total serum cholesterol level below 238.

    (b)   Five people or more will have a total serum cholesterol level below 238.

6.44   A retailer decides that he will reject a large shipment of light bulbs if there is more than one defective bulb in a sample of size 10. If the defective rate is .10, what is the probability that the retailer will reject the shipment?

6.45   A person has a 5% chance of winning a free ticket in a state lottery. If she plays the game 25 times, what is the probability she will win one or more free tickets?

6.46   Five percent of the cans of handballs purchased at a sporting goods store are unacceptable. If 12 cans are purchased, find the probability that

    (a)   All of the cans are acceptable.

    (b)   More than two cans are unacceptable.

    Suppose 200 cans were bought. What is the expected number of unacceptable cans?

6.47   A screening examination is required of all applicants for a technical writing position. The examination consists of 16 questions. Each question has five choices, consisting of the correct answer and four incorrect answers. A curious applicant wonders about some probabilities if she were to randomly guess at each question.

    (a)   What is the probability of getting three correct?

    (b)   What is the probability of getting two or more correct?

    (c)   If 50 applicants took the exam and each guessed randomly at all the questions, what would you guess the mean number of correct answers to be?

6.48   Thirty-eight percent of the people have blood type A. In a random sample of 20 people, find the probability that

    (a)   One will have type A.

    (b)   Two or three will have type A.

    (c)   One or more will not have type A.

    Suppose 100 samples of size 20 were selected, and the number of people in each sample with type A was recorded.

    (d)   What should be the approximate mean number of people with type A?

6.49   Ten percent of the people have blood type B. In a random sample of 20 people, find the probability that

    (a)   Three will have type B.

    (b)   More than five will have type B.

    (c)   Fewer than two will have type B.

    Suppose 100 samples of size 20 were selected, and the number of people in each sample with type B was recorded.

    (d)   What should be the approximate mean number of people with type B?

6.50   There are 4,230,000 eligible voters in a state, of whom 147,000 are black. A sample of 100 voters is to be selected. Let x be the number of blacks. Assume a binomial experiment. Find (a) the mean, (b) the variance, and (c) the standard deviation of x.

6.51   Between 1972 and 1974, 15 out of 405 teachers (3.7%) hired in Hazelwood, St. Louis County, Missouri, were black. In St. Louis County *plus* the nearby city of St. Louis, 15.4% of teachers were black. The Equal Employment Opportunity Commission (EEOC) sued Hazelwood for discrimination against blacks and won the case in the court of appeals. Assuming that the 405 teachers hired constitute a random sample from a population of teachers, 15.4% of whom are black, answer the following:

    (a)   What is the mean (or expected) number of black teachers?

    (b)   What is the standard deviation?

    (c)   In the case of *Castenada* v. *Partida,* 430 U.S. 482 (1977), the "Standard Deviation Rule" was advanced. This states that if the observed value (15 teachers in the Hazelwood case) is more than 2 or 3 standard deviations from the expected value, discrimination may be present. How many standard deviations away from the expected value is the observed value of 15?

(d) On appeal to the Supreme Court, the decision of the court of appeals was vacated. The Supreme Court noted that the relevant job market for teachers might well be St. Louis County alone (which does not include the city of St. Louis), where the percentage of black teachers is 5.7%. Redo parts (a), (b), and (c) using this percentage.

(e) This analysis assumes that the selection of the 405 teachers is a random process (with respect to race). Can the selection of teachers be considered a random process?

For a discussion, see DeGroot, M., S. Fienberg, and J. Kadane, *Statistics and the Law,* New York: Wiley, 1986, pp. 1–48.

6.52 Seven percent of printed circuit boards made by the SKC company are defective. A company official wishes to see whether the percentage of defective boards in a current batch has decreased. A sample of size 50 is to be selected. Let x be the number of defectives. Assume a binomial experiment. If there is no change from the 7% figure, find (a) the mean, (b) the variance, and (c) the standard deviation of x.

6.53 Consider a binomial experiment with $n = 4$. Construct probability histograms when

(a) $p = .3$ and $p = .7$. Comment on the relationship between the two.

(b) $p = .4$ and $p = .6$. Comment on the relationship between the two.

6.54 Consider a binomial experiment with $p = .5$. Construct probability histograms when $n = 3$ and $n = 5$. Comment on the shapes of the distributions.

6.55 Consider a binomial experiment with $n = 3$. Construct probability histograms when $p = .2$ and $p = .4$. You will see that each distribution is skewed to the right. Compare the amount of skewness in the two histograms.

6.6

USING MINITAB (OPTIONAL)

PDF Command

The PDF (probability distribution function) command can be used to find probabilities for a variety of probability distributions. In Example 6.15, we found the binomial probability $P(4)$ when there are 5 trials and the probability of success is .6. We can obtain this probability as follows:

Session Commands	**Dialog Box**
MTB > PDF 4; SUBC> BINOMIAL 5 .6.	**Calc ▶ Probability Distributions ▶ Binomial** Type 5 for **Number of trials** Type .6 for **Probability of success** Click **Input constant.** Type 4 in box Click **OK**

Output

```
          Probability Density Function

   Binomial with n = 5 and p = 0.600000

            x         P( X = x)
          4.00           0.2592
```

We see that $P(4) = .2592$. To store this probability for later use, the main command in the Session window would be

PDF 4, STORE IN K1

In the Dialog box, click **Optional storage**, and type *K1* in the box.

We can find several probabilities at a time. Suppose we want $P(4)$ and $P(5)$. Put the values 4, 5 in column 1. The following program would return the values of $P(4)$ and $P(5)$:

Session Commands	Dialog Box
MTB > PDF C1; SUBC> BINOMIAL 5 .6.	**Calc ▶ Probability Distributions ▶ Binomial** Type *5* for **Number of trials** Type *.6* for **Probability of success** Type *C1* for **Input column** Click **OK**

If we wanted to store $P(4)$ and $P(5)$ in, say, column 2, the Session window command would have been

PDF C1, STORE IN C2;

In the Dialog box, we would have typed C2 in the **Optional storage** box. Column 2 would then contain the probabilities:

$$\begin{array}{ll} \text{C2} & \\ 0.25920 & \leftarrow P(4) \\ 0.07776 & \leftarrow P(5) \end{array}$$

We have seen these probabilities in Example 6.15 (where a hunter shoots at five pheasants). We were interested in the probability of at least four hits:

$$P(x = 4 \ or \ x = 5) = P(4) + P(5)$$

To obtain this, we would just type in the Session window:

SUM C2

Minitab would print the value 0.33696. In Example 6.15, we found the probability of at least one hit by computing $1 - P(0)$. To compute this using Minitab, first compute $P(0)$ and store it as K1 using the techniques described previously. Then in the Session window type

LET K2 = 1 − K1
PRINT K2

Other distributions can be specified by a subcommand or by appropriate choices in the Dialog box. For example, consider the distribution

x	P(x)
1	.4
2	.4
3	.1
4	.1

Suppose we put the x values in column 1 and the probabilities in column 2. The following program would return the value of $P(2)$:

Session Commands

MTB > PDF 2;
SUBC> DISCRETE C1 C2.

Dialog Box

Calc ▶ **Probability Distributions** ▶ **Discrete**
Type *C1* for **Values in**
Type *C2* for **Probs in**
Click **Input constant**. Type *2* in box
Click **OK**

Output

Probability Density Function

Discrete distribution using values in C1 and probabilities in C2

```
        x         P( X = x)
     2.00           0.4000
```

CDF Command

Whereas PDF gives probabilities $P(x = k)$, the CDF (cumulative distribution function) gives **cumulative probabilities** $P(x \leq k)$. For example, to find $P(x \leq 4)$ for the binomial distribution discussed previously,

Session Commands

MTB > CDF 4;
SUBC> BINOMIAL 5 .6.

Dialog Box

Calc ▶ **Probability Distributions** ▶ **Binomial**
Click **Cumulative probability**
Type *5* for **Number of trials**
Type *.6* for **Probability of success**
Click **Input constant** and Type *4* in box
Click **OK**

Output

Cumulative Distribution Function

Binomial with n = 5 and p = 0.600000

```
        x        P( X <= x)
     4.00           0.9222
```

We see from this that $P(x \leq 4) = .9222$.

INVCDF Command

We have seen that CDF gives probabilities of the form $P(x \leq k)$. For example, we saw that for a binomial distribution with $n = 5$, $p = .6$, CDF 4 gave .9222:

$$P(x \leq 4) = .9222$$

INVCDF .9222 would give the value 4. In summary, CDF answers the question

$$P(x \leq k) = \underline{\quad ? \quad}$$

for a given value of k, whereas INVCDF answers the question

$$P(x \leq \underline{\quad ? \quad}) = p$$

for a given probability p where $0 < p < 1$. Actually, this is a bit of an oversimplification. Sometimes there will not be an x value having the exact cumulative probability specified. In this case, Minitab prints the two x values with the closest cumulative probabilities to the one specified. Even when there is an x value having the cumulative probability specified, Minitab prints that x value and the next lower x value, as shown here:

Session Commands	Dialog Box
MTB > INVCDF .9222;	**Calc ▶ Probability Distributions ▶ Binomial**
SUBC> BINOMIAL 5 .6.	Click **Inverse cumulative probability**
	Type *5* for **Number of trials**
	Type *.6* for **Probability of success**
	Click **Input constant** and Type *.9222* in box
	Click **OK**

Output

Inverse Cumulative Distribution Function

```
Binomial with n = 5 and p = 0.600000

        x      P( X <= x)              x      P( X <= x)
        3        0.6630               4        0.9222
```

We see from this that $P(x \leq 4) = .9222$.

If we think of probability distributions as abstract descriptions of populations, the INVCDF command gives percentiles. For example, if for some distribution

$$P(x \leq 46) = .90$$

then the percentage of values in the population less than or equal to 46 is 90%. So 46 is the 90th percentile.

Reminder PDF, CDF, and INVCDF can all store results instead of printing them. Just remember to store constants as constants and columns as columns. For example,

INVCDF .43, STORE IN K1;

and

INVCDF C1, STORE IN C2;

Similar remarks apply to the Dialog box.

PRACTICE QUIZ (Answers follow the Review Exercises.)

For the problems in Questions 1–4, give the approximate values that will be returned, without using Minitab.

1. PDF 4;
   BINOMIAL N = 14, P = .3.
2. SET C1
   3, 5
   END
   PDF C1;
   BINOMIAL N = 8, P = .7.
3. CDF 2, STORE IN K1;
   BINOMIAL N = 5, P = .1.
   LET K2 = 1 − K1
   PRINT K2
4. READ INTO C1 C2
   0 .1
   1 .2
   2 .3
   3 .4
   END
   INVCDF .6;
   DISCRETE, VALUES IN C1, PROBS IN C2.
5. Write a program to find μ, σ^2, and σ for the distribution in Question 4. (*Note:* The Minitab command for finding square roots is SQRT; it works just like the MEAN command.)

EXERCISES

Suggested exercises for use with Minitab are 6.77, 6.78, 6.79, 6.80, and 6.81.

6.7

SUMMARY

In this chapter, we introduced numbers into the setting of a sample space by means of a **random variable,** which is a rule by which we can assign a number to each outcome. Presumably the number will describe some numerical property of the outcome that will be of interest.

A random variable is **continuous** if it can assume any value on some interval or continuous scale; it is **discrete** if the values it can assume constitute a sequence of isolated or separated points on the number axis.

We also studied the notion of the **probability distribution** for a discrete random variable x. We said $P(x)$ is the probability of observing the value x. We then studied the **mean** μ and **variance** σ^2 for a discrete random variable:

$$\mu = \sum x \cdot P(x)$$

The mean μ is also called the **expected value** of x, $E(x)$.

$$\sigma^2 = \sum (x - \mu)^2 \cdot P(x) = \left[\sum x^2 \cdot P(x)\right] - \mu^2$$

We call σ the **standard deviation**.

We then studied a particular discrete random variable—the binomial random variable. This counts the number of successes in a **binomial experiment** consisting of n repeated independent trials or repetitions of some basic experiment, which has two possible outcomes called success (S) and failure (F). If the probability of success on a given trial is p and the probability of failure is q, the probability of exactly x successes in n trials is given by the binomial distribution

$$P(x) = \frac{n!}{x!(n-x)!} \cdot p^x \cdot q^{n-x}$$

Finally, for the binomial random variable x,

$$\mu = n \cdot p$$
$$\sigma^2 = n \cdot p \cdot q$$

REVIEW EXERCISES

6.56　A fair die is to be tossed. Let $x =$ the number of tosses up to and including the first time a 6 appears.

(a)　What values can x assume?

(b)　Is x a discrete or continuous random variable?

(c)　Is this a binomial experiment? Why?

6.57　A medical doctor is interested in studying the effect of a low-cholesterol diet on people with high blood cholesterol levels (measured in milligrams per 100 milliliters). To study this, she obtains 50 volunteers with high blood cholesterol levels to try the diet.

(a)　Describe a random variable of possible interest to the medical doctor. Is it discrete or continuous?

(b)　Describe the population and sample of interest.

In Exercises 6.58–6.61, determine whether a probability distribution is given. Give a reason for your answer.

6.58

x	$P(x)$
0	$\frac{1}{4}$
4	$\frac{3}{4}$

6.59

x	$P(x)$
2	$\frac{2}{3}$
-4	$\frac{1}{6}$
6	$\frac{1}{6}$

6.60

x	$P(x)$
0	$\frac{1}{2}$
1	$\frac{1}{2}$
2	$\frac{1}{2}$

6.61

x	$P(x)$
0	$\frac{1}{5}$
1	$\frac{2}{5}$
2	$\frac{3}{5}$
3	$\frac{1}{5}$
4	$-\frac{2}{5}$

6.62 Determine (a) the mean, (b) the variance, and (c) the standard deviation of the following probability distribution:

x	$P(x)$
2	$\frac{4}{6}$
3	$\frac{1}{6}$
13	$\frac{1}{6}$

6.63 Determine (a) $P(0)$, (b) the mean, (c) the variance, and (d) the standard deviation of the following probability distribution:

x	$P(x)$
0	?
2	$\frac{1}{2}$
5	$\frac{2}{5}$

6.64 Determine (a) $P(3)$, (b) the mean, (c) the variance, and (d) the standard deviation of the following probability distribution:

x	$P(x)$
1	$\frac{2}{12}$
2	$\frac{5}{12}$
3	?
6	$\frac{2}{12}$

6.65 Find the value of c so that a probability distribution is determined:

$$P(x) = \begin{cases} c, & \text{for } x = 1 \\ 2c, & \text{for } x = 2 \\ 3c, & \text{for } x = 3 \\ 4c, & \text{for } x = 4 \end{cases}$$

6.66 Find the value of c so that a probability distribution is determined:

$$P(x) = \begin{cases} c, & \text{for } x = 0 \\ 2c, & \text{for } x = 1 \end{cases}$$

6.67 Find the value of c so that a probability distribution is determined:

$$P(x) = \frac{cx}{6}, \quad \text{for } x = 1, 2$$

6.68   Three cards are numbered 1, 2, 3, and the experiment consists of turning the cards over one by one. A match occurs if the number of the card matches the number of the turn the card appears. So if the cards turn up in the order 2–1–3, there is one match, namely, the 3. Let x be the number of matches.

  (a)   Find the probability distribution. (*Hint:*   List the six possible outcomes.)

  (b)   If 60 people were to independently perform the experiment, what would you expect the approximate mean to be?

6.69   In the past year, 10% of RGH Airlines flights violated one or more safety codes. A government inspector decided to monitor one flight per day for the next 3 days. Let x be the number of flights that violate one or more safety codes. Find each of the following:

  (a)   The probability distribution

  (b)   The mean of x

  (c)   The variance of x

  (d)   The standard deviation of x

6.70   The probability distribution for the number of incoming phone calls x over a 5-minute period at a switchboard for a small business is

x	$P(x)$
0	.3679
1	.3679
2	.1839
3	.0613
4	.0153
5	.0031
6	.0005
7	.0001

In parts (a)–(c), find each of the following:

  (a)   The mean of x

  (b)   The variance of x

  (c)   The standard deviation of x

  (d)   Construct a probability histogram.

  (e)   Over a 5-minute period, what is the probability of one or more incoming phone calls?

6.71   A *binomial* probability distribution for the number of successes x is

x	$P(x)$
0	.2401
1	.4116
2	.2646
3	.0756
4	.0081

In parts (a)–(c), find each of the following:

(a) The mean of x

(b) The variance of x

(c) The standard deviation of x

(d) Construct a probability histogram.

[*Hint:* Find q from the fact that $q^4 = P(0)$. Now use the binomial shortcut formulas for μ and σ^2.]

6.72 A *binomial* probability distribution for the number of successes x is

x	$P(x)$
0	.36
1	.48
2	.16

In parts (a)–(c), find each of the following:

(a) The mean of x

(b) The variance of x

(c) The standard deviation of x

(d) Construct a probability histogram.

[*Hint:* Use the binomial shortcut formulas and the fact that $q^2 = P(0)$.]

6.73 Match the three binomial probability histograms shown here with the correct p: $p = .3$, $p = .5$, $p = .8$.

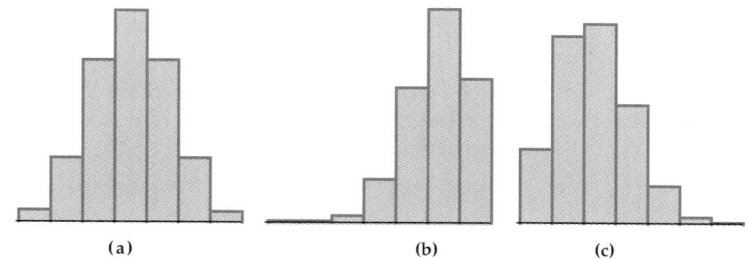

(a)   (b)   (c)

6.74 A roulette wheel has 37 equally spaced slots that are numbered $0, 1, 2, \ldots, 36$. Before the wheel is spun, a player picks one of the numbers. If the wheel is spun and stops on the number, the player wins \$35. If the wheel stops on one of the other numbers, the player pays \$1. What are the player's expected winnings (per game)?

6.75 In the game of craps, a player rolls two dice. If the first roll results in a sum of 7 or 11, the player wins. If the first roll results in a 2, 3, or 12, the player loses. If the sum on the first roll is 4, 5, 6, 8, 9, or 10, the player keeps rolling until he throws a 7 or the original value. If the outcome is a 7, the player loses. If it is the original value, the player wins. The probability that a player will win the game is .493. If the player nets \$4 for a win, what should he pay to play the game so that the game favors neither the player nor the casino?

6.76 A friend proposes the following game. He is to select one card from an ordinary deck of cards. You are to pay him \$10 if he selects an ace and \$5 if he selects a 2 or 3. What should he pay you so that the game does not favor either person?

6.77 The probability that a new flu vaccine prevents the flu is .80. Twelve people are vaccinated with the new vaccine at a local clinic. What is the probability that

(a) Eight or more people will not get the flu?

(b) Two of the people will get the flu?

6.78 Assume that the probability of a boy being born is .50. If a couple plan on having six children, find the probability that

(a) Exactly half are boys.

(b) All are boys.

(c) All are boys or all are girls.

(d) One or more are boys.

(Assume that the gender of any child is independent of the genders of the other children.)

6.79 Thirty percent of all voters in a large city are Independents. If 15 voters are to be selected by chance, find the probability that

(a) Exactly four are Independents.

(b) No more than three are Independents.

(c) Ten or more are Independents.

6.80 Seventy percent of the complaints received by a consumer protection agency are investigated by the agency. For the next seven complaints received by the agency, find the probability that

(a) All will be investigated.

(b) One will be investigated.

(c) No more than two will be investigated.

6.81 For an electronic system to function, each of 12 components must work. Assume that the components function independently of each other, and each has probability .99 of not breaking down for 1 year, when new. Suppose you buy a new system. Find the probability that the system does not break down in the first year.

6.82 Eighty-five percent of the dishwashers manufactured by a large company do not need repairs for the first 2 years. If five of the dishwashers are to be selected by chance, find the probability that

(a) None of the five will need repairs within 2 years.

(b) Three or more will need repairs within 2 years.

In Exercises 6.83–6.86, find (a) the mean, (b) the variance, and (c) the standard deviation of x.

6.83 Use Exercise 6.77 with x = the number of the 12 people who do not get the flu.

6.84 Use Exercise 6.80 with x = the number of complaints that will be investigated.

6.85 Use Exercise 6.79 with x = the number of the 15 voters who are Independents.

6.86 Use Exercise 6.82 with x = the number of dishwashers that will not need repairs in the next 2 years.

ANSWERS TO PRACTICE QUIZ

1. .229

2. .047

 .254

3. .009

4. 2

5. LET K1 = SUM(C1*C2)
   LET K2 = SUM(C1**2*C2) − K1**2
   LET K3 = SQRT(K2)
   PRINT K1 − K3
   (*Note:* K1 = μ, K2 = σ^2, K3 = σ.)

Notes

DeGroot, M. H., S. E. Fienberg, and J. B. Kadane, eds., *Statistics and the Law.* New York: John Wiley, 1986.

Koshy, T., *Finite Mathematics and Calculus with Applications.* Santa Monica, Calif.: Goodyear, 1979.

Larsen, R. J., and M. L. Marx, *Introduction to Mathematical Statistics and Its Applications.* Englewood Cliffs, N.J.: Prentice-Hall, 1986.

The 1994 Information Please Almanac. Boston: Houghton Mifflin, 1994.

Paulos, J. A. *Innumeracy—Mathematical Illiteracy and Its Consequences.* New York: Vintage Books, 1990.

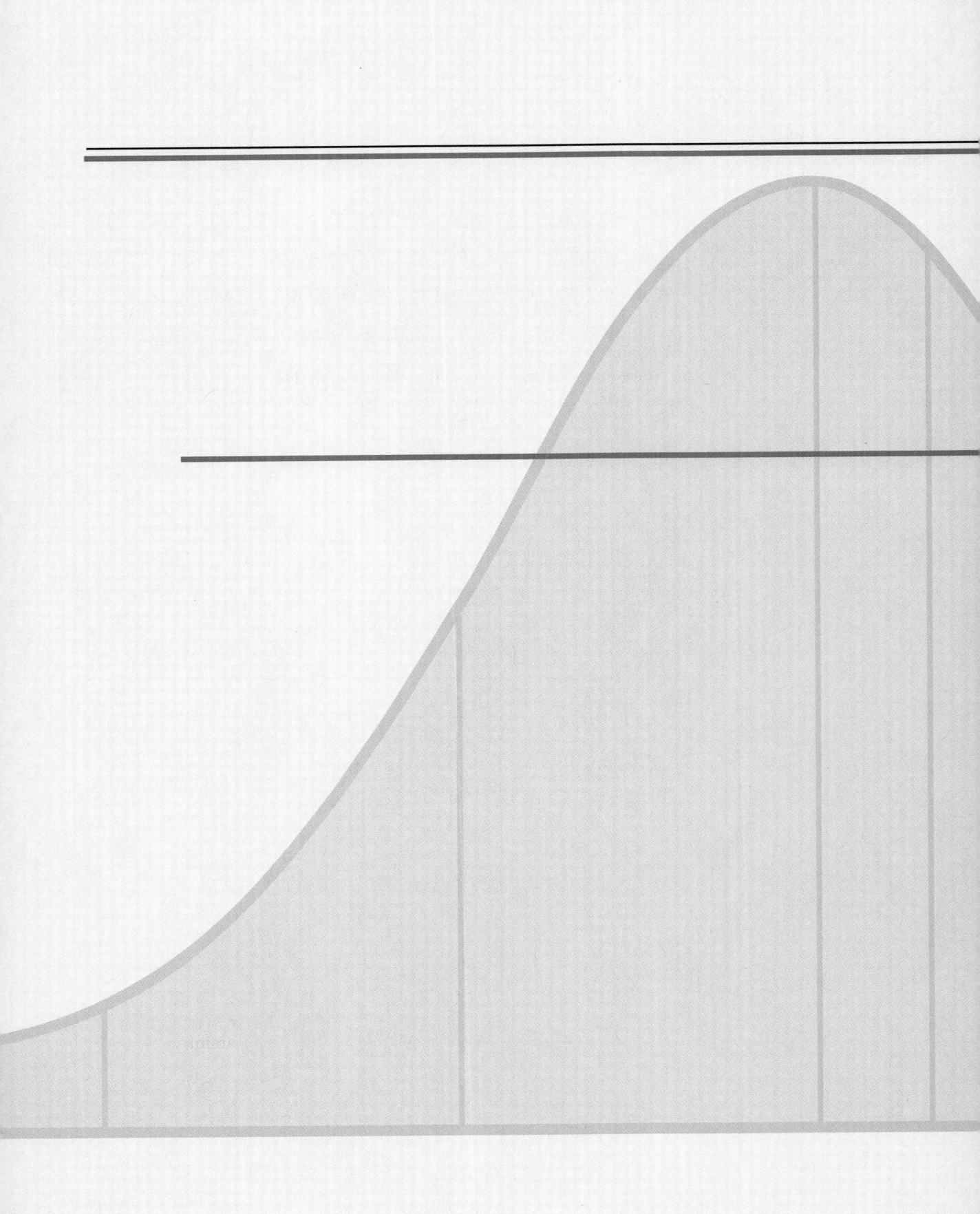

CHAPTER 7

PROBABILITY DISTRIBUTIONS FOR CONTINUOUS RANDOM VARIABLES; THE NORMAL DISTRIBUTION

7.1 INTRODUCTION

7.2 CONTINUOUS PROBABILITY DISTRIBUTIONS

7.3 THE NORMAL DISTRIBUTION

7.4 THE STANDARD NORMAL DISTRIBUTION

7.5 MORE ON NORMAL PROBABILITY

7.6 NORMAL APPROXIMATION TO THE BINOMIAL DISTRIBUTION

7.7 THE CENTRAL LIMIT THEOREM

7.8 USING MINITAB (OPTIONAL)

7.9 SUMMARY

REVIEW EXERCISES

NOTES

7.1

INTRODUCTION

As we have said a number of times, inferential statistics is concerned with making judgments about populations, and we carry on this study by examining samples from the populations. In Chapter 6, we indicated that we would find it convenient to introduce a concept that summarizes the essential features of a particular population of data values. This was called a "probability distribution."

In Chapter 6, we dealt with probability distributions for discrete random variables. In this chapter, we deal with *probability distributions for continuous random*

267

variables (also called continuous probability distributions). We then study a very important class of continuous random variables—**normal random variables**—along with their probability distributions. We show how a probability associated with a binomial random variable may be quickly approximated by a probability associated with an appropriate normal random variable. Finally, we study an important theorem that is useful in statistical inference: the **Central Limit Theorem.**

_____ **7.2**

CONTINUOUS PROBABILITY DISTRIBUTIONS

Recall that a continuous random variable is one that can theoretically take on any value on some line interval (see Section 6.2). Its probability distribution should somehow enable us to find probabilities associated with the random variable. The way this information is conveyed, however, is somewhat different for continuous random variables than for discrete random variables.

We saw in Chapter 6 that if b is some value of a discrete random variable, $P(b)$ is the probability that the value b would be observed. If we have a continuous random variable whose values are represented by the symbol x, we often use a symbol such as $f(x)$, read "f of x," to represent the probability distribution. We can think of $f(x)$ as some mathematical expression involving x so that for each value of x, the expression determines some number $f(x)$. But how does this number relate to probability? Unfortunately, $f(x)$ does *not* give us the probability that the value x will be observed.

To understand how a probability distribution for a continuous random variable enables us to find probabilities, it is important to understand a certain relationship between probability and area. Figure 7.1(a) is a histogram for a grouped frequency distribution for 25 values of a certain continuous random variable. The frequencies are displayed above each bar.

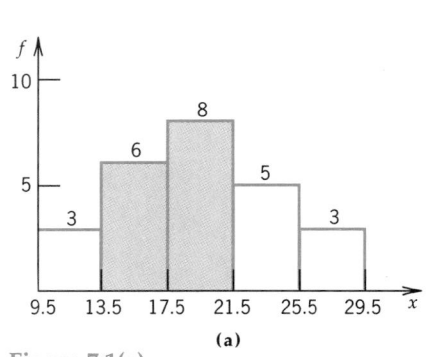

(a)

Figure 7.1(a)

Histogram for the Sample

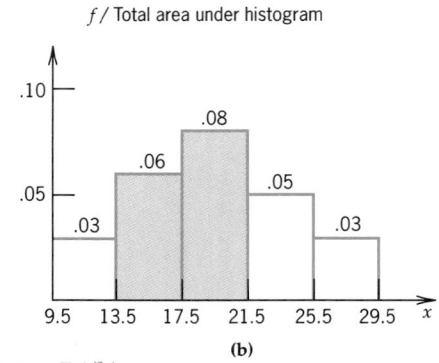

f / Total area under histogram

(b)

Figure 7.1(b)

Adjusted Histogram: Probability = Area

Suppose that we were interested in the probability that a new randomly observed value of x will fall between 13.5 and 21.5. We denote this probability by $P(13.5 < x < 21.5)$. In our sample, there are 14 data values between 13.5 and 21.5, out of a total of 25 data values. Therefore, it would be natural to estimate this probability by $\frac{14}{25} = .56$.

Observe that the width of each bar (the class width) is 4 units. The area of any bar is the frequency times the class width. The area of the bars between 13.5 and 21.5 is

$$(6)(4) + (8)(4) = 56$$

The total area of all the bars is

$$(3)(4) + (6)(4) + (8)(4) + (5)(4) + (3)(4) = 100$$

Notice that

$$P(13.5 < x < 21.5) \doteq .56 = \frac{56}{100} = \frac{\text{area of bars between 13.5 and 21.5}}{\text{total area of all the bars}}$$

To avoid dividing by the total area each time we find a probability, we could adjust the histogram so that this is unnecessary. To do this, divide each frequency by the total area of 100. The **adjusted histogram** is in Figure 7.1(b). Notice that the area under the adjusted histogram between 13.5 and 21.5 is

$$(.06)(4) + (.08)(4) = .56$$

which is our estimate of the probability. The area of all the bars of the adjusted histogram is

$$(.03)(4) + (.06)(4) + (.08)(4) + (.05)(4) + (.03)(4) = 1$$

The value .56 is only a very rough estimate of the desired probability, since we are dealing with a sample of only 25 data values. Now suppose that we obtained more and more data values and made the class width smaller and smaller. The adjusted histogram in Figure 7.1(b) could be expected to smooth out and approach some smooth curve, as in Figure 7.2.

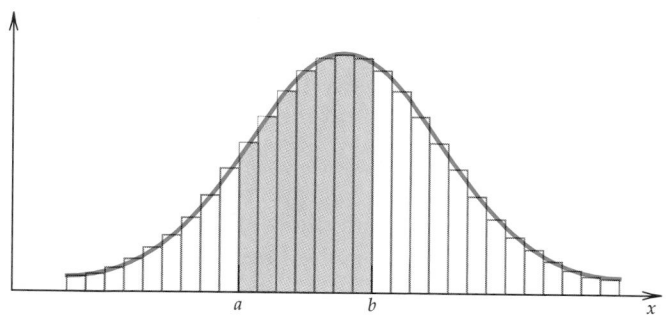

Figure 7.2

Based on the foregoing discussion, we see that a probability $P(a < x < b)$ can be approximated by the area of the bars between a and b. (See Figure 7.2.) Figure 7.2 suggests that this probability can also be obtained by calculating the area between a and b under the curve. (See Figure 7.3 on page 270.) Assuming that there are mathematical techniques for finding such a curve and areas such as the ones discussed (and there are such techniques), this curve can be quite useful in obtaining probabilities associated with the random variable x.

Suppose that the curve in Figure 7.3 has the equation $y = f(x)$, where $f(x)$ is some mathematical expression involving x. This means that this curve is the graph of the equation; that is, it is the collection of all points (x, y) that satisfy the equation.

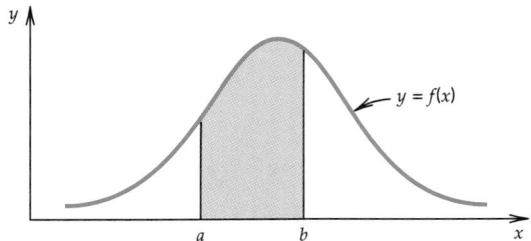

Figure 7.3
$P(a < x < b) = $ **Area of Shaded Region**

Then the expression $f(x)$ is called the **probability distribution** (or *probability density function*) for the continuous random variable.

The particular curve that we get and the form that the expression $f(x)$ takes will depend on the random variable under discussion. The technique for finding the probability distribution $f(x)$ for a continuous random variable is beyond the scope of this book. Suffice it to say that statisticians have found a number of such commonly encountered probability distributions and have developed tables containing probabilities associated with some of these distributions. Part of our task in statistics is learning which table applies in a given situation.

The following example is one that can be worked out "from scratch" without the use of tables.

EXAMPLE 7.1

Let x represent the amount of ice cream (in hundreds of gallons) sold by the Kenmore drive-in restaurant on any selected day. Because of storage limitations, the maximum amount of ice cream that can be kept on hand on any given day is 200 gallons. Thus, $0 \le x \le 2$. Further, it is known that the probability distribution for x is given by the formula $f(x) = x/2$. Sketch the graph of this probability distribution, and find the probability that on a selected day less than 100 gallons of ice cream will be sold; that is, find the probability that x falls between 0 and 1.

Solution

First we will sketch the graph of the equation $y = x/2$. This graph will be a straight line so that we need to find only two points to determine its location. When $x = 0$, $y = 0$, so $(0, 0)$ is on the line. Also, when $x = 2$, $y = 1$, so $(2, 1)$ is on the line. The line is shown in Figure 7.4. The desired probability $P(0 < x < 1)$ is the area under

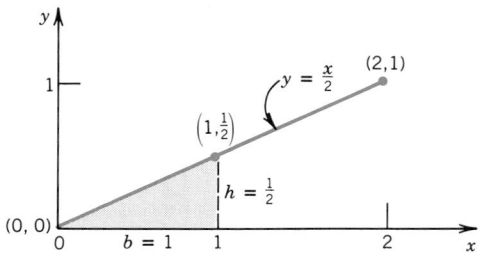

Figure 7.4
Probability Distribution for x, the Amount of Ice Cream Sold in Hundreds of Gallons (Example 7.1)

the graph between 0 and 1; it is shown as the shaded region in Figure 7.4. Since this region is a triangle, its area is one-half the base times the height, that is, $\frac{1}{2}b \cdot h$. It should be clear from Figure 7.4 that $b = 1$ and $h = \frac{1}{2}$. Hence

$$P(0 < x < 1) = \tfrac{1}{2}b \cdot h = \left(\tfrac{1}{2}\right)(1)\left(\tfrac{1}{2}\right) = \tfrac{1}{4}$$

Therefore, the probability of selling less than 100 gallons of ice cream is .25.

We summarize in the box some of the important properties of a continuous probability distribution.

1. For a continuous probability distribution, $f(x) \geq 0$ for all values x of the random variable.

2. The total area under the graph of the probability distribution [i.e., under the graph of the equation $y = f(x)$] is 1.

3. The probability that an observed value of x falls between a and b, $P(a < x < b)$, is the area between a and b under the graph. We can generalize this result. Sometimes we work with regions of x values that are not just single intervals (e.g., we may be interested in a region that consists of two separate intervals). For the regions that interest us, the probability that x falls in the region is equal to the area directly above the region and under the graph.

Note that for a continuous random variable x,

$$P(a \leq x \leq b) = P(a < x < b)$$

This is because including the endpoints a and b in the interval does not increase the area directly above the interval. Another way of putting this is that $P(x = a)$ and $P(x = b)$ are zero.

EXERCISES

7.1   Find these probabilities using the following graph of a continuous probability distribution.

(a) $P(x < \frac{1}{2})$ (b) $P(\frac{1}{4} < x < \frac{7}{4})$ (c) $P(x \geq \frac{3}{5})$

(d) $P(x < \frac{1}{5}$ or $x > \frac{2}{5})$ (e) $P(x < 2)$ (f) $P(x = \frac{3}{4})$

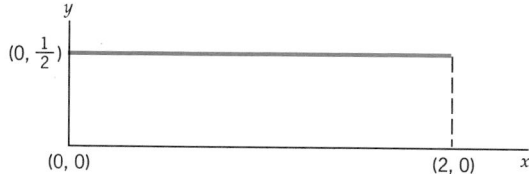

7.2   Assume that the time of birth of a New Year's baby at a city hospital will be some random time between midnight and 2:00 A.M. Let x be the number of minutes after midnight that the baby will be born. So $0 \leq x \leq 120$. The graph of the probability distribution is shown at the top of page 272. Note that x is said to be uniformly distributed.

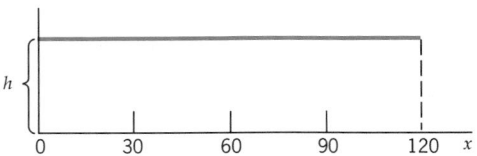

(a)   What is the area of the rectangle? What is the value of h?

(b)   What is the probability that the New Year's baby will be born
   (i)   Before 12:30 A.M.?
   (ii)   After 1:15 A.M.?
   (iii)   Between 12:45 A.M. and 1:00 A.M.?
   (iv)   Before 12:15 A.M. or after 1:30 A.M.?

(c)   Express parts (i), (ii), and (iii) of part (b) in one of the following forms:
   $P(a < x < b)$, $P(x < a)$, or $P(x > a)$.

7.3   Scores on a standardized test have a mean of 500 and a standard deviation of 100. Let x represent a student's test score. In the following probability distribution, assume a symmetric distribution.

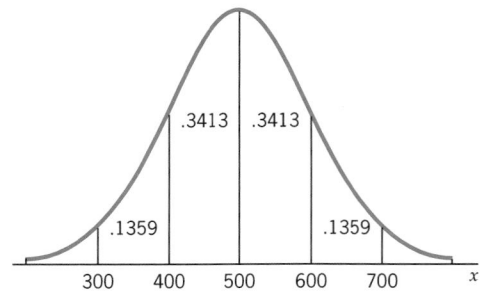

What is the probability that a randomly selected student will score

(a)   Higher than 700 or less than 300?

(b)   Higher than the mean?

(c)   Between 600 and 700?

(d)   Lower than 600?

(e)   Between 300 and 500?

(f)   Within 1 standard deviation of the mean?

(g)   Within 2 standard deviations of the mean?

7.4   A psychologist studied the length of time x, in seconds, required for completion of a project by first graders in a large city. The probability distribution is as follows:

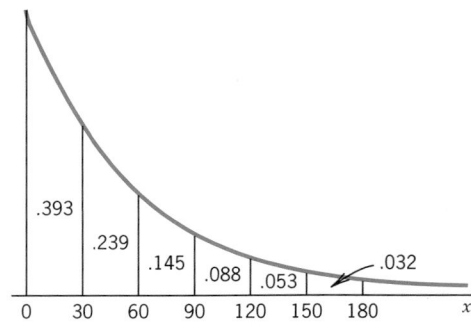

In parts (a)–(d), what percentage of students completed the project in the specific time?

(a)   Less than 60 seconds

(b)   Between 60 and 120 seconds

(c)   More than 180 seconds

(d)   More than 90 seconds

(e)   Now suppose that the psychologist is going to give the problem to a new group of first graders. She is going to allow them 2 minutes. About what percentage of these children are not expected to complete the project?

7.5   The graph of a continuous probability distribution is shown here.

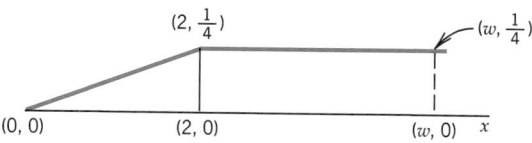

(a)   Find the value of w.

(b)   Find $P(x < 1)$.

(c)   Find $P(x > 3)$.

(d)   Find $P(x > \frac{3}{2})$.

7.3

THE NORMAL DISTRIBUTION

Perhaps the most important class of continuous random variables in statistics is the class of **normal random variables.** The probability distribution of a normal random variable is called a **normal distribution.** Many naturally occurring random variables are normal or very nearly so. For example, IQs, heights of humans, and Scholastic Aptitude Test scores all have approximately normal distributions. We often say they are *normally distributed* or have *normal populations.* The fact that many variables occurring in nature are normally distributed is no accident, and we will attempt to show why this is so later in the chapter. For now, we discuss some properties of normal distributions and investigate how to find probabilities associated with normal random variables.

Properties of a Normal Distribution

A normally distributed random variable x with mean μ and standard deviation σ has the following properties:

1.   Its probability distribution is given by the formula

$$f(x) = \frac{e^{-(x-\mu)^2/(2\sigma^2)}}{\sigma \sqrt{2\pi}}$$

where x can take on any numerical value. Also $\pi \doteq 3.1416$ and $e \doteq 2.7183$. This formula may appear threatening, but there is no need for concern because we will not have to deal with it directly. Normal probabilities can be obtained by the use of a table, as we shall see in the next section.

2.   The graph of a normal probability distribution is a bell-shaped curve that has its peak above the value $x = \mu$. Also, it is symmetric with respect to this value; that is, the portion of the curve to the right of μ is a mirror image of the portion to the left of μ. The shape of a normal distribution is given in Figure 7.5.

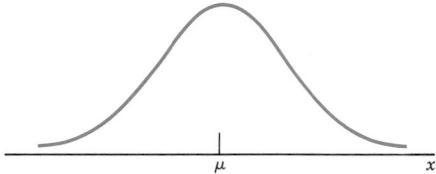

Figure 7.5
A Normal Probability Distribution

3.   The mean and median for a normal population both have the same value.

Some additional normal curves are displayed in Figure 7.6. The systolic blood pressure curves in Figure 7.6(a) indicate that younger males tend to have lower blood pressure, and the variability within the younger group is less than that of the older group.

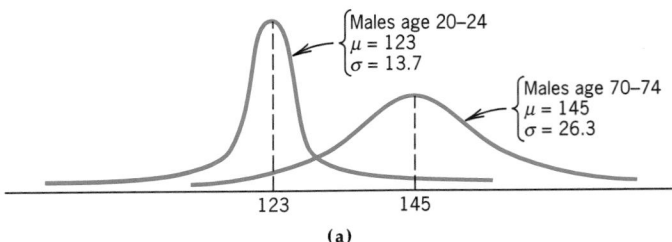

(a)

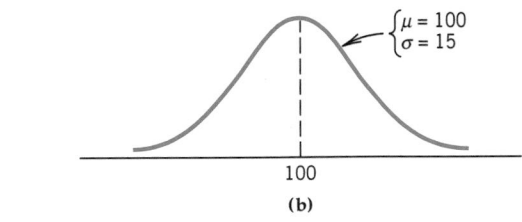

(b)

Figure 7.6
Some Normal Distributions: (a) Systolic Blood Pressure
(Source for Parameters: Lasser, R. P., and A. M. Master,
Geriatrics, **Vol. 14, p. 347, 1959); (b) IQ Scores**

_____ **7.4**

THE STANDARD NORMAL DISTRIBUTION

There is a normal random variable that stands out in importance above all other normal variables. It is important because we can use it to find probabilities associated with any normal variable. This random variable is called the **standard normal variable,** which we now define.

> **Definition** The *standard normal random variable* is that normal variable with mean 0 and standard deviation 1. Its values are usually represented by the symbol z.

Probabilities associated with the standard normal variable can be found by the use of Appendix Table B.3. Suppose we want to find the probability that a value of the standard normal variable will fall between 0 and some specific positive value of z. This is the area under the standard normal curve in Figure 7.7. Appendix Table B.3 gives the value of such areas for various values of z. The following examples show how to find probabilities associated with a standard normal variable.

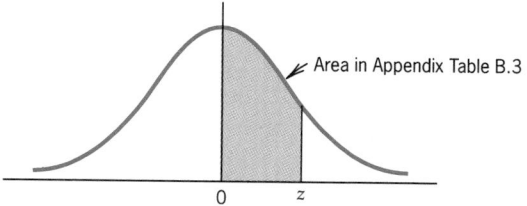

Figure 7.7
The Standard Normal Distribution

EXAMPLE 7.2

The Barton Company manufactures automobile charge indicator gauges. Under test conditions, these gauges are supposed to read 0 volts. However, some gauges read slightly more than 0 volts and some slightly less. Let z = voltage reading of a gauge under test conditions. So each gauge has a value of z. Past experience has shown that z is approximately normally distributed with a mean of 0 volts and a standard deviation of 1 volt. If one of these gauges is selected, find the probability that its voltage reading will be anywhere between 0 and 1.43 volts.

Solution

Notice that z has the standard normal distribution. We want to find $P(0 < z < 1.43)$, which is the area under the curve from 0 to 1.43. Using Appendix Table B.3, locate the number in the left-hand column that contains the same units and tenths digits as 1.43. This is 1.4. In the row across the top, locate the number that has the same hundredths digit. This is .03. Simply put, this corresponds to decomposing 1.43 as follows:

$$1.43 = 1.4 + .03$$

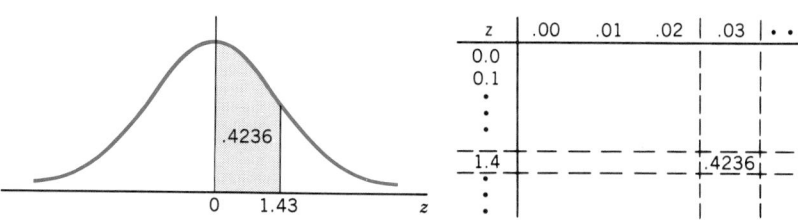

Figure 7.8
$P(0 < z < 1.43) = .4236$

Now look at the intersection of the row containing 1.4 and the column containing .03. This number is .4236. (See Figure 7.8.) This means that

$$P(0 < z < 1.43) = \text{area under curve from 0 to 1.43}$$
$$= .4236$$

EXAMPLE 7.3

For the random variable of Example 7.2, find

(a) $P(z < 1.43)$ **(b)** $P(-1.43 < z < 0)$

Solution

(a) The probability $P(z < 1.43)$ is the area to the left of 1.43. This is the same as the area to the left of 0 plus the area from 0 to 1.43. See Figure 7.9(a). In Example 7.2, we saw that the area from 0 to 1.43 was .4236. The total area under the curve is 1. The area to the left of 0 equals the area to the right of 0, and hence each has area .5. Therefore

$$P(z < 1.43) = .5 + .4236 = .9236$$

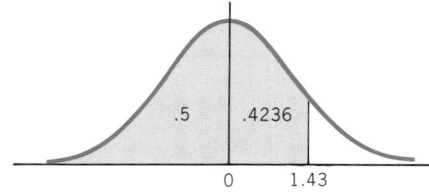

Figure 7.9(a)
$P(z < 1.43) = .5 + .4236 = .9236$

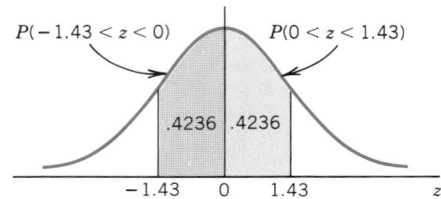

Figure 7.9(b)

(b) Note that -1.43, being negative, is not one of the values of z in the table. However, we can use the symmetry of the normal distribution to obtain the desired probability. The probability $P(-1.43 < z < 0)$ is equal to the area under the standard normal distribution between -1.43 and 0. But by symmetry, this area is the same as the area under the curve between 0 and 1.43. See Figure 7.9(b). This latter area is equal to the probability $P(0 < z < 1.43)$, which by Example 7.2 is .4236. Thus

$$P(-1.43 < z < 0) = P(0 < z < 1.43) = .4236$$

EXAMPLE 7.4

For the random variable of Example 7.2, find the probability $P(-.57 < z < 1.12)$.

Solution

As long as you identify probabilities with areas, the following steps should be clear on the basis of geometric intuition. (See Figure 7.10.) Now the area under the curve from $-.57$ to 1.12 is the area from $-.57$ to 0 plus the area from 0 to 1.12:

$$P(-.57 < z < 1.12) = (\text{area from } -.57 \text{ to } 0) + (\text{area from 0 to 1.12})$$

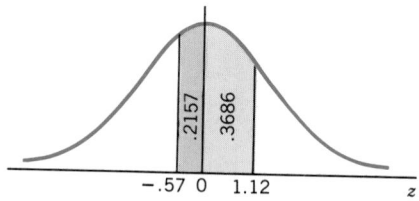 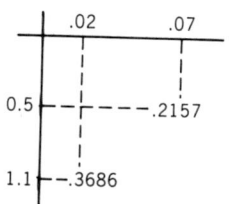

Figure 7.10
P(−.57 < z < 1.12) = .2157 + .3686 = .5843

By symmetry, the area from −.57 to 0 is the same as the area from 0 to .57. In Appendix Table B.3, the area from 0 to 0.57 is .2157 and the area from 0 to 1.12 is .3686. Hence

$$P(-.57 < z < 1.12) = .2157 + .3686 = .5843$$

EXAMPLE 7.5
For the random variable of Example 7.2, find $P(1.12 < z < 1.41)$.

Solution
From Figure 7.11, we see that the area from 1.12 to 1.41 is equal to the area from 0 to 1.41 minus the area from 0 to 1.12. Using this fact and Appendix Table B.3, we get

$$P(1.12 < z < 1.41) = \text{(area from 0 to 1.41)} - \text{(area from 0 to 1.12)}$$
$$= .4207 - .3686$$
$$= .0521$$

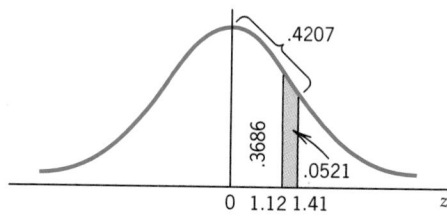 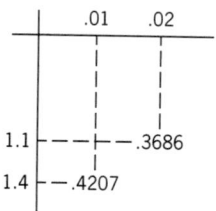

Figure 7.11
P(1.12 < z < 1.41) = .4207 − .3686 = .0521

EXAMPLE 7.6
For the random variable of Example 7.2, find

(a) $P(z > 1.28)$ **(b)** $P(z > 1.28 \text{ or } z < -1.28)$

Solution

(a) The area to the right of 0 is .5. Therefore, the area to the right of 1.28 (which is what we want) is equal to .5 minus the area from 0 to 1.28. (See Figure 7.12.)

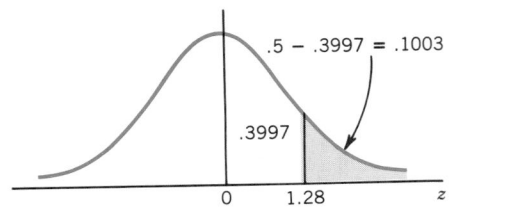 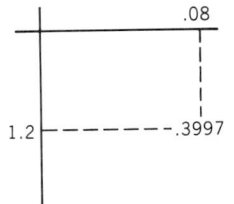

Figure 7.12
$P(z > 1.28) = .5 - .3997 = .1003$

Thus

$$P(z > 1.28) = .5 - (\text{area from 0 to 1.28})$$
$$= .5 - .3997 = .1003$$

(b) $P(z > 1.28 \text{ or } z < -1.28)$ is the probability that a value of z will be either greater than 1.28 or less than -1.28. This probability will be the area under the curve directly above the region (on the z-axis) consisting of z values to the left of -1.28 together with z values to the right of 1.28. (See Figure 7.13.)

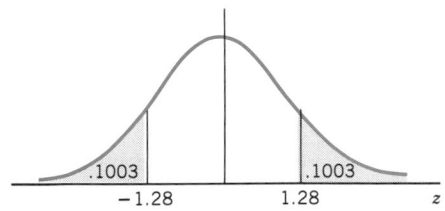

Figure 7.13
$P(z > 1.28 \text{ or } z < -1.28) = .2006$

To find this area, we just add the areas of the two tails (shaded). We have already found the area of the right tail in part (a) of this example to be .1003. By symmetry, the left tail has the same area, so

$$P(z > 1.28 \text{ or } z < -1.28) = .1003 + .1003 = .2006$$

EXAMPLE 7.7
Find the value on the z-axis such that the area under the curve to the right of it is .025. In other words,

$$P(z > \underline{\quad ? \quad}) = .025$$

Solution
If the area to the right of the desired z value is .025, then the area from 0 to this value is $.5 - .025 = .475$. (See Figure 7.14.) Therefore,

$$P(0 < z < \underline{\quad ? \quad}) = .475$$

Now in Appendix Table B.3, we locate the area .475 (not .025). The desired z value is $1.9 + .06 = 1.96$. (See Figure 7.14.)

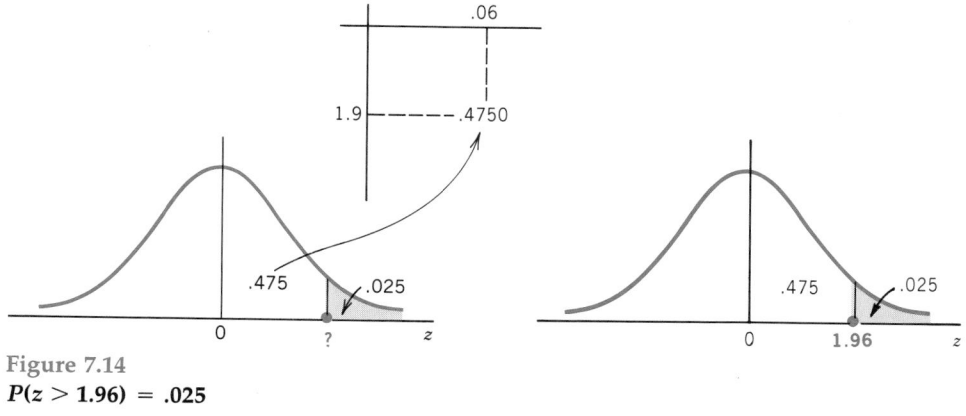

Figure 7.14
$P(z > 1.96) = .025$

Notation

In future work, it will be helpful to be able to relate a value of z to an area (or probability) under the standard normal curve by means of notation. The area we use is the area under the standard normal curve to the right of the z value. For example, the value of z such that the area under the curve to the right of it is .025 is denoted by $z_{.025}$.

$$z_{.025} = \text{that value of } z \text{ such that the area}$$
$$\text{under the standard normal curve}$$
$$\text{to the right of it is .025}$$

From Figure 7.14, we can see that this value is 1.96:

$$z_{.025} = 1.96$$

EXAMPLE 7.8

Find the following values of z:

(a) $z_{.10}$ **(b)** $z_{.05}$ **(c)** $z_{.975}$ **(d)** $z_{.80}$

Solution

(a) $z_{.10}$ is displayed in Figure 7.15.

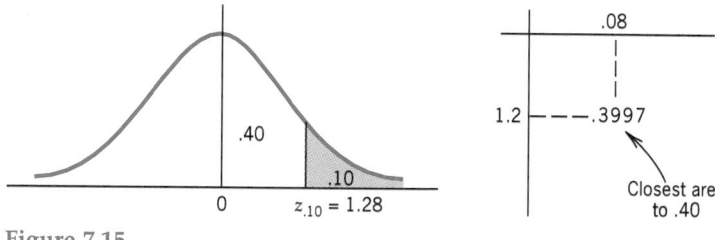

Figure 7.15

We will use Appendix Table B.3 to find the value. But remember that Appendix Table B.3 relates a specific value of z to the area under the curve from 0 to that specific value. The area from 0 to $z_{.10}$ is .40, so we must look up the value of z corresponding to the area .40 in Appendix Table B.3. The area closest to .40 is .3997. The z value corresponding to .3997 is 1.28, so

$$P(0 < z < 1.28) = .3997$$

Therefore $z_{.10} = 1.28$.

(b) $z_{.05}$ is displayed in Figure 7.16. The area between 0 and $z_{.05}$ is .45. Therefore, we look up the z value corresponding to .45. In Appendix Table B.3, the area .45 is halfway between .4495 and .4505. When this occurs, it is customary to use the larger value of z, so $z_{.05} = 1.65$.

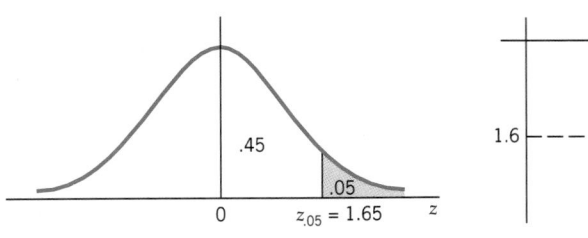

Figure 7.16

(c) Keeping in mind the symmetry of the standard normal distribution, we see from Figure 7.17 that $z_{.975} = -z_{.025}$.

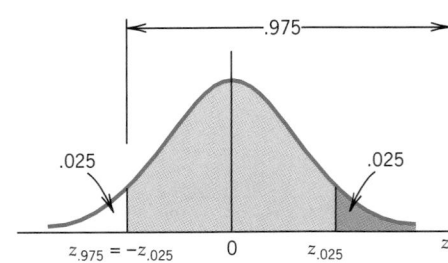

Figure 7.17

We have already seen that $z_{.025} = 1.96$; therefore

$$z_{.975} = -1.96$$

(d) $z_{.80}$ is displayed in Figure 7.18.

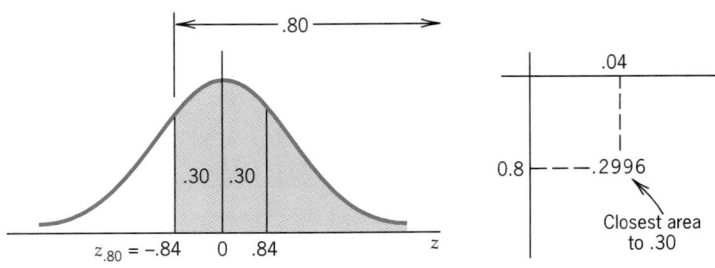

Figure 7.18

Because of the symmetry of the standard normal distribution, we look up the z value corresponding to .30 in Appendix Table B.3 and then take the negative of this value. The closest area to .30 in Appendix Table B.3 is .2996. The value of z corresponding to this is .84. Thus

$$z_{.80} = -.84$$

Remark   All the examples in this section were solved by drawing the normal curve and the area corresponding to the desired probability. When working a normal probability problem, **always draw a picture:** One picture is worth a thousand words.

EXERCISES

7.6   Let z represent the standard normal variable. Suppose a value of z is randomly selected. To find each of the following probabilities, (i) draw the standard normal curve and indicate the area representing the probability, (ii) express the probability in terms of areas from 0 to appropriate values (obtained from Appendix Table B.3), and (iii) calculate the answer.

   (a) $P(z < 1.41)$ **(b)** $P(z < -1.72)$

   (c) $P(z > 1.51)$ **(d)** $P(z > -2.43)$

7.7   Let z represent the standard normal variable, and suppose a value of z is randomly selected. To find each of the following probabilities, (i) draw the standard normal curve and indicate the area representing the probability, (ii) express the probability in terms of areas from 0 to appropriate values (obtained from Appendix Table B.3), and (iii) calculate the answer.

   (a) $P(0 < z < 1.63)$ **(b)** $P(-2.48 < z < 0)$

   (c) $P(-2.02 < z < 1.74)$ **(d)** $P(1.02 < z < 1.84)$

   (e) $P(-.58 < z < -.10)$

7.8   Suppose z represents the standard normal variable. If a value is selected at random from the z distribution, find the probability that z is

   (a)   Less than 0   **(b)**   Between $-.67$ and 0

   (c)   Between -2.3 and -1.45 **(d)**   Between $-.73$ and 2.31

   (e)   Less than 1.96

   (f)   Within 1 standard deviation of the mean

   (g)   Within 3 standard deviations of the mean

7.9   Suppose z is the standard normal variable. If a value is selected at random from the z distribution, find the probability that z is

   (a)   Between 0 and .67

   (b)   Between 1.65 and 2.1

   (c)   Between -2.1 and 1.7

   (d)   Larger than -1.86

   (e)   Larger than 2 or less than -2

   (f)   Within 2 standard deviations of the mean

7.10   Assume the standard normal distribution. Fill in the blanks.

   (a) $P(z < \underline{\hspace{1cm}}) = .9772$ **(b)** $P(z < \underline{\hspace{1cm}}) = .0668$

   (c) $P(z > \underline{\hspace{1cm}}) = .5$ **(d)** $P(z > \underline{\hspace{1cm}}) = .9599$

7.11   Assume the standard normal distribution. Fill in the blanks.

    (a) $P(z < \underline{\hspace{1cm}}) = .9573$ **(b)** $P(z < \underline{\hspace{1cm}}) = .1075$

    (c) $P(z > \underline{\hspace{1cm}}) = .0793$ **(d)** $P(z > \underline{\hspace{1cm}}) = .9929$

    (e) $z_{.02} = \underline{\hspace{1cm}}$ **(f)** $z_{.75} = \underline{\hspace{1cm}}$

    (g) $z_{.90} = \underline{\hspace{1cm}}$ **(h)** $z_{.35} = \underline{\hspace{1cm}}$

7.12   Evaluate each of the following:

    (a) $z_{.01}$ **(b)** $z_{.95}$

    (c) $z_{.005}$ **(d)** $z_{.20}$

7.13   The standard normal curve is shown here. Find the areas A, B, C, and D.

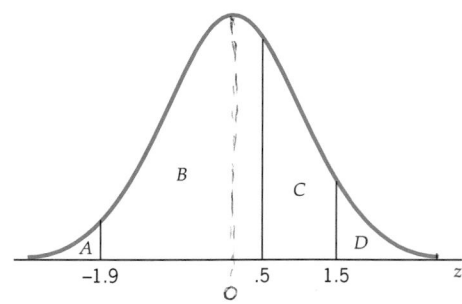

7.14   The figure shows the standard normal curve and some areas under the curve. Find the z values for a, b, and c.

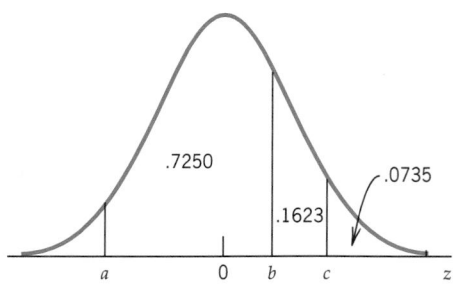

<hr>

7.5

MORE ON NORMAL PROBABILITY

We will now show how probabilities associated with any normal variable may be found by the use of a standard normal variable. To see how this is done, consider a normal variable x with mean μ and standard deviation σ. We define the **standard score** (or z score) by the formula

$$z = \frac{x - \mu}{\sigma}$$

Each value of x determines a value of z, so that z is itself a random variable. For example, if x is normal with mean 60 and standard deviation 10, then

$$z = \frac{x - 60}{10}$$

If $x = 70$, the corresponding z score is

$$z = \frac{70 - 60}{10} = \frac{10}{10} = 1$$

Notice that this corresponds to the fact that 70 is 1 standard deviation above the mean. If $x = 35$, its z score is

$$z = \frac{35 - 60}{10} = \frac{-25}{10} = -2.5$$

The minus sign means that 35 is below the mean; in fact it is 2.5 standard deviations below the mean. So all z does is measure whatever x is measuring in different units—namely, the number of standard deviations that x is above or below the mean μ. It follows that z should have the same type of probability distribution as x. Also, if we let μ_z represent the mean of z, it seems reasonable that μ_z can be obtained by replacing x by its mean in the formula for z:

$$\mu_z = \frac{\mu - \mu}{\sigma} = 0$$

It can also be shown that if we let σ_z be the standard deviation of z, then $\sigma_z = 1$.

Putting all these ideas together, we can say that if x is normal with mean μ and standard deviation σ, then

$$z = \frac{x - \mu}{\sigma}$$

is a normal random variable with mean 0 and standard deviation 1; that is, it is a standard normal variable. The following example shows how we can use this fact to find probabilities associated with any normal variable.

EXAMPLE 7.9

The scores of males on the 1974 Mathematical Scholastic Aptitude Test (MSAT) were approximately normally distributed with mean $\mu = 500$ and standard deviation $\sigma = 100$ points (approximately). Find the proportion of males who received the following scores.

(a) Between 500 and 600   **(b)** Between 400 and 600

Solution

(a) If we keep in mind that proportions and probabilities are really the same thing, it should be clear that we will have the proportion of scores between 500 and 600 if we simply find the probability that a randomly selected score falls between 500 and 600, that is, $P(500 < x < 600)$. Consider the z score of x:

$$z = \frac{x - \mu}{\sigma} = \frac{x - 500}{100}$$

When $x = 500$,

$$z = \frac{500 - 500}{100} = 0$$

When $x = 600$,

$$z = \frac{600 - 500}{100} = 1$$

Therefore, saying that a value of x is between 500 and 600 is the same as saying that its z score is between 0 and 1. Hence the probability that an x value is between 500 and 600 is the same as the probability that its z score is between 0 and 1:

$$P(500 < x < 600) = P(0 < z < 1)$$

This is shown in Figure 7.19(a).

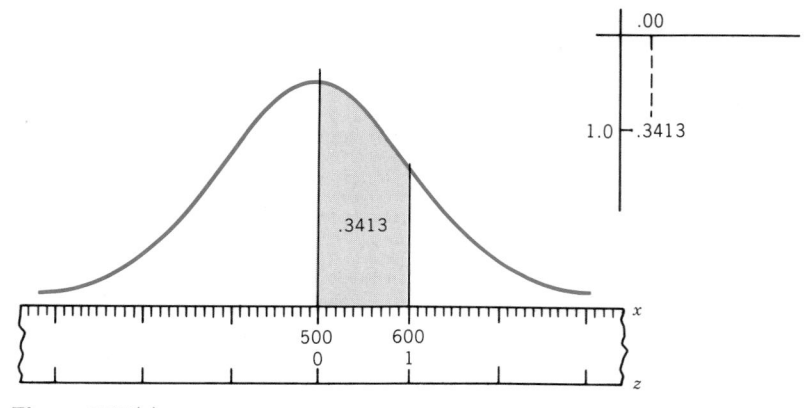

Figure 7.19(a)
$P(500 < x < 600) = .3413$

Keep in mind that changing from x to z is just changing to different units of measurement, from points to standard deviations:

($x = 600$ points) → ($z = 1$ standard deviation above the mean)

We may now look up the probability $P(0 < z < 1)$ in Appendix Table B.3. We find

$$P(500 < x < 600) = P(0 < z < 1) = .3413$$

Therefore, about 34% of scores were between 500 and 600.

(b)   Whereas 600 is 100 points above the mean, 400 is 100 points below the mean. Examining Figure 7.19(b), we see that because of symmetry of the normal distribution, the area from 400 to 500 is the same as the area from 500 to 600. We computed this area in part (a) to be .3413. Hence,

$$P(400 < x < 600) = 2(.3413) = .6826$$

Therefore, about 68% of the MSAT scores fall between 400 and 600, which is within 1 standard deviation (100 points) of the mean.

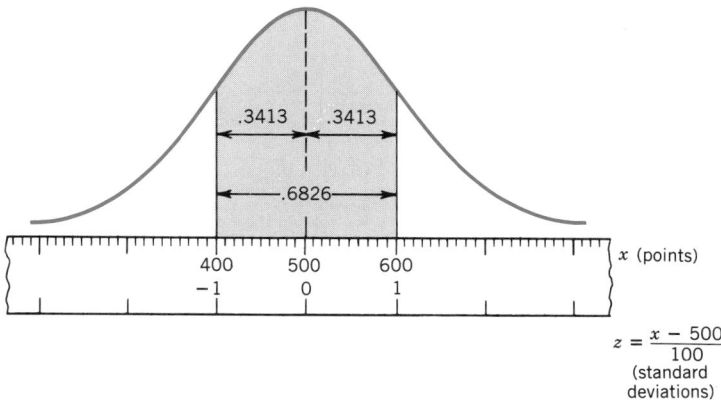

Figure 7.19(b)
$P(400 < x < 600) = .6826$

Example 7.9 shows how we can find probabilities associated with a normal variable x. We use the standard score for x:

$$z = \frac{x - \mu}{\sigma}$$

which enables us to express the values of x in terms of standard deviations, z. Using this, we can take a probability statement involving x and change it to an equivalent statement in terms of z. Since z is a standard normal variable, we can then use Appendix Table B.3 to find the desired probability.

EXAMPLE 7.10   Probability and Insurance Eligibility
The length of a pregnancy is a normal random variable with a mean of 266 days and standard deviation of 16 days.

(a)   Find the proportion of pregnancies that are between 285 and 305 days.

(b)   A health insurance company's family plan contained a clause that said that the company may refuse to cover hospital costs for a birth that is less than 217 days from the date of marriage. Find the probability that a pregnancy will last less than 217 days, and explain the logic behind the refusal of coverage by the insurance company.

Solution

(a)   Let x be the length of a randomly selected pregnancy. The proportion we are looking for is the probability $P(285 < x < 305)$. Now the standard score

$$z = \frac{x - 266}{16}$$

is a standard normal random variable. The z scores corresponding to $x = 285$ and $x = 305$ are

$$z = \frac{285 - 266}{16} \doteq 1.19 \qquad z = \frac{305 - 266}{16} \doteq 2.44$$

To say that x is between 285 and 305 is equivalent to saying that z is between 1.19 and 2.44. Therefore

$$P(285 < x < 305) = P(1.19 < z < 2.44)$$

This is shown in Figure 7.20(a).

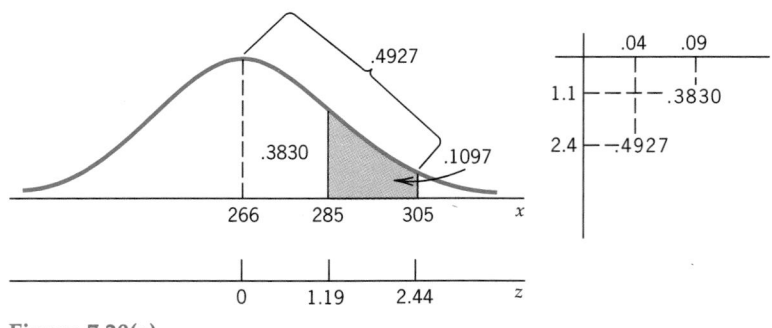

Figure 7.20(a)
$P(285 < x < 305) = .4927 - .3830 = .1097$

From Appendix Table B.3, we find

$$P(1.19 < z < 2.44) = \text{(area from 0 to 2.44)} - \text{(area from 0 to 1.19)}$$
$$= .4927 - .3830 = .1097$$

This means that about 11% of pregnancies last between 285 and 305 days.

(b)   We now find $P(x < 217)$. When $x = 217$

$$z = \frac{217 - 266}{16} \doteq -3.06$$

So

$$P(x < 217) = P(z < -3.06)$$

See Figure 7.20(b).

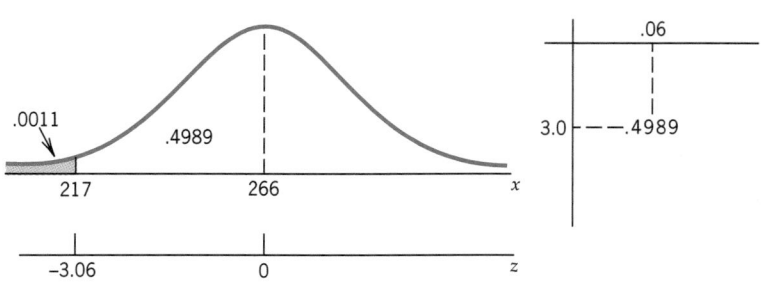

Figure 7.20(b)
$P(x < 217) = .5 - .4989 = .0011$

The area to the left of −3.06 can be found by subtracting the area under the curve from −3.06 to 0 from .5. The area from −3.06 to 0 is the same as the area from 0 to 3.06, which from Appendix Table B.3 is .4989. See Figure 7.20(b). Thus

$$P(x < 217) = P(z < -3.06)$$
$$= .5 - .4989 = .0011$$

This means that a pregnancy of less than 217 days is very unlikely (a chance of about 1 in 1000). It is so unlikely that the insurance company refuses to believe it. The company prefers to believe that the pregnancy was a pre-existing condition at the time of marriage, and thus is not covered under the terms of the policy.

EXAMPLE 7.11

Recall that, in Example 7.9, the 1974 MSAT scores for males were approximately normal with $\mu = 500$ and $\sigma = 100$. For this population, find the following:

(a)   The 90th percentile, P_{90}

(b)   The 30th percentile, P_{30}

(c)   The percentile rank of the score 567

Solution

(a)   We will first find P_{90} in terms of z and then, using the relation

$$z = \frac{x - 500}{100}$$

we will solve for x, thus getting the 90th percentile in terms of x. Now P_{90} separates the top 10% of scores from the bottom 90%. Look at Figure 7.21(a).

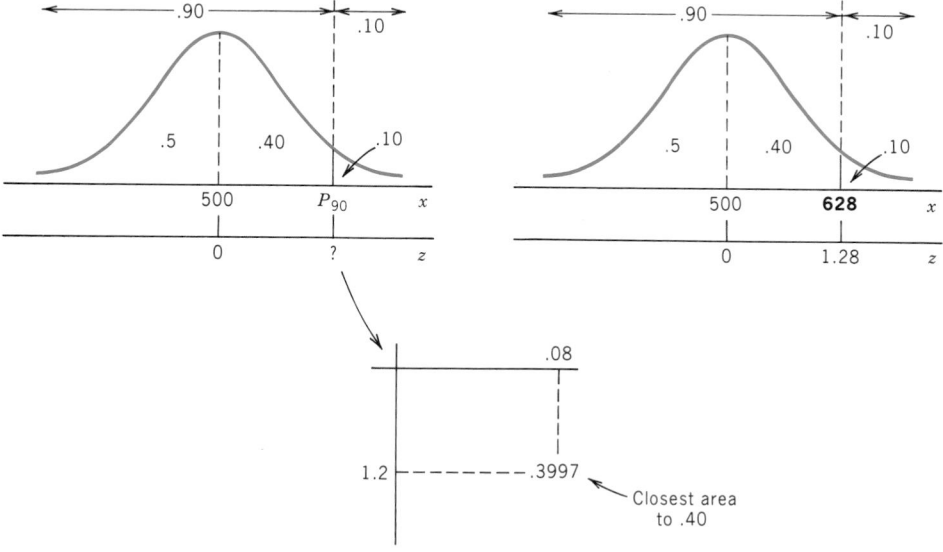

Figure 7.21(a)
The 90th Percentile = 628.

First find the number that satisfies

$$P(0 < z < \underline{\quad ? \quad}) = .40$$

In Appendix Table B.3, the closest probability to .40 is .3997. The corresponding z value is 1.28. This is the 90th percentile expressed in terms of z. We want this in terms of x. So we substitute and solve for x:

$$1.28 = \frac{x - 500}{100}$$

$$128 = x - 500$$

$$500 + 128 = x$$

$$x = 628$$

So $P_{90} = 628$.

(b)   The situation for P_{30} is shown in Figure 7.21(b). First use Appendix Table B.3 to find the number that satisfies

$$P(0 < z < \underline{\quad ? \quad}) = .20$$

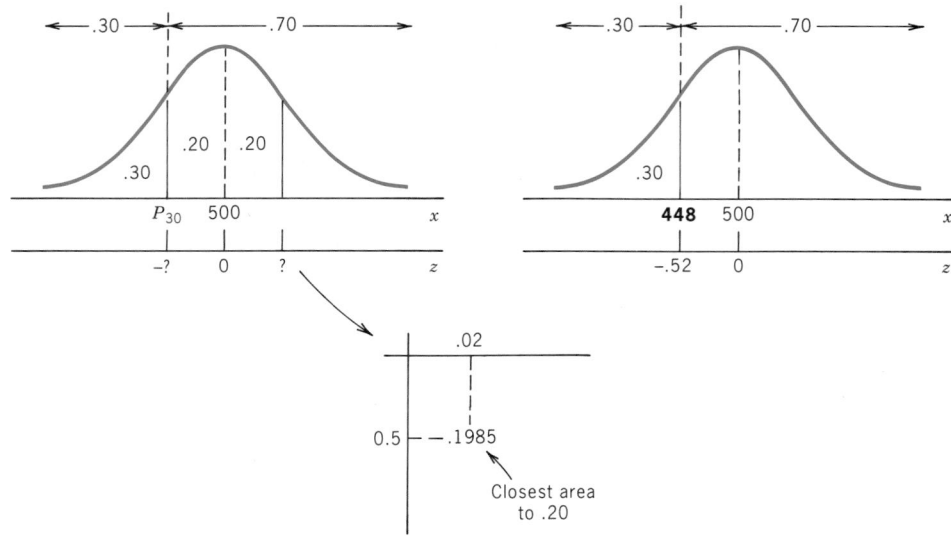

Figure 7.21(b)
The 30th Percentile = 448.

The z score we want will be the negative of the one found. The closest probability to .20 is .1985, which corresponds to a z score of .52. So the value we want is $z = -.52$. We substitute and solve for x:

$$-.52 = \frac{x - 500}{100}$$

$$-52 = x - 500$$

$$500 - 52 = x$$

$$x = 448$$

So $P_{30} = 448$.

(c)   To find the percentile rank of 567, we must find the proportion of scores less than 567:

$$P(x < 567) = \underline{\quad ? \quad}$$

When $x = 567$,

$$z = \frac{567 - 500}{100} = .67$$

Figure 7.21(c) shows that

$$P(x < 567) = P(z < .67) = .5 + .2486 = .7486$$

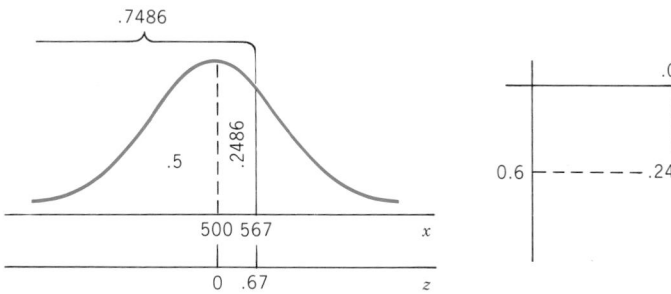

Figure 7.21(c)
The Percentile Rank of 567 Is Approximately 75.

This means that the percentile rank of 567 is 74.86 or approximately 75. Thus 567 is approximately the 75th percentile or third quartile.

EXAMPLE 7.12

A large brass company had a labor contract that required any employee layoffs to be based on the employee's years of service with the company (seniority). A cutoff value is determined, and any employee whose seniority is less than the value is laid off.

(a)   At one plant, seniority is normal with mean $\mu = 15$ years and $\sigma = 5$ years. If 18% are to be laid off, what is the cutoff value?

(b)   At another plant, seniority is normal with $\sigma = 3$ years. If 35% are laid off and the cutoff value is 9 years, what is the mean seniority μ?

Solution

(a)   The standard score for x years of seniority is

$$z = \frac{x - 15}{5}$$

The situation is depicted graphically in Figure 7.22(a) on page 290. Find the value in Appendix Table B.3 that satisfies

$$P(0 < z < \underline{\quad ? \quad}) = .32$$

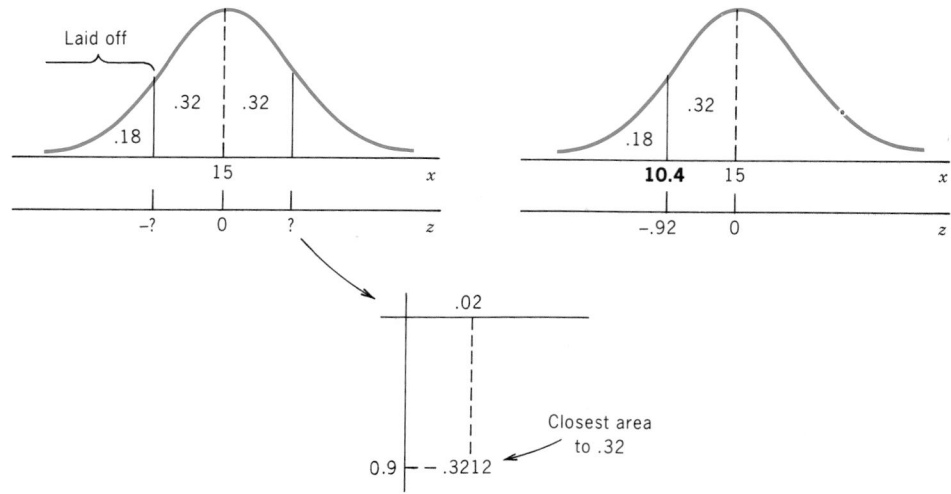

Figure 7.22(a)
Employees with Less than 10.4 Years of Seniority (18%) Are Laid Off.

From Figure 7.22(a), we see that this value is .92. Then take the negative of this value, getting $z = -.92$. Substitute and solve for x:

$$-.92 = \frac{x - 15}{5}$$

$$-4.6 = x - 15$$

$$15 - 4.6 = x$$

$$x = 10.4$$

So those with less than 10.4 years of seniority are laid off.

(b)   In this case, the standard score for x years of seniority is

$$z = \frac{x - \mu}{3}$$

We will find μ. We know that those with less than 9 years of seniority are laid off, and this constitutes 35% of employees. See Figure 7.22(b). As indicated in Figure 7.22(b), we use Appendix Table B.3 to find the value that satisfies

$$P(0 < z < \underline{\quad ? \quad}) = .15$$

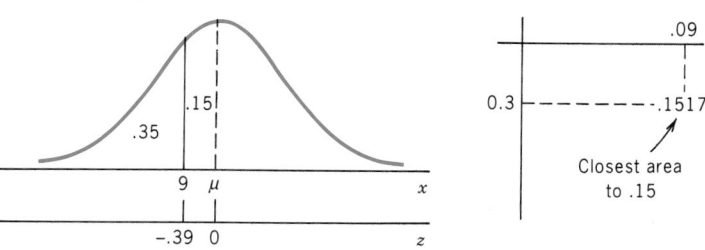

Figure 7.22(b)

From Figure 7.22(b), we see that this value is .39. We take the negative of this, $z = -.39$. Now we know that this corresponds to a seniority of $x = 9$ years. If we substitute $z = -.39$ and $x = 9$ in the equation, we can solve for μ:

$$z = \frac{x - \mu}{3}$$

$$-.39 = \frac{9 - \mu}{3}$$

$$-1.17 = 9 - \mu$$

$$\mu - 1.17 = 9$$

$$\mu = 9 + 1.17 = 10.17 \text{ years}$$

In Example 7.9, we saw that the 1974 MSAT scores for men were normally distributed with $\mu = 500$ and $\sigma = 100$. If x represents an arbitrary score, we showed

$$P(400 < x < 600) = .6826$$

Now

$$400 = 500 - 100 = \mu - \sigma$$
$$600 = 500 + 100 = \mu + \sigma$$

Thus

$$P(\mu - \sigma < x < \mu + \sigma) = .6826$$

This means that about 68% of the MSAT scores will fall within 1 standard deviation of the mean. If we were to calculate the probability of a score being within 2 standard deviations of the mean, that is, the proportion of scores between $\mu - 2\sigma$ and $\mu + 2\sigma$, we would find it to be .9544. If we calculated the proportion of scores within 3 standard deviations of the mean, that is, between $\mu - 3\sigma$ and $\mu + 3\sigma$, we would find it to be .9974.

It turns out that these results hold for any normal random variable. For example, no matter what values we have for μ and σ, 1 standard deviation above the mean corresponds to $z = 1$ and 1 standard deviation below the mean corresponds to $z = -1$. So the proportion of data within 1 standard deviation of the mean is

$$P(-1 < z < 1) = .6826$$

as we saw in Example 7.9. Therefore, if x is any normal variable with mean μ and standard deviation σ, then

$$P(\mu - \sigma < x < \mu + \sigma) = .6826$$
$$P(\mu - 2\sigma < x < \mu + 2\sigma) = .9544$$
$$P(\mu - 3\sigma < x < \mu + 3\sigma) = .9974$$

So for a normal population we expect:

Between			Percentage of data
$\mu - \sigma$	and	$\mu + \sigma$	68.26
$\mu - 2\sigma$	and	$\mu + 2\sigma$	95.44
$\mu - 3\sigma$	and	$\mu + 3\sigma$	99.74

This is the basis for the **Empirical Rule.** This rule says that if we have a large sample from a normal population and we use $\bar{x}$ and s as estimates for μ and σ, then the same proportions should hold for the sample, at least approximately. If a sample satisfies the Empirical Rule and has a mound-shaped histogram, this suggests that the sample came from a normal population.

EXERCISES

7.15 Let x be a normal random variable with mean 46 and standard deviation 4. What percentage of values are

   (a) Larger than 46?   **(b)** Larger than 50?

   (c) Larger than 40?   **(d)** Less than 38?

   (e) Less than 49?   **(f)** Between 45 and 49?

   (g) Between 50 and 54?   **(h)** Larger than 56 or less than 46?

   (i) Within 1.5 standard deviations of the mean?

   (j) Outside of 2.3 standard deviations of the mean?

7.16 Let x be a normal random variable with mean 80 and standard deviation 12. If a value is randomly selected from the x distribution, find each of the following probabilities:

   (a) $P(80 < x < 92)$ **(b)** $P(71 < x < 80)$

   (c) $P(x > 83)$ **(d)** $P(x > 56)$

   (e) $P(x < 92)$ **(f)** $P(x < 62)$

   (g) $P(89 < x < 95)$ **(h)** $P(53 < x < 59)$

   (i) $P(65 < x < 98)$ **(j)** $P(x = 80)$

7.17 Consider a normal population with mean 200 and standard deviation 25. Find the following:

   (a) The third quartile

   (b) The 35th percentile

   (c) The percentile rank of the data value 211

   (d) The percentile rank of the data value 150

7.18 Consider a normal population with mean 150 and standard deviation 10. Find the following:

   (a) The first quartile

   (b) The 65th percentile

   (c) The percentile rank of the data value 165

   (d) The percentile rank of the data value 145

7.19 Here is a normal curve for a random variable x with mean 70 and standard deviation 10. Find the areas A, B, C, and D.

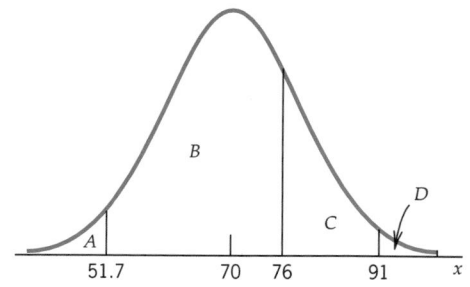

7.20   Here is a normal curve for a random variable x with mean 85 and standard deviation 8. Find the x values a and b.

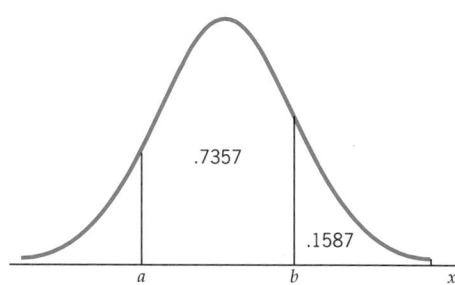

\7.21   The lengths x of the nails in a large shipment received by a carpenter are approximately normally distributed with mean 2 inches and standard deviation .1 inch.

   (a)   If a nail is randomly selected, find $P(1.8 < x < 2.07)$.

   (b)   What proportion of nails have lengths that lie within 1 standard deviation of the mean?

   (c)   The carpenter cannot use a nail shorter than 1.75 inches or longer than 2.25 inches. What percentage of the shipment of nails will the carpenter be able to use?

7.22   The length of time it takes for a ferry to reach a summer resort from the mainland is approximately normally distributed with mean 2 hours and standard deviation 12 minutes. Over many past trips, what proportion of times has the ferry reached the island in

   (a)   Less than 1 hour, 45 minutes?

   (b)   More than 2 hours, 5 minutes?

   (c)   Between 1 hour, 50 minutes and 2 hours, 20 minutes?

\7.23   Scores of males on the 1974 Mathematical Scholastic Aptitude Test (MSAT) were normally distributed with mean 500 and standard deviation 100.

   (a)   What score indicates a percentile rank of 95?

   (b)   The middle 40% of the distribution is bounded by what two scores?

   (c)   If 1000 of these students are randomly selected, how many are expected to score higher than 650?

\7.24   Some auto companies design emission sensors so that they must be replaced after 100,000 miles. One such company found that the service life x (in months) of these sensors is approximately normal with mean 48 months and standard deviation 9 months.

   (a)   The company decided to guarantee the sensors for 3 years. What percentage of the sensors will not satisfy the guarantee?

   (b)   The company decided to replace only 1% of all sensors. What should be the length (in months) of the guarantee?

7.25   Let x be the number of minutes after 11 o'clock that a bus leaves the bus station. Assume that the distribution of times is approximately normal with mean 15 and standard deviation 4 minutes.

   (a)   If a person gets to the bus station at 11:10, what is the probability that the person has missed the bus?

(b)   If a person is willing to risk a 20% chance of not making the bus, what is the maximum number of minutes after 11 o'clock that the person can reach the station?

(c)   What time should the person reach the station to have a 50–50 chance of catching the bus?

7.26   A diastolic blood pressure reading of less than 90 mm is considered normal; a reading of 90 or more indicates hypertension. Assume that the distribution of diastolic blood pressure readings of people 30 to 39 years old in the Framingham Heart Study is approximately normal with mean 79 and standard deviation 11. What proportion of this population has

   (a)   Normal diastolic blood pressure?

   (b)   Hypertensive diastolic readings?

7.27   Assume that the number of hours a product will function before needing service is approximately normally distributed.

   (a)   If the standard deviation were 70 and 10% of the product will break down before 700 hours, what would the mean be?

   (b)   If the mean time were 800 hours and 20% will function for more than 850 hours, what would the standard deviation be?

7.28   The sample mean and sample standard deviation of 35 data values are 250.77 and 6.62, respectively. The data and frequency histogram are given here.

236	238	238	241	244	246	246
247	247	247	248	248	248	249
251	251	251	251	251	252	252
252	253	253	254	254	255	256
256	256	259	260	261	263	263

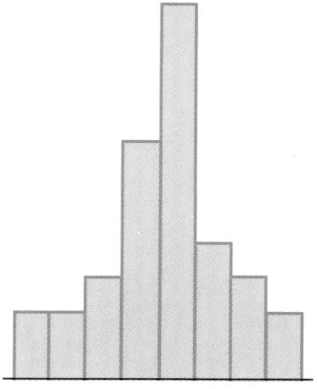

   (a)   Find the percentage of data values within 1, 2, and 3 standard deviations of the mean. Compare with the Empirical Rule.

   (b)   Are the results of part (a) and the histogram consistent with sampling from a normal population?

7.6

NORMAL APPROXIMATION TO THE BINOMIAL DISTRIBUTION

Recall that in Section 6.5, we discussed the binomial probability distribution

$$P(x) = \frac{n!}{x!(n-x)!} \cdot p^x \cdot q^{n-x} \qquad x = 0, 1, 2, \ldots, n$$

Values of $P(x)$ are given in Appendix Table B.2. But notice that this table goes up only to $n = 25$. For large values of n, the formula for $P(x)$ can be quite unpleasant to work with. Even hand calculators are not much help; they do not have the capacity to handle factorials of large numbers. However, there is a way to approximate values of $P(x)$ for large values of n using normal probabilities. We illustrate with the following example.

A sociologist conducted interviews with 16 registered voters. The voters were randomly selected from a list of voters. Assume that half the voters on the list are Democrats. The process of selecting the 16 voters can be viewed as a binomial experiment. A trial is randomly selecting a voter. Let a success consist of selecting a Democrat. The probability of a success is the proportion of voters who are Democrats, in this case $\frac{1}{2}$. So

$$P(S) = p = \tfrac{1}{2}$$

The trial is repeated 16 times, and x is the number of Democrats selected. Assume that the list is large enough that the probability of success does not change appreciably from one trial to the next. So $p = \frac{1}{2}$ for each trial. This means that the trials are independent. Therefore, we have a binomial experiment with $n = 16$ and $p = q = \frac{1}{2}$.

Figure 7.23(a) shows the probability distribution for x. The area of each bar represents the probability of observing the value at the base of the bar. Together, the bars resemble a bell-shaped curve; we have superimposed a normal curve to emphasize this. But which normal curve is this? It is the normal curve of the distribution that has the same mean and standard deviation as the binomial variable. Now recall that for the binomial random variable

$$\mu = np = (16)\left(\tfrac{1}{2}\right) = 8$$

$$\sigma = \sqrt{npq} = \sqrt{(16)\left(\tfrac{1}{2}\right)\left(\tfrac{1}{2}\right)} = \sqrt{4} = 2$$

How can the normal curve be used to find binomial probabilities? Let us examine the probability of 12 successes, that is, $P(12)$. This is the area of the bar whose base stretches from 11.5 to 12.5. If you wish to look up the answer in Appendix Table B.2, you will find that it is .028. But let's see if we can get the answer using the normal curve. It would seem natural to estimate the area of the bar by the area under the normal curve from 11.5 to 12.5. See Figure 7.23(b).

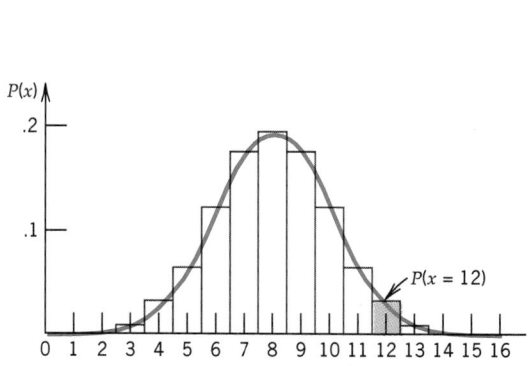

Figure 7.23(a)
Normal Approximation to a Binomial Distribution with $n = 16$, $p = q = \frac{1}{2}$

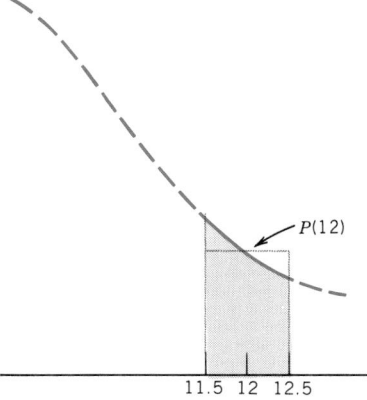

Figure 7.23(b)
Estimating $P(12)$ by Area Under a Normal Curve (Shaded)

Therefore, let us regard the binomial variable x as approximately normal, and compute the normal probability $P(11.5 < x < 12.5)$ to see how close we come to the answer of .028. Now the standard score for x is

$$z = \frac{x - \mu}{\sigma} = \frac{x - 8}{2}$$

When $x = 11.5$,

$$z = \frac{11.5 - 8}{2} = 1.75$$

When $x = 12.5$,

$$z = \frac{12.5 - 8}{2} = 2.25$$

Thus $11.5 < x < 12.5$ is equivalent to $1.75 < z < 2.25$. Hence

$$P(11.5 < x < 12.5) = P(1.75 < z < 2.25)$$

See Figure 7.23(c).

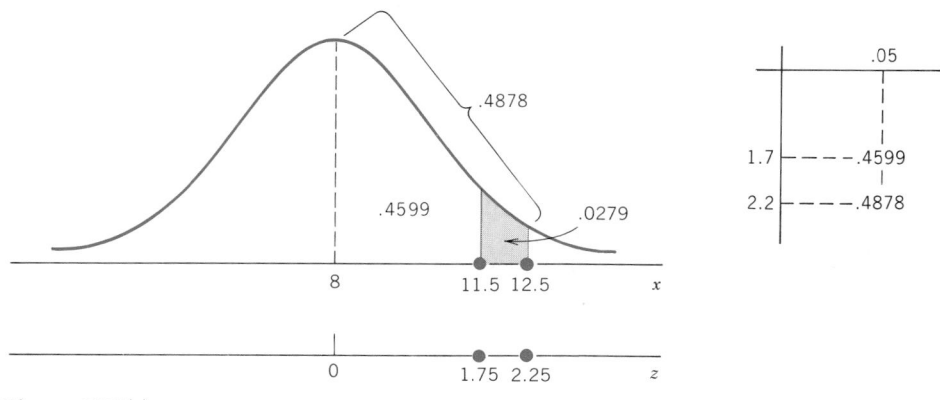

Figure 7.23(c)
$P(11.5 < x < 12.5) = .4878 - .4599 = .0279$

Using Appendix Table B.3, we see that

$$P(1.75 < z < 2.25) = \text{(area from 0 to 2.25)} - \text{(area from 0 to 1.75)}$$
$$= .4878 - .4599 = .0279$$

Therefore,

$$P(11.5 < x < 12.5) = .0279$$

Rounded to three places, this gives the same result as Appendix Table B.2.

This shows how a binomial distribution may be approximated by an appropriate normal distribution. However, it can be shown that the approximation is valid only when n is sufficiently large. It is known that n will be sufficiently large if $np \geq 5$ and $nq \geq 5$. For example, if $p = \frac{1}{2}$, then we would want n to be such that $np = n(\frac{1}{2}) \geq 5$ and $nq = n(\frac{1}{2}) \geq 5$. Therefore, we would want to have $n \geq 10$.

We summarize and generalize these results as follows:

---

1. A binomial random variable x may be thought of as having an approximately normal distribution with mean np and standard deviation $\sqrt{npq}$ if n is sufficiently large. Note that n will be sufficiently large if both np and nq are at least 5.

2. When approximating a binomial probability with a normal probability, we must use the so-called *continuity correction*. Thus, for example, to find the probability of 12 successes, calculate the normal probability $P(11.5 < x < 12.5)$. To find the probability of 9, 10, or 11 successes, calculate the normal probability $P(8.5 < x < 11.5)$.

Warning The continuity correction should be used only when approximating a binomial probability with a normal probability. **Do not use the continuity correction with other normal probability problems.**

EXAMPLE 7.13
Find the probability that between 30 and 35 of the next 50 births at a particular hospital will be boys. (By this we mean more than 30 but less than 35.)

Solution
Notice that the 50 births can be thought of as a binomial experiment:

$$\text{trial} = \text{a birth}$$
$$\text{success} = \text{child is a boy}$$
$$p = P(\text{success}) = .5$$
$$q = 1 - p = .5$$
$$n = 50$$
$$x = \text{number of successes (boys)}$$

We want to find the probability that x is between 30 and 35 (i.e., 31 or 32 or 33 or 34). Now

$$np = (50)(.5) = 25 \quad \text{and} \quad nq = (50)(.5) = 25$$

Since np and nq are both at least 5, we may view x as approximately normal with

$$\mu = np = (50)(.5) = 25$$
$$\sigma = \sqrt{npq} = \sqrt{(50)(.5)(.5)} = \sqrt{12.5} \doteq 3.54$$

The desired probability is the sum of the areas of the rectangles above 31, 32, 33, and 34. This is approximated by the area under the normal curve between 30.5 and 34.5. So we must find the probability $P(30.5 < x < 34.5)$. See Figure 7.24 (page 298). Let

$$z = \frac{x - \mu}{\sigma} = \frac{x - np}{\sqrt{npq}} = \frac{x - 25}{3.54}$$

This is approximately standard normal. When $x = 30.5$,

$$z = \frac{30.5 - 25}{3.54} \doteq 1.55$$

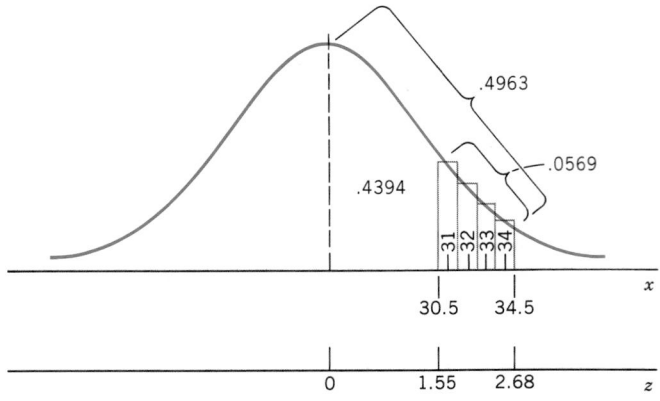

Figure 7.24
$P(30.5 < x < 34.5) = .4963 - .4394 = .0569$

When $x = 34.5$,

$$z = \frac{34.5 - 25}{3.54} \doteq 2.68$$

Therefore,

$$P(30.5 < x < 34.5) = P(1.55 < z < 2.68)$$
$$= (\text{area from 0 to 2.68}) - (\text{area from 0 to 1.55})$$
$$= .4963 - .4394 = .0569$$

This is the desired probability.

EXAMPLE 7.14

A state health official wished to study the death rate from cancer in a Massachusetts town situated near a toxic waste dump. The death certificates of 200 randomly selected individuals in this town were examined, and it was found that 58 had died of cancer. It is known that 23% of all deaths in the state are due to cancer. If the death rate from cancer in this town were the same as for the state, find the probability that more than 57 out of 200 people in the town would die of cancer. What conclusions would you draw?

Solution

Checking each death certificate is a trial. Success is a death from cancer. If the death rate from cancer in the town is the same as for the state, then $p = P(S) = .23$ and $q = .77$. The trial is repeated $n = 200$ times, so we have a binomial experiment. You may verify that both np and nq are at least 5. Thus the number of successes x may be viewed as approximately normal with

$$\mu = np = (200)(.23) = 46$$
$$\sigma = \sqrt{npq} = \sqrt{(200)(.23)(.77)} = \sqrt{35.42} \doteq 5.95$$

Therefore,

$$z = \frac{x - \mu}{\sigma} = \frac{x - 46}{5.95}$$

is approximately standard normal.

Let us find the probability of observing more than 57 deaths from cancer out of 200 deaths. Using the continuity correction, we want $P(x > 57.5)$. When $x = 57.5$,

$$z = \frac{57.5 - 46}{5.95} \doteq 1.93$$

Then using Appendix Table B.3,

$$P(x > 57.5) = P(z > 1.93) = .5 - .4732 = .0268$$

See Figure 7.25.

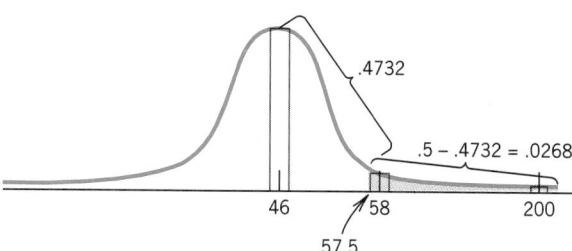

.4732

.5 − .4732 = .0268

46   58   200

57.5

Figure 7.25
$P(x > 57.5) = .5 - .4732 = .0268$

Therefore, it would be very unlikely (less than a 3% chance) that we would observe more than 57 out of 200 deaths from cancer if the death rate from cancer in this town were really only 23%. Since the observed number of deaths was 58, it would seem that the death rate from cancer in this town is higher than the rate for the entire state.

Note: You may ask why we did not calculate $P(57.5 < x < 200.5)$. The reason we did not is that the area under the curve to the right of 200.5 is practically 0. Therefore, including this area (probability) by calculating $P(x > 57.5)$ does not lead to a serious error. Also, it is easier to calculate $P(x > 57.5)$.

EXERCISES

In Exercises 7.29–7.34, assume that the experiment is a binomial experiment. Using (a) Appendix Table B.2 and (b) the normal approximation to the binomial, do the following.

7.29   Find the probability of 10 or more successes, where $n = 13$ and $p = .5$.

7.30   Find the probability of no more than 7 successes, where $n = 16$ and $p = .4$.

7.31   Find the probability of exactly 14 successes, where $n = 20$ and $p = .7$.

7.32   Find the probability of 9 or fewer successes, where $n = 14$ and $p = .4$.

7.33   Find the probability of between 5 and 7 successes inclusive, where $n = 15$ and $p = .6$.

7.34   Find the probability of exactly 10 successes, where $n = 12$ and $p = .5$.

7.35   A circuit board retailer receives a shipment of 800 boards. The manufacturer claims that only 1% of the boards are defective. If the claim is true, find the probability that the shipment contains 15 or more defective circuit boards.

7.36   A civil service multiple-choice examination consists of 100 questions with four choices per question. Suppose an applicant randomly guesses the answer to every question. Find the probability that the applicant will answer 35 or more questions correctly.

7.37   A city planning board denied a developer's request to increase the size of an existing mall. The board members claimed that they had the support of 60% of the voters.

(a) Suppose that 400 voters are selected and the planning board's claim is true. What is the probability that fewer than 211 voters will support the board's decision?

(b) Suppose that a sample of 400 voters shows that 210 voters supported the board's decision. Do you think the board's claim is valid? Why? (*Hint:* If the board is correct, would it be unlikely that fewer than 211 voters would support the board's decision?)

7.38   Suppose 65% of 45-year-olds with a diagnosed illness die between the ages of 45 to 50. Assume that 500 45-year-olds have the disease.

(a) What is the probability that between 305 and 345 inclusive will die within the next 5 years?

(b) The 500 were given a new treatment, and 295 died instead of the expected 325. Do you think 65% is still a plausible percentage for a population receiving the treatment? (*Hint:* If 65% were still correct, how likely is it that fewer than 296 would die?)

7.39   A hospital administrator claimed that an unusually large number of girls were born at the hospital in the preceding year. A check of the records showed that 120 girls and 75 boys had been born at the hospital the previous year. Do you think the administrator's claim is reasonable? Why?

7.40   A diastolic blood pressure reading of less than 90 mm is considered normal. Assume that $\frac{2}{3}$ of the participants in the Framingham Heart Study have diastolic blood pressure readings of less than 90 mm. In a random sample of 75 participants, what is the probability that 45 or more will have normal diastolic readings?

7.41   Between 1972 and 1974, 15 out of 405 teachers (3.7%) hired in Hazelwood, St. Louis County, Missouri, were black. The Equal Employment Opportunity Commission (EEOC) sued Hazelwood for discrimination under Title VII of the Civil Rights Act of 1964.

(a) The percentage of black school teachers in St. Louis County, plus the city of St. Louis, was 15.4%. Assuming a random sample of size 405 from a population of qualified teachers containing 15.4% blacks, find the approximate probability of observing fewer than 16 black teachers. Does your answer support the decision of a court of appeals that found discrimination against blacks?

(b) The Supreme Court vacated the decision of the court of appeals. It noted that the relevant job market might be St. Louis County alone (which does not include the city of St. Louis), where the percentage of black teachers was only 5.7%. Redo part (a) using this percentage.

For a discussion, see DeGroot, M., S. Fienberg, and J. Kadane, *Statistics and the Law,* New York: Wiley, 1986, pp. 1–48.

7.7

THE CENTRAL LIMIT THEOREM

Suppose that a company is considering publishing a book that prepares students for the Mathematical Scholastic Aptitude Test (MSAT). Let the variable x represent individual scores on the test. To investigate the effectiveness of the book, 50 students are selected by chance and are asked to use the book to study for the examination. Their scores are then obtained and the sample mean $\bar{x}$ is computed. Now the average for all students on the MSAT is 478 (as of 1993). If the 50 students had an average score of, say, 750 on the test, we would conclude that the book was quite effective. Of course, we might have gotten 50 very bright students by chance, but this seems unlikely. In other words, we concluded that the book is effective because it seems highly unlikely that the average score of the 50 students would be so high if the book were not effective.

In the previous discussion, we had to know something about what values of $\bar{x}$ were unlikely, based on general knowledge we had about SAT scores. However, it is not always so easy. We would like to have a better way of determining which values of $\bar{x}$ are likely and which are not.

The value of $\bar{x}$ could change from one sample of 50 students to the next. The fact is that $\bar{x}$ is a random variable. *What we are really interested in is the probability distribution of $\bar{x}$.* There are many situations in statistical inference similar to the one just discussed, where we need to know about the probability distribution of a sample mean $\bar{x}$ to make inferences about a random variable x.

For any random variable x, the **Central Limit Theorem** enables us to find probabilities associated with $\bar{x}$, because it tells us that under suitable conditions $\bar{x}$ will be approximately normal (even when x is not normal). Before stating this result more precisely, we present an example.

Suppose we have a box containing three tags labeled 1, 3, and 5. Consider the experiment of selecting a tag at random, that is, in such a way that each tag has equal likelihood of being selected. Let $x =$ the number on the tag selected. Since each number has an equal likelihood of being selected, $P(x) = \frac{1}{3}$ for $x = 1$, 3, and 5. Now consider the mean of each sample of size $n = 2$ that can be drawn with replacement. To obtain such a sample, we randomly select a tag, record its value, return it to the box, and then repeat the process. Let us find the probability distribution for $\bar{x}$. [To distinguish the distribution of $\bar{x}$ from that of x, we will use the symbol $Q(\bar{x})$ when dealing with the probability distribution of $\bar{x}$.] There are nine possible samples:

Possible Samples	$\bar{x}$
1, 1	1
1, 3	2
1, 5	3
3, 1	2
3, 3	3
3, 5	4
5, 1	3
5, 3	4
5, 5	5

Each sample has an equal likelihood of occurring and so has probability $\frac{1}{9}$. Using this fact, we may compute the probabilities associated with various values of $\bar{x}$. For example, the value $\bar{x} = 4$ can occur in two ways; therefore, $Q(4) = \frac{2}{9}$. The probability distribution of $\bar{x}$ is

$\bar{x}$	$Q(\bar{x})$
1	$\frac{1}{9}$
2	$\frac{2}{9}$
3	$\frac{3}{9}$
4	$\frac{2}{9}$
5	$\frac{1}{9}$

The probability histogram for $\bar{x}$ is shown in Figure 7.26.

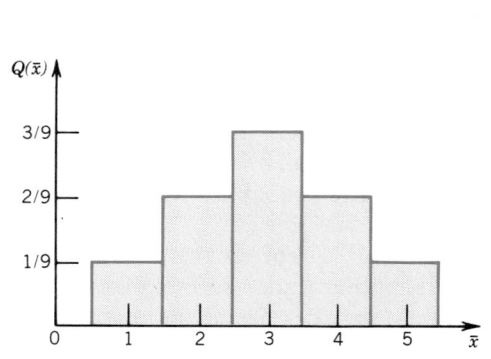

Figure 7.26
Probability Histogram for $\bar{x}$

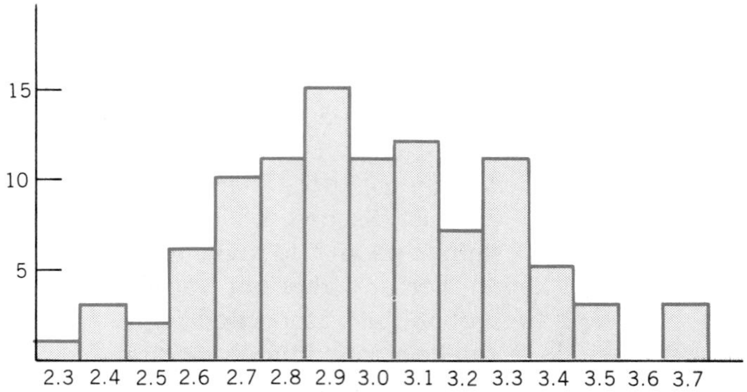

Figure 7.27
Histogram of 100 Sample Means for Samples of Size $n = 30$

Now we find the mean μ and variance σ^2 for x, and compare them with the mean $\mu_{\bar{x}}$ and variance $\sigma^2_{\bar{x}}$ for $\bar{x}$:

$$\mu = \sum x \cdot P(x) = (1)\left(\tfrac{1}{3}\right) + (3)\left(\tfrac{1}{3}\right) + (5)\left(\tfrac{1}{3}\right) = 3$$

$$\sigma^2 = \sum (x - \mu)^2 \cdot P(x) = (1-3)^2\left(\tfrac{1}{3}\right) + (3-3)^2\left(\tfrac{1}{3}\right) + (5-3)^2\left(\tfrac{1}{3}\right)$$

$$= \frac{4}{3} + 0 + \frac{4}{3} = \frac{8}{3}$$

$$\mu_{\bar{x}} = \sum \bar{x} \cdot Q(\bar{x})$$

$$= (1)\left(\tfrac{1}{9}\right) + (2)\left(\tfrac{2}{9}\right) + (3)\left(\tfrac{3}{9}\right) + (4)\left(\tfrac{2}{9}\right) + (5)\left(\tfrac{1}{9}\right)$$

$$= \frac{1+4+9+8+5}{9} = \tfrac{27}{9} = 3$$

$$\sigma^2_{\bar{x}} = \sum (\bar{x} - \mu_{\bar{x}})^2 \cdot Q(\bar{x})$$

$$= (1-3)^2\left(\tfrac{1}{9}\right) + (2-3)^2\left(\tfrac{2}{9}\right) + (3-3)^2\left(\tfrac{3}{9}\right) + (4-3)^2\left(\tfrac{2}{9}\right) + (5-3)^2\left(\tfrac{1}{9}\right)$$

$$= \frac{4}{9} + \frac{2}{9} + 0 + \frac{2}{9} + \frac{4}{9} = \frac{12}{9} = \frac{4}{3}$$

Note that

- $\mu_{\bar{x}} = \mu$
- $\sigma^2_{\bar{x}} = \sigma^2/2$. Since $n = 2$ was the sample size, we can say that $\sigma^2_{\bar{x}} = \sigma^2/n$. (So $\sigma_{\bar{x}} = \sigma/\sqrt{n}$.)
- The probability histogram in Figure 7.26 is somewhat bell-shaped. If the sample size were to increase, the values of $\bar{x}$ would start to fill in a portion of the axis like continuous data. For example, for samples of size $n = 3$ drawn from the three tags, the possible values of $\bar{x}$ are 1, $1\tfrac{2}{3}$, $2\tfrac{1}{3}$, 3, $3\tfrac{2}{3}$, $4\tfrac{1}{3}$, and 5. A histogram would more and more resemble a normal curve as the sample size increased. This suggests that when n is large enough, $\bar{x}$ will be approximately normal. Figure 7.27 depicts a computer-generated frequency histogram describing 100 sample means for samples of size 30. (The values on the horizontal axis are the midpoints of the classes.)

These ideas generalize to other random variables.

> **Central Limit Theorem**   Let x represent data values from a population with mean μ and standard deviation σ, and let $\bar{x}$ represent the sample mean defined for random samples of size n. Then $\bar{x}$ is a random variable with the following properties:
>
> 1. The mean of $\bar{x}$ is $\mu_{\bar{x}} = \mu$.
> 2. The standard deviation of $\bar{x}$ is $\sigma_{\bar{x}} = \sigma/\sqrt{n}$.
> 3. $\bar{x}$ will be approximately normal when n is sufficiently large ($n \geq 30$ will usually be sufficient). The larger the value of n, the closer the distribution of $\bar{x}$ will be to normality.

Figure 7.28 illustrates the Central Limit Theorem for a particular population.

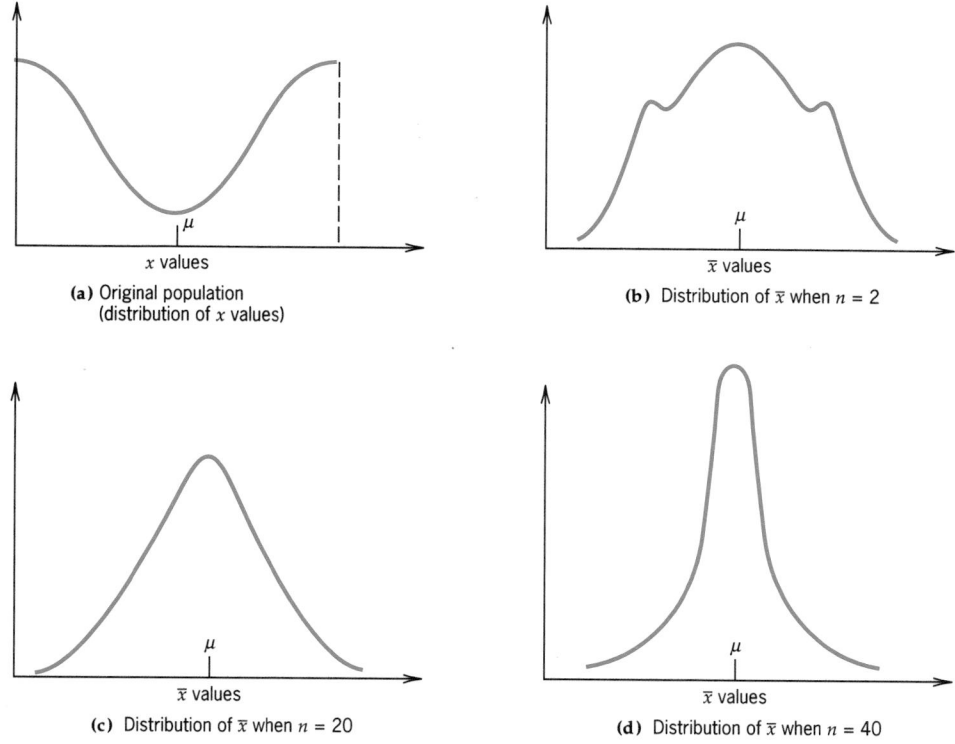

(a) Original population
(distribution of x values)

(b) Distribution of $\bar{x}$ when $n = 2$

(c) Distribution of $\bar{x}$ when $n = 20$

(d) Distribution of $\bar{x}$ when $n = 40$

Figure 7.28
As the Sample Size n Becomes Larger, the Distribution of $\bar{x}$ Approaches Normality and $\sigma_{\bar{x}}$ Becomes Smaller.

Two points should be mentioned in connection with the Central Limit Theorem:

1. The quantity $\sigma_{\bar{x}}$ is sometimes called the *standard error of the mean*.
2. The Central Limit Theorem states that $\bar{x}$ will be approximately normal for "n sufficiently large." We said that $n \geq 30$ will usually suffice. We use 30 as a

dividing point between large and small samples. So if $n \geq 30$, the sample is said to be *large*. If $n < 30$, the sample is *small*. Note that we do not require x to be normal for $\bar{x}$ to be (approximately) normal. We do not even require x to be continuous. However, if x happens to be normal (or approximately normal), then $\bar{x}$ will be normal (or approximately normal) for all values of n.

The Central Limit Theorem can be offered as a possible explanation of the fact that so many variables encountered in nature are normal. Consider the variable "Height of an adult male American." Height is influenced by many factors: the height of one's ancestors as well as other genetic and environmental factors. Perhaps we can think of height as a type of mean of all these factors. If height is a mean, this would explain why it is approximately normal.

Here is another example: Let x be the number of dots showing on the toss of a die. The probability histogram for x is shown in Figure 7.29. Now look at the data in Table 7.1. This table contains 25 random samples of size $n = 10$ obtained by tossing the die. Each sample is obtained by tossing the die 10 times and recording the number (x) on the face showing each time. A frequency histogram for the sample means is given in Figure 7.30. The shape suggests normality, even though the sample size $(n = 10)$ is less than 30.

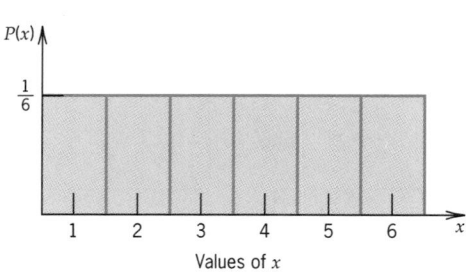

Figure 7.29
Probability Histogram for x = Number of Dots Observed When a Die Is Tossed

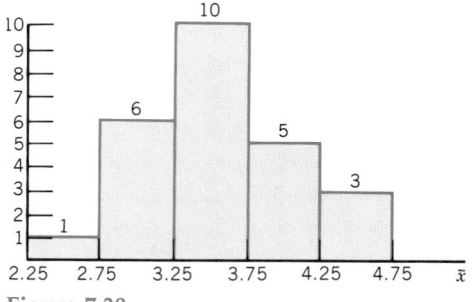

Figure 7.30
Frequency Histogram for the Sample Means of Table 7.1

The mean of the 25 values of $\bar{x}$ in Table 7.1 is 3.52 and the standard deviation is .53. The 25 samples in Table 7.1 do not constitute all possible random samples. (There are over 60 million possibilities.) But we can think of 3.52 and .53 as estimates for the mean and standard deviation of *all* the possible values of $\bar{x}$, denoted by $\mu_{\bar{x}}$ and $\sigma_{\bar{x}}$, respectively. Let's see how these estimates check with the values predicted by the Central Limit Theorem.

For the random variable x = the number of dots showing on the die, the probability distribution is

$$P(x) = \tfrac{1}{6} \quad \text{for } x = 1, 2, 3, 4, 5, 6$$

Now

$$\mu = \sum x \cdot P(x)$$
$$= (1)\left(\tfrac{1}{6}\right) + (2)\left(\tfrac{1}{6}\right) + (3)\left(\tfrac{1}{6}\right) + (4)\left(\tfrac{1}{6}\right) + (5)\left(\tfrac{1}{6}\right) + (6)\left(\tfrac{1}{6}\right) = 3.5$$
$$\sigma^2 = \left[\sum x^2 \cdot P(x)\right] - \mu^2 = (1)\left(\tfrac{1}{6}\right) + (4)\left(\tfrac{1}{6}\right)$$
$$+ (9)\left(\tfrac{1}{6}\right) + (16)\left(\tfrac{1}{6}\right) + (25)\left(\tfrac{1}{6}\right) + (36)\left(\tfrac{1}{6}\right) - (3.5)^2 \doteq 2.92$$

Table 7.1
Sample Obtained by Tossing a Die

Sample Number	Samples of Size $n = 10$										Sample Mean $\bar{x}$
1	1	3	2	5	3	3	6	5	2	1	3.1
2	3	5	6	3	4	6	3	5	4	6	4.5
3	5	1	1	3	2	2	4	4	5	3	3.0
4	4	2	4	5	6	4	4	3	2	6	4.0
5	2	3	2	2	5	6	1	5	5	3	3.4
6	3	4	6	4	3	5	3	3	6	6	4.3
7	1	2	5	2	3	6	1	5	3	3	3.1
8	3	1	1	3	1	1	6	5	4	3	2.8
9	4	4	3	6	2	6	5	1	2	1	3.4
10	3	6	1	4	6	4	3	2	3	6	3.8
11	6	5	3	5	1	1	6	1	2	1	3.1
12	1	6	3	3	6	2	6	5	4	1	3.7
13	3	4	2	6	3	6	6	3	1	6	4.0
14	5	1	3	3	5	1	1	1	2	1	2.3
15	3	1	6	1	5	4	5	5	1	2	3.3
16	4	6	3	5	3	3	4	2	6	1	3.7
17	4	6	4	3	2	3	4	3	3	1	3.3
18	5	2	6	6	2	2	5	1	6	2	3.7
19	2	6	6	6	5	4	1	3	5	3	4.1
20	2	4	1	6	2	3	5	6	3	3	3.5
21	3	2	1	3	5	5	3	2	5	4	3.3
22	4	5	5	3	5	5	4	2	4	6	4.3
23	2	3	4	1	2	6	2	4	3	6	3.3
24	4	5	5	3	3	2	6	4	3	5	4.0
25	3	2	2	6	3	2	3	4	1	3	2.9

so that

$$\sigma = \sqrt{2.92} \doteq 1.71$$

Therefore, according to the Central Limit Theorem,

$$\mu_{\bar{x}} = \mu = 3.5$$

$$\sigma_{\bar{x}} = \frac{\sigma}{\sqrt{n}} = \frac{1.71}{\sqrt{10}} \doteq .54$$

These true values and the estimates agree quite closely.

Probabilities associated with values of a sample mean may be found by viewing $\bar{x}$ as normal (when the sample size n is at least 30) and using the mean and standard deviation given in the Central Limit Theorem. You may have noted a similarity between this section and the last section, where we said that a binomial variable may be viewed as (approximately) normal under certain conditions. There is an important difference, however: *When finding probabilities associated with $\bar{x}$, we will not make any continuity correction.* The only time we will make a continuity correction in this book is when we approximate binomial probabilities by using a normal distribution.

EXAMPLE 7.15

Let x represent the scores on a mathematics achievement test given to eighth-grade students. Suppose that for the population of all scores on the test, the mean is $\mu = 50$ and the standard deviation is $\sigma = 15$. If a random sample of 100 values of x is to be obtained, find the probability that the sample mean $\bar{x}$ will be between 51 and 53; that is, find $P(51 < \bar{x} < 53)$.

Solution

According to the Central Limit Theorem, we may view $\bar{x}$ as approximately normal with

$$\mu_{\bar{x}} = \mu = 50 \quad \text{and} \quad \sigma_{\bar{x}} = \frac{\sigma}{\sqrt{n}} = \frac{15}{\sqrt{100}} = 1.5$$

Therefore,

$$z = \frac{\bar{x} - \mu_{\bar{x}}}{\sigma_{\bar{x}}} = \frac{\bar{x} - \mu}{\sigma/\sqrt{n}} = \frac{\bar{x} - 50}{1.5}$$

is approximately standard normal. When $\bar{x} = 51$,

$$z = \frac{51 - 50}{1.5} \doteq .67$$

When $\bar{x} = 53$,

$$z = \frac{53 - 50}{1.5} = 2$$

Therefore, using Appendix Table B.3,

$$P(51 < \bar{x} < 53) = P(.67 < z < 2)$$
$$= (\text{area from 0 to 2}) - (\text{area from 0 to .67})$$
$$= .4772 - .2486 = .2286$$

See Figure 7.31.

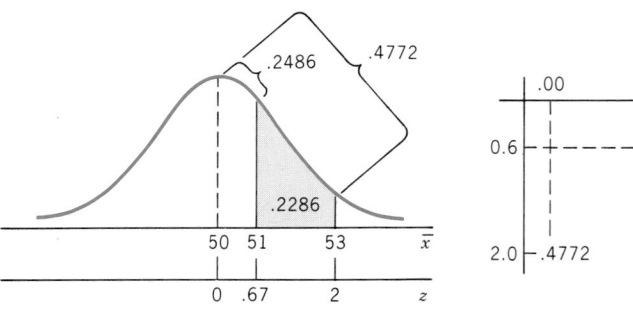

Figure 7.31
$P(51 < \bar{x} < 53) = .4772 - .2486 = .2286$

EXAMPLE 7.16

A company has been producing a 60-watt light bulb with a mean life of 750 hours and a standard deviation of 30 hours. An engineer developed a new process for producing the bulb. It was believed that bulbs produced by the new process would

$n = 36$

show the same standard deviation but possibly a longer mean lifetime. Thirty-six bulbs produced by the new process were tested and showed a (sample) mean lifetime of 765 hours.

$\mu_{\bar{x}} = 765$

(a) If the (population) mean lifetime μ of bulbs produced by the new process were still 750 hours, find the probability of getting a value of the sample mean as large as or larger than 765.

(b) What conclusions might be drawn from the answer to part (a)?

Solution

(a) We use x to represent the lifetime of an arbitrary bulb produced by the new process. A sample of size $n = 36$ gave $\bar{x} = 765$. We must find the probability of getting a value of $\bar{x} \geq 765$. We are assuming for the moment that $\mu = 750$. We are also given that $\sigma = 30$. By the Central Limit Theorem, $\bar{x}$ is approximately normal with

$$\mu_{\bar{x}} = \mu = 750 \quad \text{and} \quad \sigma_{\bar{x}} = \frac{\sigma}{\sqrt{n}} = \frac{30}{\sqrt{36}} = \frac{30}{6} = 5$$

so that

$$z = \frac{\bar{x} - \mu_{\bar{x}}}{\sigma_{\bar{x}}} = \frac{\bar{x} - 750}{5}$$

is approximately standard normal. When $\bar{x} = 765$,

$$z = \frac{765 - 750}{5} = 3$$

From Appendix Table B.3,

$$P(\bar{x} \geq 765) = P(z \geq 3) = .5 - P(0 < z < 3) = .5 - .4987 = .0013$$

See Figure 7.32.

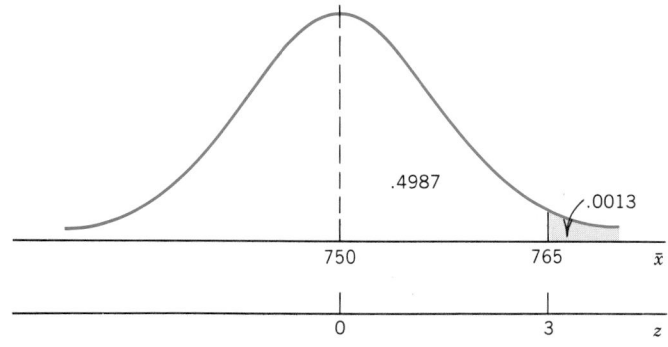

Figure 7.32
$P(\bar{x} \geq 765) = .5 - .4987 = .0013$

(b) Notice that the probability obtained in part (a) is very small. It tells us that if the mean lifetime μ were only 750 hours, it would be very unlikely that we would observe a sample mean lifetime as large as or larger than 765 hours (only about a .1% chance). Therefore, since we did observe such a large value for $\bar{x}$, we would be inclined to conclude that μ is not really 750 hours but in fact more. In other words, the new process appears to increase the mean lifetime. So we have decided that a value of $\bar{x} = 765$ hours should not be regarded as a routine chance fluctuation above an average of 750 hours, but instead should be interpreted as reflecting a real difference between the old and new processes.

Remark In Example 7.16, we used a probability value to make a decision about a population. We concluded that the mean lifetime μ for the population of bulbs produced by the new process would be more than 750 hours. (We used a similar technique in Example 7.14.) The probability .0013 used to make our decision is called a *P*-value. We will have more to say about *P*-values in Chapter 8, including a formal definition.

EXERCISES

7.42 Consider the following probability distribution.

x	$P(x)$
1	$\frac{1}{6}$
2	$\frac{2}{6}$
3	$\frac{3}{6}$

(a) Verify that $\mu = \frac{7}{3}$ and $\sigma^2 = \frac{5}{9}$.

Now consider the sample mean $\bar{x}$ for random samples of size 49.

(b) What is the largest value that $\bar{x}$ can assume? The smallest?

(c) According to the Central Limit Theorem, what are the values of $\mu_{\bar{x}}$ and $\sigma_{\bar{x}}^2$?

(d) What can be said about the distribution of sample means? Why?

7.43 This exercise illustrates the concept of $\bar{x}$ as a random variable. Suppose that a large urn contains a collection of balls, $\frac{1}{3}$ of them numbered 0, $\frac{1}{3}$ of them numbered 2, and $\frac{1}{3}$ of them numbered 4. An experiment consists of selecting a ball, noting its number, putting the ball back into the urn, selecting another ball, and noting its number. There are nine distinct ordered pairs of numbers that can be obtained, namely, $(0, 0)$, $(0, 2)$, $(0, 4)$, $(2, 0)$, $(2, 2)$, $(2, 4)$, $(4, 0)$, $(4, 2)$, and $(4, 4)$. For example, $(2, 4)$ means that a 2 was selected first, followed by a 4. Note that $\bar{x} = 3$ for the pair $(2, 4)$.

(a) Obtain the probability distribution for $\bar{x}$.

(b) Find $\mu_{\bar{x}}$ and $\sigma_{\bar{x}}^2$.

Let $x =$ the number of the ball obtained on any selection. Then the probability distribution for x is given by

x	$P(x)$
0	$\frac{1}{3}$
2	$\frac{1}{3}$
4	$\frac{1}{3}$

(c) For this distribution, find (i) μ and (ii) σ^2 with formulas from Chapter 6. Compare with part (b), and note that $\mu_{\bar{x}} = \mu$ and $\sigma_{\bar{x}}^2 = \sigma^2/n$, where $n = 2$ is the sample size.

7.44   A population has mean 325 and variance 144. Suppose the distribution of sample means is generated by random samples of size 36.

(a)   Find $\mu_{\bar{x}}$ and $\sigma_{\bar{x}}$.   (b)   Find $P(\bar{x} < 323)$.

(c)   Find $P(320 \leq \bar{x} \leq 322)$.   (d)   Find $P(\bar{x} > 328)$.

(e)   Find $P(321 < \bar{x} < 327)$.

7.45   A normal population has mean 200 and standard deviation 100. Suppose that the distribution of sample means is generated by samples of size $n = 100$.

(a)   Find $\mu_{\bar{x}}$.   (b)   Find $\sigma_{\bar{x}}$.

(c)   Find $P(195 < \bar{x} < 205)$.   (d)   Find $P(\bar{x} > 210)$.

(e)   If one x value is selected, find $P(195 < x < 205)$. Compare with part (c).

(f)   If one x value is selected, find $P(x > 210)$. Compare with part (d).

7.46   Refer to Exercise 7.45. Suppose that the distribution of sample means is generated by samples of size $n = 400$.

(a)   Find $\mu_{\bar{x}}$.   (b)   Find $\sigma_{\bar{x}}$.

(c)   Without calculating, do you believe that $P(195 < \bar{x} < 205)$ is smaller, equal to, or larger than the answer obtained in Exercise 7.45, part (c)? Now calculate $P(195 < \bar{x} < 205)$.

(d)   Without calculating, do you believe that $P(\bar{x} > 210)$ is smaller, equal to, or larger than the answer obtained in Exercise 7.45, part (d)? Now calculate $P(\bar{x} > 210)$.

7.47   At a city high school, past records indicate that the MSAT scores of students have a mean of 510 and a standard deviation of 90. One hundred students in the high school are to take the test. What is the probability that their mean score will be

(a)   More than 530?

(b)   Less than 500?

(c)   Between 495 and 515?

7.48   At a large factory, the mean wage is $42,500 and the standard deviation is $2000. What is the probability that the mean wage of 75 randomly selected workers will exceed $43,000?

7.49   An appliance manufacturer claimed that the mean life of his product is 1200 hours. Assume that the standard deviation is 120 hours. A consumer agency decides to randomly select 35 items and will reject the claim if $\bar{x} < 1160$ hours. If the manufacturer's claim is true, what is the probability that the claim will be rejected?

7.50   A computer simulated samples of size 50 from a distribution with mean 226 and standard deviation 45. One hundred mean values were obtained.

(a)   What should be the approximate mean of the 100 sample means?

(b)   What should be the approximate standard deviation of the 100 sample means?

(c)   About how many of the 100 means should be larger than 230?

7.51   A grocery store produce manager is told by a wholesaler that the apples in a large shipment have a mean weight of 6 ounces and a standard deviation of 1 ounce. The manager is going to randomly select 100 apples.

(a)   Assuming the wholesaler's claim is true, find the probability that the mean weight of the sample is more than 5.9 ounces.

(b)   The manager decides to return the shipment if the mean weight of the sample is less than 5.75 ounces. Assuming the wholesaler's claim is true, find the probability that the shipment of apples will be returned.

(c)   Suppose the retailer is willing to risk a 1% chance of returning the shipment if the wholesaler's claim is true. Let W be the mean weight of the sample below which the shipment will be returned. Find the value of W.

7.52   A biology teacher had noted that the scores on a standardized examination attained by students from her past classes had a mean of 74 and a standard deviation of 14. The teacher decided to use a new book. She believed this would increase the mean, but that the standard deviation would remain at 14. Using the new book, a class of 50 students had a mean of 76 on the standardized examination.

(a)   Find the probability that a class of 50 students using the new book will have a (sample) mean as large as or larger than 76 if the new book were equivalent to the old book (i.e., if $\mu = 74$ and $\sigma = 14$ for all students using the new book).

(b)   Do you think that there is evidence to support the teacher's claim that the new book is superior? [*Hint:*   Use part (a).]

7.53   In Section 7.7, we considered the distribution of sample means obtained by sampling from the probability distribution $P(x) = \frac{1}{3}$ for $x = 1, 3, 5$. Recall that $\mu = 3$ and $\sigma^2 = \frac{8}{3}$. This problem concerns samples of size $n = 100, 25,$ and 10. In each case, 1000 samples were generated and the sample means computed. Boxplots for each case are given here.

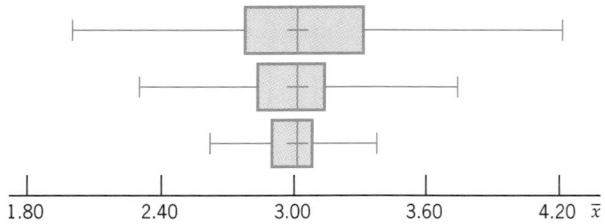

(a)   For each sample size $(100, 25, 10)$, what is the approximate mean of the 1000 samples in each case? The approximate variance?

(b)   Identify the boxplot that most likely corresponds to the case for $n = 100, n = 25, n = 10$.

7.8

USING MINITAB (OPTIONAL)

For discrete distributions, PDF gives values of the probability distribution $P(x)$, which are probabilities. For continuous distributions, PDF also gives values of the probability distribution, represented by the symbol $f(x)$. We have seen, however, that values of $f(x)$ are not probabilities. Probabilities are areas under the graph. Hence, the PDF command is not quite as useful for continuous distributions.

However, the CDF command is quite useful. Figure 7.33 shows the area computed from a normal distribution by the CDF command.

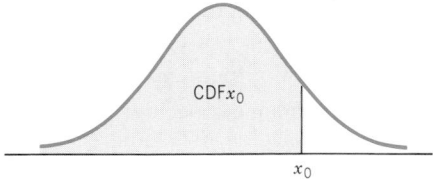

Figure 7.33
CDFx_0 Is the Area Under the Curve to the Left of x_0.

The heights of adult females are approximately normal with $\mu = 64$ inches and $\sigma = 2.5$ inches. To find the proportion of females shorter than 68 inches:

Session Commands

MTB > CDF 68;
SUBC> NORMAL 64 2.5.

Dialog Box

Calc ▶Probability Distributions ▶Normal
Click **Cumulative probability**
Type *64* for **Mean**
Type *2.5* for **Standard deviation**
Click **Input constant** and Type *68* in box
Click **OK**

Minitab would give the value .9452.

Suppose we wanted the proportion of females with heights between 65 and 68 inches. Figure 7.34 suggests how to do this using Minitab.

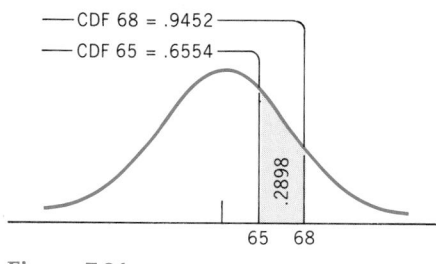

—CDF 68 = .9452—
—CDF 65 = .6554—

.2898

65   68

Figure 7.34
$P(65 < x < 68) = .9452 - .6554 = .2898$

The following Minitab program computes the desired probability. Note the abbreviated form of the subcommand—we need only the word NORMAL plus two numbers: the mean and standard deviation. Assume the values 65 and 68 are in column 1.

Session Commands

MTB > CDF C1 STORE IN C2;
SUBC>   NORMAL 64 2.5.
MTB > LET K1 = C2(2) − C2(1)
MTB > PRINT K1

C2
0.655422
0.945201

Dialog Box

Calc ▶Probability Distributions ▶Normal
Click **Cumulative probability**
Type *64* for **Mean**
Type *2.5* for **Standard deviation**
Type *C1* for **Input column**
Type *C2* for **Optional storage column**
Click **OK**

Calc ▶Mathematical Expressions
Type *K1* in **Variable** box
Type *C2(2) - C2(1)* in **Expression** box
Click **OK**

File ▶Display Data
Type *K1* in **Display** box
Click **OK**

Output

Data Display

K1   0.289779

We have seen in Figure 7.34 that the proportion of females shorter than 68 inches is .9452. So CDF 68 = .9452. Therefore, according to the definition of the INVCDF command described in Chapter 6,

$$INVCDF\ .9452 = 68$$

Another way to look at this is that 68 is the 94.52 percentile. Thus the INVCDF command can be used to find percentiles.

In Example 7.11, we considered percentiles for the scores of males on the MSAT. The following program gives the 90th percentile, 628:

Session Commands	Dialog Box
MTB > INVCDF .90; SUBC> NORMAL 500 100.	Calc ▶Probability Distributions ▶Normal Click **Inverse cumulative probability** Type *500* for **Mean** Type *100* for **Standard deviation** Click **Input constant**, and type *.90* in box Click **OK**

Output

Inverse Cumulative Distribution Function

Normal with mean = 500.000 and standard deviation = 100.000

```
P( X <= x)              x
   0.9000        628.1552
```

INVCDF can also be used to find values of the standard normal variable such as $z_{.025}$. We have seen that $z_{.025} = 1.96$. The area to the right of $z_{.025}$ under the standard normal curve is .025. (See Figure 7.14.) Hence the area to the left of $z_{.025}$ is $1 - .025 = .975$. This means that

$$z_{.025} = INVCDF\ .975$$

The following program returns the value of $z_{.025}$:

$$INVCDF\ .975$$

Note: If no subcommand is used with PDF, CDF, or INVCDF, Minitab assumes a standard normal distribution.

Simulation

The RANDOM command can be used 'to generate samples from various distributions (populations). The distribution to be used is specified by a subcommand. The following program generates a sample of 100 values of a binomial variable for which $n = 16$ and $p = .5$. Recall that $\mu = 8$ and $\sigma = 2$ for such a binomial variable. In Section 7.6, we examined this binomial distribution and noted that it is approximated by a normal distribution. The following reflects this.

Session Commands	**Dialog Box**
MTB > RANDOM 100 VALUES INTO C1;	**Calc ▶Random Data ▶Binomial**
SUBC> BINOMIAL N = 16, P = .5.	Type *100* after **Generate**
MTB > DESCRIBE C1	Type *C1* after **Store in column**
MTB > HISTOGRAM C1;	Type *16* for **Number of trials**
SUBC> MIDPOINTS 0:16.	Type *.5* for **Probability of success**
	Click **OK**

Stat ▶Basic Statistics ▶Descriptive Statistics
Type *C1* in **Variable** box
Click **OK**

Graph ▶Histogram
Type *C1* under **X**
Click **Options**
Click **Midpoint/cutpoint positions**
Type *0:16* in box
Click **OK** twice

Output

Descriptive Statistics

Variable	N	Mean	Median	TrMean	StDev	SEMean
C1	100	7.980	8.000	7.967	2.193	0.219

Variable	Min	Max	Q1	Q3
C1	4.000	13.000	6.000	10.000

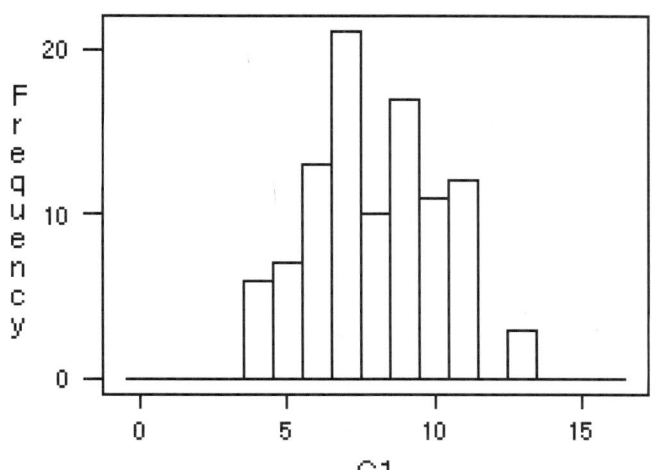

Note the bell-shaped histogram.

The RANDOM command can place data in several columns at once. Consider the following printout:

Session Commands	Dialog Box
MTB > RANDOM 10 VALUES INTO C1 - C5;	Calc ▶Random Data ▶Normal
SUBC> NORMAL MU = 60, SIGMA = 4.	Type *10* after **Generate**
MTB > PRINT C1 - C5	Type *C1 − C5* after **Store in columns**
	Type *60* for **Mean**
	Type *4* for **Standard deviation**
	Click **OK**
	File ▶**Display Data**
	Type *C1 − C5* in box
	Click **OK**

Output

Data Display

ROW	C1	C2	C3	C4	C5
1	56.4312	60.8153	49.8243	57.9456	59.7937
2	53.1379	68.4529	55.1153	63.0129	67.7372
3	64.8729	61.1107	61.2268	63.6500	62.0051
4	61.7565	60.5206	62.4910	67.2951	65.1568
5	58.6765	60.5093	60.4830	60.2945	55.3945
6	59.3649	54.5494	57.1270	62.5233	59.1065
7	66.5755	61.5291	63.1417	61.2651	64.9362
8	55.6163	66.3027	62.5761	62.4052	57.1530
9	61.8896	56.2025	51.5280	56.2052	58.5584
10	54.5946	53.6515	58.8242	61.5699	62.0890

There are two ways to look at this. We can view this as 5 columns, each containing a sample of size 10 or as 10 rows, each containing a sample of size 5. In some ways, the latter interpretation is more useful, because Minitab has some very nice commands that operate on rows. The row mean command RMEAN is one of these. We could have added the following command after the subcommand:

$$\text{RMEAN FOR C1} - \text{C5 PUT IN C6}$$

This command computes the mean for each row and puts it in C6. Column 6 then contains 10 values of $\bar{x}$ for samples of size 5.

In Section 7.7, we simulated 25 samples of 10 rolls of a die and then looked at the 25 sample means. Let's use Minitab to generate 50 samples of size 40. We could then obtain 50 values of $\bar{x}$ using the RMEAN command. According to the Central Limit Theorem, $\bar{x}$ should be approximately normal. First we store the values for x (the number on the roll of a die) in C1 and the probabilities $P(x)$ in C2. Note that $P(x) = 1/6 \doteq .16667$. Assume columns 1 and 2 are:

C1	C2
1	.16667
2	.16667
3	.16667
4	.16667
5	.16667
6	.16667

We then generate 40 columns (C3–C42), each containing 50 values of x. The 50 row means are stored in column 43. We then describe C43 and produce a histogram.

Session Commands

MTB > RANDOM 50 C3 − C42;
SUBC>   DISCRETE C1 C2.
MTB > RMEAN C3 − C42, PUT IN C43
MTB > DESCRIBE C43

Dialog Box

Calc ▶Random Data ▶Discrete
Type *50* after **Generate**
Type *C3 − C42* after **Store in ...**
Type *C1* after **Values in**
Type *C2* after **Probabilities in**
Click **OK**

Calc ▶Row Statistics
Click **Mean**
Type *C3 − C42* in **Input** box
Type *C43* in **Store results in**
Click **OK**

Stat ▶Basic Statistics ▶Descriptive Statistics
Type *C43* in **Variables** box
Click **OK**

Output

Descriptive Statistics

Variable	N	Mean	Median	TrMean	StDev	SEMean
C43	50	3.4285	3.4500	3.4295	0.3265	0.0462

Variable	Min	Max	Q1	Q3
C43	2.7500	4.1000	3.1750	3.6500

MTB> HISTOGRAM C43

Graph ▶Histogram
Type *C43* under **X**
Click **OK**

Output

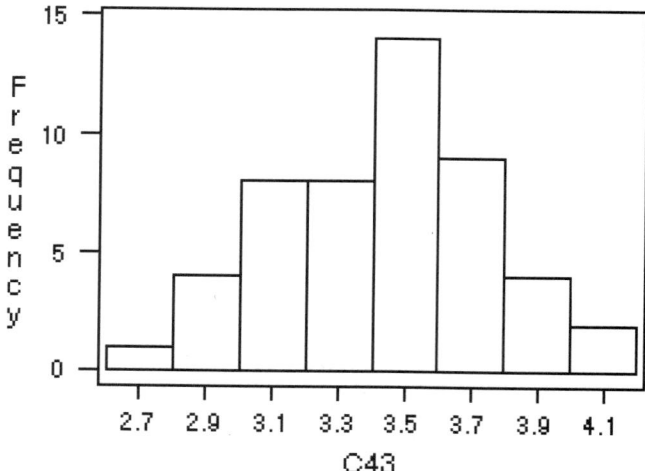

In Section 7.7, we saw that for the number observed on the roll of a die,

$$\mu_{\bar{x}} = \mu = 3.5$$

$$\sigma_{\bar{x}} = \frac{\sigma}{\sqrt{n}} = \frac{1.71}{\sqrt{40}} \doteq .27$$

We see that the mean for C43 is 3.4285 and the standard deviation is .3265. This is consistent with the Central Limit Theorem. So is the histogram, which looks fairly normal.

PRACTICE QUIZ (Answers are after the Review Exercises.)

Without using Minitab, give the approximate values that will be returned by the programs in Questions 1–4. Also indicate what the values represent.

1. CDF 70, STORE IN K1;
       NORMAL 50 10.
    LET K2 = 1 - K1
    PRINT K2

2. SET C1
    60 70
    END
    CDF C1, STORE IN C2;
       NORMAL 50 10.
    LET K1 = C2(2) - C2(1)
    PRINT K1

3. INVCDF .75;
       NORMAL 50 10.

4. INVCDF .90

5. Write a single program to compute $z_{.01}$, $z_{.025}$, $z_{.05}$, and $z_{.10}$.

EXERCISES

Suggested exercises for use with Minitab are 7.62, 7.63, 7.64, 7.65, and 7.80.

7.9

SUMMARY

In this chapter, we studied **continuous probability distributions** (i.e., probability distributions for continuous random variables). The most important class of continuous probability distributions is the class of **normal distributions**. The **standard normal random variable** z is the normal variable that has mean 0 and standard deviation 1. Appendix Table B.3 can be used to find probabilities associated with z. If x is a normal variable with mean μ and standard deviation σ, we can find probabilities associated with x by using the standard score of x, $z = (x - \mu)/\sigma$, which has the standard normal distribution.

We showed how a binomial distribution may be approximated by a normal distribution with mean $\mu = np$ and standard deviation $\sigma = \sqrt{npq}$ when both np and nq are at least 5.

Finally, we studied the **Central Limit Theorem**. This important theorem tells us that if x is a random variable with mean μ and standard deviation σ, then the sample mean $\bar{x}$ for random samples of size n has the following properties:

1. $\mu_{\bar{x}} = \mu$
2. $\sigma_{\bar{x}} = \sigma/\sqrt{n}$
3. When $n \geq 30$, $\bar{x}$ will be approximately normal.

We will see in later chapters that the Central Limit Theorem is extremely important in the study of statistical inference.

REVIEW EXERCISES

7.54 Let x represent the time in hours required to repair a machine. The probability distribution follows.

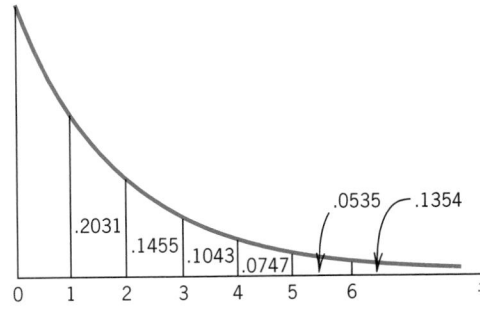

What is the probability that the machine will be repaired in

(a) Less than 1 hour?   (b) More than 6 hours?

(c) Between 1 and 3 hours?   (d) More than 1 hour?

(e) Either less than 2 hours or more than 3 hours?

7.55 Let x be a continuous random variable with the following probability distribution.

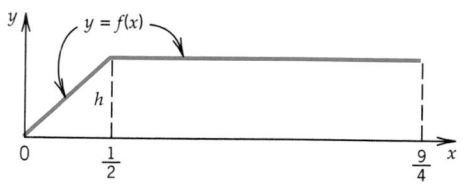

Assume that $P(0 < x < \frac{1}{2}) = \frac{1}{8}$.

(a) What is the value of h?

(b) Find the expression $f(x)$. [*Hint:* Find $f(x)$ when $0 \le x < \frac{1}{2}$, then $f(x)$ when $\frac{1}{2} \le x \le \frac{9}{4}$.]

(c) Find $P(\frac{1}{2} < x < \frac{9}{4})$.   (d) Find $P(1 < x < \frac{9}{4})$.

(e) Find $P(0 < x < \frac{7}{4})$.   (f) Find $P(0 \le x < \frac{1}{4})$.

7.56 Let x be a continuous random variable with the following probability distribution.

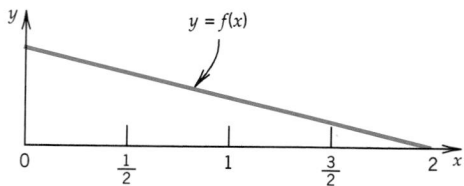

Suppose that $f(0) = 1, f(\frac{1}{2}) = \frac{3}{4}, f(1) = \frac{1}{2}, f(\frac{3}{2}) = \frac{1}{4}, f(2) = 0$. An x value is randomly selected. Find the following:

(a) $P(0 < x < 1)$ (b) $P(\frac{1}{2} < x < 1)$

(c) $P(x > \frac{3}{2})$ (d) $P(x < \frac{1}{2})$

[*Hint:* Use the idea of area under the curve representing probability. Then use the formula for the area of a triangle.]

7.57 Let x be the number of years a person teaches in a public school system. The probability distribution follows.

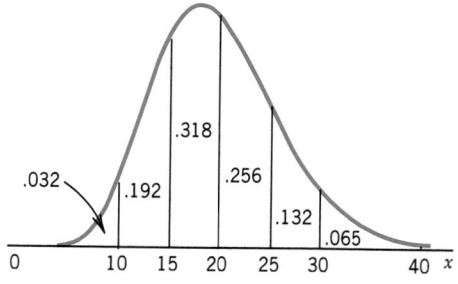

Find the percentage of teachers who teach in the system

(a) At most 15 years

(b) Between 10 and 25 years

(c) More than 30 years

7.58　Let x represent the length of life (in years) for an electrical component. The probability distribution for x follows.

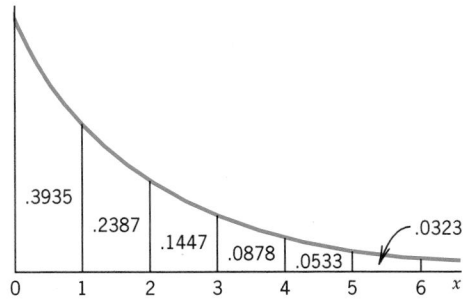

(a)　What is the total area under the curve?

What is the probability that a randomly selected component will last

(b)　Longer than 6 years?　(c)　Between 2 and 4 years?

(d)　Longer than 1 year?　(e)　Less than 2 years?

7.59　Let z represent the standard normal variable, and suppose a value of z is randomly selected. To find each of the following probabilities, (i) draw the standard normal curve and indicate the area representing the probability, (ii) express the probability in terms of areas from 0 to appropriate values of z, and (iii) calculate the answer obtained from Appendix Table B.3.

(a)　$P(0 < z < 1.86)$　(b)　$P(-1.48 < z < 0)$

(c)　$P(-1.02 < z < 2.74)$　(d)　$P(1.09 < z < 1.34)$

(e)　$P(-.99 < z < -.30)$

7.60　Let z represent the standard normal variable, and suppose a value of z is randomly selected. To find each of the following probabilities, (i) draw the standard normal curve and indicate the area representing the probability, (ii) express the probability in terms of areas from 0 to appropriate values of z, and (iii) calculate the answer obtained from Appendix Table B.3.

(a)　$P(z < 1.71)$　(b)　$P(z < -1.92)$

(c)　$P(z > 1.11)$　(d)　$P(z > -2.55)$

7.61　A computer program simulates random sampling from the standard normal distribution. Suppose that 1000 random values are to be obtained. Approximately how many of these values would you expect to be

(a)　Larger than 2?　(b)　Smaller than 1.5?

(c)　Between -1.2 and -1.1?　(d)　Larger than 2.5 or less than -2.5?

7.62　Evaluate each of the following:

(a)　$z_{.025}$　(b)　$z_{.25}$

(c)　$z_{.50}$　(d)　$z_{.85}$

7.63　Let x be a normal random variable with mean 44 and standard deviation 6. If a value is randomly selected from the x distribution, find each of the following probabilities:

(a)　$P(38 < x < 47)$　(b)　$P(48 < x < 54)$

(c)　$P(x > 59)$　(d)　$P(x < 52)$

7.64　Let x be a normal random variable with mean 180 and standard deviation 20. Find the following:

(a)　The 10th percentile　(b)　The 95th percentile

(c)　The percentile rank of $x = 190$　(d)　The percentile rank of $x = 140$

7.65 The IQs of kindergarten children in a school district are approximately normally distributed with mean 105 and standard deviation 16. Find the probabilities corresponding to A, B, C, and D under the accompanying probability curve. Note that x represents an IQ score.

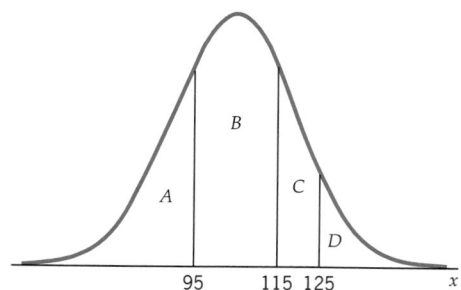

7.66 A plumber has found that the length of time x, in minutes, for installing a bathtub is approximately normally distributed with mean 160 and standard deviation 25.

(a) What percentage of bathtubs are installed within 3 hours?

(b) Find the length of time T so that only 5% of the bathtubs take longer than T to install.

7.67 The weights of chicken lobsters sold by a wholesale seafood company are approximately normally distributed with a mean of 1.5 pounds and a standard deviation of .2 pound. Find the proportion of lobsters

(a) Weighing more than 2 pounds

(b) Weighing between 1.5 and 2 pounds

(c) Weighing less than 1.75 pounds

7.68 You intend to buy wire cable of either brand A or brand B. The breaking strength of brand A is approximately normal with mean 1000 pounds and standard deviation 30 pounds. For brand B, the breaking strength is approximately normal with mean 990 pounds and standard deviation 10 pounds. Assume that you would be completely satisfied if the cable holds more than 970 pounds. Which cable should you buy? Why?

In Exercises 7.69–7.74, assume a binomial experiment. Using (a) Appendix Table B.2 and (b) the normal approximation to the binomial, find the following:

7.69 The probability of no more than 3 successes, where $n = 18$ and $p = .3$

7.70 The probability of at least 8 successes, where $n = 16$ and $p = .6$

7.71 The probability of exactly 7 successes, where $n = 15$ and $p = .5$

7.72 The probability of between 8 and 12 successes inclusive, where $n = 20$ and $p = .7$

7.73 The probability of fewer than 6 successes, where $n = 12$ and $p = .5$

7.74 The probability of between 8 and 11 successes inclusive, where $n = 16$ and $p = .5$

7.75 Assume a binomial experiment with $p = .5$ and $n = 400$. Let x be the number of successes. Approximate each of the following probabilities:

(a) $P(x \geq 210)$ **(b)** $P(180 \leq x \leq 220)$

(c) $P(170 \leq x \leq 230)$ **(d)** $P(x < 185)$

(e) $P(x = 200)$ **(f)** $P(x = 210)$

7.76 Using past data, an airline believes that 8% of the people who make reservations for a certain flight will not appear. The seating capacity for the flight is 300; the airline sells 315 tickets. What is the probability that everyone who shows up has a seat on the flight?

7.77   It was estimated that 13.9% of the United States population in 1990 had no health insurance (*Source: The 1994 Information Please Almanac,* 1994, p. 92). Find the probability that fewer than 70 of 400 randomly selected people will have no health insurance.

7.78   In 1990, it was estimated that 9.1% of residents in Massachusetts had no health insurance (*Source: The 1994 Information Please Almanac,* 1994, p. 92).

    (a)   Find the probability that 30 or more of 200 randomly selected people will have no health insurance.

    (b)   Would 9.1% uninsured seem reasonable if 30 people were uninsured in a sample of size 200?

7.79   The heights (x) of players in a division of high school football teams are approximately normal with mean 71 inches and standard deviation 2.5 inches. Consider the distribution of sample means with sample size $n = 100$.

    (a)   Find $\mu_{\bar{x}}$.

    (b)   Find $\sigma_{\bar{x}}$.

    (c)   What percentage of sample means are larger than 70.5?

    (d)   What percentage of heights are more than 70.5?

7.80   The treatment time x of patients with an eye disease is approximately normal with mean 70 minutes and standard deviation 9 minutes. In parts (a) and (b), find the proportion of treatment times

    (a)   Less than 79 minutes

    (b)   Between 58 and 82 minutes

For parts (c) and (d), assume that a sample of 36 treatment times is selected. Find the following.

    (c) $P(67 < \bar{x} < 73)$

    (d) $P(\bar{x} > 73)$

7.81   A dairy claimed that the mean amount in its milk containers was 128 ounces. Let x be the number of ounces of milk per container, and assume that x is normally distributed with standard deviation 1 ounce. If the claim is true, what percentage of containers will have

    (a)   Less than 126 ounces?

    (b)   More than 129 ounces?

    (c)   Between 127.5 and 130.5 ounces?

A random sample of 25 containers gave a sample mean of 127.4 ounces.

    (d)   Find $P(\bar{x} < 127.4)$.

    (e)   Using part (d), do you think that there is evidence that the true mean is less than 128 ounces? Why?

7.82   A digit from 0 to 9 is to be randomly selected. Let x be the value of the digit selected. The probability distribution for x is given by $P(x) = \frac{1}{10}$ for $x = 0, 1, 2, 3, 4, 5, 6, 7, 8,$ and 9.

    (a)   Find μ and σ^2. (You may already have computed these in Exercise 6.28.) Suppose n digits are to be randomly selected. Let $\bar{x}$ be the mean of these x values.

    (b)   Find $\mu_{\bar{x}}$ and $\sigma_{\bar{x}}^2$ for each of the following values of n.
       (i) $n = 36$ **(ii)** $n = 49$ **(iii)** $n = 100$

    (c)   For each of the following values of n, find $P(4 < \bar{x} < 5)$.
       (i) $n = 36$ **(ii)** $n = 49$ **(iii)** $n = 100$

       Compare and explain your results.

    (d)   For each of the following values of n, find $P(\bar{x} > 4.75)$.
       (i) $n = 36$ **(ii)** $n = 49$ **(iii)** $n = 100$

       Compare and explain your results.

ANSWERS TO PRACTICE QUIZ

1. .0228. This is the normal probability $P(x > 70)$.
2. .1359. This is the normal probability $P(60 < x < 70)$.
3. 56.7. $P(x \leq 56.7) = .75$. So 56.7 is the 75th percentile.
4. 1.28. There is no subcommand, so Minitab assumes a standard normal distribution. Note that $P(z \leq 1.28) = .90$, so $P(z \geq 1.28) = 1 - .90 = .10$. Hence, $z_{.10} = 1.28$.
5. SET C1
    .99, .975, .95, .90
    END
    INVCDF C1
    Note: z_α = INVCDF of $(1 - \alpha)$.

Notes

DeGroot, M. H., S. E. Fienberg, and J. B. Kadane, eds., *Statistics and the Law.* New York: Wiley, 1986.

Lasser, R. P., and A. M. Master, *Geriatrics,* Vol. 14, 1959, pp. 345–360.

The 1994 Information Please Almanac. Boston: Houghton Mifflin, 1994.

PART THREE

STATISTICAL INFERENCE

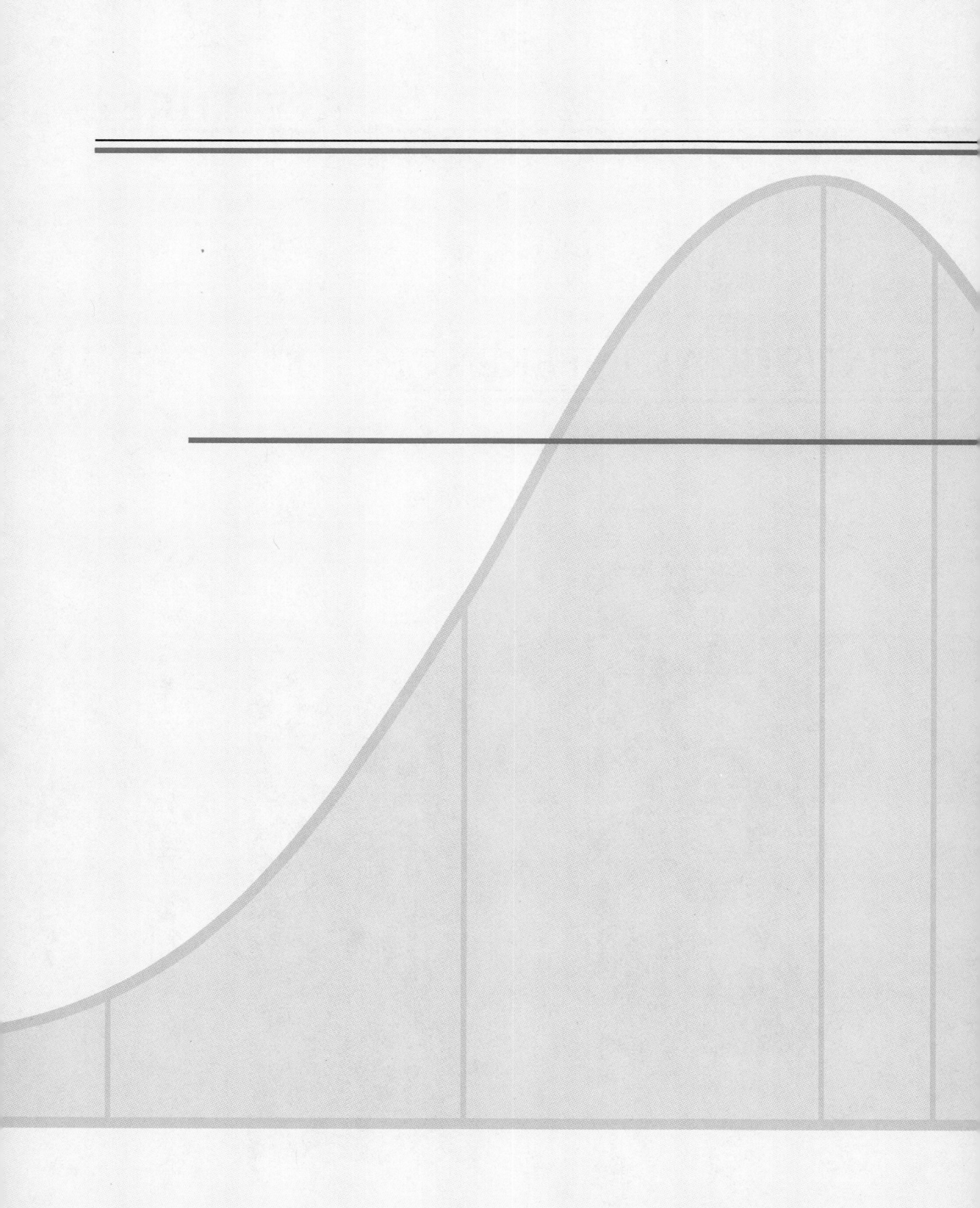

CHAPTER 8

STATISTICAL INFERENCE CONCERNING MEANS AND PROPORTIONS

8.1 INTRODUCTION

8.2 ESTIMATING A POPULATION MEAN (Large-Sample Case)

8.3 HYPOTHESIS TESTING CONCERNING A POPULATION MEAN (Large-Sample Case)

8.4 *P*-VALUES

8.5 INFERENCE CONCERNING A POPULATION MEAN (Small-Sample Case)

8.6 INFERENCE CONCERNING A POPULATION PROPORTION

8.7 USING MINITAB (OPTIONAL)

8.8 WORKING WITH DATA (OPTIONAL)

8.9 SUMMARY

REVIEW EXERCISES

NOTES

8.1

INTRODUCTION

We have seen that **statistical inference** is the process of making judgments about a population based on properties of a sample from the population. There are two types of statistical inference. **Estimation** involves approximating the value of an unknown parameter. (Recall that a parameter is a number describing some numerical property of a population.) For example, we might be interested in obtaining an estimate of the mean value of all homes in Cleveland.

The other type of inference is **hypothesis testing.** This involves choosing between two opposing statements concerning a population. These statements are called **hypotheses.** For example, we may wish to decide whether the mean value of all homes in Cleveland is more than $90,000 or whether it is not more than $90,000. In this chapter, we introduce these two types of inference. The Central Limit Theorem (see Section 7.7) plays an important part in this study.

8.2

ESTIMATING A POPULATION MEAN (Large-Sample Case)

The methods developed in this and the next section are based on the Central Limit Theorem, which requires that the sample size be large ($n \geq 30$).

Let us investigate how a population mean may be estimated from a sample of data values representing blood pressures. Blood pressure is measured in millimeters. A reading of 120 millimeters corresponds to a blood pressure that will support a column of mercury 120 millimeters high. In measuring blood pressure, two readings are important. The *systolic* pressure is the blood pressure when the heart muscle is contracting. The *diastolic* pressure is the blood pressure when the heart muscle is relaxed (between beats). Both these values are important. For young adults, the mean systolic pressure is about 120 millimeters, and for diastolic it is about 74 millimeters. This combination is expressed as 120/74. Blood pressure tends to increase with age. For males age 35–59 years, mean blood pressure readings are about 133/84.

Researchers Haskell, Stern, Lewis, and Perry at the Stanford University School of Medicine have studied blood pressure and various other characteristics of male and female runners (Haskell et al., 1977, p. 148). A sample of 41 male runners age 35–59 years showed a sample mean systolic blood pressure of $\bar{x} = 123$. These 41 runners can be thought of as a sample from the population consisting of all male runners age 35–59 years.[*] Suppose we wish to find the mean systolic blood pressure μ for this population. Since it is not feasible to obtain all the data values in this population, it would seem natural to use the sample mean 123 for the 41 runners as an estimate for the population mean μ. This is called a **point estimate.**

> **Definition**   The sample mean $\bar{x}$ is called a *point estimate* for the population mean μ.

Sometimes we hear statements such as "The average price of all new automobiles is between $13,000 and $15,000," or "The average age of all Americans is between 25 and 30." These are examples of **interval estimates.** Actually, in statistics it is customary to give not only an interval estimate for a parameter, but also the probability that the method used to find this interval will lead to an interval that contains the parameter. This probability is called the **level of confidence** and the resulting interval is called a **confidence interval.**

---

[*] All runners in the sample lived in the Palo Alto, California, area, so we should probably restrict the population to male runners age 35–59 in this geographic area.

We will explore this idea with results of the Stanford study already discussed. Suppose we want to find an interval that contains the mean systolic pressure μ of all male runners age 35–59 with a level of confidence .95. This is a 95% confidence interval. Now by the Central Limit Theorem (see Section 7.7), the values of the sample mean $\bar{x}$ for random samples of size n have a distribution that is approximately normal with

$$\mu_{\bar{x}} = \mu \quad \text{and} \quad \sigma_{\bar{x}} = \sigma/\sqrt{n}$$

when n is sufficiently large ($n \geq 30$ will usually suffice). Hence the standard score

$$z = \frac{\bar{x} - \mu_{\bar{x}}}{\sigma_{\bar{x}}} = \frac{\bar{x} - \mu}{\sigma/\sqrt{n}}$$

is approximately standard normal. We are dealing with the case where $n = 41$. We will assume that, although μ is unknown, the (population) standard deviation σ for the runners is no different from that of other apparently healthy males age 35–59. This value is about 17 millimeters. (In fact, the standard deviation for the sample of 41 runners was quite close to this at 15.4 mm.) It follows that $\sigma_{\bar{x}} = \sigma/\sqrt{n} = 17/\sqrt{41} \doteq 2.65$. Therefore,

$$z = \frac{\bar{x} - \mu}{2.65}$$

is approximately standard normal. Recall that z measures the number of standard deviations by which a value of $\bar{x}$ is above or below the mean. (A positive value indicates that $\bar{x}$ is above the mean; a negative value indicates that $\bar{x}$ is below the mean.)

Perhaps if we found a type of confidence interval for z, we could use the relation between z and μ to find a confidence interval for μ. From Figure 8.1, we see that

$$P(-1.96 < z < 1.96) = .95$$

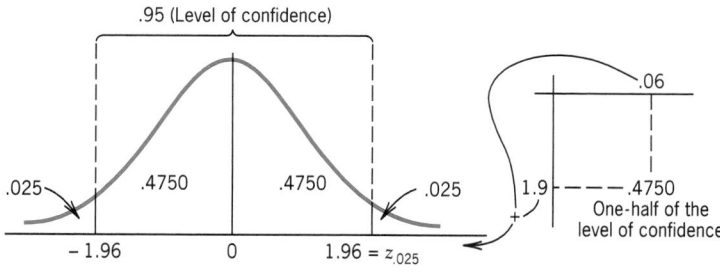

Figure 8.1

To understand this, it may help to recall that the area under the standard normal curve to the right of 1.96 is .025; that is, $z_{.025} = 1.96$ (see Example 7.7). Therefore, 95% of all values of z will be between -1.96 and 1.96. This means that 95% of all values of $\bar{x}$ will be within 1.96 standard deviations of the mean μ. One standard deviation is $\sigma_{\bar{x}} = 2.65$ millimeters. Therefore, 1.96 standard deviations is $(1.96)(2.65) \doteq 5.19$ millimeters. So for any randomly obtained value of $\bar{x}$, the probability is .95 that $\bar{x}$ will be within 5.19 millimeters of μ. The probability is .95 that the distance from $\bar{x}$

to μ is less than 5.19, that is, μ is between $\bar{x} - 5.19$ and $\bar{x} + 5.19$:

$$\bar{x} - 5.19 < \mu < \bar{x} + 5.19$$

For any randomly obtained value of $\bar{x}$, we are 95% sure that this inequality is correct. In particular, we can substitute the value of $\bar{x}$, namely, 123 millimeters, obtained from the Stanford study, into this inequality, getting

$$123 - 5.19 < \mu < 123 + 5.19$$

$$117.81 < \mu < 128.19$$

This is our desired 95% confidence interval. This confidence interval is shown in Figure 8.2.

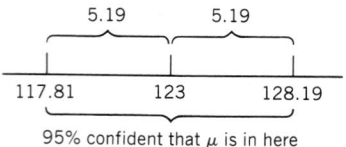

Figure 8.2

Recall that we said that the mean systolic blood pressure of *all* males age 35–59 is 133. Notice that our confidence interval for the mean pressure for runners (117.81 to 128.19) does not contain 133; it is below 133. Thus we can conclude that the mean systolic blood pressure of male runners age 35–59 is less than the mean for males in general (of comparable age).

Formula for Confidence Interval for μ

Suppose we wish to find a confidence interval for the mean μ for a random variable x. It is customary to call the level of confidence $1 - \alpha$. (For example, if our level of confidence is .95, then $1 - \alpha = .95$. So $\alpha = .05$.) Let's examine the 95% confidence interval we developed in the preceding discussion, and see whether we can use this to find out what a $1 - \alpha$ confidence interval should look like, in general. We will proceed by analogy. The 95% confidence interval was

$$123 - 5.19 < \mu < 123 + 5.19$$

For this confidence interval, recall that

$$\text{level of confidence} = .95 = 1 - \alpha \quad (\text{so } \alpha = .05)$$
$$123 = \bar{x}$$
$$5.19 = (1.96)(2.65)$$

where

$$1.96 = z_{.025} = z_{\alpha/2} \quad \text{and} \quad 2.65 = \sigma_{\bar{x}} = \frac{\sigma}{\sqrt{n}}$$

Therefore,

$$5.19 = z_{\alpha/2} \cdot \frac{\sigma}{\sqrt{n}}$$

Now we can rewrite the above confidence interval symbolically as

$$\bar{x} - z_{\alpha/2} \cdot \frac{\sigma}{\sqrt{n}} < \mu < \bar{x} + z_{\alpha/2} \cdot \frac{\sigma}{\sqrt{n}}$$

This, in fact, is the general form for a $1 - \alpha$ confidence interval for μ.

A $1 - \alpha$ confidence interval for a population mean μ when the sample size n is large ($n \geq 30$) is

$$\bar{x} - z_{\alpha/2} \cdot \frac{\sigma}{\sqrt{n}} < \mu < \bar{x} + z_{\alpha/2} \cdot \frac{\sigma}{\sqrt{n}}$$

Sometimes the interval is described by its endpoints: $\bar{x} \pm z_{\alpha/2} \cdot \dfrac{\sigma}{\sqrt{n}}$

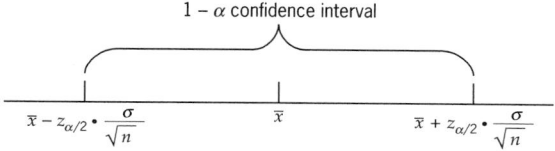

The level of confidence $1 - \alpha$ is the probability that an interval constructed in this manner will contain μ. If σ is unknown, use the sample standard deviation s as an estimate.

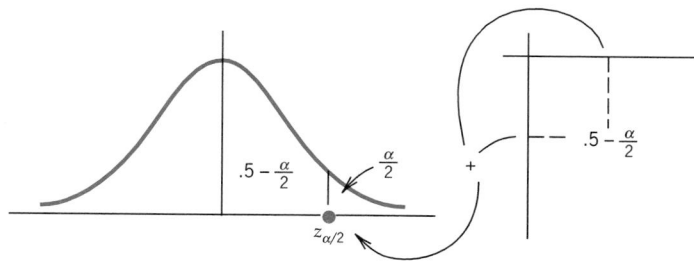

Figure 8.3
Finding $z_{\alpha/2}$

Remark If you are unsure about the meaning of the symbol $z_{\alpha/2}$, review Example 7.8. Some common values of $z_{\alpha/2}$ are as follows:

Level of Confidence $1 - \alpha$	$z_{\alpha/2}$
90%	1.65
95%	1.96
98%	2.33
99%	2.58

Since the Central Limit Theorem was the basis of our confidence interval, we should be sure that the sample size n is sufficiently large before we use it. That is, we should have $n \geq 30$. *If σ is unknown, we can use the sample standard deviation s as an estimate for σ as long as the sample size is large ($n \geq 30$).* If the random variable x is normal or approximately so, then this confidence interval may be used even when the sample size is small ($n < 30$). But in this case, σ should be known because it would be inappropriate to estimate it by s when n is small.

When these conditions are not met, it may still be possible to obtain a confidence interval for μ, as we shall see in Section 8.5.

EXAMPLE 8.1

Thirty-six automobiles of the same model are driven and the gas mileage for each is recorded. The results give $\bar{x} = 18$ miles per gallon and $s = 3$ miles per gallon. Give a 90% confidence interval for the mean mileage μ for all autos of this model.

Solution

$1 - \alpha = .90 \qquad \alpha = .10$

$z_{\alpha/2} = z_{.05} = 1.65$

$\bar{x} = 18$

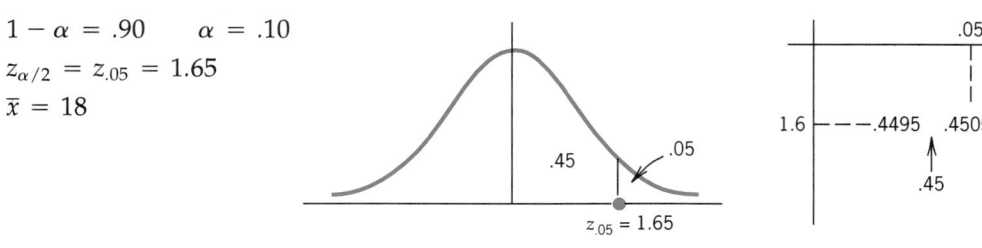

Figure 8.4

σ is unknown, but since n is large, we can use $s = 3$ as an estimate. Therefore,

$$\frac{\sigma}{\sqrt{n}} \doteq \frac{s}{\sqrt{n}} = \frac{3}{\sqrt{36}} = \frac{3}{6} = .5$$

Thus the confidence interval

$$\bar{x} - z_{\alpha/2} \cdot \frac{\sigma}{\sqrt{n}} < \mu < \bar{x} + z_{\alpha/2} \cdot \frac{\sigma}{\sqrt{n}}$$

becomes

$$18 - (1.65)(.5) < \mu < 18 + (1.65)(.5)$$
$$18 - .83 < \mu < 18 + .83$$
$$17.17 < \mu < 18.83$$

Therefore, we are 90% confident that the mean gas mileage μ is between 17.17 and 18.83 miles per gallon.

The following question often arises at this point: Why settle for a 90% or 95% confidence interval when we can find a 99% or even a 99.99% confidence interval? The answer is that the higher our level of confidence, the wider the confidence interval. Obviously, the wider the confidence interval, the less useful it will be as an estimate for μ. For example, if we had asked for a 99% confidence interval in Example 8.1, then $1 - \alpha = .99$, $\alpha = .01$, $z_{\alpha/2} = z_{.005} = 2.58$. The 99% confidence interval is then

$$16.71 < \mu < 19.29$$

There is a trade-off between level of confidence and accuracy: The higher the confidence, the less accuracy; the more accuracy, the lower the confidence. A 95% level of confidence is often used; this is regarded in many situations as a happy medium.

Maximum Error of Estimate

If we obtain a sample of data values of a random variable x, we have said that a natural point estimate for the mean μ is the sample mean $\bar{x}$. We can get an idea of how good an estimate this is by examining a confidence interval for μ.

We have said that a $1 - \alpha$ confidence interval for μ is described by the endpoints

$$\bar{x} \pm z_{\alpha/2} \cdot \frac{\sigma}{\sqrt{n}}$$

In Example 8.1, this gave us the 90% confidence interval

$$18 \pm .83$$

We display this graphically in Figure 8.5(a).

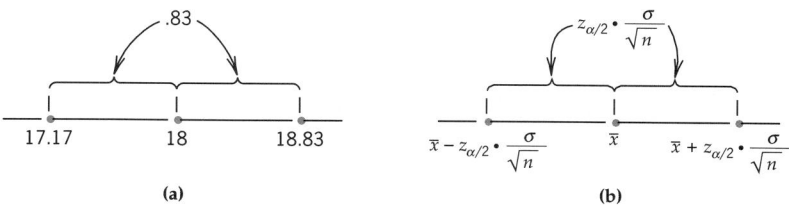

(a)   (b)

Figure 8.5
Confidence Intervals: (a) 90% Confidence Interval for Mean Gas Mileage in Example 8.1; (b) $1 - \alpha$ Confidence Interval for μ

If we estimate the mean gas mileage μ to be 18 miles per gallon (the sample mean), we can be 90% confident that the amount by which our estimate is in error will be less than .83 mile per gallon. We say that .83 is the maximum error of the estimate with 90% level of confidence. This idea can be generalized, as suggested by Figure 8.5(b).

Definition When estimating μ by $\bar{x}$ from a large sample, the *maximum error of the estimate*, with level of confidence $1 - \alpha$, is

$$E = z_{\alpha/2} \cdot \frac{\sigma}{\sqrt{n}}$$

Here again, when σ is unknown, we can estimate it by s, as long as $n \geq 30$. Note that the endpoints of the confidence interval can be written

$$\bar{x} \pm E$$

EXAMPLE 8.2

Let x = the amount of suspended impurities in the air in micrograms per cubic meter as measured by an Environmental Protection Agency sampling station. Forty-five readings of x were randomly obtained over a 1-year period, giving $\bar{x} = 52.1$ and $s = 5.3$. If $\bar{x}$ is used to estimate μ, give the maximum error of the estimate with 95% level of confidence.

Solution

$$1 - \alpha = .95 \qquad \alpha = .05$$

We have seen that $z_{\alpha/2} = z_{.025} = 1.96$. It is given that

$$\frac{\sigma}{\sqrt{n}} \doteq \frac{s}{\sqrt{n}} = \frac{5.3}{\sqrt{45}} \doteq .79$$

Note that we have estimated σ by s. Now

$$E = z_{\alpha/2} \cdot \frac{\sigma}{\sqrt{n}} \doteq (1.96)(.79) \doteq 1.55$$

measured in micrograms per cubic meter.

Determining the Sample Size

A professor wanted to estimate the mean score μ of all students at her university on a national mathematics placement test that was being considered for use at the school. The national mean was 70 and the standard deviation was 10 points. She believed that the standard deviation for her institution would be the same (so $\sigma = 10$), but that the mean would be higher. She intended to give the exam to a sample of students at her institution, and use the result ($\bar{x}$) to estimate the mean score μ for all students at the school. She wanted to decide how many students should be tested, so that the maximum error of the estimate (E) would be 2 points with 95% confidence. Now

$$E = z_{\alpha/2} \cdot \frac{\sigma}{\sqrt{n}}$$

where

$$E = 2$$
$$\sigma = 10$$
$$1 - \alpha = .95 \quad (\alpha = .05)$$
$$z_{\alpha/2} = z_{.025} = 1.96$$
$$n = \underline{\quad ? \quad}$$

We can substitute the known values in the equation for E and solve for n:

$$2 = (1.96) \cdot \frac{10}{\sqrt{n}}$$

$$2 = \frac{19.6}{\sqrt{n}}$$

Multiplying both sides by $\sqrt{n}$ and dividing both sides by 2, we get

$$\sqrt{n} = \frac{19.6}{2} = 9.8$$

Now we square both sides:

$$n = (9.8)^2 = 96.04$$

The custom is to round *up* to get the sample size. Thus the professor should test 97 students.

If we trace each of the previous steps backward, we find that

$$n = (9.8)^2 = \left(\frac{19.6}{2}\right)^2 = \left[\frac{(1.96)(10)}{2}\right]^2 = \left[\frac{z_{\alpha/2} \cdot \sigma}{E}\right]^2$$

This observation enables us to generalize our result as follows:

When estimating μ by $\bar{x}$, if we want our level of confidence to be $1 - \alpha$ that our error is less than an amount E, the sample size should be at least

$$n = \left[\frac{z_{\alpha/2} \cdot \sigma}{E}\right]^2$$

To use this formula, we must know the value of σ. Unfortunately, this quantity is usually not known. (Obviously, we cannot estimate σ by s in this situation because we do not have the sample on hand yet.) However, based on past experience, the researcher might have an idea of the approximate value of σ. If so, this value would be used in the previous formula.

EXAMPLE 8.3

A machine is designed to produce rubber gaskets with a mean thickness of .125 inch; the standard deviation is $\sigma = .01$ inch. It is thought that the mean has changed, but σ is the same. How many gaskets should be measured to be able to estimate the new mean μ by the sample mean $\bar{x}$ with maximum error of the estimate .001 inch and 90% level of confidence?

Solution

$$1 - \alpha = .90 \quad (\alpha = .10)$$

In Example 8.1, we saw that $z_{\alpha/2} = z_{.05} = 1.65$. Now

$$\sigma = .01$$
$$E = .001$$
$$n = \left[\frac{z_{\alpha/2} \cdot \sigma}{E}\right]^2 = \left[\frac{(1.65)(.01)}{.001}\right]^2 = 272.25$$

Thus the sample size should be 273. Again, we rounded up to the next integer.

EXERCISES

8.1 In each part, (i) find the maximum error of the estimate, and (ii) construct a confidence interval for the population mean μ. Note that n refers to the sample size.

		$\bar{x}$	s	n	Percentage Confidence Interval
(a)		125	16	64	95
(b)		206	25	100	99
(c)		154	3	81	90
(d)		309	50	225	95
(e)		40	7	49	99
(f)		78	6	144	90

8.2 Consider a computer simulation that samples 100 values from a population with mean 50 and standard deviation 5. The procedure is repeated 1000 times.

(a) On average, how many of the 1000 95% confidence intervals will contain the true mean value of 50?

(b) On average, what is the width of the 95% confidence intervals?

8.3 Fifty samples were randomly selected from a population with mean $\mu = 200$ and variance $\sigma^2 = 100$. For each sample, 80%, 90%, 95%, and 99% confidence intervals for μ were constructed.

(a) For each level of confidence (80%, 90%, 95%, and 99%), about how many of the 50 confidence intervals should contain the number $\mu = 200$?

(b) The following table gives the 11 samples in which the 80% confidence interval did not contain the value $\mu = 200$. (*Note:* N = interval did not contain $\mu = 200$; Y = interval did contain $\mu = 200$.) Fill in the 99% column with a Y, N, or ? (cannot be determined from the information given).

Sample #	80%	90%	95%	99%
11	N	N	Y	
14	N	N	N	
17	N	N	Y	
22	N	N	Y	
24	N	N	Y	
30	N	N	N	
35	N	N	Y	
40	N	N	Y	
46	N	Y	Y	
48	N	Y	Y	
50	N	Y	Y	

8.4 A physician wanted to estimate the mean length of time μ that a patient had to wait to see him after arriving at the office. A random sample of 50 patients showed a mean waiting time of 23.4 minutes and a standard deviation of 7.1 minutes. Find a 95% confidence interval for μ.

8.5 (a) Sixty pieces of a plastic are randomly selected, and the breaking strength of each piece is recorded in pounds per square inch. Suppose that $\bar{x} = 26$ and $s = 1.5$ pounds per square inch. Find a 99% confidence interval for the mean breaking strength μ.

(b) If you were to obtain 200 99% confidence intervals for μ, about how many can be expected to contain μ?

8.6 A study was done to estimate the mean annual growth μ in a population of *Conus pennaceus* trees in Hawaii. For those with an initial size of 2.41–2.60 centimeters, a sample of size 33 yielded a mean annual growth of .72 centimeter and a standard deviation of .31 centimeter. Find a 90% confidence interval for the population mean μ of annual growth (of those with an initial size of 2.41–2.60 centimeters) (*Source:* Perron, 1983, p. 55).

8.7 A city assessor wished to estimate the mean income per household. The previous mean income was $25,300. A random sample of 40 households in the city showed a mean income of $29,400 and a standard deviation of $6325.

   (a) Find a 95% confidence interval for μ, the population mean income per household in the city.

   (b) Based on your answer in part (a), would the assessor conclude the mean income had increased over the previous estimate of $25,300?

8.8 An electrical company tested a new type of oil to be used in its transformers. Thirty-five readings of dielectric strength were obtained. Dielectric strength is the potential (in kilovolts per centimeter of thickness) necessary to cause a disruptive discharge of electricity through an insulator. The results of the test gave $\bar{x} = 77$ kv, $s = 8$ kv.

   (a) Find a 95% confidence interval for the mean dielectric strength of the oil.

   (b) The old transformer oil had a mean dielectric strength of 75 kv. Would you conclude that the new oil has a higher mean dielectric strength on the basis of your answer in part (a)? $n = 40$

8.9 Noise level tests were done on 40 new light rail vehicles (LRVs—the new name for trolley cars). The results of the test gave a sample mean of 65 decibels and a sample standard deviation of 6 decibels. $\mu_s = 65$ $s = 6$

   (a) Find a 90% confidence interval for the mean decibel level μ for this type of transit vehicle.

   (b) What is the maximum error of the estimate at the 90% level?

   (c) Based on your answer in part (a), would you conclude that the new LRVs are quieter on the average than older-type trolley cars that had a mean decibel level of 80?

8.10 A transit official wanted to estimate the mean time μ for a bus trip between two cities. A random sample of 50 such trips gave $\bar{x} = 150$ minutes and $s = 15$ minutes.

   (a) Find a 90% confidence interval for μ.

   (b) Find a 99% confidence interval for μ.

   (c) If you were to construct a 95% confidence interval for μ (do not construct it), would the interval be longer or shorter than the 99% confidence interval? Longer or shorter than the 90% confidence interval?

8.11 A union official wanted to estimate the mean hourly wage μ of its members. A random sample of 100 members gave $\bar{x} = \$18.30$ and $s = \$3.25$ per hour.

   (a) Find an 80% confidence interval for μ.

   (b) Find a 95% confidence interval for μ.

   (c) If you were to construct a 90% confidence interval for μ (do not construct it), would the interval be longer or shorter than the 80% confidence interval? Longer or shorter than the 95% confidence interval?

8.12 A newspaper article stated that a random sample of size 144 from a population gave $\bar{x} = 150$ and $s = 36$. The article gave an interval estimate of the population mean μ as 150 ± 4.95 but did not mention the level of confidence. What is the level of confidence?

8.13 Match the confidence interval with the appropriate level of confidence. Assume the same sample size and sample standard deviation in each case.

Confidence Interval	Level of Confidence
10 ± 3	90%
10 ± 4.5	95%
10 ± 5	80%
10 ± 8	99%

8.14 A 7-day study of the diets of 34 males living in an area of Greece called Montegiorgio gave a sample mean of 23.9% and a sample standard deviation of 4.6% calories from fats (*Source:* Keys, 1970, p. I-166).

(a) Find a 95% confidence interval for the mean μ of the population from which the men were selected.

(b) What is the maximum error of estimate for μ?

8.15 A 7-day study of the diets of 33 males living on the island of Crete gave a sample mean of 41.8% and a sample standard deviation of 5.7% calories from fats (*Source:* Keys, 1970, p. I-166).

(a) Find a 95% confidence interval for the mean μ of the population from which the men were selected.

(b) What is the maximum error of estimate for μ?

8.16 An educator wishes to estimate the mean number of hours μ that 10-year-old children in a city watch television per day. How large a sample is needed if the educator wants to estimate μ to within .5 hour with 90% confidence? Use $\sigma = 1.75$.

8.17 How many households in a large town should be randomly sampled to estimate the mean number of dollars spent per household (per week) on food supplies to within $3 with 80% confidence? Assume a standard deviation of $15.

8.18 Consider a population with unknown mean μ and population standard deviation $\sigma = 20$.

(a) How large a sample size is needed to estimate μ to within 4 units with 90% confidence?

(b) Suppose that you wanted to estimate μ to within 4 units with 95% confidence. Without calculating, would the sample size required be larger or smaller than that found in part (a)?

(c) Suppose that you wanted to estimate μ to within 2 units with 90% confidence. Without calculating, would the sample size required be larger or smaller than that found in part (a)?

8.19 Consider a population with unknown mean μ and population standard deviation $\sigma = 15$.

(a) How large a sample size is needed to estimate μ to within 5 units with 95% confidence?

(b) Suppose you wanted to estimate μ to within 5 units with 90% confidence. Without calculating, would the sample size required be larger or smaller than that found in part (a)?

(c) Suppose you wanted to estimate μ to within 6 units with 95% confidence. Without calculating, would the sample size required be larger or smaller than that found in part (a)?

8.20 A journal article stated that a random sample from a population gave a sample standard deviation of $s = 30$ and a 95% confidence interval for the population mean μ as lying between 18.58 and 26.42.

(a) What is the point estimate for μ?

(b) What is the maximum error of estimate?

(c) What is the sample size?

8.21 The main reason for deaths in the first month of life is low birth weight. An administrator at Claybak Memorial Hospital (CMH) obtained the following 37 birth weights (in ounces):

100.2	102.4	82.6	79.4	132.4	107.9	120.1	119.4	63.9	137.3
135.1	143.4	128.9	78.6	144.7	131.4	117.4	114.8	108.3	
109.8	122.0	65.4	81.6	101.1	73.6	120.8	105.8	137.6	
96.8	134.0	95.2	127.8	88.9	67.9	114.0	79.4	84.7	

(a) Find a 95% confidence interval for the mean birth weight at CMH. (*Note:* $\sum x = 3954.6$ and $\sum x^2 = 442,887.6$)

(b) Babies weighing less than 88 ounces are considered abnormally small. Can the administrator feel confident that babies born at CMH are not abnormally small on average?

8.22 Refer to Exercise 8.21. The administrator believed that the mean birth weight of babies nationwide is 120 ounces. If you have not done so, construct a 95% confidence interval for the mean birth weight at the hospital. What can the administrator conclude about the mean birth weight at CMH compared with the mean birth weight nationwide?

8.23 A podiatrist recorded the recovery time, in days, for 38 patients. He was trying out a new procedure and hoped the result would be less recovery time on average. The mean recovery time using the previous procedure was 6.5 days. The recorded times were

8	7	8	6	9	4	5	3	7	8	10	7	7	6	4	10	3	6	8
2	5	5	4	5	3	8	7	4	6	3	7	12	4	3	6	6	9	4

Note that $\sum x = 229$ and $\sum x^2 = 1581$.

(a) What is a point estimate for the population mean μ?

(b) Find a 90% confidence interval for μ.

(c) What is the maximum error of estimate for μ?

8.24 A restaurant owner believed that customer spending was below normal at tables manned by one of the waiters. The owner sampled 36 checks from the waiter's tables and got the following amounts (rounded to the nearest dollar):

47	46	56	70	52	58	48	57	49	61	52	40
60	22	74	59	60	30	61	44	62	41	53	57
50	52	57	59	69	51	58	56	44	36	47	51

Now $\sum x = 1889$ and $\sum x^2 = 103,027$.

(a) Find a 95% confidence interval for the mean amount of money μ spent at the waiter's tables.

(b) Does it appear that the mean amount spent at the waiter's tables is smaller than the restaurant average of $55?

8.25 An owner of a retail outlet sold and provided service for copying machines. One type of machine, the DW 140 model, needed service often. The owner was interested in the mean time required to service this model and decided not to carry the model if the mean repair time appeared to be more than 40 minutes. The repairman provided the following 39 times (in minutes):

23	27	28	44	33	35	37	39	39	39	39	40	40
41	42	42	41	42	43	44	44	45	46	46	46	47
47	48	49	47	50	51	52	53	53	56	57	61	62

Use $\sum x = 1718$ and $\sum x^2 = 78,398$ to construct a 90% confidence interval. Based on this, will the owner continue to carry the model?

8.26   In Exercise 2.55, we discussed the number of days from remission induction to relapse for 51 patients with acute nonlymphoblastic leukemia. A stem-and-leaf plot of the data shows that 1160 is an extreme observation. (*Note:* The last digit has been cut.)

0	2 4 5 5 6 6 8 8 9 9
1	1 1 2 4 4 5 6 7 8 9 9
2	0 2 3 4 4 5 5 6 6 7 7 8 9
3	0 0 3 4 9 9
4	8
5	1 1 1 1 3
6	0 4 9
7	
8	
9	5
10	
11	6

Note: 6 | 4 = 640

(a)   For the 51 data values, $\bar{x} = 292.39$ and $s = 230.31$. Find a 95% confidence interval for the population mean μ.

(b)   Delete 1160 and consider the remaining 50 data values, for which $\bar{x} = 275.04$ and $s = 196.10$. Find a 95% confidence interval for μ. Compare with the confidence interval obtained in part (a). Is there much difference between the two? Comment on the sample size and the effect of the extreme observation on the confidence interval. Did deleting the extreme observation make much difference in this case?

_____ **8.3**
_____

HYPOTHESIS TESTING CONCERNING A POPULATION MEAN (Large-Sample Case)

A food company produces bags of peanuts weighing 336 grams (on the average). Periodically, the quality control department takes samples of peanut bags to determine whether the packaging process is under control, that is, to decide between the two statements

$$\mu = 336 \text{ g} \quad \text{(process is under control)}$$
$$\mu \neq 336 \text{ g} \quad \text{(process is not under control)}$$

If $\mu = 336$ g, then there is *no change* or *no difference* in the mean. We call $\mu = 336$ g the **null hypothesis.**

> **Definition**   The *null hypothesis* is a statement asserting no change, or no difference, or no effect. It usually takes the form of a statement about a population parameter (or parameters) containing an equal sign. The null hypothesis is labeled H_a.

The quality control department worries that there may have been a change in the mean ($\mu \neq 336$ g). This is called the **alternate hypothesis.**

Definition   The *alternate hypothesis* is a statement that might be true instead of the null hypothesis. It usually contains the symbol >, or <, or $\neq$. The alternate hypothesis is labeled H_a.

The procedure for choosing between hypotheses is called **hypothesis testing.** In hypothesis testing, the idea is to give the benefit of the doubt to the null hypothesis. The null hypothesis will be rejected (and the alternate hypothesis accepted) only if the sample data suggest beyond a reasonable doubt that the null hypothesis is false. We will have more to say about this later.

Thus the hypotheses of interest to the quality control department are

$$H_0: \quad \mu = 336 \text{ g}$$
$$H_a: \quad \mu \neq 336 \text{ g}$$

A random sample of 40 bags of peanuts was obtained. It would seem natural to use the sample mean weight $\bar{x}$ of the 40 bags to make a decision. The value of $\bar{x}$ is a rough estimate for μ. Although we do not expect $\bar{x}$ to exactly equal μ, it is likely that it will not be too far from μ.

Now the procedure in hypothesis testing is to suppose for the moment that the null hypothesis is true. Therefore, we assume for the moment that $\mu = 336$ g. We wish to determine what values for $\bar{x}$ are so far from 336, that such values would be very unlikely to occur if μ were really 336. If it then happens that we do get one of these unlikely values for the sample mean weight, we reject the null hypothesis ($\mu = 336$); otherwise, it would not be rejected.

The way to determine which values of $\bar{x}$ are likely and which are unlikely is to use the probability distribution of $\bar{x}$. The Central Limit Theorem (Section 7.7) tells us that when $\bar{x}$ is obtained from a random sample of size n, then if n is sufficiently large (at least 30), $\bar{x}$ will be approximately normal. In addition,

$$\mu_{\bar{x}} = \mu \quad \text{and} \quad \sigma_{\bar{x}} = \frac{\sigma}{\sqrt{n}}$$

Past experience with the peanut packaging process has shown that although the mean weight may change, the variability of the weight remains the same, showing a standard deviation of $\sigma = 11$ g. So for a sample of 40 bags of peanuts, if the null hypothesis is true,

$$\mu_{\bar{x}} = \mu = 336 \text{ g} \quad \text{and} \quad \sigma_{\bar{x}} = \frac{\sigma}{\sqrt{n}} = \frac{11 \text{ g}}{\sqrt{40}} \doteq 1.74 \text{ g}$$

To say that values of $\bar{x}$ are so far from 336 as to be unlikely, we mean that such values have low probability. It is up to the one performing the test of hypotheses (the researcher) to define what is meant by "low." A value often selected is .05. We will use this value here. We call it the **level of significance** of the test. The level of significance is denoted by α and can change from one test of hypotheses to another.

It is more convenient to work with the standard z score for $\bar{x}$ rather than $\bar{x}$ itself. This is just a different unit of measurement for the sample mean weight, namely, the number of standard deviations that $\bar{x}$ is above or below the mean, instead of grams. If we assume for the moment that the null hypothesis is true ($\mu = 336$), then

$$z = \frac{\overline{x} - \mu_{\overline{x}}}{\sigma_{\overline{x}}} = \frac{\overline{x} - \mu}{\sigma/\sqrt{n}} = \frac{\overline{x} - 336}{1.74}$$

and this z score is approximately standard normal. If $\overline{x}$ were 336, z would be 0. Therefore, values of $\overline{x}$ far from 336 (either far to the right or left of 336) correspond to values of z far to the right or left of 0. We will use the z score of $\overline{x}$ to make our decision concerning the hypotheses H_0 and H_a. Such an expression is called a **test statistic**.

> **Definition**   A *test statistic* is a quantity that is used to make a decision in a test of hypotheses.

Notice from Figure 8.6(a) that the probability that $z \geq 1.96$ or $z \leq -1.96$ is $.025 + .025 = .05$. We used Appendix Table B.3 to find the value 1.96 by looking up the value of z corresponding to the area $.4750$. Observe that $.4750 = .5 - .025$ and $z_{.025} = 1.96$.

Keep in mind that

$$z = \frac{\overline{x} - 336}{1.74}$$

A value of $z \geq 1.96$ or $z \leq -1.96$ will correspond to a value of $\overline{x}$ that is so far from 336 (to the right or left) that the probability of getting such a value would be very small (only .05) if μ were 336. See Figure 8.6(b). We would now obtain the

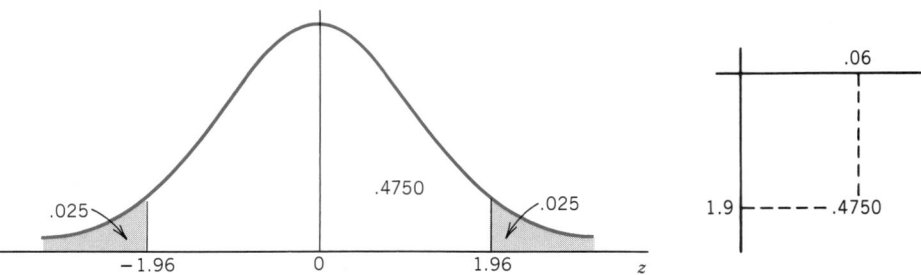

Figure 8.6(a)
$P(z \geq 1.96 \text{ or } z \leq -1.96) = .05$

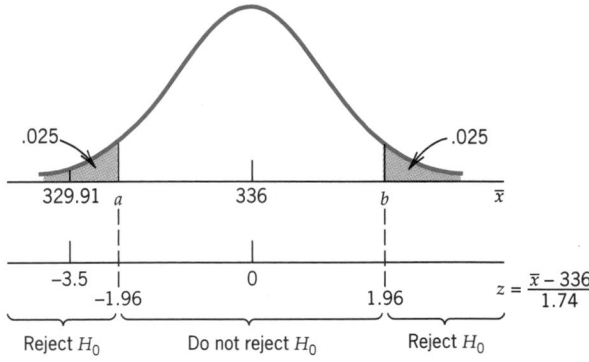

Figure 8.6(b)

value of $\bar{x}$ from the sample and calculate its z score. If $z \geq 1.96$ or $z \leq -1.96$, this would correspond to a value of $\bar{x}$ that would be very unlikely (only a 5% chance) if the null hypothesis $\mu = 336$ were correct. So if a value of $z \geq 1.96$ or $z \leq -1.96$ does occur, we would reject the null hypothesis H_0 in favor of the alternate hypothesis H_a.

One sample of 40 bags of peanuts obtained by the quality control department had a sample mean of $\bar{x} = 329.91$ g. What does this imply about the packaging process? Compute the z score:

$$z = \frac{\bar{x} - 336}{1.74} = \frac{329.91 - 336}{1.74} = -3.5$$

This is called the **observed value of** z. Since $-3.5 < -1.96$, the null hypothesis H_0 ($\mu = 336$ g) would be rejected in favor of H_a ($\mu \neq 336$ g). In fact, it would appear that $\mu < 336$ g since z was so far to the *left* of 0. See Figure 8.6(b). So the process is not under control; it appears the peanut bags are being underfilled.

Therefore, values of $z \geq 1.96$ or $z \leq -1.96$ provide strong evidence in favor of the alternate hypothesis H_a. These values of z constitute what is called the **critical region**. The values ± 1.96 are called **critical values.**

> **Definition** The *critical region* consists of those values of the test statistic that provide strong evidence in favor of the alternate hypothesis. Hence a value in the critical region leads to rejection of the null hypothesis.

Notice that it was not necessary to find the values of a and b on the $\bar{x}$-axis in Figure 8.6(b). However, these values may easily be found and would enable us to describe the critical region in terms of $\bar{x}$ values. The value a on the $\bar{x}$-axis corresponds to $z = -1.96$. Similarly, b corresponds to $z = 1.96$ so

$$-1.96 = \frac{a - 336}{1.74} \qquad 1.96 = \frac{b - 336}{1.74}$$
$$a \doteq 332.59 \qquad\qquad b \doteq 339.41$$

Therefore, a value of $\bar{x} \geq 339.41$ g or $\bar{x} \leq 332.59$ g would lead to rejection of the null hypothesis that $\mu = 336$ g.

Errors

In this discussion, we have seen that it would be very unlikely that the value of the test statistic would fall in the critical region if the null hypothesis were true. (That is why we reject H_0 when this happens.) The probability was only .05. We called .05 the level of significance of the test; it is denoted by α (alpha).

> **Definition** The probability that the test statistic will fall in the critical region if the null hypothesis is true is the *level of significance* of the test, α.

Although it is unlikely that the test statistic will fall in the critical region when H_0 is true, it is still possible. In this case, we will reject H_0 and make an error in doing so. This is called a **Type I error**—rejecting the null hypothesis when it is true. So a Type I error will occur if the test statistic falls in the critical region when H_0 is actually true. We saw that the probability of this happening is α. Thus

$$\alpha = P(\text{Type I error})$$

The other kind of error that could be made is not to reject H_0 when it is false. This is called a **Type II error**. A Type II error will occur if the test statistic does not fall in the critical region when H_0 is in fact false. We represent the probability of a Type II error by the symbol β (beta).

$$\beta = P(\text{Type II error})$$

Table 8.1
Possible Decisions in a Hypothesis Test

Null Hypothesis	Decision	
	Reject H_0	**Do Not Reject H_0**
True	Type I error	Correct decision
False	Correct decision	Type II error

Whereas the value of α is always known (in fact, the researcher chooses this value), the value of β is usually unknown. To understand why this is so, recall that in our preceding example, β is the probability that the test statistic

$$\frac{\bar{x} - 336}{1.74}$$

falls outside the critical region when H_0 is false. However, when H_0 is false, that is, when $\mu \neq 336$, we can no longer say that this expression has a standard normal distribution. Therefore, in the absence of more information, we cannot find the probability that its value will fall outside the critical region.

The following procedure will frequently be used in the remainder of this book to investigate hypotheses concerning a population. It need not be restricted to tests concerning a population mean.

Summary of the Steps in Hypothesis Testing

1. **Identify the null hypothesis H_0 and the alternate hypothesis H_a.** These will often be conjectures (or suspicions or beliefs) concerning the value of one or more population parameters. As a rule of thumb, the null hypothesis will usually contain an equal sign. The alternate hypothesis will usually contain the symbol $>$, or $<$, or $\neq$.

2. **Choose α, the level of significance.** The value of α should be small, usually $\alpha \leq .10$. But since α is the probability of a Type I error, the actual value of α chosen depends on how serious a Type I error is in a given situation. The more serious the Type I error, the smaller we should choose α.

3. **Select the test statistic and determine its value from the sample data.** This value is called the *observed value* (o.v.) of the test statistic. The test

statistic will be a quantity that has some relationship to the parameter in question. For example, when investigating μ, we could look at $\bar{x}$. Actually (when n is large), we look at the standard score for $\bar{x}$, namely, $(\bar{x} - \mu)/(\sigma/\sqrt{n})$. In this expression, we use the value of μ given in the null hypothesis H_0 because H_0 is assumed true until there is evidence to the contrary.

4. **Determine the critical region.** The critical region consists of those values of the test statistic that strongly favor the alternate hypothesis H_a. The actual size of the critical region depends on the level of significance α. This is because the critical region is chosen in such a way that the probability will be α that the test statistic will fall in the critical region (if H_0 were true).

5. **Make your decision.** If the test statistic falls in the critical region, reject H_0 in favor of H_a. When this occurs, some statisticians say the results are *statistically significant*, also giving the α level. If the test statistic does not fall in the critical region, we do not reject H_0. That is, we conclude that there is not enough evidence to reject H_0. You should interpret your decision in ordinary, nontechnical language.

Choosing H_0 and H_a

Often the statement of the problem will involve only one hypothesis, which will take the form of a claim, a belief, or a suspicion about the population. It is up to you to identify this as H_0 or H_a, and then write the other hypothesis.

For example, a nutritionist claimed that a food company's cans of soup contained more than 900 milligrams of sodium on the average.

- Write the statement in symbolic form:

$$\mu > 900 \quad \leftarrow \text{Claim}$$

- Now write the statement with an $=$ sign instead of $>$:

$$\mu = 900 \quad \leftarrow \text{Contains} = \text{sign. It is the null hypothesis.}$$

- Thus we test the hypotheses

$$H_0: \quad \mu = 900$$
$$H_a: \quad \mu > 900 \quad \leftarrow \text{Claim}$$

The preceding claim was the alternate hypothesis. Sometimes the claim is the null hypothesis. For example, an auto company claimed that the mean weight of its pickup trucks was 2 tons:

$$\mu = 2$$

This is a statement of no difference; it contains an $=$ sign. So it is H_0. What about H_a? If H_0 is false, then μ could be either more than 2 or less than 2. If we have no *prior* reason to believe which of these might be true, we should allow for either possibility and use $\mu \neq 2$ as the alternate hypothesis. So we would test

$$H_0: \quad \mu = 2 \quad \leftarrow \text{Claim}$$
$$H_a: \quad \mu \neq 2$$

The following table gives the hypothesis tests to be performed when only one statement about a population is given:

Summary of Types of Hypothesis Tests

Statement	μ is	More than 100	Less than 100	Different from 100	Equal to 100
Null Hypothesis	H_0	$\mu = 100$	$\mu = 100$	$\mu = 100$	$\mu = 100$
Alternate Hypothesis	H_a	$\mu > 100$	$\mu < 100$	$\mu \neq 100$	$\mu \neq 100$

EXAMPLE 8.4

A sports biologist claimed that female distance runners tend to be taller on the average than women in general, who have an average height of 64 inches. To study this, she obtained a random sample of 40 female distance runners and recorded their heights with the following results: $\bar{x} = 65.6$ inches and $s = 3.3$ inches. Using these results, test the claim at the 5% level of significance, that is, use $\alpha = .05$. (*Note:* Although we will need the value of σ, it is not given. However, since the sample size is large, we can use s as an estimate. Hence $\sigma \doteq 3.3$ inches.)

Solution

We will go through the five steps outlined in the box.

1. *Hypotheses:*   The claim is that $\mu > 64$. Thus our hypotheses are

$$H_0: \quad \mu = 64$$
$$H_a: \quad \mu > 64$$

2. *Level of significance:*   This is given as $\alpha = .05$.

3. *Test statistic and observed value:*   It is natural to look at the value of $\bar{x}$ or, more precisely, its standard score:

$$z = \frac{\bar{x} - \mu}{\sigma/\sqrt{n}} = \frac{65.6 - 64}{3.3/\sqrt{40}} = \frac{1.6}{.522} = 3.07$$

Recall that we are assuming for the moment that H_0 is true. Therefore, for μ we substituted 64, the value given in H_0.

4. *Critical region (favors H_a):*   Large values of $\bar{x}$ would favor the alternate hypothesis H_a. Large values of $\bar{x}$ correspond to large values of z. How large should z be to convince us to reject H_0 in favor of H_a? The answer is, so large that such a value would be unlikely (if H_0 were true). How unlikely? So unlikely that the probability is only $\alpha = .05$. See Figure 8.7.

From Appendix Table B.3, we see that $P(0 < z < 1.65) = .45$. So $P(z \geq 1.65) = .5 - .45 = .05$. Thus our critical value is $z_{.05} = 1.65$. [Recall from Section 7.4 that $z_{.05}$ is the value of z such that the area to the right of it is .05.] The critical region consists of values of $z \geq 1.65$.

5. *Decision:*   Our observed value is $z = 3.07$. Since $3.07 > 1.65$, it is in the critical region. Hence we reject H_0 in favor of H_a. Therefore, it does appear that female distance runners tend to be taller on the average than women in general.

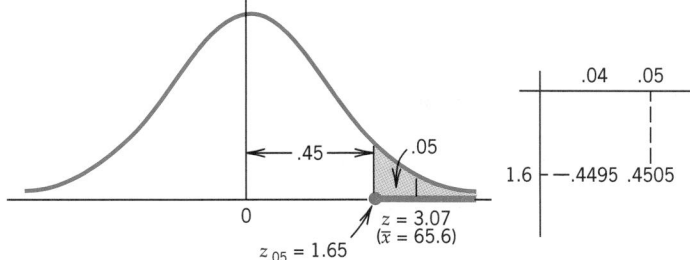

Figure 8.7

EXAMPLE 8.5

A high school mathematics department made a change in its curriculum. One of the instructors in the department suspected that the change would result in a lowering of math skills. Students in the old program showed a mean of 70 points on a mathematics proficiency exam. Forty-two students from the new program had the following scores:

62	68	85	61	54	78	63
58	65	53	57	52	76	69
65	54	58	81	76	78	82
58	68	88	61	71	59	47
61	80	78	67	75	58	73
77	75	70	66	84	79	72

Do the data indicate that the new program results in a lowering of math skills (on the average)? Use the 2% level of significance.

Solution

The population consists of current or future students in the new program. Let μ = the mean score for this population.

1. *Hypotheses:* Apparently the instructor suspects that $\mu < 70$. The hypotheses are

$$H_0: \quad \mu = 70$$
$$H_a: \quad \mu < 70$$

2. *Level of significance:* $\alpha = .02$

3. *Test statistic and observed value:* Here again, we use the standard score z as the test statistic

$$z = \frac{\bar{x} - \mu}{\sigma / \sqrt{n}}$$

For μ we substitute the value given in the null hypothesis. We must compute $\bar{x}$ from the sample data. The population standard deviation is unknown, but since the sample size is large, we can use the sample standard deviation as an estimate. To compute $\bar{x}$ and s, we will need the following sums:

$$\sum x = 62 + 58 + 65 + \cdots + 72 = 2862$$

$$\sum x^2 = 62^2 + 58^2 + 65^2 + \cdots + 72^2 = 199{,}408$$

$$\bar{x} = \frac{\sum x}{n} = \frac{2862}{42} \doteq 68.14$$

$$s = \sqrt{\frac{n\left(\sum x^2\right) - \left(\sum x\right)^2}{n(n-1)}} = \sqrt{\frac{(42)(199{,}408) - (2862)^2}{(42)(41)}}$$

$$s \doteq 10.34$$

The observed value of z is

$$z = \frac{\bar{x} - \mu}{\sigma/\sqrt{n}} = \frac{68.14 - 70}{10.34/\sqrt{42}} = -1.17$$

4. *Critical region:* This is always obtained by examining the alternate hypothesis H_a and using α. Values of $\bar{x}$ that favor H_a are those that are far to the left of 70. Since

$$z = \frac{\bar{x} - \mu}{\sigma/\sqrt{n}}$$

where $\mu = 70$, values of $\bar{x}$ far to the left of 70 correspond to values of z far to the left of 0. Values of z that lead to rejection of H_0 are those so far to the left of 0 that the probability is only $\alpha = .02$ that such values would occur if H_0 were true (Figure 8.8). Keep in mind the symmetry of the standard normal distribution. Using Appendix Table B.3, look up the z value corresponding to an area as close to .48 as possible. This value is 2.05, symbolically written $z_{.02}$. Therefore, by symmetry, the desired critical value is $-z_{.02} = -2.05$. Thus the critical region consists of values of z such that $z \le -2.05$.

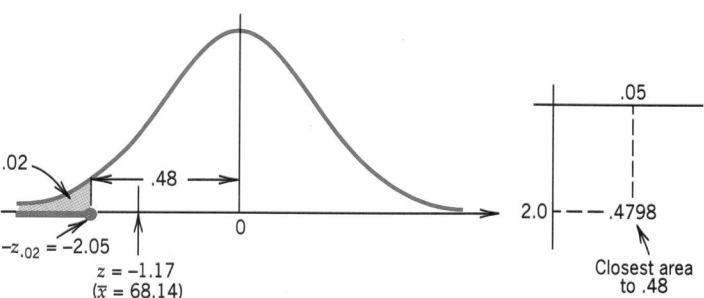

Figure 8.8

5. *Decision:* From step 3, $z = -1.17$. This is not in the critical region. Therefore, we do not reject H_0. There is not enough evidence to justify the instructor's suspicion that the new mathematics option will result in lower scores (on the average).

Minitab Printout Corresponding to Example 8.5

Z-Test

```
Test of mu = 70.00 vs mu < 70.00
The assumed sigma = 10.3

Variable      N       Mean    StDev   SE Mean       Z    P-Value
C1           42      68.14    10.34      1.57    -1.18       0.12
```

Given are the values of $N = 42$, Mean ($\bar{x} = 68.14$), StDev ($s = 10.34$), SE Mean (standard error of the mean, $s/\sqrt{n} = 1.57$), and $z = -1.18$. P-values will be discussed in Section 8.4. The observed values (-1.17 in the example and -1.18 given by Minitab) are slightly different because of different round-off procedures.

In the preceding pages, we have seen examples of three basic types of tests with their corresponding critical regions. A review of these tests follows.

1. In Example 8.4, we tested

$$H_0: \quad \mu = 64$$
$$H_a: \quad \mu > 64$$
$$\alpha = .05$$

The critical value is

$$z_\alpha = z_{.05} = 1.65$$

See Figure 8.9.

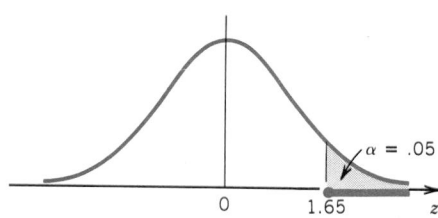

Figure 8.9
Right-Tailed Critical Region

Because of the location of the critical region, this is called a **right-tailed test.**

2. In Example 8.5, we tested

$$H_0: \quad \mu = 70$$
$$H_a: \quad \mu < 70$$
$$\alpha = .02$$

The critical value is

$$-z_\alpha = -z_{.02} = -2.05$$

See Figure 8.10.

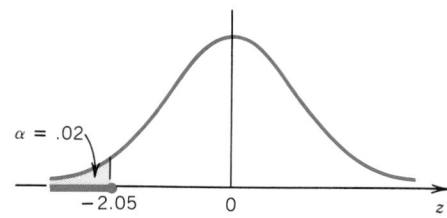

Figure 8.10
Left-Tailed Critical Region

This is called a **left-tailed test.**

3. In the introductory example of this section, we tested

$$H_0: \quad \mu = 336$$
$$H_a: \quad \mu \neq 336$$
$$\alpha = .05$$

The critical values are

$$\pm z_{\alpha/2} = \pm z_{.025} = \pm 1.96$$

See Figure 8.11.

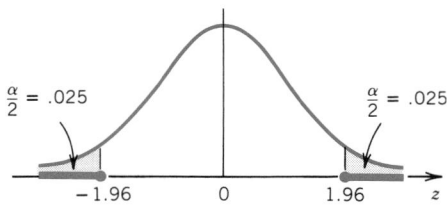

Figure 8.11
Two-Tailed Critical Region

This is called a **two-tailed test.**

All these tests used a test statistic z that had a standard normal distribution. A statistical test that uses a standard normal distribution is called a **z test.** We summarize in the box the essential features of a z test for a population mean.

The z Test for a Population Mean (Based on a Large Sample) To test hypotheses concerning μ (when sample size is at least 30), we use the test statistic

$$z = \frac{\bar{x} - \mu}{\sigma / \sqrt{n}}$$

which has the standard normal distribution (approximately). For μ, we substitute the value given in the null hypothesis. The observed value of z is computed by substituting $\bar{x}$ and n obtained from the sample data. (If σ is unknown, we use s.) If z falls in the critical region, we reject the null hypothesis H_0. Otherwise, we do not reject H_0. Assume that α is the level of significance of the test. Critical values of z are obtained in Appendix Table B.3. The possible critical regions are described as follows:

(a)   If the alternate hypothesis contains the symbol $>$, we conduct a right-tailed test. The critical region is displayed in Figure 8.12.

(b)   If the alternate hypothesis contains the symbol $<$, we conduct a left-tailed test. The critical region is displayed in Figure 8.13.

(c)   If the alternate hypothesis contains the symbol $\neq$, we conduct a two-tailed test. The critical region is displayed in Figure 8.14.

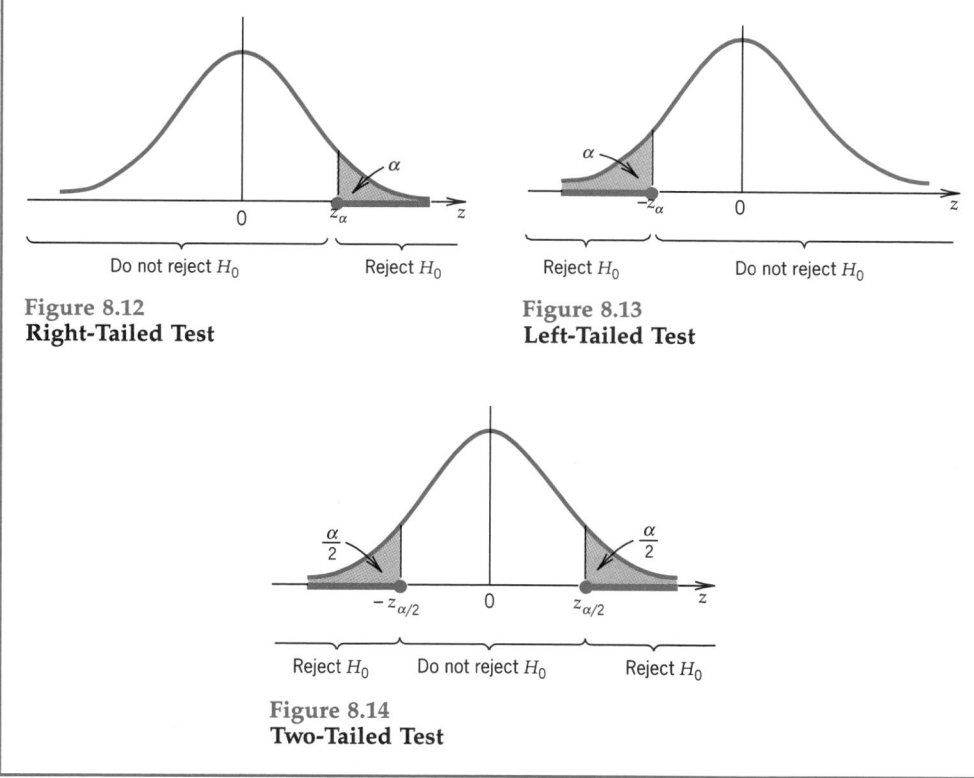

Figure 8.12
Right-Tailed Test

Figure 8.13
Left-Tailed Test

Figure 8.14
Two-Tailed Test

We can tell which type of test (i.e., which type of critical region) is to be used by examining the alternate hypothesis H_a because those values of the test statistic that strongly favor H_a constitute the critical region. We summarize this in Table 8.2 (page 350). The actual critical values will vary from one situation to the next. These can be found once the level of significance α is specified. *Note:* It is customary to write our hypotheses in such a way that the symbol for the parameter (such as μ) appears first. For example, we write

$$\mu < 70 \quad \text{rather than} \quad 70 > \mu$$

Table 8.2
Hypothesis Tests Concerning μ

If H_a Contains	>	<	$\neq$
Perform	Right-tailed test	Left-tailed test	Two-tailed test

We will follow this convention throughout the book. If we did not always follow this practice, Table 8.2 would not always be correct.

Which Hypothesis Are We Trying to "Prove"?

Our method enables us to decide whether there is sufficient evidence to "prove" the alternate hypothesis H_a but not the null hypothesis H_0. If we reject H_0, we accept H_a. In this case, we know the risk (chance) that we made an error (Type I error)—it is α, which is always known and is always chosen to be small. However, if we do not reject H_0, we have seen that the chance of an error (Type II error) is β, which is usually unknown. Sometimes β can be quite large. Therefore if we do not reject H_0, we are not prepared to say that the null hypothesis has been established, because we do not know our chance of being wrong. This is why we avoid strong language like "accept H_0," settling instead for the much weaker "do not reject H_0" or "fail to reject H_0."

Sometimes an analogy is drawn between hypothesis testing and a criminal trial. The defendant is presumed innocent unless there is evidence of his guilt beyond a reasonable doubt. In hypothesis testing, the null hypothesis is presumed to be true unless there is sufficient evidence to the contrary. This evidence consists of the test statistic falling in the critical region—something that would be unlikely to occur if H_0 were true. In a criminal trial, a verdict of "not guilty" does not necessarily mean the defendant did not commit the crime; it just means there was not sufficient evidence of guilt. In hypothesis testing, if we do not reject H_0, we do not assert that it is definitely true. The statistical evidence is just not strong enough to reject it.

The lesson for researchers is this: Formulate the statement you wish to prove as the alternate hypothesis H_a. Then hope your test will lead to rejection of H_0. In this case, you can place some faith in the truth of H_a because you know the chance that you made an error (α), and this chance is small.

Controlling Errors

Since α is the probability of a Type I error, it measures the risk of an error when we reject the null hypothesis. In general, α is chosen to be small; however, the more serious a Type I error, the smaller we would want the value of α. Determining the seriousness of a Type I error in a given situation is a subjective judgment that must be made by the researcher. In any case, *the smaller the value of α, the more confident we may feel about our decision if we reject H_0*. Some of the commonly chosen values for α are .01, .02, .025, .05, and .10. Since α measures the risk associated with a Type I error, the reader might wonder why we would settle for a value of .05 for α when we could choose .01 or something even smaller. The answer lies in the fact that when we reduce the value of α, there will be an increase in the value of β, the probability of a Type II error (not rejecting H_0 when it is false). (To get an idea of why this is true, see Exercise 8.140.)

Therefore, even though we do not usually know the value of β, we can have an influence on its size by our choice of α. For a fixed sample size, the smaller the value of α, the larger the value of β. The larger the value of α, the smaller the value of β. If a Type I error is very serious when compared to a Type II error, we should choose a rather small value of α, say, .01 or .02. However, if we are very concerned about a Type II error, we may choose a larger value for α, say, .10. One technique that can often be used to decrease the size of β is to increase the sample size.

Statistical Significance Versus Practical Significance

When the null hypothesis is rejected, we say our result is *statistically significant*. This means the data suggest that the parameter (such as the population mean) differs from the value asserted in the null hypothesis. But this difference may not be large enough to have any practical significance. The larger the sample, the more likely a statistical test is to detect a small difference that may exist between the actual value of a parameter and the value given in the null hypothesis. For example, suppose a company manufactured a diet drug and wanted the drug to produce a weight loss of 25 pounds on average. However, assume the true mean weight loss was 24.5 lb. If the company tested the drug with a large enough sample of users, the null hypothesis H_0: $\mu = 25$ lb might be rejected. But there is not much practical significance to a difference of only .5 lb. This is why confidence intervals are generally superior to tests of hypotheses: A confidence interval gives you an idea of the magnitude of the parameter.

EXERCISES

8.27 For the claims in parts (a)–(g), (i) find H_0 and H_a, (ii) give the type of critical region (right-tailed, left-tailed, or two-tailed), and (iii) explain the meaning of a Type I and Type II error.

(a) The mean amount μ of rainfall per year is more than 72 inches.

(b) The mean number μ of books borrowed per day from a library is 250.

(c) The mean temperature μ, taken at 1 P.M., in a coastal town for the month of July over a 10-year period is less than 78°F.

(d) The mean age of professors at a large university is more than 36.

(e) The mean salary of employees at an industrial plant is less than $29,500.

(f) The mean number of families per month that are below poverty level in a state is 18,000.

(g) The mean grade point average of graduating seniors at a university is greater than 2.3.

8.28 Suppose you are testing the claim that the mean μ of a population is greater than 90. Assume that the sample size is large.

(a) Give H_0 and H_a.

(b) Specify the critical region in terms of the standard normal z for the given level of significance in each of the following:

(i) $\alpha = .01$ (ii) $\alpha = .05$ (iii) $\alpha = .10$

8.29 Repeat Exercise 8.28, assuming that you are to test the claim that the population mean μ is 90.

8.30 Repeat Exercise 8.28, assuming that you are to test the claim that the population mean μ is less than 90.

8.31 The claim to be tested is that the mean μ of a population is smaller than 30. Suppose that $\bar{x} = 24$ and the population standard deviation is $\sigma = 40$. For each sample size n, determine whether H_0 would be rejected at each significance level (i) .01, (ii) .05, and (iii) .10.

(a) $n = 100$ (b) $n = 225$ (c) $n = 400$

8.32 Sometimes a critical region is given in terms of $\bar{x}$. Assume that you are to test the claim that the mean μ of a particular population is greater than 30. Assume that $\sigma = 40$ and you decide to use $n = 64$ random observations. Determine the level of significance α in each of the following, where the critical region is given in terms of $\bar{x}$.

(a) $\bar{x} \geq 36$ (b) $\bar{x} \geq 42$ (c) $\bar{x} \geq 38$ (d) $\bar{x} \geq 40$

8.33 A bus company advertised a mean time of 150 minutes for a trip between two cities. A consumer group had reason to believe that the mean time was more than 150 minutes. A sample of 40 trips showed a mean of 153 minutes and a standard deviation of 7.5 minutes. Using a 5% level of significance, is there sufficient evidence to support the consumer group's contention? What type of error has possibly been committed? Explain the error in ordinary language.

8.34 Under laboratory test conditions a handball should bounce 48 inches. The manufacturer was receiving complaints that the balls were not as lively as they should be. The manufacturer randomly sampled 50 handballs and found a mean bounce of 46.5 inches and a standard deviation of 5 inches. At the 5% level of significance, is there sufficient evidence to suggest the manufacturer's handballs are bouncing less than 48 inches on average? What type of error has possibly been committed? Explain the error in ordinary language.

8.35 To confirm her belief that abused children would show elevated levels of depression, a psychologist gave a test called the Profile of Mood States (POMS) to a sample of 50 abused children. The results showed a mean depression score of 17.3 and a standard deviation of 5.4. At the 5% level, can she conclude that abused children in general have a mean depression level of more than 15 (the mean for college students)?

8.36 Prior to expanding the facilities of a town library, it was determined that 385 books per day were loaned out. It was believed that a new addition to the building would increase the mean number of books loaned out per day. After completion of the new addition, a random sample of 35 days showed a mean of 395 and a standard deviation of 26 books loaned out per day. At the 10% level of significance, is there sufficient evidence to indicate that more books are being loaned out per day, on the average?

8.37 The owner of an artesian well-drilling company suspected that, for a large tract of development land, the average depth of water below the surface was less than 500 feet. A sample of 32 wells gave a mean depth of $\bar{x} = 486$ feet and a standard deviation of $s = 53$ feet. At the 1% level of significance, is the owner's suspicion justified?

8.38 A plastic has a mean breaking strength of 27 and a standard deviation of 6 pounds per square inch. A new process is developed and will replace the old one, provided that there is substantial evidence that it improves the strength of the product. A random sample of 40 pieces made with the new process gives a sample mean of 30 pounds per square inch. Assuming that the variability is unchanged (i.e., $\sigma = 6$), is there sufficient evidence to suggest that the strength of the product has increased at the 1% level of significance?

8.39 Repeat Exercise 8.38 using $\sigma = 15$. Comment on the relationship between the ability to detect a change and the amount of spread of data values about the mean.

8.40 A cereal is packaged to contain 16 ounces, on the average. A consumer agency has received many complaints claiming that packages of the cereal contain less than 16 ounces. To test the claim that the mean content μ is less than 16 ounces, the consumer agency randomly selects 100 packages and finds that $\bar{x} = 15.1$ and $s = 3$.

(a)   Complete the test at the 1% level of significance.

(b)   Comment on why it seems appropriate for the consumer agency to use a small level of significance.

(c)   If the mean content μ really were 16 ounces, how many times in 10,000, on the average, would a sample mean result in a value of 15.1 or less? (Use $\sigma = 3$.)

(d)   Based on your answer in part (c), does the evidence appear substantial that the population mean μ is less than 16?

8.41 A manufacturer of floor mops would like his product to last 700 hours, on the average. He hopes the mean number of hours is not a lot less than 700 (people will not continue to buy his product) nor a lot more than 700 (people would seldom have to buy the product). However, the manufacturer has reason to believe the mean may have changed. A random sample of 48 items shows that $\bar{x} = 675$ and $s = 77$ hours.

(a) Complete the test at the 5% level of significance.

(b) What type of error may have been made?

(c) What is the probability of committing this error?

8.42 A podiatrist recorded the recovery time, measured in days, for 38 patients. He was trying out a new procedure and hoped the result would be less recovery time on average. The mean recovery time using the previous procedure was 6.5 days. The recorded times were

| 8 | 7 | 2 | 6 | 9 | 4 | 5 | 3 | 7 | 8 | 10 | 7 | 7 | 6 | 4 | 10 | 3 | 6 | 8 |
| 2 | 5 | 4 | 4 | 5 | 3 | 8 | 7 | 4 | 6 | 3 | 7 | 12 | 4 | 3 | 6 | 6 | 9 | 4 |

The sample mean and standard deviation for these data are 5.84 and 2.41, respectively. Using a 5% level of significance, do the data indicate that the new procedure will require less recovery time, on average?

8.43 An owner of a retail outlet sold and provided service for copying machines. One type of machine, the DW 140 model, needed service often. The owner was interested in the mean time required to service this model, and decided not to carry the model if the mean repair time appeared to be more than 40 minutes. The repairman provided the following 39 times (in minutes):

23	27	28	33	35	37	39	39	39	39	40	40	41
42	42	42	42	43	43	44	44	45	46	46	46	47
47	47	48	49	50	51	52	53	53	56	57	61	62

Note that $\bar{x} = 44.05$ and $s = 8.45$. Use a 5% level of significance, and decide whether the owner will continue to carry the model.

8.44 A typing instructor wondered whether a new method of instruction would result in a change in the mean typing speed of students. The old method produced a mean of 64 words per minute. The results (words per minute) of 38 students using the new method were as follows:

56	60	60	76	60	59	41	66	67	33	55	43	61
71	73	60	56	77	43	58	65	67	71	56	48	90
82	46	68	36	27	52	64	54	49	69	46	68

Now $\sum x = 2233$ and $\sum x^2 = 138{,}053$. At the 5% level of significance, can the instructor conclude that the new mean is different from 64?

8.4

P-VALUES

The method of hypothesis testing discussed in the previous section is the **classical approach** to hypothesis testing, and it is the method we will emphasize in this book. However, some statisticians use a different approach. They omit the step of finding the critical region. Instead, they find the *P*-value associated with the value of the test statistic. Before giving a formal definition of this term, let us look at Example 8.4 again.

In this example, we investigated μ, the mean height of female distance runners. We tested

$$H_0: \quad \mu = 64 \text{ inches}$$
$$H_a: \quad \mu > 64 \text{ inches}$$

We used $\alpha = .05$. The critical region consisted of all $z \geq 1.65$, since $z_{.05} = 1.65$. The average height for the sample was $\bar{x} = 65.6$ inches. Its z score (the observed value of the test statistic) was

$$z = \frac{\bar{x} - \mu}{\sigma/\sqrt{n}} = \frac{65.6 - 64}{3.3/\sqrt{40}} = 3.07$$

(*Note:* We used 64 for μ. This is the value of μ if H_0 is true.) The value $z = 3.07$ is quite far into the critical region. Now the larger the value of $\bar{x}$ (or equivalently the z score), the stronger the evidence in support of the alternate hypothesis $H_a: \mu > 64$. The probability of getting a value of the test statistic z as favorable or more favorable to H_a than $z = 3.07$ (if H_0 were true) is, from Appendix Table B.3,

$$P(z \geq 3.07) = .5 - .4989 = .0011$$

Hence if H_0 were true, the chance of getting a value of $z \geq 3.07$ is only about 1 in 1000. In other words, it would be very unlikely that we would get a value of z so large if H_0 were really true. Therefore, since we did get a value this large (i.e., so favorable to H_a), we are inclined to reject H_0 in favor of H_a. The probability $P(z \geq 3.07) = .0011$ is called the **P-value** associated with $z = 3.07$. See Figure 8.15. (Often the P-value is denoted by P.)

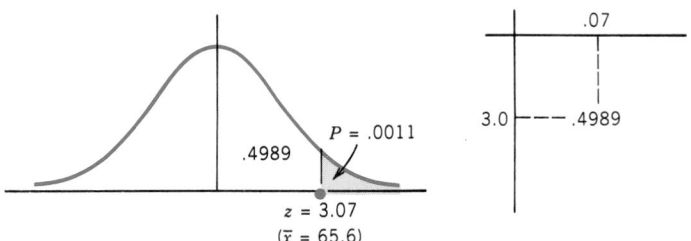

Figure 8.15
P-value = $P(z \geq 3.07) = .5 - .4989 = .0011$

> **Definition** Suppose that we are conducting a test of hypotheses and we calculate the observed value of the test statistic. The *P-value* is the probability of getting a value of the test statistic as favorable or more favorable to the alternate hypothesis than the observed value (if H_0 were true).

The importance of the P-value is that it enables us to judge just how strong (or weak) the evidence is in support of the alternate hypothesis H_a. *The smaller the P-value, the stronger the evidence is in support of the alternate hypothesis.*

How small should the P-value be for us to reject H_0 in favor of H_a? This is a subjective judgment. Some journals will not accept results as statistically significant (i.e., justifying a rejection of the null hypothesis) unless the P-value is less than or equal to .05.

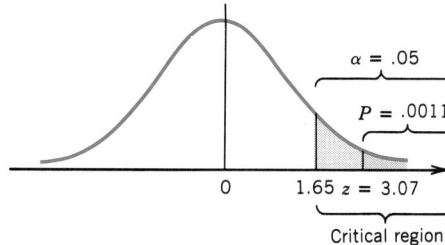

Figure 8.16

What this amounts to is using the *P*-value in conjunction with a predetermined level of significance. To see how this works, recall that the hypotheses discussed previously were tested in Example 8.4 using a level of significance $\alpha = .05$. The critical value was 1.65. In Figure 8.16, we show the relationship between α and the *P*-value associated with the observed value of $z = 3.07$.

The fact that the observed value $z = 3.07$ is in the critical region corresponds to the fact that $P = .0011$ is less than $\alpha = .05$. We could have tested the hypotheses at the 5% level of significance above *without finding the critical region*. Since P is less than .05, the observed value must be in the critical region; therefore, we reject the null hypothesis H_0.

This leads to a slightly different approach to testing hypotheses, summarized as follows:

The *P*-Value Approach to Testing Hypotheses   When testing hypotheses at a level of significance α, we reject the null hypothesis if

$$P \le \alpha$$

We would not reject H_0 if

$$P > \alpha$$

The following example shows how to compute the *P*-value for a two-tailed test.

EXAMPLE 8.6
In Section 8.3, we discussed a test of hypotheses concerning the mean weight for bags of peanuts:

$$H_0: \quad \mu = 336 \text{ g}$$
$$H_a: \quad \mu \ne 336 \text{ g}$$

The sample size was $n = 40$, $\sigma = 11$ g, and the sample mean weight of the 40 bags of peanuts was $\bar{x} = 329.91$ g. Find the *P*-value. Would the null hypothesis be rejected if the level of significance were .005?

Solution
The observed value of the test statistic is

$$z = \frac{\bar{x} - \mu}{\sigma / \sqrt{n}} = \frac{329.91 - 336}{11 / \sqrt{40}} = -3.5$$

The values of the test statistic z that are as favorable or more favorable to H_a than $z = -3.5$ are those values of $z \leq -3.5$ or $z \geq 3.5$. (Remember that values of $\bar{x}$ that favor H_a in this problem are those that are much larger than or much less than 336. These $\bar{x}$ values correspond to values of z that are much larger than or much less than 0.) Therefore, the P-value associated with $z = -3.5$ is the probability

$$P(z \leq -3.5 \text{ or } z \geq 3.5) = 2 \cdot P(z \geq 3.5)$$
$$= 2[.5 - P(0 \leq z \leq 3.5)]$$
$$= 2(.5 - .4998) = 2(.0002) = .0004$$

See Figure 8.17.

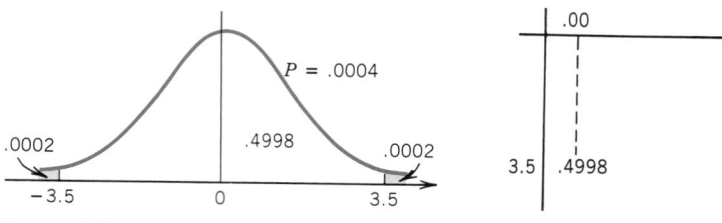

Figure 8.17

It is very unlikely (the probability is only .0004) that we would observe a value of z as favorable or more favorable to the alternate hypothesis H_a than $z = -3.5$ if the null hypothesis H_0 were really correct. Now suppose that the level of significance is $\alpha = .005$. Since the P-value is less than .005, we would reject the null hypothesis.

Figure 8.18 is a graphic display of P-values:

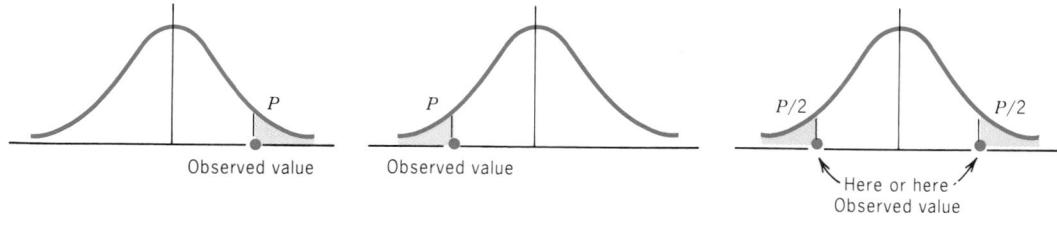

For a right-tailed test   For a left-tailed test   For a two-tailed test

Figure 8.18
P-values

EXERCISES

In Problems 8.45–8.50, find the P-value and decide whether to reject or not to reject the null hypothesis. Assume $\alpha = .05$.

8.45 H_0: $\mu = 80$; H_a: $\mu > 80$ Observed value: $z = 1.75$

8.46 H_0: $\mu = 23.5$; H_a: $\mu > 23.5$ Observed value: $z = 1.2$

8.47 H_0: $\mu = 15$; H_a: $\mu < 15$ Observed value: $z = -.83$

8.48 H_0: $\mu = 3.7$; H_a: $\mu < 3.7$ Observed value: $z = -2.95$

8.49 H_0: $\mu = 80$; H_a: $\mu \neq 80$ Observed value: $z = 1.75$

8.50 H_0: $\mu = 125.5$; H_a: $\mu \neq 125.5$ Observed value: $z = 3.5$

8.51 In parts (a)–(c), test the hypothesis that a population mean μ is more than 30. Assume $\sigma = 40$ and the sample size is $n = 64$. Determine the *P*-value for each of the following three values of $\bar{x}$:

    (a) $\bar{x} = 35$ **(b)** $\bar{x} = 37$ **(c)** $\bar{x} = 39$

    (d)   Determine the *P*-values in parts (a)–(c) for testing the hypothesis that μ is not equal to 30.

8.52 Repeat Exercise 8.51, replacing $n = 64$ with $n = 100$. Compare your results with those obtained in Exercise 8.51.

8.53 A consumer group suspected that an insecticide was effective for less than the advertised 12 days, on the average. The group used a random sample of size 36 and obtained a mean of 11.25 and a standard deviation of 3 days.

    (a)   Find the *P*-value.

    (b)   For which of the following levels of significance would H_0 be rejected?
       (i) $\alpha = .10$ **(ii)** $\alpha = .05$ **(iii)** $\alpha = .01$
       [*Hint:* These questions can be answered using your answer in part (a).]

    (c)   For each case in part (b), what type of error has possibly been committed?

8.54 A city assessor suspected that the mean income per household had increased over the old mean of $25,200. A random sample of 40 households in the city showed a mean income of $27,400 and a standard deviation of $6325.

    (a)   Find the *P*-value.

    (b)   Would H_0 be rejected at the given level of significance?
       (i) $\alpha = .05$ **(ii)** $\alpha = .01$

8.55 In Exercise 8.35, we were interested in whether abused children had a mean depression score of more than 15 on a psychological test. For the sample data, $n = 50$, $\bar{x} = 17.3$, and $s = 5.4$. The level of significance was 5%. Complete the hypothesis test using the *P*-value approach.

8.56 A vendor was concerned that a soft drink machine was not dispensing 6 ounces per cup, on average. A sample of size 40 gave a mean amount per cup of 5.95 ounces and a standard deviation of .15 ounce.

    (a)   Find the *P*-value.

    (b)   For which of the following levels of significance would H_0 be rejected?
       (i) $\alpha = .10$ **(ii)** $\alpha = .05$ **(iii)** $\alpha = .01$
       [*Hint:* These can be answered using your answer in part (a).]

    (c)   For each case in part (b), what type of error has possibly been committed?

8.57 In Exercise 8.37, we discussed a conjecture to the effect that the mean depth of water below the surface in a large development tract was less than 500 feet. For the sample data, $n = 32$ test holes, $\bar{x} = 486$ feet, and $s = 53$ feet. Complete the test using the *P*-value approach and the 1% level of significance.

8.58 A tire gauge, when tested on a machine, is designed to measure 30 pounds per square inch (psi). The manufacturer was concerned that the gauges were not meeting specifications. A sample of 50 readings gave a sample mean of 30.1 psi and a standard deviation of .35.

    (a)   Find the *P*-value.

    (b)   For which of the following levels of significance would H_0 be rejected?
       (i) $\alpha = .10$ **(ii)** $\alpha = .05$ **(iii)** $\alpha = .01$
       [*Hint:* These can be answered using your answer in part (a).]

    (c)   For each case in part (b), what type of error has possibly been committed?

8.59   In Exercise 8.44, we studied the question of whether a typing instructor could conclude that a new method of instruction gave a mean typing speed different from 64 words per minute. A partial Minitab printout follows.

Z-Test

```
Test of mu = 64.00 vs mu not = 64.00
The assumed sigma = 13.6

Variable      N      Mean      StDev    SE Mean       Z     P-Value
Speed        38     58.76     13.59       2.20    -2.38
```

(a)   Find the P-value.

(b)   Give the levels of significance for which the null hypothesis would be rejected.

8.60   Suppose that the outcome of a test of hypotheses gives a P-value of .07. For what levels of significance would the null hypothesis be rejected?

8.5

INFERENCE CONCERNING A POPULATION MEAN (Small-Sample Case)

Confidence intervals and hypothesis tests based on large samples ($n \geq 30$), discussed previously, rely on the fact that the statistic

$$\frac{\bar{x} - \mu}{\sigma/\sqrt{n}}$$

has approximately a standard normal distribution when $n \geq 30$. This follows from the Central Limit Theorem discussed in Section 7.7.

If σ is unknown (and this is usually the case), a large sample size implies that the sample standard deviation s should be a good estimate of σ. So we can use s in place of σ. Thus we are really using the statistic

$$\frac{\bar{x} - \mu}{s/\sqrt{n}}$$

When $n \geq 30$, this has approximately a standard normal distribution. But when the sample size is small ($n < 30$), we can no longer assume that this has a standard normal distribution. So if we were testing hypotheses, we could not use the table for the standard normal distribution (Appendix Table B.3) to find critical values. We would need another table.

William S. Gosset, an employee of the Guinness Brewery in Dublin, was interested in statistical inference based on small samples. Because of variability in the ingredients of beer, the samples that can reasonably be viewed as coming from the same population are usually small. Gosset called this statistic t:

$$t = \frac{\bar{x} - \mu}{s/\sqrt{n}}$$

In a paper published in 1908,* Gosset described the distribution of this expression. He published under the pen name of Student. As the story goes, the Guinness company required that Gosset not use his real name because the company did not want its competitors to know it had the advantage of having a statistician as an employee. In any case, this statistic became known as **Student's t** and its distribution as **Student's t distribution.** However, for the expression to have Student's t distribution, the population of x values must be normal or approximately normal. No such assumption was needed for the large-sample methods discussed in this chapter.

Properties of Student's t Distribution

Suppose the population of interest is normal, at least approximately. By this we mean only that the population distribution is roughly mound-shaped and not strongly skewed. For random samples of size n obtained from an approximately normal population with mean μ, the random variable

$$t = \frac{\bar{x} - \mu}{s/\sqrt{n}}$$

has Student's t distribution, which has the following properties:

1. There is not just one t distribution but, in fact, an infinite number of them. Each one has a number associated with it called its **degrees of freedom, df.** For the expression

    $$t = \frac{\bar{x} - \mu}{s/\sqrt{n}}$$

    the number of degrees of freedom, df, is $n - 1$. We will not go into the mathematical fine points involved in the notion of degrees of freedom. We will simply follow the custom of using this to identify the particular t distribution with which we are working.

2. A t distribution resembles the standard normal distribution in shape. Its curve is symmetric with respect to a vertical line through 0, and the curve extends indefinitely in the positive and negative directions. The expected value of t is 0. However, it is more spread out than the standard normal curve. (It has a larger standard deviation.) As with all continuous probability distributions, the total area under a t curve is 1. See Figure 8.19.

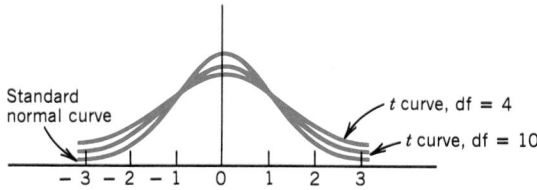

Figure 8.19

3. As the value of n gets larger and larger, Student's t curves get closer and closer to the standard normal curve. In fact, for $n \geq 30$, a t curve is approximately

---

*Student, 1908, pp. 1–25.

standard normal. This means that for $n \geq 30$

$$t = \frac{\bar{x} - \mu}{s/\sqrt{n}}$$

is approximately standard normal.

Appendix Table B.4 relates probabilities to various values of t that we will need. Specifically, for a particular t distribution, it gives the value of t such that the area under the t curve to the right of this value is equal to some desired probability. For example, suppose that we are concerned with the t distribution with df $= 15$, and we want the value of t such that the area under the curve to the right of it is .05. We denote this t value by $t_{.05}$. Locate the value of df in the left-hand column (df $= 15$). Now look at the column under $t_{.05}$. The intersection of this column with the row corresponding to df $= 15$ contains the desired value of t, namely, 1.753. Therefore, $t_{.05} = 1.753$. This means that $P(t \geq 1.753) = .05$. See Figure 8.20.

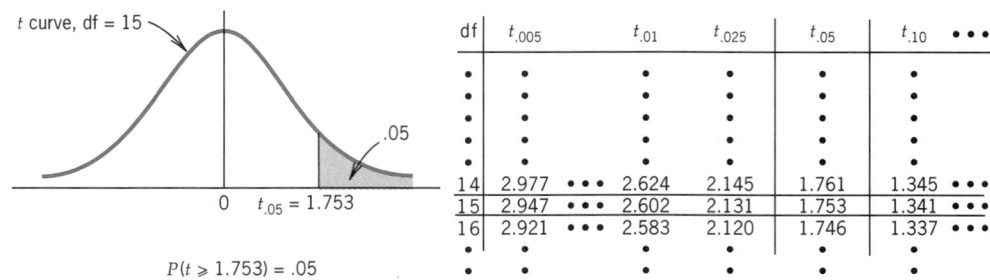

Figure 8.20

Remark   For values of df > 29 we use the last row in Appendix Table B.4. These are the same values we would get using Appendix Table B.3, since for df > 29, the t distributions are approximately standard normal.

EXAMPLE 8.7
For Student's t distribution with df $= 14$, find the value of t such that the area (probability) under the curve to the left of this value is .10.

Solution
By the symmetry of the t distribution, the desired value of t is $-t_{.10}$. (See Figure 8.21.) From Appendix Table B.4, we see that $t_{.10} = 1.345$, so the t value with the desired property is $-t_{.10} = -1.345$.

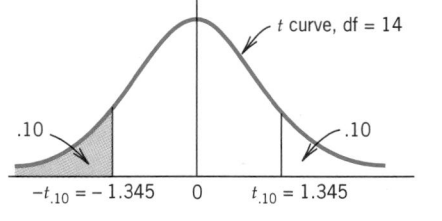
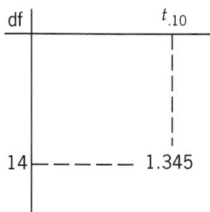

Figure 8.21
$P(t < -1.345) = .10$

When he derived the properties of the t distribution in his 1908 paper, Gosset had to assume the population was normal. As we have indicated, however, the population need be only approximately normal. For this reason, statistical procedures based on Student's t distribution are said to be **robust.**

Definition A statistical procedure that is still valid even though there may be deviations from the assumptions underlying the procedure is said to be *robust.*

Remark We will use Student's t distribution only in small-sample cases ($n < 30$). However, it can be used for large samples as well, and in this case, approximate normality is usually not a concern. Indeed some statisticians use Student's t distribution (where appropriate) whenever the population standard deviation σ is unknown. They prefer to use large-sample methods, like the z test of Section 8.3, only if σ is known, whereas when we used such large-sample methods, we estimated an unknown σ by the sample standard deviation s. The two approaches are not as different as they may seem, because when the sample size is large ($n \geq 30$), the standard normal distribution of z and the Student's t distribution are approximately the same.

Applications of Student's t Distribution

In the paper he published in 1908, Gosset (Student) discussed some data obtained by scientists A. Cushny and A. Peebles, who were studying the effects of optical isomers of hyoscyamine hydrobromide in inducing sleep. The following data give additional hours of sleep per night (x) induced in 10 patients treated with (L)-hyoscine. See Table 8.3.

The drug would be considered to increase sleep if the mean additional hours of sleep for all possible patients (μ) were greater than 0. Therefore, it would be of

Table 8.3
Student's Data

Additional Hours of Sleep Induced by (L)-Hyoscine

Patient	Additional Hours of Sleep
1	1.9
2	0.8
3	1.1
4	0.1
5	−0.1 (lost sleep)
6	4.4
7	5.5
8	1.6
9	4.6
10	3.4

$$\bar{x} = 2.33$$
$$s = 2.00$$

interest to test the hypotheses

$$H_0: \quad \mu = 0$$
$$H_a: \quad \mu > 0$$

We will complete a test of the hypotheses using the t distribution. Such a test is called a t **test.** Before applying the test, we should remember the requirement that the population be at least approximately normal (i.e., its distribution should be roughly mound-shaped and not strongly skewed). Sometimes this is known from the nature of the population being studied; for example, biological data are often normal.

But if you do not know whether the population is approximately normal, your sample data may provide a clue. To the extent that random samples may share properties of the population from which they were drawn, a picture of the data may reveal properties that would make a t test inappropriate. When a population has a skewed distribution, often a sample from the population will be skewed or have outliers. **So if the data are strongly skewed or if extreme outliers are present, a t test would not be appropriate.**

Figure 8.22 is a stem-and-leaf plot of the sleep data in Table 8.3. Such a small sample cannot be expected to mimic the population exactly. But there is nothing in Figure 8.22 that would be inconsistent with a mound-shaped population distribution. For example, the data are not strongly skewed and do not contain extreme outliers. So a t test would be appropriate. We complete the t test in Example 8.8.

```
-0 | 1
 0 | 1  8
 1 | 1  6  9
 2 |
 3 | 4
 4 | 4  6
 5 | 5              Note:   3 | 4 = 3.4
```

Figure 8.22
Stem-and-Leaf Plot for Sleep Data in Table 8.3

EXAMPLE 8.8

For the data in Table 8.3, test the claim that the drug increases sleep, on the average. Use the 5% level of significance.

Solution

1. *Hypotheses:*   The drug increases sleep if the average additional hours of sleep μ is greater than 0; therefore, we will test

    $$H_0: \quad \mu = 0$$
    $$H_a: \quad \mu > 0$$

2. *Level of significance:* $\alpha = .05$

3. *Test statistic and observed value:*

$$t = \frac{\bar{x} - \mu}{s/\sqrt{n}} = \frac{2.33 - 0}{2.00/\sqrt{10}} \doteq 3.68$$

(Note that we substitute the value 0 appearing in H_0 for μ in the test statistic.) The number of degrees of freedom is df $= n - 1 = 9$.

4. *Critical region:* Values of $\bar{x}$ far above 0 favor H_a. These correspond to values of t far to the right of 0. Therefore, we perform a right-tailed test. When df $= 9$, the critical value from Appendix Table B.4 is $t_\alpha = t_{.05} = 1.833$. Thus the critical region consists of values of $t \geq 1.833$. See Figure 8.23.

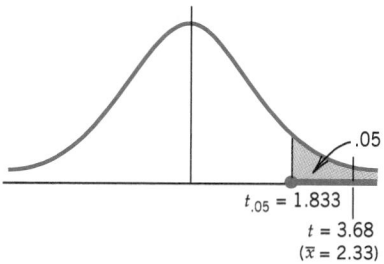
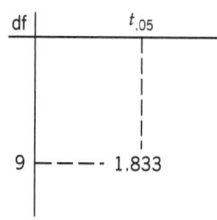

Figure 8.23

5. *Decision:* The observed value of 3.68 is in the critical region, so we reject H_0. This means that the evidence suggests that $\mu > 0$; therefore, the drug appears to increase sleep.

Data Desk Printout for Example 8.8

Test Ho: $\mu = 0$ vs Ha: $\mu > 0$
Sample Mean = 2.3300000 t-Statistic = 3.680 w/9 df
Reject Ho at Alpha = 0.0500
p = 0.0025

Data Desk allows the user to specify α. The P-value is given as .0025.

EXAMPLE 8.9

The American Heart Association recommends that an individual's cholesterol level be under 200 milligrams per 100 milliliters. The following are cholesterol readings of 16 women under age 40 randomly selected from the Framingham Heart Study:

233	197	192	179	174	217	186	221
188	209	196	167	238	179	196	191

At the 10% level of significance, do these readings suggest that women under 40 in the Framingham area have cholesterol readings below 200 on average?

Solution

1. *Hypotheses:* The question asked is whether the *population* mean is less than 200, that is, $\mu < 200$. The hypotheses are

$$H_0: \quad \mu = 200$$
$$H_a: \quad \mu < 200$$

2. *Level of significance:* $\alpha = .10$

3. *Test statistic and observed value:* Since the sample size ($n = 16$) is small, we will do a t test. The stem-and-leaf plot and modified boxplot in Figure 8.24 indicate that the sample data are slightly skewed, but not enough to prevent the use of a t test. Note that the boxplot does not show any suspected outliers.

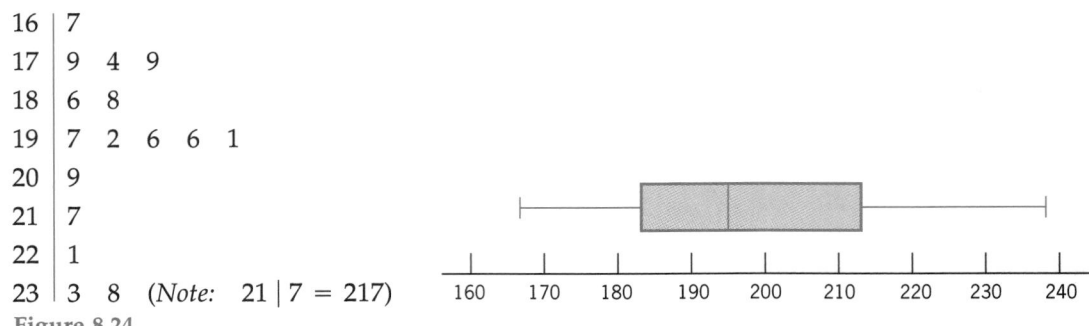

```
16 | 7
17 | 9  4  9
18 | 6  8
19 | 7  2  6  6  1
20 | 9
21 | 7
22 | 1
23 | 3  8   (Note:  21 | 7 = 217)
```

Figure 8.24
Stem-and-Leaf Plot and Modified Boxplot for Cholesterol Data

To find the observed value of t, we must first compute $\bar{x}$ and s from the sample data. The necessary sums are obtained from Table 8.4.

Table 8.4

x	x^2
233	54,289
197	38,809
192	36,864
179	32,041
174	30,276
217	47,089
186	34,596
221	48,841
188	35,344
209	43,681
196	38,416
167	27,889
238	56,644
179	32,041
196	38,416
191	36,481
Sums: 3163	631,717

$$\bar{x} = \frac{\sum x}{n} = \frac{3163}{16} \doteq 197.69$$

$$s^2 = \frac{n\left(\sum x^2\right) - \left(\sum x\right)^2}{n(n-1)} = \frac{(16)(631,717) - (3163)^2}{(16)(15)} = 428.7625$$

$$s = \sqrt{428.7625} = 20.71$$

Substituting in the test statistic, we get the observed value of t:

$$t = \frac{\bar{x} - \mu}{s/\sqrt{n}} = \frac{197.69 - 200}{20.71/\sqrt{16}} = -.45 \qquad df = n - 1 = 16 - 1 = 15$$

4. *Critical region:* Since H_a involves the symbol $<$, we do a left-tailed test. From Appendix Table B.4, we see that $t_\alpha = t_{.10} = 1.341$. Hence, $-t_{.10} = -1.341$ and the critical region consists of values of $t \leq -1.341$. See Figure 8.25.

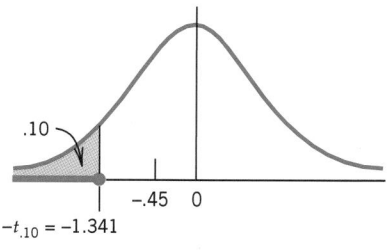
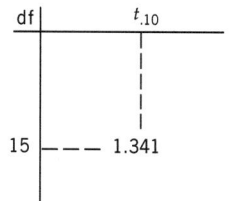

Figure 8.25

5. *Decision:* The observed value $(-.45)$ is not in the critical region. So we do not reject H_0. There is insufficient evidence to conclude that the *population* mean is below 200 (even though the sample mean is below 200).

Minitab Printout for Example 8.9

T-Test of the Mean

Test of mu = 200.00 vs mu < 200.00

Variable	N	Mean	StDev	SE Mean	T	P-Value
Chol	16	197.69	20.71	5.18	-0.45	0.33

EXAMPLE 8.10

An ice cream company claimed that its product contained 500 calories per pint (on the average). To test this claim, 24 one-pint containers were analyzed, giving $\bar{x} = 507$ calories and $s = 21$ calories. Test the claim at the 2% level of significance, using the following approaches. (Assume the population is approximately normal.)

(a) The classical approach   **(b)** The *P*-value approach

Solution

(a)   The classical approach:

   1.   *Hypotheses:*   The claim is that $\mu = 500$. Thus we will test

   $$H_0: \quad \mu = 500$$
   $$H_a: \quad \mu \neq 500$$

   2.   *Level of significance:* $\alpha = .02$

   3.   *Test statistic and observed value:*   The sample size is small (< 30), therefore we do a t test:

   $$t = \frac{\bar{x} - \mu}{s/\sqrt{n}} = \frac{507 - 500}{21/\sqrt{24}} \doteq 1.63 \qquad df = n - 1 = 23$$

   4.   *Critical region:*   Since H_a involves $\neq$, we use a two-tailed test. From Appendix Table B.4, $t_{\alpha/2} = t_{.01} = 2.500$. Thus the critical region consists of values of $t \geq 2.500$ or $t \leq -2.500$. See Figure 8.26.

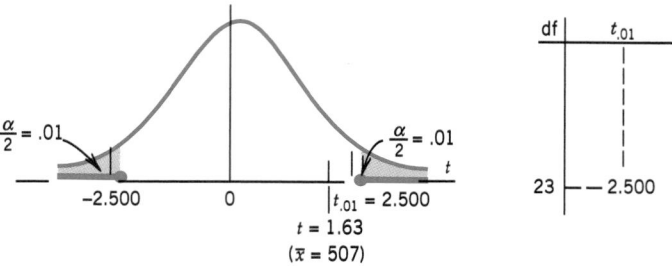

Figure 8.26

   5.   *Decision:*   The observed value $t = 1.63$ is not in the critical region; hence we do not reject H_0. This means that there is insufficient evidence to reject the company's claim at the 2% level of significance.

(b)   The *P*-value approach: Appendix Table B.4 does not lend itself to finding exact *P*-values. However, using this table we can find an interval estimate for *P*. Recall that the *P*-value is the probability of obtaining a value of the test statistic as favorable or more favorable to H_a than the observed value $t = 1.63$. This is displayed in Figure 8.27.

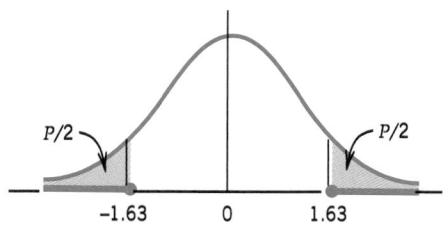

Figure 8.27
P-value

Look at the row for df $= 23$ in Appendix Table B.4. Notice that 1.63 is between the table values 1.714 and 1.319. Now $t_{.05} = 1.714$ and $t_{.10} = 1.319$. From

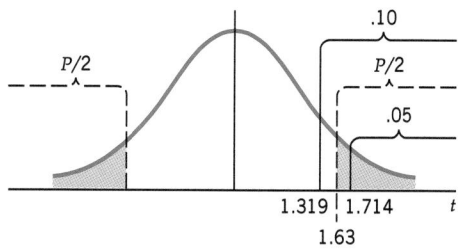

Figure 8.28
.10 < P < .20

Figure 8.28, we can see that $.05 < P/2 < .10$. Hence,

$$.10 < P < .20$$

We are testing the claim using $\alpha = .02$. Clearly, $P > .02$. Hence, we do not reject the claim H_0.

We summarize the essential features of a t test concerning a population mean in the box.

The t Test for a Population Mean (Based on a Small Sample) To test hypotheses concerning μ when the sample size n is less than 30, use the test statistic

$$t = \frac{\bar{x} - \mu}{s/\sqrt{n}}$$

This has Student's t distribution with df $= n - 1$. For μ, we substitute the value given in the null hypothesis. The observed value of t is computed using the sample data. If this falls in the critical region, reject the null hypothesis H_0. Otherwise, do not reject H_0. Suppose that α is the level of significance of the test. Critical values of t are obtained in Appendix Table B.4. The possible critical regions are described as follows:

(a) If the alternate hypothesis contains the symbol $>$, we conduct a right-tailed test. The critical region is shown in Figure 8.29.

(b) If the alternate hypothesis contains the symbol $<$, we conduct a left-tailed test. The critical region is shown in Figure 8.30.

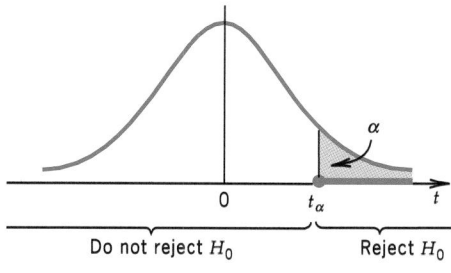

Figure 8.29
Right-Tailed Test

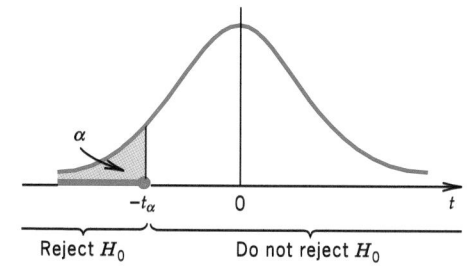

Figure 8.30
Left-Tailed Test

(c)   If the alternate hypothesis contains the symbol $\neq$, we conduct a two-tailed test. The critical region is shown in Figure 8.31.

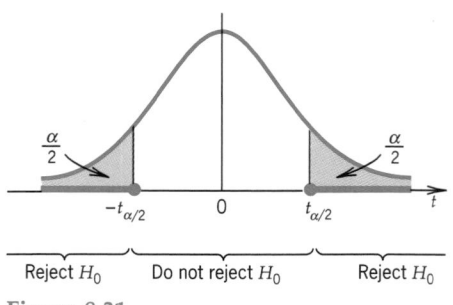

Figure 8.31
Two-Tailed Test

Assumption for the test: The population is normal or approximately normal (i.e., it has a distribution that is roughly mound shaped).

Confidence Intervals Based on Small Samples

In Section 8.2, we showed how to find a confidence interval for a population mean when the sample size is at least 30. We used the standard normal expression

$$z = \frac{\bar{x} - \mu}{\sigma / \sqrt{n}}$$

to develop the $1 - \alpha$ confidence interval with endpoints

$$\bar{x} \pm z_{\alpha/2} \cdot \frac{\sigma}{\sqrt{n}}$$

We have seen that if the sample size is small and x is approximately normal, the expression

$$t = \frac{\bar{x} - \mu}{s / \sqrt{n}}$$

has Student's t distribution with degrees of freedom, df $= n - 1$. By analogy, it seems reasonable that a $1 - \alpha$ confidence interval for μ based on a small sample would be described by the endpoints

$$\bar{x} \pm t_{\alpha/2} \cdot \frac{s}{\sqrt{n}}$$

When estimating μ by $\bar{x}$, the maximum error of the estimate with confidence $1 - \alpha$ would be

$$E = t_{\alpha/2} \cdot \frac{s}{\sqrt{n}}$$

We summarize the procedure for finding a $1 - \alpha$ confidence interval based on a small sample as follows.

For an approximately normal population, a $1 - \alpha$ confidence interval for the population mean μ (when the sample size is less than 30) is given by the endpoints

$$\bar{x} \pm t_{\alpha/2} \cdot \frac{s}{\sqrt{n}}$$

When estimating μ by $\bar{x}$, the maximum error of the estimate with confidence $1 - \alpha$ is

$$E = t_{\alpha/2} \cdot \frac{s}{\sqrt{n}}$$

EXAMPLE 8.11

In a study of college dropouts, a psychologist administered a questionnaire, designed to measure anxiety level, to 20 dropouts. Scores on the questionnaire can range from 25 (lowest anxiety level) to 100 (highest anxiety level). College students in general show a mean of about 60. The 20 scores for the dropouts gave $\bar{x} = 65.2$ and $s = 7.5$. Find a 95% confidence interval for the mean score μ for the population of dropouts from which the sample was obtained. If μ is estimated by $\bar{x}$, find the maximum error of the estimate with 95% confidence. Assume the population is approximately normal.

Solution

Since $1 - \alpha = .95$, $\alpha = .05$; df $= n - 1 = 19$. Using Appendix Table B.4, we see that $t_{\alpha/2} = t_{.025} = 2.093$. A $1 - \alpha$ confidence interval is given by

$$\bar{x} \pm t_{\alpha/2} \cdot \frac{s}{\sqrt{n}}$$

In this case, we get

$$65.2 \pm (2.093) \cdot \frac{7.5}{\sqrt{20}}$$

$$65.2 \pm 3.51$$

Therefore our 95% confidence interval for μ is

$$61.69 < \mu < 68.71$$

We are 95% confident that μ is between 61.69 and 68.71. Since the confidence interval was computed to be 65.2 ± 3.51, it follows that the maximum error of the estimate is $E = 3.51$.

Checking for Approximate Normality

We have said that Student's t procedures are not appropriate for data sets that are strongly skewed or have extreme outliers. You might well ask how strongly skewed must the data be, or how extreme must the outliers be, to render t procedures inappropriate. There is no clear-cut answer to this question. But stem-and-leaf plots

```
 1 | 1  1  2  7  8  8  9
 2 | 2  3  3  4
 3 | 1  5  7
 4 | 3
 5 |
 6 |
 7 |
 8 |
 9 | 1
10 | 3
```

(a) 91 and 103 are extreme outliers: *t* procedures inappropriate

```
 1 | 1  2
 2 | 1  3  3
 3 | 2  3  5
 4 | 1  1  7
 5 | 2  6
 6 | 4
 7 | 1
```

(b) Data are only moderately skewed: *t* procedures appropriate

```
 1 | 1
 2 | 0
 3 |
 4 | 2
 5 | 3  3
 6 |
 7 | 1  6
 8 |
 9 | 2  4  7  8
10 |
11 | 1  1  4  7  9
12 | 2  4  4  6  7  8  9
```

(c) No outliers, but data strongly skewed: *t* procedures inappropriate

```
2 | 1  3
3 | 2  2  7  8
4 | 3  4  7  9  9
5 | 1  3  8
6 | 2  8
7 |
8 |
9 | 0
```

(d) 90 is a mild outlier: *t* procedures appropriate

```
 1 | 1
 2 | 2  3  6
 3 | 1  5  7  9  9
 4 | 2  5  6  7
 5 | 1  3
 6 |
 7 |
 8 |
 9 |
10 | 3
```

(e) 103 is an extreme outlier: *t* procedures may be inappropriate

Figure 8.32
Stem-and-Leaf Plots ($4 \mid 3 = 43$)

or other graphs may help us make a decision. Figure 8.32 has some stem-and-leaf plots of data sets with comments as to whether *t* procedures would be appropriate. Modified boxplots can also be helpful because they identify suspected outliers. (See Section 3.5 for a discussion of modified boxplots and suspected outliers.)

In Figure 8.32(e), the data look fairly mound-shaped except for the outlier 103. In this situation, we could discard the outlier and perform a *t* procedure on the remaining data. Another approach is to consider a **nonparametric procedure** as an alternative to a *t* procedure. Such procedures (discussed in Chapter 13) assume little or nothing about the shape of the population distribution.

Remark In this section, we have tacitly assumed that the population standard deviation σ was unknown, because this is usually the case. Suppose, however, that the following conditions exist:

- The sample size is small ($n < 30$).
- The population is approximately normal.
- σ is known.

The Central Limit Theorem said that $\bar{x}$ is approximately normal even for small samples, if the population (of x values) is approximately normal. Hence,

$$z = \frac{\bar{x} - \mu}{\sigma/\sqrt{n}}$$

has the standard normal distribution. This was the basis of our confidence intervals and hypothesis tests using large samples (Sections 8.2, 8.3). Therefore, when $n < 30$ and σ is known, we should use the same procedures as we did in the large-sample cases, as long as the population is at least approximately normal.

Normal Quantile Plots (Optional)

Normal quantile plots are helpful in assessing normality. Suppose we have a data set, and we consider the standard score for each x value in the data set:

$$z = \frac{x - \mu}{\sigma}$$

There is a way of finding the value we would *expect* for each z score if the data came from a normal population. We label these expected z values with the symbol z^*. If the expected z values are close to the actual z values ($z^* \doteq z$), this would suggest that the data came from a normal population.

To get a rough idea how the z^* values are found, suppose we had 40 values of x listed in increasing order. Now the fourth value is greater than or equal to 4 out of 40 or 10% of the data values. And its z score would be greater than or equal to 10% of the z scores. If x is normal, z is standard normal. What value from the standard normal distribution separates the bottom 10% of z values from the top 90%? This is the 10th percentile or -1.28 (Figure 8.33), which is also the expected z score for the fourth data value. So $z^* = -1.28$.

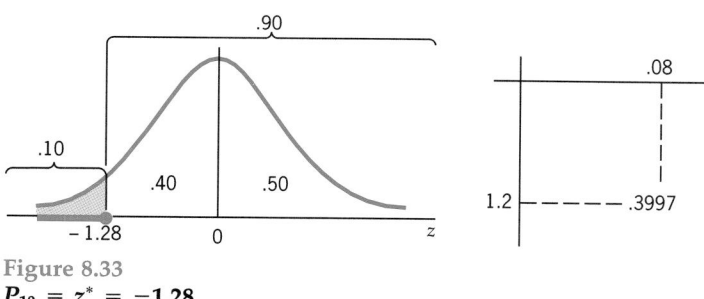

Figure 8.33
$P_{10} = z^* = -1.28$

Now the values of μ and σ are (usually) unknown, so we cannot compute the actual z scores. But there is something we do know: The relationship between x and z is linear. This is because

$$z = \frac{x - \mu}{\sigma} = \frac{x}{\sigma} - \frac{\mu}{\sigma} = \left(\frac{1}{\sigma}\right)x + \left(\frac{-\mu}{\sigma}\right)$$

So the relationship between x and z can be written as

$$z = mx + b$$

where $m = 1/\sigma$ and $b = -\mu/\sigma$. Recall from algebra that this is the equation of a straight line. Hence, for the x values in the data set, the points (x, z) lie on a straight line in the xz-plane. If the data came from a normal population, the expected z values should be close to the z values ($z^* \doteq z$), so the points (x, z^*) should be close to the points (x, z) on the line. Therefore the points (x, z^*) should be close to a straight line. A plot of the points (x, z^*) in the plane is called a **normal quantile plot.**

> When a normal quantile plot for a data set lies roughly along a straight line, we will assume the data came from an approximately normal population.

When a normal quantile plot deviates from a straight line, we can sometimes get an idea about the shape of the data distribution. Imagine a line through the main pattern of points in the normal quantile plot.

- For a right-skewed distribution, the points on the right end of the plot fall to the right of the line.

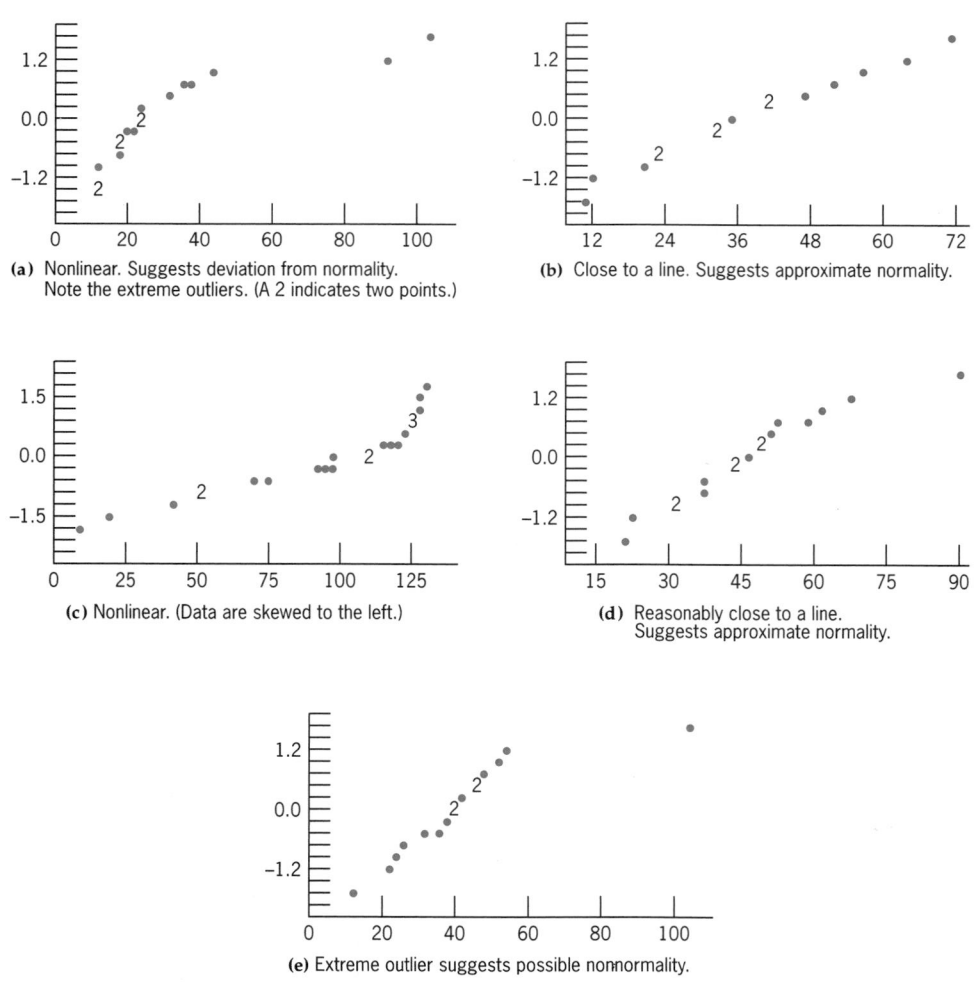

(a) Nonlinear. Suggests deviation from normality. Note the extreme outliers. (A 2 indicates two points.)

(b) Close to a line. Suggests approximate normality.

(c) Nonlinear. (Data are skewed to the left.)

(d) Reasonably close to a line. Suggests approximate normality.

(e) Extreme outlier suggests possible nonnormality.

Figure 8.34
Normal Quantile Plots for Data in Figure 8.32

● For a left-skewed distribution, the points on the left end of the plot fall to the left of the line. [See Figure 8.34(c).]

You will not be asked to compute normal quantile plots. The previous description of how the z^* values are computed is an oversimplification. It is rather more complicated. But if you have a computer with a statistical package, you can easily construct normal quantile plots. For example, suppose you are using Minitab, and your data are in column 1 (C1). Type

NSCORES C1 C2
PLOT C2*C1

Figure 8.34 contains normal quantile plots for the stem-and-leaf plots in Figure 8.32.

EXERCISES

8.61   In each part of the following, find (i) $t_{.005}$, (ii) $t_{.01}$, (iii) $t_{.025}$, (iv) $t_{.05}$, and (v) $t_{.10}$.
   (a)   Assume a t distribution with 7 degrees of freedom.
   (b)   Assume a t distribution with 12 degrees of freedom.
   (c)   Assume a t distribution with 25 degrees of freedom.

8.62   Complete each of the following.
   (a) $t_{.05} = 1.833$ df = _____   (b) $t_{\_} = 2.602$ df = 15
   (c) $t_{.10} =$ _____   df = 21   (d) $t_{.025} = 2.306$ df = _____
   (e) $t_{\_} = 2.797$ df = 24   (f) $t_{.995} =$ _____   df = 4
   (g) $t_{.01} = 2.567$ df = _____   (h) $t_{\_} = -1.319$ df = 23
   (i) $t_{.005} =$ _____   df = 3   (j) $t_{.90} = -1.328$ df = _____
   (k) $t_{\_} = -2.179$ df = 12   (l) $t_{.95} =$ _____   df = 18

8.63   In each of the following parts, (i) test the claim, and (ii) indicate the possible type of error committed (Type I or Type II). Note that n refers to the sample size.
   (a)   Test the claim that the mean μ is more than 16.

$$n = 14 \quad \alpha = .10 \quad \bar{x} = 18 \quad s = 4$$

   (b)   Test the claim that the mean μ is less than 27.

$$n = 9 \quad \alpha = .05 \quad \bar{x} = 23 \quad s = 7$$

   (c)   Test the claim that the mean μ is not 30.

$$n = 6 \quad \alpha = .01 \quad \bar{x} = 25 \quad s = 4$$

   (d)   Test the claim that the mean μ is greater than 125.

$$n = 40 \quad \alpha = .05 \quad \bar{x} = 128 \quad s = 18$$

   (e)   Test the claim that the mean μ is less than 50.

$$n = 20 \quad \alpha = .025 \quad \bar{x} = 45 \quad s = 10$$

   (f)   Test the claim that the mean μ is 60.

$$n = 8 \quad \alpha = .10 \quad \bar{x} = 70 \quad s = 16$$

8.64 Verify the conclusions reached in Exercise 8.63 by using the *P*-value approach. (*Hint:* Estimate *P* by giving an interval containing *P*, such as .025 < *P* < .05 or *P* < .005.)

8.65 At a state university, a department chairperson believed the mean salary μ of assistant professors throughout the state university system was higher than $30,750 (the mean salary of assistant professors in the chairperson's department). A random sample of nine other assistant professors gave a mean salary of $31,100 and standard deviation $420. Is there sufficient evidence to justify the chairperson's contention at the 5% level of significance? At the 1% level of significance? Assume the population is approximately normal.

    (a) Use the classical approach.

    (b) Use the *P*-value approach. (*Hint:* Estimate *P* by giving an interval containing *P* such as .025 < *P* < .05 or *P* < .005.)

8.66 A federal prison warden claimed that first-time released prisoners from a federal institution were imprisoned less than 22 months, on the average. A dot diagram of a sample of 24 first-time released prisoners follows. In this case, there is one 17, four 18's, two 19's, etc.

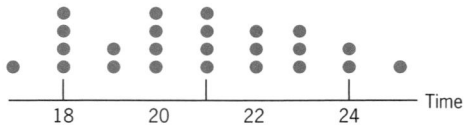

    (a) Does the *t* procedure seem appropriate for testing the warden's claim? If so, proceed to part (b).

    (b) For these data, $\sum x = 499$ and $\sum x^2 = 10,487$. At the 1% significance level, do the data support the warden's claim?

8.67 The director of admissions at a university claimed that families with an income of $30,000 a year contributed an average of $6000 per family toward a child's education. A sample of 20 such families whose children attended the university revealed a mean contribution of $6200 and a standard deviation of $300. Assume the population is approximately normal, and test the claim with a 5% level of significance.

8.68 The mean amount of money spent per customer in one department of a retail store is $30. The department manager claimed he could increase that figure by stocking a new product. The new product was put on the shelves. A stem-and-leaf plot of a sample of 25 customer amounts is given here. Note that each stem is split, with leaves 0, 1, 2, 3, 4 on the first stem and leaves 5, 6, 7, 8, 9 on the second. (The data were cut by leaving off the cents.)

$$
\begin{array}{r|l}
2 & 4 \\
2 & 557889 \\
3 & 223334 \\
3 & 55677789 \\
4 & 0033 \qquad \textit{Note:} \quad 3\,|\,2 = \$32
\end{array}
$$

    (a) Would the *t* procedure be appropriate to test the manager's claim? If so, proceed to part (b).

    (b) For the original data, the sample mean is $34.25 and the sample standard deviation is $5.48. Test the manager's claim with a 1% significance level.

8.69 A production manager noticed that the mean time to complete a job was 160 minutes. The manager made some changes in the production process in an attempt to reduce the mean time to finish the job. A stem-and-leaf plot of a sample of 11 times is as follows:

```
13 | 9
14 | 25
15 | 01356
16 | 24
17 | 0          Note:   14 | 5 = 145 minutes
```

(a)   Would a t procedure be appropriate in an attempt to determine whether the changes have decreased the mean completion time? If so, proceed to part (b).

(b)   The sample mean and standard deviation are 153.36 and 9.47, respectively. Give an interval estimate for the P-value. What values of α can be determined from your answer for which the null hypothesis would be rejected?

8.70   An alkaline battery for an AM–FM stereo cassette radio was designed to last 30 hours, on average, for FM play. There were consumer complaints that the batteries were lasting less than 30 hours. The manufacturer randomly sampled 38 batteries. The mean life was 29.3 hours and the standard deviation was 2.95 hours. Is there sufficient evidence, at the 5% level of significance, to indicate the mean battery life is less than 30 hours? (You may use a t test or a z test, since for large samples the two tests are essentially equivalent.)

8.71   A partner of a walk-in dental clinic suspected that the mean waiting time for patients had increased from the past average of 40 minutes. The partner sampled 18 patients and recorded their waiting times. She wanted to see whether the data supported her belief. Here is a stem-and-leaf plot of the 18 times.

```
2 | 79
3 | 1446
4 | 02335789
5 | 57
6 | 12          Note:   4 | 3 = 43 minutes
```

(a)   Is the t procedure appropriate in this case? If so, proceed to part (b).

(b)   The sample mean and standard deviation are 43.50 and 10.62, respectively. Give an interval estimate for the P-value using Appendix Table B.4. What values of α can be determined from your answer for which the null hypothesis would be rejected?

8.72   A sixth-grade geography teacher in a city school system gave a standardized geography test to a sample of 23 students. A stem-and-leaf plot is given here. The teacher was interested in whether the mean performance of her class differed from the national mean of 72.

```
4 | 57
5 | 46
6 | 011235558
7 | 012349
8 | 00
9 | 01          Note:   5 | 4 = 54
```

(a)   Is the teacher justified in using the t procedure? If so, proceed to part (b).

(b)   Assume $\sum x = 1552$ and $\sum x^2 = 107{,}792$. Using a 5% level of significance, can the teacher conclude the city's sixth graders' performance differs from the national mean of 72?

8.73   In a study of anxiety levels in athletes, 27 runners were given a test called the State-Trait Anxiety Inventory (STAI). The sample showed a mean trait anxiety level of 31.68 and a standard deviation of 9.27 (*Source:* Morgan, W. P., and M. L. Pollock, "Psychologic Characterization of the Elite Distance Runner," *The Long Distance Runner,* ed. P. Milvy, New York: Urizen Books, 1977, p. 106). Trait anxiety is a measure of enduring or underlying anxiety level. Do these results indicate that runners in general have a mean trait anxiety level different from 36 (the norm for college students)? Use the 5% level of significance. Assume the population is approximately normal.

8.74 Experiments conducted at the University of Michigan showed that a standing rider on a transit vehicle can withstand acceleration of up to 4.75 miles per hour per second (mphps) without experiencing discomfort, provided the acceleration is smooth. A transit official specified that a large fleet of new transit vehicles should be able to reach an acceleration rate of 4.75 mphps. An engineer thought that as a result of motor design, the vehicles' acceleration might be less than 4.75 mphps (on the average). A sample of 10 vehicles showed a mean acceleration rate of 4.58 mphps and a standard deviation of .25 mphps. At the 1% level of significance, is there evidence to justify the engineer's suspicion? Assume the population is approximately normal.

8.75 The Speedy Oil Change Company advertised a 15-minute wait for an oil change. A sample of 23 oil changes showed a mean time of 16.5 minutes and a standard deviation of 4.3 minutes. At the 5% level of significance, is there evidence that the mean time for an oil change is different from 15 minutes? Assume the population is approximately normal.

8.76 A physician suspected that smokers in the 40–45 age group with chronic bronchitis had smoked on average more than 20 years. A sample of 10 patients gave the following numbers of years of smoking:

$$22 \quad 21 \quad 19 \quad 25 \quad 24 \quad 26 \quad 23 \quad 21 \quad 23 \quad 22$$

Using a 1% significance level, is there sufficient evidence to justify the physician's belief?

8.77 A manufacturer claimed that her company's product would not require repair for more than 18 months on the average. A sample of 12 customers who had purchased her product provided the following information on how many months elapsed before repair was needed on their purchases:

$$16.5 \quad 17.0 \quad 17.5 \quad 18.0 \quad 18.5 \quad 18.5 \quad 18.5 \quad 19.0 \quad 19.0 \quad 19.5 \quad 20.0 \quad 20.5$$

(a) Construct a stem-and-leaf plot (let $18 \mid 5 = 18.5$). Proceed to part (b) if you determine that a t procedure is appropriate.

(b) The sample mean and standard deviation of times are 18.542 and 1.177, respectively. At a 5% level of significance, do the data support the belief that the mean repair time is more than 18 months?

8.78 A study of the diets of 28 men in Crevalcore, Greece, gave a sample mean of 28.7% and a sample standard deviation of 5.7% calories from fats (*Source:* Keys, 1970, p. I-166). Assume the population is approximately normal.

(a) Find a 95% confidence interval for the mean μ of the population from which the men were selected.

(b) Using the confidence interval, could you conclude that μ is different from the mean of 36.2% for American males?

(c) Find the maximum error of estimate for μ.

8.79 A psychologist wanted to estimate the mean self-esteem level μ of his patients. Fourteen patients were given a test designed to measure self-esteem. The sample mean and standard deviation were 25.3 and 5.3, respectively. Assume the population is approximately normal.

(a) Construct a 98% confidence interval for μ.

(b) Using the confidence interval, could you conclude that μ is smaller than the norm of 28.5?

(c) Find the maximum error of estimate for μ.

8.80 A group of physical education majors was discussing the heights of female runners and whether female runners tended to be tall, on the average. They decided to estimate the mean height of female runners. A sample of 12 runners showed a sample mean height of 65.80 inches and a sample standard deviation of 1.95 inches. Assume the population is approximately normal.

(a) Find a 95% confidence interval for the mean μ of the population of female runners from which the 12 runners were selected.

(b) Find the maximum error of estimate for μ.

8.81 Find a 95% confidence interval for μ using the data in Exercise 8.75. Does your result suggest that μ is different from 15 minutes?

8.82 Find a 98% confidence interval for μ using the data in Exercise 8.76. Does your result suggest that μ is more than 20 years?

8.83 Find a 90% confidence interval for μ using the data in Exercise 8.77. Does your result suggest that μ is more than 18 months?

8.84 Consider the following 16 data values:

$$11 \quad 22 \quad 23 \quad 26 \quad 31 \quad 35 \quad 37 \quad 39$$
$$39 \quad 42 \quad 45 \quad 46 \quad 47 \quad 51 \quad 53 \quad 103$$

A stem-and-leaf plot for the 16 data values follows.

```
 1 | 1
 2 | 236
 3 | 15799
 4 | 2567
 5 | 13
 6 |
 7 |
 8 |
 9 |
10 | 3
```

For the 16 data values, the mean and standard deviation are 40.62 and 20.22, respectively. With 103 removed, the mean and standard deviation are 36.47 and 11.90, respectively.

(a) Use the 16 data values and a 5% level of significance to test the hypothesis that the population mean μ is 50. Remove the data value 103, and perform the test again. Compare your results.

(b) Use the 16 data values and construct a 95% confidence interval for μ. Remove the data value 103, and construct a new 95% confidence interval. Compare your results. Comment on the maximum error of the estimates.

(c) Comment on the appropriateness of the t procedure for the two data sets.

8.85 An employee with a statistical background was asked by a supervisor to randomly sample and analyze 20 data values. The supervisor was interested in whether modifications to a piece of equipment resulted in a mean output μ of more than 78. The employee collected the data and obtained the following computer printout from JMP. Assume that the data were obtained from an approximately normal distribution.

Moments	
Mean	80.08840
Std Dev	5.12135
Std Err Mean	1.14517
upper 95% Mean	82.48525
lower 95% Mean	77.69155
N	20.00000
Sum Wgts	20.00000

Test Mean=value		
Hypothesized Value	78	
Actual Estimate	80.0884	
	t Test	Signed-Rank
Test Statistic	1.824	47.000
Prob > |t|	0.084	0.083
Prob > t	0.042	0.041
Prob < t	0.958	0.959

(a)   Specify the hypotheses H_0 and H_a. Give the value of the test statistic. Is there sufficient evidence to reject the null hypothesis at the 5% level of significance? At the 1% level?

(b)   Give a 95% confidence interval for the population mean μ.

8.86   A college graduate, looking for a job, was being interviewed by a company specializing in statistical consulting. The applicant was asked to explain the Data Desk printout given here.

Summary statistics for Data

Mean 79.9
Numeric 25 (This is the number n of data values.)
StdDev 10.5

t-Interval for Individual μ's

With 95.00% Confidence,
$75.6 < \mu(\text{Data}) < 84.2$

t-Test of Individual μ's

Individual Alpha Level 0.05
Ho: $\mu = 75$ Ha: $\mu > 75$

Data :
Test Ho: $\mu(\text{Data}) = 75$ vs Ha: $\mu(\text{Data}) > 75$
Sample Mean = 79.9 t-Statistic = 2.312 w/24 df
Reject Ho at Alpha = 0.05
p = 0.0150

(a)   Specify the hypotheses H_0 and H_a. What is the level of significance? Give the observed t value.

(b)   Report a 95% confidence interval for the population mean μ, and describe, in ordinary English, what this means.

8.6

INFERENCE CONCERNING A POPULATION PROPORTION

Estimation

In this section, we will discuss how to estimate the (unknown) proportion p of those elements in a population possessing a certain characteristic of interest. The quantity p is called a **population proportion.**

For example, a pollster wishes to estimate the proportion of all voters in a state who favor a proposal to limit property taxes (call it Proposition A). This proposition is to appear on the ballot in an upcoming election. The collection of all voters in the state constitutes a population. A voter possesses the characteristic of interest if he or she favors Proposition A, and the proportion of all voters favoring Proposition A is a population proportion p. Suppose the pollster obtains a random sample of 1000 voters from the population and finds that 540 of them favor Proposition A. A point estimate for p would be $540/1000 = .54$. This is called a **sample proportion.** This result should prove reassuring to the supporters of Proposition A. However, we should keep in mind that there will usually be an error when we use a point estimate for a population parameter. In other words, we might estimate that 54% of the voters will favor Proposition A and so it ought to pass. But if we are off by more than 4 percentage points, it may not pass.

Perhaps a confidence interval for p would be more appropriate. We can view the interviewing of the 1000 voters as a binomial experiment with

trial $=$ randomly select a voter

success $= S =$ voter selected favors Proposition A

failure $= F =$ voter selected does not favor Proposition A

$P(S) = p =$ proportion of all voters who favor Proposition A
(This is what we want to estimate.)

$P(F) = q = 1 - p =$ proportion of all voters who do not favor Proposition A

$n =$ number of trials, that is, the number of voters in the sample

$x =$ number of successes, that is, the number of voters in the sample who favor Proposition A (This can vary from one sample to the next.)

Using the observed value of x from the sample, we can estimate p by x/n. This is a **point estimate** for p and is denoted by $\hat{p}$:

$$\hat{p} = \frac{x}{n}$$

We have seen in Section 7.6 that when n is sufficiently large, the variable x may be regarded as approximately normal. We said that n will be large enough if both np and nq are at least 5. The problem here is that we do not know p (or $q = 1 - p$). If we wish to take advantage of the normal approximation in our study of p, how do we know whether the sample size is large enough? There is an alternative rule of thumb that may be used: *n will be considered large enough if the observed number of successes x and the number of failures $n - x$ are both at least* 5.[*]

We also saw in Section 7.6 that the mean value of x is np and the standard deviation is $\sqrt{npq}$. Just as x can vary from one sample to the next, so can $\hat{p}$. It seems plausible, and is indeed the case, that $\hat{p}$ is also approximately normal (when n is large enough) with

$$\text{mean} = \frac{np}{n} = p$$

$$\text{standard deviation} = \frac{\sqrt{npq}}{n} = \sqrt{\frac{npq}{n^2}} = \sqrt{\frac{pq}{n}}$$

---

[*]The reason for this is that for a given sample we may approximate p by $\hat{p}$ and q by $\hat{q}$, where $\hat{q} = 1 - \hat{p}$. Then n will be large enough if both $n\hat{p}$ and $n\hat{q}$ are at least 5. But

$$n\hat{p} = n\left(\frac{x}{n}\right) = x \quad \text{and} \quad n\hat{q} = n(1 - \hat{p}) = n\left(1 - \frac{x}{n}\right) = n - n\left(\frac{x}{n}\right) = n - x$$

So the observed x and $n - x$ should both be at least 5.

It follows that

$$z = \frac{\hat{p} - p}{\sqrt{pq/n}}$$

is approximately standard normal.

Recall that in Section 8.5 we used a standard normal expression to develop a $1 - \alpha$ confidence interval for μ. Notice the relationship

$$\frac{\bar{x} - \mu}{\sigma/\sqrt{n}} \qquad \bar{x} \pm z_{\alpha/2} \cdot \frac{\sigma}{\sqrt{n}}$$

Proceeding by analogy, we might guess what a $1 - \alpha$ confidence interval for p would look like:

$$\frac{\hat{p} - p}{\sqrt{\dfrac{pq}{n}}} \qquad \hat{p} \pm z_{\alpha/2} \cdot \sqrt{\frac{pq}{n}}$$

However, we do not know the values of p and q in this expression. Therefore, we will approximate them by $\hat{p} = x/n$ and $\hat{q} = 1 - \hat{p}$. This gives the $1 - \alpha$ **confidence interval for p**:

$$\hat{p} \pm z_{\alpha/2} \cdot \sqrt{\frac{\hat{p}\hat{q}}{n}}$$

When we are estimating p by $\hat{p}$, the **maximum error of the estimate** with confidence $1 - \alpha$ is

$$E = z_{\alpha/2} \cdot \sqrt{\frac{\hat{p}\hat{q}}{n}}$$

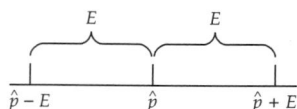

We summarize these results in the following box.

A point estimate for a population proportion p is the sample proportion $\hat{p} = x/n$. When the sample size n is sufficiently large, a $1 - \alpha$ confidence interval for p is

$$\hat{p} - z_{\alpha/2} \cdot \sqrt{\frac{\hat{p}\hat{q}}{n}} < p < \hat{p} + z_{\alpha/2} \cdot \sqrt{\frac{\hat{p}\hat{q}}{n}}$$

and if we estimate p by $\hat{p}$, the maximum error of the estimate with confidence $1 - \alpha$ is

$$E = z_{\alpha/2} \cdot \sqrt{\frac{\hat{p}\hat{q}}{n}}$$

n will be sufficiently large if both x and $n - x$ are at least 5. In terms of E, the endpoints of the confidence interval are

$$\hat{p} \pm E$$

EXAMPLE 8.12

Assume that the pollster (in the previous discussion) interviews 1000 voters and finds that 540 favor Proposition A.

(a)   Find a point estimate for p, the proportion of all voters in the state who favor Proposition A.

(b)   Find a 95% confidence interval for p.

(c)   If the point estimate is used to estimate p, find the maximum error of the estimate (with 95% confidence).

(d)   Comment on how these results should be interpreted.

Solution

Note that $x = 540$ and $n - x = 1000 - 540 = 460$ are both at least 5; therefore, we can use the procedure discussed in the box.

(a)   As we stated previously, a point estimate for p is

$$\hat{p} = \frac{x}{n} = \frac{540}{1000} = .54$$

(b)   To find a 95% confidence interval, we set

$$1 - \alpha = .95 \qquad\qquad \hat{p} = .54$$
$$\alpha = .05 \qquad\qquad\qquad \hat{q} = .46$$
$$z_{\alpha/2} = z_{.025} = 1.96 \qquad n = 1000$$

The 95% confidence interval is

$$\hat{p} - z_{\alpha/2} \cdot \sqrt{\frac{\hat{p}\hat{q}}{n}} < p < \hat{p} + z_{\alpha/2} \cdot \sqrt{\frac{\hat{p}\hat{q}}{n}}$$

or

$$.54 - (1.96) \cdot \sqrt{\frac{(.54)(.46)}{1000}} < p < .54 + (1.96) \cdot \sqrt{\frac{(.54)(.46)}{1000}}$$
$$.54 - .03 < p < .54 + .03$$
$$.51 < p < .57$$

(c)   Since the confidence interval is $.54 \pm .03$,

$$E = .03$$

(d)   Part (b) suggests that the pollster can be 95% sure that the percentage of all voters who favor Proposition A is between 51% and 57%, which indicates that Proposition A will probably pass. Another way of looking at this is given by part (c). This says that if we estimate p by $\hat{p} = (x/n) = .54$, we can be 95% sure that this estimate will be in error by less than .03. In other words, if we predict the percentage of voters favoring Proposition A to be 54%, we are 95% sure that we will be less than 3 percentage points off. Again this suggests that Proposition A will pass.

Determining the Sample Size

We can determine the sample size necessary to be able to estimate p by $\hat{p}$ in such a way that the maximum error of our estimate will be a given value E with a given level of confidence $1 - \alpha$ by solving for n in the equation

$$E = z_{\alpha/2} \cdot \sqrt{\frac{\hat{p}\hat{q}}{n}}$$

We square both sides,

$$E^2 = [z_{\alpha/2}]^2 \cdot \frac{\hat{p}\hat{q}}{n}$$

and multiply by n/E^2 to get

$$n = \left[\frac{z_{\alpha/2}}{E}\right]^2 \cdot \hat{p} \cdot \hat{q}$$

But there is a problem here. Since the sample has not yet been obtained, we do not know the values of $\hat{p}$ and $\hat{q}$ (where $\hat{q} = 1 - \hat{p}$).* However, it can be shown that regardless of the values of $\hat{p}$ and $\hat{q}$, the value of $\hat{p} \cdot \hat{q}$ will never be more than $\frac{1}{4}$. Therefore, to be on the safe side, we should take the sample size to be at least

$$n = \left[\frac{z_{\alpha/2}}{E}\right]^2 \cdot \frac{1}{4}$$

We summarize as follows:

When estimating a population proportion p by a sample proportion $\hat{p}$, if we wish the maximum error of our estimate to be (some given value) E with level of confidence $1 - \alpha$, we should choose the sample size to be at least

$$n = \left[\frac{z_{\alpha/2}}{E}\right]^2 \cdot \frac{1}{4}$$

EXAMPLE 8.13

The A. C. Nielsen Company conducts surveys to determine the proportion of households viewing various television shows. A device called an audometer is placed on a number of TV sets throughout the country, and information on which shows are watched is fed to a computer. To be able to estimate the proportion of all households viewing a certain show within 3 percentage points with 98% confidence, how many households should be surveyed if a random sample were used?

---

*If we have a rough idea of the values of p and q, we can use these values in place of $\hat{p}$ and $\hat{q}$, but often we have no such information.

Solution

In this example, the maximum error of the estimate, E, is .03 and the level of confidence, $1 - \alpha$, is .98. So

$$\alpha = .02$$

$$z_{\alpha/2} = z_{.01} = 2.33$$

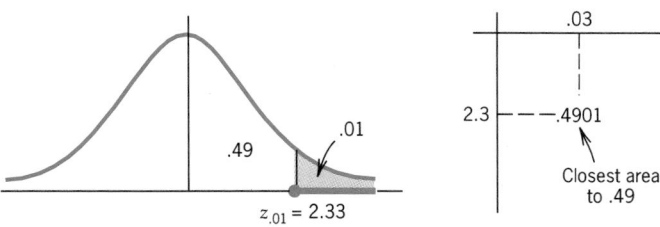

Figure 8.35

To find the necessary number of interviews, we use

$$n = \left[\frac{z_{\alpha/2}}{E}\right]^2 \cdot \frac{1}{4} = \left(\frac{2.33}{.03}\right)^2 (.25) \doteq 1508.03$$

Therefore, 1509 households should be interviewed. (Note that we round up to be on the safe side.)

Hypothesis Testing

We will use the expression

$$z = \frac{\hat{p} - p}{\sqrt{pq/n}}$$

as a test statistic when testing hypotheses concerning a population proportion p. This has approximately a standard normal distribution when n is sufficiently large. This will usually be the case if both np and nq are at least 5. The values we use for p and q are obtained from the null hypothesis. For example, suppose we were testing

$$H_0: \quad p = .20$$
$$H_a: \quad p \neq .20$$

Then we would use .20 for p and .80 for q. So we would require the sample size to be large enough so that both $(n)(.20)$ and $(n)(.80)$ are at least 5.

The Hazelwood Case

Between 1972 and 1974, 15 out of 405 teachers (3.7%) hired in Hazelwood, St. Louis County, Missouri, were black. In St. Louis County *plus* the nearby city of St. Louis, 15.4% of teachers were black. The Equal Employment Opportunity Commission (EEOC) sued the town of Hazelwood for discrimination against blacks and won in the court of appeals. The case depended largely on a test of hypotheses. But what is the population involved? In discrimination cases, the population is often conceptual or hypothetical. In the Hazelwood case, we would consider the population to be the hypothetical collection of teachers that would result if many teachers were hired using the hiring practices of Hazelwood. The 405 teachers hired can be viewed as a sample from this population. Let

$$p = \text{proportion of black teachers in this hypothetical population}$$

Now the EEOC said that the proportion of blacks in the pool of teachers from which Hazelwood recruited was 15.4% (or .154). Discriminatory hiring practices would result in a value of p less than .154. Let's test this hypothesis at the 2.5% level of significance, a value often used in discrimination cases.

EXAMPLE 8.14

Complete the test for the Hazelwood case at the 2.5% level of significance.

Solution

1. *Hypotheses:* Discrimination against blacks implies $p < .154$. Thus we test:

    $$H_0: \quad p = .154 \qquad \text{(No discrimination)}$$
    $$H_a: \quad p < .154 \qquad \text{(Possible discrimination)}$$

2. *Level of significance:* $\alpha = .025$

3. *Test statistic and observed value:* The sample consists of $n = 405$ teachers hired between 1972 and 1974. The number of blacks is $x = 15$. So

    $$\hat{p} = \frac{x}{n} = \frac{15}{405} \doteq .037$$

    $$z = \frac{\hat{p} - p}{\sqrt{\dfrac{pq}{n}}} = \frac{.037 - .154}{\sqrt{\dfrac{(.154)(.846)}{405}}} = -6.52$$

    Note that we used $p = .154$ from H_0. Hence, $q = 1 - p = .846$. Also n is sufficiently large to use this test statistic, since np and nq are at least 5:

    $$np = (405)(.154) = 62.37$$
    $$nq = (405)(.846) = 342.63$$

4. *Critical region:* The $<$ symbol in H_a implies a left-tailed test. (Low values of $\hat{p}$ relative to .154 favor H_a.) The critical region is in Figure 8.36.

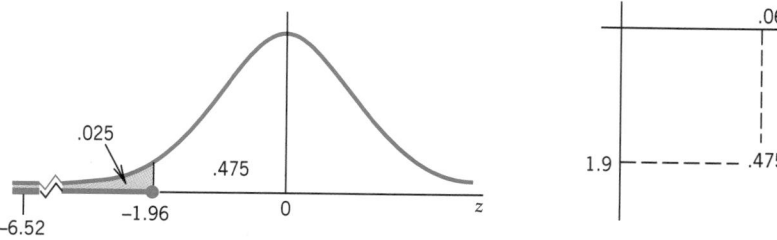

Figure 8.36

5. *Decision:* The observed value (-6.52) falls in the critical region. Thus we reject H_0 in favor of H_a. This result led the court of appeals to conclude that racial discrimination had occurred.

Discussion

There are some points about this statistical test that seem troublesome, at least on the surface. The test assumes that the hiring of the 405 teachers is a binomial experiment, with a trial being the hiring of a teacher repeated 405 times. Hiring a black on a given trial is a success. The outcome of each trial must be purely random, a matter of chance, much like getting heads or tails on the toss of a coin. However, hiring a teacher is not a chance process, like drawing a name out of a hat. But it is (or should be) a chance process as far as race is concerned.

An analogy will illustrate the point. Suppose I have a handful of coins. Four are quarters; the rest are nickels, dimes, and pennies. I throw the coins up in the air and they land on the floor. You may select any four. Naturally you would select the four quarters. This is not a chance process but rather a very deliberate selection. However, the occurrence of heads or tails on the four quarters would be a matter of chance.

Another point is more problematic. Recall that the trials in a binomial experiment must be independent. This would mean that the race of, say, the 50th teacher hired should have no bearing on the race of the 51st. (Mathematically speaking, p and q should not change from one trial to the next.) But a phenomenon called "clustering" often occurs in the hiring process. For example, suppose the 50th teacher hired (who is white) tells a friend (who is white) that Hazelwood is hiring. The friend rushes to Hazelwood and becomes the 51st teacher hired. This suggests that the trials (hiring the 405 teachers) may not be independent.

That is not the end of the Hazelwood story. The town of Hazelwood appealed the court's decision to the U.S. Supreme Court, where the lower court's decision was vacated. For more on this, see Exercise 8.119. If you wish to learn more about the Hazelwood case, including a discussion of the 2.5% significance level, see Meier, P., J. Sacks, and S. Zabell, "What Happened in Hazelwood?" in *Statistics and the Law,* edited by M. DeGroot, S. Fienberg, J. Kadane, New York: John Wiley and Sons, 1986, pp. 1–48.

The essential features of a large-sample test concerning a population proportion follow.

The z Test for a Population Proportion This test is based on a sufficiently large sample. To test hypotheses concerning p, use the test statistic

$$z = \frac{\hat{p} - p}{\sqrt{pq/n}}$$

(where $q = 1 - p$). This has the standard normal distribution (approximately) when np and nq are at least 5. For p, we use the value given in the null hypothesis. The observed value of z is computed from the sample data. If z falls in the critical region, reject the null hypothesis H_0. Otherwise, do not reject H_0. Suppose that α is the level of significance of the test. Critical values of z are obtained in Appendix Table B.3. The possible critical regions are described as follows:

(a)   If the alternate hypothesis H_a contains the symbol $>$, we conduct a right-tailed test. The critical region is shown in Figure 8.37.

(b)   If the alternate hypothesis H_a contains the symbol $<$, we conduct a left-tailed test. The critical region is shown in Figure 8.38.

(c)   If the alternate hypothesis H_a contains the symbol $\neq$, we conduct a two-tailed test. The critical region is shown in Figure 8.39.

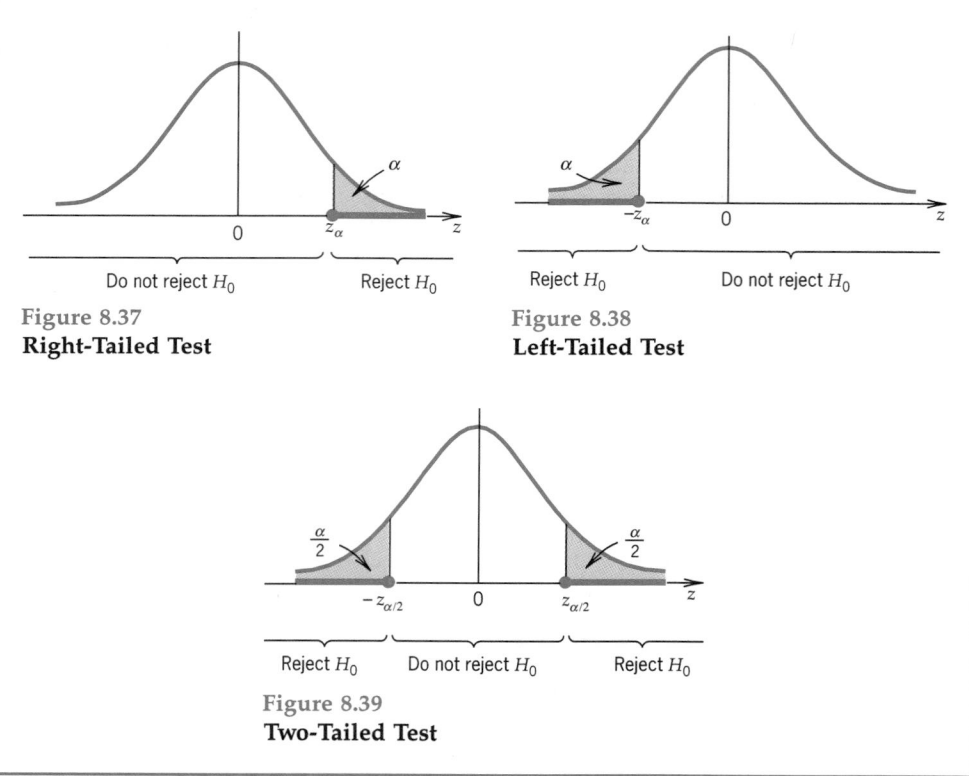

Figure 8.37
Right-Tailed Test

Figure 8.38
Left-Tailed Test

Figure 8.39
Two-Tailed Test

EXERCISES

8.87   Fill in the blanks and construct a confidence interval for a population proportion p in each of the following. Note that n is the sample size and x is the number of successes.

	$\hat{p}$	x	n	Percentage Confidence	Interval
(a)		200	400	95	
(b)	.25		900	90	
(c)		160	225	99	
(d)	.82		1250	95	
(e)		592	1600	90	
(f)	.61		1000	80	

8.88   Officials in a resort town wanted to estimate the proportion p of voters who would support a proposal restricting the number of housing starts per year. A random sample of 150 voters showed that 105 supported the proposal. Find a 99% confidence interval for p.

8.89 A psychologist gave a test measuring anxiety level, the State-Trait Anxiety Inventory (STAI), to a sample of 50 abused children, and found that 45 had above-average anxiety levels. Find a 90% confidence interval for the true proportion of abused children with above-average anxiety levels.

8.90 In a 1993 study of 614 family-business owners, 399 responded that the business was started by the current owners. Find a 90% confidence interval for the proportion p of all family businesses that were started by the current owners.

8.91 A study released in July of 1994 suggests that implanting radioactive "seeds" in men with early prostate cancer carries fewer side effects than surgery and is as effective. Dr. John Blasko, director of the Northwest Tumor Institute in Seattle, reported that 271 of 298 men were free of cancer 5 years after the implantation of radioactive seeds (*Source: The Boston Globe,* July 28, 1994). Find a 95% confidence interval for the proportion p of men with early prostate cancer, treated with radioactive seeds, who will be cancer-free after 5 years.

8.92 A dentist wanted to estimate the proportion p of patients who paid their bill within a reasonable period of time. A random sample of 90 records showed that 73 patients paid their bill to the satisfaction of the dentist. Find a 90% confidence interval for p.

8.93 In a study initiated in 1940, a research group followed the lives of 200 Harvard graduates and 400 inner-city, working-class men from Boston and Cambridge, Massachusetts (*Source: Vaillant, 1983, p. 27). Eventually, 26 from the Harvard group and 110 from the inner-city, working-class group became alcoholics. Assume that these are random samples from the collection of Harvard graduates and inner-city, working-class men from Boston and Cambridge.

(a) Find a 95% confidence interval for the proportion p of Harvard graduates that eventually became alcoholic.

(b) Find a 95% confidence interval for the proportion p of the inner-city, working-class group that eventually became alcoholic.

8.94 In the study discussed in Exercise 8.93, 96 of the 110 working-class alcoholics reported that they had experienced "family or friends' complaints." Find a 95% confidence interval for the proportion p of working-class alcoholics that have experienced "family or friends' complaints."

8.95 The Aid to Families with Dependent Children (AFDC) program has an overall error rate of 4% in determining eligibility. The state of California uses sampling to monitor its counties to see whether they exceed the 4% error rate, which can result in economic sanctions. In one county, 9 cases out of 150 were found to be in error.

(a) Find a 95% confidence interval for the error rate for the county (proportion of all cases in error).

(b) In 1982, the California legislature mandated that a 95% confidence interval be used in studying error rate. Based on your answer in part (a), would you conclude that the error rate for the county is above the 4% rate?

8.96 Candidates A and B are opponents for political office. Candidate A's pollster conducts a poll 1 week before the election and finds that 165 of 300 potential voters say they will vote for candidate A. At the time of the poll, can we be

(a) 80% confident that candidate A will win?

(b) 98% confident that candidate A will win?

Use the results of parts (a) and (b), and do not calculate, to answer the following:

(c) Can candidate A be
   (i) 70% confident that he will win?
   (ii) 99% confident that he will win?

8.97   To estimate the proportion p of passengers who had purchased tickets for more than $400 over a year's time, an airline official obtained a random sample of 75. The number of those purchasing tickets for more than $400 was 45.

    (a)   What is a point estimate for p?

    (b)   Find a 95% confidence interval for p.

    (c)   What is the maximum error of estimate for p?

8.98   A city council commissioned a statistician to estimate the proportion p of voters in favor of a proposal to build a new library. The statistician obtained a random sample of 200 voters, with 112 indicating approval of the proposal.

    (a)   What is a point estimate for p?

    (b)   Find a 90% confidence interval for p.

    (c)   What is the maximum error of estimate for p?

8.99   A union official wanted to get an idea of whether a majority of workers at a large corporation would favor a contract proposal. She surveyed 500 workers and found that 260 favored the proposal.

    (a)   Find a 95% confidence interval for the proportion of all the workers who favor the contract proposal.

    (b)   Find the maximum error of the estimate.

    (c)   Based on the results of part (a), can we conclude that the contract will be ratified by the membership?

8.100   A study of 75 lakes in Massachusetts indicated that 82% of these lakes may at some point be affected by acid rain. Assume that there are a large number of lakes in Massachusetts and that the sample can be considered random.

    (a)   Find a 95% confidence interval for the proportion p of lakes in Massachusetts that may at some point be affected by acid rain.

    (b)   What is the maximum error of estimate?

8.101   A superintendent of a city school system wants to estimate the proportion p of parents who believe the school system is providing an adequate education. How large a random sample is needed to estimate p to within 3 percentage points with 90% confidence?

8.102   A town official wants to estimate the proportion p of voters who favor the granting of a variance so that a builder can construct a health spa in a residential area. How large a random sample is required to estimate p to within 4 percentage points with 95% confidence?

8.103   To estimate the proportion p of voters favoring a nuclear freeze in your voting district, how large a random sample is needed to estimate p to within 2 percentage points with

    (a)   90% confidence?

    (b)   99% confidence?

8.104   Do parts (a)–(c) without calculating.

    (a)   Suppose that you were to estimate the proportion p in Exercise 8.103 to within 2 percentage points with 95% confidence.

        (i)   Would the required sample size be larger, the same as, or smaller than that for 90% confidence?

        (ii)   Would the required sample size be larger, the same as, or smaller than that for 99% confidence?

    (b)   Suppose that you were to estimate the proportion p of items in a population to within 1 percentage point with 90% confidence. Would the required sample size be larger, the same as, or smaller than that found in Exercise 8.103(a)?

(c) Suppose that you were to estimate the proportion p of items in a population to within 4 percentage points with 90% confidence. Would the required sample size be larger, the same as, or smaller than that found in Exercise 8.103(a)?

(d) Now calculate the sample sizes required in parts (a)–(c). Compare with the answers to Exercise 8.103.

8.105 For the claims in parts (a)–(g), **(i)** find H_0 and H_a, **(ii)** give the type of critical region (right-tailed, left-tailed, or two-tailed), and **(iii)** explain the meaning of a Type I and Type II error.

(a) The proportion p of voters in a state who favor the death penalty under prescribed conditions is .53.

(b) The proportion p of a product that breaks down before the guarantee expires is less than .06.

(c) The proportion p of full-time college students younger than 23 years of age is less than .90.

(d) The proportion p of minority students at a large university is more than .07.

(e) The proportion p of persons surviving a cancer for 5 years is .40.

(f) The proportion p of defective items from a large batch is less than .05.

(g) The proportion p of high school graduates in 1990 seeking full-time employment was more than .30.

8.106 In parts (a)–(c), specify H_0 and H_a. Also give the critical region in terms of the standard normal z for $\alpha = .10$, $\alpha = .05$, and $\alpha = .01$. Assume the claim is that the proportion p of children in a large city that watch television at least 4 hours per day is

(a) Less than .8   **(b)** .8   **(c)** More than .8

8.107 Let p be the proportion of voters in a large city who favor a restructuring of the police department. Consider the hypothesis that less than 70% of the voters are in support of the idea. In each of the following, **(i)** give the critical region, **(ii)** determine whether you would reject H_0, and **(iii)** give the type of error (Type I or Type II) that has possibly been committed. Note that n refers to the sample size; α, the level of significance; and x, the number of voters in the sample who favor the restructuring.

(a) $n = 100$, $\alpha = .10$, $x = 65$ **(b)** $n = 100$, $\alpha = .05$, $x = 60$

(c) $n = 400$, $\alpha = .01$, $x = 260$ **(d)** $n = 1600$, $\alpha = .01$, $x = 1040$

8.108 The manager of the circulation department of a newspaper claimed 75% of subscribers would renew their subscriptions. A sample of 100 subscribers showed that 63 renewed their subscriptions. At the 1% level of significance, is there sufficient evidence to conclude that the manager is wrong?

(a) Use the classical approach.   **(b)** Use the P-value approach.

8.109 A politician believed that more than half of the voters in her district support her stand on a controversial issue. Suppose that 105 registered voters in a sample of size 200 support her on this issue. Is there sufficient evidence to support the politician's belief at the 10% level of significance?

8.110 It was conjectured that a majority of recovering alcoholics exhibit abnormal levels of depression. A psychologist gave a test called the Depression Adjective Checklist (DACL) to a sample of 45 recovering alcoholics and found that 25 had above-average depression levels. At the 5% level of significance, does this result support the conjecture?

(a) Use the classical approach.   **(b)** Use the P-value approach.

8.111 An official at a large university suspected that the proportion p of their football players who have failed to receive a diploma within 4 years is more than .20. A scholarship committee obtained a random sample of 225 former players. The sample showed that 162 had received a diploma within 4 years. Using the *P*-value approach, is the spokesperson's suspicion justified at the 1% level of significance?

8.112 A retailer has received a large shipment of VCRs. He decided to accept the shipment provided there is no evidence to suggest that the shipment contains more than 5% nonacceptable items. The retailer found 14 nonacceptable items in a random selection of 160 items. At a 5% level of significance, what is the retailer's decision?

8.113 In a political discussion dealing with health care, the claim was made that more than 50% of U.S. working men were covered by employer-provided health insurance. In a random sample of 1200 working men, 660 said their employer provided health insurance. Use a 5% level of significance. Test the claim using

(a) The classical approach   (b) The *P*-value approach

8.114 The chamber of commerce of an island resort claimed that the proportion p of all automobiles transported to the island during the summer that are from out of state is different from last year's 20%. A random sample of size 40 gives 11 automobiles from out of state. At the 5% level of significance, test the claim using

(a) The classical approach   (b) The *P*-value approach

8.115 To test the claim that 60% of Americans will not buy products imported from Vietnam, 400 Americans were sampled, and 228 said they would not buy the imported products.

(a) Use a 10% level of significance and test the claim.

(b) Construct a 90% confidence interval for the population proportion p. Does your result agree with your conclusion in part (a)?

8.116 A politician claimed she has gained support since the last election. In that election, she received 52% of the vote.

(a) A poll of 100 randomly selected voters showed that 57 would vote for her at this time. Test her claim using a 5% significance level.

(b) Suppose a random sample of size $n = 4(100) = 400$ shows $4(57) = 228$ voters indicating they would vote for her at this time. Test her claim using a 5% significance level.

(c) Compare your answers in parts (a) and (b). Note that the proportion of voters who would vote for her at this time is the same in both parts. Comment.

8.117 In a *Wall Street Journal*–NBC News poll of 1005 adults published August 3, 1995, "the share of voters who say they hold 'very negative' feelings toward President Clinton has declined from 25 percent just before last fall's election to 17 percent now." (The 17% corresponds to 171 of the 1005 polled saying they have "very negative" feelings toward President Clinton.) [*Source:* *The Boston Globe*, August 4, 1995, p. 10]

(a) Let p be the proportion of all adults who have "very negative" feelings toward President Clinton. At the 1% significance level, does the sample proportion of $\hat{p} = .17$ suggest that the value of p is smaller than .25?

(b) Resampling Stats is a program that allows for approximate answers by simulation. Below is the result of simulating 5000 times a sample of size 1005 from a binomial population with $p = .25$, and counting the number of successes each time. (A success is having "very negative" feelings toward President Clinton.) The results of the simulation and a frequency histogram are given at the top of page 391. Note that the bin center is something like a class mark.

(i) The minimum value in the simulation was 205. Is it surprising that there were no observations smaller than or equal to 171, the number in the poll saying they have "very negative" feelings toward President Clinton? *Hint:*   What is the probability of finding 171 or fewer successes in 1005 trials if p were .25? Note that this is the *P*-value for the test in part (a).

(ii) In the simulation, 83.4% of the observations were smaller than or equal to 264. Does this seem reasonable? Why? *Hint:*   What is the probability of finding 264 or fewer successes in 1005 trials with $p = .25$?

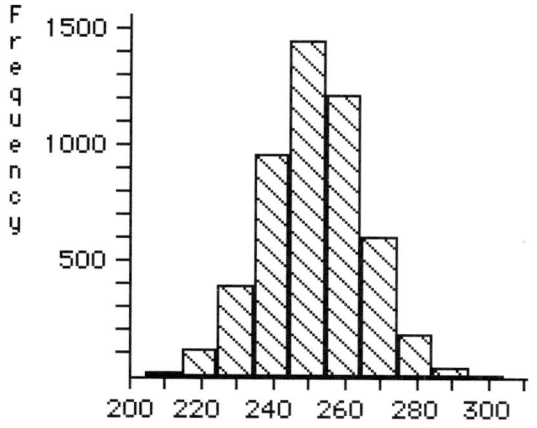

Bin Center	Freq	Pct	Cum Pct
210	20	0.4	0.4
220	119	2.4	2.8
230	392	7.8	10.6
240	964	19.3	29.9
250	1453	29.1	59.0
260	1221	24.4	83.4
270	611	12.2	95.6
280	180	3.6	99.2
290	35	0.7	99.9
300	5	0.1	100.0

```
Number of simulated values 171 or smaller = 0
Minimum simulated value = 205
```

8.118 A pain killer is known to be effective in 60% of the patients. Suppose you are the manufacturer of a new pain killer. Further suppose that you will not market the pill unless there is very strong evidence that the effective rate is more than 60%. Which one of the following levels of significance would you use? Justify your decision.

(a) $\alpha = .10$ **(b)** $\alpha = .05$ **(c)** $\alpha = .01$

8.119 In Exercises 6.51 and 7.41 and Example 8.14, we discussed the Hazelwood case. Out of 405 teachers hired in 2 years in Hazelwood, St. Louis County, Missouri, 15 (or 3.7%) were black. The Equal Employment Opportunity Commission (EEOC) sued Hazelwood for discrimination under Title VII of the Civil Rights Act of 1964. The EEOC won in the court of appeals. On appeal to the Supreme Court, the decision of the court of appeals was vacated. The Supreme Court noted that the relevant job market for comparison might well be St. Louis County alone (not including the city of St. Louis). Here the percentage of black teachers was only 5.7%. Redo Example 8.14 using 5.7% instead of 15.4%.

_____ **8.7**

USING MINITAB (OPTIONAL)

Minitab has commands to do a z test and a t test. The z test command requires that you specify the value of σ. For example, suppose that column 1 contained a sample of 45 values from a population with standard deviation $\sigma = 10$. Suppose you wanted to test

$$H_0: \quad \mu = 50$$
$$H_a: \quad \mu \neq 50$$

The Session command to accomplish this is

ZTEST 50 10, DATA IN C1

Most of the time we do not know the value of σ. Of course, we could estimate σ by the sample standard deviation s, but it is simpler just to do a t test. When the sample size is large ($n \geq 30$), a z test using s as an estimate for σ gives approximately the same results as a t test. The t test command for this test is

$$\text{TTEST 50, DATA IN C1}$$

If we wish to do a one-tailed test, we must use the subcommand ALTERNATIVE. For example, to test

$$H_0: \quad \mu = 50$$
$$H_a: \quad \mu < 50$$

we use the Session commands

$$\text{TTEST 50 C1;}$$
$$\text{ALTERNATIVE} = -1.$$

The subcommand ALTERNATIVE $= 1$ would give a right-tailed test.

The results of a t test on a sample of 15 data values are given in the following Minitab printout. The data represent daily production of rubber gaskets (in pounds) for 15 selected days using a new machine being tested by a company. The company wanted to test the following hypotheses:

$$H_0: \quad \mu = 200 \text{ lbs}$$
$$H_a: \quad \mu > 200 \text{ lbs}$$

Session Commands	Dialog Box
MTB > SET THE FOLLOWING DATA IN C1	**Statistics ▶ Basic Statistics ▶ 1-Sample t**
DATA> 195 210 211 197 215 187 220 203	Type *C1* in **Variable** box
DATA> 198 207 218 221 193 206 214	Click **Test mean**
DATA> END	Type *200* in box
MTB > TTEST OF MU = 200, DATA IN C1;	Click ↓ after **Alternative**. Menu drops down.
SUBC> ALTERNATIVE = 1.	Click **greater than**
	Click **OK**

Output

T-Test of the Mean

Test of mu = 200.00 vs mu > 200.00

Variable	N	Mean	StDev	SE Mean	T	P-Value
C1	15	206.33	10.54	2.72	2.33	0.018

Since the P-value is .018, we would reject the null hypothesis for any $\alpha \geq .018$.

The following produces a confidence interval for μ using the data in column 1. We have chosen the 95% level of confidence.

Session Command	Dialog Box
MTB> TINTERVAL 95, DATA IN C1	**Statistics ▶ Basic Statistics ▶ 1-Sample t**
	Type *C1* in **Variable** box
	Click **Confidence interval**
	Type *95* in box after **level**
	Click **OK**

Output

Confidence Intervals

```
Variable      N      Mean    StDev  SE Mean        95.0 % C.I.
C1           15    206.33    10.54     2.72  (  200.49,  212.17)
```

Therefore, the confidence interval is from 200.49 to 212.17.

Finding *P*-Values

We have seen that Minitab performs a statistical test by computing the *P*-value. Minitab commands work on the original data values. However, sometimes we have only summary data—the sample size, sample mean, and sample standard deviation. A Minitab command, such as ZTEST, will not work on this information. Nevertheless, we can use Minitab to find the *P*-value.

Recall that in Section 8.4 we found the *P*-value for a test concerning the mean height of female distance runners:

$$H_0: \quad \mu = 64 \text{ in.}$$

$$H_a: \quad \mu > 64 \text{ in.}$$

Our summary data were $\bar{x} = 65.6$, $s = 3.3$, and $n = 40$. Using 3.3 as an estimate for σ, we computed the observed value of our test statistic to be

$$z = \frac{\bar{x} - \mu}{\sigma/\sqrt{n}} = \frac{65.6 - 64}{3.3/\sqrt{40}} \doteq 3.07$$

We saw that the *P*-value was

$$P = P(z \geq 3.07) = .0011$$

We can use Minitab to compute the observed value and then use the CDF command to find the *P*-value. Note that CDF 3.07 would give the probability $P(z \leq 3.07)$, and hence the *P*-value is $1 - \text{CDF } 3.07$. (See Figure 8.16 in Section 8.4.) The program to compute the *P*-value is as follows:

Session Commands	**Dialog Box**

Session Commands

MTB > LET K1 = (65.6 - 64)/(3.3/SQRT(40))
MTB > CDF K1, STORE IN K2;
SUBC> NORMAL 0, 1.
MTB > LET K3 = 1 - K2 #THIS IS THE P VALUE
MTB > PRINT K3

Dialog Box

Calc ▶ **Mathematical Expressions**
Type *K1* in **Variable** box
Type $(65.6 - 64)/(3.3/SQRT(40))$ in
  Expression box
Click **OK**

Calc ▶ **Probability Distributions**
  ▶ **Normal**
Click **Cumulative probability**
Click **Input constant** and type *K1* in box
Click **Optional storage** and type *K2* in
  box
Click **OK**

> **Calc ▶ Mathematical Expressions**
> Type *K3* in **Variable** box
> Type *1 − K2* in **Expression** box
> Click **OK**
>
> **File ▶ Display Data**
> Type *K3* in **Display** box
> Click **OK**

Output

Data Display

K3   0.00108314

In this program, K1 = 3.07. CDF 3.07 is computed and stored as K2. K3 is the *P*-value. We used the square root function (SQRT) to compute $\sqrt{40}$.

For this right-tailed test, the *P*-value was the area of the right tail of the standard normal distribution. For a left-tailed test, the *P*-value is the area of a left tail (to the left of the observed value). The CDF command gives the area of a left tail directly. For a right tail, we must subtract the CDF value from 1, as in the previous printout. For a two-tailed test, we find the area of a tail and double it. The tail we find will be a right tail if the observed value is positive, and a left tail if the observed value is negative. For example, if we had wanted to do a two-tailed test instead of a right-tailed test, the LET command used to compute the *P*-value would be

$$\text{LET K3} = 2 * (1 - K2)$$

You might argue that it is just as easy to find the *P*-value using Appendix Table B.3. However, we shall see that tables for other statistical tests (such as the *t* test) are not as convenient for finding *P*-values. The CDF command can then be quite useful.

EXERCISES

The following exercises are suggested for use with Minitab: 8.24, 8.69, 8.77(b), 8.83, 8.124, and 8.138.

8.8

WORKING WITH DATA (OPTIONAL)

Refer to the Framingham Heart Study data sets in Section 2.8.

1. Using a 5% level of significance, test the claim that the population mean systolic blood pressure for

   (a)   Males is larger than 120   (b)   Females is 120

   Note: You may have already calculated the sample means and sample standard deviations. See Problems 1 and 4 of Section 3.7.

2. Construct a 95% confidence interval for the population mean systolic blood pressure for

   (a)   Males   (b)   Females

Note: You may have already calculated the sample means and sample standard deviations. See Problems 1 and 4 of Section 3.7.

(c)   The mean systolic blood pressure for all males in Appendix Table B.11 is 135 mm. Thinking of these males as the population, does the confidence interval you computed in part (a) "capture" the mean of 135 mm?

(d)   Approximately what percentage of the confidence intervals constructed by your classmates should contain the value 135 mm? (You might want to check with your class to see how close they come to this percentage.)

3.   The American Heart Association advises that a person's serum cholesterol level not exceed 200. Using a 5% level of significance, test that the population mean serum cholesterol level for

(a)   Males is larger than 200   (b)   Females is larger than 200

Note: You may have already calculated the sample means and sample standard deviations. See Problems 2 and 5 of Section 3.7.

4.   Construct a 95% confidence interval for the population mean serum cholesterol level for

(a)   Males   (b)   Females

Note: You may have already calculated the sample means and sample standard deviations. See Problems 2 and 5 of Section 3.7.

5.   Refer to your data from Problem 8 of Section 2.8.

(a)   Using these data, find a 95% confidence interval for the population mean diastolic blood pressure. It is thought that for men age 30–39, $\mu = 79$ mm. Does your confidence interval support this belief?

(b)   Do you believe that a confidence interval based on Student's t distribution is appropriate in this case? Explain.

8.9

SUMMARY

In this chapter, we introduced estimation and hypothesis testing concerning a population mean μ and a population proportion p. These results are summarized in the following table:

Inference Concerning Population Means and Population Proportions

Parameter	Assumptions	$1 - \alpha$ Confidence Interval	Test Statistic for a Hypothesis Test
(1) μ	Sample Size $n \geq 30$	$\bar{x} \pm z_{\alpha/2} \cdot \dfrac{\sigma}{\sqrt{n}}$	$z = \dfrac{\bar{x} - \mu}{\sigma/\sqrt{n}}$
		If σ is unknown, use s.	
	$n < 30$ x approximately normal	$\bar{x} \pm t_{\alpha/2} \cdot \dfrac{s}{\sqrt{n}}$ df $= n - 1$	$t = \dfrac{\bar{x} - \mu}{s/\sqrt{n}}$ df $= n - 1$
(2) p	$np, nq \geq 5$ $(x, n - x \geq 5$ in case of confidence intervals)	$\hat{p} \pm z_{\alpha/2} \cdot \sqrt{\dfrac{\hat{p}\hat{q}}{n}}$	$z = \dfrac{\hat{p} - p}{\sqrt{pq/n}}$

A **point estimate** for μ is $\bar{x}$, and a **point estimate** for p is $\hat{p} = \frac{x}{n}$. To obtain a point estimate for a parameter with a specified accuracy (maximum error of estimate to be E with confidence $1 - \alpha$), the sample size should be at least as large as indicated in the table:

Parameter	Sample Size
μ	$n = \left[\dfrac{z_{\alpha/2} \cdot \sigma}{E} \right]^2$
p	$n = \left[\dfrac{z_{\alpha/2}}{E} \right]^2 \cdot \dfrac{1}{4}$

The five steps in a test of hypotheses are as follows:

1. Determine the null hypothesis H_0 and the alternate hypothesis H_a. The null hypothesis will usually contain the symbol $=$. The alternate hypothesis will usually contain one of the following symbols: $>$, $<$, or $\neq$.

2. Determine the level of significance α.

3. Select the test statistic and compute its observed value from the sample data. When the parameter being tested occurs in the formula for the test statistic, we substitute the value appearing in the null hypothesis.

4. Find the critical region. This consists of values of the test statistic that strongly favor the alternate hypothesis.

5. Make your decision. If the observed value of the test statistic falls in the critical region, reject the null hypothesis H_0 in favor of the alternate hypothesis H_a. Otherwise, do not reject H_0.

The **P-value** is the probability of obtaining a value of the test statistic as favorable or more favorable to the alternate hypothesis than the observed value if the null hypothesis were true. The smaller the P-value, the stronger the evidence in favor of the alternate hypothesis. Using the P-value, we can test hypotheses without finding the critical region. We reject H_0 if $P \leq \alpha$ and do not reject H_0 if $P > \alpha$.

REVIEW EXERCISES

8.120   Suppose that 100 95% confidence intervals for a population mean μ were obtained. Approximately how many of these intervals should contain the value μ? Approximately how many 99% confidence intervals should contain μ if 1000 such intervals were constructed?

8.121   A golf ball was tested under laboratory conditions to estimate the mean distance μ the ball travels when subjected to a particular force. A random sample of 60 golf balls showed that the distances they moved had a mean of 210 yards and a standard deviation of 6 yards. Find

   (a)   A 95% confidence interval for μ

   (b)   The maximum error of estimate

8.122   A city assessor needed an estimate of the mean income per household. A random sample of 40 households in the city showed a mean income of $29,400 and a standard deviation of $6325. Find a 99% confidence interval for μ. Can the assessor conclude that the mean income per household has increased over last year's figure of $25,100?

8.123 A supermarket meat manager believed that the mean weight of meat obtained from beef cattle was around 210 pounds. The manager obtained the following 30 weights:

$$
\begin{array}{cccccccccc}
204.0 & 205.1 & 214.9 & 222.6 & 222.8 & 198.4 & 222.2 & 230.9 & 220.0 & 222.4 \\
215.9 & 207.6 & 208.2 & 228.0 & 208.4 & 219.5 & 194.2 & 192.9 & 196.4 & 202.1 \\
212.9 & 203.8 & 208.9 & 206.3 & 210.6 & 195.9 & 235.9 & 228.5 & 216.9 & 189.8
\end{array}
$$

(a) Construct a 90% confidence interval for the population mean weight μ. Use the fact that $\sum x = 6346$ and $\sum x^2 = 1{,}346{,}680.26$.

(b) Based on these data, can the manager conclude that there is no reason to believe the mean weight is different from 210 pounds?

8.124 On a stretch of interstate highway with a speed limit of 55 miles per hour, an unusual number of accidents were being reported. Forty cars were randomly clocked for speed by the state police. The speeds were

$$
\begin{array}{cccccccccccccc}
66 & 79 & 58 & 65 & 64 & 71 & 70 & 67 & 55 & 67 & 70 & 60 & 66 & 66 \\
60 & 63 & 75 & 60 & 57 & 63 & 72 & 61 & 70 & 72 & 72 & 67 & 68 \\
59 & 71 & 64 & 69 & 77 & 61 & 74 & 59 & 51 & 56 & 75 & 58 & 66
\end{array}
$$

(a) Estimate the mean speed of all cars with a 95% confidence interval. Assume $\sum x = 2624$ and $\sum x^2 = 173{,}804$.

(b) If anything above 62 miles per hour is considered excessive, can the police conclude that there is excessive speeding (on the average)?

8.125 A psychologist wanted to obtain an estimate of the average reaction time to a stimulus. Prior to the experiment, she thought the true mean time would be about 2.5 seconds. A stem-and-leaf plot of 50 reaction times is shown here. Note that each stem is split, with leaves 0, 1, 2, 3, 4 on the first stem and leaves 5, 6, 7, 8, 9 on the second.

```
0 | 9
1 | 334
1 | 566778
2 | 012334
2 | 5666777889
3 | 0111223333444
3 | 5677788
4 | 0
4 | 55
5 |
5 |
6 | 4            Note:  3 | 5 = 3.5 seconds
```

(a) For the 50 data values, $\sum x = 142.3$ and $\sum x^2 = 453.79$. Find a 95% confidence interval for the population mean μ. Should the psychologist revise her thinking that the mean value is about 2.5?

(b) The data value 6.4 is a possible outlier. For the other 49 data values, $\sum x = 135.9$ and $\sum x^2 = 412.83$. Find a 95% confidence interval for μ. Compare with the confidence interval obtained in part (a). Is there much difference between the two? Comment on the sample size and the effect of the outlier on the confidence interval. Did deleting the outlier make much difference in this case?

(c) Based on the data, can the psychologist conclude that there is no reason to believe the mean time is different from 2.5 seconds?

8.126 Consider a computer simulation that samples 100 values from a normal distribution with mean 50. The procedure is to be repeated 1000 times. Let x be the number of the 1000 95% confidence intervals that contain the true mean 50. Find the probability that between 940 and 960 (inclusive) intervals will contain the mean value 50. (*Hint:* Use the normal approximation to the binomial.)

8.127   An economist estimated the mean salary μ of a household head as between $27,170 and $27,830. The sample size was 225 and the sample standard deviation was $3000.

   (a)   What is the value of the sample mean?

   (b)   What level of confidence is being used?

8.128   Researchers in a large metropolitan area were studying systolic blood pressures of male runners, and they wished to obtain an estimate of the mean μ. Assume that $\sigma = 17$. How large a random sample is needed to estimate μ to within 2 units with 95% confidence?

8.129   A company was working on a new liquid diet, and an official wanted to estimate the mean weight loss μ. How large a random sample is required to estimate μ to within .5 pound with 98% confidence? Use $\sigma = 3$.

8.130   Consider a population with unknown mean μ and standard deviation $\sigma = 10$. How large a random sample is required to estimate μ to within 2 units with

   (a)   90% confidence?   **(b)**   99% confidence?

8.131   Refer to Exercise 8.130. Suppose you were to find the required sample size to estimate the population mean μ to within 2 units with 95% confidence. Assume that $\sigma = 10$.

   (a)   Without finding the sample size, would the required sample size be larger or smaller than that needed for
      (i)   90% confidence?   **(ii)**   99% confidence?

   (b)   Now find the required sample size and compare with your answers to Exercise 8.130.

8.132   Refer to Exercise 8.130. Suppose you were to find the required sample size to estimate the population mean μ to within 1 unit with 90% confidence. Assume that $\sigma = 10$.

   (a)   Without finding the sample size, would the required sample size be larger or smaller than that required to estimate μ to within 2 units with 90% confidence?

   (b)   Now find the required sample size and compare with your answer to Exercise 8.130(a).

8.133   A manufacturer of transparent tape was worried that the mean length of the tape was not 450 inches. The price and length of the tape were designed to yield a maximum profit. A random sample of 43 rolls of tape gave a sample mean length of 450.4 inches and a sample standard deviation of .95 inch. Complete the test at the 1% significance level.

   (a)   Use the classical approach.   **(b)**   Use the *P*-value approach.

8.134   A sample of 40 recovering alcoholics was given the State-Trait Anxiety Inventory test (STAI). The state anxiety score showed a mean of 38 and a standard deviation of 7. A psychologist suspected that recovering alcoholics in general had a higher mean state anxiety than the norm of 35. Do the sample data justify the suspicion? Complete the test with a 5% significance level.

   (a)   Use the classical approach.   **(b)**   Use the *P*-value approach.

8.135   The manager of a bicycle factory believed he was being supplied spokes that were less than the desired 12 inches in length, on the average. A random sample of 38 spokes gave a mean length of 11.85 inches and a standard deviation of .65 inch. Test the manager's claim with a 5% level of significance.

8.136   A manufacturer of flashlight bulbs claimed the mean life μ of his product is more than 500 hours. A random sample of 100 items gave a mean of 504 and a standard deviation of 20.

   (a)   Find the *P*-value.

(b) Is the test statistically significant at the 10% level of significance? At the 1% level of significance?

8.137 Cans of motorcycle oil are supposed to contain 16 ounces of oil (on the average). To test this, 36 cans were obtained, and the results showed a mean of 15.5 ounces and a standard deviation of 1 ounce.

(a) Find the P-value.

(b) What conclusion is reached at the 10% level of significance? At the 1% level of significance?

8.138 Health clinic officials believed that, on average, patients were waiting more than 1 year between physical examinations. Here are the times (in years) between physical exams for 32 patients. Can the officials be confident of their conclusion at the 5% level? Assume $\sum x = 44.9$ and $\sum x^2 = 67.73$. The data are

$$\begin{array}{cccccccccc} .6 & .7 & .8 & .8 & .8 & .9 & 1.1 & 1.2 & 1.2 & 1.3 & 1.3 \\ 1.3 & 1.3 & 1.3 & 1.4 & 1.4 & 1.5 & 1.5 & 1.5 & 1.5 & 1.6 & 1.6 \\ 1.7 & 1.7 & 1.8 & 1.8 & 1.8 & 1.8 & 1.9 & 1.9 & 1.9 & 2.0 \end{array}$$

8.139 The director of a computing center claimed that the mean down time per week (when the computer is not operating) is less than 60 minutes. The following down times (in minutes) for 32 weeks were recorded.

$$\begin{array}{ccccccccccc} 61 & 50 & 53 & 55 & 52 & 42 & 53 & 56 & 49 & 53 & 51 \\ 61 & 55 & 65 & 61 & 70 & 61 & 64 & 51 & 56 & 46 & 53 \\ 55 & 54 & 60 & 53 & 56 & 47 & 52 & 66 & 49 & 57 \end{array}$$

Use $\sum x = 1767$ and $\sum x^2 = 98{,}755$ to test the claim at the 5% level of significance.

8.140 Assume that you are testing the hypotheses H_0: $\mu = 150$ and H_a: $\mu = 146$. Further assume that $\sigma = 20$ and use a left-tailed test.

(a) For level of significance $\alpha = .05$ and sample size $n = 100$, calculate the probability of a Type II error, β. (*Hint:* Express the critical region in terms of $\bar{x}$. From the definition of β, it follows that $\beta = $ the probability that $\bar{x}$ does *not* fall in the critical region when the alternate hypothesis is true.)

(b) For $\alpha = .10$ and $n = 100$, calculate β.

(c) Comment on the relationship between the magnitudes of α and β, assuming the same sample size.

(d) Calculate β for level of significance $\alpha = .01$ and sample size $n = 100$.

(e) Calculate β for $\alpha = .01$ and $n = 400$.

(f) Comment on the relationship between the sample size and β, assuming a fixed level of significance.

8.141 Find the following values:

(a) $t_{.01}$ when df $= 11$ **(b)** $t_{.05}$ when df $= 23$

(c) $t_{.10}$ when df $= 14$ **(d)** $t_{.975}$ when df $= 21$

8.142 Assuming a t distribution with 16 degrees of freedom, find each of the following probabilities. (*Hint:* A diagram of the required area might help.)

(a) $P(-1.337 < t < 1.337)$ **(b)** $P(1.746 < t < 2.583)$

(c) $P(t < 2.12)$ **(d)** $P(-1.337 < t < 1.746)$

8.143 The mean number of calories μ per 6-ounce can of tomato paste is supposed to be 150. A weight watchers group thought that μ was larger than 150. A random sample of 14 cans yielded a sample mean of 151.2 calories and a sample standard deviation of 2.4 calories. Do the sample results support the weight watchers' contention at the 5% significance level? Assume the distribution is approximately normal.

(a) Use the classical approach.   **(b)** Use the P-value approach.

8.144   The mean percentage of sodium carbonate μ per 21-ounce can of a cleanser is supposed to be 11%. The manufacturer thinks that the mean percentage may have changed. A random sample of 20 cans showed a mean percentage of sodium carbonate as 11.5% and a standard deviation of 1.5%. At a 10% level of significance, is there sufficient evidence indicating that the mean percentage of sodium carbonate μ is different from 11? Assume the distribution is approximately normal.

8.145   A method of manufacturing a ball bearing produced a mean diameter μ of .120 inch and a standard deviation σ of .015 inch. A new process to manufacture the ball bearing was developed, and it was believed that there would be no change in the variance. To test the hypothesis of no change in the mean μ, 18 ball bearings produced by the new process were selected and the mean diameter was .114 inch. Complete the test at the 10% significance level. Assume the distribution is approximately normal.

8.146   A transit authority believed that introduction of its new rail transit vehicles would increase patronage. Past records showed an average of 2200 passengers per day on the number 10 transit line. With the new transit vehicles, a sample of 20 days showed an average of 2315 passengers per day and a standard deviation of 115. At the 5% level of significance, does it appear that there has been an increase in mean daily patronage for this route? Assume the population is approximately normal.

(a)   Use the classical approach.   (b)   Use the P-value approach.

8.147   Twenty-seven runners were given a psychological test called the Profile of Mood States (POMS). The sample showed a mean tension score of 10.46 and a standard deviation of 5.57 (*Source:* Morgan, W. P., and M. L. Pollock, "Psychologic Characterization of the Elite Distance Runner," in *The Long Distance Runner,* ed. P. Milvy, New York: Urizen Books, 1977). Do these results indicate that runners in general have a mean tension level different from 13 (the norm for college students)? Use the 5% level of significance. Assume the population is approximately normal.

8.148   The turkey bologna produced by a meat-processing company had a mean fat content of 10%. The quality control department at the company tested a sample of size 25 and found a sample mean fat content of 10.3% and a standard deviation of .83%. At the 5% level of significance, test the claim that the mean μ is no longer 10%. Assume the population is approximately normal.

8.149   An economist claimed that the mean tax deduction for charities was less than $600 for families with an income of about $35,000. A stem-and-leaf plot of a sample of 18 tax returns of families with an income of $35,000 is as follows.

```
2 | 8
3 | 49
4 | 3589
5 | 0255778
6 | 136
7 | 1        Note:   4 | 5 = $450
```

(a)   Is the t procedure appropriate for testing the claim? If so, proceed to part (b).

(b)   With a 5% significance level, do the sample data support the economist's claim? Use both the classical and P-value approaches. Note that the mean and standard deviation of the deductions are 517.22 and 110.87, respectively.

8.150   Consider the following 16 data values:

    12   83   92   92   97   98   103   104
   107 109 109 111 113 118 122   128

Here is a stem-and-leaf plot for the 16 data values.

```
 1 | 2
 2 |
 3 |
 4 |
 5 |
 6 |
 7 |
 8 | 3
 9 | 2278
10 | 34799
11 | 138
12 | 28
```

For the 16 data values, the mean and standard deviation are 99.88 and 26.19, respectively. With the data value 12 removed, the mean and standard deviation are 105.73 and 12.12, respectively.

(a) Use the 16 data values and a 5% level of significance to test the hypothesis that the population mean μ is 93. Remove the data value 12 and repeat. Compare your results.

(b) Use the 16 data values and construct a 95% confidence interval for μ. Remove the data value 12 and repeat. Compare your results.

(c) Comment on the appropriateness of the t procedure for the two data sets.

8.151 Consider the data in Exercise 8.149.

(a) Find a 90% confidence interval for the mean tax deduction μ.

(b) Find the maximum error of the estimate for μ with 90% level of confidence.

8.152 Consider the data in Exercise 8.148. Find a 95% confidence interval for the mean fat content μ. Does your result suggest that μ is different from 10%?

8.153 Use Exercise 8.147 and construct a 95% confidence interval for the mean tension level.

8.154 Consider a computer simulation that samples 15 values from a normal distribution with mean 50 and standard deviation 5. The computer repeats the procedure 1000 times, and computes a 95% confidence interval based on the t distribution each time.

(a) About how many of the 1000 95% confidence intervals would you expect to contain the mean of 50?

(b) On average, what is the width of the 95% confidence intervals?

8.155 Fill in the blanks and construct a confidence interval for a population proportion p in each of the following. Note that n refers to the sample size and x to the number of successes.

	$\hat{p}$	x	n	Percentage Confidence Interval
(a)	.50		100	95
(b)		50	125	90
(c)	.72		400	99
(d)		45	225	95
(e)	.60		60	90
(f)		30	50	99

8.156 There was concern among health officials in a community that an unusually large percentage of babies with abnormally low birth weight were being born. Abnormal low birth weight here is defined as less than 88 ounces. A sample of 180 births showed 18 babies with abnormally low birth weight.

(a) Find a 95% confidence interval for the true proportion of babies with abnormally low birth weight.

(b) Suppose the true proportion is 5%. Would the health officials conclude that the percentage of abnormally low birth weights in the community is larger than 5%?

8.157   A June 17–19, 1994, poll of 499 adults statewide in Minnesota was undertaken to gather opinions regarding the possible sale of the National Basketball Association Timberwolves to a buyer in another state (*Source: Star Tribune,* June 22, 1994). Of those polled, 54% responded that "It would really hurt Minnesota's image if the Timberwolves left the state right now." Find a 95% confidence interval for the proportion p of all adults who believed Minnesota's image would be hurt.

8.158   In Exercise 8.157, we discussed a poll of 499 adults regarding the possible sale of the National Basketball Association Timberwolves to a buyer in another state. In the poll, 37% strongly agreed that "The state has no business getting involved in the Timberwolves deal." Find a 90% confidence interval for the proportion p of all adults who strongly agree on this issue.

8.159   How large a random sample is required to estimate the proportion p of women employed in a large city with 95% confidence to within

(a) 5 percentage points?

(b) 3 percentage points?

(c) 1 percentage point?

8.160   A poll of 450 residents in a large city was conducted to estimate the proportion p of residents who believed "the federal government was not doing enough about the air pollution problem." Of those polled, 306 residents agreed that the federal government was not doing enough.

(a) Estimate p with a 95% confidence interval.

(b) What is the maximum error of estimate for p?

8.161   A lottery game consists of selecting six numbers (no repetitions) from a collection of 45 numbers, $\{1, 2, 3, 4, \ldots, 44, 45\}$. A regular player believed that too many single-digit numbers were being drawn. The player looked at 480 numbers drawn, and there were 108 single-digit numbers. Was the player justified in his assertion at the 5% level of significance?

8.162   A city planning board denied a developer's request to increase the size of an existing mall. The board members claimed that they had the support of more than 60% of the voters. In a random sample of 300 city voters, 192 supported the board's position. Test the board's claim by finding a P-value. At what levels of significance is the board justified in claiming that they have the support of more than 60% of the voters?

8.163   Over the past year, 85% of customers at a clothing store spent more than $45. The owner sampled 36 receipts from customers served by one of the clerks. The amounts (rounded to the nearest dollar) are

```
47  46  56  70  52  58  48  57  49  61  52  40
60  22  74  59  60  30  61  44  62  41  53  57
50  52  57  59  69  51  58  56  44  36  47  51
```

Using a 1% level of significance, can the owner conclude that the clerk is not living up to expectations?

8.164   In a political discussion dealing with health care, the claim was made that less than 40% of U.S. working women were covered by employer-provided health insurance. In a random sample of 1200 working women, 37% said their employer provided health insurance.

(a) Use a 5% level of significance and test the claim.

(b) Would your decision be the same as in part (b) if the level of significance were 1%?

8.165 A large box is filled with red and blue marbles. Let p be the proportion of red marbles and consider the hypotheses $H_0: p = .4$ and $H_a: p = .7$. A sample of size 5 is to be selected. Let x be the number of red marbles obtained, and consider x as a binomial random variable. Suppose that H_0 is to be rejected if the number x of red marbles selected is 4 or 5.

(a) Find the probability of a Type I error, α. (*Hint:* Use Appendix Table B.2.)

(b) Find the probability of a Type II error, β. (*Hint:* β = probability that x is not in the critical region when H_a is true.)

8.166 Consider Exercise 8.165, replacing the critical region {4, 5} with {3, 4, 5}.

(a) Without calculating α, will it be larger, smaller, or the same as the α in Exercise 8.165(a)? Now calculate α and compare it with the α in Exercise 8.165(a).

(b) Without calculating β, will it be larger, smaller, or the same as the β in Exercise 8.165(b)? Now calculate β and compare it with the β in Exercise 8.165(b).

Notes

The Boston Globe, Boston, 1994 and 1995.

Haskell, W. L., S. Lewis, C. Perry, P. Stern, and P. D. Wood, "Plasma Lipoprotein Distributions in Male and Female Runners," in P. Milvy, ed., *The Long Distance Runner.* New York: Urizen Books, 1977. Originally published as part of Volume 301 of the *Annals of the New York Academy of Sciences* under the title "The Marathon: Physiological, Medical, Epidemiological and Psychological Studies."

Keys, A., ed., "Coronary Heart Disease in Seven Countries." *Circulation,* Vol. 41, Suppl. 1:1, 1970.

Meier, P., J. Sacks, and S. Zabell, "What Happened in Hazelwood?" in *Statistics and the Law,* eds. M. DeGroot, S. Fienberg, J. Kadane. New York: Wiley, 1986.

Morgan, W. P., and M. L. Pollock, "Psychological Characterization of the Elite Distance Runner," in Paul Milvy, ed., *The Long Distance Runner.* New York: Urizen Books, 1977.

Perron, F. E., "Growth, Fecundity and Mortality of *Conus Pennaceus* in Hawaii." *Ecology,* Vol. 64, No. 1, 1983.

Star Tribune, Minneapolis, 1994.

Student, "The Probable Error of a Mean." *Biometrika,* Vol. 6, 1908.

Vaillant, G., *The Natural History of Alcoholism: Causes, Patterns and Paths to Recovery.* Cambridge: Harvard University Press, 1983.

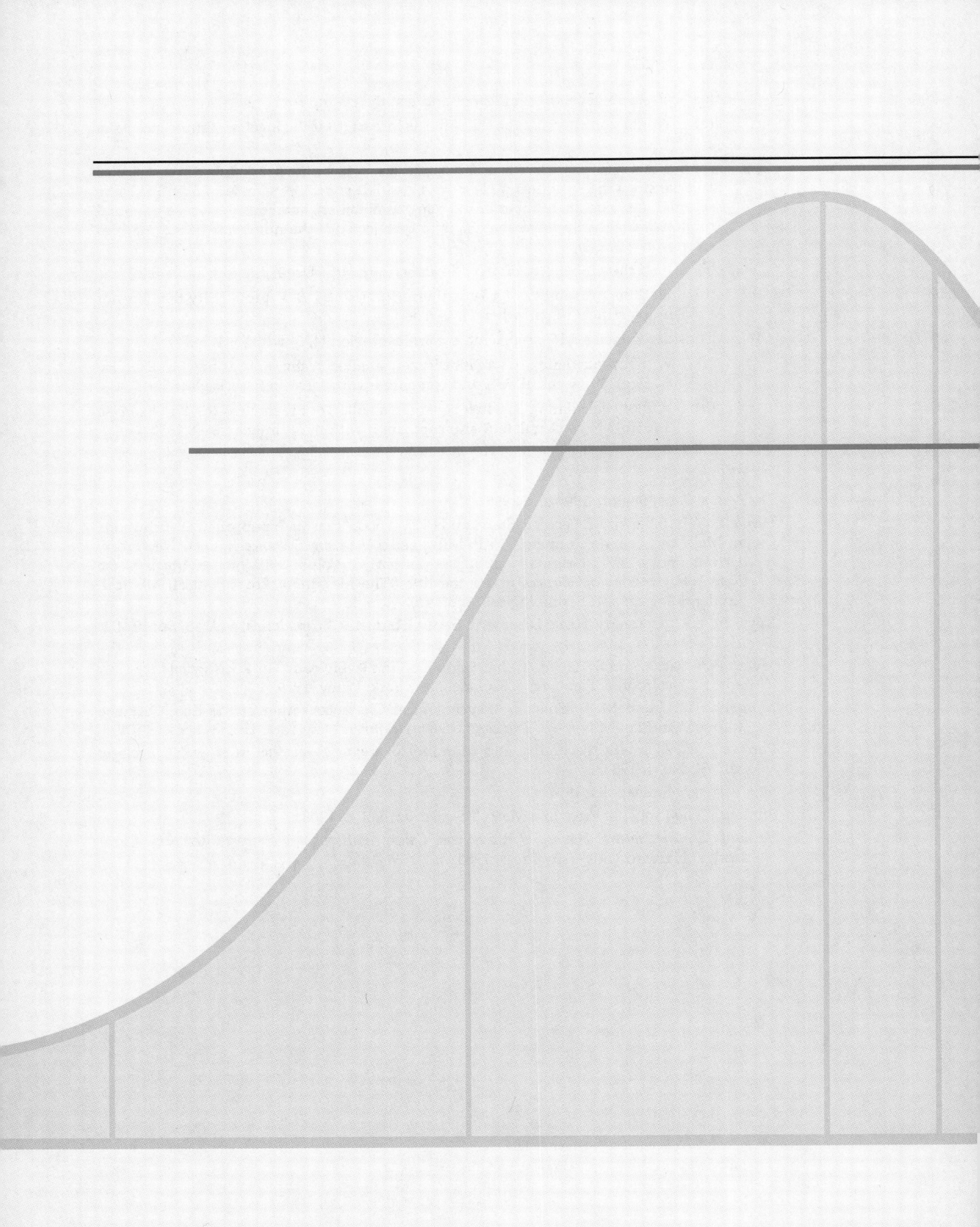

CHAPTER 9

INFERENCE CONCERNING TWO POPULATION PARAMETERS

9.1 INTRODUCTION

9.2 INFERENCE CONCERNING TWO POPULATION MEANS: DEPENDENT SAMPLES

9.3 INFERENCE CONCERNING TWO POPULATION MEANS BASED ON INDEPENDENT SAMPLES: Large-Sample Case

9.4 INFERENCE CONCERNING TWO POPULATION MEANS BASED ON INDEPENDENT SAMPLES: Small-Sample Case

9.5 INFERENCE CONCERNING TWO POPULATION PROPORTIONS

9.6 USING MINITAB (OPTIONAL)

9.7 WORKING WITH DATA (OPTIONAL)

9.8 SUMMARY

REVIEW EXERCISES

NOTES

9.1

INTRODUCTION

In many situations in statistics, the primary objective is to study how one parameter compares with another parameter rather than to study the particular value of some parameter. For example, suppose there are two medications used in the treatment of the same illness, and we let p_1 and p_2 represent the proportion of people who will be cured with medication 1 and medication 2, respectively. Then we would want to know which proportion is larger. Or we may wish to find out which of two types of automobiles has the greater mean gas mileage.

In this chapter, we develop methods for comparing two means or two proportions for a pair of populations.

405

_____ **9.2**

INFERENCE CONCERNING TWO POPULATION MEANS: DEPENDENT SAMPLES

The test statistic used to test hypotheses concerning two population means depends on a number of factors. One of these is the method of obtaining samples. Let us look at this idea more closely.

A high school developed a course in reading comprehension for its freshmen. The question is whether the course will be effective. Will the mean reading level for freshmen who are given the course be higher than that of those who are not given the course?

One way to study this question would be to select a group of freshmen, give them the course, and then compare their scores on a reading exam with the scores of a group of freshmen who have not taken the course. The two samples of scores in this case would be **independent.** Another method would be to select one group of students and compare their scores on a reading test *before* they take the course with their scores on a test *after* they take the course. In this case, the two samples of scores would be **dependent.**

It is not always feasible to obtain dependent samples, but when we can obtain them, there are certain advantages. Dependent samples tend to reduce the effects of variability among the elements in a sample. For example, suppose we obtain independent samples of students, and one of the students who did not take the course has an extremely high level of reading comprehension. If we look at the sample means of the scores for each group, this student's score might distort the results, thus making the sample mean for the students who have not taken the course unrealistically high. However, suppose we have dependent samples. We would have a "before" and "after" score for each student. If a student in the study has a tendency to score high, this should appear in both samples and therefore will not distort just one of the samples. In other words, things will balance out; the effects of variability among the subjects in the sample (which can confound the results) will be reduced.

> **Definition**   Two samples are *independent* if the data values obtained from one are unrelated to the values from the other. The samples are *dependent* if each data value from one sample is paired in a natural way with a data value from the other sample.

In this chapter, when we conduct tests for means involving small sample sizes (less than 30), the population must be approximately normal. That is, the population should have a roughly mound-shaped distribution.

Inference from Dependent Samples

Suppose that we are interested in comparing the means μ_1 and μ_2 of populations 1 and 2 whose data values are represented by the symbols x_1 and x_2, respectively. Further, assume that the samples we obtain to investigate μ_1 and μ_2 are dependent. For example, an experimental automobile emission-control system was developed, and we wish to find out whether it will increase gas mileage. Let μ_1 = mean gas mileage for cars using the experimental emission controls and μ_2 = mean gas mileage for cars with the standard emission controls. We are interested in whether $\mu_1 > \mu_2$. To compare the two emission-control systems, eight cars are selected. Each car is driven using one system and then the other. The gas mileage in each case is recorded in miles per gallon. The results are listed in Table 9.1.

Table 9.1

	Cars							
	1	2	3	4	5	6	7	8
x_1 (mileage with experimental emission controls)	17	23	27	14	28	21	29	13
x_2 (mileage with standard emission controls)	9	17	21	16	22	17	25	13
$x = x_1 - x_2$ (difference)	8	6	6	-2	6	4	4	0

We should look at the difference

$$x = x_1 - x_2$$

for each car. As one might expect, the mean of a population of differences is the difference of the means

$$\mu = \mu_1 - \mu_2$$

This is sometimes called the **mean difference.** We are asking whether $\mu_1 > \mu_2$. This is the same as $\mu > 0$. Therefore the hypotheses we wish to investigate are

$$H_0: \quad \mu = 0$$
$$H_a: \quad \mu > 0$$

But this is a hypothesis test for a single mean, μ. We investigated this subject in Chapter 8.

When investigating two population means using dependent samples, let

$$x = x_1 - x_2$$
$$\mu = \mu_1 - \mu_2$$

We can then conduct our investigation by studying μ using the methods developed in Chapter 8 to study a single mean.

For example, if the sample size is large ($n \geq 30$), the test statistic in a hypothesis test is

$$z = \frac{\bar{x} - \mu}{\sigma / \sqrt{n}}$$

where σ is usually estimated by the sample standard deviation s. If the sample size is small (less than 30) and if the variable x is approximately normal, then we use Student's t:

$$t = \frac{\bar{x} - \mu}{s/\sqrt{n}} \qquad df = n - 1$$

EXAMPLE 9.1

Do the data of Table 9.1 provide sufficient evidence to conclude that the experimental emission-control system will increase gas mileage? Use the 5% level of significance. Assume the population of differences is approximately normal.

Solution

1. *Hypotheses:*   We have seen that an increase in gas mileage will mean $\mu_1 > \mu_2$, which is the same as $\mu > 0$. Our hypotheses are

$$H_0: \quad \mu = 0$$
$$H_a: \quad \mu > 0$$

2. *Level of significance:* $\alpha = .05$

3. *Test statistic and observed value:*   The sample values of x in Table 9.1 are 8, 6, 6, -2, 6, 4, 4, 0. Since the sample size is small and the population is approximately normal, we can use the t statistic:

$$t = \frac{\bar{x} - \mu}{s/\sqrt{n}}$$

We need the values of $\bar{x}$ and s. Table 9.2 will help us compute these values.

Table 9.2

x	x^2
8	64
6	36
6	36
-2	4
6	36
4	16
4	16
0	0
Sums: 32	208 $n = 8$

$$\bar{x} = \frac{\sum x}{n} = \frac{32}{8} = 4$$

$$s = \sqrt{\frac{n(\sum x^2) - (\sum x)^2}{n(n-1)}}$$

$$= \sqrt{\frac{8(208) - (32)^2}{(8)(7)}} \doteq 3.38$$

Therefore, the observed value of t is

$$t = \frac{4-0}{3.38/\sqrt{8}} \doteq 3.35 \qquad df = n - 1 = 7$$

4. *Critical region:* Since the alternate hypothesis is $\mu > 0$, we will perform a right-tailed test. Using Appendix Table B.4, we find $t_{.05} = 1.895$. The critical region consists of values of $t \geq 1.895$. (See Figure 9.1.)

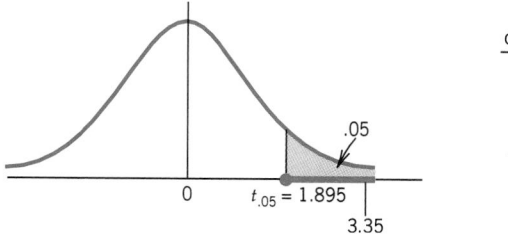

Figure 9.1

5. *Decision:* Since the observed value, $t = 3.35$, is in the critical region, we reject H_0. Therefore, it does appear that the experimental emission controls will increase gas mileage.

Minitab Printout for Example 9.1

```
        T-Test of the Mean

    Test of mu = 0.00 vs mu > 0.00

    Variable   N   Mean   StDev   SE Mean      T   P-Value
    x          8   4.00    3.38      1.20   3.35   0.0062
```

Confidence Intervals

We can find confidence intervals for the mean difference μ in the same way we found confidence intervals for a population mean in Chapter 8. For example, a $1 - \alpha$ confidence interval based on a large sample is

$$\bar{x} \pm z_{\alpha/2} \cdot \frac{\sigma}{\sqrt{n}}$$

where σ is usually estimated by s. A small-sample confidence interval is given by

$$\bar{x} \pm t_{\alpha/2} \cdot \frac{s}{\sqrt{n}} \qquad df = n - 1$$

EXAMPLE 9.2
Using the data in Table 9.1, find a 95% confidence interval for the mean difference in gas mileage (μ) between the two emission-control systems.

Solution

Since $1 - \alpha = .95$, $\alpha = .05$. Now df $= n - 1 = 8 - 1 = 7$. Using Appendix Table B.4, we see that $t_{\alpha/2} = t_{.025} = 2.365$. For the data in Table 9.1, $\bar{x} = 4$ and $s \doteq 3.38$. Our $1 - \alpha$ confidence interval is described by the endpoints:

$$\bar{x} \pm t_{\alpha/2} \cdot \frac{s}{\sqrt{n}}$$

Thus a 95% confidence interval is described by the endpoints:

$$4 \pm (2.365) \left(\frac{3.38}{\sqrt{8}} \right)$$

or

$$4 \pm 2.83$$

Therefore, we are 95% confident that

$$1.17 < \mu < 6.83$$

This means that we can be 95% confident that the new emission controls will increase gas mileage on the average between 1.17 and 6.83 miles per gallon, with a point estimate of 4 miles per gallon.

Minitab Printout for Example 9.2

Confidence Intervals

Variable	N	Mean	StDev	SE Mean	95.0 % C.I.
x	8	4.00	3.38	1.20	(1.17, 6.83)

EXERCISES

9.1 For the following data, (i) test the given claims and (ii) indicate the possible type of error committed (I or II). Assume that the samples are dependent. The mean difference is $\mu = \mu_1 - \mu_2$, where $x = x_1 - x_2$. Assume approximate normality for the population of differences.

(a) Use a 5% level of significance and test the claim that the mean difference μ is not 0. Note that $\bar{x} = 1.25$ and $s = 3.37$.

x_1	x_2
37	36
42	41
34	38
37	40
43	39
44	38
42	40
48	45

(b) Test the claim that the mean difference μ is larger than 0. Use a 5% level of significance.

x_1	x_2
23	25
19	14
22	16
20	17
25	22
33	25

9.2 For the following data, (i) test the given claims and (ii) indicate the possible type of error committed (I or II). Assume that the samples are dependent. The mean difference is $\mu = \mu_1 - \mu_2$, where $x = x_1 - x_2$. Assume that the population differences are approximately normal.

(a) Test the claim that the mean difference μ is less than 0. Use a 5% level of significance. Note that $\bar{x} = -1.86$ and $s = 3.72$.

x_1	x_2
76	79
81	83
75	78
73	77
76	72
70	77
68	66

(b) Test the claim that the mean difference is 10. Use a 10% level of significance.

x_1	x_2
49	30
41	27
38	32
39	31
47	33
47	38
44	29
38	20
41	21

9.3 Twenty-four males age 25–29 were selected from the Framingham Heart Study. Twelve were smokers and 12 were nonsmokers. The subjects were paired, with one being a smoker and the other a nonsmoker. Otherwise, each pair was similar with regard to age and physical characteristics. Systolic blood pressure readings were as follows:

A Smokers	B Nonsmokers
122	114
146	134
120	114
114	116
124	138
126	110
118	112
128	116
130	132
134	126
116	108
130	116

List the differences $x = A - B$ and verify that $\bar{x} = 6$ and $s = 8.40$. Use a 5% level of significance to determine whether the data indicate a difference in mean systolic blood pressure levels for the populations from which the two groups were selected. You may assume that the population of differences is approximately normal.

9.4 The management of a large chain of stores wished to study whether advertising tends to increase sales of a product. Six pairs of stores, each pair of comparable size and comparable sales relative to the product, were selected. For each pair, one of the stores was randomly selected to advertise the product while the other store did not advertise the product. The following results represent the numbers of cases of the product sold over a week's period of time.

A Stores Advertising the Product	B Stores Not Advertising the Product
12	9
17	12
8	10
20	18
7	8
13	10

Note that $\sum x = 10$ and $\sum x^2 = 52$. Is there sufficient evidence to suggest that the advertising program is effective? Use a 10% significance level. Assume approximate normality for the population of differences.

9.5 A salesman for a shoe company claimed runners would record quicker times, on the average, with the company's brand of sneaker. A track coach decided to test the claim. The coach selected eight runners. Each runner ran two 100-yard dashes on different days. In one 100-yard dash, the runners wore the sneakers supplied by the school; in the other, the sneakers supplied by the salesman. Each runner was randomly assigned the sneakers to wear for the first run. Their times, measured in seconds, were as follows:

A With Shoe Company's Sneakers	B With School's Sneakers
10.8	11.4
12.3	12.5
10.7	10.8
12.0	11.7
10.6	10.9
11.5	11.8
12.1	12.2
11.2	11.7

For the differences $x = A - B$, $\bar{x} = -.225$ and $s = .276$. Assume the population of differences is approximately normal.

(a) Find the P-value. (You will not be able to find an exact P-value, but indicate a possible range for the P-value, such as $.05 < P < .10$ or $P > .25$.)

(b) For which of the following levels of significance would H_0 be rejected?
(i) $\alpha = .10$ (ii) $\alpha = .05$ (iii) $\alpha = .01$

[*Hint:*   These can be answered using your answer in part (a).]

9.6   A teacher was interested in finding out whether a special study program would increase the scores of students on a national exam. Fourteen students were selected and paired according to IQ and scholastic performance. One student from each pair was randomly selected to participate in the special program, while the other student participated in the standard program. Both programs ended at the same time. Shortly thereafter, the students took the national exam. The results were

A Participated in the Special Program	B Participated in the Standard Program
66	60
82	79
96	92
72	73
78	75
82	80
67	69

At a 5% significance level, is there sufficient evidence to indicate that the special study program is more effective in raising the national exam scores, on the average? Assume approximate normality for the population of differences.

9.7   Allied Foods, Inc. suspected that a new recipe for chocolate cake mix would result in a thicker cake. Thirty-four cooks were asked to use the new recipe (A) and the old recipe (B). The difference (x) between thicknesses was recorded in each case ($x = x_A - x_B$). The results were $\bar{x} = .15$ inch and $s = .09$ inch. At the 1% level of significance, does recipe A result in thicker cakes?

9.8   A random sample of 50 GMAT (Graduate Management Aptitude Test) scores gave a mean difference $\bar{x} = -1.12$ (x = verbal score − quantitative score) and standard deviation $s = 5.95$.

(a)   With a 5% level of significance, is there sufficient evidence to indicate a difference between the mean verbal and quantitative scores?

(b)   Construct a 95% confidence interval for $\mu = \mu_1 - \mu_2$, where μ_1 and μ_2 are the population means for verbal and quantitative scores, respectively. Does the confidence interval support the conclusion reached in part (a)?

9.9   Use the data in the corresponding parts of Exercise 9.1 to construct confidence intervals for μ ($\mu = \mu_1 - \mu_2$, where $x = x_1 - x_2$). The confidence level is as follows:

(a)   95%   (b)   90%

9.10   (a)   Use the data in Exercise 9.4 to construct a 98% confidence interval for the difference in projected mean sales of the product between those stores advertising and those not advertising ($\mu_A - \mu_B$).

(b)   Use the data in Exercise 9.3 to construct a 95% confidence interval for the difference in population mean systolic blood pressures between males age 25–29 who are smokers and those who do not smoke ($\mu_A - \mu_B$).

(c)   Use the data in Exercise 9.6 to construct a 90% confidence interval for the difference in projected mean scores on the national examination between future participants in the special study program and the standard program ($\mu_A - \mu_B$).

9.11   A typing instructor thought that a new method of instruction (B) would result in a faster mean typing speed. The instructor tested her 10 students under the current method (A). A typing test was then given following 4 weeks of instruction (B). The results, measured in words per minute, are as follows:

A	58	63	66	69	70	70	70	76	77	86
B	60	64	67	69	71	72	74	76	75	85
A − B	−2	−1	−1	0	−1	−2	−4	0	2	1

(a)   Construct a dot diagram for the differences. Is a t procedure appropriate? If so, go to part (b).

(b)   Find a 90% confidence interval for the difference between the population means of methods A and B, respectively. Interpret your results.

(c)   Use a 5% level of significance and test the hypothesis that the mean typing speed for B is faster than that for A. Is your decision consistent with your results in part (b)?

9.12   Suppose we are testing the hypotheses:

$$H_0: \quad \mu_A - \mu_B = 0$$
$$H_a: \quad \mu_A - \mu_B > 0$$

with a 5% level of significance. Two samples, each consisting of six pairs of data values, are given here. (*Note:* x is the difference between corresponding scores from A and B.)

A	32	29	29	30	31	29
B	28	25	24	27	28	24
x	4	4	5	3	3	5

A	32	29	29	30	31	29
B	34	20	21	38	20	23
x	−2	9	8	−8	11	6

In both cases, $\bar{x} = \bar{x}_A - \bar{x}_B = 4$. One of the two data sets leads to a rejection of the null hypothesis. Assume that the population of differences is approximately normal.

(a) Without testing, which of the two data sets leads to rejecting H_0? [*Hint:* A sketch of the data (perhaps a dot diagram) might be helpful.]

(b) Now complete the test using each data set and compare with part (a).

9.3

INFERENCE CONCERNING TWO POPULATION MEANS BASED ON INDEPENDENT SAMPLES: Large-Sample Case

We will use the notation in Table 9.3.

Table 9.3

Population	Sample Size	Sample Mean	Sample Standard Deviation	Population Mean	Population Standard Deviation
1	n_1	$\bar{x}_1$	s_1	μ_1	σ_1
2	n_2	$\bar{x}_2$	s_2	μ_2	σ_2

Consider the following situation: A statistics instructor had two textbooks in mind (call them texts 1 and 2), one of which would be adopted by the mathematics department as the standard text for its introductory statistics course. The department wondered whether there was any real difference in results between the two textbooks. In other words, if μ_1 is the mean numerical grade for the population of future students who may use textbook 1 and μ_2 is the mean grade for future students using textbook 2, will these means be different? The instructor, who was teaching a large lecture class divided into two recitation sections, decided to investigate this by using text 1 in section 1 and text 2 in section 2. Students were randomly selected for assignment to the two sections. These sections can be viewed as samples from the populations of interest. The class results are summarized in Table 9.4.

Table 9.4
Mean Course Grades

Textbook	Number of Students	Sample Mean	Sample Standard Deviation
1	$n_1 = 35$	$\bar{x}_1 = 78$	$s_1 = 8$
2	$n_2 = 40$	$\bar{x}_2 = 75$	$s_2 = 6$

We are interested in whether $\mu_1 = \mu_2$ or $\mu_1 \neq \mu_2$. This is equivalent to testing

$$H_0: \quad \mu_1 - \mu_2 = 0$$
$$H_a: \quad \mu_1 - \mu_2 \neq 0$$

It would seem natural to look at the difference $\bar{x}_1 - \bar{x}_2$. We can think of $\bar{x}_1 - \bar{x}_2$ as a rough estimate for $\mu_1 - \mu_2$. If H_0 were true, $\bar{x}_1 - \bar{x}_2$ should not be too far away from 0.

If the value of $\bar{x}_1 - \bar{x}_2$ is so far from 0 that such a value would be unlikely (if H_0 were true), we would reject H_0. To find out what values of $\bar{x}_1 - \bar{x}_2$ are likely (i.e., consistent with H_0) and what values are not likely, we need to know the probability distribution of $\bar{x}_1 - \bar{x}_2$.

Now $\bar{x}_1 - \bar{x}_2$ is a random variable, and it can be shown that when n_1 and n_2 are at least 30, it is approximately normal. Further, the mean and standard deviation of $\bar{x}_1 - \bar{x}_2$ are given by the formulas

$$\mu_{\bar{x}_1 - \bar{x}_2} = \mu_1 - \mu_2 \qquad \sigma_{\bar{x}_1 - \bar{x}_2} = \sqrt{\frac{\sigma_1^2}{n_1} + \frac{\sigma_2^2}{n_2}}$$

It follows that

$$z = \frac{(\bar{x}_1 - \bar{x}_2) - \mu_{\bar{x}_1 - \bar{x}_2}}{\sigma_{\bar{x}_1 - \bar{x}_2}} = \frac{(\bar{x}_1 - \bar{x}_2) - (\mu_1 - \mu_2)}{\sqrt{(\sigma_1^2/n_1) + (\sigma_2^2/n_2)}}$$

is approximately standard normal. We can use this to test the hypotheses given here in much the same way we did for a single mean. We would calculate the value of z, substituting the value of $\mu_1 - \mu_2$ appearing in H_0 (0 in this case). Values of z near 0 favor H_0. Values of z far to the right or left of 0 favor H_a.

Now we complete the test for the data in Table 9.4 using the 5% level of significance.

1. *Hypotheses:*

$$H_0: \quad \mu_1 - \mu_2 = 0$$
$$H_a: \quad \mu_1 - \mu_2 \neq 0$$

2. *Level of significance:* $\alpha = .05$

3. *Test statistic and observed value:* Note that σ_1 and σ_2 are unknown but we can use s_1 and s_2 as estimates, since n_1 and n_2 are large:

$$z = \frac{(\bar{x}_1 - \bar{x}_2) - (\mu_1 - \mu_2)}{\sqrt{(\sigma_1^2/n_1) + (\sigma_2^2/n_2)}} = \frac{(78 - 75) - 0}{\sqrt{\dfrac{8^2}{35} + \dfrac{6^2}{40}}} \doteq 1.82$$

4. *Critical region:* Values of z far to the right or left of 0 favor H_a. The critical region consists of two tails, each of size $\alpha/2 = .025$. From Appendix Table B.3, $z_{.025} = 1.96$. Therefore, the critical region consists of values of $z \geq 1.96$ or $z \leq -1.96$ (Figure 9.2).

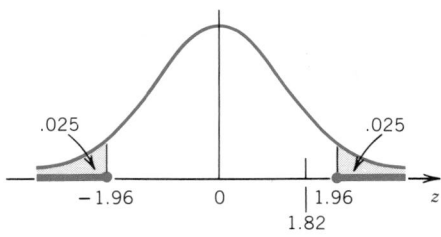

.025   .025

−1.96   0   1.96 z

1.82

Figure 9.2

5. *Decision:* The observed value of z is 1.82. This is not in the critical region. Hence we do not reject H_0. This means that there is not enough evidence to conclude that the texts produce different results.

> **Statistic for Tests Concerning Two Population Means μ_1 and μ_2:**
> **Large-Sample Case**
> When both sample sizes n_1 and n_2 are large (at least 30), use the test statistic
>
> $$z = \frac{(\bar{x}_1 - \bar{x}_2) - (\mu_1 - \mu_2)}{\sqrt{(\sigma_1^2/n_1) + (\sigma_2^2/n_2)}}$$
>
> This is approximately standard normal. When σ_1 and σ_2 are unknown, use the sample standard deviations s_1 and s_2 as estimates.

The term $\mu_1 - \mu_2$ appears in the z statistic. As usual, we will use the value of $\mu_1 - \mu_2$ given in the null hypothesis, since the null hypothesis is assumed true until there is strong evidence to the contrary. In general, if the null hypothesis were H_0: $\mu_1 - \mu_2 = k$, we would substitute the value of k for $\mu_1 - \mu_2$. (The value of k need not always be 0. For example, if we were testing the claim that μ_1 was 10 more than μ_2, the null hypothesis would be $\mu_1 - \mu_2 = 10$.) To complete the test at a given level of significance, we evaluate the test statistic and conduct a z test. The critical region for the test looks the same as the z test for a single population mean. (See Section 8.3.)

In the example discussed at the beginning of this section, the alternate hypothesis was $\mu_1 \neq \mu_2$ and we did a two-tailed test. We can formulate a rule for determining critical regions in tests for two means similar to the one we used for single-mean tests. If we keep the order of μ_1 and μ_2 in H_a the same as the order of $\bar{x}_1$ and $\bar{x}_2$ in the test statistic, we can use the following rule:

> H_a: $\mu_1 \neq \mu_2$ implies a two-tailed test
> H_a: $\mu_1 < \mu_2$ implies a left-tailed test
> H_a: $\mu_1 > \mu_2$ implies a right-tailed test

Confidence Interval for $\mu_1 - \mu_2$

In Chapter 8, we discussed a statistic to be used for testing hypotheses about a single mean μ when the sample size is large ($n \geq 30$). This was the same statistic we used to develop a $1 - \alpha$ confidence interval for μ (Section 8.2). The statistic and the confidence interval are as follows:

Test Statistic	**$1 - \alpha$ Confidence Interval for μ**
$z = \dfrac{\bar{x} - \mu}{\sigma/\sqrt{n}}$	$\bar{x} \pm z_{\alpha/2} \cdot \dfrac{\sigma}{\sqrt{n}}$

By examining these relationships, we ought to be able to guess a confidence interval for $\mu_1 - \mu_2$, knowing the test statistic for testing hypotheses concerning $\mu_1 - \mu_2$. For example, we saw that the test statistic for investigating $\mu_1 - \mu_2$, when the sample sizes are large and the samples are independent, is

$$z = \frac{(\bar{x}_1 - \bar{x}_2) - (\mu_1 - \mu_2)}{\sqrt{(\sigma_1^2/n_1) + (\sigma_2^2/n_2)}}$$

Reasoning by analogy, a $1 - \alpha$ confidence interval for $\mu_1 - \mu_2$ is

$$(\bar{x}_1 - \bar{x}_2) \pm z_{\alpha/2} \cdot \sqrt{\frac{\sigma_1^2}{n_1} + \frac{\sigma_2^2}{n_2}}$$

If σ_1 and σ_2 are unknown, use s_1 and s_2 as estimates.

EXAMPLE 9.3

A manufacturer of small engines concerned with the issue of noise pollution developed a new engine that would, it was hoped, be quieter than the standard model. Forty-one of the new models were tested for noise level and compared with 65 of the standard models. The results are given in Table 9.5 (with noise measured in decibels).

Table 9.5

Sample	Sample Size	Sample Mean (Decibels)	Sample Standard Deviation (Decibels)
Standard model	65	84	11.6
New model	41	72	9.2

(a) Find a 95% confidence interval for the difference in mean decibel levels $\mu_1 - \mu_2$, where μ_1 is the mean decibel level for the standard engine and μ_2 is the mean decibel level for the new engine.

(b) Do the population means appear to be different?

Solution

(a) The sample sizes are large, so we use

$$(\bar{x}_1 - \bar{x}_2) \pm z_{\alpha/2} \cdot \sqrt{\frac{\sigma_1^2}{n_1} + \frac{\sigma_2^2}{n_2}}$$

Now $1 - \alpha = .95$, so $\alpha = .05$; $z_{\alpha/2} = z_{.025} = 1.96$. We will use s_1 and s_2 for σ_1 and σ_2. We get

$$(84 - 72) \pm (1.96) \cdot \sqrt{\frac{(11.6)^2}{65} + \frac{(9.2)^2}{41}}$$

or

$$12 \pm 3.99$$

So we are 95% sure that the difference $\mu_1 - \mu_2$ is between 8.01 and 15.99 decibels. Therefore, we are 95% confident that the mean decibel level for the standard model is between 8.01 and 15.99 decibels louder than the mean level for the new model.

(b) Since 0 is not contained in the confidence interval for $\mu_1 - \mu_2$, this suggests that $\mu_1 - \mu_2 \neq 0$. Hence, $\mu_1 \neq \mu_2$. In fact, we can say more. Since the confidence interval consists of positive numbers, $\mu_1 - \mu_2 > 0$ or $\mu_1 > \mu_2$.

EXERCISES

9.13 It was claimed that the mean of population A was not the same as the mean of population B. Assume independent samples and consider the following sample information:

	n	$\bar{x}$	s^2
A	40	175	360
B	50	165	350

(a) Complete the test at the 5% level of significance.

(b) Suppose that you had used the 1% level of significance in part (a). Without calculating, answer the following:
  (i) Would the value of the test statistic change?
  (ii) Would the critical values change?
  (iii) Might the decision you reached in part (a) change?

(c) Now complete the test at the 1% level of significance and compare with part (b).

9.14 It was claimed that the mean of population A was larger than the mean of population B. Assume independent samples and consider the following sample information:

	n	$\bar{x}$	s^2
A	35	400	210
B	35	396	105

(a) Complete the test at the 5% level of significance.

(b) Suppose that you had used the 10% level of significance in part (a). Without calculating, answer the following:
  (i) Would the value of the test statistic change?
  (ii) Would the critical value change?
  (iii) Might the decision you reached in part (a) change?

(c) Now complete the test at the 10% level of significance and compare with the results of part (b).

9.15 Business schools A and B reported the following summary of GMAT (Graduate Management Aptitude Test) verbal scores:

	n	$\bar{x}$	s^2
A	201	34.75	48.59
B	115	33.74	30.68

At a 5% level of significance, is there sufficient evidence to believe there is a difference in the population means?

(a)   Use the classical approach.   **(b)**   Use the P-value approach.

9.16   The personnel officer of a large corporation claimed that college graduates applying for jobs with the firm in the current year tended to have higher grade point averages than those applying in the previous year. Samples from the groups of applicants gave the following results:

	n	$\bar{x}$	s
Preceding year (A)	52	2.80	.50
Current year (B)	60	2.98	.40

Is there sufficient evidence to justify the claim at a 5% level of significance?

9.17   A sociologist believed that average family size in a neighboring state (A) was smaller than average family size in his state (B). Random samples from the two states gave the following information:

	n	$\bar{x}$	s
State (A)	48	3.04	.39
State (B)	55	3.26	.36

At a 10% level of significance, is there sufficient evidence to justify the belief?

(a)   Use the classical approach.   **(b)**   Use the P-value approach.

9.18   **(a)**   A biologist suspected that males age 20–24 have a higher mean systolic blood pressure than females in the same age group. Independent random samples of males and females were selected from the Framingham Heart Study. The data are as follows:

	n	$\bar{x}$	s
A (Males)	31	125	13.9
B (Females)	41	117	12.1

At a 1% level of significance, is there sufficient evidence to justify the biologist's suspicions? Use (i) the classical approach and (ii) the P-value approach.

(b)   The biologist also suspected that in the 20–24 age group, males have a higher mean diastolic blood pressure than females. The data are summarized in the table.

	n	$\bar{x}$	s
A (Males)	45	75	10.1
B (Females)	45	70	9.8

At a 1% level of significance, is there sufficient evidence to justify the biologist's suspicions? Use (i) the classical approach and (ii) the P-value approach.

9.19   Two types of sports cars were compared for acceleration rates. Forty test runs were done for each car, and elapsed time from 0 to 60 miles per hour was recorded for each run. The results in seconds are shown here.

	$\bar{x}$	s
Car A	7.4	1.5
Car B	7.1	1.8

Construct a 98% confidence interval for the difference in mean elapsed time for the two types of cars. Using the confidence interval, can you conclude that there is a difference in the mean elapsed times?

9.20   A manager of a boat line that services a resort island wanted to know whether more passengers, on a per-trip average, travelled on the 8 A.M. or the 10 A.M. boat. Independent random samples were obtained. Note that n refers to the number of trips.

	n	$\bar{x}$	s^2
A (8 A.M. boat)	35	820	4900
B (10 A.M. boat)	40	850	6900

At a 1% level of significance, what can the manager conclude?

9.21   **(a)**   Use the data in Exercise 9.15 to construct a 95% confidence interval for the difference ($\mu_A - \mu_B$). From this, can you conclude that $\mu_A \neq \mu_B$?

(b)   Use the data in Exercise 9.17(a) to construct an 80% confidence interval for the difference ($\mu_A - \mu_B$). From this, can you conclude that $\mu_A < \mu_B$?

9.22   An administrator at a large university stated there was a difference in the mean grade point averages of graduating males and females. Independent random samples of graduating males and females gave the following information:

	n	$\bar{x}$	s^2
A (Males)	45	2.10	.64
B (Females)	50	2.45	.70

(a)   Construct a 95% confidence interval for the difference ($\mu_A - \mu_B$).

(b)   Using the confidence interval obtained in part (a), do the data support the administrator's belief? (*Hint:*   Does the confidence interval contain 0?)

9.4

INFERENCE CONCERNING TWO POPULATION MEANS BASED ON INDEPENDENT SAMPLES: Small-Sample Case

Suppose that either or both of the sample sizes are small (less than 30). In this case, we must require that the populations of x_1 and x_2 values be approximately normal. **If σ_1 and σ_2 are known, we may use the very same procedures based on the standard normal distribution given in Section 9.3.** However, if σ_1 and/or σ_2 are unknown, we cannot reliably estimate them by s_1 and s_2 when the sample sizes are small. In practice, we usually do not know the values of σ_1 and σ_2, so let us concentrate on this situation.

Although we will use the t procedures of this section only when small samples are involved, these procedures are valid for samples of any size. When the samples are large, approximate normality is not as much of a concern. In fact, for large samples, the t distribution approximates the standard normal distribution; therefore, large-sample t procedures are comparable to the standard normal procedures in Section 9.3.

Two-Sample t Procedures

Assumption: The populations are approximately normal.

To test hypotheses concerning population means μ_1 and μ_2, use the test statistic

$$t = \frac{(\bar{x}_1 - \bar{x}_2) - (\mu_1 - \mu_2)}{\sqrt{(s_1^2/n_1) + (s_2^2/n_2)}}$$

This may be treated as having (approximately) a Student's t distribution with df equal to the smaller of $n_1 - 1$ and $n_2 - 1$. As usual, the value for $\mu_1 - \mu_2$ in this formula is obtained from the null hypothesis. A $1 - \alpha$ confidence interval for $\mu_1 - \mu_2$ is

$$(\bar{x}_1 - \bar{x}_2) \pm t_{\alpha/2} \cdot \sqrt{\frac{s_1^2}{n_1} + \frac{s_2^2}{n_2}}$$

Remark   It would be more accurate to require that the population be normal. But as with the one-sample t procedures in Chapter 8, it has been found that the two-sample t procedures are robust to this assumption. In other words, only approximate normality is needed. If you are not sure about this, examine a graph for the data (stem-and-leaf plot, dot diagram, etc.) for clues to nonnormality, such as strong skewness or extreme outliers.

EXAMPLE 9.4

A component of cholesterol called high-density lipoprotein (HDL) is known as the "good cholesterol" because high levels of HDL are thought to lower the risk of coronary heart disease (Gordon et al., 1977, p. 707). It is believed that runners have increased HDL levels. The data in Table 9.6 give details of an HDL study comparing young male elite runners* with a control group of young male nonrunners. At the 5% level of significance, test the claim that young male elite runners have a higher (population) mean HDL level than young male nonrunners. Assume the populations are approximately normal.

---

*The term *elite runner* refers to one of the top 2.5% runners in the world.

Table 9.6
HDL Data (in milligrams per 100 milliliters)

Samples	n	$\bar{x}$	s
Elite runners	20	56	12.1
Nonrunners	72	49	10.5

Source: Martin, R., W. Haskell, and P. Wood, "Blood Chemistry and Lipid Profiles of Elite Distance Runners," in *The Long Distance Runner*, ed. P. Milvy, New York: Urizen Books, 1977, p. 88.

Solution

1. *Hypotheses:*   We will let μ_1 and μ_2 refer to the population mean HDL levels of the runners and nonrunners, respectively. The claim is that $\mu_1 > \mu_2$. So we test

$$H_0: \quad \mu_1 = \mu_2 \qquad (\text{or } \mu_1 - \mu_2 = 0)$$
$$H_a: \quad \mu_1 > \mu_2 \qquad (\text{or } \mu_1 - \mu_2 > 0)$$

2. *Level of significance:* $\alpha = .05$

3. *Test statistic and observed value:*   One of the sample sizes ($n_1 = 20$) is small, and the populations are assumed to be approximately normal. Thus we will do a t test based on the statistic in the previous box. This is called a **two-sample t test:**

$$t = \frac{(\bar{x}_1 - \bar{x}_2) - (\mu_1 - \mu_2)}{\sqrt{\dfrac{s_1^2}{n_1} + \dfrac{s_2^2}{n_2}}} = \frac{(56 - 49) - 0}{\sqrt{\dfrac{(12.1)^2}{20} + \dfrac{(10.5)^2}{72}}} = \frac{7}{\sqrt{8.85175}} \doteq 2.35$$

df: smaller of $n_1 - 1$ and $n_2 - 1$; so df $= 19$

4. *Critical region:*   Since H_a is $\mu_1 > \mu_2$, we do a right-tailed test. The critical region is in Figure 9.3.

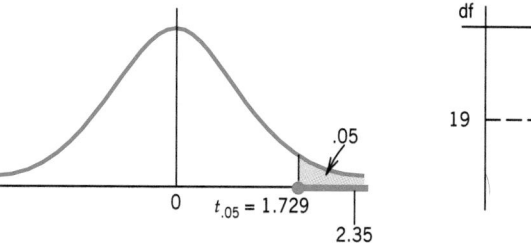

Figure 9.3

5. *Decision:*   The observed value (2.35) is in the critical region, therefore we reject H_0 in favor of H_a. Thus the data suggest that $\mu_1 > \mu_2$.

In Example 9.4, we used the minimum of $n_1 - 1$ and $n_2 - 1$ as the degrees of freedom, and we will continue to do so in this book. Some statisticians, however, think this approach is too conservative. It gives a rather small value for the degrees of freedom. The smaller the degrees of freedom, the larger the critical value of t, meaning the larger in magnitude the observed value of t must be for us to reject H_0. This may give too much of an advantage to H_0. An alternative value for degrees of freedom preferred by some statisticians and used in statistical software is

$$\text{df} = \frac{(s_1^2/n_1 + s_2^2/n_2)^2}{\frac{(s_1^2/n_1)^2}{n_1 - 1} + \frac{(s_2^2/n_2)^2}{n_2 - 1}}$$

In Example 9.4, we said that the data indicated that $\mu_1 > \mu_2$. A confidence interval can give us more information than a hypothesis test, since it gives us a range for the difference $\mu_1 - \mu_2$.

EXAMPLE 9.5

Find a 95% confidence interval for the difference of the population means $(\mu_1 - \mu_2)$ discussed in Example 9.4.

Solution

The level of confidence is

$$1 - \alpha = .95 \qquad \alpha = .05 \qquad \alpha/2 = .025$$
$$\text{df: smaller of } n_1 - 1, \ n_2 - 1; \text{ so df} = 19$$

From Appendix Table B.4, we see that when df $= 19$

$$t_{\alpha/2} = t_{.025} = 2.093$$

So our 95% confidence interval is

$$(\bar{x}_1 - \bar{x}_2) \pm t_{\alpha/2} \cdot \sqrt{\frac{s_1^2}{n_1} + \frac{s_2^2}{n_2}} = (56 - 49) \pm 2.093 \cdot \sqrt{\frac{(12.1)^2}{20} + \frac{(10.5)^2}{72}}$$

$$\doteq 7 \pm 6.23$$

So we are 95% sure that

$$.77 < \mu_1 - \mu_2 < 13.23$$

Example 9.5 points out a weakness of confidence intervals when one or both samples are small: These confidence intervals can be quite wide, making them less useful than large-sample confidence intervals. The reason for this is that sample sizes appear as denominators; the smaller the denominator, the larger the fraction. Also large-sample confidence intervals use $z_{\alpha/2}$, which is smaller than the $t_{\alpha/2}$ for small samples. These things tend to make small-sample confidence intervals wider, since the width is twice the error term

$$t_{\alpha/2} \cdot \sqrt{\frac{s_1^2}{n_1} + \frac{s_2^2}{n_2}}$$

Pooled t Procedures (Optional)

There is another two-sample statistic called the **pooled t statistic,** which, when appropriate, gives somewhat better results than the procedures discussed previously.

For example, in a test of hypotheses, this statistic usually has a smaller probability of a Type II error (not rejecting H_0 when it is false). However, for the pooled t statistic to have a Student's t distribution, the population standard deviations must be equal ($\sigma_1 = \sigma_2$). The two-sample procedures discussed previously work whether $\sigma_1 = \sigma_2$ or $\sigma_1 \neq \sigma_2$. In this section, we assume that σ_1 and σ_2 are unknown. So you might well ask how we are to know whether $\sigma_1 = \sigma_2$. This is a legitimate objection and indeed a weakness of pooled t procedures. We will have more to say about this later.

Suppose $\sigma_1 = \sigma_2$. We call this common value σ ($\sigma = \sigma_1 = \sigma_2$). We define the **pooled sample standard deviation** to be

$$s_p = \sqrt{\frac{(n_1 - 1)s_1^2 + (n_2 - 1)s_2^2}{n_1 + n_2 - 2}}$$

This is an estimate of σ. The pooled t procedures are as follows:

Assumptions: The populations are approximately normal, and the population standard deviations are equal ($\sigma_1 = \sigma_2$).

To test hypotheses concerning μ_1 and μ_2, use the test statistic

$$t = \frac{(\bar{x}_1 - \bar{x}_2) - (\mu_1 - \mu_2)}{s_p \sqrt{\dfrac{1}{n_1} + \dfrac{1}{n_2}}}$$

This has a Student's t distribution with df $= n_1 + n_2 - 2$. A $1 - \alpha$ confidence interval for the difference ($\mu_1 - \mu_2$) is

$$(\bar{x}_1 - \bar{x}_2) \pm t_{\alpha/2} \cdot s_p \cdot \sqrt{\frac{1}{n_1} + \frac{1}{n_2}}$$

EXAMPLE 9.6

Researchers Morganroth and Maron have studied various heart abnormalities that occur in male athletes. One characteristic studied was left ventricular end diastolic volume (the volume of the left lower chamber of the heart when it is filled with blood). Do the data in Table 9.7 (page 426) indicate a significant difference in volume between wrestlers and a control group of nonathletes (at the 5% level of significance)? The measurements are in milliliters.

Solution

1. *Hypotheses:* There will be a significant difference in heart volume for the two groups, if the mean volumes for the two populations from which the samples were drawn are different ($\mu_1 \neq \mu_2$). So we test

$$H_0: \quad \mu_1 = \mu_2 \qquad (\text{or } \mu_1 - \mu_2 = 0)$$
$$H_a: \quad \mu_1 \neq \mu_2 \qquad (\text{or } \mu_1 - \mu_2 \neq 0)$$

Table 9.7
Heart Sizes

Wrestlers	Controls
83	64
91	83
97	83
97	85
108	91
111	97
111	97
117	97
117	103
125	108
125	111
140	111
	117
	117
	125
	125

$\bar{x}_1 = 110.17$	$\bar{x}_2 = 100.87$
$s_1 = 16.19$	$s_2 = 17.01$
$n_1 = 12$	$n_2 = 16$

The data are estimated from a graph in Morganroth, J., and B. Maron, "The Athlete's Heart Syndrome: A New Perspective," in *The Long Distance Runner*, P. Milvy, ed., New York: Urizen Books, 1977, p. 218.

2. *Level of significance:* $\alpha = .05$
3. *Test statistic and observed value:* Since the sample sizes are small, we will do a *t* test. A side-by-side stem-and-leaf plot for the samples is given in Figure 9.4.

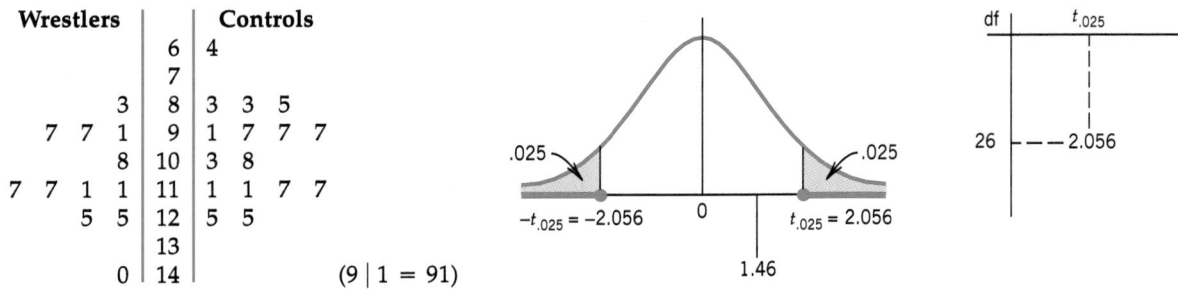

Wrestlers			Controls
	6	4	
	7		
3	8	3 3 5	
7 7 1	9	1 7 7 7	
8	10	3 8	
7 7 1 1	11	1 1 7 7	
5 5	12	5 5	
	13		
0	14		

(9 | 1 = 91)

Figure 9.4
Stem-and-Leaf Plots of Heart Sizes

Figure 9.5

$-t_{.025} = -2.056$ 0 $t_{.025} = 2.056$

$.025$ $.025$

1.46

df	$t_{.025}$
26	2.056

There are no indications that suggest departure from approximate normality for the populations (such as strong skewness or extreme outliers). Therefore, a *t* test would be appropriate. Also the sample standard deviations are quite close. So we will assume $\sigma_1 = \sigma_2$ and use the pooled statistic:

$$s_p = \sqrt{\frac{(n_1 - 1)s_1^2 + (n_2 - 1)s_2^2}{n_1 + n_2 - 2}} = \sqrt{\frac{(12 - 1)(16.19)^2 + (16 - 1)(17.01)^2}{12 + 16 - 2}} = 16.668001$$

$$t = \frac{(\bar{x}_1 - \bar{x}_2) - (\mu_1 - \mu_2)}{s_p\sqrt{\frac{1}{n_1} + \frac{1}{n_2}}} = \frac{(110.17 - 100.87) - 0}{16.668001\sqrt{\frac{1}{12} + \frac{1}{16}}} = \frac{9.3}{6.365198} \doteq 1.46$$

$$df = n_1 + n_2 - 2 = 12 + 16 - 2 = 26$$

4. *Critical region:* H_a involves $\neq$, so we do a two-tailed test. The critical region is in Figure 9.5.

5. *Decision:* The observed value (1.46) is not in the critical region. So we do not reject H_0. There is insufficient evidence to conclude that the population means are different.

Statistica Printout for Example 9.6

Statistica, a statistical software package produced by Statsoft, provides for the two-sample (unpooled) t test or the pooled t test. Here is the output for the pooled test:

t	df	2-Tailed p	1. N	2. N	1. Mean	2. Mean	1. Std.Dev.	2. Std.Dev.
1.460161	26	.1562247	12	16	110.1667	100.8750	16.18548	17.00539

The P-value is .1562247.

Remark With the pooled t test, df is sometimes more than 29 (the largest entry for df in Appendix Table B.4). In this case, just look up your critical value in the last row (for df large).

Moderate departures from the requirement that $\sigma_1 = \sigma_2$ do not seriously affect the validity of pooled t procedures if the sample sizes are approximately the same. In other words, pooled t procedures are fairly robust to the requirement that $\sigma_1 = \sigma_2$ when n_1 and n_2 are not very different. But if there is a big difference between n_1 and n_2, pooled procedures can be inaccurate when $\sigma_1 \neq \sigma_2$.

Which t Procedures Should Be Used? In general, we prefer the two-sample unpooled t procedures over the pooled t procedures. The problem with the pooled procedures is that you usually cannot be sure whether $\sigma_1 = \sigma_2$. Some people use a procedure called an **F test** to investigate this. It is a test of the hypothesis $\sigma_1 = \sigma_2$ versus $\sigma_1 \neq \sigma_2$. This test is described in Appendix C. The trouble with this F test is that it is applicable only when the two populations are normal. Approximate normality will not suffice—the F test is not robust to the requirement of normality, severely limiting this test.

EXERCISES

Use the two-sample t procedures in the following problems. Do not use pooled procedures unless specifically asked to do so.

9.23   **(a)**   Do the following data support the belief that the mean of population A is less than the mean of population B? Assume that the populations are approximately normal and complete the test using the 10% level of significance.

	n	$\bar{x}$	s^2
A	10	180	70
B	7	200	340

   (b)   Do the following data support the belief that the mean of population A is different from the mean of population B? Assume approximate normality for the populations and complete the test using the 5% level of significance.

	n	$\bar{x}$	s^2
A	8	83	21
B	12	80	5

9.24   The mayor of city A claimed that there was no difference in mean air quality between cities A and B, based on a measurement of air quality. Independent samples for each city gave the following data:

	n	$\bar{x}$	s^2
City A	11	3.8	.39
City B	11	3.5	.10

Assume that the populations are approximately normal. Using a 5% level of significance, test the claim.

9.25   In previous exercises (2.37, 3.5, 4.15) we discussed O-ring damage and temperature at time of launch for 23 space shuttle flights that preceded the *Challenger* (which exploded due to O-ring failure). The data are reproduced below.

Launch Temperatures (°F)

A: Flights with   53   57   58   63   70   70   75
O-ring Damage

B: Flights with   66   67   67   67   68   69   70   70   72   73   75   76   76   78   79   81
No O-ring Damage

Note: $\bar{x}_A = 63.71$, $s_A = 8.16$, $\bar{x}_B = 72.13$, $s_B = 4.84$

   (a)   Is the mean launch temperature for flights with O-ring damage significantly less than for flights with no O-ring damage? Use the 5% level of significance. Assume t procedures are appropriate.

   (b)   Find a 95% confidence interval for the difference between μ_A and μ_B.

9.26   Researchers Morganroth and Maron have studied various heart abnormalities that occur in male college athletes. One characteristic studied was left ventricular end diastolic volume (the volume of the left lower chamber of the heart when it is filled with blood). Do the following data show a significant difference in volume between runners and nonrunners (at the 5% level of significance)? The measurements are in milliliters. Biological measurements for groups of similar individuals tend to be approximately normal, so t procedures would be appropriate here.

	n	$\bar{x}$	s
Runners	15	160.1	33.1
Nonrunners	16	100.8	17.6

The data are estimated from a graph in J. Morganroth and B. Maron, "The Athletes Heart Syndrome: A New Perspective," in *The Long Distance Runner*, P. Milvy, ed., New York: Urizen Books, 1977, p. 218.

9.27 A town engineer suspected that a power plant was substantially increasing the air pollution in the vicinity of the plant. A sample of 1-hour measurements of carbon monoxide in the vicinity of the plant was obtained for comparison with another sample obtained from other locations in the town. The results follow: (Measurements are in milligrams per cubic meter of air.)

Near plant:
```
40  16  44  47  36  64  35  53
45  52  31  38  44  29  45  47
```

Other locations:
```
34  28  15  43  26  27  35
 9  32  25  27  35  44  18
```

(a) Construct a side-by-side stem-and-leaf plot. Is a t procedure appropriate? If so, go to part (b).

(b) At the 5% level of significance, is the engineer's suspicion justified?

(c) Find a 90% confidence interval for $\mu_1 - \mu_2$, where μ_1 = mean near the plant and μ_2 = mean elsewhere.

9.28 A typing instructor wondered whether a new method of instruction would result in a higher mean typing speed. The instructor randomly assigned 10 students to the new method of instruction B. The other 10 students received the usual instruction method A. A typing test was given following 4 weeks of instruction. The results, measured in words per minute, are given in a side-by-side stem-and-leaf plot. Note that the stems are split with leaves 0, 1, 2, 3, 4 on the first stem and leaves 5, 6, 7, 8, 9 on the second stem.

```
            1 | 5 |
          69 | 5 | 9
Method A  233 | 6 | 4     Method B
          59 | 6 | 79
           0 | 7 | 013
           9 | 7 | 55
             | 8 | 1     (Note:  6 | 4 = 64)
```

The sample means are 63.7 and 70.4, and the standard deviations are 7.82 and 6.20 for method A and method B, respectively.

(a) Is a t procedure appropriate?

(b) Based on the side-by-side stem-and-leaf plot, do you believe that the population mean for method B is higher than that for method A?

(c) If you answered Yes in part (a), use a 5% level of significance and test the hypothesis that the mean typing speed for method B is higher than that for method A.

9.29 Use the data in the following exercises to construct confidence intervals for the difference $(\mu_A - \mu_B)$. Interpret your results. The percent confidence is as follows:

(a) 90% [Exercise 9.23(a)]

(b) 95% [Exercise 9.24]

Exercises 9.30–9.34 are designed for the optional section on pooled t procedures. Unless otherwise stated, assume that the populations are approximately normal with equal standard deviations.

9.30 Do the following data support the belief that the means of populations A and B are different? Complete the test with a 5% level of significance.

	n	$\bar{x}$	s^2
A	6	120	100
B	10	125	81

9.31 A new actuarial test (A) was developed as a possible replacement for test B. An actuary claimed that the mean time to complete the new test was more than the mean time required to complete test B. To test the claim, seven people were selected to take test A and nine people selected to take test B. The summary data for completion time (in minutes) are as follows:

	$\bar{x}$	s^2
Test A	166	240
Test B	150	205

Complete the test with a 10% level of significance.

9.32 Assume that the following data were obtained with independent random samples from populations A and B.

A	B
27.2	28.5
19.7	27.7
14.6	30.9
20.4	23.1
23.1	24.8
	24.0
	22.3

The results are summarized as follows:

$$\sum x_A = 105 \quad \sum x_A^2 = 2290.86 \quad \sum x_B = 181.3 \quad \sum x_B^2 = 4756.29$$

(a) Test the hypothesis that the means of populations A and B are different using a 5% level of significance.

(b) Based on your conclusion in part (a), will a 95% confidence interval for $\mu_A - \mu_B$ contain the value 0? Now find a 95% confidence interval for $\mu_A - \mu_B$.

9.33 The finishing times of 15 males and 15 females under 40 years of age in the 1986 Boston Marathon were selected. The sample means are 182.55 and 206.16 minutes and the standard deviations are 17.66 and 17.69 minutes for the men and women, respectively.

(a) At a 10% level of significance, test the hypothesis that the mean difference between women's and men's mean finishing times is 30 minutes.

(b) Construct a 90% confidence interval for the mean difference between finishing times for women and men. Does the confidence interval support the conclusion reached in part (a)?

9.34 Consider the following dialogue between two students in a statistics class:

Joe: I thought our textbook said that dependent sampling is often more desirable than independent sampling (when possible).

Mary: It did.

Joe: I take it that this implies that dependent sampling might make it easier to reject a false null hypothesis.

Mary: So do I.

Joe: Well, how do you account for this? Dependent samples of size n result in degrees of freedom $n - 1$, whereas independent samples of size n (each) result in degrees of freedom $n + n - 2 = 2n - 2 = 2(n - 1)$ if $\sigma_1 = \sigma_2$.

Mary: So what?

Joe: Critical values in the t table get smaller as n increases. Therefore, it will be easier to reject H_0.

Mary: Maybe. But didn't the authors say something about sample variability?

Now repeat Exercise 9.4. Assume the population variances are equal and that the samples are independent. Comment on this dialogue.

9.35 In Exercise 9.27, we discussed an engineer's suspicion that a power plant was substantially increasing air pollution in the vicinity. A sample of 1-hour measurements of carbon monoxide in the vicinity of the plant was obtained for comparison with another sample obtained from other locations in the town. The results from Data Desk are given here. The measurements are in milligrams per cubic meter of air. Assume that the data were obtained from approximately normal populations. (Data Desk calculates the degrees of freedom in a different way than we did in the text.)

Near plant (1):	40	16	44	47	36	64	35	53
	45	52	31	38	44	29	45	47
Other locations (2):	34	28	15	43	26	27	35	
	9	32	25	27	35	44	18	

Near_Plant - Other_Locations :
Test Ho: μ(Near_Plant)-μ(Other_Locations) = 0 vs Ha: μ(Near_Plant)-μ(Other_Locations) > 0
Difference Between Means = 13.2 t-Statistic = 3.441 w/27 df
Reject Ho at Alpha = 0.0500
p = 0.0009

2-Sample t-Interval for $\mu 1$-$\mu 2$

With 95.00% Confidence, 5.33 < μ(Near_Plant)-μ(Other_Locations) < 21.1

(a) Give the observed t value from the accompanying output. At the 5% level of significance, is the engineer's suspicion justified?

(b) Give the 95% confidence interval for the difference in population means.

9.36 Sixteen observations were randomly sampled from each of two approximately normal populations. Consider the hypotheses H_0: $\mu_1 - \mu_2 = 0$ and H_a: $\mu_1 - \mu_2 \neq 0$. Use the Minitab printout to answer the following questions. (Note that Minitab calculates the degrees of freedom using the formula given on page 424.)

Two Sample T-Test and Confidence Interval

```
Twosample T for x1 VS x2
        N       Mean      StDev    SE Mean
x1     16      76.19      5.19       1.3
x2     16      73.19      5.68       1.4

95% C.I. for mu x1 - mu x2: (-0.9, 6.9)
T-Test mu x1 = mu x2 (vs not =): T= 1.56   P=0.13   DF=   29
```

(a) Give the observed t value. At what levels of significance would the test be statistically significant?

(b) Give a 95% confidence interval for $\mu_1 - \mu_2$.

9.5

INFERENCE CONCERNING TWO POPULATION PROPORTIONS

Sometimes we are interested in comparing two (unknown) population proportions. For example, we may wish to know whether in a voting district the proportion of men favoring health care reform is different from the proportion of women favoring health care reform. To study a topic such as this, we might obtain random samples from each population and record the number in each sample who favor health care reform. Obtaining each sample is a binomial process, so the number in a sample who favor health care reform is the number of successes in a binomial experiment.

In general, when studying (unknown) population proportions p_1 and p_2 for populations 1 and 2, respectively, suppose we obtain independent random samples of size n_1 and n_2 and record the number of successes x_1 and x_2 from populations 1 and 2, respectively. Now we can estimate p_1 and p_2 with

$$\hat{p}_1 = \frac{x_1}{n_1} \qquad \hat{p}_2 = \frac{x_2}{n_2}$$

For example, if 100 women and 100 men are interviewed and 80 of the women and 75 of the men favor health care reform, then

$$\hat{p}_1 = \frac{80}{100} = .80 \qquad \hat{p}_2 = \frac{75}{100} = .75$$

We can formulate hypotheses concerning p_1 and p_2 as statements involving $p_1 - p_2$. For example, if H_0 is $p_1 = p_2$, we can rewrite this as $p_1 - p_2 = 0$. We can think of $\hat{p}_1 - \hat{p}_2$ as a rough estimate for $p_1 - p_2$. Hence if H_0 is true, $\hat{p}_1 - \hat{p}_2$ should not be too far from 0. To know what values of $\hat{p}_1 - \hat{p}_2$ would be reasonable or likely if H_0 is indeed true, we must know something about the probability distribution of $\hat{p}_1 - \hat{p}_2$.

It can be shown that when n_1 and n_2 are sufficiently large, the variable quantity $\hat{p}_1 - \hat{p}_2$ is approximately normal. Further, the mean and standard deviation are given by the formulas

$$\mu_{\hat{p}_1 - \hat{p}_2} = p_1 - p_2 \qquad \sigma_{\hat{p}_1 - \hat{p}_2} = \sqrt{\frac{p_1 q_1}{n_1} + \frac{p_2 q_2}{n_2}}$$

Thus

$$z = \frac{(\hat{p}_1 - \hat{p}_2) - (p_1 - p_2)}{\sqrt{(p_1 q_1 / n_1) + (p_2 q_2 / n_2)}}$$

will possess an approximately standard normal distribution. This will be the case if n_1 and n_2 are large enough so that x_1, x_2, $n_1 - x_1$, and $n_2 - x_2$ are all at least 5.

When testing hypotheses concerning $p_1 - p_2$, we can use the expression in the box as a test statistic. The value of $p_1 - p_2$ is obtained from the null hypothesis H_0. The value of $\sigma_{\hat{p}_1 - \hat{p}_2}$ (the denominator) must be estimated from the sample data (since we do not know the values of the population parameters p_1, q_1, p_2, and q_2). The form of $\sigma_{\hat{p}_1 - \hat{p}_2}$ depends on the form of the null hypothesis.

1. Suppose that the null hypothesis is $H_0: p_1 = p_2$ (or $p_1 - p_2 = 0$). Assuming that H_0 is true, we will use the symbol p to represent the common value of p_1 and p_2; then $p = p_1 = p_2$. We pool the data in both samples to estimate p. It would seem reasonable to estimate p by

$$\hat{p} = \frac{x_1 + x_2}{n_1 + n_2} = \frac{\text{total number of successes in both samples}}{\text{total size of both samples taken together}}$$

We then estimate $\sigma_{\hat{p}_1 - \hat{p}_2}$ by

$$\sigma_{\hat{p}_1 - \hat{p}_2} \doteq \sqrt{\frac{\hat{p}\hat{q}}{n_1} + \frac{\hat{p}\hat{q}}{n_2}} = \sqrt{\hat{p}\hat{q}\left(\frac{1}{n_1} + \frac{1}{n_2}\right)}$$

The test statistic then becomes

$$z = \frac{(\hat{p}_1 - \hat{p}_2) - 0}{\sqrt{\hat{p}\hat{q}\left(\dfrac{1}{n_1} + \dfrac{1}{n_2}\right)}} = \frac{\hat{p}_1 - \hat{p}_2}{\sqrt{\hat{p}\hat{q}\left(\dfrac{1}{n_1} + \dfrac{1}{n_2}\right)}}$$

2. Suppose that the null hypothesis is $H_0: p_1 - p_2 = D$ (where $D \neq 0$). This can occur, for example, if H_0 said that the proportion p_1 of women in favor of health care reform is 10 percentage points higher than the proportion p_2 of men in favor. In this case, H_0 is $p_1 - p_2 = .10$. In a situation like this, we will replace p_1 and p_2 in $\sigma_{\hat{p}_1 - \hat{p}_2}$ by the sample proportions $\hat{p}_1$ and $\hat{p}_2$. The test statistic will then be

$$z = \frac{(\hat{p}_1 - \hat{p}_2) - D}{\sqrt{(\hat{p}_1 \hat{q}_1 / n_1) + (\hat{p}_2 \hat{q}_2 / n_2)}}$$

In the examples and exercises of this section, the sample sizes will be large enough so that we may use these statistics where they apply.

If we keep the order of p_1 and p_2 in the alternate hypothesis the same as the order of $\hat{p}_1$ and $\hat{p}_2$ in the test statistic, then we can use the following rule for determining the critical region:

H_a: $p_1 \neq p_2$ implies a two-tailed test
H_a: $p_1 < p_2$ implies a left-tailed test
H_a: $p_1 > p_2$ implies a right-tailed test

EXAMPLE 9.7   Discrimination and the 80% Rule

In the discrimination case *Connecticut v. Teal*, 457 U.S. 440 (1982), the following data were given concerning a Connecticut state agency's record of employees rejected or selected for promotion:

	Selected	**Rejected**
Blacks	26	22
Whites	206	53

Source: Meier, P., J. Sacks, and S. Zabell, "What Happened in Hazelwood?" in *Statistics and the Law*, DeGroot, M., S. Fienberg, and J. Kadane, eds., New York: Wiley, 1986, p. 38.

(a)   In discrimination cases, sometimes the blacks and whites described in such a table are viewed as samples from theoretical populations that might result if large numbers of blacks and whites were considered for promotion by the agency. Test the claim that the population proportion of blacks selected (p_B) is less than the population proportion of whites selected (p_W) at the 2.5% level of significance. (This level is frequently used in discrimination cases.)

(b)   Sometimes results are statistically significant (i.e., lead to rejection of H_0) but of no practical or legal significance. For example, p_B might be less than p_W but by only a very small amount. Recognizing this, the courts have sometimes used the "80% rule," which was developed by the Equal Employment Opportunities Commission (EEOC). This rule says that a substantial disparity between groups can ordinarily be shown only when the results are statistically significant *and* the selection rate for the minority group ($\hat{p}_B$) is less than 80% of the selection rate for the highest group ($\hat{p}_W$). Do the data meet the standards of the "80% rule"?

Solution

(a)

1. *Hypotheses:* The claim is that $p_B < p_W$. This is H_a.

$$H_0: \quad p_B = p_W \quad (p_B - p_W = 0)$$
$$H_a: \quad p_B < p_W \quad (p_B - p_W < 0) \quad \leftarrow \text{Suggests possible discrimination}$$
$$\text{according to EEOC}$$

2. *Level of significance:* $\alpha = .025$

3. *Test statistic and observed value:* H_0 is $p_B - p_W = 0$; hence 0 is the value we will use for $p_B - p_W$. This means that we use the test statistic (1) in the outline preceding this example (with subscripts B and W instead of 1 and 2).

Number of blacks who applied, $n_B = 26 + 22 = 48$

Number of blacks selected, $x_B = 26$

$$\hat{p}_B = \frac{x_B}{n_B} = \frac{26}{48} = .542$$

Number of whites who applied, $n_W = 206 + 53 = 259$

Number of whites selected, $x_W = 206$

$$\hat{p}_W = \frac{x_W}{n_W} = \frac{206}{259} = .795$$

$$\hat{p} = \frac{x_B + x_W}{n_B + n_W} = \frac{26 + 206}{48 + 259} = .756$$

$$\hat{q} = 1 - \hat{p} = .244$$

$$z = \frac{\hat{p}_B - \hat{p}_W}{\sqrt{\hat{p}\hat{q}\left[\dfrac{1}{n_B} + \dfrac{1}{n_W}\right]}} = \frac{.542 - .795}{\sqrt{(.756)(.244)\left[\dfrac{1}{48} + \dfrac{1}{259}\right]}} = -3.75$$

4. *Critical region:* Since H_a is $p_B - p_W < 0$, we do a left-tailed test. The critical region is shown in Figure 9.6.

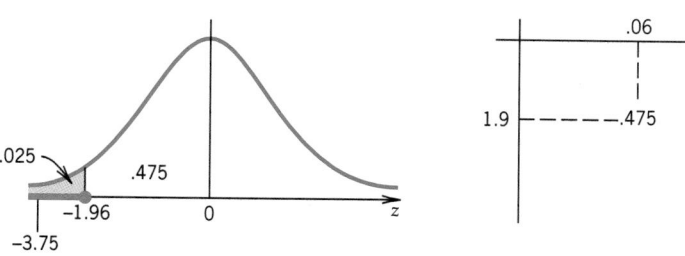

Figure 9.6

5. *Decision:* The observed value (-3.75) is in the critical region, so we reject H_0. This suggests there may be discrimination in promotion according to EEOC.

(b) The selection ratio is $\hat{p}_B/\hat{p}_W = .542/.795 = .682 < .80$, and the results are significant (from part (a)). Therefore, the data meet the requirements of the

80% rule, indicating that a substantial disparity exists between the promotion rates for blacks and for whites. The Supreme Court let stand a finding of discrimination by a lower court.

Historical Note A precedent in civil rights law was set by the Supreme Court in the case of *Griggs v. Duke Power Company*, 401 U.S. 424 (1971): If it can be shown statistically that the selection rate for blacks is "substantially" less than that of whites, then a prima facie case has been established showing "disparate impact" on a group protected under Title VII of the Civil Rights Act of 1964. (The Court held that it is not necessary to establish discriminatory intent, which is called disparate *treatment*.) The burden of proof then shifts to the employer. The employer must show that the selection procedure used (an examination in the case of *Teal*) is a "business necessity."

In 1989, the Supreme Court reversed the 1971 disparate impact analysis of *Griggs*. In the case of *Wards Cove v. Antonio*, the Court ruled that a statistical disparity alone was insufficient to establish a prima facie case of discrimination. Then in 1991 Congress reinstated the ruling of *Griggs* by codifying it in the form of law in the Civil Rights Act of 1991.

Confidence Interval for $p_1 - p_2$

We can use the following procedure to find a $1 - \alpha$ confidence interval for $p_1 - p_2$:

A $1 - \alpha$ confidence interval for the difference in two population proportions $p_1 - p_2$ is

$$(\hat{p}_1 - \hat{p}_2) \pm z_{\alpha/2} \cdot \sqrt{\frac{\hat{p}_1 \hat{q}_1}{n_1} + \frac{\hat{p}_2 \hat{q}_2}{n_2}}$$

This confidence interval will be valid if x_1, x_2, $n_1 - x_1$, and $n_2 - x_2$ are all at least 5.

EXAMPLE 9.8

Democrats and Republicans in Boston were interviewed by a sociologist and asked whether they favor mandatory minimum sentencing for violent crimes. The results are presented in Table 9.8.

Table 9.8

Political Party	Number Interviewed (n)	Number Favoring Mandatory Sentences (x)
Republicans	400	280
Democrats	300	180

Find a 95% confidence interval for the difference $p_1 - p_2$ between the population proportions of Republicans and Democrats in Boston favoring mandatory sentences.

Solution

$$x_1 = 280 \qquad\qquad x_2 = 180$$
$$n_1 = 400 \qquad\qquad n_2 = 300$$
$$\hat{p}_1 = \frac{x_1}{n_1} = .70 \qquad \hat{p}_2 = \frac{x_2}{n_2} = .60$$
$$\hat{p}_1 - \hat{p}_2 = .10$$
$$1 - \alpha = .95 \qquad \alpha = .05$$
$$z_{\alpha/2} = z_{.025} = 1.96$$

Therefore, the 95% confidence interval is

$$(\hat{p}_1 - \hat{p}_2) \pm z_{\alpha/2} \cdot \sqrt{\frac{\hat{p}_1\hat{q}_1}{n_1} + \frac{\hat{p}_2\hat{q}_2}{n_2}} = .10 \pm (1.96) \cdot \sqrt{\frac{(.7)(.3)}{400} + \frac{(.6)(.4)}{300}}$$
$$= .10 \pm .071$$

Therefore, we are 95% sure that the difference is between .029 and .171 (i.e., from 2.9 to 17.1 percentage points higher for Republicans).

EXERCISES

9.37   In each of the following parts, assume independent samples. Note that n refers to sample size and x is the number of successes.

(a)   It is claimed that proportions p_1 and p_2 for populations A and B, respectively, are the same. Consider the following sample information:

	n	x
A	250	175
B	175	135

Complete the test with a 5% level of significance.

(b)   It is believed that proportion p_1 for population A is larger than proportion p_2 for population B. Consider the following sample information:

	n	x
A	375	195
B	325	150

Complete the test with a 10% level of significance.

(c)   It is suspected that the proportion p_1 for population A is .05 more than the proportion p_2 for population B. Consider the following sample information:

	n	x
A	400	205
B	425	175

Complete the test with a 5% level of significance.

9.38   Use the data in the corresponding parts of Exercise 9.37 to construct confidence intervals for the difference $(p_1 - p_2)$. The percent confidence is as follows:

(a)   95%   **(b)**   80%   **(c)**   90%

9.39   Angioplasty and atherectomy are medical procedures for correcting blockages in heart arteries. Angioplasty uses a balloon to open blockages; atherectomy involves scraping away fatty deposits. Experts expected no essential difference in outcomes between the two procedures. But a study called CAVEAT I followed 1012 randomly selected patients, with half undergoing each procedure. The following data were obtained:

Procedure	Number of Patients (n)	Number Who Died Within 1 Year (x)
A: Atherectomy	506	11
B: Angioplasty	506	3

Source: The Boston Globe, April 18, 1995.

Recall that the methods of this section require the frequencies x_1, x_2, $n_1 - x_1$, $n_2 - x_2$ all to be at least 5. But here one of the frequencies is 3. Resampling Stats is a program that allows for answers by simulation and is not bound by these requirements. With this exercise, Resampling Stats uses the sample data to generate additional samples. Under the null hypothesis H_0 ($p_A = p_B = p$), the 506 + 506 = 1012 values are pooled and assumed to be from the same population. The null hypothesis says that the two samples came from essentially the same population. If this is true, we want to estimate how likely it is that we would get such a large difference in number of deaths as was observed (11 − 3 = 8). Resampling Stats assumes that the collection of 14 deaths and 998 who survived is representative of the population. Five hundred six values are sampled with replacement from these 1012 values (coded so that 14 of these values represent deaths and the other 998 represent survivals). These represent 506 people having undergone the atherectomy procedure. Similarly, 506 values are sampled and represent 506 people having undergone the angioplasty procedure. The difference in the number of deaths (larger − smaller) is recorded. The process is repeated 5000 times. Out of these 5000 differences, our simulation recorded 205 as large as or larger than 8, which was the observed difference in the study. From this, would you conclude that the difference of 8 would be unlikely if the null hypothesis were true, as the simulation assumes? If so, how unlikely? Based on your conclusion, would you reject the null hypothesis?

9.40   At a large university, A, a poll of 150 faculty members showed that 50 had a salary exceeding $32,000. At another large university, B, a study showed that 95 of 200 sampled faculty members had salaries exceeding $32,000.

(a)   What is the estimated proportion of faculty members at universities A and B combined earning more than $32,000?

(b) Does there appear to be a difference in the population proportions between faculty members at the two universities earning more than \$32,000? Use a 1% level of significance.

9.41 In the case of *Jackson v. Nassau County Civil Service Commission*, 424 F. Supp. 1162, 1167 (E.D.N.Y. 1976), the following information was given concerning the results of an examination taken by job applicants:

	Passed	Failed
Blacks	40	15
Whites	99	14

Source: Data reported in DeGroot, M., S. Fienberg, and J. Kadane, *Statistics and the Law,* New York: Wiley, 1986, p. 38.

(a) Test the claim that the population proportion of blacks who pass is less than that of whites at the 2.5% level of significance.

(b) The "80% rule" says that a "substantial" disparity between groups can ordinarily be shown only when the data are significant (i.e., lead to rejection of the null hypothesis) *and* the pass rate for the protected group (blacks in this case) is less than 80% of the pass rate of the group with the highest pass rate. Do the data meet the requirements of the 80% rule?

9.42 A retailer received a large shipment of air conditioners. A sample of size 100 yielded 20 that did not conform to specification. The manufacturer believed that modifications in the production process would improve the quality of the product. Later the retailer received another shipment made with the modified process, and 10 of 100 sampled pieces did not conform to specification. At the 5% level, is there sufficient evidence supporting the manufacturer's belief?

(a) Use the classical approach. **(b)** Use the P-value approach.

9.43 A railroad company used two types of wheel mounts that differ in the way they handle track irregularities: Type A (spring equalized) and Type B (frame equalized). The following data give the repair records for the two types over a 1-year period:

	Number of Cars	Number Needing Service
Type A	150	20
Type B	180	18

(a) Find a 95% confidence interval for the difference in the population proportions $p_A - p_B$.

(b) Based on your results in part (a), do you think there is a difference between p_A and p_B?

9.44 An appliance dealer sells two brands of washing machines, each with a 1-year warranty. The dealer suspected that the proportion p_1 of brand 1 washing machines that would need servicing under the warranty was smaller than the proportion p_2 for brand 2. A random sample of sales of each brand was obtained and checked to see how many of each need service under the warranty. The results were as follows:

	Number Checked (n)	Number Serviced (x)
Brand 1	100	5
Brand 2	120	9

Is there sufficient evidence (at the 5% level of significance) to bear out the dealer's suspicion?

9.45   (a)   Use the data in Exercise 9.40 to construct a 99% confidence interval for the difference in the population proportion p_A of faculty members earning more than $32,000 at university A, and the population proportion p_B of faculty members earning more than $32,000 at university B.

(b)   Use the data in Exercise 9.41 to construct a 95% confidence interval for the difference in pass rates between whites and blacks ($p_W - p_B$).

9.6

USING MINITAB (OPTIONAL)

Inference Concerning Means Based on Dependent Samples

In Table 9.1, we gave gas mileages for eight cars using experimental emission controls (x_1 values) and for the same cars with standard emission controls (x_2 values). We looked at the differences $x = x_1 - x_2$ for each car. In Example 9.1, we carried out a t test to see whether the (population) mean difference μ was greater than 0, which would indicate an improvement in mileage with the experimental system:

$$H_0: \quad \mu = 0$$
$$H_a: \quad \mu > 0$$

In the following Minitab printout, we read the x_1 values into column 1 (C1) and the x_2 values into C2. We then place the differences (x) in C3 by the command

$$\text{LET C3} = \text{C1} - \text{C2}$$

We then perform a t test with 0 as the value of μ appearing in H_0. The 1 is a code for the symbol $>$ appearing in H_a. The data are in C3. Hence the Session commands for the test are

$$\text{TTEST OF MU} = 0, \text{DATA IN C3};$$
$$\text{ALTERNATIVE} = 1.$$

```
MTB > READ THE FOLLOWING DATA INTO C1 C2
DATA> 17  9
DATA> 23 17
DATA> 27 21
DATA> 14 16
DATA> 28 22
DATA> 21 17
DATA> 29 25
DATA> 13 13
DATA> END
        8 ROWS READ
MTB > LET C3 = C1 - C2
MTB > TTEST OF MU = 0, DATA IN C3;
SUBC>   ALTERNATIVE = 1.
```

T-Test of the Mean

```
Test of mu = 0.00 vs mu > 0.00
```

Variable	N	Mean	StDev	SE Mean	T	P-Value
C3	8	4.00	3.38	1.20	3.35	0.0062

The *P*-value is .0062, so we would reject H_0 for any value of $\alpha \geq .0062$.

Inference Concerning Means Based on Independent Samples

A company planning a large purchase of computer terminals was interested in the temperature at which a computer terminal would malfunction for each of two brands under consideration (A and B). Ten brand A terminals and 11 brand B terminals were tested. In the accompanying printout, we place the breakdown temperatures for brand A and brand B into columns C1 and C2, respectively. We then conduct a hypothesis test to compare the (population) mean breakdown temperatures for the two brands:

$$H_0: \quad \mu_1 = \mu_2$$
$$H_a: \quad \mu_1 \neq \mu_2$$

The command used is the TWOSAMPLE command. This command uses the test statistic

$$t = \frac{(\bar{x}_1 - \bar{x}_2) - (\mu_1 - \mu_2)}{\sqrt{(s_1^2/n_1) + (s_2^2/n_2)}} = \frac{\bar{x}_1 - \bar{x}_2}{\sqrt{(s_1^2/n_1) + (s_2^2/n_2)}}$$

The degrees of freedom used is different from the one we used in this chapter. Whereas we used the smaller of $n_1 - 1$ and $n_2 - 1$ for df, Minitab uses

$$df = \frac{(s_1^2/n_1 + s_2^2/n_2)^2}{\dfrac{(s_1^2/n_1)^2}{n_1 - 1} + \dfrac{(s_2^2/n_2)^2}{n_2 - 1}}$$

where df is rounded down to a whole number.

Session Commands	Dialog Box
MTB > SET DATA FOR BRAND A IN C1	**Stat ▶ Basic Statistics ▶ 2-Sample t**
DATA> 100 103 97 112 99 94 109 95 99 105	Click **Samples in different columns**
DATA> END	Type *C1* in **First** box, *C2* in **Second** box
MTB > SET DATA FOR BRAND B IN C2	Click ↓ after **Alternative.** (Menu drops
DATA> 100 102 99 98 100 101 96 103 102 99 97	down)
DATA> END	Click **not equal to**
MTB > TWOSAMPLE 90, DATA IN C1 C2	Type *90* for **Confidence level**
	Click **OK**

Output

Two Sample T-Test and Confidence Interval

```
Twosample T for C1 vs C2
        N       Mean      StDev    SE Mean
C1     10      101.30      5.91       1.9
C2     11       99.73      2.20       0.66

90% C.I. for mu C1 - mu C2: ( -2.0,   5.13)
T-Test mu C1 = mu C2 (vs not =): T= 0.79   P=0.44   DF=   11
```

Notice that the command called for a 90% confidence interval for $\mu_1 - \mu_2$. If we do not specify a confidence level, a 95% confidence interval is automatically given. A two-tailed test is performed unless we request otherwise with the usual ALTERNATIVE subcommand. The two-tailed *P*-value is .44. If $\alpha < .44$, we do not reject H_0. So if $\alpha = .05$, we do not reject H_0, and we conclude there is no difference in mean breakdown temperature. The code

$$\text{TWOSAMPLE, DATA IN C1 C2;}$$
$$\text{ALTERNATIVE} = 1.$$

would produce a right-tailed test (a *P*-value of .22) and a 95% confidence interval for $\mu_1 - \mu_2$.

The two-sample *t* test is appropriate for both large and small samples. Therefore, you should use the TWOSAMPLE command in either large- or small-sample cases.

In Section 9.4, we pointed out that if $\sigma_1 = \sigma_2$, a test using the pooled standard deviation (s_p) can be done. The test statistic given was

$$t = \frac{(\bar{x}_1 - \bar{x}_2) - (\mu_1 - \mu_2)}{s_p\sqrt{\dfrac{1}{n_1} + \dfrac{1}{n_2}}} \qquad \text{df} = n_1 + n_2 - 2$$

To perform this test, we must use the POOLED subcommand. For example, to conduct a pooled right-tailed test, type

$$\text{TWOSAMPLE, DATA IN C1 C2;}$$
$$\text{ALTERNATIVE} = 1;$$
$$\text{POOLED.}$$

The developers of Minitab point out that this pooled test can be seriously in error if σ_1 is not the same as σ_2, hence the POOLED subcommand should not be used in most cases.

Minitab provides a procedure for comparing two (or more) proportions, which we discuss in Chapter 12.

EXERCISES

Suggested exercises for use with Minitab are 9.3, 9.10(b), 9.27, 9.28(c), and 9.32.

9.7

WORKING WITH DATA (OPTIONAL)

Problems 1–4 refer to the Framingham Heart Study data sets you obtained in Section 2.8.

1. **(a)** Using a 5% level of significance, test that the mean population systolic blood pressure for males is different from that of females.
    (b) Construct a 95% confidence interval for the difference in population mean systolic blood pressure between males and females.
    Note: You may have already calculated the sample means and sample standard deviations. See Problems 1 and 4 of Section 3.7.
2. **(a)** Using a 5% level of significance, test the claim that there is no difference in population mean serum cholesterol levels between males and females.
    (b) Construct a 95% confidence interval for the difference in population mean serum cholesterol levels between males and females.
    Note: You may have already calculated the sample means and sample standard deviations. See Problems 2 and 5 of Section 3.7.
3. Do your data suggest a significant difference in proportion of males and females who are smokers? Use a 5% level of significance.
4. **(a)** Find a 95% confidence interval for the mean difference between systolic and diastolic blood pressures for females.
    (b) Find a 95% confidence interval for the mean difference between systolic and diastolic blood pressures for males.
5. Obtain random samples of 20 female smokers and 20 female nonsmokers from Table B.11. Record their systolic blood pressures and serum cholesterol levels.
    (a) Do the data suggest a difference in population mean systolic blood pressures for the two groups? Use the 5% level of significance.
    (b) Give a 95% confidence interval for the difference in population mean cholesterol level between the smokers and nonsmokers. How would you interpret this confidence interval? For example, is there a difference in population means? If so, which is larger?
    (c) Construct stem-and-leaf plots for the blood pressure samples. Is a *t* test appropriate for these samples? Explain.
    (d) Construct stem-and-leaf plots for the cholesterol samples. Is a confidence interval based on Student's *t* distribution appropriate for these samples? Explain.

9.8

SUMMARY

In this chapter, we developed methods for comparing two population means or two population proportions. In Table 9.9, we give the parameter being investigated,

Table 9.9

Parameter	Assumptions	$1 - \alpha$ Confidence Interval	Test Statistic
(1) Single mean μ	Sample size $n \geq 30$	$\bar{x} \pm z_{\alpha/2} \cdot \dfrac{\sigma}{\sqrt{n}}$	$z = \dfrac{\bar{x} - \mu}{\sigma/\sqrt{n}}$
		If σ is unknown, use s.	
	$n < 30$ x approximately normal	$\bar{x} \pm t_{\alpha/2} \cdot \dfrac{s}{\sqrt{n}}$ df $= n - 1$	$t = \dfrac{\bar{x} - \mu}{s/\sqrt{n}}$ df $= n - 1$
(2) Single proportion p	$np, nq \geq 5$ $(x \geq 5, n - x \geq 5$ in case of confidence intervals)	$\hat{p} \pm z_{\alpha/2}\sqrt{\dfrac{\hat{p}\hat{q}}{n}}$ where $\hat{p} = x/n$	$z = \dfrac{\hat{p} - p}{\sqrt{pq/n}}$ where $\hat{p} = x/n$
(3) Two means (equivalent to testing $\mu_1 - \mu_2$)	Dependent samples	Let $x = x_1 - x_2$; then $\mu = \mu_1 - \mu_2$. Now use methods for single mean in (1).	
	Independent samples $n_1, n_2 \geq 30$	$(\bar{x}_1 - \bar{x}_2) \pm z_{\alpha/2} \cdot \sqrt{\dfrac{\sigma_1^2}{n_1} + \dfrac{\sigma_2^2}{n_2}}$	$z = \dfrac{(\bar{x}_1 - \bar{x}_2) - (\mu_1 - \mu_2)}{\sqrt{(\sigma_1^2/n_1) + (\sigma_2^2/n_2)}}$
		If σ_1, σ_2 unknown, use s_1, s_2.	
	$n_1 < 30$ and/or $n_2 < 30$, x_1, x_2 approx. normal	$(\bar{x}_1 - \bar{x}_2) \pm t_{\alpha/2} \cdot \sqrt{\dfrac{s_1^2}{n_1} + \dfrac{s_2^2}{n_2}}$ df: smaller of $n_1 - 1$ and $n_2 - 1$	$t = \dfrac{(\bar{x}_1 - \bar{x}_2) - (\mu_1 - \mu_2)}{\sqrt{(s_1^2/n_1) + (s_2^2/n_2)}}$ df: smaller of $n_1 - 1$ and $n_2 - 1$
	$n_1 < 30$ and/or $n_2 < 30$, x_1, x_2 approx. normal and $\sigma_1 = \sigma_2$	$(\bar{x}_1 - \bar{x}_2) \pm t_{\alpha/2} \cdot s_p \cdot \sqrt{\dfrac{1}{n_1} + \dfrac{1}{n_2}}$ df $= n_1 + n_2 - 2$	$t = \dfrac{(\bar{x}_1 - \bar{x}_2) - (\mu_1 - \mu_2)}{s_p \sqrt{(1/n_1) + (1/n_2)}}$ df $= n_1 + n_2 - 2$ $s_p = \sqrt{\dfrac{(n_1 - 1)s_1^2 + (n_2 - 1)s_2^2}{n_1 + n_2 - 2}}$
(4) Two proportions (equivalent to testing $p_1 - p_2$)	The number of successes and the number of failures should in each case be at least 5. Independent samples	$(\hat{p}_1 - \hat{p}_2) \pm z_{\alpha/2} \cdot \sqrt{\dfrac{\hat{p}_1\hat{q}_1}{n_1} + \dfrac{\hat{p}_2\hat{q}_2}{n_2}}$	When $H_0: \quad p_1 - p_2 = 0$ $z = \dfrac{\hat{p}_1 - \hat{p}_2}{\sqrt{\hat{p}\hat{q}[(1/n_1) + (1/n_2)]}}$ $\hat{p} = \dfrac{x_1 + x_2}{n_1 + n_2}, \ \hat{q} = 1 - \hat{p}$ When $H_0: \quad p_1 - p_2 = D, \ D \neq 0$ $z = \dfrac{(\hat{p}_1 - \hat{p}_2) - D}{\sqrt{(\hat{p}_1\hat{q}_1/n_1) + (\hat{p}_2\hat{q}_2/n_2)}}$

the assumptions needed, the test statistic to be used in hypothesis testing about the parameter, and the form of a $1 - \alpha$ confidence interval for the parameter. For completeness, we include the parameters studied in Chapter 8. It is understood that when the parameter being tested (such as μ or $\mu_1 - \mu_2$) appears in the formula for the test statistic, we substitute for this parameter the specific value appearing in the null hypothesis.

REVIEW EXERCISES

9.46   Computer programmer A always drove to work, whereas programmer B took the bus. Programmer A claimed that it was quicker, on the average, to go by car. The programmers recorded the following travel times in minutes for each of 10 days:

Day	A Time by Car	B Time by Bus
1	18.9	19.9
2	15.9	18.3
3	17.9	16.9
4	19.2	18.9
5	15.7	20.2
6	16.9	19.5
7	16.4	16.7
8	16.8	19.1
9	19.0	17.9
10	17.1	20.3

List the differences $x = A - B$ and verify that $\bar{x} = -1.390$ and $s = 1.896$. With a 5% significance level, is there enough evidence to support programmer A's claim? Assume the population of differences is approximately normal.

(a)   Use the classical approach.   (b)   Use the P-value approach.

9.47   A producer of corn wanted to know which of two fertilizers, A or B, was better for growing corn. To study this, seven plots of land were selected. Each plot was divided in half. For each plot, fertilizer A was assigned to one half and fertilizer B to the other using the toss of a coin. The yield of corn in bushels after a period of time gave the following data:

Plot	Fertilizer A	Fertilizer B
1	42	40
2	38	42
3	41	36
4	43	39
5	42	41
6	38	40
7	41	36

List the differences $x = A - B$, and verify that $\sum x = 11$ and $\sum x^2 = 91$. At a 5% level of significance, is there sufficient evidence to conclude that one of the fertilizers is more effective? Assume approximate normality for the population of differences.

9.48   **(a)**   Use the data in Exercise 9.46 to construct a 90% confidence interval for the difference in mean times between driving a car and taking the bus to work. Interpret your result.

(b)   Use the data in Exercise 9.47 to construct a 95% confidence interval for the difference in mean yields between the use of fertilizer A and fertilizer B. Interpret your result.

9.49   In parts (a) and (b), assume the information was obtained with independent random samples from populations A and B.

(a)   Test the claim that the means of populations A and B are the same. Use a 5% level of significance. The sample information is given in the table.

	n	$\bar{x}$	s^2
A	40	315	400
B	60	324	360

(b)   At the 1% significance level, is there sufficient evidence to believe the mean of population B is larger than the mean of population A? The sample information is summarized in the table.

	n	$\bar{x}$	s^2
A	60	400	540
B	50	410	800

9.50   In a winter and spring study of men's diets on the island of Crete, the results of independent samples of percent calories from fats were as follows (*Source:* Keys, A., ed., 1970, p. I-166):

	n	$\bar{x}$	s
A (Winter)	30	37.4	4.9
B (Spring)	33	41.8	5.7

Is there sufficient evidence to indicate a difference in population means? Use a 1% level of significance.

9.51   The union president of factory A employees wanted to compare the wages of his union members with those of employees at factory B. Both factories manufactured the same product, and the union president thought workers at his factory had lower wages, on the average. Forty members were sampled from each factory and asked their hourly wage. The results were as follows:

	$\bar{x}$	s
A	13.10	1.90
B	13.95	1.65

(a) Find the *P*-value. Using this value, complete the test at the 1% level of significance.

(b) Construct a 98% confidence interval for the mean difference in wages between factory A and factory B. Interpret your results.

9.52 In Exercises 2.5 and 2.6, we looked at the leading number of home runs hit in the American and National Leagues for the years 1954–1993. The means for the American and National League are 41.47 and 42.80, respectively. The respective standard deviations are 7.11 and 5.32.

(a) Find a 95% confidence interval for the mean difference in the number of home runs per year between the American and National Leagues. Interpret your results.

(b) Use a 5% level of significance and test that the mean leading number of home runs is the same for both leagues. Is the difference statistically significant at the 5% significance level? Is your result consistent with your conclusion in part (a)?

9.53 The personnel office of an auto company believed that if workers were rotated to different positions on an assembly line, it would improve their psychological outlook. A sample of such workers was compared to a control group of workers who stayed at the same position. The following data relate to depression scores on a psychological inventory called the Depression Adjective Checklist (DACL):

	n	$\bar{x}$	s^2
A: Rotated Group	18	4.8	4.3
B: Control Group	16	6.9	12.7

Test the claim that rotated workers have lower mean depression level than nonrotated workers. Use the 5% level of significance. You may assume that the populations are approximately normal.

(a) Use the classical approach. (b) Use the *P*-value approach.

9.54 A study was done of trained distance runners. Measurements (in millimeters) were obtained on six-site skin fold [tricep, subscapular, suprailiac, umbilical, pectoral, and mid-thigh (anterior)] (*Source:* Daniels, J., et al., 1977, p. 142). The results of the study were as follows:

	n	$\bar{x}$	s
Males	10	39.6	6.8
Females	10	48.1	4.4

A track coach suspected that for trained distance runners, the female six-site skin fold was 5 millimeters more than for males, on the average. Assuming independent samples from approximately normal populations, complete the test with a 2% level of significance.

9.55 In Exercises 2.33 and 2.34, we discussed test scores for introductory evening and afternoon economics classes. The data and summary results are shown here.

Evening:

60 42 61 70 59 65 68 67
78 68 67 74 61 74 61 71

Afternoon:

59 63 63 63 64 60 71 55 70
54 65 66 69 69 60 52 61

	n	Mean	Standard Deviation
Evening (E)	16	65.37	8.38
Afternoon (A)	17	62.59	5.59

(a)   At a 5% level of significance, does the evening class seem to perform better than the afternoon class, on average? Assume the t procedure is appropriate.

(b)   Resampling Stats is a program that allows for approximate answers by simulation. With this exercise, Resampling Stats uses the sample data to generate additional samples. Under the null hypothesis H_0 ($\mu_E = \mu_A$), the $16 + 17 = 33$ values are pooled and assumed to be from the same population. Resampling Stats assumes these 33 data values to be representative of the population. Sixteen values are sampled with replacement from the 33 values; these represent a hypothetical evening school class. Similarly, 17 values are sampled and represent an afternoon class. The mean for each class is computed, and the difference between evening mean and afternoon mean is recorded and compared with the observed difference, $\bar{x}_E - \bar{x}_A = 2.78$. The process is repeated 1000 times. The accompanying printout gives a frequency histogram for the differences and a count of the number of differences that are 2.78 or larger. Is the proportion of times the difference of the means was the same or larger than 2.78 consistent with the actual P-value of .142?

NUMBER OF TIMES MEAN DIFFERENCES AS LARGE OR LARGER THAN 2.78 = 138

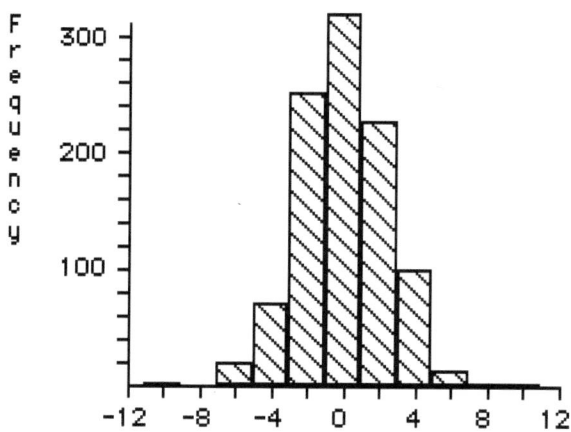

9.56   A drug was tested on rats to see whether the mean time in completing a maze was reduced. Thirty-two rats were randomly separated into groups A and B of 16 each. Each rat in group A was injected with the drug. The results of completing the maze, measured in seconds, were as follows:

	$\bar{x}$	s^2
A	9.1	1.05
B	9.9	3.63

Using a 1% level of significance, is there sufficient evidence to indicate that the drug reduces the mean time for rats to complete the maze? Assume the populations are approximately normal.

    (a)   Use the classical approach.   **(b)**   Use the P-value approach.

9.57   Construct confidence intervals for $\mu_A - \mu_B$ in parts (a) and (b).

    (a)   Use the data in Exercise 9.53 to construct a 90% confidence interval. Can you conclude that $\mu_A < \mu_B$?

    (b)   Use the data in Exercise 9.56 to construct a 98% confidence interval. Can you conclude that $\mu_A < \mu_B$?

9.58   Assume independent samples from approximately normal populations with equal variances. The data are given here.

	n	$\bar{x}$	s^2
A	10	74	60
B	13	81	40

Using pooled t procedures,

    (a)   Is there sufficient evidence to conclude that the mean of A is smaller than the mean of B? Use the 5% significance level.

    (b)   Find a 95% confidence interval for the difference in means between populations A and B.

9.59   At a large university, 200 students and 100 faculty members were selected and asked whether an additional science course should be required of all students. Seventy students and 45 members of the faculty supported the additional requirement. Do the populations of students and faculty members at the university appear to be in agreement? Use a 5% level of significance.

9.60   A pollster randomly sampled 250 men and 260 women in Massachusetts and asked whether they believed a capital punishment law should be reinstated. Of these people, 130 men and 104 women believed that the law should be reinstated. At the 1% significance level, is there sufficient evidence to indicate a difference in population proportions of Massachusetts men and women favoring capital punishment?

    (a)   Use the classical approach.   **(b)**   Use the P-value approach.

9.61   A study showed that 70 of 125 workers sampled in a large factory A were satisfied with their job, whereas 130 of 200 workers sampled from a large factory B said they were satisfied. Using the 1% level of significance, does the evidence indicate a difference in population proportions p_A and p_B of workers satisfied in factories A and B, respectively?

    (a)   Use the classical approach.   **(b)**   Use the P-value approach.

9.62   A manufacturer wanted to compare the quality of work produced by two shifts. From each shift 300 items were selected. Six percent of the items manufactured by shift A were found to be defective, and 4% of the items manufactured by shift B were defective. Is there sufficient evidence to indicate a difference in the population proportions of defectives produced by the two shifts? Use a 5% level of significance.

9.63   Construct confidence intervals for $p_A - p_B$ in parts (a) and (b). Explain why these confidence intervals suggest that you cannot conclude that $p_A \neq p_B$.

    (a)   Use the data in Exercise 9.59 to construct a 95% confidence interval.

    (b)   Use the data in Exercise 9.61 to construct a 99% confidence interval.

9.64   A state politician wanted to determine whether there was any difference in her support between the eastern and western parts of the state. In samples of size 150 from each region, 90 of the voters in the east and 80 in the west were satisfied with her performance.

    (a)   What is the estimated proportion of voters (combined) that are satisfied with her performance?

    (b)   Using a 5% level of significance, is there sufficient evidence to indicate a difference in her support between the eastern and western parts of the state?

9.65   In Exercise 9.44 we considered the following data:

	Number Checked (n)	Number Serviced (x)
Brand 1	100	5
Brand 2	120	9

Also, p_1 and p_2 represented the proportion of washing machines of brands 1 and 2, respectively, that would need servicing under the warranty. Recall H_a was $p_1 - p_2 < 0$ and the value of the test statistic z was $-.76$.

    Now consider the data:

	Number Checked (n)	Number Serviced (x)
Brand 1	600	30
Brand 2	720	54

    (a)   Compute and compare $\hat{p}_1$ and $\hat{p}_2$ for both sets of data.

    (b)   Using the second set of data, can we conclude that $p_1 - p_2 < 0$ at the 5% significance level? Note that in Exercise 9.44 we did not reject H_0. Comment.

9.66   Suppose that you are testing $H_0: p_A - p_B = 0$, where p_A and p_B are proportions for populations A and B, respectively. Consider the following three sample results. Note that x is the number of successes.

(i)

	n	x
A	100	40
B	100	50

(ii)

	n	x
A	200	80
B	200	100

(iii)

	n	x
A	500	200
B	500	250

    (a)   Calculate the value of z for each sample and compare.

    (b)   What do you notice about $\hat{p}_A - \hat{p}_B$ in each case?

    (c)   Comment on your findings.

Notes

The Boston Globe, Boston, 1995.

Daniels, J., G. Krakenbuhl, C. Foster, J. Gilbert, and S. Daniels, "Aerobic Responses of Female Distance Runners to Submaximal and Maximal Exercise," in P. Milvy, ed., *The Long Distance Runner*, New York: Urizen Books, 1977.

DeGroot, M. H., S. E. Fienberg, and J. B. Kadane, eds. *Statistics and the Law,* New York: Wiley, 1986.

Gordon, T., W. Castelli, M. Hjortland, W. Kannel, and T. Dawber, "High Density Lipoprotein as a Protective Factor Against Coronary Disease: The Framingham Study." *The American Journal of Medicine,* Vol. 62, 1977.

Keys, A., ed., "Coronary Heart Disease in Seven Countries." *Circulation,* Vol. 41, No. 1, (Suppl. 1), 1970.

Martin, R., W. Haskell, and P. Wood, "Blood Chemistry and Lipid Profiles of Elite Distance Runners," in P. Milvy, ed. *The Long Distance Runner,* New York: Urizen Books, 1977.

Morganroth, J., and B. Maron, "The Athlete's Heart Syndrome: A New Perspective," in P. Milvy, ed. *The Long Distance Runner,* New York: Urizen Books, 1977.

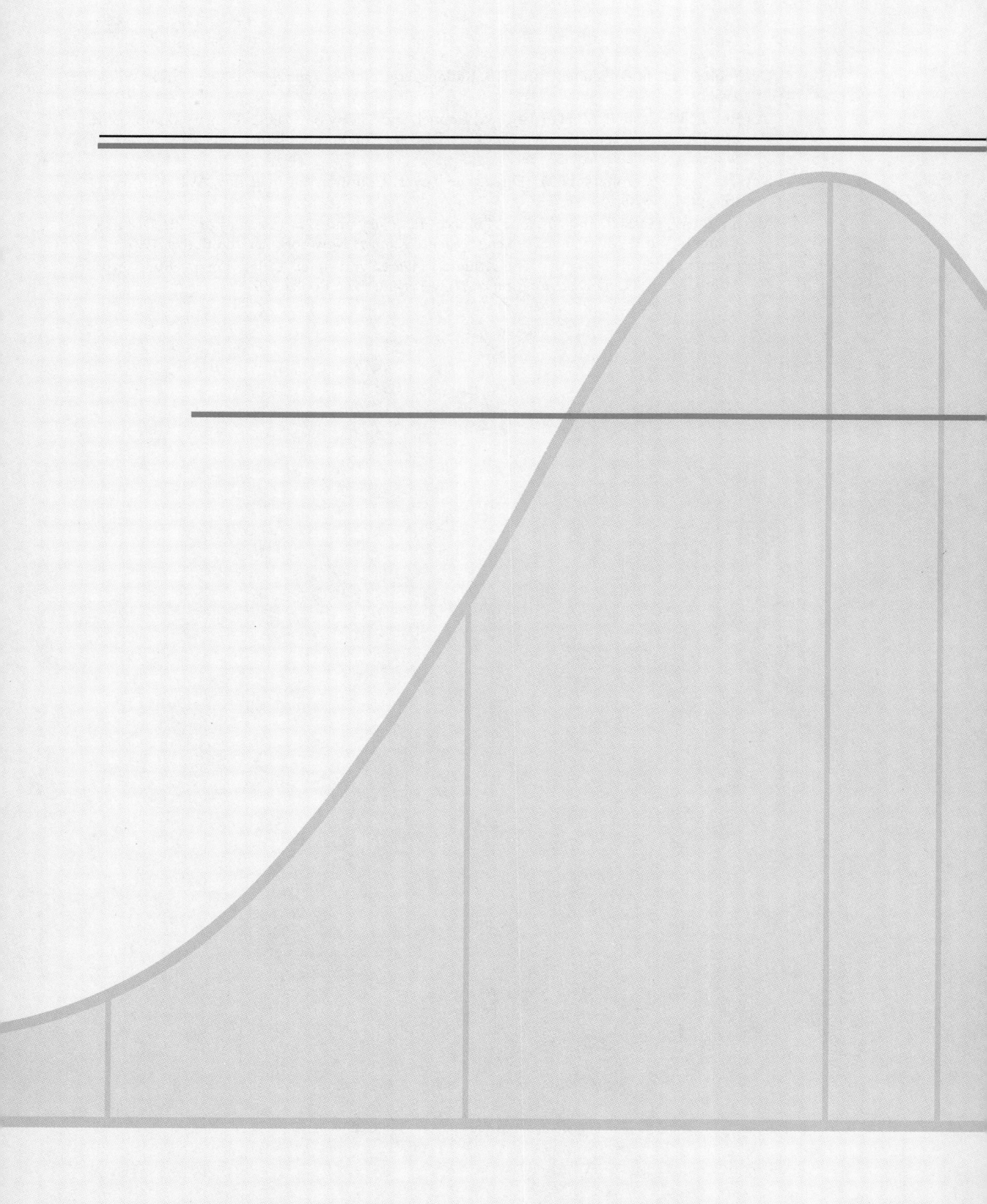

CHAPTER 10

INFERENCE CONCERNING REGRESSION AND CORRELATION

10.1 INTRODUCTION

10.2 INFERENCE CONCERNING SLOPE

10.3 INFERENCE CONCERNING CORRELATION

10.4 PREDICTION INTERVALS AND CONFIDENCE INTERVALS (OPTIONAL)

10.5 USING MINITAB (OPTIONAL)

10.6 WORKING WITH DATA (OPTIONAL)

10.7 SUMMARY

REVIEW EXERCISES

NOTES

10.1

INTRODUCTION

In Chapter 4, we studied relationships between variables, such as years of work experience (x) and salary (y), focusing on samples of subjects. In this chapter, we try to draw inferences about the population from which a sample was obtained.

10.2

INFERENCE CONCERNING SLOPE

Linear Regression Model

In Chapter 4, we discussed how to find the line of best fit and the linear correlation coefficient for a collection of (x, y) values in a scatter diagram. When we wish to generalize our results, we often consider a large population of (x, y) values from which the points in our scatter diagram were obtained. This population of (x, y) values is called a **bivariate population.** The points in the scatter diagram are thought of as a sample from this population.

In Example 4.3, we examined data from seven companies producing fertilizer. In that example, x represented number of tons produced in a year (in thousands) and y represented cost per ton in dollars. The regression line was

$$\hat{y} = 65.78 - 6.62x$$

The population could be viewed as a whole industry of companies in the same size range as the original seven. The population regression line is represented as

$$y = \beta_0 + \beta_1 x$$

This is usually unknown, but the sample regression line $\hat{y} = 65.78 - 6.62x$ can be thought of as an estimate of the population line.

For the inference methods of this chapter to be valid, the properties of the **linear regression model** must be satisfied.

Properties of the Linear Regression Model

1. **Normality**   For each x value, the collection of all possible y values corresponding to that x value has a normal distribution.[*] For example, let $x =$ a person's high school grade point average (GPA) and $y =$ college GPA. The collection of all the college GPAs for all students with a high school average of 2.50 has a normal distribution.

2. **Linearity**   There is a population regression line with equation

    $$y = \beta_0 + \beta_1 x$$

    where β_0 and β_1 are constants. (β is the Greek letter beta.) For a particular x value substituted into this equation, the resulting y value gives the mean for all the y values corresponding to that x value. This is sometimes denoted by $\mu_{y|x}$.

3. **Homoscedasticity**   This means the variance from the regression line of all the y values corresponding to a specific x value will be the same no matter what x value we choose. We denote this common variance by σ^2.

4. **Independence**   This means the y values in the scatter diagram are unrelated. In other words, these y values deviate above and below the regression line in a random fashion. This property is sometimes violated for measurements taken over time. For example, the exchange rate of the dollar in terms of German marks today is likely to be close to what it was yesterday. In this sense, the values are related.

The linear regression model is shown in Figure 10.1(a). The population regression line is usually unknown. However, if we obtain a sample, we can estimate the population regression line by the sample regression line $\hat{y} = b_0 + b_1 x$.

The linear model can also be described by the equation

$$y = \beta_0 + \beta_1 x + \epsilon$$

---

[*]Moderate departures from normality are not very serious. In fact, departures from normality become less important as the sample size increases.

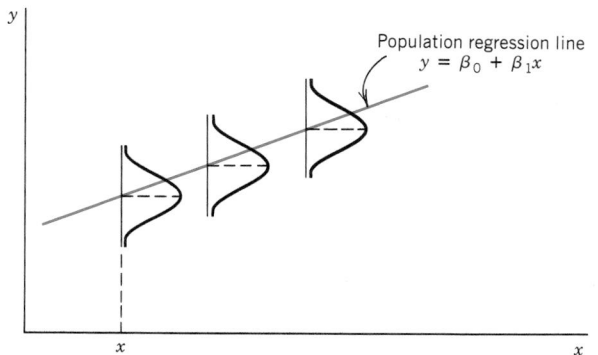

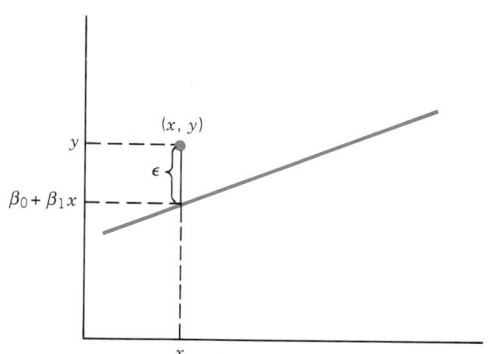

Figure 10.1(a)

Linear Model: For Each Value of x, the Population of Corresponding y Values Is Normal with the Mean on the Regression Line and with the Same Variance σ^2.

Figure 10.1(b)

$y = \beta_0 + \beta_1 x + \epsilon$

where ϵ is the Greek letter epsilon. Each point (x, y) in the population satisfies this equation for some value of ϵ. See Figure 10.1(b). When $\epsilon = 0$, the point is exactly on the population regression line

$$y = \beta_0 + \beta_1 x$$

For a fixed x, ϵ can assume a variety of values, each corresponding to a different y value. For the linear model, we assume:

- ϵ is normal. (Hence, for each x, the y values are normal.)
- The mean of ϵ is 0. (Hence the mean of the y values is $\beta_0 + \beta_1 x$.)
- The variance of ϵ (and hence of the y values) is σ^2. This is the same for each value of x.
- The ϵ's corresponding to the points in the scatter diagram are independent (unrelated). See Figure 10.1(b) for the ϵ corresponding to a point.

Inference Concerning β_1

If for the population regression line

$$y = \beta_0 + \beta_1 x$$

the slope β_1 is different from 0, then the line is nonhorizontal. This means the points (x, y) for the population are grouped about a nonhorizontal regression line, indicating at least some degree of linear relationship between x and y for the population. So if we wish to investigate linearity for the population, we could test:

$$H_0: \quad \beta_1 = 0 \quad \text{(There is no linear relationship.)}$$
$$H_a: \quad \beta_1 \neq 0 \quad \text{(There is a linear relationship.)}$$

If we reject H_0, we conclude that $\beta_1 \neq 0$. This means there is a linear relationship between x and y for the population.

The sample regression line computed from the points in a scatter diagram is

$$\hat{y} = b_0 + b_1 x$$

Here b_1 is an estimate of β_1. If b_1 is far enough from 0 so that such a value would be unlikely if H_0 were true, we reject H_0 and conclude there is a linear relationship for the population. For a test statistic, we use a standardized form of b_1. This is obtained by dividing b_1 by an estimate of the standard deviation of b_1, which is denoted by s_{b_1}. (In repeated samplings, b_1 could have different values. So it is a random variable, and therefore it makes sense to talk about its standard deviation.)

$$\text{Test statistic:}\quad t = \frac{b_1}{s_{b_1}} = \frac{b_1}{S/\sqrt{\left(\sum x^2\right) - \left(\sum x\right)^2 / n}}$$

where

$$S = \sqrt{\frac{SSE}{n-2}} = \sqrt{\frac{\sum (y - \hat{y})^2}{n-2}}$$

S is computed from the sample data and is called the **standard deviation from the regression line.** It is an estimate of the standard deviation (σ) of y values from the population regression line. Under appropriate conditions, the test statistic t has a Student's t distribution with df $= n - 2$.

Test Statistic for Testing H_0: $\beta_1 = 0$ versus H_a: $\begin{cases} \beta_1 > 0 \\ \beta_1 < 0 \\ \beta_1 \neq 0 \end{cases}$

$$t = \frac{b_1}{S/\sqrt{\left(\sum x^2\right) - \left(\sum x\right)^2 / n}}$$

This has a Student's t distribution with df $= n - 2$ when H_0 is true.

Assumptions: The properties of the linear regression model are satisfied.

EXAMPLE 10.1

In Example 4.2, we discussed the relationship between experience (x) and salary (y) for a sample of 12 technicians. Do the data (reproduced in Table 10.1) support the belief that there is a positive linear relationship between experience and salary for the population of technicians from which the sample was obtained? Use the 1% level of significance.

Solution

1. *Hypotheses:*   There will be a positive linear relationship if the slope $\beta_1 > 0$. Therefore we test

$$H_0:\quad \beta_1 = 0$$
$$H_a:\quad \beta_1 > 0$$

2. *Level of significance:* $\alpha = .01$

3. *Test statistic and observed value:*   In Example 4.2, we found that $\sum x = 176, \sum x^2 = 3162$, and the regression line was $\hat{y} = 19.47 + .71x$. (Hence, $b_1 = .71$.) In Table 10.1, we give the original data, the $\hat{y}$ values, and the residuals $(y - \hat{y})$. The predicted or estimated salary ($\hat{y}$) for a given value of years (x) is obtained by substituting the x value into the equation for $\hat{y}$. Thus when $x = 12$, $\hat{y} = 19.47 + (.71)(12) = 27.99$.

Table 10.1
Salary Data

Years of Experience (x)	Salary in Thousands (y)	Predicted Salary ($\hat{y}$)	Residual $e = y - \hat{y}$	$(y - \hat{y})^2$
12	29	27.99	1.01	1.0201
16	31	30.83	.17	.0289
6	23	23.73	−.73	.5329
23	34	35.80	−1.80	3.2400
27	38	38.64	−.64	.4096
8	24	25.15	−1.15	1.3225
5	22	23.02	−1.02	1.0404
19	34	32.96	1.04	1.0816
23	36	35.80	.20	.0400
13	27	28.70	−1.70	2.8900
16	33	30.83	2.17	4.7089
8	27	25.15	1.85	3.4225
				19.7374 = SSE

Therefore

$$S = \sqrt{\frac{SSE}{n - 2}} = \sqrt{\frac{19.7374}{12 - 2}} = \sqrt{1.97374} \doteq 1.40$$

The observed value of t is

$$t = \frac{b_1}{S/\sqrt{(\sum x^2) - (\sum x)^2 /n}} = \frac{.71}{1.40/\sqrt{3162 - (176)^2/12}} \doteq 12.22$$

and

$$df = n - 2 = 12 - 2 = 10$$

4. *Critical region:* H_a involves $>$. We perform a right-tailed t test. The critical region is given in Figure 10.2.

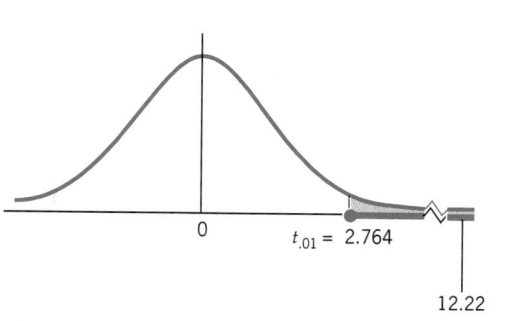
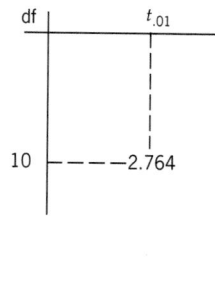

Figure 10.2

5. *Decision:* The observed value (12.22) is in the critical region, so we reject H_0. The data indicate that $\beta_1 > 0$, so there is a positive linear relationship between the x and y values for the population.

Alternate Formula for t

If you already know the value of the linear correlation coefficient r, the following alternative formula will enable you to compute t quickly:

$$t = r\sqrt{\frac{n-2}{1-r^2}}$$

For the data in Example 10.1, the value of r (computed in Example 4.4) is .9676674. The value of t obtained by substituting r in the previous formula is

$$t = .9676674\sqrt{\frac{12-2}{1-(.9676674)^2}} \doteq 12.13$$

This value is slightly different from the value of t computed in Example 10.1, namely, 12.22. This is due to round-off.

   If you know the value of r, you should definitely consider using the alternate formula for t. In fact, even if you do not know r, it could be argued that it is easier to compute r and use the alternate formula rather than the original formula.

Confidence Interval for β_1

Confidence intervals often take the general form

$$(\text{estimate}) \pm t \cdot (\text{standard deviation})$$

For example, we have seen that a confidence interval for a mean based on Student's t distribution is

$$\bar{x} \pm t_{\alpha/2} \cdot \frac{s}{\sqrt{n}}$$

The estimate (for μ) is $\bar{x}$, and the standard deviation of $\bar{x}$ is estimated by $s/\sqrt{n}$. This suggests what a $1 - \alpha$ confidence interval for β_1 should look like.

$1 - \alpha$ Confidence Interval for β_1

$$b_1 \pm t_{\alpha/2} \cdot \frac{S}{\sqrt{(\sum x^2) - (\sum x)^2/n}}$$

where $t_{\alpha/2}$ is based on degrees of freedom df $= n - 2$.
Assumptions: The properties of the linear regression model are satisfied.

EXAMPLE 10.2
Refer to the salary data of Example 10.1. Find a 90% confidence interval for β_1.

Solution
We are given $1 - \alpha = .90$, so $\alpha = .10$. For df $= n - 2 = 10$, Appendix Table B.4 gives $t_{\alpha/2} = t_{.05} = 1.812$. From Example 10.1, $\sum x = 176$, $\sum x^2 = 3162$, $S = 1.40$, and $b_1 = .71$. Our 95% confidence interval is

$$b_1 \pm t_{\alpha/2} \cdot \frac{S}{\sqrt{(\sum x^2) - (\sum x)^2/n}} = .71 \pm 1.812 \cdot \frac{1.40}{\sqrt{3162 - 176^2/12}}$$

$$= .71 \pm .1052744$$

This gives endpoints .5947256 and .8152744. So we are 90% sure that (after rounding off)

$$.59 < \beta_1 < .82$$

Checking Properties of the Regression Model

Sometimes a glance at a scatter diagram will indicate that the properties of the regression model are not met. Figure 10.3(a) suggests nonlinearity; this should certainly deter you from calculating the regression line, much less using inference methods on such data. Likewise Figure 10.3(b) suggests nonconstant variance.

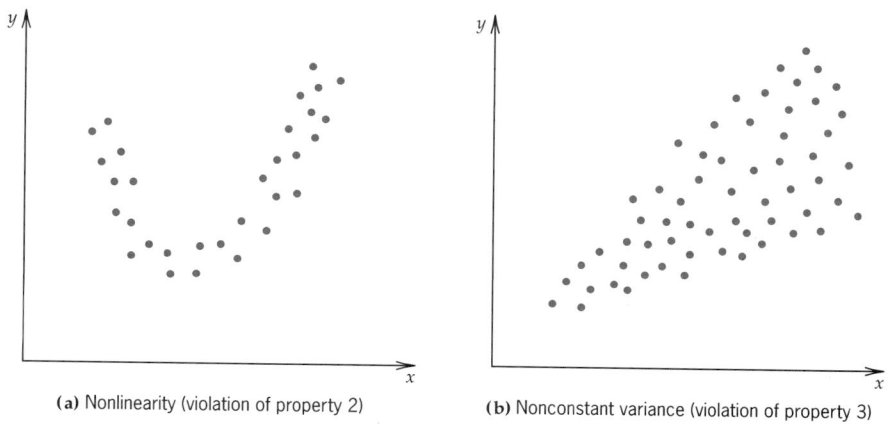

(a) Nonlinearity (violation of property 2)   (b) Nonconstant variance (violation of property 3)

Figure 10.3
Departures from the Linear Regression Model

Residuals can often be used to check properties of the regression model. Suppose we compute the regression line from the sample data:

$$\hat{y} = b_0 + b_1 x$$

This is an estimate of the population regression line, since $b_0 + b_1 x$ is an estimate of $\beta_0 + \beta_1 x$. The residual for a point (x, y) in our scatter diagram is

$$e = y - \hat{y} = y - (b_0 + b_1 x)$$

This is an estimate of the value ϵ for (x, y), since according to the regression model

$$y = \beta_0 + \beta_1 x + \epsilon$$

and hence

$$\epsilon = y - (\beta_0 + \beta_1 x)$$

We saw that the properties of the linear regression model can be stated in terms of the variable ϵ, which is an unknown quantity. But since the residuals (e) are estimates of the values of ϵ, we should be able to check the properties of the regression model by examining the residuals. For example, the variable ϵ is required to be normal. It turns out that only approximate normality is necessary. Since the residuals approximate the values of ϵ, a graph of the residuals (a histogram, stem-and-leaf plot, etc.*) should not indicate departures from approximate normality (such as strong skewness or extreme outliers).

---

*For those who have read the optional material on normal quantile plots in Chapter 8 and have access to statistical software, a normal quantile plot is a good tool for assessing approximate normality.

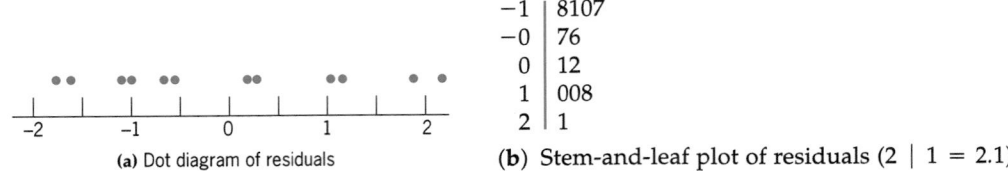

(a) Dot diagram of residuals

(b) Stem-and-leaf plot of residuals (2 | 1 = 2.1)

Figure 10.4

Graphs of Residuals for the Salary Data (No Indications of Serious Departures from Normality)

In this section, we examined years of experience (x) and salary in thousands (y) for 12 technicians. These data along with residuals can be found in Table 10.1. Figure 10.4 gives a dot diagram and a stem-and-leaf plot of the residuals. The stem-and-leaf plot was obtained by "cutting the data." The last digit was dropped: Thus 2.17 became 2.1. (If we did not cut the data, there would be too many stems. You may prefer to round off the data.) In any case, Figure 10.4 shows that although the data are slightly skewed to the right, there are no indications of serious departures from normality.

A **residual plot** is a plot of the residuals (e) against values of some other variable, such as x. Figure 10.5 contains hypothetical residual plots of e against x. When the points in the scatter diagram cluster about a line (suggesting linearity), the points in the residual plot will cluster about the horizontal axis as in Figure 10.5(a). Figure 10.5(b) is the residual plot corresponding to Figure 10.3(a) and suggests nonlinearity.

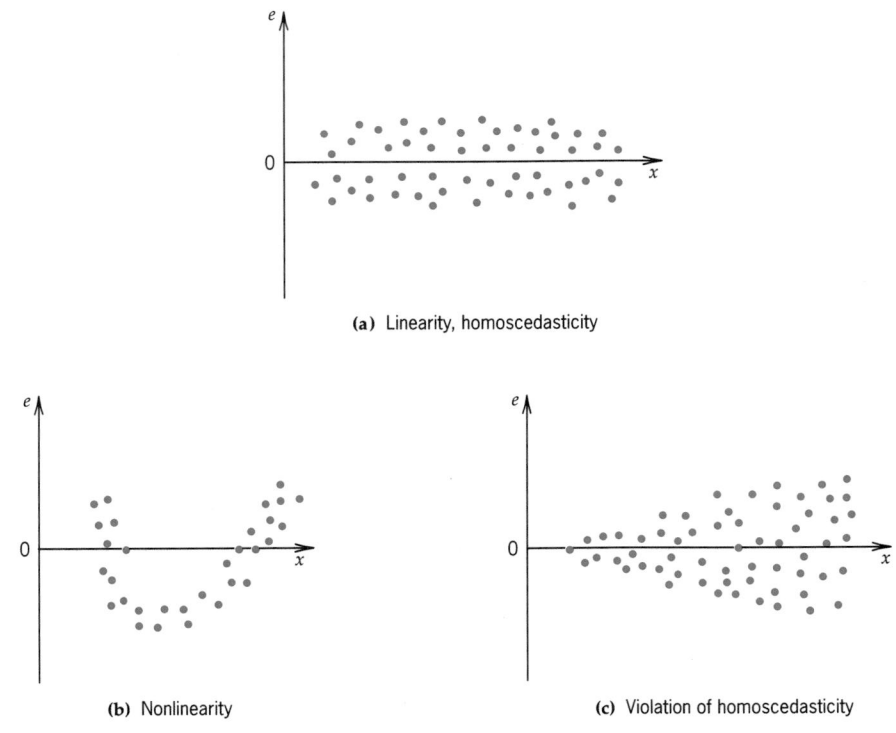

(a) Linearity, homoscedasticity

(b) Nonlinearity

(c) Violation of homoscedasticity

Figure 10.5

Some Hypothetical Residual Plots

Figure 10.5(a) does not suggest any departure from homoscedasticity. Figure 10.5(c) shows the variance increasing as x increases—a violation of the homoscedasticity requirement. Figure 10.6 is a residual plot for the salary data in Table 10.1. There do not appear to be any systematic departures from linearity or homoscedasticity.

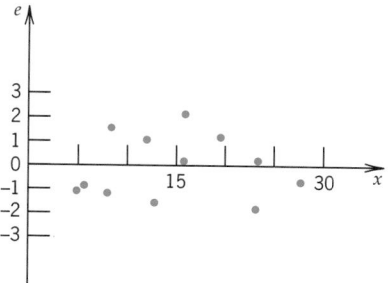

Figure 10.6
Residual Plot for the Salary Data
(No Departures from the Linear
Regression Model Are Indicated.)

If you know that the data were randomly obtained, there should be no problem with independence. But sometimes data obtained sequentially over time are dependent. A good way to check for independence is to plot the residuals against time or order in which the data were obtained. When the y values are independent, the residuals will be more or less randomly distributed above and below the zero line with no apparent pattern. (See Figure 10.7(a) for a hypothetical residual plot suggesting independence.) However, a pattern in the residual plots would suggest dependence.

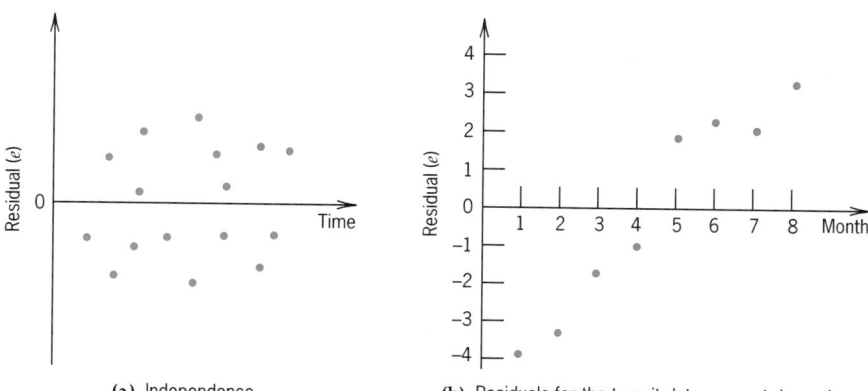

(a) Independence

(b) Residuals for the transit data suggest dependence.

Figure 10.7
Residuals Versus Time

The data in Table 10.2 represent ridership data collected by a transit authority sequentially over an 8-month period for one of its transit lines. During this period, the entire fleet of vehicles was gradually being replaced by a fleet of modern, fast, climate-controlled vehicles. The variables are

x = average total accumulation of commuters downtown at 5:00 P.M. (in thousands)
y = average number of rush-hour transit riders on the line (in thousands)

Table 10.2
Transit Data. Regression Line: $\hat{y} = -3.16 + .476x, r = .81$

Month	Average Total Accumulation of Commuters (x) in Thousands	Average Rush-Hour Ridership (y) in Thousands	Expected $(\hat{y})$	Residual $(e = y - \hat{y})$
1	40	12	15.89	−3.89
2	43	14	17.32	−3.32
3	50	19	20.65	−1.65
4	36	13	13.98	−.98
5	55	25	23.03	1.97
6	50	23	20.65	2.35
7	40	18	15.89	2.11
8	31	15	11.60	3.40

Figure 10.7(b) is a graph of the residuals in Table 10.2 against time. This shows a clear pattern for the residuals, indicating dependence of the y values. The residuals are negative in the early months, gradually increasing until they are positive in later months. Since $e = y - \hat{y}$, actual ridership (y) was below expected ridership $(\hat{y})$ in earlier months and above expected ridership in later months. There is a simple explanation for this: As more of the old vehicles were replaced by the new vehicles, riding on the line became more attractive, and more of the available commuters were drawn to the line, thus increasing ridership above the expected level.

Since the pattern of the residuals suggests that the y values are dependent, the inference techniques of this chapter would not be appropriate for the data in Table 10.2.

EXERCISES

Unless otherwise stated, assume that the assumptions of the linear regression model are satisfied.

10.1   Consider the following table:

x	y
0	0
0	3
0	6
1	6
2	6
2	9
2	12

(a)   Use a 5% level of significance and test the hypotheses $H_0: \beta_1 = 0$ and $H_a: \beta_1 > 0$.
(b)   Find a 95% confidence interval for the slope β_1.

10.2   Consider the following table:

x	y
1	2
1	4
3	6
3	8
5	10
5	12
7	14
7	16

(a)   At the 1% level of significance, would you conclude that there is a positive linear relationship between the x and y values of the population?

(b)   Find a 99% confidence interval for the slope β_1 of the population regression line.

10.3   Consider the following table:

x	y
1	11
1	10
1	9
5	8
5	6
9	5
9	4
9	3

(a)   At the 5% level of significance, would you conclude that there is a negative linear relationship between the x and y values of the population?

(b)   Find a 95% confidence interval for the slope β_1 of the population regression line.

10.4   Consider the following table:

x	y
4	12
4	11
6	10
6	9
8	7
8	6

(a)   At the 1% level of significance, would you conclude that there is a negative linear relationship between the x and y values of the population?

(b)   Find a 99% confidence interval for the slope β_1 of the population regression line.

10.5 Consider the following data:

x	y
3	11
4	13
6	9
7	10
9	8
10	6
12	10

At the 5% level of significance, would you conclude that there is a linear relationship between the x and y values of the population?

10.6 A retailer wanted to investigate the relationship between the intensity of advertising (x) and the number of big-ticket items (y) sold per week. The intensity of advertising was indexed from 1 for no advertising to 5 for the most intensive advertising. The data are given in the following table.

Intensity of Advertising (x)	Number of Items Sold (y)
1	6
2	9
3	13
4	16
5	21

At the 5% level of significance, does there appear to be a positive linear relationship between sales and intensity of advertising?

10.7 A developer intended to build a racquetball club in a city of 135,000 people but was undecided as to the number of courts to build. The data in the following table concern a flourishing chain of racquetball clubs. The data represent the population of a city (x) and the number of courts (y) the chain has in that city.

Population in Thousands (x)	Number of Courts (y)
150	13
230	16
265	21
90	8
75	6
190	12
105	8
175	14

(a)   Is there sufficient evidence to indicate a linear relationship between the x and y values for the population? Use a 1% level of significance. The value of the linear correlation coefficient is $r = .963741$.

(b)   The line of best fit is given by $\hat{y} = 1.08 + .07x$. What number of courts would you recommend the developer build?

(c)   Check to see whether any assumptions of the linear regression model are violated. Do your results in parts (a) and (b) appear to be reliable?

10.8   The data in the following table represent 18 high school grade point averages (x) and final introductory statistics grades (y). Note that $\sum x = 49.6$, $\sum y = 1441$, $\sum x^2 = 142.10$, $\sum y^2 = 117{,}909$, $\sum xy = 4070.7$, and SSE $= 707.486$.

Grade Point Average (x)	Final Grade (y)
2.0	54
2.0	69
2.1	53
2.1	73
2.1	78
2.4	72
2.4	83
2.7	76
2.7	82
2.7	85
3.0	86
3.0	88
3.3	85
3.3	87
3.3	88
3.3	90
3.6	95
3.6	97

(a)   Use a 5% level of significance and test the hypothesis that there is a positive linear relationship between the x and y values of the population.

(b)   What is the estimated increase in y given an increase of .5 in x?

(c)   Check to see whether any assumptions of the linear regression model are violated. Do your results in parts (a) and (b) appear to be reliable?

10.9   In Exercise 4.51, we discussed 38 automobiles with gas mileage in miles per gallon (y) and number of cylinders (x). The linear correlation coefficient is $r = -.81$, and the line of best fit is given by $\hat{y} = 42.509 - 3.290x$.

(a)   Use a 5% level of significance and test whether there is a negative linear relationship between miles per gallon and number of cylinders.

(b)   What is the estimated difference in gas mileage between 4-cylinder and 8-cylinder cars?

10.10   A scatter diagram of time in minutes (y) to finish the 1986 Boston Marathon versus age (x) for 20 randomly selected male runners under 40 years of age is given at the top of page 466. This problem was discussed in Exercise 4.52.

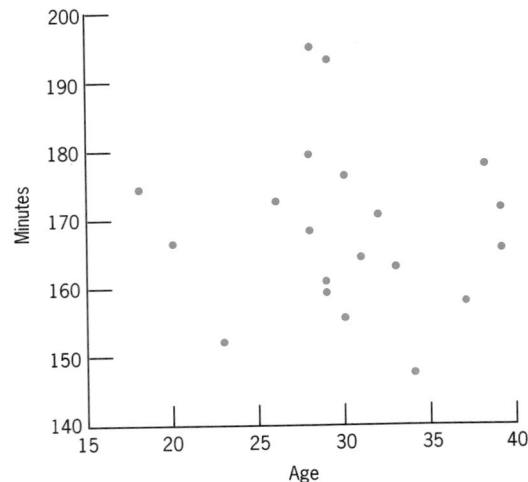

Consider the following summary information:

$$\sum x = 601 \quad \sum x^2 = 18{,}689 \quad \sum y = 3380.99 \quad \sum y^2 = 574{,}386.6793 \quad \sum xy = 101{,}462.51$$

Comment on whether there appears to be a linear relationship between y and x. Use a 5% significance level and test the hypotheses of no linear relationship versus a linear relationship. (Use the alternate formula for t.)

10.11   The accompanying Data Desk output represents measurements, discussed in Exercise 4.19, on 38 1978–1979 model automobiles. Gas mileage (MPG) in miles per gallon (y) was measured by Consumers' Union on a test track. The variable weight (x) was reported by the automobile manufacturer. Use the printout to answer the following questions. Notice that the last line in the printout gives b_1, s_{b_1}, observed value of t, and an upper bound for the P-value. Statistical packages usually give a P-value for a two-tailed test in regression output. The P-value for a one-tailed test is obtained by dividing the two-tailed P-value by 2.

Dependent variable is: MPG
R squared = 81.6%   R squared (adjusted) = 81.1%
s = 2.851 with 38 - 2 = 36 degrees of freedom

Variable	Coefficient	s.e. of Coeff	t-ratio	prob
Constant	48.7075	1.954	25.0	≤ 0.0002
Weight	-8.36459	0.6631	-12.6	≤ 0.0002

(a)   To test the hypotheses H_0: $\beta_1 = 0$, H_a: $\beta_1 < 0$ at the 1% significance level, give the observed t value. Is the test statistically significant at the 1% level?

(b)   Find a 95% confidence interval for the slope β_1 of the population regression line.

10.12   The following data were used in Exercise 10.3:

x	1	1	1	5	5	9	9	9
y	11	10	9	8	6	5	4	3

Use the partial Minitab printout to answer the following questions. Notice that the next-to-last line in the printout gives b_1, s_{b_1}, observed value of t, and the P-value.

Regression Analysis

Predictor	Coef	Stdev	t-ratio	p
Constant	10.7500	0.6208	17.32	0.000
x	-0.7500	0.1021	-7.35	0.000

s = 1.000   R-sq = 90.0%

(a)   Give the equation of the sample regression line.

(b)   Consider the hypotheses H_0: $\beta_1 = 0$ and H_a: $\beta_1 < 0$. Give the observed t value. Is the test statistically significant at the 5% level?

(c)   Obtain the residual for the observation $x = 5$, $y = 8$.

10.3

INFERENCE CONCERNING CORRELATION

In Section 10.2, we saw that we can investigate linearity in a bivariate population of (x, y) values by studying the slope β_1 of the population regression line. We can also consider the linear correlation coefficient for the population. This is denoted by ρ (the Greek letter rho). If $\rho = 0$, there is no linear relationship between the variables x and y. But if $\rho \neq 0$, there is at least some degree of linear relationship. In other words, the pairs of (x, y) values for the population are scattered about a nonhorizontal line—the population regression line.

When investigating linearity for a population, we can test

$$H_0: \quad \rho = 0 \quad \text{(There is no linear relationship.)}$$
$$H_a: \quad \rho \neq 0 \quad \text{(There is a linear relationship.)}$$

The sample correlation coefficient r may be thought of as a rough estimate for ρ. If $\rho = 0$, the value of r should not be too far from 0. But if r is too far from 0 (i.e., too close to 1 or -1) to be consistent with H_0, we reject H_0 in favor of H_a.[*] The value of r will be considered too far from 0 if it is unlikely that we would observe a value so far from 0 (if H_0 were true).

To test these hypotheses, we can find critical values of r from Appendix Table B.7. The table enables us to use either of two levels of significance: .01 or .05. Suppose that we decided to conduct a test using $\alpha = .01$ based on a sample of 12 pairs of (x, y) values. From Appendix Table B.7, we see that for $n = 12$, the critical value (call it c) is .708. This is the right critical value for a two-tailed test. See Figure 10.8.

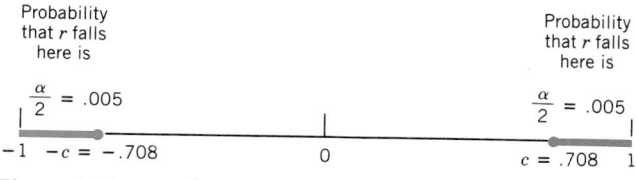

Figure 10.8
Critical Region for r When $\alpha = .01$ and $n = 12$

---

[*]Keep in mind that $-1 \leq r \leq 1$.

The critical region consists of the values of r from .708 to 1 and from $-.708$ to -1. If the value of r computed from the sample data falls in the critical region, we reject H_0 and conclude that the variables x and y tend to show a linear relationship ($\rho \neq 0$). In this case, we say that the x and y values for the sample data showed a *significant degree of linear relationship*.

Recall the salary data discussed in Section 10.2 (see Table 10.1). In Example 4.4, it was shown that for these data $r = .97$. We concluded that this value is quite close to 1 and does seem to indicate a strong linear relationship. Figure 10.8 seems to confirm this for the population because $r = .97$ falls in the critical region. That is, we reject H_0 (which asserts no linear relationship) in favor of H_a (which asserts a linear relationship for the population). The value of .97 is quite close to 1, but sometimes it is not so obvious whether a significant linear relationship exists. The hypothesis-testing procedure discussed in this section can be very useful in making a decision in these cases.

We now summarize the steps in a test for a linear relationship between two variables.

---

1. *Hypotheses:*

    $$H_0: \quad \rho = 0 \qquad \text{(There is no linear relationship.)}$$
    $$H_a: \quad \rho \neq 0 \qquad \text{(There is a linear relationship.)}$$

2. *Level of significance:*   We use $\alpha = .01$ or $\alpha = .05$.

3. *Test statistic:*   We use the linear correlation coefficient r, obtained from the sample data.

4. *Critical region:*   We perform a two-tailed test. Using Appendix Table B.7, we find the right critical value c. The critical region consists of values of $r \geq c$ or $r \leq -c$, as shown in Figure 10.9.

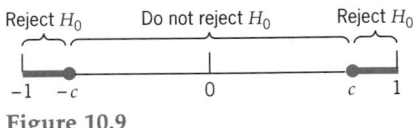

Figure 10.9

5. *Decision:*   If the value of r from step 3 is $r \geq c$ or $r \leq -c$, reject H_0 and conclude that there is a linear relationship between the variables x and y. Otherwise, we do not reject H_0; in this case, there is no evidence of a linear relationship.

Assumptions: The properties of the linear regression model are satisfied.

EXAMPLE 10.3

For each student in a computer science seminar, a computer science professor recorded the number of hours logged on the computer (x) while preparing for a final exam, along with the score on the final examination (y). The results are given in Table 10.3.

Table 10.3

Student	Hours on Computer (x)	Score on Final Examination (y)
1	5	60
2	8	60
3	10	70
4	12	65
5	14	85
6	15	70
7	18	80
8	20	90

Do these data indicate a significant degree of linear relationship between the variables x and y? Use the 5% level of significance.

Solution

The question is whether there would be a linear relationship between the x and y values for the population of all possible students who have taken, or will take, this course or a similar course. We are asking whether the population correlation coefficient ρ is different from 0.

1. *Hypotheses:*

   H_0: $\rho = 0$ (There is no linear relationship.)

   H_a: $\rho \neq 0$ (There is a linear relationship.)

2. *Level of significance:* $\alpha = .05$

3. *Test statistic and observed value:*   We must compute the value of r, the linear correlation coefficient for the sample.

Table 10.4

x	y	xy	x^2	y^2
5	60	300	25	3,600
8	60	480	64	3,600
10	70	700	100	4,900
12	65	780	144	4,225
14	85	1190	196	7,225
15	70	1050	225	4,900
18	80	1440	324	6,400
20	90	1800	400	8,100
Sums: 102	580	7740	1478	42,950 $n = 8$

$$r = \frac{n(\sum xy) - (\sum x)(\sum y)}{\sqrt{n(\sum x^2) - (\sum x)^2} \cdot \sqrt{n(\sum y^2) - (\sum y)^2}}$$

$$= \frac{(8)(7740) - (102)(580)}{\sqrt{(8)(1478) - (102)^2} \cdot \sqrt{(8)(42{,}950) - (580)^2}}$$

$$= \frac{2760}{\sqrt{1420} \cdot \sqrt{7200}} = .8631746 \doteq .86$$

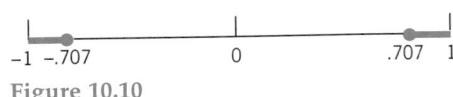

Figure 10.10

4. *Critical region:* From Appendix Table B.7, we see that for sample size $n = 8$ and $\alpha = .05$, the critical values are $\pm.707$, as shown in Figure 10.10.

5. *Decision:* Since the observed value $r = .86$ is in the critical region, we reject H_0 in favor of H_a. This means that there is a linear relationship.

Remark   The test in Example 10.3 of $\rho = 0$ versus $\rho \neq 0$ is actually equivalent to a test of $\beta_1 = 0$ versus $\beta_1 \neq 0$. One advantage of the test of ρ is that it involves less computation than a test involving β_1. A disadvantage is that Appendix Table B.7 gives critical values for a two-tailed test with only two values of α (.01 and .05). The test of β_1 we have described can be left-, right-, or two-tailed. Using the .01 and .05 critical values, you can do a one-tailed test at the .005 and .025 levels, respectively. If you want more flexibility, you can do a t test (right-, left-, or two-tailed) using the t statistic

$$t = r\sqrt{\frac{n-2}{1-r^2}}$$

This has $n - 2$ degrees of freedom.

Statistical Significance Does Not Necessarily Imply Practical Significance

Some assume that a significant value for r implies a strong linear relationship. For example, when testing the hypotheses

$$H_0: \quad \rho = 0$$
$$H_a: \quad \rho \neq 0$$

the value of r for the sample data is *statistically significant* if we reject H_0. This implies that there is some degree of linear relationship between the x and y values for the population but not necessarily a *strong* relationship. For example, if we had $n = 100$ pairs of (x, y) values and we were using the 5% level of significance, a value of $r = .2$ would lead to the rejection of H_0, indicating a linear relationship between the variables x and y. (See Appendix Table B.7. The critical values of r are $\pm.196$ when $n = 100$.) Therefore, there is some degree of linear relationship. But notice that the coefficient of determination is $r^2 = .04$. This means that only 4% of the variability of the y values (in the sample) can be accounted for by the linear relationship. In this case, the regression line may not be a reliable predictor of y values. Therefore, there is no *practical* significance to the linear relationship.

EXERCISES

In the following exercises, assume that the properties of the linear regression model are satisfied.

In Exercises 10.13–10.16, do the sample data indicate a linear relationship between the x and y values for the population? First, calculate the linear correlation coefficient r. Then test the hypotheses $H_0: \rho = 0, H_a: \rho \neq 0$.

10.13 Use $\alpha = .05$. **10.14** Use $\alpha = .05$.

x	y
2	1
2	4
2	7
3	7
4	10
4	13
4	16

x	y
3	13
3	12
3	11
4	9
4	8
5	4
5	3
5	2

10.15 Use $\alpha = .01$. **10.16** Use $\alpha = .05$.

x	y
1	2
2	2
3	1
4	0
5	0

x	y
0	3
2	5
4	6
6	4

10.17 The data in the following table represent percent sugars (x) and cost (y) for eight hot cereals (*Source: Consumer Reports,* 1982, p. 71).

Percent Sugars (x)	Cost per Serving (in cents) (y)
5	4
31	11
3	9
4	6
11	6
29	11
8	8
5	4

Do the sample data indicate a linear relationship between the x and y variables? Use a 5% level of significance.

10.18 The data in the table at the top of page 472 represent domestic (x) and export (y) factory sales, in millions, of passenger cars for the years 1982–1987 (*Source: The 1989 Information Please Almanac,* p. 76).

Domestic (x)	Exports (y)
4.70	35
6.20	54
7.03	59
7.34	67
6.87	65
6.49	60

Is there sufficient evidence to indicate a linear relationship between the x and y variables? Use a 5% level of significance.

10.19 In Exercise 4.31, we discussed the *Index of Exposure* to contaminants in the Columbia River from the Hanford Atomic Storage Preserve and *Cancer Incidence* (cancer deaths per 100,000 people) for nine counties downriver from Hanford. *Index of Exposure* is a measure of exposure to the river and proximity to Hanford; the higher the index, the more exposure to contaminants. The data are reproduced here.

County	Index of Exposure (x)	Cancer Incidence (y)
Umatilla	2.49	147.1
Morrow	2.57	130.1
Gilliam	3.41	129.9
Sherman	1.25	113.5
Wasco	1.62	137.5
Hood River	3.83	162.3
Portland	11.64	207.5
Columbia	6.41	177.9
Clatsop	8.34	210.3

The summary statistics are

$$\sum x = 41.56 \quad \sum y = 1416.1 \quad \sum xy = 7439.37 \quad \sum x^2 = 289.4222 \quad \sum y^2 = 232,498.97$$

Do the data suggest a linear relationship between the variables? Use the 1% significance level.

10.20 A college admissions officer wanted to determine whether a linear relationship existed between SAT math (x) and SAT verbal (y) scores for entering students with an undeclared major. The official had data for 104 students. Do the data presented here indicate a linear relationship between the x and y variables? Use a 1% level of significance.

$$\sum x = 45,210 \quad \sum x^2 = 20,242,300 \quad \sum y = 56,760 \quad \sum y^2 = 31,169,200 \quad \sum xy = 24,794,300$$

10.21 The following JMP printout uses the number of home runs hit by American League home run leaders in the years 1954–1993 (y) and the number of home runs hit by National League home run leaders in the years 1954–1993 (x).

(a) Find the linear correlation coefficient r.

(b) Is there sufficient evidence to indicate a linear relationship between the x and y variables? Use a 5% level of significance.

Summary of Fit

RSquare	0.037730
Observations (or Sum Wgts)	40

Parameter Estimates

Term	Estimate	Std Error	t Ratio	Prob>|t|
Intercept	30.360331	9.173952	3.31	0.0021
NL	0.2596885	0.212747	1.22	0.2297

10.22   In Example 10.1, we discussed the relationship between years of experience (x) and salary in thousands (y) for the technicians' data. We now look at the same data but with salary as x and years of experience as y. Consider the Maple V printout shown here:

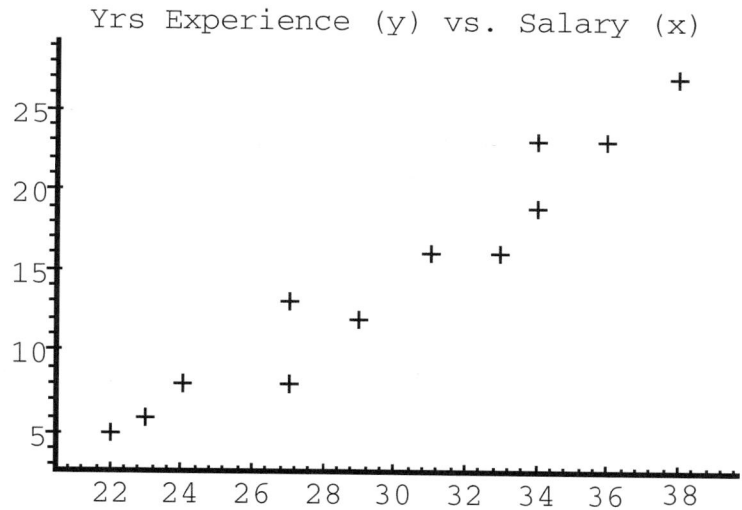

Yrs Experience (y) vs. Salary (x)

linearcorrelation (x, y); .968

$$\text{fit[leastsquare[x,y]];} \quad y = -\frac{46199}{1858} + \frac{1231}{929}x$$

(a)   Does there appear to be a strong linear relationship between salary (x) and years of experience (y)?

(b)   Estimate the number of years experience for a technician with a salary of $30,000.

10.4

PREDICTION INTERVALS AND CONFIDENCE INTERVALS (OPTIONAL)

We have seen that the regression line for a sample of (x, y) values is often used to estimate or predict an unknown y value corresponding to a given x value. For example, in Section 10.2, we looked at salary data for 12 technicians (Table 10.1). The equation of the regression line was

$$\hat{y} = 19.47 + .71x$$

An estimate of the salary for a technician with 15 years experience is

$$\hat{y} = 19.47 + (.71)(15) = 30.12$$

(This is equivalent to $30,120.) If we wanted to predict the salary of a technician with 15 years experience, we would use this figure. The actual value of y will be hopefully not too far from $\hat{y}$. We can calculate a type of confidence interval for y called a **prediction interval.** We select a level of confidence $1 - \alpha$. Then we use a procedure to find an interval such that the confidence is $1 - \alpha$ that the procedure will yield an interval containing y.

To estimate the mean salary of *all* technicians with 15 years experience in the field ($\mu_{y|15}$), we use the same figure, $30,120. We can also find an interval that hopefully contains the mean, a **1 − α confidence interval.** Since individual y values can be quite variable, we can expect prediction intervals to be wider than confidence intervals.

Prediction intervals and confidence intervals are both types of interval estimates, and we have seen that interval estimates often take the general form

$$(\text{estimate}) \pm t \cdot (\text{standard deviation})$$

Prediction intervals and confidence intervals take this same general form. In fact, they differ from one another only in the standard deviation. We will have more to say about the structure of these intervals at the end of this section.

Let's first consider prediction intervals.

---

1 − α Prediction Interval for y When $x = x_0$ Calculate the value of

$$S = \sqrt{\frac{\text{SSE}}{n-2}} = \sqrt{\frac{\sum(y - \hat{y})^2}{n-2}}$$

This is called the *standard deviation from the regression line* and is an estimate of the standard deviation (σ) of y values from the population regression line. Using the regression line, calculate the predicted value of y when $x = x_0$,

$$\hat{y}_0 = b_0 + b_1 x_0$$

Now use Appendix Table B.4 to find the t value, $t_{\alpha/2}$, based on df $= n - 2$. Then a $1 - \alpha$ prediction interval for y when $x = x_0$ is defined by the endpoints

$$\hat{y}_0 \pm t_{\alpha/2} \cdot S \cdot \sqrt{1 + \frac{1}{n} + \frac{(x_0 - \bar{x})^2}{(\sum x^2) - (\sum x)^2/n}}$$

Assumptions: The properties of the linear regression model are satisfied.

EXAMPLE 10.4

Refer to the salary data of Example 10.1. Find a 95% prediction interval for the annual salary of a technician with 15 years experience.

Solution

We have seen that the regression equation is

$$\hat{y} = 19.47 + .71x$$

and the predicted salary for a technician with $x = x_0 = 15$ years experience is

$$\hat{y}_0 = 19.47 + (.71)(15) = 30.12 \text{ (thousand dollars)}$$

From Example 10.1,

$$n = 12 \qquad \sum x^2 = 3162 \qquad \sum x = 176 \qquad S \doteq 1.40$$

Hence, $\bar{x} = 176/12 \doteq 14.67$. Our level of confidence is 95%. So $1 - \alpha = .95$ and $\alpha = .05$. Using Appendix Table B.4, we find that when df $= n - 2 = 10$,

$$t_{\alpha/2} = t_{.025} = 2.228$$

The prediction interval has endpoints

$$\hat{y}_0 \pm t_{\alpha/2} \cdot S \cdot \sqrt{1 + \frac{1}{n} + \frac{(x_0 - \bar{x})^2}{(\sum x^2) - (\sum x)^2/n}}$$

or

$$30.12 \pm (2.228)(1.40)\sqrt{1 + \frac{1}{12} + \frac{(15 - 14.67)^2}{3162 - (176)^2/12}}$$

$$30.12 \pm (2.228)(1.40)\sqrt{1.0835209}$$

$$30.12 \pm (2.228)(1.40)(1.0409231)$$

$$30.12 \pm 3.25$$

or 26.87 to 33.37. Hence our confidence is 95% that the actual value of y will be between \$26,870 and \$33,370.

In Example 10.4, we found an interval estimate for the salary of an *individual* technician with 15 years of experience. But we may also be interested in estimating the mean salary for *all* technicians in the population with 15 years of experience, $\mu_{y|15}$. We said that the point estimate for the mean is the same as the point estimate for an individual y (\$30,120). We construct a $1 - \alpha$ **confidence interval** for the mean as follows:

$1 - \alpha$ **Confidence Interval for** $\mu_{y|x_0}$ (the mean of all y values corresponding to $x = x_0$) The point estimate for $\mu_{y|x_0}$ is obtained from our computed regression line

$$\hat{y}_0 = b_0 + b_1 x_0$$

The $1 - \alpha$ confidence interval is defined by the endpoints

$$\hat{y}_0 \pm t_{\alpha/2} \cdot S \cdot \sqrt{\frac{1}{n} + \frac{(x_0 - \bar{x})^2}{(\sum x^2) - (\sum x)^2/n}}$$

where $t_{\alpha/2}$ is obtained from Appendix Table B.4 based on df $= n - 2$ and S is the standard deviation from the regression line.

Assumptions: The properties of the linear regression model are satisfied.

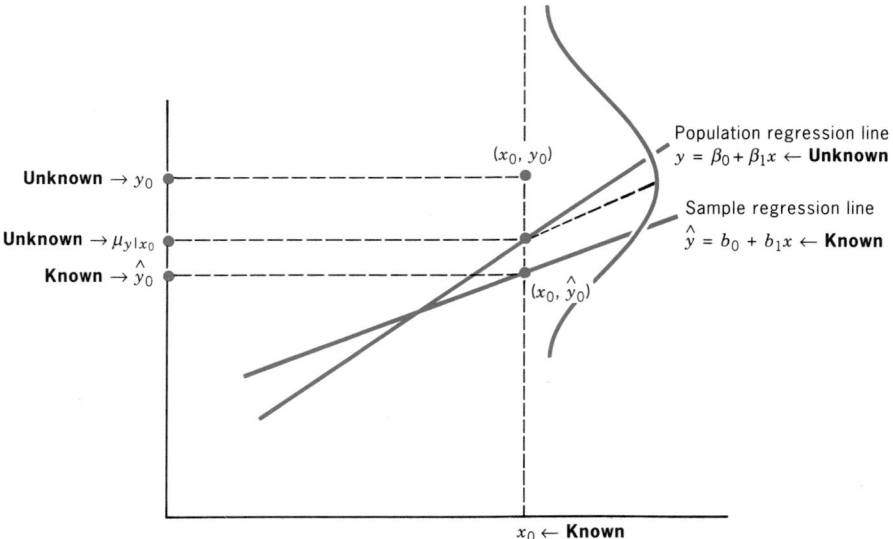

Figure 10.11
$\hat{y}_0$ **Is a Point Estimate for Both an** *Individual y* **Value (y_0) and the Mean of** *All y* **Values Corresponding to the Value** x_0 **($\mu_{y|x_0}$).**

Figure 10.11 shows the relationship between the estimate $\hat{y}_0$ and the quantities being estimated.

EXAMPLE 10.5
Referring to the salary data in Example 10.4, find a 95% confidence interval for the mean salary of all technicians with 15 years experience ($\mu_{y|15}$).

Solution
As noted, the point estimate is obtained from the computed regression line when $x = x_0 = 15$:

$$\hat{y}_0 = 19.47 + (.71)(15) = 30.12 \text{ (thousand dollars)}$$

From Example 10.4, $S \doteq 1.40, t_{\alpha/2} = t_{.025} = 2.228, \sum x^2 = 3162, \sum x = 176$, and $\bar{x} = 14.67$. Thus the $1 - \alpha$ confidence interval for $\mu_{y|15}$ is

$$\hat{y}_0 \pm t_{\alpha/2} \cdot S \cdot \sqrt{\frac{1}{n} + \frac{(x_0 - \bar{x})^2}{(\sum x^2) - (\sum x)^2/n}}$$

or

$$30.12 \pm (2.228)(1.40)\sqrt{\frac{1}{12} + \frac{(15 - 14.67)^2}{3162 - (176)^2/12}}$$

$$30.12 \pm (2.228)(1.40)\sqrt{.0835209}$$

$$30.12 \pm (2.228)(1.40)(.2889998)$$

$$30.12 \pm .90$$

or 29.22 to 31.02. Thus we are 95% confident that the mean salary for those with 15 years experience is between \$29,220 and \$31,020.

In Example 10.4, we found that a 95% prediction interval for the salary of a technician with 15 years experience went from 26.87 to 33.37 (thousand dollars). If you were to find a 95% prediction interval for the salary of a technician with $x_0 = 25$ years experience, you would obtain the endpoints

$$33.71 \text{ to } 40.73$$

The width of this interval is 7.02. In Example 10.4, where the number of years of experience was $x_0 = 15$, the width of the prediction interval was 6.50. We can understand this difference by examining the formula for the prediction interval. Note the term

$$\frac{(x_0 - \bar{x})^2}{(\sum x^2) - (\sum x)^2 / n}$$

As the value of x_0 gets farther from $\bar{x}$, this term gets larger, producing a wider prediction interval. In Example 10.4, the value of x_0 was 15, which is quite close to $\bar{x} = 14.67$. But the value 25 is farther from $\bar{x}$, accounting for the wider prediction interval.

The same is true of the confidence interval: It gets wider the farther x_0 is from $\bar{x}$. See Figure 10.12. We can also see in Figure 10.12 that a prediction interval is wider than a confidence interval. In the previous examples, we found that a prediction interval for an individual salary for 15 years experience went from $26,870 to $33,370. But a confidence interval for the mean salary (for 15 years experience) went from $29,220 to $31,020. The reason for this can be seen by comparing the formulas. The formula for a prediction interval has an additional term (1) under the radical, making the prediction interval wider than the confidence interval.

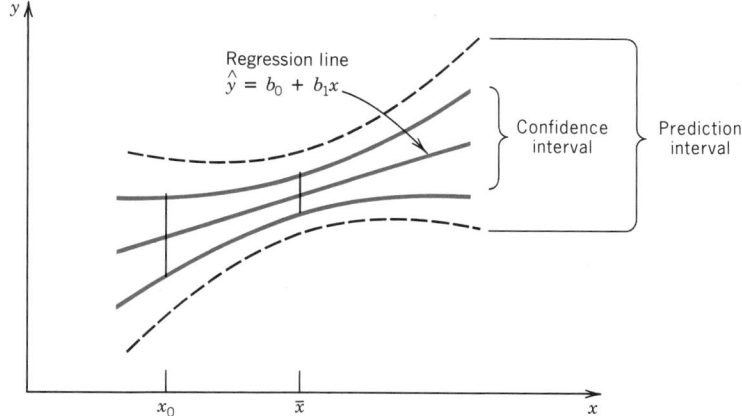

Figure 10.12
Prediction Intervals Are Wider than Confidence Intervals. The Width of Both Intervals Increases as x_0 Gets Farther from $\bar{x}$.

Background Discussion

We noted previously that our prediction and confidence intervals take the form

$$(\text{estimate}) \pm t \cdot (\text{standard deviation})$$

Here we mean the standard deviation of the distance between the estimate and that which is being estimated. We used $\hat{y}_0$ to estimate $\mu_{y|x_0}$. See Figure 10.11. Now $\hat{y}_0$ can be thought of as a variable. (In repeated sampling, its value could change because the regression line could change.) It can be shown that an estimate of the variance of $\hat{y}_0$ from the population regression line is

$$S_{\hat{y}_0}^2 = S^2 \left[\frac{1}{n} + \frac{(x_0 - \bar{x})^2}{(\sum x^2) - (\sum x)^2/n} \right]$$

Therefore

$$S_{\hat{y}_0} = S \sqrt{\frac{1}{n} + \frac{(x_0 - \bar{x})^2}{(\sum x^2) - (\sum x)^2/n}}$$

Thus our $1 - \alpha$ confidence interval for $\mu_{y|x_0}$ is

$$\hat{y}_0 \pm t_{\alpha/2} S \sqrt{\frac{1}{n} + \frac{(x_0 - \bar{x})^2}{(\sum x^2) - (\sum x)^2/n}}$$

What about the prediction interval? In Figure 10.11, the distance from y_0 to $\hat{y}_0$ consists of two components: the distance from y_0 to the population regression line, and the distance from the population regression line to $\hat{y}_0$. The variance of the first distance is estimated by S^2, the second by $S_{\hat{y}_0}^2$. The overall variance is the sum of these:

$$S^2 + S_{\hat{y}_0}^2 = S^2 + S^2 \left[\frac{1}{n} + \frac{(x_0 - \bar{x})^2}{(\sum x^2) - (\sum x)^2/n} \right]$$

$$= S^2 \left[1 + \frac{1}{n} + \frac{(x_0 - \bar{x})^2}{(\sum x^2) - (\sum x)^2/n} \right]$$

$$\text{standard deviation} = \sqrt{S^2 + S_{\hat{y}_0}^2}$$

$$= S \sqrt{1 + \frac{1}{n} + \frac{(x_0 - \bar{x})^2}{(\sum x^2) - (\sum x)^2/n}}$$

Thus our $1 - \alpha$ prediction interval is

$$\hat{y}_0 \pm t_{\alpha/2} S \sqrt{1 + \frac{1}{n} + \frac{(x_0 - \bar{x})^2}{(\sum x^2) - (\sum x)^2/n}}$$

EXERCISES

In the following exercises, assume that the properties of the linear regression model are satisfied.

10.23   Consider the data

x	y
2	12
4	9
5	8
6	6
8	5

(a)   Find the line of best fit.

(b)   Estimate y when $x = 7$.

(c)   Find a 95% prediction interval for y when $x = 7$.

(d)   Find a 95% confidence interval for $\mu_{y|7}$.

10.24   Consider the data

x	y
4	2
4	2
4	5
6	6
8	7
8	9
15	9

(a)   Find the line of best fit.

(b)   Estimate y when $x = 5$.

(c)   Find a 95% prediction interval for y when $x = 5$.

(d)   Find a 95% confidence interval for $\mu_{y|5}$.

10.25   An automotive engineer, interested in the relationship between miles per gallon y and horsepower x, sampled 30 cars and obtained the following information:

$$\sum x = 2444 \qquad \sum x^2 = 204,232$$

Assume $r \doteq -.777$, $\hat{y} = 56.90 - .31x$, and SSE $= 315.11$.

(a)   Is there sufficient evidence to indicate a linear relationship between the x and y values for the population? Use a 5% level of significance.

(b)   Find a 95% prediction interval for miles per gallon for a car with 90 horsepower.

(c)   Find a 95% confidence interval for $\mu_{y|90}$.

10.26   Refer to Exercise 10.8 and find

(a)   A 90% prediction interval for the final statistics grade, given a grade point average of 2.5

(b)   A 90% confidence interval for $\mu_{y|2.5}$

10.27   Refer to Exercise 10.7. Assume that $n = 8$, SSE $= 12.069$, $\sum x = 1280$, $\sum x^2 = 237,100$, and $\hat{y} = 1.08 + .07x$. Recall that x is population in thousands. Find

(a)   A 90% prediction interval for the number of racquetball courts when the city size is 200,000

(b)   A 90% confidence interval for $\mu_{y|200,000}$

10.5

USING MINITAB (OPTIONAL)

In this chapter, we discussed years of experience (x) and salary in thousands of dollars (y) for 12 technicians. We entered the data in columns C1 and C2:

C1	C2
12	29
16	31
6	23
23	34
27	38
8	24
5	22
19	34
23	36
13	27
16	33
8	27

The regression equation and other information are produced as follows:

Session Command	**Dialog Box**
MTB > REGRESS C2 ON 1 PRED IN C1	**Stat ▶ Regression ▶ Regression** Type *C2* in **Response** box and *C1* in **Predictors** box Click **OK**

Output

Regression Analysis

```
The regression equation is
C2 = 19.5 + 0.707 C1

Predictor        Coef        Stdev      t-ratio        p
Constant      19.4690       0.9455        20.59    0.000
C1            0.70666       0.05825       12.13    0.000

s = 1.404        R-sq = 93.6%       R-sq(adj) = 93.0%

Analysis of Variance

SOURCE         DF          SS           MS         F        p
Regression      1       289.97       289.97    147.18    0.000
Error          10        19.70         1.97
Total          11       309.67

MTB > CORRELATION BETWEEN DATA IN C1 C2
```

Correlations (Pearson)

```
Correlation of C1 and C2 = 0.968
```

In addition to the regression equation, the REGRESS command gives other information, including b_0 and b_1 displayed under Coef. The output also lists t ratios. A t ratio is a coefficient (b_0 or b_1) divided by an estimate of its standard deviation. The t ratio of the coefficient of C1 (that is, the coefficient of x) is the most important. This is the t ratio of b_1:

$$t = \frac{b_1}{\text{standard deviation of } b_1}$$

This was studied in Section 10.2. We saw that this has Student's t distribution with df $= n - 2$. In this case, df $= 12 - 2 = 10$. In the printout, the t ratio for the coefficient of x is 12.13. When b_1 (or equivalently its t ratio) is sufficiently far from 0, we conclude that the slope (β_1) of the *population* regression line is different from 0. This in turn implies a nonhorizontal population regression line, which means that there is a linear relationship between x and y. So a two-tailed t test would be appropriate:

$$H_0: \quad \beta_1 = 0$$
$$H_a: \quad \beta_1 \neq 0$$

The P-value for $t = 12.13$ is approximately 0, indicating we should reject the null hypothesis and conclude that there is a significant linear relationship.

The value of S, the standard deviation from the regression line, is given as 1.404. We computed this in Example 10.1 from the formula

$$S = \sqrt{\frac{\text{SSE}}{n - 2}} = \sqrt{\frac{\sum (y - \hat{y})^2}{n - 2}}$$

We think of S as an estimate of σ, the standard deviation from the *population* regression line. This is the standard deviation of all y values corresponding to any fixed x value.

The coefficient of determination r^2 is given (R-sq) and (except for a difference in roundoff) agrees with the value we found in Example 4.6. The printout also gives r^2 adjusted for degrees of freedom, R-sq(adj). (For a complete discussion of this, consult a Minitab reference manual.) It suffices to say that R-sq(adj) is a certain type of estimate for the *population* coefficient of determination—an *unbiased estimator*.

Under Analysis of Variance, we see the breakdown of the total sum of squares (TSS) into sum of squares for regression (SSR) and sum of squares for residual or error (SSE). Observe that the proportion of variation explained by regression is

$$\frac{\text{SSR}}{\text{TSS}} = \frac{289.97}{309.67} \doteq .936 \quad \text{or} \quad 93.6\%, \text{which is } r^2$$

Under Analysis of Variance, we also see columns for DF (degrees of freedom) and MS (mean square). When discussed in connection with a sum of squares, degrees of freedom can be thought of as a number by which we divide a sum of squares to get a quantity called a "mean square." A mean square can be thought of as an estimate of some sort of variance, in this case the variance σ^2 from the population regression line. The **mean square for error** (or residual) is

$$\text{MSE} = \frac{\text{SSE}}{n - 2} = \frac{19.70}{10} = 1.97$$

This is an estimate for σ^2. The **mean square for regression** is

$$\text{MSR} = \frac{\text{SSR}}{1} = 289.97$$

This will be a good estimate for σ^2 only if there is no linear relationship between x and y, that is, if the population regression line is horizontal ($\beta_1 = 0$). If $\beta_1 \neq 0$, MSR will overestimate σ^2 and be much larger than MSE. This indeed appears to be the case for these data. Sometimes the ratio

$$F = \frac{\text{MSR}}{\text{MSE}} = \frac{289.97}{1.97} \doteq 147.19$$

is used to decide whether there is a linear relationship (an F test). In the case of simple regression (with one independent variable), this test is equivalent to the t test just described. In fact,

$$F = 147.19 \doteq (12.13)^2 = t^2$$

Notice that the CORRELATION command produces the value of r (.968), which agrees with the value we found in Example 4.4.

The Subcommand PREDICT

In Section 10.4, we estimated the salary of a technician with 15 years experience to be 30.12 thousand dollars. We also obtained prediction and confidence intervals. If we typed the following in the Session window:

> REGRESS C2 ON 1 PREDICTOR IN C1;
> PREDICT FOR 15.

Minitab would have given the output displayed previously as well as the following:

```
    Fit   Stdev.Fit        95% C.I.          95% P.I.
  30.069       0.406   ( 29.165, 30.973)  ( 26.813, 33.325)
```

The "fit" is $\hat{y}_0$ when $x_0 = 15$. The standard deviation of the fit is calculated from

$$S_{\hat{y}_0} = S \sqrt{\frac{1}{n} + \frac{(x_0 - \bar{x})^2}{(\sum x^2) - (\sum x)^2/n}} \doteq .47$$

The prediction and confidence intervals are approximately those we found in Examples 10.4 and 10.5.

Minitab automatically gives 95% intervals unless you specify otherwise. If we had wanted 90% intervals instead of 95%, we would need another subcommand. Type

> REGRESS C2 ON 1 PREDICTOR IN C1;
> PREDICT FOR 15;
> CONFIDENCE LEVEL 90.

We can accomplish this using dialog boxes as follows:

Stat ▶ **Regression** ▶ **Regression**
Type *C2* in **Response** box and *C1* in **Predictors** box
Click **Options**
Type *15* in box after **Prediction intervals** . . .
Type *90* in **Confidence level** box
Click **OK** twice

EXERCISES

Suggested exercises for use with Minitab are 10.1, 10.3, 10.5, 10.17, 10.18, and 10.23.

10.6

WORKING WITH DATA (OPTIONAL)

Refer to the data you obtained in Section 4.6.

1. At a 5% level of significance, does there appear to be a population linear relationship between systolic blood pressure (y) and age (x)? You may answer this by investigating the slope (β_1) or the population correlation coefficient (ρ). (You may have already computed the regression line and the correlation coefficient for the sample in Problem 1 of Section 4.6.)

2. Make a residual plot (of the residuals versus age) and a stem-and-leaf plot of the residuals. Are there any indications of departures from the properties of the linear regression model that would render the procedure in Problem 1 inappropriate? (In practice, this question should be investigated before answering the question posed in Problem 1.)

3. At a 5% level of significance, does there appear to be a population linear relationship between serum cholesterol (y) and age (x)? You may answer this by investigating the slope (β_1) or the population correlation coefficient (ρ). (You may have already computed the regression line and the correlation coefficient for the sample in Problem 3 of Section 4.6.)

4. Make a residual plot (of the residuals versus age) and a stem-and-leaf plot of the residuals. Are there any indications of departures from the properties of the linear regression model that would render the procedure in Problem 3 inappropriate? (In practice, this question should be investigated before answering the question posed in Problem 3.)

5. **(a)** Give a 95% prediction interval for the cholesterol level of a woman 45 years old.

   (b) Give a 95% confidence interval for the mean cholesterol level of women 45 years old.

10.7

SUMMARY

In this chapter, we discussed inference concerning the slope β_1 of the population regression line. A test statistic for testing hypotheses about β_1 is

$$t = \frac{b_1}{s_{b_1}} = \frac{b_1}{S / \sqrt{(\sum x^2) - (\sum x)^2 / n}}$$

where

$$S = \sqrt{\frac{\sum (y - \hat{y})^2}{n - 2}}$$

The t statistic has Student's t distribution with df $= n - 2$. A $1 - \alpha$ confidence interval for β_1 is

$$b_1 \pm t_{\alpha/2} \cdot S / \sqrt{(\sum x^2) - (\sum x)^2 / n}$$

We also discussed inference concerning correlation. To test the following hypotheses concerning a population correlation coefficient ρ:

$$H_0: \quad \rho = 0 \qquad \text{(There is no linear relationship.)}$$
$$H_a: \quad \rho \neq 0 \qquad \text{(There is a linear relationship.)}$$

we compute the correlation coefficient r for the sample data. Look up the critical value c in Appendix Table B.7. If $r \geq c$ or $r \leq -c$, reject H_0 in favor of H_a and conclude that the evidence suggests a linear relationship for the population.

A $1 - \alpha$ **prediction interval** for a y value corresponding to the x value x_0 is obtained as follows: Find the value $\hat{y}_0$ corresponding to the value x_0 from the regression line: $\hat{y}_0 = b_0 + b_1 x_0$. The $1 - \alpha$ prediction interval is

$$\hat{y}_0 \pm t_{\alpha/2} \cdot S \cdot \sqrt{1 + \frac{1}{n} + \frac{(x_0 - \bar{x})^2}{(\sum x^2) - (\sum x)^2/n}}$$

A $1 - \alpha$ **confidence interval** for the mean of *all* y values corresponding to the value x_0 is

$$\hat{y}_0 \pm t_{\alpha/2} \cdot S \cdot \sqrt{\frac{1}{n} + \frac{(x_0 - \bar{x})^2}{(\sum x^2) - (\sum x)^2/n}}$$

The methods of this chapter are appropriate when the following properties of the **linear regression model** are satisfied:

1. The y values corresponding to a particular x value constitute a normal population.

2. There is a population regression line

$$y = \beta_0 + \beta_1 x$$

3. The variance of all y values corresponding to a particular x value is the same for each x value.

4. The y values of the points in the scatter diagram are independent.

REVIEW EXERCISES

Unless otherwise indicated, assume the properties of the linear regression model are satisfied.

10.28   In Exercise 4.12, the line of best fit was found to be $\hat{y} = -15.474 + 2.355x$ for predicting lung cancer mortality rate (y) from cigarette consumption (x). The data are given in the following table:

Cigarette Consumption per Capita in Hundreds (x)	Mortality Rate per 100,000 (y)
11.8	10.4
12.5	16.5
15.7	22.9
19.2	26.6
21.9	33.8
23.3	42.8

(a) Is there sufficient evidence to indicate a positive linear relationship between the variables x and y? Use a 1% level of significance. Assume SSE = 38.804.

(b) Estimate the lung cancer mortality rate when the cigarette consumption per capita is 2000.

10.29 In Exercise 4.16, the line of best fit was found to be $\hat{y} = 3.175 + .654x$ for predicting the prime lending rate (y) from the inflation rate (x). The data are listed in the following table:

Inflation Rate (x)	Prime Lending Rate (y)
3.3	5.2
6.2	8.0
11.0	10.8
9.1	7.9
5.8	6.8
6.5	6.9
7.6	9.0

Summary data are

$$\sum x = 49.5 \qquad \sum y = 54.6 \qquad \sum x^2 = 386.79 \qquad \sum y^2 = 444.94 \qquad \sum xy = 410.14$$

(a) Is there sufficient evidence to indicate a positive linear relationship between the variables x and y? Use a 5% level of significance.

(b) Estimate the prime lending rate when the inflation rate is 7.0.

10.30 The data in the following table represent the total number of Ph.D.s in statistics (x) and the total number of Ph.D.s in mathematics (y) awarded over a 12-year period (*Source:* Moore and Olkin, 1984, p. 2). Note that $\sum x = 26.9$, $\sum y = 123.6$, $\sum x^2 = 61.69$, $\sum y^2 = 1323.08$, $\sum xy = 272.42$, and SSE = 34.435.

Number of Ph.D.s in Statistics (in Hundreds) (x)	Number of Ph.D.s in Mathematics (in Hundreds) (y)
1.5	12.2
1.6	12.4
2.1	12.8
2.5	12.2
2.2	12.0
2.3	11.5
2.5	10.0
2.5	9.6
2.6	8.4
2.3	7.7
2.3	7.5
2.5	7.3

(a) Is there sufficient evidence to indicate a negative linear relationship between the variables x and y? Use a 5% level of significance.

(b) The observations were obtained over a 12-year period. Plot the residuals against time. Which properties, if any, of the linear regression model may be violated? Would your conclusion in part (a) seem reliable?

10.31 A high school administrator wished to study the relationship between the number of years teaching (x) and the teacher's effectiveness rating (y). The effectiveness ratings are on a scale of 0 to 10. The administrator obtained the following data:

Number of Years Teaching (x)	Effectiveness Rating (y)
2	6.7
3	5.8
5	8.8
9	7.7
12	9.1
12	7.9
14	9.0

Do the sample data indicate a linear relationship between x and y? Use a 5% level of significance. (*Note:* $r = .729$)

10.32 In Exercise 4.44, we discussed average cholesterol intake (x) and male population death rate (y) from arteriosclerotic and degenerative heart disease. The data are given in the table.

Country	Cholesterol Intake in Tens of mg/day (x)	Death Rate per 10,000 (y)
United States	59	72
Finland	31	65
Holland	30	30
Italy	19	21
Greece	15	9
Yugoslavia	12	9
Japan	8	12

(a) Do the sample data indicate a linear relationship between the variables x and y? Use a 5% level of significance. (*Note:* $r = .893$)

(b) Which properties, if any, of the linear regression model may be violated? Would your conclusion in part (a) seem reliable? (*Hint:* Do any of the residuals appear to be outliers?)

10.33 In Exercise 4.13, we discussed the relationship between the temperature (x) in degrees Fahrenheit at 11 A.M. and the number (y) of customers using the health spa facilities at that time for randomly selected days during the summer.

Temperature (x)	Number of Customers (y)
65	27
67	25
75	20
81	22
85	16
87	10

(a)   Find the linear correlation coefficient.

(b)   Do the sample data indicate a linear relationship between the x and y values of the population? Use a 5% level of significance.

10.34   In Exercise 4.14, we discussed the relationship between the amount of fertilizer (x) and the number of bushels (y) of soybeans. The data are shown in the table.

Hundreds of Pounds per Acre (x)	Bushels per Acre (y)
1.0	25
2.5	32
3.0	35
3.0	32
3.4	35
4.0	39
4.0	41
4.5	40

Do the sample data indicate a linear relationship between the x and y values of the population? Use a 1% level of significance.

10.35   In Exercise 4.45, we looked at the problem of the owner of a one-bedroom apartment trying to determine what to charge per month. The apartment was located 1.5 miles from a rapid transit station. The variables x and y represent the distance from a rapid transit station (x) and the rent (y).

Distance in Miles (x)	Rent in Hundreds of Dollars (y)
.3	8.5
.5	8.0
.7	8.2
1.1	7.1
1.2	7.6
2.3	6.8
2.9	7.0
3.0	6.8

Do the sample data indicate a linear relationship between the x and y values of the population? Use a 5% level of significance.

10.36   *Fortune* magazine gave a ranking of industrial firms (based on sales, assets, profits, etc.) and then ranked the same firms 5 years later. A sample of 30 of these firms had the following summary information concerning initial rank (x) and rank 5 years later (y):

$$\sum x = 4571 \quad \sum x^2 = 941{,}239 \quad \sum y = 3860 \quad \sum y^2 = 648{,}562 \quad \sum xy = 771{,}472$$

Do the data indicate a linear relationship between the x and y variables? Use a 5% level of significance.

10.37 In Exercise 4.55, we discussed the number of home runs (y) and the total number of hits (x) for 14 American League baseball teams in the 1993 season. Consider the following Mathematica printout:

```
        Estimate    SE          TStat        PValue
  1     -151.07     161.608     -0.934792    0.368326

  x     0.202748    0.109432    1.85274      0.0886627

RSquared -> 0.222427
```

Alongside x are the values of b_1, the standard deviation of b_1, the observed value of t, and the P-value.

(a) Use the P-value approach and test the hypotheses H_0: $\beta_1 = 0$, H_a: $\beta_1 \neq 0$ at the 10% significance level.

(b) Find a 90% confidence interval for β_1. [*Hint:* The confidence interval for β_1 can be written $b_1 \pm t_{\alpha/2} \cdot s_{b_1}$, where s_{b_1} is the standard deviation of b_1, also called the standard error (SE) of b_1.] Explain why this confidence interval supports your conclusion in part (a).

10.38 In Exercise 4.56, we discussed the number of home runs (y) and the total number of hits (x) for 14 National League baseball teams in the 1993 season. Consider the following Mathematica printout:

```
        Estimate    SE          TStat         PValue
  1     -9.39694    142.216     -0.0660753    0.948406

  x     0.102196    0.0973812   1.04944       0.314651

RSquared -> 0.0840625
```

Alongside x are the values of b_1, the standard deviation of b_1, the observed value of t, and the P-value.

(a) Use the P-value approach and test the hypotheses H_0: $\beta_1 = 0$, H_a: $\beta_1 \neq 0$ at the 10% significance level.

(b) Find a 90% confidence interval for β_1. [*Hint:* The confidence interval for β_1 can be written $b_1 \pm t_{\alpha/2} \cdot s_{b_1}$, where s_{b_1} is the standard deviation of b_1, also called the standard error (SE) of b_1.] Explain why this confidence interval supports your conclusion in part (a).

10.39 Refer to Exercise 10.33. Assume $\hat{y} = 66.29 - .60x$ and SSE = 38.234. Find

(a) A 99% prediction interval for the number of customers using the facilities at 11 A.M. when the temperature is 70°F

(b) A 99% confidence interval for $\mu_{y|70}$

10.40 Refer to Exercise 10.34. Assume $\hat{y} = 20.094 + 4.655x$ and SSE = 12.501. Find

(a) A 95% prediction interval for the number of bushels per acre when $x = 3.5$

(b) A 95% confidence interval for $\mu_{y|3.5}$

10.41 Refer to Exercise 10.35. Assume $\hat{y} = 8.314 - .543x$ and SSE = .730. Find

(a) A 90% prediction interval for the amount of rent when the apartment is located 1.5 miles from a rapid transit

(b) A 90% confidence interval for $\mu_{y|1.5}$

Notes

Consumer Reports, Buying Guide Issue, 1982.

Fortune magazine; Data compiled by Donoho, D. and L. Kulwarski, in Donoho, A., D. Donoho, M. Gasko, A. Ledbetter, and C. Olsen, *MacSpin Release* 1.1, Austin, TX: D^2 Software, Inc.

Information Please Almanac, Boston: Houghton Mifflin Company, 1989.

Moore, D. S., and I. Olkin, "Academic Statistics: Growth, Change and Federal Support." *The American Statistician,* Vol. 38, No. 1, Feb. 1984, pp. 1–7.

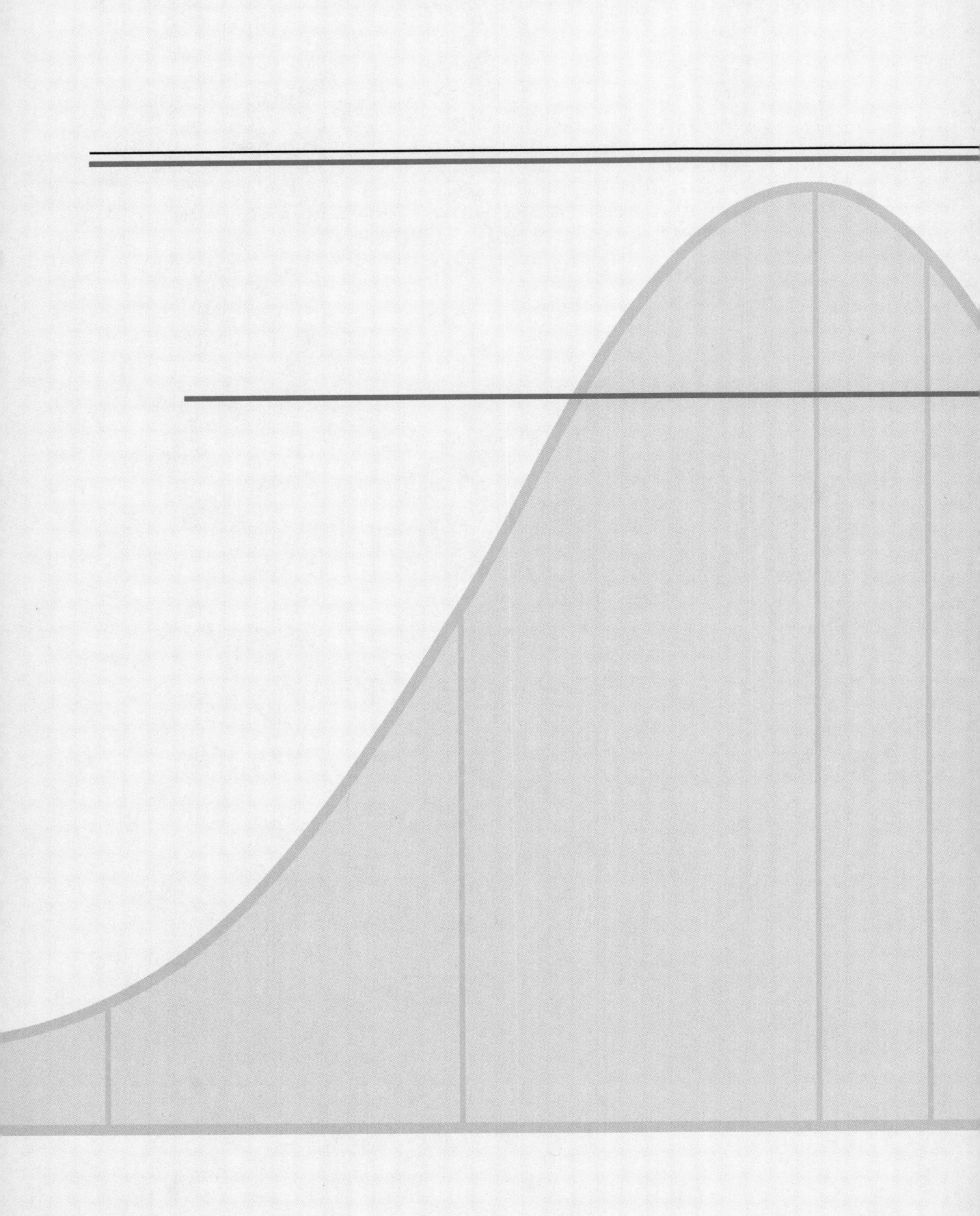

CHAPTER 11

ANALYSIS OF VARIANCE

11.1 INTRODUCTION

11.2 THE IDEA BEHIND ANALYSIS OF VARIANCE; THE CASE OF EQUAL SAMPLE SIZES

11.3 ANALYSIS OF VARIANCE WHEN SAMPLE SIZES ARE NOT NECESSARILY EQUAL; CONVENTIONAL TERMINOLOGY

11.4 ALTERNATE FORMULAS (OPTIONAL)

11.5 USING MINITAB (OPTIONAL)

11.6 WORKING WITH DATA (OPTIONAL)

11.7 SUMMARY

REVIEW EXERCISES

NOTES

11.1

INTRODUCTION

In Chapter 8, we studied inference methods (hypothesis testing and confidence intervals) concerning a single population mean. In Chapter 9, we showed how to compare two population means. In this chapter, we develop a method for comparing several population means at the same time. This method is called **analysis of variance,** abbreviated ANOVA.

Suppose that there are k populations of interest. The method of *analysis of variance* enables us (under suitable conditions) to test the hypotheses

$$H_0: \quad \mu_1 = \mu_2 = \cdots = \mu_k$$
$$H_a: \quad \text{Not all the means are equal.}$$

You may think we could use the methods of Chapter 9 to compare each possible pair of means. For example, if we are interested in the three means μ_1, μ_2, and μ_3, we could test

$$\begin{Bmatrix} \mu_1 = \mu_2 \\ \mu_1 \neq \mu_2 \end{Bmatrix} \quad \begin{Bmatrix} \mu_2 = \mu_3 \\ \mu_2 \neq \mu_3 \end{Bmatrix} \quad \begin{Bmatrix} \mu_1 = \mu_3 \\ \mu_1 \neq \mu_3 \end{Bmatrix}$$

The trouble with this approach is that each time we conduct a test, there is a chance we will make an error. The chance of making at least one error when we conduct all these tests is usually unacceptably large. The usual approach is to use analysis of variance to conduct a single test concerning all the means

$$H_0: \quad \mu_1 = \mu_2 = \mu_3$$
$$H_a: \quad \text{Not all the means are equal.}$$

11.2

THE IDEA BEHIND ANALYSIS OF VARIANCE; THE CASE OF EQUAL SAMPLE SIZES

Analysis of variance is widely used in many different fields. In manufacturing, for example, quality control engineers can use it to compare the output from different assembly lines or different plants. To get an idea of how analysis of variance works, we will consider the following hypothetical example.

A large chemical company uses four manufacturing plants to produce the same fertilizer. The plants were designed to be equivalent, so theoretically they should each have the same mean output (and the same variability). The company wished to see whether each of the four plants does have the same mean output. The output from a given plant is measured in terms of weekly production (tons of fertilizer produced during 1 week). This will, of course, vary somewhat from week to week. We are interested in the true mean weekly production for a plant. This would be the mean of the conceptual population consisting of weekly production figures for the plant for many, many weeks. Suppose that we let μ_1 represent the true (population) mean weekly production for plant 1. Similarly, μ_2, μ_3, μ_4 represent the true mean weekly productions for plants 2, 3, 4. The company wishes to test the hypotheses

$$H_0: \quad \mu_1 = \mu_2 = \mu_3 = \mu_4$$
$$H_a: \quad \text{Not all the means are equal.}$$

To investigate this situation, the company obtains the weekly production figures for 5 weeks for each plant. The results are given in Table 11.1.

Table 11.1
Weekly Production Figures for 5 Weeks for Four Fertilizer Plants

Plant	1	2	3	4
	574	566	580	573
Weekly	578	576	570	570
production	573	569	577	569
in tons	568	571	575	577
(x)	572	573	573	576
$\bar{x}$	573	571	575	573
s^2	13	14.5	14.5	12.5

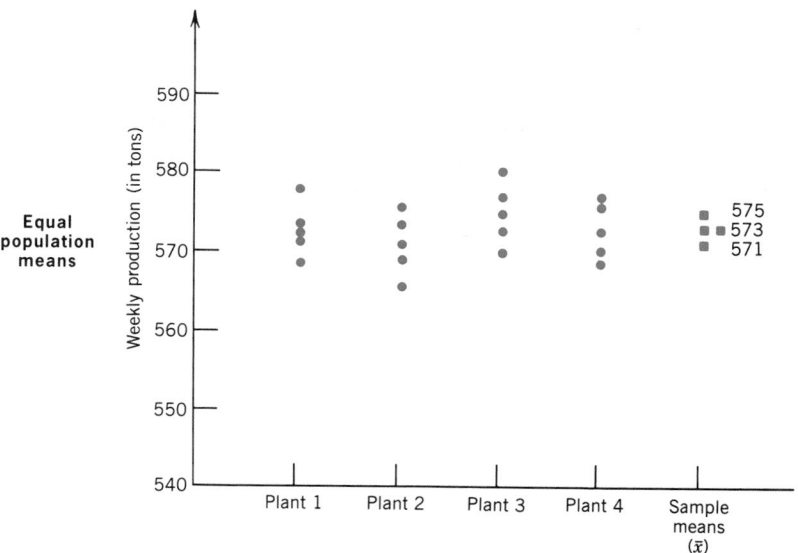

Figure 11.1
Weekly Production from Four Commercial Fertilizer Plants for 5 Weeks

The data from Table 11.1 are displayed in Figure 11.1, where the data values are represented by dots and the sample means are represented by squares. We can think of the sample means as very rough estimates for the population means. In Figure 11.1, the sample means are clustered fairly close together, which tends to support H_0.

A great deal of variability between the sample means would suggest that not all the population means were equal, thus supporting H_a. To appreciate this, look at the data in Table 11.2 and its display in Figure 11.2 (page 494). To obtain these data, we used the data in Table 11.1, except that we subtracted 20 from each figure for plant 2 and added 12 to each figure for plant 4. Note the greater variability in the sample means, suggesting that the true means are not all the same.

A key to testing for equality of several population means is to look at the variability between the sample means. A large amount of variability between the sample

Table 11.2
Revised Weekly Production Figures for the Four Plants of Table 11.1

Plant	1	2	3	4
	574	546	580	585
Weekly	578	556	570	582
production	573	549	577	581
in tons	568	551	575	589
(x)	572	553	573	588
$\bar{x}$	573	551	575	585
s^2	13	14.5	14.5	12.5

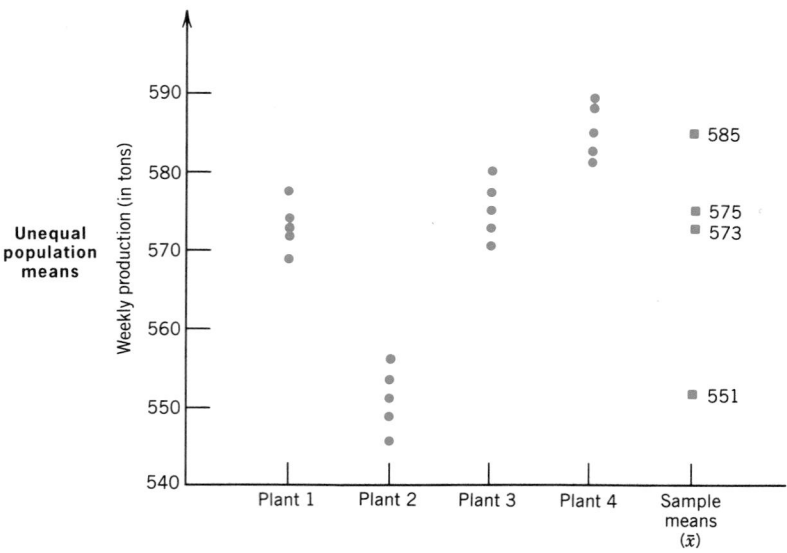

Figure 11.2
Weekly Production for the Four Plants in Figure 11.1 Obtained by Subtracting 20 from the Figures for Plant 2 and Increasing the Figures for Plant 4 by 12. Note How the Variability Between the Sample Means Has Increased.

means suggests that not all the population means are equal. Hence we would reject H_0 in favor of H_a. If this variability is not large, we would not reject H_0. Of course, "large" is a relative term. Variability must be measured in relation to something. When we say that the variability between the sample means is large, we will mean that it is large in comparison with the variability of the data values within the samples. Therefore, when the variability *between* the sample means is large in relation to the variability *within* the samples, we will reject the null hypothesis and conclude that not all the population means are equal. In the example under discussion, this would mean that not all the plants have the same productive capacity.

Throughout this discussion, we will assume that each plant has the same (true) variance σ^2 (whether the means are equal or not). The variance σ^2 is a measure of the variability we can expect within each sample. From the data in Table 11.1, we will obtain two estimates of σ^2. The first estimate is based on the variability within the samples of weekly production figures and is called the **within-samples estimate of σ^2**. The second estimate of σ^2 is based on the variability between the sample means and is called the **between-samples estimate of σ^2**. These two estimates are all we need to test the hypothesis H_0, which asserts that each plant has the same true mean output ($\mu_1 = \mu_2 = \mu_3 = \mu_4$). The reason for this is that the first estimate (within samples) gives us a valid estimate of σ^2 whether H_0 is true or not. However, the second estimate (between samples) gives a valid estimate of σ^2 only if H_0 is true. If H_0 is false, the relatively large amount of variability between the sample means causes the second estimate (between samples) to be an inflated estimate of σ^2, as we will see shortly. Thus by comparing the two estimates, we can get an idea of whether H_0 is true or not: If H_0 is true, we expect the two estimates of σ^2 to be comparable in size. But if the second estimate is much larger than the first, we would conclude that H_0 is false.

Estimate 1: Within-Samples Estimate

All four sample variances in Table 11.1 can be thought of as estimates of the common variance σ^2. It would be natural to pool these estimates by averaging them. This gives us our first estimate of σ^2:

$$\text{estimate 1} = \frac{s_1^2 + s_2^2 + s_3^2 + s_4^2}{4}$$

$$= \frac{13 + 14.5 + 14.5 + 12.5}{4} = 13.625$$

Estimate 2: Between-Samples Estimate

Let us assume (for the moment) that all four plants are equivalent and hence that H_0 is true. We may then view the samples of production figures as four samples of size 5 from the same population. The four sample means are four values of the random variable $\bar{x}$. We studied this random variable in Chapter 7. Recall that the Central Limit Theorem (Section 7.7) told us that for random samples of size m, the mean and standard deviation of $\bar{x}$ are

$$\mu_{\bar{x}} = \mu \qquad \sigma_{\bar{x}} = \frac{\sigma}{\sqrt{m}}$$

so

$$\sigma_{\bar{x}}^2 = \frac{\sigma^2}{m}$$

This means that

$$\sigma^2 = m \cdot \sigma_{\bar{x}}^2$$

This gives us another way of estimating σ^2: We can obtain an estimate of $\sigma_{\bar{x}}^2$ from our four values of $\bar{x}$. Then multiply this by the sample size m of the production samples (which in this case is 5). We will use the sample variance of the four values of $\bar{x}$, which we call $s_{\bar{x}}^2$, as an estimate of $\sigma_{\bar{x}}^2$. The mean of the four values of $\bar{x}$ in Table 11.1 is called the *grand mean* and is denoted by $\bar{\bar{x}}$:

$$\bar{\bar{x}} = \frac{573 + 571 + 575 + 573}{4} = 573$$

Now we find the sample variance $s_{\bar{x}}^2$:

$\bar{x}$	$\bar{x} - \bar{\bar{x}}$	$(\bar{x} - \bar{\bar{x}})^2$
573	0	0
571	−2	4
575	2	4
573	0	0
$\bar{\bar{x}} = 573$		8 $\leftarrow \sum (\bar{x} - \bar{\bar{x}})^2$

$$s_{\bar{x}}^2 = \frac{\sum (\bar{x} - \bar{\bar{x}})^2}{4 - 1} = \frac{8}{3}$$

We can now obtain our second estimate of σ^2 by multiplying the value of $s_{\bar{x}}^2$ by the sample size, $m = 5$. (Remember that we have four samples, each of size $m = 5$.)

$$\text{estimate 2} = m \cdot s_{\bar{x}}^2 = (5)\left(\frac{8}{3}\right) \doteq 13.333$$

Note that the two estimates of σ^2 (13.625 and 13.333) appear to be quite close together. Estimate 2 will be an estimate of σ^2 only if H_0 is true. However, estimate 1 will be a valid estimate of σ^2 whether H_0 is true or not. The fact that both estimates appear to be close, therefore, seems to support the truth of H_0. That is, the (true) means for the assembly lines appear equal.

To get an idea of what happens when H_0 is not true, look at the data in Table 11.2 and Figure 11.2. Recall that these data were obtained from the original data in Table 11.1 by subtracting 20 from the production figures for plant 2 and adding 12 to the figures for plant 4. For the new data, it appears that the variability between the sample means is large in relation to the variability within the samples, suggesting that H_0 is not true. The variability within the samples for the new data has not changed. If you want to go to the trouble of calculating estimate 1 for the new data, you will get precisely the same answer we got for the original data, 13.625. What about estimate 2? Estimate 2 will give an estimate of σ^2 when the four samples come from essentially the same population, but this does not appear to be the case for the new data. It does not appear that each plant has the same productive capacity. Notice how far apart the sample means are. The variance for the new sample means will therefore be larger than for the original sample means. The new sample means are 573, 551, 575, and 585. You may wish to verify that $\bar{\bar{x}} = 571$; the sample variance for these values is

$$s_{\bar{x}}^2 = \frac{\sum(\bar{x} - \bar{\bar{x}})^2}{4 - 1} = \frac{616}{3}$$

This means that estimate 2 (for the new data) is

$$\text{estimate 2} = m \cdot s_{\bar{x}}^2 = (5)\left(\frac{616}{3}\right) \doteq 1026.667$$

This is much larger than estimate 1. Thus, when the null hypothesis H_0 is false, estimate 2 overestimates σ^2.

We can summarize our findings as follows: When H_0 is true, estimate 1 and estimate 2 should be roughly the same size. If estimate 2 is much greater than estimate 1, we reject H_0. In practice, we usually look at the ratio of estimate 2 to estimate 1. Let

$$F = \frac{\text{estimate 2}}{\text{estimate 1}} = \frac{m \cdot s_{\bar{x}}^2}{(s_1^2 + s_2^2 + s_3^2 + s_4^2)/4}$$

If H_0 is true (i.e., the population means are equal), we expect the value of F to be not too far from 1. If F is too large, we reject H_0. We consider F "too large" if it would be unlikely that we would observe such a large value of F if H_0 were true. To assess this, we must know something about the probability distribution of F. It can be shown that under appropriate conditions, F has what is called an **F distribution.** The more general form of F for k populations is

$$F = \frac{m \cdot s_{\bar{x}}^2}{(s_1^2 + s_2^2 + \cdots + s_k^2)/k}$$

Suppose we have random samples of size m from each of k normal populations. Then if the null hypothesis of equal population means is true, F has an F distribution.

Properties of an F Distribution

1. For each F distribution, we have a pair of degrees of freedom: the degrees of freedom of the numerator, df_1, and the degrees of freedom of the denominator, df_2. For the ratio

$$F = \frac{m \cdot s_{\bar{x}}^2}{(s_1^2 + s_2^2 + \cdots + s_k^2)/k}$$

    $df_1 = k - 1$ and $df_2 = n - k$, where $k =$ the number of populations and $n =$ total number of data values in all the samples. We often express the degrees of freedom as an ordered pair of numbers,

$$df = (k - 1, n - k)$$

2. The graph of an F distribution (an F curve) starts at 0 and extends indefinitely to the right. It is skewed to the right. Of course, the total area under the curve is 1. (See Figure 11.3.)

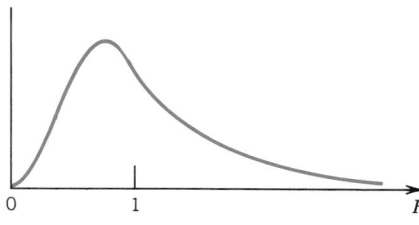

Figure 11.3
An F Curve

Appendix Table B.6 enables us to find critical values of F for the three probabilities .01, .025, and .05. Suppose that we are interested in the F distribution with degrees of freedom df $= (24, 16)$, and we want the value of F such that the area under the F curve to the right of it is .05. We denote this value by $F_{.05}$. Use the table for .05. In the row across the top, find the degrees of freedom for the numerator, 24. In the column on the left, locate the degrees of freedom of the denominator, 16. The intersection of the column under 24 and the row next to 16 contains the desired value of F, namely, 2.24. Thus $F_{.05} = 2.24$. This means $P(F \geq 2.24) = .05$. In Figure 11.4, we have included a portion of the F table (with the right tail area .05).

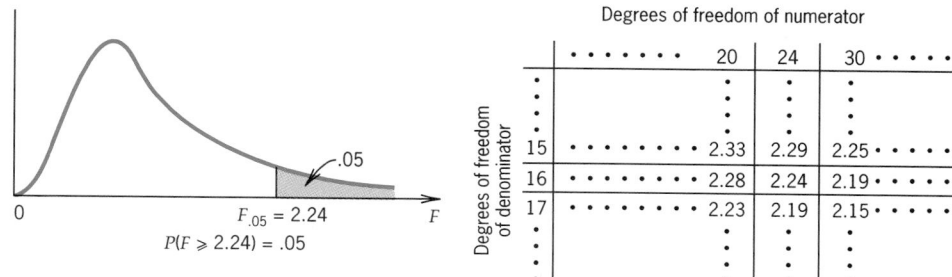

Figure 11.4

We said that the null hypothesis H_0 (of **equal** population means) will be rejected if the value of F is so large that it is unlikely that we would observe such a large value if H_0 were true. ("Unlikely" **means** having a low probability, which we call α, the level of significance. The **researcher** chooses this value.) This means that we perform a right-tailed F test.

For example, we said that the new production data in Table 11.2 seemed to suggest unequal true population means. The F value for these data is

$$F = \frac{\text{estimate } 2}{\text{estimate } 1} = \frac{1026.667}{13.625} \doteq 75.35$$

For these data, $k = 4$, and the total number of data values is $n = 20$. Hence df $= (k-1, n-k) = (3, 16)$. Suppose that we decided on the 5% level of significance. From Appendix Table B.6, we find that $F_{.05} = 3.24$. It would be unlikely (only a 5% chance) that we would observe a value of $F \geq 3.24$ if the null hypothesis were true. Since the observed value of 75.35 is greater than 3.24, we reject the null hypothesis of equal population means. This is precisely what we expected by examining Figure 11.2, which portrays these data.

We summarize the essential features of a test for equality of means as follows.

ANOVA Test   To test the hypotheses

$$H_0: \quad \mu_1 = \mu_2 = \cdots = \mu_k$$
$$H_a: \quad \text{Not all the means are equal.}$$

we perform a right-tailed F test. The test statistic is

$$F = \frac{m \cdot s_{\bar{x}}^2}{(s_1^2 + s_2^2 + \cdots + s_k^2)/k}$$

with df $= (k - 1, n - k)$. Suppose that the level of significance of the test is α. Calculate the value of F and find the critical value F_α in Appendix Table B.6. If $F \geq F_\alpha$, we reject H_0. Otherwise we do not reject H_0. (See Figure 11.5.)

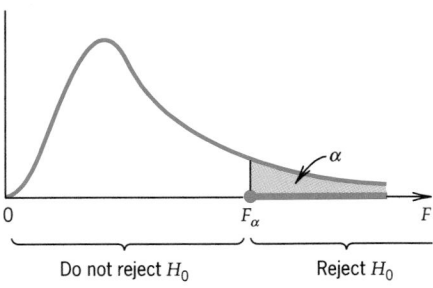

Figure 11.5
Critical Region

Assumptions: Populations are normal with equal variances and the samples are independent.

Thus the analysis of variance uses an F test for equality of population means. Note, however, that the following properties of the populations were assumed:

1. Normality
2. Equality of the population variances

Property 2 is called *homoscedasticity*. (The inequality of population variances is called *heteroscedasticity*.) Moderate departures from properties 1 and 2 do not seriously affect the test. In the next section, we discuss the analysis of variance when the sample sizes are unequal. In this case, the test is more sensitive to departures from homoscedasticity, but moderate departures are still acceptable as long as the sample sizes do not differ by very large amounts.

EXAMPLE 11.1

For the (original) production data of Table 11.1, test the hypothesis that the true mean weekly production is the same for all four plants. Use the 5% level of significance.

Solution
We use the usual five steps to complete the test.

1. *Hypotheses:*

$$H_0: \quad \mu_1 = \mu_2 = \mu_3 = \mu_4$$
$$H_a: \quad \text{Not all the means are equal.}$$

2. *Level of significance:* $\alpha = .05$
3. *Test statistic and observed value:*   We use the test statistic

$$F = \frac{m \cdot s_{\bar{x}}^2}{(s_1^2 + s_2^2 + s_3^2 + s_4^2)/4}$$

In the previous discussion, we evaluated the numerator and denominator of F. The numerator is estimate 2 of σ^2 and has the value 13.333. Similarly, the denominator (estimate 1) is 13.625. Therefore,

$$F = \frac{13.333}{13.625} \doteq .98$$

Degrees of freedom $= (k - 1, n - k)$:

$$k = \text{number of means} = 4$$
$$n = \text{total number of data values} = 20$$

so

$$\text{degrees of freedom} = \text{df} = (3, 16)$$

4. *Critical region:* We perform a right-tailed test with $\alpha = .05$. From Appendix Table B.6, we find $F_{.05} = 3.24$. (See Figure 11.6 on page 500.)
5. *Decision:* The value of the test statistic ($F = .98$) is not in the critical region; therefore, we do not reject H_0. This means that there is no evidence to conclude that there is a difference in the true mean output levels of the four plants.

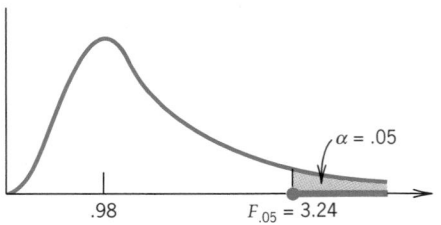

Figure 11.6

EXAMPLE 11.2

A sociologist, studying the living habits of young adults, obtained the data in Table 11.3 on the percentage of budgets used for recreation for three groups of subjects grouped by social class. There were $m = 8$ subjects in each group.

Table 11.3

	Lower Working Class	Middle Class	Upper Class
$\bar{x}$	4.3	5.4	10.1
s	3.0	3.6	4.0

Do the data indicate that the mean percentages for the populations from which the three groups were obtained are different? Use the 1% level of significance.

Solution

1. *Hypotheses:* Let μ_1, μ_2, and μ_3 represent the (population) mean percentages for the three groups.

$$H_0: \quad \mu_1 = \mu_2 = \mu_3$$
$$H_a: \quad \text{Not all the means are equal.}$$

2. *Level of significance:* $\alpha = .01$

3. *Test statistic and observed value:* Before we evaluate the F statistic, we need the value of $s_{\bar{x}}^2$. Using the alternative formula for variance of Section 3.3, we get

$$s_{\bar{x}}^2 = \frac{3\left(\sum \bar{x}^2\right) - \left(\sum \bar{x}\right)^2}{(3)(2)} = \frac{3\left[(4.3)^2 + (5.4)^2 + (10.1)^2\right] - [4.3 + 5.4 + 10.1]^2}{6}$$

$$= \frac{448.98 - 392.04}{6} = \frac{56.94}{6} \doteq 9.49$$

$$F = \frac{m \cdot s_{\bar{x}}^2}{(s_1^2 + s_2^2 + s_3^2)/3} = \frac{(8)(9.49)}{\left[(3)^2 + (3.6)^2 + (4)^2\right]/3} = \frac{75.92}{12.653} \doteq 6$$

Degrees of freedom $= (k - 1, n - k) = (3 - 1, 24 - 3) = (2, 21)$.

4. *Critical region:* The analysis of variance always uses a right-tailed test. From Appendix Table B.6, we see that $F_{.01} = 5.78$. (See Figure 11.7.)

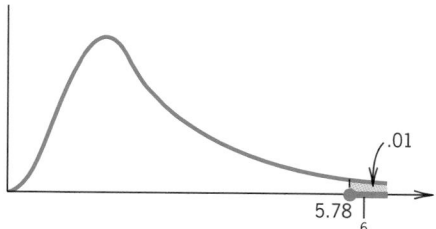

Figure 11.7

5.   *Decision:*   The observed value of F is in the critical region; thus we reject H_0. Therefore, there is sufficient evidence to conclude that the means of percentages are not the same for the three populations.

Before closing this section, we should address a point that may have occurred to you. Suppose we conclude that not all the population means are equal. Then which is the largest, or the smallest? Which pairs of means are different? Such questions can be trickier than they may seem, and we will not treat them in this book. We refer you to Neter et al. (1990, Chapter 15) for a discussion of these issues. This reference also has an excellent discussion of the questions of normality and homoscedasticity (Chapter 18).

The analysis of variance procedure used in this section requires that all the sample sizes be equal. However, the analysis of variance may also be used when the sample sizes are unequal, as we will see in the next section.

EXERCISES

11.1   In parts (a)–(d), find (i) $F_{.01}$, (ii) $F_{.025}$, and (iii) $F_{.05}$.
    (a)   Assume an F distribution with (5, 8) degrees of freedom.
    (b)   Assume an F distribution with (8, 5) degrees of freedom.
    (c)   Assume an F distribution with (20, 10) degrees of freedom.
    (d)   Assume an F distribution with (1, 7) degrees of freedom.

11.2   Assume an F distribution. Fill in the blanks.
    (a) $P(F > \underline{\quad}) = .01$,   df $= (15, 12)$
    (b) $P(F \leq \underline{\quad}) = .95$,   df $= (9, 5)$
    (c) $P(F \geq \underline{\quad}) = .025$,   df $= (6, 20)$
    (d) $P(F > \underline{\quad}) = .05$,   df $= (12, 9)$

11.3   Consider the hypothesis $H_0 : \mu_1 = \mu_2 = \cdots = \mu_k$. Random samples of size m are selected from each of the k populations. Complete the following table. (*Note:*   df $=$ degrees of freedom.)

	m	k	α	$s_{\bar{x}}^2$	$(s_1^2 + s_2^2 + \cdots + s_k^2)$	Observed F	df	F_α	Decision
(a)	5	3	.05	50	100				
(b)	5	3	.05	20	100				
(c)	6	2	.01	25	50				
(d)	6	2	.01	25	25				
(e)	4	5	.05	40	200				
(f)	4	5	.05	40	400				

11.4 For each of the following parts, assume that random samples of size 4 were selected from each of six populations. Determine whether there is sufficient evidence to reject the hypothesis of equal population means using a 5% significance level.

	$s_{\bar{x}}^2$	$(s_A^2 + s_B^2 + s_C^2 + s_D^2 + s_E^2 + s_F^2)$
(a)	5	40
(b)	4	40
(c)	10	40
(d)	5	60
(e)	5	20

11.5 A psychologist was interested in the effects of three different kinds of drugs upon the mean time to complete a task. The psychologist used 15 subjects and randomly assigned 5 of them to each drug, A, B, and C. The data represent the time in minutes to complete the task. Use a 5% level of significance to test that the population mean times to complete the task are the same with each drug. The data are given in the table.

A	B	C
20	21	30
22	26	24
25	26	26
24	27	25
19	25	30

11.6 The owner of a large company wanted to compare the mean daily output of a particular item for five plants. For each plant, a random sample of 4 days gave the data listed in the following table. Do the sample data indicate a difference in the population means for the five plants? Use a 5% level of significance.

Plants	A	B	C	D	E
	29	22	24	23	15
	18	17	16	15	8
	18	12	14	14	9
	18	11	12	10	4
$\bar{x}$	20.75	15.50	16.50	15.50	9
s^2	30.25	25.67	27.67	29.67	20.67

11.7 A biology professor was interested in whether there was a difference in the mean heart rate maximum after exercise on a treadmill between highly trained male and female distance runners. Do the following data indicate a difference in the population means? Use the analysis of variance with a 1% level of significance.

	Sample Size	$\bar{x}$	s
Males	10	180.3	7.2
Females	10	190.8	10.7

Source: Daniels et al., 1977, p. 142.

11.8   Consider the sample data from populations A and B:

A	B
52	54
42	63
32	51
46	52
55	50
50	60

Suppose that you are to test H_0: $\mu_A = \mu_B$ with a 1% level of significance.

(a)   Use the analysis of variance.
    (i)   Find the degrees of freedom.
    (ii)   Find the critical value.
    (iii)   Find the observed value.
    (iv)   Is there sufficient evidence to reject H_0?

For those who have covered the pooled t procedures in Section 9.4, go on to parts (b) and (c).

(b)   Use the pooled t test.
    (i)   Find the degrees of freedom.
    (ii)   Find the critical values.
    (iii)   Find the observed value.
    (iv)   Is there sufficient evidence to reject H_0?

(c)   Compare each item of part (a) with the corresponding item of (b). Comment. [*Hint:*   The square (or square root) is involved in the comparison of items (ii) and (iii).]

11.9   Consider the sample data from populations A, B, C, D, and E in the following table.

	A	B	C	D	E
	28	19	30	29	19
	27	28	23	26	19
	30	28	30	35	24
	22	27	16	24	16
	18	19	29	33	27
	19	29	22	33	27
$\bar{x}$	24	25	25	30	22
s	5.02	4.69	5.66	4.38	4.65

Suppose that you are to test H_0: $\mu_A = \mu_B = \mu_C = \mu_D = \mu_E$ with a 5% level of significance.

(a)   **(i)**   Find the degrees of freedom.
    (ii)   Find the critical value.
    (iii)   Find the observed value.
    (iv)   Is there sufficient evidence to reject H_0?

(b)   Decrease each observed value in population E by 4.
    (i)   Without calculating, how does the variability within the samples compare with that obtained in part (a)? (Does it increase, decrease, or remain the same?)

    (ii)   Without calculating $s_{\bar{x}}^2$, how does the variability between sample means compare with that obtained in part (a)?

    (iii)   Without calculating, and using your answers in parts (b)(i) and (b)(ii), how does the observed F value compare with that obtained in part (a)?

    (iv)   Now calculate the new value of F. Is there sufficient evidence to reject H_0 using a 5% significance level?

11.10 Consider the sample data from populations A, B, C, and D.

A	B	C	D
27	27	27	23
19	32	19	27
18	31	21	26
20	34	25	20

Suppose that you are to test $H_0 : \mu_A = \mu_B = \mu_C = \mu_D$ with a 1% level of significance.

(a)   **(i)**   Find the degrees of freedom.

    (ii)   Find the critical value.

    (iii)   Find the observed value.

    (iv)   Is there sufficient evidence to reject H_0?

(b)   Increase each observed value in population A by 5.

    (i)   Without calculating, how does the variability within the samples compare with that obtained in part (a)? (Does it increase, decrease, or remain the same?)

    (ii)   Without calculating $s_{\bar{x}}^2$, how does the variability between sample means compare with that obtained in part (a)?

    (iii)   Without calculating, and using your answers in parts (b)(i) and (b)(ii), how does the observed F value compare with that obtained in part (a)?

    (iv)   Now calculate the new value of F. Is there sufficient evidence to reject H_0 using a 1% significance level?

11.11 Officials in a large company wanted to look at the issue of job satisfaction for three shifts. The quality of work from one of the shifts had appeared to slip over a period of time. Thirty-five employees from each shift were randomly selected and asked to fill out a questionnaire. Low scores indicated a large degree of job satisfaction. The Minitab computer output follows.

One-Way Analysis of Variance

```
Analysis of Variance
Source      DF         SS          MS           F          p
Factor       2       881.0       440.5       43.79      0.000
Error      102      1026.0        10.1
Total      104      1907.0
                                     Individual 95% CIs For Mean
                                     Based on Pooled StDev
  Level      N       Mean       StDev   ----+---------+---------+---------+--
Shift_1     35     27.686       3.945   (----*---)
Shift_2     35     31.598       2.911                   (---*----)
Shift_3     35     34.769       2.478                              (---*---)
                                        ----+---------+---------+---------+--
Pooled StDev =      3.172               27.5      30.0      32.5      35.0
```

(a)   Let μ_1, μ_2, and μ_3 represent the population means of the three shifts. Write the null and alternate hypotheses.

(b)   Give the observed F value. Is the test statistically significant at the 1% level of significance?

11.12   Four companies (A, B, C, D), each a manufacturer of handballs, were trying to convince the handball association that their ball should be recognized as the official ball. The association sampled 100 balls from each company. Each ball was tested for overall quality and assigned a number on a scale of 1 to 10. Higher scores correspond to higher quality. The output that follows is from Data Desk. The last two values in the Grp row give information on the ANOVA F statistic and its P-value.

Source	df	Sums of Squares	Mean Square	F-ratio	Prob
Const	1	16392.4	16392.4	57808	≤ 0.0002
Grp	3	49.5787	16.5263	58.280	≤ 0.0002
Error	396	112.294	0.283569		
Total	399	161.872			

(a)   Use the modified boxplots to compare the results of the samples between the four companies. Does it appear that, on average, the handballs manufactured by company D are of better quality than those manufactured by the other companies?

(b)   Consider a test of the hypothesis H_0: $\mu_A = \mu_B = \mu_C = \mu_D$ with a 5% level of significance. Give the observed F value. Is the test statistically significant at the 5% level?

11.3

ANALYSIS OF VARIANCE WHEN SAMPLE SIZES ARE NOT NECESSARILY EQUAL; CONVENTIONAL TERMINOLOGY

Until now our analysis of variance technique required that the size of the sample from each population be the same. But analysis of variance may still be carried out when the sample sizes are unequal. We now give the appropriate formula for F that will work regardless of whether the sample sizes are equal.

The F statistic used to test for equality of population means is still based on the two estimates of the common population variance σ^2.

$$F = \frac{\text{estimate 2}}{\text{estimate 1}} = \frac{\text{between-samples estimate of } \sigma^2}{\text{within-samples estimate of } \sigma^2}$$

Now assume that we have samples from k populations. We represent the data values from the first population by x_1, those from the second population by x_2, and so on. We represent the size of the sample from the first population by n_1, the sample size from the second population by n_2, and so on. We let n denote the total number of data values $(n = n_1 + n_2 + \cdots + n_k)$.

We will give general formulas for estimate 1 and estimate 2, and we will show how these formulas apply to the production data in Table 11.1.

Estimate 1

First calculate the *sum of squares* for each sample. For example, the sum of squares for the first sample is

$$\sum (x_1 - \bar{x}_1)^2$$

In Table 11.1, we were given the sample variances. It would be a simple matter to obtain the sum of squares for each sample from these. But since we usually are not given the sample variance, we will calculate the sum of squares for each sample from scratch, as shown in Table 11.4.

Table 11.4

Plant 1			Plant 2		
x_1	$x_1 - \bar{x}_1$	$(x_1 - \bar{x}_1)^2$	x_2	$x_2 - \bar{x}_2$	$(x_2 - \bar{x}_2)^2$
574	1	1	566	−5	25
578	5	25	576	5	25
573	0	0	569	−2	4
568	−5	25	571	0	0
572	−1	1	573	2	4
$\bar{x}_1 = 573$		$\sum(x_1 - \bar{x}_1)^2 = 52$	$\bar{x}_2 = 571$		$\sum(x_2 - \bar{x}_2)^2 = 58$

Plant 3			Plant 4		
x_3	$x_3 - \bar{x}_3$	$(x_3 - \bar{x}_3)^2$	x_4	$x_4 - \bar{x}_4$	$(x_4 - \bar{x}_4)^2$
580	5	25	573	0	0
570	−5	25	570	−3	9
577	2	4	569	−4	16
575	0	0	577	4	16
573	−2	4	576	3	9
$\bar{x}_3 = 575$		$\sum(x_3 - \bar{x}_3)^2 = 58$	$\bar{x}_4 = 573$		$\sum(x_4 - \bar{x}_4)^2 = 50$

We now add the sum of squares for each sample. The result is called the **sum of squares within,** denoted by SSW.

$$\text{SSW} = \sum (x_1 - \bar{x}_1)^2 + \sum (x_2 - \bar{x}_2)^2 + \cdots + \sum (x_k - \bar{x}_k)^2$$

The number of degrees of freedom for SSW is defined to be $n - k$. Think of degrees of freedom as a number by which we divide a sum of squares to get an estimate for a population variance, in this case the common population variance, σ^2. For the production data (in Table 11.4)

$$SSW = 52 + 58 + 58 + 50 = 218$$

The number of degrees of freedom is $n - k = 20 - 4 = 16$. To find estimate 1, we divide SSW by its degrees of freedom, $n - k$. The result is sometimes called the **mean square within,** denoted by MSW.

$$\text{estimate 1} = MSW = \frac{SSW}{n - k}$$

For the production data,

$$\text{estimate 1} = MSW = \frac{218}{16} = 13.625$$

This is the same value we obtained in Section 11.2.

Estimate 2

First we find the mean of *all* the data values in the study. This is called the *grand mean* and is denoted by $\bar{\bar{x}}$. (For the data in Table 11.1, $\bar{\bar{x}} = 573$.) Now we calculate the **sum of squares between,** denoted by SSB. This is defined to be

$$SSB = n_1\left(\bar{x}_1 - \bar{\bar{x}}\right)^2 + n_2\left(\bar{x}_2 - \bar{\bar{x}}\right)^2 + \cdots + n_k\left(\bar{x}_k - \bar{\bar{x}}\right)^2$$

The number of degrees of freedom for SSB is defined to be $k - 1$. For the production data, $n_1 = 5$, $n_2 = 5$, and so on. Therefore,

$$SSB = 5(573 - 573)^2 + 5(571 - 573)^2 + 5(575 - 573)^2 + 5(573 - 573)^2 = 40$$

(Note that the sample sizes happen to be equal for these data sets, but this need not be the case.) The degrees of freedom $= k - 1 = 4 - 1 = 3$.

To obtain estimate 2, divide SSB by its degrees of freedom, $k - 1$. The result is sometimes called the **mean square between,** denoted by MSB.

$$\text{estimate 2} = MSB = \frac{SSB}{k - 1}$$

This will be an estimate of σ^2 only when the population means are equal. For the production data,

$$\text{estimate 2} = MSB = \frac{40}{3} \doteq 13.333$$

This is the same value we obtained in Section 11.2.

> The test statistic used to test for the equality of several population means (for normal populations with equal variances) is
>
> $$F = \frac{\text{MSB}}{\text{MSW}}$$
>
> If the means are equal, this has the F distribution with $k - 1$ numerator degrees of freedom and $n - k$ denominator degrees of freedom. If the level of significance of the test is α, we reject the null hypothesis of equality of population means if $F \geq F_\alpha$.

For our analysis of variance procedure to be applicable, the populations need be only approximately normal. Also, moderate departures from the requirement of equal variances is permissible, as long as the sample sizes are not very different.

Notes

1. When calculating SSW, we use the sum of squares for each sample. Sometimes the sample variances are known, and when this is the case, we can calculate the sum of squares for each sample quickly. For example,

$$s_1^2 = \frac{\sum (x_1 - \bar{x}_1)^2}{n_1 - 1}$$

Multiplying both sides by $n_1 - 1$, we get

$$(n_1 - 1)s_1^2 = (n_1 - 1) \cdot \frac{\sum (x_1 - \bar{x}_1)^2}{(n_1 - 1)} = \sum (x_1 - \bar{x}_1)^2$$

If we multiply the sample variance by 1 less than the sample size, we get the sum of squares for the sample. For instance, the production data for plant 1, discussed previously, gave a sum of squares of 52. From Table 11.1, we saw that $s_1^2 = 13$ and $n_1 = 5$; thus

$$(4)(13) = 52 = \text{sum of squares}$$

2. The grand mean $\bar{\bar{x}}$ is the mean of all the data values in the samples. If we know each sample mean, we can use these to find $\bar{\bar{x}}$. But we must be careful not to average the sample means unless the sample sizes are equal. What we can do is multiply each sample mean by the sample size. For example,

$$n_1 \bar{x}_1 = \cancel{n_1} \cdot \frac{\sum x_1}{\cancel{n_1}} = \sum x_1$$

This gives the sum of the data values in the first sample. Now we just add these sums and divide by the total number of data values to get $\bar{\bar{x}}$.

EXAMPLE 11.3

In a study of various heart characteristics of male athletes, the data in Tables 11.5, 11.6, and 11.7 were obtained concerning heart size for samples of swimmers, wrestlers, and a control group of nonathletes.* The characteristic measured was left

---

*Data estimated from a graph in Morganroth, J., and B. Maron, 1977, p. 218.

Table 11.5
Swimmers ($n_1 = 15$)

x_1	$x_1 - \bar{x}_1$	$(x_1 - \bar{x}_1)^2$
140	−41.733	1741.643
140	−41.733	1741.643
140	−41.733	1741.643
148	−33.733	1137.915
148	−33.733	1137.915
175	−6.733	45.333
185	3.267	10.673
194	12.267	150.479
194	12.267	150.479
203	21.267	452.285
203	21.267	452.285
214	32.267	1041.159
214	32.267	1041.159
214	32.267	1041.159
214	32.267	1041.159

$\sum x_1 = 2726$
$\bar{x}_1 = 181.733$
$\sum (x_1 - \bar{x}_1)^2 = 12{,}926.929$

Table 11.6
Wrestlers ($n_2 = 12$)

x_2	$x_2 - \bar{x}_2$	$(x_2 - \bar{x}_2)^2$
83	−27.167	738.046
91	−19.167	367.374
97	−13.167	173.370
97	−13.167	173.370
108	−2.167	4.696
111	.833	.694
111	.833	.694
117	6.833	46.690
117	6.833	46.690
125	14.833	220.018
125	14.833	220.018
140	29.833	890.008

$\sum x_2 = 1322$
$\bar{x}_2 = 110.167$
$\sum (x_2 - \bar{x}_2)^2 = 2881.668$

Table 11.7
Controls ($n_3 = 16$)

x_3	$x_3 - \bar{x}_3$	$(x_3 - \bar{x}_3)^2$
64	−36.875	1359.766
83	−17.875	319.516
83	−17.875	319.516
85	−15.875	252.016
91	−9.875	97.516
97	−3.875	15.016
97	−3.875	15.016
97	−3.875	15.016
103	2.125	4.516
108	7.125	50.766
111	10.125	102.516
111	10.125	102.516
117	16.125	260.016
117	16.125	260.016
125	24.125	582.016
125	24.125	582.016

$\sum x_3 = 1614$
$\bar{x}_3 = 100.875$
$\sum (x_3 - \bar{x}_3)^2 = 4337.756$

ventricular end diastolic volume, in milliliters. (This is the volume of the left lower chamber when the heart is filled with blood.) Test the hypothesis that the mean size is the same for the three populations of swimmers, wrestlers, and controls. Use the 1% level of significance.

Solution

1. *Hypotheses:*

$$H_0: \quad \mu_1 = \mu_2 = \mu_3$$
$$H_a: \quad \text{Not all the population means are equal.}$$

2. *Level of significance:* $\alpha = .01$

3. *Test statistic and observed value:*

$$F = \frac{MSB}{MSW}$$

$$\text{degrees of freedom} = (k - 1, n - k)$$

To find MSW and MSB, we first find SSW and SSB. The sum of squares within is

$$SSW = \sum (x_1 - \bar{x}_1)^2 + \sum (x_2 - \bar{x}_2)^2 + \sum (x_3 - \bar{x}_3)^2$$
$$= 12{,}926.929 + 2881.668 + 4337.756 = 20{,}146.353$$

$$\text{degrees of freedom} = n - k = 43 - 3 = 40$$

To find the sum of squares between, we first find $\bar{\bar{x}}$, the mean of all 43 data values. We have already added the data values in each group. Hence, we add these three sums and divide by 43:

$$\bar{\bar{x}} = \frac{2726 + 1322 + 1614}{43} = \frac{5662}{43} = 131.674$$

$$SSB = n_1 \left(\bar{x}_1 - \bar{\bar{x}}\right)^2 + n_2 \left(\bar{x}_2 - \bar{\bar{x}}\right)^2 + n_3 \left(\bar{x}_3 - \bar{\bar{x}}\right)^2$$
$$= 15(181.733 - 131.674)^2 + 12(110.167 - 131.674)^2$$
$$+ 16(100.875 - 131.674)^2$$
$$= 37{,}588.552 + 5550.613 + 15{,}177.254 = 58{,}316.419$$

$$\text{degrees of freedom} = k - 1 = 3 - 1 = 2$$

$$MSW = \frac{SSW}{n - k} = \frac{20{,}146.353}{40} = 503.659$$

$$MSB = \frac{SSB}{k - 1} = \frac{58{,}316.419}{2} = 29{,}158.210$$

$$F = \frac{MSB}{MSW} = \frac{29{,}158.210}{503.659} = 57.89$$

Degrees of freedom $= (2, 40)$

4. *Critical region:* From Appendix Table B.6, we see that $F_{.01} = 5.18$. (See Figure 11.8.)

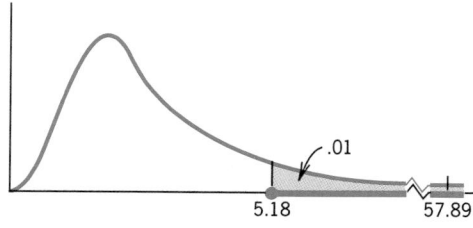

$.01$

5.18   57.89

Figure 11.8

5. *Decision:* The observed value ($F = 57.89$) is in the critical region; thus we reject H_0. Therefore, we conclude that not all three populations have the same (mean) heart size.

Checking the Requirements of Approximate Normality and Homoscedasticity

Figure 11.9 gives stem-and-leaf plots for the three samples. The plots for the wrestlers and controls do not suggest any departure from approximate normality, but the plot for the swimmers is a little strange. Values seem to load up on the highest and lowest stems. This might in part be due to the fact that the data were estimated from a graph that did not have good resolution. One dot in the graph covered 2 or 3 milliliters. Thus it could well be that the three 140's were really 139, 140, and 141.

```
14 | 00088
15            8 | 3          6 | 4
16            9 | 177        7 |
17 | 5       10 | 8          8 | 335
18 | 5       11 | 1177       9 | 1777
19 | 44      12 | 55        10 | 38
20 | 33      13 |           11 | 1177
21 | 4444    14 | 0         12 | 55
```

(a) Swimmers   (b) Wrestlers   (c) Controls

Figure 11.9
Stem-and-Leaf Diagrams of Heart Sizes
(14 | 8 = 148 milliliters)

In Chapter 8, we discussed normal quantile plots (as optional material in Section 8.5). The essential point about normal quantile plots is that when the plot roughly follows a straight line, this suggests approximate normality. To construct a normal quantile plot, you need access to statistical software. If you are using Minitab and your data (for the swimmers) are in column 1 (C1), type

NSCORES C1 C2
PLOT C2*C1

Figure 11.10 (page 512) is a normal quantile plot for the swimmers. A 2 in the plot means there are two points there. The normal quantile plot does not deviate substantially from a straight line. This suggests approximate normality for the population from which the swimmers were selected.

As for the requirement of homoscedasticity (equal population standard deviations), there is a rule for checking this.

Rule for Checking Homoscedasticity
Compute the ratio of the largest sample standard deviation to the smallest sample standard deviation. If the ratio is less than 2, this suggests that the population standard deviations are close enough so that our results will be approximately correct.

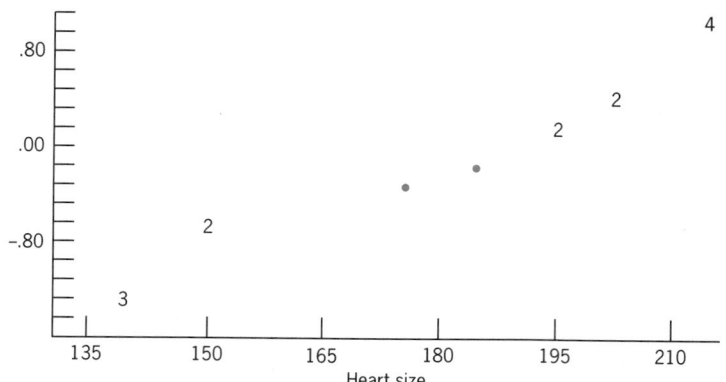

Figure 11.10
Normal Quantile Plot for Swimmers (Note That a 2 Indicates Two Points.)

Let's compute the standard deviations for the three groups.

Swimmers:
$$\sum (x_1 - \bar{x}_1)^2 = 12{,}926.929$$

$$s_1 = \sqrt{\frac{\sum (x_1 - \bar{x}_1)^2}{n_1 - 1}} = \sqrt{\frac{12{,}926.929}{14}} = 30.39$$

Wrestlers:
$$\sum (x_2 - \bar{x}_2)^2 = 2881.668$$

$$s_2 = \sqrt{\frac{\sum (x_2 - \bar{x}_2)^2}{n_2 - 1}} = \sqrt{\frac{2881.668}{11}} = 16.19$$

Controls:
$$\sum (x_3 - \bar{x}_3)^2 = 4337.756$$

$$s_3 = \sqrt{\frac{\sum (x_3 - \bar{x}_3)^2}{n_3 - 1}} = \sqrt{\frac{4337.756}{15}} = 17.01$$

$$\frac{\text{Largest SD}}{\text{Smallest SD}} = \frac{30.39}{16.19} = 1.88 < 2$$

Since 1.88 is less than 2, we may assume that the property of homoscedasticity is not violated.

ANOVA Tables

The various quantities used in the analysis of variance can be summarized in an *ANOVA table*. Computer statistical packages often print out such tables. Before explaining the table, we need to introduce one more term, the **total sum of squares,** denoted by TSS. To compute this, we calculate the mean of *all* the data values in our samples, the grand mean $\bar{\bar{x}}$. We then compute the difference between each data value x and $\bar{\bar{x}}$, and add the squares of these differences.

$$\text{TSS} = \sum (x - \bar{\bar{x}})^2$$

The number of degrees of freedom for TSS is $n - 1$. It can be shown that

$$TSS = SSB + SSW$$

For the data in Example 11.3,

$$TSS = 58{,}316.419 + 20{,}146.353 = 78{,}462.772$$

This relationship shows us that the total variation among all the data values is broken down into two components: one representing the variability between samples, the other the variability within samples.

An ANOVA table takes the general form shown in Table 11.8. The ANOVA table for Example 11.3 is given in Table 11.9.

Table 11.8
ANOVA Table

Source	Sum of Squares (SS)	Degrees of Freedom (df)	Mean Square MS $\left(= \dfrac{SS}{df}\right)$	F Statistic
Between samples	SSB	$k - 1$	$MSB\left(= \dfrac{SSB}{k - 1}\right)$	$F\left(= \dfrac{MSB}{MSW}\right)$
Within samples	SSW	$n - k$	$MSW\left(= \dfrac{SSW}{n - k}\right)$	
Total	TSS	$n - 1$		

Table 11.9
ANOVA Table for Example 11.3

Source	Sum of Squares (SS)	Degrees of Freedom (df)	Mean Square (MS)	F Statistic
Between samples	58,316.419	2	29,158.210	57.89
Within samples	20,146.353	40	503.659	
Total	78,462.772	42		

Terminology

Some statisticians refer to the populations of interest in the analysis of variance as *treatments*. They refer to the sum of squares between (SSB) as the *sum of squares for treatments*, denoted by SSTR. The deviations of the data values from their sample means (such as $x_1 - \bar{x}_1$) are referred to as *errors*, and SSW is referred to as the *sum of squares for error*, denoted by SSE. Table 11.10 (page 514) shows the correspondence between the two types of terminology.

Table 11.10
Terminology

SSB (Sum of squares between)	=	SSTR (Sum of squares for treatments)
SSW (Sum of squares within)	=	SSE (Sum of squares for error)
MSB (Mean square between)	=	MSTR (Mean square for treatments)
MSW (Mean square within)	=	MSE (Mean square for error)

Statistical packages usually print all or part of an ANOVA table, plus the P-value for the F statistic.

JMP Printout for Example 11.1

Analysis of Variance				
Source	DF	Sum of Squares	Mean Square	F Ratio
Model	3	40.00000	13.3333	0.9786
Error	16	218.00000	13.6250	Prob>F
C Total	19	258.00000		0.4274

Here "Model" refers to treatment. The P-value is given as .4274.

Statistica Printout for Example 11.3

df Effect	MS Effect	df Error	MS Error	F	p-level
2	29158.55	40	503.6588	57.89346	.0000000

"Effect" refers to treatment.

EXERCISES

In Exercises 11.13–11.16, compute the sums of squares to find SSW and SSB. Then complete the ANOVA table and the test for equality of population means using a 5% significance level.

11.13

A	B
30	35
27	37
24	33
	30
	40

11.14

A	B
29	26
38	31
25	25
36	18

11.15

A	B	C
10	9	8
16	3	10
10	6	4
		6

11.16

A	B	C	D
12	10	6	22
2	2	6	16
4		14	16
		6	13
			13

11.17 Consider H_0: $\mu_A = \mu_B = \mu_C = \mu_D = \mu_E = \mu_F$.

(a) Complete the following ANOVA table.

Source	Sum of Squares (SS)	Degrees of Freedom (df)	Mean Square (MS)	F
Between samples	250			
Within samples				
Total	400	30		

(b) Using a 5% significance level, would you reject H_0?

11.18 Consider H_0: $\mu_A = \mu_B = \mu_C = \mu_D$.

(a) Complete the following ANOVA table.

Source	Sum of Squares (SS)	Degrees of Freedom (df)	Mean Square (MS)	F
Between samples	180			
Within samples	120	12		
Total				

(b) Using a 1% significance level, would you reject H_0?

11.19 Consider H_0: $\mu_A = \mu_B = \mu_C = \mu_D = \mu_E$.

(a) Complete the following ANOVA table.

Source	Sum of Squares (SS)	Degrees of Freedom (df)	Mean Square (MS)	F
Between samples	128			
Within samples	160		16	
Total				

(b) Using a 5% significance level, would you reject H_0?

11.20 Consider H_0: $\mu_A = \mu_B = \mu_C$. Sample sizes are $n_A = 26$, $n_B = 11$, and $n_C = 6$.

(a) Complete the following ANOVA table.

Source	Sum of Squares (SS)	Degrees of Freedom (df)	Mean Square (MS)	F
Between samples	100			
Within samples				
Total	260			

(b) Using a 1% significance level, would you reject H_0?

11.21 The data in the following table represent final grades given by three professors in an advanced statistics course.

	A	B	C
	63	67	97
	45	45	97
	73	76	87
	77	80	87
	72	70	84
		70	74
			74
			64
$\bar{x}$	66	68	83
s	12.806	12.215	11.637

Does the difference in sample means appear to be due to chance variation, or is there sufficient evidence to indicate that not all population means are the same? Use a 5% level of significance.

11.22 Refer to Exercise 11.21. Prior to obtaining the data, the chairperson suspected that there might be a difference in grading between professors A and C. Test H_0: $\mu_A = \mu_C$ using a 5% significance level.

(a) Use the analysis of variance procedure.

For those who have covered the pooled t procedures in Section 9.4, go on to part (b).

(b) Use the pooled t test.

Compare the observed values in parts (a) and (b). [*Hint:* The square (or square root) is involved.]

11.23 The data in the following table represent the starting weekly wages (in hundreds of dollars) for skilled workers in selected companies in the regions. Do the data indicate a difference in population means? Use a 5% level of significance.

	Pacific	East North-Central	West North-Central	South Atlantic
	7.6	7.3	6.4	6.6
	7.2	7.2	7.0	6.6
	6.4	6.8	6.2	6.7
	5.9	8.1	5.5	5.1
		6.7	5.2	6.7
			5.8	4.5
				4.7
				4.9
				5.0
$\bar{x}$	6.775	7.220	6.017	5.644
s	.768	.554	.652	.970

11.24   A physical fitness expert claimed that there was a difference in the mean HDL cholesterol (milligrams per 100 milliliters) between elite runners, good runners, and nonrunners. Do the following data support the claim? Use a 1% level of significance.

	Sample Size	$\bar{x}$	s
Elite runners	20	56	12.1
Good runners	8	52	10.9
Nonrunners	72	49	10.5

Source: Martin, 1977, p. 93.

11.25   Test the claim that there is no difference in the mean percent of calories from fats between men in the Crevalcore, Montegiorgio, and Corfu areas of Greece. Use a 1% level of significance with the following data:

	Sample Size	$\bar{x}$	s
Crevalcore	28	26.5	4.5
Montegiorgio	34	25.5	4.6
Corfu	34	31.2	5.2

Source: Keys, 1970, p. I-166.

11.26   Consider the following data from populations A, B, and C:

A	B	C
0	7	6
4	6	7
5	2	8

Now SSB = 24 and SSW = 30.

(a) Complete the ANOVA table and test $H_0 : \mu_A = \mu_B = \mu_C$ with a 5% level of significance.

Source	Sum of Squares (SS)	Degrees of Freedom (df)	Mean Square (MS)	F
Between samples				
Within samples				
Total				

(b) Replace the sample data $\{6, 7, 8\}$ from population C with $\{12, 13, 14\}$. Note that 6 has been added to each of the sample values in population C.
   (i) Without calculating, which (if any) of the nine entries in the new ANOVA table would be larger than the corresponding entry from part (a)? Smaller? The same?
   (ii) Compute and complete the new ANOVA table.

(c) Replace the sample data $\{0, 4, 5\}$ from population A with $\{3, 7, 8\}$. Note that 3 has been added to each of the sample values in population A. (Use the original values from population C.)
   (i) Without calculating, which (if any) of the nine entries in the new ANOVA table would be larger than the corresponding entry from part (a)? Smaller? The same?
   (ii) Compute and complete the new ANOVA table.

11.4

ALTERNATE FORMULAS (OPTIONAL*)

In Example 11.3, you may have noticed that there were a large number of calculations, many of which involved rounding off. There are some shortcut formulas that can simplify the computations considerably. Also, since these formulas involve less rounding off, accuracy is improved. We will introduce these formulas in an example.

A cereal producer wanted to find out whether the market shelf position of the cereal boxes had any effect on sales. The company made an arrangement with the owner of a chain of 14 supermarkets (similar in sales and clientele) to conduct an experiment to investigate this problem. Each supermarket placed the cereal boxes on one of four shelves. We number the shelves from 1 for the bottom to 4 for the top shelf. Table 11.11 contains 14 numbers representing the number of cases of cereal sold by each store during the experimental period. Each figure is recorded under the shelf position assigned to the store. Notice that three stores were assigned shelf 1, four stores were assigned shelf 2, and so on. In Table 11.11, we also include the total sales for each shelf position: T_1 = total sales for shelf 1, T_2 = total sales for shelf 2, and so on.

---

*The formulas in this section can simplify the calculations in analysis of variance. The increasing use of computers has made it less important to cover these formulas, however.

Table 11.11 contains a sample of sales for each of the four shelf positions. (Not all sample sizes are equal.) The company is interested in whether the (true population) mean sales for each shelf are equal.* The hypotheses to be tested are

$$H_0: \quad \mu_1 = \mu_2 = \mu_3 = \mu_4$$
$$H_a: \quad \text{Not all the means are equal.}$$

Table 11.11
Number of Cases of Cereal Sold at Each Shelf Position During an Experimental Time Period

| | Shelf Position | | | |
	1	2	3	4
Cases	20	24	39	33
sold	23	25	44	39
	17	29	47	27
		22	38	
Total	$T_1 = 60$	$T_2 = 100$	$T_3 = 168$	$T_4 = 99$ $k = 4$
Number of stores	$n_1 = 3$	$n_2 = 4$	$n_3 = 4$	$n_4 = 3$ $n = 14$

Our shortcut formulas will be stated in terms of the following symbols:

n = total number of data values in all the samples
k = number of samples or groups of data
T_i = sum of data values in sample i (i may be 1, 2, 3, etc.)
n_i = number of data values in sample i

The alternate formulas for SSW and SSB are

$$SSB = \sum \frac{T_i^2}{n_i} - \frac{(\sum T_i)^2}{n}$$

$$SSW = \sum x^2 - \sum \frac{T_i^2}{n_i}$$

The symbol $\sum x^2$ represents the sum of the squares of all the data values in the study.

Let us see how these formulas work for the data in Table 11.11:

$$\sum \frac{T_i^2}{n_i} = \frac{T_1^2}{n_1} + \frac{T_2^2}{n_2} + \frac{T_3^2}{n_3} + \frac{T_4^2}{n_4}$$

$$= \frac{60^2}{3} + \frac{100^2}{4} + \frac{168^2}{4} + \frac{99^2}{3}$$

$$= 1200 + 2500 + 7056 + 3267 = 14{,}023$$

---

*The population for position 1, for example, would be the collection of data values representing the cases sold for each store that might in the future use that shelf position for the same experimental time period.

$$\frac{(\sum T_i)^2}{n} = \frac{(T_1 + T_2 + T_3 + T_4)^2}{n}$$

$$= \frac{(60 + 100 + 168 + 99)^2}{14} = \frac{(427)^2}{14}$$

$$= \frac{182{,}329}{14} = 13{,}023.5$$

$$\sum x^2 = 20^2 + 23^2 + 17^2 + 24^2 + 25^2 + 29^2 + 22^2 + 39^2 + 44^2$$
$$+ 47^2 + 38^2 + 33^2 + 39^2 + 27^2$$

$$= 14{,}193$$

$$\text{SSB} = \sum \frac{T_i^2}{n_i} - \frac{(\sum T_i)^2}{n}$$

$$= 14{,}023 - 13{,}023.5 = 999.5$$

Degrees of freedom for SSB: $k - 1 = 4 - 1 = 3$

$$\text{SSW} = \sum x^2 - \sum \frac{T_i^2}{n_i}$$

$$= 14{,}193 - 14{,}023 = 170$$

Degrees of freedom for SSW: $n - k = 14 - 4 = 10$

We can now complete the test for the equality of means. We use the 5% level of significance.

1. *Hypotheses:*

$$H_0: \quad \mu_1 = \mu_2 = \mu_3 = \mu_4$$
$$H_a: \quad \text{Not all the means are equal.}$$

2. *Level of significance:* $\alpha = .05$
3. *Test statistic and observed value:*

$$F = \frac{\text{MSB}}{\text{MSW}} = \frac{\text{SSB}/(k-1)}{\text{SSW}/(n-k)} = \frac{999.5/3}{170/10} \doteq 19.60$$

Degrees of freedom = (3, 10).

4. *Critical region:* From Appendix Table B.6, we see that $F_{.05} = 3.71$. (See Figure 11.11.)

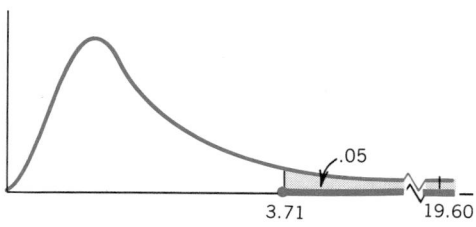

Figure 11.11

5. *Decision:* The observed value of $F = 19.60$ is in the critical region; thus we reject H_0. Therefore, it appears that the (population) means for the four shelf positions are not all equal.

EXERCISE

11.27 In each of the following parts, use the alternate formulas of Section 11.4 to find SSB and SSW.

  (a) Use the data in Exercise 11.13.

  (b) Use the data in Exercise 11.14.

  (c) Use the data in Exercise 11.15.

  (d) Use the data in Exercise 11.16.

11.5

USING MINITAB (OPTIONAL)

The following Minitab printout is a computerization of the analysis of variance we carried out on the data in Table 11.11. This table reported the sales of cases of cereal for four shelf positions over an experimental time period. The question was whether shelf position has an effect on sales. More precisely, we are interested in whether the mean sales for each shelf position are the same.

Fourteen similar stores were involved in the study; some placed the cereal in shelf position 1, some in position 2, and so on. The number of cases sold was recorded for each store (in Table 11.11). The type of analysis of variance discussed in this chapter is sometimes called *one-way analysis of variance,* and the command that performs this test is the AOVONEWAY command. The data are in columns 1–4:

C1	C2	C3	C4
20	24	39	33
23	25	44	39
17	29	47	27
	22	38	

Session Command	Dialog Box
MTB > AOVONEWAY C1 - C4	**Stat ▶ ANOVA ▶ Oneway [Unstacked]** Type *C1-C4* in box under **Responses [in separate columns]** Click **OK**

Output

One-Way Analysis of Variance

```
Analysis of Variance
Source      DF        SS        MS        F        p
Factor       3       999.5    333.2    19.60    0.000
Error       10       170.0     17.0
Total       13      1169.5
```

```
                                   Individual 95% CIs For Mean
                                   Based on Pooled StDev
 Level       N       Mean      StDev  ------+---------+---------+---------+
 C1          3      20.000     3.000      (----*----)
 C2          4      25.000     2.944          (----*----)
 C3          4      42.000     4.243                            (----*----)
 C4          3      33.000     6.000                   (----*----)
                                          ------+---------+---------+---------+
 Pooled StDev =     4.123                       20        30        40        50
```

The Minitab ANOVA table looks slightly different from the ones displayed previously in this chapter—the printout uses the term *factor* where we used *between*, and the term *error* where we used *within*. The P-value is approximately 0, so we should reject the null hypothesis of equal sales (on the average). This means that shelf position does appear to affect sales.

The printout also gives some statistics for the data in columns C1, C2, C3, and C4 (the data for the four shelf positions). Also, 95% confidence intervals are displayed graphically for the (population) mean sales for the four shelf positions (for the length of time studied). These confidence intervals give a rough idea of the location of the population means. The intervals are of the form

$$\bar{x}_i \pm t_{.025} \cdot S_p / \sqrt{n_i} \qquad \text{df for } t: \quad n - k = 10$$

where the $\bar{x}_i$ is the sample mean for sample i ($i = 1, 2, 3$, or 4), n_i is the size of sample i, and S_p is the pooled standard deviation given in the printout. This is an estimate of the common standard deviation σ. We saw that MSW is an estimate of σ^2 (estimate 1). Minitab computes S_p as follows:

$$S_p = \sqrt{\text{MSW}} = \sqrt{\text{MSError}} = \sqrt{17} \doteq 4.12$$

Great care must be taken in interpreting these confidence intervals *together*. Whereas each one taken *individually* has a 95% level of confidence, we cannot be 95% sure that *all* of them will *simultaneously* be correct. (Each time you toss a coin, you are 50% sure of getting heads. But if you toss 4 coins, you cannot be 50% sure of getting four heads. In fact, your level of confidence in four heads should be only 6.25%.)

EXERCISES

Suggested exercises for use with Minitab are 11.33, 11.35–11.38, and 11.40.

11.6

WORKING WITH DATA (OPTIONAL)

1. Subjects can be classified on the basis of blood pressure in the following way: *normotensive*—blood pressure levels below 140/90; *hypertensive*—blood pressure

levels 160/95 or higher; *borderline*—all others. Note, for example, that 126/80 represents a systolic blood pressure of 126 and a diastolic reading of 80. Using the Framingham Heart Study data in Appendix Table B.11, randomly select 15 males age 50–59 from each of the four categories. For each subject, record serum cholesterol level.

(a) At a 5% level of significance, is there sufficient evidence to indicate a difference in population mean serum cholesterol levels between the three groups for males?

(b) Do you think the ANOVA procedure used in part (a) is appropriate for your data sets? If not, which condition(s) appear to be violated?*

In Problems 2–3 use the following categories:

Number of Cigarettes Per Day	Category
0	Nonsmoker
1–19	Light smoker
20 and above	Moderate to heavy smoker

From Table B.11, obtain a random sample of at least 10 subjects in each category. Record the systolic blood pressure and serum cholesterol.

2. (a) At the 5% level of significance, does there appear to be a difference in population mean systolic blood pressures for the three categories of smokers?

(b) Do you think the ANOVA procedure used in part (a) is appropriate for your data sets? If not, which condition(s) appear to be violated?*

3. (a) At the 5% level of significance, does there appear to be a difference in population mean cholesterol levels for the three categories of smokers?

(b) Do you think the ANOVA procedure used in part (a) is appropriate for your data sets? If not, which condition(s) appear to be violated?*

11.7

SUMMARY

In this chapter, we discussed how one investigates the question of whether several population means are equal. That is, we learned how one tests the hypotheses

$$H_0: \quad \mu_1 = \mu_2 = \cdots = \mu_k$$
$$H_a: \quad \text{Not all the means are equal.}$$

The method used to test these hypotheses is called **analysis of variance** (ANOVA). The test statistic is computed as follows. Let

k = number of means to be tested

n_i = number of data values in sample i from population i ($i = 1, 2, 3,$ etc.)

x_i = any data value from sample i

T_i = sum of the data values in sample i

---

*In practice, this issue should be investigated before applying the analysis of variance procedure.

x = any data value in the study

n = total number of data values in the study

$\overline{\overline{x}}$ = grand mean (mean of all the data values in the study)

1. Find the **sum of squares within, SSW:**

$$SSW = \sum (x_1 - \overline{x}_1)^2 + \sum (x_2 - \overline{x}_2)^2 + \cdots + \sum (x_k - \overline{x}_k)^2$$

A formula that is sometimes more convenient is

$$SSW = \sum x^2 - \sum \frac{T_i^2}{n_i}$$

The number of degrees of freedom for SSW is defined to be $n - k$.

2. Find the **sum of squares between, SSB:**

$$SSB = n_1 (\overline{x}_1 - \overline{\overline{x}})^2 + n_2 (\overline{x}_2 - \overline{\overline{x}})^2 + \cdots + n_k (\overline{x}_k - \overline{\overline{x}})^2$$

A formula that is sometimes more convenient is

$$SSB = \sum \frac{T_i^2}{n_i} - \frac{(\sum T_i)^2}{n}$$

The number of degrees of freedom for SSB is defined as $k - 1$.

3. Find the **mean square within, MSW:**

$$MSW = \frac{SSW}{n - k}$$

4. Find the **mean square between, MSB:**

$$MSB = \frac{SSB}{k - 1}$$

5. Find the value of F:

$$F = \frac{MSB}{MSW}$$

This is our test statistic. Large values of F favor H_a.

The statistic F has the F distribution with df $= (k - 1, n - k)$. Appendix Table B.6 contains critical values of F. If α is the level of significance of the test, find F_α from this table. If the calculated value of F is greater than or equal to F_α, we reject H_0. Otherwise, we do not reject H_0.

REVIEW EXERCISES

11.28   For each of the following parts, assume that random samples of size 6 were selected from each of four populations. Determine whether there is sufficient evidence to reject the hypothesis of equal population means using a 1% significance level.

	$s_{\overline{x}}^2$	$s_A^2 + s_B^2 + s_C^2 + s_D^2$
(a)	4	24
(b)	2.5	24
(c)	6	24
(d)	4	48
(e)	4	12

In Exercises 11.29–11.30, compute the sums of squares to find SSW and SSB. Then complete the ANOVA table and test the hypothesis of equal population means with a 5% significance level.

11.29

A	B	C
5	15	20
15	20	20
	25	25
		30
		30

11.30

A	B	C	D
0	5	12	13
0	10	12	21
9	15	6	
		2	

11.31 Consider H_0: $\mu_A = \mu_B = \mu_C = \mu_D = \mu_E$.

(a) Complete the following ANOVA table.

Source	Sum of Squares (SS)	Degrees of Freedom (df)	Mean Square (MS)	F
Between samples	132			
Within samples				
Total	532	44		

(b) At a 5% level of significance, would you reject H_0?

11.32 Consider H_0: $\mu_A = \mu_B = \mu_C = \mu_D$. Sample sizes are $n_A = n_B = 5$, $n_C = 6$, $n_D = 8$.

(a) Complete the following ANOVA table.

Source	Sum of Squares (SS)	Degrees of Freedom (df)	Mean Square (MS)	F
Between samples	54			
Within samples	240			
Total				

(b) At a 1% level of significance, would you reject H_0?

11.33 Use the following data to test H_0: $\mu_A = \mu_B = \mu_C$ with a 5% significance level.

A	B	C
72	47	50
48	55	40
60	60	30
60		40

11.34 Consider the following data to test H_0: $\mu_A = \mu_B$ with a 5% significance level. Use the analysis of variance method. The data are given in the table.

A	B
25	15
45	15
50	20
	30
	40

11.35 A college administrator claimed that there was no difference in (population) mean college grade point averages for students coming from three high schools A, B, and C. Use the following data to test the administrator's claim with a 5% significance level.

A	B	C
1.9	2.3	2.8
2.3	2.7	2.8
2.8	3.2	2.9
2.4	2.8	3.5
2.5	2.9	3.0
2.5	2.9	

11.36 A production plant manager claimed that there was no difference in mean times to complete an assembly line job between plants A, B, C, and D. Samples from each of the plants yielded the following data, where a data value represents the time in minutes to complete the job.

A	B	C	D
18	20	23	12
11	14	16	18
14	16	21	17
12	18		13
15			

Test the claim using a 5% level of significance.

11.37 A corporation owned three large department stores, A, B, and C, located in three cities. The manager of store A claimed that the mean daily percentage of sales over $50 was the same for the three stores. A sample yielded the following data, where each data value represents the percentage of sales over $50 for a particular day. The data are

A	B	C
32	38	64
40	42	46
24	26	42
48	44	48
36	40	50

Test the manager's claim using a 5% level of significance.

11.38 Refer to Exercise 11.37. Before the data were obtained, the manager of store C claimed that there was a difference in population means between stores B and C. Test the claim using the analysis of variance procedure. Use a 5% level of significance.

11.39 Test the claim that there is a difference in mean LDL cholesterol (mg/100 ml)[*] between elite runners, good runners, and nonrunners using the following data:

	Sample Size	$\bar{x}$	s
Elite runners	20	108	24.5
Good runners	8	121	29.5
Nonrunners	72	124	35.6

(*Source:* Martin, 1977, p. 93).

Use a 5% level of significance.

11.40 Test the claim that there is no difference in the mean percent of calories from protein between men in the Crevalcore and the Montegiorgio areas of Greece and Crete using a 5% level of significance with the following data:

	Sample Size	$\bar{x}$	s
Crevalcore	28	13	1.7
Montegiorgio	34	11.7	1.7
Crete	30	11.2	2.2

Source: Keys, 1970, p. I-166.

11.41 Suppose that you are to test the hypothesis that the means of populations A, B, C, D, E, and F are the same with a 5% level of significance. Consider the following sample data:

A	B	C	D	E	F
0	4	8	4	5	5
7	10	15	11	12	12
20	22	28	24	25	22

(a) Sketch the data (as in Figure 11.1). Based on the sketch of the data, do you believe that the hypothesis of equal population means should be rejected?

(b) Carry out the test. Does this substantiate your conclusion in part (a)?

11.42 Suppose that you are to test the hypothesis that the means of populations A, B, and C are the same with a 5% level of significance. Consider the sample data given in the table at the top of page 528.

---

[*]LDL stands for low-density lipoprotein.

A	B	C
0	5	17
2	8	20
8	13	25
2	9	21
3	9	23
3	10	20

(a)   Sketch the data (as in Figure 11.1). Based on the sketch of the data, do you believe that the hypothesis of equal population means should be rejected?

(b)   Carry out the test. Does this substantiate your conclusion in part (a)?

11.43   Using the data in Exercise 11.42, the following ANOVA table is obtained:

Source	Sum of Squares (SS)	Degrees of Freedom (df)	Mean Square (MS)	F
Between samples	1008	2	504	70
Within samples	108	15	7.2	
Total	1116	17		

Suppose that 2 is added to each data value. The following data are obtained:

A	B	C
2	7	19
4	10	22
10	15	27
4	11	23
5	11	25
5	12	22

(a)   Construct an ANOVA table for these data and compare with the previous ANOVA table.

(b)   Explain why such a relationship holds between the two ANOVA tables.

11.44   The following JMP printout uses the data in Exercise 11.9. Note that the horizontal line in the diagram represents an overall mean of 25.2 for the combined five groups. Also Prob > F is the P-value.

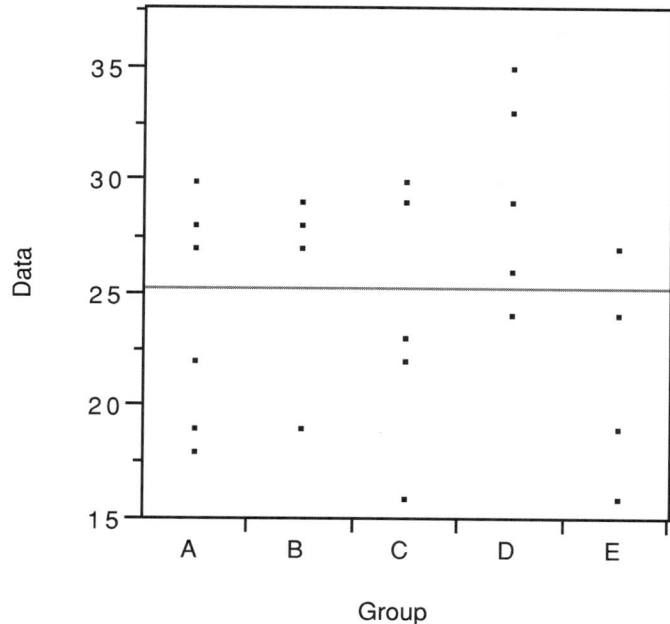

Analysis of Variance				
Source	**DF**	**Sum of Squares**	**Mean Square**	**F Ratio**
Model	4	208.80000	52.2000	2.1750
Error	25	600.00000	24.0000	**Prob>F**
C Total	29	808.80000		0.1011

(a) Consider a test of the hypothesis $H_0: \mu_A = \mu_B = \mu_C = \mu_D = \mu_E$ with a 5% level of significance. Does the diagram suggest considerable overlap among the five groups? Do you expect a P-value larger than .05?

(b) Give the observed F value. At what levels of significance would the null hypothesis be rejected?

Notes

Daniels, J., G. Krakenbuhl, C. Foster, J. Gilbert, and S. Daniels, "Aerobic Responses of Female Distance Runners to Submaximal and Maximal Exercise," in P. Milvy, ed. *The Long Distance Runner*, New York: Urizen Books, 1977.

Keys, A., ed., "Coronary Heart Disease in Seven Countries." *Circulation*, Vol. 1, No. 1 (Suppl. 1), 1970.

Martin, R., W. Haskell, and P. Wood, "Blood Chemistry and Lipid Profiles of Elite Distance Runners," in P. Milvy, ed. *The Long Distance Runner*, New York: Urizen Books, 1977.

Morganroth, J., and B. Maron, "The Athlete's Heart Syndrome: A New Perspective," in P. Milvy, ed. *The Long Distance Runner*, New York: Urizen Books, 1977.

Neter, J., W. Wasserman, and M. H. Kutner, *Applied Linear Statistical Models*, 3rd ed. Homewood, Ill.: Richard D. Irwin Inc., 1990.

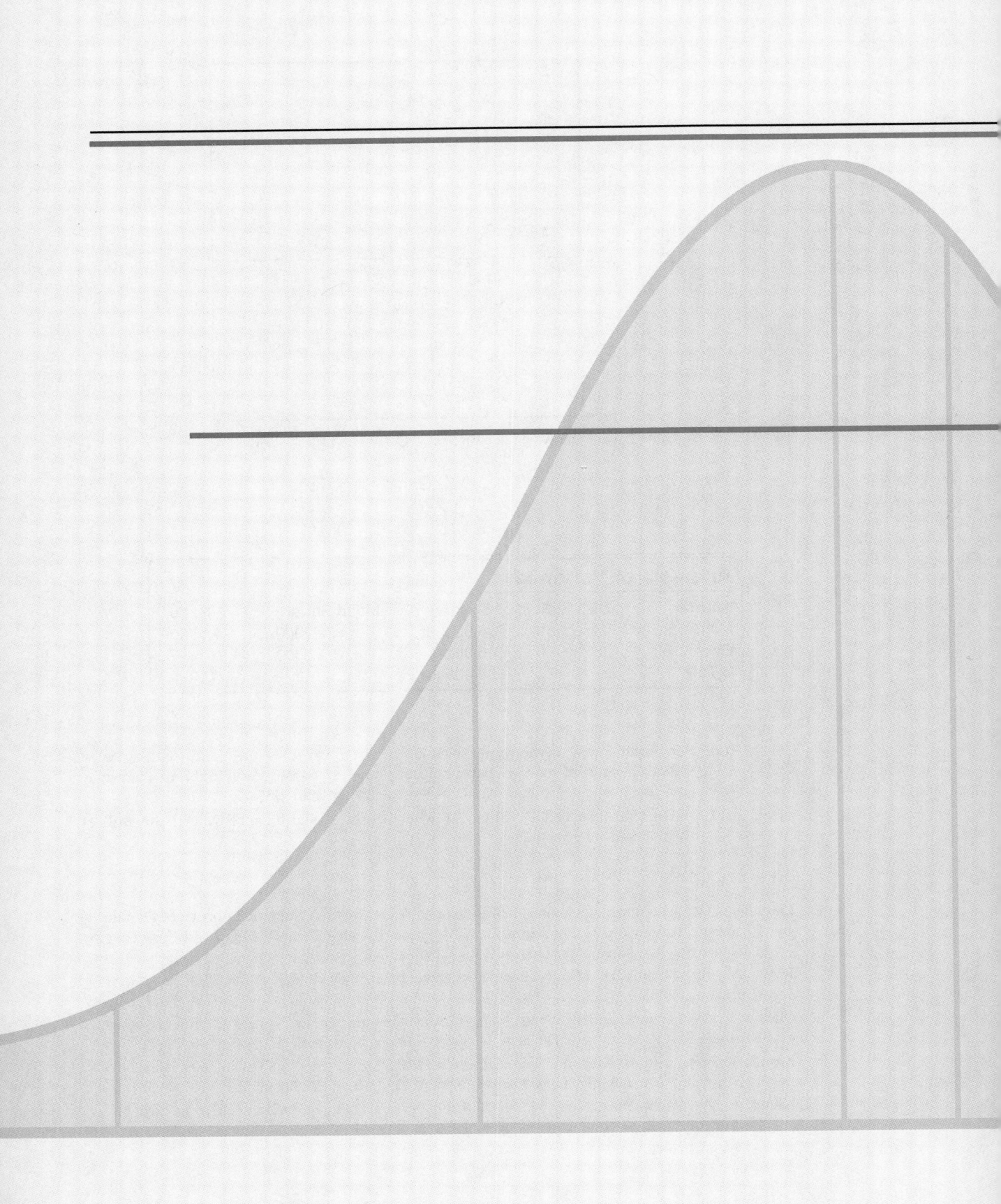

CHAPTER 12

ANALYSIS OF CATEGORICAL DATA

12.1 **INTRODUCTION**

12.2 **THE CHI-SQUARE TEST FOR GOODNESS-OF-FIT**

12.3 **TESTS OF INDEPENDENCE; CONTINGENCY TABLES**

12.4 **TESTS OF HOMOGENEITY**

12.5 **USING MINITAB (OPTIONAL)**

12.6 **WORKING WITH DATA (OPTIONAL)**

12.7 **SUMMARY**

   REVIEW EXERCISES

   NOTES

12.1

INTRODUCTION

In Chapter 8, we discussed inference problems concerning a population proportion. For example, we learned how to test a claim that the proportion of all voters favoring a candidate is more than .5. This was done by sampling a certain number of voters and placing them into two categories (also called cells), namely, those in favor of the candidate and those not in favor of the candidate. We then calculated the appropriate test statistic and carried out the test. The important data in this study are the numbers of voters placed in each category. Frequency data of this type are sometimes called **categorical data.**

In some situations, we may wish to study several proportions. For example, we might be interested in questions concerning the proportion of television viewers watching each of the three major networks: ABC, CBS, and NBC. In this chapter, we discuss such questions. The technique we introduce to study these questions is called the **chi-square test for goodness-of-fit.** A variation of this test will also be used to conduct **tests of independence.** Such tests can be used to determine whether two characteristics (such as political preference and income) are related or independent. Another variation of the chi-square test for goodness-of-fit that we will consider is a **test of homogeneity.** Such a test is used to study whether different populations are similar (or homogeneous) with respect to some characteristic. For example, we may wish to decide whether several different countries have the same incidence of coronary heart disease.

12.2

THE CHI-SQUARE TEST FOR GOODNESS-OF-FIT

To understand how the chi-square test for goodness-of-fit works, consider the following example: A department store decided to market a new toy that comes in three different color schemes. The manufacturer claimed that each color scheme should sell in the same proportion. The department store wanted to check this claim and decided to randomly observe 300 sales to see how many of each color scheme were sold. (The color schemes are the categories in this study.)

We are actually interested in the proportion of each color scheme that will be sold in the population consisting of all these toys that may be sold by the store. The 300 toys sold may be thought of as a sample from this population. We are interested in three proportions associated with this population: p_1 is the proportion of all the toys sold in color scheme 1; p_2 is the proportion sold in color scheme 2; and p_3 is the proportion sold in color scheme 3. If each color scheme is equally popular, then each proportion has the value $\frac{1}{3}$. The department store wanted to test the hypotheses

H_0: $p_1 = p_2 = p_3 = \frac{1}{3}$

H_a: H_0 is not true (not all the color schemes will sell in the same proportion).

In this case, H_0 states that the proportions are equal, but the technique we develop will enable us to test for any values of the proportions as long as they add up to 1. For example, if the situation warranted, we could check to see whether $p_1 = \frac{1}{2}$ and $p_2 = p_3 = \frac{1}{4}$.

Now if H_0 is true, we can expect about one-third of the sample of 300 sales to be in color scheme 1, one-third in color scheme 2, and one-third in color scheme 3. Therefore, we expect about $(300)(\frac{1}{3}) = 100$ sales for each color scheme. The idea is to compare these expected frequencies with the actual observed frequencies (number of sales) for each color scheme. In the second and third columns of Table 12.1, we display the observed frequencies of sales (denoted by the symbol O) and the

Table 12.1

Color Scheme	O	$E = np$	$O - E$	$(O - E)^2$	$\dfrac{(O - E)^2}{E}$
1	89	100	-11	121	1.21
2	107	100	7	49	.49
3	104	100	4	16	.16
Totals:	300	300	0	186	1.86

$$\chi^2 = \sum \frac{(O - E)^2}{E} \uparrow$$

expected frequencies (denoted by E) for each color scheme. The formula for E is

$$E = np$$

where n is the sample size and p is the proportion specified in the null hypothesis for a particular category.

If the observed frequencies deviate too much from the expected frequencies, we reject the null hypothesis. Hence our first impulse would be to calculate the differences $O - E$. If H_0 is true, then these differences taken together should not be too large. We want to calculate one number (a test statistic) that will measure this. Note, however, that the sum of these differences (column 4 of Table 12.1) is 0. This is always the case. Therefore, the sum of the differences will not help us.

If we square the differences and look at $(O - E)^2$, we eliminate negative signs so that we will not have some terms canceling or diminishing other terms when we add these terms. (See the fifth column in Table 12.1.)

However, one thing to keep in mind when looking at differences or squares of differences is that these should be assessed in relation to some standard. For example, a difference in weight of 5 pounds between two men is not much, but a difference of 5 pounds between two mice is a great deal. If we measure such differences in relation to the average weight of men and the average weight of mice, we get a more accurate measure of these differences. We could accomplish this by dividing the difference by the average or expected weight.

A similar situation occurs with the terms $(O - E)^2$. We should divide by the expected frequency E. That is, we should look at the terms $(O - E)^2/E$. (See column 6 of Table 12.1.) We will use the sum of these terms (which we denote by χ^2) as our test statistic:

$$\chi^2 = \sum \frac{(O - E)^2}{E}$$

From Table 12.1, we see that $\chi^2 = 1.86$. If H_0 is true, we expect the observed frequencies to be not too far from the expected frequencies. This means that the terms $(O - E)^2/E$, and therefore χ^2, should not be too large. Note that the strongest possible evidence in favor of H_0 would occur if each observed frequency were the same as the expected frequency ($O = E$) for each case. When this occurs, $\chi^2 = 0$.

Very large values of χ^2 would constitute evidence against H_0. If the value of χ^2 is "too large," we reject H_0. This would mean that not all three color schemes are equally popular. The value of χ^2 will be considered too large if it is unlikely that we would observe such a large value of χ^2 if H_0 were true. To assess this, we must know something about the probability distribution of χ^2. It can be shown that, under appropriate conditions, χ^2 has (approximately) what is known as a chi-square distribution.

Properties of a Chi-Square Distribution

1. There is not just one chi-square distribution but, in fact, an infinite number of them. Each one has a number associated with it called its degrees of freedom, df. For the previous expression, df $= k - 1$ where $k =$ number of categories. We use the degrees of freedom to specify which chi-square distribution we are using.

2. The shape of a chi-square curve is not symmetric but is skewed to the right. It begins at 0 and extends indefinitely in a positive direction. The total area under the curve is 1 (see Figure 12.1 on page 534).

3. The expected value of χ^2 is the degrees of freedom, df.

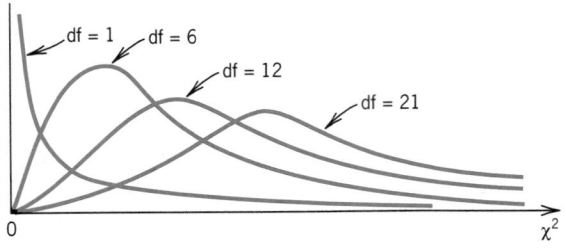

Figure 12.1
Chi-Square Curves

Appendix Table B.5 relates probabilities to various values of χ^2. For a particular chi-square distribution, it gives the value of χ^2 such that the area under the chi-square curve to the right of this value is equal to some desired probability. For example, suppose that we are concerned with the chi-square distribution with df = 10, and we want the value of χ^2 such that the area under the curve to the right of it is .05. We denote this value by $\chi^2_{.05}$. Locate the value of the degrees of freedom in the far left column of the table (df = 10). Now look at the column under $\chi^2_{.05}$. The intersection of this column with the row corresponding to df = 10 contains the desired value of χ^2, namely, 18.307. Thus $\chi^2_{.05}$ = 18.307. This means that $P(\chi^2 \geq 18.307) = .05$. See Figure 12.2.

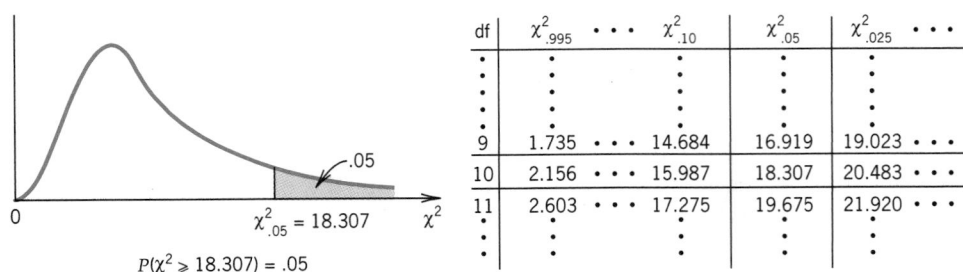

df	$\chi^2_{.995}$	$\cdots$	$\chi^2_{.10}$	$\chi^2_{.05}$	$\chi^2_{.025}$	$\cdots$
9	1.735	$\cdots$	14.684	16.919	19.023	$\cdots$
10	2.156	$\cdots$	15.987	18.307	20.483	$\cdots$
11	2.603	$\cdots$	17.275	19.675	21.920	$\cdots$

$\chi^2_{.05} = 18.307$

$P(\chi^2 \geq 18.307) = .05$

Figure 12.2
A Portion of Appendix Table B.5

The following box gives the conditions under which χ^2 has a chi-square distribution.

If the null hypothesis (specifying values for certain proportions) is true, the expression

$$\chi^2 = \sum \frac{(O - E)^2}{E}$$

has an approximate chi-square distribution provided the sample size n is sufficiently large. We will consider n sufficiently large if it is large enough so that the expected frequency (E) of each category is at least 5. The number of degrees of freedom is

$$df = k - 1$$

where k = number of categories. The expected frequency of a category is

$$E = np$$

where p is the proportion for the category specified in the null hypothesis.

We said that the null hypothesis H_0 will be rejected when the value of χ^2 is so large that it is unlikely that we would observe such a large value if H_0 were true. "Unlikely" means having a low probability. We denote this probability by the symbol α; this is the level of significance. (As we stated previously, the researcher usually chooses this value.) This means that we perform a right-tailed chi-square test. For example, suppose that we had decided on the value $\alpha = .05$ for this problem. Now df $= k - 1 = 3 - 1 = 2$. We find the critical value from Appendix Table B.5 to be

$$\chi^2_\alpha = \chi^2_{.05} = 5.991$$

Therefore, it would be unlikely (only a 5% chance) that we would observe a value of $\chi^2 \geq 5.991$ if H_0 were true. This means that the critical region consists of values of $\chi^2 \geq 5.991$. We have seen in Table 12.1 that the observed value of χ^2 is 1.86. This is not in the critical region; thus we do not reject H_0. Hence there is no evidence that the three color schemes will not sell in the same proportions.

We can now summarize the essential features of this chi-square test for goodness-of-fit.

Chi-Square Test for Goodness-of-Fit   To test the null hypothesis, which specifies certain (population) proportions associated with each category, we perform a right-tailed chi-square test. Suppose that the level of significance of the test is α. We calculate the value of χ^2 and find the critical value χ^2_α in Appendix Table B.5. If $\chi^2 \geq \chi^2_\alpha$, we reject H_0. Otherwise, we do not reject H_0.

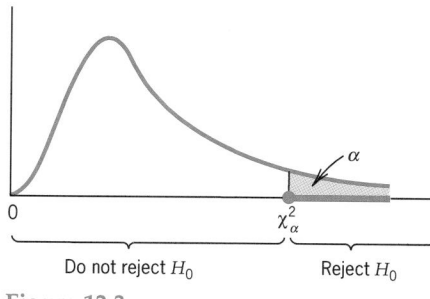

Figure 12.3
Critical Region

Assumption: The expected frequency of each category is at least 5.

We should keep in mind the following nomenclature: We said that the categories into which the elements of the sample are classified are sometimes called *cells*. Therefore, the observed frequencies are also called the **observed cell frequencies.** The expected frequencies are also called the **expected cell frequencies.**

EXAMPLE 12.1

A manufacturer of electronic instruments uses four assembly lines to produce the same instrument. Each assembly line is theoretically equivalent; hence all should have the same rate of production of instruments needing service under the warranty. The company wished to check this. Therefore, a decision was made to look at the next 100 instruments returned to the factory as defective and determine how many came from each line. Now assembly line 1 is used for two work shifts per day, whereas assembly lines 2, 3, and 4 are each used for one shift per day. The defectives attributed to lines 1, 2, 3, and 4, respectively, are 53, 18, 14, and 15. Carry out the test for equivalence of the assembly lines at the 10% level of significance.

Solution

The population of interest is all defective instruments produced by the four assembly lines. Suppose the assembly lines are equivalent; that is, they produce defectives at the same rate. Since assembly lines 2, 3, and 4 are used for one shift and assembly line 1 is used for two shifts, we would expect the proportion of all defectives produced to be the same for assembly lines 2, 3, and 4 but twice this proportion for assembly line 1. Another way to look at it is this: There are a total of five work shifts per day using the four assembly lines. Assembly line 1 is used for two of these shifts; lines 2, 3, and 4 are each used for one shift. Therefore, the proportion p_1 of all defectives from line 1 should be $\frac{2}{5}$ and the proportions p_2, p_3, and p_4 from lines 2, 3, and 4 should be $\frac{1}{5}$ each. This is the null hypothesis.

1. *Hypotheses:*

$$H_0: \quad p_1 = \tfrac{2}{5} = .4, \ p_2 = p_3 = p_4 = \tfrac{1}{5} = .2$$
$$H_a: \quad H_0 \text{ is not true.}$$

2. *Level of significance:* $\alpha = .10$

3. *Test statistic and observed value:* We have a sample of $n = 100$ defectives. To calculate the expected cell frequencies, we multiply this total by the cell probabilities (proportions) asserted in the null hypothesis H_0. The expected frequencies are given in Table 12.2.

Table 12.2

Assembly Line	p	$np = E$
1	.4	$(100)(.4) = 40$
2	.2	$(100)(.2) = 20$
3	.2	$(100)(.2) = 20$
4	.2	$(100)(.2) = 20$

Table 12.3, which is used to calculate χ^2, follows.

4. *Critical region:* We perform a right-tailed test. From Appendix Table B.5, we find that for df $= 3$, $\chi^2_{.10} = 6.251$. The critical region is sketched in Figure 12.4.

5. *Decision:* The observed value of χ^2 is in the critical region; thus we reject H_0. This means that the evidence suggests that the assembly lines are not equivalent.

Table 12.3

Assembly Line	O	E	$O - E$	$(O - E)^2$	$\dfrac{(O - E)^2}{E}$
1	53	40	13	169	4.225
2	18	20	−2	4	.200
3	14	20	−6	36	1.800
4	15	20	−5	25	1.250

$$\chi^2 = \sum \frac{(O - E)^2}{E} = 7.475$$

degrees of freedom $= k - 1 = 4 - 1 = 3$

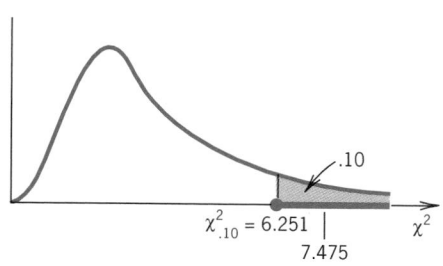

Figure 12.4

Sometimes the expected frequencies will not be whole numbers, which is perfectly all right, as the following example illustrates.

EXAMPLE 12.2
The manager of a theater complex with four theaters wanted to see whether there was a difference in popularity of the four movies currently showing for Saturday afternoon matinees. The number of customers for each movie was recorded for one Saturday afternoon with the following results: 63, 55, 75, and 77 customers viewed movies 1, 2, 3, and 4, respectively. Complete the test to see whether there is a difference at the 5% level of significance.

Solution

1. *Hypotheses:*   If the four movies are equally popular, the proportion of the population of moviegoers in town who favor movie 1 is .25. Hence $p_1 = .25$. Similarly, $p_2 = p_3 = p_4 = .25$. Thus the hypotheses are

$$H_0:\quad p_1 = p_2 = p_3 = p_4 = .25$$
$$H_a:\quad H_0 \text{ is not true.}$$

2. *Level of significance:* $\alpha = .05$

3. *Test statistic and observed value:*   Our sample size is the sum of the observed frequencies:

$$n = 63 + 55 + 75 + 77 = 270$$

The proportion specified for each movie in the null hypothesis happens to be the same, namely, .25. The expected frequency of each movie is

$$E = np = (270)(.25) = 67.5$$

Table 12.4, which is used to calculate χ^2, follows on page 538.

4. *Critical region:*   We perform a right-tailed test. From Appendix Table B.5, we find that for df $= 3$, $\chi^2_{.05} = 7.815$. See Figure 12.5 on page 538.

5. *Decision:*   The observed value ($\chi^2 = 4.78$) is not in the critical region; thus we do not reject H_0. This means that there is insufficient evidence to conclude that the four movies will not be equally popular.

Table 12.4

Movie	O	E	$O - E$	$(O - E)^2$	$\dfrac{(O - E)^2}{E}$
1	63	67.5	−4.5	20.25	.30
2	55	67.5	−12.5	156.25	2.31
3	75	67.5	7.5	56.25	.83
4	77	67.5	9.5	90.25	1.34

$$\chi^2 = \sum \frac{(O - E)^2}{E} = 4.78$$

degrees of freedom = 3

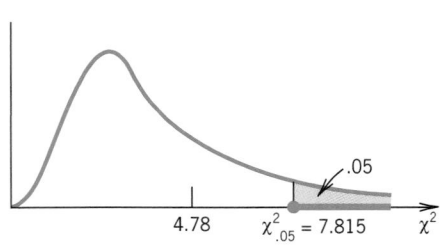

Figure 12.5

We said that to apply the chi-square test for goodness-of-fit, the sample size should be large enough so that each expected cell frequency is at least 5. When this condition is not met, it may be possible to combine two or more cells into one cell for which the expected frequency is of the required size.

The requirement that the expected cell frequencies be at least 5 is thought by some statisticians to be overly conservative. It has been observed that when the sample size is about four or five times the number of cells, the chi-square test is still applicable even when some of the expected cell frequencies are much smaller than 5 (Lindgren, 1976, p. 424).

EXERCISES

12.1   In each of the following parts, find **(i)** $\chi^2_{.01}$, **(ii)** $\chi^2_{.025}$, **(iii)** $\chi^2_{.05}$, **(iv)** $\chi^2_{.95}$, and **(v)** $\chi^2_{.99}$.

   (a)   Assume a chi-square distribution with 9 degrees of freedom.

   (b)   Assume a chi-square distribution with 15 degrees of freedom.

   (c)   Assume a chi-square distribution with 25 degrees of freedom.

12.2   Assume a chi-square distribution with 6 degrees of freedom. Fill in the blanks.

   (a) $P(\chi^2 \geq \underline{\quad}) = .01$ **(b)** $P(\chi^2 \geq \underline{\quad}) = .99$

   (c) $P(\chi^2 > \underline{\quad}) = .05$ **(d)** $P(\chi^2 < \underline{\quad}) = .90$

   (e) $P(\chi^2 \leq \underline{\quad}) = .01$ **(f)** $P(\chi^2 < \underline{\quad}) = .05$

12.3   Complete each of the following underlined parts.

   (a) $\chi^2_{.10} = 17.275$,   df = _____

   (b) $\chi^2_{\underline{\quad}} = 2.167$,   df = 7

   (c) $\chi^2_{.95} = $ _____,   df = 10

   (d) $\chi^2_{.01} = 44.314$,   df = _____

   (e) $\chi^2_{\underline{\quad}} = 18.549$,   df = 12

   (f) $\chi^2_{.05} = $ _____,   df = 17

   (g) $\chi^2_{.90} = $ _____,   df = 20

   (h) $\chi^2_{.99} = $ _____,   df = 11

12.4   Assuming a χ^2 distribution with 18 degrees of freedom, find each of the following probabilities:

   (a) $P(\chi^2 > 25.989)$ **(b)** $P(\chi^2 < 7.015)$

   (c) $P(7.015 < \chi^2 < 9.390)$ **(d)** $P(10.865 < \chi^2 < 28.869)$

In Exercises 12.5–12.7, you are given the null hypothesis H_0, the level of significance α, and the observed frequency for each of k categories. Complete the test in each exercise.

12.5 $H_0 : p_1 = p_2 = p_3 = p_4 = \frac{1}{4}; \alpha = .05$

Category	O
1	68
2	65
3	77
4	90

12.6 $H_0 : p_1 = p_2 = p_3 = \frac{1}{5}; p_4 = \frac{2}{5}; \alpha = .01$

Category	O
1	68
2	65
3	77
4	90

12.7 $H_0 : p_1 = p_2 = \frac{1}{10}; p_3 = p_4 = \frac{1}{5}; p_5 = \frac{2}{5}; \alpha = .10$

Category	O
1	12
2	20
3	20
4	30
5	38

12.8   Two friends were playing a board game in which a die played a big role. One of the players believed the die was not fair. Sixty tosses of the die produced the following results. Test the hypothesis that the die is fair. Use a 5% level of significance.

Number of Dots	O
1	7
2	6
3	7
4	18
5	15
6	7

12.9   An official of a plastics industry claimed that the industry employed 30% white women, 5% minority women, 50% white men, and 15% minority men. To test the claim, an affirmative action committee randomly sampled 150 employees and obtained the information given in the table at the top of page 540.

Category	O
White females	40
Minority females	15
White males	80
Minority males	15

Test the official's claim at a 5% level of significance.

12.10   The accompanying table gives the percent distribution of U.S. exports:

Bought by	Percent
Canada	22
European Community	23.6
Japan	11.7
Newly industrialized countries	10.8
Other	31.9

Source: U.S. News & World Report, Feb. 5, 1990, p. 54.

A computer executive wondered whether exports of the company's newest computer model would differ from the distribution in the table. Exports of 200 units were as follows: Canada, 62; European Community, 58; Japan, 15; Newly industrialized countries, 14; Other, 51. At the 5% level of significance, will the company's sales differ from U.S. export distribution?

12.11   The owner of a large company claimed that $\frac{1}{10}$ of the personnel earned less than $25,000; $\frac{3}{10}$ earned at least $25,000 but less than $30,000; $\frac{3}{10}$ earned at least $30,000 but less than $35,000; and $\frac{3}{10}$ earned at least $35,000. At a 10% level of significance, do the following sample data give sufficient evidence to refute the owner's claim?

Category	O
Less than $25,000	19
At least $25,000 but less than $30,000	56
At least $30,000 but less than $35,000	51
At least $35,000	40

12.12   A sports enthusiast theorized that 50% of college basketball games are decided by less than 10 points; 25% are decided by at least 10 and not more than 19 points; 20% by at least 20 and not more than 29 points; and 5% by more than 29 points. A survey of 112 games gave the following information:

Category	O
Less than 10 points	70
At least 10 but not more than 19 points	20
At least 20 but not more than 29 points	13
More than 29 points	9

At a 5% significance level, is there sufficient evidence to refute the claim?

12.13   A computer science major claimed to have written a program that would randomly generate integers from 1 to 100. The program generated the following data. Use a 5% level of significance to test the claim.

Integers	O
1–10	6
11–20	6
21–30	13
31–40	9
41–50	13
51–60	11
61–70	8
71–80	12
81–90	10
91–100	12

12.14   Test the hypothesis that the following data were sampled from the standard normal distribution. Use a 10% level of significance. The data, which have been rounded to two decimal places, are as follows:

Interval	O
Less than or equal to -1.16	7
More than -1.16 but not more than $-.68$	7
More than $-.68$ but not more than $-.32$	6
More than $-.32$ but not more than 0	7
More than 0 but not more than .32	13
More than .32 but not more than .68	5
More than .68 but not more than 1.16	9
More than 1.16	6

(*Hint:*   For a standard normal variable, what proportion of the data would you expect to be less than -1.16, at least -1.16 but not more than $-.68$, etc.?)

12.3

TESTS OF INDEPENDENCE; CONTINGENCY TABLES

At the beginning of this chapter, we said that the chi-square test for goodness-of-fit can be used to study the question of whether two characteristics are related (dependent) or independent.

Now we examine what is meant by the *independence of two characteristics*. Suppose that two candidates, call them A and B, are running for political office and that in fact 75% of all the voters favor candidate A and 25% favor candidate B. Consider the two characteristics: the choice of candidates and the gender of the voter. These characteristics are independent if the percentages favoring candidates A and B are the same for male voters as for female voters (in other words, if 75% of male voters favor candidate A and 75% of female voters favor candidate A, etc.). If the percentage of men favoring a particular candidate is greater than the percentage of women favoring the same candidate, the characteristics are related—men are more attracted to that candidate than are women. Note that the two characteristics

Table 12.5

	Favor Candidate A	**Favor Candidate B**
Females	Female and favoring A	Female and favoring B
Males	Male and favoring A	Male and favoring B

enable us to place voters in four classes or cells: those who are female and favor candidate A, female and favor candidate B, male and favor candidate A, male and favor candidate B. See Table 12.5.

Suppose that 60% of the voters in this election are female. What proportion of voters would we expect in each cell if the two characteristics are independent? If 100 voters are randomly selected, we expect about 60 to be women. If candidate preference is independent of gender, and 75% of all the voters favor candidate A, then we expect about 75% of the 60 women, or 45 of them, to be in favor of candidate A. This reasoning leads us to the conclusion that if the two characteristics are independent, 45% of all voters will be both female and in favor of candidate A. Suppose that we let

p_F = proportion of voters who are female

p_A = proportion of voters who favor candidate A

p_{FA} = proportion of voters who are female and favor candidate A

We said that $p_F = .60, p_A = .75$, and if the two characteristics of gender and choice of candidate are independent, $p_{FA} = .45$. Note that $.45 = (.60)(.75)$, so when we have independence

$$p_{FA} = p_F \cdot p_A$$

We call this a **multiplication rule for independent characteristics.**[*]

Now let us calculate the proportions for the other three cells. We will call p_M the proportion of male voters, p_B the proportion of voters favoring candidate B, p_{MB} the proportion of voters who are male and favor B, and so on. Then, if the two characteristics are independent, the multiplication rule says that

$$p_{MA} = p_M \cdot p_A = (.40)(.75) = .30$$
$$p_{FB} = p_F \cdot p_B = (.60)(.25) = .15$$
$$p_{MB} = p_M \cdot p_B = (.40)(.25) = .10$$

The various proportions are displayed in Table 12.6.

If the multiplication rule does not hold for each cell, the two characteristics (gender and choice of candidate in this case) are not independent—they are related. As an extreme example of a situation where the characteristics would be related, consider Table 12.7. In this table, we observe that, although the overall proportions favoring candidates A and B remain the same as in Table 12.6, all of the men, who constitute 40% of the voting population, favor candidate A. Note that the

---

[*]You may recognize this as equivalent to the multiplication rule for independent events. Keep in mind that proportions can be viewed as probabilities. Now suppose that we let F be the event that a voter selected is a female and A be the event that the voter favors A. In Section 5.4, we saw that when the two events are independent, the multiplication rule for independent events tells us that

$$p(F \text{ and } A) = p(F) \cdot p(A)$$

Table 12.6
Independent Characteristics

	Favor Candidate A	Favor Candidate B	
Females	$p_{FA} = p_F \cdot p_A = .45$	$p_{FB} = p_F \cdot p_B = .15$	$p_F = .60$
Males	$p_{MA} = p_M \cdot p_A = .30$	$p_{MB} = p_M \cdot p_B = .10$	$p_M = .40$
	$p_A = .75$	$p_B = .25$	

Table 12.7
Dependent Characteristics

	Favor Candidate A	Favor Candidate B	
Females	$p_{FA} = .35$	$p_{FB} = .25$	$p_F = .60$
Males	$p_{MA} = .40$	$p_{MB} = 0$	$p_M = .40$
	$p_A = .75$	$p_B = .25$	

multiplication rule does not hold here. For example,

$$p_{FA} = .35 \neq (.60)(.75) = p_F \cdot p_A$$

When testing for independence of two characteristics, our null hypothesis will be that the characteristics are independent. (This is equivalent to asserting that the multiplication rule holds for each category.) The alternate hypothesis will be that the characteristics are related.

A Test of Independence

To see how a chi-square test may be used to determine whether two characteristics are related, we will examine data obtained in a survey of 100 students at Framingham State College. We will try to determine whether there is a relationship between students' political views and their opinion about nuclear power for production of consumer energy. The population would be all students at the college (and at similar colleges). The questions asked of the students were as follows:

Question 1. What label most closely describes your political views?

Democratic   Republican   Independent

Question 2. What is your opinion of nuclear power for production of consumer energy?

Approve   Disapprove   Undecided

Table 12.8 (page 544), called a *contingency table,* summarizes the result of the survey. In the cell in the upper left-hand corner of Table 12.8, we see the value 10, meaning that 10 students in the survey see themselves as Democrats and favor nuclear power. The number in the lower left-hand corner means that a total of 10+9+8 = 27 students see themselves as Democrats. The row total of 45 in the upper right-hand corner means that a total of 45 students approve of nuclear power. The total number of students in the survey (grand total), 100, appears in the lower right-hand corner. This number can be obtained by adding either the row or the column totals.

Table 12.8
Survey of Students' Political Views Versus Their Opinions on Nuclear Power

	Political View			
Opinion	**Democrat**	**Republican**	**Independent**	**Row Total**
Approve	10	15	20	45
Disapprove	9	2	16	27
Undecided	8	2	18	28
Column Total	27	19	54	100 ← Grand Total

The hypotheses we wish to test for the student population are

H_0: Political view and opinion about nuclear power are independent.

H_a: Political view and opinion of nuclear power are related.

We will use the 5% level of significance and apply a chi-square test. We must calculate the expected frequencies for the nine cells in Table 12.8. The expected frequencies are the frequencies we would expect if H_0 were true. Recall that independence is equivalent to saying that the multiplication rule for independent characteristics holds. For example, this means that the proportion of students (in the population) who approve of nuclear power and are also Democrats is equal to the product of the proportion of students who approve of nuclear power (p_A) times the proportion of students who are Democrats (p_D). Therefore, if the characteristics are independent,

$$\text{proportion who approve and are Democrats} = p_A \cdot p_D$$

Using this proportion, we can find the expected frequency of the cell (assuming independence) by multiplying the proportion by the sample size of 100. The problem is that the proportions discussed (p_A and p_D) are the proportions for the entire population (of all students at similar colleges). These proportions are unknown.

We will estimate the proportions from the sample data. A total of 45 out of a grand total of 100 students in the survey said they approved of nuclear power. (See Table 12.8.) Hence we will estimate the proportion of the population who approve of nuclear power (p_A) as $\frac{45}{100}$. Note that

$$p_A \doteq \frac{45}{100} = \frac{\text{row total}}{\text{grand total}}$$

Similarly, a total of 27 out of 100 students interviewed were Democrats. Thus we estimate p_D by

$$p_D \doteq \frac{27}{100} = \frac{\text{column total}}{\text{grand total}}$$

Therefore, the expected proportion for the cell, assuming independence, is

proportion who approve of nuclear power and are Democrats

$$= p_A \cdot p_D \doteq \left(\frac{45}{100}\right)\left(\frac{27}{100}\right) = .1215$$

The expected cell frequency is obtained by multiplying the sample size by this proportion:

expected number who approve of nuclear power and are Democrats

$$= E = (\cancel{100})\left(\frac{45}{\cancel{100}}\right)\left(\frac{27}{100}\right) = \frac{(45)(27)}{100} = 12.15$$

For this cell, observe that the expected frequency is

$$\frac{(45)(27)}{100} = \frac{(\text{row total}) \cdot (\text{column total})}{\text{grand total}}$$

Therefore, the expected frequency E is

$$E = \frac{(\text{row total}) \cdot (\text{column total})}{\text{grand total}}$$

This same formula is used to calculate the expected frequency for each cell. For example, the expected frequency for the cell consisting of those who approve of nuclear power and are Republican is (from Table 12.8)

$$E = \frac{(45)(19)}{100} = 8.55$$

In Table 12.9, we display the observed frequencies O, along with the expected frequencies E (in parentheses).

We now calculate the observed value of the test statistic:

$$\chi^2 = \sum \frac{(O - E)^2}{E}$$

$$= \frac{(10 - 12.15)^2}{12.15} + \frac{(15 - 8.55)^2}{8.55} + \frac{(20 - 24.30)^2}{24.30}$$

$$+ \frac{(9 - 7.29)^2}{7.29} + \frac{(2 - 5.13)^2}{5.13} + \frac{(16 - 14.58)^2}{14.58}$$

$$+ \frac{(8 - 7.56)^2}{7.56} + \frac{(2 - 5.32)^2}{5.32} + \frac{(18 - 15.12)^2}{15.12}$$

$$\doteq .3805 + 4.8658 + .7609 + .4011 + 1.9097 + .1383 + .0256 + 2.0719 + .5486$$

$$\doteq 11.10$$

Table 12.9
Table of Observed (and Expected) Frequencies

Opinion	Political View			Row Total
	Democrat	Republican	Independent	
Approve	10 (12.15)	15 (8.55)	20 (24.30)	45
Disapprove	9 (7.29)	2 (5.13)	16 (14.58)	27
Undecided	8 (7.56)	2 (5.32)	18 (15.12)	28
Column Total	27	19	54	100

Normally, the number of degrees of freedom associated with χ^2 is 1 less than the number of cells $(k - 1)$. However, whenever a population proportion is estimated, as we have done, the degrees of freedom must be reduced by 1 for each proportion estimated. We estimated the row and column proportions. For example, the first row proportion, the proportion who approve, was estimated as $p_A \doteq \frac{45}{100} = .45$. There are three row proportions. However, since they must add up to 1, when we know two, the third is known. So, in effect, we estimated two row proportions and two column proportions. This means that we must reduce the usual degrees of freedom by 4:

$$\text{df} = (k - 1) - (\text{number of proportions estimated})$$
$$= (9 - 1) - (4) = 4$$

If we let

$$r = \text{number of rows} = 3$$
$$c = \text{number of columns} = 3$$

then we can write

$$\text{df} = 4 = (2)(2) = (3 - 1)(3 - 1) = (r - 1)(c - 1)$$

This formula holds in general for contingency tables.* If r is the number of rows and c is the number of columns

$$\text{df} = (r - 1)(c - 1)$$

As usual, large departures of the observed frequencies from the expected frequencies favor the alternate hypothesis. These large departures also cause the value of χ^2 to be large; hence we reject H_0 when χ^2 is very large. This means that we perform a right-tailed test. From Appendix Table B.5, we see that the critical value of χ^2 when $\alpha = .05$ and df $= 4$ is $\chi^2_{.05} = 9.488$. The critical region is shown in Figure 12.6. The observed value $\chi^2 = 11.10$ is in the critical region, so we reject the null hypothesis of independence. Thus the characteristics of political viewpoint and opinion on nuclear power seem to be related.

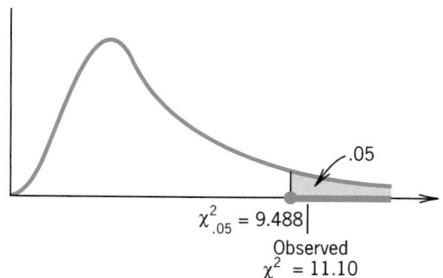

Figure 12.6

We can now summarize the essential features of a test for independence of two characteristics.

---

*When counting the number of rows and columns, we do not include the last row and column that contain the column and row totals.

Chi-Square Test for Independence of Two Characteristics   To test the null hypothesis H_0, which states that the two characteristics are independent, against an alternate hypothesis, which states that the characteristics are dependent, we conduct a right-tailed chi-square test. The number of observations (O) in each category is obtained and placed in a contingency table (such as Table 12.8). The expected frequency of a cell is

$$E = \frac{(\text{row total}) \cdot (\text{column total})}{\text{grand total}}$$

The test statistic is

$$\chi^2 = \sum \frac{(O - E)^2}{E}$$

This has an approximate chi-square distribution. If the contingency table has r rows and c columns, the degrees of freedom is

$$\text{df} = (r - 1)(c - 1)$$

If α is the level of significance, find the critical value χ_α^2 in Appendix Table B.5. If $\chi^2 \geq \chi_\alpha^2$, we reject H_0. Otherwise, do not reject H_0. See Figure 12.7.

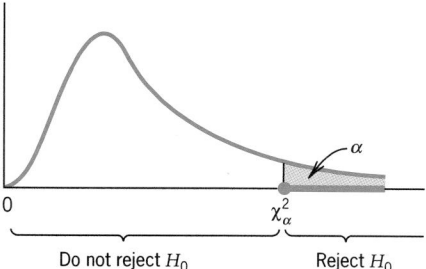

Figure 12.7
Critical Region

Assumption: Each expected frequency E is at least 5.

EXAMPLE 12.3

Prior to the time that the germ theory of disease was established (around 1870), the mortality rate from surgery was very high because of infection. Louis Pasteur and Joseph Lister were largely responsible for the germ theory. Lister believed that if carbolic acid were used as a disinfectant, the patient's chance of survival might be improved. He used it to scrub everything in the operating room that came in contact with the patient. He even sprayed the air with carbolic acid and used it on the patient's dressing. Lister compared 40 operations (amputations) in which this procedure was used with 35 amputations in which it was not used. The results are summarized in the contingency table (Table 12.10 on page 548). At the 1% level of significance, test whether the outcome of the surgery (patient lived or died) is independent of the use of carbolic acid.

Table 12.10
Results of Carbolic Acid Used in 40 out of 75 Amputations

	Patient Lived	Patient Died	Row Total
Carbolic Acid Used	34	6	40
Carbolic Acid Not Used	19	16	35
Column Total	53	22	75

Source: Winslow, C., *The Conquest of Epidemic Disease.* Princeton, N.J.: Princeton University Press, 1943, p. 303.

Solution

1. *Hypotheses:*

     H_0: A patient's survival (or death) does not depend on whether carbolic acid is used in surgery.

     H_a: A patient's survival is related to whether carbolic acid is used.

2. *Level of significance:* $\alpha = .01$

3. *Test statistic and observed value:* We will use the chi-square statistic. We must first calculate the expected cell frequencies; these are the frequencies that we would expect if the null hypothesis of independence were true. Using the multiplication rule, we calculate these frequencies from the formula

$$E = \frac{(\text{row total}) \cdot (\text{column total})}{\text{grand total}}$$

For example, the expected number of patients who lived and for whom carbolic acid was used (assuming independence) is

$$E = \frac{(40)(53)}{75} \doteq 28.27$$

Table 12.11 lists the observed frequencies, with the expected frequencies in parentheses.

$$\chi^2 = \sum \frac{(O - E)^2}{E} = \frac{(34 - 28.27)^2}{28.27} + \frac{(6 - 11.73)^2}{11.73}$$
$$+ \frac{(19 - 24.73)^2}{24.73} + \frac{(16 - 10.27)^2}{10.27}$$
$$\doteq 1.1614 + 2.7991 + 1.3277 + 3.1970$$
$$\doteq 8.49$$
$$\text{df} = (r - 1)(c - 1) = (2 - 1)(2 - 1) = 1$$

4. *Critical region:* Large values of χ^2 indicate large deviations of the observed values from the expected values and therefore favor the alternate hypothesis; thus we perform a right-tailed test. From Appendix Table B.5, we find that with df = 1, $\chi^2_{.01} = 6.635$. The critical region with observed value is shown in Figure 12.8. (Note that chi-square distributions with df = 1 or df = 2 have somewhat different shapes from other chi-square distributions.)

Table 12.11
Observed (and Expected) Frequencies for Lister's Data

	Patient Lived	Patient Died	Row Total
Carbolic Acid Used	34 (28.27)	6 (11.73)	40
Carbolic Acid Not Used	19 (24.73)	16 (10.27)	35
Column Total	53	22	75

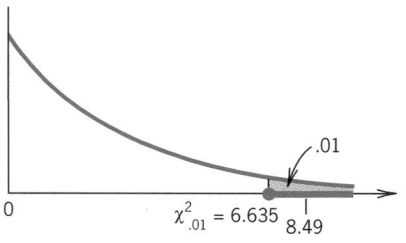

Figure 12.8

5.   *Decision:*   The observed value of χ^2 is in the critical region. Therefore, we reject H_0. This means that there does appear to be a relation between the use of carbolic acid and the survival of a patient.

EXERCISES

12.15   A sample of 50 moviegoers was taken to see whether the rating of a controversial movie and age of viewer were related. The following data were obtained:

	Excellent	Fair	Poor
Less than 30	6	12	8
30 or more	10	6	8

Test whether the characteristics of rating and age are independent using a 5% level of significance.

12.16   A random sample of students at Framingham State College was obtained to test the claim that gender and political affiliation were independent at this college. Test the claim with a 10% level of significance. The data follow.

	Democrat	Republican	Independent
Females	20	10	25
Males	10	9	38

12.17   A study of coronary heart disease (CHD) among diabetics age 45–74 with congestive heart failure yielded the following information (*Source:* Kannel, 1974, p. 31). Is there sufficient evidence to indicate a relationship between the absence or presence of CHD and gender? Use a 5% level of significance. The data follow.

	With CHD	Without CHD
Males	5	6
Females	10	7

12.18   A random sample of 200 voters living in a precinct of a large city was taken to see whether a dependent relationship existed between union affiliation and political preference. At a 5% level of significance, is there sufficient evidence to indicate a relationship? The data are given in the table at the top of page 550.

	Democrat	Republican	Independent
Union Member	80	15	35
Not a Union Member	25	20	25

12.19 A group of employees in a large firm claimed that gender and yearly salary were dependent. For the following data, test the claim using a 10% level of significance.

	Salaries (in Thousands of Dollars)			
	Less than 30	At Least 30 but Less than 35	At Least 35 but Less than 40	At Least 40
Female	12	30	20	13
Male	7	26	31	27

12.20 A political science professor claimed that the political affiliation of students and their belief concerning public funding of abortions were independent. Test the claim using a 5% level of significance. The sample data follow.

	Democrat	Republican	Independent
Approve	9	6	21
Disapprove	16	11	23
Undecided	6	5	15

12.21 **(a)** Calculate the observed χ^2 value for each of the following contingency tables:

(i)

	B_1	B_2	B_3
A_1	10	20	30
A_2	20	40	60

(ii)

	B_1	B_2
A_1	120	60
A_2	40	20

(iii)

	B_1	B_2
A_1	20	30
A_2	40	60
A_3	200	300

(b) Compare the observed χ^2 values in part (a). Note the relationship between the rows (and columns) in each of the contingency tables in part (a).

(c) **(i)** Complete the following contingency table so that the observed χ^2 value is zero. (There is more than one correct way to complete the table.)

	B_1	B_2	B_3
A_1	20	10	30
A_2	60		
A_3			

(ii)   In the table in item (c)(i), fill in the A_3B_1 cell with the number 30. Now complete the table so that the observed χ^2 value is zero. (There is only one correct way to complete the table.)

(d) What conclusion can you draw about contingency tables and the strongest evidence to support H_0?

12.4

TESTS OF HOMOGENEITY

In the tests of independence considered in Section 12.3, we were interested in whether two characteristics were related for individuals of the *same* population. For example, suppose we wanted to see whether there was a relationship between political affiliation (Democrat, Republican, or Independent) and work status (self-employed or employed by another). We could interview a certain number of people from the population of employed individuals and classify them as to work status and political affiliation. The number of self-employed people in the survey might be so small that we would be unable to complete the test of independence.

A test of homogeneity provides another approach to the problem. Such a test considers one characteristic for *different* populations. We could consider two populations: those who are self-employed and those who are employed by another. The issue is whether these populations are similar (homogeneous) with respect to the characteristic of political affiliation. To test for homogeneity, we would obtain a sample (of desired size) of self-employed people and a sample of workers who are not self-employed, and we would classify each person according to political affiliation. Similarity would exist if each population had the same political make-up (i.e., the same percentage of Democrats, the same percentage of Republicans, and the same percentage of Independents). Hence a test of homogeneity tests a null hypothesis that asserts that different populations are homogeneous with respect to some characteristic of interest against an alternate hypothesis that asserts that they are not.

Tests of homogeneity involve tables that are similar to contingency tables and, in fact, the procedure for carrying out such tests is exactly the same as the chi-square test used in connection with contingency tables. We illustrate the procedure in the following example.

EXAMPLE 12.4

In a study of voting characteristics of adult whites, blacks, and Hispanics in Massachusetts, samples of 100 individuals were obtained from each of these populations. Each individual was asked whether he or she voted in the midterm congressional

Table 12.12

Survey of Voting-Age Individuals from Three Racial Groups in the 1990 Midterm Congressional Elections

	Voted	Did Not Vote	Row Total
Whites	47	53	100
Blacks	40	60	100
Hispanics	27	73	100
Column Total	114	186	300 ← Grand Total

elections of 1990. The results of this survey are summarized in Table 12.12. Test to see whether the populations of white, black, and Hispanic adults in Massachusetts are similar (homogeneous) with respect to the characteristic of voting or not voting in the 1990 midterm congressional election. In other words, did the same proportion from each population vote? Use the 5% level of significance.

Solution

We will use the chi-square test for goodness-of-fit. It turns out that this test is used exactly the same way as it was used in analyzing contingency tables in Section 12.3.

1. *Hypotheses:*

   H_0: The three populations are homogeneous with respect to the proportion voting.

   H_a: The three populations are not homogeneous with respect to this characteristic.

2. *Level of significance:* $\alpha = .05$

3. *Test statistic and observed value:* We will conduct a chi-square test. We first need the expected frequencies. To show that these can be calculated the same way we did in Section 12.3, we consider the expected number of whites who voted. This is the expected frequency of the cell in the upper left-hand corner. A total of 114 individuals out of a total of 300 individuals from all three populations voted. That is,

$$\frac{114}{300} = .38 \quad \text{or 38\% voted}$$

Now if all three populations are homogeneous (i.e., if H_0 is true), we would expect the same proportion (38%) to have voted in each population. Since there are 100 whites in the survey, we expect 38% of those, or 38 whites, to have voted. We can express this expected frequency as follows:

$$E = 38 = (100)(.38) = (100)\left(\frac{114}{300}\right) = \frac{(100)(114)}{300}$$

$$= \frac{(\text{row total}) \cdot (\text{column total})}{\text{grand total}}$$

Thus we can use the same formula to calculate expected frequencies as we did in Section 12.3:

$$E = \frac{(\text{row total}) \cdot (\text{column total})}{\text{grand total}}$$

In Table 12.13 we give the observed and expected frequencies.

Table 12.13
Observed (and Expected) Frequencies

	Voted	**Did Not Vote**	**Row Total**
Whites	47 (38)	53 (62)	100
Blacks	40 (38)	60 (62)	100
Hispanics	27 (38)	73 (62)	100
Column Total	114	186	300

The test statistic is the usual chi-square statistic:

$$\chi^2 = \sum \frac{(O - E)^2}{E}$$

$$= \frac{(47 - 38)^2}{38} + \frac{(53 - 62)^2}{62} + \frac{(40 - 38)^2}{38} + \frac{(60 - 62)^2}{62} + \frac{(27 - 38)^2}{38} + \frac{(73 - 62)^2}{62}$$

$$\doteq 2.1316 + 1.3065 + .1053 + .0645 + 3.1842 + 1.9516$$

$$\doteq 8.74$$

The degrees of freedom is the same as for contingency tables:

$$df = (r - 1)(c - 1) = (3 - 1)(2 - 1) = 2$$

4. *Critical region:* As usual, large departures of the observed frequencies from the expected frequencies favor the alternate hypothesis. These large departures also cause the value of χ^2 to be large; therefore, we conduct a right-tailed test. The critical value of χ^2 when df = 2 and α = .05 is, from Appendix Table B.5, $\chi^2_{.05}$ = 5.991. The critical region and observed value are shown in Figure 12.9.

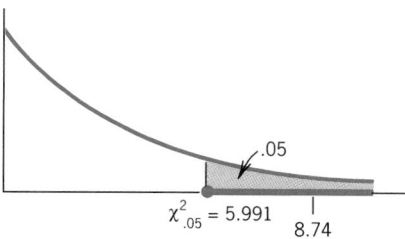

Figure 12.9

5. *Decision:* The observed value is in the critical region; thus we reject H_0. The three populations do not appear to be homogeneous with respect to the characteristic under investigation.

In the previous example, the sample size from each of the three populations happened to be the same. However, this is not a requirement in tests of homogeneity.

EXERCISES

12.22 In 1970, 1980, and 1990, women age 20–24 living in a large city were sampled and asked whether they had ever been married. Use a 5% level of significance and test whether the three populations are homogeneous with respect to the proportion of women age 20–24 who had ever married.

	Had Been Married	
	Yes	**No**
1970	54	21
1980	58	32
1990	42	38

12.23 Two dice were tossed to see whether they gave the "same results." The table gives the frequency of the number of dots.

	1	2	3	4	5	6
First Die	4	6	7	5	5	8
Second Die	7	4	8	6	5	5

At a 5% level of significance, test whether the two dice are homogeneous with respect to the number of dots showing.

12.24 A survey of medical doctors and student nurses was undertaken with the participants being asked whether they were smokers. Test whether the appropriate populations are homogeneous using a 10% significance level.

	Yes	No
Medical Doctors	18	32
Student Nurses	10	30

12.25 The results of a sample of male and female workers in a large factory are given here. Those sampled were asked whether they thought that there was discrimination in salaries between males and females. Test the hypothesis that the appropriate populations are homogeneous using a 1% level of significance.

	Yes	No
Males	55	70
Females	65	40

12.26 Former patients from four hospitals were sampled and asked whether they were satisfied with the care they received in the hospital. The results were as follows:

	Satisfied	Not Satisfied
Hospital 1	85	15
Hospital 2	82	18
Hospital 3	71	29
Hospital 4	68	32

Test the hypothesis that the appropriate populations are homogeneous with respect to satisfaction with hospital care. Use a 5% level of significance.

12.5

USING MINITAB (OPTIONAL)

In Table 12.8, we saw the results of a survey comparing political view versus opinion on nuclear power (for the production of consumer energy). The data were as follows:

Opinion	Political View		
	Democrat	Republican	Independent
Approve	10	15	20
Disapprove	9	2	16
Undecided	8	2	18

Enter this data into columns 1–3:

C1	C2	C3
10	15	20
9	2	16
8	2	18

The chi-square test for independence is carried out as follows:

Session Command	Dialog Box
MTB > CHISQUARE TEST C1–C3	**Stat ▶ Tables ▶ Chisquare test** Type C1 − C3 in box under **Columns containing the table** Click **OK**

Output

Chi-Square Test

```
Expected counts are printed below observed counts

            C1        C2        C3      Total
  1         10        15        20         45
          12.15      8.55     24.30

  2          9         2        16         27
           7.29      5.13     14.58

  3          8         2        18         28
           7.56      5.32     15.12

Total       27        19        54        100

ChiSq =   0.380 +   4.866 +   0.761 +
          0.401 +   1.910 +   0.138 +
          0.026 +   2.072 +   0.549 = 11.102
df = 4, p = 0.026
```

EXERCISES

Suggested exercises for use with Minitab are 12.32–12.36. Give the *P*-value for these exercises.

12.6

WORKING WITH DATA (OPTIONAL)

1. It has been estimated that for the population as a whole, the percentages for normotensives, borderlines, and hypertensives are 64, 27, and 9, respectively.* Obtain a random sample of 60 females from Appendix Table B.11, and classify each subject as normotensive, borderline, or hypertensive. Are these results consistent with population percentages of 64, 27, and 9 for females? Use a 5% level of significance.

2. It has been estimated that in the population of 50–59-year-olds, the percentages for normotensives, borderlines, and hypertensives are 53, 32, and 15, respectively.* Test this claim using a random sample of 40 subjects age 50–59 from Appendix Table B.11. Use a 5% level of significance.

3. Classify subjects according to presence of coronary heart disease (CHD) as follows:

   0 in column 7:   No CHD present
   Nonzero value in column 7:   CHD present

   Obtain a sample of 30 subjects with CHD and 30 subjects without CHD from Appendix Table B.11. Classify each subject according to smoking status. (See Problems 2 and 3 in Section 11.6 for these categories.) Perform a test of homogeneity to see whether there is a relationship between smoking and presence of CHD. Use $\alpha = .05$.

12.7

SUMMARY

In this chapter, we considered three types of statistical tests: the **chi-square test for goodness-of-fit,** the **test of independence,** and the **homogeneity test.** The test statistic used in all these tests is

$$\chi^2 = \sum \frac{(O - E)^2}{E}$$

where O represents the observed frequencies and E represents the expected frequencies. This statistic has approximately a chi-square distribution if each value of E is at least 5. Large departures of the observed frequencies from the expected frequencies favor the alternate hypothesis in all three tests. These large departures cause the value of χ^2 to be large; therefore, a large value of χ^2 favors the alternate hypothesis. This means that we always conduct a right-tailed test.

The expected values, E, and degrees of freedom, df, of the test statistic for each of the three tests are calculated as follows.

1. The chi-square test for goodness-of-fit:

$$E = np \qquad df = k - 1$$

where n = sample size, p = proportion for a particular category or cell stated in the null hypothesis, and k = number of cells.

2. Test of independence and homogeneity test:

$$E = \frac{(\text{row total}) \cdot (\text{column total})}{\text{grand total}} \qquad df = (r - 1)(c - 1)$$

where r = number of rows and c = number of columns in the contingency table.

---

*See Problem 1 of Section 11.6 for a definition of terms.

REVIEW EXERCISES

12.27 Discuss the differences between tests for goodness-of-fit, independence, and homogeneity.

12.28 **(a)** What is the smallest value χ^2 can be?

(b) Construct a contingency table with 2 rows and 2 columns so that $\chi^2 = 0$.

(c) Construct a contingency table with 2 rows and 4 columns so that $\chi^2 = 0$.

12.29 The distribution of final grades given by a mathematics department in the past was 10% A's, 20% B's, 30% C's, 25% D's, and 15% F's. A new teacher gave the following grades for the first semester:

Category	O
A	12
B	20
C	26
D	14
F	8

Is there sufficient evidence to suggest that the new teacher's grading policy is different from that of the department? Use a 5% level of significance.

12.30 Test the hypothesis that the following data were sampled from a normal distribution with mean 0 and standard deviation 34.92. Use a 10% level of significance. The data, rounded to two decimal places, are summarized in the table.

Interval	O
Less than or equal to -23.40	9
More than -23.40 but not more than 0	18
More than 0 but not more than 23.40	19
More than 23.40	14

(*Hint:* If the population is normal with $\mu = 0$ and $\sigma = 34.92$, what proportion of data values would you expect to be less than or equal to -23.40, more than -23.40 but not more than 0, etc.?)

12.31 A committee was formed to study traffic conditions in an industrial complex. The committee wanted to see whether the modes of transportation used to get to work had changed over the past 5 years. Five years ago, 70% of the workers had driven alone; 20% had been in a car pool; 8% had used public transportation; and the rest used other modes. The committee obtained the following information from a sample of 500 workers.

Mode of Transportation	O
Drive alone	320
Carpool	130
Public transportation	35
Other means	15

Is there sufficient evidence to indicate that the modes of transportation used to get to work have changed? Use a 5% level of significance.

12.32   A random sample of students at Framingham State College was obtained to see whether a relationship existed between political affiliation and attitude concerning racial quotas in hiring. At a 5% level of significance, is there sufficient evidence to indicate a relationship?

	Democrat	Republican	Independent
Approve	7	7	9
Disapprove	19	13	38
Undecided	6	6	12

12.33   A study of coronary heart disease (CHD) among nondiabetics age 45–74 with congestive heart failure yielded the following information (*Source:* Kannel, 1974, p. 31). Is there sufficient evidence to indicate a relationship between the absence or presence of CHD and gender? Use a 10% level of significance.

	With CHD	Without CHD
Males	54	32
Females	39	30

12.34   Refer to Exercise 12.31. The transportation committee wanted to know whether there was a relationship between the mode of transportation to work and the starting time for work. The following sample data were obtained:

	Drive Alone	Carpool	Public Transportation	Other Means
Start at 8:00	65	39	10	4
Start at 8:30	95	45	11	6
Start at 9:00	160	46	14	5

Using a 1% level of significance, determine whether the characteristics of starting time and mode of transportation to work are related.

12.35   Seventy-five male and 100 female students at a large university were randomly sampled from the populations of enrolled males and females, respectively. Use the following data to test whether the male and female populations are homogeneous with respect to age. Use a 5% level of significance.

	Less than 22	Between 22 and 30	More than 30
Males	45	20	10
Females	40	40	20

12.36 Refer to Exercise 12.31. The transportation committee wished to study the mode of transportation used by male and female employees. The following data were obtained from a sample of 250 men and 250 women:

	Drive Alone	Carpool	Public Transportation	Other Means
Men	173	58	15	4
Women	147	72	20	11

Using a 1% level of significance, determine whether male and female employees are homogeneous with respect to their choice of mode of transportation.

12.37 In Exercise 12.32, the sampling scheme consisted of selecting 117 students. It turned out that there were 32 Democrats, 26 Republicans, and 59 Independents. Suppose instead that 32 Democrats were selected from the population of all Democrats on campus. Similarly, 26 Republicans and 59 Independents were chosen from appropriate populations.

(a) What would be the appropriate hypotheses to test in this situation?

(b) Would the value of the test statistic be the same as or different from the one obtained in Exercise 12.32?

Notes

Kannel, W. B., et al., "Role of Diabetes in Congestive Heart Failure, Framingham Heart Study," *The American Journal of Cardiology*, Vol. 34, 1974, pp. 29–34.

Lindgren, B., *Statistical Theory*, 3rd ed. New York: Macmillan Publishing Company, 1976.

U.S. News & World Report, February 5, 1990.

Winslow, C., *The Conquest of Epidemic Disease.* Princeton, N.J.: Princeton University Press, 1943.

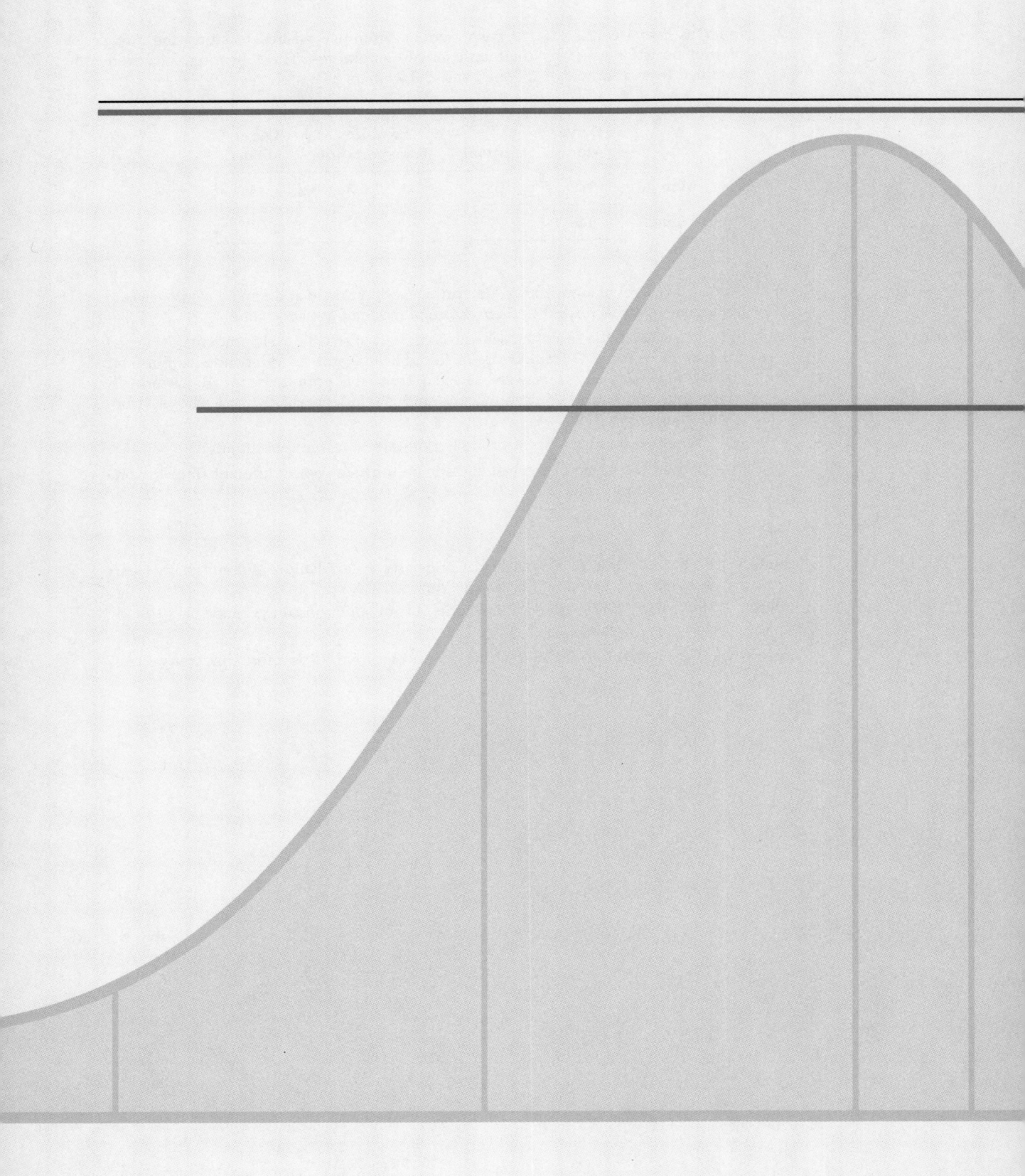

CHAPTER 13

NONPARAMETRIC STATISTICS

13.1 INTRODUCTION

13.2 THE SIGN TEST

13.3 THE WILCOXON SIGNED-RANK TEST

13.4 THE MANN–WHITNEY U TEST

13.5 THE RUNS TEST

13.6 A DISCUSSION OF PARAMETRIC VERSUS NONPARAMETRIC TESTS

13.7 USING MINITAB (OPTIONAL)

13.8 WORKING WITH DATA (OPTIONAL)

13.9 SUMMARY

     REVIEW EXERCISES

13.1

INTRODUCTION

The statistical tests we have developed thus far in this text often require that the population distributions be normal or approximately so. This is the case, for instance, with the small-sample t tests discussed in Chapters 8 and 9. Yet, in some cases, it is not known whether a distribution is approximately normal. In other cases, it is known that the distribution departs substantially from normality. For example, systolic blood pressure readings are (approximately) normally distributed with a mean of 120 (millimeters of mercury). But suppose that we consider only blood pressure readings over 140. This population has a distribution that resembles the shape of the right tail of a normal distribution, as indicated in Figure 13.1.

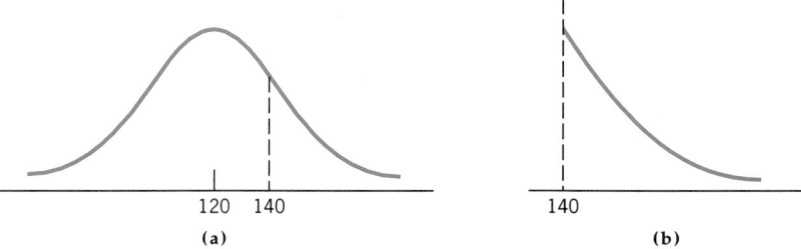

Figure 13.1
(a) Systolic Blood Pressures; (b) Systolic Blood Pressures Above 140

Nonparametric tests were developed to deal with situations where the population distributions are nonnormal or unknown, especially when the sample size is small (< 30). They make no assumptions or few assumptions about the populations under consideration.

> **Definition** Statistical methods that do not depend on a knowledge of the population distribution or its parameters are called *nonparametric* or *distribution-free* methods. All other methods are called *parametric* methods.

Actually, many nonparametric tests are not completely distribution-free, since they place some (although minimal) requirements on the distribution, such as requiring that the distribution be continuous. For this reason, some describe these methods as "distribution-freer."

Among statisticians, there is less than unanimous agreement on the definition of nonparametric methods, and the line between parametric and nonparametric tests is not a sharp one. For example, the large-sample z tests for means discussed in Chapters 8 and 9 are actually distribution-free, yet they are usually classified as parametric tests.

Even though nonparametric tests are easy to understand, simple to apply, and place minimal requirements on the form of the population distributions involved, they are not always superior to parametric tests. When the conditions on the population are met, the parametric tests are better than their nonparametric counterparts; that is, they are more likely to reject a false null hypothesis. We will have more to say about this in Section 13.6.

There are many nonparametric tests. In this chapter, we present just a few of the more commonly encountered tests.

13.2

THE SIGN TEST

We illustrate the logic behind the sign test with an example. A consulting geographer was studying various aspects of a large city. It was claimed that the median value for all homes in the city was $70,000. Recall that the median for a collection of data has the property that half the data values are larger than the median and half are smaller. The geographer wanted to check this claim. The population under consideration is the collection of the values of all the homes in the city. The question is whether the median (Md) for this population is $70,000 or not. The hypotheses to be tested are

$$H_0: \quad Md = 70,000$$
$$H_a: \quad Md \neq 70,000$$

The geographer conducted a small random survey of real estate agencies from which he obtained the selling prices of 14 recently sold homes in the city. They were arranged in increasing order, as shown in Table 13.1. For the sample of 14 homes in Table 13.1, only 2 prices are below $70,000, whereas 12 are above. If the median for the population were really $70,000, we would expect closer to one-half of the values in the sample (or 7) to be above $70,000 and one-half below. Intuitively, it seems unlikely that 12 prices would be above $70,000 and only 2 would be below $70,000 if the median were really $70,000.

Table 13.1

Selling Prices of 14 Homes (in Dollars)

61,300	87,000
66,200	95,000
71,000	96,100
76,500	99,000
77,100	125,000
77,300	140,300
81,000	190,000

In such problems, we need not rely on intuition alone. In the problem at hand, we could use x, the number of homes in the sample above $70,000 in value, as a test statistic. We may view x as a binomial random variable associated with a binomial experiment, where

$$trial = \text{randomly select a home}$$
$$success = \text{value of home is above } \$70,000$$

If the null hypothesis is true, then one-half the homes in the city should be valued above $70,000. Therefore,

$$P(success) = p = \tfrac{1}{2}$$

In the problem at hand, the number of trials is $n = 14$ and $x =$ number of successes. If the null hypothesis is true, the expected value of x is

$$E(x) = \mu = np = (14)(\tfrac{1}{2}) = 7$$

If we observe a value of x so far from 7 (above or below) that such a value would be unlikely if H_0 were true, we reject H_0. "Unlikely" means having a low probability. This probability is called the level of significance of the test (α), and we choose its value. Suppose that *prior* to obtaining our data, we had decided to choose α to be as close to .01 as possible. The critical region will consist of values of x so far from 7 that there would be only about a 1% chance of observing a value of x in this region if H_0 were true.

We can use Appendix Table B.2 to find the critical region. We find the column corresponding to $n = 14, p = .5$. This gives probabilities corresponding to the various possible values of x. Certainly, the extreme values of 0 and 14 should be in the critical region. We keep adding values of x near both extremes until the probabilities of these x's add up to approximately .01. If we choose for our critical region the x values

$$0 \quad 1 \quad 2 \quad 12 \quad 13 \quad 14$$

their probabilities add up to

$$0 + .001 + .006 + .006 + .001 + 0 = .014$$

This is reasonably close to .01. Hence we will use these values of x as our critical region. See Figure 13.2. (If we took 2 and 12 away from the critical region, the probability would be only .002. If we added 3 and 11 to the critical region, the probability would be .058.)

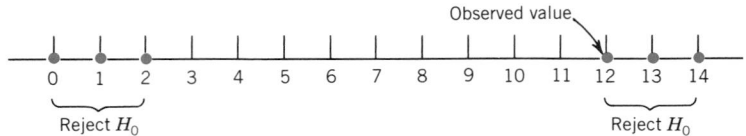

Figure 13.2

Since the observed value, $x = 12$, is in the critical region, we reject H_0. This means that the median home value does not appear to be $70,000. In fact, it appears to be higher. This test is called a **sign test** because sometimes we label the values in the sample above the (conjectured) value of the median with a plus sign, and those below with a minus sign. We then count the number of pluses.

You may be wondering why we did not use a t test in this problem. A t test was not used because the sample data are strongly skewed, suggesting that the population of selling prices may not be approximately normal. If the population were approximately normal (roughly mound-shaped), a t test should be used, because when it is appropriate, a t test is more sensitive than the sign test. This means that with a t test, there is a better chance of detecting (and rejecting) a false null hypothesis. If a t test could have been used in the previous problem, the hypotheses to be tested would have been

$$H_0: \quad \mu = \$70,000$$
$$H_a: \quad \mu \neq \$70,000$$

[*Note:* When the population is approximately normal, its distribution is approximately symmetric, so $\mu \doteq$ median. (See Figure 3.3(c).) It is also worth pointing out here that parametric tests involving central tendency are used to study means whereas nonparametric tests are often used to study medians.]

It should be no surprise that, when appropriate, a t test is more sensitive than the sign test. The sign test throws away a great deal of information—it considers only whether a data value is above the conjectured value for the median, ignoring the magnitude of the data value. The t test uses the magnitudes of all the data values.

We can summarize our findings as follows:

Sign Test To conduct this test concerning the value of the median of a population, we use the test statistic:

$$x = \text{number of data values in the sample above the value}$$
$$\text{of the median given in the null hypothesis } H_0$$

When H_0 is true, x has a binomial distribution with $n =$ the sample size and $p = .5$. We use Appendix Table B.2 to find the critical region.

- If the alternate hypothesis H_a involves the symbol $\neq$, we find a two-tailed critical region.
- If H_a involves the symbol $>$, we find a right-tailed critical region.
- If H_a involves the symbol $<$, we find a left-tailed critical region.

If α is the desired level of significance, we choose critical values so that the probability that x falls in the critical region is as close to α as possible. *Assumption:* The data are continuous.

The sign test may be used to compare two populations when the samples are dependent (i.e., the values from the two samples occur in pairs). The following example illustrates this. It also illustrates the use of a one-tailed test.

EXAMPLE 13.1

A seed company considered marketing a new variety of wheat seed that it believed would produce a greater yield than its current variety. Thirteen farmers agreed to use the new type of seed on one acre and the old variety on another acre. The resulting yields in bushels are given in Table 13.2.

Table 13.2
Bushels of Wheat from Two Types of Seed

Farm	New Variety (y_1)	Old Variety (y_2)	Difference $D = y_1 - y_2$	Sign of D
1	34	27	7	+
2	45	25	20	+
3	30	38	−8	−
4	30	42	−12	−
5	48	21	27	+
6	35	22	13	+
7	32	37	−5	−
8	46	30	16	+
9	41	32	9	+
10	23	38	−15	−
11	42	26	16	+
12	43	33	10	+
13	65	68	−3	−

The company was unsure about the distributions for the two varieties of wheat, and so decided to use the sign test instead of a t test. Complete the test, using a level of significance as close to 5% as possible.

Solution

Let

$$y_1 = \text{yield from the new variety (in bushels)}$$

$$y_2 = \text{yield from the old variety (in bushels)}$$

$$D = y_1 - y_2$$

The new variety will be considered an improvement if the (population) median of D is positive: $\text{Md}_D > 0$. This is the alternate hypothesis.

1. *Hypotheses:*

$$H_0: \quad \text{Md}_D = 0$$
$$H_a: \quad \text{Md}_D > 0$$

2. *Level of significance:* $\alpha = .05$

3. *Test statistic and observed value:*   We use the number of values of D from the sample that are above 0 (the number of pluses next to the D values in Table 13.2). Note that it was not necessary to calculate the values of D. We need know only the signs of the D values. From Table 13.2,

$$x = \text{number of pluses}$$
$$= 8$$

4. *Critical region:*   We perform a right-tailed test. Looking at Appendix Table B.2, when $n = 13$ and $p = .5$, we see that if we use the values 10, 11, 12, and 13 for the critical region, then

$$\alpha = P(10) + P(11) + P(12) + P(13)$$
$$= .035 + .010 + .002 + 0 = .047$$

which is close to .05. Hence the critical region will consist of the following x values: 10, 11, 12, and 13. (See Figure 13.3.)

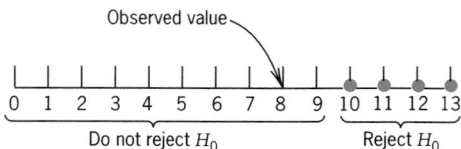

Figure 13.3

5. *Decision:*   The observed value ($x = 8$) is not in the critical region; thus we do not reject H_0. This means that there is insufficient evidence to conclude that the new variety of seed is more effective than the old one.

The following question may have occurred to you: What happens if one (or more) of the data values in the sample is exactly equal to the value of the median in the null hypothesis? How is it classified? If we encounter a data value equal to the median, the usual procedure is to remove it from the sample and reduce the sample size by 1.

Normal Approximation

Appendix Table B.2 can be used in the sign test to find the critical region for values of x when the sample size n is 25 or less. For values of n greater than 25, we may use the normal approximation to the binomial variable x. We have seen in Chapter 7 that x may be viewed as approximately normal with

$$\mu = np = n \cdot \tfrac{1}{2} \quad \text{since } p = \tfrac{1}{2} \text{ if } H_0 \text{ is true}$$

$$\sigma = \sqrt{npq} = \sqrt{n \cdot \tfrac{1}{2} \cdot \tfrac{1}{2}} = \tfrac{1}{2}\sqrt{n}$$

Therefore,

$$z = \frac{x - \mu}{\sigma} = \frac{x - n/2}{\sqrt{n}/2}$$

is approximately standard normal. The following example illustrates the use of the normal approximation.

EXAMPLE 13.2

A sports enthusiast claimed that the median weight of college football players was less than 250 pounds. A sample of 28 such players showed 16 weighing less than 250 pounds, 11 weighing more than 250 pounds, and one weighing 250 pounds. Test the claim at the 10% level of significance.

Solution

1. *Hypotheses:* It is claimed that Md < 250. The hypotheses are

$$H_0: \quad \text{Md} = 250$$
$$H_a: \quad \text{Md} < 250$$

2. *Level of significance:* $\alpha = .10$
3. *Test statistic and observed value:* One observation is 250 pounds. Since this equals the value in question, we discard it. Of the remaining $n = 27$ values, $x = 11$ are above 250. We use the standardized form of x:

$$z = \frac{x - n/2}{\sqrt{n}/2} = \frac{11 - 27/2}{\sqrt{27}/2} \doteq -.96$$

4. *Critical region:* Since H_a contains the symbol $<$, we do a left-tailed test. From Appendix Table B.3, we find that $z_{.10} = 1.28$. Therefore, the critical region, shown in Figure 13.4 (page 568), consists of values of $z \le -1.28$.
5. *Decision:* The observed value ($z = -.96$) is not in the critical region; thus we do not reject H_0. This means that there is insufficient evidence to support the claim that Md < 250.

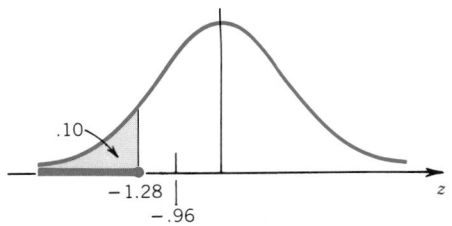

Figure 13.4

EXERCISES

13.1   In parts (a)–(l), assume a sign test is used. Complete the following table by finding either an appropriate critical region or the level of significance α. Note that n refers to the sample size.

	Hypothesis	n	Critical Region	α
(a)	Md $= 100$	12		.038
(b)	Md > 100	7	$\{6, 7\}$	
(c)	Md < 100	9		.090
(d)	Md $\neq 100$	8	$\{0, 1, 7, 8\}$	
(e)	Md > 100	15		.059
(f)	Md < 100	13	$\{0, 1, 2, 3\}$	
(g)	Md < 100	17		.071
(h)	Md > 100	11	$\{9, 10, 11\}$	
(i)	Md $= 100$	4	$\{0, 4\}$	
(j)	Md < 100	5	$\{0\}$	
(k)	Md $\neq 100$	16		.078
(l)	Md > 100	19		.031

13.2   The median time for runners in a specific age group to complete a 3-mile run is 30 minutes. A runner in this age group claimed to have a faster median time. A sample of this runner's past 3-mile runs gave the following times:

28.5   28.0   29.5   28.5   29.0   29.5   32.0   30.5   29.0   29.5   30.5

Is there sufficient evidence to justify the runner's claim? Use the sign test with a 5% significance level.

13.3   A shift in a factory was being evaluated on the basis of the number of hours to complete a job. The median time, set by management, to complete the job was 2.8 hours, but the plant manager believed that the median time of the shift was longer. A sample of 10 completed jobs gave the following times:

2.0   3.2   3.7   3.4   3.3   2.5   4.1   3.1   3.6   3.5

Use the sign test with a 5% significance level to test the manager's belief.

13.4   (a)   A newspaper reported that the median age for drivers issued tickets for speeding in a large town was less than 20 years. A sample of 13 tickets gave the following ages of the drivers:

27   17   19   18   43   18   19   17   26   36   19   34   19

Use the sign test and a 5% significance level to test the newspaper's report.

(b) Suppose that a sample of size $n = 42$ had been obtained and 15 tickets were issued to drivers over 20 years old, 24 to drivers under 20, and 3 to drivers age 20. Now use the normal approximation to test the hypothesis discussed in part (a) at the 5% level of significance.

13.5 To test the claim of a nutritionist that a new diet was effective, eight people were selected and their weights before and after the diet were recorded. The data follow.

Weight Before Diet	171	183	162	196	151	209	198	215
Weight After Diet	166	187	155	198	140	206	192	210

Test the claim using the sign test and a 5% level of significance.

13.3

THE WILCOXON SIGNED-RANK TEST

Although the sign test discussed in Section 13.2 is very simple to use, it is not a very sensitive test. Sometimes it will not reject a false null hypothesis when another test would be successful in detecting the falsity of the null hypothesis. This is not very surprising, since the sign test throws away a good deal of information about the data. The only information the sign test uses about a data value is whether it is above the conjectured value of the median; it ignores the magnitude of the data value.

In this section, we study another nonparametric test that is better than the sign test because it uses more information: the **Wilcoxon signed-rank test.** We illustrate this test with an example.

A public school official believed that high school seniors in a large school system would tend to score higher on a standard reading examination than the national median of 50. She randomly selected 13 seniors and gave them the examination. The results were as follows:

57 70 42 48 77 63 45 64 59 39 73 78 47

Since the official wanted to see whether the median for the school system (the population median) was higher than the national median, she wished to test the hypotheses

$$H_0: \quad Md = 50$$
$$H_a: \quad Md > 50$$

If we were to conduct a right-tailed sign test at an (approximate) level of significance of 5%, we would not reject H_0. (This is not hard to see. Notice that the number of scores above 50 is 8 out of 13, so that the value of the test statistic would be 8. But recall that Example 13.1 was also a right-tailed sign test at the 5% level with a sample of size 13. The value of the test statistic was also 8. In Example 13.1, we did not reject the null hypothesis; thus we would come to the same conclusion in the present case.)

The school official still thought that the null hypothesis should be rejected. There is a more sensitive test that does not throw away as much information as the sign test. This test can be applied because, based on scores on similar tests, it seemed that the seniors' test scores would have a distribution that was symmetric (although the distribution itself was unknown). When the distribution is symmetric, the Wilcoxon signed-rank test (for a single population) may be applied. (Symmetry means that a vertical line through the median will divide the distribution curve into halves that are mirror images of one another.) See Figure 13.5.

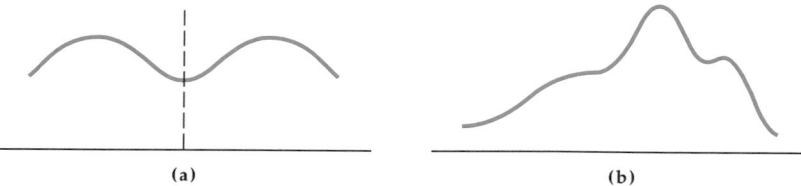

(a)   (b)

Figure 13.5
(a) Symmetric; (b) Not Symmetric

When applying the Wilcoxon signed-rank test, we also require that the data be continuous. (Even though the test scores are whole numbers, we regard these scores as continuous data that have been rounded off.)

Table 13.3 gives the data values in the sample, and the difference between each data value (x) and the value of the median appearing in the null hypothesis, namely, 50. We then rank the absolute value of these differences. We put a minus sign ($-$) in front of those ranks that correspond to data values below the median of 50. See column 4 of Table 13.3.

Table 13.3

Score x	Difference $D = x - 50$	Magnitude $\|D\|$	Signed Rank
57	7	7	4
70	20	20	10
42	-8	8	-5
48	-2	2	-1
77	27	27	12
63	13	13	8
45	-5	5	-3
64	14	14	9
59	9	9	6
39	-11	11	-7
73	23	23	11
78	28	28	13
47	-3	3	-2

Note: The minus sign ($-$) means that the rank corresponds to a difference for a data value to the left of 50.

Suppose for the moment that the population median is actually 50. Since the sample comes from a population of scores that are symmetric with respect to the population median, we expect the sample itself to be more or less symmetrically distributed about this median. This means that if we look at the ranks of the magnitudes of the differences (D), the ranks corresponding to the data values on one side of 50 should be comparable in magnitude to those corresponding to data values on the other side. Thus the sum of the ranks for one side should be comparable in magnitude to the sum of the ranks for the other side. Looking at the fourth column of Table 13.3, we let

$$W^+ = \text{sum of positive ranks} = 73$$

$$W^- = \text{absolute value of sum of negative ranks} = 18$$

As we said, if the true median is 50, we expect these two values to be of comparable size. If W^+ were much smaller than W^-, this would suggest that the data values were spread farther below 50 than above 50, implying that Md < 50. If, on the other hand, W^- were much smaller than W^+, this would suggest that the data values were spread farther above 50 than below 50, implying that Md > 50.

Small values of W^+ suggest Md < 50.

Small values of W^- suggest Md > 50.

For the data under consideration, the value $W^- = 18$ seems small (in relation to $W^+ = 73$). Figure 13.6 does seem to suggest that Md > 50.

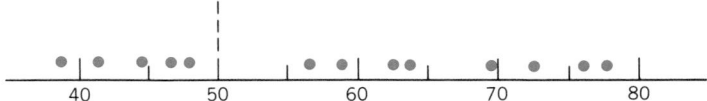

Figure 13.6
Spread of the Data Suggests Md > 50

If we were to test

$$H_0: \quad \text{Md} = 50$$

$$H_a: \quad \text{Md} > 50$$

we could use W^- as a test statistic. If this is "too small," we reject H_0 in favor of H_a. We consider W^- to be too small if it would be unlikely that we would observe such a small value if H_0 were true. "Unlikely" means having a low probability. As usual, this probability is denoted by α and is specified by the researcher. It is the level of significance of the test. Appendix Table B.8 enables us to determine the values of W^- that are too small. This table give us critical values for various values of α and the sample size. When W^- is less than or equal to the critical value, it is too small and therefore leads to rejection of the null hypothesis. A portion of Appendix Table B.8 is reproduced in Table 13.4. (This table is also used to find critical values of W^+.)

Table 13.4
Some Critical Values for the Wilcoxon Signed-Rank Test. The shaded value is the critical value c for a one-sided test with $\alpha = .05$ and sample size $n = 13$.

One-Sided α	Two-Sided α	$n = 11$	$n = 12$	$n = 13$	$n = 14$	$n = 15$	$n = 16$
.05	.10	14	17	21	26	30	36
.025	.05	11	14	17	21	25	30
.01	.02	7	10	13	16	20	24
.005	.01	5	7	10	13	16	19

We will use this table while completing the test in question at the 5% level of significance.

1. *Hypotheses:*

$$H_0: \quad \text{Md} = 50$$
$$H_a: \quad \text{Md} > 50$$

2. *Level of significance:* $\alpha = .05$
3. *Test statistic and observed value:*

$$W^- = |(-5) + (-1) + (-3) + (-7) + (-2)| = |-18| = 18$$

4. *Critical region:* Values of W^- that are too small lead to rejection of H_0. From Table 13.4, we see that when $n = 13$ and $\alpha = .05$ with a one-sided test, the critical value is $c = 21$. Therefore, the critical region consists of (integral) values of W^- less than or equal to 21: $W^- \leq 21$. (See Figure 13.7.)

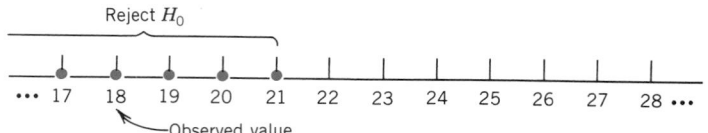

Figure 13.7

5. *Decision:* The observed value of W^- is 18 and is in the critical region; thus we reject H_0. This means that the median does appear to be greater than 50.

We can now summarize the procedure for the Wilcoxon signed-rank test. Assume that the null hypothesis involves some specific value M for the median. Keep in mind that small values of W^- favor Md $> M$, whereas small values of W^+ favor Md $< M$.

Wilcoxon Signed-Rank Test for a Population Median   Suppose that M is the value of the median in question that appears in the null hypothesis. Calculate $D = x - M$ for each data value x. We then rank the values of $|D|$ and place a minus sign in front of each rank corresponding to a negative difference D (as in Table 13.3). Let

$$W^+ = \text{sum of the positive ranks}$$

$$W^- = \text{absolute value of sum of negative ranks}$$

(a) To test the hypotheses

$$H_0: \quad \text{Md} = M$$
$$H_a: \quad \text{Md} > M$$

use W^- as a test statistic. Find the critical value c for a one-sided test with desired significance level in Appendix Table B.8. If $W^- \leq c$, reject H_0. Otherwise, do not reject H_0.

(b) To test

$$H_0: \quad Md = M$$
$$H_a: \quad Md < M$$

use W^+ as a test statistic. Find the critical value c for a one-sided test with desired significance level in Appendix Table B.8. If $W^+ \le c$, reject H_0. Otherwise, do not reject H_0.

(c) To test

$$H_0: \quad Md = M$$
$$H_a: \quad Md \ne M$$

find the critical value c for a two-sided test with desired significance level in Appendix Table B.8. If either $W^+ \le c$ or $W^- \le c$, reject H_0. This means that we can use the minimum of W^+ or W^- as a test statistic. We denote this value by W. If $W \le c$, reject H_0. Otherwise, do not reject H_0.

Assumptions:

1. The data are continuous.

2. The data come from a population with an approximately symmetric distribution.

Tied Ranks

A potential problem with the Wilcoxon signed-rank test exists. When we calculate the magnitude of the differences $|D|$ and rank them, what happens if some values of $|D|$ are the same? For example, if we list the values of $|D|$ in increasing order, what happens if, say, the fifth and sixth values are the same? In this case, we assign the rank 5.5 to both of them (the average of ranks 5 and 6). The next higher value of $|D|$ is assigned the rank 7. If the fifth, sixth, and seventh values of $|D|$ are the same, we assign the rank 6 to each (the average of the ranks 5, 6, and 7), and so on.

Zero Differences

If any of the values of D are 0, we will use the following procedure: If there are an even number of zeros, each zero is assigned the average rank for the set and then half of them are assigned a plus sign and half a minus sign. For example, if there are four zeros, we would average the ranks 1, 2, 3, 4, getting 2.5. Then we would end up with the signed ranks: $-2.5, -2.5, 2.5, 2.5$. If there are an odd number of zero values for D, we discard one of them and reduce the sample size by 1. We then have an even number of zeros and we can proceed as described above.

Comparing Two Populations Using a Paired Experiment

The Wilcoxon signed-rank test can be used to compare two populations when the data values from the two populations are obtained in pairs. In this case, the samples are dependent. In addition to requiring that the data be continuous, the two populations must have distributions with similar shapes. We illustrate the procedure with an example.

Two experimental drugs were developed for the treatment of hypertension; call them drug 1 and drug 2. The drugs were administered to seven pairs of patients with hypertension. Each pair of subjects was matched for medical history, age, and level of blood pressure. One subject in each pair was given drug 1, the other drug 2. For each patient, the drop in diastolic blood pressure was recorded. The two drugs were chemically similar, and so it was thought that their distributions (representing drop in diastolic pressure) would have similar shapes, but it was not known whether their medians would be the same. Two distributions may have the same *shape* but a different *location* (Figure 13.8).

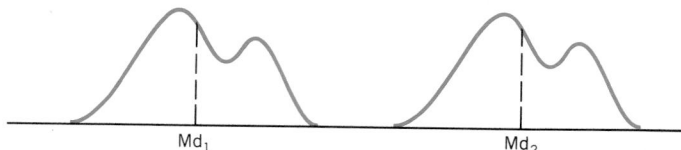

Figure 13.8

Table 13.5

Drop in Diastolic Blood Pressure for Seven Pairs of Patients

Drug 1	Drug 2
10	6
16	20
10	8
4	12
2	8
14	4
4	15

In Table 13.5, the drop in diastolic pressure for each patient (in millimeters of mercury) is given.

Suppose that we use the symbol x_1 to represent the drop in diastolic pressure for a patient given drug 1 and x_2 to represent the drop for a patient given drug 2. For each pair in the sample we look at the difference

$$D = x_1 - x_2$$

This gives rise to a new variable D associated with a conceptual population of differences.

If the researchers studying the drugs wanted to see whether there was any difference in the effectiveness of the drugs, they would test the hypotheses

$$H_0: \quad Md_D = 0$$
$$H_a: \quad Md_D \neq 0$$

This test concerns a single median (where the value in question is $M = 0$). We have seen that the Wilcoxon signed-rank test may be applied if the population of D values is symmetric. It turns out that as long as the x_1 values and x_2 values have similarly shaped distributions, it can be shown that the distribution of D values is symmetric (even if the populations of x_1 and x_2 values are not symmetric).[*] Therefore, the Wilcoxon signed-rank test can be applied.

In the following example, we complete the test of the hypotheses discussed above. Note that D plays the same role as it did before.

---

[*]In fact, it can also be shown that the median of the differences D is the difference of the medians, $Md_D = Md_1 - Md_2$ (assuming that the x_1 values and x_2 values have similarly shaped distributions).

EXAMPLE 13.3

We will now apply the Wilcoxon signed-rank test to the data in Table 13.5. Use the 10% level of significance.

Solution

1. *Hypotheses:* The question is whether drug 1 and drug 2 are equally effective. The hypotheses concern the difference D between the drop in blood pressure for drug 1 versus drug 2.

$$H_0: \quad Md_D = 0$$
$$H_a: \quad Md_D \neq 0$$

2. *Level of significance:* $\alpha = .10$

3. *Test statistic and observed value:* If *either* W^+ or W^- is very small, we reject H_0. Therefore, we can use the minimum of these values, called W, as a test statistic. Table 13.6 is used to compute W.

Table 13.6

x_1	x_2	$D = x_1 - x_2$	$\lvert D \rvert$	Signed-Rank	
10	6	4	4	2.5 ⎫	tied for second
16	20	−4	4	−2.5 ⎭	and third ranks
10	8	2	2	1	
4	12	−8	8	−5	
2	8	−6	6	−4	
14	4	10	10	6	
4	15	−11	11	−7	

If we rank the values of $\lvert D \rvert$, we get 2, 4, 4, 6, 8, 10, 11. Since the 4's occupy the second and third positions, we assign them the rank 2.5.

$$W^+ = 2.5 + 1 + 6 = 9.5$$
$$W^- = \lvert (-2.5) + (-5) + (-4) + (-7) \rvert = \lvert -18.5 \rvert = 18.5$$
$$W = \text{minimum of } W^+ \text{ and } W^-$$
$$= 9.5$$

4. *Critical region:* Using Appendix Table B.8, we find that when $n = 7$ and $\alpha = .10$, the critical value c for a two-sided test is 4. So the critical region consists of values of $W \leq 4$.

5. *Decision:* The observed value 9.5 is not in the critical region, so we do not reject H_0. This means that there is no evidence that the drugs have different effects.

EXAMPLE 13.4

A college professor developed an English course for college students in need of remediation. All students entering the college are given a screening examination. Of those receiving scores below 50, 25 students agreed to take the course. Their scores on the pretest and on a posttest given after completing the course are given in Table 13.7 (page 576), along with the differences D and the signed-ranks of $\lvert D \rvert$.

Table 13.7
Before and After Scores for 25 Students

Pretest (x_1)	Posttest (x_2)	Difference $D = x_1 - x_2$	$|D|$	Signed Rank
46	76	−30	30	−25
27	36	−9	9	−7
37	53	−16	16	−12.5
34	55	−21	21	−18
20	12	8	8	6
38	50	−12	12	−10
10	36	−26	26	−22
24	18	6	6	4
20	21	−1	1	−1
39	57	−18	18	−15
16	27	−11	11	−9
20	48	−28	28	−23
47	70	−23	23	−19
45	25	20	20	17
40	50	−10	10	−8
46	39	7	7	5
32	51	−19	19	−16
49	33	16	16	12.5
45	69	−24	24	−20
49	52	−3	3	−2
44	60	−16	16	−12.5
45	20	25	25	21
16	12	4	4	3
41	70	−29	29	−24
48	64	−16	16	−12.5

Do these data justify the professor's claim that the course improves English skills? Use the 5% level of significance.

Solution

1. *Hypotheses:*   The professor's claim is that scores on the pretest (x_1) tend to be lower than scores on the posttest (x_2). This means that values of the differences $D = x_1 - x_2$ tend to be less than 0 ($Md_D < 0$). Therefore, the hypotheses to be tested are

$$H_0: \quad Md_D = 0$$
$$H_a: \quad Md_D < 0$$

2. *Level of significance:* $\alpha = .05$

3. *Test statistic and observed value:*   We use W^+ as a test statistic. From Table 13.7,

$$W^+ = 68.5$$

4. *Critical region:*   From Appendix Table B.8, we find that the critical value for a one-tailed test with $\alpha = .05$ and $n = 25$ is $c = 101$. Hence the critical region would consist of values of $W^+ \leq 101$.

5. *Decision:*   The observed value of 68.5 is in the critical region, so we reject H_0. This means that the professor's claim ($Md_D < 0$) appears to be correct. In other

words, scores on the pretest tend to be lower than on the posttest, suggesting that the course is effective.

The following is a summary of the procedure for a Wilcoxon signed-rank test for a paired experiment.

Wilcoxon Signed-Rank Test for a Paired Experiment

Let $D = x_1 - x_2$ for each pair of data values. To test a null hypothesis $\text{Md}_D = 0$, we proceed by conducting the Wilcoxon test for a single median (where $M = 0$). Here D plays the same role as before.

Assumptions:

1. The data are continuous.

2. The two sets of data (the x_1 values and the x_2 values) come from distributions with similar shapes.

Normal Approximation

Appendix Table B.8 is applicable for sample sizes up to $n = 50$. We may wish to apply the Wilcoxon signed-rank test for larger sample sizes. It turns out that the test statistic used in this test is approximately normal when n is sufficiently large (greater than or equal to 15). Suppose that we let W represent the test statistic. This will be either W^+ or W^-, depending on the situation. It can be shown that

(a) $\quad \mu_W = \dfrac{n(n + 1)}{4}$

(b) $\quad \sigma_W = \sqrt{\dfrac{n(n + 1)(2n + 1)}{24}}$

(c) Since W is approximately normal when $n \geq 15$,

$$z = \frac{W - \mu_W}{\sigma_W} = \frac{W - n(n + 1)/4}{\sqrt{n(n + 1)(2n + 1)/24}}$$

is approximately standard normal. Therefore, when the sample size is large enough, we can find the critical region in terms of z.

We will show how this works by repeating Example 13.4, this time using the normal approximation. Steps 1 and 2 will be the same as in Example 13.4. The remaining steps are as follows.

- *Test statistic:* Use the standardized form of W^+ to calculate z:

$$z = \frac{W^+ - n(n + 1)/4}{\sqrt{n(n + 1)(2n + 1)/24}} = \frac{68.5 - (25)(26)/4}{\sqrt{(25)(26)(51)/24}} \doteq -2.53$$

- *Critical region:* Small values of W^+ favor H_a. These values correspond to values of z far to the left of 0, so we perform a left-tailed test. The critical region consists of values of $z \leq -z_{.05} = -1.65$. (See Figure 13.9 on page 578.)

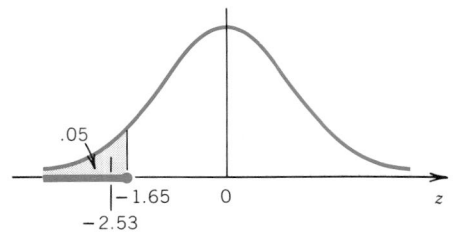

Figure 13.9

- *Decision:* The observed value -2.53 is in the critical region. Therefore, we reject the null hypothesis. This is the same conclusion we reached in Example 13.4.

If we had been testing

$$H_0: \quad Md_D = 0$$
$$H_a: \quad Md_D > 0$$

we would have used W^- when calculating z. Since small values of W^- favor H_a, we would still conduct a left-tailed test. The rejection region would consist of values of $z \le -z_\alpha$. If we had been interested in testing

$$H_0: \quad Md_D = 0$$
$$H_a: \quad Md_D \ne 0$$

we would reject H_0 if $z \ge z_{\alpha/2}$ or $z \le -z_{\alpha/2}$. But since we have agreed to deal with the minimum of W^+ or W^- when conducting a two-tailed test, it can be shown that the value of z will always be less than or equal to 0; therefore, we will reject H_0 if $z \le -z_{\alpha/2}$.

EXERCISES

13.6   In parts (a)–(j), assume a Wilcoxon signed-rank test is used. Complete the following table. Note that n and α refer to the sample size and level of significance, respectively.

	Hypothesis	n	α	Observed Value	Critical Value	Decision
(a)	Md > 50	6	.05	$W^- = 4$		
(b)	Md < 50	6	.025	$W^+ = 4$		
(c)	Md = 50	7	.05	$W = 2$		
(d)	Md < 50	8	.01	$W^+ = 3$		
(e)	Md = 50	8	.10	$W = 5$		
(f)	Md > 50	10	.01	$W^- = 5$		
(g)	Md = 50	11	.05	$W = 13$		
(h)	Md < 50	15	.05	$W^+ = 24$		
(i)	Md > 50	16	.01	$W^- = 22$		
(j)	Md ≠ 50	20	.10	$W = 68$		

In Exercises 13.7–13.9, you are given the alternate hypothesis, the level of significance α, and the sample data.

   (a)   Complete the table.
   (b)   Use the Wilcoxon signed-rank test and complete the test.

13.7 H_a : Md $> 10, \alpha = .05$

Sample Data x	Difference D = x − 10	Magnitude |D|	Signed Rank
18			
12			
4			
1			
15			
17			
26			
0			
14			

13.8 H_a : Md $\neq 60, \alpha = .10$

Sample Data x	Difference D = x − 60	Magnitude |D|	Signed Rank
49			
54			
68			
72			
65			
51			
45			
58			

13.9 H_a : Md $< 50, \alpha = .05$

Sample Data x	Difference D = x − 50	Magnitude |D|	Signed Rank
42			
39			
37			
55			
46			
52			
33			

13.10 A real estate salesman claimed that the median price of house lots in a remote resort area was $30,000. A sample of 10 lots for sale gave the following prices (in thousands of dollars):

28.9   31.5   42.5   28.0   34.9   32.5   36.9   38.5   37.9   32.9

Test the salesman's claim using the Wilcoxon signed-rank test with a 5% level of significance.

13.11 A lotion was advertised as relieving muscular pain in 10 minutes, on average. Believing that it might take longer, a "truth in advertising" group tested 15 people and obtained the following data. A data value represents the time in minutes that the symptom was relieved after application of the lotion.

10.3	9.2	10.6	11.1	9.5	12.0	12.2	9.1
10.7	13.1	12.1	10.1	10.2	11.3	11.0	

Use the Wilcoxon signed-rank test with a 1% significance level to complete the test.

13.12 An appliance dealer was concerned that the median time before an appliance must be serviced might be less than 3 years. A survey of 12 such appliances gave the following times (in years) to the first repair:

2.7	3.4	3.2	1.8	2.5	2.4
4.0	2.3	2.2	3.1	1.1	1.5

Use the Wilcoxon signed-rank test with a 5% level of significance to investigate the dealer's concern.

13.13 Past records at an eastern college indicated that the median MSAT score was 520 for incoming mathematics majors. The chairperson believed that a strong advertising campaign would help recruit majors with a higher median score. Following the advertising campaign, the MSAT scores of incoming mathematics majors were noted. Do the following data provide sufficient evidence to conclude that such advertising campaigns are effective? Use the Wilcoxon signed-rank test with a 1% level of significance.

535	560	500	550	560	540	610	490	545	550
510	620	460	575	485	630	600	515	640	650

13.14 A nutritionist claimed that a liquid diet was effective in reducing weight. A paired experiment gave the following data:

Weight Before Diet	Weight After Diet
171	166
183	187
162	155
196	198
151	140
209	206
198	192
215	210

(a) Use the Wilcoxon signed-rank test for a paired experiment with a 5% level of significance to test the claim.

(b) Test the claim using the sign test with a 5% significance level. (*Note:* You may have already done this in Exercise 13.5.)

(c) Compare your answers in parts (a) and (b). Comment on the different conclusions reached using the two tests.

13.15 An official of an athletic competition believed that judge A tended to give lower performance ratings than judge B. A sample of 26 pairs of ratings was obtained. Let x_1 and x_2 be the evaluation of judges A and B, respectively.

x_1	5.9	7.0	9.1	4.3	3.8	8.0	3.3	6.6	9.3	7.6	8.4	7.3	7.4
x_2	5.8	7.2	9.8	3.9	3.3	8.3	4.7	5.6	8.0	6.5	8.6	6.5	9.0

x_1	5.1	4.0	3.3	4.5	3.9	7.0	6.5	8.1	3.8	6.5	4.5	3.0	7.7
x_2	7.0	4.3	2.3	6.8	5.4	6.8	8.6	8.9	4.7	8.3	6.2	3.1	8.3

Using the Wilcoxon signed-rank test with a 5% level of significance, test the official's belief by using:

(a) Appendix Table B.8 to obtain a critical value

(b) The normal approximation

13.4

THE MANN–WHITNEY U TEST

In the previous section, we showed how the Wilcoxon signed-rank test can be used to compare two populations when the sample data from the populations are paired, with one value in the pair coming from each population. In this case, the samples are *dependent*. Such samples were discussed in Chapter 9. We also discussed *independent* samples in Chapter 9. When the samples are independent, we simply have a collection of data values from each population, and there is no natural way to pair the data values. F. Wilcoxon also proposed a test for dealing with independent samples in 1945. This test is called the *Wilcoxon rank-sum test.* Instead of treating this test, we discuss a test that is equivalent to the Wilcoxon rank-sum test, namely, the **Mann–Whitney U test.** This test enables us to compare two population medians. We illustrate this test with the following example.

A feed and grain company wanted to compare the effectiveness of two types of fertilizer it stocked. Four farmers who were using fertilizer 1 and six farmers who were using fertilizer 2 agreed to cooperate in the study. Each farmer reported the yield in corn obtained (in bushels per acre). The results are given in Table 13.8.

Table 13.8
Yields in Bushels per Acre for Two Types of Fertilizer

Fertilizer 1 (x)	Fertilizer 2 (y)
103	89
85	101
92	108
110	93
	90
	82

We will assume at the outset that the yields for both fertilizers have similar distributions, although the distributions may differ in location. That is, they may have different medians.

The Mann–Whitney test is based on a ranking of all the sample data taken together. The following is a list of all the data values ranked in ascending order, with x and y representing yields from fertilizers 1 and 2, respectively.

82	85	89	90	92	93	101	103	108	110
y	x	y	y	x	y	y	x	y	x

The fertilizer yields and ranks are given in Table 13.9.

Low ranks for the x values would suggest that fertilizer 1 was less effective than fertilizer 2. That is, the median for fertilizer 1 is less than that of fertilizer 2, $\text{Md}_x < \text{Md}_y$. Low ranks for the y values would suggest that fertilizer 2 was less effective than fertilizer 1 ($\text{Md}_y < \text{Md}_x$). We ought to look at the sum of the ranks for each fertilizer. These are given in Table 13.10.

Table 13.9
Fertilizer Yields with Overall Rankings

Fertilizer 1	Rank	Fertilizer 2	Rank
103	8	89	3
85	2	101	7
92	5	108	9
110	10	93	6
		90	4
		82	1

Table 13.10
Rank Sums

Ranks for Fertilizer 1	Ranks for Fertilizer 2
8	3
2	7
5	9
10	6
$S_x = 25$	4
	1
	$S_y = 30$

Small values of S_x suggest that fertilizer 1 is less effective than fertilizer 2. Small values of S_y suggest that fertilizer 2 is less effective than fertilizer 1. But we should be careful in using the word *small*. This should be measured in relation to something. The rank sum S_x can be smaller than S_y just because there are fewer x values and therefore fewer ranks for x values. We should look at how close S_x comes to the smallest possible value it could conceivably assume. The worst-case scenario for fertilizer 1 would occur if all the x values were less than all the y values:

	x	x	x	x	y	y	y	y	y	y
Ranks:	1	2	3	4	5	6	7	8	9	10

For this arrangement, $S_x = 1 + 2 + 3 + 4 = 10$. This is the smallest possible value for S_x. You may verify that the smallest possible value for S_y is 21. If we let n_1 = the number of x values and n_2 = number of y values, the following expressions give the smallest possible values for S_x and S_y, respectively:

$$\frac{n_1(n_1 + 1)}{2} = \frac{(4)(5)}{2} = 10 \qquad \frac{n_2(n_2 + 1)}{2} = \frac{(6)(7)}{2} = 21$$

It would seem reasonable to look at the amount by which S_x (and S_y) actually exceed their smallest possible values. To this end, we define

$$U_x = S_x - \frac{n_1(n_1 + 1)}{2} = 25 - 10 = 15 \qquad \left\{ \begin{array}{l} \text{Amount by which } S_x \text{ exceeds} \\ \text{its smallest possible value} \end{array} \right.$$

$$U_y = S_y - \frac{n_2(n_2 + 1)}{2} = 30 - 21 = 9 \qquad \left\{ \begin{array}{l} \text{Amount by which } S_y \text{ exceeds} \\ \text{its smallest possible value} \end{array} \right.$$

In general, the Mann–Whitney test makes use of U_x or U_y when comparing two population medians Md_x and Md_y according to the following principle:

> Small values of U_x suggest $\text{Md}_x < \text{Md}_y$.
> Small values of U_y suggest $\text{Md}_x > \text{Md}_y$.

We must further clarify the meaning of the word *small* in this context. Therefore, we continue the fertilizer discussion. Suppose that before gathering the data, the company suspected that perhaps fertilizer 1 was more effective than fertilizer 2 ($\text{Md}_x > \text{Md}_y$). The company decided to test

$$H_0: \quad \text{Md}_x = \text{Md}_y$$
$$H_a: \quad \text{Md}_x > \text{Md}_y$$

We would use U_y as a test statistic. Small values of U_y favor H_a. But how small should U_y be for us to reject H_0 in favor of H_a? We answer in the usual way: so small that it would be unlikely that we would observe such a small value if H_0 were true. Appendix Table B.9 contains critical values for U_x or U_y. We can determine how small U_y must be for us to reject H_0 because Appendix Table B.9 enables us to find a critical value c for a given level of significance. We reject H_0 if $U_y \leq c$.

A portion of Appendix Table B.9 is shown in Table 13.11. Note that Table 13.11 gives critical values for the following:

1. A one-tailed test with: $\alpha = .05$ in lightface type
                              $\alpha = .025$ in boldface type

Table 13.11
Some Critical Values for the Mann–Whitney Test. The Shaded Value Is for the One-tailed Test with $\alpha = .05$.

n_2 \ n_1	1	2	3	4	6	7	8	...	19	20
.	.	.	.	.	.	.	.			
.	.	.	.	.	.	.	.			
.	.	.	.	.	.	.	.			
4	—a	—	0	1	2	3				
	—	—	—	0	1	2				
5	—	0	1	2	4	5				
	—	—	0	1	2	3				
6	—	0	2	3	5	7				
	—	—	1	2	3	5				
.	.		.							
.	.		.							
.	.		.							

aBlanks indicate that the table is not applicable for these values of n_1 and n_2.

2. A two-tailed test with: $\alpha = .10$ in lightface type
$\alpha = .05$ in boldface type

(*Note:* Appendix Table B.9 includes additional values of α as well.)

To use this table, we determine the values of n_1 and n_2, the two sample sizes. For the fertilizer problem, $n_1 = 4$ and $n_2 = 6$. If we are interested in the one-tailed test previously discussed with, say, $\alpha = .05$, we read the value in lightface type in column 4 and row 6, namely, 3. Hence we reject H_0 if $U_y \leq 3$. But the observed value of U_y is 9, so we do not reject H_0. This means that there is insufficient evidence that fertilizer 1 is more effective than fertilizer 2.

EXAMPLE 13.5

An educator wanted to see whether college physics majors tended to have different quality point averages (QPAs) from chemistry majors. He obtained 10 students majoring in physics and 10 majoring in chemistry. Although the QPAs of *all* students tended to be normally distributed, the educator thought that the QPAs for students in a given discipline might not be normal. Therefore, he decided to use a nonparametric test: the Mann–Whitney test. The sample data values along with their ranks are given in Table 13.12.

Table 13.12
Quality Point Averages for Physics and Chemistry Majors

Physics (x)	Ranks	Chemistry (y)	Ranks
2.72	11	3.10	13.5
3.10	13.5	2.10	5
3.75	19	2.62	9
1.92	3	1.62	2
2.41	8	2.85	12
3.72	18	1.95	4
2.35	6	3.28	16
3.80	20	1.50	1
3.25	15	3.71	17
2.71	10	2.37	7
	$S_x = 123.5$		$S_y = 86.5$

The value 3.10 occurs twice, occupying the 13th and 14th positions in a ranked list. The rank assigned to each QPA is therefore the average of these two positions, namely, 13.5. The next rank assigned is 15, and so on. We will complete the test at the 5% level of significance.

Solution

1. *Hypotheses:*

$$H_0: \quad Md_x = Md_y$$
$$H_a: \quad Md_x \neq Md_y$$

2. *Level of significance:* $\alpha = .05$

3. *Test statistic and observed value:*   Small values of *either* U_x or U_y favor H_a. Therefore, we can use the minimum of these values as our test statistic. From Table 13.12,

$$U_x = S_x - \frac{n_1(n_1 + 1)}{2} = 123.5 - \frac{(10)(11)}{2} = 123.5 - 55 = 68.5$$

$$U_y = S_y - \frac{n_2(n_2 + 1)}{2} = 86.5 - 55 = 31.5$$

Our test statistic is

$$U = \text{minimum of } U_x \text{ and } U_y$$
$$= 31.5$$

4. *Critical region:*   Find the critical value c for a two-tailed test when $n_1 = 10$, $n_2 = 10$, and $\alpha = .05$. From Appendix Table B.9, this value is $c = 23$. The critical region consists of values of $U \leq 23$.

5. *Decision:*   Since the observed value ($U = 31.5$) is not in the critical region, we do not reject H_0. This means that there is no evidence that QPAs of physics majors have a different median from that of chemistry majors.

We can now summarize the essential features of the Mann–Whitney test. Keep in mind that small values of U_x favor the relation $\text{Md}_x < \text{Md}_y$, whereas small values of U_y favor $\text{Md}_x > \text{Md}_y$.

Mann–Whitney Test   This test is used for comparing two population medians based on independent samples.

- Decide on the hypotheses to be tested and the level of significance α.
- Rank all the data values in the two samples taken *together*. Call S_x the sum of the ranks of the x values and S_y the sum of the ranks of the y values.

(a)   To test the hypotheses

$$H_0: \quad \text{Md}_x = \text{Md}_y$$
$$H_a: \quad \text{Md}_x > \text{Md}_y$$

the test statistic U is

$$U = U_y = S_y - \frac{n_2(n_2 + 1)}{2} \qquad n_2 = \text{number of } y \text{ values}$$

Find the critical value c for a one-tailed test in Appendix Table B.9. If $U \leq c$, reject H_0. Otherwise, do not reject H_0.

(b)   To test

$$H_0: \quad \text{Md}_x = \text{Md}_y$$
$$H_a: \quad \text{Md}_x < \text{Md}_y$$

the test statistic U is

$$U = U_x = S_x - \frac{n_1(n_1 + 1)}{2} \qquad n_1 = \text{number of } x \text{ values}$$

Find the critical value c for a one-tailed test in Appendix Table B.9. If $U \leq c$, reject H_0. Otherwise, do not reject H_0.

(c) To test

$$H_0: \quad \text{Md}_x = \text{Md}_y$$
$$H_a: \quad \text{Md}_x \neq \text{Md}_y$$

small values of either U_x or U_y favor H_a. Therefore, we define the test statistic to be

$$U = \text{minimum of } U_x \text{ and } U_y$$

Find the critical value c for a two-tailed test in Appendix Table B.9. If $U \leq c$, reject H_0. Otherwise, do not reject H_0.

Assumptions:

1. The data are continuous.
2. The x and y values come from distributions with similar shapes.

Normal Approximation

Appendix Table B.9 allows sample sizes up to 20. We can still perform the Mann–Whitney test for larger sample sizes because of the following result: Let U represent either U_x or U_y. Then

(a) The mean is $\mu_U = \dfrac{n_1 n_2}{2}$.

(b) The standard deviation is $\sigma_U = \sqrt{\dfrac{n_1 n_2 (n_1 + n_2 + 1)}{12}}$.

(c) If $n_1 \geq 10$ and $n_2 \geq 10$, U is approximately normal. Therefore,

$$z = \frac{U - \mu_U}{\sigma_U} = \frac{U - \dfrac{n_1 n_2}{2}}{\sqrt{\dfrac{n_1 n_2 (n_1 + n_2 + 1)}{12}}}$$

is approximately standard normal. This means that when the sample sizes are large enough, we can find the critical region in terms of z.

Now we will see how the normal approximation would work if it were used in the previous example. Here the sample sizes are $n_1 = n_2 = 10$; therefore we may use the normal approximation. Steps 1 and 2 will be the same. The remaining steps are as follows:

- *Test statistic:* First find the value of U. We saw in Example 13.5 that $U = 31.5$. Now calculate the value of the test statistic z:

$$z = \frac{U - \dfrac{n_1 n_2}{2}}{\sqrt{\dfrac{n_1 n_2 (n_1 + n_2 + 1)}{12}}} = \frac{31.5 - \dfrac{(10)(10)}{2}}{\sqrt{\dfrac{(10)(10)(10 + 10 + 1)}{12}}}$$

$$= \frac{-18.5}{\sqrt{175}} \doteq -1.40$$

- *Critical region:* We are conducting a two-tailed test with $\alpha = .05$. Usually, the critical values for a two-tailed z test are (from Appendix Table B.3): $\pm z_{\alpha/2} = \pm z_{.025} = \pm 1.96$. Normally the critical region would consist of values of $z \geq 1.96$ or $z \leq -1.96$. But since we have used the minimum of U_x and U_y to compute z, there will not be any question of z falling in the right tail (≥ 1.96). Hence, in effect the critical region consists of values of z such that $z \leq -z_{\alpha/2} = -1.96$.

- *Decision:* Our decision is the same as that in Example 13.5: We do not reject the null hypothesis because the observed value ($z = -1.40$) is not in the critical region.

When using z to conduct a two-tailed Mann–Whitney test, we reject H_0 if $z \leq -z_{\alpha/2}$. For a one-tailed test, we reject H_0 if $z \leq -z_\alpha$.

EXERCISES

13.16 In parts (a)–(i), assume a Mann–Whitney U test is used. Complete the following table. Note that n_1 and n_2 refer to the x and y sample sizes, respectively, and α refers to the level of significance.

	Hypothesis	n_1	n_2	α	Observed Value U	Critical Value	Decision
(a)	$Md_x = Md_y$	6	10	.05	14		
(b)	$Md_x < Md_y$	9	12	.01	18		
(c)	$Md_x > Md_y$	15	20	.025	79		
(d)	$Md_x < Md_y$	14	8	.05	36		
(e)	$Md_x \neq Md_y$	13	13	.05	41		
(f)	$Md_x > Md_y$	17	11	.01	49		
(g)	$Md_x \neq Md_y$	5	7	.01	4		
(h)	$Md_x < Md_y$	16	12	.05	55		
(i)	$Md_x > Md_y$	9	5	.025	5		

In Exercises 13.17 and 13.18, you are given the alternate hypothesis, the level of significance α, and the sample data.

    (a) Complete the table.

    (b) Use the Mann–Whitney U test and complete the test.

13.17 $H_a : Md_x \neq Md_y, \alpha = .10$

x	Rank (x)	y	Rank (y)
43		55	
47		62	
51		68	
59		75	
65			
71			

13.18 $H_a : \mathrm{Md}_x > \mathrm{Md}_y, \alpha = .05$

x	Rank (x)	y	Rank (y)
33		20	
36		23	
42		28	
45		34	
49		37	

13.19   A high school soccer coach believed that the median endurance level of soccer players was greater than that for football players. The data in the following table represent the results (in minutes) of an endurance test taken by seven football players (x) and eight soccer players (y). Test the coach's belief using the Mann–Whitney U test with a 5% level of significance.

x	y
14.7	17.3
15.3	17.9
17.2	20.5
13.6	14.5
13.9	18.4
15.2	19.2
18.1	16.1
	17.5

13.20   A consumer protection agency wanted to test the hypothesis that the median cost of an automobile repair was the same in two nearby cities. The agency obtained estimates (x and y) from garages in the two cities for a particular job. The estimates (in dollars) were

x	y
77	68
80	71
85	73
90	97
92	101
	106
	108

Do the data provide sufficient evidence to indicate a difference in the median cost? Use the Mann–Whitney U test with a 10% level of significance.

13.21   A spokesman for an automobile manufacturer claimed that gas mileage (x) for its new model was better than gas mileage (y) for a competitor's model. Ten cars from each manufacturer were tested. The following data represent miles per gallon.

x	y
36.2	34.7
36.5	34.9
36.9	35.8
37.3	36.3
37.6	36.6
37.7	36.8
37.9	37.1
38.3	37.5
38.5	38.0
38.8	38.2

Test the claim using the Mann–Whitney U test with a 5% level of significance.

13.22   A teacher was assigned to teach two sections of a calculus course. Section A was to meet twice a week with 2-hour classes, and section B was to meet four times a week with 1-hour classes. Twenty-seven students were taking the course; 13 were randomly assigned to section A. The chairperson claimed that there would be no statistically significant difference in median performance. The final grades x and y for sections A and B, respectively, were as follows:

x	y
40	34
54	52
55	58
59	63
62	68
64	70
67	71
77	73
78	76
88	79
90	84
91	86
92	89
	95

With a 5% level of significance, test the claim using

(a)   Appendix Table B.9 to select a critical value

(b)   The normal approximation

13.5

THE RUNS TEST

The **runs test** is a test for randomness. We use the following example to illustrate the test: It was decided to conduct a survey of workers in a town, the purpose of which was to estimate the proportion of union members and to compare views of union members versus nonunion members on various issues. Each employee of the survey firm was instructed to randomly interview 12 workers and record whether the worker was a member of a union (*M*) or not (*N*), along with various other items of information. In addition, the interview forms were to be numbered in the order interviewed. Suppose union members (*M*) and nonunion members (*N*) were interviewed in the following order:

$$M \quad M \quad M \quad M \quad M \quad M \quad N \quad N \quad N \quad N \quad N \quad N$$

This means that six union members were interviewed followed by six nonunion members. Such a process does not appear to be random. On the other hand, suppose that the interviewer had obtained the following sequence:

$$M \quad N \quad M \quad N \quad M \quad N \quad M \quad N \quad M \quad N \quad M \quad N$$

This process is not random either. The interviewer carefully alternated interviews, interviewing a union member followed by a nonunion member. Both of these interviewing procedures involve a systematic procedure and are nonrandom.

We can investigate such nonrandomness by examining the number of **runs** in a sequence.

Definition   A *run* is a sequence of the same letter written one or more times. There is a different letter (or no letter) before and after the sequence.

For the sequences discussed previously, the numbers of runs are

$$\underline{M\,M\,M\,M\,M\,M} \qquad \underline{N\,N\,N\,N\,N\,N} \qquad R = \text{total number of runs} = 2$$

$$\underline{M\,N\,M\,N\,M\,N\,M\,N\,M\,N\,M\,N} \qquad R = 12$$

A very large or very small number of runs would imply nonrandomness. As usual, we would conclude nonrandomness if the number of runs is so large or small that it would be unlikely that we would observe such a large or small number, if the process were truly random. "Unlikely" means having a low probability, which we denote by α.

Appendix Table B.10 contains critical values for R, the number of runs, when $\alpha = .05$. For example, in the interviewing process, $n_1 = $ number of M's $= 6$ and $n_2 = $ the number of N's $= 6$. Then, if $\alpha = .05$, the left critical value for R is 3 and the right critical value is 11. See Appendix Table B.10. In general, we denote the left critical value by c_1 and the right critical value by c_2.

This means that if we are considering the hypotheses

$$H_0: \quad \text{The process is random.}$$
$$H_a: \quad \text{The process is not random.}$$

then we would reject H_0 if $R \leq 3$ or $R \geq 11$. For example, for the sequence

$$M \quad M \quad M \quad M \quad M \quad M \quad N \quad N \quad N \quad N \quad N \quad N$$

the number of runs is $R = 2$. This value is in the critical region; therefore, we would reject H_0.

The procedure for testing for randomness is called the **runs test** and is summarized as follows:

The Runs Test Suppose that a process results in a sequence of observations and that each observation can be placed in either one of two categories (such as M for union member or N for nonunion member).

1. *Hypotheses:*
$$H_0: \quad \text{The process is random.}$$
$$H_a: \quad \text{The process is not random.}$$

2. *Level of significance:* For this test, we will use .05.

3. *Test statistic:*
$$R = \text{number of runs in the sequence}$$

4. *Critical region:* Let n_1 = number of occurrences of one of the symbols and n_2 = number of occurrences of the other. Using these values of n_1 and n_2, find the lower and upper critical values c_1 and c_2 from Appendix Table B.10.

5. *Decision:* If $R \le c_1$ or $R \ge c_2$, reject H_0 and conclude nonrandomness. Otherwise, do not reject H_0.

One of the applications of the runs test in the area of industrial quality control involves **time series.**

Definition A *time series* is a sequence of numerical measurements obtained over a period of time.

If we were studying some measurable characteristic of an industrial product obtained over time (such as the thickness of automobile rocker gaskets selected from a production line), deviations of these measurements above or below their mean could be examined to detect a possible departure from randomness. For example, we could label a gasket A if its measurement is above the mean, and B if it is below the mean. The sequence of A's and B's can then be examined for nonrandomness. Departures from randomness involving occasional surges of A's, for example, might be caused by a machine that periodically malfunctions.

EXAMPLE 13.6

Every 5 minutes, a gasket is selected from a production line and its thickness measured. Twenty-three such measurements are obtained. An A is recorded if the gasket measures above the (sample) mean, and a B is recorded if it measures below, with the following results:

$$A \quad B \quad A \quad B \quad B \quad B \quad B \quad A \quad A \quad B \quad B \quad B \quad A \quad A \quad B \quad B \quad A \quad A \quad A \quad B \quad A \quad A \quad B$$

Do these values indicate a lack of randomness? Use the 5% level of significance.

Solution

1. *Hypotheses:*

    H_0:   The process (occurrence of A's and B's) is random.

    H_a: The process is not random.

2. *Level of significance:* $\alpha = .05$

3. *Test statistic and observed value:* R equals the number of runs in

    $$\underbrace{A}\,\underbrace{B}\,\underbrace{A}\,\underbrace{B\,B\,B\,B}\,\underbrace{A\,A}\,\underbrace{B\,B\,B}\,\underbrace{A\,A}\,\underbrace{B\,B}\,\underbrace{A\,A\,A}\,\underbrace{B}\,\underbrace{A\,A}\,\underbrace{B}$$

    Therefore, $R = 12$.

4. *Critical region:*   Let n_1 = number of A's = 11; n_2 = number of B's = 12. Using Appendix Table B.10, we find that the left and right critical values are $c_1 = 7$ and $c_2 = 18$, respectively, so the critical region consists of values of $R \leq 7$ or $R \geq 18$.

5. *Decision:*   The observed value ($R = 12$) is not in the critical region. Therefore, we do not reject H_0. This means that the results do not indicate a departure from randomness.

Normal Approximation

Appendix Table B.10 gives values of n_1 and n_2 up to 15. We can still apply the runs test for larger values of n_1 and n_2 because of the following result:

(a) $\mu_R = \dfrac{2n_1 n_2}{n_1 + n_2} + 1$

(b) $\sigma_R = \sqrt{\dfrac{2n_1 n_2(2n_1 n_2 - n_1 - n_2)}{(n_1 + n_2)^2(n_1 + n_2 - 1)}}$

(c)   If n_1 and n_2 are both greater than 10, then R is approximately normal, so

$$z = \frac{R - \mu_R}{\sigma_R}$$

is approximately standard normal.

This means that for sufficiently large values of n_1 and n_2, we can accomplish the runs test by means of a z test.

We will show how the normal approximation can be used in the previous example. Steps 1 and 2 will be the same. The remaining steps are as follows:

*   *Test statistic and observed value:*   First find μ_R and σ_R.

$$\mu_R = \frac{2n_1 n_2}{n_1 + n_2} + 1 = \frac{(2)(11)(12)}{11 + 12} + 1 \doteq 12.48$$

$$\sigma_R = \sqrt{\frac{2n_1 n_2(2n_1 n_2 - n_1 - n_2)}{(n_1 + n_2)^2(n_1 + n_2 - 1)}} = \sqrt{\frac{(2)(11)(12)[(2)(11)(12) - 11 - 12]}{(11 + 12)^2(11 + 12 - 1)}}$$

$$= \sqrt{\frac{63{,}624}{11{,}638}} \doteq 2.34$$

so

$$z = \frac{R - \mu_R}{\sigma_R} = \frac{12 - 12.48}{2.34} \doteq -.21$$

- *Critical region:*   Large or small values of R favor H_a. These correspond to values of z far to the right or left of 0. Therefore, we conduct a two-tailed test. Since $\alpha = .05$, the critical region will consist of values of

$$z \le -z_{\alpha/2} = -1.96 \quad \text{or} \quad z \ge z_{\alpha/2} = 1.96$$

(See Figure 13.10.)

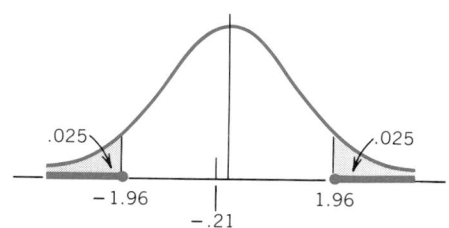

Figure 13.10

- *Decision:*   The observed value, $z = -.21$, is not in the critical region, thus we do not reject H_0. (This is the same conclusion that was reached in Example 13.6.)

EXERCISES

13.23   A plant manager is to test a hypothesis that a process is random. In a sequence of observations, each observation is recorded as A (acceptable) or B (not acceptable). For each sequence of observations given, complete the table. Use a 5% level of significance. Note that R is the number of runs; c_1 and c_2 are the lower and upper critical values, respectively.

		c_1	c_2	R	Decision
(a)	A A A A A B B B B				
(b)	A B A B A B A B A B A B				
(c)	A A A B B B A A A B B B B				
(d)	B A A B B B A B B A B A				
(e)	B B A B B A B A A A A B B B				
(f)	A A B B A A B B A A B B A B A				

13.24   The owner of a small business computed the average revenue per day over a period of 12 days. For each day, an L was recorded if the revenue was less than the average. Otherwise, an M was recorded. Do the following data indicate a lack of randomness at the 5% level of significance?

$$L \quad L \quad L \quad L \quad M \quad M \quad L \quad L \quad L \quad L \quad M \quad M$$

13.25   The following data represent a sample of 15 electrical components inspected at 5-minute intervals. A D was recorded if the component failed to meet the required specifications. Otherwise, an N was recorded. Do the data indicate that the process is not random? Use a 5% level of significance.

$$N \quad N \quad N \quad N \quad N \quad N \quad D \quad D \quad D \quad N \quad N \quad N \quad N \quad N \quad N$$

13.26   Students evaluated a college professor over a period of 25 classes. An S was recorded if more than 50% of the class indicated the teacher's performance was satisfactory. Otherwise, a U was recorded. Using a 5% level of significance, test the hypothesis that the following data indicate a lack of randomness by

(a)   Obtaining critical values from Appendix Table B.10

(b)   The normal approximation

$$U \quad S \quad S \quad S \quad S \quad U \quad U \quad U \quad S \quad S \quad S \quad S \quad S$$
$$S \quad S \quad S \quad U \quad U \quad U \quad S \quad U \quad S \quad U \quad U \quad U$$

13.6

A DISCUSSION OF PARAMETRIC VERSUS NONPARAMETRIC TESTS

Two statistical tests are often assessed by comparing the **power** of each test. To understand this concept, we should recall the types of errors that can occur in hypothesis testing. A Type I error occurs if we reject the null hypothesis, H_0, when it is true; a Type II error consists of not rejecting H_0 when it is false. The probabilities of committing these errors are denoted by

$$\alpha = P(\text{Type I error}) \quad \leftarrow \text{ Level of significance of the test}$$
$$\beta = P(\text{Type II error})$$

The researcher selects the level of significance α. If two statistical tests have the same level of significance α, then the one with the smaller value for β is a better test. Suppose that for some test the probability of not rejecting H_0 when it is false is $\beta = .10$. Then the probability of rejecting H_0 when it is false is .90 ($= 1 - .10$). We call this the **power of the test.**

> **Definition**   For a statistical test applied in a given situation, the *power of the test* is the probability of rejecting a false null hypothesis H_0:
>
> $$\text{power} = 1 - \beta$$

If two statistical tests have the same level of significance α, then the one with the greater power is the better test.

In Chapters 8 and 9, we considered various parametric tests concerning population means: t tests for small samples and z tests for large samples. The t tests required that the populations involved be approximately normal. (The z tests involving large samples did not require normality, but, still, the closer the population distributions are to normality, the better these tests are in the sense that they have greater power.) When we are considering any tests involving measures of central tendency, we should certainly consider the parametric tests because when conditions are appropriate, these tests are more powerful than nonparametric tests. It is not surprising that these tests (when appropriate) would be better tests than the sign test, or the Wilcoxon signed-rank test, or the Mann–Whitney test. After all, they use more information. For example, a t test uses the magnitudes of the data values, whereas the Mann–Whitney test uses only the ranks of the data values. However, when the population(s) departs substantially from normality, nonparametric tests should be considered, especially when the sample sizes are small. Even when the populations are normal, the Wilcoxon signed-rank test and the Mann–Whitney tests are almost as good as their parametric counterparts. When the populations depart considerably from normality, the Wilcoxon signed-rank test and the Mann–Whitney test can be better tests.

13.7

USING MINITAB (OPTIONAL)

We will illustrate Minitab commands for nonparametric tests in the context of some of the examples discussed in this chapter. One-sided tests are done by means of the usual ALTERNATIVE subcommand.

1. Sign Test

With a sample of new home prices in column 1, we can test the following hypotheses concerning median price for a new home:

$$H_0: \quad Md = 70,000$$
$$H_a: \quad Md \neq 70,000$$

Session Command	**Dialog Box**
MTB > STEST MEDIAN = 70000 C1	Stat ▶ Nonparametrics ▶ 1-Sample Sign Type *C1* in **Variables** box Click **Test median** and type *70000* in box Click **OK**

If the value of the median is not specified, Minitab assumes the value 0. A two-sided test is automatically done if no ALTERNATIVE subcommand is given. Among other things, Minitab will print the *P*-value.

In Example 13.1, we used a sign test to compare the yield for two types of seed based on dependent samples. Thirteen farms used both types of seed. We could place the yields for the two types of seed in columns C1, C2. We then conduct the following test on the median of the differences (*D*):

$$H_0: \quad Md_D = 0$$
$$H_a: \quad Md_D > 0$$

Session Commands	**Dialog Box**
MTB > LET C3 = C1 − C2 MTB > STEST C3; SUBC > ALTERNATIVE = 1.	(Assume C3 = C2 − C1) Stat ▶ Nonparametrics ▶ 1-Sample Sign Type C3 in **Variables** box Click **Test median** Click ↓ and click **greater than** Click **OK**

2. Wilcoxon Signed-Rank Test

With the test scores in Table 13.3 placed in column C1, we can conduct the following test:

$$H_0: \quad Md = 50$$
$$H_a: \quad Md > 50$$

Session Commands	**Dialog Box**
MTB > WTEST 50 C1; SUBC > ALTERNATIVE = 1.	**Stat ▶ Nonparametrics ▶ 1-Sample Wilcoxon** Type *C1* in **Variables** box Click **Test median** and type *50* in box Click ↓ and click **greater than** Click **OK**

Minitab will print an estimate of the median and a *P*-value.

As in the case of the sign test, we can do a test involving dependent samples with data values in columns C1 and C2. For example, to conduct the following test on the median of the differences (D), use the steps indicated:

$$H_0: \quad Md_D = 0$$
$$H_a: \quad Md_D \neq 0$$

Session Commands	**Dialog Box**
MTB > LET C3 = C1 − C2 MTB > WTEST C3	**Stat ▶ Nonparametrics ▶ 1-Sample Wilcoxon** Type *C3* in **Variables** box Click **Test median** Click **OK**

(If the value of the median is not specified, Minitab uses 0.)

3. Mann–Whitney U Test

This test compares two population medians based on independent samples. In Section 13.4, we compared median yield for two fertilizers in Table 13.8. We tested

$$H_0: \quad Md_1 = Md_2$$
$$H_a: \quad Md_1 > Md_2$$

The Minitab code is

MANN-WHITNEY, ALTERNATIVE = 1, DATA IN C1, C2

Assume values for fertilizer 1 are in column 1 and those for fertilizer 2 are in column 2:

C1	C2
102	89
85	101
92	108
110	93
	90
	82

Session Command	Dialog Box
MTB > MANN 1 C1 C2	**Stat** ▶ **Nonparametrics** ▶ **Mann-Whitney**

Stat ▶ **Nonparametrics** ▶ **Mann-Whitney**
Type *C1* in **First sample** box and *C2* in **Second sample** box
Click on **greater than** in **Alternative** box
Click **OK**

Output

Mann-Whitney Confidence Interval and Test

```
C1            N =   4      Median =        97.00
C2            N =   6      Median =        91.50
Point estimate for ETA1-ETA2 is          2.50
95.7 Percent C.I. for ETA1-ETA2 is (-16.00,20.00)
W = 25.0
Test of ETA1 = ETA2  vs.  ETA1 > ETA2 is significant at 0.2970

Cannot reject at alpha = 0.05
```

Note that an approximate 95% confidence interval is given for ETA1−ETA2. This is $Md_1 - Md_2$.

The printout states that the test is significant at .2970. This means that .2970 is the smallest level of significance for which the null hypothesis can be rejected. This is another way of describing the *P*-value, because we reject H_0 for any $\alpha \geq P$.

In this chapter, we used the test statistic *U* for the Mann–Whitney test (*U* is either U_x or U_y, depending on the situation). Minitab uses *W*. This is the sum of the ranks in the first sample (the *x* values, in this case). We called this S_x.

4. Runs Test

The Minitab Runs test assumes that the observations are numbers. So in a situation like the one discussed at the beginning of Section 13.5, where the observations were *M* (union member) and *N* (not a union member), we would convert these symbols to numbers. For example, we could use 1 for *M* and 0 for *N*. Choose a value in the middle of the data, say, .5. A **run** can then be defined as one or more consecutive observations above .5 or one or more consecutive observations below .5. For example, the sequence

$$1,1,0,1,1,1,0,0,1,1,0$$

has six runs. To do a Runs test, we set the observations in a column, say, C1.

Session Command	Dialog Box
MTB > RUNS .5, DATA IN C1	**Stat** ▶ **Nonparametrics** ▶ **Runs test**

Stat ▶ **Nonparametrics** ▶ **Runs test**
Type *C1* in **Variables** box
Click **Above and below** and type *.5* in box
Click **OK**

If the .5 is omitted, Minitab automatically uses the average of the data values in C1. Minitab prints out the observed and expected number of runs, the number of runs above and below *K* (we used *K* = .5), and the *P*-value.

A word of caution about using Minitab for nonparametric tests: For most of these tests, Minitab uses the normal approximation to find P-values. (One exception is the sign test, which uses the normal approximation only if $n > 50$.) Remember that there are some minimum requirements on sample sizes to use the normal approximations.

EXERCISES

Suggested exercises for use with Minitab are 13.2, 13.5, 13.15(b), 13.22(b), 13.26(b). (*Note:* Minitab will automatically use the normal approximation for the last three exercises.)

13.8

WORKING WITH DATA (OPTIONAL)

1. Obtain a sample of at least 15 males and 15 females with systolic blood pressure above 140 from Appendix Table B.11. Conduct a test to see whether there is a difference in the population medians for these groups.

2. Repeat the previous exercise with samples of males and females with cholesterol readings above 210.

13.9

SUMMARY

Nonparametric tests are useful when little is known about the distributions of the populations under investigation, or when these distributions do not meet the requirements necessary for the use of parametric tests (such as approximate normality).

In this chapter, we studied only a few nonparametric tests. These tests, along with their test statistics, were as follows:

1. Sign Test

We used this test to study the median of a population and to compare two populations when the samples are dependent.

Test statistic:

$$x = \text{number of data values in the sample that are greater than}$$
$$\text{the value of the median appearing in the null hypothesis}$$

We treat x as a binomial variable with $p = .5$ and $n = $ sample size.

2. Wilcoxon Signed-Rank Test

We used this test to investigate a single population median and to compare two populations using a paired experiment.

Test statistic:

For a left-tailed test (with $<$ in the alternate hypothesis), use

$$W^+ = \text{sum of the positive ranks}$$

For a right-tailed test (with $>$ in alternate hypothesis), use

$$W^- = \text{absolute value of sum of negative ranks}$$

For a two-tailed test (with $\neq$ in alternate hypothesis), use

$$W = \text{minimum of } W^+, W^-$$

Look up the critical value c in Appendix Table B.8. Reject H_0 if the test statistic is less than or equal to c.

3. Mann–Whitney Test

We used this to compare two population medians when the samples are independent. Let n_1 = sample size of x values and n_2 = sample size of y values.

Test statistic:

When the alternate hypothesis is $\text{Md}_x > \text{Md}_y$, use

$$U = U_y = S_y - \frac{n_2(n_2 + 1)}{2}$$

where S_y = sum of the ranks of the y values.
When the alternate hypothesis is $\text{Md}_x < \text{Md}_y$, use

$$U = U_x = S_x - \frac{n_1(n_1 + 1)}{2}$$

where S_x = sum of ranks of x values.
When the alternate hypothesis is $\text{Md}_x \neq \text{Md}_y$, use

$$U = \text{minimum of } U_x, U_y$$

Look up the critical value c in Appendix Table B.9. Reject H_0 if $U \leq c$.

4. Runs Test

This is a test for randomness. The test statistic is

$$R = \text{number of runs}$$

Look up critical values c_1 and c_2 in Appendix Table B.10. Reject H_0 (which asserts randomness) if $R \leq c_1$ or $R \geq c_2$.

REVIEW EXERCISES

13.27   A real estate agent in a large city claimed that the median rent for two-bedroom apartments was more than $625. To test this claim, a tenants' organization sampled 20 such apartments and obtained the following rents (in dollars):

635	660	670	615	620	660	600	610	700	675
615	605	650	600	665	670	645	640	655	680

At a 5% level of significance, test the claim.
   (a)   Use the sign test.
   (b)   Use the Wilcoxon signed-rank test.
   (c)   Compare parts (a) and (b) and comment.

13.28   A government official believed that the median prime interest rate for banks in Massachusetts was 9.3%. A sample of 10 banks gave the following rates (in percent):

| 9.6 | 9.8 | 9.1 | 10.2 | 10.1 | 9.7 | 8.5 | 10.3 | 9.9 | 10.0 |

Use a 5% level of significance to test the official's belief.

(a) Use the sign test.

(b) Use the Wilcoxon signed-rank test.

13.29 A sports reporter commented that the median heart rate (beats/minute) of marathoners is less than 200, when the rate is measured after exercise on a treadmill. Eight marathoners were tested, and the following data were obtained:

$$193 \quad 203 \quad 196 \quad 192 \quad 187 \quad 206 \quad 190 \quad 195$$

Use a 5% level of significance to test the reporter's comment with

(a) The sign test

(b) The Wilcoxon signed-rank test

(c) Compare parts (a) and (b) and comment.

13.30 Refer to Exercise 13.27. Test the claim that the median rent is more than $625. Use the Wilcoxon signed-rank test with the normal approximation and a 5% level of significance.

13.31 A first-grade teacher claimed that girls tend to read with more comprehension than boys upon entering the fourth grade. The results of a test designed to measure comprehension (with x for boys' scores and y for girls' scores) were as follows:

x	y
84	82
57	55
74	88
70	76
72	78
71	77
65	92
40	
45	

Test the teacher's claim using a nonparametric test and a 5% level of significance.

13.32 A type of electrical component was made by competing companies A and B. Four components were sampled from A and five sampled from B. The time to failure (in months) was recorded for each component. Use a nonparametric test with a 10% level of significance to test the hypothesis that the population medians are the same. The data are given in the table.

Company A	Company B
7.4	8.9
8.7	7.8
7.5	8.2
8.0	8.8
	8.5

13.33 The Chamber of Commerce in a resort area A claimed that the median price of building lots was less in area A than building lots in another resort area B. A survey of the costs of comparable lots from the two resorts gave the following data (in thousands of dollars):

Resort A	Resort B
39.5	42.5
48.9	47.9
35.0	40.9
32.5	61.0
30.9	53.9
44.3	36.0

Test the claim using a nonparametric test with a 1% level of significance.

13.34 A city bus was scheduled to reach a particular stop at noon each day. The bus was considered on time if it reached the stop within 2 minutes of noon. Over a 15-day period, an *A* was recorded if the bus was on time. Otherwise, a *B* was recorded. The results were as follows:

$$A \quad A \quad A \quad B \quad B \quad A \quad B \quad A \quad A \quad B \quad B \quad B \quad A \quad B \quad A$$

Do the data indicate a lack of randomness? Use a 5% level of significance.

13.35 A college basketball team played 25 games. The following data represent the sequence of wins (*W*) and losses (*L*) for the season:

$$L \quad L \quad W \quad W \quad W \quad L \quad L \quad L \quad L \quad L \quad W \quad L \quad L$$
$$L \quad W \quad W \quad W \quad W \quad W \quad W \quad L \quad L \quad W \quad W \quad W$$

Do the data indicate a lack of randomness at the 5% level?

(a) Use the critical values from Appendix Table B.10.

(b) Use the normal approximation.

13.36 Complete the test in Exercise 13.21 using the normal approximation.

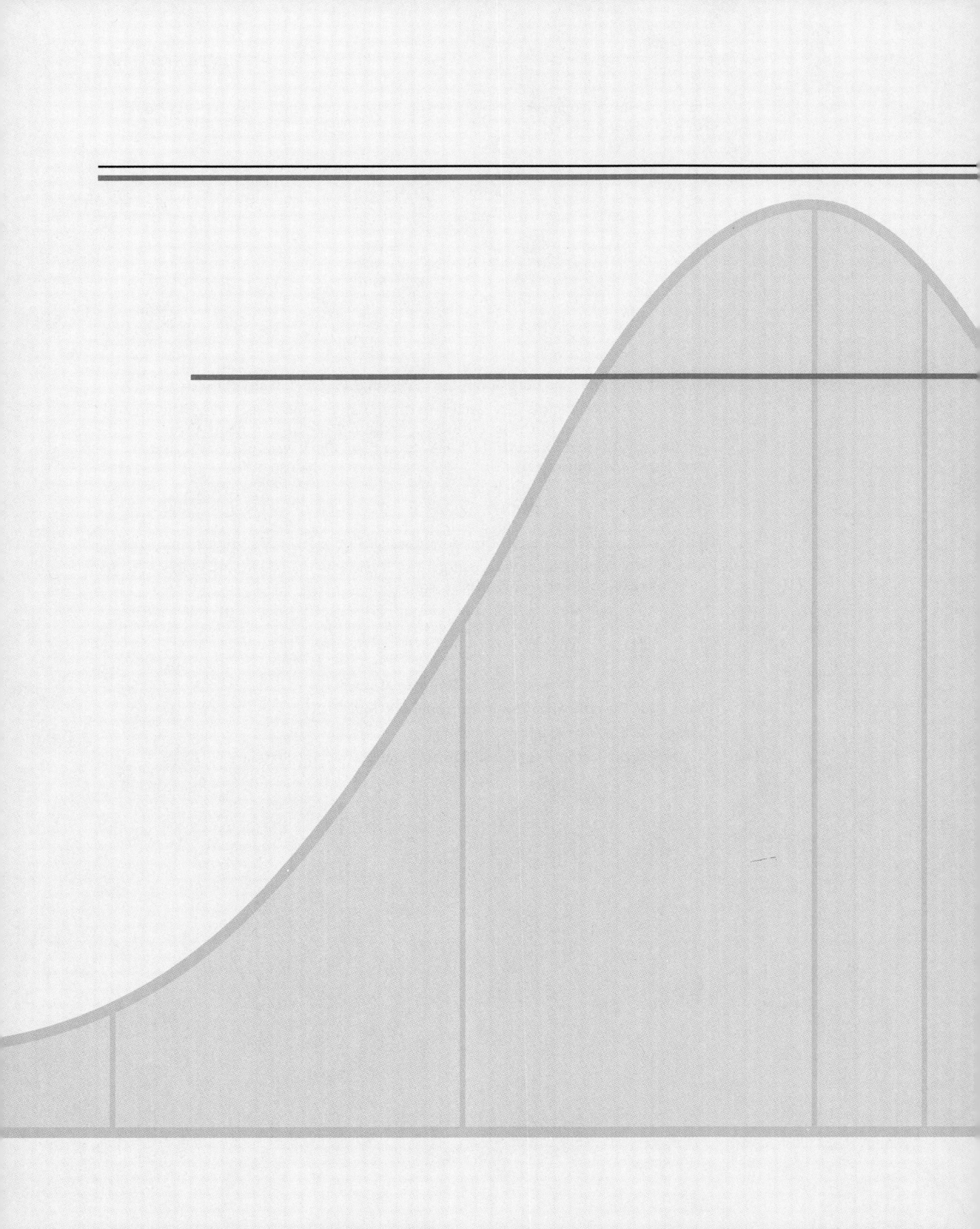

APPENDIX A

USE OF THE RANDOM NUMBER TABLE

Random numbers can be obtained from Appendix Table B.1. Suppose that we wish to choose a random sequence of 5 four-digit numbers. Randomly choose some starting point in the table. You could toss your pencil on the page and choose the nearest four digits. Then read down the table until you have 5 four-digit numbers. If you come to the bottom of the page, go to the top of the next column of four digits. The process is displayed in Figure A.1.

Often the elements of a population are assigned identification numbers. When this is the case, we can obtain a random sample from the population by choosing the desired ID numbers from the random number table. Suppose, for example, that we wanted a random sample of five students from some university with 9000 students with ID numbers ranging from 0001 to 9000. We could select the students with ID numbers that we obtained above:

2406
5692
7048
4778
8607

A random sample of five quality point averages (QPAs) could be obtained by looking up the QPAs of these students. If we had obtained a four-digit number in the random number table that was out of range (such as 9500), we would just ignore it and continue until the desired number of IDs is obtained. When we do not want any repetitions in our sample, we ignore any IDs that repeat.

34	07	27	68	50
43	57	18	24	06
02	05	16	56	92
05	32	54	70	48
03	52	96	47	78
14	90	56	86	07
39	80	82	77	32

Figure A.1
A Portion of Appendix Table B.1 Showing a Random Sample of 5 Four-Digit ID Numbers

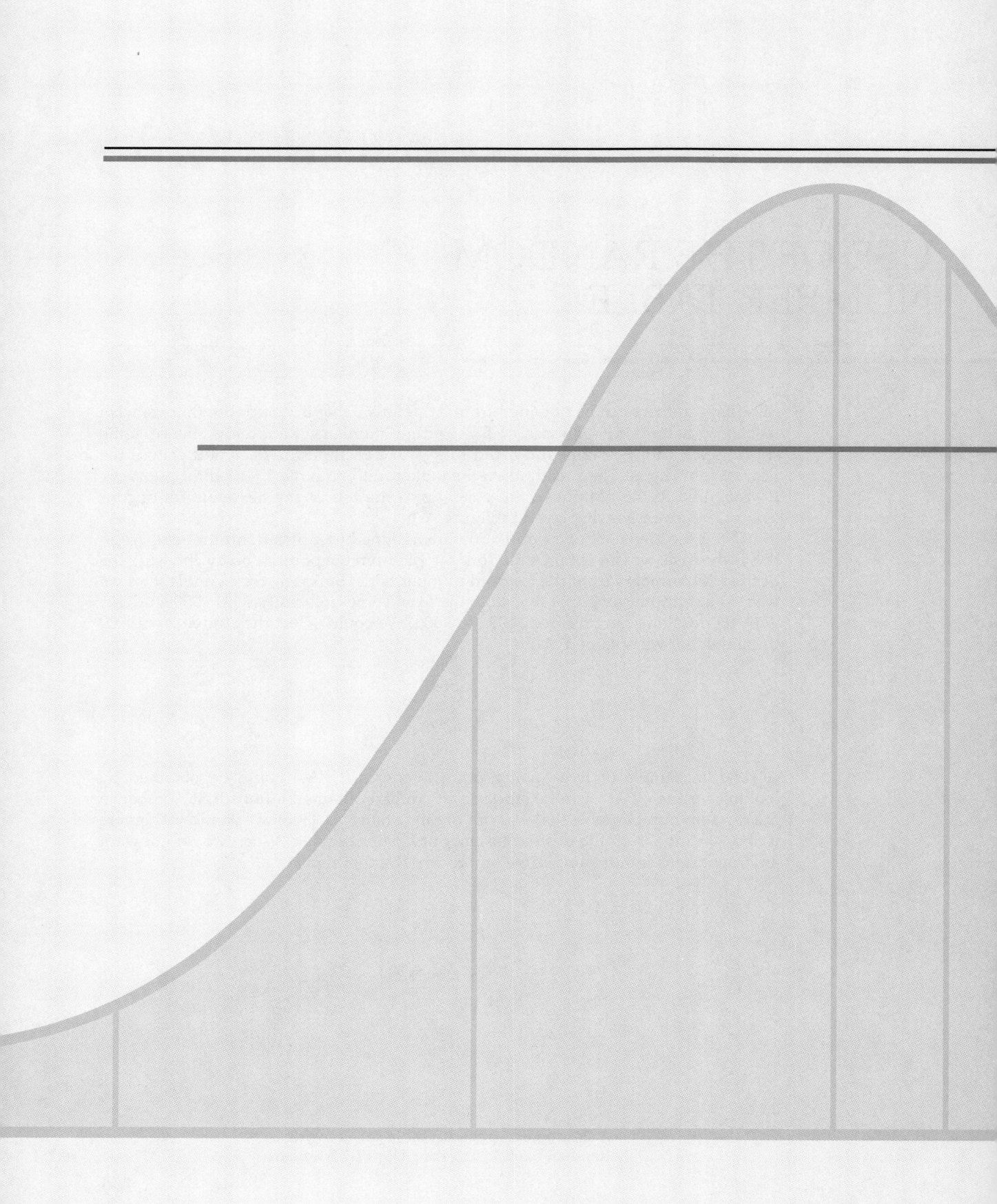

APPENDIX B

TABLES

B.1 RANDOM NUMBERS

B.2 BINOMIAL PROBABILITIES

B.3 THE STANDARD NORMAL DISTRIBUTION

B.4 STUDENT'S t DISTRIBUTION

B.5 THE CHI-SQUARE DISTRIBUTION

B.6 THE F DISTRIBUTION

B.7 CRITICAL VALUES OF r

B.8 CRITICAL VALUES FOR THE WILCOXON SIGNED-RANK TEST

B.9 CRITICAL VALUES FOR A MANN–WHITNEY TEST

B.10 CRITICAL VALUES FOR A RUNS TEST

B.11 FRAMINGHAM HEART STUDY DATA

Table B.1
Random Numbers

10	09	73	25	33	76	52	01	35	86	34	67	35	48	76	80	95	90	91	17	39	29	27	49	45
37	54	20	48	05	64	89	47	42	96	24	80	52	40	37	20	63	61	04	02	00	82	29	16	65
08	42	26	89	53	19	64	50	93	03	23	20	90	25	60	15	95	33	47	64	35	08	03	36	06
99	01	90	25	29	09	37	67	07	15	38	31	13	11	65	88	67	67	43	97	04	43	62	76	59
12	80	79	99	70	80	15	73	61	47	64	03	23	66	53	98	95	11	68	77	12	17	17	68	33
66	06	57	47	17	34	07	27	68	50	36	69	73	61	70	65	81	33	98	85	11	19	92	91	70
31	06	01	08	05	45	57	18	24	06	35	30	34	26	14	86	79	90	74	39	23	40	30	97	32
85	26	97	76	02	02	05	16	56	92	68	66	57	48	18	73	05	38	52	47	18	62	38	85	79
63	57	33	21	35	05	32	54	70	48	90	55	35	75	48	28	46	82	87	09	83	49	12	56	24
73	79	64	57	53	03	52	96	47	78	35	80	83	42	82	60	93	52	03	44	35	27	38	84	35
98	52	01	77	67	14	90	56	86	07	22	10	94	05	58	60	97	09	34	33	50	50	07	39	98
11	80	50	54	31	39	80	82	77	32	50	72	56	82	48	29	40	52	42	01	52	77	56	78	51
83	45	29	96	34	06	28	89	80	83	13	74	67	00	78	18	47	54	06	10	68	71	17	78	17
88	68	54	02	00	86	50	75	84	01	36	76	66	79	51	90	36	47	64	93	29	60	91	10	62
99	59	46	73	48	87	51	76	49	69	91	82	60	89	28	93	78	56	13	68	23	47	83	41	13
65	48	11	76	74	17	46	85	09	50	58	04	77	69	74	73	03	95	71	86	40	21	81	65	44
80	12	43	56	35	17	72	70	80	15	45	31	82	23	74	21	11	57	82	53	14	38	55	37	63
74	35	09	98	17	77	40	27	72	14	43	23	60	02	10	45	52	16	42	37	96	28	60	26	55
69	91	62	68	03	66	25	22	91	48	36	93	68	72	03	76	62	11	39	90	94	40	05	64	18
09	89	32	05	05	14	22	56	85	14	46	42	75	67	88	96	29	77	88	22	54	38	21	45	98
91	49	91	45	23	68	47	92	76	86	46	16	28	35	54	94	75	08	99	23	37	08	92	00	48
80	33	69	45	98	26	94	03	68	58	70	29	73	41	35	53	14	03	33	40	42	05	08	23	41
44	10	48	19	49	85	15	74	79	54	32	97	92	65	75	57	60	04	08	81	22	22	20	64	13
12	55	07	37	42	11	10	00	20	40	12	86	07	46	97	96	64	48	94	39	28	70	72	58	15
63	60	64	93	29	16	50	53	44	84	40	21	95	25	63	43	65	17	70	82	07	20	73	17	90
61	19	69	04	46	26	45	74	77	74	51	92	43	37	29	65	39	45	95	93	42	58	26	05	27
15	47	44	52	66	95	27	07	99	53	59	36	78	38	48	82	39	61	01	18	33	21	15	94	66
94	55	72	85	73	67	89	75	43	87	54	62	24	44	31	91	19	04	25	92	92	92	74	59	73
42	48	11	62	13	97	34	40	87	21	16	86	84	87	67	03	07	11	20	59	25	70	14	66	70
23	52	37	83	17	73	20	88	98	37	68	93	59	14	16	26	25	22	96	63	05	52	28	25	62
04	49	35	24	94	75	24	63	38	24	45	86	25	10	25	61	96	27	93	35	65	33	71	24	72
00	54	99	76	54	64	05	18	81	59	96	11	96	38	96	54	69	28	23	91	23	28	72	95	29
35	96	31	53	07	26	89	80	93	54	33	35	13	54	62	77	97	45	00	24	90	10	33	93	33
59	80	80	83	91	45	42	72	68	42	83	60	94	97	00	13	02	12	48	92	78	56	52	01	06
46	05	88	52	36	01	39	09	22	86	77	28	14	40	77	93	91	08	36	47	70	61	74	29	41
32	17	90	05	97	87	37	92	52	41	05	56	70	70	07	86	74	31	71	57	85	39	41	18	38
69	23	46	14	06	20	11	74	52	04	15	95	66	00	00	18	74	39	24	23	97	11	89	63	38
19	56	54	14	30	01	75	87	53	79	40	41	92	15	85	66	67	43	68	06	84	96	28	52	07
45	15	51	49	38	19	47	60	72	46	43	66	79	45	43	59	04	79	00	33	20	82	66	95	41
94	86	43	19	94	36	16	81	08	51	34	88	88	15	53	01	54	03	54	56	05	01	45	11	76
98	08	62	48	26	45	24	02	84	04	44	99	90	88	96	39	09	47	34	07	35	44	13	18	80
33	18	51	62	32	41	94	15	09	49	89	43	54	85	81	88	69	54	19	94	37	54	87	30	43
80	95	10	04	06	96	38	27	07	74	20	15	12	33	87	25	01	62	52	98	94	62	46	11	71
79	75	24	91	40	71	96	12	82	96	69	86	10	25	91	74	85	22	05	39	00	38	75	95	79
18	63	33	25	37	98	14	50	65	71	31	01	02	46	74	05	45	56	14	27	77	93	89	19	36
74	02	94	39	02	77	55	73	22	70	97	79	01	71	19	52	52	75	80	21	80	81	45	17	48
54	17	84	56	11	80	99	33	71	43	05	33	51	29	69	56	12	71	92	55	36	04	09	03	24
11	66	44	98	83	52	07	98	48	27	59	38	17	15	39	09	97	33	34	40	88	46	12	33	56
48	32	47	79	28	31	24	96	47	10	02	29	53	68	70	32	30	75	75	46	15	02	00	99	94
69	07	49	41	38	87	63	79	19	76	35	58	40	44	01	10	51	82	16	15	01	84	87	69	38

Table B.1 (Continued)

09	18	82	00	97	32	82	53	95	27	04	22	08	63	04	83	38	98	73	74	64	27	85	80	44
90	04	58	54	97	51	98	15	06	54	94	93	88	19	97	91	87	07	61	50	68	47	66	46	59
73	18	95	02	07	47	67	72	62	69	62	29	06	44	64	27	12	46	70	18	41	36	18	27	60
75	76	87	64	90	20	97	18	17	49	90	42	91	22	72	95	37	50	58	71	93	82	34	31	78
54	01	64	40	56	66	28	13	10	03	00	68	22	73	98	20	71	45	32	95	07	70	61	78	13
08	35	86	99	10	78	54	24	27	85	13	66	15	88	73	04	61	89	75	53	31	22	30	84	20
28	30	60	32	64	81	33	31	05	91	40	51	00	78	93	32	60	46	04	75	94	11	90	18	40
53	84	08	62	33	81	59	41	36	28	51	21	59	02	90	28	46	66	87	95	77	76	22	07	91
91	75	75	37	41	61	61	36	22	69	50	26	39	02	12	55	78	17	65	14	94	54	13	74	08
89	41	59	26	94	00	39	75	83	91	12	60	71	76	46	48	94	97	23	06	94	54	13	74	08
77	51	30	38	20	86	83	42	99	01	68	41	48	27	74	51	90	81	39	80	72	89	35	55	07
19	50	23	71	74	69	97	92	02	88	55	21	02	97	73	74	28	77	52	51	65	34	46	74	15
21	81	85	93	13	93	27	88	17	57	05	68	67	31	56	07	08	28	50	46	31	85	33	84	52
51	47	46	64	99	68	10	72	36	21	94	04	99	13	45	42	83	60	91	91	08	00	74	54	49
99	55	96	83	31	62	53	52	41	70	69	77	71	28	30	74	81	97	81	42	43	86	07	28	34
33	71	34	80	07	93	58	47	28	69	51	92	66	47	21	58	30	32	98	22	93	17	49	39	72
85	27	48	68	93	11	30	32	92	70	28	83	43	41	37	73	51	59	04	00	71	14	84	36	43
84	13	38	96	40	44	03	55	21	66	73	85	27	00	91	61	22	26	05	61	62	32	71	84	23
56	73	21	62	34	17	39	59	61	31	10	12	39	16	22	85	49	65	75	60	81	60	41	88	80
65	13	85	68	06	87	64	88	52	61	34	31	36	58	61	45	87	52	10	69	85	64	44	72	77
38	00	10	21	76	81	71	91	17	11	71	60	29	29	37	74	21	96	40	49	65	58	44	96	98
37	40	29	63	97	01	30	47	75	86	56	27	11	00	86	47	32	46	26	05	40	03	03	74	38
97	12	54	03	48	87	08	33	14	17	21	81	53	92	50	75	23	76	20	47	15	50	12	95	78
21	82	64	11	34	47	14	33	40	72	64	63	88	59	02	49	13	90	64	41	03	85	65	45	52
73	13	54	27	42	95	71	90	90	35	85	79	47	42	96	08	78	98	81	56	64	69	11	92	02
07	63	87	79	29	03	06	11	80	72	96	20	74	41	56	23	82	19	95	38	04	71	36	69	94
60	52	88	34	41	07	95	41	98	14	59	17	52	06	95	05	53	35	21	39	61	21	20	64	55
83	59	63	56	55	06	95	89	29	83	05	12	80	97	19	77	43	35	37	83	92	30	15	04	98
10	85	06	27	46	99	59	91	05	07	13	49	90	63	19	53	07	57	18	39	06	41	01	93	62
39	82	09	89	52	43	62	26	31	47	64	42	18	08	14	43	80	00	93	51	31	02	47	31	67
59	58	00	64	78	75	56	97	88	00	88	83	55	44	86	23	76	80	61	56	04	11	10	84	08
38	50	80	73	41	23	79	34	87	63	90	82	29	70	22	17	71	90	42	07	95	95	44	99	53
30	69	27	06	68	94	68	81	61	27	56	19	68	00	91	82	06	76	34	00	05	46	26	92	00
65	44	39	56	59	18	28	82	74	37	49	63	22	40	41	08	33	76	56	76	96	29	99	08	36
27	26	75	02	64	13	19	27	22	94	07	47	74	46	06	17	98	54	89	11	97	34	13	03	58
91	30	70	69	91	19	07	22	42	10	36	69	95	37	28	28	82	53	57	93	28	97	66	62	52
68	43	49	46	88	34	47	31	36	22	62	12	69	84	08	12	84	38	25	90	09	81	59	31	46
48	90	81	58	77	54	74	52	45	91	35	70	00	47	54	83	82	45	26	92	54	13	05	51	60
06	91	34	51	97	42	67	27	86	01	11	88	30	95	28	63	01	19	89	01	14	97	44	03	44
10	45	51	60	19	14	21	03	37	12	91	34	23	78	21	88	32	58	08	51	43	66	77	08	83
12	88	39	73	43	65	02	76	11	84	04	28	50	13	92	17	97	41	50	77	90	71	22	67	69
21	77	83	09	76	38	80	73	69	61	31	64	94	20	96	63	28	10	20	23	08	81	64	74	49
19	52	35	95	15	65	12	25	96	59	86	28	36	82	58	69	57	21	37	98	16	43	59	15	29
67	24	55	26	70	35	58	31	65	63	79	24	68	66	86	76	46	33	42	22	26	65	59	08	02
60	58	44	73	77	07	50	03	79	92	45	13	42	65	29	26	76	08	36	37	41	32	64	43	44
53	85	34	13	77	36	06	69	48	50	58	83	87	38	59	49	36	47	33	31	96	24	04	36	42
24	63	73	87	36	74	38	48	93	42	52	62	30	79	92	12	36	91	86	01	03	74	28	38	73
83	08	01	24	51	38	99	22	28	15	07	75	95	17	77	97	37	72	75	85	51	97	23	78	67
16	44	42	43	34	36	15	19	90	73	27	49	37	09	39	85	13	03	25	52	54	84	65	47	59
60	79	01	81	57	57	17	86	57	62	11	16	17	85	76	45	81	95	29	79	65	13	00	48	60

From tables of the RAND Corporation. Reprinted from Dixon, W. J., and J. Massey, Jr., *Introduction to Statistical Analysis,* 3rd ed., New York: McGraw-Hill, 1969, pp. 446–447. With permission of the Rand Corporation.

Table B.2
Binomial Probabilities

n	x	.01	.05	.10	.20	.30	.40	p .50	.60	.70	.80	.90	.95	.99	x
2	0	980	902	810	640	490	360	250	160	090	040	010	002	0+	0
	1	020	095	180	320	420	480	500	480	420	320	180	095	020	1
	2	0+	002	010	040	090	160	250	360	490	640	810	902	980	2
3	0	970	857	729	512	343	216	125	064	027	008	001	0+	0+	0
	1	029	135	243	384	441	432	375	288	189	096	027	007	0+	1
	2	0+	007	027	096	189	288	375	432	441	384	243	135	029	2
	3	0+	0+	001	008	027	064	125	216	343	512	729	857	970	3
4	0	961	815	656	410	240	130	062	026	008	002	0+	0+	0+	0
	1	039	171	292	410	412	346	250	154	076	026	004	0+	0+	1
	2	001	014	049	154	265	346	375	346	265	154	049	014	001	2
	3	0+	0+	004	026	076	154	250	346	412	410	292	171	039	3
	4	0+	0+	0+	002	008	026	062	130	240	410	656	815	961	4
5	0	951	774	590	328	168	078	031	010	002	0+	0+	0+	0+	0
	1	048	204	328	410	360	259	156	077	028	006	0+	0+	0+	1
	2	001	021	073	205	309	346	312	230	132	051	008	001	0+	2
	3	0+	001	008	051	132	230	312	346	309	205	073	021	001	3
	4	0+	0+	0+	006	028	077	156	259	360	410	328	204	048	4
	5	0+	0+	0+	0+	002	010	031	078	168	328	590	774	951	5
6	0	941	735	531	262	118	047	016	004	001	0+	0+	0+	0+	0
	1	057	232	354	393	303	187	094	037	010	002	0+	0+	0+	1
	2	001	031	098	246	324	311	234	138	060	015	001	0+	0+	2
	3	0+	002	015	082	185	276	312	276	185	082	015	002	0+	3
	4	0+	0+	001	015	060	138	234	311	324	246	098	031	001	4
	5	0+	0+	0+	002	010	037	094	187	303	393	354	232	057	5
	6	0+	0+	0+	0+	001	004	016	047	118	262	531	735	941	6
7	0	932	698	478	210	082	028	008	002	0+	0+	0+	0+	0+	0
	1	066	257	372	367	247	131	055	017	004	0+	0+	0+	0+	1
	2	002	041	124	275	318	261	164	077	025	004	0+	0+	0+	2
	3	0+	004	023	115	227	290	273	194	097	029	003	0+	0+	3
	4	0+	0+	003	029	097	194	273	290	227	115	023	004	0+	4
	5	0+	0+	0+	004	025	077	164	261	318	275	124	041	002	5
	6	0+	0+	0+	0+	004	017	055	131	247	367	372	257	066	6
	7	0+	0+	0+	0+	0+	002	008	028	082	210	478	698	932	7
8	0	923	663	430	168	058	017	004	001	0+	0+	0+	0+	0+	0
	1	075	279	383	336	198	090	031	008	001	0+	0+	0+	0+	1
	2	003	051	149	294	296	209	109	041	010	001	0+	0+	0+	2
	3	0+	005	033	147	254	279	219	124	047	009	0+	0+	0+	3
	4	0+	0+	005	046	136	232	273	232	136	046	005	0+	0+	4
	5	0+	0+	0+	009	047	124	219	279	254	147	033	005	0+	5
	6	0+	0+	0+	001	010	041	109	209	296	294	149	051	003	6
	7	0+	0+	0+	0+	001	008	031	090	198	336	383	279	075	7
	8	0+	0+	0+	0+	0+	001	004	017	058	168	430	663	923	8

Table B.2 (Continued)

n	x	.01	.05	.10	.20	.30	.40	p .50	.60	.70	.80	.90	.95	.99	x
9	0	914	630	387	134	040	010	002	0+	0+	0+	0+	0+	0+	0
	1	083	299	387	302	156	060	018	004	0+	0+	0+	0+	0+	1
	2	003	063	172	302	267	161	070	021	004	0+	0+	0+	0+	2
	3	0+	008	045	176	267	251	164	074	021	003	0+	0+	0+	3
	4	0+	001	007	066	172	251	246	167	074	017	001	0+	0+	4
	5	0+	0+	001	017	074	167	246	251	172	066	007	001	0+	5
	6	0+	0+	0+	003	021	074	164	251	267	176	045	008	0+	6
	7	0+	0+	0+	0+	004	021	070	161	267	302	172	063	003	7
	8	0+	0+	0+	0+	0+	004	018	060	156	302	387	299	083	8
	9	0+	0+	0+	0+	0+	0+	002	010	040	134	387	630	914	9
10	0	904	599	349	107	028	006	001	0+	0+	0+	0+	0+	0+	0
	1	091	315	387	268	121	040	010	002	0+	0+	0+	0+	0+	1
	2	004	075	194	302	233	121	044	011	001	0+	0+	0+	0+	2
	3	0+	010	057	201	267	215	117	042	009	001	0+	0+	0+	3
	4	0+	001	011	088	200	251	205	111	037	006	0+	0+	0+	4
	5	0+	0+	001	026	103	201	246	201	103	026	001	0+	0+	5
	6	0+	0+	0+	006	037	111	205	251	200	088	011	001	0+	6
	7	0+	0+	0+	001	009	042	117	215	267	201	057	010	0+	7
	8	0+	0+	0+	0+	001	011	044	121	233	302	194	075	004	8
	9	0+	0+	0+	0+	0+	002	010	040	121	268	387	315	091	9
	10	0+	0+	0+	0+	0+	0+	001	006	028	107	349	599	904	10
11	0	895	569	314	086	020	004	0+	0+	0+	0+	0+	0+	0+	0
	1	099	329	384	236	093	027	005	001	0+	0+	0+	0+	0+	1
	2	005	087	213	295	200	089	027	005	001	0+	0+	0+	0+	2
	3	0+	014	071	221	257	177	081	023	004	0+	0+	0+	0+	3
	4	0+	001	016	111	220	236	161	070	017	002	0+	0+	0+	4
	5	0+	0+	002	039	132	221	226	147	057	010	0+	0+	0+	5
	6	0+	0+	0+	010	057	147	226	221	132	039	002	0+	0+	6
	7	0+	0+	0+	002	017	070	161	236	220	111	016	001	0+	7
	8	0+	0+	0+	0+	004	023	081	177	257	221	071	014	0+	8
	9	0+	0+	0+	0+	001	005	027	089	200	295	213	087	005	9
	10	0+	0+	0+	0+	0+	001	005	027	093	236	384	329	099	10
	11	0+	0+	0+	0+	0+	0+	0+	004	020	086	314	569	895	11
12	0	886	540	282	069	014	002	0+	0+	0+	0+	0+	0+	0+	0
	1	107	341	377	206	071	017	003	0+	0+	0+	0+	0+	0+	1
	2	006	099	230	283	168	064	016	002	0+	0+	0+	0+	0+	2
	3	0+	017	085	236	240	142	054	012	001	0+	0+	0+	0+	3
	4	0+	002	021	133	231	213	121	042	008	001	0+	0+	0+	4
	5	0+	0+	004	053	158	227	193	101	029	003	0+	0+	0+	5
	6	0+	0+	0+	016	079	177	226	177	079	016	0+	0+	0+	6
	7	0+	0+	0+	003	029	101	193	227	158	053	004	0+	0+	7
	8	0+	0+	0+	001	008	042	121	213	231	133	021	002	0+	8
	9	0+	0+	0+	0+	001	012	054	142	240	236	085	017	0+	9

Table B.2 (Continued)

n	x	.01	.05	.10	.20	.30	.40	p .50	.60	.70	.80	.90	.95	.99	x
12	10	0+	0+	0+	0+	0+	002	016	064	168	283	230	099	006	10
	11	0+	0+	0+	0+	0+	0+	003	017	071	206	377	341	107	11
	12	0+	0+	0+	0+	0+	0+	0+	002	014	069	282	540	886	12
13	0	878	513	254	055	010	001	0+	0+	0+	0+	0+	0+	0+	0
	1	115	351	367	179	054	011	002	0+	0+	0+	0+	0+	0+	1
	2	007	111	245	268	139	045	010	001	0+	0+	0+	0+	0+	2
	3	0+	021	100	246	218	111	035	006	001	0+	0+	0+	0+	3
	4	0+	003	028	154	234	184	087	024	003	0+	0+	0+	0+	4
	5	0+	0+	006	069	180	221	157	066	014	001	0+	0+	0+	5
	6	0+	0+	001	023	103	197	209	131	044	006	0+	0+	0+	6
	7	0+	0+	0+	006	044	131	209	197	103	023	001	0+	0+	7
	8	0+	0+	0+	001	014	066	157	221	180	069	006	0+	0+	8
	9	0+	0+	0+	0+	003	024	087	184	234	154	028	003	0+	9
	10	0+	0+	0+	0+	001	006	035	111	218	246	100	021	0+	10
	11	0+	0+	0+	0+	0+	001	010	045	139	268	245	111	007	11
	12	0+	0+	0+	0+	0+	0+	002	011	054	179	367	351	115	12
	13	0+	0+	0+	0+	0+	0+	0+	001	010	055	254	513	878	13
14	0	869	488	229	044	007	001	0+	0+	0+	0+	0+	0+	0+	0
	1	123	359	356	154	041	007	001	0+	0+	0+	0+	0+	0+	1
	2	008	123	257	250	113	032	006	001	0+	0+	0+	0+	0+	2
	3	0+	026	114	250	194	085	022	003	0+	0+	0+	0+	0+	3
	4	0+	004	035	172	229	155	061	014	001	0+	0+	0+	0+	4
	5	0+	0+	008	086	196	207	122	041	007	0+	0+	0+	0+	5
	6	0+	0+	001	032	126	207	183	092	023	002	0+	0+	0+	6
	7	0+	0+	0+	009	062	157	209	157	062	009	0+	0+	0+	7
	8	0+	0+	0+	002	023	092	183	207	126	032	001	0+	0+	8
	9	0+	0+	0+	0+	007	041	122	207	196	086	008	0+	0+	9
	10	0+	0+	0+	0+	001	014	061	155	229	172	035	004	0+	10
	11	0+	0+	0+	0+	0+	003	022	085	194	250	114	026	0+	11
	12	0+	0+	0+	0+	0+	001	006	032	113	250	257	123	008	12
	13	0+	0+	0+	0+	0+	0+	001	007	041	154	356	359	123	13
	14	0+	0+	0+	0+	0+	0+	0+	001	007	044	229	488	869	14
15	0	860	463	206	035	005	0+	0+	0+	0+	0+	0+	0+	0+	0
	1	130	366	343	132	031	005	0+	0+	0+	0+	0+	0+	0+	1
	2	009	135	267	231	092	022	003	0+	0+	0+	0+	0+	0+	2
	3	0+	031	129	250	170	063	014	002	0+	0+	0+	0+	0+	3
	4	0+	005	043	188	219	127	042	007	001	0+	0+	0+	0+	4
	5	0+	001	010	103	206	186	092	024	003	0+	0+	0+	0+	5
	6	0+	0+	002	043	147	207	153	061	012	001	0+	0+	0+	6
	7	0+	0+	0+	014	081	177	196	118	035	003	0+	0+	0+	7
	8	0+	0+	0+	003	035	118	196	177	081	014	0+	0+	0+	8
	9	0+	0+	0+	001	012	061	153	207	147	043	002	0+	0+	9

Table B.2 (Continued)

n	x	.01	.05	.10	.20	.30	.40	p .50	.60	.70	.80	.90	.95	.99	x
15	10	0+	0+	0+	0+	003	024	092	186	206	103	010	001	0+	10
	11	0+	0+	0+	0+	001	007	042	127	219	188	043	005	0+	11
	12	0+	0+	0+	0+	0+	002	014	063	170	250	129	031	0+	12
	13	0+	0+	0+	0+	0+	0+	003	022	092	231	267	135	009	13
	14	0+	0+	0+	0+	0+	0+	0+	005	031	132	343	366	130	14
	15	0+	0+	0+	0+	0+	0+	0+	0+	005	035	206	463	860	15
16	0	851	440	185	028	003	0+	0+	0+	0+	0+	0+	0+	0+	0
	1	138	371	329	113	023	003	0+	0+	0+	0+	0+	0+	0+	1
	2	010	146	275	211	073	015	002	0+	0+	0+	0+	0+	0+	2
	3	0+	036	142	246	146	047	009	001	0+	0+	0+	0+	0+	3
	4	0+	006	051	200	204	101	028	004	0+	0+	0+	0+	0+	4
	5	0+	001	014	120	210	162	067	014	001	0+	0+	0+	0+	5
	6	0+	0+	003	055	165	198	122	039	006	0+	0+	0+	0+	6
	7	0+	0+	0+	020	101	189	175	084	019	001	0+	0+	0+	7
	8	0+	0+	0+	006	049	142	196	142	049	006	0+	0+	0+	8
	9	0+	0+	0+	001	019	084	175	189	101	020	0+	0+	0+	9
	10	0+	0+	0+	0+	006	039	122	198	165	055	003	0+	0+	10
	11	0+	0+	0+	0+	001	014	067	162	210	120	014	001	0+	11
	12	0+	0+	0+	0+	0+	004	028	101	204	200	051	006	0+	12
	13	0+	0+	0+	0+	0+	001	009	047	146	246	142	036	0+	13
	14	0+	0+	0+	0+	0+	0+	002	015	073	211	275	146	010	14
	15	0+	0+	0+	0+	0+	0+	0+	003	023	113	329	371	138	15
	16	0+	0+	0+	0+	0+	0+	0+	0+	003	028	185	440	851	16
17	0	843	418	167	023	002	0+	0+	0+	0+	0+	0+	0+	0+	0
	1	145	374	315	096	017	002	0+	0+	0+	0+	0+	0+	0+	1
	2	012	158	280	191	058	010	001	0+	0+	0+	0+	0+	0+	2
	3	001	041	156	239	125	034	005	0+	0+	0+	0+	0+	0+	3
	4	0+	008	060	209	187	080	018	002	0+	0+	0+	0+	0+	4
	5	0+	001	017	136	208	138	047	008	001	0+	0+	0+	0+	5
	6	0+	0+	004	068	178	184	094	024	003	0+	0+	0+	0+	6
	7	0+	0+	001	027	120	193	148	057	009	0+	0+	0+	0+	7
	8	0+	0+	0+	008	064	161	185	107	028	002	0+	0+	0+	8
	9	0+	0+	0+	002	028	107	185	161	064	008	0+	0+	0+	9
	10	0+	0+	0+	0+	009	057	148	193	120	027	001	0+	0+	10
	11	0+	0+	0+	0+	003	024	094	184	178	068	004	0+	0+	11
	12	0+	0+	0+	0+	001	008	047	138	208	136	017	001	0+	12
	13	0+	0+	0+	0+	0+	002	018	080	187	209	060	008	0+	13
	14	0+	0+	0+	0+	0+	0+	005	034	125	239	156	041	001	14
	15	0+	0+	0+	0+	0+	0+	001	010	058	191	280	158	012	15
	16	0+	0+	0+	0+	0+	0+	0+	002	017	096	315	374	145	16
	17	0+	0+	0+	0+	0+	0+	0+	0+	002	023	167	418	843	17

Table B.2 (Continued)

n	x	.01	.05	.10	.20	.30	.40	p .50	.60	.70	.80	.90	.95	.99	x
18	0	835	397	150	018	002	0+	0+	0+	0+	0+	0+	0+	0+	0
	1	152	376	300	081	013	001	0+	0+	0+	0+	0+	0+	0+	1
	2	013	168	284	172	046	007	001	0+	0+	0+	0+	0+	0+	2
	3	001	047	168	230	105	025	003	0+	0+	0+	0+	0+	0+	3
	4	0+	009	070	215	168	061	012	001	0+	0+	0+	0+	0+	4
	5	0+	001	022	151	202	115	033	004	0+	0+	0+	0+	0+	5
	6	0+	0+	005	082	187	166	071	015	001	0+	0+	0+	0+	6
	7	0+	0+	001	035	138	189	121	037	005	0+	0+	0+	0+	7
	8	0+	0+	0+	012	081	173	167	077	015	001	0+	0+	0+	8
	9	0+	0+	0+	003	039	128	185	128	039	003	0+	0+	0+	9
	10	0+	0+	0+	001	015	077	167	173	081	012	0+	0+	0+	10
	11	0+	0+	0+	0+	005	037	121	189	138	035	001	0+	0+	11
	12	0+	0+	0+	0+	001	015	071	166	187	082	005	0+	0+	12
	13	0+	0+	0+	0+	0+	004	033	115	202	151	022	001	0+	13
	14	0+	0+	0+	0+	0+	001	012	061	168	215	070	009	0+	14
	15	0+	0+	0+	0+	0+	0+	003	025	105	230	168	047	001	15
	16	0+	0+	0+	0+	0+	0+	001	007	046	172	284	168	013	16
	17	0+	0+	0+	0+	0+	0+	0+	001	013	081	300	376	152	17
	18	0+	0+	0+	0+	0+	0+	0+	0+	002	018	150	397	835	18
19	0	826	377	135	014	001	0+	0+	0+	0+	0+	0+	0+	0+	0
	1	159	377	285	068	009	001	0+	0+	0+	0+	0+	0+	0+	1
	2	014	179	285	154	036	005	0+	0+	0+	0+	0+	0+	0+	2
	3	001	053	180	218	087	017	002	0+	0+	0+	0+	0+	0+	3
	4	0+	011	080	218	149	047	007	001	0+	0+	0+	0+	0+	4
	5	0+	002	027	164	192	093	022	002	0+	0+	0+	0+	0+	5
	6	0+	0+	007	095	192	145	052	008	001	0+	0+	0+	0+	6
	7	0+	0+	001	044	153	180	096	024	002	0+	0+	0+	0+	7
	8	0+	0+	0+	017	098	180	144	053	008	0+	0+	0+	0+	8
	9	0+	0+	0+	005	051	146	176	098	022	001	0+	0+	0+	9
	10	0+	0+	0+	001	022	098	176	146	051	005	0+	0+	0+	10
	11	0+	0+	0+	0+	008	053	144	180	098	017	0+	0+	0+	11
	12	0+	0+	0+	0+	002	024	096	180	153	044	001	0+	0+	12
	13	0+	0+	0+	0+	001	008	052	145	192	095	007	0+	0+	13
	14	0+	0+	0+	0+	0+	002	022	093	192	164	027	002	0+	14
	15	0+	0+	0+	0+	0+	001	007	047	149	218	080	011	0+	15
	16	0+	0+	0+	0+	0+	0+	002	017	087	218	180	053	001	16
	17	0+	0+	0+	0+	0+	0+	0+	005	036	154	285	179	014	17
	18	0+	0+	0+	0+	0+	0+	0+	001	009	068	285	377	159	18
	19	0+	0+	0+	0+	0+	0+	0+	0+	001	014	135	377	826	19
20	0	818	358	122	012	001	0+	0+	0+	0+	0+	0+	0+	0+	0
	1	165	377	270	058	007	0+	0+	0+	0+	0+	0+	0+	0+	1
	2	016	189	285	137	028	003	0+	0+	0+	0+	0+	0+	0+	2
	3	001	060	190	205	072	012	001	0+	0+	0+	0+	0+	0+	3
	4	0+	013	090	218	130	035	005	0+	0+	0+	0+	0+	0+	4

Table B.2 (Continued)

n	x	.01	.05	.10	.20	.30	.40	p .50	.60	.70	.80	.90	.95	.99	x
20	5	0+	002	032	175	179	075	015	001	0+	0+	0+	0+	0+	5
	6	0+	0+	009	109	192	124	037	005	0+	0+	0+	0+	0+	6
	7	0+	0+	002	055	164	166	074	015	001	0+	0+	0+	0+	7
	8	0+	0+	0+	022	114	180	120	035	004	0+	0+	0+	0+	8
	9	0+	0+	0+	007	065	160	160	071	012	0+	0+	0+	0+	9
	10	0+	0+	0+	002	031	117	176	117	031	002	0+	0+	0+	10
	11	0+	0+	0+	0+	012	071	160	160	065	007	0+	0+	0+	11
	12	0+	0+	0+	0+	004	035	120	180	114	022	0+	0+	0+	12
	13	0+	0+	0+	0+	001	015	074	166	164	055	002	0+	0+	13
	14	0+	0+	0+	0+	0+	005	037	124	192	109	009	0+	0+	14
	15	0+	0+	0+	0+	0+	001	015	075	179	175	032	002	0+	15
	16	0+	0+	0+	0+	0+	0+	005	035	130	218	090	013	0+	16
	17	0+	0+	0+	0+	0+	0+	001	012	072	205	190	060	001	17
	18	0+	0+	0+	0+	0+	0+	0+	003	028	137	285	189	016	18
	19	0+	0+	0+	0+	0+	0+	0+	0+	007	058	270	377	165	19
	20	0+	0+	0+	0+	0+	0+	0+	0+	001	012	122	358	818	20
21	0	810	341	109	009	001	0+	0+	0+	0+	0+	0+	0+	0+	0
	1	172	376	255	048	005	0+	0+	0+	0+	0+	0+	0+	0+	1
	2	017	198	284	121	022	002	0+	0+	0+	0+	0+	0+	0+	2
	3	001	066	200	192	058	009	001	0+	0+	0+	0+	0+	0+	3
	4	0+	016	100	216	113	026	003	0+	0+	0+	0+	0+	0+	4
	5	0+	003	038	183	164	059	010	001	0+	0+	0+	0+	0+	5
	6	0+	0+	011	122	188	105	026	003	0+	0+	0+	0+	0+	6
	7	0+	0+	003	065	172	149	055	009	0+	0+	0+	0+	0+	7
	8	0+	0+	001	029	129	174	097	023	002	0+	0+	0+	0+	8
	9	0+	0+	0+	010	080	168	140	050	006	0+	0+	0+	0+	9
	10	0+	0+	0+	003	041	134	168	089	018	001	0+	0+	0+	10
	11	0+	0+	0+	001	018	089	168	134	041	003	0+	0+	0+	11
	12	0+	0+	0+	0+	006	050	140	168	080	010	0+	0+	0+	12
	13	0+	0+	0+	0+	002	023	097	174	129	029	001	0+	0+	13
	14	0+	0+	0+	0+	0+	009	055	149	172	065	003	0+	0+	14
	15	0+	0+	0+	0+	0+	003	026	105	188	122	011	0+	0+	15
	16	0+	0+	0+	0+	0+	001	010	059	164	183	038	003	0+	16
	17	0+	0+	0+	0+	0+	0+	003	026	113	216	100	016	0+	17
	18	0+	0+	0+	0+	0+	0+	001	009	058	192	200	066	001	18
	19	0+	0+	0+	0+	0+	0+	0+	002	022	121	284	198	017	19
	20	0+	0+	0+	0+	0+	0+	0+	0+	005	048	255	376	172	20
	21	0+	0+	0+	0+	0+	0+	0+	0+	001	009	109	341	810	21
22	0	802	324	098	007	0+	0+	0+	0+	0+	0+	0+	0+	0+	0
	1	178	375	241	041	004	0+	0+	0+	0+	0+	0+	0+	0+	1
	2	019	207	281	107	017	001	0+	0+	0+	0+	0+	0+	0+	2
	3	001	073	208	178	047	006	0+	0+	0+	0+	0+	0+	0+	3
	4	0+	018	110	211	096	019	002	0+	0+	0+	0+	0+	0+	4

Table B.2 (Continued)

n	x	.01	.05	.10	.20	.30	.40	p .50	.60	.70	.80	.90	.95	.99	x
22	5	0+	003	044	190	149	046	006	0+	0+	0+	0+	0+	0+	5
	6	0+	001	014	134	181	086	018	001	0+	0+	0+	0+	0+	6
	7	0+	0+	004	077	177	131	041	005	0+	0+	0+	0+	0+	7
	8	0+	0+	001	036	142	164	076	014	001	0+	0+	0+	0+	8
	9	0+	0+	0+	014	095	170	119	034	003	0+	0+	0+	0+	9
	10	0+	0+	0+	005	053	148	154	066	010	0+	0+	0+	0+	10
	11	0+	0+	0+	001	025	107	168	107	025	001	0+	0+	0+	11
	12	0+	0+	0+	0+	010	066	154	148	053	005	0+	0+	0+	12
	13	0+	0+	0+	0+	003	034	119	170	095	014	0+	0+	0+	13
	14	0+	0+	0+	0+	001	014	076	164	142	036	001	0+	0+	14
	15	0+	0+	0+	0+	0+	005	041	131	177	077	004	0+	0+	15
	16	0+	0+	0+	0+	0+	001	018	086	181	134	014	001	0+	16
	17	0+	0+	0+	0+	0+	0+	006	046	149	190	044	003	0+	17
	18	0+	0+	0+	0+	0+	0+	002	019	096	211	110	018	0+	18
	19	0+	0+	0+	0+	0+	0+	0+	006	047	178	208	073	001	19
	20	0+	0+	0+	0+	0+	0+	0+	001	017	107	281	207	019	20
	21	0+	0+	0+	0+	0+	0+	0+	0+	004	041	241	375	178	21
	22	0+	0+	0+	0+	0+	0+	0+	0+	0+	007	098	324	802	22
23	0	794	307	089	006	0+	0+	0+	0+	0+	0+	0+	0+	0+	0
	1	184	372	226	034	003	0+	0+	0+	0+	0+	0+	0+	0+	1
	2	020	215	277	093	013	001	0+	0+	0+	0+	0+	0+	0+	2
	3	001	079	215	163	038	004	0+	0+	0+	0+	0+	0+	0+	3
	4	0+	021	120	204	082	014	001	0+	0+	0+	0+	0+	0+	4
	5	0+	004	051	194	133	035	004	0+	0+	0+	0+	0+	0+	5
	6	0+	001	017	145	171	070	012	001	0+	0+	0+	0+	0+	6
	7	0+	0+	005	088	178	113	029	003	0+	0+	0+	0+	0+	7
	8	0+	0+	001	044	153	151	058	009	0+	0+	0+	0+	0+	8
	9	0+	0+	0+	018	109	168	097	022	002	0+	0+	0+	0+	9
	10	0+	0+	0+	006	065	157	136	046	005	0+	0+	0+	0+	10
	11	0+	0+	0+	002	033	123	161	082	014	0+	0+	0+	0+	11
	12	0+	0+	0+	0+	014	082	161	123	033	002	0+	0+	0+	12
	13	0+	0+	0+	0+	005	046	136	157	065	006	0+	0+	0+	13
	14	0+	0+·	0+	0+	002	022	097	168	109	018	0+	0+	0+	14
	15	0+	0+	0+	0+	0+	009	058	151	153	044	001	0+	0+	15
	16	0+	0+	0+	0+	0+	003	029	113	178	088	005	0+	0+	16
	17	0+	0+	0+	0+	0+	001	012	070	171	145	017	001	0+	17
	18	0+	0+	0+	0+	0+	0+	004	035	133	194	051	004	0+	18
	19	0+	0+	0+	0+	0+	0+	001	014	082	204	120	021	0+	19
	20	0+	0+	0+	0+	0+	0+	0+	004	038	163	215	079	001	20
	21	0+	0+	0+	0+	0+	0+	0+	001	013	093	277	215	020	21
	22	0+	0+	0+	0+	0+	0+	0+	0+	003	034	226	372	184	22
	23	0+	0+	0+	0+	0+	0+	0+	0+	0+	006	089	307	794	23

Table B.2 (Continued)

n	x	.01	.05	.10	.20	.30	.40	p .50	.60	.70	.80	.90	.95	.99	x
24	0	786	292	080	005	0+	0+	0+	0+	0+	0+	0+	0+	0+	0
	1	190	369	213	028	002	0+	0+	0+	0+	0+	0+	0+	0+	1
	2	022	223	272	081	010	001	0+	0+	0+	0+	0+	0+	0+	2
	3	002	086	221	149	031	003	0+	0+	0+	0+	0+	0+	0+	3
	4	0+	024	129	196	069	010	001	0+	0+	0+	0+	0+	0+	4
	5	0+	005	057	196	118	027	003	0+	0+	0+	0+	0+	0+	5
	6	0+	001	020	155	160	056	008	0+	0+	0+	0+	0+	0+	6
	7	0+	0+	006	100	176	096	021	002	0+	0+	0+	0+	0+	7
	8	0+	0+	001	053	160	136	044	005	0+	0+	0+	0+	0+	8
	9	0+	0+	0+	024	122	161	078	014	001	0+	0+	0+	0+	9
	10	0+	0+	0+	009	079	161	117	032	003	0+	0+	0+	0+	10
	11	0+	0+	0+	003	043	137	149	061	008	0+	0+	0+	0+	11
	12	0+	0+	0+	001	020	099	161	099	020	001	0+	0+	0+	12
	13	0+	0+	0+	0+	008	061	149	137	043	003	0+	0+	0+	13
	14	0+	0+	0+	0+	003	032	117	161	079	009	0+	0+	0+	14
	15	0+	0+	0+	0+	001	014	078	161	122	024	0+	0+	0+	15
	16	0+	0+	0+	0+	0+	005	044	136	160	053	001	0+	0+	16
	17	0+	0+	0+	0+	0+	002	021	096	176	100	006	0+	0+	17
	18	0+	0+	0+	0+	0+	0+	008	056	160	155	020	001	0+	18
	19	0+	0+	0+	0+	0+	0+	003	027	118	196	057	005	0+	19
	20	0+	0+	0+	0+	0+	0+	001	010	069	196	129	024	0+	20
	21	0+	0+	0+	0+	0+	0+	0+	003	031	149	221	086	002	21
	22	0+	0+	0+	0+	0+	0+	0+	001	010	081	272	223	022	22
	23	0+	0+	0+	0+	0+	0+	0+	0+	002	028	213	369	190	23
	24	0+	0+	0+	0+	0+	0+	0+	0+	0+	005	080	292	786	24
25	0	778	277	072	004	0+	0+	0+	0+	0+	0+	0+	0+	0+	0
	1	196	365	199	024	001	0+	0+	0+	0+	0+	0+	0+	0+	1
	2	024	231	266	071	007	0+	0+	0+	0+	0+	0+	0+	0+	2
	3	002	093	226	136	024	002	0+	0+	0+	0+	0+	0+	0+	3
	4	0+	027	138	187	057	007	0+	0+	0+	0+	0+	0+	0+	4
	5	0+	006	065	196	103	020	002	0+	0+	0+	0+	0+	0+	5
	6	0+	001	024	163	147	044	005	0+	0+	0+	0+	0+	0+	6
	7	0+	0+	007	111	171	080	014	001	0+	0+	0+	0+	0+	7
	8	0+	0+	002	062	165	120	032	003	0+	0+	0+	0+	0+	8
	9	0+	0+	0+	029	134	151	061	009	0+	0+	0+	0+	0+	9
	10	0+	0+	0+	012	092	161	097	021	001	0+	0+	0+	0+	10
	11	0+	0+	0+	004	054	147	133	043	004	0+	0+	0+	0+	11
	12	0+	0+	0+	001	027	114	155	076	011	0+	0+	0+	0+	12
	13	0+	0+	0+	0+	011	076	155	114	027	001	0+	0+	0+	13
	14	0+	0+	0+	0+	004	043	133	147	054	004	0+	0+	0+	14
	15	0+	0+	0+	0+	001	021	097	161	092	012	0+	0+	0+	15
	16	0+	0+	0+	0+	0+	009	061	151	134	029	0+	0+	0+	16
	17	0+	0+	0+	0+	0+	003	032	120	165	062	002	0+	0+	17
	18	0+	0+	0+	0+	0+	001	014	080	171	111	007	0+	0+	18
	19	0+	0+	0+	0+	0+	0+	005	044	147	163	024	001	0+	19

Table B.2 (Continued)

n	x	.01	.05	.10	.20	.30	.40	p .50	.60	.70	.80	.90	.95	.99	x
25	20	0+	0+	0+	0+	0+	0+	002	020	103	196	065	006	0+	20
	21	0+	0+	0+	0+	0+	0+	0+	007	057	187	138	027	0+	21
	22	0+	0+	0+	0+	0+	0+	0+	002	024	136	226	093	002	22
	23	0+	0+	0+	0+	0+	0+	0+	0+	007	071	266	231	024	23
	24	0+	0+	0+	0+	0+	0+	0+	0+	001	024	199	365	196	24
	25	0+	0+	0+	0+	0+	0+	0+	0+	0+	004	072	277	778	25

From Mosteller, F., R. E. K. Rourke, and G. B. Thomas, *Probability with Statistical Applications*, Reading, Mass.: Addison-Wesley, 1961, pp. 371–379. Reprinted with permission.

Table B.3
The Standard Normal Distribution:
Areas under the Standard Normal Curve from 0 to z for Various Values of z

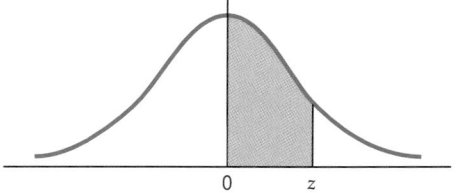

z	.00	.01	.02	.03	.04	.05	.06	.07	.08	.09
0.0	.0000	.0040	.0080	.0120	.0160	.0199	.0239	.0279	.0319	.0359
0.1	.0398	.0438	.0478	.0517	.0557	.0596	.0636	.0675	.0714	.0754
0.2	.0793	.0832	.0871	.0910	.0948	.0987	.1026	.1064	.1103	.1141
0.3	.1179	.1217	.1255	.1293	.1331	.1368	.1406	.1443	.1480	.1517
0.4	.1554	.1591	.1628	.1664	.1700	.1736	.1772	.1808	.1844	.1879
0.5	.1915	.1950	.1985	.2019	.2054	.2088	.2123	.2157	.2190	.2224
0.6	.2258	.2291	.2324	.2357	.2389	.2422	.2454	.2486	.2518	.2549
0.7	.2580	.2612	.2642	.2673	.2704	.2734	.2764	.2794	.2823	.2852
0.8	.2881	.2910	.2939	.2967	.2996	.3023	.3051	.3078	.3106	.3133
0.9	.3159	.3186	.3212	.3238	.3264	.3289	.3315	.3340	.3365	.3389
1.0	.3413	.3438	.3461	.3485	.3508	.3531	.3554	.3577	.3599	.3621
1.1	.3643	.3665	.3686	.3708	.3729	.3749	.3770	.3790	.3810	.3830
1.2	.3849	.3869	.3888	.3907	.3925	.3944	.3962	.3980	.3997	.4015
1.3	.4032	.4049	.4066	.4082	.4099	.4115	.4131	.4147	.4162	.4177
1.4	.4192	.4207	.4222	.4236	.4251	.4265	.4279	.4292	.4306	.4319

Table B.3 (Continued)

z	.00	.01	.02	.03	.04	.05	.06	.07	.08	.09
1.5	.4332	.4345	.4357	.4370	.4382	.4394	.4406	.4418	.4429	.4441
1.6	.4452	.4463	.4474	.4484	.4495	.4505	.4515	.4525	.4535	.4545
1.7	.4554	.4564	.4573	.4582	.4591	.4599	.4608	.4616	.4625	.4633
1.8	.4641	.4649	.4656	.4664	.4671	.4678	.4686	.4693	.4699	.4706
1.9	.4713	.4719	.4726	.4732	.4738	.4744	.4750	.4756	.4761	.4767
2.0	.4772	.4778	.4783	.4788	.4793	.4798	.4803	.4808	.4812	.4817
2.1	.4821	.4826	.4830	.4834	.4838	.4842	.4846	.4850	.4854	.4857
2.2	.4861	.4864	.4868	.4871	.4875	.4878	.4881	.4884	.4887	.4890
2.3	.4893	.4896	.4898	.4901	.4904	.4906	.4909	.4911	.4913	.4916
2.4	.4918	.4920	.4922	.4925	.4927	.4929	.4931	.4932	.4934	.4936
2.5	.4938	.4940	.4941	.4943	.4945	.4946	.4948	.4949	.4951	.4952
2.6	.4953	.4955	.4956	.4957	.4959	.4960	.4961	.4962	.4963	.4964
2.7	.4965	.4966	.4967	.4968	.4969	.4970	.4971	.4972	.4973	.4974
2.8	.4974	.4975	.4976	.4977	.4977	.4978	.4979	.4979	.4980	.4981
2.9	.4981	.4982	.4982	.4983	.4984	.4984	.4985	.4985	.4986	.4986
3.0	.4987	.4987	.4987	.4988	.4988	.4989	.4989	.4989	.4990	.4990
3.1	.4990	.4991	.4991	.4991	.4992	.4992	.4992	.4992	.4993	.4993
3.2	.4993	.4993	.4994	.4994	.4994	.4994	.4994	.4995	.4995	.4995
3.3	.4995	.4995	.4995	.4996	.4996	.4996	.4996	.4996	.4996	.4997
3.4	.4997	.4997	.4997	.4997	.4997	.4997	.4997	.4997	.4997	.4998
3.5	.4998	.4998	.4998	.4998	.4998	.4998	.4998	.4998	.4998	.4998
3.6	.4998	.4998	.4999	.4999	.4999	.4999	.4999	.4999	.4999	.4999
3.7	.4999	.4999	.4999	.4999	.4999	.4999	.4999	.4999	.4999	.4999
3.8	.4999	.4999	.4999	.4999	.4999	.4999	.4999	.4999	.4999	.4999
3.9	.49995	.49995	.49996	.49996	.49996	.49996	.49996	.49996	.49997	.49997
4.0	.49997									
4.5	.499997									
5.0	.4999997									

Adapted from *Standard Mathematical Tables,* 25th ed., Boca Raton: Chemical Rubber Company Press, 1978, p. 524. Reprinted with permission.

Table B.4
Student's *t* Distribution

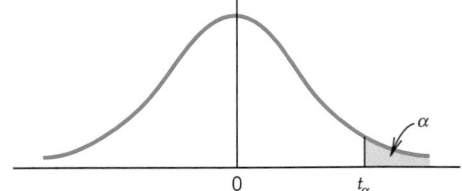

df	$t_{.005}$	$t_{.01}$	$t_{.025}$	$t_{.05}$	$t_{.10}$	$t_{.25}$
1	63.657	31.821	12.706	6.314	3.078	1.000
2	9.925	6.965	4.303	2.920	1.886	0.816
3	5.841	4.541	3.182	2.353	1.638	.765
4	4.604	3.747	2.776	2.132	1.533	.741
5	4.032	3.365	2.571	2.015	1.476	0.727
6	3.707	3.143	2.447	1.943	1.440	.718
7	3.499	2.998	2.365	1.895	1.415	.711
8	3.355	2.896	2.306	1.860	1.397	.706
9	3.250	2.821	2.262	1.833	1.383	.703
10	3.169	2.764	2.228	1.812	1.372	0.700
11	3.106	2.718	2.201	1.796	1.363	.697
12	3.055	2.681	2.179	1.782	1.356	.695
13	3.012	2.650	2.160	1.771	1.350	.694
14	2.977	2.624	2.145	1.761	1.345	.692
15	2.947	2.602	2.131	1.753	1.341	0.691
16	2.921	2.583	2.120	1.746	1.337	.690
17	2.898	2.567	2.110	1.740	1.333	.689
18	2.878	2.552	2.101	1.734	1.330	.688
19	2.861	2.539	2.093	1.729	1.328	.688
20	2.845	2.528	2.086	1.725	1.325	0.687
21	2.831	2.518	2.080	1.721	1.323	.686
22	2.819	2.508	2.074	1.717	1.321	.686
23	2.807	2.500	2.069	1.714	1.319	.685
24	2.797	2.492	2.064	1.711	1.318	.685
25	2.787	2.485	2.060	1.708	1.316	0.684
26	2.779	2.479	2.056	1.706	1.315	.684
27	2.771	2.473	2.052	1.703	1.314	.684
28	2.763	2.467	2.048	1.701	1.313	.683
29	2.756	2.462	2.045	1.699	1.311	.683
Large	2.576	2.326	1.960	1.645	1.282	.674

Adapted from Pearson, E. S., and H. O. Hartley, *Biometrika Tables for Statisticians*, Vol. 1, 1958, p. 146. With permission of the Biometrika Trustees.

Table B.5
The Chi-Square Distribution

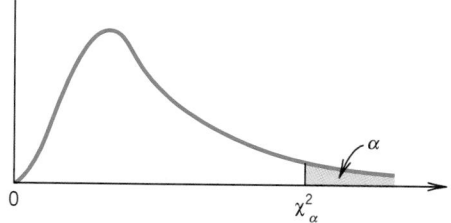

df	$\chi^2_{.995}$	$\chi^2_{.99}$	$\chi^2_{.975}$	$\chi^2_{.95}$	$\chi^2_{.90}$	$\chi^2_{.10}$	$\chi^2_{.05}$	$\chi^2_{.025}$	$\chi^2_{.01}$	$\chi^2_{.005}$
1	—	—	0.001	0.004	0.016	2.706	3.841	5.024	6.635	7.879
2	0.010	0.020	0.051	0.103	0.211	4.605	5.991	7.378	9.210	10.597
3	0.072	0.115	0.216	0.352	0.584	6.251	7.815	9.348	11.345	12.838
4	0.207	0.297	0.484	0.711	1.064	7.779	9.488	11.143	13.277	14.860
5	0.412	0.554	0.831	1.145	1.610	9.236	11.071	12.833	15.086	16.750
6	0.676	0.872	1.237	1.635	2.204	10.645	12.592	14.449	16.812	18.548
7	0.989	1.239	1.690	2.167	2.833	12.017	14.067	16.013	18.475	20.278
8	1.344	1.646	2.180	2.733	3.490	13.362	15.507	17.535	20.090	21.955
9	1.735	2.088	2.700	3.325	4.168	14.684	16.919	19.023	21.666	23.589
10	2.156	2.558	3.247	3.940	4.865	15.987	18.307	20.483	23.209	25.188
11	2.603	3.053	3.816	4.575	5.578	17.275	19.675	21.920	24.725	26.757
12	3.074	3.571	4.404	5.226	6.304	18.549	21.026	23.337	26.217	28.299
13	3.565	4.107	5.009	5.892	7.042	19.812	22.362	24.736	27.688	29.819
14	4.075	4.660	5.629	6.571	7.790	21.064	23.685	26.119	29.141	31.319
15	4.601	5.229	6.262	7.261	8.547	22.307	24.996	27.488	30.578	32.801
16	5.142	5.812	6.908	7.962	9.312	23.542	26.296	28.845	32.000	34.267
17	5.697	6.408	7.564	8.672	10.085	24.769	27.587	30.191	33.409	35.718
18	6.265	7.015	8.231	9.390	10.865	25.989	28.869	31.526	34.805	37.156
19	6.844	7.633	8.907	10.117	11.651	27.204	30.144	32.852	36.191	38.582
20	7.434	8.260	9.591	10.851	12.443	28.412	31.410	34.170	37.566	39.997
21	8.034	8.897	10.283	11.591	13.240	29.615	32.671	35.479	38.932	41.401
22	8.643	9.542	10.982	12.338	14.042	30.813	33.924	36.781	40.289	42.796
23	9.260	10.196	11.689	13.091	14.848	32.007	35.172	38.076	41.638	44.181
24	9.886	10.856	12.401	13.848	15.659	33.196	36.415	39.364	42.980	45.559
25	10.520	11.524	13.120	14.611	16.473	34.382	37.652	40.646	44.314	46.928
26	11.160	12.198	13.844	15.379	17.292	35.563	38.885	41.923	45.642	48.290
27	11.808	12.879	14.573	16.151	18.114	36.741	40.113	43.194	46.963	49.645
28	12.461	13.565	15.308	16.928	18.939	37.916	41.337	44.461	48.278	50.993
29	13.121	14.257	16.047	17.708	19.768	39.087	42.557	45.722	49.588	52.336
30	13.787	14.954	16.791	18.493	20.599	40.256	43.773	46.979	50.892	53.672
40	20.707	22.164	24.433	26.509	29.051	51.805	55.758	59.342	63.691	66.766

Table B.5 (Continued)

df	$\chi^2_{.995}$	$\chi^2_{.99}$	$\chi^2_{.975}$	$\chi^2_{.95}$	$\chi^2_{.90}$	$\chi^2_{.10}$	$\chi^2_{.05}$	$\chi^2_{.025}$	$\chi^2_{.01}$	$\chi^2_{.005}$
50	27.991	29.707	32.357	34.764	37.689	63.167	67.505	71.420	76.154	79.490
60	35.534	37.485	40.482	43.188	46.459	74.397	79.082	83.298	88.379	91.952
70	43.275	45.442	48.758	51.739	55.329	85.527	90.531	95.023	100.425	104.215
80	51.172	53.540	57.153	60.391	64.278	96.578	101.879	106.629	112.329	116.321
90	59.196	61.754	65.647	69.126	73.291	107.565	113.145	118.136	124.116	128.299
100	67.328	70.065	74.222	77.929	82.358	118.498	124.342	129.561	135.807	140.169

From Owen, D. B., *Handbook of Statistical Tables*, Reading, Mass.: Addison-Wesley, 1962, pp. 50–55. Reprinted with permission.

Table B.6
The F Distribution: Values of $F_{.05}$

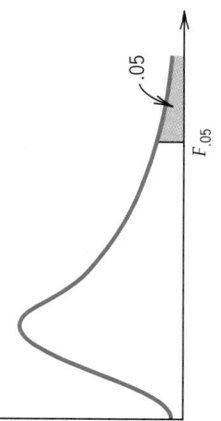

$F_{.05}$ .05

Degrees of freedom of the numerator

df_1 / df_2	1	2	3	4	5	6	7	8	9	10	12	15	20	24	30	40	60	120	∞
1	161.4	199.5	215.7	224.6	230.2	234.0	236.8	238.9	240.5	241.9	243.9	245.9	248.0	249.1	250.1	251.1	252.2	253.3	254.3
2	18.51	19.00	19.16	19.25	19.30	19.33	19.35	19.37	19.38	19.40	19.41	19.43	19.45	19.45	19.46	19.47	19.48	19.49	19.50
3	10.13	9.55	9.28	9.12	9.01	8.94	8.89	8.85	8.81	8.79	8.74	8.70	8.66	8.64	8.62	8.59	8.57	8.55	8.53
4	7.71	6.94	6.59	6.39	6.26	6.16	6.09	6.04	6.00	5.96	5.91	5.86	5.80	5.77	5.75	5.72	5.69	5.66	5.63
5	6.61	5.79	5.41	5.19	5.05	4.95	4.88	4.82	4.77	4.74	4.68	4.62	4.56	4.53	4.50	4.46	4.43	4.40	4.36
6	5.99	5.14	4.76	4.53	4.39	4.28	4.21	4.15	4.10	4.06	4.00	3.94	3.87	3.84	3.81	3.77	3.74	3.70	3.67
7	5.59	4.74	4.35	4.12	3.97	3.87	3.79	3.73	3.68	3.64	3.57	3.51	3.44	3.41	3.38	3.34	3.30	3.27	3.23
8	5.32	4.46	4.07	3.84	3.69	3.58	3.50	3.44	3.39	3.35	3.28	3.22	3.15	3.12	3.08	3.04	3.01	2.97	2.93
9	5.12	4.26	3.86	3.63	3.48	3.37	3.29	3.23	3.18	3.14	3.07	3.01	2.94	2.90	2.86	2.83	2.79	2.75	2.71
10	4.96	4.10	3.71	3.48	3.33	3.22	3.14	3.07	3.02	2.98	2.91	2.85	2.77	2.74	2.70	2.66	2.62	2.58	2.54
11	4.84	3.98	3.59	3.36	3.20	3.09	3.01	2.95	2.90	2.85	2.79	2.72	2.65	2.61	2.57	2.53	2.49	2.45	2.40
12	4.75	3.89	3.49	3.26	3.11	3.00	2.91	2.85	2.80	2.75	2.69	2.62	2.54	2.51	2.47	2.43	2.38	2.34	2.30
13	4.67	3.81	3.41	3.18	3.03	2.92	2.83	2.77	2.71	2.67	2.60	2.53	2.46	2.42	2.38	2.34	2.30	2.25	2.21
14	4.60	3.74	3.34	3.11	2.96	2.85	2.76	2.70	2.65	2.60	2.53	2.46	2.39	2.35	2.31	2.27	2.22	2.18	2.13
15	4.54	3.68	3.29	3.06	2.90	2.79	2.71	2.64	2.59	2.54	2.48	2.40	2.33	2.29	2.25	2.20	2.16	2.11	2.07
16	4.49	3.63	3.24	3.01	2.85	2.74	2.66	2.59	2.54	2.49	2.42	2.35	2.28	2.24	2.19	2.15	2.11	2.06	2.01
17	4.45	3.59	3.20	2.96	2.81	2.70	2.61	2.55	2.49	2.45	2.38	2.31	2.23	2.19	2.15	2.10	2.06	2.01	1.96
18	4.41	3.55	3.16	2.93	2.77	2.66	2.58	2.51	2.46	2.41	2.34	2.27	2.19	2.15	2.11	2.06	2.02	1.97	1.92
19	4.38	3.52	3.13	2.90	2.74	2.63	2.54	2.48	2.42	2.38	2.31	2.23	2.16	2.11	2.07	2.03	1.98	1.93	1.88
20	4.35	3.49	3.10	2.87	2.71	2.60	2.51	2.45	2.39	2.35	2.28	2.20	2.12	2.08	2.04	1.99	1.95	1.90	1.84
21	4.32	3.47	3.07	2.84	2.68	2.57	2.49	2.42	2.37	2.32	2.25	2.18	2.10	2.05	2.01	1.96	1.92	1.87	1.81
22	4.30	3.44	3.05	2.82	2.66	2.55	2.46	2.40	2.34	2.30	2.23	2.15	2.07	2.03	1.98	1.94	1.89	1.84	1.78
23	4.28	3.42	3.03	2.80	2.64	2.53	2.44	2.37	2.32	2.27	2.20	2.13	2.05	2.01	1.96	1.91	1.86	1.81	1.76
24	4.26	3.40	3.01	2.78	2.62	2.51	2.42	2.36	2.30	2.25	2.18	2.11	2.03	1.98	1.94	1.89	1.84	1.79	1.73
25	4.24	3.39	2.99	2.76	2.60	2.49	2.40	2.34	2.28	2.24	2.16	2.09	2.01	1.96	1.92	1.87	1.82	1.77	1.71
26	4.23	3.37	2.98	2.74	2.59	2.47	2.39	2.32	2.27	2.22	2.15	2.07	1.99	1.95	1.90	1.85	1.80	1.75	1.69
27	4.21	3.35	2.96	2.73	2.57	2.46	2.37	2.31	2.25	2.20	2.13	2.06	1.97	1.93	1.88	1.84	1.79	1.73	1.67
28	4.20	3.34	2.95	2.71	2.56	2.45	2.36	2.29	2.24	2.19	2.12	2.04	1.96	1.91	1.87	1.82	1.77	1.71	1.65
29	4.18	3.33	2.93	2.70	2.55	2.43	2.35	2.28	2.22	2.18	2.10	2.03	1.94	1.90	1.85	1.81	1.75	1.70	1.64
30	4.17	3.32	2.92	2.69	2.53	2.42	2.33	2.27	2.21	2.16	2.09	2.01	1.93	1.89	1.84	1.79	1.74	1.68	1.62
40	4.08	3.23	2.84	2.61	2.45	2.34	2.25	2.18	2.12	2.08	2.00	1.92	1.84	1.79	1.74	1.69	1.64	1.58	1.51
60	4.00	3.15	2.76	2.53	2.37	2.25	2.17	2.10	2.04	1.99	1.92	1.84	1.75	1.70	1.65	1.59	1.53	1.47	1.39
120	3.92	3.07	2.68	2.45	2.29	2.17	2.09	2.02	1.96	1.91	1.83	1.75	1.66	1.61	1.55	1.50	1.43	1.35	1.25
∞	3.84	3.00	2.60	2.37	2.21	2.10	2.01	1.94	1.88	1.83	1.75	1.67	1.57	1.52	1.46	1.39	1.32	1.22	1.00

Degrees of freedom of the denominator

Table B.6 (Continued)
The F Distribution: Values of $F_{.025}$

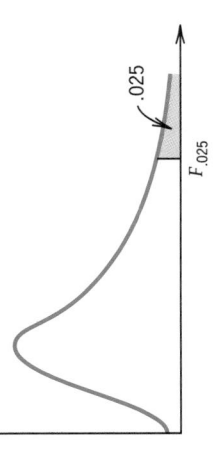

$F_{.025}$

.025

Degrees of freedom of the numerator

df_2 \ df_1	1	2	3	4	5	6	7	8	9	10	12	15	20	24	30	40	60	120	∞
1	647.8	799.5	864.2	899.6	921.8	937.1	948.2	956.7	963.3	968.6	976.7	984.9	993.1	997.2	1001	1006	1010	1014	1018
2	38.51	39.00	39.17	39.25	39.30	39.33	39.36	39.37	39.39	39.40	39.41	39.43	39.45	39.46	39.46	39.47	39.48	39.49	39.50
3	17.44	16.04	15.44	15.10	14.88	14.73	14.62	14.54	14.47	14.42	14.34	14.25	14.17	14.12	14.08	14.04	13.99	13.95	13.90
4	12.22	10.65	9.98	9.60	9.36	9.20	9.07	8.98	8.90	8.84	8.75	8.66	8.56	8.51	8.46	8.41	8.36	8.31	8.26
5	10.01	8.43	7.76	7.39	7.15	6.98	6.85	6.76	6.68	6.62	6.52	6.43	6.33	6.28	6.23	6.18	6.12	6.07	6.02
6	8.81	7.26	6.60	6.23	5.99	5.82	5.70	5.60	5.52	5.46	5.37	5.27	5.17	5.12	5.07	5.01	4.96	4.90	4.85
7	8.07	6.54	5.89	5.52	5.29	5.12	4.99	4.90	4.82	4.76	4.67	4.57	4.47	4.42	4.36	4.31	4.25	4.20	4.14
8	7.57	6.06	5.42	5.05	4.82	4.65	4.53	4.43	4.36	4.30	4.20	4.10	4.00	3.95	3.89	3.84	3.78	3.73	3.67
9	7.21	5.71	5.08	4.72	4.48	4.32	4.20	4.10	4.03	3.96	3.87	3.77	3.67	3.61	3.56	3.51	3.45	3.39	3.33
10	6.94	5.46	4.83	4.47	4.24	4.07	3.95	3.85	3.78	3.72	3.62	3.52	3.42	3.37	3.31	3.26	3.20	3.14	3.08
11	6.72	5.26	4.63	4.28	4.04	3.88	3.76	3.66	3.59	3.53	3.43	3.33	3.23	3.17	3.12	3.06	3.00	2.94	2.88
12	6.55	5.10	4.47	4.12	3.89	3.73	3.61	3.51	3.44	3.37	3.28	3.18	3.07	3.02	2.96	2.91	2.85	2.79	2.72
13	6.41	4.97	4.35	4.00	3.77	3.60	3.48	3.39	3.31	3.25	3.15	3.05	2.95	2.89	2.84	2.78	2.72	2.66	2.60
14	6.30	4.86	4.24	3.89	3.66	3.50	3.38	3.29	3.21	3.15	3.05	2.95	2.84	2.79	2.73	2.67	2.61	2.55	2.49
15	6.20	4.77	4.15	3.80	3.58	3.41	3.29	3.20	3.12	3.06	2.96	2.86	2.76	2.70	2.64	2.59	2.52	2.46	2.40
16	6.12	4.69	4.08	3.73	3.50	3.34	3.22	3.12	3.05	2.99	2.89	2.79	2.68	2.63	2.57	2.51	2.45	2.38	2.32
17	6.04	4.62	4.01	3.66	3.44	3.28	3.16	3.06	2.98	2.92	2.82	2.72	2.62	2.56	2.50	2.44	2.38	2.32	2.25
18	5.98	4.56	3.95	3.61	3.38	3.22	3.10	3.01	2.93	2.87	2.77	2.67	2.56	2.50	2.44	2.38	2.32	2.26	2.19
19	5.92	4.51	3.90	3.56	3.33	3.17	3.05	2.96	2.88	2.82	2.72	2.62	2.51	2.45	2.39	2.33	2.27	2.20	2.13
20	5.87	4.46	3.86	3.51	3.29	3.13	3.01	2.91	2.84	2.77	2.68	2.57	2.46	2.41	2.35	2.29	2.22	2.16	2.09
21	5.83	4.42	3.82	3.48	3.25	3.09	2.97	2.87	2.80	2.73	2.64	2.53	2.42	2.37	2.31	2.25	2.18	2.11	2.04
22	5.79	4.38	3.78	3.44	3.22	3.05	2.93	2.84	2.76	2.70	2.60	2.50	2.39	2.33	2.27	2.21	2.14	2.08	2.00
23	5.75	4.35	3.75	3.41	3.18	3.02	2.90	2.81	2.73	2.67	2.57	2.47	2.36	2.30	2.24	2.18	2.11	2.04	1.97
24	5.72	4.32	3.72	3.38	3.15	2.99	2.87	2.78	2.70	2.64	2.54	2.44	2.33	2.27	2.21	2.15	2.08	2.01	1.94
25	5.69	4.29	3.69	3.35	3.13	2.97	2.85	2.75	2.68	2.61	2.51	2.41	2.30	2.24	2.18	2.12	2.05	1.98	1.91
26	5.66	4.27	3.67	3.33	3.10	2.94	2.82	2.73	2.65	2.59	2.49	2.39	2.28	2.22	2.16	2.09	2.03	1.95	1.88
27	5.63	4.24	3.65	3.31	3.08	2.92	2.80	2.71	2.63	2.57	2.47	2.36	2.25	2.19	2.13	2.07	2.00	1.93	1.85
28	5.61	4.22	3.63	3.29	3.06	2.90	2.78	2.69	2.61	2.55	2.45	2.34	2.23	2.17	2.11	2.05	1.98	1.91	1.83
29	5.59	4.20	3.61	3.27	3.04	2.88	2.76	2.67	2.59	2.53	2.43	2.32	2.21	2.15	2.09	2.03	1.96	1.89	1.81
30	5.57	4.18	3.59	3.25	3.03	2.87	2.75	2.65	2.57	2.51	2.41	2.31	2.20	2.14	2.07	2.01	1.94	1.87	1.79
40	5.42	4.05	3.46	3.13	2.90	2.74	2.62	2.53	2.45	2.39	2.29	2.18	2.07	2.01	1.94	1.88	1.80	1.72	1.64
60	5.29	3.93	3.34	3.01	2.79	2.63	2.51	2.41	2.33	2.27	2.17	2.06	1.94	1.88	1.82	1.74	1.67	1.58	1.48
120	5.15	3.80	3.23	2.89	2.67	2.52	2.39	2.30	2.22	2.16	2.05	1.94	1.82	1.76	1.69	1.61	1.53	1.43	1.31
∞	5.02	3.69	3.12	2.79	2.57	2.41	2.29	2.19	2.11	2.05	1.94	1.83	1.71	1.64	1.57	1.48	1.39	1.27	1.00

Degrees of freedom of the denominator

Table B.6 (Continued)

The F Distribution: Values of $F_{.01}$

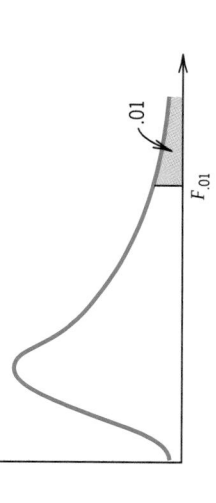

Degrees of freedom of the numerator

df_2 \ df_1	1	2	3	4	5	6	7	8	9	10	12	15	20	24	30	40	60	120	∞
1	4052	4999.5	5403	5625	5764	5859	5928	5981	6022	6056	6106	6157	6209	6235	6261	6287	6313	6339	6366
2	98.50	99.00	99.17	99.25	99.30	99.33	99.36	99.37	99.39	99.40	99.42	99.43	99.45	99.46	99.47	99.47	99.48	99.49	99.50
3	34.12	30.82	29.46	28.71	28.24	27.91	27.67	27.49	27.35	27.23	27.05	26.87	26.69	26.60	26.50	26.41	26.32	26.22	26.13
4	21.20	18.00	16.69	15.98	15.52	15.21	14.98	14.80	14.66	14.55	14.37	14.20	14.02	13.93	13.84	13.75	13.65	13.56	13.46
5	16.26	13.27	12.06	11.39	10.97	10.67	10.46	10.29	10.16	10.05	9.89	9.72	9.55	9.47	9.38	9.29	9.20	9.11	9.02
6	13.75	10.92	9.78	9.15	8.75	8.47	8.26	8.10	7.98	7.87	7.72	7.56	7.40	7.31	7.23	7.14	7.06	6.97	6.88
7	12.25	9.55	8.45	7.85	7.46	7.19	6.99	6.84	6.72	6.62	6.47	6.31	6.16	6.07	5.99	5.91	5.82	5.74	5.65
8	11.26	8.65	7.59	7.01	6.63	6.37	6.18	6.03	5.91	5.81	5.67	5.52	5.36	5.28	5.20	5.12	5.03	4.95	4.86
9	10.56	8.02	6.99	6.42	6.06	5.80	5.61	5.47	5.35	5.26	5.11	4.96	4.81	4.73	4.65	4.57	4.48	4.40	4.31
10	10.04	7.56	6.55	5.99	5.64	5.39	5.20	5.06	4.94	4.85	4.71	4.56	4.41	4.33	4.25	4.17	4.08	4.00	3.91
11	9.65	7.21	6.22	5.67	5.32	5.07	4.89	4.74	4.63	4.54	4.40	4.25	4.10	4.02	3.94	3.86	3.78	3.69	3.60
12	9.33	6.93	5.95	5.41	5.06	4.82	4.64	4.50	4.39	4.30	4.16	4.01	3.86	3.78	3.70	3.62	3.54	3.45	3.36
13	9.07	6.70	5.74	5.21	4.86	4.62	4.44	4.30	4.19	4.10	3.96	3.82	3.66	3.59	3.51	3.43	3.34	3.25	3.17
14	8.86	6.51	5.56	5.04	4.69	4.46	4.28	4.14	4.03	3.94	3.80	3.66	3.51	3.43	3.35	3.27	3.18	3.09	3.00
15	8.68	6.36	5.42	4.89	4.56	4.32	4.14	4.00	3.89	3.80	3.67	3.52	3.37	3.29	3.21	3.13	3.05	2.96	2.87
16	8.53	6.23	5.29	4.77	4.44	4.20	4.03	3.89	3.78	3.69	3.55	3.41	3.26	3.18	3.10	3.02	2.93	2.84	2.75
17	8.40	6.11	5.18	4.67	4.34	4.10	3.93	3.79	3.68	3.59	3.46	3.31	3.16	3.08	3.00	2.92	2.83	2.75	2.65
18	8.29	6.01	5.09	4.58	4.25	4.01	3.84	3.71	3.60	3.51	3.37	3.23	3.08	3.00	2.92	2.84	2.75	2.66	2.57
19	8.18	5.93	5.01	4.50	4.17	3.94	3.77	3.63	3.52	3.43	3.30	3.15	3.00	2.92	2.84	2.76	2.67	2.58	2.49
20	8.10	5.85	4.94	4.43	4.10	3.87	3.70	3.56	3.46	3.37	3.23	3.09	2.94	2.86	2.78	2.69	2.61	2.52	2.42
21	8.02	5.78	4.87	4.37	4.04	3.81	3.64	3.51	3.40	3.31	3.17	3.03	2.88	2.80	2.72	2.64	2.55	2.46	2.36
22	7.95	5.72	4.82	4.31	3.99	3.76	3.59	3.45	3.35	3.26	3.12	2.98	2.83	2.75	2.67	2.58	2.50	2.40	2.31
23	7.88	5.66	4.76	4.26	3.94	3.71	3.54	3.41	3.30	3.21	3.07	2.93	2.78	2.70	2.62	2.54	2.45	2.35	2.26
24	7.82	5.61	4.72	4.22	3.90	3.67	3.50	3.36	3.26	3.17	3.03	2.89	2.74	2.66	2.58	2.49	2.40	2.31	2.21
25	7.77	5.57	4.68	4.18	3.85	3.63	3.46	3.32	3.22	3.13	2.99	2.85	2.70	2.62	2.54	2.45	2.36	2.27	2.17
26	7.72	5.53	4.64	4.14	3.82	3.59	3.42	3.29	3.18	3.09	2.96	2.81	2.66	2.58	2.50	2.42	2.33	2.23	2.13
27	7.68	5.49	4.60	4.11	3.78	3.56	3.39	3.26	3.15	3.06	2.93	2.78	2.63	2.55	2.47	2.38	2.29	2.20	2.10
28	7.64	5.45	4.57	4.07	3.75	3.53	3.36	3.23	3.12	3.03	2.90	2.75	2.60	2.52	2.44	2.35	2.26	2.17	2.06
29	7.60	5.42	4.54	4.04	3.73	3.50	3.33	3.20	3.09	3.00	2.87	2.73	2.57	2.49	2.41	2.33	2.23	2.14	2.03
30	7.56	5.39	4.51	4.02	3.70	3.47	3.30	3.17	3.07	2.98	2.84	2.70	2.55	2.47	2.39	2.30	2.21	2.11	2.01
40	7.31	5.18	4.31	3.83	3.51	3.29	3.12	2.99	2.89	2.80	2.66	2.52	2.37	2.29	2.20	2.11	2.02	1.92	1.80
60	7.08	4.98	4.13	3.65	3.34	3.12	2.95	2.82	2.72	2.63	2.50	2.35	2.20	2.12	2.03	1.94	1.84	1.73	1.60
120	6.85	4.79	3.95	3.48	3.17	2.96	2.79	2.66	2.56	2.47	2.34	2.19	2.03	1.95	1.86	1.76	1.66	1.53	1.38
∞	6.63	4.61	3.78	3.32	3.02	2.80	2.64	2.51	2.41	2.32	2.18	2.04	1.88	1.79	1.70	1.59	1.47	1.32	1.00

Degrees of freedom of the denominator

From Pearson, E. S., and H. O. Hartley, *Biometrika Tables for Statisticians*, Vol. 1, 1958, pp. 171–173. With permission of the Biometrika Trustees.

A-21

Table B.7
Critical Values of r
The Given Values of α Are for a Two-Tailed Test.

n	$\alpha = .05$	$\alpha = .01$	n	$\alpha = .05$	$\alpha = .01$
4	.950	.999	20	.444	.561
5	.878	.959	22	.423	.537
6	.811	.917	24	.404	.515
7	.754	.875	26	.388	.496
8	.707	.834	28	.374	.479
9	.666	.798			
			30	.361	.463
10	.632	.765	40	.312	.402
11	.602	.735	50	.279	.361
12	.576	.708	60	.254	.330
13	.553	.684	80	.220	.286
14	.532	.661			
			100	.196	.256
15	.514	.641	250	.124	.163
16	.497	.623	500	.088	.115
17	.482	.606	1000	.062	.081
18	.468	.590			
19	.456	.575			

Adapted from Dixon, W. J., and J. Massey, Jr., *Introduction to Statistical Analysis,* 3rd ed., New York: McGraw-Hill, 1969, p. 569. With permission.

Critical Values for the Wilcoxon Signed-Rank Test for n = 5 to 50

One-Sided	Two-Sided	n = 5	n = 6	n = 7	n = 8	n = 9	n = 10	n = 11	n = 12	n = 13	n = 14	n = 15	n = 16
α = .05	α = .10	1	2	4	6	8	11	14	17	21	26	30	36
α = .025	α = .05		1	2	4	6	8	11	14	17	21	25	30
α = .01	α = .02			0	2	3	5	7	10	13	16	20	24
α = .005	α = .01				0	2	3	5	7	10	13	16	19

One-Sided	Two-Sided	n = 17	n = 18	n = 19	n = 20	n = 21	n = 22	n = 23	n = 24	n = 25	n = 26	n = 27	n = 28
α = .05	α = .10	41	47	54	60	68	75	83	92	101	110	120	130
α = .025	α = .05	35	40	46	52	59	66	73	81	90	98	107	117
α = .01	α = .02	28	33	38	43	49	56	62	69	77	85	93	102
α = .005	α = .01	23	28	32	37	43	49	55	61	68	76	84	92

One-Sided	Two-Sided	n = 29	n = 30	n = 31	n = 32	n = 33	n = 34	n = 35	n = 36	n = 37	n = 38	n = 39
α = .05	α = .10	141	152	163	175	188	201	214	228	242	256	271
α = .025	α = .05	127	137	148	159	171	183	195	208	222	235	250
α = .01	α = .02	111	120	130	141	151	162	174	186	198	211	224
α = .005	α = .01	100	109	118	128	138	149	160	171	183	195	208

One-Sided	Two-Sided	n = 40	n = 41	n = 42	n = 43	n = 44	n = 45	n = 46	n = 47	n = 48	n = 49	n = 50
α = .05	α = .10	287	303	319	336	353	371	389	408	427	446	466
α = .025	α = .05	264	279	295	311	327	344	361	379	397	415	434
α = .01	α = .02	238	252	267	281	297	313	329	345	362	380	398
α = .005	α = .01	221	234	248	262	277	292	307	323	339	356	373

From Wilcoxon, F., and R. A. Wilcox, *Some Rapid Approximate Statistical Procedures*, Pearl River, N.Y.: Lederle Laboratories of the American Cyanamid Company, 1964, p. 28. Reproduced with permission of the American Cyanamid Company.

Table B.9
Critical Values for a Mann–Whitney Test[a]

Critical values for a one-tailed test at $\alpha = .01$ (lightface type) and $\alpha = .005$ (boldface type) and for a two-tailed test at $\alpha = .02$ (lightface type) and $\alpha = .01$ (boldface type).

n_2 \ n_1	1	2	3	4	5	6	7	8	9	10	11	12	13	14	15	16	17	18	19	20
1	—[b]	—	—	—	—	—	—	—	—	—	—	—	—	—	—	—	—	—	—	—
2	—	—	—	—	—	—	—	—	—	—	—	—	0	0	0	0	0	0	1	1
2 (bold)	—	—	—	—	—	—	—	—	—	—	—	—	—	—	—	—	—	—	**0**	**0**
3	—	—	—	—	—	—	0	0	1	1	1	2	2	2	3	3	4	4	4	5
3 (bold)							—	—	**0**	**0**	**0**	**1**	**1**	**1**	**2**	**2**	**2**	**2**	**3**	**3**
4	—	—	—	—	0	1	1	2	3	3	4	5	5	6	7	7	8	9	9	10
4 (bold)					—	**0**	**0**	**1**	**1**	**2**	**2**	**3**	**3**	**4**	**5**	**5**	**6**	**6**	**7**	**8**
5	—	—	—	0	1	2	3	4	5	6	7	8	9	10	11	12	13	14	15	16
5 (bold)				—	**0**	**1**	**1**	**2**	**3**	**4**	**5**	**6**	**7**	**7**	**8**	**9**	**10**	**11**	**12**	**13**
6	—	—	—	1	2	3	4	6	7	8	9	11	12	13	15	16	18	19	20	22
6 (bold)				**0**	**1**	**2**	**3**	**4**	**5**	**6**	**7**	**9**	**10**	**11**	**12**	**13**	**15**	**16**	**17**	**18**
7	—	—	0	1	3	4	6	7	9	11	12	14	16	17	19	21	23	24	26	28
7 (bold)			—	**0**	**1**	**3**	**4**	**6**	**7**	**9**	**10**	**12**	**13**	**15**	**16**	**18**	**19**	**21**	**22**	**24**
8	—	—	0	2	4	6	7	9	11	13	15	17	20	22	24	26	28	30	32	34
8 (bold)			—	**1**	**2**	**4**	**6**	**7**	**9**	**11**	**13**	**15**	**17**	**18**	**20**	**22**	**24**	**26**	**28**	**30**
9	—	—	1	3	5	7	9	11	14	16	18	21	23	26	28	31	33	36	38	40
9 (bold)			**0**	**1**	**3**	**5**	**7**	**9**	**11**	**13**	**16**	**18**	**20**	**22**	**24**	**27**	**29**	**31**	**33**	**36**
10	—	—	1	3	6	8	11	13	16	19	22	24	27	30	33	36	38	41	44	47
10 (bold)			**0**	**2**	**4**	**6**	**9**	**11**	**13**	**16**	**18**	**21**	**24**	**26**	**29**	**31**	**34**	**37**	**39**	**42**
11	—	—	1	4	7	9	12	15	18	22	25	28	31	34	37	41	44	47	50	53
11 (bold)			**0**	**2**	**5**	**7**	**10**	**13**	**16**	**18**	**21**	**24**	**27**	**30**	**33**	**36**	**39**	**42**	**45**	**48**
12	—	—	2	5	8	11	14	17	21	24	28	31	35	38	42	46	49	53	56	60
12 (bold)			**1**	**3**	**6**	**9**	**12**	**15**	**18**	**21**	**24**	**27**	**31**	**34**	**37**	**41**	**44**	**47**	**51**	**54**
13	—	0	2	5	9	12	16	20	23	27	31	35	39	43	47	51	55	59	63	67
13 (bold)		—	**1**	**3**	**7**	**10**	**13**	**17**	**20**	**24**	**27**	**31**	**34**	**38**	**42**	**45**	**49**	**53**	**56**	**60**
14	—	0	2	6	10	13	17	22	26	30	34	38	43	47	51	56	60	65	69	73
14 (bold)		—	**1**	**4**	**7**	**11**	**15**	**18**	**22**	**26**	**30**	**34**	**38**	**42**	**46**	**50**	**54**	**58**	**63**	**67**
15	—	0	3	7	11	15	19	24	28	33	37	42	47	51	56	61	66	70	75	80
15 (bold)		—	**2**	**5**	**8**	**12**	**16**	**20**	**24**	**29**	**33**	**37**	**42**	**46**	**51**	**55**	**60**	**64**	**69**	**73**
16	—	0	3	7	12	16	21	26	31	36	41	46	51	56	61	66	71	76	82	87
16 (bold)		—	**2**	**5**	**9**	**13**	**18**	**22**	**27**	**31**	**36**	**41**	**45**	**50**	**55**	**60**	**65**	**70**	**74**	**79**
17	—	0	4	8	13	18	23	28	33	38	44	49	55	60	66	71	77	82	88	93
17 (bold)		—	**2**	**6**	**10**	**15**	**19**	**24**	**29**	**34**	**39**	**44**	**49**	**54**	**60**	**65**	**70**	**75**	**81**	**86**
18	—	0	4	9	14	19	24	30	36	41	47	53	59	65	70	76	82	88	94	100
18 (bold)		—	**2**	**6**	**11**	**16**	**21**	**26**	**31**	**37**	**42**	**47**	**53**	**58**	**64**	**70**	**75**	**81**	**87**	**92**
19	—	1	4	9	15	20	26	32	38	44	50	56	63	69	75	82	88	94	101	107
19 (bold)		**0**	**3**	**7**	**12**	**17**	**22**	**28**	**33**	**39**	**45**	**51**	**56**	**63**	**69**	**74**	**81**	**87**	**93**	**99**
20	—	1	5	10	16	22	28	34	40	47	53	60	67	73	80	87	93	100	107	114
20 (bold)		**0**	**3**	**8**	**13**	**18**	**24**	**30**	**36**	**42**	**48**	**54**	**60**	**67**	**73**	**79**	**86**	**92**	**99**	**105**

[a] Discussed in Section 13.4. To be significant for any given n_1 and n_2, observed U must be *equal to* or *less than* the value shown in the table.

[b] Dashes in the body of the table indicate that no decision is possible at the stated level of significance.

Table B.9 (Continued)

Critical values for a one-tailed test at $\alpha = .05$ (lightface type) and $\alpha = .025$ (boldface type) and for a two-tailed test at $\alpha = .10$ (lightface type) and $\alpha = .05$ (boldface type).

n_2 \ n_1	1	2	3	4	5	6	7	8	9	10	11	12	13	14	15	16	17	18	19	20
1	—	—	—	—	—	—	—	—	—	—	—	—	—	—	—	—	—	—	0	0
2	—	—	—	—	0	0	0	1	1	1	1	2	2	2	3	3	3	4	4	4
	—	—	—	—	—	—	—	**0**	**0**	**0**	**0**	**1**	**1**	**1**	**1**	**1**	**2**	**2**	**2**	**2**
3	—	—	0	0	1	2	2	3	3	4	5	5	6	7	7	8	9	9	10	11
	—	—	—	—	**0**	**1**	**1**	**2**	**2**	**3**	**3**	**4**	**4**	**5**	**5**	**6**	**6**	**7**	**7**	**8**
4	—	—	0	1	2	3	4	5	6	7	8	9	10	11	12	14	15	16	17	18
	—	—	—	**0**	**1**	**2**	**3**	**4**	**4**	**5**	**6**	**7**	**8**	**9**	**10**	**11**	**11**	**12**	**13**	**13**
5	—	0	1	2	4	5	6	8	9	11	12	13	15	16	18	19	20	22	23	25
	—	—	**0**	**1**	**2**	**3**	**5**	**6**	**7**	**8**	**9**	**11**	**12**	**13**	**14**	**15**	**17**	**18**	**19**	**20**
6	—	0	2	3	5	7	8	10	12	14	16	17	19	21	23	25	26	28	30	32
	—	—	**1**	**2**	**3**	**5**	**6**	**8**	**10**	**11**	**13**	**14**	**16**	**17**	**19**	**21**	**22**	**24**	**25**	**27**
7	—	0	2	4	6	8	11	13	15	17	19	21	24	26	28	30	33	35	37	39
	—	—	**1**	**3**	**5**	**6**	**8**	**10**	**12**	**14**	**16**	**18**	**20**	**22**	**24**	**26**	**28**	**30**	**32**	**34**
8	—	1	3	5	8	10	13	15	18	20	23	26	28	31	33	36	39	41	44	47
	—	**0**	**2**	**4**	**6**	**8**	**10**	**13**	**15**	**17**	**19**	**22**	**24**	**26**	**29**	**31**	**34**	**36**	**38**	**41**
9	—	1	3	6	9	12	15	18	21	24	27	30	33	36	39	42	45	48	51	54
	—	**0**	**2**	**4**	**7**	**10**	**12**	**15**	**17**	**20**	**23**	**26**	**28**	**31**	**34**	**37**	**39**	**42**	**45**	**48**
10	—	1	4	7	11	14	17	20	24	27	31	34	37	41	44	48	51	55	58	62
	—	**0**	**3**	**5**	**8**	**11**	**14**	**17**	**20**	**23**	**26**	**29**	**33**	**36**	**39**	**42**	**45**	**48**	**52**	**55**
11	—	1	5	8	12	16	19	23	27	31	34	38	42	46	50	54	57	61	65	69
	—	**0**	**3**	**6**	**9**	**13**	**16**	**19**	**23**	**26**	**30**	**33**	**37**	**40**	**44**	**47**	**51**	**55**	**58**	**62**
12	—	2	5	9	13	17	21	26	30	34	38	42	47	51	55	60	64	68	72	77
	—	**1**	**4**	**7**	**11**	**14**	**18**	**22**	**26**	**29**	**33**	**37**	**41**	**45**	**49**	**53**	**57**	**61**	**65**	**69**
13	—	2	6	10	15	19	24	28	33	37	42	47	51	56	61	65	70	75	80	84
	—	**1**	**4**	**8**	**12**	**16**	**20**	**24**	**28**	**33**	**37**	**41**	**45**	**50**	**54**	**59**	**63**	**67**	**72**	**76**
14	—	2	7	11	16	21	26	31	36	41	46	51	56	61	66	71	77	82	87	92
	—	**1**	**5**	**9**	**13**	**17**	**22**	**26**	**31**	**36**	**40**	**45**	**50**	**55**	**59**	**64**	**67**	**74**	**78**	**83**
15	—	3	7	12	18	23	28	33	39	44	50	55	61	66	72	77	83	88	94	100
	—	**1**	**5**	**10**	**14**	**19**	**24**	**29**	**34**	**39**	**44**	**49**	**54**	**59**	**64**	**70**	**75**	**80**	**85**	**90**
16	—	3	8	14	19	25	30	36	42	48	54	60	65	71	77	83	89	95	101	107
	—	**1**	**6**	**11**	**15**	**21**	**26**	**31**	**37**	**42**	**47**	**53**	**59**	**64**	**70**	**75**	**81**	**86**	**92**	**98**
17	—	3	9	15	20	26	33	39	45	51	57	64	70	77	83	89	96	102	109	115
	—	**2**	**6**	**11**	**17**	**22**	**28**	**34**	**39**	**45**	**51**	**57**	**63**	**67**	**75**	**81**	**87**	**93**	**99**	**105**
18	—	4	9	16	22	28	35	41	48	55	61	68	75	82	88	95	102	109	116	123
	—	**2**	**7**	**12**	**18**	**24**	**30**	**36**	**42**	**48**	**55**	**61**	**67**	**74**	**80**	**86**	**93**	**99**	**106**	**112**
19	0	4	10	17	23	30	37	44	51	58	65	72	80	87	94	101	109	116	123	130
	—	**2**	**7**	**13**	**19**	**25**	**32**	**38**	**45**	**52**	**58**	**65**	**72**	**78**	**85**	**92**	**99**	**106**	**113**	**119**
20	0	4	11	18	25	32	39	47	54	62	69	77	84	92	100	107	115	123	130	138
	—	**2**	**8**	**13**	**20**	**27**	**34**	**41**	**48**	**55**	**62**	**69**	**76**	**83**	**90**	**98**	**105**	**112**	**119**	**127**

From Kirk, R., *Introductory Statistics*, pp. 423–424. Copyright © 1978 by Wadsworth, Inc. Reprinted by permission of Brooks/Cole Publishing Company, Monterey, California 93940.

Table B.10
Critical Values for a Two-tailed Runs Test with $\alpha = .05$

n_1 \ n_2	5	6	7	8	9	10	11	12	13	14	15
2	*	*	*	*	*	*	*	2, 6	2, 6	2, 6	2, 6
3	*	2, 8	2, 8	2, 8	2, 8	2, 8	2, 8	2, 8	2, 8	2, 8	3, 8
4	2, 9	2, 9	2, 10	3, 10	3, 10	3, 10	3, 10	3, 10	3, 10	3, 10	3, 10
5	2, 10	3, 10	3, 11	3, 11	3, 12	3, 12	4, 12	4, 12	4, 12	4, 12	4, 12
6	3, 10	3, 11	3, 12	3, 12	4, 13	4, 13	4, 13	4, 13	5, 14	5, 14	5, 14
7	3, 11	3, 12	3, 13	4, 13	4, 14	5, 14	5, 14	5, 14	5, 15	5, 15	6, 15
8	3, 11	3, 12	4, 13	4, 14	5, 14	5, 15	5, 15	6, 16	6, 16	6, 16	6, 16
9	3, 12	4, 13	4, 14	5, 14	5, 15	5, 16	6, 16	6, 16	6, 17	7, 17	7, 18
10	3, 12	4, 13	5, 14	5, 15	5, 16	6, 16	6, 17	7, 17	7, 18	7, 18	7, 18
11	4, 12	4, 13	5, 14	5, 15	6, 16	6, 17	7, 17	7, 18	7, 19	8, 19	8, 19
12	4, 12	4, 13	5, 14	6, 16	6, 16	7, 17	7, 18	7, 19	8, 19	8, 20	8, 20
13	4, 12	5, 14	5, 15	6, 16	6, 17	7, 18	7, 19	8, 19	8, 20	9, 20	9, 21
14	4, 12	5, 14	5, 15	6, 16	7, 17	7, 18	8, 19	8, 20	9, 20	9, 21	9, 22
15	4, 12	5, 14	6, 15	6, 16	7, 18	7, 18	8, 19	8, 20	9, 21	9, 22	10, 22

From Owen, D. B., *Handbook of Statistical Tables,* Reading, Mass.: Addison-Wesley, 1962, as adapted in Weiss, N., and M. Hassett, *Introductory Statistics,* Reading, Mass.: Addison-Wesley, 1982, p. 594. Reprinted with permission.

Description of the Data

Below is a description of the Framingham Heart Study data which is displayed in the table that starts on page A-28.

Framingham Heart Study Data

Column	Name	Description of Variable
1	ID	I.D. number 0001 to 1000
2	GEN	Sex 1 Male 2 Female
3	AGE	Age 30–64 years
4	SBP	Systolic Blood Pressure 082–300 mm. 9999–systolic blood pressure unknown
5	DBP	Diastolic Blood Pressure 020–148 mm. 9999–diastolic blood pressure unknown
6	CHL	Total Serum Cholesterol 115–568 mg/100 ml. 9999–total serum cholesterol unknown
7	CHD	First evidence of coronary heart disease (CHD) 0 No evidence of CHD 1 Pre-existing CHD at time of entry to study 2–10 Exam at which CHD was first diagnosed
8	CIG	Number of cigarettes smoked per day 9999–number unknown

Table B.11
Framingham Heart Study Data

I D	G E N	A G E	S B P	D B P	C H L	C H D	C I G	I D	G E N	A G E	S B P	D B P	C H L	C H D	C I G
0001	2	59	170	98	250	0	10	0055	2	42	115	75	186	0	20
0002	1	35	150	96	188	0	0	0056	1	39	121	82	196	0	0
0003	1	46	136	88	292	0	30	0057	1	52	118	82	292	0	40
0004	2	43	96	54	194	0	0	0058	1	49	164	114	255	0	0
0005	1	53	120	80	223	0	20	0059	2	40	120	70	213	0	15
0006	1	50	110	84	292	0	30	0060	2	52	130	76	275	0	20
0007	1	33	130	80	186	0	30	0061	1	41	124	90	221	0	0
0008	1	57	145	95	242	10	15	0062	1	50	134	78	242	0	20
0009	2	41	132	90	161	0	0	0063	2	44	120	80	198	0	0
0010	2	40	112	84	226	0	0	0064	2	36	140	80	209	0	0
0011	1	54	140	90	246	0	0	0065	2	35	115	85	180	0	15
0012	1	53	148	84	225	1	5	0066	1	56	128	84	179	0	0
0013	2	53	165	90	230	0	0	0067	2	49	152	87	284	0	0
0014	1	49	100	64	167	0	0	0068	1	52	156	100	173	0	5
0015	2	61	156	94	246	10	0	0069	1	36	126	90	209	8	20
0016	2	49	170	84	305	7	0	0070	1	42	110	70	188	0	25
0017	1	32	155	80	159	0	30	0071	1	43	130	80	242	0	20
0018	2	54	162	80	339	0	0	0072	1	54	140	90	301	5	0
0019	2	33	110	80	163	0	0	0073	2	41	118	80	225	0	5
0020	2	41	145	95	242	0	15	0074	2	48	126	72	200	0	10
0021	1	56	134	94	292	9	0	0075	2	38	118	70	180	0	0
0022	2	36	104	65	165	0	0	0076	2	47	136	80	230	0	0
0023	1	56	126	82	267	2	10	0077	2	37	110	75	163	0	1
0024	2	40	100	74	265	0	5	0078	2	50	152	80	200	0	0
0025	2	37	116	78	233	0	15	0079	1	41	136	84	242	0	40
0026	1	38	132	100	167	0	0	0080	2	47	118	80	330	0	25
0027	2	46	132	84	234	0	5	0081	1	55	144	82	220	0	20
0028	1	38	124	84	228	0	0	0082	2	40	110	70	248	0	20
0029	2	36	144	104	242	0	0	0083	1	40	102	58	229	0	20
0030	2	48	154	88	221	0	0	0084	2	43	138	92	200	0	15
0031	2	50	110	80	288	0	0	0085	2	55	170	94	268	0	20
0032	2	45	110	70	188	0	0	0086	2	35	130	84	175	0	0
0033	1	53	142	92	196	0	25	0087	2	34	175	100	263	0	15
0034	2	44	114	80	188	0	10	0088	1	32	142	96	173	0	0
0035	1	50	120	80	221	3	40	0089	1	52	128	84	250	7	15
0036	2	42	180	108	211	0	0	0090	2	59	118	82	276	0	0
0037	1	48	135	85	234	5	0	0091	2	46	138	86	278	0	0
0038	2	47	158	100	225	0	0	0092	2	41	125	75	246	0	0
0039	2	48	220	130	276	0	0	0093	2	57	154	78	334	10	0
0040	2	33	108	70	196	0	0	0094	2	56	128	70	292	0	0
0041	1	44	136	106	205	0	0	0095	2	42	122	88	238	0	10
0042	1	57	124	88	188	0	0	0096	1	36	108	70	234	0	20
0043	2	51	172	108	217	2	0	0097	2	42	128	82	167	10	0
0044	2	53	110	70	307	0	0	0098	1	43	124	86	250	0	20
0045	2	44	128	80	250	0	0	0099	2	54	115	80	296	6	5
0046	1	42	160	100	205	0	20	0100	2	41	130	85	219	0	0
0047	2	52	154	90	184	5	0	0101	1	49	130	80	198	0	30
0048	1	45	135	95	228	7	0	0102	2	42	134	80	234	0	15
0049	2	35	110	70	159	0	0	0103	2	59	180	98	173	5	0
0050	1	43	136	96	221	0	0	0104	1	51	130	100	221	0	40
0051	1	33	128	92	200	0	20	0105	1	46	110	68	199	0	0
0052	2	61	195	125	301	8	0	0106	2	44	130	86	217	0	0
0053	1	49	142	90	255	0	15	0107	2	48	122	80	315	0	0
0054	2	39	138	72	199	0	0	0108	2	50	140	90	276	0	0

Table B.11 (Continued)

ID	GEN	AGE	SBP	DBP	CHL	CHD	CIG	ID	GEN	AGE	SBP	DBP	CHL	CHD	CIG
0109	2	43	145	92	224	0	0	0163	2	44	122	70	284	0	20
0110	2	41	126	80	184	0	5	0164	2	59	144	82	228	0	0
0111	2	52	224	142	213	0	0	0165	2	38	120	85	181	0	20
0112	2	59	136	76	321	0	0	0166	1	41	130	85	225	0	20
0113	2	42	132	80	200	0	5	0167	2	54	155	85	223	0	0
0114	1	38	136	96	250	7	40	0168	1	52	135	95	188	0	0
0115	2	45	149	90	230	0	0	0169	2	42	160	110	275	0	0
0116	2	44	100	70	242	0	5	0170	2	57	140	80	234	0	0
0117	1	37	114	66	209	8	15	0171	1	46	132	84	209	0	0
0118	1	50	152	98	265	3	40	0172	2	32	126	66	184	0	0
0119	1	47	142	74	234	0	20	0173	1	51	200	102	271	7	25
0120	2	51	135	90	238	0	1	0174	2	36	120	72	238	0	15
0121	1	34	146	96	326	0	20	0175	2	43	124	68	209	0	15
0122	2	48	154	114	263	0	5	0176	2	55	136	84	209	0	5
0123	1	38	160	96	284	9	20	0177	2	47	186	102	223	0	10
0124	2	62	162	96	255	0	0	0178	1	56	165	110	211	0	0
0125	2	47	128	90	238	0	0	0179	1	42	148	78	228	0	0
0126	1	46	126	76	238	0	10	0180	1	51	112	70	178	0	30
0127	2	38	112	68	209	0	15	0181	2	60	118	70	263	0	0
0128	1	47	140	100	196	0	0	0182	2	47	126	84	301	0	0
0129	1	34	134	90	176	0	0	0183	2	51	112	78	250	0	0
0130	1	41	110	68	184	0	0	0184	2	49	164	88	317	0	0
0131	1	50	180	98	255	0	40	0185	2	43	124	84	200	0	0
0132	1	50	192	100	233	0	5	0186	2	46	154	88	209	0	0
0133	2	53	126	74	234	0	0	0187	1	59	130	90	250	0	5
0134	1	41	130	70	221	0	0	0188	1	39	128	84	178	0	0
0135	1	61	108	74	255	0	0	0189	1	55	140	82	150	0	20
0136	2	50	126	80	213	3	0	0190	1	42	126	88	255	0	30
0137	1	44	118	84	186	0	0	0191	2	55	142	84	182	0	0
0138	1	46	122	68	267	0	5	0192	2	44	174	82	200	0	20
0139	1	47	142	90	200	0	0	0193	1	60	130	80	196	1	20
0140	1	61	124	84	221	0	0	0194	2	48	146	87	248	0	0
0141	2	37	140	80	234	0	5	0195	2	47	166	98	276	0	0
0142	1	45	144	96	209	0	20	0196	1	52	132	93	213	0	20
0143	1	38	106	72	150	0	0	0197	2	40	155	96	225	0	20
0144	2	54	136	82	225	0	5	0198	2	47	112	76	225	0	0
0145	2	52	108	68	250	0	0	0199	2	49	146	84	246	0	0
0146	1	43	144	84	167	0	5	0200	1	54	128	70	196	1	0
0147	2	54	124	84	255	0	0	0201	1	52	142	80	225	8	25
0148	2	53	135	80	246	0	20	0202	1	37	125	75	292	0	0
0149	1	60	140	85	171	1	20	0203	1	37	130	90	282	0	0
0150	2	44	178	100	263	0	0	0204	2	43	146	89	171	0	20
0151	2	32	108	70	138	0	5	0205	2	49	130	85	305	0	5
0152	2	39	132	84	228	0	0	0206	2	40	154	96	255	0	25
0153	2	58	152	100	317	0	0	0207	2	50	130	76	9999	0	0
0154	2	37	148	90	309	0	20	0208	2	44	116	68	178	0	0
0155	2	33	102	74	209	0	20	0209	2	51	138	82	267	0	0
0156	2	52	142	86	267	0	0	0210	2	32	122	82	200	0	20
0157	2	56	125	85	246	0	0	0211	1	48	120	76	221	0	20
0158	2	43	108	72	184	0	0	0212	1	33	110	74	161	0	0
0159	1	41	130	88	250	2	0	0213	1	53	148	96	194	0	30
0160	1	39	148	90	209	0	5	0214	2	47	192	108	238	8	0
0161	1	46	132	90	255	0	0	0215	2	41	118	74	246	0	5
0162	1	42	120	75	171	0	0	0216	1	47	142	100	250	0	0

Table B.11 (Continued)

I D	G E N	A G E	S B P	D B P	C H L	C H D	C I G	I D	G E N	A G E	S B P	D B P	C H L	C H D	C I G
0217	2	55	166	108	196	0	0	0271	2	32	144	84	173	0	0
0218	1	54	195	112	192	3	0	0272	1	58	130	78	228	5	20
0219	2	48	142	82	167	0	0	0273	1	50	150	100	232	0	0
0220	1	54	127	80	199	6	0	0274	2	49	136	80	200	0	0
0221	1	34	136	90	192	0	20	0275	1	57	154	92	209	10	20
0222	2	57	152	96	221	0	0	0276	1	37	134	70	171	0	0
0223	1	49	170	110	243	5	0	0277	1	54	138	76	255	0	25
0224	2	49	136	76	198	0	0	0278	2	40	128	80	200	0	0
0225	2	56	124	64	209	0	0	0279	2	38	112	78	9999	0	30
0226	1	59	144	90	259	0	0	0280	2	50	146	88	271	9	0
0227	2	38	130	88	263	0	0	0281	1	31	132	89	248	0	20
0228	2	36	114	72	236	0	10	0282	1	39	110	80	173	0	0
0229	2	35	132	82	9999	0	0	0283	2	47	160	94	233	0	0
0230	2	36	128	84	179	0	5	0284	2	56	172	94	276	0	1
0231	1	58	110	68	234	0	20	0285	2	45	130	88	180	0	1
0232	1	57	137	78	242	0	0	0286	2	37	122	66	192	0	5
0233	1	51	140	82	300	0	5	0287	2	47	126	68	217	0	30
0234	1	60	137	88	9999	0	20	0288	2	32	108	76	150	0	5
0235	1	34	142	78	233	0	0	0289	1	32	122	84	253	0	20
0236	2	60	144	89	334	0	0	0290	1	42	212	110	182	0	50
0237	2	55	108	64	292	0	0	0291	2	55	138	84	267	0	0
0238	2	51	118	76	179	9	0	0292	1	50	146	98	224	0	0
0239	1	60	130	80	238	0	0	0293	2	44	96	56	205	0	25
0240	2	60	124	70	296	5	0	0294	2	54	156	78	317	0	20
0241	2	43	100	64	242	0	10	0295	1	48	162	96	238	0	0
0242	1	41	146	100	180	0	5	0296	2	40	120	78	292	0	20
0243	1	50	130	72	242	0	40	0297	2	33	104	70	194	0	10
0244	2	61	190	108	376	8	0	0298	1	47	150	102	259	0	0
0245	1	56	200	140	238	0	20	0299	1	41	123	78	167	0	0
0246	2	47	130	94	326	3	0	0300	1	56	164	108	196	1	0
0247	2	58	160	94	323	0	0	0301	2	60	128	76	216	0	0
0248	2	36	104	54	163	0	1	0302	2	44	124	80	280	0	1
0249	2	39	128	78	209	0	5	0303	2	43	150	108	200	0	10
0250	2	60	152	88	255	0	5	0304	1	46	122	84	196	0	0
0251	1	44	112	84	250	0	5	0305	1	46	142	88	184	9	20
0252	2	49	132	84	356	0	0	0306	2	57	132	80	288	6	0
0253	1	33	122	78	234	0	5	0307	1	50	134	84	259	0	0
0254	1	51	138	76	238	0	0	0308	2	53	132	84	243	0	5
0255	2	50	136	94	223	0	5	0309	2	44	124	84	196	0	0
0256	2	34	102	66	209	0	20	0310	2	46	124	86	200	0	0
0257	2	45	130	80	238	0	20	0311	1	36	130	94	217	0	0
0258	2	51	154	90	227	0	0	0312	2	57	216	120	255	3	0
0259	1	48	108	68	173	0	0	0313	2	33	104	62	148	0	0
0260	1	52	114	80	179	0	20	0314	2	47	158	96	219	0	0
0261	2	54	178	92	301	0	0	0315	1	51	124	78	192	0	0
0262	2	51	112	88	188	0	0	0316	2	44	104	66	171	6	0
0263	2	58	144	66	342	0	15	0317	1	54	132	82	236	0	0
0264	1	51	128	78	230	0	0	0318	1	35	158	86	271	0	20
0265	2	35	130	80	302	0	15	0319	1	54	130	75	244	2	20
0266	2	31	124	74	192	0	0	0320	2	59	146	78	315	0	0
0267	1	45	130	88	246	0	35	0321	2	36	134	68	175	0	20
0268	1	53	135	78	217	6	15	0322	1	44	102	80	207	9	30
0269	2	56	164	106	267	0	1	0323	2	38	106	68	175	0	0
0270	2	37	116	74	180	0	15	0324	2	46	120	80	209	0	15

Table B.11 (Continued)

ID	GEN	AGE	SBP	DBP	CHL	CHD	CIG	ID	GEN	AGE	SBP	DBP	CHL	CHD	CIG
0325	2	46	120	76	292	0	5	0379	1	55	160	100	267	1	5
0326	2	34	120	80	224	0	25	0380	1	37	112	68	210	0	20
0327	2	45	160	120	274	0	20	0381	2	44	112	56	222	0	20
0328	2	42	140	88	186	0	0	0382	2	32	110	70	232	0	15
0329	1	59	140	90	252	0	20	0383	2	32	118	88	184	0	0
0330	1	44	116	74	209	0	15	0384	1	33	138	90	204	0	20
0331	2	56	130	80	278	0	1	0385	1	48	154	96	192	0	0
0332	2	44	128	84	188	0	0	0386	1	34	134	78	217	0	0
0333	2	58	152	94	192	0	0	0387	1	53	104	70	250	0	20
0334	1	53	208	108	173	0	0	0388	2	47	190	104	317	0	20
0335	1	41	116	88	230	0	20	0389	2	41	126	100	242	0	0
0336	1	56	134	72	250	0	0	0390	1	45	142	90	294	0	0
0337	2	54	114	74	310	0	5	0391	2	61	158	94	258	0	0
0338	2	35	142	90	203	0	0	0392	2	41	104	70	234	0	0
0339	1	35	134	90	250	0	0	0393	2	36	114	78	277	0	0
0340	2	44	176	90	288	0	0	0394	2	39	138	100	250	0	0
0341	2	61	138	94	9999	0	0	0395	1	46	108	72	238	0	0
0342	2	34	120	78	173	0	1	0396	1	58	134	82	228	0	1
0343	1	35	170	100	217	0	20	0397	1	36	148	100	234	0	30
0344	1	52	186	114	226	0	30	0398	2	33	96	70	200	0	5
0345	1	36	124	86	196	0	0	0399	1	42	144	90	250	0	5
0346	1	48	152	78	204	0	40	0400	1	39	142	96	209	0	5
0347	2	36	128	70	307	0	15	0401	2	54	132	86	288	0	0
0348	2	44	270	148	209	0	0	0402	2	54	214	104	204	0	0
0349	2	44	130	78	236	0	10	0403	2	32	124	80	217	0	0
0350	2	34	108	54	192	0	0	0404	2	57	154	78	216	0	0
0351	2	54	164	96	267	0	0	0405	1	54	140	92	219	0	10
0352	2	34	128	74	184	0	0	0406	1	56	155	90	228	0	20
0353	2	35	128	78	207	0	1	0407	2	43	120	72	271	0	0
0354	2	32	116	70	242	0	20	0408	2	62	164	82	227	0	0
0355	1	37	134	70	255	0	0	0409	1	42	154	90	267	4	20
0356	1	46	142	96	234	0	0	0410	2	48	140	76	271	0	0
0357	2	41	132	76	243	0	20	0411	1	59	110	66	162	4	15
0358	2	45	142	70	255	0	0	0412	2	42	140	80	180	0	0
0359	2	51	225	95	227	10	0	0413	2	53	146	80	184	0	0
0360	2	59	126	84	250	0	0	0414	2	53	136	88	267	0	20
0361	1	34	126	94	238	6	25	0415	2	44	178	100	238	0	0
0362	2	52	130	80	190	0	0	0416	1	53	140	102	256	7	25
0363	2	46	142	76	236	0	5	0417	1	55	126	60	259	0	10
0364	2	57	180	104	198	0	0	0418	2	47	120	85	209	0	0
0365	2	39	148	90	154	0	0	0419	1	34	148	88	250	0	40
0366	1	32	138	82	250	0	0	0420	2	55	144	90	233	0	0
0367	1	42	184	118	492	5	15	0421	1	54	210	130	184	0	20
0368	1	49	134	88	245	5	25	0422	2	41	108	74	234	0	0
0369	1	49	120	74	184	7	15	0423	1	55	132	86	209	3	60
0370	2	50	122	72	184	0	0	0424	2	60	148	80	242	0	0
0371	2	46	146	94	278	9	0	0425	2	38	112	68	167	0	5
0372	1	56	148	94	209	0	0	0426	2	38	110	70	229	0	40
0373	2	43	112	74	129	0	0	0427	1	35	116	70	227	0	0
0374	1	32	144	98	243	0	5	0428	2	44	100	62	280	0	0
0375	1	32	136	76	196	10	0	0429	2	44	112	70	204	0	0
0376	2	51	140	90	256	0	20	0430	2	42	118	72	150	0	0
0377	2	61	112	68	200	6	0	0431	1	46	118	70	242	4	20
0378	1	34	106	74	234	0	15	0432	2	58	130	80	175	0	0

Table B.11 (Continued)

I D	G E N	A G E	S B P	D B P	C H L	C H D	C I G	I D	G E N	A G E	S B P	D B P	C H L	C H D	C I G
0433	2	55	208	104	198	0	0	0487	1	59	118	84	292	0	0
0434	2	46	108	72	200	0	5	0488	1	49	122	74	271	0	35
0435	2	32	120	78	215	0	0	0489	2	54	130	80	322	0	0
0436	1	39	126	88	234	0	30	0490	1	42	136	90	197	0	25
0437	1	47	117	70	239	0	0	0491	1	38	122	84	159	0	0
0438	2	51	134	84	263	0	0	0492	2	51	142	110	205	0	5
0439	2	45	135	78	259	0	0	0493	1	40	114	76	194	0	0
0440	1	52	145	105	248	0	0	0494	2	49	112	74	184	0	0
0441	1	40	112	82	258	5	30	0495	2	40	144	86	479	5	0
0442	1	47	160	58	263	0	40	0496	2	45	136	92	197	0	10
0443	1	33	124	82	161	0	40	0497	2	38	134	84	213	0	5
0444	1	35	118	80	221	0	20	0498	1	45	126	88	317	0	15
0445	1	36	134	82	179	0	15	0499	2	42	126	82	184	0	0
0446	1	50	144	94	9999	4	30	0500	1	52	160	94	228	0	0
0447	1	41	106	64	234	0	20	0501	2	50	150	90	250	0	0
0448	2	37	124	84	221	0	15	0502	1	48	132	80	233	0	20
0449	2	60	186	124	219	8	0	0503	2	57	174	80	238	5	0
0450	1	47	142	94	242	3	20	0504	2	46	90	62	196	0	0
0451	2	49	124	80	209	0	15	0505	2	54	134	96	317	0	0
0452	1	50	120	80	217	0	0	0506	1	36	118	72	196	0	25
0453	1	42	112	82	154	0	20	0507	2	45	118	66	219	0	5
0454	1	46	112	80	204	5	20	0508	1	52	96	68	200	0	20
0455	2	35	104	80	221	0	0	0509	2	57	136	80	201	0	0
0456	2	37	134	80	234	0	0	0510	1	32	154	100	175	0	0
0457	2	39	140	95	200	0	0	0511	2	48	110	70	9999	0	0
0458	1	57	166	90	304	0	0	0512	1	45	112	76	200	0	1
0459	1	56	142	70	204	0	15	0513	1	48	120	90	242	6	5
0460	2	46	122	82	209	5	0	0514	2	37	108	72	234	0	0
0461	1	59	188	108	219	0	0	0515	1	42	112	78	233	0	10
0462	2	44	116	70	267	0	1	0516	1	36	136	100	363	0	0
0463	2	41	155	90	200	0	0	0517	2	41	120	80	258	0	0
0464	1	56	142	90	219	0	0	0518	2	60	132	80	288	0	5
0465	2	36	136	72	196	0	5	0519	2	47	122	76	192	0	0
0466	1	42	112	70	163	0	20	0520	2	49	134	84	276	0	10
0467	2	60	192	110	228	0	0	0521	2	61	136	86	276	0	0
0468	2	48	154	84	271	0	0	0522	2	35	110	68	185	0	0
0469	2	44	114	76	200	0	15	0523	2	33	122	66	221	0	20
0470	1	44	164	122	235	0	0	0524	1	47	108	68	204	0	20
0471	2	61	132	80	234	1	1	0525	2	45	118	68	146	0	0
0472	2	47	158	94	296	0	0	0526	2	48	112	80	200	0	0
0473	1	61	156	94	255	0	0	0527	1	36	152	78	195	0	25
0474	2	56	158	90	278	0	5	0528	2	52	116	80	9999	4	10
0475	2	63	152	102	219	0	0	0529	2	37	126	84	167	0	10
0476	1	32	104	74	226	0	40	0530	1	34	112	74	209	0	25
0477	2	53	144	80	304	0	0	0531	2	39	108	64	194	0	0
0478	1	41	140	90	276	7	20	0532	1	55	112	76	197	0	25
0479	2	43	102	52	226	0	15	0533	1	43	126	80	277	0	0
0480	2	40	114	54	309	0	20	0534	1	40	112	76	252	0	20
0481	1	41	132	92	242	0	0	0535	2	54	145	90	267	0	0
0482	2	47	172	114	234	0	0	0536	2	62	134	82	306	0	0
0483	1	58	138	84	192	0	20	0537	2	39	142	80	228	0	15
0484	1	38	120	92	217	0	20	0538	2	54	118	76	219	0	0
0485	2	49	114	70	209	0	0	0539	1	44	108	80	194	0	40
0486	2	51	104	68	210	0	0	0540	1	53	138	88	213	0	20

Table B.11 (Continued)

I D	G E N	A G E	S B P	D B P	C H L	C H D	C I G	I D	G E N	A G E	S B P	D B P	C H L	C H D	C I G
0541	2	44	170	108	255	0	0	0595	2	47	148	88	308	0	20
0542	2	38	110	72	179	0	5	0596	2	50	140	90	282	0	20
0543	1	38	125	75	243	0	20	0597	1	40	134	84	309	0	40
0544	2	51	146	80	238	0	0	0598	2	45	174	98	330	0	20
0545	1	33	118	85	162	0	20	0599	1	44	130	85	310	0	20
0546	1	37	150	92	234	0	50	0600	1	43	116	74	229	0	40
0547	2	40	120	80	188	0	20	0601	1	48	122	78	292	0	20
0548	2	45	110	70	260	0	10	0602	2	35	100	70	9999	0	10
0549	2	44	124	78	217	0	15	0603	2	40	176	110	213	0	0
0550	2	56	122	86	368	0	0	0604	2	38	120	82	197	0	0
0551	2	41	112	78	209	0	0	0605	2	36	110	78	197	0	5
0552	1	45	154	90	359	0	15	0606	1	47	120	74	274	0	25
0553	1	57	134	92	217	0	0	0607	2	57	118	75	244	0	5
0554	2	53	114	90	234	0	1	0608	2	46	118	70	157	0	20
0555	2	44	148	78	194	0	20	0609	2	44	118	80	203	0	0
0556	1	34	120	75	284	0	40	0610	1	62	144	80	220	0	0
0557	2	44	115	75	259	0	5	0611	2	54	130	80	221	0	0
0558	1	34	122	84	205	0	0	0612	2	34	110	78	255	0	5
0559	1	44	130	95	216	10	0	0613	2	33	122	66	244	0	0
0560	2	61	148	90	277	0	5	0614	2	50	110	60	234	0	25
0561	1	46	116	78	244	0	30	0615	2	34	105	65	241	0	0
0562	2	58	146	74	338	0	0	0616	2	37	110	60	9999	0	20
0563	2	51	175	105	320	0	0	0617	2	59	172	94	225	0	0
0564	2	60	134	80	260	0	0	0618	2	34	126	82	155	0	5
0565	1	54	150	100	175	4	0	0619	2	55	152	90	9999	0	0
0566	1	55	110	70	171	0	30	0620	2	37	110	70	190	0	0
0567	1	49	124	66	214	0	40	0621	2	34	112	64	200	9	0
0568	1	58	120	70	242	0	0	0622	2	37	102	68	170	0	1
0569	1	43	160	105	242	0	0	0623	1	36	118	84	183	0	15
0570	1	36	115	60	234	8	30	0624	2	41	108	72	209	0	15
0571	1	45	148	90	296	0	0	0625	1	34	138	94	328	4	30
0572	1	54	135	80	284	0	0	0626	1	50	138	94	250	4	30
0573	2	50	140	80	255	0	0	0627	1	49	112	68	244	0	0
0574	2	48	166	110	238	0	20	0628	1	35	135	95	210	0	20
0575	1	38	120	80	244	0	20	0629	2	42	122	78	221	0	0
0576	2	59	152	84	278	8	1	0630	1	34	134	90	177	0	0
0577	1	47	150	100	248	0	0	0631	2	53	280	130	308	1	20
0578	1	37	142	82	258	0	40	0632	2	38	110	76	182	0	0
0579	1	36	120	70	190	0	20	0633	1	55	132	82	289	1	0
0580	2	38	98	72	200	0	20	0634	2	32	118	80	175	0	20
0581	2	39	116	74	199	0	0	0635	2	63	128	70	308	0	0
0582	2	45	184	88	213	0	15	0636	2	36	124	86	267	0	0
0583	2	56	132	70	267	0	15	0637	2	42	112	80	234	0	0
0584	1	52	114	76	192	0	0	0638	1	42	136	92	214	0	20
0585	2	47	114	88	209	0	20	0639	2	62	170	98	425	1	0
0586	2	49	128	92	326	0	5	0640	1	47	160	85	209	0	20
0587	2	48	150	95	225	0	5	0641	2	46	152	102	243	0	0
0588	2	43	140	80	223	0	0	0642	2	60	140	82	368	0	0
0589	2	34	125	85	208	0	0	0643	1	37	108	74	213	0	30
0590	2	57	126	64	309	0	0	0644	1	52	130	90	192	0	0
0591	1	56	114	74	204	0	20	0645	1	56	138	70	267	0	20
0592	2	33	108	60	134	0	0	0646	2	39	108	84	213	0	0
0593	2	44	110	70	247	0	20	0647	1	36	112	76	195	0	0
0594	1	40	125	80	233	10	25	0648	1	39	138	94	244	0	20

Table B.11 (Continued)

I D	G E N	A G E	S B P	D B P	C H L	C H D	C I G	I D	G E N	A G E	S B P	D B P	C H L	C H D	C I G
0649	2	37	112	74	155	0	20	0703	1	60	115	78	280	0	1
0650	2	54	228	144	246	7	0	0704	1	45	134	94	244	0	20
0651	2	35	112	70	169	0	0	0705	2	39	106	76	196	0	20
0652	2	40	105	65	221	0	0	0706	2	41	112	74	233	0	20
0653	1	38	132	98	167	0	30	0707	2	33	118	72	201	0	15
0654	2	60	152	96	206	0	0	0708	2	47	110	75	219	0	0
0655	1	33	128	96	150	0	0	0709	1	63	158	92	9999	5	10
0656	2	36	124	80	183	0	0	0710	2	37	120	82	231	0	0
0657	2	33	95	50	180	0	0	0711	1	56	128	78	238	10	0
0658	1	36	140	86	195	0	0	0712	2	56	140	82	177	0	5
0659	1	40	138	100	248	0	0	0713	2	37	132	84	221	0	20
0660	1	36	118	70	170	0	20	0714	2	38	145	85	219	0	20
0661	2	50	118	80	180	0	0	0715	1	38	148	98	221	0	30
0662	1	33	105	65	206	0	10	0716	1	50	110	78	240	0	0
0663	2	50	135	90	245	6	0	0717	2	52	132	82	197	0	0
0664	1	36	135	85	301	6	50	0718	2	49	156	90	142	0	5
0665	1	55	186	114	250	1	10	0719	1	61	135	80	350	4	0
0666	2	38	158	100	169	0	0	0720	1	39	130	80	237	0	20
0667	1	47	135	85	263	4	40	0721	1	54	162	84	219	0	5
0668	2	51	174	80	197	4	0	0722	2	59	138	80	296	0	0
0669	2	36	108	68	153	0	0	0723	2	47	145	93	292	0	0
0670	1	60	174	102	242	0	0	0724	1	48	108	68	270	0	30
0671	2	39	138	80	167	0	20	0725	2	50	108	66	334	0	20
0672	2	42	105	65	169	0	0	0726	1	46	118	80	150	0	25
0673	1	35	146	100	242	0	0	0727	2	53	136	88	252	0	0
0674	1	49	180	112	223	5	10	0728	1	38	132	70	268	1	20
0675	1	55	130	88	240	0	20	0729	2	37	106	68	167	0	0
0676	2	61	104	65	250	0	20	0730	2	46	132	82	208	0	20
0677	1	35	154	108	267	0	30	0731	1	62	186	120	245	0	20
0678	2	35	112	70	200	0	0	0732	1	59	184	128	250	0	0
0679	2	55	145	92	171	0	0	0733	1	47	130	80	213	0	0
0680	1	39	114	72	245	0	20	0734	2	36	112	80	230	0	15
0681	1	57	158	100	296	4	30	0735	2	51	176	98	245	0	0
0682	2	47	100	60	206	0	0	0736	2	33	122	78	174	0	1
0683	1	56	115	75	9999	0	0	0737	2	60	144	100	242	0	0
0684	2	62	180	108	217	0	0	0738	2	35	102	60	150	0	20
0685	2	58	240	98	272	0	0	0739	2	47	126	90	193	0	0
0686	2	56	180	102	296	8	0	0740	2	44	128	74	9999	0	0
0687	1	56	184	110	183	1	0	0741	2	54	125	80	260	0	0
0688	2	37	148	84	238	0	15	0742	1	38	135	95	221	0	15
0689	2	34	110	72	9999	0	15	0743	2	43	160	85	230	0	5
0690	2	56	108	84	259	0	0	0744	2	40	104	74	196	0	0
0691	1	47	120	85	197	0	0	0745	1	34	135	95	230	0	20
0692	1	57	146	82	209	0	20	0746	2	54	134	85	338	0	25
0693	2	35	102	56	239	0	40	0747	2	39	110	74	217	0	1
0694	2	50	126	86	245	0	0	0748	2	35	132	88	197	0	0
0695	1	39	120	80	192	0	0	0749	2	49	124	80	259	0	0
0696	2	55	175	105	277	7	10	0750	2	49	110	70	331	0	10
0697	2	50	130	65	225	0	0	0751	2	34	114	74	204	0	1
0698	1	53	150	100	217	0	0	0752	2	39	128	85	205	0	0
0699	1	42	142	84	568	8	20	0753	2	47	138	94	231	0	0
0700	1	38	130	80	184	0	20	0754	1	40	148	88	343	1	40
0701	1	47	100	60	174	0	20	0755	1	38	128	88	212	0	20
0702	1	37	112	70	277	0	0	0756	1	46	134	84	249	0	0

Table B.11 (Continued)

ID	GEN	AGE	SBP	DBP	CHL	CHD	CIG	ID	GEN	AGE	SBP	DBP	CHL	CHD	CIG
0757	2	37	118	80	153	0	5	0811	1	36	154	84	210	0	20
0758	1	36	130	80	206	0	20	0812	2	37	114	68	191	0	0
0759	1	47	100	64	9999	0	20	0813	1	36	144	96	420	0	10
0760	2	45	168	86	234	0	0	0814	1	40	145	90	184	10	0
0761	2	36	115	60	206	0	10	0815	2	36	110	70	225	0	20
0762	2	52	142	70	170	0	0	0816	1	34	122	80	151	0	0
0763	2	50	100	70	158	0	0	0817	2	34	144	92	167	0	5
0764	2	41	144	94	197	0	10	0818	1	37	115	70	220	0	20
0765	2	41	150	105	200	0	0	0819	1	53	122	74	252	0	1
0766	1	42	142	105	285	0	40	0820	2	58	155	95	274	0	0
0767	2	36	122	86	289	0	20	0821	2	38	150	82	240	0	0
0768	2	35	100	68	195	0	0	0822	2	57	144	94	290	0	0
0769	1	55	114	76	9999	0	20	0823	1	58	130	84	179	0	20
0770	2	49	140	85	211	0	20	0824	1	46	150	80	215	0	0
0771	1	45	105	80	230	0	20	0825	2	62	165	85	250	0	0
0772	2	53	195	115	260	8	40	0826	1	38	108	70	230	0	20
0773	1	36	155	100	175	0	0	0827	2	45	118	80	200	0	30
0774	2	34	110	70	170	0	0	0828	2	53	130	82	9999	0	0
0775	2	35	135	75	192	0	0	0829	1	46	110	62	249	0	0
0776	1	32	132	84	160	0	0	0830	2	47	146	86	254	10	0
0777	1	58	120	72	263	10	0	0831	1	49	115	70	283	5	25
0778	1	59	146	80	9999	8	5	0832	2	45	118	74	245	0	0
0779	2	44	100	66	9999	0	0	0833	2	43	192	110	165	10	0
0780	1	52	150	100	220	6	0	0834	2	44	172	118	9999	0	0
0781	1	39	126	86	435	0	0	0835	2	41	124	70	188	0	20
0782	1	38	130	96	204	0	0	0836	2	58	210	120	231	1	0
0783	1	57	106	72	240	0	0	0837	2	44	122	80	175	0	0
0784	1	49	115	75	290	0	5	0838	1	38	138	88	282	0	0
0785	2	56	122	78	242	0	0	0839	2	33	120	80	206	0	20
0786	2	51	120	84	295	0	10	0840	1	46	145	85	225	0	15
0787	2	60	160	86	235	7	0	0841	1	36	145	90	270	0	5
0788	1	56	135	75	276	1	0	0842	1	34	120	75	280	0	20
0789	1	51	120	64	230	0	0	0843	1	42	128	82	250	0	25
0790	2	56	126	70	324	10	20	0844	2	43	155	95	205	0	0
0791	1	58	116	70	220	0	20	0845	1	39	125	80	244	0	5
0792	2	60	168	94	233	8	0	0846	1	57	255	130	242	0	25
0793	2	57	120	58	202	0	0	0847	1	41	136	85	300	0	15
0794	2	37	110	68	233	0	10	0848	2	35	124	80	203	0	0
0795	2	53	125	75	276	0	0	0849	1	33	120	50	200	0	15
0796	1	62	145	85	190	0	0	0850	2	38	148	80	157	0	0
0797	1	46	118	68	195	7	20	0851	1	48	148	90	240	0	20
0798	2	37	134	72	206	0	0	0852	1	38	140	95	222	0	30
0799	1	53	136	92	198	0	20	0853	2	58	170	95	230	0	0
0800	2	45	114	78	245	10	0	0854	2	37	114	70	173	0	0
0801	1	64	92	58	175	0	15	0855	1	52	162	106	180	8	0
0802	1	54	144	85	283	0	20	0856	2	53	138	80	291	0	0
0803	2	56	142	74	235	0	35	0857	1	53	142	98	266	0	20
0804	1	49	150	104	224	2	20	0858	2	54	95	58	284	0	0
0805	1	36	110	60	210	0	0	0859	1	42	145	108	195	0	20
0806	1	48	112	78	185	0	0	0860	1	33	104	68	230	0	20
0807	1	43	136	88	185	3	10	0861	1	47	145	80	256	6	20
0808	2	45	116	84	230	0	0	0862	1	48	154	108	267	0	50
0809	2	42	132	88	206	0	0	0863	2	47	140	84	179	0	0
0810	2	61	158	80	223	3	0	0864	1	43	155	75	234	0	20

Table B.11 (Continued)

I D	G E N	A G E	S B P	D B P	C H L	C H D	C I G	I D	G E N	A G E	S B P	D B P	C H L	C H D	C I G
0865	2	40	130	78	163	0	5	0919	2	53	134	82	275	9	0
0866	2	47	128	82	346	0	0	0920	1	52	116	76	249	0	0
0867	2	33	112	74	240	0	10	0921	1	36	155	95	268	0	20
0868	2	44	110	70	230	0	20	0922	1	34	150	75	175	0	0
0869	1	38	110	68	147	0	20	0923	2	62	130	64	342	5	0
0870	1	59	150	84	200	7	5	0924	1	40	144	102	160	0	40
0871	2	36	118	70	9999	0	30	0925	2	38	120	70	207	0	20
0872	2	36	125	75	175	0	1	0926	1	38	110	70	185	0	0
0873	2	61	165	95	9999	0	0	0927	2	36	122	78	186	0	40
0874	1	48	140	80	233	6	30	0928	2	35	125	80	9999	0	20
0875	1	61	120	78	250	0	0	0929	1	62	140	78	175	0	20
0876	1	39	130	90	271	0	0	0930	2	40	130	75	165	0	20
0877	1	47	120	70	173	0	30	0931	2	45	98	60	238	0	15
0878	1	46	145	90	203	10	50	0932	1	37	145	95	265	0	20
0879	2	56	154	60	246	4	0	0933	1	35	128	72	241	0	20
0880	1	39	130	85	252	0	20	0934	2	39	115	70	198	0	20
0881	1	38	138	87	260	0	0	0935	2	46	115	65	210	0	0
0882	2	61	102	78	258	0	0	0936	2	63	160	98	200	0	0
0883	1	46	160	95	9999	10	30	0937	1	45	115	75	248	0	40
0884	2	41	110	70	9999	0	15	0938	1	43	140	100	162	0	20
0885	1	42	140	60	183	0	20	0939	2	38	126	74	280	0	15
0886	2	35	110	70	9999	0	0	0940	2	47	154	90	183	0	0
0887	1	34	125	85	240	0	20	0941	1	47	122	86	218	0	0
0888	2	41	136	88	350	0	0	0942	1	54	168	92	197	10	0
0889	2	43	115	68	185	0	0	0943	2	41	115	75	9999	0	1
0890	2	60	190	94	330	0	0	0944	1	46	166	116	175	0	0
0891	2	43	126	80	243	0	0	0945	1	48	167	104	215	8	0
0892	2	63	124	70	260	0	0	0946	1	44	165	100	9999	0	20
0893	1	62	130	84	268	0	0	0947	2	55	186	108	295	2	20
0894	1	35	125	70	179	0	0	0948	2	62	120	88	225	0	0
0895	2	38	120	80	170	0	10	0949	1	43	156	98	197	0	5
0896	1	57	172	98	268	0	0	0950	1	39	115	85	172	0	10
0897	2	52	142	92	230	0	0	0951	1	53	135	85	299	0	35
0898	2	61	152	94	265	5	0	0952	1	56	145	95	219	0	20
0899	1	41	125	85	235	8	25	0953	2	44	105	65	252	0	0
0900	2	36	124	82	158	0	0	0954	2	46	124	84	261	0	0
0901	1	36	125	95	212	0	0	0955	2	42	120	70	192	0	0
0902	2	58	176	82	264	10	0	0956	2	39	126	76	240	0	20
0903	1	51	106	64	241	9	20	0957	1	46	130	88	287	8	0
0904	1	55	148	96	322	3	20	0958	2	46	150	94	220	0	0
0905	1	39	122	82	235	0	0	0959	1	48	158	98	317	0	35
0906	2	36	108	74	204	0	0	0960	2	59	135	85	9999	0	0
0907	2	47	105	65	9999	0	1	0961	1	38	112	60	215	0	30
0908	1	56	216	122	210	0	0	0962	2	40	132	86	190	0	20
0909	1	50	108	78	180	0	20	0963	1	43	186	112	246	0	40
0910	2	33	110	70	155	0	5	0964	2	47	134	80	284	0	1
0911	2	45	124	84	215	0	0	0965	2	38	115	75	9999	0	30
0912	1	62	150	88	197	6	20	0966	1	49	130	85	287	0	50
0913	2	60	185	95	305	0	5	0967	2	56	158	96	9999	0	20
0914	2	61	138	80	145	0	0	0968	1	46	140	96	280	4	20
0915	2	40	126	78	235	0	0	0969	1	33	110	70	172	0	30
0916	2	39	105	65	210	0	0	0970	2	37	104	70	278	0	15
0917	2	36	90	60	170	0	0	0971	2	44	154	96	207	0	15
0918	2	49	120	80	316	0	0	0972	2	51	150	72	435	7	0

Table B.11 (Continued)

I D	G E N	A G E	S B P	D B P	C H L	C H D	C I G	I D	G E N	A G E	S B P	D B P	C H L	C H D	C I G
0973	1	46	126	88	226	8	20	0987	2	37	120	78	183	0	0
0974	2	40	115	65	235	10	15	0988	1	44	112	76	155	0	0
0975	1	48	148	93	218	0	20	0989	2	36	96	40	188	0	0
0976	2	42	110	82	9999	0	0	0990	1	36	108	72	174	0	0
0977	2	34	94	68	175	0	0	0991	1	35	118	78	235	0	30
0978	1	58	134	78	165	0	40	0992	1	37	128	84	205	0	0
0979	1	40	108	68	254	9	0	0993	2	35	116	80	9999	0	0
0980	1	39	126	88	246	0	15	0994	2	49	120	85	9999	0	0
0981	2	42	112	76	240	0	0	0995	1	41	134	76	218	0	0
0982	2	47	134	82	265	0	0	0996	2	53	138	70	282	0	0
0983	1	53	120	80	157	0	0	0997	1	38	150	96	196	0	0
0984	2	45	158	98	248	0	20	0998	2	55	140	90	255	0	0
0985	2	36	94	70	178	0	0	0999	2	48	110	60	165	0	20
0986	1	36	108	70	223	0	25	1000	2	34	130	72	179	0	5

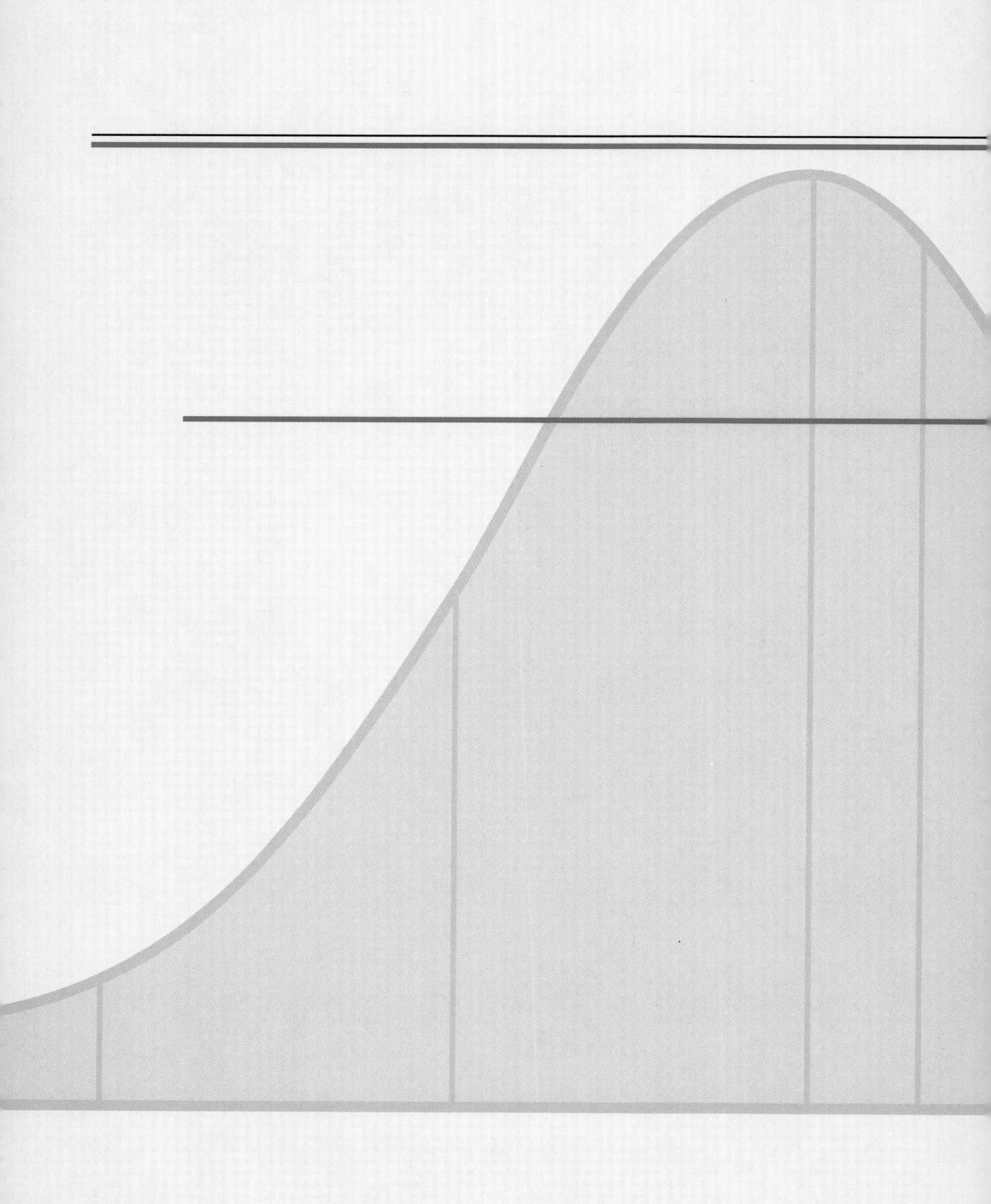

INFERENCE CONCERNING VARIANCES

C.1 **THE CHI-SQUARE DISTRIBUTION**

C.2 **INFERENCE CONCERNING A POPULATION VARIANCE**

C.3 **THE *F* DISTRIBUTION**

C.4 **INFERENCE CONCERNING TWO POPULATION VARIANCES**

C.1

THE CHI-SQUARE DISTRIBUTION

In some situations, we are concerned with making judgments about a population variance σ^2 (or standard deviation σ). For example, the variance of scores on an examination is very important. If the variance is too small, it will be difficult to differentiate between scores.

A college mathematics professor developed a mathematics examination to screen incoming students for the purpose of placing them in the appropriate mathematics course. The new examination was to be used in place of a previously used examination that showed a variance of 100. The professor wanted to compare the variance of the new examination with the old variance. He believed that the new examination would show a larger variance than the old examination ($\sigma^2 > 100$). Therefore, he wished to test the hypotheses

$$H_0: \quad \sigma^2 = 100$$
$$H_a: \quad \sigma^2 > 100$$

To investigate this, the professor decided to give the examination to a sample of 20 students and examine the sample variance s^2. The value of s^2 will influence the decision in the hypothesis test. After all, s^2 can be thought of as a rough estimate of σ^2. The 20 scores are given in Table C.1 (page A-40).

A-39

Table C.1
Scores on a Mathematics Screening Exam

Student	Score	Student	Score
1	70	11	88
2	80	12	50
3	73	13	70
4	64	14	65
5	91	15	75
6	52	16	50
7	48	17	90
8	92	18	53
9	75	19	68
10	67	20	89

$$s^2 = 217.63$$

If the observed value of s^2 is too large to be consistent with the hypothesis H_0, then H_0 will be rejected and H_a accepted. "Too large" means that the value of s^2 is so much larger than 100 that it would be unlikely that we would observe such a large value if H_0 were true. "Unlikely" means having a low probability. The researcher selects this value. As before, it is called the *level of significance* of the test and is denoted by the symbol α.

Instead of working with the quantity s^2, statisticians prefer to use a standardized form of s^2 when investigating σ^2. (This is analogous to using the standard score of $\bar{x}$ when investigating μ.) The quantity statisticians use is called **chi-square,** denoted by χ^2:

$$\chi^2 = \frac{(n-1)s^2}{\sigma^2}$$

where n is the sample size. If we assume for the moment that H_0 is true ($\sigma^2 = 100$), then

$$\chi^2 = \frac{(20-1)s^2}{100} = .19s^2$$

Large values of s^2 correspond to large values of χ^2. Therefore, we will reject H_0 if the value of χ^2 is too large—so large that it would be unlikely that we would observe so large a value if H_0 were true.

To determine the values of χ^2 that are so large as to be unlikely, we must know something about the probability distribution of χ^2. Under appropriate conditions, the quantity χ^2 has a probability distribution known as a **chi-square distribution.**

Properties of a Chi-Square Distribution

For random samples of size n from a normal population with variance σ^2, the probability distribution of the quantity

$$\chi^2 = \frac{(n-1)s^2}{\sigma^2}$$

is a chi-square distribution that has the following properties:

1.   There is not just one chi-square distribution but, in fact, an infinite number of them. Each one has a number associated with it called its degrees of freedom, df. For the above expression, df = $n - 1$. We use the degrees of freedom to specify which chi-square distribution we are using.

2.   The shape of a chi-square curve is not symmetric but is skewed to the right. It begins at 0 and extends indefinitely in a positive direction. The total area under the curve is 1. See Figure C.1.

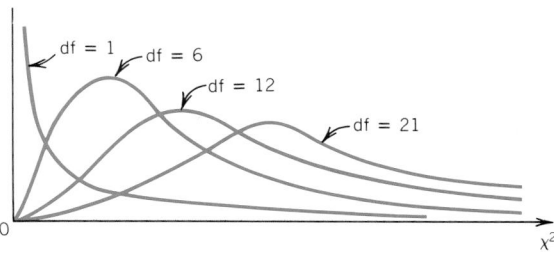

Figure C.1
Chi-Square Curves

3.   The expected value of x^2 is the degrees of freedom, df.

Appendix Table B.5 relates probabilities to various values of x^2. For a particular chi-square distribution, it gives the value of x^2 such that the area under the chi-square curve to the right of this value is equal to some desired probability. For example, suppose that we are concerned with the chi-square distribution with df = 10, and we want the value of x^2 such that the area under the curve to the right of it is .05. We denote this value by $x^2_{.05}$. Locate the value of the degrees of freedom in the far left column of the table (df = 10). Now look at the column under $x^2_{.05}$. The intersection of this column with the row corresponding to df = 10 contains the desired value of x^2, namely, 18.307. Thus $x^2_{.05}$ = 18.307. This means that $P(x^2 \geq 18.307)$ = .05. See Figure C.2.

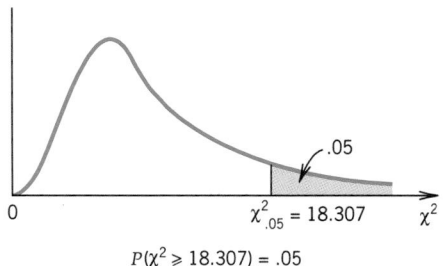

df	$x^2_{.995}$ $\cdots$	$x^2_{.10}$	$x^2_{.05}$	$x^2_{.025}$ $\cdots$
$\vdots$	$\vdots$	$\vdots$	$\vdots$	$\vdots$
9	1.735 $\cdots$	14.684	16.919	19.023 $\cdots$
10	2.156 $\cdots$	15.987	18.307	20.483 $\cdots$
11	2.603 $\cdots$	17.275	19.675	21.920 $\cdots$
$\vdots$	$\vdots$	$\vdots$	$\vdots$	$\vdots$

Figure C.2
A Portion of Appendix Table B.5

EXAMPLE C.1
For the chi-square distribution with df = 11, find the value of x^2 such that the area under the chi-square curve to the left of this value is .005.

Solution

The total area under the curve is 1. So the area to the right of the desired value is $1 - .005 = .995$. This means that the desired value will be $\chi^2_{.995}$ with df $= 11$. In Appendix Table B.5, we see that $\chi^2_{.995} = 2.603$. This means that $P(\chi^2 < 2.603) = .005$. See Figure C.3.

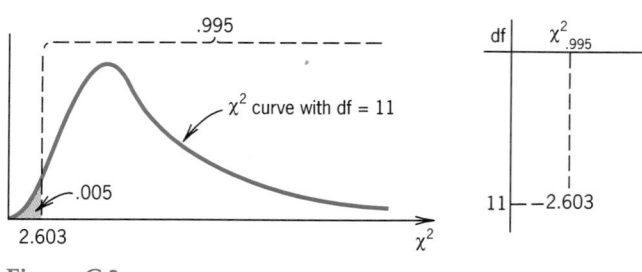

Figure C.3
$P(\chi^2 < 2.603) = .005$

Before turning to applications of the chi-square distribution, we should mention that there are no requirements on the sample size n in the expression

$$\chi^2 = \frac{(n-1)s^2}{\sigma^2}$$

Therefore, our methods will apply with small or large samples. However, for this expression to have a chi-square distribution, the population (of x values) must be normal. Chi-square procedures are not robust with respect to this condition—approximate normality will not suffice. Contrast this with the requirement on the population in applications of Student's t distribution in Section 8.5, where we said that the population need be only approximately normal—actually its distribution need be only roughly mound-shaped. The requirement of normality when applying the chi-square distribution in the study of variance is a severe limitation that you should keep in mind.

In the examples and exercises of this appendix where the chi-square distribution is used, we will assume that the populations involved are normal.

EXERCISES

C.1 In each of the following parts, find (i) $\chi^2_{.01}$, (ii) $\chi^2_{.025}$, (iii) $\chi^2_{.05}$, (iv) $\chi^2_{.95}$, and (v) $\chi^2_{.99}$.

    (a) Assume a chi-square distribution with 9 degrees of freedom.

    (b) Assume a chi-square distribution with 15 degrees of freedom.

    (c) Assume a chi-square distribution with 25 degrees of freedom.

C.2 Assume a chi-square distribution with 6 degrees of freedom. Fill in the blanks.

    (a) $P(\chi^2 \geq \underline{\hspace{1cm}}) = .01$ **(b)** $P(\chi^2 \geq \underline{\hspace{1cm}}) = .99$

    (c) $P(\chi^2 > \underline{\hspace{1cm}}) = .05$ **(d)** $P(\chi^2 < \underline{\hspace{1cm}}) = .90$

    (e) $P(\chi^2 \leq \underline{\hspace{1cm}}) = .01$ **(f)** $P(\chi^2 < \underline{\hspace{1cm}}) = .05$

C.3 Complete each of the following.

    (a) $\chi^2_{.10} = 17.275$, df $= \underline{\hspace{1cm}}$ **(b)** $\chi^2_{\underline{\hspace{0.3cm}}} = 2.167$, df $= 7$

    (c) $\chi^2_{.95} = \underline{\hspace{1cm}}$, df $= 10$ **(d)** $\chi^2_{.01} = 44.314$, df $= \underline{\hspace{1cm}}$

(e) $\chi^2_{\_\_\_} = 18.549$,   df $= 12$ **(f)** $\chi^2_{.05} = \_\_\_\_$,   df $= 17$

(g) $\chi^2_{.90} = \_\_\_\_$,   df $= 20$ **(h)** $\chi^2_{.99} = \_\_\_\_$,   df $= 11$

C.4   Assuming a χ^2 distribution with 18 degrees of freedom, find each of the following probabilities:

(a) $P(\chi^2 > 25.989)$ **(b)** $P(\chi^2 < 7.015)$

(c) $P(7.015 < \chi^2 < 9.390)$ **(d)** $P(10.865 < \chi^2 < 28.869)$

C.2

INFERENCE CONCERNING A POPULATION VARIANCE

In Section C.1, we noted that inference concerning a population variance may be conducted using the quantity

$$\chi^2 = \frac{(n-1)s^2}{\sigma^2}$$

which has a chi-square distribution with df $= n - 1$ when the population is normal. In hypothesis testing concerning σ^2, we use this expression as a test statistic. The value we use for σ^2 in this quantity is the value appearing in the null hypothesis.

When a statistic that has a chi-square distribution is used in a statistical test, we call it a **chi-square test.**

EXAMPLE C.2

For the data in Table C.1 on page A-40, we saw that a sample of size $n = 20$ gave a sample variance of $s^2 = 217.63$. Test the claim that the variance σ^2 for the new examination is larger than the variance for the old examination (which was 100). Use the 1% level of significance.

Solution

1.   *Hypotheses:*   We have seen that the hypotheses are

$$H_0:\ \ \sigma^2 = 100$$
$$H_a:\ \ \sigma^2 > 100$$

2.   *Level of significance:* $\alpha = .01$

3.   *Test statistic and observed value:*

$$\chi^2 = \frac{(n-1)s^2}{\sigma^2} = \frac{(20-1)(217.63)}{100} \doteq 41.35$$
$$df = n - 1 = 20 - 1 = 19$$

4.   *Critical region:*   Very large values of s^2 favor H_a. These correspond to very large values of χ^2, so large that it would be unlikely (only 1% chance) that we would observe such large values if H_0 were true. Hence, we perform a right-tailed test. The right critical value obtained from Appendix Table B.5 is $\chi^2_\alpha = \chi^2_{.01} = 36.191$. The critical region shown in Figure C.4 (page A-44) consists of values of $\chi^2 \geq 36.191$.

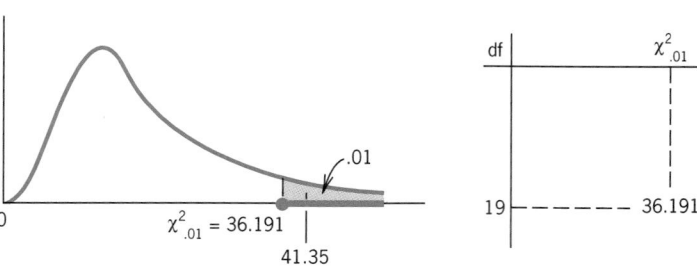

Figure C.4

5.   *Decision:*   The observed value of 41.35 is in the critical region, so we reject H_0. This means that the new test does appear to have a larger variance than the old one.

EXAMPLE C.3

A machine is designed to fill 32-ounce milk containers. The actual measurements of milk will vary somewhat from 32 ounces; it is said that for this machine the standard deviation is .1 ounce. To test this claim, 28 containers are randomly selected and the actual amount of milk in each is measured. This results in a sample standard deviation of $s = .13$ ounce. Complete the test of the claim at the 5% level of significance using

(a)   The classical approach
(b)   The P-value approach

Solution

(a)   The classical approach:

1.   *Hypotheses:*   It is claimed that $\sigma = .1$ ounce or equivalently $\sigma^2 = (.1)^2 = .01$. Therefore, we will test

$$H_0: \quad \sigma^2 = .01$$
$$H_a: \quad \sigma^2 \neq .01$$

2.   *Level of significance:* $\alpha = .05$
3.   *Test statistic and observed value:*

$$\chi^2 = \frac{(n-1)s^2}{\sigma^2} = \frac{(27)(.13)^2}{.01} \doteq 45.63 \qquad df = 27$$

4.   *Critical region:*   The fact that H_a contains the symbol $\neq$ implies that this will be a two-tailed critical region. From Appendix Table B.5, we find that the right critical value is

$$\chi^2_{\alpha/2} = \chi^2_{.025} = 43.194$$

The area under the curve to the right of the left critical value is $1 - \alpha/2 = 1 - .025 = .975$. Thus the left critical value is $\chi^2_{1-\alpha/2} = \chi^2_{.975} = 14.573$. The critical region is displayed in Figure C.5(a). The critical region consists of values of $\chi^2 \leq 14.573$ or $\chi^2 \geq 43.194$.

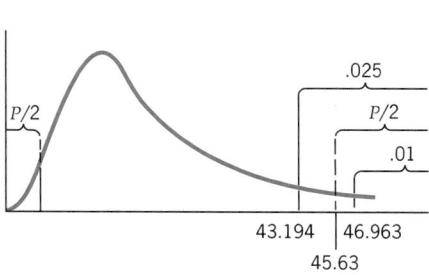

Figure C.5
(a) Critical Region   **(b) P-value: .02 < P < .05**

5.   *Decision:*   Since the observed value $\chi^2 = 45.63$ is in the critical region, we reject H_0. Therefore, it would seem that the claim is untrue.

(b)   The *P*-value approach:

We are using a two-tailed test. Thus the *P*-value is twice the area under the curve to the right of the observed value 45.63. See Figure C.5(b). Examining the df = 27 row of Appendix Table B.5, we see that 45.63 is between 43.194 and 46.963:

Area of Right Tail	.025	P/2 ↓	.01
χ^2 value	43.194	↑ 45.63	46.963

Thus $.01 < P/2 < .025$. Hence, $.02 < P < .05$. Now $\alpha = .05$, and since $P < .05$, we reject the null hypothesis.

EXAMPLE C.4

The systolic blood pressure readings of males between the ages of 35 and 59 show a standard deviation of about 17 millimeters. A sample of 41 male runners (age 35–59) showed a (sample) standard deviation of 15 millimeters (Wood et al., 1977, p. 149). Test the claim that runners in this age group show less variability in their systolic blood pressures. Use the 5% level of significance. What can be said about the *P*-value?

Solution

1.   *Hypotheses:*   Let σ = the standard deviation of systolic blood pressures of male runners age 35 to 59. The claim is $\sigma < 17$ (or $\sigma^2 < 289$). The hypotheses are

$$H_0: \quad \sigma^2 = 289$$
$$H_a: \quad \sigma^2 < 289$$

2.   *Level of significance:* $\alpha = .05$

3. *Test statistic and observed value:*

$$\chi^2 = \frac{(n-1)s^2}{\sigma^2} = \frac{(40)(15)^2}{289} = 31.14 \qquad df = n - 1 = 40$$

4. *Critical region:* Since H_a says that $\sigma^2 < 289$, values of s^2 much smaller than 289 strongly favor H_a. These correspond to small values of χ^2, so we use a left-tailed test. From Appendix Table B.5, we find $\chi^2_{1-\alpha} = \chi^2_{1-.05} = \chi^2_{.95} = 26.509$. Hence the critical region consists of values of $\chi^2 \leq 26.509$. See Figure C.6(a).

5. *Decision:* The observed value $\chi^2 = 31.14$ is not in the critical region; hence we do not reject H_0. This means that there is not enough evidence to conclude (at the 5% level) that there is less variability in systolic blood pressures for the population.

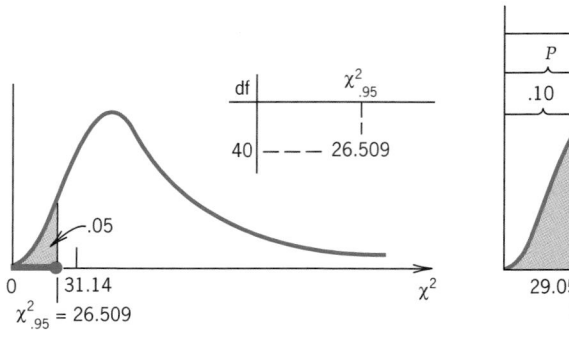

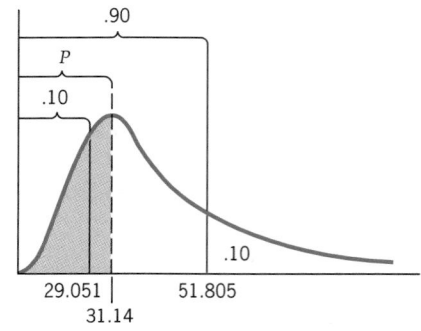

Figure C.6
(a) Critical Region   **(b) P-value: .10 < P < .90**

P-value: Since we are dealing with a left-tailed test, the P-value is the area under the curve to the *left* of 31.14. In Appendix Table B.5, locate the row for df $= 40$. Notice that 31.14 is between the values 29.051 and 51.805. The table relates χ^2 values to *right*-tail areas. For example, $\chi^2_{.90} = 29.051$. So the area to the right of 29.051 is .90. Thus the area to the left is $1 - .90 = .10$. Also, $\chi^2_{.10} = 51.805$, so the area to the *left* of 51.805 is .90. See Figure C.6(b).

	P	
Area of Left Tail	**↓**	
	.10	.90
χ^2 value	29.051	51.805
	↑	
	31.14	

Thus .10 < P < .90. Therefore we cannot reject H_0 when $\alpha = .05$ since P > .05.

We summarize the essential features of a chi-square test concerning a population variance as follows:

Chi-Square Test for a Population Variance   To test hypotheses concerning σ^2, the test statistic is

$$\chi^2 = \frac{(n-1)s^2}{\sigma^2}$$

This has a chi-square distribution with df $= n - 1$. For σ^2, we substitute the value given in the null hypothesis. The observed value of χ^2 is computed using the sample data. If it falls in the critical region, we reject the null hypothesis H_0. Otherwise, we do not reject H_0. Suppose that α is the level of significance of the test. Critical values of χ^2 are found in Appendix Table B.5. The possible critical regions are described as follows:

(a)   If the alternate hypothesis contains the symbol $>$, we conduct a right-tailed test. The critical region is shown in Figure C.7.

(b)   If the alternate hypothesis contains the symbol $<$, we conduct a left-tailed test. The critical region is shown in Figure C.8.

(c)   If the alternate hypothesis contains the symbol $\neq$, we conduct a two-tailed test. The critical region is shown in Figure C.9.

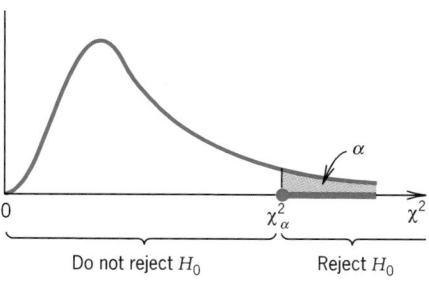

Figure C.7
Right-Tailed Test

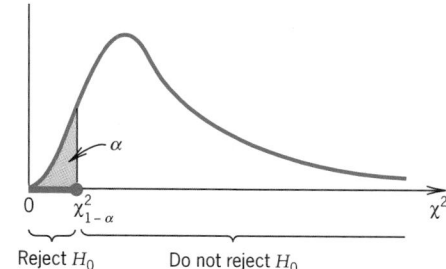

Figure C.8
Left-Tailed Test

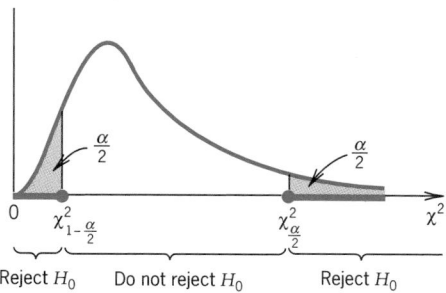

Figure C.9
Two-Tailed Test

Assumption: The population is normal.

Confidence Intervals (Optional)

Let us now turn to the subject of estimating a population variance σ^2. We will omit the derivation of the formula for a $1 - \alpha$ confidence interval for σ^2 and give only the final result.

- We use the sample variance s^2 as a point estimate for σ^2.
- A $1 - \alpha$ confidence interval for σ^2 for a normal population is

$$\frac{(n-1)s^2}{\chi^2_{\alpha/2}} < \sigma^2 < \frac{(n-1)s^2}{\chi^2_{1-\alpha/2}}$$

The values appearing in the denominators of this inequality are shown in Figure C.10.

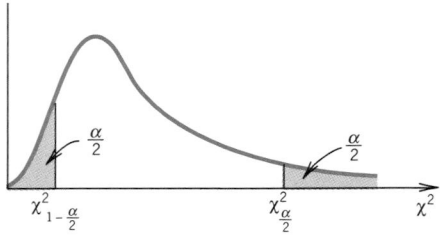

Figure C.10

EXAMPLE C.5

In Example C.2, we discussed a new mathematics screening examination. The test scores of a sample of 20 students showed a sample variance of $s^2 = 217.63$. Find a 95% confidence interval for the (population) variance σ^2 for all future test scores on the exam.

Solution

$$1 - \alpha = .95 \qquad \alpha = .05$$

Now df $= n - 1 = 20 - 1 = 19$. Using Appendix Table B.5, we see that

$$\chi^2_{\alpha/2} = \chi^2_{.025} = 32.852$$

$$\chi^2_{1-\alpha/2} = \chi^2_{.975} = 8.907$$

Therefore, a 95% confidence interval for σ^2 is

$$\frac{(19)(217.63)}{32.852} < \sigma^2 < \frac{(19)(217.63)}{8.907}$$

or

$$125.87 < \sigma^2 < 464.24$$

If we want a 95% confidence interval for the standard deviation σ, we just take the square root of each term:

$$11.22 < \sigma < 21.55$$

Therefore, we are 95% confident that σ is between 11.22 and 21.55.

EXERCISES

C.5   In each of the following parts, **(i)** test the claim, and **(ii)** indicate the possible type of error committed (Type I or Type II). Note that n refers to the sample size.

   (a)   Test the claim that the variance σ^2 is more than 100.

$$n = 16 \qquad \alpha = .05 \qquad s^2 = 173$$

   (b)   Test the claim that the variance σ^2 is less than 70.

$$n = 12 \qquad \alpha = .01 \qquad s^2 = 12.7$$

   (c)   Test the claim that the variance σ^2 is not 50.

$$n = 19 \qquad \alpha = .10 \qquad s^2 = 33.3$$

   (d)   Test the claim that the variance σ^2 is greater than 30.

$$n = 9 \qquad \alpha = .10 \qquad s^2 = 45$$

   (e)   Test the claim that the variance σ^2 is less than 65.

$$n = 22 \qquad \alpha = .05 \qquad s^2 = 40.2$$

   (f)   Test the claim that the variance σ^2 is 20.

$$n = 26 \qquad \alpha = .01 \qquad s^2 = 38.4$$

C.6   Verify the conclusions reached in Exercise C.5 by using the P-value approach. (*Hint:* Estimate the P-value by giving an interval such as $.025 < P < .05$ or $P < .005$.)

C.7   A dispenser of soft drinks is designed to fill containers with a mean μ of 16 ounces and a variance σ^2 of .0001. The manufacturer is concerned that the variability of the amount being dispensed has increased. A random sample of size 15 gives a sample variance of .0002. Is there sufficient evidence to indicate that the variability has increased? Use a 1% level of significance.

   (a)   Use the classical approach.

   (b)   Use the P-value approach.

C.8   A tablet is supposed to have a mean weight μ of 325 milligrams and a standard deviation σ of .70 milligram. A physician suspected that the standard deviation was larger than .70 milligram. A sample of 20 tablets showed a sample standard deviation of .94 milligram. At the 5% significance level, is there sufficient evidence to justify the physician's suspicion?

C.9   Under test conditions, one brand of golf ball, manufactured by the Avex company, moves a mean distance μ of 200 yards with a variance σ^2 of 4. The company decided to modify the golf ball with a tougher cover with the belief that the variance would remain the same. Twenty balls with the tougher cover are tested and found to have a sample variance of 6. Is there sufficient evidence to suggest the variance has changed? Use a 5% level of significance.

   (a)   Use the classical approach.

   (b)   Use the P-value approach.

C.10   A company has a policy of not marketing a speedometer if it believes the standard deviation σ of measurements is greater than 3 miles per hour. Twelve speedometers were tested, and the sample variance was 23. At a 1% level of significance, will the company decide to market the speedometer?

C.11   An automobile company specified that replacement of a defective head gasket should take 2 hours on the average, with a standard deviation of 20 minutes. On warranty work, the company stated that it would pay a dealership for labor up to 1 standard deviation above the mean (up to 2 hours and 20 minutes). One dealer suspected that the standard deviation σ was more than 20 minutes. A sample of 20 jobs gave a sample standard deviation of 32 minutes. At the 1% level of significance, is the dealer's suspicion justified?

C.12   In the Crevalcore area of Greece, a study of 28 men's diets showed a sample standard deviation of 1.6% of calories from proteins (*Source:* Keys, 1970, p. I-166). Find a 90% confidence interval for the variance σ^2 of the population from which the men were selected.

C.13   A medical doctor claimed that the variance σ^2 is less than 156 for diastolic blood pressure of males age 60–64 in the Framingham Heart Study. A sample of nine such males gave the following readings:

80   82   102   84   88   86   88   98   106

Test the claim using a 1% level of significance.

C.14   The following data are the lengths of time (in minutes) of six randomly selected minor league baseball games. The times are

153   137   127   143   152   148

Find a 95% confidence interval for the variance σ^2 of the population from which the times were selected.

C.15   **(a)**   Using the data in Exercise C.7, find a 98% confidence interval for the population variance σ^2.

(b)   Using the data in Exercise C.8, find a 90% confidence interval for the population variance σ^2.

(c)   Using the data in Exercise C.10, find a 99% confidence interval for the population variance σ^2.

C.3

THE *F* DISTRIBUTION

Suppose that we wish to compare two (unknown) population variances σ_1^2 and σ_2^2. It would seem natural to obtain samples from each population and examine the sample variances s_1^2 and s_2^2. For example, two fertilizer companies that marketed a fertilizer for wheat merged to form a new company that would market only one of the fertilizers. Both fertilizers result in about the same yield (in bushels of wheat per acre), on the average, but the variability is unknown. It is, of course, desirable for the variability of such a product to be at a minimum. Hence the company wishes to compare the population variances σ_1^2 and σ_2^2 for the two fertilizers. (The population for a given fertilizer can be viewed as the collection of data representing the yields in bushels per acre of wheat for each farm that has used or will use the fertilizer.)

To study this situation, the company obtained the yields of some farms that used the fertilizers. Eleven farms used fertilizer A, and 11 farms used fertilizer B. The resulting data are given in Table C.2.

You probably think that the sample variances shown are *significantly different*; that is, they are far enough apart to indicate that the population variances are

Table C.2
Wheat Yields for Two Types of Fertilizer (Bushels per Acre)

Fertilizer A	Fertilizer B
74	70
61	69
74	71
80	70
70	69
71	71
60	70
79	69
64	68
70	73
67	70
$\bar{x}_1 = 70.0$	$\bar{x}_2 = 70.0$
$s_1^2 = 44.0$	$s_2^2 = 1.8$

different. After all, s_1^2 is almost 25 times larger than s_2^2, since $s_1^2/s_2^2 = 24.44$. Often, however, it is not so easy to decide whether $\sigma_1^2 = \sigma_2^2$ by simply looking at s_1^2 and s_2^2. Hence we need some method other than intuition to investigate these issues.

In general, suppose that we are investigating two population variances σ_1^2 and σ_2^2, and we wish to test

$$H_0: \quad \sigma_1^2 = \sigma_2^2$$
$$H_a: \quad \sigma_1^2 \neq \sigma_2^2$$

If we divide by σ_2^2, we can rewrite these hypotheses as

$$H_0: \quad \frac{\sigma_1^2}{\sigma_2^2} = 1$$

$$H_a: \quad \frac{\sigma_1^2}{\sigma_2^2} \neq 1$$

Now if we obtain samples from each population, we may think of the sample variances s_1^2 and s_2^2 as rough estimates of σ_1^2 and σ_2^2, respectively. Therefore, if H_0 is true ($\sigma_1^2 = \sigma_2^2$), the values of s_1^2 and s_2^2 should not be too far apart. This means that the ratio s_1^2/s_2^2 should not be too far from 1. Now the smallest possible value such a ratio can assume is 0 (if $s_1^2 = 0$), and there is no limit to how large the ratio can be. If the ratio s_1^2/s_2^2 is so far from 1 (i.e., so large or so small) that it would be unlikely that we would observe such a value if σ_1^2 and σ_2^2 were equal, we would be inclined to reject H_0 in favor of H_a.

If we are to know what values of s_1^2/s_2^2 are unlikely, we should know something about the probability distribution of this expression. We use the symbol F to represent this ratio.

$$F = \frac{s_1^2}{s_2^2}$$

Under suitable conditions this ratio has a probability distribution known as an **F distribution.**

Properties of an *F* Distribution

Suppose that we obtain random samples from two populations. We will use the notation in Table C.3.

Table C.3

Population	Sample Size	Sample Variance	Population Variance
1	n_1	s_1^2	σ_1^2
2	n_2	s_2^2	σ_2^2

We assume that the populations are normal. Further, we assume that the samples are obtained *independently* of one another. That is, the individual data values we get in one sample are not related to any of the values in the other sample.* Then if $\sigma_1^2 = \sigma_2^2$, the ratio

$$F = \frac{s_1^2}{s_2^2}$$

has an *F* distribution. An *F* distribution has the following properties:

1. For an *F* distribution, we have a pair of degrees of freedom: the degrees of freedom of the numerator, df_1, and the degrees of freedom of the denominator, df_2. For the ratio s_1^2/s_2^2, $df_1 = n_1 - 1$ and $df_2 = n_2 - 1$. We often express the degrees of freedom as an ordered pair of numbers, writing

$$df = (n_1 - 1, n_2 - 1)$$

   There are an infinite number of *F* distributions, one for each possible pair of degrees of freedom.

2. The graph of an *F* distribution (an *F* curve) starts at 0 and extends indefinitely to the right. It is skewed to the right. Of course, the total area under the curve is 1. See Figure C.11.

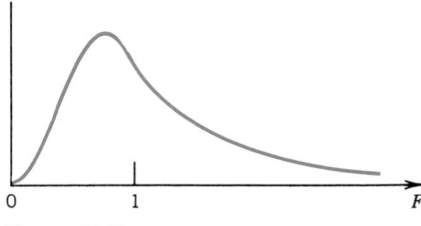

Figure C.11
An *F* Curve

---

*For example, we have independent samples if a group of farmers tries fertilizer A and a *different* group tries fertilizer B. If only one group of farmers is selected, and each farmer tries both fertilizers, the samples would be *dependent*. There is more discussion of this topic in Section 9.2.

Appendix Table B.6 relates probabilities to various values of F. The table enables us to find the value of F such that the area under the curve to the right of this value is some desired value (probability). Appendix Table B.6 actually consists of three different tables corresponding to three such probabilities (.05, .025, and .01). Suppose that we are interested in the F distribution with degrees of freedom df = (24, 16), and we want the value of F such that the area under the F curve to the right of it is .05. We denote this value by $F_{.05}$. Locate the appropriate table for .05. In the row across the top, find the degrees of freedom for the numerator, 24. In the column on the left, locate the degrees of freedom of the denominator, 16. The intersection of the column under 24 and the row next to 16 contains the desired value of F, namely, 2.24. Thus $F_{.05} = 2.24$. This means $P(F \geq 2.24) = .05$. In Figure C.12, we have included a portion of the F table (with the right tail area .05).

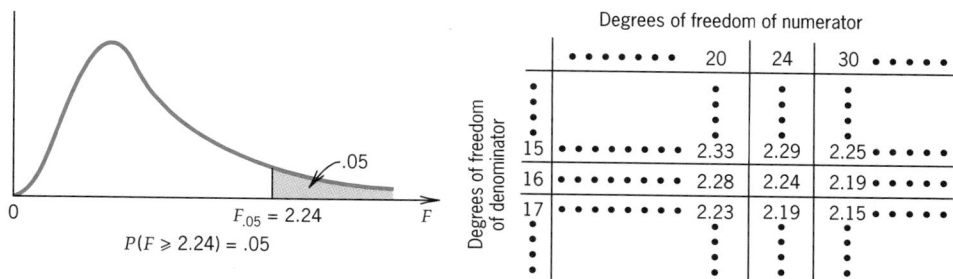

Figure C.12

Before turning to applications of the F distribution, we should note the following concerning the quantity

$$F = \frac{s_1^2}{s_2^2}$$

The sample sizes n_1 and n_2 need not be large for this expression to have the F distribution; it has an F distribution regardless of the sample sizes. However, we do require the populations to be normal, and the F distribution procedures are not robust to departures from normality. This rather severely limits the use of this expression in the study of variances. In the examples and exercises of this appendix where the F distribution is used, we will assume that the normality condition is met.

EXERCISES

C.16 In parts (a)–(d), find **(i)** $F_{.01}$, **(ii)** $F_{.025}$, and **(iii)** $F_{.05}$.

(a) Assume an F distribution with (5, 8) degrees of freedom.

(b) Assume an F distribution with (8, 5) degrees of freedom.

(c) Assume an F distribution with (20, 10) degrees of freedom.

(d) Assume an F distribution with (1, 7) degrees of freedom.

C.17 Assume an F distribution. Fill in the blanks.

(a) $P(F > \underline{\hspace{1cm}}) = .01, \quad df = (15, 12)$

(b) $P(F \leq \underline{\hspace{1cm}}) = .95, \quad df = (9, 5)$

(c) $P(F \geq \underline{\hspace{1cm}}) = .025, \quad df = (6, 20)$

(d) $P(F > \underline{\hspace{1cm}}) = .05, \quad df = (12, 9)$

_____ **C.4**

INFERENCE CONCERNING TWO POPULATION VARIANCES

In Section C.3, we said that we could compare two (unknown) population variances using the quantity

$$F = \frac{s_1^2}{s_2^2}$$

where s_1^2 and s_2^2 are sample variances for independent random samples of size n_1 and n_2, respectively, obtained from two normal populations. If the variances of the populations are equal ($\sigma_1^2 = \sigma_2^2$), then the expression F has an F distribution with degrees of freedom df $= (n_1 - 1, n_2 - 1)$.

To test hypotheses concerning variances, we can use this expression as a test statistic. We call such a test an **F test**. Critical values of F may be found in Appendix Table B.6. This table enables us to find the values of $F_{.01}$, $F_{.025}$, or $F_{.05}$. Notice that these are right critical values. In testing hypotheses, we will see that it will not be necessary to find left critical values if we use the following rule: *Label so that the numerator s_1^2 represents the larger of the two sample variances.* However, a word of caution about this: If your alternate hypothesis is H_a: $\sigma_1^2 < \sigma_2^2$, and yet for the sample data $s_1^2 > s_2^2$, then do not do an F test because there is clearly no evidence to support the alternate hypothesis.

Remark   If you do not care to follow the labeling convention discussed here, just remember to put the larger sample variance in the numerator.

_____

EXAMPLE C.6
A manufacturer of 6-volt batteries is considering two different production processes: process A and process B. In either process, we can expect some degree of variability of individual batteries from the advertised 6 volts. An engineer claims that the variance in voltages of all batteries produced by process B is greater than that of process A. To investigate this claim, samples of voltages from batteries produced by each process are obtained with the following results:

	n	s^2
A	21	.15
B	25	.33

Complete the test at the 5% level of significance. What can be said about the *P*-value?

Solution
By our labeling convention, s_1^2 will denote the larger sample variance, so $s_1^2 = .33$ and $s_2^2 = .15$. We now proceed with the usual five steps.

1. *Hypotheses:*   It is claimed that the population variance for process B is greater than the population variance for process A. Because the sample variance s_1^2 refers to process B, we denote the population variance for process B by σ_1^2. Therefore, the claim is that $\sigma_1^2 > \sigma_2^2$. This is the alternate hypothesis. Hence the hypotheses are

$$H_0: \quad \sigma_1^2 = \sigma_2^2$$
$$H_a: \quad \sigma_1^2 > \sigma_2^2$$

2. *Level of significance:* $\alpha = .05$

3. *Test statistic and observed value:*

$$F = \frac{s_1^2}{s_2^2} = \frac{.33}{.15} = 2.20$$

$$\text{df} = (n_1 - 1, \, n_2 - 1) = (24, \, 20)$$

4. *Critical region:*   Values of s_1^2 much larger than s_2^2 favor H_a. But when s_1^2 is much larger than s_2^2, s_1^2/s_2^2 will be very large. Therefore, large values of F favor H_a. Thus we will conduct a right-tailed test. We will find the appropriate right critical value from Appendix Table B.6. From Appendix Table B.6, $F_{.05} = 2.08$ when df $= (24, 20)$. The critical region, shown in Figure C.13(a), consists of values of $F \geq 2.08$.

5. *Decision:*   The observed value $F = 2.20$ lies in the critical region, so we reject H_0. Thus it does appear that process B shows more variability than process A.

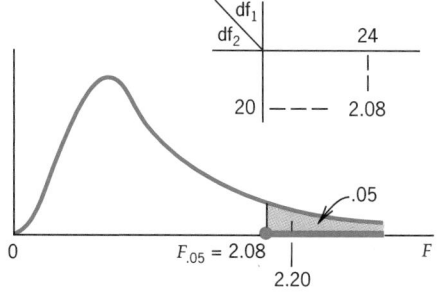

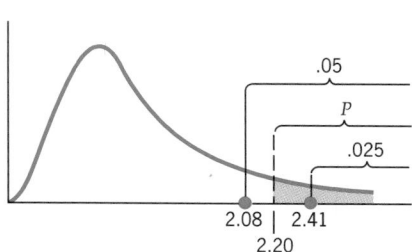

Figure C.13
(a) Critical Region   **(b) .025 < P < .05**

P-value: Since this is a right-tailed test, the P-value is the area to the right of the observed value, 2.20. Information about the P-value can be obtained by examining F values in Appendix B.6 when df $= (24, 20)$. From this table we see that

$$F_{.05} = 2.08 \qquad F_{.025} = 2.41 \qquad F_{.01} = 2.86$$

Thus

Area of Right Tail	.05	$\underset{\downarrow}{P}$	.025	.01
F value	2.08	$\underset{2.20}{\uparrow}$	2.41	2.86

See Figure C.13(b). This means

$$.025 < P < .05$$

Even when we conduct a two-tailed F-test, it will be unnecessary to find a left critical value. The reason for this is that since we are labeling so that $s_1^2 > s_2^2$, then

$$F = \frac{s_1^2}{s_2^2} > 1$$

But left critical values are less than 1. Hence our value of F will not fall in the left end of the distribution. Therefore, when conducting a two-tailed test, we will not have to find the left critical value (even though there is a left tail to the critical region). The following example illustrates this point.

EXAMPLE C.7

Cholesterol in the blood can lead to fatty deposits in the arteries, which in turn can lead to coronary heart disease. Recently, there has been a great deal of interest in a component of (total) cholesterol called "high-density lipoprotein" (HDL). HDL cholesterol is known as the "good cholesterol" because high levels of HDL are thought to lower the risk of coronary heart disease (Gordon et al., 1977, p. 707). Runners tend to have higher levels of HDL than nonrunners. This issue is examined more carefully in Example 9.4. Here we investigate the question of whether the variability in HDL readings is the same for runners and nonrunners. Table C.4 gives some data obtained concerning HDL (measured in milligrams per 100 milliliters) for elite runners[*] versus nonrunners.

Table C.4
HDL Data

Samples	n	$\bar{x}$	s
Elite runners	20	56	12.1
Nonrunners	72	49	10.5

Source: Martin, R., W. Haskell, and P. Wood, "Blood Chemistry and Lipid Profiles of Elite Distance Runners," in *The Long Distance Runner*, P. Milvy, ed., New York: Urizen Books, 1977, p. 88.

Both groups were young males (30 and under), so we should restrict our attention to this category. (The nonrunners are referred to as the *control group*.) Test the claim that the (population) variance of HDL readings for young male elite runners is the same as that of young male nonrunners. Use the 5% level of significance.

Solution

Since s_1 will represent the larger sample standard deviation, $s_1 = 12.1$ and $s_2 = 10.5$. Thus, σ_1^2 and σ_2^2 will represent the population variances for young male elite runners and young male nonrunners, respectively.

---

[*]The term *elite runner* refers to one of the top 2.5% runners in the world.

1. *Hypotheses:*   The question is whether the population variances are equal or not. Thus the hypotheses are

$$H_0: \quad \sigma_1^2 = \sigma_2^2$$
$$H_a: \quad \sigma_1^2 \neq \sigma_2^2$$

2. *Level of significance:* $\alpha = .05$

3. *Test statistic and observed value:*

$$F = \frac{s_1^2}{s_2^2} = \frac{(12.1)^2}{(10.5)^2} = \frac{146.41}{110.25} \doteq 1.33$$

$$df = (19, \ 71)$$

4. *Critical region:*   Since the alternate hypothesis is $\sigma_1^2 \neq \sigma_2^2$, we conduct a two-tailed test. (Very large or very small values of F favor H_a.) The right critical value is found in Appendix Table B.6. Note that this table does not contain the values 19 and 71 under degrees of freedom. In a case like this, it is customary to use the next *lower* values for degrees of freedom: (15, 60). The right critical value is $F_{\alpha/2} = F_{.025} = 2.06$. The left critical value, $F_{1-\alpha/2} = F_{.975}$, is less than 1. But since our observed value of F is greater than 1, there is no question of its falling in the left part of the critical region. Therefore, we will not have to know the value of $F_{.975}$. The critical region is shown in Figure C.14.

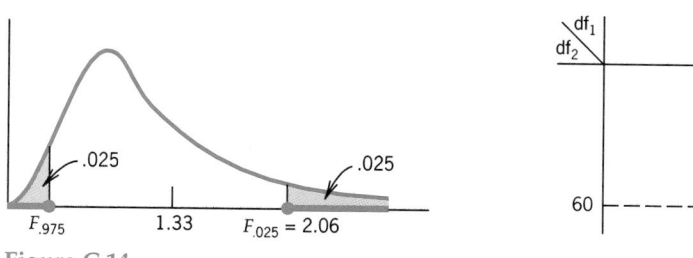

Figure C.14

5. *Decision:*   The observed value ($F = 1.33$) does not fall in the critical region, so we do not reject H_0. This means that there is no evidence to conclude that σ_1^2 and σ_2^2 are different for the nonrunners and runners.

In the previous two examples, we performed a two-tailed test and a right-tailed test. What about a left-tailed test? We need not worry about left-tailed F tests. To understand this, suppose the alternate hypothesis were $\sigma_A^2 < \sigma_B^2$. This looks like a left-tailed test, but we can write this as $\sigma_B^2 > \sigma_A^2$. We would then use the statistic s_B^2/s_A^2 and do a right-tailed test. Of course, we perform the test only if $s_B^2 > s_A^2$; otherwise there would be no evidence to support the alternate hypothesis ($\sigma_B^2 > \sigma_A^2$).

Some people do not follow the convention of putting the larger sample variance in the numerator. But if you do not, it may be necessary to find a left critical value. Although these values are not in Appendix Table B.6, there is a way of finding them that is discussed on page A-59.

We can summarize the essential features of an F test for variances as follows:

F Test for Variances   To test hypotheses concerning two population variances, we use the test statistic

$$F = \frac{s_1^2}{s_2^2}$$

where we label so that $s_1^2 > s_2^2$. This expression has degrees of freedom $df = (n_1 - 1, n_2 - 1)$, where n_1 and n_2 are the sample sizes associated with s_1^2 and s_2^2, respectively. Assume that α is the level of significance of the test.

(a)   One-tailed test: Because of our labeling convention, the only one-tailed test we will conduct is a right-tailed test. To test

$$H_0: \quad \sigma_1^2 = \sigma_2^2$$
$$H_a: \quad \sigma_1^2 > \sigma_2^2$$

we compute the (observed) value of F from the sample data and find the critical value F_α in Appendix Table B.6. If $F \geq F_\alpha$, we reject H_0. Otherwise, do not reject H_0. The critical region is shown in Figure C.15.

(b)   Two-tailed test: To test the hypotheses

$$H_0: \quad \sigma_1^2 = \sigma_2^2$$
$$H_a: \quad \sigma_1^2 \neq \sigma_2^2$$

compute the value of F from the sample data and find the value of $F_{\alpha/2}$ in Appendix Table B.6. If $F \geq F_{\alpha/2}$, we reject H_0. Otherwise, do not reject H_0. (There is no need to find the left critical value, because F will not fall in the left tail as a result of our labeling convention. Nevertheless, this is a bona fide two-tailed test.) The critical region is shown in Figure C.16.

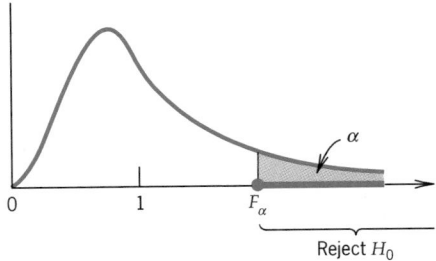

Figure C.15
Right-Tailed Test

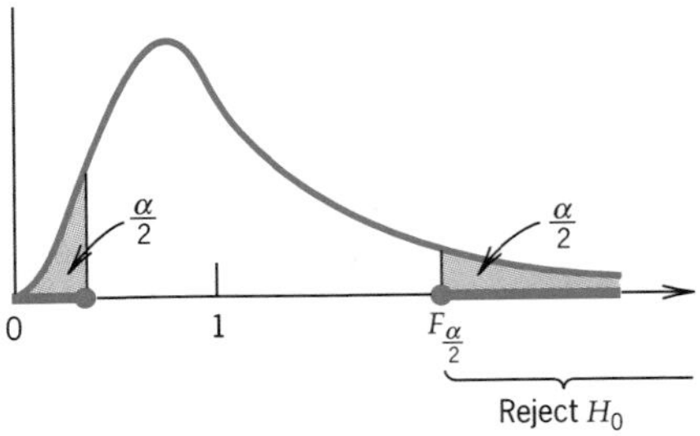

Figure C.16
Two-Tailed Test

Assumptions: The populations are normal, and the samples are obtained independently.

Confidence Intervals for σ_1^2/σ_2^2 (Optional)

To estimate the relative sizes of σ_1^2 and σ_2^2, we can obtain a confidence interval for the ratio σ_1^2/σ_2^2. Using the F distribution, we can establish the following confidence interval. (We omit the proof.)

A $1 - \alpha$ confidence interval for σ_1^2/σ_2^2 is

$$\frac{s_1^2}{s_2^2} \cdot \frac{1}{F_{\alpha/2}} < \frac{\sigma_1^2}{\sigma_2^2} < \frac{s_1^2}{s_2^2} \cdot \frac{1}{F_{1-\alpha/2}}$$

For the F values, df $= (n_1 - 1, n_2 - 1)$.

Assumptions: The samples are obtained independently, and the populations are normal.

When finding confidence intervals, it is not necessary to label so that s_1^2 is greater than s_2^2. The only time we follow this practice is when testing hypotheses concerning variances.

If our level of confidence is $1 - \alpha = .95$, then $\alpha/2 = .025$. So the critical values of F needed in the denominators in the box are $F_{\alpha/2} = F_{.025}$ and $F_{1-\alpha/2} = F_{1-.025} = F_{.975}$, with df $= (n_1 - 1, n_2 - 1)$. There is no F table corresponding to .975 in Appendix B.6. However, we can find $F_{.975}$ indirectly as follows: Suppose that df $= (6, 8)$. To find $F_{.975}$, that is, $F_{1-.025}$, we look up $F_{.025}$ for the F distribution with degrees of freedom for the numerator and denominator interchanged, namely, df $= (8, 6)$. We then take the reciprocal of this. Using Appendix Table B.6, we see that when df $= (8, 6)$, $F_{.025} = 5.60$. Therefore, when df $= (6, 8)$,

$$F_{.975} = \frac{1}{5.60} \doteq .18$$

In general, to find $F_{1-\alpha/2}$ when df $= (a, b)$, we find $F_{\alpha/2}$ for df $= (b, a)$ and take the reciprocal of this.

EXAMPLE C.8

A college mathematics department was considering two mathematics screening examinations for the purpose of placing students. Students in two sections of an introductory mathematics course required of all students were given the test with the following results.

Examination	n	s^2
A	21	121
B	16	64

Let $s_1^2 = 121$ and $s_2^2 = 64$. Thus σ_1^2 is the population variance for exam A and σ_2^2 is the population variance for exam B. Find a 95% confidence interval for σ_1^2/σ_2^2.

Solution

The level of confidence is $1 - \alpha = .95$, so $\alpha = .05$. From Appendix Table B.6, $F_{\alpha/2} = F_{.025} = 2.76$ when df $= (20, 15)$. To find $F_{1-\alpha/2} = F_{.975}$, we look up $F_{.025}$ for df $= (15, 20)$ and take the reciprocal of this value. From Appendix Table B.6, when df $= (15, 20)$, $F_{.025} = 2.57$. Therefore, for df $= (20, 15)$,

$$F_{.975} = \frac{1}{2.57} \doteq .39$$

Our desired 95% confidence interval is

$$\left(\frac{121}{64}\right)\left(\frac{1}{2.76}\right) < \frac{\sigma_1^2}{\sigma_2^2} < \left(\frac{121}{64}\right)\left(\frac{1}{.39}\right)$$

$$.69 < \frac{\sigma_1^2}{\sigma_2^2} < 4.85$$

Thus we are 95% confident that σ_1^2/σ_2^2 is between .69 and 4.85. We can translate this into a 95% confidence interval for σ_1/σ_2 by taking the square root of each term:

$$.83 < \frac{\sigma_1}{\sigma_2} < 2.20$$

Note that the confidence interval for σ_1^2/σ_2^2 (and the confidence interval for σ_1/σ_2) includes 1. When $\sigma_1^2/\sigma_2^2 = 1$, $\sigma_1^2 = \sigma_2^2$. Therefore, we cannot reject the possibility that $\sigma_1^2 = \sigma_2^2$.

EXERCISES

C.18 For the sample data given, **(i)** test the given claims and **(ii)** indicate the possible type of error committed (Type I or Type II).

(a) Test the claim that the variances of populations A and B are different. Use a 5% level of significance.

	n	s^2
A	11	43
B	8	10

(b) Test the claim that the variances of populations A and B are the same. Use a 5% level of significance.

	n	s^2
A	8	43
B	11	10

(c) Test the claim that the variance of population A is smaller than the variance of population B. Use a 1% level of significance.

	n	s^2
A	21	5
B	31	20

(d) Test the claim that the variance of population A is larger than the variance of population B. Use a 5% level of significance.

	n	s^2
A	31	20
B	21	8

(e) Test the claim that the variances of populations A and B are different. Use a 10% level of significance.

	n	s^2
A	5	100
B	10	10

(f) Test the claim that the variance of population A is larger than the variance of population B. Use a 1% level of significance.

	n	s^2
A	10	100
B	5	10

C.19 Use the data in the corresponding parts of Exercise C.18 to construct confidence intervals for σ_A^2 / σ_B^2. The percent confidence is as follows:

(a) 95%   **(b)** 95%   **(c)** 98%

(d) 90%   **(e)** 90%   **(f)** 98%

C.20 Brands A and B of racquetballs were known to bounce to about the same height (in inches), on the average, under test conditions. The manufacturer of brand A claimed that the variability of bounce of brand A was smaller than that of brand B. Use the following sample data to test the manufacturer's claim at the 5% significance level:

	n	s^2
A	25	.50
B	25	1.10

C.21 An automobile executive was undecided about which odometer to adopt: brand A or brand B. The executive was convinced that the brands measured correct mileage, on the average, but that there may be a difference in their measurement variability. The executive had odometers of each brand tested on 100-mile automobile runs with the following results:

	n	s^2
A	21	.60
B	16	1.50

At a 10% level of significance, can the executive conclude that there is a difference in population variability between brands A and B?

(a) Use the classical approach.   **(b)** Use the *P*-value approach.

C.22 A manager of a supermarket wanted to compare the abilities of clerks A and B to service customers at the check-out line. The manager believed that both clerks serviced the customers with approximately the same mean time. However, there were complaints that clerk A spent too much time with some customers and rushed with others. The manager timed the check-out times of nine customers for each clerk. Use the following data and a 1% level of significance to see whether the data support the complaints.

	n	s^2
A	9	6
B	9	3

C.23 A biologist claimed that in the 20–24 age group, variability in systolic blood pressure is larger for males than females. Independent random samples of males and females in this age group were selected from the Framingham Heart Study. The data were as follows:

	n	$\bar{x}$	s
A (Males)	31	125	13.9
B (Females)	41	117	12.1

Test the biologist's claim using a 5% level of significance.

C.24 Consider the claim that the variance of population A is more than the variance of population B. With a 5% level of significance, one of the following two tables contains enough information to reject the null hypothesis; the other does not.

(a) Without testing, which table leads to rejection of H_0?

(b) Now complete the test for both cases and compare with part (a).

	n	s^2
A	41	100
B	41	50

	n	s^2
A	11	100
B	11	50

C.25 The purpose of this exercise is to demonstrate a relationship between the *t* and *F* distributions. To illustrate the relationship, complete the following table. Round off $(t_{.025})^2$ to two decimal places.

df for *F*	df for *t*	$F_{.05}$	$t_{.025}$	$(t_{.025})^2$
(1, 3)	3			
(1, 6)	6			
(1, 8)	8			
(1, 10)	10			
(1, 14)	14			
(1, 20)	20			

Note that $P[F > F_{.05}] = .05$. Also note that $t^2 > (t_{.025})^2$ if $t > t_{.025}$ or $t < -t_{.025}$. So $P\{t^2 > (t_{.025})^2\} = .05$. Conjecture a relationship between the F distribution with $(1, k)$ degrees of freedom and the t distribution with k degrees of freedom.

Notes

Gordon, T., W. Castelli, M. Hjortland, W. Kannel, and T. Dawber, "High Density Lipoprotein as a Protective Factor Against Coronary Disease: The Framingham Study," in *The American Journal of Medicine* 62 (1977).

Keys, A., ed., "Coronary Heart Disease in Seven Countries," in *Circulation* 41 (Suppl. 1):1 (1970).

Martin, R., W. Haskell, and P. Wood, "Blood Chemistry and Lipid Profiles of Elite Distance Runners," in *The Long Distance Runner*, P. Milvy, ed., New York: Urizen Books, 1977.

Wood, P., W. Haskell, M. Stern, S. Lewis, and C. Perry, "Plasma Lipoprotein Distributions in Male and Female Runners," in *The Long Distance Runner*, P. Milvy, ed., New York: Urizen Books, 1977.

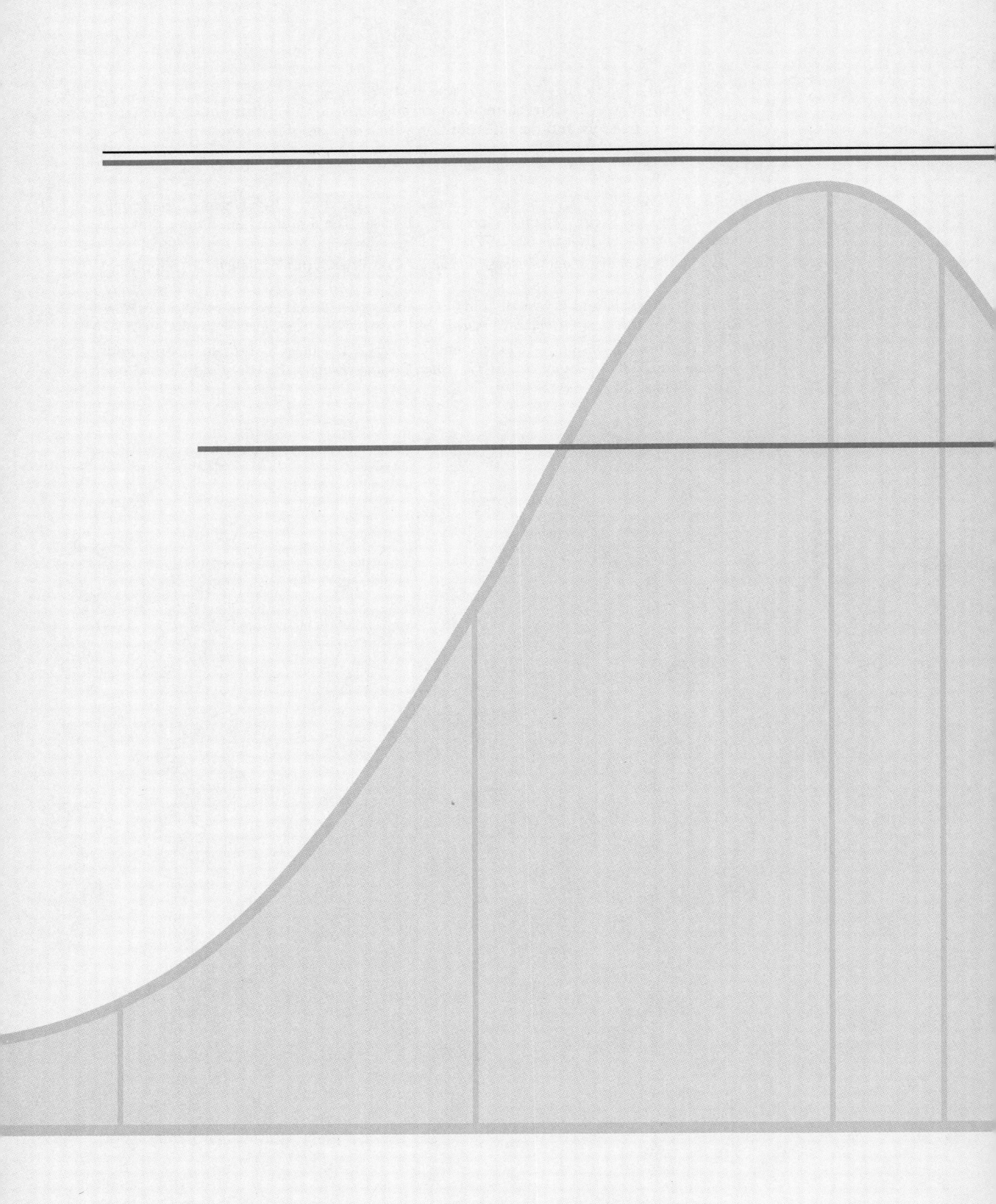

BIBLIOGRAPHY

1. Berenson, M., D. Levine, and M. Goldstein, *Intermediate Statistical Methods and Applications* (Englewood Cliffs, NJ: Prentice-Hall, 1983).

2. Bradley, J., *Distribution-Free Statistical Tests* (Englewood Cliffs, NJ: Prentice-Hall, 1968).

3. Conover, W., *Practical Nonparametric Statistics* (New York: John Wiley, 1971).

4. Daniel, W., *Applied Nonparametric Statistics* (Boston: Houghton Mifflin, 1978).

5. Draper, N., and H. Smith, *Applied Regression Analysis,* 2nd ed. (New York: John Wiley, 1981).

6. Ehrenberg, A., *A Primer in Data Reduction* (New York: John Wiley, 1982).

7. Fairley, W., and F. Mosteller, *Statistics and Public Policy* (Reading, MA: Addison-Wesley, 1977).

8. Freedman, D., R. Pisani, and R. Purves, *Statistics* (New York: W. W. Norton, 1978).

9. Haack, D., *Statistical Literacy: A Guide to Interpretation* (North Scituate, MA: Duxbury, 1979).

10. Hawkins, C., and J. Weber, *Statistical Analysis* (New York: Harper & Row, 1980).

11. Hoaglin, D., and Moore, D., eds. *Perspectives on Contemporary Statistics* (Washington, D.C.: Mathematical Association of America, 1992).

12. Hollander, M., and D. Wolfe, *Nonparametric Statistical Methods* (New York: John Wiley, 1973).

13. Huff, D., *How to Lie with Statistics* (New York: W. W. Norton, 1954).

14. Kirk, R., *Statistical Issues: A Reader for the Behavioral Sciences* (Monterey, CA: Brooks/Cole, 1982).

15. Kleinbaum, D., and L. Kupper, *Applied Regression Analysis and Other Multivariable Methods* (North Scituate, MA: Duxbury, 1978).

16. Koopmans, L., *An Introduction to Contemporary Statistics* (Boston: Duxbury, 1981).

17. Loftus, G., and E. Loftus, *Essence of Statistics* (Monterey, CA: Brooks/Cole, 1982).

18. Marascuilo, L., and M. McSweeney, *Nonparametric and Distribution-Free Methods for the Social Sciences* (Monterey, CA: Brooks/Cole, 1977).

19. Meyers, L., and N. Grossen, *Behavioral Research: Theory, Procedure, and Design* (San Francisco: Freeman, 1978).

20. Moore, D., and G. McCabe, *Introduction to the Practice of Statistics,* 2nd ed. (New York: Freeman, 1993).

21. Morrison, D., *Applied Linear Statistical Methods* (Englewood Cliffs, NJ: Prentice-Hall, 1983).

22. Mosteller, F., and R. Rourke, *Sturdy Statistics* (Reading, MA: Addison-Wesley, 1973).

23. Mosteller, F., R. Rourke, and G. Thomas, *Probability with Statistical Applications,* 2nd ed. (Reading, MA: Addison-Wesley, 1970).

24. Neter, J., W. Wasserman, and M. Kutner, *Applied Linear Statistical Models,* 3rd ed. (Homewood, IL: Richard D. Irwin, 1990).

25. Neter, J., W. Wasserman, and M. Kutner, *Applied Linear Regression Models* (Homewood, IL: Richard D. Irwin, 1983).

26. Neter, J., W. Wasserman, and G. Whitmore, *Applied Statistics* (Boston: Allyn and Bacon, 1978).

27. Phillips, J., *Statistical Thinking* (San Francisco: Freeman, 1982).

28. Ryan, B., B. Joiner, and T. Ryan, *Minitab Handbook,* 2nd ed. (Boston: Duxbury, 1985).

29. Snedecor, G., and W. Cochran, *Statistical Methods,* 7th ed. (Ames, IA: The Iowa State University Press, 1980).

30. Tanur, J., ed. *Statistics: A Guide to the Unknown* (San Francisco: Holden-Day, 1972).

31. Tufte, E., *Data Analysis for Politics and Policy* (Englewood Cliffs, NJ: Prentice-Hall, 1974).

32. Tukey, J., *Exploratory Data Analysis* (Reading, MA: Addison-Wesley, 1977).

33. Velleman, P., and D. Hoaglin, *Applications, Basics, and Computing of Exploratory Data Analysis* (Boston: Duxbury, 1981).

34. Weisberg, H., and B. Bowen, *An Introduction to Survey Research and Data Analysis* (San Francisco: Freeman, 1977).

35. Wheeler, M., *Lies, Damn Lies, and Statistics* (New York: Dell, 1976).

36. Wonnacott, T., and R. Wonnacott, *Introductory Statistics* (New York: John Wiley, 1977).

ANSWERS

Chapter 1

1.1 A sample is a subset of a population, so they have common elements. However, a population may contain elements that are not part of a sample.

1.3 True   **1.5** False   **1.7** Inferential

1.9 Descriptive   **1.11** Statistic   **1.13** Parameter

1.15 **(a)** The collection of 750 seniors. There are 750 data values in the population.

    (b) The average GPA   **(c)** 2.81

    (d) No. The two samples would consist of different data values and most likely the average values would be different. However, the value of the parameter would remain the same.

1.17 **(a)** A family is an element of the population, and the population size is 1000.

    (b) The sample consists of 50 families.

    (c) **(i)** 440   **(ii)** 430   **(d)** **(i)** .72   **(ii)** .87

1.19 {a, b, c}, {a, b, d}, {a, c, d}, {b, c, d}

1.21 **(a)** If the starting point is 00, we get {00, 10, 20, 30, 40, 50, 60, 70, 80, 90}

    (b) **(i)** {10, 37, 08, 99, 12, 66, 31, 85, 63, 73}
        (ii) {10, 37, 08, 99, 12, 66, 31, 85, 63, 44}
        (iii) {99, 66, 85, 63, 73, 98, 83, 88, 65, 80}

1.23 **(a)**

	Shift I	Shift II	Shift III	Totals
Males	11	9	5	25
Females	7	4	4	15
Totals	18	13	9	40

    (b)

	Shift I	Shift II	Shift III	Totals
Males	12	8	4	24
Females	8	4	4	16
Totals	20	12	8	40

(c) 16 females; 20 are in Shift I   **(d)** 24 from Shift II; 16 from Shift III

1.25 **(a)** The substance abuse program

(b) Treatment group is those who participated. Control group is those who did not participate.

(c) No   **(d)** Higher motivation of the volunteers

(e) Select 2 groups of alcoholics on SSI. Assign one group to participate in the program. Then track both groups.

1.27 **(a)** No. Although *U.S. News* did not specify whether this was a cross-sectional study or longitudinal study, it was in all probability a cross-sectional study. The heavier drinkers probably dropped out, or flunked out along the way, lowering the average consumption figure for upper-class students.

(b) Select a sample of freshmen and track them through four years, recording their drinking habits. Use in your study only those who completed all four years.

1.29 Longitudinal   **1.31** Cross-sectional   **1.33** Longitudinal

1.35

Job Applicants	A M	A F	B M	B F	C M	C F	D M	D F	Total M	Total F
Accepted	50	8	40	2	2	60	3	50	95	120
Rejected	100	16	60	3	10	300	24	400	194	719
Total	150	24	100	5	12	360	27	450	289	839
% accepted	33	33	40	40	17	17	11	11	33	14

Chapter 2

2.1 **(a)**

x	1	4	6	8	9	10	12
f	5	6	3	3	2	2	4

(b) Use 25 distinct data values.

2.3 **(a)**

x	2	3	4	5	6	7	8	9	10	12
f	1	5	6	3	6	6	4	2	2	1

(b) 41.7

2.5 **(a)**

x	22	32	33	36	37	39	40	41	42	43	44	45	46	48	49	51	52	61
f	1	5	1	2	2	3	3	1	4	2	4	2	2	1	4	1	1	1

(b)

Class	Class Limits	Frequency f
1	22–26	1
2	27–31	0
3	32–36	8
4	37–41	9
5	42–46	14
6	47–51	6
7	52–56	1
8	57–61	1

2.7 **(a)**

Class	Class Limits	Frequency f
1	1–2	1
2	3–4	11
3	5–6	9
4	7–8	10
5	9–10	4
6	11–12	1

(b) 5.5

(c) 4.5

(d) .278

2.9

Class Limits	Class Boundaries	Class Mark X
61–63	60.5–63.5	62
64–66	63.5–66.5	65
67–69	66.5–69.5	68
70–72	69.5–72.5	71
73–75	72.5–75.5	74
76–78	75.5–78.5	77
79–81	78.5–81.5	80
82–84	81.5–84.5	83

2.11 **(a)**

Class	Class Boundaries	Frequency f
1	189.75–196.75	5
2	196.75–203.75	2
3	203.75–210.75	9
4	210.75–217.75	4
5	217.75–224.75	6
6	224.75–231.75	3
7	231.75–238.75	1

(b) 207.25 **(c)** 7

2.13 **(a)**

Class	Class Limits	Frequency f
1	15–17	2
2	18–20	5
3	21–23	3
4	24–26	12
5	27–29	4
6	30–32	4

(b) 3

(c) 14.5

(d) .167

2.15

(a)　　　(b)

2.17

(a)　　　(b)

(c) 5

2.19

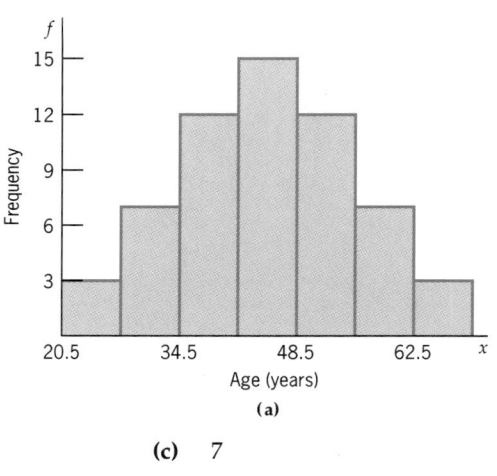

(a)

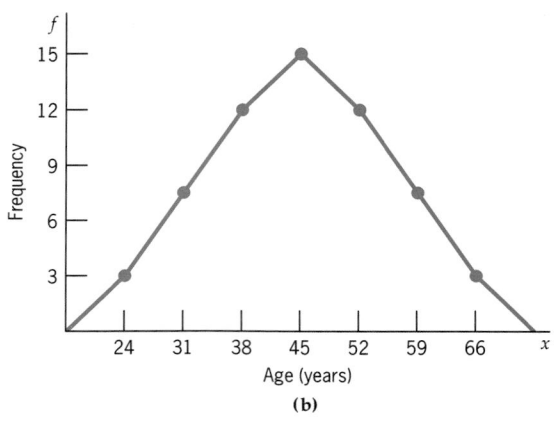

(b)

(c)   7

2.21

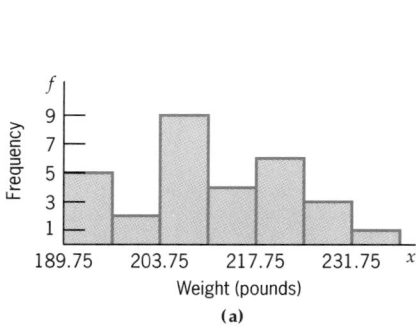

(a)

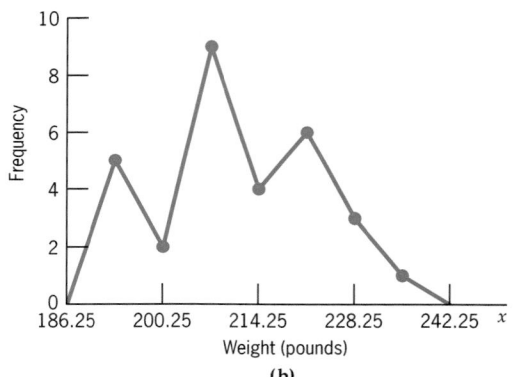

(b)

2.23

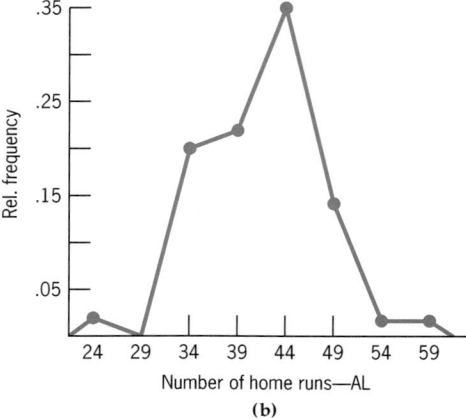

2.25   **(a)**   25   **(b)**   2–3   **(c)**   Fourth   **(d)**   5   **(e)**   0

2.27

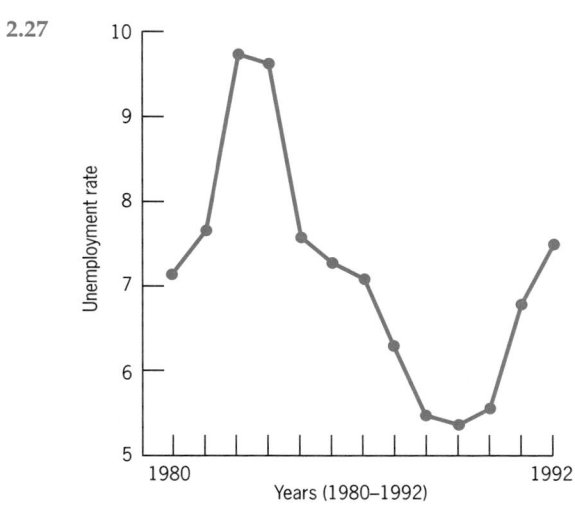

2.29

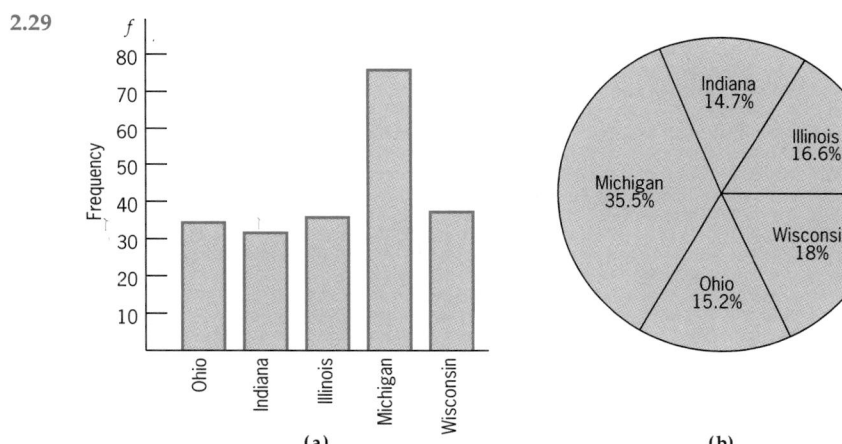

(a)   (b)

2.31   **(2.17)**   Skewed to the left   **(2.18)**   Skewed to the right
       (2.19)   Bell-shaped   **(2.20)**   Uniform

2.33   **(a)**   4 | 2   **(b)**   4 | 2
              5 | 9   4 |
              6 | 011158787   5 |
              7 | 04418   5 | 9
                                          6 | 0111
                                          6 | 58787
                                          7 | 0441
                                          7 | 8

       Skewed to the left; typical score is 67 or 68; 42 appears to be an outlier.

2.35   **(a)**   1 | 9   **(b)**   32.6   **(c)**   26.1
              2 | 1110000
              2 | 333222
              2 | 54
              2 | 76
              2 | 9
              3 |
              3 | 2

2.37   Damage   3 | 5 | No damage
                  78 | 5 |
                   3 | 6 |
                     | 6 | 677789
                  00 | 7 | 0023
                   5 | 7 | 56689
                     | 8 | 1

2.39   **(a)**   18 | 9   **(b)**   Symmetric   **(c)**   No apparent outliers
                  19 | 24
                  19 | 568
                  20 | 234
                  20 | 567888
                  21 | 024
                  21 | 569
                  22 | 02222
                  22 | 88
                  23 | 0
                  23 | 5

2.41   **(a)**   −1 | 41022   **(b)**   Skewed to the right   **(c)**   62.9 and possibly 49.9
                  −0 | 766557568
                  −0 | 1420
                   0 | 32424103
                   0 | 6697
                   1 | 120
                   1 | 7976885
                   2 | 4412
                   2 | 65
                   3 | 44
                   3 |
                   4 |
                   4 | 9
                   5 |
                   5 |
                   6 | 2

2.43   **(a)**

x	4.1	4.3	4.4	4.5	4.6	4.7	4.8	4.9	5.1	5.5	5.7
f	1	3	1	3	2	4	1	1	2	1	1

   (b)   80

(c)

2.45   For each variable, most data values occur with frequency 1. In each case, it would not be worthwhile to construct a frequency distribution.

2.47

Class	Class Limits	Frequency f
1	0–6	3
2	7–13	4
3	14–20	4
4	21–27	5
5	28–34	4

2.49

Class	Class Limits	Frequency f
1	10–19	1
2	20–29	3
3	30–39	5
4	40–49	3
5	50–59	2
6	60–69	3
7	70–79	2
8	80–89	1

2.51 **(a)**

Class	Class Boundaries	Frequency f	Relative Frequency
1	23.5–26.5	10	.05
2	26.5–29.5	30	.15
3	29.5–32.5	12	.06
4	32.5–35.5	47	.235
5	35.5–38.5	50	.25
6	38.5–41.5	28	.14
7	41.5–44.5	5	.025
8	44.5–47.5	18	.09

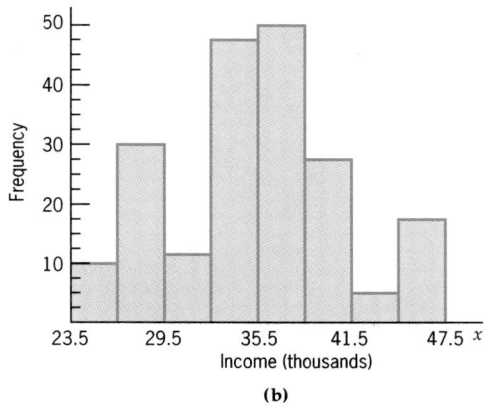

(b)

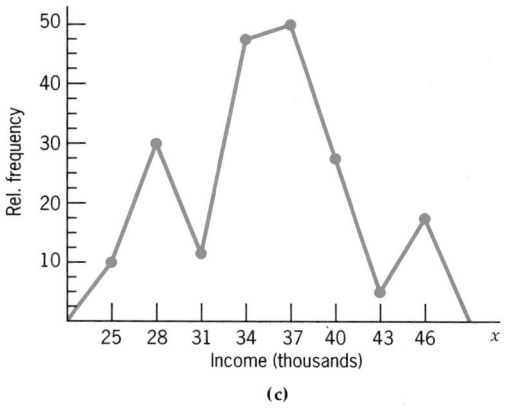

(c)

(d) **(i)** .505 **(ii)** .235

2.53 **(b)** Each integer should occur about 1/10 of the time. The approximate shape should be uniform.

2.55 **(a)**

Class Limits	Frequency f
24–213	22
214–403	18
404–593	6
594–783	3
784–973	1
974–1163	1

(b)

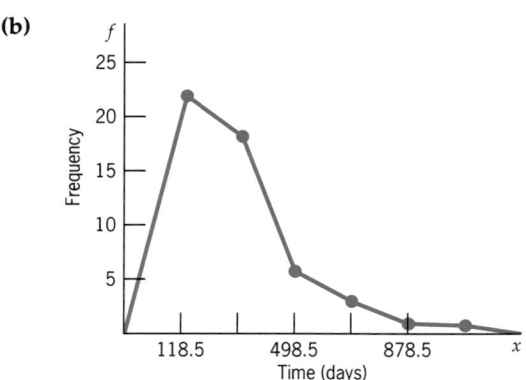

(c) Skewed to the right

(d) 21.6

2.57 **(a)**

```
1 | 5
1 | 7
1 | 89
2 | 0001
2 | 33
2 | 4444455555
2 | 6677
2 | 89
3 | 001
3 | 2
```

(b) Symmetric

2.59 **(a)**

```
 1 | 7
 2 | 477257
 3 | 14782
 4 | 32521
 5 | 0720468
 6 | 6398891732
 7 | 89149
 8 | 3978
 9 | 21
10 |
11 | 30
12 | 15
13 | 4
```

(b) Skewed to the right

(c)

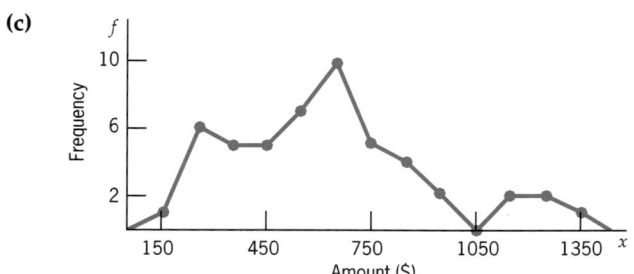

2.61

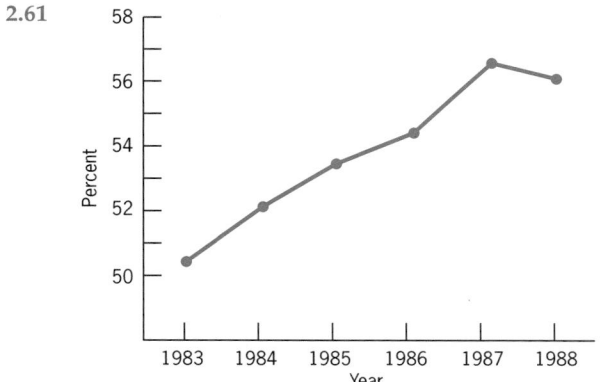

2.63

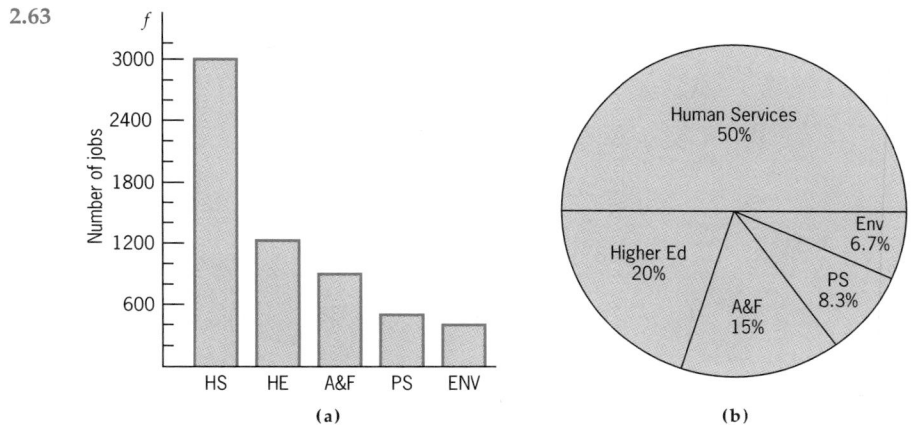

2.65

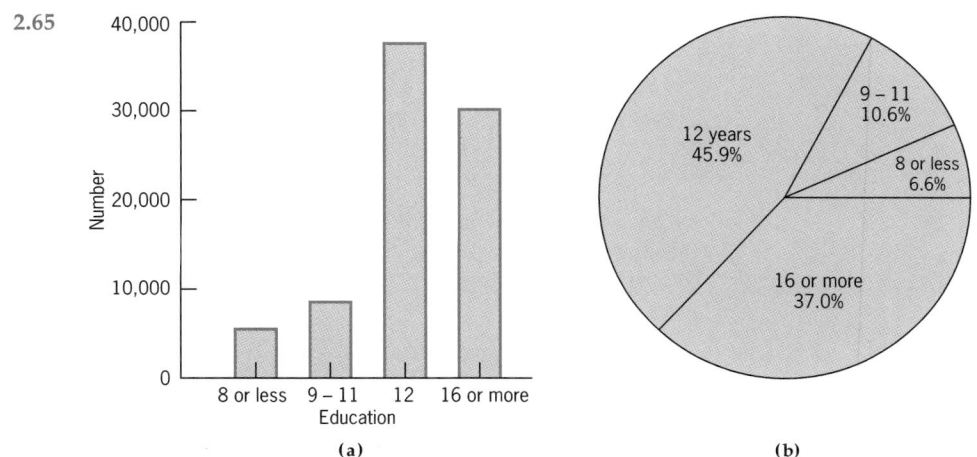

2.67

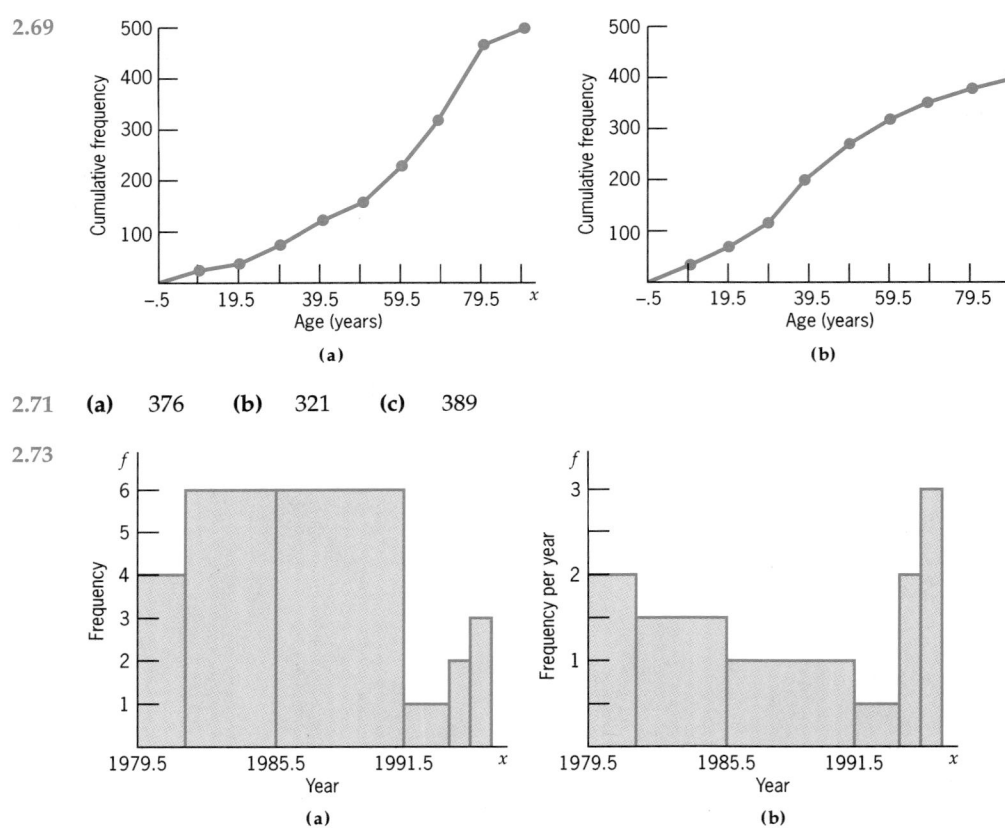

(c) The graphs are quite different after the age of 45, as the numbers of admittances are much higher at the Florida hospital. Many more older people live in Florida than in Massachusetts.

2.69

2.71 **(a)** 376 **(b)** 321 **(c)** 389

2.73

In part (a), the areas of the rectangles are not proportional to the frequency of the appropriate class. The frequency histogram in part (b) gives a more accurate description of profits.

Chapter 3

3.1 **(a)** 8 **(b)** 3.5 **(c)** 8
3.3 **(a)** 18 **(b)** 4 **(c)** 19
3.5 **(a)** Damage: 63.71; No damage: 72.13 **(b)** Damage: 63; No damage: 71

3.7 **(a)**

```
5 | 9
6 | 0111
6 | 57788
7 | 0144
7 | 8
```

(b) **(i)** 66.93 **(ii)** 67

3.9 **(a)**

```
1 | 5789
2 | 0112
2 |
3 | 4
3 | 8
```

(b) **(i)** 22.5 **(ii)** 20.5

3.11 **(a)** 292.39 **(b)** 249

3.13 About half of the families in the United States reported an income of less than $35,776.

3.15 **(a)** 15 **(b)** 0 **(c)** 24 **(d)** 69 **(e)** 225 **(f)** 105

3.17 **(b)** Median **(c)** 9.4; 5

3.19 **(a)** 13 **(b)** 14.44 **(c)** 3.80

3.21 **(a)** 24 **(b)** 87.07 **(c)** 9.33

3.23 **(a)** 22 **(b)** 53.21 **(c)** 7.29

3.25 0

3.27 Since both cans of balls bounce the same height on average, choose the can of balls with the smaller variability in the bounce.

3.29 **(b)**

```
  8 | 0 |
 46 | 1 |
 59 | 2 |
    | 3 |
 37 | 4 |
 48 | 5 | 688
 49 | 6 | 02389971
  1 | 7 | 1
```

(c) Bismarck: $\bar{x} = 41.5$ $s = 22.46$
San Diego: $\bar{x} = 63.5$ $s = 5.11$

3.31 **(a)** 49 **(b)** 4 **(c)** 4.56

3.33 **(a)** 66 **(b)** 92 **(c)** 65 **(d)** 87
(e) 22 **(f)** 36.67 **(g)** 65.5

3.35 **(a)** 6 **(b)** 19 **(c)** 6 **(d)** 30

3.37 **(a)** **(i)** 4.3 **(ii)** 4.6 **(iii)** 4.9
(b) .6 **(c)** 5.2 **(d)** 98.5

3.39 **(a)** Median and interquartile range. Data are strongly skewed to the right.
(b) Mean and standard deviation. Data are nearly symmetric.
(c) Median and interquartile range. Data are strongly skewed to the left.

3.41 **(a)** $Q_1 = 37$ $Q_3 = 45.75$ **(b)** 8.75

3.43

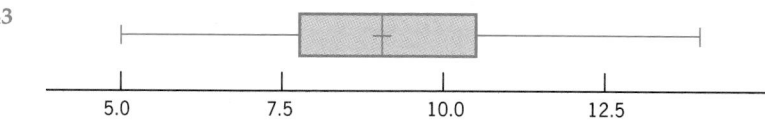

The distribution of data is nearly symmetric.

3.45 **(a)**

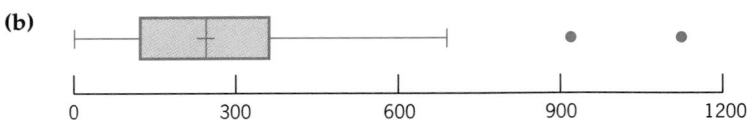

(b)

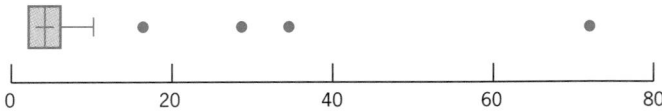

Suspected outliers are 955 and 1160.

(c) The distribution of data is skewed to the right.

3.47 Suspected outliers are 16, 16, 28, 35, 73.

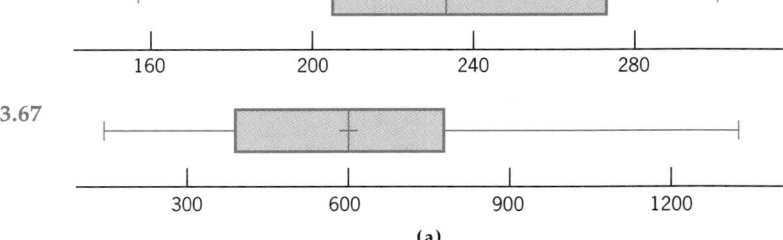

3.49 **(a)** Yes **(b)** Yes

3.51 **(a)** Median is about the same for soprano and alto, but tenor median is larger and bass median is largest. (Note that the median is very close to Q_3 for the sopranos.)

(b) 25% **(c)** No

3.53 **(a)** 9 **(b)** 8.5 **(c)** 13 **(d)** 15.09 **(e)** 3.88

(f) $Q_1 = 6$, $Q_3 = 11.5$ **(g)** 5.5 **(h)** 41.7

(i) There are no extreme observations, so use $\bar{x}$ and s.

3.55 **(a)** **(i)** 727 **(ii)** 1124 **(b)** 397

(c) **(i)** 545 **(ii)** 1289 **(d)** **(i)** 50 **(ii)** 68.1

3.57 $Q_1 = 74$ $Q_2 = 171/2$ $Q_3 = 357/4$ $P_{30} = 761/10$ $P_{80} = 477/5$

3.59 **(a)** 31 **(b)** 15

3.61 **(a)** Skewed to the right. The median appears to be a better measure and is likely to be smaller than the mean.

(b) 443,559.23 thousand **(c)** 227,030 thousand

(d) 132,130 thousand **(e)** 115,522.5 thousand

3.63 **(b)** 15.08; 13.8 **(c)** 9.4; 19.3

(d) 9.9 **(e)** 4.5 **(f)** Buffalo

3.65 No suspected outliers

3.67

(a)

(b) Skewed to the right

3.69

	Within	No. of Data	%	Empirical Rule %
1 SD	(34.36–48.58)	26	65	68
2 SDs	(27.25–55.69)	38	95	95
3 SDs	(20.14–62.80)	40	100	99.7

3.71 **(a)** $3/4$ **(b)** $11/36$ **(c)** $15/16$

3.73 **(a)** 4 **(b)** 4

3.75 **(a)** 12 **(b)** $8 + c$ **(c)** 16 **(d)** $k\bar{x} = k(8)$ **(e)** 31

Chapter 4

4.1

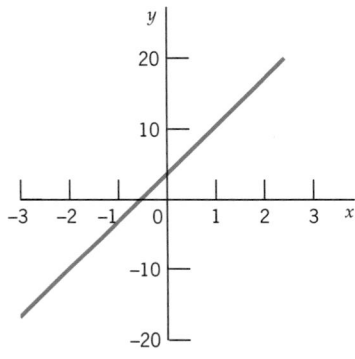

(a) $b_0 = 4, b_1 = 7$

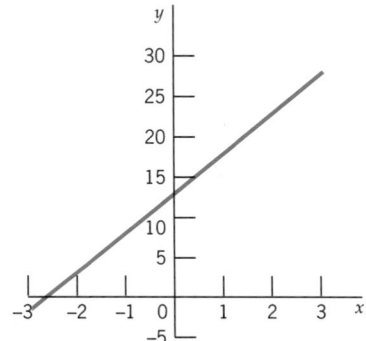

(b) $b_0 = 13, b_1 = 5$

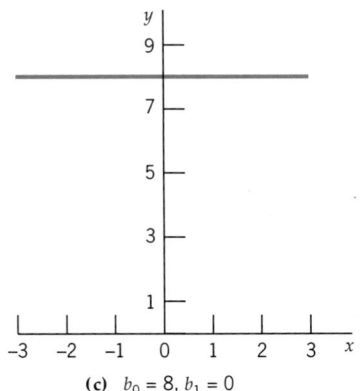

(c) $b_0 = 8, b_1 = 0$

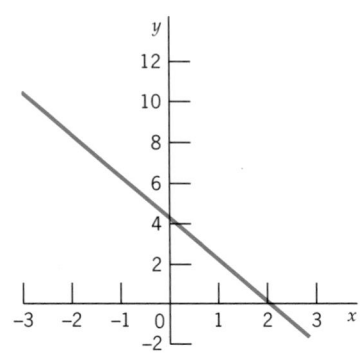

(d) $b_0 = 9/2, b_1 = -2$

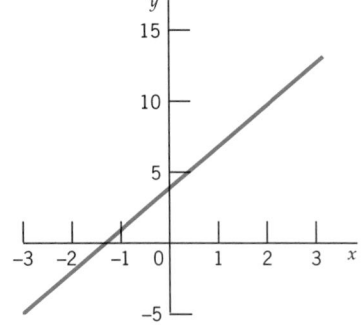

(e) $b_0 = 4, b_1 = 3$

4.3

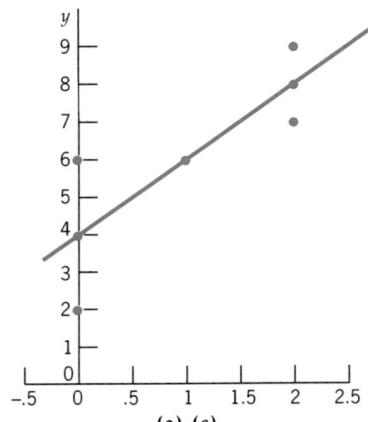

(a), (c)

(b) $\hat{y} = 4 + 2x$

4.5

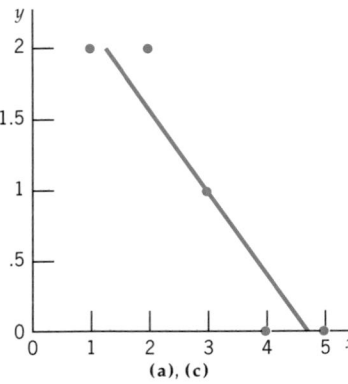

(a), (c)

(b) $\hat{y} = 2.8 - .6x$

4.7 **(a)** 10 **(c)** 34

4.9

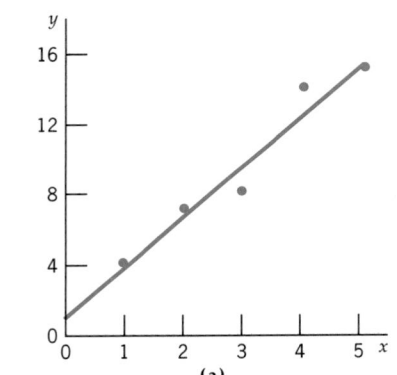

(a)

(b) $\hat{y} = .9 + 2.9x$ **(c)** 11.05

4.11

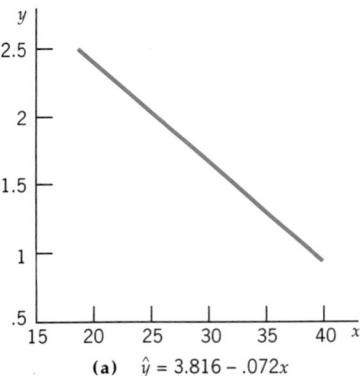

(a) $\hat{y} = 3.816 - .072x$

(b) 1.728

4.13

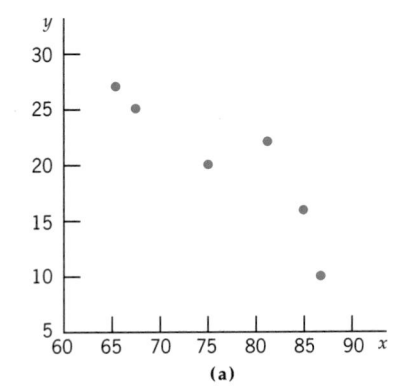

(a)

(b) $\hat{y} = 66.29 - .60x$

(c) 24.29

4.15

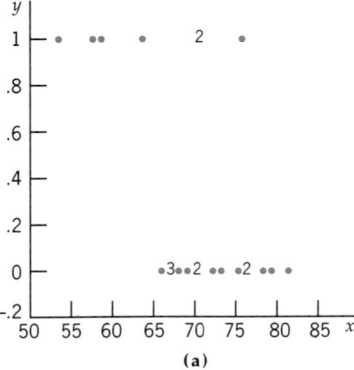

(a)

(b) $\hat{y} = 2.90 - .0374x$

(c) .92

4.17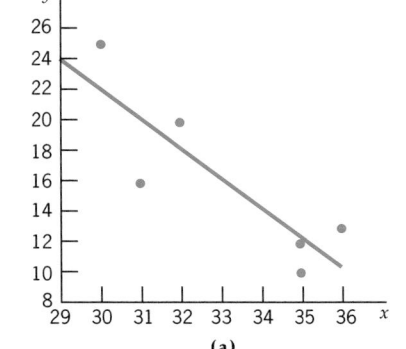

(a)

(b) $\hat{y} = 80.54 - 1.95x$ **(c)** 14.24

4.19 **(b)** $\hat{y} = 51.26 - 9.24x$ **(c)** -9.24 **(d)** 28.16

4.21 **(a)** $\hat{y} = 128.95 + 1.63x$ **(b)** $\hat{y} = 42.01 + 1.96x$

4.23 **(a)** $\hat{y} = 48.7075 - 8.36459x$ **(b)** 23.6 MPG

4.25 **(a)** .840 **(b)** .706. About 71% of the variation in y is explained by the linear relationship with x.

4.27 **(a)** $-.949$ **(b)** .901. About 90% of the variation in y is explained by the linear relationship with x.

4.29 .74

4.31 **(a)** .926 **(b)** .857. About 86% of the variation in the incidence of cancer is explained by the linear relationship with the index of exposure.

4.33 **(a)** .74. About 74% of the variation in the 1991 per capita tax collection is explained by the linear relationship with the 1980 per capita tax collection for the 50 states.

(b) .77. About 77% of the variation in the 1991 per capita tax collection is explained by the linear relationship with the 1980 per capita tax collection for the 49 states.

4.35 **(b)** Approximately 81.4% of the variation in PRO is explained by the linear relationship with UNEMP.

(c) $-.902$

4.37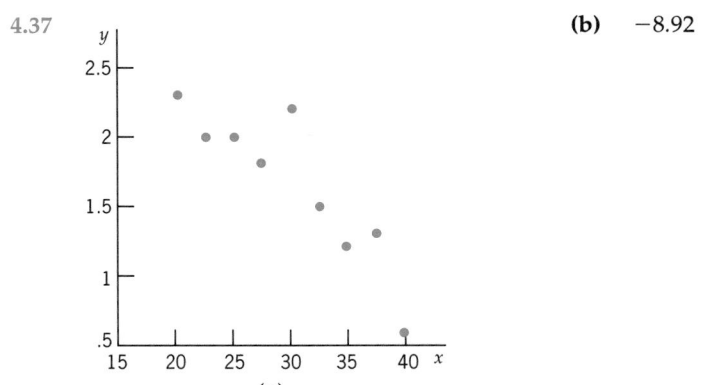

(a)

(b) -8.92

(c) .796. About 80% of the variation in number of absences is explained by the linear relationship with salary.

4.39 **(a)** TSS $= 100$; $r^2 = .40$ **(b)** SSE $= 200$; $r^2 = .33$

(c) SSE $= 120$; TSS $= 200$ **(d)** SSR $= 63$; TSS $= 90$

4.41 **(a)** $s_x = 2.121320$ $s_y = 2.915476$ **(b)** .687184 **(c)** $\hat{y} = 1.17 + .94x$

4.43 **(a)** $\hat{y} = 8.17 - .83x$ **(b)** 3.5022 **(c)** 16

(d) The line of best fit minimizes SSE.

4.45

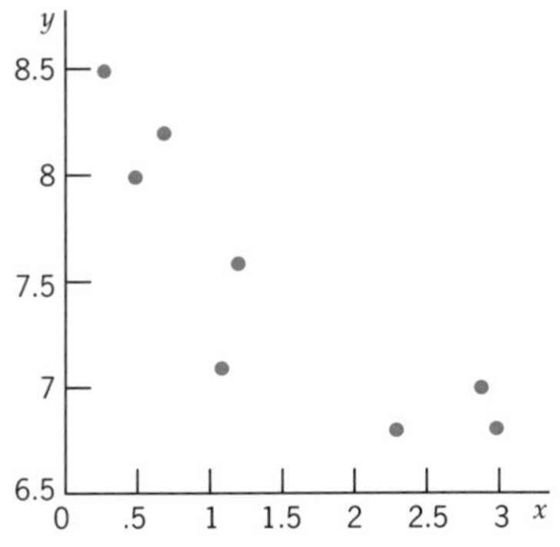

(a)

(b) $r = -.876$; $r^2 = .768$. About 77% of the variation in rent is explained by the linear relationship with distance from a rapid transit station.

(c) $\hat{y} = 8.314 - .543x$ **(d)** $750

4.47

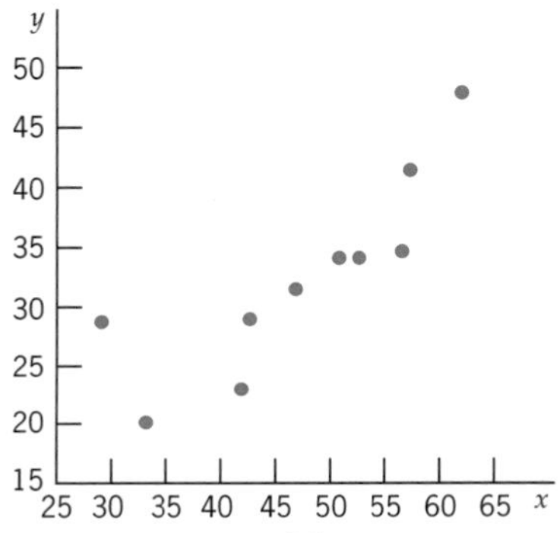

(a)

(b) $r = .839$; $r^2 = .704$. About 70% of the variation in median household income is explained by the linear relationship with percentage of residents who are college graduates.

(c) $\hat{y} = 2.446 + .634x$ **(d)** $27,806

4.49

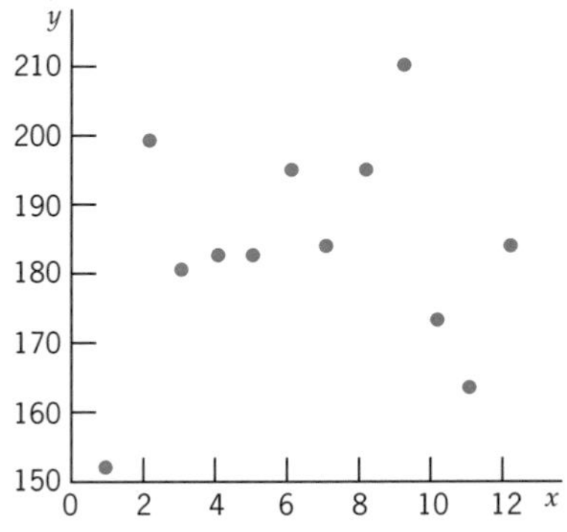

(a)

(b) $r = .115$; $r^2 = .013$. About 1% of the variation in mean number of days called into service per month is explained by the linear relationship with months.

4.51 **(b)** $r = -.806$; $r^2 = .65$. About 65% of the variation in miles per gallon is explained by the linear relationship with the number of cylinders.

(c) $\hat{y} = 42.509 - 3.290x$

4.53

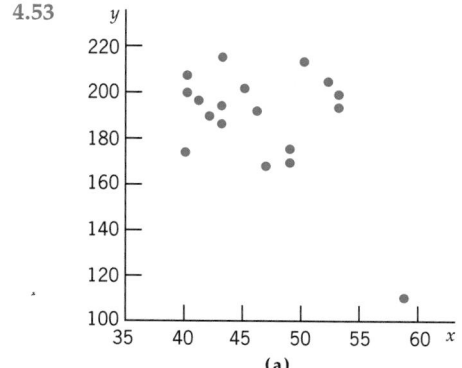

(a)

(b) $r = -.485846$; $r^2 = .2360$ **(c)** $r = -.041027$; $r^2 = .001683$

4.55 **(a)** $r^2 = .222427$. About 22% of the variation in number of home runs is explained by the number of hits.

(b) $\hat{y} = -151.07 + .202748x$; 153 **(c)** 5

4.57 **(a)** $\hat{y} = -3.25 + 1.25x$

(b)

x	y	$\hat{y}$	$\bar{y}$	$(y - \bar{y})^2$	$(\hat{y} - \bar{y})^2$
2	0	$-.75$	3	9	14.0625
5	0	3.00	3	9	0.0000
5	3	3.00	3	0	0.0000
6	4	4.25	3	1	1.5625
6	4	4.25	3	1	1.5625
6	7	4.25	3	16	1.5625

(c) TSS = 36 SSR = 18.75

(d) $r^2 = .52$, so about 52% of the variation in y is explained by the linear relationship with x.

4.59 **(a)** TSS = 100; $r^2 = .5$ **(b)** SSE = 300; $r^2 = .25$

(c) SSR = 10; $r^2 = .2$ **(d)** SSE = 60; TSS = 150

(e) SSR = 12; TSS = 40 **(f)** SSR = 32; SSE = 8

(g) SSE = 0; TSS = 50 **(h)** SSR = 75; $r^2 = 1$

Chapter 5

5.1 **(a)** {O, A, B, AB}

(b) {OO, OA, OB, O̲A̲B, AO, AA, AB, A̲A̲B, BO,

BA, BB, B̲A̲B, A̲B̲O, A̲B̲A, A̲B̲B, A̲B̲ AB}

5.3 **(a)** {4260, 4261, 4262, 4263, 4264, 4265, 4266, 4267, 4268, 4269}

(b) {2468, 2648, 4268, 4628, 6248, 6428}

5.5 {xX, xY, XX, XY}

5.7 {0A, 0B, 0C, 0D, 0E, 1A, 1B, 1C, 1D, 1E}

(a) {0D, 0E} **(b)** {1A, 1B, 1C, 1D}

(c) {0A, 0B, 1A, 1B} **(d)** {1A, 1B, 1C, 1D, 1E}

5.9 **(a)** {M1, M2, M3, F1, F2, F3}

(b) {F1, F2, F3, F4, F5, F6, M4, M5, M6}

(c) {M6} **(d)** {M3}

5.11   (a)   1/6   (b)   11/36   (c)   25/36   (d)   2/9

5.13   (a)   {0, 1, 2, 3, 4, 5, 6, 7, 8, 9}

     (b)   {1, 3, 5, 7, 9}   1/2   (c)   {7, 8, 9}   3/10

5.15   (a)   3/8   (b)   1/4   (c)   1/16   (d)   15/16

5.17   (a)   .2072   (b)   .3710

5.19   17,576,000

5.21   (a)   8,100,000,000   (b)   9,000,000   (c)   10,000

5.23   (a)   .0012   (b)   .0046   (c)   .25

5.25   (b)   4/13

5.27   (a)   .477   (b)   .387   (c)   .197

5.29   (a)   (i)   .0059   (ii)   .1538   (b)   .0055

5.31   .3439   5.33   .0043   5.35   .9750

5.37   (a)   .0045   (b)   .0769; no   (c)   .1493

5.39   (a)   1/2   (b)   0   5.41   .4286

5.43   (a)   .6250   (b)   .5385   (c)   .6316   (d)   .3

5.45   (a)   .5119   (b)   .1961   (c)   No   5.47   (a)   1/2   (b)   1/3

5.49   (a)   720   (b)   1320   (c)   120   (d)   220   (e)   220   (f)   1

5.51   3,628,800

5.53   (a)   .0333   (b)   1/2

5.55   (a)   .0014   (b)   .0083   (c)   1/3

5.57   (a)   .0026   (b)   .000005

5.59 S = {11, 12, 13, 14, 21, 22, 23, 24, 31, 32, 33, 34, 41, 42, 43, 44}

5.61   Let events W = won and L = lost

     (a) S = {WW, WL, LW, LL}

     (b)   (i)   {WW}   (ii)   {WL, LW}

5.63   (a)   1/365   (b)   31/365   (c)   12/365   (d)   92/365

5.65   (a)   .0211   (b)   .8313   (c)   13

5.67   (a)   .1875   (b)   .3750   (c)   .0625   (d)   .4375

5.69   (a)   .06   (b)   .44   (c)   .38

5.71   (a)   .1111   (b)   .3333   (c)   .2222

5.73   (a)   .3   (b)   .63   (c)   .97

5.75   (a)   .495   (b)   .33   (c)   .695

5.77   (a)   .4   (b)   .5667   (c)   .8

     (d)   .4706   (e)   .7   (f)   No

5.79   (a)   479,001,600   (b)   6840   (c)   1140   (d)   9900

5.81   (a)   10. {A, B}, {A, C}, {A, D}, {A, E}, {B, C}, {B, D}, {B, E}, {C, D}, {C, E}, {D, E}

     (b)   20. AB, BA, AC, CA, AD, DA, AE, EA, BC, CB, BD, DB, BE, EB, CD, DC, CE, EC, DE, ED

5.83   792

5.85   (a)   .000018   (b)   .0005   (c)   .000009

5.87   The exact probability is .8144. The simulated probability is .825.

Chapter 6

6.1   (a)   Discrete   (b)   Continuous   (c)   Continuous

    (d)   Discrete   (e)   Continuous   (f)   Discrete

6.3 **(a)** 3, 4, 5, 6, 7, 8, 9, 10, 11, 12, 13, 14, 15, 16, 17, 18

(b) 1, 2, 3, 4, 5, 6 **(c)** 2, 4, 6, 8, 10, 12

6.5 **(a)** Nonnegative numbers; that is, $x \geq 0$ **(b)** Continuous

6.7 **(a)** 0, 1, 2, ..., 500 **(b)** Discrete

6.9

x	25	25.7	26.6	27.2	27.3	27.8	28.4	29
$P(x)$	1/15	2/15	1/15	1/15	4/15	2/15	2/15	2/15

6.11

x	1	2	3	4	5	6	7	8	9
$P(x)$	20/50	12/50	4/50	5/50	5/50	1/50	1/50	1/50	1/50

6.13 **(a)**

x	0	1
$P(x)$	.468	.532

(b)

x	0	1
$P(x)$	.623	.377

6.15

x	0	1	2	3
$P(x)$	.49	.38	.10	.03

6.17 No; $P(x)$ cannot be negative

6.19 Yes

6.21

x	0	1	2	3
$P(x)$	.34	.38	.12	.16

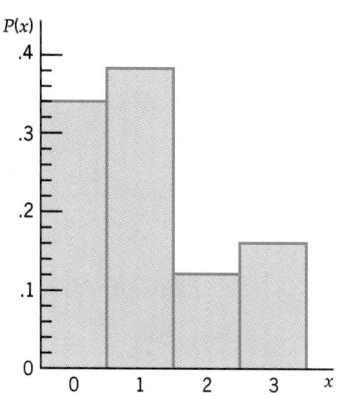

6.23 **(a)** 1 **(b)** 1 **(c)** 1 **(d)** Skewed to the right

6.25 **(a)** 3.5 **(b)** 1.25 **(c)** 1.118 **(d)** Symmetric

6.27 **(a)** 2.65 **(b)** 1.028 **(c)** 1.014

6.29 **(a)** 2.167 **(b)** .472

6.31 **(a)** 56.3 cents per game **(b)** $5.63

6.33 Expected loss is 86.25 cents

6.35 **(a)** Yes **(b)** No **(c)** No **(d)** Yes **(e)** No

6.37 **(a)** .309 **(b)** .360 **(c)** .168

6.39 **(a)** .004 **(b)** .021 **(c)** .074 **(d)** .267 **(e)** .960

6.41 **(a)** .177 **(b)** .090 **(c)** .973

6.43 **(a)** .177 **(b)** .991

6.45 .723

6.47 **(a)** .246 **(b)** .859 **(c)** 3.2

6.49 **(a)** .190 **(b)** .011 **(c)** .392 **(d)** 2

6.51 **(a)** 62.37 **(b)** 7.26 **(c)** 6.52

(d) $\mu = 23.09$ $\sigma = 4.67$ 1.73

6.53

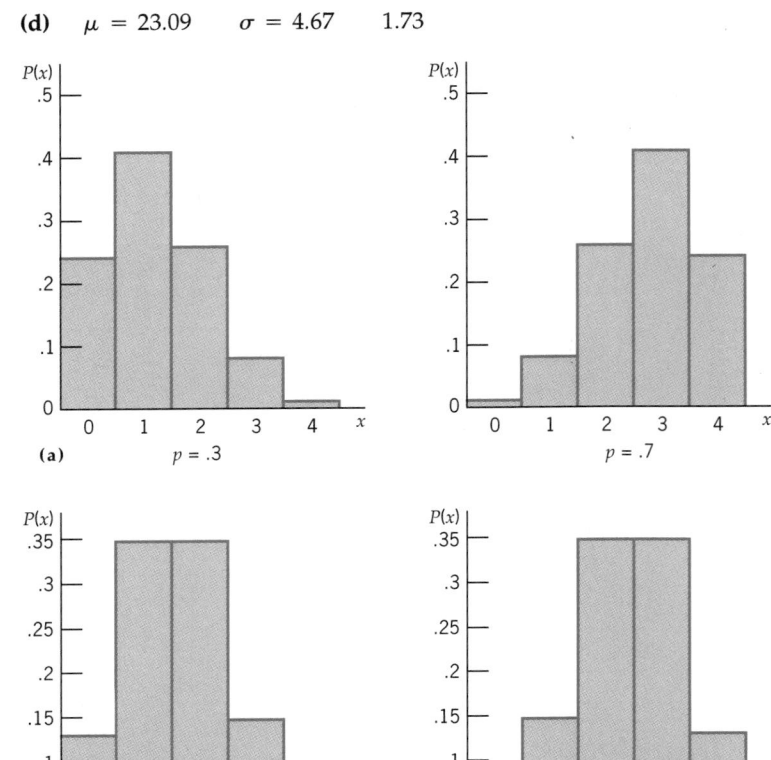

In both (a) and (b), the distributions are mirror images of each other.

6.55

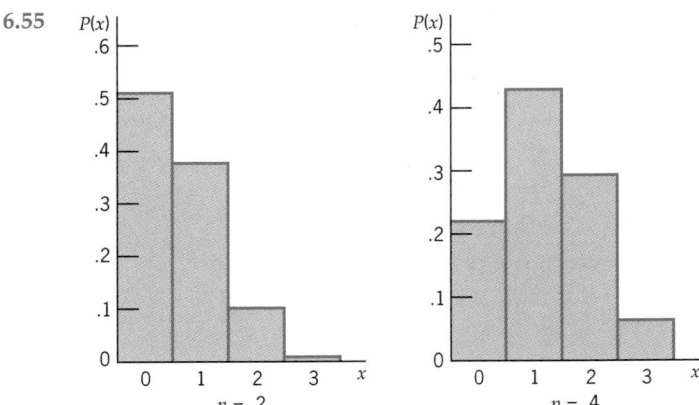

The degree of skewness lessens as p increases to $p = .5$. When $p = .5$, the binomial distribution, for any n, is symmetric. Then as p increases from $p = .5$ toward $p = 1$, the distributions become more skewed (and are skewed to the left).

6.57 **(a)**   The blood cholesterol level; continuous.

(b)   The population (conceptual) is the collection of all blood cholesterol levels of people who will use the diet. The sample is the collection of 50 readings.

6.59   Yes   **6.61**   No, because $P(4)$ is less than zero

6.63 **(a)**   1/10   **(b)**   3   **(c)**   3   **(d)**   1.732

6.65   1/10   **6.67**   2

6.69 **(a)**

x	0	1	2	3
$P(x)$	.729	.243	.027	.001

(b)   .3   **(c)**   .27   **(d)**   .52

6.71 **(a)**   1.2   **(b)**   .84   **(c)**   .917

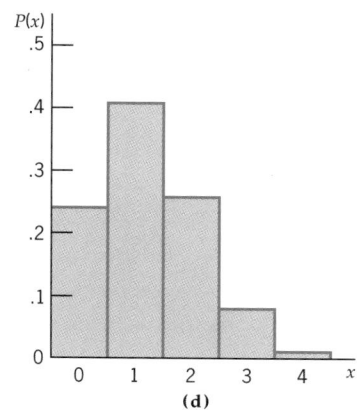
(d)

6.73 **(a)**   .5   **(b)**   .8   **(c)**   .3   **6.75** $3.89

6.77 **(a)**   .927   **(b)**   .283

6.79 **(a)**   .219   **(b)**   .298   **(c)**   .004   **6.81**   .886

6.83 **(a)**   9.6   **(b)**   1.92   **(c)**   1.386

6.85 **(a)**   4.5   **(b)**   3.15   **(c)**   1.775

Chapter 7

7.1 **(a)**   .25   **(b)**   .75   **(c)**   .7

(d)   .9   **(e)**   1   **(f)**   0

7.3 **(a)**   .0456   **(b)**   .5   **(c)**   .1359   **(d)**   .8413

(e)   .4772   **(f)**   .6826   **(g)**   .9544

7.5 **(a)**   5   **(b)**   1/16   **(c)**   1/2   **(d)**   55/64

7.7 **(a)**   .4484   **(b)**   .4934   **(c)**   .9374   **(d)**   .1210   **(e)**   .1792

7.9 **(a)**   .2486   **(b)**   .0316   **(c)**   .9375

(d)   .9686   **(e)**   .0456   **(f)**   .9544

7.11 **(a)**   1.72   **(b)**   −1.24   **(c)**   1.41   **(d)**   −2.45

(e)   2.05   **(f)**   −.67   **(g)**   −1.28   **(h)**   .39

7.13   A: .0287   B: .6628   C: .2417   D: .0668

7.15 **(a)**   50%   **(b)**   15.87%   **(c)**   93.32%   **(d)**   2.28%

(e)   77.34%   **(f)**   37.21%   **(g)**   13.59%

(h)   50.62%   **(i)**   86.64%   **(j)**   2.14%

7.17   **(a)**   216.75   **(b)**   190.25   **(c)**   67   **(d)**   2.28

7.19   A: .0336   B: .6922   C: .2563   D: .0179

7.21   **(a)**   .7352   **(b)**   .6826   **(c)**   98.76%

7.23   **(a)**   665   **(b)**   (448, 552)   **(c)**   67

7.25   **(a)**   .1056   **(b)**   11.64 minutes   **(c)**   11:15

7.27   **(a)**   789.6   **(b)**   59.52   7.29   **(a)**   .047   **(b)**   .0485

7.31   **(a)**   .192   **(b)**   .1896   7.33   **(a)**   .203   **(b)**   .2059   7.35   .0104

7.37   **(a)**   .0013

       (b)   If the claim were true, only about 13 in 10,000 times would fewer than 211 voters be observed in a random sample of 400. The evidence suggests that the board's claim is false.

7.39   .0008. If the chances of a boy or girl being born were equally likely, only about 8 in 10,000 times, on average, would 120 or more girls be born out of 195 births. The administrator's claim appears justified.

7.41   **(a)**   About 0   **(b)**   .0516

7.43   **(a)**

$\bar{x}$	0	1	2	3	4
$P(\bar{x})$	1/9	2/9	3/9	2/9	1/9

       (b)   **(i)**   2   **(ii)**   4/3

       (c)   **(i)**   2   **(ii)**   8/3

7.45   **(a)**   200   **(b)**   10   **(c)**   .3830

       (d)   .1587   **(e)**   .0398   **(f)**   .4602

7.47   **(a)**   .0132   **(b)**   .1335   **(c)**   .6648   7.49   .0244

7.51   **(a)**   .8413   **(b)**   .0062   **(c)**   5.767

7.53   **(a)** $n = 100$:   3   .0267

             $n = 25$:   3   .1067

             $n = 10$:   3   .2667

       (b)   Notice that the variance of $\bar{x}$ increases as n decreases. We would expect the width of the boxplots to increase as n decreases.

7.55   **(a)**   1/2

       (b)   For $0 \le x \le 1/2$, $y = f(x) = x$. For $1/2 \le x \le 9/4$, $y = f(x) = 1/2$.

       (c)   7/8   **(d)**   5/8   **(e)**   3/4   **(f)**   1/32

7.57   **(a)**   22.4   **(b)**   76.6   **(c)**   7

7.59   **(a)**   .4686   **(b)**   .4306   **(c)**   .8430   **(d)**   .0478   **(e)**   .2210

7.61   **(a)**   23   **(b)**   933   **(c)**   21   **(d)**   12

7.63   **(a)**   .5328   **(b)**   .2039   **(c)**   .0062   **(d)**   .9082

7.65   A: .2643   B: .4714   C: .1587   D: .1056

7.67   **(a)**   .0062   **(b)**   .4938   **(c)**   .8944

7.69   **(a)**   .166   **(b)**   .1635

7.71   **(a)**   .196   **(b)**   .1985

7.73   **(a)**   .387   **(b)**   .3859

7.75   **(a)**   .1711   **(b)**   .9596   **(c)**   .9978

       (d)   .0606   **(e)**   .0398   **(f)**   .0242

7.77   .9778

7.79   **(a)**   71   **(b)**   .25   **(c)**   97.72%   **(d)**   57.93%

7.81 **(a)** 2.28% **(b)** 15.87% **(c)** 68.53% **(d)** .0013

(e) There is strong evidence to suggest that the true mean is smaller than 128. If the population mean were 128, the chance of observing a sample mean of 127.4 or smaller is only about 13 in 10,000.

Chapter 8

8.1 **(a)** **(i)** 3.92 **(ii)** $121.08 < \mu < 128.92$

(b) **(i)** 6.45 **(ii)** $199.55 < \mu < 212.45$

(c) **(i)** .55 **(ii)** $153.45 < \mu < 154.55$

(d) **(i)** 6.53 **(ii)** $302.47 < \mu < 315.53$

(e) **(i)** 2.58 **(ii)** $37.42 < \mu < 42.58$

(f) **(i)** .83 **(ii)** $77.17 < \mu < 78.83$

8.3 **(a)** 80%; 40 90%; 45 95%; 47 or 48 99%; 49 or 50

(b) The 99% confidence interval contains $\mu = 200$ in 9 of the 11 samples in the table. We cannot decide for the 14th and 30th samples. If a confidence interval at a level smaller than 99% contains $\mu = 200$, then so will a 99% confidence interval. But if a confidence interval at a level smaller than 99% does not contain $\mu = 200$, we cannot determine whether or not a 99% confidence interval contains $\mu = 200$.

8.5 **(a)** $25.5 < \mu < 26.5$ **(b)** 198

8.7 **(a)** $27{,}439.86 < \mu < 31{,}360.14$ **(b)** Yes

8.9 **(a)** $63.43 < \mu < 66.57$ **(b)** 1.57 **(c)** Yes

8.11 **(a)** $17.88 < \mu < 18.72$ **(b)** $17.66 < \mu < 18.94$

(c) Longer than the 80% confidence interval, and shorter than the 95%

8.13 10 ± 3, 10 ± 4.5, 10 ± 5, and 10 ± 8 are matched with 80, 90, 95, and 99 percent respectively

8.15 **(a)** $39.86\% < \mu < 43.74\%$ **(b)** 1.94% **8.17** 41

8.19 **(a)** 35 **(b)** Smaller **(c)** Smaller

8.21 **(a)** $99.245 < \mu < 114.517$ **(b)** Yes

8.23 **(a)** 6.03 **(b)** $5.41 < \mu < 6.65$ **(c)** .62

8.25 $41.81 < \mu < 46.29$; no

8.27 **(a)** **(i)** $H_0: \mu = 72$; $H_a: \mu > 72$ **(ii)** Right-tailed

(iii) Type I: The data suggest that the mean amount of rainfall per year is more than 72, when it is not.
Type II: The data do not suggest that the mean amount of rainfall per year is more than 72, when it is.

(b) **(i)** $H_0: \mu = 250$; $H_a: \mu \neq 250$ **(ii)** Two-tailed

(iii) Type I: The data suggest that the mean number of books borrowed per day is not 250, when it is.
Type II: The data suggest that the mean number of books borrowed per day is 250, when it is not.

(c) **(i)** $H_0: \mu = 78$; $H_a: \mu < 78$ **(ii)** Left-tailed

(iii) Type I: The data suggest that the mean July temperature is less than 78, when it is not.
Type II: The data do not suggest that the mean July temperature is less than 78, when it is.

(d) **(i)** $H_0: \mu = 36$; $H_a: \mu > 36$ **(ii)** Right-tailed

(iii) Type I: The data suggest that the mean age is more than 36, when it is not.
Type II: The data do not suggest that the mean age is more than 36, when it is.

(e) **(i)** $H_0: \mu = 29{,}500$; $H_a: \mu < 29{,}500$ **(ii)** Left-tailed
(iii) Type I: The data suggest that the mean salary is less than \$29,500, when it is not.
Type II: The data do not suggest that the mean salary is less than \$29,500, when it is.

(f) **(i)** $H_0: \mu = 18{,}000$; $H_a: \mu \neq 18{,}000$ **(ii)** Two-tailed
(iii) Type I: The data suggest that the mean number of families below poverty level is not 18,000, when it is.
Type II: The data suggest that the mean number of families below poverty level is 18,000, when it is not.

(g) **(i)** $H_0: \mu = 2.3$; $H_a: \mu > 2.3$ **(ii)** Right-tailed
(iii) Type I: The data suggest that the mean grade point average is more than 2.3, when it is not.
Type II: The data do not suggest that the mean grade point average is more than 2.3, when it is.

8.29 **(a)** $H_0: \mu = 90$; $H_a: \mu \neq 90$

(b) **(i)** $z \leq -2.58$ or $z \geq 2.58$
(ii) $z \leq -1.96$ or $z \geq 1.96$
(iii) $z \leq -1.65$ or $z \geq 1.65$

8.31 **(a)** **(i)** No **(ii)** No **(iii)** Yes

(b) **(i)** No **(ii)** Yes **(iii)** Yes

(c) **(i)** Yes **(ii)** Yes **(iii)** Yes

8.33 $H_0: \mu = 150$; $H_a: \mu > 150$ $\alpha = .05$ Observed value: $z = 2.53$
Critical value: $z = 1.65$ Decision: Reject H_0 Type I
If an error has been made, then the data suggest that the mean time is more than 150 minutes, when it is not.

8.35 $H_0: \mu = 15$; $H_a: \mu > 15$ $\alpha = .05$ Observed value: $z = 3.01$
Critical value: $z = 1.65$ Decision: Reject H_0
The data suggest that the mean depression level is more than 15.

8.37 $H_0: \mu = 500$; $H_a: \mu < 500$ $\alpha = .01$ Observed value: $z = -1.49$
Critical value: $z = -2.33$ Decision: Do not reject H_0
The data do not suggest that the mean depth is less than 500 feet.

8.39 $H_0: \mu = 27$; $H_a: \mu > 27$ $\alpha = .01$ Observed value: $z = 1.26$
Critical value: $z = 2.33$ Decision: Do not reject H_0
The data do not suggest that the mean breaking strength is more than 27 pounds per square inch. Notice that a smaller standard deviation improves the chances of rejecting a false hypothesis.

8.41 **(a)** $H_0: \mu = 700$; $H_a: \mu \neq 700$ $\alpha = .05$ Observed value: $z = -2.25$
Critical values: $z = \pm 1.96$ Decision: Reject H_0
The data suggest that the mean number of hours is not 700.

(b) Type I **(c)** .05

8.43 $H_0: \mu = 40$; $H_a: \mu > 40$ $\alpha = .05$ Observed value: $z = 2.99$
Critical value: $z = 1.65$ Decision: Reject H_0
There is strong evidence that the true mean is more than 40 minutes.

8.45 .0401. Reject H_0

8.47 .2033. Do not reject H_0

8.49 .0802. Do not reject H_0

8.51 $H_0: \mu = 30$; $H_a: \mu > 30$

(a) .1587 **(b)** .0808 **(c)** .0359

(d) $H_0: \mu = 30$; $H_a: \mu \neq 30$ .3174 .1616 .0718

8.53 H_0: $\mu = 12$; H_a: $\mu < 12$

(a) .0668

(b) (i) Yes (ii) No (iii) No

(c) (i) Type I (ii) Type II (iii) Type II

8.55 H_0: $\mu = 15$; H_a: $\mu > 15$ $\alpha = .05$ Observed value: $z = 3.01$
P-value $= .0013$ Decision: Reject H_0
The data suggest that the mean depression level is more than 15.

8.57 H_0: $\mu = 500$; H_a: $\mu < 500$ $\alpha = .01$ Observed value: $z = -1.49$
P-value $= .0681$ Decision: Do not reject H_0
The data do not suggest that the mean depth is less than 500 feet.

8.59 H_0: $\mu = 64$; H_a: $\mu \neq 64$ Observed value: $z = -2.38$

(a) .0174 (b) All levels of significance greater than or equal to .0174

8.61 (a) (i) 3.499 (ii) 2.998 (iii) 2.365 (iv) 1.895 (v) 1.415

(b) (i) 3.055 (ii) 2.681 (iii) 2.179 (iv) 1.782 (v) 1.356

(c) (i) 2.787 (ii) 2.485 (iii) 2.060 (iv) 1.708 (v) 1.316

8.63 (a) (i) H_0: $\mu = 16$; H_a: $\mu > 16$ $\alpha = .10$ Observed value: $t = 1.87$
df $= 13$ Critical value: $t = 1.350$ Decision: Reject H_0
.025 $<$ P-value $<$ .05

(ii) Type I

(b) (i) H_0: $\mu = 27$; H_a: $\mu < 27$ $\alpha = .05$ Observed value: $t = -1.71$
df $= 8$ Critical value: $t = -1.860$ Decision: Do not reject H_0
.05 $<$ P-value $<$ .10

(ii) Type II

(c) (i) H_0: $\mu = 30$; H_a: $\mu \neq 30$ $\alpha = .01$ Observed value: $t = -3.06$
df $= 5$ Critical values: $t = \pm 4.032$ Decision: Do not reject H_0
.02 $<$ P-value $<$ .05

(ii) Type II

(d) (i) H_0: $\mu = 125$; H_a: $\mu > 125$ $\alpha = .05$ Observed value: $z = 1.05$
Critical value: $z = 1.65$ Decision: Do not reject H_0
P-value $= .1469$

(ii) Type II

(e) (i) H_0: $\mu = 50$; H_a: $\mu < 50$ $\alpha = .025$ Observed value: $t = -2.24$
df $= 19$ Critical value: $t = -2.093$ Decision: Reject H_0
.01 $<$ P-value $<$ .025

(ii) Type I

(f) (i) H_0: $\mu = 60$; H_a: $\mu \neq 60$ $\alpha = .10$ Observed value: $t = 1.77$
df $= 7$ Critical values: $t = \pm 1.895$ Decision: Do not reject H_0
.10 $<$ P-value $<$ .20

(ii) Type II

8.65 (a) H_0: $\mu = 30{,}750$; H_a: $\mu > 30{,}750$ Observed value: $t = 2.50$ df $= 8$
Critical value: $t = 1.860$ for $\alpha = .05$, and $t = 2.896$ for $\alpha = .01$
Decision: Reject H_0 at the 5% level; Do not reject H_0 at the 1% level

(b) .01 $<$ P-value $<$ .025; Reject H_0 at the 5% level
Do not reject H_0 at the 1% level.

8.67 H_0: $\mu = 6000$; H_a: $\mu \neq 6000$ $\alpha = .05$ Observed value: $t = 2.98$
df $= 19$ Critical values: $t = \pm 2.093$ Decision: Reject H_0 P-value $<$ .01
The data suggest that the mean contribution is not $6000.

8.69 (b) H_0: $\mu = 160$; H_a: $\mu < 160$ Observed value: $t = -2.33$ df $= 10$
.01 $<$ P-value $<$ .025 $\alpha \geq .025$

8.71 (b) H_0: $\mu = 40$; H_a: $\mu > 40$ Observed value: $t = 1.40$ df $= 17$
.05 $<$ P-value $<$ .10 $\alpha \geq .10$

8.73 $H_0: \mu = 36; H_a: \mu \neq 36$ $\alpha = .05$ Observed value: $t = -2.42$
df $= 26$ Critical values: $t = \pm 2.056$ Decision: Reject H_0
$.02 < P\text{-value} < .05$ The data suggest that the mean trait anxiety level is not 36.

8.75 $H_0: \mu = 15; H_a: \mu \neq 15$ $\alpha = .05$ Observed value: $t = 1.67$
df $= 22$ Critical values: $t = \pm 2.074$ Decision: Do not reject H_0
$.10 < P\text{-value} < .20$ The data do not suggest that the mean time is unequal to 15 minutes.

8.77 **(a)**
16	5
17	05
18	0555
19	005
20	05

(b) $H_0: \mu = 18; H_a: \mu > 18$ $\alpha = .05$ Observed value: $t = 1.60$
df $= 11$ Critical value: $t = 1.796$ Decision: Do not reject H_0
$.05 < P\text{-value} < .10$
The data do not suggest that the mean time is more than 18 months.

8.79 **(a)** $21.55 < \mu < 29.05$ **(b)** No   **(c)** 3.75

8.81 $14.64 < \mu < 18.36$ **8.83** $17.932 < \mu < 19.152$

8.85 **(a)** $H_0: \mu = 78; H_a: \mu > 78$ Observed value: $t = 1.824$ df $= 19$
$\alpha = .05$ Critical value: $t = 1.729$ Decision: Reject H_0
$\alpha = .01$ Critical value: $t = 2.539$ Decision: Do not reject H_0

(b) $77.692 < \mu < 82.485$

8.87 **(a)** $\hat{p} = .50$ $.45 < p < .55$ **(b)** $x = 225$ $.23 < p < .27$
(c) $\hat{p} = .71$ $.63 < p < .79$ **(d)** $x = 1025$ $.80 < p < .84$
(e) $\hat{p} = .37$ $.35 < p < .39$ **(f)** $x = 610$ $.59 < p < .63$

8.89 $.83 < p < .97$ **8.91** $.88 < p < .94$

8.93 **(a)** $.08 < p < .18$ **(b)** $.24 < p < .32$

8.95 **(a)** $.02 < p < .10$ **(b)** No

8.97 **(a)** $.60$ **(b)** $.49 < p < .71$ **(c)** $.11$

8.99 **(a)** $.48 < p < .56$ **(b)** $.04$ **(c)** No   **8.101** 757

8.103 **(a)** 1702   **(b)** 4161

8.105 **(a)** **(i)** $H_0: p = .53; H_a: p \neq .53$ **(ii)** Two-tailed
(iii) Type I: The data suggest that p is not .53, when it is.
Type II: The data suggest that p is .53, when it is not.

(b) **(i)** $H_0: p = .06; H_a: p < .06$ **(ii)** Left-tailed
(iii) Type I: The data suggest that p is less than .06, when it is not.
Type II: The data do not suggest that p is less than .06, when it is.

(c) **(i)** $H_0: p = .90; H_a: p < .90$ **(ii)** Left-tailed
(iii) Type I: The data suggest that p is less than .90, when it is not.
Type II: The data do not suggest that p is less than .90, when it is.

(d) **(i)** $H_0: p = .07; H_a: p > .07$ **(ii)** Right-tailed
(iii) Type I: The data suggest that p is more than .07, when it is not.
Type II: The data do not suggest that p is more than .07, when it is.

(e) **(i)** $H_0: p = .40; H_a: p \neq .40$ **(ii)** Two-tailed
(iii) Type I: The data suggest that p is not .40, when it is.
Type II: The data suggest that p is .40, when it is not.

(f) **(i)** $H_0: p = .05; H_a: p < .05$ **(ii)** Left-tailed
(iii) Type I: The data suggest that p is less than .05, when it is not.
Type II: The data do not suggest that p is less than .05, when it is.

(g) **(i)** $H_0: p = .30; H_a: p > .30$ **(ii)** Right-tailed

(iii) Type I: The data suggest that p is more than .30, when it is not.

Type II: The data do not suggest that p is more than .30, when it is.

8.107 $H_0: p = .70; H_a: p < .70$

(a) **(i)** $z \leq -1.28$

(ii) Observed value: $z = -1.09$

Decision: Do not reject H_0 P-value $= .1379$

(iii) Type II

(b) **(i)** $z \leq -1.65$

(ii) Observed value: $z = -2.18$

Decision: Reject H_0 P-value $= .0146$

(iii) Type I

(c) **(i)** $z \leq -2.33$

(ii) Observed value: $z = -2.18$

Decision: Do not reject H_0 P-value $= .0146$

(iii) Type II

(d) **(i)** $z \leq -2.33$

(ii) Observed value: $z = -4.36$

Decision: Reject H_0 P-value $= .00003$

(iii) Type I

8.109 $H_0: p = .50; H_a: p > .50$ $\alpha = .10$ Observed value: $z = .71$
Critical value: $z = 1.28$ Decision: Do not reject H_0 P-value $= .2388$
The data do not suggest that the proportion p is more than .5.

8.111 $H_0: p = .20; H_a: p > .20$ $\alpha = .01$ Observed value: $z = 3$
P-value $= .0013$ Decision: Reject H_0
The data suggest that the proportion p is more than .20.

8.113 **(a)** $H_0: p = .50; H_a: p > .50$ $\alpha = .05$ Observed value: $z = 3.46$
Critical value: $z = 1.65$ Decision: Reject H_0

(b) P-value $= .0003$ There is strong evidence suggesting that the true proportion is more than 50%.

8.115 **(a)** $H_0: p = .60; H_a: p \neq .60$ $\alpha = .10$ Observed value: $z = -1.22$
Critical values: $z = \pm1.65$ Decision: Do not reject H_0
P-value $= .2224$
At the 10% level, the data do not indicate that the percentage of Americans who refuse to buy imported products from Vietnam is different from 60%.

(b) $.53 < p < .61$

8.117 **(a)** $H_0: p = .25; H_a: p < .25$ $\alpha = .01$ Observed value: $z = -5.86$
Critical value: $z = -2.33$ Decision: Reject H_0 P-value $= 0$
At the 1% level, the data suggest that there is a decline in the percentage of adults who say they hold "very negative" feelings toward President Clinton.

(b) **(i)** 0; it is not surprising   **(ii)** .834; it is reasonable

8.119 $H_0: p = .057; H_a: p < .057$ $\alpha = .025$ Observed value: $z = -1.73$
Critical value: $z = -1.96$ Decision: Do not reject H_0 P-value $= .0418$
The data do not suggest that the proportion p is less than .057.

8.121 **(a)** $208.48 < \mu < 211.52$ **(b)** 1.52

8.123 **(a)** $207.869 < \mu < 215.197$ **(b)** Yes

8.125 **(a)** $2.569 < \mu < 3.123$ **(b)** $2.531 < \mu < 3.015$ **(c)** No

8.127 **(a)** \$27,500   **(b)** 90%   8.129 196

8.131 **(a)** **(i)** Larger   **(ii)** Smaller

(b) 97

8.133 **(a)** $H_0: \mu = 450; H_a: \mu \neq 450$ $\alpha = .01$ Observed value: $z = 2.76$
Critical values: $z = \pm 2.58$ Decision: Reject H_0
(b) *P*-value $= .0058$ The data suggest that the mean length is not 450 inches.

8.135 $H_0: \mu = 12; H_a: \mu < 12$ $\alpha = .05$ Observed value: $z = -1.42$
Critical value: $z = -1.65$ Decision: Do not reject H_0 *P*-value $= .0778$
The data do not suggest that the mean length is less than 12 inches.

8.137 $H_0: \mu = 16; H_a: \mu \neq 16$ Observed value: $z = -3$
(a) *P*-value $= .0026$ **(b)** Reject H_0 at the 10% level and at the 1% level.

8.139 $H_0: \mu = 60; H_a: \mu < 60$ $\alpha = .05$ Observed value: $z = -4.38$
Critical value: $z = -1.65$ *P*-value $\doteq 0$ Decision: Reject H_0
The data suggest that the mean down time per week is less than 60 minutes.

8.141 **(a)** 2.718   **(b)** 1.714   **(c)** 1.345   **(d)** -2.080

8.143 **(a)** $H_0: \mu = 150; H_a: \mu > 150$ $\alpha = .05$ Observed value: $t = 1.87$
df $= 13$ Critical value: $t = 1.771$ Decision: Reject H_0
(b) $.025 < P\text{-value} < .05$. The data suggest that the mean number of calories is more than 150.

8.145 Notice that the *z* test is used, because we are assuming that the population standard deviation is known. $H_0: \mu = .120; H_a: \mu \neq .120$ $\alpha = .10$
Observed value: $z = -1.70$ Critical values: $z = \pm 1.65$ Decision: Reject H_0
P-value $= .0892$ The data suggest that the mean diameter is not .120.

8.147 $H_0: \mu = 13; H_a: \mu \neq 13$ $\alpha = .05$ Observed value: $t = -2.37$
df $= 26$ Critical values: $t = \pm 2.056$ Decision: Reject H_0
$.02 < P\text{-value} < .05$ The data suggest that the mean tension score is not 13.

8.149 **(b)** $H_0: \mu = 600; H_a: \mu < 600$ $\alpha = .05$ Observed value: $t = -3.17$
df $= 17$ Critical value: $t = -1.740$ Decision: Reject H_0
The data suggest that the mean tax deduction for charities is less than $600.
P-value $< .005$.

8.151 **(a)** $471.75 < \mu < 562.69$ **(b)** 45.47   8.153 $8.26 < \mu < 12.66$

8.155 **(a)** $x = 50$ $.40 < p < .60$ **(b)** $\hat{p} = .40$ $.33 < p < .47$
(c) $x = 288$ $.66 < p < .78$ **(d)** $\hat{p} = .20$ $.15 < p < .25$
(e) $x = 36$ $.50 < p < .70$ **(f)** $\hat{p} = .60$ $.42 < p < .78$

8.157 $.50 < p < .58$ 8.159 **(a)** 385   **(b)** 1068   **(c)** 9604

8.161 $H_0: p = .20; H_a: p > .20$ $\alpha = .05$
Observed value: $z = 1.37$ Critical value: $z = 1.65$
Decision: Do not reject H_0 *P*-value $= .0853$
The data do not suggest that the proportion p is more than .20.

8.163 $H_0: p = .85; H_a: p < .85$ $\alpha = .01$ Observed value: $z = -.75$
Critical value: $z = -2.33$ Decision: Do not reject H_0 *P*-value $= .2266$
The data do not suggest that the proportion p is less than .85.

8.165 $H_0: p = .4; H_a: p = .7$
(a) .317   **(b)** .162

Chapter 9

9.1 **(a)** **(i)** $H_0: \mu = 0; H_a: \mu \neq 0$ $\alpha = .05$ Observed value: $t = 1.05$
df $= 7$ Critical values: $t = \pm 2.365$
Decision: Do not reject H_0 $.20 < P\text{-value} < .50$
(ii) Type II
(b) **(i)** $H_0: \mu = 0; H_a: \mu > 0$ $\alpha = .05$ Observed value: $t = 2.74$
df $= 5$ Critical value: $t = 2.015$ Decision: Reject H_0
$.01 < P\text{-value} < .025$
(ii) Type I

9.3 $H_0: \mu = 0; H_a: \mu \neq 0$ $\alpha = .05$ Observed value: $t = 2.47$ df $= 11$
Critical values: $t = \pm 2.201$ Decision: Reject H_0 $.02 < P$-value $< .05$
The data suggest that the mean systolic blood pressure is different between smokers and nonsmokers.

9.5   **(a)** $H_0: \mu = 0; H_a: \mu < 0$ Observed value: $t = -2.31$
           df $= 7$ $.025 < P$-value $< .05$

       (b)   Reject H_0 at the 5% and 10% levels, but do not reject H_0 at the 1% level of significance.

9.7 $H_0: \mu = 0; H_a: \mu > 0$ $\alpha = .01$ Observed value: $z = 9.72$
Critical value: $z = 2.33$ Decision: Reject H_0 P-value $\doteq 0$
The data suggest that the mean thickness of cake A is larger.

9.9   **(a)** $-1.57 < \mu < 4.07$ **(b)** $1.01 < \mu < 6.66$

9.11   **(b)** $-1.78 < \mu < .18$

(a)

       (c) $H_0: \mu = 0; H_a: \mu < 0$ $\alpha = .05$ Observed value: $t = -1.50$
Critical value: $t = -1.833$ Decision: Do not reject H_0
$.05 < P$-value $< .10$
Yes, as the 90% confidence interval contains 0

9.13   **(a)** $H_0: \mu_A - \mu_B = 0; H_a: \mu_A - \mu_B \neq 0$ $\alpha = .05$
Observed value: $z = 2.50$ Critical values: $z = \pm 1.96$
Decision: Reject H_0 P-value $= .0124$

       (b)   **(i)**   No   **(ii)**   Yes   **(iii)**   Yes

       (c)   Observed value $z = 2.5$ $\alpha = .01$ Critical values: $z = \pm 2.58$
Decision: Do not reject H_0

9.15   **(a)** $H_0: \mu_A - \mu_B = 0; H_a: \mu_A - \mu_B \neq 0$ $\alpha = .05$ Observed value: $z = 1.42$
Critical values: $z = \pm 1.96$ Decision: Do not reject H_0

       (b) P-value $= .1556$ Do not reject H_0 at the 5% level.   The data do not suggest that the mean GMAT scores for A and B are different.

9.17   **(a)** $H_0: \mu_A - \mu_B = 0; H_a: \mu_A - \mu_B < 0$ $\alpha = .10$
Observed value: $z = -2.96$ Critical value: $z = -1.28$
Decision: Reject H_0

       (b) P-value $= .0015$ Reject H_0 The data suggest that the average family size is smaller in state A.

9.19 $-.56 < \mu_A - \mu_B < 1.16$ Cannot conclude there is a difference in the mean elapsed times, as the confidence interval contains 0.

9.21   **(a)** $-.39 < \mu_A - \mu_B < 2.41$ **(b)** $-.32 < \mu_A - \mu_B < -.12$

9.23   **(a)** $H_0: \mu_A - \mu_B = 0; H_a: \mu_A - \mu_B < 0$ $\alpha = .10$
Observed value: $t = -2.68$ df $= 6$ Critical value: $t = -1.440$
Decision: Reject H_0 $.01 < P$-value $< .025$
The data suggest that the mean of population A is less than the mean of population B.

       (b) $H_0: \mu_A - \mu_B = 0; H_a: \mu_A - \mu_B \neq 0$ $\alpha = .05$
Observed value: $t = 1.72$ df $= 7$ Critical values: $t = \pm 2.365$
Decision: Do not reject H_0 $.10 < P$-value $< .20$
The data do not suggest that the population means are different.

9.25 **(a)** $H_0: \mu_A - \mu_B = 0; H_a: \mu_A - \mu_B < 0$ $\alpha = .05$
Observed value: $t = -2.54$ df $= 6$ Critical value: $t = -1.943$
Decision: Reject H_0

(b) $-16.53 < \mu_A - \mu_B < -.31$

9.27 **(a)**

	0	9
6	1	58
9	2	86757
6518	3	4525
0475457	4	34
32	5	
4	6	

(b) Let A = Near plant and B = Other locations
$H_0: \mu_A - \mu_B = 0; H_a: \mu_A - \mu_B > 0$ $\alpha = .05$
Observed value: $t = 3.44$ df $= 13$ Critical value: $t = 1.771$
Decision: Reject H_0 P-value $< .005$
The data suggest that the power plant was substantially increasing the air pollution in the vicinity of the plant.

(c) $6.41 < \mu_A - \mu_B < 19.99$

9.29 **(a)** $-34.48 < \mu_A - \mu_B < -5.52$

(b) $-.17 < \mu_A - \mu_B < .77$

9.31 $H_0: \mu_A - \mu_B = 0; H_a: \mu_A - \mu_B > 0$ $\alpha = .10$ Observed value: $t = 2.141$
df $= 14$ Critical value: $t = 1.345$ Decision: Reject H_0
P-value $\doteq .025$ The data suggest that test A has a longer mean completion time.

9.33 **(a)** Let A = women and B = men.
$H_0: \mu_A - \mu_B = 30; H_a: \mu_A - \mu_B \neq 30$ $\alpha = .10$
Observed value: $t = -.99$ df $= 28$ Critical values: $t = \pm1.701$
Decision: Do not reject H_0 $.20 < $ P-value $< .50$
There is no evidence to suggest that the difference in the population mean times is different from 30 minutes.

(b) $12.63 < \mu_A - \mu_B < 34.59$

9.35 **(a)** $H_0: \mu_1 - \mu_2 = 0; H_a: \mu_1 - \mu_2 > 0$ $\alpha = .05$
Observed value: $t = 3.441$ df $= 27$ Critical value: $t = 1.703$
Decision: Reject H_0 P-value $< .005$
The data support the engineer's suspicion that the power plant was substantially increasing the air pollution in the vicinity of the plant.

(b) $5.33 < \mu_1 - \mu_2 < 21.1$

9.37 **(a)** $H_0: p_1 - p_2 = 0; H_a: p_1 - p_2 \neq 0$ $\alpha = .05$
Observed value: $z = -1.63$ Critical values: $z = \pm1.96$
Decision: Do not reject H_0 P-value $= .1032$
The data do not suggest that the population proportions p_1 and p_2 are different.

(b) $H_0: p_1 - p_2 = 0; H_a: p_1 - p_2 > 0$ $\alpha = .10$
Observed value: $z = 1.54$ Critical value: $z = 1.28$
Decision: Reject H_0 P-value $= .0618$
The data suggest that the population A proportion p_1 is larger than the population B proportion p_2.

(c) $H_0: p_1 - p_2 = .05; H_a: p_1 - p_2 \neq .05$ $\alpha = .05$
Observed value: $z = 1.47$ Critical values: $z = \pm1.96$
Decision: Do not reject H_0 P-value $= .1416$
The data do not suggest that p_1 is .05 more than p_2.

9.39 Let p_A and p_B be the death rates for two populations of patients, one treated with atherectomy (p_A), the other with angioplasty (p_B).
$H_0 : p_A - p_B = 0; H_a: p_A - p_B \neq 0$ $205/5000 = .041$
The data suggest that there is a difference in the population proportions.

9.41 **(a)** $H_0: p_B - p_W = 0; H_a: p_B - p_W < 0$ $\alpha = .025$
Observed value: $z = -2.40$ Critical value: $z = -1.96$
Decision: Reject H_0 P-value $= .0082$

    (b) $\hat{p}_B/\hat{p}_W = .83$; The data do not meet the requirements of the 80% rule.

9.43 **(a)** $-.037 < p_A - p_B < .103$ **(b)** No

9.45 **(a)** $-.277 < p_A - p_B < -.007$ **(b)** $-.281 < p_B - p_W < -.016$

9.47 $H_0: \mu = 0; H_a: \mu \neq 0$ $\alpha = .05$ Observed value: $t = 1.19$ df $= 6$
Critical values: $t = \pm 2.447$ Decision: Do not reject H_0 $.20 < P$-value $< .50$

9.49 **(a)** $H_0: \mu_A - \mu_B = 0; H_a: \mu_A - \mu_B \neq 0$ $\alpha = .05$
Observed value: $z = -2.25$ Critical values: $z = \pm 1.96$
Decision: Reject H_0 P-value $= .0244$
The data suggest that the population means are different.

    (b) $H_0: \mu_A - \mu_B = 0; H_a: \mu_A - \mu_B < 0$ $\alpha = .01$
Observed value: $z = -2$ Critical value: $z = -2.33$
Decision: Do not reject H_0 P-value $= .0228$
The data do not suggest that population mean B is larger than population mean A.

9.51 **(a)** $H_0: \mu_A - \mu_B = 0; H_a: \mu_A - \mu_B < 0$ $\alpha = .01$
Observed value: $z = -2.14$ P-value $= .0162$
Decision: Do not reject H_0

    (b) $-1.78 < \mu_A - \mu_B < .08$ We cannot conclude that $\mu_A < \mu_B$.

9.53 **(a)** $H_0: \mu_A - \mu_B = 0; H_a: \mu_A - \mu_B < 0$ $\alpha = .05$
Observed value: $t = -2.07$
df $= 15$ Critical value: $t = -1.753$
Decision: Reject H_0

    (b) $.025 < P$-value $< .05$. The data suggest that rotated workers have lower mean depression levels than nonrotated workers.

9.55 **(a)** $H_0: \mu_E - \mu_A = 0; H_a: \mu_E - \mu_A > 0$ $\alpha = .05$
Observed value: $t = 1.11$ df $= 15$ Critical value: $t = 2.131$
Decision: Do not reject H_0 $.10 < P$-value $< .25$
The data do not suggest that the population means are different.

    (b) $.114$, yes

9.57 **(a)** $-3.88 < \mu_A - \mu_B < -.32$ Yes
    (b) $-2.21 < \mu_A - \mu_B < .61$ No

9.59 $H_0: p_S - p_F = 0; H_a: p_S - p_F \neq 0$ $\alpha = .05$ Observed value: $z = -1.68$
Critical values: $z = \pm 1.96$ Decision: Do not reject H_0 P-value $= .0930$

9.61 **(a)** $H_0: p_A - p_B = 0; H_a: p_A - p_B \neq 0$ $\alpha = .01$
Observed value: $z = -1.62$ Critical values: $z = \pm 2.58$
Decision: Do not reject H_0

    (b) P-value $= .1052$. Do not reject the null hypothesis. The data do not suggest a difference in population proportions.

9.63 **(a)** $-.218 < p_A - p_B < .018$ (p_A refers to students; p_B refers to faculty)
    (b) $-.234 < p_A - p_B < .054$

9.65 **(a)** $\hat{p}_1 = .05, \hat{p}_2 = .075$ for both sets of data
    (b) $H_0: p_1 - p_2 = 0; H_a: p_1 - p_2 < 0$ $\alpha = .05$ Observed value: $z = -1.85$
Critical value: $z = -1.65$ Decision: Reject H_0 P-value $= .0322$

Chapter 10

10.1 **(a)** $H_0: \beta_1 = 0; H_a: \beta_1 > 0$ $\alpha = .05$ Observed value: $t = 2.74$
df $= 5$ Critical value: $t = 2.015$ Decision: Reject H_0
$.01 < P\text{-value} < .025$ The data suggest that there is a positive linear relationship between the x and y values for the population.

(b) $.18 < \beta_1 < 5.82$

10.3 **(a)** $H_0: \beta_1 = 0; H_a: \beta_1 < 0$ $\alpha = .05$ Observed value: $t = -7.35$
df $= 6$ Critical value: $t = -1.943$ Decision: Reject H_0
$P\text{-value} < .005$ The data suggest that there is a negative linear relationship between the x and y values for the population.

(b) $-1.00 < \beta_1 < -.50$

10.5 $H_0: \beta_1 = 0; H_a: \beta_1 \neq 0$ $\alpha = .05$ Observed value: $t = -1.79$
df $= 5$ Critical values: $t = \pm 2.571$ Decision: Do not reject H_0
$.10 < P\text{-value} < .20$ The data do not suggest that there is a linear relationship between the x and y values for the population.

10.7 **(a)** $H_0: \beta_1 = 0; H_a: \beta_1 \neq 0$ $\alpha = .01$ Observed value: $t = 8.85$
df $= 6$ Critical values: $t = \pm 3.707$ Decision: Reject H_0
$P\text{-value} < .01$ The data suggest that there is a linear relationship between the x and y values for the population.

(b) $\hat{y}_0 = 10.53$; Would recommend 10 or 11 courts be built.

(c) The scatter diagram and plot of residuals versus x do not indicate any problems with the assumptions of the linear regression model.

10.9 **(a)** $H_0: \beta_1 = 0; H_a: \beta_1 < 0$ $\alpha = .05$ Observed value: $t = -8.29$
df $= 36$ Critical value: $z = -1.65$ Decision: Reject H_0
$P\text{-value} \doteq 0$ The data suggest that there is a negative linear relationship between miles per gallon and number of cylinders.

(b) 13.16

10.11 **(a)** $\hat{y} = 10.75 - .75x$ **(b)** Observed value: $t = -7.35$; Yes **(c)** 1

10.13 $H_0: \rho = 0; H_a: \rho \neq 0$ $\alpha = .05$ $n = 7$ Observed value: $r = .873$
Critical values: $r = \pm .754$ Decision: Reject H_0
The data indicate a linear relationship between the x and y values for the population.

10.15 $H_0: \rho = 0; H_a: \rho \neq 0$ $\alpha = .01$ $n = 5$ Observed value: $r = -.949$
Critical values: $r = \pm .959$ Decision: Do not reject H_0
The data do not indicate a linear relationship between the x and y values for the population.

10.17 $H_0: \rho = 0; H_a: \rho \neq 0$ $\alpha = .05$ $n = 8$ Observed value: $r = .767$
Critical values: $r = \pm .707$ Decision: Reject H_0
The data indicate a linear relationship between the x and y values for the population.

10.19 $H_0: \rho = 0; H_a: \rho \neq 0$ $\alpha = .01$ $n = 9$ Observed value: $r = .926$
Critical values: $r = \pm .798$ Decision: Reject H_0
The data indicate a linear relationship between the x and y values for the population.

10.21 **(a)** $r = .194$

(b) $H_0: \rho = 0; H_a: \rho \neq 0$ $\alpha = .05$ $n = 40$
Observed value: $r = .194$ Critical values: $r = \pm .312$
Decision: Do not reject H_0. The data do not indicate a linear relationship between the x and y values for the population.

10.23 **(a)** $\hat{y} = 14 - 1.2x$ **(b)** 5.6 **(c)** 3.22 to 7.98 **(d)** 4.33 to 6.87

10.25 **(a)** $H_0: \rho = 0; H_a: \rho \neq 0$ $\alpha = .05$ $n = 30$ Observed value: $r = -.777$
Critical values: $r = \pm .361$ Decision: Reject H_0 The data suggest that there is a linear relationship between the x and y values for the population.

(b) 21.97 to 36.03 **(c)** 27.50 to 30.50

10.27 **(a)** 12.09 to 18.07 **(b)** 13.93 to 16.23

10.29 **(a)** $H_0: \beta_1 = 0; H_a: \beta_1 > 0$ $\alpha = .05$ $n = 7$ Observed value: $t = 4.85$
df $= 5$ Critical value: $t = 2.015$ Decision: Reject H_0
P-value $< .005$ The data indicate a positive linear relationship between the x
and y values for the population.

(b) 7.8

10.31 $H_0: \rho = 0; H_a: \rho \neq 0$ $\alpha = .05$ $n = 7$ Observed value: $r = .729$
Critical values: $r = \pm.754$ Decision: Do not reject H_0 The data do not suggest
that there is a linear relationship between the x and y values for the population.

10.33 **(a)** $r = -.896$

(b) $H_0: \rho = 0; H_a: \rho \neq 0$ $\alpha = .05$ $n = 6$
Observed value: $r = -.896$ Critical values: $r = \pm.811$ Decision: Reject H_0
The data suggest that there is a linear relationship between the x and y values
for the population.

10.35 $H_0: \rho = 0; H_a: \rho \neq 0$ $\alpha = .05$ $n = 8$ Observed value: $r = -.876$
Critical values: $r = \pm.707$ Decision: Reject H_0 The data suggest that there is
a linear relationship between the x and y values for the population.

10.37 **(a)** $H_0: \beta_1 = 0; H_a: \beta_1 \neq 0$ $\alpha = .10$ P-value $= .0886627 \leq .10$ Reject H_0

(b) $.008 < \beta_1 < .398$

10.39 **(a)** 8.24 to 40.34 **(b)** 16.88 to 31.70

10.41 **(a)** 6.781 to 8.219 **(b)** 7.260 to 7.740

Chapter 11

11.1 **(a)** **(i)** 6.63 **(ii)** 4.82 **(iii)** 3.69

(b) **(i)** 10.29 **(ii)** 6.76 **(iii)** 4.82

(c) **(i)** 4.41 **(ii)** 3.42 **(iii)** 2.77

(d) **(i)** 12.25 **(ii)** 8.07 **(iii)** 5.59

11.3

	Observed F value	**df**	F_α	**Decision**
(a)	7.5	(2, 12)	3.89	Reject H_0
(b)	3	(2, 12)	3.89	Do not reject H_0
(c)	6	(1, 10)	10.04	Do not reject H_0
(d)	12	(1, 10)	10.04	Reject H_0
(e)	4	(4, 15)	3.06	Reject H_0
(f)	2	(4, 15)	3.06	Do not reject H_0

11.5 $H_0: \mu_A = \mu_B = \mu_C; H_a:$ Not all the means are equal $\alpha = .05$
Observed value: $F = 4.75$ df $= (2, 12)$ Critical value: $F = 3.89$
Decision: Reject H_0 $.025 < P$-value $< .05$
The data suggest that not all the means are the same.

11.7 $H_0: \mu_M = \mu_F; H_a: \mu_M \neq \mu_F$ $\alpha = .01$ Observed value: $F = 6.63$
df $= (1, 18)$ Critical value: $F = 8.29$ Decision: Do not reject H_0
$.01 < P$-value $< .025$ The data do not suggest that the means are different.

11.9 $H_0: \mu_A = \mu_B = \mu_C = \mu_D = \mu_E; H_a:$ Not all the means are equal $\alpha = .05$

(a) **(i)** df $= (4, 25)$ **(ii)** $F = 2.76$ **(iii)** $F = 2.17$
(iv) Decision: Do not reject H_0 P-value $> .05$

(b) **(i)** Same **(ii)** Larger **(iii)** Larger
(iv) $F = 4.57$ Decision: Reject H_0 P-value $< .01$

11.11 **(a)** $H_0: \mu_1 = \mu_2 = \mu_3; H_a:$ Not all the means are equal

(b) Observed value: $F = 43.79$; The test is statistically significant, as P-value $=$
.000.

11.13

Source	SS	df	MS	F Statistic
Between samples	120	1	120	9.47
Within samples	76	6	12.667	
Total	196	7		

$H_0: \mu_A = \mu_B$; $H_a: \mu_A \neq \mu_B$ $\alpha = .05$ Observed value: $F = 9.47$
$df = (1, 6)$ Critical value: $F = 5.99$ Decision: Reject H_0
$.01 < P\text{-value} < .025$; The data suggest that the means are different.

11.15

Source	SS	df	MS	F Statistic
Between samples	63.6	2	31.8	3.59
Within samples	62	7	8.857	
Total	125.6	9		

$H_0: \mu_A = \mu_B = \mu_C$; H_a: Not all the means are equal $\alpha = .05$
Observed value: $F = 3.59$ $df = (2, 7)$.   Critical value: $F = 4.74$
Decision: Do not reject H_0 $P\text{-value} > .05$ The data do not suggest that there is a difference in means.

11.17   (a)

Source	SS	df	MS	F Statistic
Between samples	250	5	50	8.33
Within samples	150	25	6	
Total	400	30		

(b) $H_0: \mu_A = \mu_B = \mu_C = \mu_D = \mu_E = \mu_F$; H_a: Not all the means are equal
$\alpha = .05$ Observed value: $F = 8.33$ $df = (5, 25)$
Critical value: $F = 2.60$ Decision: Reject H_0 $P\text{-value} < .01$
The data suggest that not all the means are the same.

11.19   (a)

Source	SS	df	MS	F Statistic
Between samples	128	4	32	2
Within samples	160	10	16	
Total	288	14		

(b) $H_0: \mu_A = \mu_B = \mu_C = \mu_D = \mu_E$; H_a: Not all the means are equal $\alpha = .05$
Observed value: $F = 2$ $df = (4, 10)$ Critical value: $F = 3.48$
Decision: Do not reject H_0 $P\text{-value} > .05$ The data do not suggest that there is a difference in means.

11.21 $H_0: \mu_A = \mu_B = \mu_C$; H_a: Not all the means are equal $\alpha = .05$
Observed value: $F = 4.03$ df $= (2, 16)$ Critical value: $F = 3.63$
Decision: Reject H_0 $.025 < P\text{-value} < .05$ The data suggest that not all the means are the same.

11.23 $H_0: \mu_P = \mu_E = \mu_W = \mu_S$; H_a: Not all the means are equal $\alpha = .05$
Observed value: $F = 4.97$ df $= (3, 20)$ Critical value: $F = 3.10$
Decision: Reject H_0 $P\text{-value} < .01$ The data suggest that not all the means are the same.

11.25 $H_0: \mu_{CR} = \mu_M = \mu_{CO}$; H_a: Not all the means are equal $\alpha = .01$
Observed value: $F = 13.49$ df $= (2, 93)$ Critical value: $F = 4.98$
Decision: Reject H_0 $P\text{-value} < .01$ The data suggest that not all the means are the same.

11.27   **(a)**   SSB $= 120$ SSW $= 76$ **(b)**   SSB $= 98$ SSW $= 196$
(c)   SSB $= 63.6$ SSW $= 62$ **(d)**   SSB $= 275.714$ SSW $= 190$

11.29

Source	SS	df	MS	F Statistic
Between samples	322.5	2	161.25	5.64
Within samples	200	7	28.571	
Total	522.5	9		

$H_0: \mu_A = \mu_B = \mu_C$; H_a: Not all the means are equal $\alpha = .05$
Observed value: $F = 5.64$ df $= (2, 7)$ Critical value: $F = 4.74$
Decision: Reject H_0 $.025 < P\text{-value} < .05$ The data suggest that not all the means are the same.

11.31   **(a)**

Source	SS	df	MS	F Statistic
Between samples	132	4	33	3.3
Within samples	400	40	10	
Total	532	44		

(b) $H_0: \mu_A = \mu_B = \mu_C = \mu_D = \mu_E$; H_a: Not all the means are equal $\alpha = .05$
Observed value: $F = 3.3$ df $= (4, 40)$ Critical value: $F = 2.61$
Decision: Reject H_0 $.01 < P\text{-value} < .025$ The data suggest that not all the means are the same.

11.33 $H_0: \mu_A = \mu_B = \mu_C$; H_a: Not all the means are equal $\alpha = .05$
Observed value: $F = 5.82$ df $= (2, 8)$ Critical value: $F = 4.46$
Decision: Reject H_0 $.025 < P\text{-value} < .05$ The data suggest that not all the means are the same.

11.35 $H_0: \mu_A = \mu_B = \mu_C$; H_a: Not all the means are equal $\alpha = .05$
Observed value: $F = 6.01$ df $= (2, 14)$ Critical value: $F = 3.74$
Decision: Reject H_0 $.01 < P\text{-value} < .025$ The data suggest that not all the means are the same.

11.37 $H_0: \mu_A = \mu_B = \mu_C$; H_a: Not all the means are equal $\alpha = .05$
Observed value: $F = 4.30$ df $= (2, 12)$ Critical value: $F = 3.89$
Decision: Reject H_0 $.025 < P\text{-value} < .05$ The data suggest that not all the means are the same.

11.39 $H_0: \mu_E = \mu_G = \mu_N; H_a$: Not all the means are equal $\quad \alpha = .05$
Observed value: $F = 1.81 \quad$ df $= (2, 97) \quad$ Critical value: $F = 3.15$
Decision: Do not reject $H_0 \quad$ P-value $> .05 \quad$ The data do not suggest that there is a difference in means.

11.41

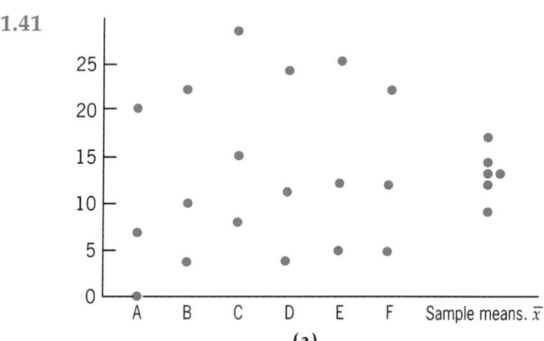

(a)

(b) $H_0: \mu_A = \mu_B = \mu_C = \mu_D = \mu_E = \mu_F; H_a$: Not all the means are equal; $\alpha = .05$
Observed value: $F = .22 \quad$ df $= (5, 12) \quad$ Critical value: $F = 3.11$
Decision: Do not reject $H_0 \quad$ P-value $> .05 \quad$ The data do not suggest that there is a difference in means.

11.43 **(a)** The ANOVA table is identical with the table in Exercise 11.42.

(b) When 2 is added to each data value, the variance of the means and the variance within each sample remain the same.

Chapter 12

12.1 **(a)** **(i)** 21.666 **(ii)** 19.023 **(iii)** 16.919 **(iv)** 3.325 **(v)** 2.088

(b) **(i)** 30.578 **(ii)** 27.488 **(iii)** 24.996 **(iv)** 7.261 **(v)** 5.229

(c) **(i)** 44.314 **(ii)** 40.646 **(iii)** 37.652 **(iv)** 14.611 **(v)** 11.524

12.3 **(a)** 11 **(b)** .95 **(c)** 3.940 **(d)** 25

(e) .10 **(f)** 27.587 **(g)** 12.443 **(h)** 3.053

12.5 $H_0: p_1 = p_2 = p_3 = p_4 = 1/4; H_a: H_0$ is not true $\quad \alpha = .05$
Observed value: $\chi^2 = 5.04 \quad$ df $= 3 \quad$ Critical value: $\chi^2 = 7.815$
Decision: Do not reject $H_0 \quad$ P-value $> .10$

12.7 $H_0: p_1 = p_2 = 1/10, p_3 = p_4 = 1/5, p_5 = 2/5; H_a: H_0$ is not true $\quad \alpha = .10$
Observed value: $\chi^2 = 9.58 \quad$ df $= 4 \quad$ Critical value: $\chi^2 = 7.779$
Decision: Reject $H_0 \quad .025 <$ P-value $< .05$

12.9 Let A, B, C, and D represent white females, minority females, white males, and minority males, respectively.
$H_0: p_A = .30, p_B = .05, p_C = .50, p_D = .15; H_a: H_0$ is not true. $\alpha = .05$
Observed value: $\chi^2 = 10.89 \quad$ df $= 3 \quad$ Critical value: $\chi^2 = 7.815$
Decision: Reject $H_0 \quad .01 <$ P-value $< .025 \quad$ The data suggest that the official's claim is not true.

12.11 Let A, B, C, and D represent less than \$25,000, between \$25,000 and \$30,000, between \$30,000 and \$35,000, and more than \$35,000, respectively.
$H_0: p_A = 1/10, p_B = p_C = p_D = 3/10; H_a: H_0$ is not true $\quad \alpha = .10$
Observed value: $\chi^2 = 3.08 \quad$ df $= 3 \quad$ Critical value: $\chi^2 = 6.251$
Decision: Do not reject $H_0 \quad$ P-value $> .10 \quad$ The data do not dispute the owner's assertion.

12.13 $H_0: p = 1/10$ for each category; $H_a: H_0$ is not true. $\quad \alpha = .05$
Observed value: $\chi^2 = 6.40 \quad$ df $= 9 \quad$ Critical value: $\chi^2 = 16.919$
Decision: Do not reject $H_0 \quad$ P-value $> .10 \quad$ The data do not dispute the claim.

12.15 H_0: Characteristics of ratings and age are independent.
H_a: Characteristics of ratings and age are related $\quad \alpha = .05$
Observed value: $\chi^2 = 2.92$ $\quad$ df $= 2$ $\quad$ Critical value: $\chi^2 = 5.991$
Decision: Do not reject H_0 $\quad$ P-value $> .10$ $\quad$ The data do not suggest that the characteristics of rating and age are related.

12.17 H_0: Characteristics of gender and CHD are independent
H_a: Characteristics of gender and CHD are related $\quad \alpha = .05$
Observed value: $\chi^2 = .48$ $\quad$ df $= 1$ $\quad$ Critical value: $\chi^2 = 3.841$
Decision: Do not reject H_0 $\quad$ P-value $> .10$ $\quad$ The data do not suggest that the characteristics of gender and CHD are related.

12.19 H_0: Characteristics of sex and salaries are independent
H_a: Characteristics of sex and salaries are related $\quad \alpha = .10$
Observed value: $\chi^2 = 7.40$ $\quad$ df $= 3$ $\quad$ Critical value: $\chi^2 = 6.251$
Decision: Reject H_0 $\quad$ $.05 < P$-value $< .10$ $\quad$ The data suggest that the characteristics of sex and salary are related.

12.21 **(a)** **(i)** $\quad \chi^2 = 0$ $\quad$ **(ii)** $\quad \chi^2 = 0$ $\quad$ **(iii)** $\quad \chi^2 = 0$

(c) **(i)** **(ii)**

	B_1	B_2	B_3		B_1	B_2	B_3
A_1	20	10	30	A_1	20	10	30
A_2	60	30	90	A_2	60	30	90
A_3	180	90	270	A_3	30	15	45

12.23 H_0: The two dice are homogeneous with respect to the number of dots showing.
H_a: H_0 is not true $\quad \alpha = .05$ $\quad$ Observed value: $\chi^2 = 2.07$
df $= 5$ $\quad$ Critical value: $\chi^2 = 11.071$ $\quad$ Decision: Do not reject H_0
P-value $> .10$ $\quad$ There is insufficent evidence to conclude that the dice are not homogeneous.

12.25 H_0: The appropriate populations of males and females are homogeneous with respect to belief of discrimination in salaries; H_a: H_0 is not true $\quad \alpha = .01$
Observed value: $\chi^2 = 7.34$ $\quad$ df $= 1$ $\quad$ Critical value: $\chi^2 = 6.635$
Decision: Reject H_0 $\quad$ $.005 < P$-value $< .01$ $\quad$ The data suggest that the appropriate populations are not homogeneous.

12.29 H_0: $p_A = .10$, $p_B = .20$, $p_C = .30$, $p_D = .25$, $p_F = .15$; H_a: H_0 is not true
$\alpha = .05$ $\quad$ Observed value: $\chi^2 = 6.30$ $\quad$ df $= 4$ $\quad$ Critical value: $\chi^2 = 9.488$
Decision: Do not reject H_0 $\quad$ P-value $> .10$ $\quad$ The data do not suggest the new teacher's grading policy is different from that of the department.

12.31 Let A, B, C, and D represent the categories drive alone, carpool, public transportation, and other means, respectively.
H_0: $p_A = .70$, $p_B = .20$, $p_C = .08$, $p_D = .02$; H_a: H_0 is not true $\quad \alpha = .05$
Observed value: $\chi^2 = 14.70$ $\quad$ df $= 3$ $\quad$ Critical value: $\chi^2 = 7.815$
Decision: Reject H_0 $\quad$ P-value $< .005$ $\quad$ The data suggest that the modes of transportation to work have changed.

12.33 H_0: Characteristics of gender and CHD are independent
H_a: Characteristics of gender and CHD are related $\quad \alpha = .10$
Observed value: $\chi^2 = .63$ $\quad$ df $= 1$ $\quad$ Critical value: $\chi^2 = 2.706$
Decision: Do not reject H_0 $\quad$ P-value $> .10$ $\quad$ The data do not suggest that the characteristics of gender and CHD are related.

12.35 H_0: The appropriate male and female populations are homogeneous with respect to age; H_a: H_0 is not true $\quad \alpha = .05$ $\quad$ Observed value: $\chi^2 = 6.86$
df $= 2$ $\quad$ Critical value: $\chi^2 = 5.991$ $\quad$ Decision: Reject H_0
$.025 < P$-value $< .05$ $\quad$ The data suggest that the male and female populations are not homogeneous with respect to age.

12.37 **(a)** H_0: The attitudes concerning racial quotas in hiring are homogeneous with respect to appropriate populations of Democrats, Republicans, and Independents; H_a: H_0 is not true

(b) Same

Chapter 13

13.1 **(a)** {0, 1, 2, 10, 11, 12} **(b)** .063 **(c)** {0, 1, 2} **(d)** .07

(e) {11, 12, 13, 14, 15} **(f)** .047 **(g)** {0, 1, 2, 3, 4, 5}

(h) .032 **(i)** .124 **(j)** .031

(k) {0, 1, 2, 3, 4, 12, 13, 14, 15, 16} **(l)** {14, 15, 16, 17, 18, 19}

13.3 H_0: Md = 2.8; H_a: Md > 2.8 α = .05
Let x be the number of data values larger than 2.8. Observed value: $x = 8$
Critical region: {8, 9, 10} Decision: Reject H_0 The data support the manager's claim.

13.5 H_0: Md = 0; H_a: Md > 0 α = .05 Let x be the number of differences (weight before − weight after) larger than 0. Observed value: $x = 6$
Critical region: {7, 8}
Decision: Do not reject H_0 The data do not suggest that the diet is effective.

13.7 **(a)**

Sample Data x	Difference $D = x - 10$	Magnitude $|D|$	Signed Rank
18	8	8	6
12	2	2	1
4	−6	6	−4
1	−9	9	−7
15	5	5	3
17	7	7	5
26	16	16	9
0	−10	10	−8
14	4	4	2

(b) H_0: Md = 10; H_a: Md > 10 α = .05 Observed value: $W^- = 19$
Critical value: $c = 8$ Decision: Do not reject H_0

13.9 **(a)**

Sample Data x	Difference $D = x - 50$	Magnitude $|D|$	Signed Rank
42	−8	8	−4
39	−11	11	−5
37	−13	13	−6
55	5	5	3
46	−4	4	−2
52	2	2	1
33	−17	17	−7

(b) H_0: Md = 50; H_a: Md < 50 α = .05 Observed value: $W^+ = 4$
Critical value: $c = 4$ Decision: Reject H_0

13.11 H_0: Md = 10; H_a: Md > 10 α = .01 Observed value: $W^- = 19$
Critical value: $c = 20$ Decision: Reject H_0 The data suggest that the lotion does not perform as advertised.

13.13 H_0: Md = 520; H_a: Md > 520 α = .01 Observed value: $W^- = 39.5$
Critical value: $c = 43$ Decision: Reject H_0 The data suggest that the advertising campaign was successful.

13.15 Let $D = x_1 - x_2$. H_0: $Md_D = 0$; H_a: $Md_D < 0$ $\alpha = .05$

(a)   Observed value: $W^+ = 101$ Critical value: $c = 110$
Decision: Reject H_0

(b)   Observed value: $z = -1.89$ Critical value: $z = -1.65$
Decision: Reject H_0 The data suggest that judge A tended to give lower performance ratings than judge B.

13.17 (a)

x	Rank (x)	y	Rank (y)
43	1	55	4
47	2	62	6
51	3	68	8
59	5	75	10
65	7		
71	9		
Sums:	27		28

(b) H_0: $Md_x = Md_y$; H_a: $Md_x \neq Md_y$ $\alpha = .10$
Observed value: $U = 6$ Critical value: $c = 3$
Decision: Do not reject H_0

13.19 H_0: $Md_x = Md_y$; H_a: $Md_x < Md_y$ $\alpha = .05$ Observed value: $U = 10$
Critical value: $c = 13$ Decision: Reject H_0 The data suggest that the median endurance level of soccer players is greater than that for football players.

13.21 H_0: $Md_x = Md_y$; H_a: $Md_x > Md_y$ $\alpha = .05$ Observed value: $U = 26$
Critical value: $c = 27$ Decision: Reject H_0 The data support the spokesman's claim.

13.23

	c_1	c_2	R	Decision		c_1	c_2	R	Decision
(a)	2	9	2	Reject H_0	(b)	3	11	12	Reject H_0
(c)	3	12	4	Do not reject H_0	(d)	3	11	8	Do not reject H_0
(e)	3	12	7	Do not reject H_0	(f)	4	13	9	Do not reject H_0

13.25 H_0: The process is random; H_a: The process is not random $\alpha = .05$
Observed value: $R = 3$ Critical values: $c_1 = 2$, $c_2 = 8$
Decision: Do not reject H_0 There is insufficient evidence to conclude that the process is not random.

13.27 H_0: $Md = 625$; H_a: $Md > 625$ $\alpha = .05$

(a)   Let x be the number of data values larger than 625.
Observed value: $x = 13$ Critical region: {14, 15, 16, 17, 18, 19, 20}
Decision: Do not reject H_0

(b)   Observed value: $W^- = 40$ Critical value: $c = 60$ Decision: Reject H_0

(c)   The Wilcoxon signed-rank test is a more sensitive test than the sign test.

13.29 H_0: $Md = 200$; H_a: $Md < 200$ $\alpha = .05$

(a)   Let x be the number of data values larger than 200
Observed value: $x = 2$ Critical region: {0, 1}
Decision: Do not reject H_0

(b)   Observed value: $W^+ = 5$ Critical value: $c = 6$
Decision: Reject H_0

(c)   The Wilcoxon signed-rank test is a more sensitive test than the sign test.

13.31 H_0: $Md_x = Md_y$; H_a: $Md_x < Md_y$ $\alpha = .05$ Observed value: $U = 11$
Critical value: $c = 15$ Decision: Reject H_0 The data suggest that girls tend to read with more comprehension than boys upon entering the fourth grade.

13.33 Let x and y represent resorts A and B, respectively.
H_0: Md_x = Md_y; H_a: Md_x < Md_y α = .01   Observed value: U = 8
Critical value: c = 3   Decision: Do not reject H_0 The data do not support the claim that the median price of building lots was less in resort area A than building lots in resort area B.

13.35 H_0: The process is random; H_a: The process is not random α = .05

(a) Observed value: R = 8   Critical values: c_1 = 8, c_2 = 19
Decision: Reject H_0

(b) Observed value: z = -2.25 Critical values: z = ±1.96
Decision: Reject H_0 The data suggest a lack of randomness.

Appendix C

C.1 **(a)** **(i)** 21.666   **(ii)** 19.023   **(iii)** 16.919   **(iv)** 3.325   **(v)** 2.088

(b) **(i)** 30.578   **(ii)** 27.488   **(iii)** 24.996   **(iv)** 7.261   **(v)** 5.229

(c) **(i)** 44.314   **(ii)** 40.646   **(iii)** 37.652   **(iv)** 14.611   **(v)** 11.524

C.3 **(a)** 11   **(b)** .95   **(c)** 3.940   **(d)** 25

(e) .10   **(f)** 27.587   **(g)** 12.443   **(h)** 3.053

C.5 **(a)** **(i)** H_0: σ^2 = 100; H_a: σ^2 > 100 α = .05   Observed value: χ^2 = 25.95
df = 15   Critical value: χ^2 = 24.996   Decision: Reject H_0
.025 < P-value < .05

(ii) Type I

(b) **(i)** H_0: σ^2 = 70; H_a: σ^2 < 70 α = .01   Observed value: χ^2 = 2.00
df = 11   Critical value: χ^2 = 3.053   Decision: Reject H_0
P-value < .005

(ii) Type I

(c) **(i)** H_0: σ^2 = 50; H_a: σ^2 ≠ 50 α = .10   Observed value: χ^2 = 11.99
df = 18   Critical values: χ^2 = 9.390, χ^2 = 28.869
Decision: Do not reject H_0 P-value > .20

(ii) Type II

(d) **(i)** H_0: σ^2 = 30; H_a: σ^2 > 30 α = .10   Observed value: χ^2 = 12
df = 8   Critical value: χ^2 = 13.362   Decision: Do not reject H_0
P-value > .10

(ii) Type II

(e) **(i)** H_0: σ^2 = 65; H_a: σ^2 < 65 α = .05   Observed value: χ^2 = 12.99
df = 21   Critical value: χ^2 = 11.591   Decision: Do not reject H_0
.05 < P-value < .10

(ii) Type II

(f) **(i)** H_0: σ^2 = 20; H_a: σ^2 ≠ 20 α = .01   Observed value: χ^2 = 48
df = 25   Critical values: χ^2 = 10.520, χ^2 = 46.928
Decision: Reject H_0 P-value < .01

(ii) Type I

C.7 **(a)** H_0: σ^2 = .0001; H_a: σ^2 > .0001 α = .01
Observed value: χ^2 = 28   df = 14   Critical value: χ^2 = 29.141
Decision: Do not reject H_0 The data do not suggest that the variance is more than .0001.

(b) .01 < P-value < .025   Do not reject H_0

C.9 **(a)** H_0: σ^2 = 4; H_a: σ^2 ≠ 4 α = .05   Observed value: χ^2 = 28.5
df = 19   Critical values: χ^2 = 8.907, χ^2 = 32.852
Decision: Do not reject H_0 The data do not suggest that the variance is different from 4.

(b) .10 < P-value < .20   Do not reject H_0

C.11 $H_0: \sigma^2 = (20)^2 = 400; H_a: \sigma^2 > (20)^2 = 400$ $\alpha = .01$
Observed value: $\chi^2 = 48.64$ df = 19   Critical value: $\chi^2 = 36.191$
Decision: Reject H_0 P-value < .005   The data suggest that the standard devia-
tion is more than 20.

C.13 $H_0: \sigma^2 = 156; H_a: \sigma^2 < 156$ $\alpha = .01$
Observed value: $\chi^2 = 4.40$ df = 8   Critical value: $\chi^2 = 1.646$
Decision: Do not reject H_0 P-value > .10   The data do not suggest that the
variance is less than 156.

C.15   **(a)** $.000096 < \sigma^2 < .000601$ **(b)** $.56 < \sigma^2 < 1.66$ **(c)** $9.46 < \sigma^2 < 97.20$

C.17   **(a)**   4.01   **(b)**   4.77   **(c)**   3.13   **(d)**   3.07

C.19   **(a)** $.90 < \frac{\sigma_A^2}{\sigma_B^2} < 16.99$ **(b)** $1.09 < \frac{\sigma_A^2}{\sigma_B^2} < 20.47$ **(c)** $.10 < \frac{\sigma_A^2}{\sigma_B^2} < .70$

(d) $1.23 < \frac{\sigma_A^2}{\sigma_B^2} < 4.83$ **(e)** $2.75 < \frac{\sigma_A^2}{\sigma_B^2} < 60.00$ **(f)** $.68 < \frac{\sigma_A^2}{\sigma_B^2} < 64.20$

C.21   **(a)** $H_0: \sigma_A^2 = \sigma_B^2; H_a: \sigma_A^2 \neq \sigma_B^2$ $\alpha = .10$ Observed value: $F = 2.5$
df = (15, 20)   Critical value: $F = 2.20$ Decision: Reject H_0
The data suggest that there may be a difference in the measurement variability.

(b) $.05 < $ P-value $< .10$

C.23 $H_0: \sigma_A^2 = \sigma_B^2; H_a: \sigma_A^2 > \sigma_B^2$ $\alpha = .05$ Observed value: $F = 1.32$
df = (30, 40)   Critical value: $F = 1.74$ Decision: Do not reject H_0
P-value > .05   The data do not suggest that the variability of males' systolic blood
pressure is larger than females.

C.25

df for F	df for t	$F_{.05}$	$t_{.025}$	$(t_{.025})^2$
(1, 3)	3	10.13	3.182	10.13
(1, 6)	6	5.99	2.447	5.99
(1, 8)	8	5.32	2.306	5.32
(1, 10)	10	4.96	2.228	4.96
(1, 14)	14	4.60	2.145	4.60
(1, 20)	20	4.35	2.086	4.35

The F distribution with (1, k) degrees of freedom is the same as a t^2 distribution,
where t has k degrees of freedom.

INDEX

Addition rule, 199
  general form, 206–208
  for mutually exclusive events, 199
Alternate hypothesis
  accepting, 341
  choosing, 342–344
  definition, 339
  homogeneity test, 551
  P-value in testing, 354
ALTERNATIVE subcommand, 392, 440, 442, 595–597
Analysis of variance. *See* ANOVA
ANOVA (analysis of variance)
  alternate formulas, 518–521
  equal sample sizes, 492–505
  Minitab program, 521–522
  principles, 492–505
  steps in, 523–524
  tables, 512–513, 522
  terminology, 513–514
AOVONEWAY command, 521

Bar graph, 32
  frequency histogram, 33
  truncated, 47
Between-samples estimate, 494–495
Bias
  nonresponse, 9
  response, 9
Binomial experiment, 379
  to compare two population proportions, 432
  definition, 245
  probability of success, 252
Binomial probability distribution, 245–255
  formula for calculating, 247, 249
  histograms, 247
  normal approximation to, 294–300
  in statistical inference, 251
Bivariate population, linear correlation coefficient, 454
Boxplot, 102–106
  Minitab command, 116
  modified, 104
Box-and-whisker plot, 102

Categorical data, 531
CDF command, 257, 310–311, 393
Cell frequencies
  chi-square test, 535–538
  expected, 535, 538, 545
  independence test, 544
  observed, 535, 545

Central Limit Theorem, 300–310
  graphic representation, 303
  normal sample criteria, 339
  procedure, 303
  for random samples, 495
  for small samples, 358
Central tendency measures, 76–85; *see also* Mean; Median
CHISQUARE command, 555
Chi-square distribution, 533–534
  degrees of freedom, 533–534, 546
  normality requirement, 534
  properties of, 533–534
  shape of curve, 533–534
Chi-square test
  confidence intervals, A-48
  for goodness-of-fit, 532–541
    principles, 535
  for independence of two characteristics, 547
  Minitab program, 554–555
  for population variance, A-47
  right-tailed, 533
Class(es)
  boundaries, 26
  class mark of, 27
  frequency of, 25
  in grouped frequency distributions, 23
Class limits, 23, 25
Class width, 24-25
  grouped frequency distributions, 24–25
Coefficient of determination, 157–162
  definition, 160
  error terms, 159
  Minitab program, 172
Combinations, 215–216
Combinatorics, 213–218
Confidence interval, 326–328
  chi-square distribution, A-48
  F tests, A-59
  for mean differences, 409
  for means, 473–479
    of random variables, 328–330
  for population proportions, 380–381, 436–437
  small sample, 368–369
  tests for two means, 417–419, 422
  width of, 330–331, 477
Confounding factor, 12
Contingency tables, 543
  estimating row and column proportions, 546
Continuity correction, 297, 305

Continuous probability distribution, 268–273
  Minitab command, 310–311
  properties of, 271
Continuous random variable, probability distribution, 270
Control group, 12
COPY command, 115
Correlation analysis, 132
Correlation coefficient (linear), 141, 152–169
  bivariate populations, 467
  to calculate SSR/TSS, 160
  definition, 153
  Minitab command, 170
  properties of, 154–157
CORRELATION command, 170, 173, 482
COUNT command, 115
Critical region, 341, 343
  chi-square test, 535
  left-tailed test, 348–349, 367, 386
  right-tailed test, 347, 349, 367, 386, 546
  sign test, 563–564
  tests for two means, 416–417
  two-tailed test, 348–349, 368, 386, 467
Critical values, 341, 349–350
  in F test, A-54
  Student's t distribution, 358

Data, 2
  ranking, 24
  summarizing, 22–31
Data Desk printouts, 104, 363, 378, 431, 466, 505
Data value, 2
  percentile rank, 96–97
  of random variables, 228
Decimals
  in data, 27
    graphic representation, 43
  rounding off, 76
Decision making, errors in, 341–342
Degrees of freedom
  chi-square test, 533-534, 546
  F distribution, A-52
  with SSW, 507
  t distribution, 359
DESCRIBE command, 113
Descriptive statistics, 2
  organization of data, 21–73
Deviation
  from the mean, 87
  square of, 87

I-1

Discrete probability distribution, 231–237
  definition, 231
  expected value, 240–243
  Minitab program, 310
  properties satisfying, 233
  random variables, 230
Discrete random variable
  mean, 238
  probability distribution, 230
  variance, 238
Dispersion, measures of, 75, 85–94, 98; *see also* Range
  and resistance, 92
Dot diagram, 31
  to determine range, 86

Empirical Rule, 292
Error of the estimate (*see also* Maximum error of the estimate)
  least squares regression line, 135
Estimation, 325
Events, 189–190
  complement of, 198
  complementary, 202
  compound, 197–205
  definition, 189
  independent, 200
  mutually exclusive, 198–199
  probability of, 191–197
  simple, 189
Expected proportion, 192
Expected value of discrete probability distributions, 240–243
Experiment(s), 186
  binomial, 245
    mathematical components, 246
    probability of success, 252
  controlled, 12–13
  cross-sectional, 13
  design of, 12–15
  double-blind randomized controlled, 13
  longitudinal, 13
  observational, 12
  possible outcomes, 186–187
  randomized controlled, 12
Explained variation. See Sum of squares for regression (SSR)

F distribution, 496
  analysis of variance, 498, 524
  graphic representation, area under the curve, 497
  normality requirement, 499
  properties of, 497
F test
  confidence interval, A-59
  labeling convention, A-54
  left-tailed, A-57
  for population means, 498
  steps in, A-55
  two-tailed, A-57
Factorials, 214
Failure, probability of, 246

Framingham Heart Study, 61–63, 118, 173, 394, 443, 483, 522, 556, 598
Frequency distribution, 22
  graphic representation, 33, 268–269
  grouped, 23, 25
    constructing, 24
    estimating sample variance, 90
    histogram, 33, 268–269
    mean, 77
    relative, 25
  for nonnumerical data, 23
  skewed, 81
  symmetric, 40, 81
Frequency polygon, 33
  area under the graph, 268–270
  relative, 34
  shape of, 39, 81, 269–270
Fundamental Principle of Counting, 194–195
  for more than two tasks, 194

Game show paradox, 202
Gosset, William S., *t* distribution, 358–360
Graphic representations
  F distributions, A-52
  of grouped frequency distributions, 33
  mean, 77
  misleading, 46–49
  of probability distributions, 234–235, 274, 295
  types of, 31–39

Hazelwood Case, 383–385
Heteroscedasticity, 499
Hinges, 102
Histogram (*see also* Probability histogram)
  cutpoints, 56
  dotplot, 58
  frequency, 33
  grouped frequency, 268–269
  mean, 77
  Minitab, 54–56
  relative frequency, 33
  shape of, 39
HISTOGRAM command, 55
Homogeneity test, 532, 551–554
Homoscedasticity, 454, 461, 499, 511
Hypothesis, 326; *see also* Alternate hypothesis; Null hypothesis
Hypothesis testing, 326, 339–344
  classical approach, 353
  controlling errors, 350–351
  for population means, 338–353
  for population proportions, 383–386
  P-value approach, 355
  selecting hypothesis to prove, 350
  steps in, 342–343
  Type I error, 342, 350–351, 594
  Type II error, 342, 350–351, 594
  types of, 344

Independence tests, 532, 543–549
  principles, 546–547
Independent characteristics, 541
  multiplication rule, 542, 544
  testing for, 543–549
Inference
  with two population means, dependent samples, 406–415
  with two population variances, A-54
Inferential statistics, 2–3
  binomial distributions in, 251
  probability, 3, 185–186
Interquartile range, 98
Interval estimate, 326
Interval segment, 229
INVCDF command, 258–259, 312

JMP printouts, 98, 102, 140, 377, 473, 514

Least squares criterion, 135
Least squares regression line, 132–152
  dependent and independent variables, 133
  intercept, 133
  slope of line, 133
Left-tailed test, 348–349, 367
  chi-square, A-47
  t test, 386
LET command, 109, 111–112, 394
Level of confidence, 326
Level of significance, 339, 341
  chi-square distribution, 535
  P-value and, 355
  sign test, 563
  Type I errors and, 342
Line of best fit, 152
  equation, 136
  for least squares regression line, 133–134
Line segment, 229
Linear regression model, 453–455
  assumptions, 455
  properties of, 454, 459–462
Linear relationships
  between two variables, 468–470
  degree of, 157, 468
  F test, 482
  negative, 155
  nonlinear, 154–155
  perfect, 154
  positive, 155
  strength of, 154–155

Mann–Whitney *U* test, 581–589
  critical values, 583
  Minitab command, 596–597
  normal approximation, 586–587
  purpose and procedures, 585–586
Maximum error of the estimate
  for means, 331
  for proportions, 380
  small samples, 368–369

Mean(s) (*see also* Population mean)
  comparison of median to, 81
  definition, 76
  deviations from, 87
  equality of, 518–521
  grand, 495, 507–508
  graphic representation, 77
  Minitab command, 112–113, 314
  of population, 76
  of random variables, 238, 241
    binomial, 252
    confidence interval, 328–330
    discrete, 238
  standard error of, 114, 303
  summation convention, 77
  trimmed, 114
MEAN command, 112–113
Mean difference, 406–407
  confidence intervals, 409
Mean square between (MSB), 507,
    513–514
Mean square for error, 481
Mean square for regression, 481
Mean square within (MSW), 507,
    513–514
Median
  comparison of mean to, 81
  definition, 78
Minitab commands
  ALTERNATIVE subcommand, 392,
    440, 442, 595–597
  AOVONEWAY, 521
  BOXPLOT, 116
  CDF, 257, 310–311, 393
  CHISQUARE, 555
  COPY, 115
  CORRELATION, 170, 173, 482
  COUNT, 115
  DESCRIBE, 113
  HISTOGRAM, 55
  INVCDF, 258–259, 312
  LET, 109, 111–112, 394
  MEAN, 112–113
  NAME, 60
  NSCORES, 511
  PDF, 255–257, 310
  PLOT, 170, 511
  POOLED subcommand, 442–443
  PREDICT subcommand, 482
  RANDOM, 314
  READ, 109–110
  REGRESS, 170, 480–481
  RMEAN, 314
  SET, 51, 110, 392
  SQRT, 394
  subcommands, 52
  TINTERVAL, 392
  TTEST, 392, 440
  TWOSAMPLE, 441–442
  ZTEST, 391
Minitab computer program (*see also*
    Minitab commands)
  alpha data value, 52
  analysis of variance, 521–522
  annotating, 60
  arithmetic operations, 110–111
  bar graphs, 53

Minitab computer program
    (*continued*)
  chi-square test, 554–555
  correlation, 170
  describing data, 112–113
  dotplots, 58
  entering data, 51
  evaluating expressions, 111
  finding *P*-values, 393–394
  frequency polygons, 56–57
  histograms, 54–56
  independence tests, 554–555
  Mann–Whitney *U* test, 596–597
  naming columns, 60
  for normal distributions, 310–316
  percentiles, 114–115
  pie charts, 54
  population means
    dependent samples, 440–441
    independent samples, 441–443
  regression analysis, 170–173
  runs test, 597
  sign test, 595
  simulation, 312–313
  stem-and-leaf plots, 58–59
  stored constants, 59
  t test, 392
  Wilcoxon signed-rank test, 595–596
  for Windows, 50
  worksheet, 51
  z test, 391–392
Multiplication rule
  general form, 208–211
  for independent characteristics,
    542, 544
  for independent events, 200
Multistage cluster sampling, 7

Nonparametric tests, 562
  vs. parametric tests, 594–595
Normal distribution, 273–282
  graphic representation, 274, 280
  properties of, 273–274
  shape of, 274
  standard, 274–282, 433
Normal quantile plots, 371–373
  Minitab command, 511
Normal random variable
  probability distribution, 273–274,
    282–294
  standard, 275, 282–283
  Minitab command, 314
  probabilities associated with, 275
Normality requirement
  for ANOVA test, 499, 511
  chi-square distribution, A-47
  F distribution, A-58
  for linear regression model, 454
  t distribution, 369
Notation, 22, 279
NSCORES, 511
Null hypothesis
  ANOVA test, 496–498
  chi-square test, 532–535
  choosing, 342–344
  definition, 338

Null hypothesis (*continued*)
  homogeneity test, 551
  independence tests, 547
  sign test, 563–564
  testing, 339–344
Numbers Game, 241

Observational study, 12
Observations
  extreme, 78
  influential, 142–143
  unusual, 142
Observed value of test statistic,
    341–342
One-tailed test, 583
Outliers, 78, 104

Paired population
  Mann–Whitney *U* test, 581–589
  Wilcoxon signed-rank test,
    573–577
Parameter, 3
Parametric tests, 562
  vs. nonparametric tests, 594–595
PDF command, 255–257, 310
Percentiles, 95–97
  Minitab command, 114–115,
    311–312
  procedure for finding, 95–96
  rank, 96–97
Permutation, 214–215
Pictogram, 34, 48
Pie chart, 32
PLOT command, 170, 511
Point estimate, 326, 476
  for population proportions,
    379–381
POOLED subcommand, 442–443
Population, 2
  estimating sample size, 332–333
  infinite, 231
  mean, 76
  polygon shape for, 40
  probability distribution, 227
  sampling, 2
Population distribution
  nonnormal or unknown, 562–595
  normal, 561
  symmetric, Wilcoxon signed-rank
    test, 570, 574
Population mean
  confidence interval, 329, 475
  estimating
    with large samples, 326–338
    with small samples, 358–378
  F test, 498, 506, 508
  hypothesis testing with large
    samples, 338–353
  inference with small samples,
    358–378
  Minitab program
    dependent samples, 440–441
    independent samples, 441–443
  two-mean tests
    confidence interval, 417–419, 422
    dependent samples, 406–415

Population mean (*continued*)
two-mean tests (*continued*)
independent samples,
large-sample case, 415–421
independent samples,
small-sample case, 421–432
z test, 348–349
Population median, comparing two,
572–573, 581
Population proportion(s), 252
comparing two unknowns,
432–440
confidence interval, 436–437
estimating, 378–382
hypothesis testing, 383–386
inference concerning, 378–391
large-sample test, 385–386
multiple, 531–532
z test, 385–386
Population regression line, 172,
454–455
slope of, 172, 455
Population samples
dependent, 406–409
vs. independent, 406
sign test, 565
independent
large-sample case, 415–421
small-sample case, 421–432
Population variance(s), 88
alternative formulas for computing,
90–91
chi-square test, A-47
comparing two, A-58
testing significant difference, A-51
Position, measures of, 76, 95–102
Power of test, 594
PREDICT subcommand, 482
Prediction interval, 473–479
Primary sampling units, 7
Probability, 3, 185–186
of *A*, 192
area and, 268–269
conditional, 208–211
of an event, 191–197
normal, 273–294
Probability density function, 270
Probability distribution, 227, 359;
see also Binomial probability
distribution; Chi-square
distribution; Continuous
probability distribution;
Discrete probability
distribution
F, 496
graphic representations, 234–235
area under the curve, 269–270,
295, 327
Minitab commands, 255–259
of random variables, 230–231
Probability histogram, 234–235
of binomial distributions, 247
of a sample mean, 302
Probability value. *See* P-value
P-value, 308
definition, 354
graphic representation, 356
in hypothesis testing, 353–358

P-value (*continued*)
Minitab program, 393–394
right- vs. left-tailed tests, 394

Quadratic relationship, 154
Quartiles, 97
Quintiles, 13

RANDOM command, 314
Random sample, 6
lottery method, 6
random number method, 6
Random variable, 227; *see also* Normal
random variable
binomial, 245, 297
mean and variance, 252
continuous, 229
definition, 228
discrete, 229, 231
mean, 238
probability distribution, 230–231
standard deviation, 495
variance, 238
Range, 85–86
Ranked data, 24
median, 78
percentile, 96–97
READ command, 109–110
REGRESS command, 170, 480–481
Regression analysis, 132
Minitab commands, 170–173
Regression line. *See* Line of best fit
Residual, 135, 459
plot, 460
Resistant measure, 78, 80–81
Right-tailed test, 347, 349, 367
chi-square, 533, 547, A-47
F testing, A-58
Minitab program, 392
P-value, A-55
t testing, 386
RMEAN command, 314
Robust procedure, 361
Run, 590
Runs test, 589–594
Minitab command, 597
normal approximation, 592–593
procedure, 591
randomness vs. nonrandomness,
590–591

Sample means, variability between,
493–494
Sample proportion, 379
Sample size
with Central Limit Theorem,
303–304, 330
chi-square distribution, 538
comparing population proportions,
379, 382–383, 434
equal, for analysis of variance,
492–505
F distribution, A-53
homogeneity tests, 553
unequal, for analysis of variance,
505–518
when estimating population mean,
332–333

Sample space, 187
Sample standard deviation, 89
pooled, 425
Sample variance, 89
alternative formulas, 90–91
Samples (*see also* Random sample)
bias, 9
cluster, 6–7
of convenience, 8
population, 2
probability, 8
random, 5–6
representative, 22
stratified, 6
systematic, 7–8
Scatter diagram, 133–134, 141
high leverage points in, 143
for nonlinear relationships, 155–156
SET command, 51, 110, 392
Sign test, 562–569
to compare two populations, 565
Minitab command, 595
normal approximation, 567–568
steps in, 565
Significance, statistical vs. practical,
351, 470
Simple random sample, 6
Simpson's paradox, 15
SQRT command, 394
Square root, Minitab command, 394
Standard deviation
of the distribution, 238
for estimating means, 327
for normal random variables, 291
pooled sample, 425
population, 89
from regression line, 172, 456, 474
sample, 89
Standard error of the mean, 114, 303
Standard score, 285
standard normal, 327
Statistica printouts, 427, 514
Statistical inference
large samples, 348–349, 385–386
small samples, 358–368
types of, 325–326
Statistics (*see also* Descriptive
statistics; Inferential statistics)
in decision making, 326
definition, 2
nature of, 1–5
Stem-and-leaf plot, 41–46
choosing stems and leaves, 42
Minitab, 58–59
ordered, 41
splitting stems, 43
Stratified sample, 6
proportional, 6
Student's *t* distribution, 358–368
applications, 361–367
graphic representation, area under
the curve, 359
history, 358–359
properties of, 359–360
standard normal distribution and,
359
Success, probability of, 246, 295
in binomial experiments, 252

Sum of squares, analysis of variance, 506
Sum of squares between (SSB), 507
    alternate formula, 519
Sum of squares for error (SSE), 159, 513–514
    line of best fit, 159–160
Sum of squares for regression (SSR), 159–160
Sum of squares for treatments (SSTR), 513–514
Sum of squares within (SSW), 506, 508
    alternate formula, 519

t distribution. *See* Student's *t* distribution
t statistic, pooled, 424
t test, 358–368
    five-step procedure, 362–363
    Minitab program, 292
    for population means, 367, 425–427, 441
    power of, 594
    vs. sign test, 564
    small samples, 367
    two-sample, 422–423
Tables, 240
    of frequency distributions, 22–23
Test statistic, 340
Tied ranks, 573
Time series, 591

TINTERVAL command, 392
Total sum of squares (TSS), 159–160, 512
Total variation. *See* Total sum of squares (TSS)
Treatment, 12
    in analysis of variance, 513
Treatment group, 12
Tree diagram, 211
TTEST command, 392, 440
TWOSAMPLE command, 441–442
Two-tailed test, 348–349, 368, 386
    critical region, 587, 593
    for linear relationship, 467
    Mann–Whitney *U*, 584
    P-value, 355
    t testing, 386

Unexplained variation. *See* Sum of squares for error (SSE)

Variables, comparing two, 132–133
Variance
    alternative formula, 239
    of random variables, 238
        binomial, 252
        discrete, 238
Venn diagram, 198
    depicting mutually exclusive events, 199

Whiskers, 102
Wilcoxon rank-sum test, 581
Wilcoxon signed-rank test, 569–581
    to compare two populations, 573–577
    continuous data, 570
    magnitudes of the differences, 570
    Minitab command, 595–596
    normal approximation, 577–578
    paired experiment, 573–577
    procedure
        for a paired experiment, 577
        for a population median, 572–573
    tied ranks, 573
    zero differences, 573
Windows with Minitab, 50
Within-samples estimate, 494–495

z score, 285
z test, 327, 368
    Minitab program, 391–392
    for population means, 348–349
    for population proportions, 385–386
    power of, 594
    two-tailed, 586–587
Zero differences, 573
ZTEST command, 391